Ordeal of the Union

President Abraham Lincoln

Ordeal of the Union

VOLUME 4

The War for the Union:

THE ORGANIZED WAR
1863–1864

THE ORGANIZED WAR TO VICTORY
1864–1865

by ALLAN NEVINS

With a new Introduction by
James M. McPherson

Collier Books
MACMILLAN PUBLISHING COMPANY
NEW YORK

MAXWELL MACMILLAN CANADA
TORONTO

MAXWELL MACMILLAN INTERNATIONAL
NEW YORK   OXFORD   SINGAPORE   SYDNEY

Collier Books
Macmillan Publishing Company
866 Third Avenue
New York, NY 10022

Maxwell Macmillan Canada, Inc.
1200 Eglinton Avenue East
Suite 200
Don Mills, Ontario M3C 3N1

Macmillan Publishing Company is part of the Maxwell Communication Group of Companies.

Library of Congress Cataloging-in-Publication Data
Nevins, Allan, 1890–1971.
    Ordeal of the union / by Allan Nevins; with a new introduction by James M. McPherson.—1st Collier Books ed.
        p.   cm.
    Vol. 1 originally published: Ordeal of the Union. New York: Scribner, 1947; v. 2 originally published: The emergence of Lincoln. New York: Scribner, c1978; v. 3–4 originally published: The war for the Union. New York: Scribner, 1959–1971.
    Includes bibliographical references and indexes.
    ISBN 0-02-035441-X (v. 1).—ISBN 0-02-035442-8 (v. 2).—ISBN 0-02-035443-6 (v. 3).—ISBN 0-02-035445-2 (v. 4)
    1. United States—History.   I. Title.
E468.N428   1992   92–3522   CIP
973—dc20

Macmillan books are available at special discounts for bulk purchases for sales promotions, premiums, fund-raising, or educational use. For details contact:

Special Sales Director
Macmillan Publishing Company
866 Third Avenue
New York, NY 10022

First Collier Books Edition 1992

10   9   8   7   6   5   4   3   2   1

Printed in the United States of America

GENERAL INTRODUCTION

ALLAN NEVINS's life illustrated the American dream of upward mobility that he wrote about in many of his books. Born on an Illinois farm, Nevins became America's foremost historian and the recipient of the top honors of his profession, including two Pulitzer prizes, a National Book award, and the presidency of both the American Historical Association and the American Academy of Arts and Letters. In an active career that spanned sixty years, he wrote at least fifty books, edited seventy-five others, and authored uncounted hundreds of articles and reviews. At the time of his death in 1971, fourteen different publishers had books written by Nevins in print.

This prodigious output was achieved not only by inspiration but also by the ninety-nine percent perspiration that Thomas A. Edison defined as genius. Nevins did not have armies of research assistants and collaborators to do his work. The twelve-to-fourteen-hour days he had put in on the farm as a youth trained him for even longer hours as a journalist and historian. Stories abound of missed appointments, skipped lunches, and disappearances into his study during dinner parties at his home where bemused guests would soon hear his typewriter clacking away. Nevins learned how to write under the pressure of deadlines during nearly two decades as a journalist before he joined the faculty of Columbia University as DeWitt Clinton Professor of American History in 1931. But it would be far from accurate to characterize his historical writings as "journalism." The prose flows lucidly and pulses with energy—and, admittedly, with an occasional tinge of purple. But Nevins's books were the product of exhaustive research, thorough mastery of sources, and a professional command of the historiography of his subject.

The subject was most often biography, of the life-and-times genre, which won him Pulitzer prizes in 1932 and 1937 for biographies of Grover Cleveland and Hamilton Fish. But Nevins's crowning achievement was his eight-volume series on the era of the Civil War, published from 1947 to 1971. The final two volumes won Nevins a posthumous National Book award in 1972. The title originally intended for the whole series, *Ordeal of the Union*, became the title for the first two volumes, covering the period from the Mexican War to the Inauguration of James Buchanan in 1857. The next two, with the title *The Emergence of Lincoln*, carry the story down to Lincoln's Inauguration in 1861. The final four volumes,

one for each year of the Civil War, bear the general title of *The War for the Union*.
The grandeur and sweep of these eight volumes—four thousand pages, one
million, seven hundred thousand words—are worthy of the great theme they
treat, the drama and trauma of internecine conflict, the *ordeal* of American nationality
in which the United States was preserved and purged of its great anomaly,
slavery, in a war that cost nearly as many American lives as all the rest of the
nation's wars combined. The Civil War was America's *Iliad* and Allan Nevins
was its Homer. Befitting Nevins's skill at biography as well as the Homeric
model, the narrative and interpretation are carried forward by the story of the
dominant individuals of the age, chiefly Abraham Lincoln who makes brief
appearances in the first two volumes and "emerges" in the next two, becoming in
the final four the Agamemnon of this American *Iliad*.

Each of the two pairs of volumes in the original series has been combined into
one volume for this edition, and the whole given the main title originally
intended, *Ordeal of the Union*.

INTRODUCTION TO THIS VOLUME

The National Book Award that Nevins won posthumously for this final volume
was intended to recognize the whole series. Volume 4, standing alone, would
have merited such an honor, to be sure. The courage Nevins demonstrated in
completing it paralleled that of Civil War soldiers who fought on in the face of
discouragement and death. Like Ulysses S. Grant writing his memoirs nearly a
century earlier, Nevins wrote much of this volume amid the pain of a serious
illness and approaching death. That fate overtook him at the age of eighty, before
he could give this volume the final polish that characterized the previous ones.
Thus an occasional error, inconsistency, or infelicity creeps into these pages.
Nevertheless, they measure up to the standard of comprehensive, rich, perspicuous
exposition that gives such distinction to this series.

The main theme, once again, is expressed by the subtitle. The improvised
war of 1861 became the organized war of 1864–1865. "The invertebrate
country of Bull Run days, goaded by necessity, gathered its energies, submitted
to system, and became the partially structured country which heard the news of
Five Forks," writes Nevins. "To organize armies, to organize the production of
arms, munitions, clothing, and food, to organize medical services and finance, to
organize public sentiment—all this required unprecedented attention to plan, and

an unprecedented amount of cooperative effort. The resultant alteration in the national character was one of the central results of the struggle."

As in Volume 3, the main focus is on the North. Nevins devotes more attention to strategy and leadership than to tactics and battles in his narrative of military campaigns. This volume marks the emergence of Grant and Sherman as the Union's winning team; Nevins's analysis of their qualities is trenchant and discerning. But his main contribution concerns the economics and logistics of war. He brings to light unsung heroes such as Daniel McCallum, superintendent of the U.S. Military Railroads, whose genius kept the trains rolling right up to the rear of Sherman's advancing army, and Herman Haupt, chief of construction for U.S. Military Railroads in Virginia, whose men constructed from green timber a trestle eighty feet high and four hundred feet long in less than two weeks, eliciting from Lincoln this appreciative comment: "I have seen the most remarkable structure that human eyes ever rested upon. That man, Haupt, has built a bridge over which loaded trains are running every hour, and upon my word, gentlemen, there is nothing in it but beanpoles and cornstalks." Above all, Nevins admires Quartermaster General of the Union Army Montgomery Meigs, whose brilliant organizational talents kept an army of one million men abundantly supplied. "In any just view of the Civil War," insists Nevins, Meigs "should stand as one of the central figures"—and the array of data that Nevins summons forth will convince the reader that he is right.

Nevins does not neglect the logistical problems and achievements of the Confederacy—especially of Ordnance Chief Josiah Gorgas, who almost literally turned plowshares into swords, building from scratch an arms and ammunition industry that kept Confederate armies better supplied than had seemed possible at the outset. But this is mainly a story of how northern superiority in resources—more accurately, superiority in organization of resources—won the war and set the stage for postwar emergence of the American economy as the world's most productive.

To an astonishing degree the northern economy produced plenty of both guns and butter by 1864. An extraordinary blitz of laws passed during the war helped promote this phenomenon: the Homestead Act, which opened up three million acres to farming by the war's end and eighty million ultimately; the Pacific Railroad Act, which launched the first transcontinental railroad on which construction began before Appomattox; the Morrill Land–Grant College Act, which laid the groundwork for great state universities; the National Bank Act, which rationalized and modernized the chaotic antebellum banking structure; and several other laws that facilitated westward expansion and economic growth. A few weeks after Appomattox, Senator John Sherman wrote to his brother William Tecumseh Sherman: "The close of the war with our resources unimpaired gives an elevation, a scope to the ideas of leading capitalists, far higher than anything ever undertaken in this country before. They talk of millions as confidently as formerly of thousands." Thus, writes Nevins in the concluding chapter, "from the flame and ashes of the Civil War emerged . . . a new country. . . . The sense of Americans in 1865 that they stood at the close of one era and the beginning of another . . . was confirmed and strengthened by the evident fact that the perspective of all mankind had been sharply and decisively revolutionized by Union victory in the war."

Two subthemes run through this final volume. One focuses on a sphere in which the North's organizational revolution failed: justice for the freed slaves. "Few chapters are as unhappy as that which deals with the slaves to whom the nation owed so great a debt, and for whom it did so little, both tardily and grudgingly," Nevins maintains. "The story of the freedmen in wartime is one of gross mismanagement and neglect." If this conclusion is too harsh, giving too little credit to those northerners who did try to help the freedmen and too little recognition of the difficulties they faced amid the destructive chaos of war, it nevertheless points to a crucial aspect of the conflict neglected in many accounts. Curiously, though, just as Nevins's antebellum volumes depreciated the abolitionists whose position on slavery agreed with his own, this volume disparages the radical Republicans who demanded justice for the freedmen and tried to overcome the very neglect of them that Nevins condemns.

The second subtheme concerns presidential leadership. Though it is conventional to compare Abraham Lincoln favorably to Jefferson Davis, Nevins offers substance and incisive analysis to support this conventional wisdom. Lincoln was more eloquent than Davis in expressing war aims, more successful in communicating with the people, more skillful as a political leader in keeping factions working together, better able to endure criticism and work with his critics to achieve a common goal. Lincoln was flexible, pragmatic, with a sense of humor to help him survive the stress of his job; "the primary faults of Davis were narrowness, frigidity, and pride; he had little breadth, little warmth or imagination." In this as in his other judgments, Nevins will not win universal agreement. But this volume, as do all that go before it in this monumental series, compels universal attention from all those interested in America's shaping experience, the Civil War.

JAMES M. MCPHERSON

CONTENTS

ILLUSTRATIONS

xi

ACKNOWLEDGMENT

The author wishes to express his appreciation for material aid given in the preparation of these last volumes of *The War for the Union* to the Guggenheim Foundation, the National Foundation on the Arts and Humanities, and Columbia University. He is deeply indebted to the staffs of the Library of Congress and of the Henry E. Huntington Library at San Marino, California. Without the active support of his colleagues Ray Billington, E. B. Long and John Niven, these volumes would never have been completed. The greatest debt is to Lillian K. Bean whose untiring effort can never be repaid. He also acknowledges gratefully the assistance of his daughters Anne Loftis and Meredith Mayer and his wife Mary Nevins. Finally, he would like to express his gratitude to Joseph G. E. Hopkins of Charles Scribner's Sons for his unflagging patience and devotion to the task of editing these volumes.

Allan Nevins

PART I

The War for the Union

THE ORGANIZED WAR

1863–1864

1

Balance Sheet at Mid-War

MANY AMERICANS realized by the spring of 1863 that the country was in the throes of a revolution, and all astute men comprehended that it would leave the nation radically changed in a great variety of respects. Although the people and governments of the North and the South counted the penalties of civil war with the same sorrow, they confronted the future with divergent gaze. A goodly number of Northerners mingled flashes of exhilaration with their anxieties, and looked to the next chapter of national history with as much optimism as apprehension, for already they could enumerate some clear gains. No matter what the ending of the war, for both sections it would mark a beginning rather than a termination, and for supporters of the Union in especial a fresh and fruitful beginning. But just how would it end? That, after Chancellorsville, was still the all-important question.

From the outset the antagonists had been aware of a fundamental difference in position. The North had to fight for a decisive victory in the field; for the destruction or hopeless crippling of the Confederate armies, and the subjugation of the rebellious areas and their inhabitants. The South could pursue a less difficult objective, well short of an elimination of the main Union forces. If it fought the war to a clear draw, a deadlock, that would suffice, for then Northern war-weariness would compel acquiescence in Confederate independence, boundaries and other terms then becoming merely matters for negotiation. To be sure, important Northern elements were determined, in Senator Henry Wilson's words, to crush the rebellion beneath an iron heel, but these elements had a fluctuating strength, and many people would consider a less heroic eventuality. In short, Northern success demanded total victory; Southern success only a paralysis of Northern determination.

This did not mean that the South was free to wage a purely defensive war, for such a passive strategy would increase the chances of shattering defeat. General E.P. Alexander[1] was unquestionably right when he wrote that a decisive defeat of Lee's army in any summer campaign of 1862, 1863, or 1864—and particu-

1. Alexander, E.P., *Military Memoirs of a Confederate*, New York, 1907, VII, 363.

larly a defeat on the defensive, well within Southern boundaries—would have meant the end of the struggle. It might seem that in trying to weary the North into an acceptance of disunion, the Confederacy would do best to entrench itself in a "Fortress Slavedom," fight off all attacks, and develop a program of self-sufficiency. But complete entrenchment was impossible, for along thousands of miles of land and sea the frontiers lay open. Defensive strategy would simply facilitate Northern application of the anaconda plan of concentric pressures from every quarter. Secretary of War James Seddon wrote in mid-1863 of the need for local defense troops, realizing the impossibility of guarding all points, a method causing weakness everywhere. As Lee perceived, the South had to take bold blows whenever opportunity offered, and to indulge at times in desperate gambles, or it, and not the North, would finally be exhausted by grinding erosion. Then too, Southern armies in moving northward, East or West, hoped to relieve pressure on the South by feeding its armies on Northern crops, enlisting Border-State pro-Confederates, and furnishing the folks at home something to cheer about.

In taking the offensive, the South made the most of three great advantages: the superior élan of its cavalry, the admirable management of its artillery, unequalled by the Union forces until late in 1863, and above all, the superior generalship of Lee and his Eastern lieutenants. Obviously, however, it compromised its supposed advantage in the use of interior lines. When Lee threw his army above the Potomac to Antietam in 1862, and to Gettysburg in 1863, it was the North which held the interior lines, or an approach to them. Lee had to invade if he were to intensify the war-weariness of many Northerners, or prompt Britain and France to intervene, but the deeper he pushed his lines the more precarious became his communications. It was increasingly doubtful, anyhow, whether the South held any real advantage in interior lines. The Northern command of sea and rivers, and the steady deterioration of Southern railroads, made transportation a far easier problem for the Union than for the Confederacy.

Another obvious difference in the situation of the two antagonists lay in the fact that the longer the war was protracted, the greater became the disparity of strength. By the spring of 1863 Union military lines were dividing Tennessee, cutting deep into Mississippi, and were being pushed north and west from New Orleans into Louisiana and Texas. The armies, with naval support, bit into the flanks of the Carolinas and Georgia, while west of the Mississippi, Arkansas was seriously threatened. At sea, the navy, month by month, tightened the blockade. The Confederacy shrank, the Union expanded. Meanwhile, the partially industrialized North, lifting its population by natural increase and immigration, importing commodities freely, and developing fresh Western areas, gained by steady strides in economic power. Not so the agricultural South; it felt every death list;

every sinking of a steamboat,[2] and every loss of a gun was usually irretrievable. This spring, herds of beeves from the southwestern plains and shipments of foreign munitions from Matamoros still crossed the Mississippi eastward, but in dwindling and uncertain driblets.

The North *might* conceivably have ended the war in the spring of 1862 when McClellan advanced upon ill-fortified Richmond, and when Halleck after Shiloh could have moved irresistibly upon Vicksburg or Chattanooga. A little later, the South could conceivably have broken the spine of Northern determination when Lee marched into Maryland to face McClellan and force the South Mountain passes, while Bragg simultaneously led his host through Kentucky to threaten Louisville. But, as Lincoln said later, the Almighty had His own purposes, and apparently one of them was that the war should not close until slavery was doomed.

[I]

Two years of fighting had taught both sides a great deal of realism. They at last comprehended that no fairly recent conflict, not even those of Louis XIV and Napoleon, had cost so much in life and treasure as this one threatened to cost. Malplaquet, Blenheim, Talavera, Austerlitz, and Waterloo had been sanguinary, but not bloodier than Shiloh, the Seven Days, Fredericksburg, Antietam, Murfreesboro, and Chancellorsville. By the morrow of Second Manassas the groans of the dying had drowned out the fifes, and the weeping of mothers the drums. Even if editors and politicians muted the fact that a peaceful adjustment before Sumter would have saved hundreds of thousands of sturdy young men, every sensible citizen understood it. Benjamin Franklin's dictum that there never was

2. One illusion, however, had a long life; the illusion that the Confederate government in the spring of 1861 could have obtained a large number of vessels, and at once shipped abroad great quantities of cotton to afford a basis for future purchases of arms and other supplies. Jefferson Davis dealt with this visionary idea, among others, in the *North American Review* of October, 1889; so, previously, did C.F. Memminger in the Charleston *News and Courier* of March 27, 1874. It was said that four million bales could have been obtained and hurried abroad. Those who propagated this idea forgot that such a movement would have required a fleet of 4,000 vessels. The actual facts were stated by G.A. Trenholm, Memminger's successor as head of the Treasury, in the same Charleston paper. What was the cotton crop of 1860-61, he asked, the only crop available?—"Up to the 28th of February, the month that gave birth to the infant government, 3,000,000 bales had been received at the seaports, and the great bulk of it had been exported to Europe, or been sold to the New England spinners. By the 1st of May, 586,000 bales more had been received and sold. England and the Continent took 3,127,000 bales; the New England spinners 654,000 bales. It will thus be seen that before the new government was fairly organized, *the entire crop was already beyond its reach!* Another crop followed, but the exportation in any quantity was an absolute impossibility. There were no vessels in the ports of the Confederacy... The only vessels that took cotton after that time were the foreign steamers that ran the blockade to procure cargoes for the owners. They came in small numbers, and one or two at a time." Trescot Papers, South Caroliniana Library, Seddon to Gov. Bonham of S.C., Richmond, June 6, 1863. Davis, Jefferson, "Lord Wolseley's Mistake," *North American Review*, Oct., 1889, Vol.149, No.4,472-482.

a good war nor a bad peace applied particularly to a civil war. As the hospital ships and boats anchored at Alexandria, Va., and Cairo, Ill., onlookers could grasp the truth of what H.G. Wells later put into a pregnant sentence—that those who win wars are the dead and wounded; the dead can't parade and the wounded usually don't wish to or cannot.[3]

The young writer Rebecca Harding, later Rebecca Harding Davis, knew old Virginia, the Deep South, New England, and the Keystone State. One gloomy autumn day in 1861 she crossed the Pennsylvania mountains to Philadelphia. The train halted at a wayside station in the hills. "Nobody was in sight but a poor, thin country girl in a faded calico gown and sunbonnet. She stood alone on the platform, waiting. A child was playing beside her. When we stopped the men took out from a freight car a rough, unplaned pine box and laid it down, baring their heads for a moment. Then the train steamed away. She sat down on the ground and put her arms around the box and leaned her head on it. The child went on playing."[4] A little later Rebecca Harding stood on the Staten Island porch of Robert Gould Shaw's mother, who held up his watch, shattered by a bullet. "It saved his life," she said. "I think he will come back to me. But if he does not—," and her eyes burned. The sorrow of Mrs. Shaw was assuaged by the fame which her son won before he died at Battery Wagner; but what of the grief of the poor mountain girl?

For each section a film of illusions had long since evaporated under the heat of actualities. The Southern dream that Europe would intervene to obtain cotton for its starving factories had faded as rapidly as the Northern dream that the South would collapse for want of arms, goods, and money. Confederate fancies of a political revolt by tax-maddened Yankees had proved as absurd as the Union fancies of a wide slave insurrection. The cardinal illusions, however, had been military in character. Countless rebels had cherished the notion that anemic Yankee counter-jumpers and mill-hands would "cave in" as soon as they faced the intrepid Southerners. Countless Federal officers had scoffed at the idea that slave-breeding braggarts, good only for drinking juleps and fighting duels, could match the tough Northerners. Where were such conceits now?

After Malvern Hill, the South ceased to fulminate about cowardly Yankee storekeepers, just as after Fredericksburg and Chancellorsville the Union recalled with a grimace the bluster of Pope and Hooker about an irresistible march to Richmond. Everybody saw that if Southern commanders outgeneralled their adversaries in Virginia, the Northern leaders showed an equally clear superiority

3. Wells, H.G., Introduction to *The Outline of History: the Story and Aim of the Outline*, New York, 1927. "There were many reasons to move a writer to attempt a world history in 1918 . . . everywhere there was mourning. . . the tale of the dead and mutilated had mounted to many millions . . . men felt they had come to a crisis in the world's affairs. . . ."
4. Davis, Rebecca Blain Harding, *Bits of Gosssip*, New York, 1904, 120.

in Tennessee and Mississippi. By 1863, few informed Confederates retained much hope that Napoleon III could seduce Lord John Russell and Palmerston into a costly American adventure; for one reason, they had read of the mighty response of the British middle classes to emancipation. By that date, even Senators Charles Sumner and Zachariah Chandler knew that the South would somehow supply itself, in part at least, by blockade-running, extemporized factories, and the invention of substitutes for everything from coffee to needles. It was also clear that the South could somehow manage to get along on far less than normal means of existence and still fight a war. Even arch-Southerner Robert Toombs realized that Lake Michigan would freeze in August about as soon as the farmers of Illinois and Iowa would turn to an alliance with slaveholders. In short, the romantic delusions that had helped beguile the two sections into mutual butchery had been replaced by hard truths.

"Neither party," Lincoln was soon to say in his second Inaugural address, "expected for the war, the magnitude, or the duration, which it has already attained. . . Each looked for an easier triumph. . ." The Rev. Mr. H.A. Tupper of Washington, Georgia, Toombs's home, used a Thanksgiving discourse in 1862 to list the early self-deceptions of his people. "Had it not been for our ignorance of the immense resources of the enemy—the men he could bring into the field, the damage he could do to us, and the vast proportions the war would assume —had it not been for our delusive hopes of dissensions among their parties; the uprising of their populace, their succumbing to national bankruptcy, of the necessity for European interference for King Cotton, and the efficiency of our 'militia of the seas' which were to penetrate into every ocean. . .would we have been so ready to plunge ourselves into the billows of blood?" Although Tupper declared it providential that they did not know the facts, his auditors must have regretted their ignorance.[5] Even the fiery Toombs, his left hand shattered by a bullet, his public career ended by his quarrel with the Davis Administration, and his hopes of victory fading, could well have felt regret.

Neither side had foreseen the greatest single result of the war in its first two years—emancipation, and the enlistment of colored troops. Yet already it was clear that the liberation of the blacks would have the profoundest effect not only upon the war, but on national life afterward. Many a Southerner on the morrow of Lincoln's proclamation looked upon his Negro hands with a new vision; for the first time he saw at his elbow not a chattel, but a man. Many a Northerner looked upon the refugee freedman with a fresh and startled glance; he saw not only a man, but a Problem. Not for a single day was the proclamation a mere piece of paper. It instantly stimulated the flow of Negroes into Union lines, many

5. Tupper, Henry Allen, "A Thanksgiving Discourse Delivered at Washington, Georgia, Thursday, September 18, 1862", Macon, Ga., 1862, 7.

of them destitute of food and proper clothing, and nearly all piteously eager for employment. Before January ended in 1863, the War Department had authorized the governor of Massachusetts to raise colored regiments; before March ended it had sent Adjutant-General Lorenzo Thomas west to organize such units among the men flocking to Union camps; before June ended, black men had fought intrepidly at Milliken's Bend and Port Hudson. Southerners might scoff at the proclamation, but they knew in their hearts that no Negro who walked down the road to freedom would ever walk back again to the hoe and the lash. And how the proclamation affected the moral standing of the combatants! It threw a dazzling burst of light upon the figure of the Union as it appealed to the wide world, and by contrast left the Confederacy in inkier darkness.

But in their new realism the two combatants took nothing for granted about ultimate victory. They knew that wars were not won until the last shot was fired, and that it required ponderables, imponderables, and luck to bring about a Yorktown or Waterloo. To estimate strength was difficult, and to measure nerve and resolution was impossible.

[II]

On muster-sheets, the Union armies by 1863 were decidedly larger than the Confederate forces. Enlisted men and officers present for duty when the year opened totalled well over half-a-million; at least 555,958. While figures are not exact, the Federal army totaled around 918,000 with about 698,000 present or accounted for. The Union numbers present for duty were about 230,000 more than the Confederates, and increasing continually. Confederate figures are less exact, but records available show by the end of 1862 at least 325,000 effectives out of a total army of 473,000, and beginning to decline steadily. Yet the margin of the North, as events showed, was actually inadequate, for its task was much the heavier. The Union had to push the offensive month-in and month-out, from countless places around the thousands of miles of perimeter, to occupy broad conquered areas in part at least, to succor and drill large numbers of liberated slaves, and to guard a long frontier and extensive lines of communication. It had to man an ever-increasing navy, primarily for blockading duty. The greater part of the Union forces was disposed in four all-important arrays: the Army of the Potomac under Joseph Hooker, the Army of the Cumberland under William S. Rosecrans, the Army of the Tennessee under Ulysses S. Grant, and the Army of the Gulf under Nathaniel P. Banks. But additional troops had to be kept active, from Cape Hatteras to Missouri, some facing Confederate units, and some guarding rivers, railroads, and towns. A single June day in 1863 brought news of rebel raids upon Elizabethtown, Ky., Triune, Tenn., Middletown, Va., and Milliken's Bend, La., each a probing thrust that had to be countered.[6]

The greatest weakness of the Northern armies lay in their lack of skillful coordination. They marched not as parts of a well-organized machine, each general assisting and supporting his fellow generals, but largely as individual entities, each general acting alone. This defect was not to be cured until early in 1864, when Lincoln appointed Grant Lieutenant-General in command of all the armies of the North, and Grant and Sherman agreed upon a plan of cooperative action.

The Union strength by land and sea was rising all too slowly toward the aggregate of about a million, which it was to reach by Appomattox. Although Lincoln's call for "300,000 more" in July, 1862, to serve three years, eventually brought in 421,465 volunteers, his simultaneous draft upon the militia for 300,000 nine-months men yielded fewer than 90,000.[7] This total of slightly more than a half-million men tardily and imperfectly replaced expirations, battle-losses, and wastage by illness. The North commenced the fighting of 1863 with many veteran regiments reduced to a pitiful remnant, and that spring the battles before Vicksburg and Port Hudson, and the grapple at Chancellorsville, tore new gaps in the ranks. "The nation needs not new regiments nor more officers," Henry Wilson told the Senate in mid-February; "it needs new recruits in the war-wasted ranks of the veteran regiments."[8] With labor scarce, wages high, and the lengthening casualty lists a deterrent to volunteering, it appeared that nothing less than conscription could supply the men required.

This was indeed a fact. The War Department had gambled on a one-year or two-year conflict; it had accepted many regiments recruited by the States for short periods; and it had failed to stop the widespread desertions. Short-term enlistments would be largely replaced by three-year enlistments, however, and some 2,036,700 enlistments out of a total of 2,778,304 were for three years. When McClellan's advance upon Richmond failed, editors like Horace Greeley demanded that the North at once follow the Confederate example in instituting a draft. Congress responded in time with the Act of March 3, 1863. But, as enroll-

6. For troop figures see R.N. Scott et al., eds., *War of the Rebellion. . . . Official Records*, Washington, 1880-1901 (hereafter cited *"O.R."*), Ser. III, II, 957; Series IV, II, 278,380; Kreidberg, Marvin A., and Henry, Merton G., *History of Military Mobilization in the United States Army, 1775–1945*, Washington, 1955, 95; from Provost Marshall General's Report, I, 102, New York *Tribune*, June 13, 1863.

7. Lerwill, Leonard W., *Personnel Replacement System in the United States Army*, Washington, 1954, 90. While the draft and manpower problem is covered in Nevins, Allan, *The War for the Union: War Becomes Revolution, 1862-1863*, 462-466, it deserves some reiterating and enlargement when looked at in the light of the spring of 1863, and the change in war attitude.

8. *Congressional Globe*, 37th Cong., 3rd Session, 976. See Nevins, *op.cit.*, 463.

ment was a slow process, the law was not applied until July, 1863, and then proved effective only in an indirect fashion:[9] that is, in the fresh stimulus it gave volunteering, not in its own immediate fruits.

Remaining effective well into 1864, this first draft law brought fewer than 36,000 men to the colors, out of a quota of nearly 195,000 "drafted for." Of these 36,000 new soldiers, some 26,000 were substitutes. Over 52,000 others paid commutation, nearly 40,000 others failed to report, over 81,000 were exempt for physical disability, and 83,500 exempt for other causes. The law broke down because some State governments deliberately impeded it; because it created a horde of professional substitutes intent upon collecting bounties and then deserting; and above all, because it was riddled by a score of loopholes. General Henry W. Halleck wrote Sherman in the fall of 1863 that its enforcement really demanded more soldiers than it supplied. "A more complicated, defective, and impractical law could scarcely have been framed."[10] Colonel James B. Fry, head of the draft's administrative bureau as Provost-Marshal General, informed one Congressman it was a splendid law for enrolling men, but worthless for recruiting and keeping them. Angry complaints arose over State quotas, over the willingness of local provost-marshals to wink at fraud, and over the glaring inequalities of the system. The commutation clause, allowing any drafted man to escape by paying $300 in cash, made the law appear a device for raising money rather than troops.

But the draft was basically intended to encourage volunteering, and in this it was a success. Fry wrote flatly that men had ceased to come forward of their own free will, and would not have proved their patriotism again "without the spur of the draft."[11] In the end, the four successive draft calls did their work. But three of them waited until 1864, and in the spring of 1863 it was the paralysis that was most evident.[12]

Meanwhile, what of Confederate strength and its augmentation?

"We shall need a million men in the spring," a Georgian had declared in 1862, asserting that nothing short of this array could save ten million Southern freemen from subjugation by twenty million Yankees.[13] But the fact was that the South could not keep even a half million in the field. The Confederate armies reached their maximum fighting strength late in 1862 and early 1863, the aggregate total of the present-for-duty army was about 473,000 at that time, thereafter declining

9. Lerwill, *op.cit.*, 91-93; War Dept. General Orders 82, pp.462, 463; the first district was in Massachusetts. Fox, William F., *Regimental Losses in the American Civil War, 1861-1865*, Albany, N.Y., 1889, 525.

10. *O.R.*, I, liii, Pt.1, 718 Oct. 1, 1863; *O.R.*, III, iv, 927.

11. Lerwill, *op.cit.*, 94-96; *O.R.*, III, iii, *passim;* for large numbers of complaints from congressmen, governors and others.

12. *O.R.*, III, iii, 1080; the militia was a minor element in both numbers and efficiency.

13. Coulter, E. Merton, *The Confederate States of America, 1861-1865*, Baton Rouge, 1950, 313.

steadily. Although insufficient data makes exact figures dubious, effectives probably never reached over 325,000, if that. Even as the Southern authorities were making every effort to strengthen Lee's army for the invasion of Pennsylvania, Robert Garlick Kean of the War Department in Richmond wrote that it "is smaller than I supposed . . . aggregate effectives say 70,000."[14] This was a close estimate, and Gettysburg proved that the total was not enough. In middle Tennessee, Bragg had 47,000 effectives at Tullahoma when Rosecrans began advancing upon him in June, 1863, with 50,000 or more troops in his forward columns and 12,575 in reserve, or about 63,000 in all.[15] On the Mississippi, Grant and his corps commanders never failed to muster forces superior to those of Joseph E. Johnston and John Pemberton, and were more expert in concentrating their troops. At Champion's Hill, for example, McPherson and McClernand brought up 29,000 men to defeat Pemberton's about-20,000, and a week later Grant closed around Vicksburg with over 45,000 against Pemberton's approximate 22,000.[16]

Some dubious partial estimates of the soldiers present-for-duty around Dec. 31, 1862, assigned about 10,000 Confederate effectives to the fumbling Theophilus H. Holmes west of the Mississippi; troops ill-trained, ill-armed, and ill-aligned; other reports give Holmes up to 50,000 spread over a vast area. The lesser Confederate armies early in 1863 included about 20,500 effective fighters under Beauregard in South Carolina, Georgia, and Florida; some 34,000 effectives under Gustavus W. Smith on the James, and in North Carolina; and E.K. Smith's little force of 7,300 effectives guarding East Tennessee. All the other so-called armies were even tinier.

By mid-war, the Confederacy had, in fact, reached the limits of its manpower. The Secretary of War, in the autumn of 1862, George Wythe Randolph, wisely pointed out that if the entire white population was estimated at five millions, an army of one one-tenth that number would constitute a larger proportion of the adult males than European nations placed in the field in war. Perhaps his figure of five millions was too small, for he did not include Kentucky, Missouri, Maryland, and the enemy-occupied parts of Virginia, which probably gave 150,000 recruits to the Confederacy; but in broad terms his statement was sound.[17] Actu-

14. Kean, Robert Garlick Hill, *Inside the Confederate Government, the Diary of Robert Garlick Hill Kean,* ed. Edward Younger, New York, 1957, 78; *O.R.,* IV, ii, 278, 380, 1073.

15. Lamers, William E., *The Edge of Glory, a Biography of General William S. Rosecrans,* New York, 1961, 275.

16. Livermore, Thomas L., *Numbers and Losses in the Civil War,* Boston, 1901, 99, 100; Pemberton, John C., Account of Vicksburg, in Pemberton Letters, New York Public Library; *O.R.,* I, xxiv, Pt.1, 273; Pt.2, 324-325; Pt.3, 452-453; Everhart, William G., *Vicksburg National Military Park, Mississippi,* Washington, 1954, passim.; E.B. Long Papers, private, Edwin Bearss to Long, Feb. 16, 1962; and other sources on Vicksburg which give conflicting figures.

17. *O.R.,* IV, ii, 132, 278, 280-81, 380. The numerical strength of the Confederate army is discussed by Joseph T. Derry (a Southern view), and A.B. Casselman (Northern rejoinder) in *Century,* Vol.22,

ally, a Consolidated Report of the Confederate Army in January, 1863, computed the aggregate muster-rolls of the twelve principal commands at 473,000, and the effectives at 325,120.[18] This represented a heroic effort quite as great as Southern resources warranted.[19] Randolph was correct in believing that additional strength could be more surely attained by careful attention to arms, diet, general equipment, and medical care than by mere numerical additions, for the armies must not be allowed to bleed agriculture and industry to the point of fatal weakness.

For one simple reason the erosion of battle affected the Southern armies much more gravely than the Northern: the problem of replacements was more difficult. Our best figures for Lee's strength on the eve of Gettysburg give his Department of Northern Virginia 88,756 men present, and 68,352 present for battle-duty. In August, after his return to Virginia soil, his army was sharply diminished, for although he had collected many stragglers, restored his slightly wounded, and obtained some reinforcements, he had not quite 72,000 men present, and only 56,372 ready for battle-duty.[20] As Lee retreated, President Davis issued a proclamation summoning absentees to return immediately to the ranks, and another calling out all men between eighteen and forty-five liable to bear arms, but the response was bitterly disappointing.[21] When Lee detached Longstreet's corps on

New Series, 1892, 954-960, following an earlier article by Casselman who had stated it would not be hard to prove that the whole number of men enrolled in the Confederate army came close to 1,500,000. Derry maintains that the total strength of the Confederate army could not have been above 800,000. But he excludes West Virginia, Kentucky, Missouri, and Maryland, which Casselman thinks must have furnished about 180,000 men to the rebs as they gave 180,000 to the Union.

Derry writes that the principal ex-Confederate historians who held high military or civil rank estimate the Confederate strength at about 700,000 men, a conclusion that he believes much nearer the mark than Casselman's estimate. Derry adds: "The Confederate armies reached their maximum strength for the field during 1862. After that year there was a steady decline in their numbers, and all the efforts of the Confederate government to fill up their depleted ranks were unavailing. Adjutant-General S. Cooper says that for the last two years of the war the active force present in the field was nearly one-half less than the returns called for.

The Richmond *Dispatch* called Randolph, Apr. 5, 1867, the best Secretary of War the Confederacy had had, but others regarded him as merely a clerk for President Davis. See Jones, J.B., *A Rebel War Clerk's Diary*, New York, 1935, Vol.I, 120.

18. This captured document, without signature or indication of origin, is in the Stanton Papers, LC; *O.R.* IV, ii, 380.

19. During the war, the Confederate armies were augmented by more than 125,000 sympathizers from sister slave states in the Union; Ropes thinks 150,000. Ropes, John Codman, *The Story of the Civil War*, New York, 1933, Chap.VII, "The Opposing Parties," 28-99.

See C.F. Adams, *Resources of North and South*, Mass. Hist. Soc., Proc. XIX, 311-356. During the war, one-eighth of a generation reached arms-bearing age. But the original body of 1,350,000 whites of arms-bearing age, 17-50, was being cut down by battle losses, conquest of several states, and other causes. And as the young men came on, the older men passed the 50-year limit.

The South, in 1861, had at least 500,000 able-bodied Negroes fit for semi-military service—cooks, teamsters, pioneers—but now, since the Emancipation Act, many had fled, others had become insubordinate, and many were in occupied areas. See also: Letter to Jefferson Davis, Oct. 20, 1862, *O.R.*, IV, ii, 132.

20. Southern Historical Society Papers, II, 16, 17 (July to Dec., 1876) based on Archives in Washington.

21. Lossing, Benson J., *Pictorial History of the Civil War*, Hartford, 1881, III, 96, 97.

September 9 to reinforce Bragg's army, the Army of Northern Virginia was reduced to 37,806 effectives, not including cavalry. Although the Union forces also had their difficulties, by the beginning of October, Meade headed about 74,000 men ready for active duty, for the volunteering that the draft inspired had restored his ranks.[22]

The exigencies of the Confederacy in Tennessee were just as great. Braxton Bragg had emerged from the battle of Murfreesboro with about 20,000 effective fighters left in his infantry, and 1500 in his artillery. Some of his regiments even before Murfreesboro contained hardly a hundred men ready for the firing-line.[23] Moreover, while Bragg could obtain but slender reinforcements, Rosecrans's decidedly stronger army was soon happy in the arrival of some 14,000 fresh troops by rail and boat through Nashville.[24] "The appearance of the fleet approaching Nashville," wrote a Northern witness, "was exceedingly imposing. The river below the city is tortuous, and the line of gunboats and steamboats, whose decks were covered with troops with arms and banners revealing its winding length, formed a pageant of wonderful grandeur. The unfriendly citizens of Nashville were forced to contrast this revelation of power and splendor with the confusion and dismay which reigned when the retreat of Johnston's army through their streets left them defenceless."[25] When Rosecrans advanced on Tullahoma in midsummer of 1863 with the force of 63,000 that we have noted, including reserves but not rear garrisons, he easily outflanked Bragg with fewer than 47,000 defenders.

In Mississippi and Eastern Louisiana, Pemberton had found not more than 25,000 scattered troops available when he took command in the autumn of 1862. Both Secretary Randolph and General Joseph E. Johnston, who was now made

22. Comte de Paris, *History of the Civil War in America*, Philadelphia, 1876, III, 751–753.

23. Seitz, Don C., *Braxton Bragg, General of the Confederacy*, Columbia, S.C., 1924, 203-205.

24. The Confederates destroyed their conscription records by official action, and some of the periodic reports of total military strength are open to question, but are the best records available as to Southern military strength. One paper which did survive from the bureau of conscription affords proof that in January, 1864, the six states of Virginia, Georgia, the Carolinas, Alabama, and Mississippi, had put 566,456 men in the field. In addition, the Confederacy had 296 regiments from other states, and 98,000 men in various irregular organizations. These facts reduce to absurdity the assertions of some Southerners after the war that they had only 600,000 men in the field. The South, as Col. T.L. Livermore shows in his standard work on numbers and losses, had 1,440,000 men of conventional age available for war. It swept into the army, with iron rigor, nearly all the useful men from this population; by an early date in 1864 the military age had been extended to run from seventeen to fifty, and before the war ended, the number of exemptions had been brought down to the low total of 87,863. Although the Union had an aggregate of 2,898,304 enlistments in the army and navy, over two-thirds of them were for three years, while the Confederacy prolonged the service of its first-year volunteers until the end of the conflict. In comparing numbers, it should be noted that the Union authorities listed all men not sick or absent in its battle strength, even if they were guarding communications or handling supplies; but the Confederates listed as "effectives" only men immediately employable on the firing line. However, they also listed aggregate present. New York *Nation*, Feb. 23, 1905 (Vol.LXXX, 149, 150); Livermore, Thomas L., *Numbers and Losses in the Civil War, op.cit.*, 2-46.

25. Van Horne, Thomas B., *History of the Army of the Cumberland*, Cincinnati, 1875, I, 290.

the chief general in the West, thought it desperately necessary to concentrate the rebel forces to save Vicksburg. Not so Jefferson Davis. The only important shift which the President would permit was a transfer, on May 9, 1863, of 3000 men from Bragg's army to the Mississippi front. The move was belated; Mississippi needed a far heavier reinforcement, and Bragg's army was already too weak. It was from Arkansas that troops ought to have been brought. Two days before the transfer was ordered, Joe Johnston had sent Davis an accurate survey of the numerical position. "We are too much outnumbered everywhere," he wrote. "Burnside may go through E. Tennessee to the Ga. Railroad. The enemy is fortified in front of Bragg, who for that reason can't attack. Mississippi is invaded by an army 50 per cent greater than ours, and our general[Pemberton]... can't comprehend that by attempting to defend all valuable points at once he exposes his troops to being beaten everywhere."[26] Davis had urged reinforcement of Confederates at Vicksburg by Holmes's force west of the Mississippi, but Holmes had refused to act, and Davis had not pushed the matter hard enough.

Outnumbered everywhere! And everywhere was a broad word, for by the spring of 1863 the Confederacy was in anguish over the power of the North to attack simultaneously at many points. Not only were there threats from the main armies, but from the Atlantic and Gulf Coasts as well, where the people of the Confederacy were just as much in fear of invasion as in Virginia and Tennessee. Beauregard wrote to D.H. Hill in mid-June: "I can hardly believe the enemy contemplate to take the offensive in N.C. when he has so much need of troops in Va. and Miss., but after all he has a singular way of operating, and then anaconda may not be entirely dead, dead!"[27] Indeed, anaconda was very much alive. In March, Union troops with gunboats to aid them were fighting at New Bern, N.C.; Banks's army and Farragut's fleet were delivering an assault upon Port Hudson; W.W. Averell's cavalry were launching a swift blow at Kelly's Ford in Virginia, (the action which cost Lee the gallant Pelham); Grant was attempting to get at Vicksburg via Steele's bayou, and the Federals struck once more against Fort McAllister south of Savannah. April saw the bombardment of Fort Sumter by the South Atlantic Blockading Squadron, the smart Union stroke at Bayou Teche, La., which almost trapped Dick Taylor, Benjamin Grierson's famous raid, one less famous by A.J. Steight, Stoneman's Federal cavalry activities in Virginia, operations around Suffolk, Va., and by the end of the month the major moves at Chancellorsville and Vicksburg. No wonder that the new Secretary of War in Richmond, James A. Seddon, was insisting just before Gettysburg on the mobili-

26. Govan, Gilbert E., and James W. Livingood, *A Different Valor, The Story of General Joseph E. Johnston, C.S.A.*, New York, 1956, 163, 196. Rowland, Dunbar, *Jefferson Davis, Constitutionalist*, Jackson, Miss., 1923, V, 387, Davis to Holmes, Vicksburg, Miss., Dec. 21, 1862. Davis had shown real concern for Vicksburg by visiting the area, and wrote Holmes: "It seems to me then unquestionably best that you should reinforce Genl. Johnston. . . ."

27. D.H. Hill Papers, Virginia State Libr., Richmond.

zation of home-guard units to repel "transient invasions," and looking desperately for more men.[28]

Conscription had worked as lamely in the Confederacy as in the North. Bragg complained that in its first seven months the draft act yielded him not a single recruit.[29] When Chief Justice Richmond Pearson of North Carolina pronounced the law unconstitutional, weary Carolina boys deserted in squads with arms, deeming themselves safe from arrest. The draft ages of eighteen to forty-five were wide enough; even too wide. But the exempted groups were at first excessive, the plan of letting conscripts purchase substitutes aroused ill-feeling, and medical examinations were often shockingly lax.[30] Worst of all, the exemption of owners or overseers of twenty or more slaves looked like a gross class distinction. It has resulted, wrote the novelist Augusta J. Evans to J.L.M. Curry, "in the creation of an anti-slavery element among our soldiers who openly complain that they are torn from their homes, and their families consigned to starvation, solely in order that they may protect the property of slaveholders. . . in quiet enjoyment of luxuriant ease."[31] She heard of one band of three hundred Alabama soldiers who had thrown down their arms, vowing never to return to the front.

Moreover, the population upon which the Southern draft could operate was not merely limited; as the Northern armies advanced, it ebbed lower and lower. In the gloom after Gettysburg the diarist Kean in the War Department pronounced the prospect of reinvigorating the wasted armies very poor. "The conscription up to 40 is about exhausted," he wrote. "Between 40 and 45 it will not yield probably over 50,000 men and will take 6 months to get them out. We are almost exhausted."[32] And for the South as for the North, desertion, upon which we shall have more to say, was an open wound through which the lifeblood of armies trickled away; it was bad enough in the spring of 1863, and, as losses and privations increased, it was certain to grow worse.[33]

28. Seddon, J.A., June 6, 1863; Trescot Papers, So. Caroliniana Library, Columbia, S.C. This ability of the North to attack at will always worried the South. First Confederate conscription act passed April 16, 1862, all whites 18-35. Second act, Sept. 27, 1862, all whites 35-45 added in service for three years. Third act, Feb. 11, 1864, extended to embrace all between 17 and 50. By this time almost all Tennessee was lost. Gov. Brown of Georgia told a visiting agent of Davis, William M. Browne, late in 1862, that he would offer no obstacle to enforcement of the national Conscription Act, but he would also give no aid. Browne to Davis, Dec. 23, 1862, Davis Papers, Duke Univ.
The Bureau of Conscription held powers so broad in enrolling male citizens and assigning them to duty anywhere that it might have acted as a priorities agency, deciding which skilled mechanics should go to factories and railroads, which skilled clerks should go into government departments, which men should be assigned to other essential labors. It never interpreted its authority so broadly, with the result that some essential services were starved of experts simply to add privates to the armies. The Secretary of War might have cured this, but he was afraid of the hot and angry resistance of army commanders.
29. Seitz, *Bragg, op.cit.*, 204.
30. Coulter, E.M., *The Confederate States, op.cit.*, 319, 392
31. Augusta Evans (novelist) to Curry, Dec. 20, 1862; J.L.M. Curry Papers, LC.
32. Coulter, E.M., *ut supra*, 316, gives this figure.
33. Kean, *Diary*, 81. Lincoln's remark that moving Union armies was like shovelling fleas could

[III]

And yet the lack of numbers was not the only major problem of the South. Manpower in excess of the needed supplies of clothing, rations, and arms was an encumbrance, not a source of strength. The devitalization of the Confederacy by the blockade, by the destruction of railroads and bridges, by the capture of mines and factories, and by sheer wear and wastage, was a process that, by the spring of 1863, produced consternation in the South. In contrast, the vitality of Northern economic life never flagged.

Union troops were so much better fed than Southern armies, especially after the first year, that a few hungry men left the Confederate ranks for the Northern units partly to get better "grub."[34] In the spring of 1863 all the principal Federal commands enjoyed fairly full, if sometimes irregular, rations of pork or beef, bread or hardtack, beans, and coffee. But primarily because of flagging transportation and secondarily because of the shortage of salt, many Southern regiments often felt lucky to obtain a little flour or cornmeal to be mixed with water for baking, and a little meat to be cooked on the end of a stick. Scurvy was rare on both sides, but it was actually reported in Lee's army in the winter of 1862-63. Beyond question, a good many Southern soldiers, as the war continued, were weakened by the lack of a well-rounded diet; in the spring they hungrily searched for greens to boil with bacon, using wild mustard and the leaves of the poke-weed. Northern horses or mules usually had a sufficiency of baled hay and sacked corn or oats; Southern horses rarely got them. In clothing, the Yankee soldier again held a clear advantage. He had overcoats, blankets, stout uniforms, and good shoes, all rarities in most Confederate camps.[35] The rebel troops would have fared

---

have been applied equally to the Southern armies. After the evacuation of Corinth in 1862, Buell's pursuing forces found that many thousands of raw levies, hurriedly brought together under the conscription law in the interior of Mississippi and Alabama and assigned to Beauregard, disbanded and scattered to their homes. The Confederate generals had never considered them really a part of their fighting strength. Cincinnati *Daily Commercial*, July 1, 1862. Spec. Corr. dated Corinth, June 12; *O.R.*, IV, ii, 619, July 9, 1863; 721, Aug. 15, 1863.

34. *O.R.*, IV, ii, 762, Aug. 10, 1863. In March, 1863, a rough-looking party of about fifty men came into the camp of the 114th New York at Alexandria, Louisiana, some in Confederate uniforms, and all with rifles or double-barrelled shotguns. They said they were draft-evaders or deserters; some had not visited their homes in two years. When hard-pressed by draft officers, a hundred men might get together to fight them, and no quarter was shown on either side. Brig.-Gen. Alfred Mouton, CSA, on June 15, ordered a battalion to hunt down the "bands of outlaws, deserters, conscripts, and stragglers" from several parishes, and exterminate them: "No prisoners are to be taken." The fifty, with grievances to avenge, came in to offer their services as scouts and spies, and some of them did good work. Elias P. Pellet, *A History of the 114th New York State Volunteers*, Norwich, N.Y., 1866, 183-186.

35. Clothing in the first year of the war was relatively easy to get, although A.C. Myers early pointed out that the resources of the Confederacy could not supply the army with the essential cloth for uniforms, blankets, stockings, and flannel, and suggested immediate importations from Europe. (To L.P. Walker, May 13, 1861, *O.R.*, IV, 1, 314.) He took steps to get Major J.B. Ferguson, alert, efficient, sent abroad as purchasing agent with Major Caleb Huse. Myers to J.P. Benjamin, Oct. 10,

badly indeed after 1862 had they not captured large supplies of shoes and blankets in Union depots, and obtained garments by stripping the Union dead on the battlefield.

And in how many other respects were the Northern soldiers better girded and guarded! A Virginia observer[36] noted that if they stayed in camp a few days they usually constructed beds off the ground, on forked sticks, something the Southerners rarely troubled to do. Perhaps the little comforts and conveniences in the Northern camps reflected their home life—but this was not the full explanation. The Yankees lifted their beds because they had better blankets, sometimes with rubber covers; they dug deeper latrines because they had abundant spades; they took greater care of their tents because they had well-woven canvas. The Union columns possessed more wagons—indeed, often too many. They were

1861, *Ibid.*, 688; Thompson, S.B., *Confederate Purchasing Operations Abroad*, Chapel Hill, N.C., 1935, 22, 25-27, 29. Conscription soon interfered with home manufacture of cloth. Myers to G.W. Randolph, May 23, 1862, *O.R.*, IV, i, 1127.

By the end of 1862, supplies of various raw materials and manufactured products were becoming difficult to obtain. An agent sent by Davis on an inspection trip in the spring of 1863 found some 3,000 women sewing busily in an Atlanta factory, using both wool and cotton cloths. Output was rising, and so long as materials could be found, the factory would run energetically. *O.R.*, I, xxiii, Pt. 2, 764-769.

The Southern textile mills of the time, laboring hard, are described in Mitchell, Broadus, *William Gregg, Factory Master of the Old South*, Chapel Hill, 1928, dealing with the Graniteville, S.C. mill. See also Fleming, W.L., "Labor and Labor Conditions in the Confederacy," in *The South in the Building of the Nation*, Richmond, 1909-13, V, 146-151; Reid, John C., "Economic Conditions in the South During the Civil War," *Ibid.*, V, 668-672; Clark, Victor S., "Manufacturing During the Ante-Bellum and War Periods," *Ibid.*, V, 324-334. But C.W. Ramsdell, "Confederate Control of Manufacturing in the Mississippi Valley," *Mississippi Valley Hist. Rev.*, VIII, Dec. 1921, 231-249, paints a darker picture.

The weekly capacity of such mills in the two States, as the Quartermasters of Augusta and Columbus, Ga., knew, amounted to about 22,000 yards of woolen and 215,000 yards of cotton goods. The Augusta Quartermaster had contracted for more than 100,000 yards of cotton shirting, and 23,000 osnaburg (wool). One factory in Columbus was furnishing 7,000 yards of jeans and 2,500 yards of duck weekly; a large quantity of raw wool was on the way from Texas. Gov. J.E. Brown to Jefferson Davis, Davis Papers, Duke Univ.

Senator C.C. Clay in the autumn of 1862 sponsored legislation for the admission of textile machinery duty-free; and—a somewhat ominous sign of the trend—an act suspending previous laws to fix the kinds and grades of army apparel, and permitting the use of such garb "as it may be practicable to obtain." *Journal of the Congress of the Confederate States of America*, Washington, 1904, II, 415; V, 459, 477, 483, 504.

Much clothing, especially shoes, blankets, and overcoats, was captured in Union depots or obtained from stripping Union dead on battlefields. See Tables of materials and equipment taken in middle quarters of 1862 in the Valley district; *O.R.*, I, xii, 723, 724. Bell Wiley in *The Life of Johnny Reb*, Indianapolis, 1943, 108-122, "From Finery to Tatters," gives a good account of the Confederate soldier's difficult experiences with shoes and clothing.

For a time in the winter of 1861-62 the Confederacy seemed to have a plethora of shoes. Several large shoe-manufacturers from the South went home from Richmond at Christmas convinced that shoes would not sell, for the market was overstocked. "The Confederate Government has six hundred cases of army shoes on hand, over and above the demand," wrote the Richmond correspondent of the Charleston *Courier* in the issue of Jan. 7, 1862, "and the Government contractors are now furnishing it with a constant supply of two hundred additional pairs per diem." Soon the South sang a different tune.

36. George W. Randolph, June 17, 1862; Misc. Letters, LC. Quartermaster-General.

uniform in size and shape, were much stronger and roomier than Confederate wagons, and were kept dry under stout canvas marked in black with the numerals of the corps, division, and brigade. Southern wagons were in great part simply picked up about the countryside, where they had been made by local smiths or carriage-makers. The eyes of a Southern farm-boy would have glistened as he saw the shining harness on many Union horses, the unworn shoes on their feet, and the heavy doubletrees and tires. They would have glistened still more had he seen the driver lifting an armful of tools out of his wagon.

Yet, in one requirement of warfare, the provision of arms, the Confederacy wrote an astonishingly proud record. When Sumter fell, the seceding States by careful count had about 143,000 serviceable muskets and rifles,[37] the best of them stored in eight arsenals from Richmond to Baton Rouge and Texas. Battle losses and wear and tear took their toll. Yet so ably did the authorities cope with the situation that by January 7, 1863, nearly 300,000 small arms, rifles, muskets, carbines, and pistols had been issued, with nearly 10,000 more on hand. By fall, despite the severe losses of arms at Vicksburg, Port Hudson, and Gettysburg, the supply was steadily increasing, with armories at Richmond, Virginia, Fayetteville and Asheville, N.C., turning out about 28,000 small arms "within the year." In addition, there were private production, imports, and battlefield pickups. Secretary of War Seddon, in his report of November 26, 1863, said: "It is gratifying to be able to report that during the past year the Ordnance and Mining Bureaux have steadily increased the production and supply of arms and munitions." Although they were obtained from a variety of sources, many of the arms had been manufactured under the direction of a remarkable leader—a West Pointer in the class of 1841 who had previously been stationed at the Watervliet, N.Y., Mount Vernon, Ala., and Charleston arsenals; a Pennsylvanian by birth, but married to a Southerner and a secessionist by conviction. His name was Josiah Gorgas. Few men served the Confederacy so well as this brisk, blackbearded, sharp-eyed executive, a veteran of the Mexican War approaching his middle forties when appointed Chief of Ordnance.[38]

For lack of money and ships, Gorgas was unable to obtain small arms from Europe until early in 1862. Yet, with the aid of machinery captured at Harper's Ferry, he quickly established armories at Richmond and Fayetteville which made

37. The North had seven really important arsenals which worked hard through the war—Watertown, near Boston, Watervliet near Troy, Bridgeburg at Philadelphia, Allegheny at Pittsburgh, and others at Washington, St. Louis, and Fort Monroe. They employed at capacity about 5,200 hands; were equipped with excellent labor-saving machinery; and distributed their work effectively. Watervliet, at the height of the war, could make 150,000 cartridges a day.DeChenal, François, *The American Army in the War of Secession,* Fort Leavenworth, 1894, 140-142. But the whole number of government arsenals, foundries, and armories in the United States rose before the end of the war to twenty-eight.

38. *O.R.,* IV, ii, 299, 955-959, 1007; for biography see Vandiver, Frank, *Ploughshares into Swords,* Austin, Tex., 1952.

rifled muskets and rifles respectively; he created in the fall of 1861 a factory at Nashville which soon turned out 3,000 pounds of powder a day; and he prodded the existing Southern arsenals—those at Augusta, Charleston, Mount Vernon, Baton Rouge—into frenzied effort.[39] Even the Virginia Military Institute turned out cartridges. By the spring of 1863 Gorgas and his resourceful lieutenant, the North Carolinian George W. Rains, were converting lead from Virginia, copper from East Tennessee, and iron from Virginia and Alabama into ammunition.[40] Heavy coast-defense guns meanwhile came from Britain, and excellent small arms were captured from the Union forces and run in through the blockade.[41] But the manufacture of small arms, cannon, and powder, maintained at a high level to the very end of the conflict, was indispensable to the cause. Throughout the war the Richmond armory, which drew the best part of its equipment from the Tredegar Iron Works, remained the principal small-arms factory.[42]

The South had more iron furnaces, rolling mills, and factories when the war began than the world realized. During the 1850s the Tredegar Works not only supplied bridge castings, locomotive axles, car wheels, and rail-chairs for many of the nation's principal railroads, but earned renown for the high quality of its

39. According to the Kean Diary, 66, May 26, 1863, the Chief of Ordnance of the Army of Northern Virginia shortly after Chancellorsville reported 26,000 small arms taken from the field and counted, with small lots still coming in; he deducted 10,600 as the Confederates' own arms, a number that some subordinates thought excessive, "since many of our men exchange on the fields."

40. Col. George W. Rains carried out this undertaking; he also launched the collection of nitre from caves; see his *History of the Confederate Powder Works*, Augusta, 1882, *passim*.

41. First and last, nearly 200,000 small arms came to the Confederacy through the blockade between September 30, 1862, and the end of 1864. Important shipments of saltpetre and lead also came, though not enough to meet the critical lead shortage. Official figures for September 30, 1862, to September 30, 1863, give 113,504 arms; November 1, 1863, to December 8, 1864, about 69,000 more arms. One and a half million pounds of lead came in during this period. See Frank E. Vandiver, "Makeshifts of Confederate Ordnance," *Journal of Southern History*, XVII, No. 2, May, 1951, 180. The War Department gave Gorgas a free hand in arranging for imports through the blockade. He bought four ships for his bureau under Seddon's orders: the *Columbia*, the *R.E. Lee*, the *Merrimac*, and the *Eugenia*, at home, and the steamer *Phantom*, running to Bermuda and Nassau. *O.R.* IV, ii, 955-959; IV, iii, 733-734.

42. Dew, Charles B., *Ironmaker to the Confederacy*, New Haven, 1966, *passim*; Bruce, Kathleen, *Virginia Iron Manufacture in the Slave Era*, New York, 1930, 281, 282. One of the ablest men serving Gorgas was Captain John Mallet, a British subject married to a Southern girl, whom Gorgas made chemist to the bureau in May, 1862, and superintendent of Confederate Ordnance Laboratories in September 1863. Mallet erected the Confederate Central Laboratories at Macon, Ga., as a permanent installation for making sulphuric and nitric acids, friction tubes, and uniform ammunition for field guns and small arms—for the troublesome variety of ammunition made uniformity a crying need. Mallet carried on experimental work, and invented several important devices, including a new shell with polygonal cavities which would burst into a planned number of fragments.

Another resourceful officer, Col. Isaac M. St. John, meanwhile made the Nitre and Mining Bureau one of the most powerful arms of the government, for it commandeered mines, caves, and slave labor. He could have borne an autocratic hand, but he was considerate and benevolent. Still another able man, the master armorer James H. Burton, who had helped erect the Enfield factory in England before the war, took charge of the expansion of facilities for making Enfields in the South. In due course, in the summer of 1863, he went to England to buy machinery in Leeds for a central armory at Macon, Georgia.

products.[43] Beside it stood other important Virginia enterprises; the Richmond Foundry had been one of the earliest American shops to build locomotives, and Talbott & Brothers, though specializing in portable steam engines and saw-mills executed a wide range of railway orders. By 1860, according to the Tredegar owners, the iron companies of Richmond represented an investment of nearly four millions,[44] and employed more than a thousand workers. As early as 1851 they had cast sixty-four cannon for South Carolina.[45] Elsewhere in Virginia—at Lynchburg, Petersburg, and Alexandria[46]—were important concerns making railway cars, farm machinery, nails, saws, and miscellaneous ironware. Thriving foundries and machine shops would also be found at various points in Tennessee, Georgia, Alabama, and other States.

These Southern establishments were hampered by the paucity of skilled mechanics, so that antebellum ironmasters had to bring them in from Pennsylvania and other well-developed areas in the North. However, slaves from Revolutionary times had proved their capacity to mold and cast cannon and other large pieces, and to perform work demanding high mechanical skill. By 1860 the best ironmasters, like the heads of tobacco factories and cotton mills, were accustomed to using slave labor.[47] The difficulty was that when the war drained off the most expert white hands, no adequate replacement was possible. As Lee moved north to Gettysburg, the government ordered that all the able-bodied white men in the Midlothian and Westmoreland coal mines be sent to the Richmond fortifications; and this brought a vehement protest from the ironmasters.

Thus one large and vital area in which the Confederacy kept fairly abreast of the Union, in fact, was in arming its troops. It did not have breechloading rifles, which one expert after the war rated as worth three times as much as muzzle-loaders; but then even the North failed to produce them in quantity before the war ended. It did not have repeating rifles, but not until 1864 did the North prove the destructive potentialities of the limited number it possessed. Nevertheless, by Gorgas's mobilization of every shop and arsenal, by the erection of new plants, by the development of niter beds, by captures, and by the blockade-running which Gorgas helped to place on an efficient basis, the South kept a sufficient body of arms and ammunition in the hands of its sons. Grant, as we have noted, thought the Confederates on the Mississippi better armed in 1862 than his own forces. Meade at Gettysburg found that Lee was nearly as well supplied as the Union host in everything except for laboriously-hauled ammunition.[48] The waste-

43. *Ibid.*, 286-294.
44. *Ibid.*, 323, quoting J.R. Anderson & Co. Catalogue.
45. *Ibid.*, 279-280.
46. *Ibid.*, 290-309
47. *Ibid.*, 231-258; very illuminating.
48. Freeman, Douglas Southall, *R.E. Lee*, New York, 1934, III, Chs. IV-IX, *passim.* notes no grave handicap. Gorgas, on March 31, 1863, changed the distribution policy of his bureau. Thereafter

ful Federal armies at every advance and retreat threw away arms and equipment that the South had to husband painfully—and its losses often enriched the rebel forces.

A steady food supply is as vital to troops as Napoleon asserted, even though one of the world's greatest armies, the Soviet forces, lived in the winters of 1942 and 1943 on unthreshed grain and horsemeat, while their draft animals ate roof-thatch. The Northern commissary, after the large harvests of 1861 and 1862, had every advantage in resources, and Commissary-General Joseph P. Taylor, a Mexican War veteran, made forceful use of them.[49] By contrast, the picture below the border was dark indeed. The fundamental difficulty lay in the paradoxical fact that, although the South was far more heavily agricultural than the North, it was far feebler in subsistence. Its tillage was concentrated on staples that filled no mouths. Crippled transportation and shortages of salt complicated the Southern problem. But men like to find a personal scapegoat, and Southern commanders concentrated their irritation on the unpopular Commissary-General Lucius B. Northrop.[50]

It is clear that Northrop, a headstrong, quarrelsome West Pointer from South Carolina who enjoyed a favored position with President Davis which many found

---

requisitions for ammunition and stores should be addressed to the arsenals and depots nearest the armies in the field. Alabama troops would draw arms and munitions from the arsenals in Selma and Montgomery; Mississippi and West Tennessee troops with those west of the Mississippi from Jackson, Miss.; North Georgia, North Alabama, and East Tennessee from the Atlantic arsenal.

49. *O.R.*, III, ii, 738-739.

50. Many Southerners, poor fellows, had always been ill-fed. In that generally dubious book, *Among the Pines*, New York, 1862, Edmund Kirke (J.R. Gilmore) relates how, in the Waccamaw Valley in South Carolina, he stayed overnight with poor whites in an unfloored log-cabin. A Negro told him not many such people lived thereabouts, but in the up-country plenty of them were "pore and no-account," for "none ob dem kin read, and dey all eat clay"; they began eating clay as toddlers, and continued into old age. (p.82); *O.R.*, IV, ii, 1007-1009.

The report of the Confederate Secretary of War covering the year 1863 confessed that "the Quarter-master and Commissary Generals, in the administration of their respective departments, have had, during the past year, extraordinary difficulties and embarrassments to encounter." Seddon added: "nothing has given so much trouble as the purchase and transportation of sufficient forage and subsistence for the army." These armies had been kept "moderately supplied," but he was not sure of the future.—For this, he felt "grave anxiety." "The consumption of all animal life in the war has been very great, and in addition, during the past few months, destructive and widespread disease has prevailed among the swine, which constitutes the most serviceable as well as the largest resource for meat. Bacon and beef, in view of the needs of both the army and the people, must be scarce during the coming year." New York *Tribune*, April 27, 1864, offers comment.

Lack of forage was felt by growers as well as by army commanders. A Mississippi planter wrote Gov. John J. Pettus from Irindian, Sept. 29, 1862, that he understood from government agents that "there are hundreds of cattle that have been refused by the inspectors on account of their being too poor to eat"; the agents say they will die this winter; he suggests the Confederate Government sell these cattle to farmers. Pettus Papers, Miss. State Archives.

Twelve officers of the Fourth Mississippi State Volunteers sent Gov. Pettus a petition from Camp West, Panola County, Sept. 18, 1862, that "in view of the increasing prevalence of intermittent fever and other malarious diseases in this encampment, and the approach of the harvest season," they be allowed to go home to get the crops in until "the frosts of autumn" had made the country healthy. Pettus Papers, Miss. State Archives.

quite incomprehensible, had grave faults of aggressiveness and tactlessness. Beauregard hated him, asserting that his troops had been unable to take the field in the summer of 1862 for want of decent food to prevent an outbreak of scurvy. Both Lee and Johnston pronounced him inefficient.[51] Davis was right, however, in saying that he was a man of integrity and sense; and only a miracle-worker could have surmounted his endless impediments. At the outset, he appointed commissary agents in the various States, who soon found that they had to impress supplies because of currency inflation, the steady rise of prices, the activities of speculators, and the reluctance of growers to sell their crops at what seemed low rates. At first, these military seizures were unsystematic. Later, in March, 1863, Congress passed an Impressment Act regulating them and providing a system of price-fixing. Many and loud were the complaints against the arbitrary seizures by government agents; against the taking of corn at a dollar a bushel when the market price was $3; against the impounding of flour at $45 a barrel when it sold for twice that sum; and against the low appraisal of bacon and beef. While farmers and planters declared they were being robbed, army commanders made the air resonant with protests over the lack of rations. Thus, the spring of 1863 found Northrop almost in despair.

The Impressment Act was based on the assumption that the South had an abundance of meat and grain for both the army and people, an assumption that proved untenable. As it stipulated that the people must have a full supply for the year, the troops were the principal sufferers from the shortages. The Cotton Kingdom had never produced its own bread or pork or beef. In large degree it had purchased them from the Border and Northern States; according to Northrop's estimates, early in 1861, bacon representing 1,200,000 hogs had been brought into the seceded States.[52] An increasing deficiency became certain when the North closed its gates, and it was aggravated by the Union occupation of meat-producing areas in Tennessee and Mississippi. The pinch was severely felt by the middle of 1863. Selfishness was flagrantly displayed by growers and consumers alike.[53] "The citizens individually, and in corporations," wrote Northrop, "are eager to secure an abundant supply—and more eager to convert depreciated currency into appreciating commodities—while holders and producers are in a natural league with buyers, to sell to them all surplus at unlimited prices, rather than to the agents of the government powerless to give more than the prices fixed by the state commissaries." Moreover, the agents were restricted, under War

51. Eaton, Clement, *A History of the Southern Confederacy*, New York, 1954, 140.

52. L.B. Northrop, Richmond, Dec. 7, 1863, to General Samuel Cooper, ms., New York Public Library.

53. For a lucid account of the abuses rife in impressment in 1863-64, see the report of Asst. Inspector-General George B. Hodges to Jefferson Davis, July 14, 1864, upon the "wrong and injustice in the seizure of horses and crops" in Eastern Louisiana and Southern Mississippi. *O.R.* I, iii, Pt.2, 695-700.

Department regulations, to that part of the surplus not in transit to markets, or sold to consumers.[54]

"The officers in charge of collecting supplies in all the States this side of the Mississippi," added Northrop, "unite in describing these obstacles as insupera-ble." Virginia, Georgia, South Carolina, and Florida had hardly enough meat to supply the civilian population, much less afford an excess for troops. Government agents were helpless to enter the open market because of the price limitation fixed by Congress. The generals could impress stores under the plea of military necessity, if only they chose their commissary officers from Northrop's personnel[55]—for some centralization of control was necessary; and Northrop wondered why grumblers like Beauregard did not do this, and cease their complaints.[56]

At times, unquestionably, numerous Confederate commands were gaunt and half-starved. A veteran of Lee's army reported that famine and abundance alternated, that two days of tramping and fighting without rations was not uncommon, and that one artillery battalion had no issue of food for an entire week of marching, so that it lived on the corn for the horses. Circumstances, however, rather than the crotchety Northrop, were responsible for the deficiencies.[57] The Northern conquest of the very districts of Kentucky, Tennessee, and Mississippi richest in corn and pork, the spoiling of ill-salted meat on the railway cars moving at snail's speed, and the competition of women, children, and plantation Negroes with the soldiers for food, made the problem frustrating. Lieut.-Col. Frank G. Ruffin of the Bureau of Subsistence declared in the fall of 1862 that the Confeder-

54. Lucius Northrop, to Gen. Samuel Cooper, Richmond, Va., Dec. 7, 1863, NYPL; *O.R.* IV, ii, 968-972. To obtain meat, flour, and other needed foodstuffs held by Northern speculators and whole-salers, Confederate officials resorted to a barter of cotton for supplies. An efficient if uneven system of smuggling between the lines had sprung up. By 1863, a special office or bureau at Shreveport, La., dealt exclusively in this exchange; illegal, of course, but so advantageous to both parties that the authorities winked at it. A bale of cotton floated on the Mississippi into Memphis or New Orleans could readily be traded for a bag of salt or a box of well-cured bacon.

55. Braxton Bragg, Hdq. Confed. States, Richmond, to Jefferson Davis, March 29, 1864; New York Public Library.

56. Governor Brown of Georgia, authorized by his legislature to employ summary means to prevent extortion, had his agents seize, on December 4, 1862, all cotton and woolen goods and all shoes except those made for the Confederate Government, paying holders what he thought a fair compensation. An angry chorus of wails smote the Georgia skies. President Davis had just asked William M. Browne to go down to look into the situation. Leaving Richmond November 30, Browne reached Milledgeville December 5, at once calling on the Governor, and talking with manufacturers and other businessmen. His verdict was emphatic. The power of impressment as exercised by the Governor, he wrote President Davis, was anything but satisfactory. "Many owners of cotton and woolen mills told me that if he persisted in his seizures, they would abandon their mills rather than trust to his caprice in fixing the prices of their goods. But had a fair scale of prices been established, I believe that the industrial energies of the State would have received an impetus instead of the check Governor Brown's action has given. . ." W.M. Browne, to Jefferson Davis, Dec. 23, 1862, Davis Papers, Duke Univ.

57. Johnston, Joseph E., *Narrative of Military Operations,* New York, 1874, 67-144, and *passim;* Roman, Alfred, *The Military Operations of General Beauregard,* New York, 1884, I, 73, 120, 128.

acy was "completely exhausted of supplies,"[58] an exaggeration, but a natural impression. The summer of 1863 found the food shortage acute for all the main armies, and growing worse.[59]

Almost equally serious for the South, since the effectiveness of a command depends upon its mobility, was the faltering supply of horses and mules. Again we meet the familiar difficulties. The loss of border territory deprived the Confederacy of its best sources of supply, the deterioration of the railroads impeded the flow from distant points, and Cotton Kingdom staples included as little hay as grain. It was necessary for the War Department in the spring of 1863 to order horses taken from the supply-wagons to keep the artillery equipped.[60] While Confederate officers and cavalrymen usually furnished their own mounts in the first part of the war, Secretary Seddon saw this year that future replacements would have to come from the government.[61]

The Army of Tennessee was in one of the better horse-growing areas. But when President Davis's aide, Col. W.P. Johnston, inspected it at Tullahoma in the spring of 1863, he found its transportation in poor condition. The mules and horses, he wrote, were suffering from want of long forage, which could not be obtained, and artillery horses were in equally distressing condition for the same reason. In Virginia the situation was still sadder. "Where," Colonel John R. Chambliss of Lee's cavalry asked A.R. Boteller just after Gettysburg, "am I to get another horse, and how can I buy one at present prices after I have lost so many without compensation from the government?"[62] General W. N. Pendle-

58. Eaton, *Confederacy, op.cit.*, 140.

59. Although huge supplies of corn were to be had in Georgia and Alabama, want of transportation immobilized it; so W.M. Browne reported to President Davis as 1862 closed. The Gulf & Albany Railroad from Savannah to Thomasville, Georgia, for example, had hauled no corn whatever; it did not have the necessary cars. It was difficult to accumulate and store large stocks of corn for want of sacks; difficult to find teams to haul corn to the railway. Then, also, some men were obstructive. "I regret to state that the planters in Southwest Georgia, infected with the same greed of gain which has pervaded all other classes, evince an unwillingness to sell their corn at present prices." W.M. Browne to Davis, Richmond, Dec. 23, 1862, Jefferson Davis Papers, Duke Univ.

60. *G.O.* 60, *A. & I.G.O.*, May 13, 1863.

61. *O.R.*, IV, ii, 552; see Annual Report, Nov. 26, 1863, *O.R.*, IV, ii, 1002-1003. Secretary Seddon, who felt it his duty in his annual reports to put as favorable a face on Confederate affairs as possible, had to confess late in 1863 that the difficulties in buying and transporting forage had become— particularly for Lee's forces—appalling. The enlistment of able-bodied farmers, the ravages of the enemy, and the unfavorable crop season had depressed production to wretched levels, and the greed of many holders and speculators had intensified the shortages. "The scarcity, too, was greatest in one or two of the States nearest to our large armies, and the necessity for months of sustaining almost entirely the armies of northern Virginia from supplies of corn drawn from North Carolina and Georgia, will strikingly illustrate both the dearth and the difficulty of supplying it." *Annual Report*, Nov. 26, 1863; *O.R.*, IV, ii, 990-1018.

62. Charles W. Ramsdell's article in the *American Historical Review*, Vol.XXXV, 1929-30, 758-777, "General Robert E. Lee's Horse Supply, 1862-1865," is indispensable. At first the Confederate cavalry was superior—Ashby, Forrest, Stuart; the North had heavier plodding horses. But a dramatic change took place by the middle of 1863. The Northern horses—rather Western horses, lithe, fast, sturdy— now surpassed the Southern; in the South horses were overworked by hard riding and pulling, with forage scarce.

ton, Lee's artillery chief, found on visiting the remount depot at Lynchburg that more than a fifth of the three thousand horses there had been lost by disease and poor feeding, forage again being scarce. In 1864 the rebel war clerk who kept such an enlightening diary, J.B. Jones, recorded that the cause was in danger of defeat for want of horses and mules, and this shortage, like all others, worsened. The Union met occasional difficulties and complained of high prices, but with effort it could find a plentiful stock of sound animals.[63]

[IV]

The point of perhaps the greatest and most rapidly growing disparity between Northern and Southern strength, however, lay elsewhere: in the railroads. Vital both to economic life and military activity, the iron highways steadily contracted and broke down in the Confederacy, while they expanded, grew better equipped, and adopted better operating methods in the Union. Some 4,000 miles of new track were laid in the North during the war years. This included a trunk line of capital importance, the Atlantic & Great Western, connecting the Erie with Cleveland, central Ohio, and (by the Ohio & Mississippi) St. Louis, and tapping the Oil Regions. During 1863, this road, carrying nearly 220,000 passengers and 470,000 tons of freight, including well over half-a-million barrels of petroleum, made no small contribution to the Northern war-boom.

As for the betterment of operating methods, it was many-sided. The war witnessed an uneven but healthy substitution of coal for wood as locomotive fuel; the laying of heavier rails for larger and faster trains; the purchase of stronger cars and engines; and a widespread shift toward the standard gauge of 4 feet 8½ inches —the New York Central, for one, adopting it. Steel rails began to come in from abroad. Armored cars appeared; hospital cars, for which the Sanitary Commission drew up plans, better mail cars, baggage cars, and sleeping cars. Business arrangements became more efficient, and government demands enforced a novel cooperation among different lines. In 1863, representatives of nearly a score of railroads,

---

Everywhere in the South, by the summer of 1863, the Confederacy was robbing Peter to pay Paul; everywhere it was searching for workable substitutes. The army needed more manpower; very well, it was taken from the ordnance works, railroads, and textile factories that could not afford to give it. The country was running short of woolen cloth; it turned to cotton cloth soaked in alum or sulphate of ammonia, and then coated with a mixture of hot beeswax and tallow. Shoes were being made with leather soles and cloth uppers. Even paper was growing so scarce that people thought twice before writing a letter. Southern courage and determination, however, never flagged.

Replacements were poor. Some field artillery had to be dropped by Lee's army in 1864 because— says Ramsdell—horses could not be found to pull it. The artillery horses were bony skeletons. The Medical Corps had to get along with fewer ambulances, the army with fewer wagons. The remount service worried itself sick. *O.R.*, I, xxiii, Pt.2, 759.

63. *O.R.*, I, xxiii, Pt.2, 1188-1189; Feb. 18, 1864; see Ramsdell, "General Robert E. Lee's Horse Supply, 1862-1865," *op.cit.*, 758, 759; Jones, John B., *A Rebel War Clerk's Diary*, ed. by Earl S. Miers, New York, 1958, 418, Sept. 13, 1864.

led by officers of the New York Central and Erie, decided that the east-west lines should establish union ticket offices in Boston and New York. The North possessed not only a strong network of railroads, but a technological and managerial capacity for making the most of it.

Alas the South! Hard as men, weapons, ammunition, and foodstuffs were to get, they could be found more readily than they could be moved to the point of need. To talk of expanding or improving the railways was absurd; they could not even be maintained.[64] The railroads of the South were cursed by too many gauges; too little fresh equipment; lack of repair facilities; excessive corporation selfishness and other weaknesses—all compounded by the want of any thoughtful, coherent system for their utilization. The so-called director of railroad transportation was pretty much a nullity. Hence the South limped along in a shortsighted, hand-to-mouth fashion, when intelligent direction would have hammered out a priorities plan under which the most essential lines would have been given a preference in rails, locomotives, and skilled mechanics; so that better roundhouses and repair shops would have been manned and stocked. The Secretaries of War, unfortunately, knew all too little about railroads, which were a novelty in some parts of the South. The North did far better. Not only did it have far more miles of track, far better repair facilities, a steady supply of new rails and locomotives; it did have a *plan.* It controlled the railways, it possessed far more efficiency, and it laid down new trackage with vigor and dispatch. President P. V. Daniel of the Richmond, Fredericksburg & Potomac, who knew as much about the situation as anybody, estimated in the spring of 1863 that to sustain the 6,300 miles of railroad then in use, at least 4,125 tons of rails ought to be obtained each month—or 49,500 tons a year. Yet the only available rolling mills, those at Richmond and Atlanta, could not provide more than 20,000 tons a year even if devoted solely to this end. Well might Daniel ask Secretary Seddon, "Where are the rails to come from?"[65] In point of fact, a few rails were rolled in Atlanta in 1861, and after that not a single rail was produced in the whole Confederacy during the war.[66] Nor was any substantial importation through the blockade feasible.

Yet, of the 6,300 miles of railroad mentioned by Daniel, about 5,500 miles were in military use, they were of the highest value to the Confederacy. How could they be kept part of the war apparatus? In just one way: the most vital lines were preserved by borrowing rails from the lesser roads—whenever they could.

Lee repeatedly voiced his anxiety over the deterioration of the system. "Our

64. The whole dreary picture of Confederate railroads may be obtained from Black, R.C., *The Railroads of the Confederacy,* Chapel Hill, 1952. For Northern railroads, see Weber, Thomas, *The Northern Railroads in the Civil War, 1861-1865,* New York, 1952.

65. *O.R.,* IV, ii, 512; Daniel to Seddon, April 23, 1863.

66. Report, Col. Frederick W. Sims to Brig-Gen. A.R. Lawton, April 1, 1864, *O.R.,* IV, iii, 227, for general conditions. For lack of rails see Black, R.C., *The Railroads of the Confederacy, op.cit.,* 124.

railroads are our principal lines of communication," he warned Seddon in the spring of 1863, "necessary for the transportation of munitions of war, and to the maintenance of our defensive lines and works. . . . We cannot retain our position unless the railroads can afford sufficient transportation, which they cannot do in their condition."[67] Other officers noted with anguish how often the soldiers abused rolling stock, and how little protection some careless commanders gave to railway lines. They would abandon strips for which they should have fought to the last. Union forces, for example, were allowed to capture a segment of the Memphis & Charleston. In the spring of 1863, the Confederate authorities moved 3,000 men of Bragg's army, as we have seen, to Jackson, Miss., Joseph E. Johnston leaving Chattanooga for the same destination. Because the direct line was closed, the force and general had to make a long circuit by way of Atlanta, Montgomery, Mobile, and Meridian to reach the capital of Mississippi; and the service was so poor that the trip took more than three weeks, or almost as long as the passage of the wagon-train by road. In other instances, however, movements were carried out which surpassed even the Federal movement from Virginia to Tennessee. These were the transfer of Bragg to Chattanooga after the pull-out from Corinth in 1862, and equally remarkable the movement of Longstreet's men from Virginia to Chickamauga in the fall of 1863. Considering the difficulties involved, these were uniquely expeditious movements.[68]

Mistakes both of government and railway management added to the difficulties. For a time Richmond ordered rolling stock from line to line, keeping it in constant movement, and wearing it out. At least fifty locomotives in the Confederacy, by the fall of 1863, were worthless for lack of tires.[69] The managers early in the war, fearing bankruptcy, retrenched expenses by encouraging their employes to enlist, and reducing their workshops to minimum strength. Then came the conscription law, cutting further into manpower; and some generals, including even Lee, kept skilled mechanics in their armies who would have been better employed in repair work. Friction between army men and railroad presidents or superintendents was all too common, for the only law making the railway heads amenable to military authorities was so full of loopholes as to be almost inoperable.[70] When a cordial cooperation was achieved it sometimes worked wonders. It was largely because of the zeal and energy of managers that Bragg was able to win his victory at Chickamauga, and for weeks thereafter the head of the railroad bureau in Richmond, Frederick W. Sims, lauded the patriotism

67. *O.R.*, I, xxv, Pt.2, 704, April 4, 1863.

68. For detailed summary see Black, *op.cit.*, passim; and Coulter, E.M., *The Confederate States of America, 1861-1865*, Baton Rouge, 1950, Chap.XIII, "Transportation and Communication," 169-184, for details.

69. *O.R.*, IV, ii, 882, F.W. Sims to Quartermaster General A.R. Lawton, Oct. 23, 1863.

70. F.W. Sims to A.R. Lawton, Feb. 10, 1865, So. Hist. Soc. Papers, II, July to December, 1876, 121.

of the lines.[71] But such cooperation was seldom achieved.

Month by month, Southern trains became slower, sound locomotives fewer, good mechanics rarer, and breakdowns and wrecks more numerous. Some thought that one reason why the Confederacy lost the powerful ironclad *Mississippi*, which it was hurriedly building for the defense of New Orleans, was that, although the Richmond and Atlanta ironworks toiled overtime to finish plates and machinery, trains carried them west so slowly that the city surrendered a few days before they approached it. In February, 1863, an officer was trying to take three regiments to Savannah. "Three hours after the arrival of the 25th Georgia at the depot at Wilmington," he reported, "the train upon which it was placed attempted to leave, but in consequence of the weakness of the engine could not proceed." The English officer Arthur James Lyon Fremantle, crossing the Confederacy from Texas to Virginia this spring, met one delay after another.[72] The eighty-mile run from Montgomery to Columbus, Ga., now occupied a whole day. By the spring of 1864, the fastest train on the vital 170-mile line from Wilmington to Richmond travelled at an average speed of ten and a quarter miles an hour.[73] Meanwhile, the Union cavalry, as the war continued, slashed at every line within reach.

The capable Colonel Sims, armed by Congress with belated and inadequate powers over the railroads, pressed what few constructive measures he could devise.[74] He cancelled passenger trains; he tried to give government freight precedence over private freight, which was often speculators' goods; he borrowed rails from Peter to pay Paul; and he did what he could to compose such quarrels as that between General Bragg, who threatened to seize the Western & Atlantic in the spring of 1863 for failing to bring certain guns from Atlanta, and Governor Joseph E. Brown, who responded that Georgia troops would halt such an unwarranted aggression. Sims also pushed the construction of lines to fill two glaring gaps in the Confederate system: the Piedmont Railroad to link Danville, Va., with Greensboro, N.C., and the line connecting Selma, Ala., with Meridian, Miss. The Piedmont line was finished across forty miles of rough country in time (May, 1864) to give invaluable aid to Lee in the last months of the war. But the Selma line, which might have been highly useful, was never completed across the Tombigbee, where a bridge was left unbuilt.[75]

Looking at the railroads, Secretary of War Seddon hopefully declared in the autumn of 1863, "The lowest point of depression has probably been passed"—but

71. Black, *op.cit.*, 192.
72. *Ibid.*, 193.
73. *Ibid.*, 217, 333.
74. Weber, Thomas, *The Northern Railroads in the Civil War, 1861-1865*, New York, 1962, 104, 105, 127, 128, 130, 131.
75. Black, *op.cit.*, 149-153; 227-230.

he was quite mistaken.[76] The odds against the indomitable Sims continued to lengthen. Meanwhile, in the North, the more and more efficient railways, enjoying an unprecedented prosperity, expanded as need arose, and served the government without friction or hesitation. In the year of Donelson and Shiloh the Illinois Central had net earnings of $1,830,000 of which almost a fourth came from troop transportation.[77] Such a line could well afford to improve its services. The rare organizational talents of Daniel C. McCallum, Herman Haupt, and Lewis B. Parsons in running government railroads and in moving troops over the entire northern railroad system had a scope which the equal talents of Sims could not command. McCallum directed military railroads from February, 1862, until September, 1864, while Haupt was chief of construction and transportation, making a splendid record in a little over a year of military service. Parsons, after managing rail and river transport in the West for much of the war, took over the national job in August, 1864. These men, and others, accomplished many astonishing feats.[78] The North commanded the seas; to a greater and greater extent it commanded the rivers; but it was command of a vigorous and energetically-managed network of railways which gave it crowning advantage over the South.[79]

On the seas and rivers, the North had a formidable advantage from the start, but soon assumed overwhelming naval supremacy. From forty-two vessels in service in March, 1861, out of a total of ninety ships, the Federal fleet had increased to 427 vessels by the end of 1862 through purchase and new construction. As Secretary of the Navy Gideon Welles stated, "The annals of the world do not show so great an increase in so brief a period to the naval power of any country."[80]

Whereas, for the Confederacy, the naval situation had been radically different from the start. It had no navy whatsoever to begin with, not even a weak one, while the North had but the nucleus of a fighting fleet. As in so many other cases of wartime necessity, however, the North had superior materiel, manpower, and industrial skills. The Southern sea forces were never any match for the Union Navy in numbers or guns, and did not really expect to be. The few ships of the Confederate Navy were of necessity scattered about, and by 1863 not many useful ports remained open to them. By November, 1863, the Confederate Navy num-

76. *O.R.*, IV, ii, 1013.
77. Weber, Thomas, *op.cit.*, 88.
78. *Ibid.*, 99.
79. *O.R.*, III, iii, 795-796; III, iv, 957; III, v, 941-942, 974-1005; I, iii, Pt.i, 459-466; Weber, *Northern Railroads, op.cit.*, 117, 164, 178, 191, 195, 199, 200, 201; Nevins, *War for the Union: War Becomes Revolution, 1862-1863*, New York, 1960, 458-462; Haupt, Herman, *Reminiscences*, Milwaukee, 1901, 189-190; Perkins, Jacob R., *Trails, Rails and War: the Life of General G.M. Dodge*, Indianapolis, 1929, 92; Grant, Ulysses S., *"Chattanooga,"* *Battles and Leaders*, New York, 1887, III, 692-693; Grant, U.S., *Personal Memoirs*, New York, 1885, II, 46-48, 398-399; Wilson, James Harrison, *The Life of John A. Rawlins*, New York, 1916, 390.
80. *Congressional Globe*, 37th Cong., 3rd Sess., Pt.2, Appendix, Report of Secretary of the Navy, Dec. 1, 1862, 11-21.

bered only twenty-nine vessels of all classes, of which ten were considered iron-clads. Navy personnel numbered 2,943 officers and men. Most of the ships were small, with few and light guns. A goodly number of supposedly powerful vessels were building, but most of them awaited machinery, armor, or guns. Efforts to purchase or build ships of war abroad were being frustrated, except for the unarmored cruisers obtained in Britain. A few other vessels and men were employed on the rivers by the Army and by the States.[81]

Commerce raiders such as the *Alabama, Florida,* and *Georgia* had perturbed Northern shipping to an extent out of proportion to the actual threat of these vessels, although by striking fear into Yankee commanders they had been a nuisance of some propagandist value. Occasionally the Confederate Navy carried out sorties from their few ports. The James River Squadron, aided by shore batteries, became of protective value at Richmond. Forced to experiment in an effort to make up their numerical deficiencies, they had been quite successful considering the difficulties in development of torpedoes, mines, and submersibles. But the time had gone, if it had ever really existed, for the Southern Navy to offer a challenge on ocean or river.

Navy Secretary Stephen R. Mallory had estimated in March, 1862, that his navy needed fifty light-draft, armored steam propellers, four ironclad ten-gun frigates, and ten "clipper propellers." In addition, marine engines, ironplate, iron bar, ordnance, powder, and seamen were needed to supply and man this dream fleet.[82]

Such a mythical fleet might have made a difference, and very well could have wrecked the primary naval weapon of the Union, the blockade. As it was, by 1863, the blockade was strengthening rapidly, and while runners still broke through, they were growing fewer in number almost monthly. The best available figures, which may be open to question, show that one out of ten blockade runners was taken in 1861, one out of eight in 1862, and one out of four in 1863.[83] Secretary of State Judah Benjamin wrote in December, 1862, that "The almost total cessation of external commerce for the last two years has produced the complete exhaustion of the supply of all articles of foreign growth and manufacture. . ." Benjamin claimed that it was not so much the blockade itself, but the cruising of Federal vessels on the coast, operating against commerce, that was causing most of the shortage.[84]

81. *O.R.N.,* II, ii, 528-538, Mallory's report, Nov. 30, 1863.
82. *O.R.N.,* II, i, 796, Mallory to Davis, March 4, 1862.
83. Owsley, Frank Lawrence, *King Cotton Diplomacy,* 2nd ed., Chicago, 1959, 261. Owsley's famous figures are based on as sound research as possible, but actual figures and size of cargoes brought in remain in doubt. Owsley used them to disprove the effectiveness of the blockade, while other historians believe that his figures can be used to prove the opposite.
84. *O.R.N.,* II, iii, 620, 625, Benjamin to J.M. Mason, Dec. 11, 1862.

While the ocean-going Federal fleet was mainly occupied in the often dreary blockade duty, in staging occasional combined operations with the Army against coastal points, and in tracking down wary cruisers, the river boats were meanwhile contributing mightily to the Northern invasion of Confederate territory in the West. Not only were the gunboats and their officers and men cooperating effectively in the main with the army, and serving Grant at Vicksburg as well, but river-freight traffic shared with the railroads the task of supplying such advanced bases as Memphis and Nashville.

Admiral Farragut had proved that seagoing vessels could be used in at least the deeper channels of the Mississippi, while the experimental Northern ironclad riverboats and rams in time introduced a larger aspect to the river war.

[V]

Increasingly terrible was the picture of devastation and ruin over broad reaches of the South. The farmers of Pocahontas County in Virginia petitioned Governor Letcher in the summer of 1863 for special consideration, declaring that the destruction of property by both armies had left but little land under fence; that enlistments, disease, and removal had taken all but a few of the men needed to gather the scanty crops; and that if any new levy were made on the destitute families, they would be left "in a hopeless condition for sustenance."[85] Many a community from the James to the Sabine now faced actual beggary, for whenever the armies fought, the civil population suffered pillage and wanton destruction. Under John Pope in Virginia, who had issued the first orders sanctioning looting and outrage, Sherman in Mississippi, and James Montgomery on the South Atlantic coast, Union behavior came closest to the example of Tilly in Germany, and Bonaparte in Spain. Some of these excesses can be laid to the fact that the soldiers-in-blue were the invaders, all too ready to forage liberally on the country. Outrageous plundering also marked the activities of Western or border guerrillas of Confederate attachment.

James Montgomery of the Second South Carolina, a ruthless religious fanatic heading a Negro regiment, was responsible for the burning of Darien, Ga. He had a liking for what Robert Gould Shaw called a "barbarous sort of warfare." Steaming up the Altamaha River, he threw shells among plantation buildings without regard for women and children. When he reached Darien he ordered all movable property to be put aboard the boats, and having thus dismantled the place, said to Shaw with a smile, "I shall burn this town." Of the pretty settlement not a plank remained standing. Firing the last buildings with his own hands, Montgomery explained that the Southerners must be made to feel the wrath of

85. John Letcher Papers, Virginia State Library, Richmond; date conjectural.

God for their misdeeds; but he also indulged what Thomas Wentworth Higginson called a "western" taste for seizures of private property.[86] Easterners, however, could be just as harsh.[87] The burning of Jacksonville, Florida, a favorite resort for Northern invalids, with the pillage of houses and shops, was charged by the Sixth Connecticut upon the Eighth Maine, and by the Maine boys upon their Connecticut comrades.[88]

Many Northern soldiers by 1863 made no distinction between the confiscation of property by disciplined commands for war purposes, and random plunder for individual profit.[89] General N.P. Banks, hearing a private say in Virginia, "The protection of secesh [secessionists] property has been played out," concluded that this attitude toward the interpretation of Pope's order was so widely accepted that the troops needed sharp admonition.[90] General John M. Palmer was equally shocked by the wanton ravaging of Tennessee. The Union forces there should have encouraged agricultural production by fair prices and protective measures; instead, they burned fences and barns, seized horses, and killed livestock without compensation. "It is a wonder that we maintain an army at all," he wrote, "and we shall probably be driven out of the South by starvation." In Nashville he was appalled by the moral degradation which attended penury.

"The war has undermined and demoralized the whole foundation of society in Tennessee," he wrote his wife. "Two years ago everything was prosperous; almost every family had the comforts and many the luxuries of life. Now many families are deprived of both, and at the same time of the care of husbands and fathers absent in the rebel army without any prospect of a speedy return. The natural consequence of this state of things is that many families have no choice but between want and shame, and between the surrender of indulgences to which they have been accustomed and crime. Pride is a hard taskmaster, and I need not describe the consequences. Many officers and men are spending their all in supporting *persons* of this description."[91]

It was primarily Western troops who devastated large parts of Tennessee, Mississippi, and the so-called garden of Louisiana. A special report compiled from sworn testimony under the direction of Governor Henry W. Allen of Louisiana described how this region, rich in cotton plantations, small farms, herds of cattle, and fields of cane, with costly sugar-refining machinery, was laid waste in 1863 through purely wanton destruction. N.P. Banks's army, despite his opposition,

86. Higginson, Thomas Wentworth, *Army Life in a Black Regiment,* Boston, 1870, 114.
87. Robert Gould Shaw, St. Simon's Island, Ga., June 9, 1863, Robert Gould Shaw Papers, Mrs. Pierre Jay.
88. New York *Herald,* April 8, 1863.
89. Redfield, H.V., "Union and Confederate Equipment," Philadelphia *Weekly Times,* Feb. 16, 1888.
90. Francis Lieber Papers, HEH, Nov. 23, 1862.
91. John M. Palmer Papers, Illinois State Hist. Libr., Nov. 22, 1862, April 26, 1863.

converted a plenteous district into a desert. One woman described in vivid terms how a Federal column suddenly debouched upon her place, troopers shooting down the livestock, officers pursuing her boys' ponies, squads stripping the yards of poultry and the garden of vegetables, and men invading the kitchen to carry off cooking pots and the day's food. When such columns passed, the people were left destitute.[92] In vain did Banks threaten the severest penalties; the looting was uncontrollable.[93] General Grenville M. Dodge later this year expressed sorrow over the excesses of his troops in Tennessee; but at the same time he declared his determination to ravage the country, so that if the rebels ever regained possession, they would be unable to exist a day. He regarded all their possessions as legitimate Federal property. If brought to him freely, he would offer compensation, but "If I go after it I never pay."[94]

Although New Englanders assumed an air of superior virtue, they could be as pitiless as any others. The historian of the 1st Massachusetts, describing the vigor with which his regiment denuded Virginia plantations of all they possessed, quoted the lamentation of one impoverished citizen: "I was Union; I never got any protection; it's no use to be a Union man, you suffer from both sides." The chronicler of the 37th Massachusetts told of seeing a flock of 300 fine sheep turned in one night into 300 bloody pelts. When Henry Wilson's Regiment, the 22nd Massachusetts, camped at the fine Carter mansion on the James, everything removable or drivable outdoors vanished, and only a special guard saved the house. The historian of the 1st Massachusetts frankly declared that under the influence of Pope's order, "large numbers of houses were entered, females insulted, private property was plundered, and many grievous outrages were perpetrated."[95]

Women insulted?—even so. C.C. Coffin of the Boston *Journal* confidentially wrote Governor Andrew in February, 1863: "I am sorry to say that the Massachusetts 24th has been acting outrageously here—robbing, burning houses, killing cattle, etc.,—ravishing negro women—beating their husbands who attempted protection. Butler has some of them in irons. I hear that the Col. when appealed to for a guard to prevent the outrages *refused* the request!"[96] Governor Joseph E. Brown later this year informed the Georgia legislature that Northern soldiers

92. Official Report Relative to the Conduct of Federal Troops in Western Louisiana during the Invasions of 1863 and 1864, Compiled from Sworn Testimony, Henry M. Allen, 1865.

93. Orders, April 21, 1863, New York *Tribune*, May 8, 1863.

94. Bennett, A.J., *Story of the First Massachusetts Light Battery*, Boston, 1886, 85ff.; *O.R.* I, xxxi, Pt.3, 261-262.

95. Bowen, James Lorenzo, *History of Thirty-seventh Regiment Massachusetts Volunteers*, Holyoke, Mass., 1884, 92-93; Parker, John Lord, *History of the Twenty-second Massachusetts Infantry*, Boston, 1887, 179ff.; Cudworth, Warren Handel, *History of the First Regiment Massachusetts Infantry*, Boston, 1866, 255.

96. John A. Andrew Papers, Mass. Hist. Soc.

had in numerous instances violated white women.[97] Doubtless he could have specified few such occurrences, and doubtless also the victims were usually camp followers. It was in property destruction that the Union page was blackest—so black that it produced consternation among judicious officers.

The violence, which Pope had sanctioned, did more to demoralize and weaken the army, one New Englander asserts, than most unsuccessful campaigns. Unquestionably, the Union forces suffered morally as grievously as the civilian population of the South suffered materially; and beyond question Charles Francis Adams, Jr., who was emphatic on this loss of discipline, was correct in stating that the severe officer, who meted out a few condign punishments for the first offenses, was less cruel than the slack commander who, in the end, had to chastise many harshly. General Jesse L. Reno became so incensed that he finally ordered the first man caught stealing even an ear of green corn shot—but only after the countryside about him had been reduced almost to a primal wilderness.[98] A soldier of the 45th Massachusetts found foraging in North Carolina full of what he called "charm", for its excitement and its utter lawlessness.[99] A more honest Yankee, who helped spread havoc in Georgia, equated charm with mere greed. The men of his Negro regiment came in by twos, threes, and dozens, he writes, laden with every variety of portable goods: sofas, tables, pianos, chairs, mirrors, carpets, beds, tools, books, family papers, and even sets of china.[100]

After depredations and brigandage on both sides in 1862, in the main by the Confederate guerrillas, Missouri was relatively quiet in the first few months of 1863. After the battle of Prairie Grove, Arkansas, in December, 1862, no operations on a large scale were carried out by either side. The winter of 1862-1863 had been particularly severe, and Federal troops were needed to help Grant advance against Vicksburg in the spring. The scattered Northern forces remaining in the State were restricted to patrol duty against bushwhackers and other lawless men. General Samuel Curtis of the Department of the Missouri issued detailed general orders setting forth descriptions of proscribed bandits and outlaw groups of guerrilla, insurgent, partisan, or brigand character, and the like, stating the punishment they could expect if caught.[101] But orders and strongly worded threats were never enough in Missouri. The savagery continued on what seemed its inevitable and unstoppable course, in a vindictive and cruelly savage series of

97. Fielder, Herbert, *Sketch of the Life and Times and Speeches of Joseph E. Brown*, Springfield, Mass., 1883, 287.

98. Walcott, Charles F., *History of the Twenty-first Regiment Massachusetts Volunteer Militia*, Boston, 1882, 128, 188; Adams, Charles F., Jr., *A Cycle of Adams Letters*, I, 263-4 and II, 8, 14, 217.

99. Mann, A.W., *The Campaign of the Forty-fifth Regiment Massachusetts Volunteer Militia*, Boston 1882, 33.

100. Emilio, Luis F., *A Brave, Black Regiment: History of the Fifty-fourth Regiment of Massachusetts Volunteer Infantry*, Boston, 1891, 42.

101. *O.R.*, I, xxii, Pt.2, 237-244.

blows and retaliations. Brig. Gen. J.S. Marmaduke raided beyond Fredericktown to Cape Girardeau in late April. Smaller but even harder outbreaks of violence had occurred earlier in many parts of the State. In one ebullition of savagery on March 28, guerrillas attacked the steamer *Sam. Gaty* on the Missouri River, and a number of persons were killed before the affray ended.

In April, William Clarke Quantrill's notorious guerrilla band moved north-ward, striking rapidly with murder, fire, and robbery. Bridges were burned, homes and farms ransacked, patrols ambushed, and Missouri again became an unsafe place for person or property. General John M. Schofield replaced Curtis in late May, and took new steps to cope with this uncivil warfare but Missouri in its devastation began to resemble a kind of no-man's land.

The four States of Virginia, Tennessee, Mississippi, and Louisiana, down to the time of Sherman's seaward march, were, along with Missouri, scenes of the most malign destruction. The Mississippi planter Julian Alcorn has poignantly depicted the way in which the Northern army, in the months before the fall of Vicksburg, laid waste the northwestern part of his State, seizing mules and horses, killing cattle, burning gin-houses, smashing machinery, and breaking up hand-some furniture. Too often they left farmers without seed-corn or cotton-seed, necessary draft animals, plows or hoes—helpless to begin anew. It is true that, as Grant informed Halleck,[102] ostensibly quiet citizens sometimes gave real provocation for such spoliation, for the moment they had a safe chance they would shoot Union soldiers from ambush.[103] But ill-controlled troops seldom waited for an excuse. Such areas as Alcorn's, which grew increasingly numerous, soon presented what the postbellum traveller, J.T. Trowbridge, called a dismal scene of torpor.

The ruin which was thus spread across the face of the South was to cripple its production for the whole war period and longer. Moreover, it sent a burden-some stream of refugees flowing into the untouched districts.[104] Some who could demonstrate their attachment to the Union, like East Tennesseans, found assist-ance on reaching the North. A few more enlisted under the national colors, like the loyal whites whom General Mason Brayman embodied in the 1st Alabama Infantry. Hundreds from the lower Mississippi Valley reached Cairo in the spring of 1863, and were distributed by the commander there to various Illinois cities; some were cordial, some not. The mayor of one town, who was later suitably rebuked, wrote the commander: "By what authority do you force upon

102. Corinth, Aug. 9, 1862, Grant-Halleck Papers, Ill. State Hist. Library; Julian Alcorn to his wife, Mound Place, Miss., Dec. 18, 1862, Alcorn Papers, Univ. of N.C. Library.

103. Bokum, Herman, *Wanderings North and South: the Testimony of a Refugee from East Tennessee,* Philadelphia, 1863, *passim.*

104. E.L. Acee to Gov. Pettus, July 29, 1862, Pettus Papers, Miss. State Archives, Jackson, Miss.

the people of Centralia the 120 paupers you sent here by yesterday's train? You are respectfully requested to arrange for their transportation south." The general movement, however, was a headlong search by farmers, planters, overseers, and many slaves, for asylum in the safer South. Groups of women, like Sidney Harding of Old Brier Plantation in St. Mary's Parish, La., with her mother and sister, wandered across country, camping in the pine woods at night and begging from families as poor as themselves.[105]

Federal authorities, by decree or pressure, compelled many partially helpless people to leave cities and towns. When Banks and his provost-marshal in New Orleans ordered all registered enemies of the Union to leave his department before mid-May, 1863,[106] hundreds forthwith departed. They were glad to abandon a city in which political prisoners might be put under special arrest without notice, no more than three citizens could assemble on the streets, and the stars-and-stripes flew over all public places. By President Davis's order, a commissioner was stationed in Mobile to receive the refugees, succor the penniless, and help them forward with transportation. Most effective assistance, however, came from a relief committee which collected supplies and money, and procured clothing, shelter, and travel aids. One of the women thus helped was Mrs. William B. Mumford, whose husband had been hanged by Ben Butler.[107]

However harried and impoverished, the people of invaded districts maintained a warlike spirit. One of the ablest observers of the Vicksburg region in the summer of 1863 testified that, although the people were penniless, homeless, and hungry, he found no evidence that any considerable number advocated unconditional surrender.[108] The women of New Orleans and occupied Louisiana evinced a sterner nationalism than the soldiers. They sang "The Bonnie Blue Flag" with frenzy, passed Union officers with haughty disdain, and even insulted the dead —Butler exiling to Ship Island one woman accused of laughing over a Union corpse. Rebel soldiers on furlough reported that when they wished to remain at home another week, young women urged them to hasten back to the battle-line.[109] But the pride and courage, so magnificently expressed in Sarah Morgan's famous diary, often masked a heart that ultimately came as near breaking as her own. Hardships, losses, humiliation, and the exhaustion of inflation, slowly eroded the morale of the South.

105. Harding, Sidney, Ms. Diary, La. State Univ. Archives; Mayor Samuel Storer to Buford, June 24, 1863, Mason Brayman Papers, Chicago Hist. Soc.; Dodge, Grenville M., Ms. autobiography, Iowa State Hist. Soc.
106. Banks-Bowen Correspondence, March-July, Provost-Marshal General's Records, V.309, National Archives.
107. Records of Relief Commission, May, 1863 to Oct., 1864, Chicago Hist. Soc.
108. Cadwallader, Sylvanus, *Three Years with Grant*, ed. Benjamin P. Thomas, New York, 1955.
109. An English Merchant, *Two Months in the Confederate States*, London, 1865, 46ff., 192.

[VI]

One cardinal deficiency of the Confederacy, as many Southerners vigorously asserted, lay in the lack of a chief national executive possessing some of the energy, foresight, and firm decision exhibited by those other leaders of a new-born republic at war, Washington, Cromwell, or Masaryk. It is impossible for a student of the great rebellion to avoid comparing the character, talents and sagacity of Lincoln with the parallel gifts of Jefferson Davis, greatly to the disadvantage of the latter. This broad subject of the judicious statesmanship of Lincoln and his Cabinet in Washington as compared with the type of leadership provided by Jefferson Davis in Montgomery and Richmond, must always be kept in mind as an essential element of the war, and offers some aspects that are commonly neglected in brief examinations of the conflict.

In coping with the problems of war, Jefferson Davis was handicapped by ill health, and tortured by sorrows both private and public. He suffered from dyspepsia and neuralgia, from a tendency to boils, from impaired sight of one eye, and from insomnia. His ceaseless anxieties naturally plunged him from time to time into melancholia. As his Negro coachman, William A. Jackson, stated in 1862,[110] the Northern capture of Roanoke Island depressed him greatly, and similar fits of low spirits followed other disasters.[111] The loss of his five-year-old son Joseph in April, 1864, was a cruel bereavement. The child clambered up on a banister above the piazza, fell to the brick pavement below, and was killed; his mother, having gone to the President's office with a basket of lunch, did not witness the tragedy, which became known when another youngster reported to a black mammy that "Joe wouldn't wake up."[112] Against his wife's stubborn resistance, Davis confined his table to the fare that ordinary citizens enjoyed. Visitors described breakfasts where he drank sassafras tea, and other meals when he had no meat but slices of fat pork fried crisp. The one recreation he allowed himself was horseback riding, and his frequent rides about the city and its fortifications made him more familiar than anybody else with the environs of Richmond.[113] Sometimes he rode all night. But his favorite Kentucky bay could not preserve the health of the master, who grew more and more haggard as the war advanced.

Most of the civil leaders South and North suffered in health from the overwhelming burdens of the war. Lincoln became so exhausted that near the end he said he had a tired spot which no ordinary rest could touch. Stanton, Seward,

---

110. Jefferson Davis Papers, W.I . Fleming Collection, Duke Univ., Box 5.

111. New York Weekly *Tribune*, May 31, 1862; cf. reminiscenses of Richmond neighbor, Emma L. Bryan in Jefferson Davis Papers, Duke Univ.

112. Fleming Collection, *ut supra*.

113. Davis, Varina Howell, *Jefferson Davis, ex-President of the Confederate States of America*, New York, 1890, Chap. 23, "Reminiscences of General Robert Ransom."

and Chase all worked until they shortened their days, and none of this trio long survived the war. The Confederate Secretary of War, Seddon, seemed to the author of *A Rebel War Clerk's Diary* to resemble "an exhumed corpse after a month's interment,"[114] and left the war little better than a chronic invalid.[115] Even sick and tired men, however, can work, but the central question is: what of their grasp, wisdom, and decision?

It was the opinion of Robert Garlick H. Kean of the War Department, who saw Davis at as close range as any public man, that he lacked the faculty of deputing special tasks to others, and frittered away time and energy upon unimportant details. He wished to be personally conversant with all public business, and therefore welcomed rather than repelled subordinates who ran to him for instructions on every subject. Naturally a slow worker, he held endless consultations which terminated in no clearcut conclusion. It is certainly true that he gave far too much attention to military detail when he should have fixed his gaze upon larger national problems. He was strongly addicted to the doctrine of personal leadership; both in the civil government and in military affairs *he alone* should be the controlling head. The double responsibility would have been too much for any man, and far exceeded Davis's powers. Early in 1862, the Confederate Congress wished to give Robert E. Lee general control of all the Southern military forces, with authority to take personal command of any army at any time.[116] This was a wise measure, but Davis regarded it as an invasion of his constitutional rights as commander-in-chief of the army and navy, and vetoed it. As a partial substitute, he made Lee his assistant in conducting military affairs, as a species of chief-of-staff, something more than a mere military adviser, but much less than a director of all the armies. This arrangement, satisfactory neither to Davis nor Lee, ended abruptly when Lee took charge of Johnston's army.

Thereafter Davis regarded himself as commander-in-chief in fact as well as name, and to a great extent undertook the management of the details as well as the broad lines of strategy. In directing affairs in Virginia, however, he acted in constant consultation with Lee. When not busy in the field, the General could often be found in President Davis's office (which was in the old custom-house quarters of Richmond), or the President's home. Mrs. Davis and Mrs. Lee were not intimate, but whenever a clatter of hoofs announced Lee's late-afternoon arrival, he was shown at once into Davis's study, and stayed to dinner and long afterward.[117] The supervision of the West was a different matter. In the autumn of 1862, Davis created a vast province, over which Joseph E. Johnston was to reign with practically unlimited power, including all of Tennessee, Alabama, and Mis-

114. Jones, John B., *A Rebel War Clerk's Diary, op.cit.*, I, 380.
115. *Dictionary of American Biography*, "Seddon, J.A."
116. Freeman, Douglas S., *Robert E. Lee*, New York, 1934-35, II, 5; text of bill, *O.R.* IV, i, 997-998.
117. Ross, Ishbel, *First Lady of the South*, New York, 1958, 194.

sissippi, all of unoccupied Louisiana east of the Mississippi, and part of western North Carolina and northern Georgia.[118] Secretary Seddon, who believed both in the centralization of command and the high abilities of Johnston, was largely responsible for this step. Johnston was to make his headquarters in Chattanooga, to repair in person to any part of his command whenever his presence seemed necessary, and to take command of any army there when he saw fit. Under this arrangement Davis might have relieved himself from most responsibilities.

Unfortunately, Davis in his orders to Johnston did not define the powers of the General with clarity and precision. While the too-cautious Johnston hesitated to affirm his authority vigorously, his three subordinate generals made it clear that they expected to hold autonomous positions. Certainly Johnston had no explicit power of summary removal. He concluded that, as he wrote his friend Louis T. Wigfall, he could only play the part of an inspector-general. "I am virtually laid upon the shelf with the responsibility of command." At the same time, Davis's deep affection for his own State of Mississippi gave him so anxious a concern for the preservation of Vicksburg that he opposed all proposals for extricating the garrison and uniting large Confederate forces in the open field against Grant. Dissatisfied with Johnston, and cherishing a high regard for Bragg which almost no other Southerner shared, Davis gave much time and attention to the Western theatre. His order to Pemberton in mid-May to hold both Port Hudson and Vicksburg to the last had a great deal to do with the maintenance of a desperate defense of both, and the ultimate loss of the armies which guarded them.[119]

If the President overburdened himself with details, and overemphasized his military responsibilities at the expense of his civil functions, so that Congress floundered with a painful lack of direction, he exposed a graver fault in his inability to labor amicably with other men. His path became stony with needless quarrels. One of the Rhetts declared that he was conceited, wrongheaded, wranglesome, and obstinate. Only one of these adjectives, the invented word "wranglesome," was just. He was proud rather than conceited, and firm rather than obstinate, but he had as natural a disposition to quarrel as Andrew Jackson. Had he been as selfless, patient, and generous as Abraham Lincoln, he would never have quarreled with Johnston, Beauregard, or with his War Secretary, Randolph, and Longstreet as he did.[120] He even had a tiff with the ever-loyal Judah P.

118. Rowland, Dunbar, *Jefferson Davis, Constitutionalist: His Letters, Papers, and Speeches,* Jackson, Miss. 1923, V, 557.
119. Vandiver, Frank E., "Jefferson Davis and United Army Command," *Louisiana Historical Quarterly,* Jan., 1955, Vol.38, 26-38. Davis quarreled with Secretary of War Randolph; indeed, according to Kean, he deliberately forced a quarrel because the Secretary's independence of spirit excited his jealousy. Kean, Robert, *Inside the Confederate Government, op.cit.,* 30.
120. Bradford, Gamaliel, *Confederate Portraits,* New York, 1914, 142, 143.

Benjamin. The most scathing indictments of Davis during the war and afterward came from Henry S. Foote, the former Mississippi governor who had opposed secession, and who left Confederate soil in disgust when Lincoln's proposals for peace were rejected.[121] He (and others) termed the President a dictator, charging him with originating the scheme of burning all the cotton of the South to keep it out of enemy hands, and with other irresponsible acts.[122]

In his relations with the State governors, with leaders of Congress, and with some of the principal editors, Davis's want of tact and bonhomie, his abruptness, and his glacial pride, made him an ineffective head of government. As Allan Tate writes, one large element in the defeat of the South was "the lack of a magnetic national leader."[123] The eloquence of a Lincoln or Woodrow Wilson would have helped nerve the people to meet losses and disasters; but he lacked the flaming words that rouse men to face a long ordeal of blood, sweat, and tears. The iron masterfulness of a Cromwell or Bismarck might have won a respect from such executives as Brown of Georgia and Vance of North Carolina that he never gained. Wit, humor, epigram, and a flair for apposite anecdotes could have done something to lighten anxiety and assuage grief, but he never commanded them any more than he commanded a Gladstone's moral fervor. It was Lincoln who

121. Foote, Henry S., *Casket of Reminiscences,* Washington, D.C. 1874, 388ff.

122. Yancey Papers, Alabama State Archives. Ill feeling between President Davis and those leading Alabamians, W.L. Yancey and C.C. Clay, first appeared when just after Shiloh the two men complained that their State, with forty regiments in the field, had but five brigadiers. The President, they remarked, had given a brigadiership to Col. Roger A. Pryor of Virginia, but had ignored Alabamians just as able. Davis's reply had a needless asperity that would never have crept into one of Lincoln's statements. He willingly received recommendations, he wrote, but never argued as to their propriety, and rejected as unfair Yancey's and Clay's statement upon his course and assumption of what it should be.

C.C. Clay wrote Yancey early in 1863 that Davis's character was a strange compound which he could not analyze. "He will not ask or receive counsel and, indeed, seems predisposed to go exactly the way his friends advise him not to go." Clay had resolutely maintained his good temper even when Davis seemed intent upon alienating him—all this for old friendship's sake. "If he survives this war and does not alter his course, he will find himself in a small minority party." One of his errors which distressed the Alabamian was an attempt to appoint a close friend, Dr. Cartwright of North Carolina, who was nearly seventy, totally deaf, and physically unfit for active service, to be inspector-general of hospitals on Pemberton's staff. (Undated fragment of letter, probably April 1863, to Yancey; Yancey Papers, Alabama State Archives.)

Yancey, near his end, wrote Davis in bitterly hostile terms at the time of Chancellorsville. He had learned that Davis was his enemy, he declared; he had also learned that appointments "are often conferred as rewards to friends and are refused as punishments inflicted upon enemies"; and he therefore withdrew his request that his son Dalton, a cadet in the University of Alabama, be given a commission. He followed this epistle with another acrimonious letter. When Davis assured C.C. Clay that he felt no enmity for Yancey, Clay characterized his conduct in a tart sentence: "But it is perhaps possible for a man to abuse with offensive and opprobrious epithets, innuendoes, and so on, those whom he really likes as true friends. . . ." It is clear that Yancey had reluctantly opposed some of the President's measures; that Davis had then spoken harshly of Yancey; and that Davis had earned a reputation for favoritism to friends and vengefulness to enemies which offended Clay and embittered Yancey. (Yancey to Davis, from Montgomery, May 6, 1863; June 26 to same; Clay to Yancey, from Macon, Ga., June 30, 1863; all in Yancey Papers, Alabama State Archives.)

123. Tate, Allan, *Jefferson Davis: His Rise and Fall,* New York, 1929, 271.

humorously called the rival President "that tother fellow,"[124] a phrase eloquent of his tolerant condescension and his sense of fun.

In spite of all the ill-feeling about him, Davis was unquestionably the best man who could have been chosen to guide the Confederacy; firmer than Toombs, stronger than the half-invalid Alexander H. Stephens, and far more devotedly a Southern nationalist than Howell Cobb, who had opposed secession almost to the last. He had his vision; that of a powerful and opulent new republic rising in the West to vindicate the right of an injured and insulted people to the control of their own social fabric and governmental ideals. He would at all costs uphold a priceless political principle. That he was not a *great* man in any sense of the word, all astute observers, such as the fanatical secessionist Thomas Cobb, quickly perceived.[125] Nevertheless, his unyielding determination and, according to Hendrick, his large experience as Mexican War soldier; his loyalty to his chosen appointees; his service as Pierce's Secretary of War, and as Senator; his dignity of bearing and speech; and his unshakable integrity, constituted a greater body of assets than any rival leader of the South could have offered. He was guilty of favoritism to certain pets, and this favoritism cost the South dear in the cases of Bragg and Northrop. He sometimes lost his temper in a splenetic way, and wasted time and energy in trying to prove that Johnston and Brown were in the wrong; he had a fallible grasp of human nature, but to find a better civil leader we have to move outside the Confederacy. The impetuous Pierre Soulé, spending a few summer weeks at Richmond in 1863, reached a correct conclusion upon the merits of Davis and the central defect of his government: "The President is ever the man of lofty interests, of unblemished character and pure patriotism. . . ." he wrote; "but he is unfortunately saddled with as inefficient and unpopular a cabinet as ever brought a nation's existence to the brim of its ruin."[126]

The Confederate government faced a continuous crisis, and had to leap from one desperate expedient to another to avoid collapse. The principal members of the Cabinet in the summer of 1863, Judah P. Benjamin as Secretary of State, Christopher G. Memminger as Secretary of the Treasury, and James A. Seddon and Stephen A. Mallory as heads of the War and Navy Departments, all appear weak figures in comparison with their Washington compeers, Seward, Chase, Stanton, and Gideon Welles. This is partly because they all had insuperable tasks. With the resources and confidence of the North, they would have written abler records.

If we term Seddon and Mallory the two most striking discoveries of the war in the civil leadership of the Confederacy, Benjamin was also something of a

124. Strong, George Templeton, *Diary*, ed. Allan Nevins, New York, 1962, 204-205.
125. Hendrick, Burton J., *Statesmen of the Lost Cause*, Boston, 1939, 93.
126. Mercier, Alfred, *Biographie de Pierre Soulé, Sénateur á Washington*, Paris, 1948, *passim*.

discovery (he had never been a commanding Senator), and held a place close behind them. Not only was Benjamin endowed with a quick, shrewd mind, a cheerful, ingratiating temper, and a grace of deportment and speech which soon made him Davis's most congenial associate, and won him friends; but as head of foreign affairs, he was in precisely the position he best fitted. Benjamin was always cheerful and relaxed, Davis always gloomy and tense. They could work hand in hand. The President had appointed Benjamin, after a storm of criticism fell on the man for the Roanoke Island disaster, because he felt a personal grievance in the injustice done his most faithful friend and able right hand.[127] When Benjamin became Secretary of State, the two often worked in the same office from ten in the morning until nine at night. It was then and still is impossible to determine to what extent each man was responsible for Southern policies,[128] but it seems certain that it was Benjamin who dangled before Napoleon III in the early months of 1862 a tempting proposal that the Confederacy give him 100,000 bales of cotton, and a preference for French goods in the Southern markets for a certain period, if France would recognize the Confederacy and break the blockade. Napoleon was willing, but the British would not give him their cooperation. It seems certain also that Benjamin would have advocated the arming of slaves, who would thus gain freedom at the end of the war, as early as the beginning of 1864—but neither Davis nor the Southern people were ready for so revolutionary a step.[129] Benjamin was also one of the controlling powers in the relations between the Richmond government and Confederate agents in Canada, and in arranging for the Hampton Roads conference.

The insuperable difficulty when Benjamin took over his office from the less competent R.M.T. Hunter was simply that the possibilities of any real achievement were ebbing day by day. After Antietam and emancipation, nearly all hope of British intervention (for France could not and would not act alone) had to be given up by realistic men, and Benjamin was too acute not to be realistic. Hence it is that he is best remembered in Confederate diplomatic history for ordering James Mason, in the summer of 1863, to terminate his mission to England, and later on, for persuading the Cabinet, over which he presided in the absence of President Davis, to cancel the exequaturs of British consuls and expel them from Southern cities. That is, he is best remembered for open admissions of failure. This failure, however, was in no way his fault. It was traceable to a variety of causes—to a surplus of cotton in Europe when the war broke out, to Confederate defeat in the field at critical moments, to the ever-greater risks any European Power would run in fighting the North,

127. Meade, Robert D., "The Relations between Judah P. Benjamin and Jefferson Davis," *Journal of Southern History,* Vol.V, 468-478, quoting letter by Mrs. Davis.
128. *Ibid.*
129. *Ibid.*

and above all to the rising tide of liberalism in Britain.[130]

Of Benjamin, Robert Garlick Kean wrote that he was an untrustworthy adviser. He was a clever lawyer, "but perhaps the least wise of our public men."[131] A sufficient answer to this allegation is that Benjamin advocated the arming of Negroes when that proposal took both courage and foresight, and that their enlistment and consequent liberation would have been one of the wisest possible steps for the South to take.[132]

When it became necessary to appoint a successor to Randolph as Secretary of War, Albert T. Bledsoe, the Assistant Secretary of War (and former University of Virginia professor), advised Davis that Seddon would never do. True, he was a man of fine parts, estimable character, high accomplishments, and true patriotism, but he was too feeble of physique. "The labor of the office would kill him in one month."[133] Though the first months did nearly crush him, Seddon worked to exhaustion until Appomattox, faithful and useful to the last. No one can read the Secretary's letters in the Official Records[134]—letters in which he speaks of the engrossing nature of his official engagements—without respect for his grasp of intricate issues, and his conscientious attention to manifold duties. His annual reports evince a courageous vigilance, as in his insistence that examining boards be created to purge the army of incompetent officers. His broad general policies, such as his steady pressure for a greater concentration of forces, especially in the West, his urgent demand that heavily depleted regiments be consolidated and organized anew at normal strength, and his insistence that extending the draft ages below eighteen and above forty-five would do more harm than good, were sagaciously statesmanlike. All his state papers are marked by a calm moderation of tone which is all the more striking when compared with the shrill and querulous exhortations by Davis.

Seddon quickly realized that successful maintenance of the war demanded a steady expansion of the functions of the general government. In his long official report in the fall of 1863 he asked Congress to provide for the compulsory employment of slaves for use upon public works, or as teamsters, cooks, and other camp employees. He anticipated difficulty in getting owners to agree to give up certain quotas for public service, but the labor must be obtained. He asked for authority to organize the veterans whose terms of service were about to expire in such companies and regiments as they and their officers might select. He called for the appointment of a judge-advocate specially detailed to pass upon the recommendations of examining boards for the retirement or dismissal of officers, thus

130. Eaton, Clement, *A History of the Southern Confederacy*, New York, 1954, 81.
131. Kean, *Diary, op. cit.*, August 12, 1863.
132. Eaton, *op. cit.*, 275.
133. Nov. 12, 1862, Davis Papers, Duke Univ.
134. *O.R.*, IV, Vol. II.

relieving the Executive from a heavy duty. The laws providing for volunteer home guards should be stiffened to make such service compulsory by men past forty-five, but still vigorous; for, as Seddon wrote, "the Confederacy may well be regarded as a beleaguered city, where all capable should be placed at the guns." He thought that Congress ought to place the entire business of blockade-running under equitable regulation, so as to ensure to the Confederate government a fair proportion of the profits of the trade. It should take steps to give the trans-Mississippi region, with which communications were difficult, a separate self-sustaining machinery of administration, so that in the management of conscriptions and the manufacture of arms and munitions it could carry on its own operations.[135]

In these and other recommendations for an expansion of the powers of the general government, Seddon angered the jealous State-Rights governors; and much of the criticism and detraction he received came from men like Vance and Brown. He was in the right, however, not only as to the need for an invigoration of Richmond's power, but as to the propriety of emphasizing the paramount authority of the civil over the military arm. Military orders could have met many of the purposes he defined, but they would have converted the Confederacy into a military state, a new Sparta or imperial Rome or Prussia. It is of cardinal importance, he declared, that the enforcement of all laws, including those upon military affairs, should depend not on the sanction of armed force, but upon civil and judicial procedures. He had regretted the necessity of issuing War Department directives when the same or better provisions should have rested upon legislative action.[136] This was the voice of a man imbued with the finest spirit of Anglo-American institutions. In the words of Kean, viewing the new Secretary, Seddon, staggering under his load: "He is physically weak, seems to be a man of clear head, strong sense, and firm character, but from long desuetude wanting in readiness in dispatching business." Kean added that he had just the helper he needed in Judge Campbell; that he "is invaluable; his capacity of labor infinite; his breadth of view great." His endorsements are so judicial, "deciding questions rather than cases [that] they perplex the red tapists who complain that they do not decide the *case.*"[137]

The entrance of John A. Campbell upon the Richmond scene as assistant Secretary of War in the autumn of 1862 had done much to strengthen the government. Ever since his well-intentioned and honest conversations with Seward in an effort to bring about the peaceable evacuation of Sumter, he had been the subject of unreasonable abuse in the South. Men had accused him of all kinds of

135. *O.R.*, IV, ii, 990, 1018.
136. *Ibid.*
137. Kean, *Diary, op. cit.*, Dec. 13, 1862, 33; March 15, 1863, 45.

traitorous ideas and acts. He had urged army officers not to resign their Union commissions, it was said; he had accused the South of breaking up the most splendid government in the world without adequate cause; he had constantly hoped for the defeat of Southern armies. While we were fighting for independence, declared Thomas J. Butler of Mobile, "he was clutching his Union ermine, all smeared with federal dirt, and holding on to its honor and emoluments."[138] Though Campbell was expected to give his central attention to conscription, he was broadly useful.[139]

Of Memminger and Mallory as heads of financial and administrative affairs respectively, it may be said that they were competent, earnest, and honest men struggling with insuperable difficulties. One of them had commonplace parts, the other was brilliant. A German by birth, a South Carolinian by nurture, a lawyer by profession, Memminger had no preparation or special fitness for the financial leadership of a nation. He came into office to face—and conquer—the task of floating a fifteen-million dollar bond issue; and the first measure which he recommended and carried in Congress provided for a further bond issue of fifty millions, of which twenty millions was reserved as security for that amount of redeemable paper money. Thus the bark of Confederate finance floated forth not on a sea of taxation, which was left to the States, but a marsh of paper. Memminger continued to set his sails diligently on a course as narrow as his own mind, toward a misty harbor that gradually assumed the dark lineaments of bankruptcy.

Memminger's intentions were good, but his fund of determination and pugnacity was insufficient to divert Congress from the popular preference for paper money instead of taxation. The printing presses were kept busy rolling off notes, and the women clerks of Memminger's department still busier signing and numbering them.[140] The inevitable consequences were falling credit, rising inflation, impossible prices, and a rain of abuse upon the Secretary. During 1863 alarmed and angry citizens began speaking of the plethoric paper bills as rags, fodder, oak-leaves, and assignats, and to predict for them the end that had overtaken the Continental currency. They began to speak of Memminger as a mournful expert in impecuniosity. Yet the verdict of the first thorough student of Confederate finance remains unshakable: the financial traditions of America since colonial days being so loose, and the economic predicament of the blockaded South being so harsh, probably even another Alexander Hamilton would not have managed the Confederate finances in a different way, or with greater success.[141]

Certainly Memminger was correct in saying that he had been forced to administer plans which he neither originated nor approved, and that all his

138. Thomas J. Butler to Yancey, Jan. 28, 1863, Yancey Papers, Alabama State Archives.
139. Southern Historical Society Papers, Oct. 1917, 3-81.
140. Coulter, *op. cit.*, 149-182.
141. Schwab, J.C., *The Confederate States of America, 1861-1865*, New York, 1901, 5.

anxious labors to reduce the flood of paper had been frustrated by legislators who would give him nothing else.[142] It was not his fault that, by July 1, 1863, it cost $8.00 in Confederate money to buy $1.00 in gold.[143] When he was forced to resign in 1864, his successor George A. Trenholm of Charleston was equally helpless. Perhaps the richest man in the South, he presided over a disintegrating fabric.

Mallory, who had been chairman of the Senate Committee on Naval Affairs in Buchanan's day, had a passion for the sea and ships, conceived in childhood days at Key West and on Mobile Bay. The son of a civil engineer, he had an unusual insight into the scientific and technological possibilities awaiting mankind. Before the war was a month old, he was asserting that the South should fight wood with iron. He hurried an agent off to London in the vain hope of obtaining two ironclads there. It was mainly by his enterprise and his skill in choosing able lieutenants that he had the *Merrimack* (renamed the *Virginia*) ready in Hampton Roads for use against the Union fleet; and his much stronger ironclad, the *Mississippi*, was almost ready at New Orleans when Farragut took that city and forced the builders to burn her. The stars in their courses seemed to fight against Mallory. After his promising start he never had powerful ships, or efficient navy yards.[144] But it was because of the stimulus he gave to brilliant aides that the Confederacy went further in the development of submarines and torpedoes than any other government of the time.

[VII]

No comparison between the civil leadership of the North and that of the South on the lower executive levels can be convincing, for the leaders on the two sides faced different tasks with utterly different resources. Given the advantages which the Union possessed, the departmental heads in Richmond might have written a much more lustrous record than they did. It is difficult to believe that in foreign affairs Judah P. Benjamin could have shown such capacity as Seward did after he outgrew his appalling early blunders, that in financial management Memminger could have grown in skill as expertly as Chase did, or that in military

142. *Ibid.*, 163, 164.

143. *Confederate Inflation Chart, Official Publication 13*, Richmond Civil War Centennial Committee.

144. *Dictionary of American Biography*, XII, 225. Mallory was harassed by his many enemies and critics. Rep. Conrad on Aug. 19, 1862, offered a resolution in the House instructing the Committee on Naval Affairs to inquire into the expediency of abolishing the Navy Dept. and transferring its work to the War Department. This incensed Mallory. Mallory to Davis, Aug. 27, 1862, Davis Papers, Duke Univ.

Later, a Joint Select Committee of Congress investigated the Navy Department, for various men, including the irrepressible Henry Foote, had charged general inefficiency and misuse of funds. The committee submitted a report exonerating Mallory from all censure. Ketring, Ruth A., *Clay of Alabama: Two Generations in Politics*, Duke Univ. Ph.D. Thesis, 1934, 306, 307. The report was published in the Richmond *Enquirer* of Feb. 18, 1864.

affairs Seddon could ever have displayed such a bulldog tenacity, independence of politicians, and incessant industry as Stanton. Yet these men never had full opportunity to prove their capacity.

In two cabinet posts the South held the advantage. The sturdy, courageous, straightforward John H. Reagan as postmaster-general had a simple integrity that shines by contrast with the devious, self-seeking of Montgomery Blair; and Stephen R. Mallory possessed an inventive resourcefulness in naval administration that leaped beyond the plodding but better publicized sagacity of Gideon Welles. One of the handicaps of the Confederate departments was a Congress far inferior in both brains and character to its counterpart in Washington, and far less effective in supporting the Executive. Another was the inability of the South to create in the departments such large and expert groups of assistant secretaries, bureau heads, chief clerks, solicitors, and other officers as the North possessed by 1863. Stanton's War Department, for example, by that year boasted a dozen men of high ability to superintend various interests: Peter H. Watson as Assistant Secretary, Charles A. Dana as an observer in 1863 and as Assistant Secretary in 1864, Lorenzo Thomas as Adjutant-General, Joseph G. Totten as Chief Engineer, William A. Hammond as Surgeon General, and so on. Still another Southern handicap was the lack of a reservoir of trained men available for *ad hoc* appointment to special tasks.[145]

The North in 1863 held four tremendous advantages: first, its possession of a chief of state who was indisputably the greatest American of his time; second, its ever-growing superiority in manpower, natural resources, all phases of economic life, and money; third, its open ports, largely undamaged rail and river transportation system, and its unoccupied territory; and fourth, the moral superiority that a combatant of slavery could assert over a defender of slavery, although all did not agree on the weight of this. These advantages were sternly impressive, but they were not irresistible. The valor, dash, and tenacity of the South had to be reckoned with. To the end of June in 1863 it had won more tactical victories in the East than had the North, and one of the most striking facts about the war at this period was that these traits, combined with high military leadership, might yet possibly produce a deadlock—which would mean Confederate success.

145. *O.R.*, IV, iii, 1199; iv, 1035.

2

Vicksburg: The Organized Victory

THE NATION'S attention was now drawn abruptly to a review of events that had been absorbing the West, and to a study of the prospects immediately at hand in Mississippi. To most Northerners this was a novel scene. Some visitors knew the State as a fertile land of winter greenery, mild breezes in spring and autumn, and mellow winters. Other Northerners had only a vague general knowledge that it was a wide, rich part of the great central Mississippi Valley, and that its growth in population, agricultural production, and river and railroad commerce had made it vital to the life and authority of the battling South. This was an area established upon a unique mingling of slaves and freemen, of whites, blacks and mulattoes, upon a social culture in part cultivated and liberal, and in part ill-educated and marked by decidedly reactionary views, social, economic and political. It stretched from the tawny waters of the Mississippi River on the west, to the low, rolling hills in the central area, white with cotton, and to the piney woods in the north; it stretched from the feudal traditions and principles of Natchez to the bustling, commercial activities and progressive ideas of Meridian and Waynesboro.[1] Its university town, Oxford, was to give birth to one of the greatest men in American letters, William Faulkner, and was long the home of the jurist and courageous thinker, L.Q.C. Lamar, a member of Cleveland's Cabinet. Missis-

---

1. Davis, Reuben, *Recollections of Mississippi and Mississippians*, Heston, 1889, calls attention to the picturesque interest of Mississippi towns in the half-century before the Civil War. It is dedicated by the author to the lawyers of the State, and describes Natchez in the days of the fiery Quitman, Vicksburg in times of the eloquent S.S. Prentiss, and Athens, Corinth, and Aberdeen. This had been a land of duels, and vindictive political feuds, but also a State where many men read as widely as did Jefferson Davis, and prized the arts of conversation and story-telling as much as the people described by the novelist, Stark Young, in his *So Red the Rose,* and by William Alexander Percy in his reminiscent *Lanterns on the Levee.*

Mississippi was primarily, but by no means exclusively, an agricultural state, as J.K. Bettersworth makes plain in *Confederate Mississippi,* Baton Rouge, 1943, 270; Vicksburg was, of course, the commercial metropolis, and Frederick L. Olmsted described its bustling activity in *A Journey in the Back Country,* New York, 1860. This "terraced city of the hills," as it was called, had a public school with 500 children before the war, and a public reading room. The town of Jackson drew vigor from the facts that it held the seat of government in the State, and lay at the junction of the main cross-line State railways, containing numerous people of German, Italian and French origin. Russell, W.H., *My Diary North and South,* London, 1863, *passim.*

sippi, a part of a great coastal plain widening as it stretched southward, was a muddy land like much of Alabama and Louisiana, given sporadic firmness by the gravel brought down by seasonal floods and by its abundant streams which were productive also of crops of pestiferous mosquitoes.

Mississippi had no mineral deposits comparable to Pennsylvania's, for example, or energy-producing waterfalls equal to those in New England, but students of history were aware of the importance of its strategic position on the Mississippi River, leading up to the Missouri and the Ohio. Mark Twain gives something of the flavor of the place in his *Life on the Mississippi,* including a chapter on the "art of inundation," and describing a town that would "come up to glow in the summer." This State regarded the Civil War with deep and abiding feeling. Mark Twain would later write about the multiplicity of steel-engravings of historic scenes which adorned every Mississippi home in post-war years—scenes that might be entitled: "First Interview Between Lee and Jackson," "Last Interview Between Lee and Jackson," "Jackson Accepting Lee's Invitation to Dinner," "Jackson Declining Lee's Invitation to Dinner," "Jackson Apologizing to Lee for a Heavy Defeat," "Jackson Reporting a Splendid Victory to Lee," and so forth, *ad infinitum.*

[I]

Everyone North and South knew that Vicksburg was of crucial importance. One main object of Confederate leadership in invading the North and fighting at Gettysburg was the hope that this action would compel the Union to halt its operations on the Misssissippi, where a Northern break-through would clearly be decisive. A lesser but allied attempt to divert Union pressure from the great river artery was planned at the same time by the gallant Kirby-Smith, who believed that he might act from west of the Mississippi, with the cooperation of Major-General Theophilus Holmes in Arkansas and Major-General Richard Taylor in West Louisiana. He was encouraged in this enterprise by the success of General John Bankhead Magruder, a West Pointer and veteran of the Seminole and Mexican Wars, who had fought ably in the Seven Days Battles before taking command of the Department of Texas in 1862 (a Department later enlarged to include New Mexico and Arizona). Magruder had cleared Texas of a great part of the Union invaders sent against him.[2]

Kirby-Smith's early prospects seemed bright. He found an able associate in "Dick" Taylor, the son of President Zachary Taylor, who had studied at Edinburgh, Harvard, and Yale, before fighting in the Mexican War and being commissioned Colonel of the 72nd New York. Tall, slender, finely dressed, Taylor was

2. Foote, Shelby, *The Civil War,* New York, 1958, Vol.II, 596-597 describes this ambitious plan.

so proud of his handsome countenance that he refused to wear glasses lest they mar his appearance. His gracious manners and fine courtesy, combined with his descent from Zachary Taylor, won him the complimentary appellation of "Prince Dick." Kirby-Smith himself had many gifts, but unfortunately other officers concerned in the campaign were less distinguished. Holmes proved slow and uncertain. Born late in 1804, he was now elderly, and the fact that he had been a classmate of Jefferson Davis at West Point ceased to count in his favor. He was soon sent to North Carolina to take charge of that State's reserves. The Confederate leader, John S. Marmaduke, a great favorite in Arkansas, made a raid into Missouri in the hope of capturing Helena, but he was repulsed at Cape Girardeau and defeated. Dick Taylor failed in his plans for recapturing New Orleans. Checkmate of the Confederates was to be complete when these two efforts, and Lee's desperate charge at Cemetery Hill, all broke down on July 3rd, the critical day at Gettysburg. On the morning of that day, white flags also blossomed out along the Confederate lines defending Vicksburg.[3]

After Farragut had run past New Orleans, steamed on up the river, and dropped anchor; after Mansfield Lovell had evacuated New Orleans and his retiring Confederates had fired warehouses, cotton, boats, and goods of all kinds along the levees, it was plain that Vicksburg must be the next objective of the Union forces in their drive to cut the Confederacy in two and open a waterway into the middle of the South. This first long stride must be followed by a second. Supplies from the West were plainly indispensable to the Confederacy. Admiral Porter remarked that the shipment of western supplies through Mississippi meant the steady flow of great quantities of hogs and hominy, large contingents of rebel troops, and indeed, of all the resources remaining in the Arkansas and Texas country as well as farther south and west. "Let us get Vicksburg!" Porter exclaimed, "and that country is ours!"

Grant had fully understood from the outset the exigent importance of clearing and sealing the great river. But how should it be done?

This was a war in which every road to success had to be paved with incessant efforts and frequent failures. The background of Grant's undertaking was gloomy. As he approached his great effort, Rosecrans was still recovering from the sickening losses of Murfreesboro, where, beginning with 40,000 effective troops, his brilliantly promising campaign had terminated in a drawn battle. He had moved his Army of the Cumberland out of Nashville just after Christmas Day in 1862 to attack General Bragg's troops near Murfreesboro (alternatively called Stone's River). The battle went on from December 31, 1862 to January 3, 1863. Bragg had been weakened by the despatch of an entire division of his force for the fighting in Mississippi, but he defended himself skillfully. Altogether, Rose-

3. *Ibid.*, II, 596-605.

crans lost 7,543 men wounded, and 1,294 killed. When Bragg evacuated Murfrees-boro, Rosecrans's adherents credited him with a victory, yet the Union army was not able to deliver another blow again for half-a-year.

Several events preceding the Vicksburg campaign influenced the movements of Grant at this point. After the evacuation of Corinth, General Halleck, who had gathered an army of 100,000 men, instead of pushing on to pursue the Confeder-ate army, had deliberately divided his forces, adopting a purely passive defense. Such conduct was, indeed, inexcusable.[4] On October 31, 1862, Halleck went to Washington to take command of the army, leaving Grant in control of the Department of Tennessee. Grant was holding the Mobile & Ohio Railroad from a point 25 miles south of Corinth, with about 75,000 men, divided into four groups, some of them new levies.

On the Confederate side, Pemberton held a large army—one large body at Vicksburg, and another at Port Hudson—about 30,000 at the two places. The rebels had fortified the Port Hudson area from about twenty miles above and forty miles below the Red River—the Red River being the chief channel of communication between Arkansas, Louisiana, and Texas. Most of the grain for Confederate armies came over this Red River route, and the three States named sent 100,000 troops into the Confederate armies.[5]

If the Union army could gain possession either of Vicksburg or Port Hudson, it could open the Mississippi to navigation by the superior Union naval power and thus cut the Confederacy in two.

In the East came defeat at Chancellorsville, May 2-4, 1863, but before this and other sad and weary news came in from Tennessee and Virginia, Grant and Porter had been struggling with a series of obstacles, miscalculations, and reverses that were equally depressing. They held undiscouraged hopes for a time of opening a new waterway for the Union forces from the Mississippi River to the upper part of the Yazoo River, which, with many a loop, and with numerous out-thrown bayous and lakelets, connected with the Mississippi River west of Vicksburg, and west also of the Walnut Hills bordering the Mississippi.

On January 17, 1863, Grant announced that he would take command in person of the Union forces against Vicksburg. On January 29 he arrived at Young's Point near Vicksburg, and on January 30 he assumed command. The problem was to gain a footing on the dry ground east of the river, so that his troops could move from this position against Vicksburg. The Mississippi Valley country surround-ing the city was a terrain of almost intolerable difficulty, an appalling combination of hills, wooded valleys with steep sides, superabundant water, deep bayous

4. Livermore, William R., *The Military History of Massachusetts*, Vol. XV, 541-585, says an excellent discussion of the operations before Vicksburg will be found in Major John Bigelow's book, *The Principles of Strategy*, New York, 1891, 540.

5. Livermore, *op.cit.*, 543; Church, William Conant, *Grant*, New York, 1897, 156.

infested with snakes and alligators, thicket-filled ravines, canebrakes, poisonous shrubs, and boggy paths. The previous winter of 1862-63 had witnessed heavy rains, raising streams, lakes and swamps to unusual levels, and leaving but few stretches of the land sufficiently dry to furnish a road, a camp ground, or even a burial place for dead soldiers. As fighting progressed, and disease and sharp-shooters took a heavy toll, many Northern soldiers had to be interred in the levees adjoining the Yazoo, the Mississippi and other streams. Malarial fever, small-pox and measles broke out among the men. Visitors to the camps told dismal stories of them on returning home, which Northern newspapers relayed back to the soldiers in grossly exaggerated form. Grant wrote of this time in his *Memoirs* that "the real work of the campaign and siege of Vicksburg now began."[6]

The Union leaders found that, for an army to approach Vicksburg from the north, the troops must encounter, as they neared the city, the vast bottomland known as the Yazoo Delta. This difficult stretch of land extends northward along the Mississippi and parallel to its border of Walnut Hills for 175 miles, comprising more than several thousand square miles. Much of the land is soft, very low, and wet. Were it not for the levees built along the Mississippi to hold it back, the Delta would be under water for a large part of the year. A force burdened by heavy guns and wagons would find it an obstacle almost as difficult, and in places impassable, as any large chain of timber-choked hills. If Grant threw an army across the Mississippi and tried to approach Vicksburg on the east of the river from either front or rear, north or south, he would find the approaches equally fraught with difficulties. Troops moving upward toward Vicksburg would have to be supplied by boats, and these boats would have to run the Vicksburg batteries. Hence, Grant's initial effort in November and December of 1862 to beleaguer and seize Vicksburg by a stroke combining land and water operations had been completely checked. He was compelled to keep the Union troops based on the *west* bank of the Mississippi, somewhat upstream from a point opposite the city. While he lay there, making plan after plan to get his troops into position before Vicksburg, seeing one scheme after another fail, he perceived the necessity of engaging the attention of the Confederates by diversionary enterprises. From this perception was born the dramatic raid by Col. Benjamin H. Grierson with a brigade of cavalry, moving swiftly from LaGrange, Tennessee, deep into the South in an effort to cut the Mobile & Ohio Railroad, running east from Vicksburg to Jackson, the capital of Mississippi, and on into the interior. Grierson's diversion prevented the Confederates from dispatching troops from Vicksburg to Port Hudson.

A classic narrative of Grierson's foray, written by S.H.M. Byers, explains how, after Sherman had failed to get across the Mississippi at Vicksburg, Grant

6. Livermore, *op.cit.*, 550-551; Grant, *Memoirs* I, 458.

moved the whole army in the spring of 1863 down the river to begin one of his immortal campaigns.[7] Byers writes that Grant built long stretches of corduroy roads and bridges that ran snake-like for forty miles among the black swamps, canebrakes, and lagoons on the west side of the Mississippi, bivouacking his men on the river shore while Byer's regiment remained above the city as part of a force of possibly 25,000 men holding the Union position there. He describes the momentous passage of Union vessels down the river in terms reflecting the excitement he felt. The sky was black ink, as the Confederates lighted bonfires and opened their guns. The channel became a sheet of flame. The roar of rebel guns from the bluffs, some of them big ten-inch cannon, became thunderous, as cannonballs and shells made some lucky hits, and as Union soldiers and sailors leaped from their craft into the water to escape, "Hell seemed loose." Then suddenly, at dawn came silence. The fleet under Porter had passed the city. Eleven boats had passed the river batteries safely; a twelfth boat was sunk. On the night of April 16 the cheering troops welcomed the advance vessels. Now they felt the campaign could begin in earnest.

Soldiers who had been encamped on the levees up about Milliken's Bend came tramping down through ponds and swamps on little roads, lanes, and paths, to the point where the Union vessels had anchored. The ferrying of additional troops day and night across the river at once began. Byers' force, impressed by the battle-scarred ships of the Union navy, hurried by rapid marches, punctuated by engagements, toward positions in the rear of Vicksburg and Jackson, foraging on farms as they went, and filling their canteens from creeks as they tramped roadways deep in yellow dust. Byers offers a lively description of the assault by McPherson's corps on the Vicksburg lines on the 19th, where he heard Logan's stentorian voice ring over the field, cheering on his troops as they advanced in fearful heat, until their forward ranks lay down in front of the defensive forts.[8]

Grant's intention of crossing at Grand Gulf proved infeasible after a six-hour bombardment failed to silence rebel fire, but on the next day, April 30, he made a completely successful landing on the east shore of the river at Bruinsburg, and was ready to move against the interior beyond Vicksburg. The Union army commenced its march on May 12, and after fighting sharp skirmishes at Raymond and other points, threw Northern forces into Jackson on the afternoon

7. Byers, S.H.M. *With Fire and Sword,* New York, 1911, 54-99. Major Byers of Sherman's staff, a Missourian with bristling moustaches, gives a spirited description of the hot, dusty Union march to Jackson, the long, exhausting siege of that Mississippi capital, and the climactic rebel capitulation. He credits Grant with the plan of attacking Vicksburg from the south, going down the Mississippi to win a firm foothold, and says it had occurred to nobody else. Evidence exists that Frank Blair and Charles A. Dana supported Grant in his plans for a landing at Grand Gulf, treating the possible response of the public to any failure with contempt. Lewis, Lloyd, *Sherman, Fighting Prophet,* New York, 1932, *passim.*

8. Byers, *op.cit., passim.*

of May 14. On May 16, blue-clad troops under McPherson and McClernand came into heavy collision with Confederate forces at Champion's Hill, one of the bloodiest battles of the whole Vicksburg campaign. On the 19th came the tragic assault in which Grant's troops were flung back by Pemberton's army at every point.[9]

On the 22nd Grant mistakenly repeated his assault, for he was anxious to avoid a protracted siege of Vicksburg, which would require him to withdraw needed Union troops from other points. In his second attack, Union casualties were again heavy, and Grant to the end of his days regretted his orders bitterly.[10]

The siege of Vicksburg required more than 70,000 Union troops to conduct it, and at the same time hold the Confederate defensive army under Joseph E. Johnston at bay. The people of the city and the Confederate forces were subjected to a pitiless bombardment, and suffered increasingly from a desperate shortage of food and a lengthening list of casualties from wounds and sickness. By July 3rd, the Confederate officers and men were convinced that the situation was hopeless, and they were ready to discuss terms of surrender.

In the spring of 1863, an observant British officer, Lieutenant-Colonel A.J. Lyon Fremantle, entered the Confederacy by the Matamoros gateway, and after arduous travel across Texas, reached Natchez in mid-May. He found the people of Mississippi fearfully excited and distressed by the conflict raging among them. The capital, Jackson, had just seen the Fifty-ninth Indiana unfurl the Union flag, and watched Grant briefly pace its streets. Then the Northern army had marched westward to cut off John Pemberton's force from that of Joseph E. Johnston. Striking Pemberton two quick, heavy blows, Grant's troops forced him back into Vicksburg. Reaching Jackson soon after Grant evacuated it, Fremantle found factories demolished, houses pillaged, railroads torn up, and piles of stores still burning. The citizens spoke with fury of the outrages they had undergone, and of their hope for a bloody revenge—for retaliation without quarter. But when he joined General Johnston not far from the capital, the Briton heard respectful words upon Union accomplishments. Grant, conceded Johnston, had displayed an astonishing rapidity and energy. On April 30, he had thrown a great part of his army across the river below Vicksburg in a movement of unexampled boldness; on May 14, with an enlarged force well in hand, he had driven the Confederates out of Jackson; and on May 15-19, he had routed them and put an iron investment around the river fortress. It was plain that Johnston did not expect Vicksburg to hold out long. The distant thud and roll of the bombardment was already continuous. Soldiers and civilians alike were highly critical of Pemberton

9. Jones, Jenkin L., *An Artilleryman's Diary,* Madison, 1914, *passim.,* Jones, an eminent Unitarian minister in Chicago, then an artilleryman, told how the Union officers brought up howitzers to the line of caissons before the city.

10. Grant, *Memoirs,* II, 276.

for letting himself be outmanoeuvred, and some even doubted the loyalty of the Northern-born Confederate general.

Everywhere, Fremantle found evidence of superior Union strength and a determination to use it with iron resolution. Leonidas Polk told him how heavily the Confederates had been outnumbered at Murfreesboro. Johnston, with a somewhat careless misuse of figures, but no great misrepresentation of the general situation, declared that a garrison of only 20,000 in Vicksburg was besieged by 75,000 troops under Grant; and some of the rebel soldiers, confident despite recent defeats, were clamoring to be led against "only twicet" their own numbers. A brigade, just arrived at Jackson under "States-Rights" Gist, bore good Enfield rifles, but other units were armed only with what they had captured from the enemy. Fremantle heard that Pemberton had lost much of his artillery at Champion's Hill and Edwards' Station; he had, in fact, lost 42 pieces. Johnston was eager to attack, but as he told the Englishman, he was too weak to do any good.

Crossing Mississippi and Alabama eastward, Fremantle saw these States giving up their last sons and ultimate resources in an extremity of anguish. The raid of Grierson's cavalry through nearly the whole length of Mississippi in April, and other Union forays, had left trails of destruction smoking behind them. But the Confederacy was falling into dilapidation anyway. It was painful to hear an old planter gloating over the dead bodies of Northerners in Jackson; to find an officer regretful because a Yankee "surrendered so quick I couldn't kill him"; and to see gentlewomen wild with hatred. At William J. Hardee's headquarters three ladies depressed the Englishman with their innumerable stories of Yankee brutality. Fremantle glowed when General Johnston declared that ninety-nine Southerners in a hundred would rather be subjects of Queen Victoria than return to the Union; but the effect of the statement was spoiled when another officer said they would rather be minions even of His Satanic Majesty! Everywhere he saw misery —combined with resolution.

"We slept at a farmhouse (near Jackson). All the males were absent at the war, and it is impossible to exaggerate the unfortunate condition of the women left behind in the farmhouses; they have scarcely any clothes, and nothing but the coarsest bacon to eat, and are in miserable uncertainty as to the fate of their relations, whom they can hardly ever communicate with. Their slaves, however, generally remain true to them. . . . We breakfasted at another little farmhouse on some unusually tough bacon, and coffee made out of sweet potatoes. The natives, under all their misery, were red-hot in favor of fighting for their independence to the last." The Confederate, he wrote, "has no ambition to imitate the regular soldier at all; he looks the genuine rebel; but in spite of his bare feet, his ragged clothes, his old rug, and tooth-brush stuck like a rose in his button-hole, he has a devil-may-care, reckless, self-confident look, which is decidedly taking."[11]

When Fremantle left the West, Grant's army of some 75,000 effectives had to perform the double task of besieging Vicksburg and fending off Johnston. Pemberton had around 23,000 fit for duty, plus about 5,700 ill, while Johnston had some 28,000 effectives of 36,000 present.[12] If the Confederate armies had been united during the previous three months and strengthened with troops from west of the Mississippi, they would have been a fair match for Grant's army. As it was, their divided forces stood at a hopeless disadvantage. Grant's rear was protected by the Big Black River, winding down to join the Mississippi, and by a maze of hills, minor streams, swamps, and ravines.[13] Johnston telegraphed the Confederate War Department on June 15 that he regarded Vicksburg as good as lost. On the chessboard of war, the Northern forces had been deployed with far more masterly skill than the Southern.

[II]

Two Presidents from the Mississippi Valley led the Union and the Confederacy. Both Lincoln and Davis comprehended the vital importance of holding the Mississippi, but while Davis could not do anything about it, Lincoln could. If Richmond were lost, and Virginia taken, the Confederacy would suffer no vital injury, while if the Mississippi were lost, the back of the Confederacy would be broken. All the men and supplies in the rich area of western Louisiana, Texas, Arkansas, southern Missouri, and the Yazoo district of Mississippi would be sundered from the rest of the country. Great new stores of cotton would fall within the Northern grasp. Scores of thousands of able-bodied Negro men would be turned loose to become soldiers or laborers for the North.[14] The morale of the Northwest would rise to a point at which Copperhead feeling would wither and die; the morale of the lower Valley would sink to a point at which thousands of soldiers would desert to look after their homes.

Why did President Davis, Secretary Seddon, and General Lee fail to take decisive action to protect the Mississippi? Lee, because he thought Virginia more

11. Fremantle, Lieut. Col. A.J.L., *Three Months in the Southern States, April-June, 1863,* New York, 1864, *passim.* Greene, F.V., *The Mississippi,* New York, 1882, 188-190 for numbers. *O.R.* I, xxiv, Pt.3, 452-453, 978; Bearss, Edwin C., *Decision in Mississippi,* Jackson, Miss., 1962, 425, 432. Confederate figures in the Vicksburg Campaign are subject to even more than usual controversy, and it is difficult to be really very definite. Federal figures for troops in the immediate area had increased steadily during the siege.

12. Fremantle, *op.cit.*

13. "The country in this part of Mississippi stands on edge, as it were, the roads running along the ridges except where they occasionally pass from one ridge to another"; *Military History and Reminiscences of the Thirteenth Regiment of Illinois Volunteer Infantry,* Chicago, 1892, 313.

14. *O.R.* I, xxiv, Pt.1, 227. Of the 186,000 Negro troops whom the North enlisted in the South, the Mississippi historian J.S. McNeily states that 24,000 were recruited in Louisiana, 17,800 in Mississippi, and 20,000 in Tennessee: *Mississippi Historical Society Publications, Centenary Series,* II, 174.

important than the great river, knew himself better able to handle a great army than any Confederate general in the West, and supposed the summer climate would be fatal to sustained Union activity about Vicksburg. Seddon, because he was a Virginian, did not understand the logistical advantages which the steamboat gave the Union forces on the Mississippi, and underrated Grant's strength, enterprise, and daring. Moreover, the Confederate government could not manufacture the ironclads and shipping needed. Davis failed to act because he trusted in Lee, and because he still deemed foreign intervention the best hope of victory. To his mind, a victorious invasion of Pennsylvania would be the best means of achieving intervention. All three believed Joseph E. Johnston to be a more dynamic commander than he actually was.

We must repeat that the origins of the Union campaign against Vicksburg, far from being purely military, were in substantial part political. The full conquest of the Mississippi River, always vital in the eyes of the Northwest, had become urgent by the fall of 1862. Since John A. McClernand of Illinois—a veteran Jacksonian who had been elected to four terms in the Legislature and six in the national House, and who as a resident of Springfield since 1856 knew Lincoln well —understood the Northwestern demands, he was busy in Washington in the fall of 1862 crying for energetic action. Three governors, Samuel J. Kirkwood of Iowa, Richard Yates of Illinois, and Oliver P. Morton of Indiana, supported his call for action with a vigor born of their acute apprehension of Copperhead sedition. The Mississippi never eroded its banks more dangerously than dread of the loss of free navigation and control of the river eroded the loyalty of many dwellers in the upper valley. If they ever decided that Washington was indifferent to the great artery, they would react just as Kentuckians had reacted in the days of Aaron Burr and James Wilkinson. Morton believed that an army of 100,000 men could be marched straight down the western bank. McClernand more astutely proposed an attack on the central key to the river system, Vicksburg, by a strong fleet of gunboats and an army of 60,000 men—approximately the force which finally took it.

When Lincoln threw himself behind McClernand's plans, and Stanton equipped him with confidential orders in October to raise or mobilize troops in the Northwest and forward them to Cairo, Memphis, or some other rendezvous so that "an expedition may be organized under General McClernand's command against Vicksburg," the President was not actuated by any particular faith in McClernand's generalship. He knew nothing about it. He was moved by faith in McClernand's political insight, his influence over a powerful array of Jacksonian and Douglasite Democrats in the Middle West, and his energy. The President was also exhibiting a concern for the historic waterway that had no counterpart, unfortunately for the South, in Richmond. "I feel deep interest in the success of the expedition," he endorsed on McClernand's orders, "and desire it to be pushed forward with all possible dispatch, consistently with the other parts of the military service."[15]

Could the South have held the Mississippi if it had centred its main energies upon the task? Probably it could, if a number of posts between Island No. 10 and Port Hudson had been energetically fortified and provisioned; if a powerful mobile army had been kept intact under one bold general; and if this army had been given timely strength by reinforcements from Virginia and from Arkansas. Effective defensive measures could have been taken, but the necessity was not always clear, and in taking such measures the Confederacy would have weakened other areas. The country was full of provisions; it had insufficient transport, to be sure, but determined and resourceful officers, moving in time, could have accumulated enough salt-pork, corn, beans, rice, sugar, and molasses to feed garrisons in Vicksburg, Port Gibson, and Port Hudson for long periods. The river was as much a natural barrier for defense as a natural avenue for invasion. Effectively fortified to prevent the passage of boats—unarmed transports steaming down, slow-moving ironclads struggling upstream—it would have proved a valuable bulwark. The people of the lower valley felt strongly that the defense of New Orleans had been bungled; that it should never have been possible for Farragut to make so easy a conquest. They felt equally outraged that the Confederate flotilla at Memphis should have been so swiftly annihilated.[16]

The North won its triumphs at New Orleans and Memphis by naval power alone, but in the Vicksburg-Port Hudson area such victories were impossible. The Confederacy had critical advantages if it could use them; that is, if they were not nullified by weakness of command. After Grant asserted his primacy, however, the quality of the Northern generalship was as unquestioned as the quality of the Western troops.

Splendid Union armies had been forged in both the East and West, but forged in quite diverse ways. The primary creator of the Eastern army was McClellan, whose masterly skill made it a weapon which an abler strategist might have used to achieve victory. McClellan could not use it with slashing spirit because he was palsied by fear of the defeat that a supposedly superior adversary might inflict upon him. He was succeeded by three generals, Pope, Burnside, Hooker, who failed for different reasons. It was a tribute to the Army of the Potomac that, despite bloody reverses, it never lost the sense of unity which McClellan had instilled into it by careful, methodical drill, and which Hooker strengthened by his dash and pugnacity. The Western armies, meanwhile, had been forged and tempered not by endless drill combined with long avoidance of danger, but by

15. Lincoln, *Collected Works*, V, 468; VI, 230-231; Nicolay and Hay, *Lincoln*, VII, 135-143.
16. June 6, 1862; Greene, F.V., *The Mississippi*, New York, 1882, 14-17.

early and grim fighting at close-quarters. The Western generals seasoned armies by throwing them into combat without delay. At Belmont, Forts Henry and Donelson, Shiloh, Corinth, and Iuka, the troops of Grant, Sherman, and Buell learned boldness and tenacity from action under heavy fire. Even the green regiments seldom flinched.[17]

In the West, Grant fought on the field with his men. At Belmont he was almost captured; at Donelson he was in the advance line when he learned from an examination of the Confederates' haversacks that they were trying to cut their way out; at Shiloh he risked his life again to help stay the initial rout, and was with his troops when they advanced to the attack on the second day. But McClellan's headquarters were usually so far from the battle-lines that, as a shrewd Scottish-born observer, General Peter S. Michie, says in his biography, "so far as his personal or professional influence was concerned, it may be almost completely ignored in all tactical combinations."[18] At Gaines' Mill his want of direct oversight let almost the whole weight of the Confederate attack fall upon one vastly outnumbered corps; at White Oak Swamp he supplied no effective leadership whatever; and at Malvern Hill he went aboard the gunboat *Galena* when his post of duty was ashore. The close liaison of Western troops and generals contributed to the confidence of the troops; they felt, writes one Ohio corporal under Grant, "strong faith in the sagacity of their leader."[19]

The Western armies differed from the Eastern, again, in that they were largely devoid of political coloration. The humility of Grant—untouched as yet by political ambition, fully aware of the supremacy of the civil authority, and highly deferential to Lincoln and Stanton—contrasted with the hard bright egotism which made McClellan feel himself indispensable to the army and country. McClellan felt bitter hatred for Stanton, and for Lincoln an approach to contempt; Grant held both in high regard. The various corps headquarters of the Army of the Potomac were full of political talk, and the talk in such tents as Fitz-John Porter's was dangerous. If the Western officers talked politics, it was very quietly. They had their prejudices. Some of them said at the beginning of 1863 that they would never serve with Negro regiments. But they surrendered these prejudices; three months later they declared that although Adjutant-General Lorenzo Thomas had erred in encouraging Negro recruiting, they would obey orders nonetheless.[20]

Once the Union leadership gave up the attempt to attack Vicksburg from the north, the blunders of the campaign were nearly all on the Confederate side. For months the Northern and Southern numbers in the campaign were approxi-

---

17. Except in the shock of the Shiloh surprise.
18. Michie, Peter S., *General McClellan*, New York, 1901, XV.
19. Hopkins, Owen J., *Under the Flag of the Nation*, ed. O.F. Bond, Columbus, Ohio, 1961, 54.
20. C.A. Dana, April 20, 1863, to Stanton, Dana Papers, LC.

mately equal. Moreover, at the beginning, and down to the battle of Port Gibson on May 1, 1863, the forces on each side were about equally scattered. On April 16, Porter's gunboats ran past the Vicksburg batteries. Grant was gathering his forces together on the west side of the river. As soon as he threw part of his army (the Thirteenth corps and one division of the Seventeenth) across the Mississippi to Bruinsburg,[21] confronting 8,000 rebels with 23,000 bluecoats and so making possible the capture of Port Gibson, the superior ability of the Union commanders in concentrating their forces became manifest. This was the greatest amphibious landing in American history before the Second World War. Other Union troops were quickly ferried across the river, and gained hard ground beyond it. The Confederates evacuated Grand Gulf on May 2, the gunboats taking possession next day. But at no time during April and May did Grant have more than 45,000 men available for his approach to Vicksburg.[22] Not until the first half of June, when thousands of reinforcements arrived from the North in response to an urgent plea from Grant, did the Union army outnumber the defending forces. In fact, on June 7, Grant had only 56,000 men in his ranks, while the combined armies of Pemberton and Johnston came to about 60,000. Then in less than a fortnight Grant increased his strength by more than 21,000.[23] In the end, the Federal army gained its victory by superior strength, naval and military; but in the beginning it owed its steady advance to its superior concentration and abler strategy, combined with the indispensable fleet.

And if nearly all the apparent errors, some of them readily explicable, were on the Confederate side, Pemberton was the leader most censurable for them. It was his fate, to be sure, to suffer from the radically conflicting views of his two superiors, Johnston and Davis. The president believed it vital to hold Vicksburg even at the risk of losing a powerful army. He therefore instructed Pemberton to hold the city at all costs. Johnston, knowing that Union warships ranged the river north and south of Vicksburg (which hung by but a fragile thread), thought it far more important to save the well-armed men under Pemberton. If this force were preserved intact it could be united with other troops, and await an opportunity for striking Grant a staggering blow.[24] It can be said for President Davis that he made the most strenuous efforts, by telegraph, to summon assistance for Pemberton from every quarter; from Charleston, from Arkansas, from Tennessee, from the militia and home guard of Alabama.[25] All his exertions failed. His

21. As fast as Grant's troops crossed to the West bank, they were collected at a camp about four miles below New Carthage; so wrote Porter. O.R.N., I, 410.
22. Greene, F.V., *The Mississippi*, op.cit., 136.
23. Bearss, *Decision in Mississippi*, op.cit, 372ff.
24. Johnston, *Narrative*, op.cit., 178.
25. The telegrams are in Pemberton, John C., *Pemberton, Defender of Vicksburg*, Chapel Hill, 1942, 51-56.

Confederate President Jefferson Davis

General Joseph E. Johnston of the Confederacy

insistence upon the supreme importance of the stronghold meanwhile added to Pemberton's determination to hold it.

The hour of decision for Pemberton struck on May 14. On the previous day Johnston, who was ill and exhausted, had written from Jackson a message intended to bring about an immediate concentration of their forces. Had he not been so weak, he would have gone himself to take command of Pemberton's troops. As it was, his directions were peremptory. He had learned that Sherman, with four divisions, held ground between them at Clinton. If possible, Pemberton should march against the Union rear at once, with all the men he could assemble, and Johnston's troops in Jackson would cooperate in the attack.

Had Pemberton acted instantly on this order, he might have effected a junction with Johnston somewhere near Clinton, and helped preserve the mobility of the joint force. Instead, he called his generals to a council of war, showed them the message, and argued at length against obeying it. A majority of the council voted for accepting the orders; a minority wished to strike at the communications of the advancing Union forces. Pemberton unwillingly adopted the latter plan. Johnston, however, was at this moment forced out of Jackson by Grant's brief occupation of the place, and when he directed Pemberton on the 15th to move directly to Clinton for a junction, his orders were betrayed to Grant.[26]

The Confederates were in fact in a hopeless situation. Their intelligence of the rapid movements of Grant's army, partly because of lack of cavalry, was so poor that they operated half the time in the dark. Even had they been well informed, they would have been fatally crippled by the disagreement between Davis and Pemberton on one side, determined to cling to Vicksburg, and Johnston on the other, insistent on abandoning Vicksburg so as to save the defenders. When Pemberton attempted to cut Grant's supply line, a line really fictitious, for he lived mainly on the country, and on what he had with him, the Confederates failed in the stinging defeat at Champion's Hill. The next certain news that Johnston received was that Pemberton had retreated to the Big Black River Bridge. He must not abandon his base, he explained, and doubtless Confederate sentiment would have held him a traitor had he refused to undergo a siege. In deep alarm, Johnston on May 17 sent Pemberton a final appeal, declaring that Vicksburg was now valueless, and if he were invested he must ultimately surrender. "Under such circumstances, instead of losing both troops and place, we must, if possible, save the troops. If it is not too late, evacuate Vicksburg and its dependencies, and march to the northeast." It was too late. On the evening of the 17th, as the sun sank after a day of stifling heat, the retreating

26. Johnston, *Narrative, op. cit.,* 181; Pemberton, *Pemberton, op.cit.,* XIV.

Confederates moved into the seven-mile line of fortifications about the city, and wave after wave of blue-clad infantrymen closed behind them.

The siege of Vicksburg had begun. "I still conceive it to be the most important point in the Confederacy," Pemberton wrote on the 18th.[27]

It might well have been so considered, so long as it and Port Hudson kept the intervening reach of the river open for ferrying men, livestock, and ammunition from the west shore to the eastern bank. But that era had ended. Warships now ran past the two towns with impunity. The single way left for the transfer of beeves was by smuggling them over at night. Transfers along the lower river had thus been carried on ever since New Orleans fell. Agents of the Confederate commissary bureau would gather hundreds of steers in the Red River valley or southern Arkansas, drive them by night aboard concealed steamboats or barges, and ferry them across. If the lookouts descried smoke from Federal gunboats, the steers would be hastily herded into cover. One agent got 2,250 head of cattle across in eight days.[28] "Pretty good, ain't it?" he demanded of his superiors. The Union patrol, however, an integral part of the blockade of the South, was steadily tightened.

Vicksburg was actually no longer worth defending; but Pemberton had allowed an almost invaluable army to be locked within its earthen walls with only sixty days' provisions and limited ammunition.[29]

With his long miles of trenches and redoubts to fill, Pemberton said he had an effective force of 18,500 men for the work, but he had to keep a mobile reserve of 3,000 to throw into any threatened spot. All thought of a break-out or of a relief expedition by Johnston was folly, for Grant soon had 71,000 men and 248 guns around the city. The situation was entirely different from that in which McClellan had flung his army against Richmond. Then, a strong Confederate army, superbly led and possessing full power of manoeuvre, had faced an army which, timidly led, was caught at a disadvantage in crossing the Chickahominy. Then, the defenders were full of confidence. Now the Union army alone had bold leadership and power of manoeuvre, and all the advantage of morale lay with the Northerners. The only course Pemberton could follow was to lie behind weaker fortifications than the Russians had possessed at Sebastopol, repulse assaults as heroically as they, and, like them, hold out as long as he could. Lack of transport, salt, and energetic aides had made it impossible (so he later said) to accumulate sufficient stores in the city.

27. Johnston, *Narrative, op.cit.,* 188; *O.R.* I, xxiv, Pt.I, 241, 272, 273.

28. See Andrew W. McKee, June 13, 16, 1862, to Major W.L. Lauer, Palmer Collection, Western Reserve Hist. Soc.

29. As S. H. Lockett, chief engineer of the Vicksburg defenses, states in "The Defense of Vicksburg" in *Battles and Leaders,* New York, 1887, III, 492, "We had been from the beginning short of ammunition. . ."

[III]

To Grant's admirers his movements seemed Napoleonic in their rapidity and precision. In eighteen days, to march 200 miles; to sunder Pemberton completely from Johnston; to win five fights; and to drive the main Confederate army across the Big Black and into Vicksburg—this was a grand historic feat.[30] Lincoln was delighted. He admitted later to Grant that he had not seen the full possibilities of the situation. He had thought, when Grant first reached the Vicksburg area, that the General should do just what he finally did; march the troops down the west bank, run the batteries with the empty transports, refill them, and thus set the army below. But he believed that thereafter Grant should drop farther down the river and join N.P. Banks to take Port Hudson. So thinking, wrote Lincoln, "when you turned northward, east of the Big Black, I feared it was a mistake." But Grant had been right—"and I was wrong."[31]

The Northern press was as deeply impressed as Lincoln. Greeley's *Tribune* commented a few days after the siege began: "It is hardly possible to praise too highly the extreme rapidity of Grant's operations.[32] It should be added, however, that Grant and Sherman had been exceedingly anxious, during their marches behind Vicksburg, to reach the Yazoo and reëstablish direct communications with the North. "My first anxiety," writes Grant, "was to secure a base of supplies on the Yazoo River above Vicksburg." He and Sherman impatiently accompanied the skirmishers to the point on the Walnut Hills not far from where Sherman had been repulsed the previous December. Gaining the brow, Sherman turned to Grant with the confession that until that moment he had felt no assurance of success, but now he was confident of it.[33] The soldiers were delighted for a different reason. They had missed their crackers and coffee even while feasting on fresh pork, chicken, and eggs, and as Grant came back to the main lines, they set up a chorus of "Hardtack! Hardtack!"[34] It should also be added that, swift and easy as Grant's movements seemed, the swiftness and ease owed much to the river navy, which in turn owed its efficient cooperation to skilled organization. Not numbers, but planning furnished the key to victory.

Grant depended for river transport on a finely educated colonel, later general,

30. Greene, *The Mississippi*, *op.cit.*, 170; *O.R.* I, xxiv, 273.

31. Lincoln, *Collected Works*, VI, 326, July 13, 1863. It might seem extraordinary that Grant did not inform Lincoln of his bold plan at an early date. But Grant did not determine to move across the river and take Vicksburg in the rear until March 19, 1863; a letter from Halleck then led him to consider sending one corps to cooperate with Banks against Port Hudson; and it was not until May 2 that he finally determined to throw his whole army against Jackson and Vicksburg. Of course, Lincoln did know the general plan was to take Vicksburg. Greene, *The Mississippi*, *op.cit.*, 139. For more on the campaign to Vicksburg see Nevins, Allan, *The War for the Union: War Becomes Revolution*, 399ff.

32. New York *Tribune*, May 25, 1863.

33. Rear Admiral D.D. Porter and a party of naval officers accompanied Grant, and were greatly impressed by the strength of the Confederate position.

34. Grant, *Memoirs*, *op.cit.*, I, 528-530.

Lewis B. Parsons, a New Yorker by birth who had lived in Alton, Illinois, and St. Louis before the war, and had been one of the principal executives of the Ohio & Mississippi Railroad. In December, 1861, he had been given charge of all river and rail transportation in the Department of the Mississippi, and after devising regulations for military use of the railways, he devoted his whole attention to the carriage of men and supplies, leaving only what General Peter J. Osterhaus called "gunboat soup" to the naval forces. Few assignments in the West required more ability or experience.

The tasks of river transportation were tremendous, for the boats had to carry men, medical supplies, forage, horses, rations, munitions, cannon, wagons, and an endless list of miscellanies. Parsons had to toil day and night providing all kinds of craft; tugs, barges, hospital boats, transports, mailboats, cargo boats, wood-cutting boats, and snag-removal boats, while lending a hand at times with iron-clads, tinclads, and mortarboats. He was naturally a target for criticism from steamboat owners, army officers, naval officers, and Treasury officers. When Grant expressed a passing disapprobation in hasty terms, the St. Louis quarter-master, General Robert Allen, flew to Parson's defense. "In his zeal to conduct the affairs of the transportation branch of the service with *economy,* he has drawn upon him the whole power of the steamboat interest, and by those representing this interest he has been abused and villified without stint. In this his honest effort to discharge his duty as he understood it, reckless of his personal popularity, is it not hard that he should be rewarded by a sneer from his commanding general?" Grant at once withdrew his censure.[35]

Grant, in fact, repeatedly expressed high esteem for Parsons and his work. He would have been utterly helpless without the naval forces commanded first by Flag-Officer Andrew H. Foote, Charles H. Davis, and later by Rear-Admiral David D. Porter, and the shipping mobilized by Parsons. The warships serving in the Mississippi Squadron in the critical months from the beginning of 1863 to the opening of the siege of Vicksburg numbered 64, of which 5 displaced a thousand tons or more, 12 were ironclads, and nearly all carried guns.[36] The need for a multiplicity of additional vessels large and small never slackened, and their number ran into the hundreds. Grant telegraphed Parsons from his headquarters near Vicksburg on January 30, 1863: "A move may take place at any time requiring the use of all our transports." He demanded so many small boats for his Yazoo Pass operations that he feared enough could not be drawn from the Upper Mississippi, the Cumberland, the Tennessee, and other Western rivers to meet his needs. In March, he wanted the steamboats that were sent from the north

35. Parsons Papers, Illinois State Historical Library; Fox, G.V., Correspondence, Box 6, 1863, New York Historical Society.
36. *O.R.N.*, I, xxiv, 5.

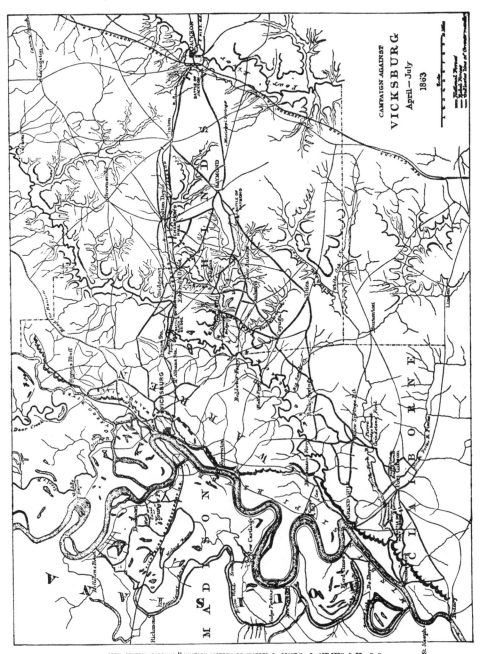

Map of the *Vicksburg Campaign, April–July, 1863*

given a double load; subsistence stores and forage below deck, and troops crowding the upper part of the vessels.

At the time when Porter took command on the Mississippi (early in October, 1862; he remained in charge until Vicksburg's fall was assured), the fighting squadron was by modern standards relatively weak. It consisted of fifteen vessels, most of them out of repair, insufficiently protected against shot and shell, and drawing too great a depth of water. Porter immediately sent for a work crew of mechanics and put the ships in efficient trim. He also began buying and arming light-draft steamboats, so that in the next few months he added 54 vessels of 324 guns to his force. The fleet of rams under Col. Alfred Ellet was converted into a marine brigade, manned by 1500 troops, to be used with the gunboats to suppress the guerrillas that had made the river banks a series of hornets' nests.[37] It was under Porter's command that a large fleet of transports had carried Sherman's army of 40,000 troops to his futile attack on the Yazoo River fortifications, and later transported McClernand's successful movement against Arkansas Post. Likewise under his command, perfectly coordinated with Grant's movements, seven gunboats and a group of provision-laden transports ran past Vicksburg on the night of April 16.

This passage of Vicksburg was planned with remarkable efficiency. Pains were taken to get the vessels into line at proper distances from each other, the flagship *Benton* leading the way. Till she was abreast of the forts, no wheel turned except to keep the ships in the four-miles-an-hour current. Even then the vessels "drifted slowly by," as Porter put it, keeping as good order as could be expected in a narrow river amid flame and smoke—so much smoke that the rear vessels had to stop firing to let the pilots see their way clear. Only one empty transport was lost, with some damage to the coal barges, and only 12 men wounded. On the evening of April 22, six more transports were sent past Vicksburg, one being sunk. However, the Union gunboats failed to knock out the Grand Gulf batteries on April 29 after five hours' bombardment. When the time came to move the Union forces from the west to the east bank, Porter was ready. "For 48 hours," he wrote, "the gunboats were employed, in conjunction with the army transports, in carrying over the large army, munitions of war, and transports. Never was there a more rapid or better-planned movement."[38] The placid stretch of waters below Grand Gulf bore a cohort of steamers, the decks covered with bluecoats; beyond the bends above and below, other transports whistled and puffed, their smoke curling over woods and levees. Thickening lines of men marched from the eastern bank toward the rising sun. Those who saw the spectacle thought the army invincible.

37. *O.R.N.*, I, xxiii, 395, 396; the marine brigade was ready for duty March 24, 1863.
38. *O.R.N.*, I, xxiii, 409; 414; xxiv, 553-554.

River-power as mobilized by Parsons, Porter, and Ellet was, in fact, as important as sea-power. It now completed the cordon of the blockade, forging with the Atlantic and Gulf squadrons a ring around the Confederacy. It made possible amphibious operations of an even more telling character than those on the Atlantic. It was not merely invaluable as an auxiliary of the Union armies; the naval elements were equally important as an independent force. Admiral Porter was insistent in his reports that his forces, and not the army's, deserved by far the major share of credit for the capture of Arkansas Post and Grand Gulf. In three hours, he wrote, possibly exaggerating his own role, the gunboats dismounted every gun in the former stronghold with a terrific destruction of men, artillery, and horses. "This has been a naval fight."[39] He agreed with Captain Guild that the Navy alone should be credited with the taking of Grand Gulf. The Army never fired a gun there; and when Grant rode into the place all its guns were out of action and lying at the water's edge, while the sailors were busy dismantling the fortifications. The Confederate forces under Bowen had evacuated Grand Gulf without a fight because of Grant's army to the south marching inland toward Port Gibson, and the Navy did the occupying job.[40] Even when acting in a supporting capacity, the river navy had an enterprise all its own. The suppression of guerrillas was an especially dangerous activity, and required constant alertness. Not only the Mississippi, but all the tributaries had to be kept clear of irregular partisans. "Whenever you hear of a musket fired at a transport," Porter wrote the head of the marine brigade who had been sent to scour the White and the lower Arkansas, "dash in there and clean them out; take every musket you can find . . . The important object is to make continual dashes into the enemy's country, then disappear, to turn up somewhere else. In this way the guerrillas will soon disappear, especially when they find that their style of warfare is not looked upon as civilized."[41]

The lamentations of the Confederates over their difficulties with transportation, among other things, help to illuminate the advantages enjoyed by the Union leaders. General Johnston harped considerably upon this chord. He was bemired while the Federal armies moved with ease. "The whole of the Mississippi Valley is said to be impassable for large wagon trains," he wrote Wigfall from Chattanooga March 4, 1863.[42] When he penned his final report to the Adjutant-General that fall, he declared that he had been completely fettered. Late spring reinforcement, he stated, had brought his army up to about 24,000 infantry and artillerymen, but it had been deficient in guns, ammunition, and above all, in transport.

39. To Fleet Captain A. M. Pennock, Cairo, January 11, 1863; *O.R.N.*, I, xxiv, 114, 115; C.F. Guild to Gustavus V. Fox, Fox Correspondence, Box 6, 1863, NYHS.
40. *O.R.N.*, I, xxiii, 414, 415; *O.R.* I, xxiv, Pt. I, 666.
41. March 26, 1863; *O.R.N.*, I, xxiv, 513, 514.
42. Letters of J.E. Johnston to L.T. Wigfall, and others; copies in Univ. of Texas.

"The draft upon the country had so far reduced the number of horses and mules, that it was not until late in June that draught animals could be obtained from distant points for the artillery and trains. There was no want of commissary supplies in the department, but the limited transportation caused a deficiency for a moving army. . . The want of field transportation rendered any movement for the relief of Port Hudson impossible, had a march in that direction been admissible."[43]

It was inferior transportation, in the opinion of Johnston, which really made Vicksburg untenable, for sufficient stores could not be collected to hold it. And it was plain to the Confederates as to the Federals that movement by highway or railroad was far less safe than by steamboat. A railway could always be cut by a few lurking men, as Buell had found when he tried to repair the Corinth-Chattanooga line after Shiloh; it could be raided to shut off supplies, as Grant had learned when he tried to march south from Grenada along the Mississippi Central. No river could be cut, and no steamboat derailed. It was true that the stages of water in any stream had to be watched carefully; Grant's advance against Forts Henry and Donelson were necessarily undertaken in a wet season. The Federal Navy did lose three major vessels in the long campaign around Vicksburg, however. The *Cairo* hit a torpedo in the Yazoo, Dec. 12, 1862; the *Cincinnati* was sunk by Vicksburg batteries May 27, 1863; and the *Baron DeKalb* hit a torpedo below Yazoo City in July, 1863. There was also considerable damage to the ironclads in Porter's abortive daylight attack at Grand Gulf, but on the whole the celerity of river transportation was matched by its security.[44]

[IV]

On May 22nd, when the siege of Vicksburg was but four days old, Grant made the most tragic error of the campaign, a foretaste of Cold Harbor. He ordered a frontal attack, launching about 40,000 men over difficult ground against a total garrison 32,000 strong, which held powerful fortifications. He had already been repulsed on the 19th with heavy losses. Now he was almost certain to be repulsed again, although he well knew that if he merely held his lines and continued his bombardment, victory within weeks was certain—an almost bloodless victory.

For this futile and costly assault, he later assigned a number of reasons, all fairly poor. One was that he now held better ground for launching an attack than on the 19th. Although this was to some extent true, on the 19th the Confederate defenders had been largely demoralized, while three days later they had recov-

43. *O.R.*, I, xxiv, Pt.i, 242.
44. *O.R.N.* II, i, 42, 49, 58; a good description of the *DeKalb* in New York *Herald*, July 23, 1863.

ered.[45] Another excuse was that he could not effectively besiege Vicksburg, and
at the same time fight off Johnston's army at Canton to the northeast. But
Johnston was too weak to save Vicksburg (as he wrote Pemberton on May 29),
too weak even to extricate Pemberton unless they made mutually-supporting
movements which were infeasible. He was apparently at no time able to interfere
with the siege.[46] Grant, too, felt that success then would close the campaign and
free his army immediately for further operations. This might have some merit,
but was the possible saving of six weeks worth the terrible risk incurred? After
all, was the time really lost? As Grant himself says in another connection, "the
siege of Vicksburg had drawn from Rosecrans's front so many of the enemy that
his chances of victory were much greater than they would be if he waited [to
attack] until the siege was over, when these troops could be returned."[47] But
Grant's main reason seemed to be that it was the beginning of the hot season,
they had won five victories, and "the Army of the Tennessee had come to believe
that they could beat their antagonist under any circumstances." He was concerned over the effect on his army of trench life during a siege. He admitted in
his *Memoirs* that he regretted two assaults, Cold Harbor in 1864, and that of the
22nd of May, 1863. But he felt there was more justification for the Vicksburg
assault, though he admits: "The only benefit we gained—and it was a slight one
for so great a sacrifice—was that the men worked cheerfully in the trenches after
that, being satisfied with digging the enemy out. Had the assault not been made,
I have no doubt that the majority of those engaged in the siege of Vicksburg
would have believed that had we assaulted it would have proven successful,
and would have saved life, health and comfort." Perhaps some officers and some
civilians might have felt so, but would this have been true of the men in the ranks?

"As our troops came in fair view," wrote Sherman later, "the enemy rose
behind their parapet and poured a furious fire upon our lines; and, for about two
hours, we had a severe and bloody battle, but at every point we were repulsed."[48]
The Confederates had dug exterior ditches eight to twelve feet deep, erected
ramparts and parapets behind them for their troops, mounted 102 guns, and
protected parts of their front by an abattis of felled trees and telegraph-wire

45. In February, 1863, President Davis expressed astonishment that the army was not more efficient
in interrupting the Union navigation of the Mississippi; T.C. Reynolds, Jacksonport, June 1, 1863, to
Lt.-Gen. T.H. Holmes; Reynolds Papers, LC.
46. Johnston, Joseph E., "Jefferson Davis and the Mississippi Campaign," *Battles and Leaders*, III,
478, 479.
47. Grant, Ulysses S., "Chattanooga," in *Battles and Leaders*, III, 679. Grant, of course, meant that
the siege had kept Johnston's army, including troops sent from Bragg, in Mississippi. Moreover, it
should be noted that after Vicksburg did surrender, no effective use was made of Grant's released
command. By a decision apparently Halleck's, they were "dissipated over other parts of the country,"
as Grant put it; some going to Banks, some to Schofield, some to Kentucky, some to Natchez. *Battles
and Leaders*, III, 680; Grant, *Memoirs*, I, 530-531; II, 276-277.
48. Sherman, William T., *Memoirs of General Sherman*, New York, 1875, I, 326.

entanglements. Three times the Union soldiers poured forward to the assault, and thrice they were thrown back with heavy loss. At two points McClernand's troops crossed the ditches, scaled the ramparts, and planted their colors on the Southern parapets; at one they even seized a detached work, driving out the defenders, and held it—their colonel standing on the parapet and shouting for help—until they were slowly exterminated.[49]

This limited success encouraged McClernand to call for more support. Grant ordered McPherson and Sherman to make new attacks which they did in a somewhat uncoordinated manner. The failure of the assault became a subject of much controversy. McClernand, with the ear of the press and political pipelines to Washington, claimed he had not been supported and had been wrongly condemned. Grant replied that McClernand had misled him as to the degree of his success, so causing much of the afternoon loss. In a rare burst, Grant told Halleck that McClernand "is entirely unfit for the position of corps commander." McClernand said there "appears to be a systematic effort to destroy my usefulness and reputation. . . ." That Grant was responsible for a great needless sacrifice of brave men was clear, but it is probable that all the Union commanders were overly optimistic in view of their recent triumphs. The Confederates estimated that 3,500 men were left dead and wounded between the lines; the records show 3,052 killed and wounded, and 147 missing.[50]

Once more the familiar sequel of battle was enacted. The dead and wounded lay untended on the field as one chill night passed, one hot day, another chill night, and a second hot day. By that time the dead stank, and the living, wrote the chief engineer of the Vicksburg defenses, "were suffering fearful agonies." Not Grant, but Pemberton, proposed a brief truce to succor the Union wounded, and from 6 in the evening until 8:30 a tardy mercy was extended the prostrate men.

Not only was Grant disturbed by what he believed to be McClernand's faults in the assault of May 22; he was further disconcerted by a dispatch of McClernand stating that he had held two of the enemy's forts, and claiming great things for his troops and himself. Charles A. Dana wrote Stanton May 24 that Grant was determined to relieve McClernand at once, but concluded it would be better to

49. Lockett, S.H., *Battles and Leaders,* III, 489.

50. The controversy between McClernand and Grant is so deep and involved that it requires very intensive study to even make a reasoned judgment. For two modern and somewhat opposing opinions, see: Bearss, *Decision in Mississippi, op.cit.* Unfortunately, there is no modern biography of McClernand. For casualties on May 22, see Livermore, *Numbers and Losses in the Civil War,* Boston, 1901, 100. For Grant to Halleck regarding McClernand's ability, *O.R.* I, 37, May 24, 1863. Much material in his own defense will be found in the McClernand Papers, Illinois State Historical Library, including a draft of a letter of McClernand to Grant, June 4, 1863. Also, Grant, *Memoirs,* I, Chap.XXXVIII; Sherman, *Memoirs,* I, 355; New York *Herald,* July 1, 1863. Jones, Jenkin Lloyd, *An Artilleryman's Diary,* Madison, 1914, 91-93.

wait and try to induce him to ask for leave. Dana wrote, "My own judgment is that McClernand has not the qualities necessary for a good commander, even of a regiment." In June, McClernand's orders of congratulation to his troops, a very bombastic statement, found its way into the press. Grant, Sherman, and McPherson were furious, inasmuch as McClernand had not cleared this release with headquarters as required. On June 18, Grant relieved McClernand from command of the Thirteenth Corps and sent him home. E.O.C. Ord, a more stable commander, took over the corps. McClernand, however, would not let things rest. Prior to his dismissal he had written Governor Richard Yates of Illinois, praising his own corps and blaming others. After dismissal, McClernand wrote Lincoln protesting Grant's action: "Is it not hard that I should be dismissed from command and Sherman and McPherson complimented by promotion in the regular army when it will hardly be said that they have done more or better than myself?" He bluntly asked for restoration. He also wrote Stanton and Halleck. This only tended to augment the bitterness.[51]

As the siege continued, the city was given no peace. From the river, hour after hour, came the thud of cannon on the gunboats, and from the western shore the boom of mortars planted on the bank; shells tore through the air with a scream, while bombs rose as black balls in an arc, hung suspended an instant like poised eagles, and then plunged down to fling up earth and debris in an angry roar. Along the waterless valleys and their yellow clay banks the Northern troops pushed their zigzag approaches a little forward every day, every night. Lean, sun-tanned squads, perspiring, grunting, and cursing, flung the dirt to right and left. Where the Union trenches ran close to the Confederate redoubts, hand grenades and shells would be lobbed back and forth, and limbs and bloody lumps of flesh hurled in air. Sometimes quiet would descend and, to the tune of friendly voices, "Time to surrender, Reb!" "Ain't you lost enough men, Yank?", hardtack or bacon, wrapped in paper, would be tossed across in exchange for tobacco. Toiling Union gangs labored stealthily on mines, and Confederates on countermines, men catching the faint clang of enemy picks and spades far underground. Above the river and city hung buzzards awaiting their opportunity, for they could find carrion aplenty if they braved the shot and shell.

Had the Confederate leaders shown more foresight, they would have expelled almost the whole civil population from Vicksburg before its investment. It was no place for women and children, whose extra mouths were a serious problem. By the end of May, the incessant bombardment had forced many civilians into hastily-excavated caves, particularly during especially heavy shelling. Built into

51. Lockett, *ut supra*, 489, 490; Charles A. Dana Papers, LC, Dana to Stanton, May 24, 1863; Catton, Bruce, *Grant Moves South*, Boston, 1960, 466-468; McClernand to Yates, May 28, 1863, McClernand to Lincoln, Aug. 12, 1863, and ms. biography of McPherson, unpublished, McClernand Papers, Illinois State Historical Library.

the terraced hills on which the town sprawled, they were equipped with bedding, clothing, and food; sometimes carpets and fine furniture. One great cavern contained about two hundred people, who lived in fear that a mortar bomb would bury them alive. Even after most houses had been damaged or wrecked, many people clung to them; when church bells rang on Sunday, hardy souls still ventured to the services. It was food which became the insoluble problem. As flour, meal, and bread disappeared, mule-meat became a staple, and some men counted rats the delicacy that the besieged people of Paris would esteem them in 1870-71. However, it is probable that some accounts exaggerated the extent of the lack of food. Pemberton later denied that the garrison was starved out.[52]

"The Federals fought the garrison in part, but the city mainly," one resident records. Nowhere during the war was the heroism of the Southern women more evident. A calm endurance marked the deportment of the poorer women, a wild enthusiasm that of their wealthier sisters. Every man who could bear arms went into the trenches. Some distinguished themselves by daring feats; three, for example, floated down the river on logs to bring back a desperately-needed supply of percussion caps. But, little by little, the hardships and squalor destroyed the morale of garrison and residents alike. After the tenth day, the garrison subsisted on half-rations, later reduced; the people were glad to boil cane-sprouts. Yet a few speculators made the most of the situation, selling flour for $1,000 a barrel, meal for $140 a bushel, and molasses for $12 a gallon. A flow of Confederate deserters kept Grant informed as to conditions inside the city, as did at least one spy.[53]

As the siege continued, the Richmond authorities seemed confused, inert, and hopeless. Secretary Seddon, gaunt, cadaverous, and more toilworn than ever, was now in despair. Like his subordinate Robert Garlick Kean, he felt from the beginning that Vicksburg would fall—probably by the end of June.[54] Although he repeatedly urged Johnston to take more active steps in repelling Grant, he was unable to provide him the forces needed. Davis appealed in vain to governors and generals for help. When Johnston telegraphed on June 4 that his army was far too small to relieve Pemberton, Davis replied: "I regret inability to promise more troops, as we have drained resources even to the danger of several points. You know best concerning General Bragg's army, but I fear to withdraw more. We

52. Bell, L. McRae, "A Girl's Experiences in the Siege of Vicksburg," *Harper's Weekly*, June 8, 1912; *O.R.* I, xxiv, Pt.i, 285.

53. Gregory, Edward S., "Fall of Vicksburg," Philadelphia *Weekly Times*, March 9, 1878; Abrams, A.S., *A Full and Detailed History of the Siege of Vicksburg*, Atlanta, 1863, *passim.*; Dana to Stanton, June 20, 1863, Stanton Papers, LC. There are numerous first-hand accounts of the siege both in books and manuscripts. A good collection is Walker, Peter F., *Vicksburg, A People At War, 1860-1865*, Chapel Hill, 1960.

54. Kean, Robert G.H., *Inside the Confederate Government, op.cit.*, New York, 1957, 68, 69.

are too far outnumbered in Virginia to spare any. . ."[55] The dispatch reached Johnston in garbled form, leaving him to suppose that the government wished no troops withdrawn from Bragg. Moreover, he believed that to take a force sufficient to break the siege would involve the surrender of Tennessee. He so telegraphed the War Department June 12-15: "It is for the government to decide between this State and Tennessee."[56] In desperation, Seddon telegraphed the general to attempt the relief of Vicksburg with what force he had; to which Johnston replied that the difficulties were insuperable.[57]

Because of his concern over possible loss of the Mississippi River, Davis had not ordered Vicksburg evacuated. Yet he could find no way really to help either Johnston or Pemberton. After the siege began, he continued to urge Johnston to act, tried to assemble troops for reenforcement, and attempted every possible expedient but to go himself into the field, a course that his health did not permit. If he seemed to fumble the situation, it was because there was little effective that he could do. "The Secretary and President are at their wits' end and seem to have no plan, to be drifting along on the current of events"; so Assistant-Secretary J.A. Campbell in the War Department told Kean.[58] And Kean wrote: "This is characteristic of the President. He is not a comprehensive man. He has no broad policy, either of finance, strategy, or supply." A letter Davis wrote Bragg at Shelbyville, Tennessee, as the siege neared its inexorable climax, certainly revealed him in a state of confused indecision. The assignment of several military departments to a geographical district under Johnston as head had plainly worked badly, for Johnston protested that he could not command in Tennessee while he was absorbed in the Mississippi operations. What suggestions could Bragg make for remedying the situation? Did he have adequate means of communication to direct operations in both Tennessee and Kentucky? How much cooperation could be expected between separate forces without an actual junction? This was the almost despairing letter of a commander-in-chief fumbling in the dark while the Western front fell apart.[59]

Even after Johnston had telegraphed that an attack on Grant would almost certainly fail, that after a repulse the Big Black would cut off his retreat, and that all Mississippi and Alabama would then lie open to attack, Seddon persisted. Convinced of an almost imperative necessity for action, he replied on June 21, he was ready to take the responsibility for the most desperate course the occasion might demand. The eyes and the hopes of the Confederacy were upon Johnston,

55. Johnston, *Narrative, op.cit.*, 233; Rowland, Dunbar, *Jefferson Davis, Constitutionalist*, Jackson, 1923, V, 534 and *passim*.
56. Johnston, *Ibid.*, 247, 248.
57. Kean, *op.cit.*, 74.
58. *Ibid.*, 72.
59. Davis to Bragg, June 19, 1863, Palmer Collection, Western Reserve Hist. Soc.

he continued, and "it is better to fail nobly daring than, through prudence even, to be inactive."[60] Belatedly, for he lacked adequate supplies and transportation, Johnston advanced to the vicinity of Grant's lines on July 1. His troops spent two days in reconnaissances north of the Vicksburg-Jackson railway lines. As scouts had previously reported, no weak spots existed in the Federal position. Attack in that area would mean ghastly and futile losses. Johnston then decided to move on July 5 to the south of the road, where the Union works might be weaker. But it was too late.

Pemberton had queried his four division commanders on the 1st upon the ability of their troops to carry out a successful evacuation, and they in turn consulted brigade and regimental commanders. The unanimous opinion of senior officers was that the troops were physically too exhausted to cut their way out. After day-and-night service in the trenches for nearly a month and a half, now drenched by rains and now roasted by the subtropical sun, ill-fed, denied sleep by the storm of shot and shell, with legs cramped and swollen for lack of free movement, they had grown gaunt and weak. To expect them to march out against an enemy four times their strength, well-fed, well-armed, and full of confidence, would be folly. A petition "From many soldiers" dated June 28, 1863, had warned Pemberton of a crisis. "Our rations have been cut down to one biscuit and a small bit of bacon per day, not enough scarcely to keep soul and body together, much less to stand the hardships we are called upon to stand. . . . If you can't feed us, you had better surrender."[61]

Under a scrawny oak, on a scarred, sun-parched hillside, at three o'clock on the afternoon of July 3, two old comrades of the Mexican War greeted each other with friendly restraint. No one was aware, of course, of what was going on far to the east in Pennsylvania. Pemberton, tall, erect, dignified, his black hair and full black beard adding to the stern effect of his determined features, and Grant, short, of slouching posture, biting a cigar, but of equally resolute mien, stood for some time talking. They strolled a short distance toward the Confederate lines. Disagreeing, they sat down alone while a Northern artist named T.R. Davis remained under the tree to sketch the scene, and while two officers, General A.J. Smith on the Union side and General John S. Bowen on the Confederate, continued the conference. Finally, all agreed that Grant should send a letter with his final terms by ten that night. This he did, offering to parole the entire Southern force, the officers to keep their side-arms and one horse each. These terms seemed to Halleck excessively generous, for he feared the men would break parole and rejoin the army. Grant at the time was a bit reluctant to accept the parole idea, but agreed and later became sincerely convinced it was the right

60. Johnston, *Narrative, op.cit.*, 200, 201.
61. National Archives; *O.R.* I, xxiv, Pt.1, 280-283.

thing. As he later wrote a friend: "I was very glad to give the garrison of Vicksburg the terms I did. There was a cartel in existence at that time which required either party to exchange or parole all prisoners either at Vicksburg or at points on the James River within ten days after capture, or as soon thereafter as practicable. This would have used all the transportation we had for a month. The men had behaved so well that I did not want to humiliate them. I believed that consideration for their feelings would make them less dangerous during the continuance of hostilities, and better citizens after the war was over."[62]

Next day, the 4th, under another burning sun, the hard-faced Union veterans of Frederick Steele's division, with bands playing patriotic airs, swung into the city and garrisoned the principal points. Along the Confederate lines, the defenders filed dejectedly out of their trenches, stacked arms, and then, forming columns, marched with dignity back to their works. Union flags began to go up on buildings. An officer strode into the postoffice to reëstablish Federal postal service. In the center of the city a little group of citizens watched as two men on horseback rode up to the Court House—Pemberton in gray, Grant in blue. They alighted, climbed the steps, and stood at attention. So did the lines of blue troops, bayonets and sabers glittering in the sun, who fronted the building. All saluted while slowly the Confederate banner came down, and the national ensign rose in its stead. The naval forces had been expectantly awaiting this moment; and past the city came gunboat after gunboat, transport after transport, their decks black with men, their flags flying, their bands playing, and their guns firing salutes.[63]

[V]

The North had won its victory primarily by the superior organization of the combined naval and military forces which Admiral Porter and General Grant led, and the superb organization of the supply system for which Lewis B. Parsons was primarily responsible. This was one indispensable element in the success. A secondary but almost equally important element was Grant's generalship: his boldness, decision, and rapidity in executing his plan for flanking Vicksburg from the east.[64] Audacity was never carried further save by Stonewall Jackson in similarly daring and decisive flank movements at Second Manassas and Chancellorsville. Organization gave Grant's army its transportation and supplies up to the point at which both could be partially abandoned; to the time when, once across the river below Grand Gulf, the troops could move by rapid marches over good roads and forage on the countryside for provisions. True to his nature, in his

62. To Gen. Marcus J. Wright, Nov. 30, 1884, Eldridge Collection, HEH.
63. Pemberton, *Pemberton*, 236-239; Grant, *Memoirs*, I, ch. XXXVII; Bell, L. McRae, *Harper's Weekly*, June 8, 1912.
64. Badeau, Adam, *Military History of Ulysses S. Grant*, New York, 1868, I, 222.

dispatches to subordinates he continually emphasized speed, or as he put it in writing to Sherman on May 3, "the overwhelming importance of celerity."[65]

The river flotillas constituted in 1863 perhaps the best-organized branch of the Northern war effort, no whit inferior to the railroad system under Daniel C. McCallum and Herman Haupt. To the very end the Navy, though less conspicuous than the Army, was indispensable in the Vicksburg campaign. Transports brought Grant his indispensable reinforcements and supplies; gunboats shelled the city up to the day that Pemberton rode out to surrender; mortar boats threw their shells into Pemberton's eastern fortifications three miles away. Ellet's patrols suppressed the guerrillas who would otherwise have harassed transports and exploded ammunition boats. On the morrow of the surrender, Sherman wrote Porter a well-earned tribute:

"I can appreciate the intense satisfaction you must feel at lying before the monster that has defied us with such deep and malignant hate, and seeing your once disunited fleet again a unit; and, better still, the chain that made an enclosed sea of a link in the great river broken forever. It is so magnificent a result that I stop not to count who did it. It is done . . . God grant that the harmony and mutual respect that exist between our respective commanders, and is shared by all the true men of the joint service, continue forever, and serve to elevate our national character, threatened with shipwreck."[66]

Four days after Vicksburg, the garrison of Port Hudson surrendered. The siege had actually begun May 24, when Banks's force of possibly about 30,000 at its peak invested Major General Frank Gardner's force of approximately 6,000 at Port Hudson. As we have related previously, Banks's assault of May 27 was a tragic blunder, and, like Grant's at Vicksburg, failed, with Northern losses of 1,842 killed and wounded. The Confederates held an interior line of four to five miles, which necessitated a Federal siege line of seven to eight miles. In mid-June, Banks made some fresh dispositions of his troops, and assaulted again at daybreak on June 14. Although lines were advanced, the Confederates did not break. On July 6, news came of the surrender at Vicksburg. As a result, Port Hudson was formally surrendered July 8. Like Pemberton, Gardner had no way to escape. Also there was no chance that Port Hudson could hold out after Vicksburg was taken. According to eyewitnesses, Port Hudson was not starved out, although rations were substantially reduced.[67]

65. *O.R.*, I, xxiv, Pt.3, 268; Fuller, J.F.C., *The Generalship of Ulysses S. Grant*, New York, 1919, 140ff.
66. Guernsey, Alfred H., and Henry M. Alden, *Harper's History of the Civil War*, Chicago, 1894-1896, 480.
67. *O.R.* I, xxiv, Pt.3, 473. For Port Hudson early stages, see Nevins, *The War for the Union: War Becomes Revolution*, 402-405; Palfrey, John C., "Port Hudson," *Papers of the Military Historical Society of Massachusetts*, Vol. VIII, Boston, 1910, *passim.;* Cunningham, Edward, *The Port Hudson Campaign, 1862-1863*, Baton Rouge, 1963, *passim.;* Wright, Lieut. Howard C., *Port Hudson, Its History from an Interior Point of View*, Baton Rouge, 1861; *Report of the Joint Committee on the Conduct of the War,*

These victories were regarded by some as primarily a marine triumph. On July 16 the steamboat *Imperial* arrived at New Orleans from St. Louis, its path completely clear. A week later, Secretary Chase instructed the customs surveyor in St. Louis to clear boats and cargoes of permissible materials to New Orleans, if desired, taking care not to land goods at intermediate points, except under authorized permits.[68] The cargoes *were* needed. When, early in August, three large steamboats reached New Orleans, beef fell from 40 cents per pound to 25, potatoes from $13.50 per barrel to $3.00, and flour in proportion. Merchants looked forward to a large West-Indian trade. The Vicksburg and Port Hudson levees were lined with steamboats discharging miscellaneous supplies while the owners looked eagerly for cotton to send back by way of Cairo. Sugar and molasses began going upstream. Although Southern planters and shippers complained bitterly of the restrictions placed upon trade by the internal ("infernal") revenue officers, large profits were nevertheless made. The Father of Waters flowed unvexed by guns, but vexed instead by Treasury regulations, and occasional snipers.[69]

[VI]

Deep was the gloom which settled upon Southerners. Yet they were still defiant. "It is strange," wrote one Wisconsin soldier on entering Vicksburg, "to see a people who have suffered so much, spitting forth open defiance to us and uttering such intensified sentiments of hostility to Yankees."[70] The gloom would have been deeper and the defiance perhaps less marked, but for the fact that only high Confederate and Union officers knew the full extent of the calamity which the South had sustained. Not only was the whole trans-Mississippi region largely cut off from the rest of the Confederacy; not only was New Orleans again made a port for the Northwest; not only was Copperheadism in the prairie States dealt a prostrating blow; and not only were the troops of Grant and Sherman now free to operate in Alabama, Tennessee, and Georgia! The immediate losses of the South were staggering. At Vicksburg Grant took 29,500 prisoners, with 172 cannon, over 50,000 small arms (many of them Enfields better than the Union pieces), and much ammunition.[71] At Port Hudson the Confederates lost 6,400

1865, Vol. II, 311-315; *O.R.* IV, 1059. Numbers at Port Hudson are very much in dispute. Cunningham has made a careful study, *ut supra*, 120-124. The letters of the realistic American novelist, John W. DeForest, his fictional sketches, and his book, *A Volunteer's Adventures*, contain much upon the Port Hudson scene, and the fighting thereabouts.

68. "St. Louis During the War," Ms., James O. Broadhead Papers, Missouri Historical Society.
69. New York *Herald*, New Orleans correspondence, August 11, 12, 20, 1863.
70. J. McDonnell, Vicksburg, Aug. 15, 1863, to J.R. Doolittle, Doolittle Papers, State Hist. Soc. of Wisconsin.
71. Grant, *Memoirs*, I, 572; *O.R.*, I, xxiv, Pt.1, 62, *O.R.*, I, xxiv, Pt.2 324-325.

prisoners, 51 guns, and 5,000 small arms, with about 150,000 rounds of ammunition.[72]

Jefferson Davis, plunged into dejection, proclaimed a day of fasting for August 21. Word spread among his intimates that he despaired of success in the struggle. "Oh, for a leader with the calm heroism of a William of Orange!" exclaimed the diarist Kean.[73] A vitriolic exchange of letters between Johnston and Davis did nothing, when it became known, to improve the standing of either in the South, or to further the Confederate war effort.[74] But for Johnston's strong political following and widespread popularity, Davis might have removed him and put D.H. Hill in his place.[75] To a Mississippi friend, Davis confided that the disasters in the State were not only great, but unexpected, for he had thought that the troops at hand made a force sufficient to destroy Grant's army.[76] Yet he had known since mid-June that Johnston believed his force must at least be doubled to save Vicksburg, and that to draw sufficient reinforcements from Bragg would mean the loss of Tennessee.

Rejoicing in the North was matched by that among the friends of the Union overseas who could hail a double victory—the fall of Vicksburg and the coincident defeat of Lee at Gettysburg. "With deep, devout, and grateful joy," declared the London *Star* of July 20, "we publish today the news of victories that are the heralds of a happy peace. . . The glorious Fourth-of-July has indeed received a glorious celebration." The London *Daily News* pointed out that the fall of Vicksburg was a more serious blow to the Confederacy by far than Lee's failure. "All who understand and sympathize with the higher interests and issues of humanity at stake in the great conflict," it added, would join Meade in thanking God for giving victory to "the cause of the just."[77] The *Times* surpassed itself in malignant comment. But John Bright was transported with gratification and relief; the Confederate cotton-loan fell by one-fifth in little more than a week; and the Richmond government, seeing that all hope of British intervention was gone, recalled its unrecognized envoy James Mason from London. As it was now clear that he would never be received, wrote Judah P. Benjamin,[78] it was neither useful nor dignified for him to remain.

Under the stunted oak where Pemberton and Grant shook hands, a tree

72. Harrington, Fred H., *Fighting Politician, Major-General N.P. Banks,* Philadelphia, 1946, 124. Among the prisoners at Port Hudson marched a future chief justice of the United States, Edward D. White. *Report of the Joint Committee on the Conduct of the War,* Washington, 1865, II, 315.
73. Kean, *Inside the Confederate Government, op.cit.,* 86.
74. Davis, Varina, *Jefferson Davis, A Memoir by his Wife,* New York, 1890, Ch.XLII.
75. Kean, *op.cit.,* 83.
76. *O.R.,* IV, ii, 766; Davis to J.M. Howry, August 27, 1863.
77. July 20, 1863.
78. Trevelyan, George M., *The Life of John Bright,* Boston, 1914, 323. Adams, E.D., *Great Britain and the American Civil War,* Gloucester, Mass., 1957, II, 179.

swiftly whittled to shreds by relic-hunters, an imperishable fame was born, although Grant kept the scene undramatic, for no more modest a commander ever
lived. "I am afraid Grant will have to be reproved for want of style," Elihu
Washburne (as we have noted in *War Becomes Revolution*) had informed Lincoln
two months earlier. "On this whole march of five days he has had neither a horse,
nor an orderly or servant, a blanket, or overcoat, or clean shirt, or even a sword;
that being carried by his boy 13 years old. His entire baggage consists of a
toothbrush."[79]

Now, as the country rang with praises, his demeanor was unaltered. Charles
A. Dana went back to Washington voluble with admiration. "I tell everybody that
he is the most modest, the most disinterested, and the most honest man I have
ever known," he wrote. He assured hundreds of this, and more. "To the question
they all ask, 'Doesn't he drink?' I have been able from my own knowledge to give
a decided negative."[80] Lincoln sent him a letter eloquent with gratitude. And
while the taciturn, imperturbable general digested in grim silence the refusal of
Halleck to accept his suggestions for effective use of his army, and busied himself
in expediting the movement of troops and transports out of Vicksburg, the North
made up its mind that at long last it had what it had desperately wanted ever since
Sumter—a military hero.

[VII]

The fall of Vicksburg, coinciding with the commencement of Lee's retreat
from Gettysburg, caused widespread rejoicing in the North. Predictions that the
Confederacy would be crushed within a few months resounded on all sides, and
were echoed in England and other countries. But the extreme opponents of
Lincoln, and his Reconstruction policies did not share this exultation. They did
not wish to see the Confederacy felled immediately, and a rapid peace arranged,
for they feared that this would be a peace of delay and compromise, such as that
supported by Seward, Montgomery Blair, and Greeley in his New York *Tribune*.
The promoters of such policies, they apprehended, might be willing to retain
some form of slavery in the South—a type of serfdom with attachment to the land
similar to that found among the lower classes in Russia and the Balkans. They
believed that such a revised slaveocracy might conceivably challenge the political
and economic dominance of the new Northern alliance of freesoilers, Republicans, and industrial progressives. This group now sat safe behind tariff walls,
government bond issues, generous land policies and programs for building rail-

79. May 1, 1863; Hay Papers, Illinois State Hist. Library.
80. Dana to E. Washburne, Aug. 29, 1863, Washburne Papers, LC.

roads, canals and colleges, while exploiting to the utmost the natural resources of the land in timber, minerals, oil and agriculture. Charles Sumner declared that the recent victories were more dangerous to the ascendancy of the Republicans which had fostered this new coalition of finance, industry and railroad promotion than defeats would have been.

Sumner (and others) also feared that a compromise peace would do less than full justice to the Negro demands for unslackened progress toward social, political, and eventually economic equality. He lamented the fact that Meade had failed to follow the repulse of the Confederacy at Gettysburg by an onslaught which would have destroyed secessionist and anti-emancipationist forces. Full of abuse for the slavemongers, for the Democrats, for Copperheads and the Tory element in Britain, he violently denounced Seward, and all other Republicans who might insist upon amnesty and restoration of the Union "with no questions asked about slavery." "God save us from such calamity!" he wrote John Bright on July 21, 1864. Before Lee's army was compelled to surrender, he declared that he hoped to see 200,000 Negroes with muskets in their hands.[81] He was in a mood equally dangerous to national concord and to the maintenance of world peace. More upheaval, struggle, oceans of bloodshed, and the loss of many millions in property were as nothing if he could see a vengeance and repression achieved.

Lincoln, who, according to John Hay "was in fine whack," felt more relief than exultation. He believed that the rebel power was at last beginning to crack apart and break into fragments. If the North stood firm, this disintegration would continue, but he wished only to restore the Union, extinguish the doctrine of secession, and continue the work of liberation that he had begun. He did not wish to humiliate the South, or to establish a new dominant truce.[82]

One Illinois Republican had more faith in the President's firmness than some of his associates. Senator Lyman Trumbull awaited the development of events for some light, showing no anxiety lest Lincoln might yield any important ground upon emancipation to please the Southerners and thus hasten a peace. Senator Zach Chandler of Michigan also, to his credit, derided the notion that Lincoln might surrender any vital position. To be sure, Chandler wrote that Seward and Seward's close friend Thurlow Weed were snaky. But he added that the President fortunately had the stubbornness of a mule, and his back was as stiff as ever.[83] Some Republican radicals had become blind with rage at finding themselves helpless in dealing with the President.[84] The President's only positive move was

81. Pierce, Edward L., *Memoir and Letters of Charles Sumner,* Boston, 1877-1893, IV, 143.
82. Dennett, Tyler, *Lincoln and the Civil War in the Diaries and Letters of John Hay,* New York, 1939, 77-78.
83. *Ibid.*
84. Williams, T. Harry, *Lincoln and the Radicals,* Madison, 1941, *passim.*

mild. Lincoln had thought, when he heard that Grant had invested Vicksburg, that the moment had come for General Rosecrans to deliver a crushing blow against Bragg, or to send large reenforcements to Grant's army. But now that Grant had taken Jackson and Vicksburg in rapid succession, he felt more patient. After writing Rosecrans that he was watching what he did with no censorious or unfriendly eye, Lincoln paused to let the General decide on his own course.[85]

85. Dennett, *op.cit.*, 77-78; Staff of the Detroit Freepress, *Life of Zachariah Chandler*, Detroit, 1880, 269ff.

3

Gettysburg: The Fumbled Victory

[I]

THE VERY leaves on the trees seemed to stop growing (anxious men thought) in sympathy as the country waited during the last June days in 1863 for news of Lee's invasion of the North, and Grant's siege of Vicksburg. That the war was approaching a climax was plain to all. Like spectators in an amphitheatre watching simultaneous performances, people turned their eyes first to the great winding river of the West, and then to the Appalachian valleys in the East. For the moment, all other activities were ignored: the contest between blockaders and blockade runners, the capture of Puebla by the French in Mexico, the deadlock between Bragg and Rosecrans in Tennessee, the bickerings of a constitutional convention in Missouri, and the work of recruiting North and South. Two mighty decisions impended, either of which might determine the outcome of the war.

Of the two centers of suspense, Pennsylvania held the more portentous uncertainty. For one reason, it had become plain to informed observers by early June that Confederate weakness, and Grant's brilliant energy in handling his massive forces, had almost sealed the fate of Vicksburg. The Chattanooga *Rebel* declared on June 7th that many Mississippians deemed the city already lost. For another reason, men knew that even if desperate exertions and some stroke of genius temporarily saved this section of river to the South, the North would simply try again; it was steadily reinforcing Grant. But as Lee crossed the Potomac and swung northwest of Washington, with the laurels of Chancellorsville still fresh on his brow, nobody could predict the event, and all could see that another rebel victory, followed possibly by the seizure of Baltimore or even Washington, might have the most far-reaching consequences at home and abroad.

There had been preliminary moves by part of Lee's army from south of the Rappahannock to near Culpeper Court House. On June 9, Alfred Pleasonton's Federal cavalry corps crossed the Rappahannock in two columns, striking Stuart's Confederate horse in what became the greatest nearly all-cavalry battle

79

ever waged on this continent! After vicious, frantic fighting on horseback and on foot, Pleasonton pulled back, content that he had found Lee's army and had punished the great Jeb Stuart rather severely. Brandy Station yielded a small amount of knowledge, rumpled Stuart's exalted plume, and gave the Federal cavalry something to really cheer about. But it was on June 18 that North and South alike were startled by tidings that the Confederate storm had broken the day before upon the high Potomac and the hills beyond. On June 15, powerful forces under Richard S. Ewell had compelled the Union commander at Winchester to cut his way out and retreat to Harper's Ferry with the loss of nearly 4,000 prisoners.[1] The Southern columns had pressed on with all possible speed. By evening of the 15th, other forces of Ewell had crossed the Potomac at Williamsport with cavalry pushing on towards Chambersburg well up the Cumberland Valley of Pennsylvania, so that soon Confederates were threatening Mercersburg to the west, Gettysburg to the east, and Carlisle and Harrisburg to the north. The movement might be a feint. But Lincoln, on that ominous 15th, called out 100,000 militia for six months, half of them from Pennsylvania and the remainder from Ohio, Maryland, and West Virginia. Hooker had shifted north from the Rappahannock, after Lee got away, and was preparing to follow on Lee's heels, keeping between him and Washington.

The campaign entered a more exigent stage when, on June 23-25, the remainder of the Confederate army, following Ewell's corps, crossed the Potomac, and moved up toward Chambersburg. Panicky Washington reports declared it twice as strong as Lee's force at Chancellorsville. Lee and D.H. Hill forded the river at Williamsport and Shepherdstown, united their corps at Hagerstown, and moved along the Cumberland Valley until they entered Chambersburg on the 27th. Ewell in their front meanwhile had pushed ahead deeper into Pennsylvania, reaching Carlisle by June 27.[2] The Southerners drove ahead of them, on all roads, a pell-mell mass of fugitives; farmers in wagons, villagers with their valuables crammed into carts and buggies, bankers and merchants with saddlebags of money, herdsmen with droves of lowing cattle. A wide belt from Baltimore to Pittsburgh was filled with consternation. The militiamen that Lincoln had summoned were slow to appear, Pennsylvania mustering at most 25,000 and Maryland and West Virginia 10,000 more; but New York had taken the alarm and was sending 15,000. Men of Pittsburgh were digging trenches along the Braddock road; men of Harrisburg were drilling with fowling pieces and scythes.

Western Maryland and much of Southern Pennsylvania, indeed, felt abandoned to the foe. Instead of defending the North inch by inch, the government had apparently decided to leave a wide area open to devastation and plunder. As

1. *O.R.* I, xxvii, Pt.2, 313-314, 442ff.
2. *Ibid.*, 443.

the Southern columns advanced, the people despaired. Philip Schaff, a young professor in the theological seminary at Mercersburg, dolefully watched Ewell's infantry and cavalry occupy the town. "We fairly, though reluctantly, belong to the Southern Confederacy," he wrote. He saw that the men, though a motley, roughly-dressed array, were better equipped than in the Antietam campaign. They all had shoes; they carried many Springfield muskets captured at Harper's Ferry the previous autumn; their wagons, some marked "U.S.", were full of supplies taken from Hooker and Milroy. "Uncle Sam has to supply both armies," Schaff ruefully commented. Officers and men, veterans of Stonewall's command, were inured to hardship, in good fighting trim, and proud of the fifteen battles they had fought. Announcing that they would respect private property and pay in Confederate money for seized supplies, they politely ransacked the stores. But a detachment of guerrilla cavalry who came after them, brave, defiant, and bold, took whatever they could use without ceremony or pay.[3]

Marching Confederates in high spirits chaffed the bystanders in Pennsylvania towns. "We got back into the Union at last, you see," they sang out. Few carried knapsacks, a haversack was enough. For blanket-raincoats many used strips of carpet in which they had punched holes for their heads. Young Schaff heard one Confederate general, John D. Imboden, a handsome, commanding man with haughty mien, say bitterly: "Your army destroyed all the fences, burned towns, turned poor women out of house and home, broke pianos, furniture, and old family portraits, and committed every act of vandalism." Southern restraint shone brightly by comparison. As Charles Francis Adams, Jr., remarked, it is doubtful if a force ever operated in an enemy's country leaving behind it less cause for resentment and hatred than Lee's army in these memorable days.[4] But as it pressed on, seizures of property grew, and depredations by stragglers increased. The roads became more crowded. On the right were troops, caissons, and supply wagons; on the left, moving back, droves of cattle and sheep, and farm wagons so heavy with spoils that they frequently used six or eight horses. When rains made the highways muddy, progress became slow, and soldiers who found them impracticable streamed alongside through the fields, to the wrath of farmers. Officers who searched houses for hidden stores meanwhile excited the contumely of irate women.[5]

On and on the Confederates swung. Harrisburg dispatches on June 28 announced that they were within four miles of the city's defensive works, and had burned the Columbia bridge over the Susquehanna twenty miles downstream. Marching into York that day, Ewell demanded food, clothing, and $100,000, and

3. Schaff, Philip, "The Gettysburg Week," *Scribner's Magazine*, XVI, July, 1894, 21-30.
4. "Remarks on Rhodes's History, Vol. V," *Proceedings Massachusetts Historical Society*, XIX, 311-356.
5. Fremantle, J.A.L., *The Fremantle Diary*, ed. Walter Lord, Boston, 1954, 195.

actually obtained not only supplies, but $28,000. "We will occupy the place permanently," threatened Jubal A. Early.[6] The deepest excitement now prevailed in Philadelphia, where workshops and stores shut down or closed early to enable men to drill, the merchants began raising a million dollars for defense, and even clergymen volunteered to handle shovels on the fortifications. By the 29th, Lee had determined to concentrate his army at Cashtown, just east of the Blue Ridge (here called South Mountain), and moving his own troops through a pass toward that village, which was only eight miles from Gettysburg, he sent word to Early at York and Ewell at Carlisle to meet him there. To the puzzlement of some observers, the advance upon Harrisburg abruptly halted on the 29th, but Lee gave as a reason the news that Hooker's army had crossed the Potomac and was approaching South Mountain.

Thus it was that the Confederate columns never quite reached the Pennsylvania capital. In the trenches before Harrisburg a young volunteer named Richard Watson Gilder, later editor and poet, kept an all-night vigil as June closed, quoting bits of verse to a sergeant beside him on the parapet. At last day broke —the day of the 30th; and there in the distance, on the brow of a hill, sat a solitary gray-clad horseman. Though Gilder did not know it until later, this horseman was the cresting drop on the farthest wave of the high tide of the Confederacy.[7]

[II]

Any full rehearsal herein of the details of the Gettysburg campaign would rank high among exercises in futility, for the mountain of books piled upon the battlefield equals in weight the stone and bronze of its serried monuments. Not details but general considerations, attempted answers to the enigmas of the combat, arrest our interest. Who, on the Southern side, made the decision to invade the North, and why? How much clearcut understanding and how much hazy misunderstanding accompanied the decision? For this desperate effort, what tried officers and what numbers and quality of troops could Lee summon into his reorganized army? What were the merits and weaknesses of his plan? In its execution, how much error may be charged to Lee, to Longstreet, to Early, to Jeb Stuart, and to A.P. Hill, and what defects of temper, if any, did they show? How much of the outcome may be attributed to chance, always blindly operative in war?

On the Northern side the questions are equally pregnant. Why was it that the North, with its tremendous superiority in numbers, wealth, and resources, was not able by midsummer of 1863 to muster a weight of men and arms that would

6. The New York *Herald*, June 30, 1863, said $150,000. *O.R.* I, xxvii, Pt.2, 307-317, 466.
7. Gilder, Rosamond, *Letters of Richard Watson Gilder*, Boston, 1916, 23-24.

have made all thought of invasion preposterous? What executive mismanagement lay behind the fact that it had to change its commanders just as the crisis broke and the all-important battle loomed imminent? How much of the strategy of the campaign may be attributed to the old commander, how much to the new, and how much to the compulsion of circumstance? In battlefield tactics, was it to Meade, or Hancock, or Gouverneur K. Warren, or John Sedgwick, that the Union owed most? Why was it that a victory won well within Pennsylvania, half a hundred miles from the nearest good crossing of the Potomac, and nigh a hundred from his Staunton base, did not culminate in the total destruction of Lee's army?

The decision to invade the North was Lee's, and he took it under a sense of almost desperate compulsion. Lee reportedly told D.H. Hill that the intention was to "turn back the tide of war, that is now pressing the South." He feared another Northern advance in Virginia during the summer. The Union army might gather all its forces and loose a crushing blow against him in the Fredericksburg-Culpeper area, or it might establish a base on the James and attack Richmond on McClellan's old front. Lee wrote President Davis on May 30 indicating that he was not confident he could frustrate either move; and either, if not frustrated, could be fatal to the Confederacy.[8] He thought his chances of substituting victory for defeat would be greater if he struck first, hard, and in an unexpected quarter. Even if he won again in northern Virginia, the victory could gain him little. In a war of attrition the South was certain ultimately to lose; already, as he told Davis, he did not receive enough recruits to replace his losses.[9] A daring stroke, such as the capture of Baltimore, offered the only real hope. Knowing how savagely Virginia was being stripped of supplies, he felt the importance of the herds of cattle, the droves of horses, the wagons, shoes, clothing, and arms that Maryland or Pennsylvania might offer.

After the war Lee was said to have stated that "he had never invaded the North with an eye to holding permanently the hostile portions of it. . . . As for Gettysburg—First he did not intend to give general battle in Pa. if he could avoid it—the South was too weak to carry on a *war of invasion,* and his offensive movements against the North were never intended except as part of a defensive system. . . ." Both in his battle report and later, Lee stated that it was impossible to attack Hooker at Fredericksburg so the Federals had to be drawn away, and if practicable, the scene of hostilities transferred north of the Potomac. This

8. Lee to Hill, D.H. Hill Papers, Virginia State Library. *O.R.,* I, xxv, Pt.2, 832-833. Among the several shelves of volumes and articles on Gettysburg that might be assembled, there are a goodly number that are significant along with too many that merely repeat the familiar story. Most recent, and most outstanding of all, is Coddington, Edwin B., *The Gettysburg Campaign,* New York, 1968, which proves that new research is possible even on such a well canvassed subject.

9. *O.R.,* I, xxvii, Pt.3, 880-882.

would break up the enemy's summer plans. Of course, the movement was risky, but "everything was risky in our war." Further, Lee said he suggested that Beauregard be brought to Manassas and, with a diversionary force, threaten Washington while Lee went North. But it was never done.

In a momentous debate in Richmond in mid-May, Lee urged these considerations upon a reluctant Davis and a divided Cabinet. A victory on the Northern scene, a seizure of some great Northern city, might deepen Northern discouragement to the breaking point, or even win foreign recognition, although Lee's stated aims were considerably less than this. He carried his plan, but over the opposition of men who believed that he made a cardinal error in not consenting instead to reinforce the West.

President Davis had been specially anxious, as a Mississippian, to hold the Vicksburg-Port Hudson line, and had been fervently pressed for reinforcements by a Mississippi delegation.[10] Secretary of War Seddon had requested Lee to send Pickett's division, which had been serving under Longstreet in the region of Suffolk, Virginia, to Mississippi, but Lee on May 10 had disagreed. Longstreet himself, spending May 8 and 9 in Richmond, had urged a larger strategic plan for the succor of the West. In fact, several Confederates offered plans. Longstreet proposed a grand concentration at Murfreesboro: he himself would take 13,000 men to join Bragg's army, Joseph E. Johnston would bring 25,000 more from Jackson, and Simon Buckner 5,000 from Knoxville. Leading this host of more than 80,000, Longstreet believed that he might defeat Rosecrans's army, and advance into Kentucky to threaten Louisville; he might even compel Grant to withdraw from his position before Vicksburg.[11]

But Lee would not be moved from his purpose. The great thrust would be his, he would keep all the men he could muster under his own command, and he would attack northwest of Washington. His prestige, force of personality, and tenacity in argument compelled Davis to yield. In the Cabinet, Reagan alone, pleading to the last and even forcing a new meeting after the decision had been taken, held out for sending 25,000 or 30,000 men to the West.[12] On the evidence available, it is difficult to believe that Lee either knew or cared much about the Mississippi front. One of his arguments against sending Pickett's division thither was that it could not arrive until the last of May, "and all will then be over, as the climate in June will force the enemy to retire."[13] That statement would have raised a guffaw in Grant's camps! Lee wrote Davis June 2 that he still hoped

10. Strode, Hudson, *Jefferson Davis; Confederate President,* New York, 1959, II, 403. *O.R.,* xxvii, Pt.2, 305, Lee's Report; Col. William Allan's Collection, Univ. of N.C. Library.
11. Alexander, Edward Porter, *Military Memoirs of a Confederate,* New York, 1907, ch. XVI; *O.R.,* xxv, Pt.2, 790.
12. Strode, *op. cit.,* II, 405, 406.
13. *O.R.,* I, xxv, Pt.2, 782.

Johnston would demolish Grant, and save the Mississippi. "The enemy may be withdrawing to the Yazoo for the purpose of reaching their transports and retiring from the contest, which I hope is the case."[14] The Grant who was thus to be demolished had fought Champion's Hill on May 16 and invested Vicksburg on May 18-19. But Lee, seeing the East alone clearly and thinking only of Virginia, believed with the Richmond *Examiner* that the great opportunity of the South had come. "From the first day," said the *Examiner*, "the only reasonable hope of the Confederacy has been the transfer of hostilities to the enemy's territory."[15]

Longstreet unwillingly consented to the thrust. He asked, however, that the tactics be defensive, and that once they entered Pennsylvania they should so operate as to force the enemy to attack them. His impression was that Lee so promised. But this Lee later denied, terming the idea absurd.[16] It should have been plain to both men that, when two great armies were manoeuvring over a vast terrain of hills and streams, all too blind to each other's movements, nobody could predict where, when, or how they would collide. Chance might be the governing factor. The important fact is that, when the movement began, a misunderstanding existed between Lee and his principal lieutenant. It seemed to some observers then (and some shrewd commentators later) that the lethargic but self-confident Longstreet fancied himself Lee's mentor. The part he had played at Williamsburg, Antietam, and Fredericksburg justified his rank of lieutenant-general. But he had been balky, unmanageable, and slow at critical moments in the battle of Fair Oaks and Second Manassas, and had by no means covered himself with glory when he commanded later in the Suffolk area. Far from possessing the decision, dash, and quick intuition of Stonewall, he could sometimes be a dragging impediment.

No one can censure Lee for determining to keep the reins in his own hand and turn his columns toward Pennsylvania. He had just seen that when Longstreet was detached to the lower coast of Virginia he became very detached

14. *Ibid.*, 848-849.
15. May 21, 1863. Of Lee's consummate abilities as a commander, as of his nobility of character, there can be no doubt, but his breadth of view may be seriously questioned. In 1861, he had chosen Virginia in preference to the nation, although this involved a choice also of slavery, which he disliked, and of secession, to which he had been opposed. Now, in 1863, he chose Virginia again in preference to the Western theatre. Much may be said for his belief that at this moment an invasion of Pennsylvania was the most promising military operation. But in a man who had served before the war on the upper Mississippi and in Texas, the notion that summer fighting in the Vicksburg area would be impossible is hard to excuse. And as Joseph E. Johnston throughout May and the first three weeks of June was vigorously telegraphing Seddon in Richmond upon the realities of Grant's strength and his own weakness (*Narrative of Military Operations*, VII), Lee's supposition on June 2 that Grant was retreating to the Yazoo can be explained only on the theory of a preposterous breakdown of communications between Seddon and Lee, or a closed mind on Lee's part.
16. Swinton, William, *Campaigns of the Army of the Potomac*, New York, 1882, 340; Col. William Allan's Conversations with Lee, ms. typescript, Southern Historical Collection, Univ. of N.C. Library.

indeed; he might display the same excessive independence in Tennessee. The welding of a large body of Eastern troops into a new combination in which Johnston, Buckner, and Longstreet were all involved would take time, and time the Confederacy did not have. Lee's demeanor illustrated his sense of desperation, for this was a major occasion on which he exerted himself powerfully to determine Confederate policy, and for a time he remained apprehensive that Davis might interfere with his plans. His decision was logical. It was a mistake, however, not to have made surer of the Western situation, and of the unity of subordinate commanders and the government behind him. The demands of the Richmond press for an offensive suggested the desirability of mobilizing popular support, but he still needed warmer acquiescence in high quarters and more enthusiasm among his principal officers.

He needed them the more because he had just reorganized the Army of Northern Virginia into three corps, a step authorized by Davis and made almost imperative by Jackson's death. Lee had informed Davis on May 20 that the existing two-corps organization was manifestly defective, for 30,000 fighters, the approximate number in each, were too large a body for one commander to direct in the rough Virginia terrain. "They are always beyond the range of his vision, and frequently beyond his reach."[17] He had hesitated to create new corps earlier simply because he had been unable to recommend efficient commanders. Now he kept Longstreet as head of the First Corps, made Ewell (one of Stonewall's most trusted lieutenants) head of the Second, and placed A.P. Hill, who had succeeded Jackson at Chancellorsville, in charge of the newly-created Third.

Two-thirds of Lee's army thus passed under new chieftains; one of them, Hill, with no experience in managing more than one division at a time, though his command had distinguished itself by such celerity of movement that it was called "Hill's Light Division"; the other, Ewell, in poor health and suffering from permanent physical disability. Three of the nine divisions also went under new heads. As for the brigade commanders, the Second Corps in especial had so many new ones that it was thrown into confusion, and Ewell, himself recently absent from the corps for nine months, would find it difficult to coordinate the units. The batteries of the army were meanwhile redistributed, so that their liaison with the infantry was temporarily disrupted. The cavalry was enlarged to include two new brigades, one from western Virginia under John D. Imboden, and one from southern Virginia under A.S. Jenkins. In short, the reorganization, mingling new units with old, breaking old associations, and bringing many veteran regiments under officers unfamiliar with them or with Lee's procedures, meant temporary *dis*organization.[18] To be sure, the Federal side had also under-

17. *O.R.* I, xxv, Pt.2, 810-811.
18. Freeman, Douglas Southall, *R.E. Lee, A Biography,* New York, 1934, III, 14.

gone reorganization, and it had a new commander at the top in Meade.

To succeed in his thrust, Lee needed a well-forged thunderbolt, hurled with speed, force, and accuracy. A reluctant second in command who held a misconception of the fundamental strategy of the movement, believing that it would shift from the offensive to the defensive at the critical moment, and a redisposition of commanders and troops that impaired the army's solidarity, were hardly calculated to forge such a weapon.

[III]

Lee's plan of marching northward up the Shenandoah and Cumberland Valleys offered clear advantages over his previous Antietam invasion. He could keep the Blue Ridge on his eastern flank to shelter and partly screen his troops. While advancing through a high farming country with ripening crops, he could threaten numerous towns and cities in Maryland and Pennsylvania. He could find good roads, and some wagons and horses to haul ammunition and other necessities up from Staunton and Winchester. His movement nevertheless had flagrant weaknesses. He could not move seriously against Baltimore or even Harrisburg without abandoning his Blue Ridge rampart. The farther he penetrated, the more vulnerable his line of supply would become. From Winchester to Harrisburg as the crow flies is nearly 120 miles, and from Staunton to Harrisburg by wagon-road, according to E.P. Alexander's estimate, 200 miles. This long line would be exposed to Union cavalry raids.

When the Confederate columns first lengthened out on their march, Lincoln on June 14 wrote Hooker his famous admonition: "If the head of Lee's army is at Martinsburg, and tail of it on the Plank road between Fredericksburg and Chancellorsville, the animal must be very slim somewhere. Could you not break him?"[19] Hooker did not really try to break Lee, had not really attempted anything since Chancellorsville, and was now forced on the defensive to protect Washington as the Confederate army continued in its northward advance, despite its dependence on precarious lines of communication.

Moreover, as Lee advanced, a growing host of troops, including militia, would rise before him. If he turned westward to strike at Pittsburgh he would have to battle not only distance, but a wilder, hillier country with few roads. If he fought a drawn battle anywhere deep within Pennsylvania, he would have to retreat exhausted, and if he were defeated he would have to retreat precipitately and in badly battered condition. Even if he left ample forces to guard the fords on the Potomac and the river did not rise, he might be in dire peril. It appears that the desperate Lee was never quite certain how much, if anything, he could accom-

19. Lincoln, *Collected Works*, VI, 273.

plish. On the morning that he himself crossed the Potomac, June 25, he had written President Davis on the insufficiency of troops to maintain his communications. "I think," he added, "I can throw General Hooker's army across the Potomac and draw troops from the south, embarrassing their campaign in a measure, if I can do nothing more and have to return."[20] This statement suggests that he was belatedly daunted by difficulties he had not fully measured at the outset. Well would it have been for the Confederacy if he had contented himself with taking prisoners at Winchester, seizing easy booty across the Potomac, frightening the North, and embarrassing whatever plan of campaign the Union leaders had!

Lee's army, as it advanced into Pennsylvania, numbered about 75,000 men and 200 guns.[21] He had called in troops from every available quarter: from South Carolina; from the North Carolina forces of D.H. Hill, who spared him about 8,000 effectives; from the Virginia coast; and from inland Virginia, where recruiting was sternly pressed. He had strengthened Jeb Stuart's cavalry by fresh men and horses. Of course he had to leave Richmond adequately defended. He reassured the anxious Davis on this point, writing that he was doing his best on all exposed fronts: "The question which seems always to be presented is a mere choice of difficulties." It was sufficient, he thought, to keep the local troops and home guard ready for instant service, with advanced commands under General Arnold Elzey north and east of the city equally alert. In an emergency, D.H. Hill's force could be rushed up from North Carolina.

Lee's march was at first ably conducted. His troops found the Pennsylvania extension of the Blue Ridge an even better screen than they had anticipated. It was thickly wooded, the roads across it were narrow and difficult, and the passes could be held by small detachments.[22] The army, exultant over the ejection of the much-hated General R.H. Milroy from Winchester, was further elated by the easy occupation of Chambersburg.[23] Ewell drove with headlong vigor into Carlisle so that he could collect cattle, grain, and stores, although the town lay dangerously far east. With Early of Ewell's corps in York, Brigadier General John

20. *O.R.* I, xxvii, Pt.3, 930-931.

21. Lee's field returns of May 20, 1863, gave him an aggregate of 81,568 officers and men, with 67,567 present for duty. Much troubled by desertions, he asked Seddon to guard the fords across the James. "The deserters usually go in squads, taking their arms and equipment, and sometimes borrowing from their comrades ammunition sufficient to make 100 rounds per man." *O.R.* I, xxv, Pt.2, 814-15, 846;E.P. Alexander in *Memoirs of a Confederate* credits Lee with 76,224 men and 272 guns; the Comte de Paris, after careful study, estimated his battle forces at 68,000 to 69,000 men and 250 guns. (*History of the Civil War in America*, Philadelphia, 1875-1888, III, 692-693); Abner Doubleday gives an estimate of 73,500 men and 190 guns (*Chancellorsville and Gettysburg, Campaigns of the Civil War*, VII, New York, 1882, 123). Frederick Tilburg of the National Park System, in his handbook on the battle, offers the round figure of 75,000. Milroy's defense is in *O.R.*, I, xxvii, Pt.2, 41-52.

22. Hyde, Thomas W., *Following the Greek Cross*, Boston, 1894, 158ff, gives a graphic description.

23. Milroy's brutalities had led the Confederates to put a price on his head; Fremantle, *Diary, op.cit.*, 182, 183. Cf. Lincoln's castigation of Milroy, *Collected Works*, VI, 308, 309.

B. Gordon's brigade was sent on as far as Wrightsville on the Susquehanna. Then, with his forces scattered all too widely, Lee learned on the night of the 28th that Hooker had not only crossed the Potomac in pursuit, but was well north of that river and close to the Confederate rear. At once, the Southern leader scented danger, for part of Hooker's army might thrust west across the Blue Ridge or South Mountain, ensconce itself in the Cumberland Valley across his line of retreat, and seize the initiative. He must concentrate his troops and move them east of Gettysburg, as if closing down on Baltimore, so as to keep Hooker also on the east. On the morning of the 29th he sent hurried orders to Ewell to march from Carlisle directly to Cashtown or Gettysburg, which lie only ten miles apart; ordered Hill to march from Chambersburg toward these two towns; and ordered Longstreet to follow Hill.

Lee supposed at this moment that Gettysburg was free from Union troops. Cashtown, under the very shadow of South Mountain, would have been an excellent concentration point, for there the Confederates could take strong defensive positions and turn east or west as advantages offered. To get involved in a sudden offensive battle at Gettysburg was a different matter. Why was it, we may ask, that Hooker's passage of the Potomac took Lee by surprise? And why was he ignorant of the fact that on the 29th some Federal troops were already in Gettysburg? Because in this critical hour he lacked Jeb Stuart's cavalry or failed to use his other horsemen to bring him essential information.

The fault was primarily Lee's own. In the haste and pressure under which he began his invasion, he had committed the grave error of yielding to Stuart's suggestion that the dashing young cavalryman should sweep into the rear or flank of Hooker's army as it first moved north, and try to find an opening for a swift blow. When John S. Mosby had suggested this raid, Stuart had instantly seen that it might crown him with glory.[24] Lee, at the very least, gave his partial assent in confused and ambiguous orders on June 22 which he confirmed and enlarged the next day: "You will be able to judge whether you can pass around their army without hindrance, doing them all the damage you can, and cross the river east of the mountains. In either case, after crossing the river you must move on and feel the right of Ewell's troops"—that is, of the advance force.[25] Stuart naturally interpreted this grant of discretionary power in his own favor, and plunged forward. Lee's full commands were cloudy, indistinct and permissive, but he seems to have wished Stuart to cross into Maryland, take position on Ewell's right, guard his flank, keep him informed of enemy movements, and collect whatever supplies were available. Instead, Stuart detached himself completely from Ewell, moved into Maryland and Pennsylvania at a wide distance from the

24. Mosby, John S., in Philadelphia *Weekly Times*, December 15, 1877.
25. Lee's important orders are in *O.R.* I, xxvii, Pt.3, 823, 913, 923.

other Confederate columns—the Union forces marching north between him and Ewell—and furnished no information. On June 30, as the armies converged on Gettysburg, he was at Hanover, Pennsylvania, far over to the east. Lee should have realized that this raid could accomplish little of value under any circumstances, and would make Stuart's junction with him in time for a battle unlikely, although Lee did not intend to fight unless attacked by the enemy. When on June 28 Stuart, just across the Potomac, captured a train of 125 wagons at Rockville, Maryland, and halted to rifle them and parole 400 prisoners, the dangers of a miscarriage increased.[26]

Thus Lee was in the dark as to Union movements from the moment he forded the Potomac, and still in the dark when, about two P.M. on July 1, riding eastward from Cashtown, he suddenly came in sight of the action opening on the western and northwestern outskirts of Gettysburg. He had no idea whether he faced the whole Union army or merely a small advance detachment. Stuart had taken with him Wade Hampton and Fitzhugh Lee, who stood hardly second to him as observers and fighters, and whom the army missed sorely. It was as an uninformed commander that Lee had to make his first critical decisions. He had been anxious to avoid a general engagement at least until his whole army was concentrated—until Longstreet's corps had followed Hill's into the area. But when he saw Early's division of Ewell's corps suddenly arrive on the road leading into Gettysburg, he changed his mind, and ordered the troops forward. Under Major-General Jubal A. Early, and Rodes, Heth and Pender, the gray forces swept on. They routed the Union troops on the edge of town, hurled them back to the ridges east and south of it, occupied the streets, and took 5,000 prisoners. "A doubtful morning had ended in a smashing victory."[27] But it was an improvised and hurried victory caught out of fog and mystification, and it was not consolidated by the occupation of Cemetery Ridge beyond the town, which Gordon on the Confederate side and Winfield S. Hancock of the Union army, both on the field, thought would have been easily feasible.[28]

Clearly, in all this Lee was not at his best; not the Lee of Second Manassas and Chancellorsville. Not only had he lost Jackson, a loss that he recognized as irremediable; but the gravity of the Confederate situation, the sense that complete victory or utter ruin might hang in the balance, created an unwonted mental tension in him. Observers spoke of his anxious and excited mien. He was not a well man, for pleurisy and an infection in April had weakened him.[29] The lack

26. Davis, Burke, *Jeb Stuart, the Last Cavalier,* New York, 1957, 327; McClellan, H.B., *The Life and Campaigns of Major-General J.E.B. Stuart,* Boston, 1885, XVII; *O.R.* I, xxvii, Pt.2, 308, 692-697, 823.
27. Freeman, *Lee, op.cit.,* III, 71.
28. Gordon, John B., *Reminiscences of the Civil War,* New York, 1904, 153-156.
29. Eckenrode, H.J., and Bryan Conrad, *James Longstreet, Lee's War Horse,* Chapel Hill, 1936, 173; Freeman, *Lee, op.cit.,* II, 502-504; IV, Appendix 7, 521ff.

of positiveness and decisive clarity in his orders evidenced an inner uncertainty. Prussian officer Justus Scheibert, who accompanied the army, noted that his nervousness infected the men around him with a similar uneasiness.[30] Fretted to exasperation by Stuart's absence and lack of other information on Union movements, he lost his usual confident composure.[31]

[IV]

What, meanwhile, of Hooker and the Union army? Stanton, Halleck, and others in Washington had little or no real faith in Hooker. But the President would not go so far as to remove him until he had firm reasons, partly because the army retained confidence in Hooker, partly because Secretary Chase still championed him, and still more because, after McClellan, Pope and Burnside, a fourth removal would be discouraging to the nation.

As Lee's columns turned north in the Shenandoah, Hooker's first apprehension was that they might strike a sudden blow at Washington. He moved slowly after the Confederates, posting his army at Centreville, Manassas, and Fairfax Court House in such a position as to protect the capital. When Lee forded the Potomac, Hooker determined to cross at once and strike north on an inside line paralleling Lee's and covering the capital and Baltimore. On June 25-26, half a dozen Union corps took up their march through Maryland on a line running northwest from Frederick. Of this Lee knew nothing.

Thus far, in fact, the two armies and the whole country found the campaign mystifying. The North knew that the Confederate array was executing a movement toward Harrisburg, and might seize it, or concentrate against Baltimore, or even lunge toward Philadelphia. Just what would the rebels do?—the entire Northern press agonized over the question. And Hooker's plans were as mysterious as Lee's purpose. He would have done well, Washington thought, to start his pursuit of Lee a few days earlier.[32] Moving into Pennsylvania, he used Pleasonton's cavalry to scout Longstreet's column and make sure the Confederates were closely guarding the Blue Ridge passes. On the 26th he fixed his headquarters at Poolesville, Maryland; on the next day he ordered cavalry sent to Emmitsburg and Gettysburg to discover whether Lee's forces were in the area.[33]

At this moment, with Longstreet in Chambersburg, the high Union command presented an unhappy picture. Halleck nursed his old animosity toward Hooker, dating from California days. Stanton told Lincoln: "I have no confidence

30. Eckenrode and Conrad, *op. cit.*, 191.
31. No "correct intelligence," he later wrote; Lee, R.E. Jr., *Recollections and Letters of General Lee*, New York, 1904, 102.
32. Doubleday, Abner, *op. cit.*, 106.
33. Herbert, Walter E., *Fighting Joe Hooker*, Indianapolis, 1944, 244.

in General Hooker, though his personal courage I do not question."[34] Gideon Welles had lost whatever faith in•the general he had ever possessed; Charles Sumner, who was often in the White House, was dubious or antagonistic. Hooker himself was in an irritated frame of mind, for his recent proposals had met with one rebuff after another. When Lee began to move, Hooker had proposed using his army in a direct attack upon Richmond, but Lincoln had indicated he thought the true object was Lee's army. When on June 16 he had heard that Lee was crossing the Potomac, he had suggested that Pleasonton's cavalry be sent across the river forthwith; but this Lincoln and Halleck again vetoed. It is not strange that he burst out in a telegram to Lincoln:

"You have long been aware, Mr. President, that I have not enjoyed the confidence of the major-general commanding the army, and I can assure you so long as this continues we may look in vain for success . . ." Lincoln replied, "When you say I have long been aware that you do not enjoy the confidence of the major-general commanding, you state the case much too strongly. You do not lack his confidence in any degree to do you any harm. On seeing him, after telegraphing you this morning, I found him more nearly agreeing with you than I was myself. If you and he would use the same frankness to one another, and to me, that I use to both of you, there would be no difficulty. I need and must have the professional skill of both, and yet these suspicions tend to deprive me of both. . . . " [35]

R.E. Schenck, the erratic commander in Baltimore, and Samuel P. Heintzelman, the feeble and timid head of the Washington garrison, both clamoring for protection, added to the confusion. Into the tangle of sometimes contradictory telegrams exchanged on June 16-20 by Hooker, Halleck, Stanton, and Lincoln we need not go. At one moment on the 16th the resentful Hooker informed Lincoln that he was prepared "to move without communication with any place for ten days." In this crisis, there would be no communication between the nation's principal army and Washington! Halleck seemed to many to blow hot and cold. He explicitly assured Hooker: "You are in command of the Army of the Potomac, and will make the particular dispositions as you deem proper. I shall only indicate the objects to be aimed at."[36] Yet Hooker remained fearful that Halleck would not support him with enough troops. Herman Haupt, visiting Hooker's headquarters, found him in a morose temper; he said that all his suggestions having been rejected, he would move only when he got orders, would follow them literally, and if they resulted in failure, would let others bear the blame.[37]

34. Gorham, George C., *Life and Public Services of Edwin M. Stanton*, Boston, 1899, II, 99; precise date uncertain.

35. *O.R.* I, xxvii, Pt.I, 45; June 16, 11 a.m. 1863; Lincoln, *Collected Works*, VI, 281-282.

36. *O.R.* I, xxvii, Pt.I, 47-50.

37. Haupt, Herman, "The Crisis of the Civil War, Gettysburg," *Century Magazine*, XXII, May-Oct., 1892, 794-797.

Chase, visiting the general, did his best to dispel the man's ill humor, and as soon as he got back in Washington on the 20th assured him that he had talked with Lincoln, Chase, and Stanton, and that Hooker might count on their support.

Then Hooker, distrustful, morose, perhaps drinking, suffered three jolts. First, he issued an order to the general commanding at Alexandria. It was not obeyed. When Hooker tried to place the general under arrest, it turned out that Heintzelman had directed him to disregard all orders not coming from Halleck or the War Department.[38] Soon afterward, Hooker ordered a colonel to proceed to Harper's Ferry. The colonel sent a saucy reply that he did not belong to Hooker's command, but Heintzelman's. And third, when Lee's thrust had developed to a point of real peril, and Hooker tried to bring under his direct command the force on Maryland Heights, overlooking Harper's Ferry—some 10,000 men led by General William H. French—he was once more rebuffed.

This rebuff was so important that its story deserves a few details. On the morning of June 27, the anxious Hooker rode into Harper's Ferry and examined the Heights. He quickly saw that French's force was quite useless, for nothing remained at the Ferry worth capturing, and the river, fordable at many other points, could not be blocked. He had telegraphed Halleck the previous evening to ask if there was any reason why the Heights should not be evacuated. His answer was waiting at Harper's Ferry: since Maryland Heights had always been regarded as important, and had been fortified at great expense, it should not be abandoned except under absolute necessity. This disgusted Hooker, and he telegraphed back that the troops ought to be transferred to some point where they would be of real service: "Now they are but a bait for rebels, should they return." He asked that his plea be laid before Lincoln and Stanton.[39] Then, angry and

---

38. *O.R.* I, xxvii, Pt.1, 56-57.

39. *Ibid.*, 60. The question of Harper's Ferry and Hooker's resignation is discussed in the Horatio Woodman Papers, Mass. Hist. Soc., Boston, Document of John Codman Ropes, Boston, Feb. 8, 1870, "Conversation with Edwin M. Stanton." " . . . He said Hooker was never removed, but resigned, and that he resigned most unexpectedly. He was, said he, in Washington consulting with the President, General Halleck and myself, only a week before he resigned. Wednesday I think (24 June 1863) we talked over the matter of Maryland Heights which had been fortified and provisioned and equipped at a vast expense, and it was agreed that they should not be given up, General Hooker concurring without objection—He then went up to the front. Judge then our surprise when a dispatch came in a day or two from General French commanding Maryland Heights, stating that he had been ordered to evacuate the position. We held a brief consultation, and ordered him to hold the position. If Hooker had asked for the evacuation of the Post, he would have been granted to him [sic] to evacuate it, just as Meade had afterwards. But we supposed there might be (as I recollect the conversation) some mistake, and therefore countermanded the order to French until we could communicate with Hooker. But as soon as Hooker learned that his order had been countermanded he resigned." This of course is a bit late and second-hand, and does not take into consideration Hooker's desire to evacuate, received in Washington five minutes before his resignation was received. Halleck to Lieber, Lieber Papers, HEH, Aug 4, 1863:-Halleck stated in this letter that Lincoln "then ordered Gen. H. to report to me & obey my orders. This caused him to be asked to be relieved, which was done instantly. Had he remained in command, we certainly should have been defeated at Gettysburg." Horatio Woodman Papers, Mass. Hist. Soc., Sumner to Woodman of the Boston *Transcript,*

impatient, he waited with his old classmate French for Halleck's response.

At this moment, Hooker mistakenly believed that he was outnumbered. Two Union men who had independently counted Lee's forces on their march through Hagorstown computed them at 91,000 infantry, 6,000 cavalry, and 280 guns. If this count was accurate Lee had about 100,000 men, with more coming; and even including troops drawn from Schenck and Heintzelman, Hooker put his own army at not more than 105,000. He indicated he *must* have French's 10,000. But he did not get them, for a curt telegram from Halleck came directly to French: "Pay no attention to General Hooker's orders." Its contemptuous flavor enraged Hooker. Stepping out of French's headquarters, he encountered an old friend, Andrew T. Reynolds, of the cavalry, who remarked that a battle seemed imminent. "Yes," rejoined Hooker, "but I shall not fight it. Halleck's dispatch severs my connection with the Army of the Potomac."[40] He made good his words by instantly telegraphing Halleck:

"My original instructions require me to cover Harper's Ferry and Washington. I have now imposed on me, in addition, an enemy in my front of more than my number. I beg to be understood, respectfully, but firmly, that I am unable to comply with this condition with the means at my disposal, and earnestly request that I may at once be relieved from the position I occupy."[41]

To this angry dispatch Halleck, only too glad to get rid of a distrusted commander, replied the same day that he had referred the General's request to the President. The same day, for the emergency permitted no delay, Lincoln and Halleck agreed upon the promotion of George Gordon Meade to the command. It was a logical choice. Meade, graduating in the upper half of his West Point class in 1835, had served in both the Seminole and Mexican Wars, had performed engineering and scientific work all over the country, and had been appointed brigadier-general of Pennsylvania volunteers by Governor Curtin after Sumter. He had fought bravely and skillfully in the Seven Days and at Second Manassas, South Mountain, Antietam, and Fredericksburg. His judgment and nerve as major-general, heading the Fifth Corps at Chancellorsville, impelled two other corps leaders, D.N. Couch and John F. Reynolds, both disgusted with Hooker, to urge that he be made head of the Army of the Potomac. Halleck did not know him personally—he asked Heintzelman what kind of a man he was—but recommended him warmly to Lincoln.[42]

Halleck at once selected a tried officer who was in the War Department at

---

July 1, 1863; "Hooker complained of Halleck & asked to be relieved. I think the change has been taken well. . . . Stanton & Chase did not like it, but since Hooker asked it there was nothing to be said."

40. Herbert, *Hooker, op. cit.,* 245.
41. *O.R.* I, xxvii, Pt.1, 60; received 3 p.m., June 27, 1863.
42. Heintzelman, Samuel P., Ms. *Diary,* June 28, 1863, LC.

the moment. James A. Hardie, to notify Meade of his appointment. Riding a locomotive to Frederick, and wearing civilian clothes lest Stuart's cavalry seize him, Hardie found a driver and buggy, and hurried off on the rough streets, alive with stragglers, many of them drunk, and roads full of crippled army vehicles. It was around three A.M. June 28 when, drawing up in front of Meade's headquarters in the country, he was challenged by a sentry who reluctantly admitted him. The General, emerging in his nightshirt, was astounded and half-dismayed when told he was head of the army.[43] He would have preferred to see the place go to his comrade Reynolds. But modest and self-controlled, he could only accept. A war correspondent saw him a few minutes afterward outside his tent, standing with bowed head and downcast eyes, lost in thought; his slouch hat drawn low, his uniform stained with hard service, his boots dusty.[44] At seven A.M. he telegraphed Halleck that he would move toward the Susquehanna, would keep Washington and Baltimore, as ordered, well covered, and if Lee turned toward Baltimore, would give battle.[45]

In Washington, Meade's promotion afforded general relief, although the supersedence of Hooker shook radical Republicans who had liked his aggressiveness and his sharp criticism of McClellan. Chase, who had tried so hard to assure Hooker of Administration support, first heard of his loss of command when he attended a Cabinet meeting on Sunday, June 28. Chase could hardly believe it. Lincoln cut short his protest: "The acceptance of an army resignation is not a matter for your department." The resentful Secretary wrote his daughter Kate that Halleck, though likable and apparently capable, failed to master the situation, for "he does not *work, work, work* as if he were in earnest."[46]

43. *O.R.* I, xxvii, Pt.3, 369; Nicolay and Hay, *Lincoln, op.cit.*, VII, 226. Meade Papers, July 16, to his wife, Berlin, Md.: "They have refused to relieve me, but insist on my continuing to try to do what I know in advance it is impossible to do.—My army men and animals is exhausted—it wants rest & reorganization—it has been greatly reduced & weakened by recent operations, and no reinforcements of any practical value have been sent—Yet in the face of all these facts, well known to them I am urged, pushed & *spurred* to attempting to pursue & destroy an army nearly equal to my own falling back upon its resources and reinforcements, and increasing its morale daily. This has been the history of all my predecessors, and I clearly saw that in time my fate would be theirs—This was the reason I was dis-inclined to take the command, and it is for this reason I would gladly give it up. . . ." July 18: " . . . I am very worried, and long for rest & quiet—My temperament is not sufficiently phlegmatic for a post of such responsibility as the command of an army, which is really commanded at Washington." This type of comment appears often and is almost without exception left out of the printed version of the letters. "It is impossible to give satisfaction.—If you succeed, they claim the credit, and if anything goes wrong, you are the scape goat even tho you may be strictly carrying out orders. . . ." Aug. 1 to a Mr. Walker: " . . . The whole difficulty lay in the fact that people only looked at the *result* of a *successful* attack, but lost sight of the *consequences* of a *failure*— . . . I however am very well contented with what I have done viz-in less than 30 days defeating Lee & not only compelling him to relinquish his scheme of invasion, but compelling him to evacuate Pa. Maryland-the Valley of the Shenandoah, & return to his line behind the Rapidan. . . ."
44. Coffin, Charles Carleton, *Marching to Victory*, New York, 1889, 189.
45. *O.R.* I, xxvii, Pt.1, 60, 61; Hooker went to Baltimore, as ordered.
46. Schuckers, J.W., *The Life and Public Services of Salmon Portland Chase*, New York, 1874, 469-470.

Meade's first steps were promising. He was not a man to kindle the ardor of his troops. Tall, thin, with a large broad brow, prominent aquiline nose and grizzled beard and mustache, his bent shoulders, nearsighted eyes, and quiet, reserved manner gave him the aspect of a careworn lawyer rather than a soldier. Although his demeanor was usually icy, he frequently gave way to fierce bursts of temper, with vitriolic speeches that made many officers his enemy. He lacked the sense of conscious power, the imperious will, and the spirit of leadership that has nerved great captains from Hannibal to Allenby. It was significant that he found fault with Hooker chiefly for his lack of *caution*. He would clearly be a colorless general—but he began well. He wisely kept Hooker's staff, though he vainly tried to appoint a new chief in place of Butterfield. Harper's Ferry was now under his orders and he took part of the garrison away, but he left a force sufficient to hold Maryland Heights until, influenced by a false report of low supplies at Harper's Ferry, he temporarily evacuated it. His only important deviation from Hooker's plans was to abandon the idea of a stroke against Lee's communications which his predecessor apparently had in mind. Sending his columns forward, by June 30 he had them across the Pennsylvania boundary. His troops, following all the useful roads they could find, with adequate cavalry protection on the flanks, were spread out on a front thirty-miles wide.[47]

Halleck made every effort to assist him. "You will not be hampered by any minute instructions from these Head Quarters," he wrote in a letter accompanying Lincoln's appointment. "Your army is free to act as you may deem proper under the circumstances as they arise." The day after the appointment he thought it probable that Lee would concentrate south of the Susquehanna and so wrote Meade. That same day he exhorted the commander in Harrisburg, Couch, to hold the Confederates in check on the Susquehanna until Meade could give them battle. On July 1, he telegraphed Meade that Lee seemed moving either to turn the Union left, or to press back into Maryland along the South Mountain: "Don't let him draw you too far to the east." That day, of course, the fighting began. At six in the evening Meade had a full budget of news to send Halleck, who doubtless gave it to Lincoln before midnight; two corps had been engaged all day in front of Gettysburg, three more had been moving up, Reynolds had been killed, and Hancock had been sent to assume field command. Meade saw no alternative to hazarding a general battle next day.[48]

Everybody had been taken by surprise. Lee had hoped to give battle, if necessary at all, on the defensive, to Union attackers at or near Cashtown; Meade had hoped to open the combat, on the defensive, somewhere southeast of Gettys-

47. Cleaves, Freeman, *Meade of Gettysburg*, Norman, Okla., 1960, 129ff.; Hunt, Henry J., "The First Day at Gettysburg," *Battles and Leaders*, III, 255ff.; Doubleday, *Chancellorsville and Gettysburg, op. cit.*, 114-115; Meade to Butterfield, Feb. 4, 1864, Meade Papers, Hist. Soc. of Pennsylvania.
48. *O.R.* I, xxvii, Pt.I, 67-72; Halleck Papers, Eldredge Coll., HEH.

Edwin M. Stanton, Union Secretary of War

George Gordon Meade, Union General

burg at works he was preparing near Pipe Creek, Maryland. Lee stood in the more dangerous situation, for his communications must grow increasingly precarious, and his strength must deteriorate. By June 30 it was more urgent for him to grapple with Meade than for Meade to engage Lee. The situation was taking just the form that Longstreet had feared; the Confederates, after assuming the strategic offensive, were being compelled to adopt the tactical offensive as well. The most momentous event on the 30th possessed a significance which nobody appreciated at the time. That morning a Union cavalry division under John Buford had ridden into Gettysburg on a reconnaissance, and posted scouts on the roads leading west and northwest. Pettigrew's Confederate brigade, marching toward Gettysburg for supplies, had seen these scouts and withdrawn, for he had no orders to begin a battle. But Buford, comprehending the importance of the town as a center of nine or ten converging roads, resolved to hold the ridge on the northwest—McPherson's Ridge—and posted his troops there to make a desperate stand.

Pettigrew had done just right; Buford had done just right; and A.P. Hill did what seemed natural and right when at dawn on July 1 he ordered two brigades to march down the Chambersburg road to Gettysburg to ascertain the real Union strength. The battle was thus unexpectedly and abruptly joined in a chance encounter between the forces of subordinate officers at a village of 2400 people, which lay just north of the point where two ridges (soon to be famous) faced each other—Seminary Ridge on the west, and Cemetery Ridge on the east. Near the northern end of Seminary Ridge stood the theological school which gave it its name; opposite, at the northern end of Cemetery Ridge stood the town graveyard on a hill of its own. This was flanked on the east by the higher, rockier eminence of Culp's Hill. The two ridges, with the difficult hills, Little Round Top and Big Round Top, closing the southern end of Cemetery Ridge, would dominate the battle. Had Lee's army been able the first day to push across Cemetery Ridge, holding it and Culp's Hill, he could have flung Meade's army back in retreat. Later, when Schurz arrived to fight the battle at its fiercest, the situation was just as doubtful as he indicated. Lee had held the initial advantage and his men had fought well. His great disadvantage was the persistent, unnerving absence of Stuart, who he had hoped would find and keep a place on Ewell's right in leading the advance of the army, and would be the eyes of his gray host in a strange and much-broken country.

As the forces drew up in battle array, reflective men on both sides could ponder grave errors and shortcomings. Lee's failure to keep Stuart's cavalry in hand was a blunder heavy with misfortune. His tardy concentration of his army at Cashtown was another error for which he would pay heavily. On the Union side, the change of commanders just three days before the battle might have cost the high command a fearful penalty if the conflict had not turned out to be, in the end, a fight in which Northern corps commanders were of much more importance than the chief general. Lincoln should have removed Hooker immediately after Chancellorsville, and given his successor—either Meade or Reynolds—full control of the army before the end of May, when he would have had a golden month to acquaint himself with his forces and their leaders. What if Wellington had been moved up to the chief command of the British army just three days before the battle of Waterloo?

It was a maladroit combination of misunderstandings—with Halleck irritated by Lincoln's direct orders to Hooker, Lincoln disturbed by Halleck's attitude, Hooker angered by the repeated rejection of his proposals, and Halleck and Hooker deeply distrustful of each other—which brought about the latter's request to be relieved. Assuredly these misunderstandings and distrusts should have been terminated long before the campaign in Pennsylvania reached its climax. They endured, however, until June 28, and on July 1, the battle began with an apprehensive, uncertain Meade in charge. We find no real evidence that Meade advocated retreating, despite rumors that he favored withdrawal at a council of war on the evening of the second day. The majority of those present testified that Meade had no idea of pulling out; although other officers, some of them disgruntled with Meade personally or pro-Hooker, received an impression that he was ready to retire from the field. He was abler than Hooker, but he began his work with grave disadvantages.

Saddest of all Union delinquencies, however, was the failure of the government to bring to the field an army decisively superior to Lee's force. Deep in Pennsylvania, close to its capital, the Confederacy marshalled 75,000 men, well-armed, hopeful of still another great victory under their unmatchable leader, and happy in the possession of guns. Such was the army flung forward by an ebbing population of hardly five millions. Against them, so close to the large Northern cities and manufactories, the twenty-odd million people of the North might have been expected to array an overwhelming host. Flanking that host, it might well have placed three or four well-trained army corps in a position to cut off the retreat of the enemy.

Yet what was the fact? Meade, after his army had been strengthened by large contingents drawn from Harper's Ferry and the Washington and Baltimore garrisons, had on the field 84,000 men by one count, 88,000 by another. The two armies were so fairly matched in strength that, had the South defended the ridges and the North attacked, as Longstreet had hoped, the result might well have been different. Such were the fruits of Northern folly in temporarily halting enlistments in the spring of 1862, in letting States recruit many regiments for limited terms, and in delaying operation of a draft until this summer.

Over the errors on each side it was too late to repine—too late, that is, when Heth's and Rode's Confederates struck the first heavy blows on McPherson's Ridge, when Early followed them with a more shattering stroke, and when Hancock, rallying the Union troops on Cemetery Hill, sent word to Meade in the rear that Gettysburg was the place for the battle.

[V]

The story of Gettysburg can neither be justly written in terms of the generals who commanded important posts of the armies at critical times and places, nor in terms of the controversies which instantly arose over the sagacity or ineptness of their movements. To be sure, these controversies are often of compelling interest, and the windrows of conflicting evidence, when impartially examined, offer highly enlightening information upon the bloody three days of fighting. But the heart of the truth about the conflict—does it really lie here?

On the first day, when Heth's division, driving against the Union cavalry picket west of town, found itself hotly embattled with the First Corps of the Army of the Potomac, and, after heavy losses, swept into the central streets and beyond, the stage was set for controversy. The hot sun which shone out after an early drizzle that July 1st saw Reynolds shot dead from his horse as he rallied the Northern line. It saw Abner Doubleday take his place in command, to be quickly superseded by O. O. Howard, and he in turn by Winfield S. Hancock. The Union troops fought a stubborn delaying action until pressed back to a defensive position on Cemetery Hill and Cemetery Ridge. But why did the Confederates in their powerful onslaught, easily the victors of the day, not accomplish more? Why did not Ewell, bringing his corps from the northwest in time to help deliver the first blows and pursue the routed Federals through the town, push on to seize Cemetery Ridge and Culp's Hill while they were still thinly defended? Or were the defenses really thin when he arrived? Could he actually have seized the positions? Endless ink has been expended on these questions, yes and no. The only certainty is that if Ewell had taken Cemetery Ridge and the adjoining heights, the sun that evening would have sunk on a Union army with but one course before it—retreat.

The second day, still hot and clear but for light fleecy clouds, saw both armies curiously quiet all morning except for the early fighting on Culp's Hill. Meade, who had arrived at one A.M., tired and irritable but determined, faced Lee, who had spent part of the night conferring with Longstreet and examining what ground he could by torchlight and moonlight. Why did not Longstreet attack, as Lee expected, in the early hours? Here was the basis for another controversy. Finally, in mid-afternoon an exciting action did open. Longstreet, probing the Union line, found that the Third Corps under Daniel Sickles had pushed forward to a badly exposed position in front of Cemetery Ridge, running out to a sharp salient. The Confederates attacked, hoping to crush Sickles and break the whole Union left. Bloody fighting developed at the Peach Orchard, Devil's Den, and surrounding points, in which Sickles lost a leg, but his command held fast. Had he imperilled Meade's whole army merely in the hope of winning some special glory for himself? Whatever his motives, he had provided materials for another warm dispute. Although the evidence against him seemed clear, the theatrical strutter had never lacked partisans since he had ruthlessly murdered Philip Barton Key for being excessively attentive to his wife.

And still another controversy had meanwhile been born. In their hot thrust forward, Longstreet's troops had all but captured Little Round Top, which if seized and crowned with guns would have enabled them to enfilade the whole Union line. Why did they not take it? Because, some Southern commentators later wrote, one Confederate officer needlessly delayed ten minutes, in defiance of orders, in flinging his troops upon the invaluable height. The only certainty is that credit for the rapid Union thrust which took and fortified the hill in the nick of time belonged to General Gouverneur K. Warren—who might well claim later that his promptness had saved the battle.

Part of the basis for a much larger disputation had been laid as well. Longstreet, depressed by the fact that the Confederate army had been thrust by circumstances into a position where it must fight an offensive battle, and must attack strong positions held by an antagonist superior in numbers and guns, had pleaded with Lee, on the evening of the first day, to break off the engagement and seek new ground. The Southern army was at last well concentrated; it had won the day's fighting and taken thousands of prisoners. Why should Lee not fall back upon its superior marching ability, and manoeuvre for a fresh grapple in a better position? Why should he not swing southeast a few miles around Meade's left flank, thus placing himself between Meade and Washington, and so compel the Union army to do the attacking on ground that Lee himself would select? But to this plan Lee offered emphatic objections. With Stuart still absent, the Confederates lacked cavalry to cover their flanks as they turned, while Meade possessed strong and well led cavalry units under Buford and Kilpatrick. They would be sliced flank and rear with no Stuart to protect them; they would find their communications harried and perhaps cut. No, Lee believed that the best plan would be to attack strongly in front. The difference of opinion was less important in itself than in the indication it gave that Longstreet might, as critics later contended he did, show a lukewarm and reluctant temper throughout the second and third day of the battle—especially the third.

It was indeed true that by the evening of the second day the Confederate outlook was gloomy enough to discourage Lee and daunt Longstreet. Meade had concentrated his forces with a speed and address which astonished the Confederate leaders. Longstreet's blow against Sickles and the Union left, at one time on the verge of success, had been parried. Late in the day, a blow by part of Ewell's corps against Culp's Hill on the Union right had gained a partial and precarious success in taking some of the intrenchments, due to the absence of defenders needed elsewhere. Cemetery Hill near by had repulsed a stroke delivered by the Confederates under Early. It is not strange that Longstreet, seeing his hopes for the avoidance of an offensive lost, and his plan for a flanking movement thrown aside, became ill-tempered and uncooperative, ready to drag his sword. Nor is it strange that when Meade held his council of corps commanders that evening— a council itself the subject of controversy—they helped him maintain a decision to hold his line and strengthen all its parts, from Cemetery Hill along Cemetery Ridge to Little Round Top, against any Confederate assault on the morrow.

The third day opened again hot and fair, with drifting clouds casting shadows on hills and fields. Fighting began at dawn on the Union right, where Confederates tried to increase their hold on Culp's Hill only to meet Federal reinforcements from Slocum's Corps. Why had Ewell's forces not strengthened their ranks and position on the hill? As they had not, they were driven out of what works they held in furious fighting. The retirement depressed them, while the Northern forces felt elated by their recapture of the position, even after terrible slaughter. Then came hours of silence; and afterward, at one in the afternoon, the thunderous Confederate cannonade which heralded Pickett's charge.

We may learn a little about how the battle was directed or misdirected from an examination of the decisions of Lee and Meade—Lee, who was strangely indecisive at times, declining to impose his will firmly upon Ewell, Longstreet, and others; Meade, who counted for less in the conduct of operations than Reynolds, Howard, Hancock, and Warren. We may learn more from studying the reports of the corps commanders on both sides. But the essential character of the struggle can be grasped only when we examine the supreme effort of the troops, the unwavering courage and devotion of the plain soldiers who withstood the fiery ordeal. "A full account of *the battle as it was* will never, can never be made. Who could sketch the changes, the constant shifting of the bloody panorama?" So wrote a young officer, Frank A. Haskell, destined to die within a year at Cold Harbor, whose long letter on the conflict lives as a classic narrative.[49] The participants came nearest catching the Promethean fire of truth from the gun-bursts.

A farm boy of thirteen, picking wild raspberries near Gettysburg when the guns began to boom, gives us a vivid sketch of the foremost Confederate hosts

49. Haskell, Frank A., *The Battle of Gettysburg*, (privately printed twice before the Massachusetts Commandery of the Loyal Legion published it in 1908), 94.

pouring over the hills in clouds of dust. "The first wave swelled into successive waves, gray masses with the glint of steel as the sun struck the gun barrels, filling the highway, spreading out into the fields, and still coming on and on, wave after wave, billow after billow."[50] Reynolds's orderly, Charles H. Veil, wrote that as the General turned to look towards the Seminary "a Minnie Ball struck him in the back of the neck, and he fell from his horse dead. He never spoke a word, or moved a muscle after he was struck. I have seen many men killed in action, but never saw a ball do its work so *instantly* as did the ball which struck General Reynolds, a man who knew not what fear or danger was . . . " The gallant artillery officer Charles S. Wainwright, fighting hard by, also tells us that Reynolds was slain by a Minie ball through the top of the spine, fell from his horse, and expired instantly—that is all.[51] Wainwright then relates how his artillery was pushed off Seminary Hill, although one gun, with an oblique line of fire, cut great gaps in the oncoming lines of the enemy. The streets of the town were a confused mass of Union soldiers, "brigades and divisions pretty well mixed up," and one general drunk, but nobody panic-stricken. Posting his guns on Cemetery Hill, Wainwright fought a sharp artillery duel next day with Confederate artillery on higher ground toward Culp's Hill. Despite losses, he compelled the foe to retire.

"I saw during this artillery duel two instances of the destruction which can be caused by a single twenty-pounder shot," he wrote, "both of which happened within two yards of me . . . One of these shots struck in the center of a line of infantry who were lying down behind the wall. Taking the line lengthways, it literally ploughed up two or three yards of men, killing and wounding a dozen or more. The other was a shell which burst directly under Cooper's left gun, killed one man outright, blew another all to pieces so that he died in half an hour, and wounded the other three . . . The man who was so badly blown to pieces lost his right hand, his left arm at the shoulder, and his ribs so broken open that you could see right into him."

A United States regular with the artillery, Augustus Buell, wrote an excited description of the first day's battle just before the Union line gave way. He states that the Confederate infantry poured volley after volley into the batteries on McPherson's Ridge, while the artillery replied with double canister as fast as men could load. A burly corporal moved among the guns, helping the wounded stagger to the rear and shifting men about to fill gaps; the commanding officer cheered the gunners on with shouts of "Feed it to 'em, God damn 'em! Feed it to 'em!" The very guns took on life; every artilleryman did the work of two or three. "Up and down the line men were reeling and falling; splinters flying from

50. Miers, Earl Schenck, and Richard A. Brown, *Gettysburg*, New Brunswick, N.J., 1948, 50.
51. Wainwright Col. Charles S., *A Diary of Battle 1861-1865*, New York, 1962, 234; Charles H. Veil letter of April 7, 1864, Civil War Institute, Gettysburg College.

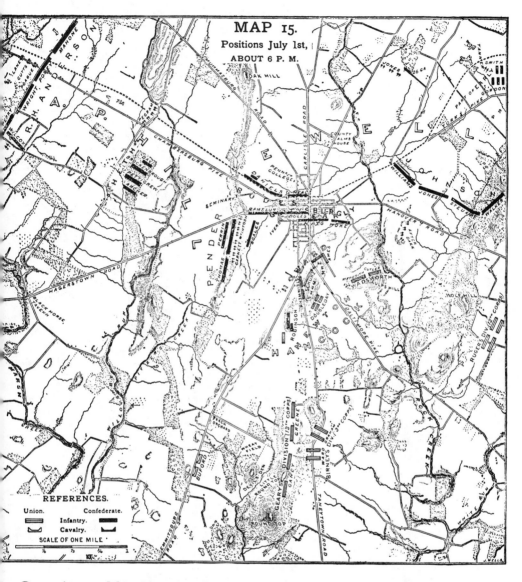

Gettysburg: Map Showing Positions of Union and Confederate Armies on July 1, about 6 P.M.

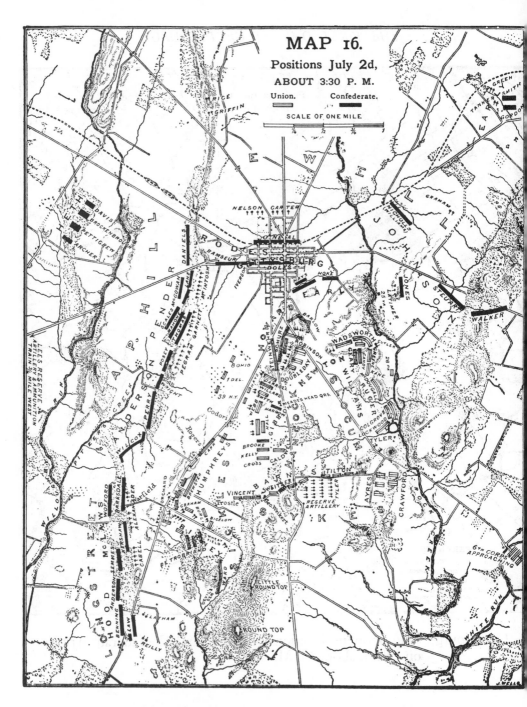

Map of Positions on July 2, about 3:30 P.M.

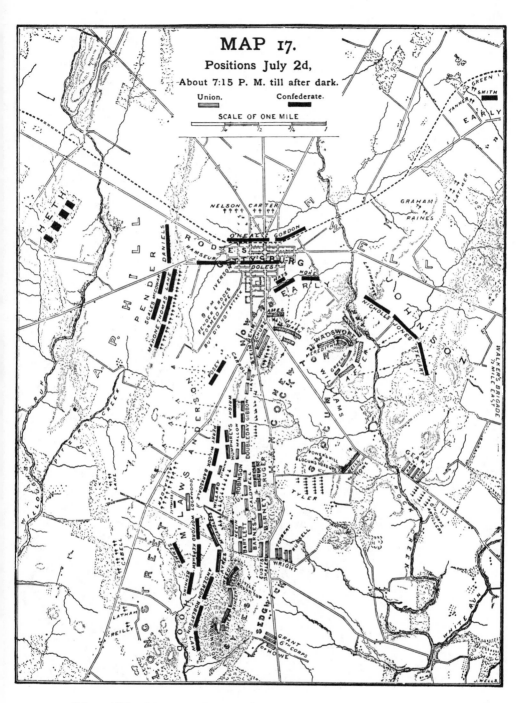

Map of Positions on July 2, from 7:15 P.M. until after dark

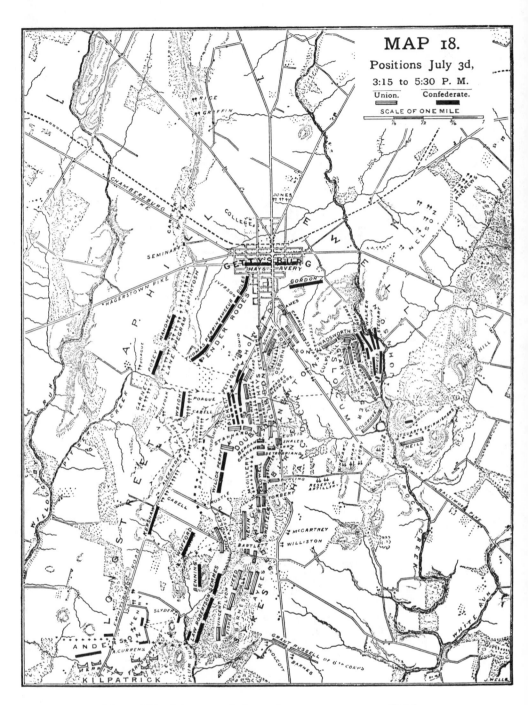

Map of Positions on July 3, from 3:15 to 5:30 P.M.

wheels and axles where bullets hit; in rear, horses tearing and plunging, drivers yelling, shells bursting, shot shrieking overhead, howling about our ears, or throwing up great clouds of dust where they struck; the musketry crashing on three sides of us; bullets hissing, humming, and whistling everywhere; cannon roaring—all crash on crash and peal on peal, smoke, dust, splinters, blood, wreck and carnage indescribable. But not a man or boy flinched or faltered."

The struggle of Union troops to hold Big Round Top, the sugar-loaf hill about 400 feet high at the extreme left of Meade's line, is described by Daniel G. McNamara of the Massachusetts Ninth. On its right, connected by a narrow wooded defile, stands Little Round Top, about 300 feet high. Both were wild, rocky, and full of brush, both had huge boulders scattered over their steep sides, some of them concealing dangerous caverns and pitfalls. Between these two heights and the Devil's Den lies a valley which, after thousands perished in it on the second day, was dubbed the Valley of the Shadow of Death. The colonel of the Ninth formed his battle line on the northeast base of Big Round Top, with a breastwork of rocks laid by the masons of the regiment. "Skirmishers from General Hood's division of Longstreet's corps, on the west side of the hill, assaulted this point at various times during the day intending to capture the hill and flank Little Round Top, but they were always driven back by our rapid infantry fire. The enemy, mostly Hood's Texans, would creep and crawl and stumble through the thickets and underbrush, that grew wild and tangled among the scrubby trees, until they appeared in sight, when the Ninth would open on them."

And Little Round Top? Porter Farley, the historian of the 140th New York, tells how, under direct orders from Warren, his regiment began ascending the wooded, rocky eastern slope of the hill just in time.[52] "As we reached the crest a never-to-be-forgotten scene burst upon us. A great basin lay before us full of smoke and fire, and literally swarming with riderless horses and fighting, fleeing, and pursuing men. The air was saturated with the sulphurous fumes of battle and was ringing with the shouts and groans of the combatants. The wild cries of charging lines, the rattle of musketry, the booming of artillery and the shrieks of the wounded were the orchestral accompaniments of a scene very like hell itself—as terrific as the warring of Milton's fiends in Pandemonium. The whole of Sickles' corps, and many other troops which had been sent to its support in that ill-chosen hollow, were being slaughtered and driven before the impetuous advance of Longstreet." Farley saw that a broad ravine between the two Round Tops led down into the basin filled with this bloody melee. Right up this ravine,

52. Farley, Porter, "Reminiscences of the 140th Regiment New York Volunteers," *Rochester Historical Society Publications,* xxii, Rochester, N.Y., 1944, *passim.* Buell, Augustus, *The Cannoneer,* Washington, 1890, 70; McNamara, Daniel George, *The History of the Ninth Regiment Massachusetts Volunteer Infantry,* Boston, 1899.

the easiest path, was advancing a rebel force which outflanked all the troops in the plain below. The 140th had no time to form a new battle line. With loud shouts they rushed down the rocky slope, their sudden appearance as formidable as if they were carrying fixed bayonets. "Coming abreast of Vincent's brigade, and taking advantage of such shelter as the huge rocks lying about there afforded, the men loaded and fired, and in less time than it takes to write it the onslaught of the rebels was fairly checked, and in a few minutes the woods in front of us were cleared except for the dead and wounded."

The melee in what Farley calls the plain or hollow was the fierce battle in which Longstreet endeavored to crush the impetuous Sickles. Whitelaw Reid of the Cincinnati *Gazette* witnessed the desperate attempt of Massachusetts and Maine batteries to hold a position with Sickles. When a fierce Southern charge put them in dire peril, Captain Bigelow received orders to hold on at every hazard short of total annihilation. He opened with double charges of grape and canister, but could not halt the oncoming line.

"His grape and canister are exhausted, and still, closing grandly up over their slain, on they come. He falls back on spherical case, and pours this in at the shortest range. On, still onward, comes the artillery-defying line, and still he holds his position. They are within six paces of the guns—he fires again. Once more, and he blows devoted soldiers from his very muzzles. And still mindful of that solemn order, he holds his place as they spring upon his carriages, and shoot down his horses! And then, his Yankee artillerists still about him, he seizes the guns by hand, and from the very front of that line drags two of them off . . . That single company, in that half-hour's fight, lost 33 of its men, including every sergeant it had. The captain himself was wounded."

Seldom did a battle of the war entail such hand-to-hand fighting; seldom was so much slaughter endured so bravely by so many companies on both sides. Who could have fought more intrepidly against odds than the South Carolinians in J. B. Kershaw's brigade, sent on the second day to drive the Union troops out of the Peach Orchard? One company went into action with forty men, of whom only four remained unhurt to bury their comrades. His losses exceeded 600 men slain or wounded, or about half the force engaged.[53] How many stories we have like that of the Texas sergeant at Devil's Den who reached a rock in advance of his line and stood erect on its top amid a storm of bullets, firing as fast as wounded men below could hand him loaded guns, until a ball in the right leg brought him down; who then, regaining the top, continued firing until a bullet in the left leg felled him again; and who then once more crawled to the top, fighting on, until

53. See J.B. Kershaw's own account, "Kershaw's Brigade at Gettysburg," in *Battles and Leaders*, III, 331ff. Whitelaw Reid of the Cincinnati *Gazette*, in Greeley, Horace, *The American Conflict*, Hartford, 1867, II, 381.

he received a bullet in the body which prostrated him, weeping because he was helpless. And how many men had the spirit of the officer who, carried through the Thirty-seventh Massachusetts to have his leg amputated, exclaimed, "I don't begrudge it a bit! We drove the graybacks a mile and a half, and it was worth a leg to see them go!"[54]

In one encounter after another, combatants wrote later, the air seemed alive with lead, but troops still rushed to the fray amid the "terrible medley of cries, shouts, cheers, groans, prayers, curses, bursting shells, whizzing rifle bullets, and clanging steel."[55] Hill's corps had numbered about eight thousand effectives when the battle began, and came out of it with fifteen hundred. The 143rd Pennsylvania had 465 men at the outset, and 253 at the end. Of the 150th Pennsylvania, which lost 264 men, the official report ran: "They all fought as if each man felt that upon his own arm hung the fate of . . . the nation."

Most dramatic and memorable of all was the final attack of the Confederates upon the Union center, where Hancock's Second and Third Corps were to bear the brunt of the assault. The Union troops had every advantage of position; a definite ridge topped along most of its crest by a wall of small stones, which they had strengthened with rails and earth to make a fair breastwork for kneeling men.[56] A second line of defenders could fire over the heads of the first. The North had the further advantage of easy reinforcements, for troops could be quickly despatched from left or right to the center. The eighty guns which they had posted along the ridge and on Cemetery Hill could spew out destruction, unless silenced, over the slope and open wheatfield before them. The Confederates had nothing but disadvantages. They nevertheless cherished a hope that by concentrated fire they might smash the Union guns before the infantry charge began, and might send to the top of Cemetery Ridge a greater number of hard-fighting men than the Union army had posted there.

From the moment that he learned of Lee's plan, Longstreet believed that defeat was certain. "It is my opinion," he declared, "that no 15,000 men ever arrayed for battle could take that position." But Lee remained immovable, believing that a heavy bombardment could clear the way. Doubtless he recalled that

54. Bowen, James Lorenzo, *History of the Thirty-seventh Regiment Mass. Volunteers,* Holyoke, Mass., 1884, 184; Polley, J.B., *Hood's Texas Brigade,* New York, 1910, 170.
55. Gerrish, Theodore, *Army Life, a Private's Reminiscences of the Civil War,* Portland, Maine, 1882, 154.
56. The inevitable clash of testimony blurs even the picture of these defenses. The correspondent of the Washington *National Republican* (July 9, 1863) stated that the front before Pickett consisted of a line of men behind hastily constructed defenses, partly stone wall, partly rifle pits, and partly natural projections of rock. Whitelaw Reid wrote the Cincinnati *Gazette* (quoted in Greeley, *American Conflict, op. cit.,* II, 386:) "We had some shallow rifle pits, with barricades of rails from the fences." But Abner Doubleday testified before the Committee on the Conduct of the War that his position was "Quite strong, and well strengthened with rails and stones." The correspondent of the Richmond *Enquirer,* writing July 8, termed the Union position "almost impregnable." *O.R.,* I, xxvii, Pt.2, 331.

Napoleon had won Austerlitz by a massive use of artillery; doubtless, also, he thought that the butchery of his own troops at Malvern Hill and Burnside's men at Fredericksburg had little relevance to the coming encounter. He hoped that when Pickett's, Pettigrew's, and Trimble's splendid body of Virginians, North Carolinians, Tennesseeans, and others swept up to the crest they could carry all before them. Longstreet, retiring from their final conference, wrote a discouraged note to artillery officer E. P. Alexander. "Colonel: If the artillery fire does not have the effect to drive off the enemy or greatly demoralize him so as to make our efforts pretty certain, I would prefer that you should not advise General Pickett to make the charge. I shall rely a great deal on your good judgment to determine the matter . . ." But Alexander pointed out that any alternative to the charge should be weighed before the bombardment, not after it, for his artillery had just sufficient ammunition to make this one test.[57]

As noon drew near, perfect silence descended upon Gettysburg. About Culp's Hill the clangor of battle had ceased, and only the groans of the wounded could be heard. Along Cemetery Ridge Hancock's troops lay perfectly quiet. From a bright sky, with a few fleecy clouds casting shadows on the grass, the sun poured burning rays upon muskets stacked in orderly array, and brass and steel artillery in perfect immobility. The wheatfield in front rippled under an occasional breeze and then was still again. The Union soldiers lay silent in the heat, some of them shielding their heads by shelter tents raised on a ramrod. The hum of bees, the noise of army wagons and caissons in the distance, and the far-off echo of commands, mingled in a drowsy murmur, so that some infantrymen went to sleep. General Meade and John Gibbon, with a few other officers, sat down at Gibbon's headquarters in the rear to a meal of stewed chicken, potatoes, buttered toast, tea, and coffee.[58]

On wooded Seminary Ridge a mile to the west the same somnolent quiet reigned. Longstreet had disposed the troops for the charge in two long lines, six brigades of perhaps 10,000 men in the first, and five brigades of 5,000 in the second. Alexander and other officers had posted the guns for the cannonade: 83 of Longstreet's First Corps, 44 of the Second Corps, and 60 of the Third, or 187 in all—but of these 56 stood idle; the whole number used by the Confederates in the battle was 172, and in the attack on Cemetery Ridge 115.[59] As the Southern troops took position in the shelter of the trees, orders came to lie down in line

57. Alexander, *Military Memoirs of a Confederate, op. cit.,* 414ff; Longstreet, James, *From Manassas to Appomattox,* Philadelphia, 1896, XXVIII, *passim.*
58. Meade, George, *The Life and Letters of George Gordon Meade,* New York, 1913, II, 104-105, calls this a hasty breakfast; Meade was busy all morning on various parts of the line, so that every possible enemy movement had been considered, "every contingency anticipated."
59. Alexander, *Military Memoirs, op. cit.,* 418. Alexander writes (p. 416): "Our artillery equipment was usually admitted to be inferior to the enemy's in numbers, calibres, and quality of ammunition."

of battle until, when the bombardment ended, they were to advance and sweep all Yankees from their path. Some composed themselves for a nap; Longstreet himself, up most of the previous night, dismounted and slept briefly.[60]

Suddenly, at one o'clock precisely, the sharp crack of a Confederate gun echoed across the field, and after it, another. Above the crest of Cemetery Ridge suddenly bloomed the smoke of two bursting shells, plainly a signal. Before men could look at each other in surprise, gun after gun rattled a thunderous staccato. From the Southern line streamed a steady bombardment; all along the opposite swell, smoke, dust, and fire traced the exploding shells. A moment more, and the Union artillery awakened in a hoarse roar of reply. Flaky streams of fire spouted from the muzzles of a hundred guns—nearly half of the 220 pieces the Union employed in the battle. Shells began exploding in the Confederate woods. The whole two miles of the Union line, Alexander tells us, was soon blazing like a volcano. The field appeared a playground of giants pelting each other with thunder, flame, and iron.

In this terrible duel Northern officers for a time feared severe losses. Shells exploding over limber-boxes blew up, one by one, eleven caissons. Solid shot struck other Union guns, throwing fragments of wood and iron in all directions. Limbs from the shattered trees fell with a crash. Mangled horses writhed and kicked while others galloped madly over the fields. Wounded men hobbled to the rear, followed by stretcher-parties carrying the more seriously injured. All the while, against the dull roar of the cannon, a horrific din filled the upper air as the various missiles shrieked, hissed, howled, and muttered. Yet the damage actually inflicted was not great. The Southern gunners, once billowing smoke shrouded the area, could aim but blindly; they fired too fast, and made the mistake of cutting their fuses so long that many shells exploded tardily and harmlessly. Doubleday exaggerated when he later testified: "They had our exact range and the destruction was fearful."[61] As General Pleasanton said, the Confederate fire should have been more closely concentrated; or as General T. W. Hyde put it, the whole of their fire directed on the Second Corps would have given their attack a better chance. Union men who were at first frightened became cool. "Let it go on," they told each other. "We are beginning to like it."[62]

Meanwhile the Confederates, as the minutes passed, themselves suffered heavily from the Union riposte, which one captain calls "very effective and deadly."[63] Both commanders came under fire. Meade's headquarters were in the thick of the falling shells, so that he rode to Slocum's safer position on Powers

60. Fremantle, *Three Months in the Southern States,* New York, 1864, 270.
61. *Report of the Joint Committee on the Conduct of the War,* Washington, 1865, Vol.I, "Army of the Potomac," 309.
62. Hyde, *Following the Greek Cross, op.cit.,* 151-154.
63. W. W. Wood in Miers and Brown, *Gettysburg, op.cit.,* 228-232.

Hill.[64] On the opposite ridge, Lee and a single companion suddenly appeared on horseback between the artillery and the troops lying behind the guns. Thrilled but horrified, for the ground was swept by Union missiles, the men shouted to him to retire, and doffing his hat in acknowledgment, he quickened the pace of Traveller to a quieter spot.

At three, Meade's chief of artillery, Henry J. Hunt, anxious to let his guns cool and conserve ammunition, ordered a cease fire. Numerous pieces were limbered up and withdrawn. Alexander on the Confederate side concluded that the Northern artillery was being silenced. He had agreed to give Pickett his signal for the charge; he thought the moment had come. As orders rang out, the gray veterans clambered to their feet, formed ranks, and swung forward. The plan was that some eleven Confederate brigades numbering perhaps 15,000 men, all under Longstreet and led by Pickett, Pettigrew, and Trimble, would attack the center of the Union lines, while other troops were to furnish support and threaten. The idea was that the Union army would be ripped apart, its two wings entirely separated. Many Southerners thought the formation a poor one, with its six brigades in the front line, plus four more in the second, and another echeloned to the right rear. "Both flanks of the assaulting column were in the air;" writes E. P. Alexander, "and the left without any support in the rear."[65] Above all, success depended on the destruction of the Union artillery, and all along Cemetery Ridge Hunt was wheeling up his reserve guns, filling his ammunition boxes, and marshalling his gunners to use shells and solid shot at distance range, shrapnel when the Southerners drew nearer, and finally canister.

"We believed that the battle was practically over," wrote one Confederate officer, "and that we had nothing to do but to march unopposed to Cemetery Heights and occupy them."[66] Pickett's men felt their first moment of dismay when they saw that the supporting columns on the flanks were not moving forward with proper alacrity. In vain did mounted officers dash up and down the line urging greater speed. Still the main advance went on. The men moved to a post-and-rail fence, climbed it, and halted beyond to reform. Just as they started forward again, a cannon shot came from the left, striking down a long line of men. At that instant the breeze lifted the smoke from the ridge in front to reveal the full panoply of Union strength in its terrifying grandeur, a double line of infantry in front, guns frowning beside them, and reserves in thick platoons farther back. The Confederates pressed on undaunted, densely crowded together, battleflags tossing in the breeze, musket barrels and bayonets gleaming in the sun. As the

64. Doubleday, *Chancellorsville and Gettysburg*, *op.cit.*, 190-191; "a very uncomfortable place," writes Colonel Thomas L. Livermore, *Days and Events, 1860-1866*, Boston, 1920, 260; "the yard later showing a dozen or score of dead horses."
65. Alexander, *op.cit.*, 419.
66. Miers and Brown, *op.cit.*, 231.

15,000 swept over meadow and wheatfield, grimly magnificent in their precision, still hardly a noise broke the silence in front. But had the Confederates halted to listen closely, they might have heard the click of locks as the Union infantry brought their pieces to the ready, the clank of cannon wheels as the guns slid a little forward, and the clatter of ammunition boxes dumped open for eager fingers.

Along the Union line rode steel-cold John Gibbon, speaking with impassive calmness to each platoon: "Don't hurry, men—Don't fire too fast. Let them come up close before you fire, and then aim low and steadily."

Thus came the swift climax, so swift that it was over almost before men comprehended the fact. In a sudden roar, the Union artillery belched forth fire and smoke. As Pickett's line, despite terrible gaps, came on without faltering, the gunners changed from shrapnel to canister. The gaps grew. The right flank of the Confederates, moving farther right than it should when the men saw Doubleday's position defended by five lines, swung close to a Vermont brigade which delivered a withering flank fire. Recoiling nearer the center, the shattered line at once resumed its charge.[67] The gray host was at last well within musket range, and a sheet of flame leaped from the Northern line toward Pickett's and Pettigrew's columns. Stung to a response, the Virginians and North Carolinians halted, fired, reloaded, and fired again. A moment more and Pickett's troops were up to the wall occupied by Alexander S. Webb's brigade of the Second Corps, which had suffered most heavily from the bombardment. A. H. Cushing's battery of regular artillery on the crest had but one serviceable gun left. Though wounded in thighs and body, and bleeding heavily, Cushing—a brother of the naval hero —pushed his piece forward, gasping to Webb, "I will give them one more shot!" As it rang out he called "Good-bye!" and fell dead.

Along the wall the red flags thickened, and the defenders, as the Southern vanguard poured up, wavered. Lewis A. Armistead, who had led his brigade with cap on upraised sword, leaped at the Union line shouting to perhaps a hundred followers, "Give them the cold steel, boys!" He fell dead over the muzzle of Cushing's cannon. One officer, Colonel James Mayo, claimed he had carried enemy intrenchments and, "At this critical juncture when seconds seemed more precious than hours of any former time, many an anxious eye was cast back to the hill from which we came in the hope of seeing supports near at hand and more than once I heard the despairing exclamation, 'Why don't they come!' But no help came." Already Webb's officers were rallying their men, and the Union defense, as reserves came on the run, was being restored. Everywhere the Confederates were falling back. Pettigrew's men had lost all but one of their field officers; they had mustered 2800 strong on the morning of July 1, and at roll call

67. Hyde, *op.cit.*, 156.

on the 4th would number but 835.[68] The rebel yell was heard no more. First the extreme left of the Confederate assault broke, and then the retreat rapidly extended to the right. For Pickett's men in particular, it was soon a case of *sauve qui peut.* Only a third of his division was left unscathed; the rest lay on the field. Trimble's and Wilcox's supporting troops had failed to grapple with the Union line, so that the brave Virginians and North Carolinians in advance were left with no choice but to face about or be overwhelmed. And as the Southern troops fell dejectedly back, fresh musket volleys and shells from newly-fetched guns sped them on their way. To the east of Gettysburg Stuart's cavalry, which arrived the day before, fought the Federal cavalry of David McM. Gregg. Stuart was repulsed in his effort to cut off Meade's communications.

Once more quiet reigned over the Gettysburg terrain. As the sun sank in the West, the sultry evening felt breaths of coolness. Before darkness came both sides had a last look at the fields and valleys. They were scarred with shells and scored with round shot; the fences were levelled, the wheat trodden into the dirt, the trees gashed and rent; the ground was littered with broken weapons, haversacks, canteens, blankets, coats, and muskets; here and there horses weltered in their blood, some dead, some alive. Everywhere lay the slain and wounded, in heaps, in lines, in single dark spots, some seeming to sleep unhurt, some writhing in the pain of frightful mutilations, some stirring slowly. The twilight deepened; the lanterns and torches of ambulance men and doctors flickered here and there; and from the ground rose the terrible symphony of thousands in agony of body and mind.

Pickett's charge, as Longstreet and other Confederate officers saw at the time, was a blunder founded on two miscalculations; first that it was possible for the Confederate guns to silence a greater number of Union cannon, and second, that a charge over a mile of ground against well-entrenched troops, superior in number, could ever succeed. It was not difficult, as the Georgian A. R. Wright wrote, to reach Cemetery Ridge—he himself had briefly penetrated it the second day; the trouble was to hold it, for the convex Union line of defense made it easy to reinforce any point, while the concave Confederate line of attack made it hard to move long enveloping arrays effectively. The Southern army was defeated because, distant from its bases, outnumbered, and limited in ammunition, it had accepted battle where it must not only attack, but attack under a grave disadvantage—the disadvantage of bringing a wide hemispheric line to bear upon a shorter, stronger inner line. Lee might have striven more vigorously to compel Meade to deliver the attack. He might even have endeavored to accomplish this, as Longstreet proposed, by a final flank movement that placed his army between

68. Greeley, *American Conflict, op.cit.,* II, 385; Col. James Mayo to Pickett, unpublished report of battle. George E. Pickett Papers, Duke Univ. Lib.

Meade and Baltimore, for Meade would never have dared to let Lee hold for long an inner position, with roads open even to Washington.

It was a glorious charge, but it was not war. Some thought it glorious that color-bearers of thirty-five regiments were shot down, and that seven Confederate colonels were buried on the battleground after Pickett fell back; glorious that a Union general could write, "I tried to ride over the field, but could not, for the dead and wounded lay too thick to guide a horse through them."[69] Yet futile carnage is never glorious. From any humanitarian point of view such losses were as horrible as they were calamitous from the Confederate standpoint. As the survivors fell back within their original lines, Lee rode toward them, and meeting General Cadmus M. Wilcox, who was on the verge of tears over the frightful losses of his brigade, exclaimed, "Never mind, general, all this has been my fault —it is I that have lost this fight, and you must help me out of it the best way you can."[70] It was a manly statement, and it was true.

[VI]

The figures can give only a most superficial idea of the horrors of any battle, particularly one of the size and length of Gettysburg. But even the figures are stark enough. While estimates and totals vary, it is probable that the official casualty toll for Gettysburg is fairly correct, although the Southern figures are possibly lower than they actually were. For the Union, 23,049 total casualties including 3,155 killed, 13,529 wounded, and 5,365 missing or captured; for the Confederacy, 20,451 total casualties including 2,592 killed, 12,709 wounded and 5,510 missing or captured.

For the first time, a bloody battle found the field medical service of the Union army adequate. Dr. Jonathan Letterman, reorganizer of this service, had proved the value of his ambulance corps and other preparations at Chancellorsville; now he did still better. He had at hand 3,000 drivers and stretchermen equipped with 1,000 ambulances; he had 650 medical officers present for duty. [71] Each night the wounded within the picket lines were picked up by stretcher parties, and carried to waiting teams; surgeons dealt with the more desperate cases on the ground. By noon of July 4th, 14,000 men had received attention. The Southern casualties fared as well as the Northern. When surgeons lifted a soldier to the table, they never stopped to see whether he wore blue trousers or gray; they looked only at his wound. The proximity of the battlefield to large Northern centers made it easy for the Sanitary Commission, Christian Commission, and other associations,

69. Hyde, op.cit., 157.
70. Fremantle, Diary, op.cit., 215.
71. OR I, xxvii, Pt.1, 187; Pt.2, 346; Adams, George W., Doctors in Blue, New York, 1952, 91.

as well as the surgeon-general's office, to pour in abundant quantities of lint, bandages, chloroform, surgical instruments, garments, bedding, food, and delicacies.[72] From fans to mosquito-bars, from fruit to brandy, everything needed was available.

The field hospitals were fated not to complete their task of caring for the total of about 21,000 wounded, nor the surgeons to cope with such a multitude of exhausted, maimed, and gangrened men. When Lee retreated and Meade began his slow pursuit, another heavy battle seemed imminent. While his immediate task was yet unfinished, therefore, Letterman detached more than 500 of his 650 medical officers for the anticipated emergency farther south. Since at Gettysburg every doctor had about 300 patients, and every operating surgeon about 900 cases, this was a costly blunder. Letterman could plead that he was counting on an influx of additional physicians and surgeons from all over the North, and on the rapid transfer of many of the wounded to Harrisburg, Baltimore, and Washington; but he should have waited until his burden was thus mitigated before dropping it.

To the poignant disappointment of the country and the President, Meade failed to pursue and destroy Lee's army when it seemed that he had repeated opportunities to bring his foe to bay. He can be excused for not ordering a vigorous advance just after the close of Pickett's charge. Lee dreaded it. The Confederate guns had an average of only five rounds left. But the hour was late, most of the Union army was exhausted, worn and severely blooded from long marches and three days' fighting. Meade feared a repulse on Seminary Ridge. Longstreet later declared that an attack by Union forces would have been thrown back. "I had Hood and McLaws, who had not been engaged; I had a heavy force of artillery; I should have liked nothing better than to have been attacked, and have no doubt that I should have given those who tried as bad a reception as Pickett got."[73] Meade was prudent, and prudence counselled inaction. If he had shown the imprudence exhibited by Lee and Jackson at Second Manassas and Chancellorsville he might have routed the Confederates and ended the war; but it is difficult to fault his caution. Far different was the situation later.[74] Lee, on July 4, ordered his trains, with many wounded, to move toward Williamsport, while after dark the army itself was put en route toward the Potomac. A number of wagons and ambulances were captured because of high water, for heavy rains had flooded the Potomac so that it was impassable except by two small ferries. While Ewell's corps did not leave the Gettysburg area until July 5, the Confederate army managed to reach Hagerstown on the 6th and 7th. Except for small

72. Sp.Correspondence of *English Medical Times*, n.d., Hall, Newman, *A Reply to the Pro-Slavery Wail*, London, 1868, *passim*.
73. Swinton, *History of the Army of the Potomac, op.cit.*, 364. Swinton quotes from memory.
74. Cf. Biddle, J.C., "Why Meade Did Not Attack Lee," Philadelphia *Weekly Times*, May 12, 1877; Gen. Alfred Pleasonton, Philadelphia *Weekly Times*, Jan. 19, 1878, censures Meade sharply.

cavalry actions, Lee had no opposition until July 12, when Meade's army approached. Lee then took up a previously selected position covering the Potomac from Williamsport to Falling Waters, remaining there during two days penned up in a highly vulnerable position, where he seemed at the mercy of Meade's advancing army, augmented by powerful reserves. For the first and only time, Alexander says, he found the General visibly anxious. After the war, Lee was quoted as saying that he would have crossed the Potomac at once if he could have done so. "He would not have been sorry if Meade had attacked him there, but he did not stop specially to invite it, but because the river was high. Meade's failure to attack showed how he had suffered." On July 15, Lee wrote his wife that the return to Virginia "is rather sooner than I had originally contemplated but having accomplished what I proposed on leaving the Rappk. (Rappahannock) viz: relieving the valley of the presence of the enemy and drawing his army north of the Potomac, I determined to recross the latter river. . . ."[75] General French, left unemployed with 7,000 Union veterans at Frederick during the battle, had shown enough energy before Lee's arrival to send a cavalry detachment to Williamsport to destroy the bridge there. It was, in fact, one of his few exhibitions of energy. Very fortunately for Lee, Meade's pursuit was preternaturally slow. By nature cautious, new to the responsibilities of chief command, aware how all his predecessors had failed, he made safety his guiding rule. He remained at Gettysburg for two days resting his troops, succoring the wounded, and burying the dead; then, turning southeast of Lee's line, he halted another day at Middletown for fresh supplies and the arrival of his trains. It was not until July 12 that Meade caught up with Lee's army, now fortified on the Potomac for a last stand. He might have attacked that day, but contented himself with a reconnaisance. Only Pleasanton's cavalry showed any spirit in the pursuit. Capturing large trains of wagons and taking many prisoners, it demonstrated that if Meade had begun a rapid march on the 4th or 5th, Lee would probably have found surrender unavoidable.[76]

As Lincoln and Halleck waited in Washington for news of some heavy blow by Meade they were tormented by alternating hopes and fears. "I presume from what the President said this morning," Montgomery Blair wrote his father on July 8, "that the Rebels will not get over the river in safety. He was much discouraged yesterday and seemed to think they would escape from Meade. He did not speak with confidence this morning, but he said he felt better . . ."[77] That same day Halleck wrote Meade that Lee was reported crossing the Potomac. "If

75. Alexander, op.cit., 439; Allan, William, "Conversations with Lee," ms. Southern Historical Collection, Univ. of N.C. Library; to his wife July 15, 1863, from Bunker Hill, Va., R.E. Lee Papers, LC.
76. Pleasonton, ut supra; Alexander, Military Memoirs, op.cit., 435.
77. Blair Papers, Princeton University.

Lee's army is so divided by the river, the importance of attacking the part on this side is incalculable. Such an opportunity may not occur again." If, on the contrary, Lee was keeping his army together, Meade should take time to concentrate —but he should still attack. General Benjamin F. Kelley was under orders from Hancock to move to strike the Confederate right; General W. T. H. Brooks was moving from Pittsburgh to reinforce Kelley; troops were being sent from New York and Fort Monroe directly to Harper's Ferry. "You will have forces sufficient to render your victory certain. My only fear now is that the enemy may escape by crossing the river." That same July 8, Meade told Halleck that the army was in high spirits, and ready and willing to push forward. He would move forward the moment he could get different commands together and supplied. However, "I expect to find the enemy in a strong position, well covered with artillery, and I do not desire to imitate his example at Gettysburg, and assault a position where the chances were so greatly against success. I wish in advance to moderate the expectations of those who, in ignorance of the difficulties to be encountered, may expect too much. All that I can do under the circumstances, I pledge this army to do."[78]

The critical hour arrived on Sunday the 12th. Lee issued a rousing address to his army that day, full of boasts and threats that were but a blind; he strengthened his long earthworks near Meade's front, which looked formidable but were merely heaped earth covering a continuous line of piled rails; he had campfires built at night to simulate a strong immobile army even while his regiments were beginning to cross the Potomac—some by a new pontoon bridge, some by rafts and boats which his engineers had constructed of boards from dwellings. That evening Meade summoned his corps commanders to a council at headquarters to determine whether the powerful Union army should attack next morning. Reynolds had been killed, Hancock badly wounded, and Warren slept in exhaustion. The majority of the corps commanders opposed an attack, but a good many other officers seemed to favor it. Meade himself was for fighting, but in such a lukewarm, hesitant mood that he yielded his will. As the war correspondent Noah Brooks wrote, Hooker would probably have listened to the council—and then would have attacked, although one has to remember Hooker's failure to continue his advance at Chancellorsville.[79] "Upon this day (July 13) the soldiers who bore muskets wished to hear the commands, 'Take arms,' and 'Charge,' because they knew, what is conceded now, that it would have captured all the cannon, *materiel*, and men from the enemy, and finished the Rebellion without a hard contest or a large loss of valuable lives. . . ."[80]

78. Halleck Papers, Eldredge Collection, HEH; *O.R.* I, xxvii, Pt.i, 84.
79. Letter dated Boonsborough, Md., July 14, 1863, in Sacramento *Union*.
80. Blake, Henry N., *Three Years in the Army of the Potomac*, Boston, 1865, 229.

Another war correspondent, Theodore C. Wilson of the New York *Herald*, had been taken prisoner by Stuart. On Monday night, the 13th, he and other prisoners were marched to Williamsport. Gray infantrymen were passing at the time, many of them singing gaily. "In the distance, toward Hagerstown, burned a long line of well-lit camp fires, illuminating the sky for miles around; yet little did the Unionists know that these campfires while they helped to deceive them, also helped to light the very path of the retreating rebel army." Southern officers had been very fearful of an attack by Meade until the evening of the 12th. Then Wilson heard them begin to laugh and make derisive remarks. "Yes," said Stuart to Rodes and Fitzhugh Lee, "the Yankees, instead of attacking us, are actually throwing up some kind of entrenchments; and they boast that they are not afraid of us and are pressing on for a fight. Well, they had better come."[81]

Of Lincoln's chagrin, grief, and anger we have abundant records. The most impressive is perhaps the statement his son made years later to a friend. "Entering my father's room right after the battle of Gettysburg," said Robert, "I found him in tears with head bowed upon his arms resting on the table at which he sat. 'Why, what is the matter, father?' I asked. For a brief interval he remained silent, then raised his head, and the explanation of his grief was forthcoming. 'My boy,' he said, 'when I heard that the bridge at Williamsport had been swept away, I sent for General Haupt and asked him how soon he could replace the same. He replied, 'If I were uninterrupted I could build a bridge with the material there within twenty-four hours, and Mr. President, General Lee has engineers as skilful as I am.' Upon hearing this I at once wrote Meade to attack without delay, and if successful to destroy my letter, but in case of failure to preserve it for his vindication. I have just learned that at a council of war of Meade and his generals, it has been determined not to pursue Lee, and now the opportune chance of ending this bitter struggle is lost."[82] The essential, if not literal, truth of this statement we can hardly doubt.

It was at Falling Waters, four miles below Williamsport, that Lee drew in his final lines to cross the river, and as the Federal forces took a threatening position on the 13th, the Confederates began crossing that night, completing the move by early afternoon of the 14th. Dashing cavalrymen under Buford and Kilpatrick seized some 2,000 prisoners here—all they could capture of an army which a general of high courage and consummate skill might have forced to a surrender as complete as that of Bazaine, a little later, at Sedan. Such a surrender would have ended the war. It is impossible not to blame Meade for the failure. But it is also impossible not to ask whether a large responsibility did not rest with the highest

81. New York *Herald*, July 18, 1863.
82. George H. Thatcher of Albany, N.Y., letter in *American Historical Review*, Jan., 1927, Vol. XXXII, No.2, 282-283; see Nicolay and Hay, *op.cit.*, VII, 280-281, for the letter he wrote Meade and suppressed.

The Battle of Gettysburg, sketched by Thomas Nast

Union command—Lincoln, Stanton, Halleck—which had not found a general for the most fateful battle of the war until three days before it began, so that Meade was still nervously uncertain of what his various corps could accomplish;[83] and which had not assembled powerful reserve forces, far surpassing those available, to cooperate with Meade as he followed the retreating rebels, and to join him in the final struggle.

83. The military historian, John Codman Ropes, who spent much time with the Twentieth Massachusetts in the field, told Thomas L. Livermore that "in the first place, General Meade was utterly unacquainted with his command and did not know what it could do"; Livermore, *op.cit.*, 271.

4

The Officers, the Soldiers, the People

WHILE CANNON pounded and muskets crackled at Vicksburg and Gettysburg, the war carried a confusing array of impressions and meanings to the millions, North and South, who were caught in its toils; to the North who felt they were fighting for Emancipation and for Union, two great causes, and to the South who believed they were fighting for Independence. It was a horrible war in that it had lasted much longer, with far more bloodshed and anguish, than anybody had anticipated. It was a depressing war in that the first passion and excitement had long since disappeared in a grim, gray ordeal of endurance. It was an unnerving war in that the two peoples descried no end to the process of flinging hundreds of thousands of young men into the work of exterminating or mutilating each other, with incalculable future penalties to the nation, or nations. Finally, it was a disillusioning war in that the more exhausting the strain became, and the deeper the churning of society went, the plainer grew evidences of the class selfishness, individual greed, and corruption which it generated.

Even while the conflict was producing its heroes, it was becoming more impersonal. It was a war of peoples; of organizations pitted against organizations —the ever stronger, better-knit organizations of the North against the desperately improvised organizations of the South. The temper of the country was changing. It was becoming tougher, harsher, and coarser; it had cast aside old romanticisms and sentimentalities. By 1863 the majority of Americans were sternly critical of everybody and everything, and swept by gusts of angry self-appraisal. Every leader, and not least Lincoln and Davis, was measured with doubt.

Hence amid the rejoicing after Gettysburg and Vicksburg, as before these battles, many Northerners asked themselves deeply anxious questions. Why had the national government ever allowed the State Militia to be so ill-organized, ill-tried and weakly officered? Why was it that Lincoln, calling for 75,000 men after Sumter, had limited their service to three months, while the Confederates fixed the term of one hundred thousand volunteers at one year? Later, why was it that, when Lee's army had marched north from the Shenandoah into the Cumberland Valley, the only Union force in front of him was the futile little garrison at Harper's Ferry? Why was it that, when Hooker's command, numbering almost 140,000 before Chancellorsville, was weakened in May by the battle and in June by desertion and the discharge of nine-months' men and two-year men, no effective steps had been taken to repair the losses? Why, in the critical year 1863, had the conscription law that was passed in chilly March not been put in operation before sultry July? Why was Hooker forced to drop his command only three days before the most sharply critical battle of the war, giving way to one of the less noted corps commanders, who had to clutch hurriedly at the reins? Was it really necessary for Grant to try seven unsuccessful approaches to Vicksburg before military and political necessities impelled him to make his final spectacularly successful movement? And why were the War Department and President not informed of his plans until after he had committed his army to the advance by way of Jackson? Why had not Rosecrans been forced into action after practically resting for nearly six months after Murfreesboro? Other questions were also involved: emancipation, the role of the freed Negroes, the elections coming up next year, reconstruction of conquered areas, personalities civil and military, and perhaps the biggest—how long was it going to last?

Southerners were meanwhile intent upon even more agonizing questions. Had it really been necessary for Lee to fight an offensive battle against a larger army entrenched upon the Pennsylvania ridges and hills? Had Pickett's charge been less rash and less ill-managed than it looked? In the West, why had no troops been brought from Arkansas and Louisiana across the Mississippi to defend Vicksburg? Why had Joseph E. Johnston and Pemberton not united for an attack on Grant when the Union army first crossed the river and still lay below the hills? Was the liaison of these two armies with those of Lee and Longstreet all that might have been expected? And what of the inadequate numbers in the Confederate ranks? When Port Hudson fell like a loosened plum from its bough, and Bragg, after evacuating Tullahoma in haste on July 1, continued a retreat that seemed likely to sacrifice the vital rail center of Chattanooga to the Union troops, the depression of Southern onlookers increased. Where in all the West, asked editors, could a general of real talent and resourcefulness be found? How could the Southern draft be made to yield more fighters? How was the invasion of the South to be halted? Was President Davis the right man? What was wrong with Congress? How could the blockade be broken? Where were food and other necessities to come from in the future? What was going to happen to their slaves? What was going to happen to themselves?

After Vicksburg and Gettysburg, there were no great battles for a while, but a lot of cleaning-up operations, reorganizations, and sparring in Virginia. Meade missed a splendid opportunity to cut Lee in two at Manassas Gap when his commanders failed him. There was considerable action along the Rappahannock between the opposed forces, and Lee carried out a movement toward Washington known as the Bristoe Campaign, but had to pull back. Then there was the abortive and mismanaged Mine Run Campaign late in the year. Meade felt he had been hampered by Halleck in offensive moves. In the West, the Tennessee front resumed great importance and activity. But, along the Mississippi, why were the forces of Grant and Banks scattered in all directions instead of being concentrated to march against Mobile or Chattanooga? Grant later placed the blame for this squandering of opportunity upon Halleck; but James Grant Wilson, an informed observer, placed it rather upon Grant himself.

And while men pondered such questions, the draft riots, which convulsed New York just after Gettysburg, revived Northern doubts about the whole recruiting system.

[II]

For twenty years Americans had been reading *Barnaby Rudge.* They little thought that the foremost American city would soon witness scenes even more shocking than those of the Gordon riots. Dickens had limned a series of lurid pictures: Newgate forced open, the Bank of England attacked, Catholic houses and chapels sacked by the mob, murdered people thrown into the Thames, the home of the Lord Chief Justice burned, the Prime Minister gazing from his rooftop at six different conflagrations, the King himself giving the order for the military to fire on rioters. Edmund Burke had written: "If one could in decency laugh, must not one laugh to see what I saw?—a boy of fifteen years at most in Queen Street, mounted on a penthouse and demolishing a house with great zeal . . . children plundering, at noonday, the City of London."[1] The New York scenes were bloodier and more brutal. Nearly a hundred years later, the eminent attorney C.C. Burlingham recalled that as a young child he had seen a Negro lynched in front of his father's parsonage while fusillades echoed across the city.[2]

When Lincoln signed the Draft Act on March 3, 1863, two years after his inauguration and the outbreak of war, all patriotic men knew that it was evoked by desperate necessity. The North had closed 1862 with only 556,000 officers and men present for duty.[3] There was an imminent manpower crisis. Nine-month and other short-term enlistments would soon expire. Some of the vast numbers absent-without-leave—more than a hundred thousand at the end of 1862—would

1. Newman, Bertram, *Edmund Burke,* London, 1927, pp.116-117.
2. Oral History dictation, Columbia University, 1959.
3. *O.R.* III, ii, 957.

be brought back by the new stringent measures, but nobody could guess how many. Althogether, very nearly 200,000 enlisted men deserted during the war, of whom 76,000 were arrested and returned to duty. Desertion is common on both sides in any bloody, gruelling war, as it was in Washington's army when homesick soldiers broke away in spring to help plant or gather crops, and as in Wellington's peninsular army, grumbling over repeated retreats in a harsh land. Meanwhile, volunteering had dried up until it yielded only a trickle of recruits.[4]

"We must see to it," declared Chairman Henry Wilson of the Senate Military Affairs Committee on February 16, "that the ranks of our armies, broken by toil, disease, and death, are again filled with the health and vigor of life." Too late, men saw that conscription should have been adopted as soon as the government realized that the conflict might be long. Senator James A. McDougall of California echoed Wilson: "The whole business has been unequal and wrong from the first." John Sherman of Ohio was more outspoken: "I believe," he told the Senate, "if this law had been passed at the beginning of this rebellion, this rebellion would now be over."[5]

The law was assuredly mild, and based partly on French practices. Aside from substitution and paying $300 for exemption, there were other ways out. A first class of unmarried men of 18 to 45 and married men of 18 to 30 must serve before a second class of married men, 30 to 45, was called. Other exemptions included the only son of aged and infirm parents, the father of motherless children under 12, or the only brother of orphaned children below that age, and any member of a family group of father and sons that had already sent two members into service. The main resentment was caused by the substitute and commutation provisions. The delays in getting the draft into operation were exasperating, as it was to be based upon a special new listing of eligible men and not upon census returns. Enrollment did not begin until May 25, 1863, or until plans were drawn, personnel chosen, and offices opened. The number enrolled, supposedly the total of males in the country between 20 and 45, was 3,115,000, which included many later exempted for physical defects, foreign allegiance, or other reasons. (Almost one-third, in fact, or 319.1 in each thousand, were dropped for physical or mental infirmities.) Colonel James B. Fry found it a thoroughly perplexing task to compute quotas for each district, for he had to make an accurate allowance for the soldiers already furnished. Controversies over the quotas flared almost as soon as the drawing of names began in this fateful Lottery.[6]

In New York City the enrollment was peculiarly difficult, for the population was highly mobile, aliens were numerous, and many men were listed twice, once

4. Lerwill, *Personnel Replacement System, op.cit.*, 74-76.
5. *Congressional Globe*, 37th Cong., 3rd Sess., Pt. 1, 976, 983, 998.
6. *Ibid.*, 983; O.R. III, iii, 1046-1049, 1175; v, 616-619.

at home and once at the place of employment. The work was completed on June 29, with a total of 54,372 names in Class 1, and 23,405 in Class 2. At last, it was announced that the wheel of chance would begin to turn on July 11, 1863. Cards listing individuals and addresses were drawn from the wheel by a blindfolded clerk. That hot Saturday morning, several hundred names were announced without special incident. This peaceable beginning was a relief to those who knew of the recent warning given Governor Horatio Seymour that a desperate gang of Copperheads and deserters were ready to attack the Seventh Regiment's armory and seize its contents to stop the draft.

But when, on Sunday, the press published lists of the men summoned to service, thousands were reminded that their names might be posted next. That night the superintendent of police, John A. Kennedy, received word that an agitator named John Andrews was making fiery speeches to longshoremen and other workers, denouncing the war, the Negroes, and the President, and calling for mob action to stop the draft at once.

Next morning, Monday, July 13, the *Herald* appeared with an ominous paragraph. The city was quivering with excitement, it declared; the Thirtieth Ward, full of Irish laborers, was threatening an outbreak; some workers were openly organizing to resist the government.[7] The paper was hardly on sale before crowds of stevedores, cartmen, porters, and factory hands assembled at what the *Herald* termed "certain specified spots" in lower Manhattan, and swept uptown, halting work in all establishments as they went. Astute organizers kept the columns moving. Obviously, mob leaders were taking advantage of the absence of militia regiments in Pennsylvania. They poured into the draft office at Third Avenue and 46th Street, smashing windows and furniture, and setting it afire in a dozen places. Seizing Superintendent Kennedy, they beat him nearly to death. At the Second Avenue Armory, another target, they found the building guarded by a detachment of militia; and as the mob increased, these troops were reinforced by a body of regulars, while cannon were placed to sweep the streets.[8] But as night came on, fires lighted up the skies. George Templeton Strong caught a glimpse of the nucleus of the riot—perhaps five hundred rough laborers, chiefly Irish, quite unarmed but furious, sacking two three-story dwellings on Lexington Avenue at their leisure, and setting them in flames. He was helpless, disgusted, and deeply alarmed.

"If a quarter one hears be true," he wrote, "this is an organized insurrection in the interest of the rebellion, and Jefferson Davis rules New York today."[9]

7. New York *Herald,* July 13, 1863; *O.R.* I, xxvii, Pt.2, 878-881; *American Annual Cyclopaedia,* 1863, 811-817.
8. Major T.P. McElrath, "The Draft Riots," Phila. *Weekly Times,* April 27, 1878; New York *Herald Tribune,* July 14, 1863.
9. Strong, George Templeton, *Diary,* New York, 1952, III, 336.

By nightfall that Monday, a detachment of veterans in the Invalid Corps, trying to fight its way through the mob on Forty-second Street, had been routed and scattered; the Colored Orphan Asylum at Lexington and Forty-third had been gutted and burned, though fortunately not until the children had been evacuated; and Horace Greeley had been driven from the *Tribune* Building to hide in the restaurant of Windust's Hotel on Ann Street until the rioters could be dispersed. Conflagrations had spread, many buildings had been plundered, and a number of Negroes had been hanged or beaten to death. Meanwhile, three elderly men, John E. Wool, head of the Department of the East, Harvey Brown, commander of the regulars in the city, and Charles Sandford, head of the militia, had engaged in a confused wrangle over military responsibility and authority, with Brown refusing to serve under Sandford in field command, and issuing his own orders. As word came that Governor Seymour was speeding to the city from Long Branch, a drenching night rain fell on the city. Mayor George Opdyke and General Wool, being short of forces, on Monday, July 13, called for troops from the Navy Yard, West Point, and Newark, N.J., and appealed to the governors of New York, New Jersey, Connecticut, Massachusetts, and Rhode Island. Navy men came in at once, as did a company from West Point, one from Newark, and, of course, men from other parts of New York State.

On Tuesday, July 14, with many shops closed and business at a standstill, the mob came into collision with bands of troops and police patrolling the streets. It attacked Mayor Opdyke's house, but was driven off; it continued to kill Negroes, plunder houses, and set fires. Rumors circulated that it would destroy the Union League Club, and hostile newspaper offices. The sub-treasury and custom house were barricaded and placed under heavy guard. Assistant Treasurer John J. Cisco even had a live shell ready to throw out of the window.[10] A police station on Twenty-second Street went up in a rich blaze. All omnibuses and street-cars had been stopped, for the mob talked of burning the stables to bring the drivers to their side. The worst outrage of the day was the murder of Colonel Henry F. O'Brien of the Eleventh New York, home on leave, who was beaten senseless, dragged through the street, and beaten again till he died. Governor Seymour issued an address that was partly a stump-speech expressing sympathy with men carried to extremes by "an apprehension of injustice," and partly an assurance that violence would be put down. Brooks's clothing store was looted. But as troops began firing on the rioters, they realized the power of law. "The people are waking up," wrote Strong, "and by tomorrow there will be adequate organization to protect property and life." E.S. Sanford of the U.S. Military Telegraph Service kept Stanton posted, stating on the second afternoon that the mob was

10. *Ibid.*, III, 339; *O.R.* I, xxvii, Pt.2, 879.

testing the government, and "If you cannot enforce the draft here, it will not be enforced elsewhere."

The reign of fear among Negroes, however, continued on the morrow. Hundreds were fleeing in utter panic to Brooklyn, Westchester, and New Jersey; others, men, women, and children, slept in station houses. Negro tenements were gutted by men who brought carts to carry off the furniture; Negro boarding houses in Roosevelt Street were burned down; Negroes were assaulted and lynched. The *Herald*, after estimating that on the second day 150 black people had been killed or wounded, added on the third: "Everywhere throughout the city they are driven about like sheep, and numbers are killed of whom no account will ever be learned." Prosperous white families joined the exodus. Meanwhile, Manton Marble's *World*, which had assailed Lincoln's "wanton exercise of arbitrary powers," and stigmatized the Draft Act as a measure which could not have been ventured upon in England even in the black days when press gangs were filling the English warships with forcibly seized conscripts, was giving all the encouragement it could to the rioters. And Ben Wood's *Daily News* was coming as close to treason as it dared, for Ben Wood, a brother of Fernando, who had bought the *Daily News* in 1860, and would soon enter the State Senate, was an audaciously virulent Democrat, who would later expose himself as a traitor.[11]

In less than four days the riots passed into history, and the draft was temporarily suspended until August 19; they guttered out on Thursday evening, like a smoky fire of rubbish, amid the crowded tenement houses of the East Side. But what a four days the people had seen! Flame and smoke, shouts and screams, rattle of musketry and boom of cannon, possessed the terrified city. In the midsummer heat, Sirius looked down on maddened thugs and viragoes committing every kind of atrocity, on robbers filling their pockets with loot, on ranks of sunburned, dust-stained soldiers from the Pennsylvania front moving down the avenues with gleaming bayonets, and on sullen cannon rolling into the squares. It saw field guns sweeping the streets with a sudden hurricane of grapeshot; snipers on tenement rooftops firing into the police and militia; veteran riflemen picking off these assailants and toppling them to the pavement. Men at the windows of brownstone mansions listened, like Herman Melville, as "fitfully from far breaks a mixed surf of muffled sound, the Atheist roar of riot," saw "Red Arson glaring balefully," and concluded, as he did, that "the town is taken by its rats."[12] In a final bloody encounter, somewhere near Third Avenue and Twenty-first Street, a stubborn fragment of the mob made its stand against a body of United States regulars which General Brown thrust against them. Some died on the street;

11. *O.R.* I, xxvii, Pt.2, 888; Nicolay and Hay, *op.cit.*, VII, 17-18; *Annual American Cyclopaedia*, 1863, 811-818.

12. Melville, Herman, "The House Top, a Night Piece, July 1863," *The Works of Herman Melville*, London, 1924, Vol.XVI.

others were bayoneted by soldiers who courageously fought their way into the houses. Altogether, thirteen men were killed and a score wounded in this final spasm. Then, as more troops poured into the city, all was silence, and the bloodiest race riots thus far known in American history ended with many lives lost, and more than a million dollars worth of property destroyed.[13]

Draco had triumphed, as Melville put it; deference to law had gained the day. But New York bore on its shield the stain of the ugliest turbulence that ever disgraced the republic. It was another evidence of the growing fury of the age of hate; of the power of anger, violence, and blood-lust (which Lincoln had eloquently denounced in his first important speech, in 1838) to seize upon and degrade a people.[14]

The riots had expressed a variety of passionate resentments and fears. Many detested the war, especially since it had embraced the extinction of slavery among its objects. Not a few believed conscription alien to the spirit of English-speaking liberty, and held it unconstitutional; all cowards dreaded the risks it offered. Most important of all, however, was the fact that large numbers of unskilled laborers dreaded the Negro as a competitor for jobs, even though at the moment the demand for labor exceeded the supply. In New York, as in other cities, many immigrants, ill-paid, ill-housed, and ill-treated, felt keenly the rise in living costs. They had suffered endless hardships and countless indignities. Now they feared that a mass of freedmen would inundate the Northern cities, snatching the bread from their mouths. A mass meeting in upper Manhattan, with a priest for chairman, passed resolutions declaring that "a great portion of the poor workingmen of this community will necessarily be compelled under the provisions of the draft, if enforced, to leave their families in abject poverty, in consequence of the odious provision exempting from military duty any citizen having $300."[15]

The aftermath of the riots was a dolorous period. For weeks the press was full of obituary notices of people who had received mortal injuries, of accounts of the recovery of stolen goods, and of court sentences for rioting and robbery. Estimates of the total deaths ran to 1,000 or 1,200, figures certainly exaggerated. Charles Nordhoff, managing editor of the *Evening Post*, in the most careful of contemporaneous studies, declared that between 400 to 500 lives had been lost. "A continuous stream of funerals flows across the East River," he wrote a week after the outbreak, "and graves are dug privately within the knowledge of the police here and there."[16] The better New Yorkers deeply resented the outrages

13. Greeley, Horace, *The American Conflict*, Hartford, 1867, II, 506, 507. Frost, James A., "The Home Front in New York During the Civil War," *New York History*, July, 1961, 273-297.
14. Lincoln's speech to young men's Lyceum, January 27, 1838; *Collected Works*, I, 108-115.
15. New York *Herald*, July 15, 1863.
16. See his 8,000-word narrative in the *Evening Post*, July 23, 1863.

visited upon the helpless Negroes—worse, commented George Templeton Strong, than those of St. Bartholomew's or the medieval pogroms. Placards appeared reading, "Sam, Organize!"—a call for a revival of Know-Nothingism. The damage to private property was later officially computed at approximately $2,000,000. Fortunately, bitter anger soon subsided among both the rioters and the supporters of law and order; but unfortunately nothing was done to remove the real grievances of the Irish immigrants, or to safeguard the rights of black people.

Angry exchanges between the Democratic and Republican editors followed the disorders. Manton Marble, in his *World*, had referred to the rioters as animated by a burning sense of wrong, and a determination not to be forced into a hopelessly mismanaged and partisan war. He and Ben Wood of the *Daily News* continued to explode in this vein. When Wood denounced the Federal troops for firing on the people, Bryant retorted that it was not the people who invited repression; it was a band of cutthroats, pickpockets, and robbers. On this Bennett's *Herald*, standing between the extremists, made a characteristically impudent comment. "Are not members of the mob people?" it asked. "Their intelligence is low, but it is at least equal to that of the niggerhead organs."

In a less acrimonious and more dignified vein, President Lincoln and Governor Seymour, a Democrat, wrote each other a set of interesting letters, those of the governor clearly addressed to the public. As might be expected, Lincoln, striving to be just and moderate, and ready to make any reasonable concession, appeared in far the better light. While Seymour was patriotic, according to his own standards, he was narrowly partisan. He believed the Administration maliciously hostile to New York, and he was convinced that the Draft Act was unconstitutional. He therefore let a note of asperity creep into his communication of August 3 to Lincoln, which denounced the draft as harsh and unfortunate, asserted that the quotas assigned to New York districts were not proportionate to their relative population, and, with a veiled threat of the consequences of a "violent" policy, asked that the conscription be suspended in his State until the courts could examine the validity of the law. Lincoln courteously pointed out that time was too important to permit of a suspension.

Thereupon Seymour, in another acrid letter, laid figures before the President purporting to show that the quotas of nine Democratic districts were unjustly high, while those of nineteen Republican districts were too low. He spoke of shameless frauds and gross wrongs. The Chief Executive, who had already reduced the quotas of several districts to meet the governor's first demands, generously responded by cutting down those of others. And later this year, after another call for recruits in the autumn, Lincoln, in his large-minded, patient way, approved the appointment of a commission of three to report upon the whole subject of the draft in New York State.[17] The dominant figure in this body was a Democratic intimate of Seymour, selected at the governor's instance. The report in effect rejected Seymour's charges of deliberate unfairness, pronouncing the draft officers men of integrity and fidelity, and finding no evidence of any gross wrongs. It did recommend, however, that the quotas should be adjusted not to the number of men of arms-bearing age newly enrolled, but to the entire population under the last census. Secretary Stanton rejected this recommendation, for as he pointed out, only Congress could change the basis of the draft, and any postponement would perhaps fatally delay the strengthening of the armies.[18]

Actually, a special enrollment was much fairer than reliance upon a census that had been faulty when taken, that was now three years out of date, and that was especially defective in mirroring any fast-growing city which experienced constant shifts in population.

But although the principal charges made by Seymour were unfounded, and although Fry had executed a task of great complexity and delicacy in admirable fashion, the draft had in some respects been mismanaged. The Provost-marshal General later admitted the fact.[19] It had been presented to the people not as opening the door to a patriotic duty, so that the conscript deserved all honor, but as a grim necessity caused by the failure of volunteering, so that drafted men bore a stigma. The lottery feature was most unfortunate; all enrolled and ablebodied citizens in the primary category should have been required to serve, not just one out of five. The $300-clause introduced an unhappy element of class distinction. Moreover, as in the South, too many loopholes were left in enforcement. Many drafted men, especially those with dependents, inevitably felt that they had been treated unfairly. When conscription was resumed in New York, the city had to be filled with so many troops that (the *Herald* complained) it looked like an armed camp.[20]

Minor disturbances meanwhile took place all over the country, even in States as law-abiding as Connecticut. "The poor," declared the Norwich *Aurora* in that State, "will never allow the rich man's money to be an equivalent for their blood."[21] Governor William A. Buckingham, anxious to avoid any clash, secretly removed rifles and ammunition from the State arsenals, and equipped responsible citizens at various points to overawe any malcontents. The possibility of trouble was avoided in some towns by action which amounted to general draft evasion, the authorities appropriating public money to pay commutation fees or to offer

17. This was in early December; Nicolay, John G., and John Hay, *op.cit.*, VII, 40, 41; *O.R.*, III, iii, 612-619, 639-640, 681; Lincoln, *Collected Works*, VI, 369-370, 381-382, 391.
18. Fry, James B., *New York and the Conscription*, 61, as in Nicolay and Hay, *op.cit.*, VII, 45.
19. Nicolay and Hay, *op.cit.*, VII, 45, 46.
20. New York *Herald*, August 24, 1863.
21. Norwich, Conn., *Aurora*, July 15, 1863.

Draft Riots in New York City.

Above, the Destruction of the Colored Orphan Asylum;
below, troops engaging the rioters in First Avenue

bounties to men from other districts. Sporadic violence occurred in the Pennsylvania anthracite fields, at Portsmouth, N.H., Boston, Troy, N.Y., and Holmes County, Ohio, in scattered communities of the Middle West—even Illinois and Wisconsin—and in Kentucky and Missouri, for the draft was especially unpopular all along the border. But even in the aggregate, these disturbances were not too serious.

The first draft was both a success and a failure. It was effective as a stimulus to volunteering; on the Friday and Saturday preceding the riots, 600 men enlisted in New York City, and in the week prior to draft resumption another thousand came forward.[22] So it was all over the North. Young men who saw that they would get both bounties and applause by freely donning the uniform, and little but the prospect of bad company by waiting to be summoned, hesitated no longer. But in furnishing a flow of conscripts, the draft was a dismal failure. Fry presently reported to Secretary Stanton that in the districts which had furnished returns, three drafted men out of ten had been excused for disability, and three more for other reasons, leaving four in ten to serve. But of these four, about half paid the $300-commutation, so that only two in ten entered the ranks or sent a substitute to do so. Fry commented that the Draft Act was good for enrolling men, but if it did anything to raise and maintain an army he could not discover what.[23]

Heads of armies in the field had dreamed of squads of sturdy, bright-faced men marching in to fill up wasted companies and shattered regiments. Instead, they saw a mere trickle of reluctant laggards. The substitutes were often worthless; they pocketed the money paid them, and watched for the first opportunity to desert. Many, wrote a Rhode Island officer, were scoundrels and thieves whom fetters could not hold.[24] Some States, which like Ohio had been credited with a previous fulfillment of their quotas and so exempted entirely from the 1863 draft, of course contributed no recruits whatever to their dwindling units. In fact, in the draft of July, 1863, only thirteen States and the District of Columbia were included. All these were in the East except Michigan and Wisconsin. In the draft of March 14, 1864, twelve States were involved, all Eastern except Ohio, Kentucky, Michigan, and Minnesota. Many more States, nineteen in all, were involved in the last two drafts of July and December, 1864. Halleck sadly informed Sherman that he could expect nothing of value from the conscription. "It takes more soldiers to enforce it than we get from its enforcement."[25] The volunteers, of course, preferred to go into entirely new companies and regiments, filled with men like themselves and commanded by officers they perhaps knew.

22. New York *Herald*, Aug. 14, 1863.
23. Fry to Stanton, Oct. 19, 1863, *O.R.*, III, iii, 893ff.
24. Lerwill, *Personnel Replacement, op.cit.*, 94; *O.R.*, III, iii, 558.
25. *O.R.*, I, iii, Pt.1, 716; III, v, 730, 733, 735, 737.

This was a great misfortune, and one that could never be remedied so long as the government placed its trust mainly in volunteering. Ambitious men were always ready to organize new units, politicians were always ready to encourage them, and governors could almost always be persuaded to grant them commissions. Local boys were kept together in one unit. The result was that while old regiments wasted away to skeletons, the new ones had to learn for themselves much that could have been taught them by veterans. Had Washington resorted earlier to conscription, had it not been so fatuously hopeful that McClellan would end the war in 1862, and Hooker in 1863, the conscripts could have been assigned to the battle-worn outfits. How much they were needed! "The old regiments," Senator Henry Wilson of the Military Affairs Committee said on February 16, 1863, "hardly average now more than four hundred men in the field fit for the stern duty of war." At Murfreesboro, Rosecrans commanded 139 regiments, but instead of 139,000 men he possessed about 45,000. Some brigades had five or six skeleton regiments in them instead of two full regiments. Grant wrote Lincoln during the siege of Vicksburg: "I would add that our old regiments, all that remains of them, are veterans equaling regulars in discipline and far superior to them in the material of which they are composed. A recruit added to them would \become an old soldier from the very contact before he was aware of it." Cost could be much less, Grant claimed. "Officers and men have to go through months of schooling and, from ignorance of how to cook and provide for themselves, the ranks become depleted one-third before valuable services can be expected. Taken in an economical point of view, one draft man in an old regiment is worth three in a new one."[26] Late in the war, Sherman burst out angrily against this perverted system of using the draft to stimulate volunteering for fresh units while the old ones sank into feebleness. It was unjust to the men, the officers, and the national cause.[27]

"I do think it has been wrong to keep our old troops so constantly under fire. Some of these old regiments that we had at Shiloh and Corinth have been with me ever since, and some of them have lost 70 percent in battle. It looks hard to put these brigades, now numbering less than 800 men, into battle. They feel discouraged, whereas, if we could have a steady influx of recruits, the living would soon forget the dead. . . . It has been a very bad economy to kill off our best men, and pay full wages and bounties to the draft and substitutes." Just how many young men scattered to the winds to avoid volunteering and enrolling for the draft will never be known, but it was undoubtedly a substantial number. In the

26. *Cong. Globe*, 37th Cong., 3rd Sess., Pt.1, 896; Pt.2, 996; Feb. 12-16, 1863; Grant to Lincoln, near Vicksburg, June 14, 1863, Nat'l. Archives; Adj.-Gen. Office, Special Civil War Collection, Generals' Papers and Books (Halleck).
27. To Halleck, Sept. 4, 1864, on the eve of a new draft, *O.R.*, I, xxviii, Pt.5, 793.

first draft in 1863, 292,441 names were drawn and 29,415 of those persons failed to report. In the entire Civil War draft, 161,244 failed to report out of 776,829 numbers drawn, or well over 20 percent. It is fairly certain also that the enrollment for the draft did not contain by any means all the names of those available. An officer charged with enrollment reported that getting competent officers to handle it was difficult because "this duty in some parts of the country [was] dangerous to life from the disaffection of the inhabitants." Some officers were attacked and even murdered. Then, too, "many men, on the approach of the enrolling officer, left their homes, and their wives, mothers, or children gave false names, or grossly misrepresented the age of the person to be enrolled." Greatest difficulty was encountered in mining districts.

Furthermore, it was comparatively easy to "get lost." There were plenty of wide open spaces where the draft could never reach, or the stigma of not volunteering did not exist. Others fled to Canada. The Toronto *Globe* reported that "our towns and villages, not only on the frontier, but inland, are crowded with motley groups of fugitives from the draft." A Chicago paper was shocked by the number of young Irishmen in St. Louis who insisted they be treated as subjects of Great Britain. The mining camps of the far West, the mountains, and the plains furnished other havens. Some effort was made to enforce enrollment and to prosecute draft evaders, but it was a far cry from the extensive later efforts of a more modern draft.[28]

Slowly and imperfectly, the situation improved. Four more draft calls were issued in 1864—February, March, July, and December. But the February call was postponed, so that three drafts were ordered in 1864, plus the first one in 1863. All together, they yielded 168,649 men, of whom 74,207 were substitutes. In addition, 86,724 more men paid commutation. Congress did change the commutation payment rule in early 1864, limiting it to conscientious objectors. All this was pitiful enough. The drafts continued, however, to maintain their primary function of impelling men to volunteer, and more and more of these recruits went into old regiments. When Lincoln called on October 17, 1863, for 300,000 volunteers, he stipulated that they should be assigned to "the various companies and regiments in the field from their respective States."[29] Moreover, old regiments were given an opportunity to send recruiting agents back to their States, and the Provost-marshal General did his utmost to direct replacements to the three-year regiments whose time would expire in 1864.[30] In the year following November

28. See the previous treatment of this subject in its earlier stages in Nevins, *The War for the Union: The Improvised War*, New York, 1959, 229-231; *O.R.*, III, v, 626, 714, 730-739; Toronto *Globe*, Aug. 11, 1863; Chicago *Morning Post*, Aug. 6, 1863.
29. *O.R.*, III, iii, 892; v, 636, 720, 722, 730-739.
30. Lerwill, *op.cit.*, 99-100.

1, 1863, thirty-seven Michigan regiments, for which we have records, received replacements, and ten of them obtained more than 500 men apiece.[31] The reform came late, but it came in time to help end the war.

Not until the late summer of 1864 did replacements in truly significant numbers begin to reach the front. Thereafter, from August and September until Appomattox, the distribution of new men to old units became continuous. These replacements were never numerous enough to raise the effective strength of veteran regiments to their full levels, but they did at least enable them to remain battle-worthy.[32]

[III]

The American soldier was many things, North and South. True, there were those who deserted, those who dragged their feet in action, those who avoided the army altogether. But they were the exceptions. The vast majority of the youths who served their respective sections acted with honor, ability, and generally with a firm sense of duty and devotion. At the same time, they maintained an individualism that was truly American. Their story is intertwined with all the events of the war, preserved in letters, diaries, and printed volumes of memoirs. It will not be rehearsed in detail here, yet it stands alone and unique.[33] It is not exceptional that a Yankee soldier on the way to prison in Richmond would exclaim, "A Confederate soldier! I believe the fellow would storm hell with a penknife."[34] At the same time the Yankee soldier himself proved pretty adept at storming both ends of the spectrum.

The composite Northern man-at-arms is said to have averaged five feet eight and one-fourth inches in height; he weighed one hundred forty-three and one-half pounds. Sixty percent were light in complexion, forty-five percent were blue-eyed, and thirty percent had brown hair. Some forty-eight percent of the Union soldiers had been farmers, with twenty-four percent listed as mechanics, sixteen percent as laborers, five percent businessmen, three percent professional people, and four percent miscellaneous. All but one and one-half percent of the men were between 18 and 46 years of age on date of enlistment. The average age at time of enlistment was 25.8 years; and 76.57 percent were under thirty years of age, with the largest group 18 to 22. Eighteen-year-olds made up 13.27 percent. However, there were recorded 127 of age 13, 330 age 14, and 2,366 fifty-years old or over.

Of the approximately two million individuals counted in one survey of the

31. *Ibid.,* 101.
32. *Ibid.,* 105.
33. The most complete treatment of the soldier is to be found in Wiley, Bell I., *Johnny Reb,* and *Billy Yank,* Indianapolis, 1943 and 1951.
34. Joseph Clay Stiles Papers, HEH.

Northern army, three-fourths were native-born Americans, while the half-million foreign-born is estimated to have been composed of 175,000 Germans, 150,000 Irish, 50,000 English, 50,000 British-Americans, and 75,000 others.[35] An officer of the 119th New York declared that in his regiment, "There are Germans who don't understand English, Frenchmen ditto, Swedes and Spaniards who don't understand anything, and Italians who are worse than all the rest together."[36]

Desertion and absence with or without leave was a constant debilitating factor in both armies. Over-generous and extended leaves also hurt the fighting potential. The absent figure for the Confederates reached as high as 186,676 on December 31, 1863, out of an aggregate army of 464,646, and by the end of 1864 was over 200,000, while the present figure was 196,000.[37] While not approaching the high percentages of absentees from which the Confederates suffered late in the war, the Federals in the last two years reached a high of about a third absent out of the aggregate in the army.[38]

The Federal Provost-marshal General stated: "There can be no cause so just or so beloved that war in its behalf will not be attended by desertion among its defenders." At first, the Adjutant General's office offered a reward of $5 for the arrest and delivery of a deserter. The later increase to $30 proved a powerful stimulus to arrests. Incomplete Federal records show 268,520 deserters, although that probably included a considerable number unavoidably absent. The total has often been pegged at 200,000. The loss per thousand from desertions is put at 62.50 for all volunteers, while among the Negro troops it was only slightly higher at 67 men per thousand. In the last three years, desertion averaged about 5,500 per month. But desertion dropped with the increased severity of punishment, including execution. One record shows that 147 men were shot or hanged for desertion out of 267 total executions by U.S. military authorities.

Provost-marshal General Fry blamed desertion on the free and independent spirit and lack of restraint enjoyed by many Americans; and ignorance of military rules was another major reason. Other contributing factors included the large bounties paid to recruits, the substitute provisions of the draft and the ease with which desertion could be accomplished. Fry concluded that: "Lives sacrificed, battles lost, and war prolonged, in consequence of the depletion of the ranks of the armies by desertion, were the natural fruits of the want of rigor in dealing

35. Fox, William F., *Regimental Losses in the Civil War,* New York, 1889, 63-65; *Ages of U.S. Volunteer Soldiers,* U.S. Sanitary Commission Statistical Bureau, New York, 1866, 2, 5, 6; Newman, Ralph G., and E. B. Long, *Civil War Digest,* New York, 1956, 239; Lonn, Ella, *Foreigners in the Union Army and Navy,* Baton Rouge, 1951, 572-584 for a lengthy discussion of numbers.

36. Letter home Nov. 21, 1862, Theodore A. Dodge Papers, LC; for more on foreign soldiers see Lonn, *op.cit.,* and also her *Foreigners in the Confederacy,* Chapel Hill, N.C., 1940.

37. *O.R.,* IV, ii, 73; iii, 989.

38. For chart of Union figures, see Kreidberg, Marvin A., and Henry, Merton C., *History of Military Mobilization in the U.S. Army,* Washington, 1955, 95.

with this evil in the early stages of the war. Undue mercy to deserters was in reality harsh cruelty to those who remained true to their flag."[39] Another estimate is that one out of every eleven Union enlistments was a deserter, although the figure may have been as high as one out of seven, at times. In the Confederate Army, desertion is put by one authority at one out of nine, but that may be low.[40]

Enforcement of laws against desertion was even harder to maintain in the South than in the North.[41] General Lee and other officers constantly cried out against the evils of desertion. After all, the South could not afford such a luxury. But, while there were deserters in large numbers on both sides, it cannot be said that all of them pulled out from fear, from criminal tendencies, or from lack of faith in the cause. Many just wanted to go home for a while, and indeed many who slunk off for a quick visit without permission did return to take up arms again. Serious though desertion was, it did not prevent the fighting of a war.

Loyalty was perhaps the keynote of the vast majority of soldiers on both sides; loyalty to a cause or several causes, loyalty to their respective nation and leaders, loyalty to their families and community, and to themselves.

[IV]

Troops, no matter how patriotic, disciplined, and courageous, are worthless unless well officered. No informed man doubted that the success of the Western armies in 1863 was in great degree attributable to superior generalship. Grant had learned strategy by patient study enforced by some stinging lessons. At Belmont, leading some 3,000 men in amateurish fashion, he had learned not to advance over unknown ground without a reconnaissance and strong reserves. At Shiloh he had learned how stunning a surprise attack may be, and how heavy can be the penalty for failing to organize a pursuit force to deal with a defeated enemy. He was fortunately given time to absorb these lessons. Halleck's transfer from the West to Washington has well been termed a providential act for the West, for it set Grant free to think and act for himself in entire command of a large strategic theater. To what good purpose he learned to think became evident at Iuka and Corinth, operations of his overall command which, in the words of a British student, proved that "he had grasped the great secret of the art of war, namely, how to develop offensive action from a defensive base."[42] How effectively he had learned to act and plan became evident in the months preceding Vicksburg. The

39. *O.R.*, III, v, 676-678, Provost-Marshal General Fry's report; Lonn, Ella, *Desertion During the Civil War*, New York, 1928, *passim.;* for execution record in detail, see U.S. Soldiers Executed by U.S. Military Authorities during the Late War, 1861-66, National Archives, War Records Division.

40. Shannon, Frederick Albert, *Organization and Administration of the Union Army, 1861-1865*, I, 179; also Lonn, *Desertion, op.cit.*, 226.

41. Lonn, *Desertion, op.cit.*, 36.

42. Fuller, J.F.C., *The Generalship of Ulysses S. Grant*, New York, 1929, 122ff.

only lesson he had not learned, though Vicksburg should have taught it to him, was the folly of throwing heavy formations against entrenched lines.

The first cardinal mistake of the North in officering its armies had been its failure to scatter regular army veterans, holding commissions or worthy of them, throughout the volunteer army. The two services should have been amalgamated; regulars should have helped train the new units, and whenever equipped, take posts of command. The best-drilled militia regiments did scatter their officers widely among the volunteers; the New York Seventh, for example, furnished about 300 officers for them, and some less famous regiments did nearly as well. These officers were often active in organizing new regiments, and some of the best colonels climbed to the rank of brigadier-general or higher. Two officers of militia who commanded larger bodies of men in field operations than almost any of the West Pointers—Nathaniel P. Banks and Ben Butler—wrote at times nearly as good war records as the ordinary regular army officers. However, they had much to learn from experience, and were regarded with jealousy. They made grave mistakes along with some creditable successes, but they were men of marked, if not superior, ability. When Butler delivered Baltimore from its early peril, no less discerning a man than Theodore Winthrop wrote in the *Atlantic Monthly* of June 1861 of this, "Gen. Butler has at least had invaluable promptness and decision."[43] In maintaining the separation of the tiny regular army from the massive volunteer army, the government deprived the great national array of what might have been an invaluable leavening force. The segregation tended to keep some of the best potential instructors out of the body that most needed instruction, and to lessen the number of regular soldiers who in time might have found shining rank and opportunity with fast-growing volunteer armies.

Not that the army lacked a sufficient number of officers! As the muster of regiments swelled, it soon had more than it needed. The French army counted 2,400 men in a regiment, and 8,000-9,000 in a brigade, with at most four colonels and one brigadier-general to 10,000 men. The American volunteer army had theoretically 1,000 men in a regiment, four regiments in a brigade, and three brigades in a division. As the regiments fell to an effective strength of perhaps 500, the volunteer army would exhibit fifteen or twenty colonels, three or four brigadier-generals, and a division commander for each body of 10,000 men. Henry Wilson explained to the Senate early in 1863 that if every army, every corps, and every division were given a major-general, the Northern forces would theoretically require 140 or 150 officers of that exalted rank. But, of course, many divisions, in the rapid growth of the army, were commanded by brigadiers, just as many brigades were commanded by colonels. Indeed, Wilson thought that

43. West, Benjamin F., *Lincoln's Scapegoat General,* Boston, 1965, Ch. IX.

four-fifths of the divisions were led by brigadiers. In point of fact, several corps commanders, even, were merely brigadiers.[44]

Early in 1863, according to Secretary Stanton, the Northern armies had 52 major-generals, and 208 brigadiers. To be sure, a number of the major-generals were out of active service. At this moment McClellan, McDowell, Cassius M. Clay, Frémont, Ben Butler, Buell, and Burnside were on the sidelines waiting for field assignments. The Army of the Potomac, however, had a minimum of ten major-generals—Hooker, his chief of staff, and the commanders of the eight corps.[45] No wonder that Wilson wished a lid kept on the roster of generals!

Although such a limitation existed, it was fragile. Congress had provided in 1862 that the President should not be authorized to appoint more than 40 major-generals and 200 brigadier-generals. As these figures just covered the men appointed up to the date of the enactment, it was not clear whether Congress intended to freeze appointments at this number, or wished rather to allow an additional 240 generals to be named! Lincoln naturally interpreted the law as giving him broad powers of appointment; particularly as it did not specifically supersede the general law of July 24, 1861, giving the President power to name as many major and brigadier generals for the volunteer army as he thought right. Congress did not like this latitude. It saw that nearly every colonel wished to be made a brigadier, and nearly every brigadier a major-general. They raised a clamor, they enlisted influential friends, and they badgered every accessible politician. Senator Fessenden noted caustically "the continual leaves-of-absence that are granted officers who come here and spend their time about this city soliciting somebody" to help them gain promotion.

After some chaffering, Congress and the President agreed early in 1863 upon a law validating 30 additional major-generalships and 75 new brigadier-generalships for the volunteer service, which Lincoln signed on March 2. This gave the North a total of 70 major-generals and 275 brigadiers. As these figures had been, or were being exceeded, some generals had to be sacrificed. One was the efficient Jacob D. Cox. In the Ohio roster a choice had to be made between him and Robert C. Schenck. Cox had no political friends, Schenck had many; Cox had no influence with Halleck, Schenck knew Halleck well; Cox had never sought Congress, but Schenck had served there and would soon return. Though far superior in brains and character, Cox was dropped.[46] Such displacements were common. The elevation of the admirable brigadier-general Charles Devens to division command cost the equally meritorious N.C. McLean an anticipated promotion, and sent him back to his old brigade; while the appointment of the

---

44. February 11, 1863; *Congressional Globe*, 3rd Sess., Pt. 2, 868ff.
45. Henry Wilson, quoting Stanton's Report of February, 1863.
46. Cox, Jacob Dolson, *Military Reminiscences of the Civil War*, New York, 1900, I, 435ff.

gallant Francis C. Barlow to brigade command similarly displaced the able Orland Smith, a colonel who had earned the rank of brigadier that (except by brevet) he never received.[47]

Yet, although politics was always a debilitating influence in the appointment of officers, it would be an error to assume that Lincoln and Congress placed political chaffering above patriotism. It seemed almost a law of nature in this era, long before the passage of civil service reform legislation, that offices of all kinds should be used to promote political ends. Many men boldly argued that the best party organizers would sometimes make the ablest governmental leaders. Clearly, military appointments should be controlled by a different rule. But, writes General Cox, most people thought it a sufficient safeguard merely to confine a majority of the promotions to officers already in the service, and to make sure that commissions of the higher grade were not given entirely to newcomers from civilian life. In the existing social and intellectual situation, tremendous pressures could be improperly exerted. James B. Fry relates that the clever and pertinacious wife of a major in the regular army beset Lincoln until he made the man a brigadier-general. "She is a saucy little woman," said the President, "and I think she will torment me until I have to do it."[48] Under a different type of pressure Lincoln raised Carl Schurz, Franz Sigel, and Julius Stahel to major-generalships, in part for real ability, but in part as a mark of appreciation of German-American support in politics and war.

The appointment of "slates" of Ohio generals, Pennsylvania generals, or New York generals by semi-political agreements between President and members of Congress, under the legislation of 1862-63, soon filled every place permitted. No high commissions were then available to reward special field service except those opened by disability, death, or dismissal. While some generals sank under bullets or disease, few indeed were dismissed, for the same influences which had obtained an appointment later offered it protection. The incompetents were quietly shifted, like Pope, to innocuous posts; given a transfer to distant points like the temperamental Rosecrans who, after Chickamauga, retired and waited until he was sent as minister to Mexico; or given opportunity to continue their blundering in less dangerous commands, as Burnside blundered in ordering the arrest of Vallandigham and in helping to lose the spectacular battle of the Petersburg crater. The most conspicuous instance of the continuance of a defective military leader in high station was offered by the retention of Butler, but it is possible that Lincoln was keeping him from becoming politically harmful by retaining him in a command which was neither highly important nor likely to incur any grave army liabilities. The penalty in the Bermuda Hundred fiasco was severe, but not

47. Schurz, Carl, *Reminiscences,* New York, 1907, II, 405-406.
48. Fry, James B., *Military Miscellanies,* New York, 1889, 280-281.

disastrous. The sad aspect of this military situation was the wearisome, provocative bickering when commissions were issued. The work done by the Popes and Frémonts on the battle-lines was sometimes better performed by men of lesser rank, who could not get the promotion they deserved because no place was open. Bad as the system was, it was not bad enough to deny the North victory. The Union armies were fortunate in that they had no higher rank than that of major-general, until Grant received a quite unique lieutenant-generalship when he took command of all the armies in 1864. Had the North given the altitudinous grades of general and lieutenant-general to a number of officers, as the Confederacy did, it would have found its high command an even more inflexible cadre.

Perhaps if Secretary Chase had been on better terms with the President, and if, ambitious politician that he was, he had steeled himself by a private self-denying resolution to avoid any show of favoritism to men who would lend support to his party groups, and to his sleepless ambitions, then he might have pressed effectively for some of the changes that were needed in the appointment of general officers—but, in view of Chase's temperament, this was asking for a great deal! Sherman saw clearly the steps needed, but Sherman at the moment was helpless. If Halleck had been a man of more force and vision, he might have done something to prod the harassed Stanton and the overworked Lincoln into the provision of remedies. Halleck did see the problem, as he wrote his friend Francis Lieber in April, 1863, "The real difficulty we have to contend with is poor, poorer, *worthless* officers. Many of them have neither judgment, sense, nor courage. And I almost despair of any improvement. Recent appointments are worse if anything than before. Politics! Politics! They are ruining the country."[49] More than a few men saw as clearly as Jacob D. Cox and W.T. Sherman what was needed, but they were helpless. Those who urged reform were opposing a powerful politico-military tradition, for army appointments were all too frequently a form of patronage, and pressures from mutually jealous States and such duographic elements as the German-Americans numerous in the Middle West, were powerful. Many faced with demands for change were always ready to echo Lord Melbourne's conservative expostulation, "Why can't they leave it alone?" As late as November 22, 1864, Grant was in Washington pleading with Stanton and Lincoln to give promotion to certain officers who had shown conspicuous gallantry and efficiency in the field, arguing that the needed vacancies would be made by mustering failed generals out of the service, and laying before Lincoln a list of eight major-generals and thirty-three brigadiers who, Grant believed, might well be dropped. It was to Grant's credit that this list, as Lincoln noted, included some of Grant's personal friends.

Lower officers—mere colonels, majors, and captains—were more easily set

---

49. Porter, Horace, *Campaigning with Grant*, New York, 1897, 328; Lieber Papers, Huntington Library, April 30, 1863.

aside if unfit, for their unfitness was difficult to conceal. Nowhere were character and ability more severely tested than in the command of companies, regiments and brigades. Every officer had the eyes of hundreds of men fixed severely upon him, and was meanwhile scrutinized sharply by superiors who had various channels of information. It was taken for granted that a good captain or colonel would show intrepidity in action, always setting an example of unflinching valor to his men. It was also taken for granted, though with less confidence, that he would prove his integrity, honesty, and self-respect on every occasion, never using his position for personal profit, never tyrannizing over inferiors, and never giving way to petty resentments.

These elementary virtues did not alone suffice to lift an officer to effectiveness. He had also to master the arts of the superior disciplinarian, keeping his men under strict control without harshness, and making them friends but not familiars. Obedience, self-sacrifice, and patient endurance are the cardinal military qualities, wrote Charles Francis Adams—obedience first.[50] No stricter disciplinarian than John Reynolds, who had been commandant of West Point cadets when Sumter surrendered, could be found in the Union armies. Yet his men thought him the beau ideal of a soldier. "His great abilities and his bravery the world has acknowledged," wrote one, "but the love we had for him is beyond expression."[51]

Even the best-disciplined regiment might behave badly unless it could trust the coolness and quickness of its commanders; coolness in action, quickness in emergency and tight predicaments. A confident resourceful leader fired the ardor of his men. "The general," wrote one soldier of 'Uncle John' Sedgwick of Connecticut, "seemed intuitively to perceive the mental condition of his troops, as to their confidence or lack of confidence . . . and he had, moreover, the gift of inspiring confidence when untoward circumstances might beget a temporary faltering." It was while Sedgwick was rallying his men that a sharpshooter finally killed him. The historian of the Tenth Massachusetts Battery wrote of one lieutenant slain at Hatcher's Run: "He fell far short of the ideal military hero, never seeming at home on parade, but in the earnestness of battle his coolness was unsurpassed." The head of the Massachusetts Forty-second earned similar praise for coolness under fire combined with thoughtfulness for his men. During one hot engagement he walked the front amid flying shot. "While risking his life in this manner, in order to be able to observe all that was taking place, he kept his men under shelter as much as possible."[52] And the men of Jesse L. Reno's brigade thought him a consummate leader, "cool, cautious, and slow, till the moment

50. Adams, Charles Franics, Jr., *An Autobiograpby*, Cambridge, 1916, 134-136.
51. Davis, Charles E., Jr., *Three Years in the Army: the 13th Massachusetts Volunteers*, Boston, 1894, 80, 231.
52. Bosson, C.P. *History of the 42nd Massachusetts Volunteers*, Boston, 1886, 114; Billings, John D., *History of the Tenth Massachusetts Battery of Light Artillery*, Boston, 1881, 289.

came to strike quick and hard, and then *with* his men, inspiring them with his own irresistible daring."

By 1863, despite political pressures, inertia, and the mistaken generosity of temper which made some generals (not least of all Grant and Lee) occasionally reluctant to censure men whose much-tried worth they knew, it was much easier to purge both the Northern and Southern armies of inefficient officers. The examining boards busy in the Union armies in the winter of 1861-62, took out of action, to the vast relief of anxious subordinates and critical associates, many hopeless amateurs and nincompoops among the lower officers, including some colonels, and at the same time instilled a healthy respect for proper military standards throughout the army. An account of these activities given by the sterling artillery officer, Charles S. Wainwright, shows what a healthy dread the boards inspired.[53] "The examining board closed up its business yesterday. It was decided that Tamblin was too old a dog to learn new tricks. Slocum too must go, but the board softened his case down with a commendation of the poor fellow's efforts to learn, and informed him that he may do better in some less responsible post. Lieutenant Gansevoort resigned sooner than stand an examination, and Lieutenant Cooper on his plea of ill health was given another trial. This finished up those from our right. We had but one other case before us, that of Captain Bunting of the Sixth New York Infantry, a case in which I took a great deal of interest as his battery is one of my new command (if I get it) and he himself has been acting chief of artillery in Hooker's division for a couple of months past. Never did man's looks belie him more than did Captain Bunting's: a fine, military-looking man, evidently well educated and of good social standing. We were surprised to see him before the board. He has been in command of a battery over four months, and most of the time of several, but did not know the first thing; could not tell the proper intervals and distance in line; nor where the different cannoneers should sit on the boxes; indeed he at last admitted that he had never studied the tactics, so his was a very short and decided case. It was astonishing to me that such a man should have taken a position where he must become known, and then not even try to fill it respectably. . . ."[54]

Indeed, the mere announcement of these tribunals frightened some "scrub" officers into resigning. A vigilant colonel or brigadier could soon find means of eliminating weak majors and captains. Robert Williams, head of the First Massachusetts Cavalry Volunteers, informed his subordinates in October, 1861, that they held their places on probation, and any who proved unfit would be dismissed. He shortly told some of them to resign, and they got out.[55] Thus he did

---

53. Wainwright, Charles S., *Diary of Battle*, ed. Allan Nevins, New York, 1962, 4ff.; Walcott, Charles Folsom, *History of the Twenty-first Regiment Massachusetts Volunteers*, Boston, 1882, 17.
54. Wainwright, *op.cit.*, p.7.
55. Crowninshield, Benjamin W., *A History of the First Massachusetts Cavalry*, Boston, 1891, 43.

some good, although this West Pointer and Virginian ("typically both," states Charles Francis Adams), a hard drinker of no character, himself soon dropped his command, an acknowledged failure.[56] The exit of a single misfit sometimes lifted the morale of a whole regiment. "There is great relief in camp," wrote a member of the Ninth Massachusetts Battery, "now that Captain De Vecchi has resigned; nearly all the rank and file were glad, and it was contagious at headquarters. Officers and men felt the change; hope sprang up where indifference had been."[57]

A new officer projected into a veteran regiment was in a particularly sensitive position. He was instantly measured against his predecessors. Dexter F. Parker of Worcester, a former brigade Quartermaster, was made a major in the Tenth Massachusetts in 1862, after that regiment had fought through the Peninsular campaign. Owing his place to political and personal influences, and aware that his appointment was unpopular, he took a defiant attitude toward his associates. "Major Parker was undoubtedly one of the bravest men in Massachusetts, and would have done honor to a new regiment," wrote the historian of the outfit; "but his qualifications and excellencies were lost when brought into the Tenth, where ninety out of every hundred men in the regiment stood his peer in bravery, and excelled him in all other requirements of the position."

Some of the highest officers stood exposed to quite ruthless treatment by superiors "dressed in a little brief authority," as the tensions of the struggle grew harsher, and both criticism and disciplinary demands mounted. Halleck and McClellan were conspicuous examples. Instances of impetuous severity are almost inevitable in a long grinding war, and need not be regarded too harshly. Wainwright was doubtless almost as unjust, writing in March, 1864, of Halleck's petty spite and Stanton's rancorous hatreds in their treatment of McClellan, as he was in speaking of Lincoln's seeming instances of obstinate conceit.

The long-hostile Halleck used ruthless and questionable tactics in bringing about Hooker's downfall. Stanton, too, could be utterly unreasonable in dealing with men he disliked; and after Sherman had granted his unwise and irritating surrender terms to Joseph E. Johnston, he instituted a campaign of resentful watchfulness and suspicion against even that gifted commander.[58] Grant was rough-handed and abrupt in relieving McClernand from active duty on June 19, 1863, before Vicksburg fell, and some spectators may have thought his just condemnation of McClernand's inefficiency and insurbordination had been intensified by a strain of jealousy over McClernand's success. Later on, we shall find

56. Adams, *An Autobiography, op.cit.,* 138, 139.

57. Letter quoted in Baker, L.W., *History of the Ninth Massachusetts Battery,* South Farmington, Mass., 1888, 8, 9.

58. Liddell Hart, B.H., *Sherman, Soldier, Realist, American,* New York, 1929, 394ff. Newell, Joseph Keith, *"Ours,"* Annals of the 10th Regiment Massachusetts Volunteers, Springfield, Mass., 1875, 139; Wainwright, *op.cit.,* 331.

Grant equally rough in his treatment of William Farrar (Baldy) Smith after the failure of the initial attack on Petersburg—Smith having criticized Grant's bloody frontal assaults. The abrupt order by which Gouverneur K. Warren, who had made Union victory at Gettysburg possible by his seizure of Little Round Top, was summarily relieved from his corps command by Sheridan at Five Forks (an episode still to be narrated) shocked the army, and was later condemned by a board of inquiry. On the Confederate side, the public humiliation of Joseph E. Johnston, which also remains to be described, has never been forgotten. For high commanders as well as ordinary soldiers, the war was growing steadily more dangerous.

[V]

A regimental officer, even a colonel, saw little and knew less of what was really occurring in a campaign; he was a minor wheel, perhaps a tiny cog, in a vast, complex machine, mainly unintelligible to him. "A well-organized staff, on the contrary, constitutes the army's brain, and everything centers at headquarters." So concluded Charles Francis Adams on the basis of his wartime experience.[59] Yet staff work was given a curiously random and uneven treatment, North and South.

Much of the efficiency of a corps commander or general of an army depended upon his ability to organize an able staff. Some leaders clearly grasped this fact, and Sherman gave the republic a conspicuous example of brilliant staff selection and organization. His staff was small, and he wanted no chief-of-staff but himself. He had acquired by the summer of 1863 a unit that satisfied his rigorous standards and impressed all observers. Keeping an "omnipresent eye" in close scrutiny of its members, he tolerated no idlers. His adjutant, his quartermaster, and his chief of artillery worked like helots to satisfy their commander. Charles A. Dana reported to Stanton that, although small, the General's staff was exceedingly capable—much of its power coming from Sherman's inspiration. "What a splendid soldier he is!" Even better was the staff of James B. McPherson—head of the Seventeenth Corps, who had begun as staff officer under Halleck and Grant, and therefore knew the requirements—which was "the most complete, the most numerous, and in some respects the most serviceable in Grant's army."

In their close attention to staffs, Sherman and McPherson followed the example of McClellan, who had taken pains to gather a well-equipped group about him. His chief-of-staff Randolph B. Marcy, was able, experienced, industrious, and conscientious, for he had served in the Seminole and Mexican Wars, and in the Utah expedition. Although his two chief quartermaster officers, Rufus Ingalls and S. Van Vliet, did not avoid controversy, they showed the remarkable skill

59. Adams, *An Autobiography, op.cit.,* 135, 136.

and energy with which McClellan credited them. Ingalls, West Pointer of Mexican War experience, only in his forties when the war began, became chief quartermaster of the Army of the Potomac in the summer of 1862. He remained with the Army of the Potomac after Hooker succeeded McClellan, and when Meade took the helm. Col. Theodore Lyman wrote in *Meade's Headquarters* that he handled his huge army trains as if they were perambulators on a smooth sidewalk. The chief signal officer, Albert J. Myer, was keenly inventive. It was Andrew Atkinson Humphreys of Pennsylvania, however, the chief topographical engineer, who gave the greatest lustre to the staff; indeed, for sheer ability and engineering skill he was indispensable to the army, as it soon found. His greatest feat, the establishment and supplying of the huge base of Grant's army at City Point on the James in 1864, was a monumental accomplishment. He was a worthy subordinate, and in due time successor to the truly illustrious, though long ill-recognized, General Montgomery C. Meigs as quartermaster-general of the Army, and one of the chief architects of Union victory.[60] In time, Meade made Humphreys his chief-of-staff, and he served in that position until the autumn of 1864, when he became a corps commander. Lyman, like others, was impressed by his quick peppery ways, his extreme neatness—"Continually washing himself and putting on paper dickeys"—and the scientific talents which in time made him one of the great engineers of the world.[61]

Sherman in time set down his views on the proper staff for a general. "I don't believe in a chief-of-staff at all," he wrote, "and any general commanding an army, corps, or division that has a staff officer who professes to know more than his chief is to be pitied." The general, he thought, should have a competent quartermaster, commissary officer, two or three medical officers, some bright young aides capable of riding under fire to give and explain his orders, and of course an adjutant-general. This last-named officer should be able to grasp the full scope of operations, to deliver orally and in writing all the orders necessary to carry out the general's policies in army management, and to keep accurately all the returns and a record of events. "A bulky staff," declared Sherman, "implies a division of responsibility, slowness of action, and indecision, whereas a small staff implies activity and concentration of purpose." In size, his and Grant's staffs were good models, while McClellan's was too large.

Grant's staff, both in Mississippi and Virginia, was a small one, numbering twelve to fifteen, or no more than some division staffs. The wisest influence upon him, as we have noted, was that exerted by John A. Rawlins, his fellow-townsman

---

60. The careers of Meigs and Ingalls are illuminatingly treated in the invaluable volume by Erma Risch, *Quartermaster Support of the Army: A History of the Corps*, Washington, 1962, *passim*.

61. Humphreys, H.A., *Andrew Atkinson Humphreys, A Biography*, Philadelphia, 1924, *passim.*; Abbot, H.L., *Memoir of Andrew Atkinson Humphreys, National Academy of Science Biographical Memoirs*, 1865, II, *passim*.; Lyman, Theodore, *Meade's Headquarters*, Boston, 1922, 34; Dana to Stanton, Cairo, July 13, 1963, Charles A. Dana Papers, LC.

in Galena, an attorney of passionate devotion both to the Union and to Grant, and a born executive of shining gifts, intellectual and moral. The worst influence in the long run was deemed by some to be that of Cyrus B. Comstock, a West Point engineer of Massachusetts birth who had served in the East through Chancellorsville, and who displayed an insatiable appetite for desperate charges against blazing entrenchments.[62] The adjutant was T. S. Bowers, a prompt, honest young man, formerly a country editor in Illinois, whom Grant specially valued. Two West Pointers were aides: Grant's brother-in-law Frederick T. Dent, who had been wounded in the Mexican War; and Orville E. Babcock, an engineer officer, conspicuous for bravery and judgment,[63] who wrote some creditable pages in a career destined, alas, to show a few blotted pages.[64] A conspicuously creditable place was also held by a full-blooded Indian, the swarthy, heavy Ely S. Parker, a Seneca leader and a graduate of Rensselaer Polytechnic Institute. After many frustrations, for he was refused admission to the bar in New York, after legal study, because he was regarded as a non-citizen, and was rebuffed by Secretary Seward while seeking a commission with the remark that the whites would win the war without Indian aid, he climbed high. He became Grant's adjutant, and resigned from the Army in 1869 to become Commissioner of Indian Affairs.

Just as clearly as Humphreys was the ablest staff officer of technical attainments under Generals McClellan and Meade, Horace Porter deservedly held such a preeminence under Grant, who had first seen this shrewd, witty West Pointer from Pennsylvania at Chattanooga in the fall of 1863. At that time, Porter, after distinguishing himself in the Port Royal expedition, had become George H. Thomas's highly valued chief-of-ordnance. Impressed by the personality of this young officer, trained at the Lawrence Scientific School as well as at West Point, and by Thomas's hearty commendation, Grant decided he was needed on the staff. Alas! Stanton was already calling him to Washington to reorganize the Ordnance Bureau, and refused to give him up. Not until Grant was made head of all the armies could he insist on Porter's services, that is, not until April, 1864, when the star of Rawlins had declined. Thus belatedly, Porter was placed in a position which enabled him later to write one of the truly thoughtful and perceptive books on the war, *Campaigning with Grant.*[65] His essay on Appomattox in *Battles and Leaders* is classic.

62. He watched these entrenchments at a safe distance; Wilson, James Harrison, *Under the Old Flag,* New York, 1912, I, 442-449. It is regrettable that Horace Porter and Adam Badeau, in their books on Grant in the field give no portraits of Comstock, Badeau, and other staff members. However, Gen. W.F. ("Baldy") Smith has left some scorching comments on Comstock's faith in murderous charges, and so have Rawlins and Emory Upton. Sherman, *Memoirs,* II, 402. New York, 1875.

63. Porter, H., *op.cit.,* 32, 311.

64. Bowers, Claude G., *The Tragic Era, passim,* for details.

65. Mende, Elsie Porter and H. G. Pearson, *An American Soldier and Diplomat,* New York, 1927, 36-98.

Of the entire group, it was Rawlins whose name is most indissolubly connected with Grant's. He was a self-made man, a poor farmer's son who, after some schooling, had won admission to the bar and the post of city attorney. He had first attracted Grant's attention by a Websterian speech at a Union meeting. He was a Douglas Democrat, and friends had advised him to stay away, but with clenched fist and flashing eye he declared he would not only go, but *speak*. He roused the audience by his eloquence, declaiming: "I know no party now! I only know that traitors have fired upon our country's flag." Then he helped organize the Forty-fifth Illinois. His oaken strength, dynamic energy, and his aptitude for business, supported by a tenacious memory, were valuable assets. The trait that gave him a preeminent distinction, however, was his watch-dog sense of guardianship over Grant, backed by vigilance and rectitude. He was the one man who dared not only to counsel the General, but, on occasion, to lecture him severely. Although totally untrained in the art of war, his instinct for strategy and his shrewd judgment of men made him an invaluable advisor. Watching Grant day and night, whenever the General was moved to drink, Rawlins reminded him peremptorily of his solemn promise never to touch a drop. No man could have been more loyal. He by no means approved all of Grant's decisions, but once they were adopted, he gave painstaking care to their execution.

Yet Grant's staff left much to be desired. Charles A. Dana reported just after Vicksburg that it was a mixture of the good, bad, and indifferent, for as Grant was neither an organizer nor a disciplinarian, he let accident and friendship dictate his choices. His staff then contained only four hardworking men, wrote Dana, with two more who could do their jobs without much toil, and others who were worthless. "If Gen. Grant had about him a staff of thoroughly competent men, disciplinarians and workers, the efficiency and fighting quality of this army would soon be much increased. As it is, things go too much by hazard and by spasms; or when the pinch comes, Grant forces through by his own energy and main strength what proper organization and proper staff officers would have done already."[66] Unquestionably, Grant's generous good nature was partly responsible for staff deficiencies, and on this Dana provides a significant comment. The General's chief of artillery, William M. Dunn, was incompetent; the siege of Vicksburg had suffered from the fact, and Grant recognized the deficiency. "But it is one of his weaknesses," wrote Dana, "that he is unwilling to hurt the feelings of a friend, and so keeps him on."[67] His excessive amiability toward loyal friends was undoubtedly one of Grant's faults, for he had suffered so many hard buffets in his toilsome, erratic early life that he naturally came to overvalue warm friend-

66. Wilson, James Harrison, *The Life of John A. Rawlins*, New York, 1916, 47; Dana to Halleck, Cairo, Ill., July 13, 1863, Dana Papers, LC.
67. *Ibid.*

ships. Dana, sharply observant, was so invincibly convinced of Grant's strategic superiority and unyielding will in combat, that he performed an invaluable service to Stanton and Lincoln in persuading them that all Grant's stumblings in the Vicksburg campaign were temporary and trivial, and that, if supported, his single-minded vision and persistence would achieve his great object. Dana, always as aggressive in temper as when he had persuaded the New York *Tribune* to blazon its "On to Richmond" slogan, and ever as independent as when he had parted company with Greeley because of the editor's vacillating and unsteady policies, was largely responsible for the sturdy, resolute acceptance of both Grant and Sherman by the leaders of the republic in the critical years 1863-1864, and helped in the recognition of their military genius by the whole nation. For Dana, as he was shortly to prove in his stimulating re-creation of the New York *Sun*, was above all a man of the people.[68]

The staff arrangements of Robert E. Lee were even more haphazard than Grant's. He wrote many of his most important orders with his own hand. Like Grant, he disliked burdening his subordinate commanders with detailed instructions, so that they sometimes misunderstood his wishes and intentions with disastrous results, as Stuart did before Gettysburg, for example. His staff, too, was small; Colonel Walter H. Taylor, his adjutant-general, was at times almost a one-man staff. The adjutant was expected to be the ears, eyes, and voice of the General, and Taylor was all that.[69] It was to Taylor that Lee turned when, on an April morning at Appomattox, he found himself confronted by overwhelming forces, and asked, "Well, Colonel, what are we to do?"—though he had already made up his mind. Lee had an able chief engineer in W. T. Wofford, who also held field command; he had capable men in charge of commissary arrangements, quartermaster work, and medical activities. Yet of trusted staff advisers he had but one—Taylor.[70]

A page of wartime photographs exhibiting Stonewall Jackson and his staff

68. Dana, *Recollections of the Civil War, 1819-1897*, New York, 1898; Wilson, James Harrison, *Life of Charles A. Dana*, New York, 1907, *passim*. Dana's own memoirs contain peppery and frankly candid sketches of many leaders of the Lincoln and Grant eras.

69. "It is he," wrote one expert Union observer concerning the corps adjutant-general, "who collects, compares, and collates the statistics of numbers from day to day, and detects the increase or diminution of the fighting strength of the corps, intercepts and digests the countless communications which ascend from twenty thousand men to their commander, conducts all the correspondence, and frames all orders. Even in the saddle, under the enemy's fire, he must, with nerves under control, and patience unruffled, catch the spirit of the commands from a general, sometimes, perhaps, inflamed with the ardor of combat, or oppressed with the weight of disaster, and translate them into clear, courteous, and orderly phrases on the instant, for transmission to subordinate commanders..." The adjutant-general of an army had similar duties on a larger scale. Munroe, James Phinney, *Life of Francis Amasa Walker*, New York, 1923, pp.62, 63, quoting from a Loyal Legion obituary; Taylor, Walter H., *Four Years with General Lee*, New York, 1877, 151, *passim*.

70. Taylor's circumstantial and detailed account of Lee's conduct and planning of numerous campaigns and battles in *Four Years with Lee, op.cit.*, is indispensable to Civil War studies. The best recent edition is that edited by James I. Robertson, Jr., for the Indiana University Press in 1962.

shows just ten men, the more striking of whom have been described by his youngest aide, Henry K. Douglas. The genial James K. Boswell, engineer officer, killed at Chancellorsville; the youthful Colonel Alexander S. Pendleton, nick-named Sandy, his adjutant-general; the ever-faithful Dr. Hunter H. McGuire, chief surgeon as well as Jackson's personal physician, mortally wounded late in the war; and William Allan, chief of ordnance—these, with Douglas, were the principal figures. Jackson was too stalwartly self-reliant to want advice, too fertile in original concepts to need suggestions. Like Lee and other Southern generals, he was too poignantly aware, after 1862, of the paucity of capable officers to call into his service those badly needed for field commands. The North could afford to set a Humphreys or a Horace Porter to staff work; the South could not.[71]

War, even for a nation as disciplined as Prussia or as patriotically united as Britain, is inevitably a blundering, confused, wasteful, chaotic field of effort. Its countless crises can never be foreseen. At the most unexpected moment, the human instruments will fail. The plans, the organization, and the leadership are never fully adequate. The United States had floundered through the little War of 1812; it would presently flounder through the little War of 1898. No rational observer could have expected a country so adolescent, loose-jointed, and individu-alistic as the North in 1861 to wage an efficient, well-coordinated war—to do more than flounder through the most colossal struggle of the century. By 1863 shrewd men could see that if the Union had raised a truly national army at the outset by a well-devised system of conscription, forgetting politics, overriding State lines, using camps of instruction to train officers, and placing a million well-trained men on the fronts in the time it actually took to raise half a million ill-trained soldiers, it could have won the war with celerity. Anyone acquainted with the United States, however, knew that in the existing political, social, and psychological situation this was utterly impossible—knew, in short, that 1861 was not yet 1917.

It was all very well for Henry Wilson and John Sherman to say in 1863 that they wished the country had used the draft from the outset, applying it to all able-bodied men. It was sound doctrine for editors like Greeley to declare that politics should have been given far less place in the appointment of generals. It was right that wise commanders like the alert cavalry leader James Harrison Wilson and Jacob D. Cox should inveigh against the poor system of promotions.

71. Although Lee and Jackson had modest staffs, complaint arose in the South that lesser generals made all too many appointments. In the spring of 1863, a bill to create a general staff in the War Department was before Congress. Confederate Governor Thomas C. Reynolds of Missouri wrote Col. W.P. Johnson May 28, 1863: "I regret extremely that the General Staff bill did not become a law; it would have destroyed those nests of intrigue and insubordination, the large permanent staffs of generals. An aide of one who wished promotion smilingly remarked to me that he supposed I knew the staff of a general felt more anxiety about his advancement than *he himself did*, as they also got promoted. It let in a flood of light to me on that subject." T. C. Reynolds Papers, LC; Douglas, Henry Kyd, *I Rode With Stonewall*, Chapel Hill, 1940, *passim*.

Wilson lamented even in the last year that "no fixed rule had yet been established for the selection of generals or their assignment to command."[72] Partly because men like Emory Upton pointed out the blunders and shortcomings with stern emphasis, the country would later avoid most of them in the titanic effort of 1917-18. General Upton, with the prestige of brilliant military service, and the support of William Tecumseh Sherman, had forced through an improved system of tactics, supported a systematic program of examinations for staff positions, and had vigorously urged the establishment of a General Staff for the Army before Secretary Elihu Root laid the cornerstone of the Army War College building in Washington in 1903. Upton was truly the remoulder of the national army. But the really remarkable fact is that, in the mid-century condition of American society North and South, the Union and the Confederacy should have done so well. In the North, particularly, great forces were working under the surface. A superficial glance showed gross errors and halting progress; but, underneath, State allegiance was losing strength, national feeling was growing, lessons of organization were being learned, and men were becoming aware that modern exigencies could not tolerate the slack improvisations of the frontier era.

The President no longer experimented with the appointment, displacement, and replacement of his chief generals; soon able to confide in Grant, Meade, Sherman, and Thomas, he was free to deal with other problems. He left military affairs to the best military leaders. (President Davis, outside Virginia, was in no such happy position.) The principal commanders on both sides now knew with accuracy the virtues and weaknesses of the generals under them. Grant, for example, revealed a clear estimate of the high capacity of General E.O. Ord, a West Pointer from Maryland who had fought against the Seminoles, who had served on the Western border before he was badly wounded in 1862, and who had later been a corps commander in the Antietam campaign—he placed Ord in charge of the Thirteenth Corps. In Washington, Lincoln and Stanton knew what Halleck was worth as well as what he was not worth, and the three could devise plans with fair unison. Although the hundreds of volunteer regiments were still nominally State regiments, the veteran units of the North, after years of service on a variety of fronts, were at last becoming a national army, led in the main by well-tested generals of national training and tremendous loyalty. The best Northern officers who worked under Montgomery C. Meigs in the quartermaster service, under Joseph P. Taylor in the office of the commissary-general of subsistence, under Lorenzo Thomas or E.E. Townsend in the adjutant-general's offices, and under William A. Hammond in the surgeon-general's office, had become very tough professional groups indeed, carrying great responsibilities with energy and precision.

72. Wilson, J.H., *Under the Old Flag*, II, 8.

Under the spur of the draft, volunteering in 1863-64 swelled the ranks of the Northern forces up toward the total of a million men which was reached by the end of the war. The Washington departments, the numerous military and naval offices scattered over the land, and headquarters in the field, all operated with growing efficiency. They still fell far short of the standards attained in a later generation, but for the young, sprawling democracy so lately giving all its energies to the solution of problems of continental expansion and growth, they represented a prodigious mobilization of strength.

Northern Morale and the Elections of 1863

[I]

THE UNION, as we have said, could win the war only by a sufficiently crushing defeat of the main Confederate armies, along with the blockade and dismemberment of the South, to end all resistance East and West. The South, however, might win independence if it held the struggle in such a prolonged deadlock that war weariness numbed the Northern will to fight, and enabled the Peace Democrats to make a successful demand for negotiations to end the slaughter. The partial victories of July, 1863, left the situation still obscure, though with new elements of Northern hope. While Grant had captured Pemberton's army on the Mississippi, Meade had signally failed to cut Lee's Army of Northern Virginia to pieces. In these circumstances, it was essential that the North make the most of two elements of inspiration, without which its spirits would flag. It must continue to find in Lincoln and his Cabinet a steadfast resolution, a hopefulness, and a patient resourcefulness which would promise eventual success. Meanwhile, it must find a few generals whose victories in the field would be sufficiently lustrous to dispel further the gloom created by the seemingly inevitable disappointments and frustrations.

Neither Lincoln's determination to maintain the Union, nor his confidence in the future, founded upon faith in the people, ever flagged despite depressing moments. By the middle of 1863 his associates, even the critical Chase and once-captious Stanton, regarded him with respect and wonderment. His tall frame had become bent; his face bore in repose a pensive, suffering expression; his public and private griefs and incessant labors had worn him almost to the breaking point. He seemed, wrote one observer, to be in mourning for all the dead of the endless battles. He had seldom taken an hour of rest; he relaxed best on his rare visits to the theatre, where he preferred "Lear" or "Macbeth." "It matters little to me," he said, "whether Shakespeare be ill or well played. The thoughts are enough."[1] Yet the tycoon, as John Hay called him, managed all his complex public duties,

1. Laugel, Auguste, *The United States During the Civil War*, ed. Allan Nevins, Bloomington, Ind., 1961, pp.211-213.

military, political, and diplomatic, with a sureness of touch, a keenness of insight, and a firmness of will that impressed men who knew his difficulties. And even those who could fairly accuse him of errors could never indict his integrity of purpose.

After all the anxieties and frustrations of McClellan's Peninsular campaign, after the heartbreaking casualty lists of Fredericksburg and the mortification of Chancellorsville, the steady though incomplete brightening of the skies lifted Lincoln's heart. In a long talk in June, 1863, with that congenial Indianian, T.J. Barnett of the Interior Department, he said that he had no fear of the Peace Democrats; that he looked upon them as an amalgam of discontented New Yorkers, men subject to the draft law, and other self-interested groups whose talk of peace overtures would hurt them worse than anybody else. The President showed himself almost excessively cheerful, perhaps for the benefit of the spiteful critics of the New York *World* with whom Barnett corresponded. "He is in great spirits about Vicksburg," Barnett reported to S.L.M. Barlow, referring to Grant's advance on the city, "and looks to that as the end of organized opposition to the war. He will not make any issues (he denies that personally he has made any) with military arrests. In short, he smokes the pipe of peace with his own conscience —and will keep 'pegging away at the Rebels' . . ." He called himself more of a chief clerk than a despot, and believed that, although malcontents and plotters would keep busy, they were too shrewd to stab themselves with their own daggers.[2]

The Administration was for the most part a unit in its determination to prosecute the war with vigor, and its disdain for Democratic criticism. It believed that what some hostile newspapers termed a dictatorship would be justified by events; resolute action always looked dictatorial.[3] In other respects, however, it remained lacking in cohesion. Lincoln had announced that each head of a department must in general "run his own machine," and most of them did so with little counsel from their colleagues. It irked Chase in particular to see so little concert of action. The country really has no Cabinet, he told friends. "The President limits his participation in the conduct of affairs very much to the War Department. His authority is of course respectfully recognized by all; Mr. Seward, I think, generally reads to him the dispatches sent to our foreign ministers, and he appoints such officers as he thinks fit. But there is almost never any consultation on matters of importance, so that what are called Cabinet Meetings have fallen pretty much into disuse."[4] The progress of the Union seemed steady and irresist-

2. Barnett to Barlow, June 10, 1863, Barlow Papers, HEH. "Mrs. Grundy will talk," Lincoln told Barnett, "but she has more sense than to scald her ass in her own pot."
3. So Chase had written Dr. H.S. Townsend, May 6, 1861. Chase Collection, Historical Society of Pennsylvania.
4. Chase to James Watson Webb, Nov. 7, 1863, *ibid.*

ible to Chase, but it was the progress of an enormous pressure of numbers and material resources rather than that of vigorous, intelligent, well-directed action.

Seldom seeing each other, and conferring still more infrequently, Cabinet members had little opportunity to compose the animosities that arose from dissimilarity of origin, thought, and oldtime party allegiances. "Part of them really hate each other," David Davis assured Lincoln's friend Leonard Swett after four days in Washington. "Mr. Blair hates Chase and speaks openly on the street—and so it is with others."[5] Chase had a temperamental dislike for Montgomery Blair that, during 1863-64, grew into hatred, for they were at swords' points on Reconstruction and other issues. The waspishly ambitious Blair not only repaid this enmity in kind, but spoke in the harshest terms, by 1863, of both Seward and Stanton, calling the former an unprincipled liar, and the latter a great scoundrel who put money into his own pocket by fraudulent contracts.[6] Attorney-General Bates believed that all three Blairs, Francis P., Montgomery, and Frank, were sly and selfish, versed in tricks, and always ready to act in cunning concert to advance their family fortunes. "I have no confidence in Seward, and very little in Stanton," he wrote in his diary; "but that does not make me confide in tricky politicians, who have not the first conception of statesmanship." Bates would write a little later, "There is, in fact, *no Cabinet*, and the show of Cabinet-councils is getting more and more a mere show—Little matters, or isolated propositions are sometimes talked over, but the great business of the country—questions of leading policy—are not mentioned in C.[abinet] C.[ouncil]—unless indeed, after the fact, and when some difficulty has arisen out of a blunder." Washington observer Adam Gurowski opined, "Littleness prevails in the thus called highest councils of the nation, and so the one-day Chase-or-Stanton-orBlair-orSeward-quarrel among themselves, the other day they make it up etc. etc. Seward as always, intrigues with all and humbugs all . . ." Halleck was to write that "there is no unity of feeling either in the cabinet or among the generals. *Self,* and that little proud 'I' are too prominent in the minds of our would-be great men. They love the country some, but themselves a great deal more. Party Politics! Party Politics! I sometimes fear they will utterly ruin the country. . . ."[7]

When Cabinet meetings did take place, the members could never have shaken hands with cordiality, and some could hardly have shaken hands at all; all Lincoln's kindly honesty and tact were needed to maintain a decent show of courtesy. Yet the more important Cabinet members, including that self-contained and busily quiet Missouri lawyer, the conservative Edward Bates, did the work of their departments well, and four, Seward, Chase, Stanton, and Welles,

5. David Davis to Leonard Swett, David Davis Papers, Ill. state Hist. Lib.
6. Bates, Edward, *The Diary of Edward Bates,* ed. Howard K. Beale, Washington, 1933, 290-291.
7. *Ibid.,* 291, 302; Gurowski to Gov. Andrew, Washington, April 10, 1863, John A. Andrew Papers, Mass. Hist. Soc.; Halleck to Lieber, April 15, 1863, Lieber Papers, HEH.

made distinguished records before they left office. Each gained the confidence of the country in his official competence, although Stanton in particular was mercilessly criticized by Democrats. The bankers and moneyed men of the East, after some doubt in dark months of 1862 when taxation yielded little return and government bonds did not sell, acquired a new confidence in Chase during the first half of 1863; for taxation began to produce a healthy revenue, bond sales rose and the Secretary's recommendation of a national banking system, which bore fruit in the epochal law passed in February, was clearly wise. Nobody could deny Chase's financial resourcefulness amid his innumerable difficulties. Seward was as facile in offhand talk as ever, as amiable in temper, as charming in manners; a pleasant contrast to the crusty Gideon Welles and harsh Stanton, though sometimes open to the charge of insincerity. We cannot accept Welles's statement that he seemed to be "universally" disliked and distrusted.[8] Rather, he was widely liked and trusted, although radical Republicans continued to deplore his conservative influence over Lincoln. After his almost incredible blunders during 1861, he trod a discreet path in foreign relations, accepting Lincoln's leadership so completely that he once called himself Abe's little clerk,[9] and faithfully drudging over his innumerable duties.

Stanton, similarly, had learned much since the spring day in 1862 when he had too optimistically halted recruiting. Emotional, often neurotic, capable of occasional acts of compassion and generosity that contrasted sharply with his roughness, and wildly inconsistent in his official policies, he had three great virtues. He cherished that sense of duty which is the foundation of Anglo-Saxon character, saying once, "In my official station I have tried to do my duty as I shall answer to God at the great day."[10] He was tirelessly industrious, slaving late into the night while his carriage waited hour after hour outside the War Department. Most important of all, he was magnificently effective in the very channel that American life had most neglected—organization. He had an instinct for system

8. Welles, Gideon, *Diary of Gideon Welles,* Boston, 1909-1911, III, 100.
9. Stanton, H.B., *Random Recollections,* New York, 1881, 223.
10. Quoted by Gamaliel Bradford, *Union Portraits,* Boston, 1916, 186, from Harriet Beecher Stowe, *The Lives and Deeds of our Self-Made Men,* 376. We can believe the story that an associate once came upon him late at night, weeping violently at his desk and crying, "God help me to do my duty!" Stanton appears so often in memoirs of the period in a disagreeable light that it is refreshing to quote what Seward's daughter Fanny wrote of him on April 5, 1862, after he (with others) had come to dinner. He was like his pictures, she noted, "except for a cheery look, and a merry twinkle of the eye. I like him very much—his manners are warm and hearty." Fanny also found Mrs. Lincoln, who was out for the first time since Willie's death, and dressed in deep mourning, "pleasant and kind. I think her most attractive point is her fondness for her children." She had remarked of Willie that he used to sit thinking dreamily, and that when she accosted him, he would reply, "Oh mother, I am thinking of a great many things!" Seward Papers, Univ. of Rochester, N.Y. It may be noted that David Dudley Field rated Stanton next to Lincoln and Chase, praising his indomitable energy, his erect front against all disaster, his unwearied industry, and his devotion to the public service. Field, E.A., *Record of the Life of David Dudley Field,* Denver, 1931, 174.

and precision that would have done credit to John Jacob Astor, a passion for detail and a foresight that resembled Rockefeller's, and a gift for selecting able, practical-minded subordinates that Carnegie might have envied. Moreover, his devotion to duty gave him a special type of courage—less thrusting and pugnacious than rocklike, an enduring courage that threw back the endless schemers about him as Maine granite with sullen roar throws back the Atlantic surf.

"You overrate my influence," Chase wrote a lieutenant-colonel who wished him to intercede with Stanton. "Indeed, I think that no one has much *influence* with the Secretary of War. His own judgment controls his decisions, and all that anyone can do for another with him is to present facts which may properly be taken in account by his judgments."[11] Those who suggested John A. Andrew or Preston King as a possible replacement spoke rashly. As Governor William Dennison of Ohio wrote F.P. Blair, Andrew lacked discretion, saying and doing foolish things, while King was untried.

From newspapers, political speeches, sketches in the *Continental Monthly,* the *Atlantic, Harper's Weekly,* and other sources, the country learned that the Cabinet was a discordant body. It knew by 1863 that Chase was a jealous contriver, ambitious to reach the White House; that Seward might sometimes be called Mr. Pliable if not Mr. Facing-Both-Ways; that Montgomery Blair was consistently, insidiously, and at times combatively active in behalf of Border State views and Blair family interests; that Stanton seemed to many people a morose bully; and that Welles appeared to need the quick businesslike assistance of G.V. Fox. But it also realized that these five men were as able and constructive a group of departmental heads as the country had ever seen. Welles, for example, had cooperated earnestly with Ericsson in building the *Monitor;* he labored steadily to give the warships heavier ordnance; step by step, he made the blockade efficient; and he foresaw that the future Navy must have speedy ironclads of the latest design to keep pace with other powers. Montgomery Blair organized both an efficient postal system for the Army, and the first free delivery system for the cities. If Seward was neither so able nor so honest-minded a head of the State Department as John Quincy Adams had been, after his early follies he labored effectively to keep the nation free from foreign embroilments.

Like Lincoln, all five had a passionate belief in the future of the republic as the archetypal democracy of the modern world. All, and Bates as well, were passionately resolved to preserve the Union as essential not only to the well-being of the American people, but to the proper molding of man's vast future. In this fervent patriotism, and in their deep respect for Lincoln, they found the two bonds they needed. Chase wrote in the autumn of 1863 that he had often been

11. Chase to Lt.-Col. G.W. Neff, Nov. 10, 1862, Chase Papers, Hist. Soc. of Penn.

tempted to resign (which, in fact, he had done or suggested doing) "but the President has always treated me with such personal kindness, and has always manifested such fairness and integrity of purpose, that I have never found myself free to throw up my trust;"[12] and other Cabinet members could have said the same. Stanton declared on one occasion that if the Union did not triumph, he did not wish to live. More than rhetoric went into the rolling periods in which Seward asserted that if he fell in a Southern capture of Washington, he wished his dust to stay there. "Let it be buried under the pavements of the Avenue, and let the chariot wheels of those who have destroyed the liberties of my country rattle over my bones until a more heroic and worthy generation shall recall that country to life, liberty, and independence."[13] Stout Gideon Welles could assert as honestly as anybody that he had but one object in life. "There is no office that I want or would accept in prospect, but my heart is in again beholding us once more United States and a united people."[14]

Despite all differences of opinion, all personal aversions, and all petty irritations, the Administration was permeated by a single spirit. Since Lincoln had defeated the effort of the Senate to force a reconstruction of his Cabinet just after Fredericksburg, it was plain that he dominated the Administration, and that he preferred variety and balance to a strict unity. Quite willing that Blair and Chase should differ sharply, he was ready to listen to either just as much as he found profitable. (Chase told Welles on a Saturday evening drive in August, 1863, that he made it a point to see the President daily and talk about the reconstruction of the South.)[15] Lincoln really expected each man to run his own machine effectively, and that was about all. He knew by the spring of 1863 that his Emancipation Proclamation had been both a masterful war blow, and an epochal step in the history of the nation. He knew that other Administration measures, such as the National Banking Act, the Morrill Tariff Act signed by Buchanan March 2, 1861, the Pacific Railroad Act, the Land Grant College Act, and the Homestead Act, would find popular support in his own time, and the acclaim of coming generations. If he kept his hold upon the country, he must shut the mouths of those who declared the war a failure by winning victories in the field. But even before Grant and Meade gained their successes, he was confident of this.

"At present," Barnett informed Sam Barlow shortly after Chancellorsville, "the President is busy arranging his program for a negro army, as a Southern reserve; he is perfectly assured, from facts which he gets from cavalry raids, that the whole available force of rebeldom is in front; that the negroes understood that

12. To James Watson Webb, Washington, Nov. 7, 1863, Chase Papers, Hist. Soc. of Pennsylvania.
13. Lincoln, *Collected Works, op.cit.,* V, 499.
14. Welles, *Diary,* I, 413.
15. *Ibid.*

they are free; that the interior of rebeldom is now helpless in view of our threatening lines everywhere—and hence he is in fine spirits for a summer and fall negro
campaign."[16] After Vicksburg and Gettysburg his confidence in the nation's
perseverance rose.

[II]

It was well that Lincoln was a shrewd politician, well that he made moderation a policy, and well that his prestige was rising. Both parties were in a state
of flux. Large numbers of Democratic voters were moving into the Republican
(or to use a name gaining favor, the Union Party) ranks. Would they stay? Would
they grow in number? Undoubtedly they would if Lincoln remained moderate
toward the South, and if Copperhead Democrats opposed vital war measures, for
then Union Democrats would have no choice but to take their stand by the
President.

The Republicans, meanwhile, were uncertain of their future road, or rather,
perplexed by a double crossroad lying ahead. Radical elements demanded war to
the bitter end, a severe peace, and a harsh reconstruction of the conquered States.
Conservative elements agreed with Lincoln when he declared privately that he
intended "if possible to carry a truce in the belly of this war, ready to be delivered
if the South call for accoucheurs. . . ." and that loyal governments should be
organized in the Southern States as rapidly as the Union armies freed them.[17]
Radicals insisted that the rebellious States had taken themselves out of the Union;
conservatives were ready to accept Lincoln's view that the wise course was to
avoid a needless debate on the constitutional status of these States. Beyond this
momentous issue lay a hazier but all-important crossroads. Was the future of the
Republican Party to belong to the old yeoman element and the idealists, or to
the business groups, financiers, and other materialists encouraged by the recent
legislation on tariffs, banking, and railroads?

Lincoln was disposed to mollify the Radicals, whose help he would need in
the elections and in Congress. He was ready to court the good will of Thaddeus
Stevens in the House and Charles Sumner in the Senate, keeping on cordial
personal terms with them. But he was as blunt in rebuking their violent language
as in telling Democrats that they would be fools to let Copperhead extremists lead
the party astray. The President liked to bait a radical leader, as when he fell upon
one of them—perhaps Ben Wade or Zach Chandler—who said that anybody who
wished to recall McClellan was a traitor:[18]

16. May 15, 1863, Barlow Papers, HEH.
17. His phrase to T.J. Barnett, *ibid.*, April, 1861.
18. Barnett, Washington, to S.L.M. Barlow, July 10, 1863, reports this colloquy, *ibid.*

Salmon P. Chase, Secretary of the Treasury under President Lincoln

Gideon Welles, Secretary of the Navy under President Lincoln

Lincoln: "What do you think Mac would do if he had the power?"

Radical Leader: "By God, he's the man that ruined us!"

Lincoln: "But what would he *do?* Would he erect a despotism with the army that he instructed to consider the civil law as paramount; the army that hates rebels, whose members write home stinging lectures to Copperheads, and whose ranks cry for vengeance for fallen comrades, and whose great discontent is that they have failed of signal successes?"

Radical Leader: "No—he would fritter the army away."

Lincoln: "But then he was on the march when he was recalled, and had staked his reputation on the issue of a big fight."

Few men would have predicted early in 1863 that the autumn elections would be one of the important turning-points in the political history of the nation, but they did prove just that. Would they establish the rising strength of the new Republican Party and the growing hold of Lincoln upon public esteem throughout the North? Would they break the grip the Democrats had held upon several of the more populous States for a full generation? Or would they offer an augury of growing opposition to the war, to culminate in 1864 in the election of a President who would regard himself as authorized to bring the conflict to an end by negotiation with the Confederacy? The answer would depend in part upon military factors: would the Union armies keep advancing, or be thrown back in defeat? It would depend in part on political factors: which party would show the greater unity, and play its cards better? It would depend in part on the role of Lincoln: could he make effective appeals to public opinion? One by one, the answers were given, and given decisively.

After weeks of discouragement early in 1863, particularly bitter as Murfreesboro proved to be a drawn battle and Grant was again foiled before Vicksburg, the skies had brightened in the spring.[19] Union men found the spring elections cheering. March opened with the Republicans holding great victory parades in New Hampshire. A Republican legislature was chosen which placed a Republican governor in the State House, although a Democrat had a plurality in the three-man race; two of the three Congressmen elected were Republicans.[20] In judicial and local elections in Michigan, the party won what Zach Chandler's Detroit *Tribune* termed a decided victory. Cleveland, Cincinnati, and Toledo in Ohio were carried by Union tickets. As for Indiana, the recently arrogant Copperheads were brought low in city after city—Indianapolis, Evansville, Terre Haute, and Kokomo. The Union Party carried Davenport in Iowa, and heavily reduced the Democratic majority in Dubuque, notorious as a focus of Copperhead sentiment. St. Louis and Kansas City put unconditional Union men in the

19. See Nevins, *The War for the Union: War Becomes Revolution,* Ch. XV, "The Darkest Hours of the Northwest."

20. New York *Tribune,* March 13, 1863; *Annual Cyclopaedia,* 1863, 681.

municipal offices. Greeley's *Tribune* lifted an exultant voice to hail these results as evidence of a determination to be rid of the desolating curse of Copperheads.[21]

The spring gains of Unionism, while mere curtain-raisers to the more important autumn campaigns, significantly confirmed other evidences of the rally against Copperhead influences.[22] They were much needed, for from Boston to Omaha a war-weary pacifism verging on disloyalty kept cropping to the surface. Like George Lunt in Massachusetts and Ira A. Eastman in New Hampshire, Thomas H. Seymour in Connecticut had insisted on a negotiated peace, declaring that he would contribute nothing to the subjugation and consequent degradation of the South.[23] He termed it a monstrous fallacy to suppose the South could be brought back into the Union by force of arms; a fallacy "that will burst with the shells that are thrown into its defenseless cities, and leave the condition of this country, after its treasures are exhausted, and its brave men on both sides consigned to hospitals and graves, a spectacle for the reproach and commiseration of the civilized world." His letter to the Hartford *Times* expressing these ideas at once guaranteed him the Democratic nomination for the governorship.[24] The large and noisy convention that nominated him could hardly have been more inimical to the Northern cause if it had met in Richmond.[25] Yet in the spring elections, the Administration triumphed. The Union Party won decisive majorities in both houses of the Connecticut legislature; it elected its Congressional nominees in three out of four districts; and William A. Buckingham defeated Seymour for the governorship by a majority which was quite reassuring, since only a small number of the more than 20,000 men enlisted had been given furloughs to return and vote—the result being Buckingham 41,032, Seymour 38,395.[26]

In New Jersey no elections for State offices were held during the spring, or that year. The Democratic legislature passed early resolutions denouncing the Emancipation Proclamation, the suspension of the writ of habeas corpus, and the creation of West Virginia, and ending in an emphatic call for negotiations, on the basis of a restoration of the Union, "to terminate peacefully and honorably to all a war unnecessary in its origin, fraught with horror and suffering in its prosecution, and necessarily dangerous to the liberties of all in its continuance."[27] This craven legislature simultaneously sent to the national Senate James W. Wall,

---

21. New York *Tribune*, April 9, 1863.
22. This rally is described in Nevins, *The War for the Union: War Becomes Revolution*, 390-398.
23. Letter, to Hartford *Times*, July 10, 1862.
24. New York *Tribune*, March 3, 1863.
25. So said the Hartford *Press*, quoted in New York *Tribune*, *ut supra*.
26. *American Annual Cyclopaedia*, 1863, 330. The legislature had passed a bill to permit voting in the field, but the State Supreme Court declared it unconstitutional. Niven, John, *Connecticut for the Union*, New Haven, 1965, Chap. 10.
27. *American Annual Cyclopaedia*, 1863, 622.

a popular leader who had been quite unnecessarily arrested for disloyalty and detained in the Old Capitol Prison.[28] New Jersey answered all calls for troops promptly, filling her quotas with volunteers who received liberal bounties. Nevertheless, a strong Copperhead feeling simmered just under the surface.

The situation was the same in Wisconsin and Indiana, in Illinois and Iowa— sentiment in support of a vigorous prosecution of the war, and of a peace which required unconditional submission to the Union and to emancipation, was rising but adverse opinion remained strong. In Indiana, partisanship rather than Copperheadism had discredited the legislature early in 1863, Republicans being as culpable as Democrats. Nearly all Democrats there stood for restoration of the Union as emphatically as did sturdy Oliver P. Morton at the head of his dictatorial government.[29] Nevertheless, Daniel W. Voorhees talked eloquently of peace and violently assailed Lincoln's policies, adding angry protests against protective tariffs and national banks which delighted his fellow agrarians in the State. At the same time, a little group in which Lambdin P. Milligan was prominent edged close to treason in its opposition to recruiting and its discouragement of material or moral support of the war effort. The military commander of the district of Indiana appealed against such men by quoting that unperturbed Democrat Reverdy Johnson of Maryland: "The sole ministers of peace at present are our gallant officers, soldiers, and sailors . . . and let us, in pressing on the foe, not halt to criticize the conduct of the government."[30]

While the Administration won the encouragement of favorable spring elections, Lincoln's mild views on Reconstruction also received the support of important newspapers throughout the country. The *National Intelligencer* gave nearly its whole editorial page, four-and-a-quarter columns, to a withering blast against the Radical thesis that seceded communities were dead as States and must be governed as Territories. It argued that as soon as Louisiana, or Tennessee, or any other State was redeemed, the people should reorganize their government on the basis of their old State Constitution. "We deny that any State can 'go out' of the Union, and therefore there can be no necessity in any event of providing for her 'readmission.' "[31] At the same early date, the voice of William Cullen Bryant was raised against treatment of the seceded States as Territories. The State governments, declared his *Evening Post,* had been perverted, but not annihilated; they were in suspense, but not annulled. "As soon as enough people loyal to the Federal Constitution are gathered to put the machinery in operation, they will

28. New York *Tribune,* Jan. 13, 1863; Milton, George Fort, *Abraham Lincoln and the Fifth Column,* New York, 1942, 125.
29. Stampp, Kenneth M., *Indiana Politics During the Civil War,* Indianapolis, 1949, Chap. VIII.
30. Steiner, B.C., *Reverdy Johnson,* Baltimore, 1914, 52, 53.
31. Washington *National Intelligencer,* March 1, 1862.

be revived."[32] The New York *Herald* enunciated the same firm doctrine in editorial after editorial.[33]

Although other moderate newspapers throughout the country took a nearly identical position, it was impossible early in 1863 to say where public opinion on the still undeveloped issues of Reconstruction stood. Two facts, however, were certain. The first was that Lincoln's initial step, the appointment of military governors in Tennessee and Louisiana, was generally agreed to be just, proper, and indeed inescapable. Andrew Johnson and George F. Shepley, the two men he named, were selected not to exercise military functions, but to provide and supervise civil agencies for the protection of loyal citizens in their persons and property, to preserve order, and to maintain law. They were also empowered, as Representative John W. Noell of Missouri put it, to assist citizens in their inter-course with the Federal Government.[34] The second fact was that practically all the Union Democrats or War Democrats, whose gravitation into Lincoln's ranks it was important to assist, detested the idea of State suicide. They would fight to the last against it. The New Jersey legislature, for example, passed by decisive majorities early in 1863 a resolution protesting against efforts to effect the subjuga-tion of any of the States with a view to their reduction to a "territorial condi-tion."[35] Lincoln and the Union Democrats agreed that generous treatment of the first Southern States to lay down their arms would encourage the others to do likewise.

As summer began, the military factor came into play on the side of the Administration. In the Northwest, the moral effect of Vicksburg was incalcula-ble; in the East, Meade's repulse of Lee, though without a proper sequel, was still a potent victory. Moreover, heartening successes ensued in the Tennessee theatre as well.

Following the battle of Murfreesboro (or Stone River) at the beginning of January, General Rosecrans spent six months in that well-fortified town stub-bornly confronting Bragg, who had retreated twenty-five miles southward to Shelbyville. Although the Union commander had improved the time by strength-ening his forces and gathering supplies, he had worsened his position in the eyes of the country and the War Department by quarreling with Stanton and Halleck over his excuses for what appeared excessive inaction. At last, on June 23-24, he began a movement which flanked Bragg, first at Shelbyville and then at Tul-lahoma, forcing him back over the rocky Cumberland mountains toward Chat-tanooga. "Thus," declared Rosecrans in his report, "ended a nine days' campaign, which drove the enemy from two fortified positions, and gave us possession of

32. New York *Evening Post*, March 7, 1862.
33. See its long editorial of Aug. 25, 1863.
34. *Congressional Globe*, 37th Cong., 3rd Sess., Pt. 1, 861; Feb. 10, 1863.
35. This passed the House, 38 to 13; *American Annual Cyclopaedia*, 1863, 682.

Middle Tennessee."[36] From Kentucky, Burnside was threatening East Tennessee, moving against Knoxville and Buckner's small army in August. It appeared that the Confederates might soon lose all of Tennessee, including the great gateway to Alabama and Georgia at Chattanooga, where the three States touch upon one another and two vital railroads, the Nashville & Chattanooga and the Memphis & Charleston, joined and hooked up with railroads into Georgia and northeastward to Knoxville and Virginia.

Throughout July and August, gratifying dispatches came from Rosecrans's army. He repaired the railroad which ran down from Nashville to Stevenson in northern Alabama. He gathered his forces all along the Tennessee River, ready to cross it and fall upon Chattanooga; by August 20, Union troops were within fifteen miles of this vital center. Rosecrans maintained his steady pressure until on September 7-8 Bragg was forced to abandon Chattanooga, which Northern troops occupied on September 9. Another of the great objectives of the Union had been gained without a battle! The exultation of Union adherents in the Middle West was unbounded. In the meanwhile, a dashing cavalry raid by John Hunt Morgan into Kentucky, Indiana, and Ohio ended in disaster for both the hard-riding Confederate horsemen and the Copperhead politicians of the Ohio Valley. Morgan had not been authorized to go beyond the Ohio River. With 2,500 men at his back, however, he crossed the stream into Indiana on July 9, thundered eastward through the suburbs of Cincinnati, and with superior Union squadrons pursuing him, and home guards swarming out to harass him, finally surrendered with the remainder of his command not far short of the Pennsylvania line. Furthermore, the Copperheads were conspicuous in their failure to aid Morgan.

To many Confederates this bold dash was what General Basil W. Duke later called "incomparably the most brilliant raid of the entire war."[37] But it cost Morgan all but about 300 of his fine command, and the panic he created had heavy political consequences. "If there was before any doubt about the Ohio election," trumpeted Lyman Trumbull, "Morgan's raid has settled it. No compaign before ever damaged a political friend so much as Morgan's has damaged Vallandigham."[38]

The rejoicings of Union men over Western success in the summer of 1863 were to be temporarily halted as autumn began with a stunning Confederate blow at Chickamauga. But the mood of victory had been too firmly fixed to be shattered. After Vicksburg and the capture of Chattanooga, it was impossible to persuade reasonable Middle Westerners that the war was a failure. The costs were

36. Lossing, Benson J., *The Pictorial Field Book of the Civil War*, Hartford, 1881, III, 126-128.
37. Duke, Basil W., *A History of Morgan's Cavalry*, Bloomington, Indiana, 1961, 458.
38. Trumbull, August 4, 1863, to Zach Chandler, Chandler Papers, LC.

appalling, but the salvation of the Union would repay all sacrifices—and that salvation now seemed certain. Nor were the victories of the day confined to the battlefields, for triumphs of policy had equal magnitude. It had become so clear that all risk of Anglo-French intervention was past, that men ceased to worry about it. The first anniversary of the Homestead Act, Land-Grant College Act, and Pacific Railroad Act found farmers, educators, land-speculators, and railway inventors breathing the hopeful air that these laws provided. Before September brought the anniversary of Emancipation, an overwhelming sentiment north of the Ohio acknowledged its wisdom.

The serenity with which Lincoln pursued his median path was illustrated by his response to a set of Radical resolutions from German citizens of St. Louis brought him by James Taussig, a leading Missouri attorney. He treated Taussig to a frank two-hour talk. It might be a misfortune, he said, as some Radicals thought, that he had been elected President; but having been chosen, he meant to perform his duty according to *his* best understanding, if he had to die for it. He would remove no general, and make no Cabinet change, to suit any particular party, faction, or set of men, whether radical or conservative. He would not disturb General Halleck, who was innocent of the ignorant charges made against him. He was not designedly keeping Frémont, Sigel, and Ben Butler out of command; on the contrary, he appreciated their merits, and was anxious to place them in the field as soon as he could find suitable openings. Unfortunately, "I have more pegs than holes to put them in."[39] The charge of disunity in the Administration did not trouble him. Without admitting its validity, he declared that each Cabinet member was responsible for his own department, and that the only man who could centralize Cabinet action was the President himself. Indeed, he returned the charge upon the Missouri Unionists, rebuking their factious spirit sharply. The "Charcoals", who advocated immediate emancipation in Missouri, and the "Claybanks", or gradual emancipationists, "ought to have their heads knocked together forthwith. Either would rather see the defeat of their adversary than that of Jefferson Davis himself." Since his removal of Samuel R. Curtis from the Missouri command that spring, Lincoln had thought first of appointing Frémont and then McDowell in his stead; but he had finally selected John M. Schofield, with his ripe military experience in Missouri and Georgia, as the man most likely to reconcile the two factions.

This position did not please the St. Louis *Democrat*, representing the Charcoals. The editor was irritated by the illustration Lincoln used to explain why gradual emancipation would be the better course in Missouri—his story of the man with a tumor on his neck, who would die if it were removed in one operation, but survive if the surgeon "tinkered it off by degrees." What about the pain of the dog whose tail was cut off by inches? Lincoln's stand seemed too advanced

39. New York *Tribune*, June 13, 1863, quoting undated letter of Taussig to Emil Pretorius.

to some Claybanks, just as it seemed tardy and hesitant to some Charcoals. The President was satisfied, however, that moderation was true statesmanship, and that the country would stand by him as he rejected both kinds of extremism— the Radical and the ultra-Conservative. Opposing with equal firmness the Ben Wades and Zach Chandlers on one side and the Horatio Seymours and Vallandighams on the other, he leaned by natural inclination toward gradual and cautious policies. T.J. Barnett, who apparently was occasionally at the White House, saw that Lincoln's moderation, his dislike of both partisan and sectional animosities, and his reluctance to hurt settled interests, would have made him even more conservative if the Copperheads and Peace Democrats had given him leeway.

"My dear fellow," Barnett wrote S.L.M. Barlow, head of the central Democratic coterie in New York,[40] as Gettysburg still raged, "Lincoln is not a madman wholly. You are mistaken if you suppose that he is blind to the mischiefs of the Radicals. Does the appointment of Meade look that way? The business of the hour is to whip the Rebels or to give up our nationality, and . . . to settle with our incendiaries afterwards . . . I am no parasite, that I am sure you know, but I do have a high respect for Mr. Lincoln's character and motives, as an honest man with sufficient discernment to read the plain ABC of the hornbook before him. He sees and knows that the North cannot afford peace and dismemberment . . . The struggle within and without, with us, is for national existence—and this the President sees; and more and more; every day, he discerns the waning power of the Radicals; so much so that, if the opposition to his Administration had not been so precipitate and so organized as to render him, at one time, afraid to trust them with the conduct of the war, he would long ago have made a sensational demonstration in their jaws.

"But what are the opposition doing? To be sure [Horatio] Seymour has acted like a patriot, as well as a good and sound politician; but the partizans are carping and yelling about dead issues, or the secondary one of constitutional law, which will keep well enough till we have the power to settle it. And this makes Mr. Lincoln timid of the very men with whom, on the absorbing question of the instant, his predispositions are. Why do not the respectable leaders of the Conservative Party present themselves here with half the energy which brings the Radicals to Washington? The answer is [that they are] selfish and unworthy. It only amounts to this, that they have failed in less imminent, and in mere party terms (comparatively) to drive him from the Chicago platform. Tempora mutantur. We have done with the negro and with everything else but the bayonets of the rebels and the intrigues of Europe. We must wipe out all, fight, win a peace, kill our dogs, and begin anew—or go into inglorious chaos. This is the only *live* idea at the moment."

And a week later Barnett wrote his Democratic friends that Lincoln's recent

40. July 2, 1863, Barlow Papers, HEH.

mild speech to serenaders,[41] and the denunciation which it evoked from Wendell Phillips, indicated again that Lincoln was naturally a conservative. So did the utterances of the Blairs. Barnett scolded Barlow, the *World,* and the Democratic leadership roundly. Couldn't they see that by an opposition, not merely partisan but personal, they were driving Lincoln into the enemy camp? "Now the. President might be aided to subserve many good ends if he did not feel that the Radicals are his only support, and that after all, he was elected by a party to whom he made certain pledges, and which, entirely to slough off, and to fall into the hands of raging lions, would hardly be a fair stewardship or a decent personal risk. I want the conservatives, on the simple issue of the conduct of the war, of the probable terms of peace, and all such questions, to offer the President a fair chance to stand on a platform more modified than that he occupies."[42]

The Democratic leadership was deaf to this plea, although many Union Democrats felt about the patient, judicious President just as Barnett did.

[III]

Effective organization for the Union cause, emancipation, and a more energetic prosecution of the war, was essential. A strong bipartisan effort was needed, rallying War Democrats alongside the Republicans. It should have a greater militancy than that of the Knights of the Golden Circle; it should put more intellectual distinction at the service of the Administration than S.F.B. Morse, George Ticknor Curtis, and Samuel J. Tilden were giving the Copperhead cause. It should have money, idealism, and vision, for its usefulness might long outlast the war. Before 1863 ended, the need was being met.

For the most important organization in rallying patriotic men and combating defeatism and sedition, born of a spontaneous movement in several States during 1862, was the Union League or Loyal League. Possibly the first unit was formed in Pekin, Illinois, in June, by a Unionist from East Tennessee who had observed the work of semi-secret loyal societies there.[43] With a ritual, oaths, and a spirit of fervent dedication, it was more than a mere antagonist of the K.G.C. Spreading rapidly through Illinois, holding a fall meeting of its council in Bloomington, and vigorously enlisting members, it laid claim by midwinter to fifty thousand members. Among its active promoters was Joseph Medill of the Chicago *Tribune,* who had devised the ritual, forms, and most of the signs the Union League used, and

---

41. July 7, 1863; Lincoln, *Collected Works,* VI, 319, 320. On the theme of human equality, with what some men took as a favorable reference to McClellan.
42. July 10, 1863; Barlow Papers, HEH.
43. Cole, Arthur Charles, *The Era of the Civil War,* Springfield, Ill., 1919, 309-310; Gray, Wood, *The Hidden Civil War,* New York, 1942, 143.

set it going.[44] It had 4,000 members in Chicago, and 75,000 in Illinois. He had called a national convention in Cleveland later that month, and felt confident that with the help of military successes the League would keep the people firmly behind the Administration.

"My labors and services may not be appreciated by you," wrote Medill, who had filled his columns with criticism and his private letters with defeatism, rather tinged with radicalism; "but no matter, if the Union is saved, the rebellion crushed, and the principles of liberty established, I will be content and die happy." The volatile Medill, a strong supporter of an all-out policy to win the war, had been particularly disconcerted by the commutation clause of the draft act, calling it an "outrage," and saying "the poor only are forced to go. . . ." In another letter Medill, early in 1863, had railed against the Administration, claiming its policy would lead to an armistice. There was no help for it; the Democrats were so hostile, the war had been conducted so long by "central imbecility." "Lincoln is only half awake, and never will do much better than he has done." Later in the year, Medill would ask, "Tell me what devil is it that prevents the Potomac Army from advancing on the rebels." He was most despondent over the forthcoming 1863 elections. The columns of the *Tribune* cried out often against slavery and the Confederacy.[45]

Branches of the Union League spread through the Middle West and into the Atlantic States. A hundred Wisconsin councils, boasting that they mustered nearly 20,000 men, sent delegates to an enthusiastic State gathering at about the same time that the Cleveland convention formed a grand council, with headquarters in Washington. Thousands in New York and tens of thousands in other Eastern cities signed the pledge of the League. An organization meeting on the evening of March 20 jammed Cooper Union with a crowd that enthusiastically cheered the speakers, and elected a council including the first citizens of the metropolis, William Cullen Bryant, George Bancroft, William E. Dodge, Francis Lieber, and A.T. Stewart. General John Cochrane announced that 1,700 policemen had joined the League.[46] Although its founders wished to keep it out of party politics, it was an arm of strength for Lincoln in most respects.

The Union League Clubs and Union Clubs, separate bodies entirely, meanwhile had their origin in Philadelphia, Boston, and New York—again in what Greeley termed a "spontaneous rising."[47] A gathering of Administration supporters in Philadelphia late in 1862 decided that as systematic propaganda must be

44. Hay Papers, Illinois State Historical Library.

45. Chicago *Tribune*, 1863, various issues; New York *Tribune*, March 3, 1863.

46. Medill to E. Washburne, Jan. 16, 1863, Washburne Papers, LC; Medill to Horace White, March 5, 1863, Robert Todd Lincoln Papers, LC; Medill to O.M. Hatch, Oct. 13, 1863, O.M. Hatch Papers, Illinois State Hist. Libr.

47. New York *Tribune*, March 3, 1863, and in other issues.

carried on, quarters should be rented for a reading room and auditorium, where patriots would hold regular meetings. The response was so lusty that a large house was leased. Many of the wealthiest and most influential citizens joined. "Its name, and the flag that floats over it, its very existence," declared William M. Meredith, the first president, "are a standing rebuke to the traitors."[48] Accepting War Democrats as willingly as Republicans, the club disclaimed any desire to influence elections beyond an opposition to disloyal or notoriously incompetent men. Meredith, Secretary of the Treasury under Taylor, had been a conservative Whig. But club membership inevitably became a symbol of social status and of Republican high tariff, sound money leanings, as well as devotion to the Union.

This tendency was clearly manifest in the Union League Club which New Yorkers organized on February 6, 1863. Its creators were the guiding spirits of the United States Sanitary Commission. The executive heads of that organization—the brilliant clergyman Henry W. Bellows, the diarist George Templeton Strong, the chemist Wolcott Gibbs, Drs. C.R. Agnew and W.H. Van Buren, and Frederick L. Olmsted, met regularly to discuss their problems. Encountering the parochialism of State medical organizations, and jealous ignorance of the army Medical Bureau and some Washington officials, they became convinced of the importance of a firmer national spirit. Gibbs, who inherited the Federalist traditions personified in Oliver Wolcott, began to talk in 1862 of forming a Loyalists' Club. The election of Horatio Seymour as governor stimulated the movement. Olmsted, with a sense of the prestige of traditions, thought the club should insist not only on absolute loyalty, but on special social qualifications; members should include men "of old colonial names well brought down," of repute in letters and science, of cleverness and wit, of wealth and promising influence. Some of his tests would have excluded Lincoln! But the primary object was to foster a sentiment of devotion to the Union, and make it politically effective. A clubhouse fronting on Union Square soon sheltered a large membership, which included a sprinkling of Union Democrats.[49]

The Union League Clubs and Union Clubs, confined to large cities, did effective work in sustaining the national war aims. The social éclat they conferred on the Republican leadership was useful. In Boston, for example, the much-respected Edward Everett presided over the meeting which early in 1863 founded the Union Club, and helped take steps to buy the Abbott Lawrence mansion on Park Street at a cost of $50,000.[50] In Philadelphia, the opening of the Union League Club in a handsome mansion on February 23 was a stately occasion, with

48. March 5, 1863, Meredith Papers, Hist. Soc. of Penn.
49. Bellows, Henry W., *Historical Sketch of the Union League Club of New York*, New York, 1879, *passim*.
50. New York *Tribune*, March 3, 1863.

speeches by Governor Curtis, Horace Binney, Jr., and others.[51] It was the plebeian Union League organization, however, which did invaluable service in educating voters on the issues of the war, stiffening popular confidence in the Administration, encouraging enlistments, and nerving men to a grim determination. In many localities they overawed knots of Copperheads. When disloyal threats were loudest in southern Illinois, an Alton friend of Lyman Trumbull assured him that men were organizing in every county to show traitors that Lincoln would be upheld. "We are *about ready and able* to take care of home troubles *in any event.* "[52] The renaissance of enthusiasm for the Union cause in the spring and summer of 1863 owed much to their efforts.

The fact that the Union League tended to support all measures of the Administration aroused the ire of Caleb Cushing. The formation of societies to back the government *quand même,* he wrote, "that is, for approving its acts however unwise they may be, and lauding its members however perverse and corrupt they may be, is a spectacle never before exhibited in any country, republican or monarchical, and which deserves to be considered as a policy of mere hopelessness and despair."[53] Theoretically, he was right. Practically, however, the utility of a thick and thin support was illustrated by the aid the League gave the government in enforcing the draft law, tax measures, and the repression of serious troublemakers. After Congress passed Lyman Trumbull's bill on habeas corpus in March, 1863,[54] much of the debate on civil liberties was academic, but it continued to rage with unabated fury.

In the flood of pamphlets on civil liberties and arbitrary arrests, several written by Union League members had conspicuous influence. Particularly able was the learned monograph of Horace Binney, leader of the Philadelphia bar, and a man of fearless principle.[55] His three-part treatise held that Lincoln clearly possessed the power to suspend the writ of habeas corpus. The Constitution, he pointed out, provided that the privileges of the writ might be withdrawn whenever invasion or rebellion precipitated a situation of public danger. "Whichever power of the constituted government can most properly decide these facts is master of the exception and competent to apply it." As the Constitution did not expressly delegate the power either to Congress or the President, it belonged, wrote Binney, to that department whose functions were most appropriate. Congress could not give executive force to the suspension, and the President could. There-

51. Philadelphia *Press,* Feb. 24, Mar. 12, Mar. 16, 1863, describes its activities.
52. H.G. McPike to Trumbull, Feb. 23, 1863, Trumbull Papers, LC.
53. Undated memorandum early 1863, Clement Clay Papers, LC.
54. *American Annual Cyclopaedia,* 1863, 257-258.
55. Binney, C.C., *Life of Horace Binney,* Philadelphia, 1903, 341ff.

fore, Binney concluded, "The President being the properest and safest depository of this power, and being the only power which can exercise it under real and effective responsibilities to the people, it is both constitutional and safe to argue that the Constitution has placed it with him."[56]

This was the view of Francis Lieber also. The Columbia College professor and adviser to Halleck wrote that the framers of the Constitution, having never contemplated a great civil war, had made no explicit statement on the means of suspending the writ. But when the ship of State was adrift, and Congress could not assemble or would not act, the President obviously had to use his authority to meet the crisis. In such emergencies the safety of the nation could not be entrusted to hairsplitting lawyers or precedent-grubbing pedants, but must be protected by patriotic officers of government—in the first instance, by the Chief Executive. Other authorities penned other pamphlets so rapidly that the Union League soon had a long list on sale. Lieber's *No Party Now but All for Our Country*, an address to the Union League of Philadelphia, April 11, 1863, went through edition after edition.[57] These defenders of the Administration outgunned such adverse pamphleteers as S.F.B. Morse, William B. Reed, and J.C. Bullitt.

One of the most effective agencies for the Union cause was the Loyal Publication Society, organized early in 1862 by George Putnam and some friends, with Lieber as head of its publications committee. Putnam, the founder of the magazine and publishing house bearing his name, the close friend of Irving and Hawthorne, and the foremost champion of international copyright, was a pillar of strength to the Administration.[58] The Society was especially anxious to frustrate Copperhead attempts to persuade troops to accept the idea of a negotiated peace. It arranged for the distribution of tens of thousands of copies of loyal newspapers among the troops in Virginia, and before the middle of 1863 scattered about 150,000 pamphlets and broadsides over the country.[59] Altogether, it issued ninety pamphlets, and was responsible for the publication in 1864 of one of the most important and effective of all the wartime books, David A. Wells's *Our Burden and Our Strength*. His study of the national balance sheet, an anticipation in some respects of Keynesian doctrine, showed that the wealth of the United States, which Wells believed would reach twenty-two and one-half billion dollars in 1865 and would rapidly increase, was amply sufficient to bear the war debts.

The Loyal National League, the Union League, the Union and Union League Clubs, and the Loyal Publication Society made up a network of interlocking

56. Binney, Horace, *The Privilege of the Writ of Habeas Corpus under the Constitution*, Philadelphia, 1862, with two sequels; copies in New York Hist. Soc.

57. Vol. I, No. 19, in pamphlets issued by Union League of Philadelphia, but also in other forms.

58. Putnam, George Haven, *A Memoir of George Palmer Putnam*, New York, 1903, 280ff.

59. Freidel, Frank, *Francis Lieber, Nineteenth-Century Liberal*, Baton Rouge, 1947, 346.

organizations whose members might work under any name. Although not ostensibly Republican, they actually became bulwarks of the party. Lieber's *No Party Now but All for Our Country* was in fact a Radical Republican manifesto, insisting that all good citizens should support the total defeat of the South, the eradication of slavery, the firm execution of the draft, and resistance to the mischievous neutrality of European powers.[60] In every large city, commercial and industrial leaders played such roles that class lines and economic interests grew increasingly prominent. The New York *Herald* called the Loyal National League simply a contractors' cabal.[61] It was not difficult to raise money for these bodies; not difficult to make entrance into the clubs a social distinction allowed to few but the wealthy, the influential, and the firmly partisan. Yet in the ticklish year 1863 they were almost invaluable to the government.

[IV]

By the end of September, the State campaigns were catching fire. Trustworthy governors were to be elected this fall. In Massachusetts, the Republicans renominated John A. Andrew and his official colleagues by acclamation. The Democrats chose Henry W. Paine for governor, with a vehement denunciation of Lincoln's usurpations of power, and a protest against continuing the bloody struggle for purposes of subjugation and emancipation. In Maine, the Republicans and War Democrats joined hands to form a Union Party which nominated Samuel Cony, a War Democrat, for governor; the Regular Democratic party selected Bion Bradbury, who sent the convention a letter assailing the fanatical radicalism which he thought rampant in the land, denouncing the inroads upon civil liberties, and calling for a restoration of the Union with all the rights of the States unimpaired. "The country is oscillating between despotism and anarchy," declared Bradbury. The convention termed the draft law unnecessary, unequal, and oppressive. In Vermont, identical lines were drawn. A Union Convention nominated John G. Smith for governor, with resolutions placing the State completely behind Lincoln; the Democrats nominated R.P. Redfield for governor on a platform of opposition to all tyrannical acts endangering the liberties of the citizens.[62]

Even in New England, it was plain the Democrats were making the cardinal error of letting the violent anti-war, anti-draft, anti-emancipation extremists go too far. Their clamor obscured the real issues of the time and discredited their party. Lincoln's moderation was preventing the Republican extremists from

60. *Ibid.*, 347. For modern analysis of Civil War pamphlets and their publication, see: *Union Pamphlets of the Civil War*, ed. Frank Freidel, 2 vols., Boston, 1967, particularly the Introduction.
61. New York *Herald*, May 20, 1863.
62. *American Annual Cyclopaedia*, 1863, 603-604, 624-625, 843.

making any like mistake. The Democrats had plenty of sage advice from cool-headed leaders. Daniel S. Dickinson of New York, a former lieutenant-governor and Senator, said in repeated speeches that he was a Jacksonian Democrat, who held that the Union must and should be preserved. He was for throwing all the national energies into the war, for enlisting Negro soldiers, and for letting slavery go down forever when the South collapsed.[63] Reverdy Johnson and Samuel J. Tilden were staunch Unionists, however acidly they might criticize certain Administration measures. In Chicago, James W. Sheehan kept the *Post* an unwavering advocate of the principles of his oldtime friend and chieftain Douglas,[64] and a relentless antagonist of Wilbur F. Storey's Copperhead *Times*. T.J. Barnett showered advice upon S.L.M. Barlow, August Belmont, and Manton Marble, assuring them that the Copperheads were political gamesters who wanted the Southern States back only as pawns on their chessboard.

When will the Democrats take the right road? Barnett asked S.L.M. Barlow. "When will they command the heart of the nation, instead of swaying with its whims and its fears? When will they discard such oracles as Fernando Wood, James Brooks, and [Charles] Ingersoll, and [James W.] Wall, and Vallandigham, and Voorhees, and not sporadically but by a general voice?"[65] This was Sheehan's view, and Reverdy Johnson's, and with petulant vacillation even Horatio Seymour's. But the party could not save itself from its hotheads, a fact which encouraged farsighted opponents. Every rash move by Vallandigham, Daniel Voorhees, and Fernando Wood shook sensible Democrats into the Republican ranks. If Lincoln had blended his real party-consciousness with more partisanship, he might have felt pleased to see the hotheads manoeuvering their party into a position where it could not regain national power for another twenty years.

The nomination of Vallandigham for governor by the Ohio Democrats on June 11 was a particularly spectacular triumph of passion and impulse over good sense. It is true that few judicious men condoned General Burnside's arrest of the former Congressman, his lodgment in a military prison in Cincinnati, and his sentence after summary military trial to close confinement in some fortress for the remainder of the war. All this constituted an indefensible invasion of fundamental civil liberties. It was questionable whether Burnside had any right to make even the arrest. Once he arrogated to himself this right, and sent the troops who on May 5, at three o'clock in the morning, haled Vallandigham out of his home in Dayton, he should instantly have reported the facts to the Federal district judge, so that a grand jury might consider an indictment. The courts were open, and as the Supreme Court later found in the famous case of *ex parte* Milligan, no

63. See speech of Feb. 22, 1863, in all New York papers, Feb. 23.
64. One of the misfortunes of history is that Sheehan's correspondence with his friend Douglas, apparently through Douglas's illness and the Chicago fire of 1871, has been irretrievably lost.
65. Washington, July 6, 1863, Barlow Papers, HEH.

military tribunal had any legal standing in their presence. Vallandigham was justified in protesting that he was subject to arrest only upon a warrant issued by an officer or court of competent jurisdiction, and was amenable to trial only after indictment by a grand jury, and in a regular court under due process of law.[66]

Ohio Democrats had an effective issue in this violation of principles well settled in Anglo-American precedent and bulwarked by the Constitution; but, in naming Vallandigham for governor, they overplayed their hand.[67] Did they have a choice? S.S. Cox believed that if McClellan had been willing to take the nomination, he could have had it by an avalanche. The sensible delegates would have seized on any feasible alternative to the frothy Vallandigham. They simply did not feel like organizing a movement against an exiled victim.[68] But why did they not nominate Cox, or former Senator George E. Pugh?

Every observer of events knew that a wide gulf separated the able, patriotic Horatio Seymour from the flighty, irresponsible Vallandigham, just as a gulf separated the conscientious Manton Marble of the New York *World*—who declared that he was for maintaining the war unflinchingly to the last extremity,[69] but within constitutional bounds—from the bitter, lying Storey of the Chicago *Times.* Vallandigham had been grossly intemperate in his language. He had told a shouting Copperhead crowd that Lincoln's war was for the liberation of the blacks and the enslavement of the whites; he had asserted that the Administration was waging the contest not for the Union but for ulterior objects, which he denounced;[70] he had said that he spat upon all arbitrary military decrees. The moderate S.S.Cox wrote Manton Marble that, while the Ohio Democrats condemned Vallandigham's arrest, they by no means endorsed his peace notions. "I think, as do our prudent men, that his nomination would be injudicious—that we would jeopardize our success."[71]

Why should the Ohio Democrats go to the worst element in the party for a candidate? The lessons of the spring election in Connecticut had been fairly plain. Had the Democrats there named a man less generally and justifiably distrusted than the venomous T.H. Seymour, the majority for William A. Buckingham would have been less decisive. Yet the June convention in Columbus not only vociferously selected Vallandigham for governor but placed him on a platform declaring that the Emancipation Proclamation was unwise, unconstitutional, and void, and denouncing as traitors "the Abolition Jacobins who are seeking to bring

66. Text of his protest in *American Annual Cyclopaedia*, 1863, 480. His term in Congress had just expired.
67. *Ibid.*, 730-731; for worthy summation see Klement, Frank L., *The Copperheads in the Middle West*, Chicago, 1960, 128-133.
68. S.S. Cox, June 14, 1863, to Manton Marble, Marble Papers, LC.
69. New York *World*, September 16, 1862.
70. *American Annual Cyclopaedia*, 1863, 474-478.
71. Cox to Marble, June 1, 1863, Manton Marble Papers, LC.

about civil war in the loyal States." At that moment the candidate was in banish-
ment in the Confederacy. C.C. Clay met him near Petersburg, Virginia, and
reported that he was at heart for peace, even at the price of Southern independence. He talked of a possible truce, and, wrote Clay: "I think his hope and aim
is to get New England sloughed off and restore the Union without her."[72] He
felt certain of election, and told Clay that the only road to peace was by a political
revolution in the North effected by "we Democrats"! It is not strange that loyal
men of both parties received the nomination with anger. The good Democrat,
T.F. Meagher of New York, organizer of the Irish Brigade, burst out:

"The importance of the coming contest in Ohio . . . cannot be exaggerated. The
triumph of the National Government in this contest . . . will be of no less (possibly
of greater) consequence, than the repulse of the armed enemy at Gettysburg
and the capitulation of Vicksburg have been. Defeated in Ohio, the malcontents and conspirators of the North are beaten everywhere. Their backbone is
broken; and the surest way to kill a copperhead or any other reptile . . . is to break
his back."[73]

The conduct of Horatio Seymour, though always defensible, was ill-advised
from the standpoint of his party's long-term interests. He delivered a raucous
Independence Day speech in Brooklyn, in which he spoke (on the morrow of
Gettysburg and Vicksburg) of broken promises of victory;[74] he talked about
Lincoln's awful despotism; and he asserted that the whole blame for the war fell
upon the Republican Party. This, with his hesitant treatment of the draft riots,
his greeting of a turbulent crowd as "my friends," and his querulous appeals to
Lincoln to suspend the draft, displeased judicious Democrats. The *Herald*
termed him a small-fry political trimmer.[75] Yet when August Belmont protested
against his second letter to Lincoln, Seymour replied with an explosion of venom.
    "I cannot explain in a letter my reasons for writing it," declared the Governor.
"In dealing with the Republican leaders it is necessary to bear in mind that they
are coarse, cowardly, and brutal. They cannot understand generous purposes.
They represent the worst phases of the Puritan character."[76] This was of a piece
with the frenzied utterances of Samuel F.B. Morse, who also publicly stigmatized
the war as a failure. Lincoln, the eccentric artist-inventor wrote his brother-in-law
just after Gettysburg, is "a President without brains, so illiterate as not to be able
to see the absurdities of his own logic, so weak and vacillating as to be swayed

    72. Clay to W.L. Yancey, Macon, Ga., June 30, 1863; Yancey Papers, Ala. State Archives; *American
Annual Cyclopaedia*, 1863, 731.
    73. Lyons, W.F., *Brigadier-General Thomas F. Meagher*, New York, 1870, 182.
    74. Mitchell, Stewart, *Horatio Seymour*, Cambridge, 1938, 303, 304.
    75. New York *Herald*, July 7, 1863.
    76. Seymour to August Belmont, Albany, Aug. 12, 1863; Belmont Papers in possession of Mrs.
August Belmont, New York.

this way and that by the vulgar cant and fanaticism of such mad zealots as Wilson, Wade, Sumner, Chandler, Wendell Phillips . . ."[77] Men and journals indulging in this vein of abuse, and State conventions responding to them, were irreparably injuring the Democratic name. A truthful view of Lincoln at this moment was given by the perceptive and by no means uncritical John Hay. "The Tycoon is in fine whack," he wrote Nicolay. "I have rarely seen him more serene and busy. He is managing the war, the draft, foreign relations, and planning a reconstruction of the Union, all at once. I never knew with what tyrannous authority he rules the Cabinet till now. The most important things he decides and there is no cavil. . . . There is no man in the country so wise, so gentle, and so firm. I believe the hand of God placed him where he is."[78]

The Democratic Party made a further effort to put its worst foot forward in nominating George W. Woodward, chief justice of Pennsylvania, for the governorship of that State. He had asserted that the Draft Act and the Legal Tender Act were unconstitutional, had tried to wreck a State enrollment law, and stood accused of saying in 1861 that, if the Union were divided, he wished the line of separation run north of Pennsylvania! It would have been impossible to find a candidate who more fiercely aroused the detestation of Republicans. They rallied with frantic energy in the struggle to reëlect Andrew G. Curtin, whose eloquence, promptness, and vision had won the respect of every Unionist outside of Simon Cameron's selfish influence. Pennsylvania soldiers in particular spared no exertion, for they idolized Curtin. He had fought for their interests against Stanton. He had organized a State agency in Washington to attend to their wants. He had visited them in hospitals, seen to the assistance of their families, and answered thousands of their letters over his own signature. They flooded the State with pleas for his retention in Harrisburg, and with denunciations of Woodward.

From the outset, it was clear that the Democrats had thrown away their chances in the Buckeye and Keystone States. What loyal Ohioan would vote for Vallandigham against the Republican nominee, John Brough? This rugged leader, son of an Englishman who had come over on the same ship with Harman Blennerhassett, was one of the true builders of Ohio. He had studied at Ohio University, had edited newspapers in Marietta and Lancaster, and had become president of the Madison & Indianapolis Railroad. As State auditor his exposure of a mass of corruption in taxation and land surveys had proved his civic vigilance. A blunt, downright, rigidly just man, he was esteemed from Cleveland to Cincinnati as were few other leaders. And what loyal Pennsylvanian would vote for

77. Morse, July 9, 1863, to William M. Goodrich, Thomas F. Madigan catalogue, Oct. 1936, 40.
78. Hay, John, *Lincoln and the Civil War in the Diaries and Letters of John Hay*, Selected by Tyler Dennett, New York, 1939, 76, 110, 112. (August 7, 1863).

Woodward against Curtin—the Curtin who had organized fourteen almost invaluable reserve regiments, who had earned the title of the "Soldiers' Friend," who had taken such prompt action after Lee's invasion? Part of the recent legislation in Harrisburg had been odious to many citizens,[79] and, with Scotch-Irish toughness, Curtin had never hesitated to make enemies. But when the overriding issue was to fight the war through to victory, few good citizens could hesitate.

All over the country, the Republicans and War Democrats closed up their ranks in a firm Union front, with full Administration support. Stanton, who knew Brough well and proclaimed him one of the ablest and most patriotic men of the time, lent his aid in reaching the Ohio soldiers—for they were allowed to vote. So did Chase, who said that no man in the country excelled Brough in executive capacity, and who went home to Ohio to make a number of speeches.[80] Lincoln sent Curtin an encouraging letter, tendering his assistance. Late in the campaign the financial straits of the Pennsylvania Republicans impelled the governor, anxious "to secure beyond peradventure the triumph of what must certainly be looked upon as the cause of the country," to make a successful appeal to the New York party for aid.[81] Other aids poured in. In Pennsylvania, George Mifflin Dallas, Vice-President under Polk and minister to Great Britain under Pierce, announced his intention of voting the Union ticket. Horace Greeley, making a hurried visit to northern Pennsylvania shortly before election day, returned convinced that thirty thousand War Democrats would come to the Governor's aid, and that he would receive another twenty thousand votes from furloughed and invalided soldiers.[82]

[V]

Lincoln's personal intervention in the battle was limited but highly effective. As he recovered from the disappointing failure of Meade to pursue and crush Lee, his faith in ultimate Union victory and buoyant self-confidence[83] carried him to the height of his powers. His interest in politics was almost untinged by selfish considerations. He had a world of responsibilities upon which to spend his thought and energies, and the country knew little of most of these cares and

79. So Greeley wrote in the New York *Tribune,* Oct. 16, 1863.
80. Chase, Sept. 7, 1863; Stanton, Oct. 15, 1863; W.H. Smith Papers, Ohio Hist. Soc.
81. Curtin, Oct. 1, 1863, to E.D. Morgan, Morgan Papers, N.Y. State Library.
82. New York *Tribune,* Oct. 18, 1863.
83. Welles writes in his *Diary* for October 13, 1863, that, although the contests in Ohio and Pennsylvania riveted close attention, "The President says, no doubts have troubled me." If he worried more than in other elections, he took more precautionary action, he authorized the grant of fifteen days' leave for government clerks from Ohio and Pennsylvania, to whom railroads gave passes, politicians assessing the clerks one per-cent of their salaries.

burdens. Officers of the government, and the great body of the people, were preoccupied with the multitudinous cares and duties of the conflict. They were imperfectly aware that during this great conflict the United States was undergoing violent and sweeping changes which were carried forward by forces operating largely outside the war. Only with the passage of time would they become plainly visible. The most important of these changes included the following:

First, the settlement and development of the Trans-Mississippi West. Second, the growing urbanization of the country, as population gravitated more and more to the towns and cities, and their influence increased. Third, the opening in the North of new sources of wealth, and new bodies of capital by the application of efficient machinery and improved methods of tillage to agriculture, and by the tapping of fresh mineral resources ranging from the gold of Nevada, the iron ore of Michigan, and the silver of Colorado to the petroleum of Pennsylvania. Fourth, the growth of organization in all fields under the pressure of war, with a resultant heightening of economic and social efficiency. But great as they were, these changes were to a large extent imperceptible, and the Administration dealt with them, if at all, in a casual and often indirect fashion.

As we have previously indicated, in the management of his Cabinet Lincoln was not a chairman, trying to weld and direct it as the chairman of the board directs a great corporation. It had no unity. He was never inclined to manage the departments; on the contrary, he let them manage themselves. He did not try even to inform himself of routine details in the Navy Department, the Interior Department, the Postoffice Department, or the Treasury; they were autonomous. He did not regard the Cabinet as a powerhouse, as later a President or Prime Minister would regard such a body in America, Britain, Canada, or Australia. It was *not* a powerhouse, and Lincoln could not have sent much voltage through it if it had been. It did not help him in managing Congress, or moulding public sentiment, or manipulating the machinery of the Republican (later the Union) Party. On the contrary, the Cabinet divisions and antagonisms hindered him.

Lincoln was too shrewd and magnanimous to worry over Chase's tendency to intrigue against him, which he had long perceived. He knew that the Secretary tried to turn executive difficulties to his own political advantage, and that when the President took steps adverse to Frémont, David Hunter, and General Butler, Chase tried to persuade supporters of these men that he would have acted differently. Radical Ben Wade was reported to say that Chase was a good man, "but his theology is unsound. He thinks there is a fourth person in the Trinity." His behavior, Lincoln told Hay, was in bad taste, but he was a strong head of the Treasury and as such should stay. "If he becomes President, all right. I hope we may never have a worse man."[84] The President had a sharp sentence for Chase

84. October 18, 1863; Hay, John, *Lincoln and the Civil War, op. cit.,* 53, 100.

—("I suppose he will, like the bluebottle fly, lay his eggs in every rotten spot he can find!")—but no sharp acts. He himself was not playing politics, he told Hay: "I wish they would stop thrusting that subject of the Presidency into my face. I don't want to hear anything about it."[85]

His replies to Horatio Seymour, which were widely publicized, showed reason and courtesy. That of August 7, explaining that he would be glad to facilitate a Supreme Court decision on the draft law, but could lose no time in strengthening the armies, was crisply phrased. "We are contending with an enemy who, as I understand, drives every able-bodied man he can reach into his ranks, very much as a butcher drives bullocks into a slaughter-pen. No time is wasted, no argument is used. This produces an army which will soon turn upon our now victorious soldiers already in the field, if they shall not be sustained by recruits, as they should be."[86] Still more important was one frank excursion into politics in behalf, not of Republicans, but Union men.

His old Springfield friend James C. Conkling, who had married one of Mrs. Lincoln's intimates, helped arrange a general meeting of unconditional Union men of Illinois at the State capital September 3, designed to counteract similar meetings of Democrats. Governor Yates, Owen Lovejoy, Jesse Dubois, W.H. Herndon, and many others signed the call. The *State Journal* predicted that it would be the largest and most inspiring popular demonstration yet held in the area.[87] Lincoln, invited to be the principal speaker, replied that he would attend or send a letter—"probably the latter." He took great pains with this letter, for he was genuinely grieved not to see old neighbors and friends. Though it has been called his last stump speech,[88] that term is unjust, for it was a calm, reasoned argument addressed not to his supporters but his opponents; condensed, cogent, and pointed, without any partisan flavor, Administration boasting, or rhodomontade. It was in fact a state paper, with so broad a view, and so fine a touch of eloquence at the end, that it ranks with his finest utterances.

With great economy of statement, he strove to establish three facts. The first was that the only way to save the Union was to suppress the rebellion by force; the second, that his Emancipation Proclamation was not only a constitutional exercise of his war powers, but a staggering blow to the Confederacy; and the third was that the use of Negroes as troops increased Northern military power while it weakened the South. Except for a reference to men who "with malignant heart, and deceitful speech," had done their utmost to crush the war effort,

85. Hay, op.cit., 112; Oct. 30, 1863.
86. Lincoln, Collected Works, op.cit., VI, 369, 370.
87. Aug. 17, 1863; quoted in Randall, James G., Lincoln the President, New York, 1952, III, 254; Selby, Paul, "The Lincoln-Conkling Letter," Transactions Illinois State Historical Society, Springfield, Ill., 1908, Vol. XIII, 217; Lincoln, Collected Works, VI, 406-410.
88. Randall, op.cit., III,257.

Lincoln said nothing of his fanatical enemies. He spoke to citizens who were entirely loyal to the Union, but doubtful whether he was alive to the deep popular yearning for peace, and who questioned whether he had not needlessly enlarged the objects of the conflict. He wished to reason them out of their objections.

But this was far from all. Confident that the coming peace would prove that among free men there can be no successful appeal from the ballot to the bullet, Lincoln could not refrain from paying tribute to the heroes who had just won such resounding victories. Characteristically, he said nothing about what his Administration had done. The letter was modesty itself. But it suddenly rose to heights of poetic emotion, lifting a jet of sparkling eloquence in the political desert:

> The signs look better. The Father of Waters again goes unvexed to the sea. Thanks to the great North-West for it. Nor yet wholly to them. Three hundred miles up, they met New-England, Empire, Key-Stone, and Jersey, hewing their way right and left. The Sunny South, too, in more colors than one, also lent a hand. On the spot, their part of the history was jotted down in black and white. The job was a great national one, and let none be banned who bore an honorable part in it. And while those who have cleared the great river may well be proud, even that is not all. It is hard to say that anything has been more bravely, and well done, than at Antietam, Murfreesboro, Gettysburg, and on many fields of lesser note. Nor must Uncle Sam's Web-feet be forgotten. At all the watery margins they have been present. Not only on the deep sea, the broad bay, and the rapid river, but also up the narrow muddy bayou, and wherever the ground was a little damp, they have been, and made their tracks.
>
> Thanks to all. For the great republic—for the principle it lives by, and keeps alive—for man's vast future—thanks to all.[89]

Lincoln had been anxious that Conkling should read his letter slowly and effectively. He was annoyed when, through a breach of faith by someone connected with the press, a mutilated version of his words—"botched up," he put it—was telegraphed to Eastern journals and thus published September 3 and 4.[90]

The President's statement that Confederate leaders had never made any peace proposals was at once questioned by Fernando Wood of New York, who on several occasions had asserted the contrary. The former mayor had written Lincoln in December, 1862, that he had been advised by an authority whom he did not identify that the Southern States would send members to the next Congress (in which Wood would sit) provided a full and general amnesty permitted them to do so. Lincoln had at once replied that if this meant the Southern States would cease all resistance and re-inaugurate the national authority within their borders,

89. Lincoln, *Collected Works*, VI, 430.
90. Conkling thought someone connected with the Chicago *Tribune* responsible; Lincoln, *Collected Works*, V, 553-554.

the war would cease, and that if an amnesty were necessary to that end, it would be granted. Wood now published this correspondence. It proved nothing except that he had been in touch with unnamed Confederates, and that they had gulled him—for the South was far indeed from submission.

Thereafter, Wood called twice at the White House. Tall, thin, solemn-looking, with dyed hair and dapper dress, he wanted amnesty for not only the Confederates, but for their Northern abettors as well, and permission for Vallandigham to return home. He and his yet more vicious brother Benjamin, owner of the New York *Daily News,*[91] stood for negotiations and a compromise peace. If Lincoln was obliging, he suggested, War Democrats and Peace Democrats would nominate two candidates in 1864! When he called the second time, the Chief Executive brusquely refused to see him. "I am sorry he is here," the President told Nicolay. "I would rather he should not come about here so much."[92]

The President's moderation of temper and language in no way detracted from his iron firmness on all issues relating to an unrelenting prosecution of the war. His utterances consistently tended to strengthen national understanding, unity, and hence vigor. The New York publishers, H.H. Lloyd & Co., delivered an effective stroke when they sold large quantities of a pamphlet, *Lincoln's Letters on National Questions,*[93] at seven-and-a-half cents a copy. Embracing various epistles to Horace Greeley, McClellan, Fernando Wood, J.C. Conkling, and the Albany group headed by Erastus Corning, this brochure presented the argument for the Administration's acts and policies with unmatchable logic and lucidity. The Corning letter, for example, discussed the constitutional issues bound up in Vallandigham's arrest and military trials with a simple directness that appealed to all minds. "Must I shoot a simple-minded soldier-boy who deserts, while I must not touch a hair of a wily agitator who induces him to desert?"[94] Lincoln's reasonableness stood in bright contrast with the angry diatribes that Secretary Chase and Frank Blair were exchanging upon Reconstruction.[95] But the steady recruitment of Union strength and the stern repression of crypto-traitors were subjects upon which Lincoln was adamant. He proved the fact by a thunder peal from the White House on September 15, 1863, his proclamation suspending the writ of habeas corpus, in certain enumerated cases, throughout the country.[96]

"We are quietly jolly over the magnificent news from all round the board," John Hay wrote Nicolay from the White House just after the occupation of

91. Pleasants, Samuel A., *Fernando Wood of New York*, New York, 1948, 137-140.

92. Nicolay, J.G., Personal Memorandum, White House, Dec. 14, 1863; Hay Papers, Illinois State Historical Library.

93. See advertisement in the New York *Press*, October-November, 1863.

94. Lincoln, *Collected Works*, VI, 260-269.

95. For continuation of the Chase-Blair conflict, see the chapter "Cement of the Union" in the succeeding volume of *Ordeal of the Union*.

96. Lincoln, *Collected Works*, VI, 451, 452.

Chattanooga, and just before this proclamation. "You may talk as you please of the Abolition Cabal directing affairs from Washington; some well-meaning news-papers advise the President to keep his fingers out of the military pie: and all that sort of thing. The truth is, if he did, the pie would be a sorry mess. The old man sits here and wields like a backwoods Jupiter the bolts of war and the machinery of government with a hand equally steady and equally firm."[97]

[VI]

By Wednesday morning, October 15, it was known throughout the country that a Union tide had flooded Ohio, Pennsylvania, and Maine. Vallandigham, still lingering in his Canadian exile, was buried beyond sight. Stout John Brough, sweeping both Cuyahoga and Hamilton Counties, with the cities of Cleveland and Cincinnati, had a majority of well over a hundred thousand. The soldier vote, though not needed, had been overwhelmingly in his favor. The lieutenant-colonel of the 116th Ohio indicated the spirit of the balloting when he reported his regimental total as "Brough, 650, The Traitor 70."[98] Secretary Chase had told Lincoln the Friday before election: "I have a great notion to go to Ohio and vote the Union ticket, and if you have nothing in particular for me to do—as the wheels of my department are running quite smoothly just now, and I have laid away $25,000,000 to pay the soldiers on the 1st of November—I believe I will go."[99] He made a stirring speech in Cincinnati, the day before the voting. The Administration was delighted by the outcome. Lincoln, when Brough tele-graphed news of his hundred thousand, flashed back the exultant reply: "Glory to God in the highest. Ohio has saved the nation."[100] Greatest of all, however, was the rejoicing among the soldiers.

"You should have heard the cheering," wrote an officer at Chattanooga on October 18, "to know how Buckeye soldiers opened their mouths and made the welkin ring again and again as one Ohio regiment after another heard the news. We have been very anxious lest. . . . Val would lay claim to the Gub'l Chair of our much-loved State. The anxiety was so great that gloom was apparent, resting on the Army. . . . Now, we are proud that we are Buckeyes; before, we were ashamed."[101]

97. Hay, *Lincoln and the Civil War, op.cit.,* 91; *American Annual Cyclopaedia,* 1863, 731.

98. New York *Tribune,* Oct. 17, 19, 1863. Vallandigham had run the blockade to Bermuda, sailed thence to Halifax, and proceeded to Windsor on Lake Erie, whence he had directed his campaign by letter.

99. Chase reported this in an Indianapolis speech Oct. 14, 1863; New York *Tribune,* October 19, 1863.

100. Lincoln, *Collected Works,* VI, 513; VIII, 524; Hertz, Emanuel, *Abraham Lincoln: A New Portrait,* New York, 1931, II, 914. There is some question of the authenticity of the telegram.

101. Turner, G.B., Chattanooga, Oct. 18, 1863, Ohio Hist. Soc.

In Pennsylvania, soldiers could vote only when given leave to return home. General George H. Thomas evinced anxiety that Pennsylvania troops in the Army of the Cumberland, and especially his own Fourteenth Corps, should get leave, for the soldiers' vote was really needed. The Democrats were restrained by few scruples. On the day before the election, squads of porterhouse politicians from New York descended upon Philadelphia, accompanied by carloads of purchasable vagabonds; and some arrested men confessed that they were expected to act as repeaters, create disturbances, and even smash ballot boxes.[102] Philadelphia, which had voted against Curtin in 1860, gave him a large majority; Pittsburgh and Lancaster increased the vote they had previously given him. Only in the discontented coal-mining counties did the governor's vote fall sharply, and his total majority exceeded 15,000. "All honor to the Keystone State," Stanton telegraphed John W. Forney. "With steel and cannon shot she drove rebel invaders from her soil; and now, in October, she has again rallied for the Union, and overwhelmed the foe at the ballot-box."[103]

In Maine, Cony defeated Bradbury by more than 17,500 votes; in Iowa, the November polling gave the Administration candidate for governor over 86,000 votes against only 56,132 cast for the Democratic candidate;[104] and in Wisconsin the Union nominee won the governorship by 24,000 majority. In Massachusetts, John A. Andrew obtained the largest of his majorities, some 41,000. Indeed, he received twice as many votes as his opponent. In New York, Thurlow Weed's young friend Chauncey M. Depew was elected secretary of state by nearly 30,000 majority, a telling reversal of Horatio Seymour's victory of the previous year. As striking as any other result was Maryland's choice of Union men for four out of five seats (three seats were uncontested) in the House. City after city went Republican. Greeley's *Tribune* listed more than forty, stretching from Augusta, Maine, to Sacramento.[105]

Most important of all, the Union forces had wrested clear control of the House of Representatives from the opposition groups. Political experts listed 90 Republicans and War Democrats, 72 old-style Democrats and John Bell Whigs, and 14 Border State men chosen by a mixed vote.[106] The figures were slightly variable, for some members were singularly nondescript, but on the whole trustworthy.

102. New York *Tribune*, Oct. 17, 1863.
103. Stanton Papers, Oct. 15, 1863, LC; *American Annual Cyclopaedia*, 1863, 740.
104. Hesseltine, William B., *Lincoln and the War Governors*, New York, 1949, 325, 336; *American Annual Cyclopaedia*, 1863, 532, 604.
105. New York *Tribune*, October 19, 1863; *American Annual Cyclopaedia*, 1863, 546, 626, 689; *National Almanac*, 1864, 527.
106. See editorial analysis in New York *Tribune*, Oct. 18, 1863. New York *Tribune Almanac*, 1864, 24, gives 102 Republicans, 75 Democrats, and 9 Border-State men. *National Almanac*, 1864, 78, says parties were so intermingled it was difficult to classify.

"Breaking That Backbone" —a cartoon lithograph by Benjamin Day, 1862

The Emancipation Proclamation, issued to become effective at the beginning of 1863, had indeed helped "break the backbone" of the Confederacy as this cartoon prophesied. It raised the determination of the North; it placed the government in a better light before Europe, thus making foreign intervention more difficult; and it dismayed many Southerners.

Such Border State men as James S. Rollins and Frank Blair of Missouri were certain to give Lincoln staunch support, and it was plain that the Republicans would elect the Speaker.

But only slowly did the voters realize that they had crested a high ridge, named "Democratic Stupidity," which parted the political waters of two generations. Back of them lay the decades stretching from Jefferson and Jackson through Polk's ascendency, when astute leadership had given the Democratic Party a long supremacy; ahead of them lay the decades stretching to Cleveland and Woodrow Wilson, when an able leadership, aided by Democratic blundering, would secure an equally long tenure for the Republicans.

Minuet in Tennessee

[I]

"SO FAR, fairly good," Union leaders could say in the early autumn of 1863 of the military campaigns after Gettysburg and Vicksburg, and "a hopeful prospect," they could add with respect to the political situation as the autumn election of 1863 approached. Yet uncertainty is the dominant note in the brazen throat of war. The Northern troops had also suffered four tragic reverses—a repulse at Battery Wagner on the approaches to Charleston in July (although it was taken in September); a bold enemy raid into Indiana and Ohio; Quantrill's savage massacre at Lawrence, Kansas, in August; and the defeat of Union land and sea forces at Sabine Pass on the Texas coast in September—all of which proved that the North still had heavy blows to take and endure. Meanwhile, under the surface from New England to Iowa, partisan malice and popular resentment of the anxieties, pains, and losses of the struggle, simmered hotly, and threatened, if any new disaster occurred, to boil up alarmingly.

In Mississippi, at last held tight in a Union vise, any such disaster was now impossible. After Lee's advance to a point fairly near Washington in the October Bristoe Station campaign had failed, and Meade once more confronted him in Virginia, a Federal disaster there was most unlikely. Neither general wished to see his artillery mired down in winter mud, and both therefore stood still. But what of Tennessee? Rosecrans and Bragg faced each other there with armies of nearly equal strength. To this theatre, all eyes turned as the storm of war suddenly broke forth over it.

At first, Rosecrans forced the gray columns backward toward the southern boundary of the State; then he pushed them round to the eastward. But the gray host turned at last, surged forward angrily, and struck at him, bringing him to a standstill. The blue-clad troops moved forward again; but once more the Confederates, having received heavy reinforcements which gave them the advantage, became a formidable foe. The Northern armies, in their turn securing immediate accretions of men and materiel, once again were possessed of dominant strength. Back and forth the armies swayed with no certain result. But to anxious onlookers it was a fascinating spectacle, and the convergence upon the scene of a half-dozen armies was highly dramatic. The fact that this scene was critically central, almost half-way between the Mississippi on the west, and the Atlantic on the east, and half-way between the Ohio on the north, and the Gulf on the south, also made the conflict one of serious consequences to both sides. It seemed possible that in this wide, slab-like State the fate of both sections might be largely decided.

The limits of the Confederacy had now been pushed well southward. But like a great rectangular mass of granite, the Volunteer State, old Tennessee, lay squarely across the whole Northern front of the Confederate domain in the West, abutting on six rebel States, and on the vital Union States of Ohio and Kentucky. It had long seemed fated to be an area of combat and slaughter. Historic memories overhung the land. It had long been contested by the Cherokees, the Chickasaws, and the bellicose frontiersmen under John Sevier and Andrew Jackson who held them at bay. Tennessee was a land of striking variegation in geography, climate, scenery, and economic production. East Tennessee, dominated by the Cumberlands, where Mount Mitchell rose higher than New England's Mount Washington, had picturesque mountain stretches full of rich coves and valleys, which gave the talented Mary N. Murfree (writing under the pen-name of Charles Egbert Craddock) the setting for her memorable novels and short stories, such as "The Prophet of the Great Smokies," and "Where the Battle Was Fought," dealing with the bloody field of Murfreesboro. Middle Tennessee, with the broad basin containing Nashville, was much like the placid Ohio country; and West Tennessee, picturesque with its river valleys, lakes, swamps and low, flat plains adapted to cotton, had a fertile warmth akin to that of the Deep South. This same variegation marked the cities of the three belts, Knoxville in the east, Nashville in the middle, and Memphis in the west, three towns nearly as diverse in ideas and customs as if they lay in far-separated sections.

Knoxville, a town which Americans had known longest, for it was named after Washington's Secretary of War, had been the first capital of the State, drawing from the valleys and misty peaks about it a highland sternness. It had long been full of pioneers with hunting shirts and long rifles, blanket-clad Indians, hard-eyed frontier hunters and gamblers, bustling fur-traders and land speculators. In this area, Andrew Johnson rose to prominence and power. Here, Baptist and Methodist exhorters preached dogmatic Scriptural injunctions; but here, too, corn-whiskey, peach brandy and the violent diversions of the frontier were in constant employment. The shallow Tennessee River rippled over its rocky bed past a business district, and at one time a little "university" that obstinately refused to yield to poverty. Even when Lincoln was elected five years after the first railroad puffed in from Chattanooga, all of Knox County had fewer than 23,000 people. A majority were simple country folk who shocked Northern visitors by their illiteracy, ignorance, uncouth manners, and grimy mountain dress. Many women "dipped" snuff, after the regional custom. The highland area, nevertheless, appealed to Northerners because most of the people detested slaveholders and slavery. They loyally supported the Union, so that, of the 32,000 Federal soldiers recorded from Tennessee, the majority came from the eastern part of the State.[1]

Memphis was the metropolis of an equally distinctive district. West Tennessee had been so promptly overrun by Union forces that by 1863 it was seldom in the news, but everybody soon knew that the cotton counties in the hot, humid Mississippi Valley had been a hotbed of rebel feeling. Although Memphis had not been laid out until 1819, rich slave-grown crops and Mississippi trade had made it strong and prosperous. Its Egyptian name was appropriate to a city on a wide muddy river which sent annual floods across alluvial lands. Here dwelt, instead of plain farmers and sturdy mountaineers, a poor-white folk who responded to such fundamentalist parsons as William G. Brownlow, together with a prouder community of steamboat owners, merchants trading with St. Louis and New Orleans, bankers who studied Liverpool prices, and such slave-traders as the brilliant Nathan Bedford Forrest. Memphis knew well the cotton-gin, the whip and hoe, the auction block, and the disruption of sad-eyed Negro families. By 1861, handsome mansions stood in well-shaded streets, well-dressed children crowded into fashionable schools, and merchants in linen and broadcloth bustled from the Cotton Exchange into the parlors of the dignified Gayoso Hotel. Since 1857, Memphis had been the terminus of a line which its citizens expected to become one of the nation's greatest railroads, the Mississippi & Charleston. Newspapers and, in time, novelists publicized its Smoky Row, a street that sheltered gamblers, thieves, prostitutes, and quarrelsome flat-boat men. Though aristocratic planters, lawyers, and traders might give a thin gilding to the motley population of nearly 23,000 people in 1860, Memphis had become noted for its frequent brawls and homicides, its bullies, racial quarrels, lynching parties, and outbreaks of disease. Forrest thwarted one Memphis mob intent on hanging a captive;[2] in post-war years the town's great yellow-fever epidemic of 1878 was to become internationally famous, and later still, the novelist Faulkner was to make it the scene of one of his most horrifying books.

---

1. So says W.R. Carter in his *History of the First Regiment of Tennessee Volunteer Cavalry,* Knoxville, 1902, raised under Robert Johnson, son of Andrew Johnson. *O.R.,* I, xxiii, Pt.2, 28-29, 572-574, 622, 873; Dyer, Frederick H., *A Compendium of the War of the Rebellion,* Des Moines, 1908, II; *Tennesseans in the Civil War,* Nashville, 1964, Pt.I, I.
2. Lytle, Andrew Nelson, *Bedford Forrest and His Critter Company,* New York, 1931, 24-27.

[II]

In the summer of 1863, it was Middle Tennessee upon which the eyes of the nation fastened—the central belt of the State, from Nashville on the winding Cumberland in the north, to Chattanooga on the mountain-girt Tennessee in the south. During the Revolution one branch of the Cherokees, rejecting a treaty with the settlers, had trudged westward to establish villages on Chickamauga Creek, and the traders who followed them first heard the name destined to be famous in military history. The basin about Nashville, and the wide lands stretching southward into the craggy Cumberlands, differed greatly in aspect from the Chickamauga country. They were alike, however, in being a district of small holdings, where the farmers worked in the fields beside their Negroes, and the typical dwelling was a "dog-run" house with a kitchen on one side, living rooms on the other, and a breezeway between. It was one happy feature of the war that it showed many soldiers a wealth of beautiful scenery they might otherwise never have viewed. The lovely Shenandoah country, with its rhododendrons, dogwood, and bright blossoms of mixed white and yellow in the spring; the flaming maples, birches, and sumac of the Blue Ridge, Alleghenies, and upper Potomac in autumn; the rugged heights above Harper's Ferry, their grandeur extolled by Jefferson; the coastal reaches of the Carolinas, with their splendid seascapes; the stretches along the fertile, tangled Yazoo, with great trees and thick bushes stretching their webs above the channel along which the gunboats struggled; the fertile prairies of western Louisiana, seamed with rivers and streamlets—all these came as revelations to the men under arms. One officer from Maine, O.O. Howard, to whom these States were Far West, writing of the great reception his troops received in Ohio and Indiana, called Richmond, Indiana, "a gem of a place!"[3] His troops previously had had no idea of the surpassing beauty of the countryside. Volunteers of manifold origin found Nashville, in spite of its clouds of blinding limestone dust, its little frame houses, its ugly and ill-managed hotels which some thought the worst in the world, a city of many fine aspects, with a lofty State capitol recalling the lines of the Parthenon, numerous well-built mansions, and thrifty outlying farmhouses. The blue-clad fighters from distant States, who carried their bayonets into the mountains and ravines about Chattanooga, realized that they had reached one of the most picturesque parts of the nation.

"In one view," Rawlins wrote his bride of a month, "you behold the mountains of several states. . . . The mountains to the east and southeast of Lookout, which stands peerless amid its neighbors, so lift themselves up from Lookout that one at first mistakes them for clouds far above the horizon. Throughout this vast

---

3. Howard, O.O., *Autobiography,* New York, 1907, I, 453-455. See also *With Sword and Olive Branch,* by John A. Carpenter, Pittsburgh, 1964, 12ff.

system of mountains, the magnificent Tennessee meanders to every point of the compass, and perhaps from no point does it present so picturesque and grandly beautiful an appearance as from the top of Lookout."[4] The Cumberland Mountains crowd in together at the point where Tennessee, Alabama, and Georgia join, several ranges clustering close to each other. Here the Tennessee breaks through scarp and ravines in a general southwest course, but with so many convolutions that, in a dozen miles as the hawk flies, it bends in almost every direction. As it dips down near the southern boundary of Tennessee as if to touch the northeast apex of Georgia, it encloses a loop of land shaped like a moccasin, and so named. Near the toe of the moccasin, south of the general course of the river, lies Chattanooga. It is belted with heights on all sides, some of the ridges rising a thousand feet above the river, while the peaks lift still higher. Missionary Ridge stands on one side, Lookout Mountain on another, and Raccoon Ridge in still a third. A bit of lofty tableland, a contracted eyrie overlooking the valley, gives room for Chattanooga, which, in the Cherokee language, meant "the hawk's nest,"—mistranslated "eagle's nest"—and in the Creek tongue was "the rock that comes to a point."[5]

It was Lookout Mountain, as Rawlins wrote, that dominated the scene, rising downstream from Chattanooga on the left bank of the Tennessee, due south from the toe of the moccasin, and hence southeast of the town. This striking natural monument was rather a long ridge than a mountain—a high, rocky, thickly-wooded wall, striking from Tennessee across the upper corner of Georgia and far on into Alabama. It abutted so closely upon the river, and made so steep a descent, that it had perplexed engineers to lay a railroad bed between it and the rushing waters. To this railway line, extending up past Chattanooga, the railroaders added a narrow wagon-track. The town was thus boxed in. The looping Tennessee flowed past it on the north and west, Lookout loomed steeply above it on the southeast, and a ridge, named for the apostles sent out by the Presbyterian-Congregational Missionary Board to convert the Indians, rose on the east. A traveller standing in the center of Chattanooga would have nonplused any citizen by asking how he could best reach the outside world by horse and buggy. "If you don't mind a rough lane of rock and gravel," he would be told, "you can get out toward Alabama across the upper end of Lookout yonder. Or there is a still worse road leading south around Missionary Ridge into Georgia, or one still more wretched going north beyond the river toward Nashville."

Before the summer of 1863, a little history had already been made hereabouts. Not far below Chattanooga lay the hamlet of Rossville, commemorating the last

4. Wilson, James Harrison, *The Life of John A. Rawlins,* New York, 1916, 389.
5. Govan, Gilbert and James Livingood, *The Chattanooga Country, 1540-1951 . . .,* New York, 1952, 21, 220.

great Cherokee chief, John Ross. Some houses built by missionaries still stood. The wild district, however, never cared much about the past. When John Howard Payne toured the Cherokee nation in northwestern Georgia to collect its folklore, the Georgia Militia arrested him, a colonel alleging that his notes upon Indian legends were treasonable. Although Payne was set free, he lost most of his papers.[6] Nashville to the north was proud of the homes of William Walker, the late filibuster, and of John Bell, a candidate in 1860 for president. It boasted above all of Jackson's Hermitage, not far distant. But since the battle of Stone River, and the capture of Vicksburg, the vital question was of the history still to be made. Could the army of the Cumberland, after taking Nashville, and pushing on to the south, while holding the Confederates at Tullahoma, push forward to unlock the gateway at Chattanooga? For here was one of the most important railway centers of the continent, with lines radiating to Montgomery, Atlanta, Wilmington, and Richmond. The two generals, Rosecrans and Bragg, would answer this question.

[III]

Nobody doubted that William S. Rosecrans was a man of remarkable talents. An Ohioan, now forty-three, his career had been marked by enterprise; he was a versatile West Pointer who had resigned from the army to engage in engineering work, coal-mining and Ohio River traffic, and who, when the war began, had quit an oil business to reënter the army. He had risen rapidly to a brigadier generalship, and commanded the Department of Western Virginia when that area became a new State. Energy stamped his erect, sturdy form, his voice, and his manner. "He had a clear, mild blue eye which lights up under excitement until it can flash fire," wrote a correspondent of the New York *Herald.* "In conversation, his face is illumined by a peculiarly winning smile, and an eye shining with mirth ... You would trust that face in a stranger as thoroughly true, full of character and reserved power. His talk is like it: direct, frank, overflowing with humor, or strong in emphasis."[7] He liked his own way, meant to have it, and being deficient in tact, was ready to bicker with anyone in authority who urged a different course.

A tremendous worker, Rosecrans was usually at his desk by ten in the morning, and stayed there until midnight, or after; on occasion until four A.M. next day. His aides sometimes dropped asleep in their chairs while he toiled on. In the field, he was often the first man in camp to spring from his blankets. Insisting on efficiency, he was also a highly systematic worker. When he took charge of the Army of the Cumberland, he at once reorganized the staff-work, which he

6. "Chattanooga And How We Held It," *Harper's Magazine,* XXXVI, Jan. 1868, 137-149.
7. New York *Herald,* April 10, 1863.

put in the hands of men quick, sharp, and toughminded; he collected military maps from every source, and sent out scouts to improve them; he called in Union men to give him information on topography, roads, and the movements of the enemy; and he established courier lines with all the camps. He made it a fixed rule that no officer might take a furlough or resign if in health. At the same time, he was inexorable in getting rid of incompetents. "I don't care for any individual," he would say. "Everything for the service; nothing for individuals." He liked young men, full of snap, who thought quickly and executed orders without delay. "Young men without experience are better than experienced old men," he would say; "young men will learn."[8] His sternness of temper sometimes blazed out in a fit of anger, particularly when slovenliness or inaccuracy offended his conviction that war should be an exact science. A subordinate who handed him an inaccurate report witnessed an explosion: "How do you know this? How did your informant know? Why didn't you get all the particulars? What are you an officer for? It's your business to know—war means killing!" He spent much time among his troops, scrutinizing their equipment with searching minuteness. Punctilious in saluting privates, he would pounce on any man with a defective canteen, knapsack, or bayonet. "Your captain wouldn't get you a better one?— that's no excuse! Demand what you need, and go to him every day till you get it. Bore him for it. Bore him in his quarters, bore him at meals, bore him on parade!" He would shame an officer in front of his command: "You make a poor statement of facts." "Your knowledge of geography is bad—you don't observe closely."[9] Such a commander was sure to whip his army into finely disciplined condition. A. D. Richardson, the New York *Tribune* correspondent, wrote his managing editor in the spring of 1863 that Rosecrans's force was in such splendid condition, so full of fight, faith, and zeal, that it did him good to look at it. "It is wonderful how enthusiastically everyone believes in him. The mere moral effect of his presence in a battle would be worth 30,000 men to this army. And he impresses me as a pure, earnest, strong man."[10]

With all his strength, he had weaknesses of temperament. Although his zeal in preparing for battle was admirable and his energy in action inspiring, he was deficient in the hard, unrelenting persistence that stamped Grant. At Iuka, Rosecrans had defeated Price, but the Confederate force had slipped away. At Corinth he was victorious in defending the important center against Van Dorn's attack, but to Grant's great dissatisfaction he made nothing of the advantages he had gained. Of Iuka, Grant wrote: "I ordered pursuit by the whole of Rosecrans's command, and went on with him a few miles in person. He followed only a few miles after I left him and then went into camp, and the pursuit was continued

8. Bickham, William D., *Rosecrans's Campaign*, Cincinnati, 1863, *passim*.
9. *Ibid.*
10. A.D. Richardson to S.H. Gay, April 11, 1863, Gay Papers, Columbia University.

no further." Of Corinth, he wrote that it was "a decided victory, though not so complete as I had hoped for, nor nearly so complete as I now think was within the easy grasp of the commanding officer."[11]

More important, and much more a key trait, was a certain nervous excitability that in ordinary moments contributed to his winning traits—his flashing eye, his overflowing talk, his irrepressible activity—but in time of crisis became a liability. This it was that caused General John M. Palmer[12] to think him "facile, easily led;" that made him now considerate, now roughly overbearing in his attitude toward subordinates, and that led him, as we shall see, to overleap a prudent goal in victory and to give way to panicky apprehension in defeat. His emotionalism found expression in a wide range of enthusiasms—for nature, which he studied closely, for science, for art, and for literature, which he read more widely than most officers. It made religion a passion; a devout Roman Catholic, converted at West Point, he tried to go to Mass twice weekly, disliked military operations on Sunday, and showed zest and skill in theological disputation. Emotionalism, however, is not a desirable trait in a general. One coldly analytical observer, Henry Villard, found him gentlemanly in manners and volubly persuasive in talk, but excessively critical of Halleck and Stanton, confident that he would yet be recognized as the ablest of all Union generals, and while vain enough to fancy himself commanding all the armies, lacking in pluck to make a prompt attack on Bragg.[13]

The character of the Confederate leader was less complicated but equally interesting. Bragg, who succeeded Beauregard as commander in Kentucky and Tennessee four months before Rosecrans succeeded Buell, was only about three years older; but he had emerged from West Point in time to fight in the Seminole and Mexican Wars, winning three brevets, and might call himself the more experienced fighter. The first pitched battle between the two generals at Stone River (or Murfreesboro) was inconclusive, neither accomplishing what he had hoped or his people had expected. The Confederates won a tactical victory on the field, but the Union army gained a strategic victory in the campaign.[14] After his enforced retreat to Tullahoma, Bragg, comprehending that his failure had angered the South, sent his corps and division commanders a pointed inquiry respecting their opinion of his strategic capacities and recent movements.[15] Lieutenant-General W.J. Hardee consulted Major-Generals John C. Breckinridge and Patrick R. Cleburne. Hardee's reply was crisp: "I feel that frankness compels me

11. Grant, *Personal Memoirs*, I, 413, 419, 420; Lamers, William E., *The Edge of Glory, A Biography of W.S. Rosecrans, U.S.A.*, New York, 1961, 122-130, 154-158, defends Rosecrans.
12. To his wife, Oct. 20, 1863; Palmer Papers, Illinois State Historical Library.
13. Villard, Henry, *Memoirs of Henry Villard*, Boston, 1904, II, 64-68.
14. Otis, Ephraim A., "The Murfreesboro Campaign," *Papers of the Military Historical Society of Massachusetts*, Vol.VII, 318-320.
15. For text, *O.R.*, I, xx, Pt.I, 699.

to say that the general officers, whose judgment you have invoked, are unanimous in their opinion that a change in the command of this army is necessary. In this opinion I concur."[16] Lieutenant-General Leonidas Polk made an equivocal answer, and then wrote President Davis that it would be well to appoint Joseph E. Johnston in place of Bragg, removing the latter to Richmond to employ his talents for organization and discipline in the War Department.[17]

The fact was that too much had been expected of the tall, ungainly, brusque officer, harsh in speech and tactless in demeanor, who had taken charge of the Army of Tennessee in the early summer of 1862. The South knew that he had distinguished himself as an artillery officer at Buena Vista, and had led the Confederate right at Shiloh with such energy that he claimed credit for most of the successes of the first day's battle. It knew that he was a stern disciplinarian and had been a hard student of the art of war; but it was not yet aware how much self-distrust underlay his notorious irascibility. He was probably too hesitant to succeed in any circumstances, but the general Confederate disability—too few men too thinly placed and too erratically controlled by the high command in Richmond—defeated one chance of success after another. He marched into Kentucky late that summer with too few men, moving too late because of shortages in transport, and he used his troops for a political object, a futile effort to bring Kentucky manpower into the Confederate ranks, when he should have concentrated upon military goals alone. When he encountered his first severe test of generalship in manoeuvring against Buell, he disappointed his fellow officers. Advancing between Buell and Louisville, he threw away a priceless opportunity to capture the city, and left Buell unharmed.[18]

When, later, a larger and better-armed Union army advanced against him at Stone River, Bragg was all too conscious that he was outnumbered and outgunned. His attacks the first day were so magnificently effective, pressing the Union troops back to their last defensive line, that Rosecrans hesitated that night whether to remain on the field. Bragg also did well on the second day of fighting. Then, apprehensive that after their sickening losses his tired men might be crushingly overpowered, he became irresolute. Richmond waited in vain for news that he had followed up his early successes. Instead, it heard that he had broken off the battle and was retreating. As he had fallen back from Perryville to northern Tennessee, so now he fell back to Tullahoma. Hence the loud chorus of southern criticism, and his petulant circular-letter to his generals.[19]

If Rosecrans was too nervously excitable, Bragg was too coldly harsh. From the day he left West Point, his reputation was that of a rough, conscientious, and brutally rigid officer. He took life with Cromwellian seriousness, and was deter-

16. *Ibid.*, 683.
17. Polk, William M., *Leonidas Polk: Bishop and General,* New York, 1915, Vol.II, 206-207.
18. *Ibid.*, II, 128ff; Polk scathingly indicts his hesitancies.
19. Seitz, Don C., *Braxton Bragg, General of the Confederacy,* Columbia, S.C., 1924, 237-270.

mined to make his associates face its responsibilities unflinchingly. His classmate Hooker spoke of his constant fault-finding: "Free to express his opinion on all occasions and all subjects. . . .he appeared to be conscious of his own rectitude, and therefore free in approving or condemning the acts of others."[20] Anecdotes of his stiff rudeness became common. While he was serving at Fort Moultrie in 1845, an officer accosted him in the sutler's quarters with the greeting: "Lieutenant Bragg! A glass of wine with you, sir!" Bragg made a surly reply: "Colonel Gates, if you order me to drink a glass of wine with you, I shall have to do it."[21] Grant relates as an illustration of Bragg's disputatious temper that once, early in his career, when he was acting company commander and acting quartermaster, he gave himself an order in one capacity, rejected it in the other, and filled up a sheet with peppery exchanges. "My God, Mr. Bragg," said the post-commander when he saw it, "you have quarreled with every officer in the army, and now you are quarreling with yourself!"[22]

Grateful though Colonel Jefferson Davis was for the aid of his guns at Buena Vista, even he viewed Bragg with some concern.[23] But the man was guilty of graver offences than censoriousness and rudeness. After Leonidas Polk, ordered to Richmond by the President, had given Davis an unfavorable report on the conduct of the Kentucky campaign, Bragg wrote to a number of generals in an abortive effort to collect evidence upon which he might base an arrest of Polk, and order a courtmartial trial for alleged disobedience to orders.[24]

Altogether, Bragg was a faithful, hardworking mediocrity, a martinet devoted to detail but totally devoid of vision, and a man of duty who liked to make duty singularly disagreeable to others. We may admire his bravery and fortitude, his cool self-possession in battle, and his capacity for routine labor, without losing our conviction that President Davis would have done far better to leave the brilliant Beauregard, for all his temperamental faults and grandiose schemes, in command of the Army of Tennessee.

[IV]

All winter and spring in 1863, Rosecrans irritated Grant and his fellow-generals in front of Vicksburg, provoked the War Department, and distressed his own chief-of-staff, James A. Garfield, by his refusal to develop an offensive. He lay inactive for nearly six months, grumbled Halleck, *preparing* to move. "When a large part of Bragg's army was detached against Grant in Mississippi, Rosecrans was repeatedly urged to attack Bragg in his weakened condition, but he would

20. *Ibid.*, 3.
21. *Ibid.*, 4.
22. Grant, U.S., "Chattanooga," *Battles and Leaders*, III, 710.
23. Seitz, *Bragg*, *op.cit.*, 18.
24. *O.R.*, I, xvi, Pt.i, 1097-1112; Polk, *Polk*, *op.cit.*, II, 164-167.

not do so, preferring to wait until Bragg was again reinforced."[25] Grant kept urging Halleck to get Rosecrans in motion, but the latter persistently made the inane response that it was a military maxim not to fight two decisive battles at the same time; as if winning two victories simultaneously would be unfortunate![26] Garfield, though a warm admirer of his chief, chafed more and more anxiously for an advance. Early in May he thought the army quite ready. "From all present indications," he wrote on the 4th, "it cannot be long before we meet the rebel army now in our front and try its strength again. When the day comes it bids fair to be the bloodiest fighting of the war. One thing is settled in my mind: direct blows at the rebel army—bloody fighting—is all that can end the rebellion."[27] He continued writing his friends in the same vein. But Rosecrans still wrangled with the War Department, and in his talks with Henry Villard abused both Stanton and Halleck in highly improper language.[28]

By early June, Rosecrans had to admit that, far from holding Bragg's entire force in leash, he had permitted that general, by his inaction, to reinforce Johnston. Yet still he found excuses for delay. He sent all his division and corps commanders on June 8 a confidential letter asking them to answer three questions which really boiled down to one: Was an immediate advance against Bragg advisable? Once more, their replies proved the truth of the military adage that councils of war never fight. The seventeen commanders agreed almost unanimously that it was unwise to give battle at this time. "No one thinks an advance advisable until Vicksburg's fate is determined," he notified Halleck.[29] Garfield was sunk in a sense of mortification and chagrin. For a fortnight he had been writing friends that before they received his letter they would hear that the army was on the march; he had been making his last personal preparations, and commending his cause and himself to God. "Now I write to tell you that I have given up all hope of either fighting or dying *at present.* . . The chessboard is indeed muddled and no man sees through it."[30] Resentfully, he prepared a memorandum showing that it would be possible to launch an effective army of 65,217 against Bragg's force of 41,680, and setting forth the reasons which made an early thrust strategically desirable. At the same time, Garfield told Rosecrans he thought it had been wise to delay a general movement hitherto, but now the army was ready for an immediate advance.[31]

Finally, the angry War Department took an imperative stand. Halleck tele-

25. Halleck to Lieber, Oct. 13, 1863, Lieber Papers, HEH.
26. Grant, *Memoirs, op.cit.,* II, 20.
27. Smith, Theodore Clarke, *The Life and Letters of James Abram Garfield,* New Haven, 1929, I, 202.
28. Villard, *Memoirs, op.cit.,* II, 66.
29. *O.R.,* I, xxiii, Pt.i, 8.
30. Smith, T.C., *Garfield, op.cit.,* I, 300-302.
31. *O.R.,* I, xxiii, Pt.2, 378-379, 420-424, 873; Smith, *Garfield,* I, 300-302.

graphed Rosecrans June 16: "Is it your intention to make an immediate movement forward? A definite answer 'Yes' or 'No' is required." The general replied that with five days more he could answer yes. He took seven, but on June 24 wired back: "The army begins to move at three o'clock this morning."[32]

For his irritating delays Rosecrans kept protesting that he had ample grounds. He wrote Lincoln that, although Stanton had assured him just after Stone's River that he and his command could have anything they wanted, the Secretary had then refused or ignored a series of requests. "I hate injustice," observed Rosecrans, who believed Stanton was personally hostile, and let Lincoln and Halleck as well as Tom, Dick, and Harry, know it. Like McClellan, he believed that his preparations for the offensive must be complete to the last axe and mule-shoe. Over and over again, he asked for cavalry horses. He employed a cloud of spies, using them and his scouts to survey minutely the roads and hills in front, and to get the last word on enemy numbers. He knew that Bragg had strongly fortified his front at Tullahoma and Shelbyville, and when he questioned his generals upon the wisdom of an advance, he let them suppose he was planning a frontal attack, although his superior numbers gave him ample means to use a flanking strategy.

With much reason, too, he constantly assured Halleck that his problems of logistics were appallingly difficult. From his base at Louisville to the area about Tullahoma, by way of Nashville, was some 260 miles. His army had to transport all its subsistence, clothing, camp equipment, ammunition, and other materiel over this half-hostile stretch of territory by rail, guarding every bridge and trestle.[33] And what a railroad! Some officers said they would as soon face another battle as a trip over the Louisville & Nashville. As he pushed beyond Tullahoma, he would confront the rough peaks and ravines of the Cumberland Mountains, for the most part threaded only by wretched cart-tracks and byways; the mountains that divide the Cumberland and Tennessee Rivers, with ridges 2,000 feet high.

These excuses may have been rationalizations to conceal his real motives. Henry Villard thought so; he wrote that a memory of the hard fighting of Stone River, the Southern valor, and the narrow escape from defeat, haunted Rosecrans, robbed him of pluck, and made him unwilling to fight without overwhelming superiority.[34] However this may be, the course of events proved Rosecrans wrong. He enjoyed a clear superiority of force in the spring and early summer, as Garfield showed. His delays gave Bragg opportunity to detach three divisions —two of infantry with artillery, one of cavalry—to reinforce Joseph E. Johnston who had been ordered to Mississippi May 9 to take command there, a loss which

32. *O.R.*, I, xxiii, Pt.1, 5-10.
33. See Rosecrans, Aug. 1, 1863, Winchester, Tenn., to Halleck in Extra-Illustrated *Battles & Leaders*, XII, facing p.678, HEH; *O.R.*, I, xxiii, Pt.2, 146-147.
34. Villard, *Memoirs, op.cit.*, II, 68; Lamers, *Edge of Glory, op.cit.*, 244-273.

Richmond later repaired by sending Longstreet with his corps from Virginia to strengthen Bragg. If Rosecrans had moved promptly, Bragg would not have helped Johnston, and the battle of Chickamauga would have been fought without Longstreet; it would therefore probably have been won, not lost, by the Union, provided Bragg would have attacked at all. No less able a strategist than General Jacob D. Cox declares: "If a brilliant victory at Chickamauga had been coincident with the fall of Vicksburg and Lee's defeat at Gettysburg, it does not seem rash to believe that the collapse of the Confederacy would have been hastened by a year."[35]

But once started, Rosecrans brilliantly executed his brief Tullahoma campaign. His department counted more than 90,000 men in infantry, cavalry, and artillery, so that even after leaving heavy garrisons in Nashville and Murfreesboro, he had about 62,500 men "present for duty, equipped"; an army inferior to the Confederates only in guns, which counted little in this rough terrain, and decisively superior in every other respect. "When we do advance," confided an Illinois colonel to his wife, "we will take all before us, and do it too, without coming in contact with their principal batteries."[36] They moved on a front of about fifty miles. Bragg had no choice but to evacuate his fortifications at Tullahoma, for Rosecrans could easily have swung his right and left wings about and bagged all the defenders. The Confederates had to abandon siege-guns, tents, and provisions. Once Tullahoma was taken on June 30, Rosecrans paused for a reorganization of his army, its supply system, and its rail facilities before a further advance on Chattanooga. The new wait seemed needless to Garfield, for while Bragg's army was utterly disheartened, the Union troops were eager to fight. After the bridges were rebuilt and the railroad from the Cumberland to the Tennessee was fully opened, Rosecrans still delayed. In vain did Garfield urge him to press forward before Johnston could send reinforcements. The future President wrote Secretary Chase that he was profoundly depressed, for his commander was incomprehensibly reluctant to grasp his rare opportunities.[37]

Washington was equally disturbed, and Halleck sent Rosecrans one of his tartest letters. He wrote that it was wrong to think, and much more to assert, that Stanton cherished some personal antagonism; he had none—but neither he nor Lincoln liked the general's incessant delays. They had manifested deep disappointment and dissatisfaction, and had repeatedly urged Halleck to push the army on into East Tennessee. After declaring that many of Rosecrans's dispatches had been highly annoying, Halleck added a sentence which contained

35. Cox, Jacob Dolson, *Military Reminiscences of the Civil War*, I, 480-482.
36. Col. James I. Davidson, 73rd Illinois Volunteers, June 11, 1863, Davidson Papers, Alabama State Archives.
37. July 27, 1863; Smith, T.C., *Garfield, op.cit.*, I, 309-310.

one of Lincoln's favorite similes. "No doubt such was not your intention, but they certainly have been calculated to convey the impression that you were not disposed to carry out the wishes of the Dept. at least in the *manner* and at the *time* desired. It is said that you do not draw straight in the traces, but are continually kicking out, or getting one leg over."[38]

Yet when Rosecrans did resume his march, it was with irresistible effect. He made full reconnaissances, repaired the roads, used his cavalry to threaten Bragg's rear, and got the railway to Stevenson and Bridgeport running smoothly. Crossing the Tennessee below Bragg's army in Chattanooga, he placed the Confederate leader in a dilemma; he could either withstand a siege in Chattanooga, or evacuate it and manoeuvre in the open. If he relinquished the city without a battle, he would face a storm of popular denunciation. But with the example of Vicksburg before his eyes, Bragg wisely did what Pemberton had failed to do: he retired in time, moving southeast into Georgia as if bound for Dalton, and protecting his rear by strong guards in the mountain passes.

Thus it was that on September 9, 1863, troops of the division commanded by Thomas L. Crittenden, son of Senator John J. Crittenden, entered Chattanooga. Seven days earlier Burnside's Army of the Ohio, about 20,000 strong, had captured Knoxville, flinging part of Buckner's defenders westward and part northward. As Rosecrans pushed on toward Ringgold in Georgia, high rose the exultation of the North. "After Chattanooga," said men, "Atlanta!" Most observers expected Rosecrans to advance directly down the Western & Atlantic Railroad to the Georgia center, and Greeley's *Tribune* led a chorus of optimists counting their chickens before they were hatched. "Atlanta is the last link which binds together the southwestern and northeastern sections of the Rebel Confederacy," it proclaimed. "Break it, and these sections fall asunder."[39] Already the conquest of Chattanooga and Knoxville had severed the northerly railway route between Montgomery and Richmond. Seize Atlanta, and the southerly line running from Montgomery through Augusta, Ga., and Weldon, N.C. into the Confederate capital would also be cut. Rosecrans would then have isolated Mississippi, Alabama, and Georgia from the Carolinas and Virginia.

The hopes of Union leaders, however, outraced their powers. Southern desperation and grit matched Northern exultation. It was in full realization that the fate of the Confederacy depended upon his next blow that, while New York and Chicago echoed to cheers for Rosecrans, Bragg struck, and struck hard. As one of the Southern officers later wrote, the Rebels were tired of running and were turning on their pursuers.[40] Along the creek that drained the deep forest south-

38. Rosecrans Papers, UCLA Library; copy in Halleck letters, Eldredge Collection, HEH.
39. Formby, John, *The American Civil War*, New York, 1910, 263.
40. Wyeth, John A., *Life of General Nathan Bedford Forrest*, New York, 1899, 242.

east of Chattanooga sounded the Rebel yell, as when Stonewall Jackson had marched his veterans in the grim devoted spirit of Cromwell's ironsides:

> Silence! ground arms! kneel all! caps off!
> Old Massa's goin' to pray!
> Strangle the fool that dares to scoff!
> Attention! it's his way.
> Appealing from his native sod,
> In *forma pauperis* to God:
> "Lay bare Thine arm; stretch forth Thy rod!
> Amen!" That's "Stonewall's way."[41]

Before this time, the high command in Washington, as Rosecrans believed, should have sent reinforcements to the perilously exposed army, but it failed to do so. After crossing three mountainous ridges and a wide river, clearing middle Tennessee of the enemy without a serious engagement, and triumphantly occupying Chattanooga, meanwhile capturing 1,600 prisoners and three guns, Rosecrans had overreached himself. Unfortunately for him, the long high block of Lookout Mountain in his front as he flanked Chattanooga had been traversable for his three corps only by three passes, spaced at intervals of about twenty-five miles in the rough country. The army had thus emerged on the far side, facing the Georgia towns of Ringgold and Dalton, divided into three parts, its right and left extremes about fifty miles asunder. In his newfound impetuosity, Rosecrans accepted as true the first reports from his extended front that Bragg was in hurried retreat through these places toward Rome, sixty miles from Chattanooga; and instead of concentrating his scattered troops to guard the vital railroad center he had won, he ordered them to keep on. It was Bragg who concentrated, and who now attacked.

Usually deliberate and careful, Rosecrans in his hour of victory fell victim to his fatal trait of nervous exaltation; he fancied himself hammering at the gates of Atlanta. His deployment upon such a broad front would have been dangerous even had he kept his superiority in strength. But he had not done this, for Bragg had been so heavily reinforced that he now possessed about 65,000 men to meet Rosecrans's 60,000. He had been reinforced, too, by veterans. Part of Buckner's troops from East Tennessee had come in; remnants of the Mississippi army, including many men who had been released from Grant's parole, were arriving by every train; and as battle ensued, two splendid divisions of Longstreet's battle-hardened corps, some 12,000 troops, reached the scene. Halleck denounced this release of Vicksburg parolees as a gross violation of the laws of war. Longstreet

41. Palmer, John W., "Stonewall Jackson's Way," from *Poems of the Civil War*, in *American Poetry*, ed. Percy H. Boynton, New York, 1918, 328.

himself had proposed this dramatic transfer over the battered railroads, pressing it earnestly upon Seddon. Lee, perhaps with regret for his veto of a similar movement in July, had approved it, bidding his best remaining lieutenant good-bye with the words: "Now, General, you beat those people out of the West."[42]

In mobilizing locomotives, cars, and other rail facilities, Frederick W. Sims made admirably thorough arrangements. Quartermaster-General Alexander R. Lawton also performed well. Hood's division led the way, and Henry L. Benning's brigade, in the van, reached Atlanta after a ride of nearly four days, the shorter route through Tennessee having been blocked by Federal seizure of Knoxville. Perforce using this roundabout southerly route, Sims divided the traffic from Virginia to Atlanta between the Raleigh-Charlotte-Columbia line, 705 miles long, and the Wilmington-Florence line, 755 miles long. Extended troop trains and horse trains rumbled over the uneven ties and tracks of varying gauges. On September 14, some 1,700 men, with mounts, rolled through Charlotte; on the 15th, some 500; on the 17th, about 2,000. Crammed into box-cars and stock-cars, sitting or lying on flatcars, or if lucky enjoying coach seats, the soldiers enlivened the hours with jest and song. The rudest jokes were at the expense of the few civilian passengers and the pretty girls who offered refreshments.

By the morning of the 18th, three brigades, or 4,500 men, had arrived at Bragg's front, marching from the trains at the wooden platform called Catoosa Station. Two o'clock the next afternoon saw Longstreet climb wearily from the cars, wait for his horses, get lost in finding Bragg's headquarters and finally arrive at 11 P.M. of the night before the major fighting. Many of the troops that were hurried out of Richmond arrived in time to fight in the battle.[43] So defective was the Northern intelligence service that on September 11, when the transfer of Longstreet's men had been under way for two days, if not three, Halleck telegraphed Rosecrans that, according to deserters, part of Bragg's army was reinforcing Lee! He exhorted Rosecrans to hold the mountain passes against the return of Bragg's troops, and to ascertain the truth about an augmentation of the Army of Northern Virginia.[44]

One of the hardest battles of the entire conflict, in which both sides fought with what seemed unsurpassable valor, thus impended—the battle of Chickamauga. It was remarkable not only for its dramatic character as a tremendous attack by the Confederates which drove the Union forces back, and seemed for a time likely to cut off their retreat and defeat them decisively, and for its

---

42. Longstreet, James, *From Manassas to Appomattox*, Philadelphia, 1896, 437.

43. See admirable account of the rail operation in Black, R.C., *Railroads of the Confederacy*, Chapel Hill, 1952, 176-192; Longstreet, *op.cit.*, 437-438.

44. Greeley, Horace, *The American Conflict*, Hartford, 1867, II, 414; Halleck's Report, *O.R.*, I, xxx, Pt.i, 34.

desperately-bloody fighting in which the total losses on both sides rose to the staggering figure of almost 38,000,[45] but also for the fact that the principal part of the battle of Chickamauga was fought almost wholly by subordinates of Rosecrans and Bragg. The most prominent and important of these subordinates were Longstreet and D.H. Hill on the Southern side, and Daniel McCook and George H. Thomas leading Northern troops.

Confederate troops went into line of battle in the valley of West Chickamauga Creek between Missionary Ridge and Pigeon Mountain, in an effort to seize the road to Chattanooga and shut Rosecrans off from the city. Bushrod Johnson's Confederates, supported by Forrest's cavalry, advanced, but were held up by Federal horsemen, as was another Confederate drive under W.H.T. Walker. Reinforcements came up, and General John Bell Hood took over, forcing the Federals west of the creek. For a time, the Confederates seemed to hold a great advantage. Rosecrans, who may have exaggerated the difficulties of the rough terrain, and had shown great strategic ability in bringing Bragg and his army out of Chattanooga, showed much less strategic skill thereafter. It was Grant's opinion that when Bragg left Chattanooga to find better ground for a great battle, Rosecrans should not have struck boldly forward, trying to show the same brilliant personal leadership that he had exhibited on the field of Stone River, but should, instead, have placed his forces in a formidable position behind entrenchments. The Union army became scattered over a front of some thirty miles, with many of its officers confused in a maze of hills and valleys, while the troops found the rough roadways very adverse to progress. The English student, Formby, wrote that "Rosecrans had made a rash and badly-calculated move, and was caught in the middle of it."[46]

The battle, raging for three days, September 18-20, began with a repulse of Bragg's efforts to turn the Union left, and enabled Rosecrans to bring up Thomas to protect the vital road to Chattanooga.[47] On the 19th, another day of furious Southern onslaughts and Northern counter-attacks left both armies maimed and exhausted, but hopeful of success on the morrow. The third day, September 20, opened with a sore Confederate disappointment in the failure of Leonidas Polk to make the dawn assault that Bragg had ordered. Yet preliminary thrusts warned Thomas that he must again meet slaughter with slaughter, and along most of the two-mile front fighting recommenced.

Never in the war had troops fought with fiercer anger or more terrible losses than in the three days now coming to a climax. This prolonged encounter made even the battle of the three emperors at Austerlitz and the duel of Napoleon and

45. Formby, John, *The American Civil War*, New York, 1910, 263.
46. *Ibid.*, 260.
47. Tucker, Glenn, *Chickamauga: Bloody Battle in the West*, Indianapolis, 1961, 110-125.

Wellington at Waterloo seem pallid in contrast. Amid billows of yellowish smoke, under a red and brazen sky, the dark forest resounded to the thud and bellow of artillery and the incessant, deadly rattle of musketry. Long rows of dead lay stretched under the trees; lines of wounded crawled moaning into the under-brush; stretchermen carried hundreds on both sides to the field hospitals where rose gory heaps of amputated arms and legs. "Bloody Pond" near the center of the battlefield became half-filled with men and horses that had groped their way to the shores only to die. Hardly able to discern the outlines of different units in the smoke, dust, and flying leaves, the men fought on like devils under what one officer called the "thunder of a thousand anvils."[48]

At last, however, came the break for which Southerners had hoped. As 11 A.M. struck, the long-delayed Confederate attack on the Union right, prepared all morning, was ready to fall like a thunderbolt; and the Confederates launched it at the precise moment that a fatal gap opened in the Union lines, caused by a misunderstanding of the positions of troops and resulting faulty orders. Bragg, perceiving the Union mistake, had kept a cavalry screen in front of the Union army until the reinforcements under Longstreet could arrive from Virginia. When they came, Bragg ordered his troops to try to cut Rosecrans off from Chattanooga. As soon as all of Longstreet's force had come in, Bragg divided his army into two parts—one to attack the Union left, and the other to seize the road to Chattanooga. Longstreet delivered a tremendous attack with five divisions, broke the Federal line in front of him, and cut the Union army in two. One Indiana soldier destined to literary fame, Ambrose Bierce, never forgot the spine-tingling sound of the bugles and the wild rebel yells. [49] Through the opening in the attenuated Union line Longstreet poured his men, until Rosecrans's right was receiving what Alexander McCook called "a most furious and impetuous assault in overwhelming numbers"; the full weight of divisions led by E. McIver Law, Bushrod Johnson, William Preston, T.C. Hindman, and A.P. Stewart. The break-through caught some of Thomas J. Wood's best regiments off balance. Before the defense understood what was happening, Longstreet was attacking in flank and rear, and throwing the troops of Cook, John M. Brannan, and Horatio P. Van Cleve into demoralized confusion. A host of fugitives rushed pell-mell back toward Chattanooga. In vain did a half-dozen generals try to stay the rout; they were carried along with it. Fearful that the whole army was being destroyed, Rosecrans, with part of his staff, was overwhelmed in the flight.

"In the midst of the confusion, which increased every instant," wrote Nicolay and Hay, "the suddenness of the catastrophe for the moment quite appalled [Rosecrans]; his spirit, usually so indomitable in battle, under the stress of the

48. Lamers, *The Edge of Glory, op.cit.,* 328-334.
49. Bierce, Ambrose, *Battle Sketches,* London, 1930, 40-47.

week's enormous labor and anxiety, his physical fatigue, his lack of sleep, and the tremendous impression of a terrible calamity suddenly occurring under his eyes, without an instant's warning, for the moment gave way, and amid the horrible wreck and confusion of his beaten army, in the tumult and disorder, and entanglement of trains of artillery, mingled foot and cavalry, he lost heart and hope."[50] This is the conventional, long-accepted statement of the General's collapse. McCook, Crittenden, Thomas Wood, even the fiery Phil Sheridan, had all given way to a greater or lesser degree; and his nerve failing, Rosecrans decided to retreat into Chattanooga and do what he could there to salvage his army.

The truth, however, especially when psychological factors are intertwined with tangled troop movements, is always complicated, and in this instance it lies at the heart of an unresolved controversy. Only a minute study of time, place, and military shifts can furnish a dubious solution to the problem. Apparently it lies not in the over-simplified narrative by Nicolay and Hay, but half-way between Rosecrans's defensive statements and the charges made by his critics on the field and by the still more critical Halleck in Washington.

"Chickamauga was not a defeat," Rosecrans wrote a Boston friend, "and never has been so regarded by me, or by the army under my command."[51] He and his defender Whitelaw Reid declared that he had not moved precipitously and loosely after Crittenden occupied Chattanooga; that he was trying to unify his three corps as soon as Thomas and McCook moved across Lookout Mountain, and to bring them between Chattanooga and Bragg's army;[52] and that in this endeavor he came into collison with Bragg. "The battle of the 20th was the only thing left for us. It was for the safety of the army and the possession of Chattanooga."[53] He denied that he had become panic-stricken on the battlefield; on the contrary, although worn out by his efforts to rally his left wing and his hurried uphill tramp of seven or eight miles to get back to his center, and grief-stricken by seeing General William H. Lytle mortally wounded at his side, he kept his head. While riding back, he made elaborate plans for reorganizing the army and maintaining the security of his reserves and trains.[54]

Yet on all counts the heaviest evidence is against him. General William B. Hazen, one of the heroes of the battle, declares that Rosecrans *had* advanced recklessly: "The excuse that Chickamauga was necessary for the possession of Chattanooga made by some of his creatures in books, and sanctioned by himself,

50. Nicolay and Hay, *Abraham Lincoln, op.cit.*, VIII, 96.

51. Rosecrans to George B. Pearson, Nov. 1, 1863, Rosecrans Papers, UCLA Library.

52. Thomas 20 miles south of the city, McCook 42 miles, so wrote Rosecrans, *Ibid.* Report of "Agate" or Whitelaw Reid, New York *Tribune*, Nov. 7, 1863.

53. In letter from Yellow Springs, Nov. 1, 1863, to George B. Pearson of Boston; Rosecrans Papers, UCLA Library.

54. See defense by Reid ("Agate") in Cincinnati *Daily Gazette* and New York *Tribune*, Nov. 7, 1863.

is destitute of the shadow of truth or reason. He expected to drive Bragg to the sea."[55] That he did lose his nerve on the battlefield is attested by many witnesses. He jumped too soon to the conclusion that nearly his whole army had been shattered, and the battle irretrievably lost, and that he must hurry back to Chattanooga to gather up the fragments. "It was the fatal mistake of his life," wrote his champion Reid.[56] The Washington authorities believed that only a man badly "stampeded" could have failed, on hearing from stragglers that James S. Negley's command had been routed on the left, to realize that much of Negley's force was still on the right, and to deduce from the continuing roar of artillery and musketry the fact that more than half of the army· was holding firm. And Rosecrans compounded his errors by too hastily pulling his forces back to Chattanooga and evacuating Lookout Mountain, so that he lost his communications along the south bank of the Tennessee and was reduced to the precarious road northward through the mountains.

One man, the "Rock of Chickamauga," did not fall back. General George H. Thomas, at the front, determined to stand his ground stubbornly, and to beat off all attacks. In this decision he displayed his characteristic combination of tenacity and fighting power (he was a man of the most unconquerable character) and thus saved the day for the Union. He held firm on the left, kept his corps under tight control, and with the assistance of Brannan, Granger's relief corps, and others, imperturbably defended his hilly position until night fell. About four o'clock, he was encouraged by the appearance of General Garfield. That high-spirited young officer, if we accept his own recollections, had accompanied Rosecrans to the rear when the right wing was swept back; but instead of sharing the trepidation and despair of his chief, he had plucked up heart when he heard the thunder of continuing battle on the left, and had finally stopped his horse and begged permission to report to Thomas.[57] He refused to believe that the battle was lost. At first Rosecrans forbade him to go, but as he continued his appeals, gave way. Garfield's treacherous hill path took him close to enemy forces and through flying bullets which killed several companions, but he hurried on. He arrived at Thomas's position shortly before orders came from Rosecrans to retreat into Rossville. How much better it would have been for Rosecrans if the chief had moved up beside Thomas, and sent Garfield to the rear to oversee such reorganization as was needed!

The morning of September 21, as gloomy a day as the Union had known since

---

55. Memorandum on Chickamauga Sept. 18, 1863, Palmer Coll., Western Reserve Historical Society.

56. Whitelaw Reid in New York *Tribune,* Nov. 7, 1863.

57. Rosecrans's story of his side in the dispute between him and Garfield as to Garfield's return to the battlefield while Rosecrans went on to Chattanooga is in *O.R.,* I, xxx, Pt.i, 60. See also Villard, Henry, *Memoirs, op.cit.,* 157.

Chancellorsville, found the whole army within Chattanooga or its environs, badly mauled and utterly dejected, but safe. On both sides the casualties had been appalling. The Northern troops had lost 16,170 men killed, wounded, and missing or captured. The South had even more in slain and wounded, for Bragg admitted a total loss of about 18,000, of whom only 2,000 were prisoners. Longstreet's command had lost nearly 44 percent of its men in one two-hour assault, and twelve Confederate regiments called the roll after the battle to find more than half their men dead, wounded, or missing.[58] One of the best students of battle casualties, T.L. Livermore, has computed the Confederate total losses at 18,454, which included 2,316 slain.

Bragg was mercilessly assailed by Southern critics, just after the battle, for not pursuing the defeated enemy into Chattanooga, just as earlier some Northern commentators had attacked Rosecrans for not following Bragg more closely out of the city. Possibly late at night on the 20th, or early on the 21st, Bragg might have recaptured Chattanooga. Part of the Union army had been reduced to a mob; Thomas's position at Rossville was so weak that Rosecrans soon ordered him to withdraw from it. Bedford Forrest, rising early on the 21st to inspect the Union lines from a treetop on Missonary Ridge, saw a scene of such hopeless Union confusion that he told Bragg: "Every hour is worth a thousand men."[59] Later on, D.H. Hill was to argue that the refusal to pursue was the greatest Confederate blunder of the war.[60] But the darkness of the night, the thickness of the forest, the exhaustion of the Southern troops, and the staggering casualties, made an attack within the first hours of the rout impossible. Perhaps Bragg did not realize how great an advantage he had won. Moreover, Thomas had seven divisions still substantially intact, and held them ready to resume fighting at once. The Rock of Chickamauga had not been moved.[61]

The Confederates had won a brilliant victory, but nothing more. Like the Union armies after Antietam and Gettysburg, they could pluck no immediate gains from their triumph. Once the Union troops were brought into order, the Southern officers knew that it would be folly to attempt to storm their entrenchments; the assailants would be mowed down. Yet the city was such a glittering prize that a determined effort must be made to gain it, and Bragg saw that while he could neither storm it nor outflank it, he might starve it into surrender. The Southern troops, retaking Lookout Mountain with its command of the railway and roads on the margin of the Tennessee, able temporarily to forbid all navigation, and holding Missionary Ridge just east of the city, seemed competent to deny any reasonable access to it. The Union forces could obtain supplies only by

58. Longstreet, *From Manassas to Appomattox*, *op.cit.*, 459; *O.R.*, I, xxx, Pt.1, 179; Livermore, Thomas L., *Numbers and Losses*, Bloomington, 1957, 105-106.
59. Tucker, *Chickamauga*, *op.cit.*, 382.
60. Lamers, *Edge of Glory*, *op.cit.*, 365.
61. *Ibid.*, 325-361, gives the best picture of the battle. See also Tucker, *op.cit.*, *passim*.

wagons coping with almost unconquerable steeps, streams, and gullies on a detestable road northward.

Thus it was that Rosecrans's recently victorious army, in this most anomalous of campaigns, was compelled to undergo the siege of Chattanooga.

[V]

Famine now became the principal foe confronting the Union army—one as deeply dreaded as any Confederate battle-line. Bragg placed his right on the Tennessee, four miles above Chattanooga, cordoned the city with camps carried along the top of Missionary Ridge, and garrisoned Lookout Mountain, its prow rising formidably only three miles from the town. His artillery controlled the railroad to Bridgeport, the river, and the highway hewn into the steep rock-cliff on the northern bank of the so-called Narrows. Rosecrans's lifeline from Stevenson, Ala., into Chattanooga, required the wagon-trains to cover sixty miles of Alpine road, and even this was exposed to swooping cavalry raids by Forrest, one of which cost the Union army nearly a thousand wagons and millions of rations. For five weary weeks the siege of the Hawk's Nest continued, while hunger grew until soldiers could be seen grubbing in the dust for grains of corn fallen from mangers where the mules were fed. Whenever a supply-train came in from Stevenson, groups of men gathered at the storehouses in the hope that a fragment of hardtack might be dropped. Some wagons arrived empty, for the guards—hungry men from the town, frantic to satisfy their gnawing stomachs—ate the food along the way. Horses and mules became shadows, dropping dead in long lines across Walden's Ridge from sheer exhaustion. After the third week, the troops went on quarter-rations.

Rosecrans faced two urgent tasks, to fortify himself against attack, and to hammer out enlarged lines of supply. General James St. Clair Morton, his chief of engineers, built the defensive works with iron hand. Through streets and gardens he drove his intrenchments; residences became blockhouses, vineyards gave way to bastions, bones were tossed out of graveyards to make way for rifle-pits. A crescent-shaped line of works soon stretched from the river above the town to the river below, an impregnable bow of iron. "Chattanooga grew suddenly old," wrote one journalist. Within a fortnight, as the troops toiled at demolition and reconstruction, it became literally a walled city. The rebels watching from above called the troops "beavers in blue." Nobody thought of yielding, for everyone comprehended the necessity of holding the rail-center.[62]

Meanwhile, Rosecrans received the reinforcements that should have been

---

62. Hannaford, Ebenezer, *The Story of a Regiment,* Cincinnati, 1868, Ch.32, gives a vivid picture of hardships in this history of the Sixth Ohio Infantry; Shanks, W.F.G., "Chattanooga, and How We Held It," *Harper's New Monthly Magazine,* XXXVI, Jan., 1868, 144-149.

sent to him earlier. Stanton, alarmed by a message from Charles A. Dana[63] that the army might abandon Chattanooga, and by Dana's equally unfounded post-script that, although it would stay and fight, it could not hold out for more than fifteen or twenty days, determined to hurry some 20,000 men from the Army of the Potomac to the West. Troops forthwith began moving from Culpeper on the long journey through Washington, Columbus, Indianapolis, Louisville, and Nash-ville to Bridgeport, Alabama. Dawn of September 25 saw the first trains steaming through the capital. The veteran organizers, Daniel C. McCallum, John W. Garrett, and Thomas A. Scott, sped them on their way. All tracks were cleared; a new floating bridge was flung across the Ohio; 8,000 Negroes hastily changed the gauge of the Louisville & Lexington. Within fourteen days, more than 23,000 men, with ten batteries, horses, ammunition, and baggage, had traversed the 1,233 miles to Bridgeport, using long stretches of track that had been repeatedly dis-rupted and rebuilt. Equipment for two corps followed. Stanton could well con-gratulate Scott on his brilliant work. This was one of the great transportation feats of the war, deserving comparison with the smaller but more difficult movement of Longstreet's corps from Virginia to the Chickamauga front. The credit for initiating the stroke belonged entirely to Stanton, who insisted upon it when Lincoln and Halleck showed reluctance. Although Hooker went too far when he assured the Secretary that he had saved Chattanooga, Stanton might well be proud of his achievement.[64]

To obtain a better supply-line for Chattanooga was not impossible. Close study of the map showed Rosecrans that if Bragg could be ejected from control of the small peninsula of Moccasin Point and Brown's Ferry near Chattanooga, where his guns commanded the area, steam boats could be sent from Bridgeport to Brown's Ferry, and then Federal supplies carried across Moccasin Point into Chattanooga, bypassing the Confederate position on Lookout Mountain. Troops under Hooker from the Army of the Potomac arrived in northeastern Alabama in early October, and later made possible a pincers movement to seize the peninsula; the soldiers had built two small but serviceable steamboats. There rose before Rosecrans's eyes a vision, soon to be realized, of vessels fetching up cargoes

63. Some students have thought this message unfounded, but Dana telegraphed Stanton at 6 o'clock on the evening of September 22: "Rosecrans is considering question of retreat from here. I judge that he thinks that unless he can have reassurance of ample reinforcements within one week, the attempt to hold this place will be much more disastrous than retreat." Then at 9:30 on September 22, Dana declared, "Rosecrans is determined to fight it out here at all hazards. . . ." *O.R.*, I, xxx, Pt.i, 197. So Dana's message may not have been unfounded. He may have had his doubts about holding out, but eventually reached a stronger decision. By September 24 Dana confidently told Stanton: "Have no doubt about this place. It will hold out. . ." *O.R.*, I, xxx, Pt.i, 199.

64. Weber, Thomas, *The Northern Railroads in the Civil War, 1861-1865*, New York, 1962, 180-192; Turner, George E., *Victory Rode the Rails*, Indianapolis, 1953, 289ff.; Kamm, Samuel R., *The Civil War Career of Thomas A. Scott*, Philadelphia, 1940, 164ff.; Thomas, Benjamin P. and Harold Hyman, *Stanton, the Life and Times of Lincoln's Secretary of War*, New York, 1962, 286-289.

of food in a single day. It was not Rosecrans, however, who saw the realization of this plan. Before Chattanooga was relieved and ere Knoxville was saved from the beleaguerment which Longstreet instituted, the same bolt fell upon the head of Rosecrans that had fallen upon Frémont, McClellan, Buell, and Hooker. Without warning, he received an order just a month after the battle (October 19) relieving him from command. Next day he quietly departed for the North. All radical Republicans, including Ben Wade in the Senate, Chase in the Cabinet, and Horace Greeley in his editorial chair, heard of his departure with consternation and regret. His removal, like that of other high officers, was long to be a theme of controversy.

The precise circumstances surrounding it have never been clarified. One decisive factor was the conviction of Stanton and Halleck that Rosecrans lacked the stamina for a dogged, well-pondered, earnest effort to meet a crisis. Another element was Grant's antipathy. Ever since the delays at Iuka, Corinth, and Stone River or Murfreesboro, Grant had distrusted Rosecrans. Now Washington had decided that Grant should head the powerful concentration to be made at Chattanooga. It was clear that the two men could not serve together amicably; Rosecrans could not even be left in a subordinate position there.[65]

Lincoln frankly told Garfield his side of the story when the recent chief of staff called at the White House on December 17, 1863. A report of the talk at once reached Rosecrans. "He said," wrote Garfield, "that the service you rendered at Stone River was, at the time it was rendered, *one* of the most if not the *most* important proofs of support the country has had since the war. If that battle had been lost it is difficult to see where our fortunes would have landed—and to you personally the country was deeply indebted for its salvation from almost fatal disaster. In the next place, he said, your support of the government in the two letters to the Indiana and Ohio legislatures at a time when treachery at home was overwhelming everything, was, if possible, more important than your service at Stone River. He then traced the progress of the Army of the Cumberland from Murfreesboro to Chattanooga, saying that while others blamed you, and he sometimes felt anxious and a little dissatisfied at the delay to move against Bragg in the Vicksburg days, yet he never lost confidence in your courage or patriotism. He referred to the letter he wrote you after the battle of Chickamauga and said he wrote as he then felt and still feels. He said that it was the tone of your dispatches from Chattanooga several days after the battle that led him to fear that you did not feel confident that you could hold the place; and hence the consolidation of the three armies to make Chattanooga sure. It was still at that time his intention to keep you at the head of the Army of the Cumberland—as before—with Grant the ranking officer in command of the whole; but Grant made it a

65. So wrote Whitelaw Reid ("Agate") in the New York *Tribune*, Nov. 7, 1863.

condition of accepting the command that you should be removed. The importance of the consolidation was so great to the cause that the President deemed it a sufficient reason for his action, but he did not want it understood that he was not still your friend."[66]

Grant in his memoirs neither affirms nor denies making the removal of Rosecrans a condition for his acceptance of the command. He writes simply that when he met the excited and apprehensive Stanton at Indianapolis en route by train to Louisville October 17, the Secretary handed him two orders with the remark that he might take his choice. One gave him command of the consolidation, leaving the three departmental heads untouched; the other gave him command with a substitution of Thomas for Rosecrans. "I accepted the latter," writes Grant, adding no comment whatever. This seems to make Stanton, not Grant, the prime mover in the displacement of a man who had long irritated the Secretary. Of course we do not know what Grant said to Stanton on the train journey to Louisville, or during their stay at the Galt House afterward. We may be sure that Lincoln was quite honest in his statement to Garfield, but we may doubt whether Stanton, in his report to the President on his return from the West, did not overstate Grant's readiness to demand the removal. Charles A. Dana told a member of the McCook family: "The Tycoon of the War Department is on the war path; his hands are red and smoking with the scalping of Rosey."[67]

Much later, Rosecrans formed an impression that Garfield had played him false, for a set of busy talebearers sprang up who planted this unpleasant idea in his mind. The fact was that numerous officers in Chattanooga were dissatisfied with Rosecrans's leadership, and freely said so. This was not playing the general false; it was telling the truth. These officers made no secret of their belief that a change in the chief command was desirable. Charles A. Dana, loitering about Chattanooga, reported this sentiment to Stanton, and with it his belief that a replacement by Thomas would be welcomed by the army. He gave his own view that Rosecrans was too hurt and confused to command efficiently. "There is no system in the use of his busy days and restless nights."[68] According to the inventor Calvin Goddard, Garfield on a visit to Cleveland at the beginning of December said just what many others were saying, picturing Rosecrans as "totally demoralized"[69] when he fled into Chattanooga, while Thomas and Garfield himself retained their calm determination. This, again, was not playing Rosecrans

66. Garfield to Rosecrans, Dec. 18, 1863, and James Roberts Gilmore to Rosecrans, Nov. 23, 1864, Rosecrans Papers, UCLA; Dana, *Recollections,* New York, 1898, 124-125; Rawlins to Mary Emma Hurlbut, Chattanooga, Tenn., Nov. 23, 1863, John A. Rawlins Papers, Chicago Hist. Soc.

67. Thomas and Hyman, *Stanton, op.cit.,* 290. And Stanton asked Dana to tell Thomas: "It is not my fault that he was not in chief command months ago." Stanton Papers, LC.

68. *Ibid.;* see Dana's numerous letters in early November in Stanton Papers, LC.

69. Samuel A. Goddard, Cleveland, Dec. 7, 1863, to Rosecrans; Rosecrans Papers, UCLA.

false, but telling the truth. Rosecrans was deeply hurt by the violent attacks of certain journalists upon him, by the criticism of friends, and by Whitelaw Reid's assurances early in 1865 that it was hopeless to expect any favor or even justice from either Secretary Stanton or Assistant Secretary Dana.[70] His next command was a troublesome and unsatisfactory assignment to Missouri, and when he resigned from the army to recommence a frustrating business career, he continued to nurse many suspicions.

As they concerned Garfield, these suspicions seemed to have little justification. Garfield's letters late in 1863 show that, while properly critical of Rosecrans's deficiencies, he was a vigorous defender of the general against exaggerated censure. He was outraged by a long attack which Henry Villard published as a review of the Chickamauga campaign in the New York *Tribune* early in December: "I sent word to Mr. Greeley that it was outrageously false and calumnious," he wrote his former chief. "I told Swinton the same."[71] George L. Andrew, an officer of the Sanitary Commission who rode into Chattanooga on an armored train just after the battle, found Garfield enthusiastically loyal to Rosecrans: "He certainly took a great deal of pains to shield Gen. R. from the criticisms which were already very freely made against him."[72] When long afterward Dana's New York *Sun* published a statement that one of Garfield's letters to Chase had made even that powerful friend assent to Rosecrans's removal, the new charge kicked up a tremendous pother. It turned out that Dana had never seen the letter, and really knew nothing of it beyond the alleged fact that Stanton had mentioned it. Various men offered what contributions of stale scuttlebut they could. Fitz-John Porter, for example, sent Rosecrans a sympathetic letter full of hearsay gossip about Garfield's treachery, Lincoln's pliability, the part that Garfield's letter played in getting both Chase and Montgomery Blair to yield, and so on—a discreditable missive even for Porter.[73]

Doubtless Garfield did tell Lincoln the facts as to Rosecrans's battlefield breakdown; he would have been remiss in his public duty had he not done so. But all our substantial evidence shows that it was Stanton, Grant, and Dana who terminated the general's leadership of the Army of the Cumberland, and that Lincoln approved the step long before he saw Garfield. Altogether, we have good reason for accepting at face value the earnest letter Garfield, then about to become President, wrote Rosecrans early in 1880. He had not seen the New York *Sun* article, he declared. "I can only say . . . that any charge, whether it came from Dana or any other liar, to the effect that I was in any sense untrue to you or

70. Reid from Washington, Feb. 18, 1865, to Rosecrans, Rosecrans Papers, UCLA.
71. Garfield to Rosecrans, Dec. 9, 1863, Rosecrans Papers, UCLA.
72. Andrews, George L., Ms. Memoirs, HEH.
73. July 13, 1880, Rosecrans Papers, UCLA. Rosecrans built up a folder of papers which he labelled as recollections of the circumstances surrounding his removal.

unfaithful to our friendship, has no particle of truth in it. On my way from your army to Washington I met Mr. Stanton at Louisville, and when he denounced you in vigorous language, I rebuked him and earnestly defended you against his assaults. I did the same as you remember in the House of Representatives very soon after I entered that body." He added that he could "fearlessly challenge all the rascals in the world" to show that he had never written an improper letter to Secretary Chase.[74]

Grant, arriving at Chattanooga October 23, found the situation of the army still critical. Supplies were still being brought by rail to Bridgeport, hauled thirty miles over the wretched roads, and then taken on their final roundabout leg under peril of sharpshooters. The men were still on half or quarter rations, the draft animals were still dying by hundreds daily, and the possibility of enforced evacuation remained. Sherman arrived at Bridgeport on the night of November 13 from Memphis—his troops, ordered up from Vicksburg in late September, following by several roads behind him—and found a dispatch from Grant hurrying him on. He reached Chattanooga by horseback on the 15th, and next morning walked out to the fortifications to see Confederate flags flying on Lookout and rebel tents all along Missionary Ridge. "Why, General Grant," he exclaimed, "you are besieged." To this Grant glumly replied, "It is too true."[75]

But it was not to be true much longer. Grant had quickly formed a plan of operations, partly his own, partly Rosecrans's, Thomas's and W.F. Smith's; he would use Thomas's troops in Chattanooga and those of Hooker at Bridgeport to reopen direct communications. To be sure, Longstreet's position on Lookout seemed to forbid this, but Grant quickly ascertained from Thomas and W.F. Smith that the forces there were weak, and that if Lookout Valley were taken, a new safe supply route across Moccasin Point into Chattanooga could be opened. The ensuing pincers operation between Hooker on one side and Smith on the other was complex, but successful. After sharp fighting at Wauhatchie in Lookout Valley, Brown's Ferry was taken and the siege really lifted. The result was electrical.

"On the way to Chattanooga," wrote Grant, "I had telegraphed back to Nashville for a good supply of vegetables and small rations, which our troops had been so long deprived of. . . .In five days from my arrival in Chattanooga the way was open to Bridgeport, and with the aid of steamers and Hooker's teams, in a week the troops were receiving full rations. It is hard for anyone not an eyewitness to realize the relief this brought. The men were soon reclothed and also well-fed; an abundance of ammunition was brought up, and a cheerfulness prevailed not before enjoyed in many weeks."[76]

74. Garfield to Rosecrans, "Confidential," Jan.19, 1880, Rosecrans Papers, UCLA.
75. Sherman, *Memoirs, op.cit.*, I, 361.
76. Grant, *Memoirs*, II, 38.

Thus, as the reinforcement of the Army of Tennessee by troops from all sides, and the weakening of Bragg's army by his ill-advised dispatch of Longstreet northeastward in an effort to destroy Burnside in Knoxville, gave the North a decisive advantage in numbers, the scene was set for the advances that made the names of Lookout Mountain and Missionary Ridge immortal in American history. Grant, Thomas, and Sherman, in councils on the night of November 16, perfected their designs. Not only was their idea to defeat Bragg, but to relieve pressure on Knoxville. They waited until Sherman's leading regiments reached Brown's Ferry on the 20th, and until unexpected rains that day and on the 21st ceased, and the ground dried. With consummate skill, Grant handled the long irregular crescent of his army as a unit. Hooker on the Union right was to attack Lookout Mountain and seize the valley beyond; Sherman on the Union left was to move against the North flank of the Confederate position on Missionary Ridge; and when the two wings had achieved success, Thomas in the center was to throw his divisions against the main enemy position on Missionary Ridge. In Grant's mind the Union army would fight a single battle. Inevitably, however, it fell into three parts—the important skirmish of Orchard Knob on November 23, the battle of Lookout Mountain on the 24th, and the battle of Missionary Ridge on the 25th.[77]

At an early hour on the 23rd, the Union guns on the fortifications about Chattanooga awoke the echoes along the heights, and the Confederate cannon on the flat top of Lookout and all along Missionary Ridge replied. It was plain to all that the final drama of the campaign was opening. As the sun grew hot and the fog rose from the valley, watchers on the Ridge above saw 20,000 bayonets gleaming in serried ranks. They supposed at first that a parade was under way; the evolutions of Northern regiments could not have been more precise, the bands could not have played more calmly. Suddenly, as the shots of Union skirmishers scattered Southern pickets, the line wheeled and swung against the wooded slope above. Troops of Thomas, pouring forward in this surprise attack, seized a strategic mound known as Orchard Knob and a line of low hills halfway between Chattanooga and Missionary Ridge. With little loss, the Northern host overran the first line of Confederate intrenchments, captured 200 prisoners, and shook the morale of the Confederates. Sherman at last managed to draw his three divisions up on the north side of the Tennessee River and started across.[78]

On the 24th came Hooker's opportunity to distinguish himself. Shrouded in the mists, his troops attacked the upper end of Lookout. Six Confederate brigades or about 7,000 men spread out to cover the entire area. "The ascent of the mountain is steep and thickly wooded," wrote Grant's aide Badeau, who knew it well. "Beetling crags peer out all over its sides from the masses of heavy foliage,

77. Grant, "Chattanooga," *Battles and Leaders*, III, 679-718; *O.R.*, I, xxxi, Pt.2, 30-31.
78. Sherman, *Memoirs, op. cit.*, final ed., I, 392-413; *O.R.*, I, xxxi, Pt.2, 572.

and at the summit, a lofty palisaded crest rises perpendicularly as high as sixty or eighty feet. On the northern slope, about midway between the summit and the Tennessee, a plateau of open and arable land belts the mountain. There, a continuous line of earthworks had been thrown up; while redoubts, redans, and rifle-pits were scattered lower down the acclivity, to repel assaults from the direction of the river."[79] Without hesitation, the Union troops swept up, and after sharp fighting began to clear the narrow plateau along the mountain side near the Craven house. In mid-afternoon, the fog or mist that had hovered over the summit settled lower and lower; the scene grew darker and darker. Finally, the progress of the battle was discernible only by the rattle of musketry, flashes of fire, and fitful glimpses of battleflags and struggling units seen through intervals in the fog. Still the troops of Peter J. Osterhaus, John W. Geary, and Charles Cruft advanced until by four o'clock Hooker could notify his superiors that they had carried the mountain. Sporadic firing continued until late in the night, but next morning the Northern flags floated above the summit.[80]

Superior numbers had triumphed. One student declares that at Lookout Mountain 10,000 Union troops attacked one portion of the defenses held by 1,295 Confederate defenders.[81] Certainly Hooker had 9,000 infantry, a small force of cavalry, and some artillery; perhaps four Northerners for every Southerner.[82] Since the Confederates found it difficult to depress the guns on the crest, their supposed advantage of position was partly illusory.[83] Grant, who disliked Hooker, later belittled the conflict, declaring: "The battle of Lookout Mountain is one of the romances of the war. There was no such battle, and no action even worthy to be called a battle on Lookout Mountain."[84] This engagement nevertheless cost the South all chance of regaining a grip on the river and waterside railroad, 1,250 men (of whom a thousand were captured), and a position which flanked the Confederate defenses east of Lookout.[85]

At the other end of the Federal line, Sherman had two divisions across the Tennessee River by daylight of November 24, with another following. Tardily, in the early afternoon, Sherman's troops moved forward against what their commander thought was the northern end of Missionary Ridge. However, all he managed to take against light opposition was a hill isolated from the main part

79. Badeau, Adam, *Military History of U.S. Grant,* New York, 1868, I, 498.

80. Hebert, Walter H., *Fighting Joe Hooker,* Indianapolis, 1944, 261-270, places the victory earlier in the afternoon.

81. Downey, Fairfax, *Storming of the Gateway: Chattanooga, 1863,* New York, 1963, *passim.*

82. Hebert, *op. cit.,* 265.

83. Col. Lewis R. Stegman, "Address at Dedication Chickamauga and Chattanooga Military Park," 1895, in Boynton, H.V., compiler, *Dedication of the Chickamauga and Chattanooga National Military Park,* Washington, 1896, 166-174.

84. So Grant told John Russell Young; *Around the World with General Grant,* New York, 1879, II, 306.

85. Hebert, *op. cit.,* 265; the phrase "battle above the clouds" was coined after the war.

of Missionary Ridge. Faulty maps had caused the mistake, but this error and the slow advance gave the Confederates time to fortify the northern end of the ridge. Both sides dug in for the night.

Grant then instructed Sherman to make ready to use his augmented force against the north end of Missionary Ridge at dawn on November 25. The center under Thomas and the right under Hooker were apparently to move simultaneously. There was some vagueness and misunderstanding in regard to these orders, and delays resulted. The Confederates had gathered about forty-thousand men in all, with a hundred guns, on the slopes and summit of the Ridge. Although Grant's army was much stronger, he had to face the supposed disadvantages of a toilsome climb with various clifflike ascents.

In the seemingly desperate charge up and over Missionary Ridge, one of the most spectacular attacks of the kind in history, about 25,000 men of the Army of the Cumberland struck at the center of Bragg's defenses, held by 15,000 men and 50 cannon. As the blue ranks of Thomas moved forward in the late afternoon, many a man thought of the fate of Burnside's troops below Marye's Heights. This time, however, the headlong onset of the army was not once checked. The panting soldiers found the steep slopes as much a protection as a hazard, they braved the musket and artillery fire without wavering, and they smashed through the Confederate lines in gap after gap, establishing footholds from which they could enfilade the remaining strong points. Part at least of the Southern works had been badly sited, so that the assailants found large intervals where they were fairly safe. Bragg also made a mistake in putting a large part of his men at the foot of the ascent, with orders to fire and then retreat; many of them were overrun before they could offer proper resistance. Hooker, though full of admiration for the Western troops, said later that if Ewell and Longstreet had held Missionary Ridge, all the Northern armies could not have taken it. We may dismiss any such idea, but Longstreet's presence would have made a difference.[86]

Grant had expected the troops to halt after storming the foot of the Ridge. To his amazement, they took control of the situation and pressed on. This was partly because their impetuous enthusiasm carried them straight on in pursuit of the flying enemy; partly because they saw that the lower intrenchments were no protection from the artillery above—that to remain would be suicide. This was a battle of the privates, of the plain soldiers, the farmboys, villagers, town clerks, and laborers of all sorts, not of the high command. The thick Union lines went steadily up without pausing to fire—they had no time. Regimental officers, caught in the onrushing wave, had nothing to do but cheer on the foremost and aid the weak-limbed. Watchers in the valley felt long minutes of anxiety in the interval between passage of the base lines and the heights above. But the suspense

86. J.H. Hammond, reporting Hooker, to McClellan, Dec. 15, 1863; Barlow Papers, HEH.

was eased as the standards went on up, and the knots of blue uniforms were glimpsed higher and higher. Soon a flag was seen flying where General Wood's division had reached the crest; then another and another. A wild burst of cheers rose from the Union ranks below[87] as the first arrivals at the top deployed right and left to clear it of rebels, and thus aid the troops still toiling on the slopes. The Confederate center had collapsed, and although there was stubborn resistance against Sherman at the north end of Missionary Ridge, Bragg could do nothing to stave off severe defeat. Remarkably, however, casualties on both sides had been comparatively low for such a major battle.

The Confederates, seeing that they had encountered a Spartan onslaught, lost the élan and confidence which they had previously exhibited. Their army had risen to its greatest height in the recent actions under Bragg. But now, as their able leader, General D.H. Hill, stated, they saw that their initial victory was proving barren, and they lost heart. They were never again to repeat their splendid exploits at Chickamauga. Bragg ruefully concluded that he had come to a dead end, a standstill, in flinging his great army against Rosecrans and Thomas. Rosecrans had returned in humiliation to his command which he was obviously no longer fit to lead, and had been relieved on October 19, and sent to command the Department of Missouri, his later career to be spent in Mexico and California.

On November 26, the Confederates were in rapid retreat toward Ringgold in Georgia, hardly to pause until they reached Dalton. Four days later still, Sherman, with more than 25,000 men at his back, was turning northeast to break the communications between Bragg and Longstreet, and relieve Knoxville. The weather had turned bitter cold, and Sherman's men had brought no baggage or provisions. The general heard from Grant, however, that Longstreet had completely invested Knoxville, that Burnside had insufficient provisions to last beyond December 3, and that although General Gordon Granger had been sent from Chattanooga, it was uncertain whether he could arrive in time. In fact, Burnside's plight was exaggerated. He had beaten off Longstreet in the fighting at Fort Sanders and some supplies were still coming in. He managed to serve Sherman a fine turkey dinner. "Seven days before," wrote Sherman, "we had left our camps on the other side of the Tennessee with two days' rations, without a change of clothing—stripped for the fight, with but a single blanket or coat per man, from myself to the private."[88] But with 12,000 fellow-soldiers besieged in Knoxville eighty-four miles away, the only course had been to hurry to their aid.

It was another dramatic moment in the history of the Western army when Sherman, on December 6, rode into Knoxville to shake hands with Burnside. The previous night Longstreet had retreated out upon the Bristol road leading into

---

87. See Hannaford, E., *The Story of a Regiment, op. cit.*, for a vivid account.
88. Sherman, *Memoirs, op. cit.*, final edition, I, 407.

Virginia. The campaign was over. Snow would fall any day on hills and plain, and it was time for all armies to give up the idea of large-scale operations and go into winter quarters. As soldiers began to build their huts, they could ponder the meaning and probable results of the recent battles.

Again and again, in this war, strategic operations had to be related to two considerations of a non-military character. One was their effect upon public sentiment, party movements, and decisions at the polls; the other was the agricultural and industrial situation. It had been highly important for the Union army to take and hold Chattanooga before the November elections. Had it lost its grip upon the city and been forced back toward Nashville, a heavy depression would have settled upon the Northwest. Now a sense of elation pervaded the great area from Ohio to Kansas. It was equally important for the powerful Western forces to gain the prospect of an early subjugation of Georgia. That State, with its resources of grain and livestock (to say nothing of mills and factories), had been one of the main supports of the Confederate armies; but now, long before a new harvest could ripen, Union forces would push their way into its very heart. These were facts upon which the sorely tried Army of Tennessee could base comforting reflections in the long winter months ahead. Northern soldiers could also reflect cheerfully upon the fact that the Union had at last a group of generals, Grant, Sherman, Thomas, and Sheridan, of whose capacity and energy no question whatever could exist.

Altogether, the desperate Tennessee campaign of 1863 was inconclusive and aroused the most intense anxiety, North and South. It had cost the lives of thousands of brave men on both sides. After sustained and often convulsive efforts which had given both Unionists and Confederates shining but delusive hopes of a climactic victory, and after both principal generals, Bragg for the South, and Rosecrans for the North, had exerted every effort, the North and South alike had lost ground and prestige. Chickamauga had seemed a stunning blow to the Union, but it had proved nugatory. General disappointment and chagrin enveloped this great central landscape, and left little but sorrow and unhappiness behind it. As the year 1863 ended, a troublesome siege of Knoxville was brought to an end by the dejected retreat of the Confederate columns from that city. Tennessee remained a solid, impregnable, and invaluable bastion of Union sentiment and of the Northern cause. However harassed and tormented by guerrilla warfare and political factionalism, that State helped maintain the cause of Lincoln, national unity, and the anti-slavery forces in the dominant position which they had gained.

7

The Great Boom in the North

[I]

IN ALMOST every field and at every point, the war had laid a profound imprint upon Northern life. Nearly every family had husbands, fathers, sons, brothers, or nephews at the front. On Beacon Street in Boston, Euclid Avenue in Cleveland, Main Street everywhere, and on the isolated farms, the same emblems of patriotism and mourning were visible. Every town had its hobbling wounded and white-faced invalids. Everywhere the traveller met anxious women who had seen service in base hospitals, the Sanitary Commission, or similar organizations. Hardly a lawyer, a doctor, or engineer of repute had failed to devote his special skills to the war effort. If the visitor talked with representative citizens, he saw at once that a demand for greater realism in the guidance of industry, agriculture, government, and the multiplying social endeavors of the land was growing imperative. The temper of the people was becoming more earnest and systematic; organization was advancing apace. Men had feared, when the war began, that the nation might become militarized. On the contrary, while war news sometimes excited intense anxiety, and military titles besprinkled the country and many people found evanescent martial heroes to admire, there remained a general hatred of battle, and a healthy suspicion of strutters in epaulets. The desire for a resumption of civil tasks and business undertakings was fierce and universal.

The mailed fist of war was smiting the republic hard, but the impact of change on many fronts, economic, cultural, and social, diverted men's attention from its blows. Meanwhile, the physical and psychological wounds that the land sustained were largely obscured by an overriding phenomenon: the Great Boom of 1863-65, following close on the heels of the economic reverses and the painful readjustments of 1861-62.

Foreign visitors, in the summer of Gettysburg, aware that a conflict of almost unparalleled magnitude had been convulsing the land for two years, asked an instinctive question: How much has the country suffered? They were taken aback when people in the North and West responded: Very little! Those who looked deeply saw this answer was untrue; those who looked superficially saw much to bear it out. They were astonished. In most of the great wars of European history —wars of religion, of conquest, of liberation, and above all, civil wars—the armies had spread general desolation; misery had stalked abroad; and the end had often descended upon peoples prostrate in appalling exhaustion. The Thirty Years' War left half of Europe ruined. In the War of the Spanish Succession, 132 battles took place in each of which more than 2,000 men were slain or wounded; in the Seven Years' War more than 110 such battles were fought;[1] and conditions of life in the embattled lands had become pitiable. The wars of Louis XIV were marked by a savagery and destructiveness that left wide areas palpitating with anguish. As the wars of Napoleon drew to a close, writes Sir Arthur Bryant, half of continental Europe was convulsed with pain, want, and despair.[2]

Yet now, in the North, from Maine to Missouri, no signs of prostration appeared, even of a civilian nature. Militarily, of course, but small portions of the Union had been touched by actual combat. One astute British observer and promotor in the North, Sir Morton Peto, found the elasticity of the free States impressive. He traversed regions where rich crops seemed to spring up spontane- ously; he rode upon trains and steamboats carrying this harvest bounty to busy ports; in the old States he saw villages springing into towns and towns into cities, while in the newest States great reaches were being opened and populated. He recalled that early in the war the London *Economist* had predicted that Northern finances must soon collapse; yet despite debts and taxes, the country boasted of fast-growing wealth. American resources seemed to him to surpass anything known in the Old World, and American opportunities to invite a thousand forms of enterprise.

Lincoln, in fact, summed up the position of the North when he wrote that the axe had enlarged the borders of settlement, and the mines had yielded more abundantly than before; that population and wealth had grown steadily despite the losses of camp, siege, and battlefield; and that the country, rejoicing in unchecked vigor, could expect "continuance of years with large increase of freedom."[3] So ran his Thanksgiving proclamation in the midst of war.

To Congress, in December of 1863, Lincoln had conveyed the correct intelli- gence that mineral riches were greater than expected in the western territories; and he had urged it to establish a system for the encouragement of immigration, remarking, "It is easy to see that, under the sharp discipline of civil war, the nation is beginning a new life."[4] A year later, he informed Congress of the advance of railroads and telegraph lines, and new discoveries of gold, silver, and

1. Bodart, Gaston, *Losses of Life in Modern War,* London, 1916, 14-20.
2. Bryant, Sir Arthur, *Years of Victory,* New York, 1945, 424-425.
3. Lincoln, *Collected Works,* VI, 496.
4. *Ibid.,* VII, 40, Dec. 8, 1863.

cinnabar, adding that the Sierra Nevada and Rocky Mountains "now teemed with enterprising labor, which was richly remunerative." He went on in broader terms to state that "we do not approach exhaustion in the most important branch of national resources—that of living men . . . we have *more* men *now* than we had when the war *began*;" and he declared, "we are not exhausted, nor in process of exhaustion; that we are *gaining* strength, and may, if need be, maintain the contest indefinitely. This as to men. Material resources are now more complete and abundant than ever. The national resources, then, are unexhausted, and, as we believe, inexhaustible."[5]

With these advantages Lincoln believed that "the public purpose to reëstablish and maintain the national authority" was unchanged and unchangeable. Had he been spared to write a state-of-the-Union message at the close of 1865, he could have amplified these truths.

Why was it, asked Peto, that the single small State of Indiana, with a population less than half that of Lancashire, had been able to contribute fully 125,000 men to the armies, raise great sums by taxes and voluntary contributions, and press forward with rising vigor? Why had Illinois done still better? Because of their natural resources, rapid improvements, energy, and devotion to the ideas of freedom and continental union. Their exertions were indicative of larger efforts to follow in wiping out all the baneful effects of the war; a fact that made Peto confident that the resources and energies of the country were more than ample to redeem her liabilities "readily, speedily, and without undue difficulty."[6]

Such Southern leaders as Laurence Keitt, Greeley's *Tribune* recalled, had predicted that a loss of Southern resources would destroy Yankee industry from turret to foundation. But while the seceding States were half ruined by battle, blockade, attribution, and depletion of labor, the North flourished. A large part of Charleston had been destroyed by fire early in 1862, and still lay in ashes; in Troy, N.Y., after a similar misfortune, the burned district had long since been covered by buildings superior to the old. A track for a city railroad on the main business street of Richmond, laid as the war opened, had just been abandoned because the company never put cars on the line; yet New York, with five street railroads to begin with, had seen new lines placed on Seventh Avenue, Ninth Avenue, Tenth Avenue, and various connecting streets, while Broadway and Madison Avenue would soon have cars. Look at the North six weeks after Gettysburg and Vicksburg!, exclaimed the *Tribune*. "Never did manufactures, commerce, the mechanic arts, and agriculture flourish as they do now."[7]

Publications of the day reflected the sense of affluence, confidence and pleni-

5. *Ibid.*, VIII, 146, 150-151.
6. Peto, Sir S. Morton, *The Resources and Prospects of America*, London, 1866, *passim*.
7. New York *Tribune*, Aug. 17, 1863.

tude in what appeared to be a dual economy—guns and butter. Writing even of the year 1862, the *Scientific American* had asserted, "It may well surprise ourselves and all other nations that, during a year of the greatest civil war on record, our country in her productive and commercial interests has been wonderfully prosperous. There has been no commercial suffering, and want has been unfelt in the land . . ." While difficulties had been encountered in 1861 and 1862, this magazine joined numerous other magazines in the exultant statement: "The great secret of our nation's wealth and strength lies in her superabundant natural products, developed by an industrious people. In this respect we stand first among the nations of the earth. A country which raises annually such immense crops of grain never can be poor. Business panics may occur occasionally, and the disasters of war may change the course of manufacture and trade; but while the elements of true wealth remain, prosperity will always succeed disaster. It is true that nearly all articles of merchandise have greatly advanced in price; still there is employment for all, and it is an old business maxim, that 'work and want do not fellowship together.' "[8]

The *American Railroad Journal* asserted that the year 1862 had probably been the most remarkable in its commercial achievements in the nation's annals. Of course, the war had altered the "even tenor of past experience," but the condition of commercial affairs when the year ended, and 1863 began, was much more favorable than the most sanguine had ventured to predict, or even hope. The great tests of national prosperity, an abundance of all the necessaries of life, and active employment for the country's population, seemed to this magazine never better fulfilled than during 1862.[9] The fact here stated was as important in its way as the successes of Shiloh and Antietam. The *American Railroad Journal* was hopeful of similar economic progress in 1863, noting that there seemed "a perfect harmony between the resources and the actual condition of the country . . ."[10] Commenting upon the war, the editor wrote: "The magnitude of the contest can scarcely be realized by us in the North, because the peculiar horrors of war have never reached our homes and firesides; little have they affected our comforts, or diminished our personal security. Our Northern cities are full of life and activity instead of death and decay; all our material interests appear to be thriving; we hear of debt and taxation, but . . . they are scarcely felt beyond the anxiety which attends a perusal of . . . statements of our indebtedness."[11]

By November, 1863, Senator John Sherman was able to declare that, "The wonderful prosperity of all classes, especially of laborers, has a tendency to secure acquiescence in all measures demanded to carry on the war. We are only another

8. *Scientific American*, Vol. VIII, No. 3, Jan. 17, 1863, 41.
9. *American Railroad Journal*, Vol. XXXVI, No. 1395, Jan. 10, 1863.
10. *Ibid.*, Vol. XXXVI, No. 1396, Jan. 17, 1863, 65-66.
11. *Ibid.*, Vol. XXXVI, No. 1400, Feb. 14, 1863, 144-146.

example of a people growing rich in a great war. And this is not shown simply by inflated prices, but by increased production, new manufacturing establishments, new railroads, houses, and other gains. . . . Indeed, every branch of business is active and hopeful." This he regarded as not a mere temporary inflation caused by paper money, but as evidence of steady progress, based almost entirely upon actual capital. "The people are prospering and show their readiness to push on the war," he continued. "Taxes are paid cheerfully, and the voluntary donations for our soldiers and their families are counted by thousands. . . ."[12] In the autumn of 1863, a leading farm journal recorded the memorable feat of the American democracy in maintaining the colossal burdens of war, while trade and manufactures thrived perhaps more vigorously than ever before.[13]

And so the confidence of enlightened and patriotic Northerners and Westerners was reiterated in even louder voices, with one magazine declaring as 1864 opened and that year of battle wore on: "The growth of the United States is the wonder of the world. Nothing like it is recorded in authentic history."[14]

Keeping harmonic pace with these cheery accounts of economic affluence were the frequent expressions in the newspapers, magazines and new books, of a new zest for life, a faster pace in a thousand activities, and a wider, more exuberant range of experience. "Never was New York so brilliant, so captivating. . . . Our élite, our aristocracy of money, our shoddy people, have run their mad race of extravagance and show at the fashionable watering places, and are returning to commence in the city a season of unparalleled display. All classes are taking advantage of the recklessness and extravagance of the day." Theater prices were up fifty percent, but the masses came in greater numbers than ever. Many people had been content with two horses; now four were in fashionable demand, and even six for carriages and tally-ho coaches. Ladies' finery, silks, satins, and laces, wrote one observer, "now [began to] cost their weight in greenbacks." And, "the wonder of it was that, in spite of these high prices, the consumption was greater than ever."[15]

One of the prominent business journals was somewhat gloomier about all the resplendent display, reminding people of "a general depression which has lain heavily upon all business since the commencement of the war," but which was showing some degree of recovery by the end of 1862.[16] Occasional pessimistic reports continued early in 1863 in the same journal, particularly with regard to

12. *The Sherman Letters, Correspondence Between General and Senator Sherman from 1827 to 1891*, ed. Rachel Sherman Thorndike, London, 1894, 215-216, John Sherman to William T. Sherman, Nov. 14, 1863.

13. *The Country Gentleman*, Vol. XXII, No. 19, Nov. 5, 1863, 304.

14. *American Railroad Journal*, Vol. XXXVII, No. 1486, Oct. 9, 1864, 988-989.

15. *Prairie Farmer*, Vol. XIV, No. 17, Oct. 22, 1864, 267, from New York *Herald*.

16. "Commercial Chronicle and Review," in *Hunt's Merchants' Magazine*, Vol. XLVII, No. 6, Dec., 1862, 537.

government debt and a fear of "national bankruptcy."[17] But these voices, expressing the traditional conservatism of a sizable segment of the more established financial world, were in the minority.

The boom was beyond all question real and effective, but it came gradually and unevenly and, as was characteristic of all great advances and hopeful changes in American life, not all the populace benefited by any means. It was not a wild, exhilarating revival, despite highly colored accounts. After all, the war was always present to throw its somber pall over everything in life. Nevertheless, most people in the Northern States were living a dual life—feeling the heartrending emotions of a nation in the throes of civil conflict, but feeling also the lusty self-confidence of an active people riding the headlong currents of agricultural, industrial, financial, and social growth.

[II]

Much of the growth and change arose from the fact that a land still primarily agricultural was being rapidly pushed forward by an industrial revolution that was just gaining momentum. North and South, the republic was as yet a nation of small farms averaging less than two hundred acres; a nation in which land was cheap, labor becoming dear, and the mechanization of farming therefore under forced stimulus.[18] It could be said when Lincoln delivered the Gettysburg Address, as when he took his oath, that half the people lived on farms, more than half the gainfully employed worked on them, and three-fourths of the population followed a rural mode of life. The Northwest from the Ohio to the far borders of Kansas and Minnesota had achieved international power and prestige.

Chicago, for example, was by 1864 showing some surprising evidences of rapid growth and continued prosperity. Never before had there been such activity and success in all branches of trade, manufactures, and commerce, far more so than in any city west of the Alleghenies up to this time.[19] When Chicago, in 1865, shipped out nearly a million barrels of flour, seven million bushels of wheat, and twenty-five million bushels of maize, with about ten million bushels of oats, rye, and barley, King Cereal was plainly mounting the throne lately occupied by King Cotton. Yet, whereas cotton had too often ruled jealously alone, King Cereal allowed crop diversification to receive a tremendous impulse from the war, giving a larger and larger place to flax and wool, sorghum and dairy products, fruit and vegetables.[20]

17. *Ibid.*, Vol. XLVIII, No. 1, Jan., 1863, 65.
18. Gates, Paul, *Agriculture and the Civil War*, New York, 1965, Chap. IX, "Farm Labor and Machinery."
19. *Hunt's Merchants' Magazine, op. cit.*, Vol. LI, No. 3, March, 1865, 239.
20. Gates, *op. cit.*, Chaps. I, VI, VII, VIII, *passim*.

In April, 1863, the perceptive editors of *Hunt's Merchants' Magazine* commented on the effects of the war on the farming and stockgrowing areas of the trans-Allegheny West and the Mississippi Valley: "It is evident that the West, rich in mineral and material wealth of every kind and with free and extensive means of communication with the markets of the world, has a future in store for it of unexampled prosperity. Its rich lands are even now feeding the world; but we think a greater source of wealth will be its manufactures. . . ; the working up of its own abundant materials. . . ."[21]

The West had outstripped other sections of the country in prosperity during the ante-war decade, and population and capital continued to flow in. Now that the population was somewhat greater than the number readily supported by agriculture, manufactures were growing and succeeding "even in spite of the advantages of capital and long experience of the East."[22] Thus, the editors concluded that the golden period for the West had arrived; the East no longer possessed the old advantage over her, and the usual outlets for capital were to a great extent cut off. *Hunt's Magazine* predicted that: "We shall soon find her expanding in this new direction and furnishing not only food but clothing for the world. . . . Now the West is about to do that business for herself, combining her own labor, material, food, and thereby becoming the center of manufactures."[23]

As manpower left the farms to enlist in the armies, the need for agricultural machinery increased. Inventors had long been busy with such labor-saving devices, and now an eager market appeared at just the right time. Industry had to produce these and other machines, and take advantage of the expansion of burgeoning agriculture. At the same time, rural America was being altered by the fact that it needed less labor, and could free even more men for the growth of railroads, river trade, and manufactures.

While the natural course of economic events in the 1850's would have meant an increase of industrialism everywhere, and particularly in the wide Middle West, and it was certain that rural America would be thus transformed, it was also self-evident that the demands of war accelerated this trend, and shaped it to meet the demands of a crisis.

Among the many natural resources of the Northern States was manpower, both from foreign and domestic sources. Since the nation's beginning its population had grown almost continuously, particularly in the Northern States; and now, with the drain of manpower for the army, it faced a new test. It is important

---

21. *Hunt's Merchants' Magazine, op. cit.,* Vol. XLVIII, No. 4, April, 1863, 278.
22. *Ibid.,* 279.
23. *Ibid.,* 280.

to note that government inquiries and statistics show that a million males would reach draft age by 1864.[24]

Some unfriendly European journals had been predicting an interruption in the manpower growth of the Union, but the optimistic *American Railroad Journal* called these anticipations absurd. At about midsummer of 1862, it announced that, "Severe as may be the losses arising from the war, a conflict of one or two years is not going to turn aside the destinies of this country, nor can it essentially retard the progress of a nation possessed of such industrious habits, such natural resources, and such newly-created elements of wealth. . . ."

The opening of public lands would, at least after the war, attract thousands from the laboring masses of Europe. As the teeming Britons, Germans and Italians settled public lands, they would furnish enlarged markets to all the busy railways, mills, and factories. For every hundred settlers in the Northwest, openings for ten inhabitants were created in the city of New York alone.[25] Moreover, even the most populous of the older States were by no means filled.

The rise of immigration in 1863-65 contributed unmistakably to the Great Boom. The total of alien newcomers, which had stood below one hundred thousand in each of the first two years of the war, soared to 176,282 the year of Gettysburg, to 193,418 in the year of Spotsylvania, and to 248,120 the year of Appomattox. Great Britain sent the largest number in the first of these boom years, Ireland in the second, and Germany in the third, these three countries being by far the largest contributors. The river of humanity included undesirable elements, the Association for Improving the Conditions of the Poor declaring that New York drew as by irresistible magnetism some elements of the dregs and feculence of every land.[26] That, in general, however, the flow brought invigoration and a sturdy body of people, there could be no doubt.

The tide of immigration had aspects of a new character. Much larger numbers than before were coming from Liverpool and Queenstown with passages prepaid by friends or relatives in America. Use of screw steamers continued to rise in competition with the slower, riskier, and less comfortable sailing ships. In 1856, the steamer passengers who landed at Castle Garden had numbered only about 5,000, or just over three percent of the whole body; in 1863, the number rose to nearly 64,000, or two-fifths of the total. This was in spite of the fact that steerage passage by steamer, Liverpool-to-New York, cost about $35 in gold, or nearly double the sailing-ship rate. Many immigrants also made their way hither by way

24. Survey compiled from: *Ages of U.S. Volunteer Soldiers*, New York, 1866, 35; *Historical Statistics of the United States*, Washington, 1860, 10; Kennedy, Joseph A , *Population of the United States in 1860*, Washington, 1864, 592-595.

25. *American Railroad Journal*, Vol. XXXVI, No. 1368, July 5, 1862, 505.

26. *Report 1864, Association for Improving the Condition of the Poor*, New York, 1865, 44, 49, 52.

of Canada. The agent in charge of landings in New York estimated the average amount of coin brought by immigrants in the first half of 1864 at $80. A contemporary writer placed each immigrant's cash value to the country at $500.

It was observed during the boom that an unusual proportion of skilled workers seemed to be entering the country, experienced mechanics and farmers, cotton and woolen hands bound for the northeastern States, coal and iron miners going mainly to Pennsylvania, and copper and lead miners to points farther west.[27] The *Tribune* found later that about one-tenth of the immigrants who landed in New York in the first five months of 1864 entered the army or navy, a fact which justified the statement of Maldwyn Allen Jones in *American Immigration,* that in the latter part of the war "numbers of foreigners became soldiers immediately on arrival."[28] But much more important was the fact that the tide of immigration, as the *Commercial and Financial Chronicle* of December 15, 1866, said, went "far toward supplying the deficiencies of the producing population caused by the casualties of war."[29]

A leading commercial paper in 1864 expressed the feeling, contrary to the report just mentioned, that, "It is pleasant to be able to state that the class of emigrants who are coming out are very superior, the majority of them being small farmers and mechanics who bring property with them, and are industrious, frugal, sober people." Tickets for transportation were sold two months in advance to residents of Irish and English villages, and "scores of agents . . . sent to England and Ireland to engage factory hands, farmers, mechanics, laborers. . . ."[30]

Of about 800,000 immigrants during the course of the Civil War, about 160,000 were less than fifteen years of age upon arrival, while nearly 631,000 were adults, from fifteen to forty, the most productive years. About two-thirds of the immigrants were male, and by far the greatest number listed as laborers, while skilled workers, farmers, and merchants held second place. However, a respectable number came from the professions.[31]

One leading immigration authority has pointed out an important shift during the Civil War period. From 1849 to 1862, the influx of immigration preceded railway construction, but the latter preceded the rise of soft-coal output; while, after the war, the relationship between these two forms of growth was reversed.[32]

27. See long editorial, "Immigration," New York *Tribune,* June 17, 1864; Hansen, Marcus Lee, *The Immigrant in American History,* Cambridge, 1940, 53ff.

28. Jones, Maldwyn Allen, *American Immigration,* Chicago, 1961, 173.

29. Wells, David A., *Our Burden and Our Strength,* Norwich, Conn., 1864, 25-26.

30. *Prairie Farmer,* Vol. XIII, No. 21, May 14, 1864, 256, in part quoting New York *Journal of Commerce.*

31. *Monthly Summary of Commerce and Finance of the United States,* Washington, June, 1903, "Immigration in the United States," 4336, 4362, 4408-4409.

32. Brinley, Thomas, *Migration and Economic Growth; A Study of Great Britain and the Atlantic Economy,* Cambridge, 1954, 93.

The war apparently witnessed the end of the predominantly Irish phase of what has been termed "the second colonization." Although the Irish continued to enter, they were not so predominant. Also, the general movement of immigration to the land was checked, for wartime prosperity had stimulated a more varied industrial activity, demanding new workers. Many foreign-born were employed, so that, by the close of the war, these new Americans "were also more a part of that spiritual entity that makes up a nation . . ."[33]

In its usual cheeriness of comment, the *American Railroad Journal* in August, 1864, said that despite efforts in the foreign press to discourage immigration, the word got through. Furthermore, agreeing with others, it pronounced the immigration to be "of a better and more desirable character than has been usual." Despite inflation, wages were still three or four times greater than in any part of Europe, and many newcomers soon grew what they ate from the land and thus were partly independent of the advance in prices.[34]

Immigrants who had imagination knew they were builders of the new America to rise after the war. The Republican Convention of 1864 adopted a cloudy resolution that immigration should be fostered by a liberal and just policy, without defining that policy. The outgrowth of this resolution and of the establishment of the American Emigrant Company as a channel between "the man in America who wants help and the man in England who wants work," was the enactment of a law permitting wages to be pledged for a year in fulfillment of immigrant engagements.[35] Strong objection was expressed, however, to any government-assisted scheme of entry on the ground that it would burden the Treasury, open the door to fraud, and above all break down the thrifty, hardworking character of the migrants. Nor did native labor view without alarm the so-called contract-labor law. Although it was patriotically endorsed in wartime by Peter Cooper, William Cullen Bryant, and others of high standing, it had slight practical value, and endured but a few years.[36]

It is beyond dispute that the Federal Union had sufficient population and manpower to deal with the exigencies of the war against the Confederacy. The question was the organization, training, and utilization of those human resources. Aside from governmental administration of the raising of armies, no thought was taken of any significant scope of a conscription of able-bodied persons, their enrollment for industry and agriculture, or upon possible wage, price, or job controls. Such measures would have been regarded as excessively restrictive, and beyond doubt would never have been tolerated. Moreover, they were not really needed, for no transcendent crisis supervened. Problems arose from time to time

33. Hansen, *op. cit.*, 167.
34. *American Railroad Journal*, Vol. XXXVII, No. 1478, Aug. 13, 1864.
35. Jones, *American Immigration, op. cit.*, 190, 251-254; *Encyclopaedia of the Social Sciences*, IV, 342-344.
36. *Ibid.*

in the enlistment of troops and the draft; shortages of agricultural workers and other employees appeared, but most of such difficulties were met by rural and industrial readjustments, the growth of population, and more efficient use of men and machines. Many farm women boldly undertook field work, and many youngsters and old folks came forward to help replace those in service.

As we have previously noted, a steadily rising demand for changes in education had made itself felt in better common schools, academies, public high schools, and colleges. More and more of the population were responding to the need for effective new methods and institutions for training youth, especially in the new courses termed "science," which were basically applied mechanics.[37]

While the Morrill College Land Grant Act, which Lincoln had signed July 2, 1862, after it had failed under Buchanan, really did not become operative and widely beneficial until after the war, it did act as an influential educational stimulus, and was heartening evidence that the nation could consider such an advanced measure even while the war raged. It was neither directly nor indirectly a war measure, but proof that the nation of Franklin, Jefferson, and Hamilton felt a loyalty to civilization.

The voices for more practical education were many, lifted by such public leaders as Seward, the editors Greeley and Bryant, and by men strictly educators like Horace Mann and Henry Barnard, successful business organizers like Ezra Cornell, eminent agriculturalists as proficient in reaching the public as Jonathan Baldwin Turner, who introduced Osage oranges into Illinois for making hedges. He formed an effective alliance with Greeley and Ezra Cornell, did much to promote the Morrill Land Grant Act, and became father of the University of Illinois.[38]

For instance, the *Cultivator* felt that practical education would be useful in agriculture, but such things as soil chemistry would be "a delusion and a snare. If the colleges turn out well-drilled lads, thoroughly grounded in an English education, knowing something of surveying, bookkeeping and mechanics, with such lessons in farming as they may learn by example and practice on a good farm, it will be well . . . But if they graduate youths, who think they know something of vegetable physiology, agricultural chemistry, and the theories of Leibig, they will merely produce a considerable number of badly educated men, who are worse than uneducated men, because they use their common sense less, and are more conceited."[39] Frequent opinions were expressed that agriculture was neither a science nor an art, but a handicraft or trade, and that "agricultural colleges then must simply be high schools for farmers. What makes a good

37. See Nevins, Allan, *The War for the Union: War Becomes Revolution 1862-1863*, 206-208; also Nevins, Allan, *The Origins of the Land-Grant Colleges and State Universities*, Washington, D.C., 1962, *passim.*
38. Turner, Carol, *Life of Turner*, Urbana, 1911, *passim.*
39. *Cultivator*, October, 1863, 319.

farmer? The same qualities which make a good mechanic or a man of business —intelligence, judgment, and industry. Can a school teach these to its pupils? To a certain extent and indirectly it can; but as it is the object of all schools to do so, your object and means will be the same as a thousand other good schools."[40]

Much thought, planning, and discussion were devoted to this new and fertile educational concept, and although much of it had a discursively random character, it ultimately gave education a more democratic and fruitful thrust. The Secretary of the Massachusetts State Board of Agriculture devoted 120 pages of his report in 1863 to a survey of useful developments in European schools, giving special attention to the British agricultural school at Cirencester. Interest was manifested in the idea of an apprentice system in agriculture, later called job-training, a system already in operation, although somewhat informally. Recruitment of the younger sons of farmers disrupted their apprenticeship. *Country Gentleman* in 1863 commented that "our farmers could afford to receive pupils or apprentices who would assist in the routine of work for a slight pecuniary compensation," though in cases where the farming was highly developed or scientific, and attention given to instructing the pupils in the various processes and details, the students "could well afford to pay a considerable fee for the benefits thus conferred . . ."[41] This system was already in practical operation in Scotland and England. Later, the same magazine quoted an educational authority as saying the physiologist, chemist, and botanist had knowledge of the general laws of agriculture, "but, though any one combined the knowledge of . . . all [these men], he would not therefore be an agriculturist." None of them could make a living farming unless he also possessed a knowledge of farm practice, "and therefore it is that no school or college will ever be . . . considered as an agricultural school or college, unless practical teaching is regarded as the aim and end of the institution."[42]

Jonathan B. Turner of Illinois, crusading for nationally endowed universities to serve the "industrial classes," exclaimed during the war, "For heaven's sake, let our boys and girls have time to breathe, at least for one-half the year, the pure air of the world that God made, if we must sentence them to the solitary confinement in our so-called culture for the other half!" He continued, "I mean what I say, the best *educated*, not simply the *most schooled*."[43]

Calls were made for early implementation of the Land Grant Act, and recognition of its purpose. "Hence an agricultural or industrial college is to differ from the institutions of learning we already possess, rather by *adding* to their present programme than by building up one that is wholly or even principally new,—

40. *Ibid.*
41. *Country Gentleman*, Vol.XXII, No. 17, Oct. 22, 1863, 266.
42. *Ibid.*, Vol. XXXIII, No. 4, Jan. 28, 1864, 65.
43. *Ibid.*, Vol. XXIII, No. 25, June 23, 1864, 400.

and by eliminating from it whatever can be spared where something must necessarily be omitted for lack of time . . ."[44]

Agricultural schools as such had found a small beginning around 1800 in Switzerland and Germany. By 1869, one hundred forty-four agricultural experiment stations, institutes, schools, and colleges were operating in Germany, while Britain had two basic agricultural colleges, and France one. The United States, though only beginning to establish such institutions, was soon second only to Germany. Oberlin College had organized an agricultural department in 1844, which was transferred as a separate college to Cleveland in 1855, and several chairs of agriculture were established at the University of Georgia, at Amherst and elsewhere. Michigan was the first state, after Ohio, to set up an independent agricultural college which was begun in 1855 with a 676-acre farm, stock-stables, botanical gardens, and other facilities. In 1859, the Farmers' High School of Pennsylvania opened, and three years later became the Agricultural College of Pennsylvania. Iowa, too, had a small institution in 1859.[45]

When the Morrill Act passed, a considerable number of embryonic schools existed and educators were inspired to grasp at the opportunity they offered. At the opening of the Civil War, the nation had twenty-one State universities and colleges, with more ready to open. The University of Michigan was strong, and the Universities of Wisconsin and California were growing. The monopoly of the small endowed college had ended.[46]

Not only were people aware of the need for practical education in agriculture and mechanics, and of the trend toward what amounted to a "trade school," but a rising revolt was evident against the long traditional and accepted type of classical pursuits in higher education. In 1864, the *Scientific American* praised Columbia College for following the pioneer example of Brown and Harvard in establishing a separate course in science. "It is a curious fact that our old institutions of learning are the most conservative element in our social life." A century earlier, the languages and literature of ancient Greece and Rome had been deemed reasonable and proper fields of learning. "But since Geology, Chemistry, and Natural History have been made known, their great and wonderful truths" have reduced classical learning to a position of less significance, although many institutions of learning still continued to teach "Grecian and Roman Literature and Language." The *Scientific American* further stated, "Among all the signs of the times, there is none more full of glorious promise than the steady progress of that reform in education which is substituting, for the puerilities of

44. *Ibid.*, Vol. XXIII, No. 6, Feb. 11, 1864, editorial.
45. Bolles, Albert S., *Industrial History of the United States,* Norwich, Conn., 1879, 27-29.
46. Nevins, Allan, *The Origins of the Land-Grant Colleges and State Universities, op. cit.,* 26-28.

ancient fable, the useful and sublime truths of modern science."[47]

The increased public interest in invention and mechanics had been in existence for some decades. For example, Lincoln himself had once prepared a lecture on invention; and numerous magazines were devoting themselves to various mechanical and agricultural subjects, such as articles on making wagon-wheels, the possibility of steam-cars on the roads, turning tools, steam-expansion, lumber seasoning, water engines in Europe, patent stone bricks, manufacture of magnesium, aluminum, improved axles, the Rhumkorff cell, Squires's fruit-jar, Porter's Sifter Shovel, and still others.[48]

While little or no mention of the war was made in scientific magazines in the 1860's, considerable attention was paid to mechanical developments brought about by the conflict, such as ironclads, artillery, special automatic guns, machines for rifling, revolving turrets, portable breastworks, and imaginative but unworkable devices such as armor for men and horses, along with improved steam-boilers, a hog-blast grain-dryer, and new rolling-mills in Pittsburgh. The numerous farmers' publications, such as *Prairie Farmer, Country Gentlemen, Cultivator,* and *Genesee Farmer,* stressed labor-saving devices, crop statistics, and more advanced methods of farming. It is impossible to determine what effect these publications had, but their number and contents indicate that they had a wide distribution. The new Federal Department of Agriculture was firm in indicating that the Land-Grant College Act was intended for all industrial classes, the mechanics, the manufacturers, and those in the carrying trades, as well as in agriculture.[49] The Department of Agriculture itself, within its limited field of crop and livestock statistics and seed distribution, was a powerful educational influence, along with the increased number of pamphlets and texts published on such subjects.

Machinery now became an integral part of agriculture, from the cotton-gin to the McCormick reaper. While some farmers resisted, or could not afford, these new inventions, an increasing number had taken advantage of them. With the sudden reduction in farm labor due to the demands of the army and increased need for food crops, the market for available farm-machinery greatly increased, as evidenced by advertisements and articles in the current farm magazines. Available were such machines as the Vaughn Power Corn Sheller, Hawkeye Corn Cultivator by Deere & Co., Ball's Ohio Reaper and Mower, Call's Canton (Ohio) Threshing Machine, and many others. "Life is too short and human strength too precious for our womenkind to be kept to the old process of Washing and

47. *Scientific American,* Vol. X, No. 16, April 16, 1864, 249.
48. Partial list from a few issues of *Scientific American,* particularly Vol. XII, No. 1, Jan. 2, 1865.
49. *Monthly Report of the United States Department of Agriculture,* January, 1865, 15–20.

Wringing," read the advertisement for the Universal Clothes Wringer with Cog Wheels, of which 53,819 were sold in 1863, and 72,083 in the first nine months of 1864. Along with announcements of a million acres of Illinois Central land available in 1865 for $8.00 to $12.00 an acre, these magazines also advertised artificial legs.[50]

The great agricultural advances of the quarter-century before 1864 were displayed at many State and County fairs for 1864, and at numerous agricultural institutions.[51]

As farm-labor became more and more scarce, the rise in wages to $3.00 per day plus board, for binding up wheat in up-state New York in 1864, encouraged farmers to cooperate with each other in harvesting their crops rather than to pay "exhorbitant" wages.[52]

The noble contribution of the farmers to the war effort enabled the country to "prosecute the war with vigor and maintain its elements of commercial greatness . . . America has reasons to be proud of her rural sons . . ."[53] A recent study said, "In the North, the Civil War gave a tremendous impetus to the adoption of new machines and techniques as manpower diminished while the demand for farm products appeared unlimited . . ."[54]

The sewing-machine, put on the market in 1849, was by 1860 a vital tool in making clothing, shoes, and other articles. Sales doubled in five years because of the need for uniforms, and many sewing-machines were exported to other countries even during the war. Before the war, most men's shirts were hand-made, but the sewing-machine drastically cut the time for making clothing. The shoe industry, likewise, was rapidly shifted from a piecework, home-industry, to a factory operation by the application of the almost universal steam-power operation, increasing the output one-hundred-fold.[55]

Shortage of manpower had created the need for machinery, thus giving the inventor the greatest opportunity he had yet known. In 1860, patents totalled 4,589 out of 7,653 applications—by far the largest number in history—and by 1865, from a total of 10,664 applications, 6,490 patents were granted.[56]

For the first time in America, to any major extent, women shared in the nation's agricultural, business, and industrial enterprises. As the men disappeared

50. *Prairie Farmer,* Vol. XV, No. 1, Jan. 7, 1865, and other farm magazines. A million acres of Illinois Central land was available in 1865 for $8 to $12 an acre.
51. *Genesee Farmer,* June, 1864, 181, 183-184; September, 1864, 288.
52. *Ibid.,* August, 1864, 258.
53. *Prairie Farmer,* April 22, 1865, 12.
54. Towne, Marvin W., and Wayne D. Rasmussen, "Farm Gross Product and Gross Investment in the Nineteenth Century," *Trends in American Economy in the Nineteenth Century,* Vol. XXIV, Princeton, 1960, 260.
55. For summary, see Fite, Emerson D., *op. cit.,* 88-90. *Social and Industrial Conditions in the North During the Civil War,* New York, 1930, 88-90.
56. *Historical Statistics of the United States, op. cit.* 608.

George H. Thomas, Union General—"The Rock of Chickamauga"

Justin Smith Morrill of Vermont,
Originator of the College Land Grant Act

from farms, wives and daughters went into the fields, one observer in Iowa reporting more women driving teams and busy on the land than men. A current song exhorted volunteers: "Just take your gun and go! For Ruth can drive the oxen, John, and I can use the hoe!" In every State, women put their shoulders to the plow.[57] Though most of these women returned to home duties after the war, they still had proved that when the crisis came, they were able and willing to share the load.

In the ranks of schoolteachers an equally sharp but more enduring change took place. Women had been replacing men in teaching the lower grades for some years, but the war rapidly augmented their numbers in all departments of education. Illinois, in 1860, had 8,223 men and 6,845 women teachers, but by 1865 the numbers were 6,170 men and 10,843 women. New York, Michigan, Pennsylvania and other states witnessed similar changes.[58]

Industry also profited from the same increased employment of women workers. In the Massachusetts cotton mills from 1860–1866, expenditures for female labor increased by 90 percent in current money, and even after allowing for inflation, by 66 percent.[59]

Although salaries of women were considerably lower than those of men, the general advance in female wages in the New England mills was 50 percent compared to 61 percent for males.[60] Despite these gains, however, the low status of women in industry finally became cause for considerable unrest, for women were now entering the stream of economic life in important new ways, especially in clerical and government work, including the Treasury Department.[61]

[III]

The Great Boom moved in an atmosphere resounding with martial music, with songs like "We'll rally round the flag, boys, we'll rally once again," and a succession of poems, editorials, essays, and stories, that nerved the hearts and strengthened the arms of all Northerners. Edward E. Hale's "The Man Without a Country," appearing in December, 1863, just after Vicksburg and Gettysburg, and just before the desperate battles of the spring and summer of 1864, was worth a division of soldiers to Grant's army; for, widely republished, it dealt a stunning blow to all the followers of Vallandigham and McClellan, who were urging upon Lincoln a negotiated peace. H. H. Brownell's stirring verses, "The Bay Fight,"

57. Fite, *op. cit.*, 8–9; Gates, *Agriculture, op. cit.*, 75, 242-243.
58. Fite, *op. cit.*, 244–246.
59. Lebergott, Stanley, *Trends in American Economy in the Nineteenth Century*, "Wage Trends, 1800-1900," 460.
60. Wells, O.A. *The Recent Financial, Industrial and Commercial Experiences of the United States*, New York, 1872, 482.
61. Massey, Mary Elizabeth, *Bonnet Brigade*, New York, 1966, *passim.*

after Farragut's victory in Mobile Bay, his "The River Fight," after the battles to seize the Mississippi; Bryant's eloquent editorials in the *Evening Post*, and Longfellow's "The Cumberland" and "A Nameless Grave," and other verses, were worth regiments to the Union. The national scene, despite all blows and losses, still had a few memorably happy scenes. George William Curtis, attending the opera in 1864, wrote that the Academy of Music was just what it used to be. "There were the bright rows of pretty women and smiling men; the floating ribbons; the marvelous chevelures; the pearl-gray, dove, and tan gloves, holding the jewelled fans and beautiful bouquets—the smile, the sparkle, the superb and irresistible dandyism that we all knew so well in the days of golden youth"—they were all there "in the thick odor of heliotrope."[62] But greed and vulgarity often ruled. George Ticknor, whose *History of Spanish Literature* reached its third edition in 1863, and who was busy gathering books, money and supporters for the Boston Public Library, recalled that Henry I. Bowditch, the unwearied public health crusader, had said to him thirty years earlier: "We are living in the best days of the republic. That the worst will follow soon does not seem to me very likely."[63] Many would have said in 1864 that the worst days *had* followed, and still more would have been tempted to say it in 1865. New York was never so crowded, its hotels never so glittering, the scale of spending never so lavish.

But Greeley's *Tribune* stated in 1864 that it did not believe that half the legal amount of income tax had been paid by individuals the previous year.[64] Evasion was flagrantly widespread. Thaddeus Stevens told the House as the year ended that, in the opinion of experts, tobacco importers and dealers had pocketed many millions by barefaced devices to avoid new taxes.[65] These same practices were prevalent in the liquor trade as well. Lobbying, log-rolling, and bribery defeated efforts to protect the Treasury, and bulging warehouses escaped the levy. The resulting profit to middlemen and market operators was estimated at $50,000,000, a gargantuan sum for that day.[66]

From the beginning of the war, the price of whisky rose from 18½ cents per gallon to $2.01 per gallon in 1865.[67] Taxes, and frantic efforts to sweep them into private pockets, unquestionably limited liquor manufacture during the boom year. During the greater part of 1865, reported the Milwaukee Chamber of Commerce, "our distilleries were lying idle, as they could not compete with the large stock of spirits made prior to passage of the law increasing the tax to the present

62. Curtis, George William, *From the Easy Chair*, New York, 1892-1894, 15-20.
63. Ticknor, George, *Life, Letters and Journals of George Ticknor*, Boston, 1876, II, 464.
64. New York *Tribune*, March 17, 1864.
65. *Congressional Globe*, 38th Cong., 2nd Sess., 1864-65, Pt. I, Dec. 8, 1864, 11.
66. Fite, Emerson David, *Social and Industrial Conditions in the North During the Civil War*, New York, 1910, 81-82.
67. *Annual Report*, Cincinnati Chamber of Commerce and Merchants' Exchange, Cincinnati, 1870, 114.

rate."[68] The heavy excise tax on liquor contributed to the corruption which gave birth to the unfortunate Ring scandal which stained the Grant Administration a few years later. However, the excise tax and resultant price increases had one healthy effect in curtailing the use of whisky among the poor, and increasing the consumption of beer.[69]

Yet the inflation that won fortunes for some made paupers of many, or increased their present pauperism. In the autumn of 1863, about 250 girls, who made a precarious living sewing umbrellas in New York, went on strike. They were paid from six to eight cents an umbrella; by steady work from 6 A.M. to midnight they could finish a dozen. Out of their pittance they had to buy their own needles and thread, so they asked in desperation for two cents more on each umbrella.[70] The strike succeeded—but the umbrella-sewers could still sing Thomas Hood's sad "Song of the Shirt." Laborers on various railroads running into New York had struck a little earlier for decent pay. Freight handlers of the Hudson River line, demanding $1.50 a day in place of the $1.13 previously received, were defeated early in 1863 by gangs of strike-breakers who marched to work under police protection. When the railroad hired a number of blacks, the strikers showed what the *Tribune* called "renewed excitement"—a fact perhaps connected with the subsequent draft riots.[71]

During the boom which gave some social groups so much luxury and leisure, many workers endured not only poor pay, but preposterously long hours. In 1862, Henry Ward Beecher devoted one sermon to a protest against the 14-hour-day, and Sunday labor required of employees on city streetcars and omnibuses. A great meeting was held at Cooper Institute in 1863, and the next year, as infantry fought at Kenesaw Mountain and Petersburg, several thousand workers gathered in Union Square in New York to demonstrate in favor of earlier closing of stores and offices. They carried transparencies reading, "Our wives and children require us," and "Clerks are no longer strangers to their families." Former Mayor Opdyke presided; Horace Greeley made a speech arguing that, while shorter hours would reduce expenses, workers would really do more in ten hours than twelve; and Beecher again demanded reform in the interests of health, education, and morals. The best newspapers supported the movement, and when angry shoe clerks mobbed several shops, a sporadic reduction was achieved.[72]

Eloquent evidence of poverty and squalor in New York appeared in the annual reports of the Sanitary Company of the Police Department. In the spring of the draft riot year of 1863, it found that of the 401,376 people living in tenements,

68. *Annual Report,* Milwaukee Chamber of Commerce, Milwaukee, 1865, 42.
69. United States Census, 1900, Vol. II, "Alcoholic Liquors," 616.
70. New York *Tribune,* Oct. 9, 1863.
71. New York *Tribune,* March 2, 1863.
72. New York *Tribune,* March 25, 1863; June 4, 17, 1864.

no fewer than 22,095 dwelt in cellars; a whole city of troglodytes. Of the 12,347 tenement houses, well over one-fourth, or 4,221, were badly ventilated. The majority of tenement houses were divided into small apartments, housing an almost incredible number of families, eight or ten people sometimes using a single sunless room as kitchen, living-room and bedroom.[73] In such crowded buildings the condition of sinks and privies was noisome. The Citizens' Association, founded in 1863 in the shock after the draft riots, lent its aid to the Association for Improving the Condition of the Poor, established nearly two decades earlier by such public-spirited merchants as James B. Lenox and Robert B. Minturn. Its reports were as appalling as the graphic picture that Arthur Young and Tobias Smollett drew of conditions in France on the eve of the Revolution. At the height of the boom, the Citizens' Association observed that the million people of New York City had about 200,000 cases of needless and preventable sickness every year, and 7,000 to 10,000 of the 25,196 people who died in 1863 could have been saved by proper sanitation. Other cities told the same story.[74]

Figures for the cost of living and wages furnish some instruction, despite discrepancies between the findings of various authorities. In consumer prices, taking 1860 as 100 in index number, prices rose in all items to 175 in 1865 before beginning to drop sharply. In 1861 the index was only 101, in 1862 it was 113, in 1863 it was 139, and in 1864, 176.[75] Food consumer prices ran a little behind the total for all items with light, fuel, and rent even somewhat lower. Clothing was the highest of all, rising from 100 in 1860 to 261 in 1864, and then down to 238 in 1865. In other words, there was 75% increase in all consumer prices in 1865 over 1860.

Wages also increased, although not at the rate of prices. Again using 1860 for an index level of 100, wages for all industries reached 152 by January of 1865. Wages of unskilled men reached 152 and skilled workers 150. Employees who rose above the top figure of 152 overall were those in city public works, in the illuminating-gas industry, and in the building trades. Below 152 were the cotton textile workers, woolen textile workers, metal workers and railroad workers.[76] Wages lagged about one year behind prices. However, at the end of the war prices broke sharply while wages continued generally to mount until the early seventies and, in fact, surpassed prices in the index comparison.[77] Income-tax returns for New York and

73. *Annual Reports of the Sanitary Company of the New York Police Department*, ed. Capt. G. B. Lord, New York, 1862, 1863, 1864.

74. *Reports of Citizens' Association*, New York, xi, xii; Atkins, Gordon, *Health, Housing and Poverty in New York City, 1865-1898*, Ann Arbor, 1947, Chs. I-III.

75. *Historical Statistics of the United States*, 127; Hoover, Ethel D., "Retail Prices After 1850," *Trends in the American Economy in the Nineteenth Century*, Vol. XXIV, *op. cit.*, 142-143; Taussig, F.W., "Disparities Between Rich and Poor in Wartime America," *Yale Review*, Vol. II, Nov., 1893, 244; Falkner, Roland P., "Report of the Statistician, Wholesale Prices, Wages and Transportation," *Senate Report No. 1394*, 52nd Cong., 2nd Sess., Washington, 1894, Pt. I, 9, 30-32.

76. *Historical Statistics of the United States*, 90; Lebergott, *op. cit.*, 466-468.

77. Taussig, *op. cit.*; Martin, Robt. F., *National Income in the United States*, New York, 1939, 6, 13.

other Northern cities showed in 1864 an astonishing increase of private revenue over the previous year, not to be accounted for by any difference in the value of currency. In one collection district of Massachusetts the taxable incomes of 1864 were nearly three times those of 1863.[78]

While some people doubtless suffered from the wage-price squeeze, and indeed in many social areas the gap between the rich and poor widened during the war, nevertheless the wartime boom was beneficial to the majority of the people. Except for occasional shutdowns and slowdowns in textiles early in the war, unemployment was very low. Jobs remained plentiful, in many instances paying rates better than in pre-war days. It was possible, because of the demand for workers, for a capable man to advance to better pay. According to a leading farm journal, "There must be something radically wrong with the farmer who does not free himself from debt. Never in the lifetime of the present generation will such another opportunity present itself. If a man's crops and livestock last year brought him a thousand dollars, and his expenses were $500, this year his receipts will be two thousand, while his expenditures, even if they doubled— which they will not in one instance in ten—will allow a profit twice that of last year. . . ."[79]

[IV]

The panic of 1857, the secession movement, and the war had taught useful lessons in economy and caution to businessmen and farmers. As the *Scientific American* remarked in 1863, noting the general prosperity, and abundance of capital and low interest: "Business is now conducted very extensively upon a cash basis," and the elements of thrift were evident on every hand.[80] Late in 1863, *The Country Gentleman* made the same assertions, noting that losses were diminished even though prices of purchased materials were enhanced, and taxation had increased.[81]

Another evidence of the general stability of capital was the sharp and real decline in business failures. In the Northern States alone, because of the disruption of the war in 1861, failures, including a large number of small businesses, reached a high of over 178½ millions in liabilities, representing nearly 6,000 individual businesses. However, between 1861 and 1864, these totals fell to a mere 510 failures, representing only 8½ millions in liabilities.[82] These figures

78. Walker, George, *The Wealth, Resources and Public Debt of the United States*, London, 1865, 17.
79. *Prairie Farmer*, Vol. XIV, No. 11, Sept. 10, 1864, 161.
80. *Scientific American*, Vol. VIII, No. 3, Jan. 17, 1863, 41.
81. *Country Gentleman*, Vol. XXII, No. 19, Nov. 5, 1863, 304.
82. *American Railroad Journal*, Vol. XXXVIII, No. 1506, Feb. 25, 1866, figures from R. G. Dun; *Hunt's Merchants' Magazine*, Vol. LII, No. 2, Feb., 1865, 146-147.

did not include speculators in gold, stock and produce, but even in those fields many unscrupulous men were rescued from time to time.

The *American Railroad Journal* attributed the spectacular decrease in failures primarily to "that rigid caution which has obtained in our business community" in granting credits, and to the increased values of stocks on hand, declaring that "the immense and general prosperity of all branches of agriculture has augmented the wealth of the trading classes, and the scarcity of labor, suitable to the requirements of the mechanical interests, has tended to increased wages, and enhanced receipts of the operating classes."[83] For 1864, business houses were said to number 168,925 with a "wealth" of $4,994,766,000. Profits ranged from twelve to fifteen percent, but even assuming low profits of ten percent, the accrued gain for the year was $494,476,600.[84]

On the farms, examples of increased production were numerous. For one, the use of artificial manures or fertilizers was being urged in all farm magazines. "The increased consumption of agricultural and horticultural products by our armies and navies, with a decreased production from the scarcity of labor, renders any means which favors a high system of cultivation of national importance. To 'Make two blades of grass grow where one grew before' should now, more than at any former time, be the aim of every American farmer. . . ."[85] This publication asserted that "At the present price of agricultural produce the use of good artificial fertilizers is more profitable than it has ever been in this country . . . and artificial manures can be so easily applied that those who have once tried them will not lightly abandon their use."[86]

In its first monthly report in July, 1863, the new Department of Agriculture stated that, "No nation has ever developed such agricultural resources as the United States. . . . The amount of capital it has invested in lands and farming implements is nearly seven billions of dollars, producing an annual value of two and a half billion dollars. It employs and directly supports about seventeen million of the population of the U.S." In addition to cereals and animals, agriculture at that time embraced the entire textile raw material field, "hence our manufacturing indirectly has been created by and is dependent on our agriculture. The *capital* invested in our manufactures exceeds two billions of dollars, yielding an annual product not much less in value. This diversified industry has created a commerce of not less proportionate magnitude, which . . . uses as its means of travel and transportation railroads, canals, and river improvements costing two and a half billions of dollars, and employs a tonnage in value about two hundred and twenty-five billions of dollars. . . . Nor is this all. The wants of Europe have

83. *Ibid.* Vol. XXXVIII, No. 1506, Feb. 25, 1866, 180.
84. *Ibid*.
85. *Rural Annual* for 1865, Rochester, New York, 1866, preface.
86. *Ibid.*, 47.

established a great and rapidly increasing dependence upon the United States for its agricultural products. . . . The world leans on us . . ."[87]

Exports of breadstuffs, for the first seven months of each year, despite the war, showed high increase in wheat, rye and corn.[88] Although exports did drop in 1864, they were still substantial.[89] The value of beef exports increased immensely from 1861 to 1863.[90] In New York, exports of agricultural produce increased in 1862, keeping a high level in spite of declines in 1863 and 1864, which were attributed to lessening of European demand and increase in prices, rather than lack of availability.[91]

Most remarkable of all, to foreign observers, was the growth of the meat trade. "At Chicago," one Briton wrote Peto, "a million pigs die every year for the benefit of the public. They are killed by machinery in the quickest and most scientific way. Within twenty minutes of the time of your hearing the pig squeal, he is killed, cut up, packed in barrels, and on his way to Europe."[92] Tongues were packed separately; the feet, which had once gone to glue-makers, went to army sutlers or poor men's tables; bristles, hides, lard, bones, and in fact everything was utilized. Centers that in pre-war days had sent salt meat down the Ohio and Mississippi to Southern markets had given way to midwestern cities supplying the East and Europe. Within a single war year, Chicago doubled her meat-packing capacity by the erection of about twenty-five packing houses. Whereas some 270,000 hogs had been slaughtered there in 1860, the number rose by the end of the war to about 900,000. Union stockyards, with pens for all the cattle and pigs brought in by various railroads, covered about five hundred acres when opened on Christmas Day in 1865. Peto marvelled to see so much space devoted to livestock, with light, drainage, and water for every pen; but he did not inquire how much food, water, and exercise the animals had gotten in their long journey to the city, nor how satisfactory were the sanitary rules for slaughtering and packing. An honest reply would have shocked him.

Exports of some meats showed large increases in 1863 over even 1862, and the value of beef exports increasing from $1,372,564 in 1861 to $2,807,042 in 1863.[93] These "rapid and extensive changes were attributed to the effects of civil war upon commerce; and to the rapid increase of settlement in the West, especially Iowa, Illinois and Missouri."[94]

87. *Monthly Report of the Condition of the Crops*, U.S. Dept. of Agriculture, Washington, July 10, 1863, 1.
88. *Ibid.*, 4.
89. *Report of the U.S. Department of Agriculture*, Sept.-Oct., 1864, Washington, 1864, 33.
90. *Ibid.*, March-April, 1864, Washington, 1864, 20.
91. *Ibid.*, Washington, January, 1865, 31.
92. Peto, *op. cit.*, 95, 96.
93. *Monthly Report of the U.S. Dept. of Agriculture*, Dec. 1863, 17, 20.
94. *Ibid.*, March-April, 1864, 23.

Actually, the numbers of cattle, oxen, and cows declined somewhat between 1860 and 1865, though much of the loss in totals was undoubtedly caused by the failure to count livestock in the Southern States. Cattle and oxen declined from 7,941,148 in 1860 to 7,072,573 in 1865. It was evident that these four years of war had drained the country of many cattle which could not be easily replaced. *The Prairie Farmer* attributed this to the fact that the nation had been largely absorbed in activities other than stock growing, and to the great army demand, supported by high prices.[95] Nevertheless, sufficient cattle remained to support the Northern civil population, to supply the army as well as export needs. While hogs showed a total decline, sheep increased sharply.[96] The government reported that "the high price of grain food and the scarcity of labor have led to less attention to stock growing."[97]

Most historians have neglected giving proper attention to the supply of horses and mules in Civil War days. One authority asserts that, next to the consumption of manpower and even more important than the cost in money, were the requirements for cavalry and draft-horses. That noble and docile animal, the horse, he rather grandiloquently states, "is intimately connected with the existence of nations, who would not know how to live . . . without him."[98] The need for the "equine race" included not only horses for agriculture, industry and civilian transportation in increased numbers, but for the cavalry, artillery, and wagon-trains. Actually, due to this demand and heavy attrition, the population of horses on the farms dropped from 4,199,141 in 1860 to 3,740,923 in 1865. Mules showed a similar drop.[99]

Livestock prices increased throughout the war, except for a drop late in 1861. For instance, No. 1 cattle in December 1860 were at $3.75, while by January 4, 1865, the price reached $6.75 to $8 for choice beeves. Hogs, which had averaged $4.75 in December, 1860, then dropped drastically through 1862 before rising to $11.50 and $12.50 for "best" on January 4, 1865.[100]

The total value of farm crops in 1862 was put at $706,887,395 by the Department of Agriculture; 1863 saw an increase to $955,764,322. In 1864 the total value reached $1,440,415,435, nearly half again as much, the rise being chiefly in crops most in demand for war purposes. The total increase in gold value from November, 1862, to January 1, 1865, was 73 per cent, while that of the value of crops about 103 per cent.[101]

95. *Prairie Farmer*, Vol. XV, No. 18, May 6, 1865, editorial.
96. *Monthly Report of the U.S. Department of Agriculture*, March, 1865, 19.
97. *Ibid.*
98. Vogeli, Felix, "Horses in the United States as Connected with the War," *Prairie Farmer*, Vol. XIV, No. 21, Nov. 19, 1864.
99. "Farm Stock," *Monthly Report of the U.S. Department of Agriculture*, March, 1865, 19.
100. From various issues of *Prairie Farmer*, Jan. 3, 1861, through Dec. 30, 1865.
101. *Monthly Report of the U.S. Department of Agriculture*, Washington, February, 1864, 31.

Men were increasingly conscious that profitable farming meant more than scattering seeds upon the ground, or allowing livestock to roam and graze for themselves. "The difference between good and bad cultivation is often the difference between a full and a half-crop; and while our best managers scarcely ever fail" to procure twenty-five or thirty bushels of wheat per acre, "poor farmers who trust to luck and hope . . . will not average half this amount." This verdict held true for corn as well as wheat. "We can point to several farmers who do not fail even in unfavorable seasons to raise sixty or seventy bushels per acre," said *The Country Gentleman*, "while others, through neglect and nothing else, either in draining, . . . manuring or other preparation, or from a want of cultivation and general management, do not average thirty bushels. . . ." They do not "receive one-half the prices obtained by some of their apparently fortunate neighbors who have long since discovered that diligence is the mother of good luck. . . ."[102]

Accepting the statement that the best wheat farmers could get 25 to 30 bushels an acre, and superior corn farmers 60 to 70 bushels an acre, it appears that in production per acre we have advanced a relatively short distance, separating good from mediocre farmers. In the fall of 1966 the Department of Agriculture reported an average yield per acre of wheat at 26.4 bushels and 69.6 for corn. Thus the best farmers of the 1860's could produce the equivalent of the average for later years.[103] The 1860's average for wheat, however, had been about 15 or 20 bushels, and for corn not more than 40 bushels.[104]

Of basic importance to agricultural production and capital development during the Civil War years, were the good weather conditions encountered in the North.[105]

The Country Gentleman stated in 1864: "The war and its results are as much the business of the farmer as of the soldier. The great questions of the demand and supply of provisions, of horses, or clothing, all immediately affect the producer. The withdrawal and diversion of labor from the soil, by the employment of our sons and brothers in the army or in service connected with the army, comes home to our farms and our firesides. The breaking up of the great system of involuntary service at the south, the sales of estates for taxes, the desolation of large portions of the States which have been the scenes of active army operations, are all opening new fields for the ambition of our young northern farmers, and offering problems difficult of solution to the land owners of the whole country. Of these great changes it is our duty to take thought, early and carefully, that we

102. *Country Gentleman*, Vol. XXII, No. 15, October 8, 1863, 102.

103. *Ibid.;* current figures from Information Office of the U.S.D.A., Chicago, Paul Ostendorf, interview.

104. *Country Gentleman*, Vol. XIII, No. 5, Feb. 4, 1864; *Monthly Report of the U.S. Department of Agriculture*, January, 1865, 28.

105. *American Annual Cyclopaedia*, 1862, 4-8; 1863, 2-6; 1864, 2-9; 1865, 2-9.

so direct our agricultural energies as to produce the best results for ourselves and our country."[106]

Some authorities place the first American agricultural revolution during the years 1850 to 1870, when real farm gross output rose from $1.4 to $2.5 billion. The new farm technology was not really felt until the Civil War period, for no substantial rise in demand for grain had occurred, and farmers generally felt no strong incentive to buy machines that would increase output, while many men resisted the adoption of new ideas. Expansion westward also played a part in increased agricultural production. In 1860, of the ten leading wheat states three were east of the Alleghenies, and only one—Iowa—was west of the Mississippi. By 1870, only one wheat state was east of the Alleghenies, and four of the leading wheat-producing states were west of the Mississippi.[107]

Furthermore, the united effort needed to fight the war, along with the increased use of railroads, was influencing agriculture in another way. It was no longer a local pursuit, supplying only its own area; products were moving more and more over the entire nation. While modern agriculture added to the capital value of farms in the 1850's, and would have continued to do so, there can be little doubt that the unique demands of the Civil War period accelerated, as in other fields, the expansion of production and the investment of capital in agriculture to a degree which benefited the North and eventually the whole nation, consumer and producer alike.

Everyone, it seemed, had an exuberant confidence in the nation's natural resources, including mineral wealth. Extremely optimistic assessments, such as those expressed by Lincoln from time to time, were repeated; and exaggerated estimates were often published. To be sure, much of the optimism was justified, for all the important major minerals were now available in the Northern States or in territory under their control. It was true that considerable copper had been imported from Chile, but local sources in Michigan were replacing importations, and new copper mines were fast developing in California, precursors of the great Arizona deposits.

Pig-iron production totaling 920,000 short tons in 1860, more than half of which was in Pennsylvania, dropped in 1861 and 1862, and then rose to 1,136,000 short tons in 1864.[108] This increase, while not sensational, was sufficient for the added pressures of the war effort, without sacrifice of civilian production. Coal, so vital to the naval warfare and blockade, was assured by ample fields, Pennsyl-

106. *Country Gentleman*, Vol. XXIII, No. 2, Jan. 14, 1864, 25, by a "Judge French;" No. 10, March 10, 1864, 160.

107. Towne, Marvin W., and Wayne D. Rasmussen, "Farm Gross Product and Gross Investment in the Nineteenth Century," *Trends in the American Economy in the Nineteenth Century*, Vol. XXIV, Princeton, N.J., 1960, 260-261.

108. *Historical Statistics of the United States, op. cit.*, 366.

vania being far the most productive state, particularly in anthracite. No real shortages of iron or coal appeared during the war. With the extension of the railroads, Michigan was developing into an iron and copper center. The newly found beds of salt brine in Michigan proved opportune as the salt works on the Kanawha in West Virginia were partially destroyed by the war, and importations into New Orleans were cut off. Thus the Union never suffered, as the South did, from a deficiency of salt. Full supplies came from New York State and the new Michigan fields.[109]

Continuously optimistic, the *American Railroad Journal* in the fall of 1863 reported: "The universal employment of iron in all branches of manufactures, is such as to make the capacity for its production a pretty accurate measure of a state's prosperity. . . . An iron foundation was being laid, and upon it a light will arise far more brilliant than that which shone upon the water, which will be reflected for ages to come upon our nation, and our nation's children. The age of iron is an age of strength and intelligence. We believe our future will be an iron age."[110] Actually, such a view required no crystal ball. It can assuredly be said that the war did no harm to the capital investment in iron, coal, copper, and other mining enterprises.

It was the field of precious metals, however, that first excited the nation. Until the late 1850's the primary source of gold ore had been California. When war came, some fears were felt in the North that somehow the Confederacy might interrupt the supply of gold to the East, or even seize the mines. While these fears proved highly exaggerated, there were those in the Confederacy, or pro-Southerners in California, who dreamed of making a strike there. In Nevada the famous Comstock Lode was discovered in 1859, and the great silver boom then underway led to the settlement of such famous communities as Virginia City, Montana Territory. Furthermore, these new northern mines relieved the Union of any fear of possible Confederate seizure or disruption. However, the war itself cannot be said to have been the primary catalyst in the discoveries of the early sixties. The lure of precious metals was enough, war or no war. In fact, no one will ever be able to even estimate with any accuracy the numbers of men, many of whom were fleeing the war, who entered mining in the West in 1860-65.

Gold production in 1860 totaled well over two million troy ounces. Production declined, particularly in California from 1861-1863, but in 1864 rose again as gold came from the Montana fields. Only small amounts of silver were mined in the United States before 1860, but by 1861 the Nevada mines were yielding large amounts. In shaky-dollar statistics, an official report of 1867 put the value of gold produced in Oregon, California, Nevada, and Washington Territory at

109. For survey, see Fite, *op. cit.*, Chap. II.
110. *American Railroad Journal,* Vol. XXXVI, No. 1433, Oct. 3, 1863, 943.

$43,391,000 in 1861, rising to $106,000,000 in 1866. In fact, production of gold and silver in 1866 exceeded all the gold and silver in the National Treasury and in all banks combined which, as of August 1, 1866, was reported to be $69,700,000.[111]

The Comstock Lode was perhaps the major topic of conversation and excitement in Far Western mining circles. The Nevada region, then generally known as Washoe, soon became a primary basis of mining speculation. Bullion sent to California from Nevada, valued at only $90,897 in 1860, had risen by 1863 to $12,486,238.[112]

Anyone remotely connected with mining owned shares in some silver mine; some even owned stock in impossible, mythical, or hopeful silver mines. Speculators would pay high prices for mines at places "of which the purchaser had never heard until a day or two before the purchase. Men seemed to have discarded all dictates of prudence. Their judgment was overwhelmed by the sudden ... wealth of a few and ... the general [fever] ... of the many to buy any kind of silver shares."[113]

Three thousand silver-mining companies were incorporated in San Francisco. Shares in the best Comstock Lode mines were considered preferred security for loans. The value of these shares, generally known as "feet" (for a share represented a lineal foot on the vein), advanced rapidly. A foot of the Gould and Curry mine, worth $500 on March 1, 1862, sold for $1,000 in June, soaring to $5,600 in July, 1863. Other advances were equally spectacular.[114]

Virginia City, Nevada Territory, suddenly became the second largest town west of the Rockies with 15,000 population. By the summer of 1863, however, stock prices began to fall. Experts wrote that management of the mines had been "grossly wasteful." Some companies were flagrant swindles. Prices dropped slowly until mid-1864, when panic hit the Washoe. Gould and Curry dropped from $5,600 to $900 per foot; Savage from $3,600 to $750, and others likewise. Spurious wildcat operations were wiped out. "The dray-men, the hod-carriers, the mechanics, the clerks, the seamstresses, the servant girls, who had cheerfully paid assessments for years, in the confidence that they would soon have a handsome income from their silver mines, were disenchanted."[115] The name of Washoe, once blessed, was now accursed. A primary trouble was that many mines had not been opened with the idea of extracting silver, but as excuses for the promotion and sale of stock. Ignorance of mining and metallurgy contributed to the slump. A primary point of debate was the question whether the Comstock

111. Browne, J. Ross, and James W. Taylor, *Report Upon the Mineral Resources of the United States*, Washington, 1867, 9.
112. *Ibid.*, 30-31.
113. *Ibid.*
114. *Ibid.*
115. *Ibid.*, 31.

had a number of connected branches, or was one of a series of separate lodes. Expenses rose as mines went deeper, timber became costly, and problems of water and ventilation increased. However, things did improve. After its low of $900 per foot in July, 1864, Gould and Curry went up again to $2,000 in April, 1865. This upward trend held true in the fields on the Esmeralda and Humboldt Rivers, and in the Columbia Basin. Strikes in Idaho and Oregon were not so large or rich, although important during the Civil War.[116]

While the Colorado gold mines encountered serious obstructions, the fields continued to be developed. In Montana Territory in the summer of 1862, some Minnesota emigrants found prospectors working on branches of the Jefferson River and in the Deer Lodge Valley tributaries of the Columbia. Various placer-mines were soon in operation, until June, 1863, when a major find about seventy miles east of Bannock on Alder Creek, a tributary of the Jefferson River, resulted in the rise over night of Virginia City in Montana Territory. In 1865, at Helena, an even richer field was discovered, known as Confederate Gulch.[117] Estimates of Montana gold production are put at $2,000,000 in 1863; $5,000,000 in 1864; $6,000,000 in 1865, and up to $12,000,000 in 1866. Some silver was also mined in Montana.[118]

One authority feels that the Montana promoters were the victims of "bad timing." They had to compete with the Civil War, the two big discoveries being obscured by war news from the Peninsula, Vicksburg, and Gettysburg. Montana did not get the publicity of Washoe or Colorado, and was a long, long way from the "States."[119]

Research indicates that a good many men who went to the Montana mines favored the Confederacy, or were at least anti-Union. This had its effect politically immediately after the war, when this element in the mining camps controlled the Democratic Party.[120] Toward the end of the war, Idaho and Montana areas were oft-times referred to as the "left wing of Price's army." After the failure of Sterling Price's invasion of Missouri in the fall of 1864, one eyewitness told of a large number of Confederate citizens heading for the mountains of the Northwest.[121]

Thus, in spite of war, the immigrant trains rolled westward, fleeing military service, seeking mining profits, escaping from prospective Northern victory.

116. *Ibid.*, 32-36.
117. *Ibid.*, 327-328.
118. *Ibid.*, 329.
119. Athearn, Robert G., "The Civil War and Montana Gold," *Montana, the Magazine of Western History*, Vol. XII, No. 2, Spring, 1962, 62-63.
120. Thane, James L., Jr., "Confederate Myth in Montana," *Montana the Magazine of Western History*, Vol. XVII, No. 2, April, 1967, 14-19.
121. Ware, Capt. Eugene F., *The Indian War of 1864*, Introduction and Notes by Clyde C. Walton, Lincoln, Neb., 1960, 280-281.

During the first year of the war, from twenty-five to one hundred teams a day crossed the Missouri at Omaha heading toward California. Mormons came into Utah by the thousands. In 1863, trains of 900 and 1,200 wagons were noted. One traveler in Kansas in 1863 reported seeing an average of 500 wagons a day heading west. Even if exaggerated, these are impressive figures, buttressed by many more.[122] It is estimated that in 1864 migration through Omaha alone totaled 75,000 people, 22,500 tons of freight, 30,000 horses and mules, and 75,000 cattle, and total migration through Kansas and Nebraska from the Missouri River was about 150,000 people.

Secretary of the Interior Usher reported that, of the two billion acres of land embraced in the territorial extent of the nation, 1,400,000,000 belonged to the public domain. Receipts of sales of public lands had been $884,887.03 for the year ending June 30, 1861, and then dropped sharply to $125,048.30 (an obvious war effect) for the year ending June 30, 1862. Sales continued slow in the year 1863, but shot upward for the fiscal year ending June 30, 1864, to $678,007.21. Secretary Usher stated, "The depressing influences of civil war have been felt during the last three years, but the results for that just closed demonstrates a revival of the annual demand for public lands, particularly for settlement and cultivation."[123] This upward trend was even more striking in the third quarter of 1864, with sales reaching a high of $341,439.23.[124]

Far less spectacular than mining, though more immediately responsive to essential needs, was the expanding lumber industry, wartime demands for lumber having been urgent.[125] Transporting of lumber was second only to grain as a Great Lakes and canal trade. Lumber from the South was completely cut off, thus stimulating the Northern lumber camps of Maine, New York, Michigan, and Wisconsin. As the war neared its end, capitalists bought larger and larger tracts of timber, not to supply the South, but to build houses, barns, factories, schools, mills, and bridges for the North and West.[126]

Second only to the lure of gold and silver was oil, in some areas even more irresistible. In the late summer of 1859, petroleum was first obtained in large quantities along Oil Creek, Pennsylvania, and within a short time the oil boom was under way. The petroleum trade "has sprung into existence with such rapidity and attained to such dimensions," wrote one observer, "that it appears almost like the work of some great wizard. A few years since, some persons, while boring for water in an obscure Pennsylvania valley, were surprised to find their

122. Fite, *op. cit.*, 34-36.
123. "Report of the Secretary of the Interior," Dec. 5, 1864, *Cong. Globe*, 38th Cong., 2nd Sess., Pt. 2, Appendix, 20.
124. *Ibid.*
125. *American Annual Cyclopaedia*, 1865, 567.
126. For summary, see Fite, *op. cit.*, 40-41.

labors culminating in an oil instead of a water spout. The event caused great excitement; other wells were soon sunk, with like results, until finally the rocky chambers of that valley have become the natural laboratory which supplies all the rural mansions and cottages in America and Europe with beautiful artificial light to cheer the long winter evening hours. Next to gas, refined petroleum gives the most clear light, while it is also the cheapest ever used by man; we therefore hope, for the good of our fellowmen, that the supply of it will long continue to be copious. Since petroleum was first introduced, great improvements have been made in refining it. . . ."[127]

For a time after discovery of petroleum, its commercial use was limited primarily to lubrication, some lighting, and heating. But the consumption of oil spread rapidly, creating a whole new field of opportunity, very little of which could be attributed to the war. Petroleum development was simply coincidental. Farmers and mill operators alike began using "rock oil" instead of lard oil for a lubricant because it was cheaper, wore well, and did not gum-up the machinery.[128] *The Scientific American* stated in November, 1862, "The rapid and extended use of petroleum has no parallel in the history of manufactures or commerce." In three years "its employment for artificial illumination has spread over all parts of the civilized world and the distant islands of the sea. The obtaining of it from the oil wells, the refining of it, the carrying of it to market and the export of it abroad, combine to form a new manufcturing and commercial business for America, of great extent, which is the source of no small amount of wealth . . ."[129] Just a few years before this, whale and lard oils had been the common fuel used for artificial light. These were superseded by a dangerous "burning fluid" made of alcohol and turpentine, and then by kerosene distilled from cannel coal. Now petroleum was rivaling coal products.[130]

By 1865 experiments in the use of petroleum for generating steam were well advanced.[131] Rails were being laid to the oil fields, and pipe-lines constructed to carry the oil to the termini by the summer of 1864.[132]

As usual in all such booms, with stock companies proliferating, it became difficult to find names for them all—Cosmopolitan, Rennekoff, Hidekoper, Inexhaustible, Maple Shade, Radiant, Revenue, Allegequi, Brilliant, Diamond, Big Tank, Tarr, Tack, Blood, Tarentum, Tionesta, Organic, Van Buren, Pit Hole, Horse Neck, Oak Ball, Sled Ford.[133] Along with the new industry went the old story as related in a scientific journal: "A lot of relentless speculators heat up the

127. *Scientific American*, Vol. X, No. 4, Jan. 23, 1864, 54-55.
128. *Ibid.*, Vol. VII, No. 22, Nov. 29, 1862, 342.
129. *Ibid.*
130. *Ibid.*, Vol. IX, No. 18, 281.
131. *Ibid.*, Vol. XI, No. 1, July 2, 1865, 19.
132. *Ibid.*, Vol. VI, No. 8, Aug. 20, 1864, 118.
133. *Ibid.*, Vol. XII, No. 1, Jan. 2, 1865, 19.

money-loving spirit of our people to a consuming fever; thousands are thus allured into the tempting snare, and lose, perhaps, their little all. It is absurd to suppose that the whole community are to be lifted suddenly upon the high places of wealth by these joint-stock petroleum-well companies."[134] At the same time, millions of dollars were being realized honestly, and thousands of people employed.

Several publications such as *Scientific American* made efforts to combat the stock schemes and wildcat swindles, and by early 1865 reported some cooling off of the ardor for petroleum stocks as, "people are beginning to realize that the windy prospectuses of Petroleum Companies are nothing more than cunningly contrived traps in which to catch the unthinking multitude. . . ."[135]

In spite of the war, people in the oil regions of Pennsylvania could talk of nothing but oil, and "life in Oil City" became "fast and peculiar." Representatives of millions in greenbacks and thousands of acres in oil lands jostled with teamsters, stage drivers, carpenters, penniless or nearly penniless adventurers, "nabobs from afar," and speculators of every class.[136] At Oil City a perplexing maze of derricks was spread helter-skelter along a stream to the base of the hills. Intermingled with the derricks were engine houses, shanties, offices, tanks, groceries, taverns, and embryonic villages. Noise, smoke and steam filled the air while sleighs and wagons filled the roads, and horsemen thronged the crooked lanes.[137]

Gushers burst on this busy scene with roaring jets of oil and flame. When oil was struck on the John Buchanan Farm near the mouth of Oil Creek on April 17, 1861, crowds ran to stare at the sheets of exploding flame, causing the tragic death of nineteen people. But the work went on. One well, about the same time, poured oil for fifteen months bringing profits of two-and-one-half millions for a Pennsylvania lumberman who had paid only $1,500 for the farm in 1859.[138]

Production leaped from about 1,200 barrels per day in 1860 to more than 5,000 in 1861. The inevitable occurred—supply outran demand. After all, relatively little use could yet be made of the oil, for it took time to develop appliances and methods of employing the new material in large quantities. The start of the war seemed to stimulate the Pennsylvania fields; it also awakened rumors of cheaper wells elsewhere. Oil selling at the wells at $10 in January, 1861, dropped to fifty cents in May, and ten cents by December.[139] With the increased flow of oil in

134. *Ibid.*, Vol. XXI, No. 2, Jan. 9, 1865, 23.
135. *Ibid.*, Vol. XII, No. 4, Jan. 21, 1865, 47.
136. Oberholtzer, Ellis Paxson, *Jay Cooke, Financier of the Civil War*, Philadelphia, 1907, Vol. I, 615; *Scientific American*, Vol. XII, No. 13, March 25, 1865, 192.
137. *Ibid.*
138. Giddens, Paul H., *The Birth of the Oil Industry*, New York, 1939, 76.
139. *Ibid.*, 83; *American Annual Cyclopaedia*, 1861, 579.

eastern Ohio, Kentucky, western Virginia, and even Canada, inventions and scientific development could not keep pace with production.

Faced with possible ruin, a group of producers met in late November, 1861, for the purpose of organizing to combat the great crisis. By the opening of 1862 the first combination of producers was well under way, refusing to sell oil under $4-a-barrel. Although there were still heavy losses due to the slowdown in production, and momentary consternation over Lee's invasion in mid-summer 1863, petroleum prices leaped to $7.25 in September, and refineries were quickly built to help utilize the surplus oil. Gradually, as petroleum was used more widely as an illuminant, old-style kerosene manufacturers were forced out of business, and the refined-oil industry became more widespread and sounder financially. One authority reports that capital invested in oil-land purchase and development by 1864 reached $100,000,000, but the exact figure is unobtainable.[140]

In May of 1860, Charles Lockhard of Pittsburgh went abroad with oil samples. At first the British were somewhat indifferent, but soon foreign demand became a major market for American oil. France, Britain, Belgium, Italy, and even Russia, were primary markets. Petroleum became by the end of the Civil War the sixth largest export, more than trebling from over ten and one-half million gallons to nearly thirty-two million between 1862 and 1864.[141] Venango County, Pennsylvania, had been one of the poorest counties in the State, with about one-third of the land purchasable at a mere $3 per acre, the best land bringing only $30. With the discovery of oil, land in this county sold generally from $300 to $500 an acre, with some going up to $45,000.[142] Oil City, Franklin, and Titusville boomed, but this was just the beginning of one of the world's greatest industries, an industry in which demand and use would have to be developed to encourage production.

[V]

Northern exports and imports in terms of dollars generally declined during the war, but still remained strong. Again, it is remarkable that a nation engaged in such devastating civil strife could nevertheless remain a producer of major exports. In 1860, total shipments of gold, silver, and merchandise abroad were valued at $400,000,000, with imports at $362,000,000, a favorable margin of $38,000,000. This dropped sharply in 1861 when imports exceeded exports by $86,000,000, a drop reflecting the loss of Southern markets. In 1862 and 1863 exports once more exceeded imports, but by 1864 imports again exceeded ex-

140. Giddens, *op. cit.*, 95-123, for summary.
141. *Monthly Report*, U.S. Department of Agriculture, January, 1865, 35; *Amer. Ann. Cyclo.*, 1865, 700; Giddens, *op. cit.*, 99-100.
142. Fite, *op. cit.*, 30.

ports, followed by other oscillations. However, throughout all these years exports remained large.[143] As one authority put it, "Contrary to the opinions of contemporaries, which have been perpetuated in textbooks, no sustained outflow of capital occurred during the Civil War. . . ."[144]

The *American Railroad Journal* complained about "excessive importations," which would continue as long as Americans were able to pay for them. A list of the cargo of vessels in May and June, 1864, showed such widely assorted imports and luxuries as beer, wool, lead, skins, grindstones, ginger, puncheons of whisky, cases of "sauce," pig lead, and iron in manufactured form. Complaint was made that "Now there is scarcely one of these articles which could not be produced at home. . . ."[145]

Some items high on the list of American exports during the war, nearly doubling from 1861 to 1865, were the following: carriages, glassware, clothing, boots and shoes. Grain exports prior to 1860 were largely nominal, but during 1863 and 1864, when British wheat prices rose rapidly, exports of American wheat averaged 33,000,000 bushels a year.[146] In 1864, about 50,000 sewing machines, valued at two million dollars, were sent abroad.[147]

Throughout the war, a number of small books and pamphlets containing articles by Americans on economic conditions in the United States were printed and distributed in Britain, with the obvious purpose of influencing political opinion, English buyers, and investors. In one such pamphlet, the author pointed out that "extra economy in living has hardly been thought of among us, leaving the large resources of $500,000,000 per annum almost, if not wholly, unimpaired and available, if the necessities of the country should require it. There is, then, no danger that we shall be exhausted financially—no danger of inability on the part of the Government to command to pay for all that can be needed." He obtained the half-billion-dollar figure from what, if necessary, could be paid in taxes merely by retrenchment in expenditures of living.[148]

In one field, particularly, British investment took a special interest—that of railroads. Before the war, British interests held very few American manufacturing stocks, and only limited investments in eastern railways, in private banks of New York and New Orleans, and in a few mining enterprises. Holdings were higher in State securities, general public securities, and canal bonds. For example, toward the construction of James McHenry's inventive enterprise, the Atlantic

143. *Historical Statistics of the U.S.*, 538.
144. Simon, Matthew, "The United States Balance of Payments, 1861-1900," *Trends in the American Economy in the Nineteenth Century*, Vol. XXIV, 699-700.
145. *American Railroad Journal*, Vol. XXXVII, No. 1469, June 11, 1864, 561-562.
146. Wells, David A., *The Recent Financial, Industrial and Commercial Experiences of the United States, op. cit.*, 486.
147. Clark, Victor S., *History of Manufactures in the United States 1607-1860*, New York, 1929, II, 11.
148. Hazard, R.G., *Our Resources*, London, 1864, 15.

& Great Western Railway from Salamanca, New York, to Cincinnati, Ohio—the longest railroad built during the Civil War—$25,000,000 was raised in Great Britain, along with other substantial amounts in Germany and Spain. Some 15,000 foreign laborers were brought in, including 5,000 from Britain. By autumn of 1864 it was possible to travel over this railway from the Hudson River to the Mississippi. It was said that all financial London believed in McHenry's project, including Sir Morton Peto, a financier and publicist whose word carried much weight. Direct competition was given to the Erie, unlocking a great part of the Oil Regions. After the war, McClellan became its president and finally the road, a financial failure, was acquired by the Erie. This was a cardinal example of British railroad investment, enterprising and highly useful, although somewhat erratic.[149] Private railroad securities in the United States held by British interests alone are estimated to have been £1,300,000 sterling in 1864, rising to £2,700,000 in 1865.[150]

From a world view, the most remarkable feature of the war period was the steadily maintained rise in production of great primary commodities, grain, meats, minerals, and lumber. Exports of grain in years of European drought were of the first importance economically, even though their political potency was much less than some later students conjectured. They saved many a poor household in Britain and Western Europe from worry about the price of bread in 1862-64. Moreover, American grains held great promise for the future. Large as the shipments of cereals overseas were, they were trifling in comparison to what the country might have sent—and would send when demand arose.[151]

Estimating their resources of gold, silver, copper, and other metals, most Americans took an exuberantly optimistic view of the future. They would have accepted Sir Morton Peto's flat statement, "We should not be unmindful that the discovery of gold in California has been one of the great causes of the recent development of the United States."[152] They would have thought Horace Greeley and Grant well warranted in predicting that the gold and silver mines would ultimately meet most of the costs of the war. The General Land Office report to Congress in 1863 asserted that Arizona was believed to possess mineral wealth beyond any territory of equal extent, and that "the richest mines are yet unfound." Successive gold rushes to Colorado, Montana, and Idaho generated the wildest hopes. The Comstock Lode attained international celebrity, and asser-

149. Jenks, Leland Hamilton, *The Migration of British Capital to 1875*, London, 1963, 255-59; Fite, *op. cit.*, 55; Hungerford, Edward, *Men of Erie*, New York, 1946, 191-199; Weber, Thomas, *The Northern Railroads in the Civil War*, New York, 1952, 15-19.
150. Jenks, *op. cit.*, 426.
151. Gates, Paul W., *Agriculture and the Civil War*, New York, 1965, Ch. IX, "Farm Labor and Machinery."
152. Peto, *op. cit.*, 173.

tions that the Gould & Curry mine alone had yielded nearly twelve million dollars worth of bullion by 1865 gave many an American a delusive elation. Not in the Far West alone were important wartime discoveries made. The Detroit *Tribune* in 1864, gloating over recent new finds of silver, copper, iron, gypsum and salt in Michigan, declared: "our population is increasing as it has never done before," and that the current growth was equal to that of Illinois in its best years of the 1850's.[153] Robert J. Walker, reminding people that the precious metals were nearly all on public lands, added, "They are the property of the Federal Government, and their intrinsic value exceeds our public debt."[154]

Far better justification existed for Sir Morton Peto's statement on the truly providential character of the wartime development of petroleum. Except for the advent of steam power, few parallels in history could be found for the rise of the oil industry—which came at just the right moment.

"This great natural development made its appearance at a period when it was of peculiar value to the United States," Peto remarked.[155] "At a moment of civil war, when the balance of trade was against the nation, gold was necessarily going out, and when there was a heavy drain upon the natural resources of the country, petroleum sprung up from lands previously considered valueless, in quantities sufficient to make a sensible diversion in the national commerce. Nor was that the only benefit it offered. While it assisted the external commerce, it also stimulated the internal industry of the United States. It gave to the railway industry of the country a prospect of large additional profits; it offered employment to capital with every prospect of abundant returns; and it afforded a more than ordinary reward for labor. It is difficult to find a parallel to such a blessing bestowed upon a nation in the hour of her direst necessity."

Then, too, if the continued strength of agriculture was obviously fundamental to American prosperity, it was the vigor of manufacturing that gave the largest hope for the future. The rapid expansion of the flour-milling and meat-packing establishments was a fact which, with armies to feed, could be taken for granted. The woolen industry obviously had to grow throughout the war to furnish uniforms and substitutes for cotton garments. The rise of the ready-made-clothing industry to new heights astonished nobody familiar with the new technological improvements in the sewing- and cloth-cutting machines of Elias Howe, Isaac Singer, and the partners A.B. Wilson and Nathaniel Wheeler. The vigorous shoe industry, built upon the ingenuity of Lyman Blake and business enterprise of Gordon McKay, and the continued growth of foundries and machine shops, were equally predictable. Developments in technology, marketing, and business orga-

153. New York *Tribune*, March 31, 1864.
154. Peto, *op. cit.*, 174.
155. *Ibid.*, 205, 206.

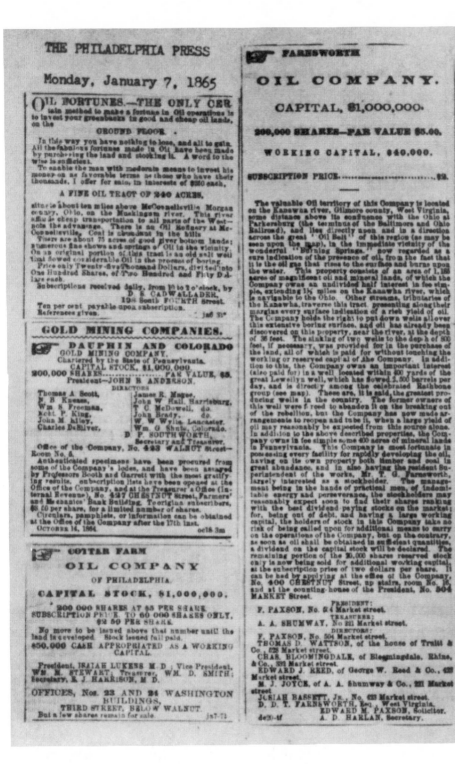

Oil Stock Advertisements

nization before the war had laid a foundation for larger structures, and careful observers believed that without a war the production of iron might have been larger than it actually was.[156] On the other hand, the wartime necessity of casting larger and more complex pieces certainly added to the technological ability of the iron industry.

Some phenomena of the war period, however, took even astute businessmen by surprise, and contributed in unforeseen ways to the emergence of the larger economic world after Appomattox. One of these was the creation of a new psychology favorable to investment, even though it was predominantly speculative rather than prudent. Next to it stood a related phenomenon, the formation of investment capital with a scope and freedom previously unknown. In the creation of this new psychology the business genius and organizing capacity of Jay Cooke, who did yeoman work in helping the government market its great bond issues, was invaluable. His feat in selling to the American people in 1865 the last of the $830,000,000 loan authorized by Congress, the seven-thirty loan, caused one Confederate leader to exclaim, "The Yankees did not whip us in the field. We were whipped in the Treasury Department."[157] These developments must be described in terms as largely psychological as statistical. While they are solid economic realities, some of their aspects have little to do with bank balances, tons of pig iron, or dollar earnings of railways. They support the statement made by John Robinson in *The Accumulation of Capital,* an inquiry into economic dynamism:[158] "Most casual elements in economic life lie partly in the beliefs and expectations (often vague and emotional) of the actors, and are very hard, if not impossible in principle, to pin down by any scientific observation. For these reasons it can be plausibly maintained that economics is not and never will be a serious scientific discipline, and that it properly belongs to a class of subjects, such as theology or aesthetic criticism, which use words to play upon sentiment rather than investigate reality."

It is assuredly true that economic exuberance in the Civil War years cannot be understood when abstracted from beliefs and expectations, uncertainties and apprehensions, of an emotional character. It is also true that capital formation as a governing element in economic development cannot be comprehended without reference to sociological forces of great complexity.

These sociological forces were indirectly manifest in many facts of life. The number of business firms alone reflected the capital wealth of a major segment of the North. In 1864, 168,923 business houses, apart from California, were listed, with a wealth of $4,944,766,000. Profits were said to average from twelve to fifteen

156. Clark, Victor S., *op. cit.,* Vol. II, 15-16.
157. Oberholtzer, E. P., *Jay Cooke, Financier of the Civil War, op. cit.,* I, 478.
158. Robinson, John, *The Accumulation of Capital,* London, 1956, *passim.*

per cent. Even taking a low figure of ten per cent this gives a sizable profit for the nation's business. In announcing these figures, the U.S. Department of Agriculture and R.G. Dun & Company in February, 1865, stated that "this in view of the unprecedented expenditure necessarily incurred, both by heavy taxation and in otherwise sustaining the government, exhibits the self-supporting character of our people, and are but one element of the strength of the country, which, when added to the other immense resources not brought into our estimates such as real estate, agriculture, mining and other interests, should inspire the most hopeful confidence in our future growth and permanent prosperity. . . ."[159]

In the fast-developing Northwest particularly, industrial expansion would have been rapid without a war, for all the conditions were favorable. The initial equipment that entrepreneurs needed cost only a few thousand dollars. Profits could then be plowed back, and any man who did not accumulate capital fast enough could take a partner. An investigator of the financing of industry in the Illinois area found that, although most of the fifty manufacturers studied came from the East or Europe, and were better educated than the average, they generally used savings taken from a variety of employments.[160] Small sums sufficed at first. This was true of the meat-packers Gurdon Saltonstall Hubbard and Gustavus Swift, of the farm machinery manufacturers John Deere and William Deering, and of many others. Twenty-three of the fifty had worked for hire, four others received money from sales of their farms, and two made it in the gold rush. In no major instance, with perhaps one exception, did money come from borrowing or inheritance. A few thousands sufficed for a start, and the growth of the country and the economy did the rest.

But while it would be a mistake to suppose that the war inaugurated many *fundamental* economic changes in the North, or that some economic results were anything but injurious, it would be a greater mistake to think that the conflict was not connected with important transformations and accelerations. Advances by the War Department to encourage arms manufacture were an old story in the United States, and became ever larger.[161] In the last year of the war, government spending to supply Army artillery, small arms, ammunition, clothing, and camp and garrison equipage alone approached $150,000,000—a sum certain to stimulate manufacturing on a hundred fronts.[162] It is also easy to point to business areas crippled by the conflict. Although the Northern cotton industry, for example, began to rise from its long depression in 1863, and continued when the capture

159. *Monthly Report of the U.S. Department of Agriculture,* February, 1865, 15, article quoting R.G. Dun & Company.
160. Kemmerer, D.L., "Financing Illinois Industry 1830-1850," *Bulletin of Business Historical Society,* XXVII, June, 1953, 97-111.
161. Clark, Victor S., *op. cit.,* 369ff.
162. *Ibid.,* II, 10.

of Vicksburg opened new Southwestern sources of raw cotton, its wounds were not easily healed. It was still convalescent early in the 1870's, although the shift of portions of the industry to woolens had helped.[163] Yankee shipbuilding and shipping suffered almost mortal blows, but it is difficult to avoid the conclusion that entries on the other side of the ledger were decidedly heavier.

The main East-West trunk-line railroads of the North, for example, had just placed themselves by 1861 in a position where they could meet the requirements of internal commerce should the Mississippi be closed. In the 1850's the Erie, the Baltimore & Ohio, the Pennsylvania, the New York Central & Lake Shore with connecting roads, and the line from Boston to Ogdensburg, had all completed fairly satisfactory facilities.[164] Their network was ready for the emergency just in time. "A miserable existence had these trunk-lines previous to the war," declared the most authoritative financial journal. "But [after Sumter] the capital which had been applied to them began to show exceedingly fruitful results, and in a few years they succeeded in emerging from a condition of penury to one of almost absolute independence."[165]

The journal estimated their total floating debt in 1861 at $4,289,518, and it was still growing. But when the first guns opened, the Northern traffic changed course. It became difficult to realize that in 1860 no fewer than 3,566 steamboats and 831 flatboats had arrived in New Orleans; vast freights now came thundering over the tracks and bridges of the Northern railroads to the seaboard. As a result, the floating debt was practically wiped out. The Erie, which had previously yielded no dividends, paid 8 percent in 1863. The Hudson River railroad, which had offered none until 1864, began semi-annual dividends of 4 or 5 percent, and the New York Central paid 7 and 9 percent in 1864. Far and wide in the North a similar story was told. According to Secretary Chase, the total commerce between East and West had a value of $1,138,000,000, and this the railroads shared with the Great Lakes and canals.

The Michigan Central earned $1,740,000 in 1864-65. Another great Midwestern railroad, hard hit by secession, was the Illinois Central, which had but recently completed connections with Memphis and New Orleans. Its managers, controlling a 365-mile line from Chicago to Cairo, and another from Centralia, Ill., to Dubuque, Iowa, had confidently expected to have trains running between Chicago and the Gulf in the spring of 1861 to compete with Mississippi River traffic.[166] The war cut off the Southern potential, and threw on the road a heavy burden of troops and supplies, carried at a very slight margin above cost. The War

163. Copeland, Melvin T., *The Cotton Manufacturing Industry of the United States*, Cambridge, Mass., 1912, 222.
164. Daggett, Stewart, *Railroad Reorganization*, New York, 1966, 2.
165. *Commercial and Financial Chronicle*, August 10, 1865.
166. Andreas, A.T., *History of Chicago*, Chicago, 1884-86, II, 130.

Department was slow in making payment. At the same time, the difficulties of Western banks which had based their notes too heavily on the securities of Southern States, the eagerness with which lake shipping reached for freight, and the precarious character of the early wartime market for Western products, embarrassed the line.[167]

But the war shortly pulled the Illinois Central out of its financial slough, traffic soon becoming so heavy that it had to expand its rolling stock greatly.[168] The broad belt of land it had received from the national government, moreover, yielded an increasing revenue. Early difficulties disappeared, debts were paid off, and an era of prosperity with few parallels in American railway history dawned, so that the road could pay annual dividends of ten percent from 1865 to 1873, and even the panic seemed to harm it little. Other Midwestern lines did nearly as well. The railroad eventually known as the Chicago & Northwestern had reached Fulton on the Mississippi in 1865; the line later called the Chicago, Burlington & Quincy, which some people liked to term "the Pennsylvania of the West," was vigorously expanding its trackage; the Chicago & Alton, its main line, running nearly 250 miles from Joliet to East St. Louis, and the Chicago, Rock Island & Pacific, likewise rode the wave of wartime prosperity; and when the first north-western railway reached the Missouri in 1865, it was evident that a huge new area would soon be brought into subordination to Chicago.[169]

"The Northwest has been developed entirely by its railroads," wrote an English expert on American railway securities, Van Oss; and he pointed out that only a quarter-century after the war the density of the network of rails in propor-tion to population in Illinois, Iowa, and Wisconsin far exceeded that of England and Belgium.[170] This development would have come had no war occurred; the standardization of the railroad gauge at four feet eight-and-one-half inches—the English norm—would have eventually taken place; railroad conventions to im-prove Western facilities, like that in Boston in the spring of 1863, would have drawn many representatives.[171]

The augmented railroad activity and rising industrialism of the land were built upon iron. As the leading American ironmaster, Abram S. Hewitt, said, the production of iron was fundamental to 19th-century civilization.[172] Peto thought in 1865 that the people of the United States were prepared to use almost any amount of iron.[173]

167. *Commercial and Financial Chronicle*, Oct. 7, 1865; Andreas, *op. cit.*, II, 130.
168. Andreas, *ut supra*.
169. Van Oss, S.F., *American Railroads as Investments*, New York, 1893, 725-732.
170. *Ibid.*, 452.
171. *Merchants' Magazine*, Vol. XLVIII, May, 1863, 403.
172. *Selected Papers of Abram S. Hewitt*, ed. Allan Nevins, New York, 1935, 19-85.
173. Peto, *op. cit.*, 179.

No doubt iron production would have had as great a growth or greater had the war not taken place. Southern railroads would have been much extended. The use of iron bridges, and of the Phoenix column, or hollow wrought-iron post, for construction, first known in the war years, would have been more extensive. In the year before the war, a record-breaking total of iron rails was rolled—205,000 tons—and after a drop in 1861, the figure climbed step-by-step until 350,000 were rolled in 1865; but would it not have climbed faster in peace, and would not Bessemer steel have been made sooner? The year 1864 saw a veritable iron famine, which at one time pushed the price of pig-iron to $126 a ton. This famine arose from demands not directly or importantly connected with the conflict.[174] Nor does it appear that the wartime tariffs on iron had any great effect in stimulating the industry, for the simple reason that demand greatly exceeded supply during most of the period. Certainly no large effects of the tariff were visible until the 1870's.

Daniel J. Morrell, head of the important Cambria Iron Works, testified just after Appomattox that the expansion of the American iron market, drawing many British iron workers overseas, had compelled British ironmasters to raise wages to keep them at home. He believed the tariff had not been effective in shutting out British exports. On the contrary, he found the domestic manufacturer in peril in 1866, with importations at New York increasing so fast as to excite alarm.[175] The rise in American prices more than offset the new tariff levies.

It was not growth in volume, however, that was the most significant feature of the iron industry during the war. It was changes in form, function, and methods that arrested the attention of observers. Concentration of production was inevitable. For example, when horseshoes, which previously had been used all over the country, now were needed in huge quantities for the armies, the Troy Nail & Iron Manufacturing Company began to supply them in hundreds of thousands, and by trainload lots. With the use of increased capital and a steady process of combination and consolidation, expansion of iron mills took place throughout the North.

Every year it required more capital and ability to establish and equip a profitable iron business. The little foundries that made pig-iron for nails, bolts, stove castings, railings, and the like, doing local business, were crowded aside by larger works. Two Vermont establishments, capitalized in 1860 at $40,000, could never compete in interstate trade with the 125 foundries in Pennsylvania capitalized at $21,725,000—the largest of them powerful by standards of the time. More ability, experience, and skill were also demanded. The locomotive works, judged by Peto as the war ended to be as efficient as those in England, would have fared ill

174. *Report,* American Iron and Steel Association, 1874, 42.
175. Morrell, Daniel J., *The Manufacture of Railroad Iron,* Philadelphia, 1866, *passim.*

without wise directors. When a slump or depression struck, or changes in demand cut off old trade channels, swift action was indispensable. Hewitt, running the Cooper-Hewitt works in Trenton, had to spend large sums in obtaining good ore, paying for his furnaces, fuel, and workmen, creating new wares like his iron beams or the wire cables for the Roebling suspension bridges, and studying new methods. He built an experimental Bessemer furnace during the war, wormed from a British maker of gun-metal his closely-guarded secrets, and eventually brought the open-hearth process of steel-making to America. His energies were taxed to the utmost, and sometimes he felt near the brink of bankruptcy.[176]

But he and others laid a foundation for the future. One of the others was Andrew Carnegie, who in 1863 organized the Keystone Bridge Company—a name appropriate to the Keystone State—as a means of supplementing wooden spans with iron. New England bridge-builders had shown ingenuity in using heavy wooden beams and trusses.[177] Carnegie, however, laughed when he heard a railroad president, viewing piles of heavy cast-iron lying about for a bridge at Steubenville, Ohio, ejaculate: "I don't believe those heavy castings can be made to stand up and carry themselves, much less carry a train across the Ohio River."[178] And Carnegie had the last laugh.

Accurate statistics on the growth of the average unit in the iron business are not obtainable for the war period. We know, however, that the capacity of the American mills rolling iron rails increased from 205,000 tons in 1860 to 735,000 tons in 1865, and that this meant an increase in average size. The Rensselaer rolling-mill at Troy, New York, the Lackawanna mill at Scranton, Pennsylvania, and the Trenton, New Jersey, iron works lifted their production from one-half to three-quarters. We know also that new techniques entailed an expansion in the size of mills. Before the war, the work of smelting and rolling iron had seldom been combined. Indeed, the first rolling-mill in Pittsburgh to smelt its own iron was the Clinton Furnace built in 1859. During the war, this combination became common. The day of the small local furnace near the mines was over. Still another evidence of growing size was the introduction of the three-high roller in making iron rails, an innovation increasing production and reducing waste. John Fritz had invented the three-high roller amid predictions that he would ruin his employers and himself. Yet, in 1865, the industry had 137 such rollers in successful operation, and reversion to the older technique was unthinkable.

One of the interesting features of the iron industry during the war was the remarkable use of technological skills by keen-minded, energetic men, some of them broadly educated. Alexander Lyman Holley of Connecticut was a graduate of Brown. Hewitt received a diploma from Columbia, and then studied law. Eben

176. Hewitt, Abram S., *Selected Papers, op. cit.,* Chapters XI-XVI.
177. Kirkland, Edward C., *Men, Cities, and Transportation: A Study in New England History, 1820-1900,* Cambridge, Mass., 1948, I, 290-292.
178. Carnegie, Andrew, *Autobiography,* ed. J.C. Van Dyke, Boston, 1920, 117.

B. Ward, Canadian-born, was trained by an uncle on the Great Lakes, made money in shipbuilding, invested in rolling-mills in Wyandotte, Michigan, and Chicago, and at an early date became keenly interested in the new Bessemer process, but failed to get full control of American rights.[179] Fritz, a farm lad of German and Scotch-Irish descent, spent precociously alert years at a rural academy before he began his apprenticeship as a machinist in Chester County, Pennsylvania. Yet more remarkable was Andrew Carnegie—not a technologist, not an inventor, but a capitalist and organizer—who perceived fresh needs and new expedients for meeting them. When he saw pig-iron go up in 1864 to $130 a ton, he obtained capital and a partner (both easy to find in that expansive year) to build a blast-furnace and rolling-mill in Pittsburgh.

Meanwhile, at Altoona, he relates, he had seen the first small bridge built of iron. Its merits convinced him that railroads could never depend upon wooden bridges for permanent use, and the burning of a wooden structure on the Pennsylvania, closing the line eight days, heightened his resolve to establish a bridge company. He invited Tom Scott of the Pennsylvania to become one of five partners who subscribed $1,250 apiece. They began by equipping the Pennsylvania with iron bridges, finding both demand and profits in the boom days satisfactory; and as imitators arose, iron bridges spread everywhere.[180]

So it was that John D. Rockefeller, after two years in the excellent Cleveland High School, and looking in the spirit of the time for "something big," launched a commission business that made the most of army orders, the growth of farm shipments to rising industrial centers, and the European demand for grain and meats. Then his firm of Clark & Rockefeller, joining hands with the English expert Samuel Andrews, showed an astute comprehension of the fact that, while Cleveland could not compete with Chicago in the Western agricultural trade, it was near enough to the oil regions to build a great and profitable refinery. The war was still raging when Rockefeller courageously bought out the Clarks and proceeded to make Rockefeller & Andrews a power in the domain of oil. He was soon to do as much as anyone to prove the truth of the observation that where consolidation is possible, competition is impossible.

In industry after industry the same story unfolded—in railroading, petroleum, ironmaking, munitions, lumbering, woolen and cotton textiles, and meatpacking. It was a story of quick profits for the enterprising and lucky, large opportunities for reinvestment, swift recovery from mishaps, and a general forward surge. What man of industry and brains could fail, asked the Boston Board of Trade of Britons in 1863. Hearing from the American consul in London that thousands of the best English and Scottish workingmen wished to settle in America, the Board took pains to assure them that, notwithstanding the war, "unexampled prosperity

179. Casson, Herbert N., *Romance of Steel*, New York, 1907, 16-17.
180. Carnegie, *Autobiography, op. cit.*, 114-117.

in agricultural, manufacturing and mining interests" prevailed. It sent circulars
to a large number of American factories and workshops, requesting information
on the number of employees, wages, demand for help, kind of dwellings occupied, and price of room and board. They were answered by eight factories,
machine shops, and other establishments. Photographs of some of the best mills
and typical bills-of-fare in boarding houses were distributed to English agencies.
One set was sent to *Lloyd's Penny Journal,* a pictorial weekly with a circulation
of 150,000 among working people, and this exhibit of the American boom met
a proper response.[181] The Northern war boom was in nearly all aspects an
epitome of the development of energetic capitalism, and doubtless would persist
for a long time.

[VI]

While historians have taken passing looks at the wartime prosperity of the
North, few have considered the fact that this was one of the primary factors in
the Federal victory. Although inflation has to be considered, the value of the
national product showed an increase from the 1860 figure of $3,804,000,000 to
$4,019,000,000 in 1864, despite the loss of the eleven Southern States.[182] A declin-
ing capital, severe economic unrest, and painful unemployment or deprivation,
would have augmented the dissident forces that did exist by hundreds of thousands of new recruits, and it is conceivable that the war itself would have been
lost through internal disruption of the Union.

Underlying financial strength was present, as has been seen, from the beginning. One authoritative source in April of 1864 estimated that about an eighth of
the personal property of the North had been consumed by the government in
the war effort, and this portion of the wealth had been largely destroyed. Yet no
crisis arose, a fact attributed to two conditions: first, the change from a credit to
a cash system of trade; and second, the backlog of savings of all kinds accumulated
in 1861 through the rapidly increasing wealth of the country. As the credit system
was practically abandoned, stocks of ready merchandise diminished, "and thus
the Government found a great reservoir of unemployed capital from which to
draw. The traders, having ceased to take notes for their goods, of course ceased
to offer notes for discount. The banks, seeing no other safe way of employing
their capital, invested it in Government notes and bonds. . . ." Individual capital,
released by the abandonment of the credit system, was invested in the same way.
Other individual capital in cash merchandise, etc., was made increasingly available for government use.[183]

181. *Tenth Annual Report, Boston Board of Trade, for 1863,* Boston, 1864, 16ff.
182. *American Railroad Journal,* Oct. 8, 1864, Vol. XXXVII, No. 1, 486, 989.
183. *Scientific American,* Vol. X, No. 18, April 30, 1864, 281.

In spite of war, personal bank savings by the public increased sharply. In January, 1860, in the State of New York, deposits in savings banks reached $60,753,396 with an average of $221.90 for each depositor, increasing January 1, 1865, to deposits of $119,341,393 for 456,403 depositors, and an average deposit of $260.38, nearly doubling in five years. Massachusetts showed similar remarkable increases.[184] The same authority pointed out that nearly all the Federal debt incurred during the war had been taken up at home, and not more than three or four hundred millions out of an estimated $2,635,000,000 in 1865 had found its way into foreign hands. People were buying government bonds, as well as depositing savings in banks more than ever before.[185]

As the effervescent *American Railroad Journal* put it, there had been those "who, as the country entered upon 'an era of national debt', saw nothing before it but widespread ruin." But, by August of 1865, some banking houses in New York found no difficulty in making payments in cash of half-a-million dollars a month, though, at the commencement of their business, fifty-thousand would have been deemed beyond their resources.[186] Bank stocks almost trebled in a period of three or four years.[187]

When war first broke out, banks felt the crisis considerably, for many had been holding out inadequate cash reserves. New York banks soon adopted a standard of holding twenty-five percent in reserve. From the time of Lincoln's election until after the start of the war, depositors and holders of bank-notes demanded specie payments. In Philadelphia, Baltimore, Washington, and St. Louis, the cities nearest the seceded states, specie payments were suspended for a time, while many wild-cat banks holding Southern securities were forced to close their doors.[188] In April, 1861, thirty-seven Illinois banks failed; Wisconsin had 39 failures, Indiana 27, and so on. Losses were enormous, with bankers forced to assume no responsibility.

With Northern banks issuing their own notes in a multitude of designs, sizes, and forms, and wild-cat banks everywhere issuing their own paper, counterfeiters had one grand heyday. No one could be quite sure what was "good" money or "bad." There was even a publication entitled *The Counterfeiter Detector*, to be used as a guide. The inconvenience of such a loose and uncertain currency is obvious.

While most states of the West strengthened and standardized their banking laws, particularly Wisconsin, the principal reform was brought about by the

184. Walker, George, *The Wealth, Resources and Public Debt of the United States,* London, 1865, 14-16. Walker was Massachusetts Bank Commissioner.
185. *Ibid.,* 5, 13-14.
186. *American Railroad Journal,* Vol. XXXVI, No. 1426, Aug. 15, 1863, 761-763.
187. *Ibid.,* Jan. 30, 1863.
188. Fite, *op. cit.,* 110-111.

National Banking Act.[189] Establishment of the national banking system under a law of February, 1863, did much to realize Secretary Chase's hopes for a general improvement of the financial mechanism of the country. The founding of a uniform banking currency, receivable for taxes, based upon securities of the national government, in place of an irregular, unstable body of local bank notes, assisted both government and private business.[190] The old banknotes, issued by about 1,500 different banks under the laws of twenty-nine States, had a wide variety of privileges, restrictions, and guarantees. The new banknote currency possessed a standard and stable character.

The national banking system began to go into effect in the spring of 1863. National banks were to be set up under their own boards of directors, but were required to deposit U.S. bonds with the Treasury before issuing notes. State bonds and other securities were not accepted for this purpose. The Federal government printed the new bank notes for the sake of uniformity, and other regulations led to stability for a national bank. However, no bank could be forced to become national. The usual protests were heard against enlargement of Federal power, which the Act undoubtedly encouraged. When put into operation, the Eastern banks were slower to become national, as they had been more stable, with established reputations. There was little for them to gain. On the other hand, the Federal Plan took quick hold in the West and Chicago led the way; the bankers and merchants agreed to discount State bank currency and accept at face value only national bank notes and greenbacks. In June, 1863, there were 66 national banks, and by 1864-65 the number rose to 1,294.[191] Banking was learning its lesson, and its new stability contributed a good measure of strength and confidence to the wartime boom, to capital development, and to the war effort itself.

Adding to the stability of the nation's finances was the issuance of greenbacks or legal tender currency begun under the Act of February, 25, 1862, which authorized $150,000,000 in national notes convertible into six-percent bonds redeemable in five to twenty years. "In no other way," Lincoln explained in his Annual Message of December, 1862, "could the payment of the troops, and the satisfaction of other just demands, be so economically, or so well provided for."[192] This flow of legal tender, with the enactments of February, 1862, and March, 1863, for long-term bonds and allied measures, inflated the currency, raised prices for all goods, and stimulated business along a wide front.

189. For a running account of banking during the Civil War, see *The Banker's Magazine* for 1861-1865; Fite, *op. cit.*, 100-127; Sharkey, Robert P., *Money, Class, and Party*, Baltimore, 1959, 221ff.; Gilchrist, David T., and W. David Lewis, editors, *Economic Change in the Civil War Era*, Greenville, Delaware, 1965, "Commercial Banking," 23-40.

190. Dewey, D.R., *Financial History of the United States*, New York, 1913, 320-322; but State-bank issues held much of the field until driven out by a tax law, March, 1865.

191. Fite, *op. cit.*, 118.

192. Lincoln, *Collected Works*, V, 522.

A slight depreciation in greenbacks and appreciation of gold began at once, never reaching the runaway conditions of the Confederate states. The rate fluctuated up or down according to military successes or setbacks to the North. In April, 1862, the premium of gold over greenbacks was around two percent, and by the end of McClellan's abortive Peninsula campaign was up to twenty percent. In the fall of 1862 and winter of 1862-63, it rose to thirty-four percent, and then climbed above fifty percent, with variations, until July, 1863. The successful campaigns of Vicksburg and Gettysburg brought it down again to twenty-four percent, but by the end of 1863 it was up to fifty percent again. A sharp rise in 1864, due in part to the failure of the war to end, and the apparent, though not actual, stalemate on the Virginia front, brought it to the highest premium of 185. The ensuing succession of victories, and the more and more evident collapse of the Confederacy pulled the premium down to 28 percent in May, 1865.[193]

In spite of these fluctuations, inflation brought about in part by the use of greenbacks was generally applauded by financial interests. "The activity which money encourages is the secret of our prosperity," observed the *American Railroad Journal.*[194]

[VII]

Sober John Doe, Esq., of Broad Street, Philadelphia, unfolded his newspaper one crisp October morning in 1863 to the usual depressing news, indicating greater military progress of late, but painful in the images of destruction and suffering evoked. He was not edified by an announcement that the current of speculation in the stock market was "sweeping on,"[195] or that a commercial convention had been held in Chicago.[196] John Doe approved of conventions to encourage commercial activity, but he knew that this gathering had been ruled by men loud in complaints that the Western farmers were being fleeced by the railroads, grain elevators, and commission brokers. When he saw that the rising price of coal had lifted quotations on stock of the Delaware & Hudson R.R. and Pennsylvania Coal Company to new heights, a shadow passed over his face, and a grimace ended his reading of an editorial, "Petrolia in a Rage," its first sentence boasting that "We live in a gay and flashing era."[197]

After the bank mania, canal mania, railway mania, and gold-rush mania had come the oil mania. John Doe knew that the lines he scanned were being read

---

193. Fite, *op. cit.*, 118-120; Sharkey, *op. cit.*, 50-55; Mitchell, Wesley C., *Gold Prices and Wages under the Greenback Standard*, Berkeley, 1908, 279.
194. *American Railroad Journal*, Vol. XXXVI, No. 1433, Oct. 3, 1863, 944-945.
195. This statement led the money column of the New York *Tribune*, May 16, 1863.
196. It had opened June 2, 1863; Chicago *Post*, Chicago *Tribune*, June 2, 1863.
197. See this editorial in New York *Herald*, Oct. 20, 1864, one of several.

just as curiously by Bridget in the kitchen and Otto in the coach-house, and were much more dangerous to them. The editorial noted that a broker named Kingsland offered stock in the Noble Well Company paying two percent a month, in the Maple Shade paying three percent, and in the Manhattan with dividends of four percent a month. These returns were tame compared with those of the Columbia Company of Pittsburgh, which had been paying monthly dividends of ten percent. Other brokers offered equally glittering prizes. Wealth—wealth fresh from the veins of Mother Earth! Who could not hope that the President Oil Company, with five millions in capital and stock at a dollar-a-share, might not do as well as the celebrated Tarr Farm Company, which for a time had paid twelve percent-a-year?

Somewhere about the oil regions, surely, was a young man who might make the greatest fortune of his time in oil. So there was, but not by buying oil stocks. America was full of men recently poor and now fast growing wealthy. Few of the new fortunes were made from Nevada mines or Pennsylvania oil wells; some of them seemed coined out of the blood and sweat of a struggling people. How much money could be made out of the purchase in the spring of 1864 of bonds of the new $200,000,000 "ten-forty" issue, which the press was urging upon patriotic citizens? A man who possessed $1,000 in coin could use it to buy $1600 to $1700 in greenbacks. If he invested $1600 in the new bonds, he would be paid $80-a-year interest in gold; his holding would be exempt from State and local taxation; interest would be subject to only half the national income tax; and when the bond was redeemed in ten to forty years, he would get $1600 in gold. Later, President Andrew Johnson in a message of 1868 asserted that holders of a large part of government securities had then received in interest a larger amount than their original investment, as measured by gold, and were still receiving six percent in coin, while they were still entitled to an ultimate return of the whole principal. One wartime expedient of the Treasury to raise money was the issue of three-year compound-interest notes. The purchaser paid $100 in greenbacks for a hundred-dollar note, for which three years later he received $119.40 in coin.

Men who took a greater risk than United States bonds might make fortunes more rapidly. For example, in the spring of 1863, as people awaited news of Vicksburg, the bonds of the guerrilla-racked State of Missouri were available at heavy discounts. Yet they were secured not only by the credit of the State, but by a first mortgage upon Missouri railroads in whose behalf they had been issued. Nearly fifteen-percent interest had accumulated upon the bonds. It was understood that the next session of the legislature would fund the unpaid coupons, and resume payment of interest. Missouri had a population roughly equal to that of Massachusetts, and far greater natural resources. How much did buyers of Missouri six-percent bonds, quoted at 71 just after Gettysburg, add to their capital?

The boom was geared in part to the speculative temper which currency and credit inflation created by holding out the possibility of quick profits. Some of the foundations for bolder speculation had been laid by the panic of 1857 and its aftermath of recovery, which brought bold adventurers upon the stage. By the date of Lincoln's nomination in Chicago, according to the banker Henry Clews, a sweeping revolution in business methods had begun. "Prior to this time, the antique element had ruled in things financial, speculative, and commercial. . . . A younger race of financiers arose and filled the places of the old conservative leaders."[198] The chronology is faulty. Daniel Drew, who in old age recalled that "I got to be a millionaire afore I knowed it, hardly," entered Wall Street in 1844 with the house of Drew, Robinson, and became a director of Erie in 1857. Jay Gould was speculating in leather and small railways in the late 1850's and was later accused of driving an associate to suicide in 1857 by sharp business tactics. Jacob Little made a historic corner in Morris Canal stock in 1835, and executed a spectacular coup in Erie Railroad stock in 1840. Although gold, silver and oil speculation had existed without special reference to the war, it was inevitable that war contracts, wartime inflation, and wartime psychology should open exciting new chapters in speculation.

"Money is pouring into Wall Street from all parts of the country," stated the New York *Herald* money column of July 29, 1863. The possibilities of market speculation are evident from a glance at security prices. New York Central stock at the opening of 1862 stood at $87.50 a share; by the end of 1863 at $130. Illinois Central stock was priced at $57.25 a share early in 1862; at the beginning of 1863 it was $125. Pacific Mail Steamship stock early in 1862 was valued at $111 a share, and early in 1863 at $236. Six weeks after Gettysburg the *Herald*, reporting an exciting day in the stock market with speculation at new heights, hailed the advent of an era of new affluence with fatuous comment. "Since the war began, all kinds of stocks and many other kinds of property have largely increased in value. . . . If there are, as is supposed, $1,200,000,000 railroad securities representing railroad property in this country, the aggregate increase in the market value of the property within the past year cannot be less than $500,000,000, and there is in this country just that amount of new wealth to be invested, to be used in speculation, to be spent in extravagance, or to be turned to good account in industry and enterprise."[199]

The writer pointed out that while this "new wealth" sprang into existence by an enhanced valuation of railroad property, and the government added greenbacks and bonds to it, no simultaneous development of money-consuming enterprises had taken place. "We are building few new railroads, opening no new mines, building few merchant steamers, carrying on very little business on

198. Clews, Henry, *Twenty-eight Years in Wall Street,* New York, 1887, 6.
199. New York *Herald,* August 18, 1863.

credit."[200] No sensible man believed that inflation in itself produced "new wealth." However, the writer's pessimism was really caused by the lack of development rather than a shortage of credit.

But the depreciation of the currency was paralleled by the rise in the price of gold and in rents, living costs, wages, and the general price level. Many members of Congress had voted for the legal-tender issues with grave doubts; and as Wesley Clair Mitchell writes, if any member held such "ideas of the beneficence of an irredeemable paper currency as afterwards animated members of the Greenback Party, he kept them to himself."[201] The impact of inflation upon the various economic groups varied widely, sometimes happy, sometimes most unhappy.

It had become plain in 1862 that some speculators, like their predecessors in Europe in the Napoleonic era, had arranged to obtain prompt and accurate knowledge of military events. Various brokers seemed better informed at times than even press or government. In the latter part of June, 1862, while the public still thought McClellan's position bright and promising, the stock market suddenly dropped, for dealers had devised ingenious plans to obtain information from the front. Frequently, states one Wall Street observer, before the government knew an important development, it was the possession of Wall Street, and a shrewd observer could predict victory or defeat on the battlefield simply by watching the action of stocks.[202] But it was impossible to be sure; numerous economic forces and endless stock-jobber manoeuvring affected the market. There also were "plants" such as the famous conspiracy by two gold speculators who managed to get a spurious Lincoln proclamation published in two anti-administration papers. This invented "proclamation" of May 17, 1864, lamented the dire condition of Union armies, proclaimed a day for prayer, and asked for 400,000 more troops. For a few days the New York *Journal of Commerce* and the New York *World* were suspended by order of the President, though the papers themselves had been victimized. The perpetrators were soon caught and forced to confess, but the incident caused many repercussions.[203] Also, for example, stock of the Harlem Railroad, which had sold as low as $8 or $9 a share in 1860, shot to $30 in January, 1863, when Cornelius Vanderbilt got full control, bounded to $92 in July of that year, and when a "corner" was effected in August, reached the astonishing figure of $179. The wartime presidents of the New York Stock Exchange—A.B. Baylis, H.G. Stebbins, William Seymour, Jr., and R.L. Cutting —set their faces against gambling on battles; and the Exchange, to assist the government, passed a resolution condemning anyone who sold United States

200. *Ibid.*
201. Mitchell, Wesley Clair, *History of the Greenbacks*, Chicago, 1903, 68.
202. Fowler, W.W., *Ten Years in Wall Street*, Hartford, 1870, 156ff.
203. Harper, Robert S., *Lincoln and the Press*, New York, 1951, 289-303.

bonds short.[204] But these efforts at self regulation were largely fruitless.

While overall dividend figures are unobtainable, fairly accurate statistics show that dividend payments to stockholders of banks increased from $39,500,000 in 1863 to $66,700,000 in 1864 and $67,100,000 in 1865 before dropping. Dividend payments to stockholders of banks, insurance companies, railroads, canals, and turnpikes totaled $78,500,000 in 1863 and rose to $124,900,000 in 1864 before declining in 1865. Bonds showed only a small increase.[205]

Early in the war every Union reverse tended to send stock prices down. As the conflict lengthened, Northern victory sometimes had the same effect, for it meant abbreviation of the war, with its contracts and inflation. Nevertheless, in the spring of 1864 the money column of the New York *Tribune* declared that stocks were inflated beyond prudent bounds, and that this was caused by "the operations of speculators, aided by the banks." The financial editor, who patriotically counselled investors to turn to Federal securities, gave a shocking table of wartime gains:[206]

	April 17, 1863	*April 14, 1864*	*Gain*
New York Central	113¾	143½	29¾
Erie Common	76¾	126	49¼
Michigan Central	100¾	157	56¼
Michigan Southern	60	115¼	55¼
Illinois Central	70	150	80
Rock Island	89¼	134	44¾

At the height of the speculative frenzy, in 1863-64, basements in Wall, William, and Broad Streets and Exchange Place, were crammed with little offices, sheltering old Oily Gammons and young Napoleons-of-finance, with a scattering of honest men among the rascals and sharpers. They dealt in bank stocks, insurance stocks, textile and mining stocks, and Federal, State, and Municipal bonds. The Stock Exchange served an indispensable function, and its best spirits tried to divorce themselves from the bedlamite atmosphere about them. They looked with suspicious eyes upon the gold speculation that, becoming visible in 1862, rose like an aureate comet, its soaring flight watched with alarm by Chase in Washington and John J. Cisco in New York, and with indignation by many conservative citizens.[207]

204. Clews, *op. cit.*, 61.
205. Schwartz, Anna Jacobson, "Gross Dividend and Interest Payments by Corporations at Selected Dates in the 19th Century" *Trends in the American Economy in the 19th Century, op. cit.*, 407, 412. An act of July 1, 1862 imposed a duty on dividends and interest paid by banks, insurance companies, railways, canals and turnpikes. They were required to report on this, and therefore we have fairly reliable figures on dividend payments in these fields.
206. New York *Tribune*, April 18, 1864.

Gold fluctuations and speculation thereon were irrepressible once the country left a specie basis, and no more censurable in themselves than the fluctuations of the grain and livestock markets. But they aroused indignation when gold gambling became a favorite occupation of some Peace Democrats and quasi-traitors. Letters of Confederate agents intercepted in 1863 revealed that Southern leaders were nearly as well pleased when their Copperhead friends forced the price of gold up as when their generals threw Rosecrans or Meade back. One Senator who accepted the treasonable character of speculators declared: "Gold gamblers as a class are disloyal men in sympathy with the South." Most of them were probably only in sympathy with their pocket nerves.[208] But as gold swayed during 1863 between $125 and $160 in greenbacks, and during 1864 between $150 and $285, suspicion and antipathy grew. Newspapers like Greeley's *Tribune* fulminated. In March, 1863, a tax was placed upon time-sales of gold. Early in April, 1864, Chase visited New York, plainly much disturbed, to announce that the Treasury would thereafter make its own daily quotations of the price of gold in greenbacks. This brought the market down sharply, and as everybody was tense with anxiety for battle news from Grant and Sherman, in the nick of time.

A sudden upward soar in the price of gold would at any time have had dire possibilities. Chase wrote the Assistant Treasurer concerning this sudden dash to the metropolis. "I have just come from New York where my arrival was most opportune. Had I stayed away, gold would certainly have gone to $200 and over, and we should have had a terrific panic. A little judicious use of the exchange I so fortunately had in London and other points has made the speculators look glum, and had not the disaster at Fort Pillow provoked discouraging forebodings and disloyal misrepresentations, gold would have gone down today to only $165. As it is, the change is very favorable."[209]

On June 17, a law to prohibit speculative contracts was passed with the apparent approval of the Secretary. Men could still use greenbacks to buy gold if they paid their money down, but they could not buy without making immediate payment, nor make contracts to sell gold they did not possess. This enactment proved totally abortive. After a wild market dance and general rise, it was shamefacedly repealed. Then the Union victories in late summer helped to place the quotations on a downward trend, and public uneasiness abated.[210]

207. Fowler, *Ten Years in Wall Street, op. cit., passim.*
208. Dewey, *Financial History, op. cit.,* 295.
209. Philadelphia, Apr. 16, 1864. George Harrington Papers, Missouri Historical Society.
210. New York *Tribune,* editorial, "The Gold Flurry," June 23, 1864; Fowler, *op. cit.,* 75ff.; Medberry, James K., *Men and Mysteries of Wall Street,* Boston, 1879, Chs. XII, XIII; Dewey, *op. cit.,* 290-297; Myers, *The New York Money Market, op. cit.,* 197, 299.

[VIII]

That the war demanded an increase in governmental activities was more than clear; it was glaringly obvious in the existence and use of the army, the tremendous sums spent in war contracts, and in the increased number of civil workers engaged in the war effort. This was planned, directed, and organized without concern over whether it was actually violating State, local, or individual rights, though the issue did sometimes demand attention, and was often in the background. The States still had much to say about recruiting and organizing troops, and little desire was expressed by the Federal government to dominate or dictate. The job had to be done, and it was done.

In other fields, governmental action was less directly tied to the war, but here too the government showed no reflective wish to invade the private sector of life with planned or directed interferences. The check on arbitrary impulses, if any existed, was still ingrained in the body politic. In a few instances, Lincoln and the Union government were called despotic, as Davis and the Confederate authorities were in many. But most of such criticisms were for political effect, and nothing more. Still, not far below the surface always lurked fears of any approach toward the mildest form of dictatorship or governmental encroachment. Some men were ready to defend their sacred civil rights, as they proved in the wide popular denunciation of military-political arrests and press suspension in the North.

When the new Department of Agriculture was set up in 1862, many conservatives cried out against the expenditure. (A little attention to agriculture had previously been given by a fraction of the Patent Office of the Interior Department.) In 1864, after a year's operation, the new department was limited to a modest seed-distribution program, publication of free crop bulletins, a six-acre propagating garden, a small museum, some translations of foreign publications, a small amount of taxidermy and chemical work, a fairly large correspondence, and the compiling of statistics.[211] *Country Gentleman* in December, 1863, could see no reason for the 632-page "Report of the Commissioner of Agriculture for the Year 1862," and much of the agricultural press agreed.[212]

But of much more immediate importance in government stimulation of the wartime economy was the issuance of bonds, the National Banking Act, the Morrill tariff, the greenbacks issue, and such new revenue measures as the income tax. All of them were planned by the national government as stimuli for the war effort and civilian economy. Most of them benefited the national economy, and served as weapons of war.

211. *Prairie Farmer*, Vol. XIV, No. 25, Dec. 17, 1864, 388.
212. *Country Gentleman*, Vol. XXII, No. 23, Dec. 3, 1863, 368; *Cultivator*, May, 1862; also *Massachusetts Ploughshare*, *New England Farmer*, March, 1865.

In iron and steel, for instance, the spokesman for the American Iron and Steel Association wrote: "With the enactment of the Morrill protective tariff on March 2, 1861, and with the added stimulus of the Civil War, our iron and steel industries at once entered upon a period of extraordinary development . . ."[213]

Although there had been much automatic stimulation of industry due to the war, and much natural growth through development and invention, there were areas where there was perforce an automatic reduction because of the war. Clearly, for example, while railroad building did not halt, the war undoubtedly did limit extension of the lines. The cotton-textile manufacturers and their work forces suffered in the early days of the war, but soon the mills converted to woolens and other products where necessary, showing the flexibility of a primary segment of industry. The husky Atlantic and Gulf Coast trade was suspended and commercial shipbuilding largely eliminated. Yet, at the same time, the Navy, through the great need of transports, and the Army as well, built up a backlog of vessels which, when sold at the end of the war, as we will see, were easily convertible to commercial purposes and were responsible for the quick renewal of the coastal trade. Every department of technology was quickened.

Thus, most of the reductions were temporary or even beneficial in opening the doors to new ventures. The nation did mobilize industrially, but without price and wage controls, quotas, immense governmental regulatory machinery or any of the paraphernalia of a later age. Mistakes and wastes were many, but the task was done largely within the philosophy of the North, although the signs of changed patterns of thought were there. Few may have read them, however, or been conscious of them.

In the area of civilian life, the pinches were present for some, but, as has been shown, they were not sufficient to wound, impede, or even discomfort most of the nation, or delay economic progress or the war effort. Some non-governmental attempts were made in the North to restrict the use of luxuries and fineries, as the war struck into daily life more deeply. But these arose more often from patriotism, or a feeling that sacrifices in the field must be matched by sacrifices at home, than from a harsh pressure of need. It was the South that felt the inexorable Laocoon-grip of dire need.

The ladies of Chicago met in the Bryant House in May, 1864, for one of numerous gatherings of the "Non-Importation Movement." They resolved that, due to the war, public debt and prices "are most seriously aggravated by the large and excessive importation of costly and luxurious apparel, decorations, and so forth, caused, in part by an unnatural, transient, and hence deceptive, prosperity, and resulting in a tendency to extravagance, not less dangerous to our social

213. Swank, James M., *Notes and Comments on Industrial, Economic, Political, and Historical Subjects,* Philadelphia, 1897, 145.

purity and well-being, than hostile to the best interests of our beloved country." They agreed to unite in "discouraging extravagance, and retrenching expenditures, especially for luxurious and costly apparel. . . ."[214]

A first effect of the war had been to emphasize the general austerity of American life, but such gestures had but little influence. Nevertheless, the efforts did not cease. About the same time as the meeting in Chicago, Greeley's *Tribune* in May, 1864, was chronicling an enthusiastic meeting in Cooper Union of the "women's patriotic association for diminishing the use of luxuries."[215] This movement, an outgrowth of the recent Sanitary Commission Fair, enlisted such men as President King of Columbia and capitalist William Dodge, as well as women like Susan B. Anthony and Louisa Lee Schuyler. It inveighed against the indecency of ladies sweeping the streets with Lyons silks and Paris velvets, flashing in jewelry, while soldiers died on the Potomac; and it carried unanimously a pledge not to purchase imported articles of luxury while those of home production could be conveniently substituted. This would conserve American funds and protect gold, yet still permit expenditures. Many, however, were genuinely economical from patriotic motives, and one British observer was impressed by the union of tight-fisted private parsimony with public generosity among American businessmen. "I know commercial men by repute who think no more of giving twenty or thirty thousand dollars for any benevolent purpose brought under their notice than if the sum were so many farthings."[216]

In a time of rising rents, taxation, food and clothing prices, and other costs, however, not many middle-class folk and still fewer of the urban working classes had much margin for economy. No adequate fact-gathering apparatus upon social change yet existed. What little was available suggests that, as in later wars, only fuller employment, more overtime labor, and the opening of new occupations to women permitted many families to ride the wild mustang of inflation.[217]

But, as indicated, most of the austerity calls went for naught, and, as such, were merely a manifestation of the most patriotic or sensitive segments of the population, or those who perhaps felt it was unseemly to indulge oneself while the boys were on the battlefield. There were still other, more substantial cries.

The American laboring man was admittedly the most prosperous in the world in the years before the war. By the standards of the day, the London *Times* was probably only slightly exaggerating when it wrote: "If ever there was a country in which labor was in clover, in which it was looked up to, petted, and humored,

214. *Prairie Farmer,* Vol. XIII, No. 22, May 28, 1864, 384.
215. New York *Tribune,* May 17, 1864.
216. Burn, James Dawson, *Three Years among the Working Classes in the United States During the War,* London, 1865, 243.
217. Cf. Marwick, Arthur, *The Deluge,* London, 1965, 123ff., for British experience in the First World War.

it certainly was this North American community." Others, like *Scientific American*, painted the same picture.[218] But this was a distinctly relative, comparative view. With paper-money, inflation, and wartime demands, discontent troubled the labor market. Jobs were plentiful, more than plentiful, but some workers were caught in the squeeze. Slowly there arose some antagonism toward employers and a trend toward experimenting with organization and strikes. A tentative movement toward unionism had existed for some time, and it increased during the war, as the effects of the Panic of 1857 wore off and the manpower shortage grew exigent. Another fact involved was a fear along the docks, on the railroads, and elsewhere in the lower echelons of labor that Negroes would take over the jobs of white laborers, an apprehension that played a part in the horrifying New York draft riots. In fact, a month before the riots, New York longshoremen had struck for higher wages and failed. Cincinnati also had difficulties of this sort. The stimulation of further immigration irritated some laborers, as did improvements in labor-saving machinery.

At the same time, the wartime scarcity of labor gave some workers a chance to move upward into better skilled and more profitable jobs. Then, too, an increasing demand appeared, as has been seen, for shorter hours and even an eight-hour-day. The average was now about ten hours, although some toiled for still longer periods.

Both capital and labor were moving toward combination, labor perhaps more slowly than capital. Strikes became commonplace, and many failed. However, it does not appear that the war effort suffered any considerable injury from these labor disturbances. Most of them were local and scattered, attracting limited attention. In a few instances, the military had to step in, but this was not general. In one strike, army deserters were compelled to load Federal transports in New York, and stoppages of work were temporarily forbidden in such cities near the war front as St. Louis and Louisville. The Reading Railroad was run for a period by the Army. But, these instances were infrequent.

Unionism was definitely mounting, however, particularly in the middle period of the war and in the larger cities. Most of the unions were small and many were single-shop organizations, but perhaps as many as 300 new unions were formed in New York alone.[219] Unionism on a national scale did not really become significant until well after Appomattox.

Many of the industrial journals sharply opposed what they believed to be unjustifiable demands and organizations. The *American Railroad Journal,* while

218. Fite, *op. cit.,* 183, quoting London *Times,* Dec. 1, 1863; *Scientific American,* Vol. VIII, No. 2, Jan. 10, 1863, 26.
219. Fite, *op. cit.,* 205.

admitting that the laborer had the right to demand for himself the best remuneration for his services in the general market, and that he might even change employers as often as he found the change beneficial, declared that "whether laborers or employees have the moral right to band themselves together, and to demand an increase of wages upon condition of resuming work, is questionable. . . . Such action can only be defended on the ground that employees are the weaker parties to the contract, and that a union of their strength is necessary in order to make labor equal in the struggle to capital. . . ." But the *Journal* also denounced the monopoly of any branch of trade by "a few wealthy men" and against excessive profits.[220]

Scientific American, in December, 1863, reporting on a machinists' strike in large shops in New York, pointed out that the owners maintained they could not afford to increase wages, "and that it would be politic for them to close their works rather than to accede to the demands of their operatives." The workmen said they could not live under the present remuneration, and that while wages had increased, purchasing power was less. "To us it is most melancholy. . . . The workmen are some $300,000 out of pocket. The winter approaches, and soon the cold weather will be felt in all its severity; with coal at $11 per ton, it seems well to take counsel for the future. . . . Not only this, but our machinists, than whom there is no class more loyal or patriotic, must see that the interests of the country suffer greatly by their action; and will, we hope, reconsider the matter and see if some understanding cannot be arrived at whereby all parties will be suited."[221]

Early in 1864 the *Scientific American* called for adjusting the interests of capital and labor harmoniously, and deplored the injuries suffered when capital combined to control or force prices upward, or when "capitalists coalesce for the purpose of cheating the laborer of his hire. . . ." On the other hand, "Labor is also exacting in its demands, at times, and when it fancies it has the sweep of the market, so to speak, takes advantage of the circumstance like other speculators, and in some instances is enabled to carry out its objects, in others not; depending principally upon the ability of Capital to withstand the demand made. . . ."[222]

Undoubtedly some pressure and demand toward labor organizations, and an increase of strikes, would have come without the war, depending on economic trends. Nevertheless, it does seem that the conditions brought about by the war did definitely affect the increase in labor discontent, and in animosity between some segments of labor and capital. It was not yet a virulent problem, but certainly one that was accelerated by the great boom of the Civil War.

220. *American Railroad Journal,* Vol. XXXVII, No. 1442, Dec. 5, 1863.
221. *Scientific American,* Vol. IX, No. 24, Dec. 12, 1863, 377.
222. *Ibid.,* Vol. X, No. 1, Jan. 2, 1864, 9.

[IX]

The question whether the Civil War advanced or retarded industrialization does not properly invite the pontifical responses it has received.[223] It did both, producing mixed results in a very mixed economy. Unquestionably the war lent direct stimulus to various industries by its flood of contracts; but it was assisted at the same time by the lift which inflation gave market demand and profits, by fresh capital formation and creation of new fortunes, by novel machinery, and by improved technological and commercial methods. It is undeniable, too, that the upward curve of industrial development had been growing more pronounced ever since the Mexican victories, and recovery from the Panic of 1857 had been rapid and strong. How far would that curve have carried the nation had war been avoided? Nobody can say.[224]

The great boom of 1863-1865 was to go down in history as one of the most remarkable phenomena of the nineteenth century; but however enjoyable to many participants at the time, and however picturesque in the materials it gave writers later, it was eventually to be remembered with very mixed feelings indeed.

Increasingly, the boom had its unhappy aspects. One price paid for it was the great debt, which the *Commercial and Financial Chronicle* estimated at the end of 1865 to stand at $2,716,581,586, or about two-thirds of the annual product of the nation's industry. J.F.D. Lanier of New York, in a widely accepted pamphlet late in 1865, estimated the aggregate wealth at $16,112 billions, and the yearly product at $4,318 millions. If this was approximately correct, the republic was in a favorable position, very similar to that of a manufacturer who, to get rid of a burden or disease which had for years fettered his progress, had mortgaged his property for a sum equal only to two-thirds of his income for one year. Such a man would not be regarded by his neighbors, and would not regard himself, as deeply in debt.[225] As soon as victory became certain, capitalists, especially in England, began purchasing American bonds with significant eagerness.

On the other hand, a deplorable price that had to be paid lay in the fact that wage increases trailed price increases at a distance that meant some hardship to millions. The most regrettable fact of all was that the great boom had infected business and political life with a recklessness and dishonesty which were to cost the nation dearly.

Inflation, according to the correspondent of the London *Times,* had filled

---

223. Andreano, Ralph, ed., *The Economic Impact of the American Civil War,* Cambridge, Mass., 1962, 148ff.

224. Gallman, Robert E., *Trends in the Size and Distribution of Wealth in the 19th Century,* N.Y., 1969, *passim.*

225. *Commercial and Financial Chronicle,* Jan. 6, 1866, 1-2.

American cities with needy men and women turned thieves and prostitutes. As 1865 closed, prices had fallen, and wages were higher, but inflation was still grievous. The country had $900,000,000 in paper currency afloat, estimated the *Chronicle*, though the largest amount that could be kept in circulation on a specie basis was probably not more than $300,000,000.[226] The greed engendered by economic fluctuations, rising prices, and the spectacle of men suddenly enriched had a natural result in cheating and speculation. The annual report of the Chamber of Commerce of New York for 1865-66, after pointing out that the boot-and-shoe industries in New York and New England had never before rolled up such huge income for the capitalists engaged in them as during the war, added that "an immense amount of trash was palmed off upon the army and navy," and that "frauds in the shoe-manufacturing line still exist to an alarming extent." As much could be said of other industries. If beggars and prostitutes grew more numerous, so did the men that Theodore Roosevelt would have called malefactors of great wealth. One entry in the diary of John Bigelow is significant.[227]

Bigelow relates that the capitalists John Murray Forbes and William H. Aspinwall came to France and took an apartment on the Champs Elysées. Aspinwall told the Minister how he had made a great deal of money by purchasing arms when the war began and later selling them to the American Government. George D. Morgan, financier, politician, and cousin of ex-Governor Morgan of New York, then told Bigelow that Aspinwall had kept the profits for a year or more, and had not surrendered them except under pressure. That is, he had given them up only when Morgan told the merchant R.B. Minturn, whose daughter was about to marry Aspinwall's son, that before long he would hear things about a distinguished friend which would astonish him. Aspinwall was one of those whom Francis Lieber called "rich fogies", and Henry W. Bellows "rich do-nothings" who used their comfortable castles to make raids upon public confidence.

Still more significant were certain pamphlets evoked by corporate malpractices of the day; such pamphlets as one written by a Dr. Ayer of Lowell, who complained of the mismanagement of the textile companies of New England. Reputed to be one of their largest shareholders, he offered shocking facts upon the tendency of the directors and officers of corporations to divert into their own pockets money that should have gone to shareholders. His statements were so persuasive that the New York *Tribune* devoted one of its longest editorials of 1863 to restating and supporting them.[228] The current newspapers abounded in such

226. London *Times*, April 18, 1864. By this date the *Times* had a correspondent friendly to the North. *Commercial and Financial Chronicle*, Jan. 6, 1863, editorial, "High Prices and inflated Currency," 2-3.
227. Bigelow, John, *Diary*, ms., New York Public Library, entry of May 13, 1863.
228. New York *Tribune*, "Manufacturing Mismanagement," April 3, 1863.

materials. Meanwhile, all unnoticed at the time, though later recalled by shocking disclosures, were public statements such as those which, in 1864, began the riot of speculation and thievery that ruined Erie stockholders, and within a few years made the names of Erie, Jay Gould, and James Fisk, Jr. infamous.

The Great Boom increased as government expenditures rose. These stood, in round numbers, at 475 millions in 1862; at 715 millions in 1863; at 865 millions in 1864; and at 1,298 millions in 1865. Financially, the country was lifted to a new, high plateau. Nearly all the huge expenditures were for war purposes, and by far the greatest part of the money needed was raised by borrowing. Total government receipts from taxes, public-land sales, and miscellaneous minor sources rose from a mere 51 millions in the second year of war to 322 millions in the last year.[229]

But despite the many black marks abounding, perhaps the nation as a whole and the world of economics at large did not grasp at the time the near phenomenon that had occurred. A nation moving rapidly out of depression and groping its way into a new industrial age had been ripped asunder by a monumental, sectional civil conflict. The whole South had been torn from the existing economic and social fabric and yet, despite setbacks, readjustments, and changes in trends, the Federal Union proved in basic terms that it could fight such a civil conflict which engrossed hundreds of thousands, and at the same time not only continue the economic life of 1860, but advance it. True, at the beginning of the war there was an optimism as to the material growth and strength of the nation; there was recovery from the downturn of 1857; there was a sufficient and growing population; technological tools were at hand, raw materials were abundant, and the North was largely uninvaded and undevastated. But, even if unplanned and with some halting steps, the Union undertook and completed the dual task. Civilian life not only went on, but everyday life in broad terms was really little disrupted by shortages, substitutes, or drastic hardships. We may repeat that no rationing was imposed, no price or wage controls were applied, no priorities were dictated by government, and, in short, regimentation was unknown. It was indeed a time of "guns and butter." We must also emphasize the fact that if a business collapse, depression, or even recession and severe unrest had interrupted the course of the war, victory would only have been postponed. It is not too much to say that no other great nation at that time, or perhaps later, could have enjoyed a similar reign of economic sunshine.

229. *Historical Statistics of the United States,* Washington, D.C., 1960, 718; various sources give slight discrepancies.

The Sweep of Organization

[I]

"THE AMERICANS, in some things at least, seem to have a good faculty of organization," the Duke of Argyll rather dubiously wrote Gladstone on September 15, 1864. Naming the U.S. Sanitary Commission as an instance of efficient management, he suggested that the freedmen might be suffering from a lack of organized care.[1] He had read enough of Tocqueville, Harriet Martineau, and others to know that Americans were a nation of individualists. The Alsatian observer Auguste Laugel, married to an American girl, stated the fact emphatically. "In the United States," he wrote, "there is a horror of all trammels, system, and uniformity." Edward Dicey, describing the looseness of the social structure as he traversed the land, believed that it was visibly receding: "The one clearest result of this war has been to bring the people of the States together—to give them common recollections, common interests, and common dangers."[2]

A shrewd native observer, a man trained in the New York militia who became one of the best Northern artillery officers, Colonel Charles S. Wainwright, laid his finger on what he regarded as the primary reason for the paucity of organizations. It was the lack of social discipline and competitive spirit in a spacious, newly settled land. "It is astonishing how little snap people have generally," he wrote. Not more than a half-dozen officers in his regiment showed alertness and energy. "This is doubtless in part owing to the miserable, sleepy, slipshod way everybody does business in our villages and small towns," he added. That is, he indicted the loose-jointed, leisurely mode of life in a rural society.[3] In the cities, however, foreigners noted that "go ahead" and "hurry up" were among the commonest American phrases. The hurry and competitive pace of life restricted friendly cooperation, although in many instances the go-spirit made use of cooperation and organization. European communities possessed more of a social spirit, wrote

---

1. Gladstone Papers, British Museum, Add. mss. 44099.
2. Laugel, Auguste, *The United States During the Civil War*, ed. Allan Nevins, Bloomington, Ind., 1961, 195; Dicey, Edward, *Six Months in the Federal States*, 2 vols., London, 1863, Vol. I, 297.
3. Wainwright, Charles S., *A Diary of Battle*, ed. Allan Nevins, New York, 1960, p. vii.

the British observer J.D. Burn. "Here it would seem that the people are mere units, and that each atom of humanity exists only for itself."[4]

On the other hand, some observers saw the situation differently. A Scottish visitor in California wrote: "The Americans have a very great advantage, for ... they are certainly of all people in the world the most prompt to organize and combine to carry out a common object."[5] A modern authority maintains that, in the period before the war, "Americans were becoming a nation of 'joiners'." Alexis de Tocqueville and other Europeans expressed astonishment at the propensity of Americans for organizing private associations for every conceivable purpose.[6] A tremendous rash of local political clubs, abolitionist groups, temperance societies, and religious organizations appeared in the 1850's and 1860's, along with churches, infant labor unions, chambers of commerce, trade organizations, professional groups, fraternal organizations, cultural organizations, sprouting social and religious societies.

While in the pre-war days many Americans did fear the encroachment of organization, particularly in the form of governmental interference, and dreaded any threat of what they believed might become organizational interference with their traditional individualism, a tremendous growth of group activity for business, professional, and social ends was inevitable as population, wealth, and general culture grew by vaulting leaps. The multiplication of organizations in a society long simple and hostile to complicated or sophisticated activities seemed to many a paradoxical and artificial new development in national life. But as Benjamin Franklin would have declared, in any comprehensive view, this quick and dynamic tendency for the people of the fast-growing nation to attempt a wide variety of organized undertakings could be described as a result of individualism. One has to look in a multitude of directions and delve into local history to see the magnitude of this craving for organization. It had not yet coalesced to gain wide national scope, although gropings toward sectionalism or national expression were abundant.

That the Civil War brought a systematic shift in American society from an unorganized society to a well-organized nation is undoubtedly much too strong a statement. But that the Civil War accentuated and acted as a catalyst to already developing local tendencies toward organization, there can be no doubt. As in so many fields of thought and endeavor, the war changed and stimulated the impulse toward organization, and served as a proving ground or experimental phase for

4. Burn, James Dawson, *Three Years among the Working Classes in the United States During the War*, London, 1865, 12.

5. Borthwick, J.D., *Three Years in California*, Edinburgh, 1857, as cited in Billington, Ray Allen, *America's Frontier Heritage*, New York, 1966, 146. Billington points out, "Even those crown princes of individualism, the ranchers and miners, depended far more on joint effort than on self-prowess." See also Jackson, W. Turrentine, *Treasure Hill, Portrait of a Silver-Mining Camp*, Tucson, Ariz., 1963.

6. Bates, Ralph S., *Scientific Societies in the United States*, New York, 1951, 37.

numerous tentative expressions of organization. There seems no doubt that this momentum sprang primarily from necessity or pragmatic impulses, rather than from philosophical devotion to organization for its own sake. That such a pragmatic trend would have occurred without wartime demands is unquestionable, but it certainly would have been different and perhaps slower. The war imposed requirements and opened opportunities. Organization met the demands and grasped many of the opportunities.

In the so-called second American Revolution, the economic transformation within the years 1860-1875, leadership was provided partly by government, while more and more of the initiative came from industrial capitalism. As time passed and national growth and the war effort demanded bold action, private, social, and governmental exertions differed in fundamental aims and psychology, often in a groping, unconscious way; but government captains, industrial leaders, and thrusting innovators came more and more to think alike. Such a leader as Abram S. Hewitt, or Jay Cooke, could use his talents alike in civic organizations, and private business. Government officials were to a large extent rural-born, rural-trained, and rural-minded; business leaders were largely urban-trained, and acted as William E. Dodge, Cornelius Vanderbilt, or Ezra Cornell did through banks, textile companies, iron mills, insurance firms, and complicated railroad corporations concentrated in Northern cities. Yet they quickly learned to be effective as organizers in the joint enterprise of industrializing the North. It was natural that Colonel Oliver Hazard Payne should come home from organizing and commanding thousands of troops in the war to join John D. Rockefeller in organizing Standard Oil, and helping to form the American Tobacco Company and Tennessee Coal & Iron. He had the gift of uniting and galvanizing strong-willed men in huge enterprises. Political leaders, many of whom depended upon voters who were soon caught up in the Greenback, Granger and Populist parties, often leaned toward what might be called the left; industrial capitalists inclined toward what was later called the right. In collisions of interest between rural and city elements, the latter held a growing advantage. The war boom of 1861-1868 was a great wave which flung industrial growth forward, and gave the factories, forges, and town offices a widening authority. When flush times were abruptly ended in 1873, a process of reorganization and consolidation ensued. It resulted in a new and more efficiently directed republic, with industry overtaking agriculture in a struggle of clashing economic interests, and disciplined cohesion replacing immaturity and slackness in center after center.[7]

Individualism had stamped nearly all American settlement, for almost all the colonists came, like John Smith and William Bradford, as stern-tempered in-

---

7. Cochran, Thomas, and William Miller, *The Age of Enterprise*, New York, 1942, *passim;* Williamson, Harold F., ed., *The Growth of the American Economy*, New York, 1951, Chaps. XXVIII-XXXI; Nevins, Allan, *The Emergence of Modern America, 1865-1878*, New York, 1927, *passim.*

dividuals, even though they did have some organizational support. Individualism was dominant in the continued immigration from the British Isles, and from northern and western Europe. Such a society best suited the shaggy continent, where the conditions of wilderness life bred an assertive independence that we can plainly trace from Cotton Mather and Samuel Sewall down to at least Andrew Jackson. Although organized politics, religion and amusements were taken for granted, they were rudimentary in form and often half-chaotic. Self-reliance, versatility, and enterprise were the traits most prized as the border moved west and new communities grew up behind the mountain men, fur-traders, and Indian-fighters. The yeasty, nebulous society was slow to develop knots and filaments of collective action. When they appeared, as they soon did, the spirit of the Victorian world reëmphasized individualism which went side by side with the new organizational tendencies, each supplementing and invigorating the other.

The spirit of *laissez-faire* liberalism was especially hostile toward government interference in organizing the forces of society. If it did not oppose organization, it opposed what was often the most convenient and effective way of realizing it. In the Civil War era, John Stuart Mill warned his Anglo-American public against "the mischief of overloading the chief functionaries of government with demands on their attention and diverting them . . . to objects which can be sufficiently well attained without them. . . . the danger of unnecessarily swelling the direct power and the indirect influence of government . . ."[8] In the same spirit, E. L. Godkin's New York *Nation,* just after the war, inveighed against the proposal to establish a Bureau of Education in Washington:

Since the war began there has been exhibited a marked tendency toward bureau-making. Some of these bureaus, like the Bureau of Navigation and the Freedmen's Bureau, are avowedly mere temporary necessities which the war created and a well-established peace will end. But others, like the Bureau of Agriculture and the so-called National Academy (of Sciences), seem to have been permanently established, and we are further threatened with a Bureau of Manufactures and a Bureau of Education. . . . Now these bureaus . . . propagate and give countenance to the grave error that government agencies have the power to foster and promote these great national interests. It should never be forgotten that all real growth and progress in agriculture, commerce, manufactures, science or education is from the people, never from the government. The government may hinder but cannot help; a bureau may record progress, but never originates or causes it. In matters touching education, science, or manufactures, the best instruction which the people could give to their chosen representatives would be, —let us alone.[9]

8. Dodd, William Edward, *Jefferson Davis,* Philadelphia, 1907, 209-214; Owsley, Frank L., *King Cotton Diplomacy,* Chicago, 1931, Ch. I.
9. New York *Nation,* June 12, 1866.

This was the voice of John Stuart Mill and Manchester liberalism.

The principle of organization, slowly albeit confusedly developing before the war, played a part in American history as yet imperfectly studied. Historians have examined the influence of the frontier upon American character, psychology, and politics.[10] They have taken due note of the fact that the wealth of natural resources, and their exploitation by the unfolding processes of science and technology, have had a vital influence upon life, progress and outlook.[11] The mobility of the American folk has been scrutinized as an element in understanding the national past, although this mobility stems from varied causes.[12] The principle of organization, however, and its manifest expansion in practical power and psychological influence, or the lack of it, has not been properly analyzed. It was of cardinal significance, and in the Civil War era received an impetus of tremendous importance.

The pre-war republic presented one of the sparsest and weakest arrays of organizations on a national basis to be found among the Western nations. It was in some respects almost as formless and inchoate as China. As yet no single railway connected the Atlantic coast with the Mississippi or Chicago, and none linked the Great Lakes to the Gulf of Mexico. However, several such lines as the Baltimore & Ohio and Illinois Central were interstate, and cooperation between various roads was growing. Many sections now had railways, although some of them presented a confusion of different gauges, ranging from three to six feet, and equipment interchange was limited. Time zones were dimly defined until the mid-sixties, and time differed wildly from place to place, Boston, Chicago, Cincinnati, and other cities marking the hours at their own sweet will. The country had no national labor union worthy of the name, though in various cities local unions were developing in such trades as those of typographers, iron workers, and hatmakers. The panic of 1857, indeed, had stunted the adolescent impulse toward labor organization. Few national associations of importance existed outside of religion and politics, although regional, state, city, and local groups in many fields were emerging. Communications by rail and telegraph were enlarging the scope of these local groups by 1860. The American Medical Association had been founded in May, 1847, and while its power was not great, it was a national group with useful activities in medicine, medical education, ethics, and professional literature. Farming and stock-growing, the central occupations of the country, encouraged numerous scattered societies and fairs of varying size and influence. The United States Agricultural Society, incorporated by Congress in 1860, was formed in 1841, but remained practically inactive until 1852. By 1861, it exercised

10. Turner, Frederick Jackson, *The Frontier in American History,* New York, 1920, the best collection of his papers.
11. Potter, David M., *People of Plenty,* Chicago, 1954, *passim.*
12. Pierson, George W., "A Restless Temper," *American Historical Review,* LXIX, July, 1964.

some influence, although Solon Robinson's proposal for even greater activity was not yet effective.[13] Industrial groups were far from powerful in influence, but they were steadily growing, and Chambers-of-Commerce and Boards-of-Trade were active in most large cities.

Although the postal system was still well behind that of Great Britain, significant advances had been made to meet problems of distance which were much greater than in the British Isles. It would be many years before the special delivery, rural free delivery, parcel post, or postal savings emerged. However, the United States did institute compulsory prepayment of postage and registered mail in 1855, free delivery in the cities in 1863, postal money orders in 1864, and railway post-offices in 1865.[14] Montgomery Blair pointed out in December, 1861, that his predecessor had the fact that large numbers of unpaid letters continued to be posted despite the compulsory prepayment law. In July, 1863, free delivery of mail by carriers was begun at forty-nine of the larger post offices, with about 450 carriers. New York had five deliveries daily from the post office, and six collections of letters from depositories. With Army mail problems having priority, the setting up of a city-carrier service did not seem to be a wartime necessity.[15] Collections of soldiers' letters bear evidence that the mail often reached them quite rapidly.

Not a single State Bar Association was in existence. Bar associations, or similar groups, projected in colonial and early national days, had soon declined. Records of these early groups are sketchy. As Roscoe Pound said, between 1836 and the Civil War, the time was not ripe for such associations.[16] Only the Association of the Bar of Milwaukee, founded in 1858, seems to have a valid claim to a continuous existence, and even that is uncertain.[17]

A very few cities had small, weak Departments of Health. The first State Department of Public Health (toward which Lemuel Shattuck had pointed the way in his sanitary survey of 1849) would be established in Massachusetts in 1869. Few cities had sewage systems deserving of the name, Philadelphia still relying upon the antiquated system of more than fifty-thousand cesspools. Boston, too, had not yet instituted an able metropolitan health administration that could equal that found in London. Although some American urban areas made initial provi-

13. Robinson, Solon, *Selected Writings,* ed. Herbert Anthony Keller, Indianapolis, 1935-1936, Vol. I, 87ff. and *passim.*

14. Van Riper, Paul P. and Keith A. Sutherland, "The Northern Civil Service, 1861-1865," *Civil War History,* Dec. 1965, Vol. XI, No. 4, 351-369.

15. Reports of the Postmaster General in *Congressional Globe,* 37th and 38th Cong.; for a brief summary of postal development and dates of various services, see *Dictionary of American History,* IV, 319-21.

16. Pound, Roscoe, *The Lawyer from Antiquity to Modern Times,* St. Paul, 1953, *passim.*

17. *Ibid.,* 246; see also Warren, Charles, *A History of the American Bar,* Boston, 1911, 83, 87, 98, 200, 210, and *passim.* Also various records in the Library of the Chicago Bar Assoc.

sions for a steady water-supply long before 1860, the City Engineer of Chicago had not even begun its labyrinth of underground works until the 1850's; water had been pumped through hollow cedar-logs as late as 1842. A municipally owned plant was finally built in 1864, and that same year Chesbrough designed the great system of water-cribs in Lake Michigan with tunnels to pumping stations which are still in use today.[18]

Nearly all manufacturing was performed on a local basis, managed in small units as family affairs or small partnerships. State laws forbade corporations to hold property outside State boundaries except by special charters seldom granted. Not one satisfactory article on the subject of organization and management could be found in financial or business magazines down to 1860, thus reflecting the fact that a land with few machines is unorganized. The British Isles, in 1860, with a population only a little less than the entire United States, were much better equipped with machine industry, and so were far better organized. Small crafts still held an important place in America, but wider organization was slowly taking hold of partially mechanized areas such as that between Boston and Philadelphia.[19]

In one broad field, it may be said, the nation had developed a considerable amount of specialized organization before 1860—the field of Westward expansion. Since the main fact of American life was the movement of population toward the setting sun, the best energies of the country were channeled into its promotion. In steamboat traffic on river and lake, the United States led the world after Fulton sent the *Clermont* to Albany, and Nicholas Roosevelt sped the *New Orleans* on its way down the Ohio and Mississippi. In railroad and canal construction, we again set new marks. Inventors were inspired by the need for ploughs and harvesters, as well as sewing-machines, shovels, and shoes, which the settlement of wide new areas soon made evident. Expeditions into new territory required some organization for the sake of protection as well as law and order.

[II]

This sprawling country, much of it in the gristle rather than the bone, suddenly had to pull itself together. The unnatural catalyst of war demanded concentration and coordination. The North alone enrolled more than two million persons before the war ended; it had to clothe, arm, transport, and feed them. Simultaneously, it had to improvise a Navy able to maintain a blockade along more than 3,500 miles of coast; to plan and execute financial measures for raising

18. Lewis, Lloyd, and Henry Justin Smith, *Chicago, The History of its Reputation,* New York, 1929, p. 264; *Illinois, a Descriptive and Historical Guide,* American Guide Series, Chicago, 1939, 242.
19. Clapham, John Harold, *An Economic History of Modern Britain,* Cambridge (Eng.), 1930-1938, Vol. II, Chs. V, VI, VII, and VIII, with references.

three billions of dollars; and to build up a directing force, a bureaucracy, to manage the gigantic war effort. The largely unorganized country of 1860, in short, had to take giant strides forward to become the partially organized country of 1865.

As the government advanced on essential fronts, an impressive panoply of volunteer agencies had to support and complement its efforts. The health and medical services of the Army would indeed have been feeble without the aid of the Sanitary Commission and other voluntary agencies. The needs of hundreds of thousands of men on the battlefield and in parole or convalescent camps could never have been met without the carloads of supplies and hundreds of workers mobilized by the Christian Commission. Within a fortnight after Sumter, the Soldiers' Aid Society of Cleveland, the Ladies' Aid Society of Philadelphia, and the Women's Central Association of Relief in New York sprang into existence. Home and foreign missionary societies of the churches, numerous Bible and tract societies, ladies' aid societies, temperance groups, organizations for assisting seamen, homeless children, and the dependent, all went to work. State agents to see to soldier needs were appointed in some areas, while the American Union Commission strove to ameliorate the condition of loyalists and refugees from the South. The American Association for the Relief of the Misery of the Battle Fields, an auxiliary to the *Comité Internationale de Secours Aux Militaires Blessés* from which the Red Cross in part grew, was active. No sooner did it become plain that the advance of Union armies in Virginia, Kentucky, and down the Mississippi would release a host of slaves than Freedmen's Relief Societies were established in all the larger Northern cities. They cooperated with religious and educational organizations in providing money, clothing, farm implements, and general supplies for the black folk, and were soon intensively busy opening schools and administering refugee camps. Home-relief organizations for soldiers' families sprang up rapidly across the continent.

It was the national government, however, that for three reasons had led the march of organization, aside from the over-riding fact that it was the prime agency in fighting the war. It commanded the greatest resources; it could most easily manage the factor of *consent,* many of its mandates becoming imperative; and in all military affairs it made effective use of the power of *hierarchy.* Citizens who by nature relished equality had learned that the emergency demanded a society amenable to the influence of status, in which governors, generals, and high industrial executives must necessarily assert firm leadership.[20]

The inexorable rise of government departments to what then appeared enormous dimensions impressed all observers, and alarmed quite a few. Significantly,

20. Cf. Boulding, Kenneth F., *The Organizational Revolution,* New York, 1953, on the sociology of organization.

real assistant secretaries had seldom before appeared in the Cabinet departments. A chief clerk had always been sufficient. But, as the war grew, the post of assistant secretary necessarily became powerful, particularly in the War and Navy Departments. Even the President augmented his two-man secretarial staff, and Noah Brooks reported early in 1864 that in many government offices the increase was fourfold: "The Treasury Department now has 1200 clerks and laborers; the Interior Department has 450; the War Department has 500."[21] A few dozen altogether had sufficed before the war. Brooks thought that the Quartermaster-General's office had upon its rolls as many as 7,000 clerks and other employees, and that the Navy Yards, Government Printing Office, and other offices hired at least 3,000 more. Actually these figures were an underestimate, and Brooks trailed behind the facts when he wrote that the whole array of workers employed at the seat of government reached 12,000 men—truly a small army.[22] The total number of civilian government employees increased from 40,651 in 1861 to 195,000 in 1865, according to one authority, with 136,236 in the War Department alone.[23] Furthermore, the Northern State governments employed thousands more in such war-born posts as the State Adjutant-Generals' offices. For such an array careful organization was needed, and the roster of executives grew proportionately.

The most important government department before the war, the Treasury, had a total of but 4,025 employes in 1861, and by 1865 this had grown to 10,390.[24] For the fiscal year 1861-62, the Treasury had a payroll of $53,800 covering the executives of the "regular staff", including the Secretary, the two Comptrollers, the Treasurer, the Solicitor, and a few others. It was a small department compared to that of 1865 or by today's standards. By 1865, what a change! Now, a formidable organization transacted the mass of new business. The Comptroller of the Currency reported a total of 1,601 national banks;[25] the Commissioner of Internal Revenue reported that income tax receipts, unknown before Sumter fell, had just reached more than $20,500,000. The Solicitor announced that during the year he had prosecuted suits netting almost two million dollars for the government. The First Auditor more impressively announced that he had handled more than $1,755,000,000 in annual expenditures, a vast sum by the government's prewar standards. In addition, the number of women in the Treasury had increased

21. Sacramento *Daily Union*, letter dated Washington, Jan. 7, 1864.
22. *Ibid.*
23. Van Riper, Paul P., and Keith A. Sutherland, "The Northern Civil Service, 1861-1865," *Civil War History*, Vol. XI, No. 4, Dec. 1965, 354-358. Another writer, Lionel V. Murphy, himself a civil servant, states that the Union civil service, by the time of Appomattox, employed as many as 100,000 civilians. That number were on the Federal payroll. Murphy, Lionel V., "The First Federal Civil Service Commission, 1871-1875," Pt. I, *Public Personnel Review*, III, January, 1942.
24. Van Riper and Sutherland, *op.cit.*, 357.
25. *Annual Report, Comptroller of Currency, 1865*, House Exec. Doc. No. 2, 39th Cong., 1st Sess.

steadily until in 1865 there were 447 in the department.[26] Altogether, the new Treasury machinery was an object-lesson in organization.

One of the best illustrations of effective organization under the stress of war was afforded by John J. Cisco, directing the Sub-Treasury in New York; he had been originally appointed to the Treasury by Pierce, and reappointed by both Buchanan and Lincoln. Too valuable to be spared, he presided over a great marble pile at Wall, Nassau, and Pine Streets, an enlarged copy in exact proportions of one of the Greek temples. Before the war, the Sub-Treasury business was modest; by the beginning of 1863 it was Gargantuan. In April of that year, its payments reached $105,000,000, and the receipts even more. Cisco insisted upon confining his appointments to experts of tested integrity in finance. He demanded also the prompt dispatch of all functions. "The business of the day must always be done on the day. Accounts are balanced every afternoon. Every letter is answered by return mail. Mistakes must not be made. Neither carelessness nor incompetence can be excused. This is the secret of the reputation of the New York Sub-Treasury." It was the boast of Cisco's aides that his organization was so efficient that it carried on larger activities than the Bank of England with a much smaller force.[27]

Other able men took charge of training the new organizers whom the government needed. One veteran in the Civil Service was George Harrington, a Yankee appointed to a clerkship in the Navy Department in the Tyler Administration, who had played an important part in establishing the Interior Department. Then, serving successive Secretaries of the Treasury from John C. Spencer and Robert J. Walker down to Chase, with the title of Chief Clerk, he finally became the principal lieutenant of subsequent heads. While Secretaries attended to policy-making and the larger measures, he controlled organization, and in Lincoln's phrase, "ran the machine." Lincoln appointed Harrington to take Chase's place when the Secretary was temporarily absent in the spring of 1862.[28] Fessenden assured Lincoln that he would hardly have dared assume the responsibilities of the Treasury without Harrington's assurances of support. His papers contain a vivid account of the new weight of detail crushing the government, the pressures to which Harrington was subjected, and the way in which he overcame them:[29]

The file of anxious applicants for attention, collectors of customs, Army and Navy paymasters, Treasury agents, private individuals, and so on, extended day after day far out from the office door into the corridor, often more than a hundred in

26. Massey, Mary Elizabeth, *Bonnet Brigades,* New York, 1966, 132, (ftn. 2) as from *Register of Officers and Agents, Civil, Military, and Naval, in the Service of the United States, 1865,* Washington, 1861-1870, pub. biennially, and chief source of information on employed, salaries, etc.

27. New York *Herald,* Aug. 3, 1863.

28. Lincoln, *Collected Works,* V., 22, 75, 221.

29. Undated and unsigned sheet in Harrington Papers, Missouri Hist. Soc.

number. Each in turn was heard and answered; and it was in this connection that the phenomenal strength and accuracy of his [Harrington's] memory was especially displayed. He stood daily on the floor of his room from nine o'clock until three, listening to these thronging applicants in succession, and determining their several cases—pronouncing decisions, making promises, disposing of claims, granting privileges, distributing money through paymasters and others, perhaps to millions in amount, and throughout the whole he never made a note; yet was never caught in a failure or mistake.

At three o'clock when office hours were over he seated himself at his desk, his several decisions and promises came vividly up to his mind in the precise order in which they had been made, and he was long busy, often into the small hours of the night, in perfecting the business pertaining to them.

Such an organizer of business was priceless. It is not astonishing to learn that Harrington's health broke down as suddenly and completely as Stanton's.

The Interior Department offered a less striking but still remarkable illustration of the incessant and multifarious work of organization. It was a grab-bag department, looking after Indian affairs, patents, pensions, public buildings, census, the General Land Office, and government printing. Before the new Department of Agriculture was set up, its activities also fell to the Patent Office. Other responsibilities included the District of Columbia's Metropolitan Police, the Washington Aqueduct, the asylums for the insane, and the Hospital for the Deaf and Dumb.[30] The Government Printing Office was established just at the start of the war, and from 1861 to 1865, its 343 employes increased to 879.[31] Operations in 1861 had been relatively simple with a small staff. Total employees in the Department of the Interior rose from 1,916 in 1861 to 2,564 in 1865.[32] The Pension Office reported that on June 30, 1861, it had 10,709 pensioners—a squad of old soldiers with a small army of widows—the nucleus of an ever-huger array emerging in 1865. The grant of multitudinous patents for war weapons constituted another heavy load.[33] The passage of the Homestead Act also threw fresh labors upon the Land Office, especially as it stimulated rather than lessened the sales of public lands. Homesteading, which fell under general Land-Office supervision, became the primary channel of land distribution. The College Land-Grant Law meant still more work in organization, for by the middle of 1864 nineteen States had taken advantage of it, receiving land and land-scrip amounting to nearly five million acres.[34]

Another interesting if transient burden of the Interior Department was its

30. *Cong. Globe,* 38th Cong., 2nd Sess., Pt. 2, Appendix, Report of the Secretary of the Interior, 20-24.
31. Fite, Emerson Davis, *Social and Industrial Conditions in the North During the Civil War,* New York, 1963, 98; Van Riper and Sutherland, *op.cit.,* 366.
32. *Ibid.*
33. Bruce, Robert, *Lincoln and the Tools of War,* Indianapolis, 1958, 64-66.
34. *House Exec. Docs.,* No. 1, 38th Cong., 2nd Sess., 4.

responsibility for suppression of the African slave-trade, in which American ships illicitly engaged, hampering humane British efforts to suppress the monstrous international traffic. Lincoln, on May 2, 1861, ordered the Department to take charge, and five vessels were seized that year. One slaver was captured off the African coast with about nine hundred Negroes, who were taken to Liberia; the captain of another was executed in New York; two mates of still another were sent to jail; and the outfitter of a vessel for the slave trade was convicted in Boston. Within little over a year the United States, under contracts made for it with Monrovia, liberated 4,500 Africans in Liberia. By 1862 this particular iniquity was dead, so that by December, 1864, Secretary of the Interior Usher could report that enforcement of Congressional laws for the suppression of the African slave trade had been crowned by the most auspicious results. The Secretary believed that not a single slaver had been fitted out in any American port. Several prizes were still before the mixed courts at Sierra Leone and the Cape of Good Hope.[35]

The new Department of Agriculture, established separately from the Pension Office in 1862, had 29 employes by 1865.[36] No evidence exists that the Agriculture Department was directly inspired by war conditions.

The State Department expanded slowly as the war went on, chiefly in diplomatic and consular personnel abroad; its most prominent invasion of new territory was in the creation of the Commissionership of Immigration in 1864 to administer the new legislation for admitting contract laborers, the first step in American history for the control of immigration. State Department employees increased about ten-fold, rising from about 33 in 1861 to 299 in 1865.[37]

The Post Office Department, always one of the better organized branches of government, had its own special problem. After the secession of the Southern States, nearly 9,000 post offices were dropped, leaving about 20,550 in operation. While mail service to the South was cut off officially early in the war, express companies continued to carry correspondence between the hostile sections until August 26, 1861. Subsequently, mail communication between North and South made use of furtive independent couriers who received high fees for getting messages through the lines. No full and accurate account of this clandestine mail delivery is possible, but we have abundant proof that at times it flourished on the eastern seaboard. An immediate task of the Post Office Department was the organization of military post offices, and as would be expected, numerous complaints arose because of poor service between the home-front and the Army.

35. Report of Sec. of Interior, *Congressional Globe*, 38th Cong., 2nd Sess., Pt. 2, Appendix, 24; Report of the Sec. of Interior, *Senate Executive Documents*, No. 1, 37th Cong., 2nd Sess., 453-454.

36. Gates, Paul W., *Agriculture and the Civil War*, New York, 1965, 307ff.

37. Van Riper and Sutherland, *op.cit.*, 357; Van Deusen, Glyndon G., *William Henry Seward*, New York, 1967, 273.

Nevertheless, examination of soldiers' letters, where envelopes and other evidence exist, often proves remarkably rapid service. Naturally, much depended on where the Army units involved were located, or what they were doing at the moment. Civilian superintendents were in charge of mail transport between armies and the nearest post offices or railway cars, while military units arranged for the appointment of their own officers or enlisted men as postmasters. In an Army corps or division the postmaster, serving in the Quartermaster's department, received and delivered mail for brigades, regiments, or other units. Personnel from these smaller units were detailed on a full or part-time basis to handle the mail and run temporary mail tents. Soldiers could send letters without postage after 1862 when endorsed by officers. The addressee paid the regular rate. Congress turned down proposals for free mail for the army that had been in effect during the Mexican War.[38]

The Post Office, as we have noted, was still having difficulty enforcing the principle of prepaid postage which had been in effect since 1855. Advances in mail service during the war, despite the many problems of the troubled time, seem praiseworthy. The free delivery by carriers in the cities in 1863, the postal money orders of 1864, and the use of railway post offices in 1865 certainly increased both the resort to organization and service given the public. The Post Office operated in debt. From 1861 through June, 1864, the deficit totaled $4,088,957.38; but considering the loss of Southern revenues and the military mail costs, this was regarded tolerantly by Postmaster-General William Dennison in his report of December, 1864.[39] An Act of March 3, 1865, repealed the old law prohibiting since 1802 the employment of Negro mail carriers.[40] The postal service had to deal with such problems as robbery of postmasters and post offices by Southern forces or guerrillas, and the damage or loss of post offices from military action.

In addition to regular postal employees, many others were working under various contracts for mail delivery and pickup. Routes under these contracts totaled 129,173 miles in 1864. Railroads and steamboats supplied more than 29,000 miles of these contract lines, and over 100,000 miles of lines were described by the Postmaster General as marked by "celerity, certainty, and security."[41] It can be safely said that the postal service met the problems of war through organization in an efficient and public-spirited manner.

38. McReynolds, Ross Allan, *History of the United States Post Office, 1607-1931*, Dissertation in Univ. of Chicago Business Library, 1935, 210, 211, 214, 217; Van Riper and Sutherland, *op.cit.;* appraisal of soldier letters made by E.B. Long for Bruce Catton's *Centennial History of the Civil War.*

39. *Congressional Globe*, 38th Cong., 2nd Sess., Pt. 2, Appendix, 15.

40. McReynolds, *op.cit.*, 218.

41. Report of the Postmaster General, Nov. 2, 1864, *Cong. Globe*, 38th Cong., 2nd Sess., Pt. 2, Appendix, 16.

Fortunately for the government, it had a number of men who, like Cisco and Harrington, possessed talent for organization, and whose devotion matched that of the best officers in the field. In the Interior Department the head of the census work, J.C.G. Kennedy, was not only one of the most distinguished statisticians of the nineteenth century, but a skillful coordinator of many talents and energies. While the volumes of the Census of 1860 which he supervised had inevitable defects, they showed how ably he and his staff had gathered an unprecedented mass of details on manufactures, commerce, and agriculture, as well as population.[42] In the State Department another remarkable talent, William Hunter, had begun his long service as Chief Clerk so aptly that Frederick W. Seward called him "the actual head of affairs departmental."[43] He had been in government service since John Quincy Adams found him a place, spoke French and Spanish fluently, and had so completely mastered diplomatic history that he was virtually a walking encyclopedia of decisions and precedents. Every Secretary of State from Seward onward trusted his knowledge, and his comprehension of the best way to organize the foreign service.

Then, too, some men not necessarily career officers added their worth to the organization of the civilian branches of the government. These included Frederick W. Seward, who often stood in for his father in the State Department; Isaac Newton, Commissioner of Agriculture; David P. Holloway in Patents; L.E. Chittenden in the Treasury; and John G. Nicolay and John Hay, who constituted a major element of the "executive department."

While our national government has nearly always held many persons of such quality and ability, their talents became more and more prominently useful under the pressure of the much heavier and more exigent tasks imposed by the wartime years.

[III]

No Navy, of whatever size, could long pretend to operate without at least rudimentary organization. Although in 1860 the nucleus of naval organization existed, it was a relatively small nucleus. Because of the limited communications at sea between ships and home authorities, naval vessels and squadrons had always sought tight, self-sufficient, autonomous organizations. An officer could not yet radio his superiors for instructions in a crisis, and he had to supply, coordinate, and manage his command much on his own responsibility. Smooth systematization of national naval policies was a difficult and nigh-impossible operation. For

42. See also his special report on the Census sent to the Senate in 1862 and published by the U.S. Civil War Centennial Commission in a re-edited edition in 1963.
43. Seward, Frederick W., *Reminiscences of a War-Time Statesman and Diplomat,* New York, 1916, 70, 142, 195.

instance, it is certainly improbable that Washington would have approved Wilkes's seizure of Mason and Slidell from a British mail ship in the late fall of 1861. But Wilkes acted on his own initiative, according to normal procedure. Not until a much later day could naval operations really be directed by an overall command. Organization was thus dependent upon, or limited by, mechanical and technological developments.

Lacking the necessary devices, the Civil War Yankee Navy operated in part under the old methods, but the exigencies of its tasks forced it to new heights of organization. Secretary Gideon Welles and Assistant Secretary Gustavus Vasa Fox; Benjamin F. Isherwood, Chief of the Navy's Bureau of Steam Engineering; Charles H. Davis, both at sea and in bureau posts; Horatio Bridge, Chief of the Bureau of Provisions and Clothing; William Whelan, Chief of the Bureau of Medicine and Surgery; ordnance expert John A. Dahlgren; A.N. Smith, Chief of the Bureau of Equipment and Recruiting; H.A. Wise, Chief of the Bureau of Ordnance; Capt. Percival Drayton, Chief of the Bureau of Navigation —all these, along with a number of others, carried out their duties with great ability.

Like the Army, or to an even greater degree, it had been impossible for the Navy to be in full readiness for the war. Preparations of any kind were politically impossible, at least in any quantity. At the same time, events made it evident that it would have been wise for the Navy Department under Buchanan to have called back some vessels from foreign stations, and that Secretary Welles might even have issued withdrawal orders when he took command on March 4, 1861, although time would not then have permitted such concentration. As of March 4, 1861, the Navy had forty-two active vessels carrying 555 guns and about 7,600 men; in addition, it had forty-eight vessels of varying degree of condition and value, laid up or out of commission, making a total of ninety vessels. The Home Squadron consisted of twelve vessels, and only four small vessels were in northern ports at the beginning of the war.[44]

By December, 1864, the Navy totaled 671 vessels. These included 113 screw steamers especially constructed for naval purposes, 52 paddle-wheel steamers especially constructed, 71 iron-clad vessels, 149 screw steamers purchased or captured and fitted for the Navy, 174 paddle-wheel steamers purchased, captured and fitted, and 112 sailing vessels of all classes.[45] In January of 1865, the blockading squadrons alone numbered 471 vessels with 2,455 guns, though this force was shortly cut down as the need for blockade lessened in the spring of 1865. From the 7,600 men at the start of the war Navy personnel had risen to 51,500. Where 3,844 men had been employed in various naval shipyards and bases, their ranks

44. Report of the Secretary of the Navy, July 4, 1861, *Cong. Globe*, 37th Cong., 1st Sess., App. 7.
45. Report of the Secretary of the Navy, Dec. 5, 1864, *Cong. Globe*, 38th Cong., 2nd Sess., App. 9.

were soon swollen by nearly 17,000 artisans and laborers.[46] The Bureau of Construction and Repair was given appropriations in 1864-65 of more than $46 million, with a diversified load of detail that burdened a hardworking staff. Steam Engineering required about forty millions a year. Yards and Docks had to look after a great variety of repair and construction facilities on all coasts, with temporary stations along the Mississippi. Meanwhile, the Bureau of Equipment and Recruiting, established in the middle of 1862, spent twenty millions during 1864 alone. More work had to be done in these various offices than that carried on in the largest private establishments, and with a tighter, more efficient organization.[47]

Horatio Bridge, Chief of the Bureau of Provisions and Clothing, reported in 1865 that when "the late rebellion was brought so suddenly to its end, the navy was in better condition to continue its efforts with vigor. . . ." than ever before. As for the physical state of naval personnel, he said: "It is a noteworthy fact that during the long, arduous cruises of blockading vessels stationed along a hostile and insalubrious coast, the health of the ships was remarkably good," due, in part, to the admirable hygienic system in the Navy, as well as to the vigilant care of the Bureau of Medicine and Surgery. But doubtless the kinds and quality of the provisions furnished were also significant.[48] Most officers agreed on the high quality of the rations. For instance, considerable improvement had been made in the quality of bread now baked under naval inspection. Supply steamers of the blockading fleet had proved invaluable, making it possible for the fighting ships to remain on station much longer. These supply steamers were roomy, fast vessels with capacious icehouses which would hold 35,000 pounds of fresh beef, and sufficient ice to preserve it for many weeks.[49] They carried in addition 600 to 700 barrels of vegetables and other stores, mail, and passengers, on a regular schedule between the squadrons and Boston, New York, and Philadelphia. A somewhat modified system was used on the rivers of the West.

The Navy Department operated its own supply system. Anthracite coal for delivery at New York to its base and hospital,[50] and to Philadelphia, was purchased through bids advertised in newspapers. After only a few days on station, blockading warships had been forced to leave their posts due to want of coal, but this situation improved as coaling stations were set up at Port Royal and other

46. Report of the Secretary of the Navy, Dec. 4, 1865, *Cong. Globe,* 39th Cong., 1st Sess., Appendix, 20-21.
47. *House Exec. Documents,* 38th Cong., 1st and 2nd Sess., and *House Miscellaneous Documents,* 38th Cong., 2nd Sess.
48. Report of the Bureau of Provisions and Clothing, Navy Dept. Reports, *House Exec. Documents,* Vol. V, 1865, serial 1253, 39th Cong., 1st Sess., 374-375.
49. *Ibid.,* 375.
50. Report of the Chief of the Bueau of Medicine and Surgery, Navy Dept. Reports, *House Exec. Documents,* Vol. V, 1865.

points along the Atlantic and Gulf Coasts.[51] The Navy also established its own medical laboratory.

Chief of the Bureau of Ordnance, H. A. Wise, reported on the full supply of cannon and ordnance available late in the war. Cast-iron, smooth-bore naval guns endured the severe service to which they were subjected, and proved of sterling quality. Not a single gun of the Dahlgren design burst prematurely; only a few of the 15-inch guns, even when fired with their heaviest charges, ever failed. Chief Wise thought that the claims for rifled cannon over smooth-bores "are in many respects visionary, and do not bear the test of actual combat, much less the more elaborate and quietly pursued experiments on the ground; and that whatever of extraordinary power or range may be obtained from them is qualified in a great degree by the danger of premature rupture, under the strain of excessive charges and heavy projectiles necessary to produce such effects, and this whether the rifles are made of cast-iron, wrought-iron, or steel." A great debate had arisen over the comparative merits of rifled cannon and smooth-bore naval guns.[52]

The tremendous increase in paper-work and duties of the Navy Department overburdened the old building in Washington which housed it, and a new floor had to be installed. In July, 1862, when Welles was authorized to reorganize and simplify the Department, only three bureaus remained unchanged—Yards and Docks, Provisions and Clothing, and Medicine and Surgery.[53] The establishment of five new bureaus of Ordnance, Navigation, Equipment and Recruiting, Construction and Repair, and Steam Engineering, caused some difficulties, particularly since some of the officers had been superseded.[54]

Innovation of ironclads and iron-built ships, the new and growing use of ironclad gunboats and amphibious forces in river warfare, the launching and support of the first major blockade in our history, the operation of fighting fleets, vital inter-service cooperation, maintenance of some semblance of world-ranging squadrons during the war, the conversion of merchant vessels to war service, the recruitment of sufficient experienced manpower, and the purchase of immense quantities of miscellaneous goods, were the responsibility of the Navy Department. Welles, in his report of December, 1862, pointed out that the war had found the Navy literally destitute of needed materials in the navy-yards, as well as warships. No other course remained, when the conflict began, but for the Department to build vessels as speedily as possible, and of such timber as could hurriedly be procured, whether up to specifications or not. As a consequence, hulls that

51. Report of the Chief of the Bureau of Equipment and Recruiting, Navy Dept. Reports, *House Exec. Documents*, Vol. V, 1865.
52. Report of the Chief of the Bureau of Medicine and Surgery, Navy Dept. Reports, *House Exec. Documents*, Vol. V, 1865, 176.
53. West, Richard S., *Gideon Welles, Lincoln's Navy Department*, Indianapolis, 1943, 188-189.
54. Welles, Gideon, *Diary of Gideon Welles*, Boston, 1909-1910, I, 74-77.

should have lasted for years with only routine maintenance were soon crowding dockyard space for urgent and expensive repairs.[55]

Naval warfare was gradually being transformed by steampower, iron vessels, improved guns, and new strategical concepts. The responsibility for accomplishing this transformation was much more exigent under the stress of war than it would have been in peacetime, and some blundering occurred as, for example, in the design and construction of the light-draft monitors. Yet mistakes were held to a minimum, considering the magnitude of the job. The Navy Department developed its organization from a small, inert bureau into an aggressive, powerful, and generally efficient agency answering the demands both of war and the current revolution in naval architecture and engineering, and the new doctrines of warfare these imposed.

The brunt of organizational labor, however, inevitably fell upon the War Department which fortunately had one of the most courageous and tireless of administrators in Secretary Edwin M. Stanton. He was quick, in his abrupt, domineering, ill-tempered way, to see what was required. "To bring the War Department up to the standard of the times, and work an army of five hundred thousand with machinery adapted to a peace[time] establishment of twelve thousand," he wrote Charles A. Dana, "is no easy task." Stern devotion to his titanic labors was inescapably the cause of many of the complaints lodged against him. "All I ask is reasonable time and patience. The pressure of much of Congress for clerk and army appointments notwithstanding the most stringent rules, and the persistent strain against all measures essential to obtain time for thought, combination, and conference, is discouraging in the extreme. It often tempts me to quit the helm in despair," he wrote in one of his desponding moods.[56]

Stanton did not quit, however, but carried out a reorganization and vast enlargement of the machinery of the War Department and Army. True, much of this was forced upon him and his aides by the fact of war, but at the same time it represented a triumph of originality and organizational skill which dwarfed all the inevitable mistakes and failures.

Five men served as Assistant Secretary of War at various times and for various terms. Thomas A. Scott and Charles A. Dana made enviable records, while Peter H. Watson, John Tucker and Christopher P. Wolcott were more than competent. Lorenzo Thomas, aided by Edward D. Townsend, filled the office of Adjutant-General capably. As superannuated men were weeded out of the Department, efficient newcomers such as Inspector-General Randolph B. Marcy, Judge-Advocate-General Joseph Holt, Chief Topographical Engineer Stephen H. Long, and

55. Report of the Secretary of the Navy, December 10, 1862, *Cong. Globe*, 37th Cong., 2d Sess., Appendix, 19.
56. Stanton to Asst. Secretary Charles A. Dana, Feb. 1, 1862, Dana Papers, LC.

Signal Officers Albert J. Myer and W. L. Nicodemus took their places. The Bureau of Topographical Engineers was merged into the Corps of Engineers in May, 1863. When Joseph G. Totten, especially proficient as Chief of Engineers, died in office April 29, 1864, he was succeeded by Richard Delafield. Much criticism arose then and later of James W. Ripley's work as Chief of Ordnance, but some of his faults were possibly exaggerated. He was finally succeeded by the more alert and modern-minded George D. Ramsey and Alexander B. Dyer.

The most important new post created during the war was that of Provost-marshal General where James B. Fry, after March 17, 1863, carried the complex duties of handling manpower and the draft with the remarkable skill and success we have previously outlined. The monumental work of Montgomery C. Meigs as Quartermaster-General deserves far more applause than he has received. From September, 1861, to his death in late June, 1864, Joseph P. Taylor was one of the modest but invaluable leaders of the Union effort as Commissary-General of Subsistence. Four men ably held the post of Paymaster-General, Timothy P. Andrews carrying the burden the longest. William A. Hammond and Joseph K. Barnes were the Surgeons-General for most of the war, both writing admirable, although controversial, records.[57]

The concept of General-in-Chief during most of the war was simply that of chief military operations officer, while the bureaus were primarily responsible to the Secretary of War who held almost complete sway. One authority believes that the bureau chiefs, freed of acting under the General-in-Chief, exercised much power. It may be only a slight exaggeration to say, "Because of the paramount authority of the bureau heads under the scrupulous oversight of a head zealous to maintain the grip of the Department upon all its prerogatives, Grant, and Sherman, and Sheridan, in turn, despite all their force, determination, and pres-tige, could not prevail against that organization."[58] While problems of conflicting authority did arise when the officers of a given bureau sometimes tended to overemphasize their duties, bureau organization was in general efficient and productive, at least by the standards of the day. General Emory Upton, the perceptive authority on military policy, feels that the various departments of supply did sound work, building upon foundations already well laid in the War Department.[59]

We cannot too strongly emphasize the signal good fortune of the War Depart-ment in having as Quartermaster-General one of the nation's truly preëminent organizers, Montgomery Cunningham Meigs. In any just view of the Civil War, he should stand as one of the central figures, although he was long almost totally

57. *O.R.* III, Vol. I, 964; II, 957; III, 1199; IV, 1035; V, 581.

58. Pound, Roscoe, "Bureaus and Bureau Methods in the Civil War Era," *Proceedings of the Massa-chusetts Historical Society*, Vol. LXVII, Oct. 1941-May 1944.

59. Upton, Emory, *The Military Policy of the United States*, Washington, 1912, 262.

ignored because few men had any clear understanding of the crushing load of pressures on his time and strength. Meigs has belatedly come into his own, partly through an excellent biography by Russell F. Weigley.[60] This tardily repairs the oversight of such earlier historians as John Bach McMaster and Edward Channing who in treating the war, except for Sumter, did not mention Meigs. Almost incredibly, F.A. Shannon in his *Organization and Administration of the Union Army* mentioned him only once. Carl Russell Fish gave him one line, misstating his initials, and James Ford Rhodes dismissed him with but cursory mention.

To say that Meigs, with the Commissary-General and the Chief of Ordnance, shouldered nearly the entire work of equipping the Union armies for camp, march, and battle, is to do little to define his responsibilities. Of these three men, Meigs played by far the chief rôle. The duties of the other two were simple compared with his tasks in procuring uniforms, shoes, tents, horses and mules, harness, forage, wagons, ambulances, blankets, hammocks, canteens, knapsacks, and a vast miscellany of other equipment. His procurement responsibilities involved at least half the field of Northern industry.

Meigs, in his 1865 report, gave his own clear definition of his work: "This department is charged with the duty of providing means of transportation by land and water for all the troops and for all the material of war. It furnishes the horses for artillery and cavalry, and the horses and mules of the wagon-trains; provides and supplies tents, camp and garrison equipage, forage, lumber, and all materials for camps and shelter of the troops. It builds barracks, hospitals, and storehouses; provides wagons and ambulances, harness, except for cavalry and artillery horses; builds or charters ships and steamers, docks and wharves; constructs and repairs roads, railroads, and their bridges; clothes the Army, and is charged generally with the payment of all expenses attending military operations not assigned by law or regulation to some other department. While the Ordnance Department procures, and issues arms and ammunition, and the Subsistence Department supplies provisions, and the Medical Department medical and hospital stores, the Quartermaster's Department is called upon to transport the stores of all these departments from the depots to the camps, upon the march, and to the battlefield, where they are finally issued to the troops. . . ."[61]

Meigs's biographer shows that the arrival of Stanton was a turning-point towards greater efficiency, but too many difficulties were rooted in the command-system and in the Quartermaster-General's Office to be completely overridden; especially certain hoary and deep-rooted traditions. The independence of the bureaus also caused problems. The work of the Quartermaster-General could not

60. Weigley, Russell F., *Quartermaster-General of the Union Army, a Biography of M.C. Meigs,* New York, 1959.
   61. *O.R.,* III, Vol. V, 213, Meigs's report of Nov. 8, 1865.

always be properly coordinated with other parts of the entire service. His biographer declares that, "If heavy responsibility rested upon the shoulders of General Meigs, his power as quartermaster-general was not always commensurate with his responsibility. The office of the Civil War quartermaster-general was not the office of a master planner, taking within his purview the logistical needs of all the armies, securing materials to meet those needs, and distributing them to the fields of battle. Such powers were not entirely lacking in Meigs's position, but by and large the procedures of the Quartermaster's Department were so decentralized that Meigs's tasks were largely advisory and supervisory, sometimes even clerical . . ."[62] The quartermasters at the major depots and departmental headquarters made contracts and obtained supplies. Then the materiel moved down the chain of command to regimental quartermasters. But it was Meigs who was comprehensively responsible.

To equip one regiment alone with uniforms in 1861 cost $20,000; to equip 500 regiments cost $10,000,000—and the uniforms lasted but a few months. In shaping government contract policy, Meigs found himself molding much of the future economy of the United States. What share of the contracts should go to small manufacturers? A memorable page in the history of the war relates how Meigs rose to the initial crisis of supply for the hundreds of thousands who rushed to the colors in 1861. He wrote Brig. Gen. Francis Laurens Vinton after First Bull Run with agonized eloquence: "The nation is in extremity. Troops, thousands, wait for clothes to take the field. Regiments have been ordered here [Washington] without clothes. Men go on guard in drawers for want of pantaloons. The necessity is far greater than I imagined when I saw you. I had no idea of this destitution, this want of preparation by this Department when I took charge of it. It has been forced upon me by gradual proof. . . . We must bear the clamor of fools who would pick flaws in a pin while the country hangs in the balance."[63]

It was Meigs and his staff who did most to set new standards for American shoe manufacture; to insist that the Army abandon for field use the large Sibley and Adams tents, which had to be transported by wagon, and employ the French shelter tent, portable on a soldier's back. It was he who adapted French mess equipment for American use. Meigs bought all horses and mules, purchasing the cavalry mounts even after the Army had a cavalry bureau. Purchases of cavalry horses from Jan. 1, 1864 to May 9, 1865 numbered 198,388; artillery horses bought Sept. 1, 1864, to June 30, 1865 were 20,714; and mules, from July 1, 1864 to June 30, 1865, numbered 58,818.[64]

When Stanton conceived the idea in August, 1863, that Western infantry might be mounted on large-sized mules, Meigs set him right. It fell to Meigs to

62. Weigley, op.cit., 215-219.
63. Meigs Papers, LC, July 24, 1861.
64. O.R., III, Vol. V, 220.

read McClellan and other generals constant lectures on the cruel and wasteful destruction of horses (averaging $120 in unit cost) by undisciplined troops. He asked Rosecrans in the spring of 1863 to compel his cavalry officers to see that horses were given proper opportunities to graze, to rest during noonday heat, and to eat corn, and were not pushed to exhaustion on the march. "We have over 126 regiments of cavalry," he declared, "and they have killed ten times as many horses for us as for the rebels."[65]

Meigs tried to drive home, as Sherman did, the fact that Northern armies were for several years over-wagoned. Twelve or thirteen wagons should suffice for a single regiment, he believed, and five hundred wagons for a full army of 40,000 on a campaign. Yet some commanders, dragging useless impedimenta, used three times as many. After all the losses of the Peninsular campaign, McClellan's Army of the Potomac, as Meigs disgustedly observed, had 2,578 wagons at Harrison's Landing in mid-August, 1862, or twenty-six for each thousand men— this for an Army with water-communication.[66] Meigs did more than buy ambulances; he put them into action. It was he, not the Surgeon-General, who, after Lee and Pope had covered the field of Second Manassas with dead and dying, fitted out a train of 280 new ambulances in such haste that time was not given to fill the water-kegs. It was Meigs and his organization who built temporary barracks, and purchased coal for Army steamers. Indeed, they performed a multitude of essential functions of the war. They took control of Grant's supply bases at Fredericksburg and Belle Plain in 1864. Meigs assumed personal charge of refitting and resupplying Sherman's army at Savannah in January, 1864.

"The army will start with fifteen days' supplies," Grant wrote Halleck as he began the campaign of 1864. A half-month's supplies for 75,000 or 80,000 men meant a veritable mountain of flour, meat, coffee, salt, sugar, and other comestibles; another mountain of blankets, shoes, clothing, tents, and miscellaneous supplies; and a third mountain of forage, meal, and grain for horses, cattle, and mules. "All the country affords will be gathered as we go along," Grant added. "This will no doubt enable us to go twenty-five or thirty days without further supplies, unless we should be forced to keep in the country between the Rapidan and Chickahominy, in which case supplies might be required by way of the York or the Rappahannock Rivers." He *was* confined to the area between the Rapidan and Chickahominy until he broke away to the James after Cold Harbor. "To provide for this contingency I would like to have about one million rations and two hundred thousand forage rations afloat to be sent whenever it may prove they

65. *O.R.*, I,xxiii, Pt.2, 300-304, Meigs to Rosecrans, May 1, 1863.
66. *O.R.*, III, ii, 797-799.

Monitor Class Warships.

Above, the gun turret of the original *Monitor* after the fight with the *Merrimac; below,* the double-turreted monitor *U.S.S. Kickapoo,* built at St. Louis in 1864 and active with the Mississippi and West Gulf blockading squadrons

will be required."[67] Until the very end of the war, Meigs continued laboring to improve his many-sided organization.

The Quartermaster-General's importance may be measured by the fact that for the year ending June 30, 1865, departmental expenditures totaled $431,706,-057.44.[68] During this same period the department purchased 3,463,858 uniform trousers, 3,708,393 drawers, and 3,268,166 flannel shirts.[69] One little-known aspect of its work was the construction of the river fleet, before such work was transferred to the Navy. Meigs reported that, as of November 17, 1862, his department had managed the assembly "by construction, purchase, or capture, of a fleet of forty-five vessels . . . of a flotilla of thirty-eight mortar boats, or rafts . . . and one wharf boat of 4,000 tons burden," this fleet including ten ironclads. It was Meigs who signed the contract with James B. Eads for the famous river ironclads.[70] It was he who recognized the larger food problem presented by the needs of horses than of men when he declared "A horse requires nearly 26 pounds per day of food and a man but three pounds."[71] Thousands of horses thus were used to transport their own food. It was Meigs who had to arrange for constructing hospitals, housing in 1862 sometimes as many as 100,000 ill and wounded.[72] He, it was, who had to search far and wide for the very cloth to make uniforms and blankets, especially at the start of the war—even importing goods from other countries to be turned over to the manufacturers, or, in some cases, having his own departmental establishments actually make the clothing.[73]

Meigs was not alone, by any means, in learning the specialized functions of purchasing and disbursement, coordinating a multitude of diverse activities. A former engineer officer himself, with no prior training in the duties of a quartermaster, he drew his staff by necessity from various walks of life, both civilian and military. To these subordinates he delegated immense responsibilities despite their junior rank. One captain in the Quartermaster's Department would disburse many millions of dollars a year, and often had on his rolls thousands of persons. Characteristically, Meigs was most generous in praising the work of associates. "Upon the faithful and able performance of the duties of the quartermaster an army depends for its ability to move. The least neglect or want of capacity on his part may foil the best conceived measures and make the best planned campaign impracticable," Meigs stated.[74]

67. Grant to Halleck, Apr. 29, 1864, from Culpeper Court House, Va., Grant-Halleck Papers, Ill. State Hist. Lib.
68. *O.R.*, III, Vol. V, 212.
69. *Ibid.*, 220.
70. *Ibid.*, Vol. II, 792-793, 816-817.
71. *Ibid.*, 797.
72. *Ibid.*, 802.
73. *Ibid.*, 802-803.
74. *Ibid.*, 805.

In his report of November, 1864, Meigs stated that not less than 220,000 separate regular accounts were due at his office in the course of the year. But he also stated, "All difficulties in providing a sufficient supply of clothing and material for our increasing Army have disappeared. The manufacturing power of the country has so expanded as to fully meet the demands. . . . and it may be said generally that while prices have advanced they have not advanced in proportion to the appreciation of the metallic currency. . . ."[75] The main supply depots of New York, Philadelphia, Cincinnati, and St. Louis, along with the branch depots, handled things well. There were hardly any complaints of defective material or workmanship, and but few cases of infidelity or fraud by inspectors.

By November, 1864, the Quartermaster's Department was operating a huge fleet of transports, including 39 ocean-steamers, and many scores of river and bay steamers, steam tug-boats, barks, brigs, and other vessels, and chartering as well 74 additional ocean-steamers, 164 river and bay steamers, and several hundred other ships.[76]

When cotton became scarce, the Department had to turn to wool, causing domestic consumption during the war to run as high as 200-million pounds, compared with 86-million pounds in 1859, much of it for the services.[77]

Meigs was especially proud of the Department's work in the Atlanta Campaign. He reported for the year ending June 30, 1865, that, as in former years of the war under the energetic and liberal administration of the War Department, the wants of the troops had been regularly supplied, and their comfort, health, and efficiency amply and regularly safeguarded. "In no other country have railroads been brought to perform so important a part in the operations of war. Scarce in any other country could be found the workmen to perform the feats of construction which have illustrated this campaign. At no time during the march from Chattanooga to Atlanta were the railroad trains five days behind the general commanding. The reconstruction of the bridges over the Etowah and the Chattahoochee are unparalleled feats of military construction. . . ." Meigs and his department made successful efforts to augment supplies for Sherman's army when it reached the sea from Atlanta. He concluded, "During the whole year—I believe I may say during the whole war—no movement was delayed, no enterprise failed, for want of means of transportation or the supplies required from the Quartermaster's Department . . ."[78]

Winfield Scott had been instrumental in placing Meigs in the Quartermaster's post over objections by Secretary Cameron, Meigs having to gain the support of long-term officers of the Department, and to resist Cameron's use of patronage

75. *O.R.* III, Vol. IV, 877, 884.
76. *Ibid.,* 890.
77. Cole, Arthur Harrison, *The American Wool Manufactures,* Cambridge, Mass., 1926, I, 337.
78. *O.R.* III, Vol. V, 213, 216.

Montgomery C. Meigs, Quartermaster-General of the Union Army

and political friends as purchasing agents. Finding much difficulty in hiring enough men for clerical work, he employed women in increasing numbers. Fraud was held to a minimum through legislation requiring stronger penalties, and well-centralized controls were established. Meigs himself often went to the field to supervise activities personally.[79] He was one of the architects of both victory and the transformed nation which emerged. He not only superintended the expenditure of one-and-a-half billion dollars, or almost half the direct cost of the war, but supervised it in such a way as to turn the nascent industrial revolution into some of the channels it was to follow during the rest of the century.[80]

It would be a sad error, however, to suppose that Meigs stood alone in the War Department as an exemplar of systematic, judicious organization, though it must be said he and his Department were the leaders as far as supply bureaus were concerned. The Commissary, headed by the Commissary-General of Subsistence, encountered especially grave problems because of antiquated methods, and yet succeeded in doing its work creditably. For forty-three years Colonel George Gibson had been in the Commissary Department, and on his death in September, 1861, Joseph Pannell Taylor, brother of General and President Zachary Taylor, took charge. Taylor, born in 1796, was admittedly somewhat elderly for his taxing post, and was sometimes stuffy and conservative. On the other hand, some innovations were undertaken by Taylor, and he must be credited with conscientious efforts to create a department many times larger than any previous commissary in the nation's history. Upon his death in late June, 1864, Brig. Gen. Amos B. Eaton took over the cumbersome duties of Commissary-General of Subsistence.

As State authorities began to gather troops in 1861, problems of provisioning the new regiments became paramount. Local officials had no experience in mass-feeding, nor did the local restaurateurs who were called in to assist. Upon leaving State recruiting centers for further training or the battlefront, the men were expected to prepare and cook their own food. The novelty of the rations, the utter lack of training in cookery, and the general newness of military life resulted in a rather hit-or-miss system for feeding the men. The Commissary or Subsistence Department did not train Army cooks, or even have much success with the one cook-book prepared for Army use. On the State level, fraud and favoritism in food purchase and distribution were very common, and for the Army out in the field, local depots retained too much independence, a fact which inevitably led to speculation. Furthermore, hundreds of tons of rations had to be contracted for at major depots in leading cities in the West and elsewhere,

79. For a thorough survey of the actual work of the Quartermaster Department, see Risch, Erna, *Quartermaster Support of the Army, a History of the Corps, 1775-1939,* Washington, 1962, 333ff.
80. Risch, *op.cit., passim.*

since they could not all be purchased or controlled by Washington.

The Army had on paper the largest and best-prescribed rations in the world, but no one would deny the wide gap between regulations and actual practise.[81] Every effort was made to advertise in newspapers of New York and other cities for bids to furnish produce and meat. Sometimes, early in the war for example at Washington, there was not always time to call for bids, so that contracts had to be made as promptly and advantageously as possible. In November, 1861, Taylor's report did not reflect the commissary situation in the West, or anywhere except in Washington where conditions respecting supply seemed to be improving.[82] Conflicts, however, had occurred between the department and General Frémont, and troops in Western Virginia had temporarily been short of subsistence. Confusion arose regarding the duties of the depots when vexatious transport problems had to be met. Taylor stated: "Some confusion has prevailed in the operations of the department from the total ignorance of their duties by many of the brigade commissaries appointed from civil life, and many irregularities in their accounts have and will continue to occur until experience has given them knowledge. Great irregularity in this department also occurred in the raising of volunteers, but less than should have been expected when the sudden uplifting of such a force in so short a time is considered. The few regular officers of the corps have had a very responsible and laborious course of duties imposed upon them, and have performed these duties in a very satisfactory manner . . ."[83] Beef for the field Army was bought on the hoof, the cattle being butchered and dressed when needed. Soldiers often complained of the stringy toughness of the meat, but any Army contains some inveterate grumblers. The department had also to furnish subsistence for political prisoners, prisoners-of-war, many contrabands, and "suffering Union inhabitants found in the march of the armies in the South . . ."[84] By the fall of 1863, marked improvement was reported in the accounts kept by volunteer officers.[85]

The new department head, John Eaton, in the fall of 1864, roughly sketched his operations. Supplies of subsistence stores for the Army had been procured chiefly in the markets of Boston, New York, Philadelphia, Washington, Chicago and other cities, he wrote, and were forwarded to the main Army depots in the field, whence they were distributed to more advanced depots, according to the wants and positions of the troops. For local issues, a limited amount of sub-

81. For capable secondary surveys of the Army food situation, see: Wiley, Bell, *The Life of Billy Yank*, Indianapolis, 1951, 1952, Ch. IX, 224-246; Boeger, Palmer H., "Hardtack and Burned Beans," *Civil War History*, Vol. IV, No. 1, March, 1958, 73-92.
82. *O.R.*, III, Vol. I, 676-678.
83. *Ibid.*
84. *Ibid.*, Vol. II, 738-739.
85. *Ibid.*, Vol. III, 944.

sistence had to be bought at many other points as circumstances dictated, where rising prices were often troublesome to purchasing officers.[86]

In his final report, Eaton echoed Meigs in declaring that during the entire war no campaign or expedition had failed because of the inability of the Subsistence Department to meet proper requirements.[87] Transportation of supplies was efficiently managed by the Quartermaster's Department, which, during 1863, shipped from the port of New York alone an average of 7,000 packages of subsistence daily,[88] and during the war spent a total of $361,796,991.83.[89]

Inevitably, some instances of food shortages appeared, as in 1862 in the West, and in Buell's armies in the Kentucky Campaign. But these shortages on the Union side were few, usually the fault of enemy action.[90] Commissary subsistence officers felt their responsibility keenly, as it was upon their work in good measure that the comfort and fighting capacity of the men depended.[91]

Some new and memorable features marked the organization of communications. The military telegraph and its managers, Anson Stager and Thomas T. Eckert, made enduring reputations. Stanton reported in 1863 that they had established a system of inestimable value, giving the 1500 telegraph operators unmatchable *esprit-de-corps*. During the year, 300 miles of lines had been constructed under Eckert's direction in the Department of the Potomac, and great lengths in other areas—another 300 miles in the Department of the Gulf alone. On July 1, 1862, the Union had 3,571 miles of military land and submarine telegraph lines, while during the fiscal year additions brought the total to 5,326 miles. Messages were sent and received at the rate of about 6,000 daily.[92]

Probably no more potent agency of communication and organization existed than the telegraph, which had opened up a sphere of rapid communications quite new to Americans. Vital military applications were in many instances logical extensions of services already familiar in civilian life. Sherman pointed out in his *Memoirs* that, "For the rapid transmission of orders in any army covering a large space of ground, the magnetic telegraph is by far the best, though habitually the paper and pencil, with good mounted orderlies, answer every purpose. I have little faith in the signal-service by flags and torches . . . but the value of the magnetic telegraph in war cannot be exaggerated, as was illustrated by the perfect concert of action between the armies in Virginia and Georgia during 1864. Hardly a day intervened when General Grant did not know the exact state of

86. *Ibid.*, Vol. IV, 782-784.
87. *Ibid.*, Vol. V, 145-148.
88. *Ibid.*
89. *Ibid.*, 1039.
90. For survey of problems and shortages, see Wiley, *Life of Billy Yank, op.cit.*, 225-231.
91. "Feeding a Great Army," author unknown, *The United Service*, Vol. II, No. 2, Feb. 1880, 148-159.
92. *O.R.* III, Vol. III, 1137; Bates, David Homer, *Lincoln in the Telegraph Office*, New York, 1907,
II.

facts with me, more than fifteen hundred miles away as the wires ran. . . ." This, of course, was before Sherman left Atlanta for the sea. He went on to write that, "on the field a thin insulated wire may be run on improvised stakes or from tree to tree for six or more miles in a couple of hours, and I have seen operators so skillful that by cutting the wire they would receive a message from a distant station. As a matter of course, ordinary commercial wires along the railways form the usual telegraph lines for an army, and are easily repaired and extended as the army advances, but each army and wing should have a small party of skilled men to put up the field-wire, and take it down when done . . . Our commercial telegraph-lines will always supply for war enough skillful operators. . . ."[93]

At the beginning of the war, a number of independent telegraph companies were busy and wires and offices were spreading rapidly. Work was well under way toward a transcontinental line completed in the fall of 1861. However, three major companies dominated the field: the American Telegraph Company, Western Union Telegraph Company, and Southwestern Telegraph Company. The American Telegraph served generally the region along the Atlantic and the Gulf from New England to New Orleans. The Southwestern met the American at Chattanooga, Mobile and New Orleans, running as far north as Louisville, and covering the lower Mississippi Valley and Southwest. Western Union primarily served the Midwest, and was building a line to San Francisco.[94]

For seven months, no organized U.S. Military Telegraph acted under a single head, railroad executives and telegraph companies handling the wires. Tom Scott and Andrew Carnegie displayed marked enterprise in the early weeks of war to assure Washington of telegraph communication, making possible close contact between Federal bureaus and buildings of the Army and Navy in the District of Columbia, the telegraph becoming almost a telephone. With E.S. Sanford, President of the American Telegraph Company, giving vigorous oversight, Washington and the army posts in Virginia were completely connected by May. But in the first Bull Run Campaign, no direct telegraph connected General Patterson in the Shenandoah area with General Scott at Washington. Reaching only to Fairfax Court House, the telegraph did, however, help keep Washington informed of the progress of the battle of Bull Run on July 21, 1861.

Eight telegraph operators were lost in battle during the war; many others died during Army service, or were captured.[95] The military telegraph service grew slowly, with Davis Strouse the first superintendent. On November 11, 1861, Anson Stager, then general superintendent of the Western Union Telegraph Company

93. Sherman, William T., *Memoirs of General William T. Sherman,* New York, 1875, II, 398.
94. Plum, William R., *The Military Telegraph During the Civil War in the United States,* Chicago, 1882, II, 349.
95. *Ibid.,* II, 353.

(a post he had held since 1856), was appointed chief of the United States military telegraphs in Washington.[96]

Since no early appropriations were granted for the telegraph, Sanford and the American Telegraph Company temporarily paid the bills. Not until early spring of 1862 was the U.S. Military Telegraph in full operation, deciphering enemy letters and codes, handling messages upon supplies and troops, and maintaining battlefield and headquarters communications. Many posts, bridgeguards, and other small units had to be effectively tied together. Then, too, numerous high-level conferences were conducted by telegraph, generals in Washington holding long conversations by clicking instruments with commanders in the West. The telegraph tent on any field became a rendezvous for men hungry to obtain the latest military and civilian news.[97] Reports of engagements and all other military events moved by wire from the field to press offices; while in countless communities scattered across the North, people gathered at the local telegraph office for the latest word on elections, battles, and casualties, particularly at the height of such great struggles as Gettysburg and Vicksburg.

In addition to supporting the military telegraphs, the regular domestic lines carried a greatly increased civil burden throughout the war. Thousands of government messages upon troops, supplies, and other business, were sent from Washington to every State. Businessmen used the telegraph much more than before, and profits of the companies rose rapidly despite losses in Southern business or from wartime destruction. The Western Union, beginning with a powerful base, expanded its lines and business until by the end of the war it was gaining a dominant rôle.[98]

The telegraph managers and operators produced a new type of adventurous hero. A mystery still hung about the electric speed of telegraphy which invested it with the peculiar aura that later hung about aviation. Telegraph executives controlled an agency which, under the stress of war, was powerful both for good or ill. Scrupulous pains had to be taken in choosing operators. Since intelligence, quick perception, and integrity were essential, employees were required to take a special oath. Many young operators went on to conspicuous careers in the continuous postwar growth of the telegraph.[99] All in all, the telegraph represented a triumph of American invention, business enterprise, and system, which

96. Bates, David Homer, *op.cit.*, 25-26. Bates and Plum, both actual operators in military service, left the best record with Bates's work being more personal and Plum's of greater historical value. Many experiences of operators do not permit a detailed record. See O'Brien, Emmett, "Telegraphing in Battle," *Century*, Vol. XXXVIII, No. 5, Sept. 1889, 782ff.

97. Paris, Comte de, *History of the Civil War in America*, Philadelphia, 1876, I, 279-280.

98. For a useful summary of civilian telegraph progress, see Thompson, Robert Luther, *Wiring a Continent: The History of the Telegraph Industry in the United States, 1832-1866*, Princeton, 1947, 372-380.

99. "Relief of Telegraph Operators who Served in the War of the Rebellion," *Senate Doc. No. 251*, 58th Cong., 2nd Sess., 1903-1904, 1-2.

more than any other mechanical device helped to knit the nation closely together.

From the first shot fired at Sumter, railroads, too, became an instrument of warfare, although it took time to organize them for such a wholly unprecedented adventure. Railroads had been little used in previous conflicts, although a short, specially built, military railway was constructed by the Allies in the Crimea. Thus, the Civil War offered the first great opportunity to rails and locomotives.

At first, quite naturally, most rail operations connected with the war were performed by existing lines, for some of them were already partially equipped to handle the movement of supplies and troops. Military railroads as such were not clearly necessary until Federal armies advanced into the Confederacy; then they became absolutely essential. For months, Assistant Secretary of War Tom Scott served to coordinate the War Department and the railroads. As a former railroad executive, Scott was in a position to enlist the aid of various lines, which was not a difficult task, and the opportunity to make profits was obvious.

On February 11, 1862, D. C. McCallum was appointed Military Director and Superintendent of the Railroads in the United States. He had authority to take possession of and use all railroads and equipment required for the war.[100] Born in 1815 in Scotland and reared in New York, McCallum was primarily an architect, engineer, and inventor, especially in connection with building railroads and bridges. Upon taking over his new post, he found that only one railroad was in government possession, a seven-mile line from Washington to Alexandria. Though McCallum was subordinate to Meigs and the Quartermaster's Department, he regarded himself as independent. His work lay chiefly in the eastern theater, with John B. Anderson in general charge of western railroads. Later, Anderson was removed and McCallum given full authority in February, 1864.[101] McCallum acted primarily as a liaison officer between the government and the private railroads, while at the same time he supervised the military railroads. Before the war ended, nearly 25,000 men were employed on these military railroads, 17,000 of them in the West.[102]

McCallum's most brilliant success was achieved in 1864 when the U.S. military railroads did so much to supply Sherman at Atlanta from Nashville and Chattanooga. He modestly described his rôle as arranging "the military railroad organization upon a basis sufficiently comprehensive to permit the extension of the system indefinitely to perfect the modus operandi for working the various lines; to determine as to the number of men to be employed in the several departments, and the compensation to be paid therefor; the amount and kind of machinery to be purchased, and the direction as to the distribution of the

100. *O.R.*, III, Vol. V, 974.

101. Weber, Thomas, *The Northern Railroads in the Civil War, 1861-1865*, New York, 1952, 136.

102. *O.R.*, III, Vol. V, 1003, gives McCallum's report of May 26, 1866, which is an excellent summation of the work of the Military Railroads.

same. . . ." He continued: "With few exceptions, the operations of military railroads have been conducted under orders issued by the Secretary of War or by army commanders in and out of the field. . . ."[103] Truly magnificent contributions were made by cantankerous Herman Haupt, the West Point graduate who had been superintendent of transportation on the Pennsylvania Railroad, and who in the spring of 1862 had become chief of construction and transportation for United States military railroads, his brief career with the Army of the Potomac being a model of military railroad engineering practice.

Government dealings with the railroads became a large and intricate business, for much of which few precedents existed. McCallum and Meigs labored in close collaboration, for Meigs had to organize the transportation of troops and war materials; and together they conducted interstate railway operations on a scale undreamed of before the war. Early in 1862, the persons and freight carried were divided into four classes, rates were fixed for each class, and the government tried to share traffic fairly among the lines. It tried also to hold the railroads to an agreement between themselves and the government, made in February, 1862, to discourage rate-wars, and to lessen the inclination toward pooling arrangements. The basic rate for troop transportation was two cents a mile per soldier, with a baggage allowance of eighty pounds. Meigs directed his subordinates to divide the shipment of goods "in such manner as to give each road carrying freight to the same destination a share of the Government patronage."[104] He insisted upon certain rules. The usual company officers were normally to direct all operations; traffic arrangements should be general, avoiding special rates; and Army commanders should not interfere with him, but leave control of business arrangements in the hands of the Quartermaster's Department.

Some idea of the magnitude of transportation needs is given by the fact that in the year ending June 30, 1865, nearly 410,000 horses and 125,000 mules had to be carried by various private and government lines. Railroads, not owned or operated by government, transported more than five million tons of stores, including subsistence, quartermaster, ordnance, medical and miscellaneous. Government railroads, boats, and barges, took huge amounts. Thus, the total body of stores forwarded by railroads, steamships and other carriers, totaled for the fiscal year 1865 nearly nine-and-a-half million tons of freight.[105]

Sherman again comments in his *Memoirs:* "The value of railways is also fully recognized in war quite as much as, if not more so than, in peace. The Atlanta campaign would simply have been quite impossible without the use of the railroads from Louisville to Nashville, from Nashville to Chattanooga, and from

103. *Ibid.*, 999-1000.
104. D.D. Tompkins, Mar. 6, 1862. Quartermaster-General, Letterbook No. 99, Nat'l. Archives, 248.
105. Parsons, Lewis B., *Reports to the War Department,* 1867, 55.

Chattanooga to Atlanta."[106] That single strand of railroad 473 miles in length, subject to constant interruptions, supplied an army of a hundred thousand men and 35,000 animals for well over a year.[107]

One authority asserts that Northern railroads proved able to handle their new loads partly because they had been overdeveloped in the previous decade, and at the opening of the war were not operating to full capacity.[108] The railroads, at any rate, did their duty. In only a few emergencies was the power of seizure exercised. Cooperation between the roads and the War Department was on a high level. The railroads not only profited monetarily, but learned a great deal about efficient methods. They made better use of rolling-stock; for example, by utilizing box cars on a round-trip basis rather than returning them empty.

It can be said that to some extent the railroads approached their maturity during the war. Some advances had certainly been made earlier, but the exigencies of the conflict stimulated these reforms, and compelled the use of organization and cooperation far more promptly than normal peacetime demands would have effected.

The management of river transportation was another great school of organization. Here, too, the existing equipment and staff were altered, enlarged and applied to war needs. Fortunately a master planner, Lewis B. Parsons, was in charge of military river and rail transportation in the West until August, 1864, when he was given control of all these facilities for the Northern armies. His only previous experience in transportation had been gained by a brief stint of service with the Ohio & Mississippi Railroad.[109]

Yet during the war, Parsons directed the greatest fresh-water flotilla the world had ever seen. He correctly wrote in his final report, "Not only has the world never before seen such vast armies so suddenly created, but it never has witnessed such *rapidity* in the movement of those armies for long distances, with their vast supplies. It is now practicable, on twenty-four hours' notice, to embark at Boston or Baltimore a larger army than those with which Napoleon won some of his most decisive victories, and landing it within three days at Cairo, twelve hundred miles distant, there embark it on transports, and, within four days' more time, disembark it at New Orleans, a thousand miles farther . . ."[110]

He justly added that "no portion of the community has been more ready to respond to the wants of the Government, more willing to make sacrifices, or has labored with a greater earnestness and efficiency in the suppression of the rebel-

106. Sherman, *Memoirs*, II, 298-399.
107. *Ibid.*
108. Murphey, Hermon King, "The Northern Railroads and the Civil War," *Mississippi Valley Historical Review*, Vol. V, Dec., 1918.
109. *In Memoriam General Lewis Baldwin Parsons*, privately published, 1909, 35.
110. Parsons, *op.cit.*, 5.

lion, than have our railroad proprietors and managers. . . ."[111] He specially noted the speedy movements of such large units as the Ninth Corps of Burnside from central Kentucky to Vicksburg; the transfer of the Twelfth and Thirteenth Corps under Hooker from Washington to Chattanooga; the transfer of the Twenty-third Corps from Tennessee to Washington; and the disbanding of the armies in 1865.

Parsons managed river transport at first entirely by chartering boats, which involved careful contracts and well-organized arrangements. When chartering proved extravagant, specific contracts were made by the hundred-weight or the piece, which proved better.[112] As the war went on, the use of water carriage to transport men for longer distances increased, much of it in enemy or former enemy territory. Parsons estimated that the entire network involved twenty-thousand miles of river navigation. "When we consider its great extent," he wrote, "the many dangers incident thereto, and the frequent occurrence of accidents from collisions, fires, and other causes in time of peace, often resulting in great loss of life . . . ," and the fact that boats "have been frequently ordered into service, in great emergencies, by officers ignorant of their safety or fitness . . . , and have often been greatly overloaded;" furthermore, when we recollect "that thousands of miles of this navigation have been along rivers whose banks, except at a few fortified points, have been in possession of the enemy [and] where batteries or guerrilla bands were almost daily brought into action for the destruction of transport. . . . I think it will not only appear extraordinary that so few accidents and losses have occurred, but remarkable that navigation, under such circumstances, could be at all maintained . . ."[113]

When Sherman launched his movement in the Vicksburg campaign, seventy to eighty steamboats were assembled within a week at Memphis and lifted his 40,000 men, with horses and artillery, down to the Vicksburg area, nearly 450 miles below, in eight days. Western commanders, who had learned to distrust railroads because guerrillas cut them so easily, felt a special faith in steamboats, which usually got through in spite of hostile volleys from the banks.[114]

Transport, manpower, and management do not suffice to fight a war. Armies and navies must have their needed weapons. From January 1, 1861 to June 30, 1865, the Ordnance Department of the Army provided huge quantities of cannon, artillery carriages, small arms, complete sets of accoutrements for infantry and cavalry, harness, ammunition and projectiles.[115] In addition, immense quantities

111. *Ibid.*, 20.
112. *Ibid.*, 6.
113. *Ibid.*, 19.
114. Murphey, *op.cit.*, 327; Parsons, *Reports, passim;* Hunter, Louis C., *Steamboats on the Western Rivers,* Cambridge, 1949, 554. Parson's Papers in the Illinois State Historical Library are a mine of valuable information, and prove him one of the redoubtable administrators of the war.
115. *O.R.*, III, Vol. V, 1042-1043, Stanton's report of Nov. 14, 1865.

of parts were supplied by States and private sources. To have furnished these varied implements of warfare in such quantity a half-century before the advent of systematic traffic-management, demanded a precision of planning and organization without parallel or precedent.

Geared to supplying armament for the tiny pre-war Army and its various, often inactive forts, along with a supposed reserve for emergencies and State militias, the Ordnance Department had been unprepared to fight any large war. Procurement and stockpiling of modern weapons would not have been tolerated. When secession came and a great quantity of military supplies fell into the hands of the Southern States and the Confederacy, an immediate need arose for arms of all kinds, modern and advanced, or old and out-of-date. The weapons on hand had to be used, while production at the arsenals was immediately increased, and purchases were made abroad. Colonel H. Craig, retiring at 70 on April 23, 1861, was succeeded as Chief of Ordnance by 66-year-old James Wolfe Ripley, who had had a long and successful career in the ordnance work of the old Army.

Both during the war and afterward, Ripley received much criticism. He was accused of a narrow hostility to innovations, new types of arms, and particularly to large-scale use of breechloading repeaters. Undoubtedly this criticism was in part well-founded, though sometimes exaggerated. He was devoted to the Union cause and army, and worked tirelessly to fill the sudden and often overwhelming requirements for ordnance. Until he was replaced in September, 1863, he made stern demands for as much uniformity as possible in weapon parts and ammunition. He and his aides performed most of their work in organization and procurement effectively. The Union armies were given a sufficiency of weapons and ammunition, and no instances of delays or halts in military operations are recorded which were caused by lack of ordnance. This fact furnishes the strongest evidence of the fundamental efficiency of the Ordnance Department.

Secretary Cameron reported on July 1, 1861, that the "embarrassment" in the early days of the war over the shortage of weapons "has been in a great measure overcome."[116] Private manufacturers were called upon at once, as the government armories were not able to provide the supply needed, despite a doubling of their manpower. In July, 1861, Ripley stated his position: "A great evil now specially prevalent in regard to arms for the military service is the vast variety of the new inventions, each having of course its advocates, insisting upon the superiority of his favorite arm over all others and urging its adoption by the Government. The influence thus exercised has already introduced into the service many kinds and calibers of arms, some in my opinion unfit for use as military weapons, and none as good as the government musket, producing confusion in the manufacture, issue, and use of ammunition, very injurious to the efficiency

116. *O.R.*, III, Vol. I, 308-309.

of troops. . . ." Ripley believed this evil could be stopped only by adhering strictly to uniformity of arms for all troops, and declared that government muskets "as now made have no superior arms in the world. . . ."[117] Ripley also questioned the ability of some men clamoring for contracts to deliver their arms, even if adopted, in quantity and on time.

He pointed out that, "Even Mr. Colt, who has the most complete private armory in the United States or probably elsewhere, and greater means and facilities for commencing the fabrication of the Government-pattern arms than anyone else, states that it will require six months for him to make the first delivery. . . ."[118] His reasons for objecting to a hasty adoption of new arms appear in his report to Cameron on December 9, 1861, after examining the Henry and Spencer rifles. "I regard the weight of the arms with the loaded magazine as objectionable," he wrote, "and also the requirement of a special ammunition, rendering it impossible to use the arms with ordinary cartridges or powder and ball. . . ." He did not see any advantages in these new rifles over other breechloaders despite their rapidity of fire. But he did not oppose other breechloaders and carbines for special use.[119]

The leading authority on Civil War ordnance, Robert V. Bruce, though highly critical of Ripley's attitude toward new weapons and inventions, points out that Union troops seldom went into battle "without a fair number of serviceable arms and a good supply of ammunition."[120] Ripley's insistence on moderate uniformity was much needed, and he helped lead the way toward mass production of arms and proper organization of their procurement.

Stanton reported in December, 1862, that the Ordnance Bureau had, despite all difficulties, armed more than 400,000 new troops. The Secretary noted that, "great diversity of opinion prevailed in respect to arms," and declared that the War Department had tried as far as possible to meet the demands of all, and that where this was impossible, the troops had in general readily acquiesced in the necessity of the case, "relying on the Department for exchange when it should be able to make one. . . ."[121] Stanton admitted that the sudden demand for arms, and the shortages, had "led to speculation and exhorbitant prices." But this situation was alleviated following an investigation which resulted in an increase in capacity of public arsenals, and the development of reliable private sources of American manufacture.[122] After the loss of the Harper's Ferry armory early in the war, the primary government manufactory of arms was at Springfield, Mass.

117. *O.R.*, III, Vol. I, 264-265, "Notes on subject of contracting for small arms."
118. *Ibid.*
119. *Ibid.*, 733-734.
120. Bruce, Robert V., *Lincoln and the Tools of War*, Indianapolis, 1956, 34, and for Ripley see 22-36.
121. *O.R.*, III, Vol. II, 906-909.
122. *Ibid.*

But Congress in 1862 approved additional armories for Columbus, Ohio, Indianapolis, and Rock Island, Illinois. By the end of 1862, foreign importations were restricted to those of high excellence, in place of the variety of arms previously bought abroad.

Lead supplies were stockpiled at the arsenals, and iron and timber proved no great problem. As Ripley stated, saltpeter had been the only article mainly dependent on foreign importations, and the Ordnance Department therefore had a large supply on hand at the outbreak of war.[123]

In 1863, Brigadier-General George D. Ramsay, who succeeded Ripley on September 15, expressed his opinion that the previous year had forcibly exposed the danger of excessive reliance on private parties, no matter how large their resources, for the principal munitions of war. "It is impossible for them to control fluctuations of the market in labor and material; and no private establishment can afford to keep a large stock of ordnance stores on hand, such as are required by the Government to meet its sudden wants."[124] Late in 1863, operations were being enlarged at arsenals in Watertown and Watervliet, N.Y., Allegheny, Pa., St. Louis, Washington, and Benecia, Calif. Every effort was being made to depend on American manufactures. The National Armory at Springfield, Mass., was by 1865 capable of producing more than 300,000 arms a year.[125]

When Ripley retired in the early fall of 1863, a controversy arose over his successor, Lincoln favoring George Douglas Ramsay and Stanton preferring a different man. A compromise was struck. Ramsay, a capable officer, was named Chief of Ordnance but had to share his authority with George Balch. This dubious division of power ended in September, 1864, when Brigadier-General Alexander B. Dyer became Chief. He brought a more advanced outlook to the Ordnance Department than Ripley's, although he retained Ripley's organizational structure.

In his report of October, 1864, Dyer stated that the increased productivity of the government arsenals and armories had already gone far toward supplying the heavy demand for arms and other ordnance stores, and, with the product of private manufacturers in America, had made the nation independent of foreign supplies. Dyer urged an increase of government manufacturing sufficient to meet all ordnance demands. This would permit greater precision in manufacture, more uniformity of arms, and better quality in the product.[126] He urged an extension of the use of breechloaders to infantry, for they had proved successful with mounted troops. As soon as the best model could be established and machinery altered, the Federal armories would begin making breechloaders. He also asked for a government powder mill.

123. *Ibid.*, 852, Ripley's report of Nov. 21, 1862.
124. *Ibid.*, 930-935.
125. *O.R.*, III, iv, 1208, Stanton's report on March 1, 1865.
126. *Ibid.*, 810.

Dyer kept urging Stanton to equip infantry with breechloaders, but wished to be certain that the best arm was chosen, and that all made by or for the army thereafter would conform to it.[127] He also emphasized the need for a greater number of specially-trained ordnance officers, lack of whom during the war had caused much embarrassment and confusion.[128]

Although space does not permit a thorough, critical survey of the weapons of the conflict, the stimulus given private arms companies was, of course, galvanic. During the Civil War, the Remington Company, for example, received nearly three million dollars for arms. The Manhattan Arms Company of New York produced machinery for making guns, later becoming the American Standard Tool Company. The New Haven Arms Company, which during the war met some success with the Henry repeater, was in 1866 renamed the Winchester Repeating Arms Company, and was soon on its way to a national reputation. Smith & Wesson were successful, primarily in making ammunition.[129]

The story of Christopher Miner Spencer and his famous rifle may properly be repeated here. While still in his twenties, Spencer designed the successful seven-shot repeating rifle and carbine that bear his name. Possibly 200,000 Spencers were made, although that figure may be excessive. Spencer got his patent in March, 1860, and put all the capital he could find into his plant. In June, 1861, trials by the Navy brought him contracts for rifles. Lively competitive jockeying accompanied the efforts of generals to induce the government to make Spencer and Henry rifles. Finally, in November, 1861, the War Department ordered 10,000 Spencer carbines for the cavalry. Lincoln is reliably said to have taken an interest in the unique Spencer although his rôle might easily have been exaggerated. At any rate, Spencer rapidly increased his production. When the war ended, he found that this production was excessive for the market, so that in 1869 his assets were sold to Oliver Winchester. Spencer, who survived until 1922, however, enjoyed a very successful later career in making machine-tools.[130]

The manufacture of successful breechloading repeaters was the most spectacular wartime development in small arms; in 1860, fifteen patents were granted for breechloaders, and many more in 1861-63.[131]

In 1855, Ambrose E. Burnside, formerly of the Army, had established the Bristol Firearms Company at Bristol, Rhode Island, to manufacture a lever-action breechloader known as the Burnside, another superior carbine much used during

---

127. Dyer to Stanton, Dec. 5, 1864. *Ibid.*, 971-972.
128. *Ibid.*, Vol. V, 145.
129. For summation see Edwards, William B., *Civil War Guns*, Harrisburg, 1962, *passim*.
130. Much has been written about the Spencer rifle; for summaries see Edwards, *op.cit.*, 144ff; Bruce, *op.cit.*, 113-116, and *passim*; Buckeridge, J.O., *Lincoln's Choice*, Harrisburg, 1956, *passim*.
131. Fite, Emerson D., *Social and Industrial Conditions in the North during the Civil War*, New York, 1930, 101.

the Civil War. However, early in the conflict, Burnside gave up his part in the firm's business.[132] Even more prominent were the Sharps rifles, developed by Christian Sharps, who patented in 1848 a breechloader still warmly commended in 1861, although eventually it lost favor and passed into obscurity. Sharps himself was not connected with the firm during the war. Most prominent in making revolvers was the Colt Armory which produced both Army and Navy models. Many individual officers and soldiers bought them directly from the Hartford firm. Although a disastrous fire destroyed production facilities for the Army pistol, this proved only a temporary deterrent.[133]

It is impossible in a limited volume to treat artillery, whether field or siege types, or the great variety of wartime accoutrements.[134] But gunpowder demands at least cursory attention. All gunpowder was produced by private firms, paramount among them the Du Pont Company of Delaware. Its owner-managers were intensely loyal, despite the situation of their plant on the margin of the Confederacy and within a slave State. The Du Pont Powder Mills at the opening of the war possessed about one-third of the nation's capacity for making gunpowder and Lammot du Pont was the youthful expert on explosives manufacture.[135]

Gunpowder, unlike arms, had not undergone any major changes until shortly before the Civil War. Improvement of powder thus became the key to the efficiency of the new guns. Most powders produced a "blasting" rather than "propelling" force. Lammot du Pont and Captain Thomas Rodman, however, developed the "Mammoth" powders of greater propulsive power. While the Hazard Company also produced sizable quantities of gunpowder for the Union, Du Pont carried the principal load. The business was, of course, dangerous. Eleven explosions at Du Pont during the war left 43 killed and scores injured; yet it was a successful industry, and Du Pont went into the postwar era well equipped for gigantic production. However, when depression struck the industry at the close of the war, the government "dumped" surplus powder for as little as five-cents a pound, so that for six years cheap powder flooded the market. Meanwhile, Du Pont and the eastern mills had lost the western market because of difficulty of wartime transport, so miners who had to have blasting powder united in opening the California Powder Works with low-cost Chinese labor, thus attaining a virtual monopoly of the Western powder market.

In other branches of the War Department, particularly the Engineers and the

132. Edwards, op.cit., 114.

133. Ibid., 304, 307, 311, 328.

134. Best summary volume on equipment is Lord, Francis A., Civil War Collector's Encyclopedia, Harrisburg, 1863.

135. See: A History of the Du Pont Company's Relations with the United States Government, 1802-1927, Wilmington, Del., 1928; Carr, William H.A., The Du Ponts of Delaware, New York, 1964; Dutton, William S., Du Pont, One Hundred and Forty Years, New York, 1942.

Signal Corps, organization played its rôle. The Federal war effort was fortunate in the talent available, both individual and industrial. Men appeared willing to take responsibility and to use it effectively. Under pressure of war, some who had thought little about organizational work discovered unexpected talents, and developed a taste for administration. Training other men, they urged business to undertake elaborate new projects.

When the Bureau of the Provost-marshal General was established in 1863 to give new vigor to the recruiting of volunteers, the enforcement of conscription, and termination of desertion, Grant made a fortunate choice in recommending James B. Fry, who had been McDowell's and Buell's Chief of Staff, and was fully experienced in war and business. This blunt Illinoisan knew plain men; at West Point he had learned administrative skill and exactness; and in five years as adjutant of the Academy, he had proved himself a man of moral intrepidity. He had exhibited this moral courage by insisting upon recognizing the contribution of Buell to victory at Shiloh in a way that Grant and Sherman never liked. As the Bureau undertook its staggering task, Fry formed its plan of efficient organization and laid down the principles that gave it distinction. A target of incessant criticism, it not only did something to systematize the composition of the armies, and still more to equalize State exertions and expenditures, but contributed to the unity between people and government. As Nicolay and Hay wrote, Fry was "an executive officer of extraordinary tact, ability, and industry." A man of like talents, Adjutant-General E.D. Townsend also became important to army administration.[136]

But despite the work of Fry and others, the ragged, uneven organization of regiments, divisions, and brigades continued to limp loosely along. From time to time they were reorganized, as Meade unwisely reorganized the Army of the Potomac, reducing its five corps to three, early in 1864. Special organizations were required for exchanged troops, militia, and Negro volunteers. Many of the soldiers discharged for disability were mustered into an invalid corps that became a reserve corps. The complexities of the task, as our narrative has implied elsewhere, were endless, but its real magnitude was seldom fully grasped.

The Army wrote not a mere story of enlistment, drill, and battle, as most people supposed, but a story also of endless paper work, the fundamental task of organization and discipline. The formation of fifteen hundred regiments meant fifteen hundred sets of clerical slaves painfully scratching pens over interminable sheets that dealt with transporting, feeding, clothing, and paying the men; with answers to complaints, promotions for achievements, and reports on successes and failures; with every aspect of life and death. Death?—that, too, was omnipres-

136. Nicolay and Hay, *Abraham Lincoln*, VII, 6; for background on Fry, see Warner, Ezra J., *Generals in Blue*, Baton Rouge, 1964, 162-163.

ent and incessant. As the Army grew from fewer than 17,000 men to 1,700,000, the Adjutant-General in Washington received reports of deaths in hospitals, mortality lists after battles, and inventories of the effects of those perishing in the service. They were promptly and carefully copied and sent to the Second Auditor. Furthermore, the Adjutant-General furnished the Second Auditor, upon the call of that officer, any information in his office relating to the military history of soldiers and officers, answering these questions within twenty-four hours after receiving them.[137] This particular paper work is continued today in the National Archives, not only to further the work of historians, but to supply data for family and pension records. Paper work pursued the soldier from the moment he crossed the sill of the recruiting office, until his name went on a record of burial which was sent to the national capital to be copied.

But if the making and remaking of armies at times furnished lessons in sound organization, more was to be learned from the woes that attended foolish neglects and vicious perversions of organization. Nearly all regiments were State organizations, and the method by which they were made and officered often illustrated organization at its worst. As early as the end of 1862, the astute Jacob D. Cox of Ohio saw clearly that the proper mode of raising a national army would have been by national conscription. He wrote Secretary Chase on the subject, giving examples of the mischief done by the impulsive and blundering effort to recruit innumerable fresh regiments of volunteers under incompetent leadership. The spectacle appalled him:

I have known a lieutenant to be forced by his captain (a splendid soldier) to resign on account of his general inefficiency. I have seen that same lieutenant take the field a few months later as lieutenant-colonel of a new regiment, whilst the captain still stood at the head of his fraction of a company in the line. This is not a singular instance, but an example of cases occurring literally by the thousand in our vast army during the year past. . . . Governor Tod of Ohio said to me some time ago, with the deepest sorrow, that he was well aware that in raising the new regiments by volunteering, the distribution of officers to the successful recruiters was filling the army with incompetents whom we should have to sift out again by such process as we could! Have we time for the sifting process?[138]

137. New York *Tribune,* January 9, 1864, Washington correspondence.
138. There is a full exposition of views of Gen. Jacob D. Cox upon the varying qualities of regular army men and volunteers in the Union forces, upon discipline and the needs for making it sterner and upon the best mode of sifting military officers, or remedying their defects, and of heightening their military aptitude, in *Military Reminiscences of the Civil War,* New York, 1900, Vol. I, Ch. IX. This chapter contains a section, p. 165ff, comparing volunteers and regulars, and dealing with the practical efficiency of soldiers, in both these categories. This chapter also discusses problems peculiar to the rapid increase of the army and emphasizes the anomaly of a double army organization, partly regular and partly volunteer. It is full of judicious comment on army organization, discipline and training, improvement, and wise conclusions on these subjects. Attacking political appointments to the army, it also emphasized the quick progress of rightly chosen young men, and points to "an excellent army at the end of the year."

A democracy has to learn by painful trial and error. The best that could be said for the formation of the great armies was that it offered a spectacle of hits-or-miss organization, bad and good, but still organization, presenting costly lessons in method to men of discrimination. Often, in such obvious situations as the formation of new regiments, local, political, and social forces operated with little heed to any practical theory of organization. Yet in this process, however blundering, thoughtful men learned much they later applied in a hundred channels, especially in business. The instances that might be cited are innumerable. The poor clerk who, quitting law studies because of precarious health, had helped organize the Crosby Guards in Chicago, returned after Perryville, Chickamauga, and a colonelcy, to found the best bookstore and publishing business in the lake city; and what Alexander C. McClurg did was done in different ways by a thousand others.[139] Any clerk could enlist and fight; but the clerk who helped organize a volunteer regiment could best organize a postwar business.

No firmer friends of systematic organization could be found than the really qualified medical officers of the government, headed after the spring of 1862 by Surgeon-General William A. Hammond, and the officers of the powerful Sanitary Commission, led by a genius for inspiring cooperative action, the well-known Unitarian minister and editor of reforming zeal, Henry W. Bellows. When Hammond made Jonathan Letterman medical director of the Army of the Potomac, he outlined the manifold problems before him with a warning that he occupied "the most arduous, responsible, and trying position" of his life, and must hold to strict accountability all officers of transport and supply, all surgeons, and all physicians and nurses.[140] The lurid record of the Crimean War gave warning that if such officers as Letterman did not institute system, the health, comfort, and lives of thousands would be lost. Bellows was meanwhile declaring that nothing could be more foolish than the usual sneer against red tape, and that the Army, government, and country needed more red tape (he meant organization) of the right kind. "If you could only have real rule carried out even to the death, you would have the surest way of attaining to the best results in military affairs."[141]

The medical services of the Army had to start from a very low point indeed.

139. McClurg's incomplete recollections are published in Mabel McIlvane's *Reminiscences of Chicago During the Civil War*, published in Chicago, 1914. See Chap. XXIV, "Demobilization for Peace," for other postwar careers.

140. Hammond to Letterman, Washington, June 19, 1862, New York *Tribune*, June 23, 1862.

141. Fisher, E.C., "The Working of the U.S. Sanitary Commission," *Journal of the Royal United Service Institution*, Vol. IX, 1866, 107ff. An excellent account of the organization of the U.S. Sanitary Commission is given by William Y. Thompson of Louisiana in *Civil War History*, Vol. II, No. 2, June, 1956, 41-63. He concludes that the Commission played a thankless but highly useful part in achieving Northern victory in the war, and that humanitarian endeavor "expanded to tremendous proportions."

All the world's armies in 1861 had medical arrangements no better than those which existed when Napoleon and Wellington fought at Waterloo; and many of them, including the United States regular Army with its 30 surgeons and 83 assistant surgeons, had arrangements that were worse. "The Civil War was fought at the end of the medical Middle Ages."[142] At the outset, North and South alike had no ambulance corps, few ambulances, and no general military hospitals. Everything had to be improvised. It was not until the Medical Bureau was reorganized by the law Lincoln signed on April 16, 1862, that a proper reorganization could be undertaken. In defence of the feeble medical facilities, it can be said that the small Army of 1861, scattered about the huge country, did not require a thousandth part of the establishment that the war did, so that the Medical Bureau could not even to a small extent be ready for the tremendous enlargement of its work demanded by rapidly expanding warfare.

With countless errors, provoking delays, the general medical ignorance of the time, and not a little outright brutality, the renovated Medical Bureau finally conquered the worst of its difficulties. Before the pompous and arbitrary but efficient Surgeon-General Hammond was unfairly court-martialled and dismissed in 1864, after many difficulties with Stanton, he had recruited about as able a body of physicians and surgeons as the low scientific level of the profession, the awkward methods of appointment, and the heavy demand permitted. He had manifested vision and zeal in introducing administrative reforms. He and his associates, with harrowing labors and anxieties, and by the aid of the Quartermaster's Department, had created by 1864 a system of hospitals with a capacity of 136,000 beds—hospitals that Dr. S. Weir Mitchell described as "unexcelled."[143] For all their deficiencies in bad diet, poor sanitation, inefficient medical attendance and nursing, their mortality rate was low. Those who witnessed the physical and mental suffering in these vast hospitals could well say with Walt Whitman that "the real war will never get in the books";[144] but, on the whole, the hospitals were a credit to the nation.

Surgeon-General Hammond was succeeded by Joseph K. Barnes, who proved

---

142. This statement was emphatically made by Dr. William A. Hammond, whom Lincoln had commissioned as Surgeon-General of the United States, April 25, 1862, and who became the ablest and most energetic officer of the U.S. Sanitary Commission on its establishment by the Act passed by Congress April 18, 1862, to reorganize and increase the efficiency of the Medical Department of the Army. His views and those of other medical experts are treated in George W. Adams, *Doctors in Blue*, New York, 1952, Chap. I, and in George Templeton Strong's *Diary of the Civil War, 1860-1865*, ed. Allan Nevins, New York, 1962, 219ff.

143. See the *Annual Reports of the Sanitary Commission*, which deal elaborately with the status and shortcomings of medicine and surgery in the war. Cf. Burr, Anna Robeson, *Dr. S. Weir Mitchell, His Life and Letters*, New York, 1929, *passim*. This latter account is useful, but inadequate, and is supplemented by his own *Catalogue of the Scientific and Literary Work of S. Weir Mitchell*, 1894, *passim*.

144. Whitman, Walt, *Specimen Days in America*, London, 1932. For a capable survey of Northern medicine, see Adams, George Worthington, *Doctors in Blue, op.cit., passim*.

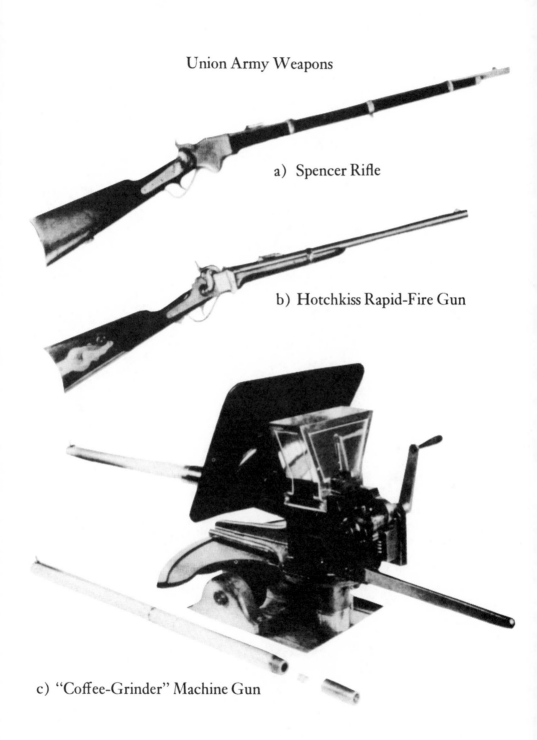

Union Army Weapons

a) Spencer Rifle

b) Hotchkiss Rapid-Fire Gun

c) "Coffee-Grinder" Machine Gun

a more capable and less cantankerous chief of service. Hammond started and Barnes ably developed several innovations, which were not only important, but daringly original.

Historians and scholars, including specialists in Civil War medicine, have paid but little attention to the procurement of medical supplies, especially in pharmacy. Actually this is a preëminent part of the story of Civil War organization and supply. It was soon found that existing pharmaceutical houses could not supply the great quantity and variety of medicines needed. One author describes conditions in the industry at the beginning of the war as "undisciplined" and "sometimes chaotic."[145] Necessarily, the Surgeon-General's Office set up what were called the Union laboratories to manufacture medicines of many kinds on a fairly large scale. For the first time in the United States, private enterprise was supplemented and in part supplanted by government-owned-and-operated manufacturing. The venture ended with the close of the war, but its effect on plans of government enterprise and on the pharmaceutical industry was tremendous. A new, revised, and enlarged Supply Table of medicines was set up, finally totaling 131 different varieties of *materia medica* and pharmaceutical preparations. These included strychnine, camphor, magnesium sulfate, numerous opium preparations, ether, chloroform, sweet spirits of nitre, various cinchona products, calomel, ipecac, licorice, and medical whiskey.[146] An eminent board of experts set up the new Supply Table, promulgated in October, 1862, and later revised.

Surgeons, particularly volunteers, often varied the standard Supply Table, clinging stubbornly to their own ideas of treatment. As Surgeon Charles S. Tripler, Medical Director of the Army of the Potomac before Letterman, put it: "The volunteer medical officers, being many of them country doctors, accustomed to a village nostrum practice, could not readily change their habits and accommodate themselves to the rigid system of the Army in regard to their supplies. To meet this difficulty I attempted within reasonable limits to disregard supply tables, and to give the surgeons articles of medicine and hospital stores to suit even their caprices, if in my judgment such articles could be of any avail in the treatment of disease. . . ."[147] Later, permission for variations in the Supply Table had to be approved in Washington, but this requirement was eventually relaxed and much independence was exhibited by surgeons in following prescribed practices.

Other problems arose in sending supplies to the front, and many surgeons began to transport them personally instead of relying on the quartermasters. Early in the war, medical officers faced a shortage of hospital tents and other

145. For a wise summary, see Smith, George Winston, *Medicines for the Union Army*, Madison, Wis., 1962, v.ff.
146. *Ibid.*, 2.
147. *O.R.*, I, Vol. V, 79.

essential equipment. Like all the volunteer officers, they committed many blunders until they learned to adapt their medical training and civilian practice to the special needs of the field. Some never did learn. Said one professional observer: "The want of military experience of the medical officers and their consequent helplessness made it extremely difficult to discover the real causes of disease, sometimes the nature of the diseases themselves, and to enforce the means of preventing these when discovered."[148]

As in other supply branches, medical purveyors at major depots purchased some of the needed supplies in the market.[149] A wide range of new depots had to be established to supplement the pre-war supply of army medical staples, all of which had come from New York. The prominent purveyors included Richard S. Satterlee in New York, and George E. Cooper in Philadelphia.[150] Pharmacists as such had no separate standing in the army, despite the pleas of the *American Journal of Pharmacy.* In May, 1862, Congress did allow the appointment of six Medical Storekeepers of unstated rank. Some supplies, such as uniforms, were obtained from the States when troops were mustered in, and on occasion the Commissary, or Quartermaster Departments purchased what was required. When necessary, as during major battles, any expedient was used.

Letterman, in 1862, designed a mobile field medicine wagon to go with the ambulance as a source of supplies. This, and the Autenrieth wagon which succeeded it in 1864, were considered eminently successful. They were supplemented by medical panniers or medicine-chests. Some of these were large chests for reserve supplies, but more useful were the lighter field panniers developed in 1863 by Edward R. Squibb and others. Every medical officer carried a packed knapsack. Hospital stewards supervised these kits and aided the surgeons in countless ways, much as the modern army medic does, even giving limited treatment.

Some losses in the course of purveying and campaigning were inevitable. And there was much grumbling over real or presumed inefficiency in furnishing medicines, and over delays or shortages in the manufacture of new drugs, medicines, or equipment. Speculation by pharmaceutical houses, inflation, and difficulty in the importation of necessities also gave much trouble. Even some cornering of the market occurred.[151] By the close of 1862, it was clear that steps had to be taken to provide greater promptness and safety in the flow of medical supplies.

Surgeon W. C. Spencer made a report that the quantity and cost of the medicines, hospital stores, dressings, bedding and clothing needed for troops had

148. *Ibid.*, 80-81.
149. *The Medical and Surgical History of the War of the Rebellion,* Washington, 1875, Pt. II, Vol. I, 964.
150. Smith, *Medicines for the Union, op.cit.,* 5.
151. *Ibid.*, 12-13.

become so great that the authorities were discussing the possibility of preparation and manufacture by the department itself.[152] Hammond wrote that transportation difficulties and the interests of the service required that the Medical Department be independent. "Much suffering," he added, "has been caused by the impossibility of furnishing supplies to the wounded, when those supplies were within a few miles of them in great abundance." He added that "the establishment of a laboratory, from which the Medical Department could draw its supplies of chemical and pharmaceutical preparations, similar to that now so successfully carried on by the Medical Department of the Navy, would be a measure of great utility and economy . . ."[153] The Navy had been manufacturing some of its medicines since 1852. For five years Assistant-Surgeon Edward R. Squibb helped in the laboratory, meanwhile developing his own processes, which he used later in founding a great drug house.[154]

The Philadelphia Army Laboratory went into operation in late April, 1863, and the Astoria (Long Island, N.Y.) laboratory in the middle of 1864. The leading authority on army pharmacy in the Civil War asserts that the laboratories provided a uniformity in medical supplies issued, but alongside their uniform packages and labels the varied products of private manufacture continued to be supplied through commercial channels. "Indeed," he declares, "the manufacturing processes in the laboratories paralleled the development of privately-owned enterprises; and the extraordinary demand for medicines during the war stimulated the pharmaceutical manufacturing of all kinds, from the cheapest nostrums to the finest official products . . ."[155] Major drug companies received a tremendous impetus from wartime business. Drug manufacturing companies added new machinery as the drug business shifted from the manual mortar-and-pestle processes to machines. New apparatus was invented and improved, especially in the preparation of fluid extracts and in counting and packaging pills. As many as 173 new pharmaceutical firms appeared in the United States in 1860, with a capital of $1,977,385. Ten years later the number had increased to 292 firms worth an invested capital of $12,750,809.[156]

In the spring of 1865, it was at last recorded that proper organization in the Surgeon-General's Department enabled Department and Field depots to receive their medical supplies in packages. This greatly facilitated their operations, and permitted the equipment of a whole division in a few hours, or the speedy establishment of a thousand-bed hospital. Under a rigid and thorough system of accountability, the Surgeon-General was informed of every issue of various items,

152. *Medical and Surgical History*, Pt. III, Vol. I, 965.
153. *O.R.*, III, Vol. II, 752-753, Nov. 10, 1862.
154. Smith, *Medicines for the Union, op.cit.*, 15-16.
155. *Ibid.*, 73.
156. *Ibid.*, 74.

and all officers receiving medical supplies were required to account for each article received.[157] The law of May 20, 1862, creating Medical Storekeepers gave them no actual rank, but the courtesy title of captain was accorded. Although they were not in the line of promotion, nor entitled to any pensions or bounties, their responsibility both for priceless supplies and for great sums in dollars and cents was incalculable. "As a new employment of Pharmaceutists, called into existence by the rebellion," wrote an observer, "the history of the medical storekeepers deserves mention in the annals of Pharmacy."[158]

One storekeeper-pharmacist has described the neat and careful organization of the dispensing and store rooms. He reported that 500 to 800 new prescriptions were filled each month at the Mower General Hospital at Chestnut Hill, Philadelphia, and that no serious mistakes occurred during his year there. The procedures would appear to have resembled those of a modern hospital pharmacy.[159]

Losses of medical stores by capture were great. Charles F. Squibb later sarcastically recalled that his chief distributor in the South was General Banks. "The Johnnies always managed to capture his well-equipped trains. Our goods went all through the Confederacy and were appreciated . . ."[160]

The year 1864 saw the adoption of improved processes from the revised Pharmacopaoeia, and the introduction of novel preparations which, as one expert of the day wrote, "are slowly effecting considerable changes in the daily routine of our operations."[161] A later scholar listed among Civil War developments a larger use of the stethoscope, percussion, and auscultation by the better-educated physicians; administration of morphine and strychnine by mouth; and better use of quinine. The medical and surgical advances during the war were attributable "not so much to the relatively slight advance in the theory and practice of medicine and surgery," he wrote, as to the improved plans of the Medical Department to develop a system with adequate authority given it to purchase and control its own supplies, to organize and equip the required medical units, and to direct them, subject only to the proper and necessary military control. "Much of the theory and practice was still wrong, but the environment was good and gave the sick and wounded a chance to respond to the curative processes of nature. The great change for the better was, therefore, almost entirely due to improved organization and adequate supplies."[162] Another result of the organization of the

157. "The Medical Purveying Department of the U.S. Army," *American Journal of Pharmacy*, Third Series, Vol. XIII, March, 1865, 97-98.

158. Rittenhouse, Henry N., "U.S. Army Medical Storekeepers," *American Journal of Pharmacy*, Third Series, Vol. XIII, March, 1865, 87-90.

159. Fell, Edward R., "The Pharmaceutical Department of a U.S.A. Hospital," *American Journal of Pharmacy*, Third Series, Vol. VIII, March, 1865, 107-112.

160. Blochman, Lawrence G., *Doctor Squibb*, New York, 1958, 136-137.

161. *Proceedings of the American Pharmaceutical Association at the Twelfth Annual Meeting held in Cincinnati*, Philadelphia, 1864, 56-57.

162. Reasoner, M.A., "The Development of the Medical Supply Service," *The Military Surgeon*, Vol. 63, No. 1, July, 1928, 4-5, 17.

Surgeon-General's Department was the eventual publication of the gigantic *Medical and Surgical History of the War of the Rebellion*, (Washington, 1870-1888), a memorable contribution both to history and to the study of medicine.

It may be safely asserted that the medical facilities of the Army scored not the least of their triumphs in the field of organization. When a man like Jonathan Letterman had to face hundreds of problems such as the provision of transports for sick and wounded, of beef stock for diets and fresh vegetables for preventing scurvy, and of sufficient drugs and sundries both on the march and during and after battles, his success in dealing with these and other tasks far too many to mention here was attributable in great part to the perfected organization through which he dealt with them.[163] We can agree with one critic that "The Medical Department of the Army was developed from an unorganized collection of surgeons at Bull Run into a splendid, reliable and efficient machine in 1864 . . ."[164] How we wish that it could have been possible to say as much for the practice of medicine itself!

[IV]

The United States Sanitary Commission, and some sister organizations such as the United States Christian Commission, were more than a national credit; they could be counted one of the minor glories of the war. More than any other institution, the Sanitary Commission systematized the benevolence of the whole North. An English officer hardly exaggerated when he wrote of its organizing power: "The Sanitary Commission has, in fine, disciplined and instructed the whole people, and enlisted every man, woman, and child in the military service of the country."[165] It was unquestionably the greatest voluntary organization of benevolent character that America had yet produced. The papers of Frederick Law Olmsted, the general secretary, contain a jotting on the members of the Commission: "personal influence—how much they helped to start and set along in Washington and at home." After mentioning the "social limpness of the country," and hence the "essentially decentralized and provincial condition of all communities," he set down a significant statement, mentioning the "constant effort to cultivate federalism, patience, and long views—value of Commission and its affiliated societies in this respect."[166]

The authorized history of the Sanitary Commission by Charles J. Stillé is one of the most interesting books produced by the war. It begins with intimations of

163. For Letterman's story see Jonathan Letterman, *Medical Recollections of the Army of the Potomac*, New York, 1866, 6-10, 17, 20, 34, 41, 50 and *passim*.

164. Duncan, Capt. Louis C., *The Medical Department of the United States Army in the Civil War*, (Series of magazine articles reprinted in book form), no place or date, 6-9, 21, 23.

165. Fisher, E.C., "The Working of the U.S. Sanitary Commission," *Journal of the Royal United Service Institution*, Vol. IX, 1866, 107ff.

166. Undated memorandum, evidently memorabilia on his work, Olmsted Papers, LC.

regret that the eight founders of the Commission received nothing like the official encouragement that Sidney Herbert of the British War Office had given Florence Nightingale's similar undertaking in Crimean War days; that it lacked the plenary powers in matters of health and sanitation that its British prototype had enjoyed; that Stanton at first fought Surgeon-General William A. Hammond tooth and nail; and that even Lincoln suggested that the Commission might be but a fifth wheel to the Medical Bureau—which rattled along, as we have seen, on one or two rickety wheels until Hammond took control. Stillé's chronicle describes the first nauseating army camps, the poisonous army diet, the demoralization of First Bull Run so plainly traceable to "radical defects of organization and discipline," and the labors of the Commission to avert the diseases that had scourged European armies and threatened to decimate Americans troops. It carries the story through the triumphant "Sanitary Fairs" late in the war, describing the hard-won plaudits for the Commission's heroic work in great battles like Chancellorsville and Gettysburg and in camps and hospitals, and happy public acceptance of the value of its inspection services.[167]

The volume, however, is more than a history, or a laudation of the work of the Commission by one of its leaders. It is a handbook of planning in methods and activities. "Organization of popular benevolence"—thus runs an early subheading. "Plan of Commission Organization," reads another; "Organization of the system of inspection," runs a third, meaning camp and hospital inspection. "Reorganization of the Medical Bureau," a cardinal event early in 1862, is followed by a line apposite to Donelson and Shiloh—"Organization of hospital steamers by the Commission." The establishment of supply depots, the enlistment of councils of women, the exciting contributions of money and gold-dust from California, the system of canvassing in Chicago and the Northwest, the establishment of soldiers' homes and convalescent camps, the conduct of systematic warfare against scurvy, the administration of hospitals during Sherman's Georgia campaign, the outfitting of the Commission's wagon-train for the siege of Petersburg—all this, and much more, had to be organized. When Commission transports in 1862 began bringing tens-of-thousands of sick and wounded soldiers up from Virginia battlefields in clean, comfortable surroundings, the North first comprehended the value of organization; when the next autumn many hundreds of Thanksgiving Day collections poured in from a thousand congregations all over the land, it realized how the heart of the nation had been touched.

Olmsted, who regarded himself as an apostle of organization, wrote the journalist W.H. Hurlbert midway in the war that few men in Washington knew what

167. Stillé, C.J., *History of the United States Sanitary Commission, Being the General Report of its Work During the War of the Rebellion,* Philadelphia, 1866, *passim.*

organization really meant, or what were the proper relations of authority and responsibility. "It is plain that the alphabet of administration is unknown to the Secretary of War, and to many others."[168] It astonished him that the bright exceptions like Quartermaster-General Meigs, Commissary-General Alexander E. Shires, and Surgeon-General Hammond, were not better recognized. But when, exhausted by his labors, Olmsted left the secretaryship of the Sanitary Commission in 1863, he might have boasted that the cause of organization had triumphed. The correspondent of the London *Daily News* thought the Commission one of the most remarkable feats of organization in the world.[169] While no real monetary value can be placed on its work, general calculation of its moral and material worth is conservatively put at $25,000,000.[170] Many glimpses into its activities and the incessant labors of its devoted officers are furnished by the fascinating wartime record in the diary of its cultivated and keenly observant treasurer, George Templeton Strong.

The Sanitary Commission has received just attention of recent years at the hands of the Civil War students, but other organizations, although admittedly of lesser importance, have remained neglected both as to their broad, general value, and their influence in the field of efficient organization. The United States Christian Commission is certainly one of these. As one authority puts it, "The United States Christian Commission, while not neglecting the physical wants of the soldiers, had as primary object their spiritual welfare, just as the Sanitary Commission attended mainly to the physical, though not entirely neglecting the spiritual."[171] The Christian Commission grew out of a meeting of the Young Men's Christian Association in New York during the first year of the war. "Delegates," as workers in the field were called, supplemented the meagre chaplain service of the Union armies. While they were generous with their Bibles, hymn-books, religious papers, and primers for the illiterate, they did much more.[172]

In organizing the work, three types of Delegates—Field, Hospital and Battle Ground—were active. The Field Delegates supplied field hospitals with clothing, bedding and stores, as well as religious tracts. They also dealt personally with individual soldiers, instructing, cheering and converting them.[173] Soldier letters still survive with printed headings of either the Christian or the Sanitary Commis-

168. Olmsted to Hurlbert, Jan. 21, 1863, Olmsted Papers, LC.
169. An admirable modern account of the U.S. Sanitary Commission is found in Maxwell, William Quentin, *Lincoln's Fifth Wheel*, New York, 1956; also, Thompson, William Y., "The U.S. Sanitary Commission," *Civil War History*, Vol. II, No. 2, June, 1956, 41ff., and by the same author, "Sanitary Fairs of the Civil War," *Civil War History*, Vol. IV, No. 1, March, 1958, 5iff.
170. Fite, *Social and Industrial Conditions in the North During the Civil War, op.cit.*, 277.
171. *Ibid.*, 284-285.
172. *Ibid.*, 286.
173. *Documents of the Christian Commission*, Philadelphia, 1862, 20.

sion. Hospital Delegates assisted chaplains and doctors, while Battle Ground Delegates aided the wounded on the field.[174] The main activities of the Christian Commission were carried on from 1863 to the close of the war, during which time it had a total of 4,859 commissioned Delegates, with 157 women managers for diet kitchens, and 108 Army agents along with 53 in home service. The Commission had offices in 31 cities, distributing tens of thousands of Bibles, knapsack books, library books, magazines, newspapers and tracts. Delegates preached over 58,000 sermons and held over 77,000 prayer meetings. More than seven million sheets of writing paper were distributed, and 92,321 letters were written by Delegates for the soldiers.[175]

During its four years, the Home Secretary of the Commission reported the receipt of over two-and-one-half million dollars, the larger part of which—about $866,500.00—was spent for hospital stores, while nearly $735,000 was used for publications. Most of the labor was furnished free. Before the organization of the Christian Commission, the YMCA had been independently active in many places. The Commission described itself as combining "piety with patriotism."[176] At first, the Commission itself admitted that it was treated with indifference. The Secretary reported that: "National feeling had not yet been sufficiently developed and hardened into unity of action; the solidity of systematic organization and effective cooperation were wanting alike in the army and at home," as the government had not yet learned to use advantageously "the spontaneous and abundant benevolence . . . so freely proffered."[177] By mid-1862 the situation was better. At first friction arose between the Commission and Stanton and Halleck. But eventually Stanton "became the steadfast friend of the Commission, as did the medical officers,"[178] many of whom at first looked askance at its activities.[179]

"The surgeons, in the beginning," wrote the Reverend Lemuel Moss, Secretary of the Commission, "were hardly favorable to the presence among their patients of men who had neither professional training nor experience, and whose only recommendation was their earnest desire to do good."[180] But, in time, the surgeons were conciliated. The response of the soldiers then became hearty and sustained. Grant is quoted as saying, "To the Commission the army felt the same gratitude that the loyal public felt for the services rendered by the army."[181]

174. *Ibid.*, 24-25.
175. Moss, Rev. Lemuel, *Annals of the United States Christian Commission*, Philadelphia, 1868, 729. Examples of their publications remain, including a primer chiefly for freedmen. The pocket hymn books contain most familiar Protestant hymns of the day. E.B. Long Collection, Univ. of Wyoming.
176. *Ibid.*, 63, 726.
177. *Ibid.*
178. *Ibid.*, 117, 124.
179. *Ibid.*, 124-125.
180. *Ibid.*
181. *Ibid.*, 125-126.

The Secretary admitted that the task of organizing the two main branches of work, supply at home and relief in the army, was not easy.[182] Efficiency was particularly shown during and after "the Pennsylvania Invasion" or Gettysburg campaign. The Commission Delegates rushed in at once to give help in hospital, in kitchens, and on battlefields. Some days a thousand loaves of bread, all of them four times larger than usual, were distributed. Countless wagonloads of supplies came in for distribution. Thousands of letters had to be written, assistance had to be provided people who sought tidings of relatives, and innumerable other tasks performed. "In short, all the work of a great establishment was . . . planned and done."[183]

The Loan Libraries were a major undertaking of the Commission, some 240 naval ships being supplied with reading material, much of it religious. Negro regiments were given special packets, Army units received libraries, and about 125 volumes each were sent to more permanent camps and hospitals. Another feature was the Special Diet Kitchen, really a government kitchen under charge of the hospital surgeon, but supplemented and managed by the Commission. The noted Mrs. Annie Wittenmyer, mainly responsible for establishing these unusual kitchens, later wrote a manual on the feeding of the sick.[184] Diet kitchens also appeared in the West, with the first at Cumberland Hospital in Nashville. The idea spread to the eastern armies, until in all the Commission operated between 50 and 60 such kitchens.[185]

No serious conflict arose between the Christian and the Sanitary Commissions, and although some healthy competition marked their work, they also offered important instances of cooperation. Behind Christian Commission workers in the field stood at least 266 chapters of the Ladies' Christian Commission in large and small communities.[186] At times, onlookers might have felt that the Commission's religious zeal was too exuberant, but certainly no more dedicated group could be found.

The two major Commissions were far from standing alone. Late in 1863, the American Association for the Relief of the Misery of the Battlefields appeared, an outgrowth of the international conference at Geneva, Switzerland, in October, 1863, from which rose the international Red Cross. The American Association was busy on eastern battlefields late in the war, and eventually became the American Red Cross. An "American Union Commission" undertook a special task in trying

182. *Ibid.*, 128.
183. *First and Second Annual Reports, United States Christian Commission*, Philadelphia, 1863, 79-80; Smith, Rev. Edward P., *Incidents of the United States Christian Commission*, Philadelphia, 1869, *passim.; Christian Work on the Battle-Field; Being Incidents of the Labours of the United States Christian Commission*, London, 1870, *passim.*
184. Moss, *op.cit.*, 665, 700.
185. *Ibid.*, 669.
186. *Ibid.*, 358, and *passim.*

to aid loyalists and refugees from the South. Some religious groups naturally took advantage of wartime emotions in pouring out tons of free publications. Thus the American Tract Society of New York distributed 63,000,000 copies of free tracts in one year to soldiers; the American Bible Society gave 800,000 volumes, the American Temperance Union issued some two million pamphlets, and many similar enterprises appeared.[187] Packages of various necessities and even luxuries for soldiers occupied the attention of another type of organization, the Massachusetts Soldiers' Relief Association, which, by December, 1862, had sent 3,790 packages to Massachusetts men.[188] Many Ladies' Societies attended to the "wants of the 'Contrabands' "—for multitudes suffered for lack of proper shelter, medical stores and attention.[189]

Individuals, church groups, abolitionist societies, and others joined in the work of numerous organizations befriending the freedmen.[190] Supplies of all kinds were gathered and sent into the areas on the fringes of the military action where the freedmen gathered. Hundreds of persons felt prompted to undertake teaching and missionary posts among them. For intance, Lewis C. Lockwood, under the auspices of the American Missionary Association, successfully launched a number of enterprises for liberated Negroes in the Fortress Monroe district. Other organizations included the National Freedmen's Relief Association of the District of Columbia, the Kansas Emancipation League, Western Freedmen's Aid Commission, Freedmen's Aid Society of Cincinnati, Northwestern Freedmen's Aid Society of Chicago, and the Western Sanitary Commission. Distinctively alert and energetic was the Western Sanitary Commission, whose field was primarily the Mississippi Valley. Freed Negroes at the North gladly lent a hand, and one of the most earnest helpers was the Contraband Relief Association of Washington.[191]

The energies, personnel, and money needed for charity and philanthropic endeavors lie just beneath the surface of society, and so it was in the United States of pre-war days. It took a cataclysm such as the Civil War to energize the latent forces and capacities of society in a forcible response to an imperative need. After the trumpet call of Sumter, and the fast advance of the armies, it became clear that here was a rich field for public service, advancement of many great patriotic causes, and the satisfaction of long-felt ambitions and aspirations. While many activities were impulsive, haphazard, ill-planned or uncoordinated, at the same

187. Fite, op.cit., 286; Aid Societies in the Civil War, (a bound volume of pamphlets, so titled in the Newberry Library, Chicago, covering various groups.)
188. Report, Massachusetts Soldiers' Relief Association, Washington, 1863, passim.
189. Register of Letters Received, Irregular Books, Record Group 107, War Records, National Archives, Nov. 7, 1862, Mrs. Julia A. Wilbur.
190. For full story see Rose, Willie Lee, Rehearsal for Reconstruction, New York, 1964, passim.
191. For summation see Quarles, Benjamin, The Negro in the Civil War, Boston, 1953, 101-131.

time the urgency of the crisis, and the necessity of seizing every opportunity with breathless speed, forced men into systematic exertions, and a slow, thoughtless people became measurably alert and purposeful. In no other way could the emergency of the hour be met. There can be no doubt that the extensive organizational lessons applied in the philanthropic activities of the war years under sheer necessity, but with exhilarating ardor, made an enduring psychological impression upon Americans which became clearly evident in the postwar years.

[V]

While the war-born philanthropic institutions made vital contributions to the social history of the Civil War, they were immediate answers to a temporary need. It will be useful, therefore, to observe the status of more permanent organizations during the war.

Few private business enterprises before the war had done more than $25,-000,000 worth of business a year. Some heads of such undertakings possessed a broad organizational experience. One of John Jacob Astor's friends remarked that he was capable of commanding an army of half-a-million men, and his manifold activities in amassing a great fortune in the fur trade, shipping, and New York real estate did not prevent him from founding, with the aid of Joseph G. Cogswell, a splendid library. Many heads of family firms in merchandising, however, like the Kingslands of New York in hardware, the Schieffelins in drugs and liquor, and the English-born Arnold and Constable in drygoods, pursued a relatively narrow range of activities. So did such a firm as Prime, Ward & King in banking and brokerage, whose interests were restricted, compared with those of Grinnell, Minturn & Co. or Howland & Aspinwall as shipping merchants. It is, indeed, curious to find how many of the "wealthy citizens of New York" listed in the ante-bellum book of that name sprang from firms whose organization and management was in the hands of an expanding family.[192]

However, a serious business journal could express the opinion that: "It is evident. . . . that by some extraordinary agency the power of production and accumulation has received an immense impulse in the present century, beyond what was ever the case in the previous history of the world, and wealth has poured in upon the people in an unprecedented degree. If we would seek the leading causes of this rapid accumulation, they will, we think, be found to be 1st, the co-operative power of capital, which has in this country been carried to a far greater extent than in any other . . ."[193] This statement was made in the year of Gettysburg, when much greater accomplishments by the cooperative power of

192. *Wealthy Citizens of New York*, New York, 6th Edition, 1845.
193. *Hunt's Merchants' Magazine and Commercial Review*, Vol. XLVIII, No. 5, May, 1863, 355.

capital were still to come. The writer cited steam transportation as a second cause; as a third, the application of many new inventions; and as a fourth, abundance of cheap and fertile land open to all comers. Implicit in the efflorescence of this array of forces was the new understanding of organization and a growing disposition to utilize it in all branches of human activity.

The business and professional world was definitely expanding by 1861, and was becoming more and more regional, and indeed national, in scope. This tendency was bound to persist, irrespective of the movements of war, in response to the innate desire of the people for such expansion and communication as had now been rendered possible by the railroads and telegraph. The practical difficulties of transportation and communication had previously restricted close inter-relationships. Henceforth, raw materials could be shipped to a central manufacturing point rather than be processed near their source. Parts that might be made more advantageously in separate plants could now be assembled in one machine-building center. Farmers could concentrate upon the crops best suited to their situation, knowing that the products they did not now grow could be obtained elsewhere, and their own yields distributed far and wide. This distribution now had the mechanisms to operate, and was rapidly developing the organization required to be operated successfully. That the war often altered, advanced, or retarded this process is undeniable, just as it is undeniable that the process was incipient at the start.

The country did not so much lack business and professional organizations as it lacked those which possessed a national scope and influence. Most of this deficiency can be ascribed to poor transportation prior to the maturity of the railroad system. Later, people could assemble more easily. The revolution wrought by air-transport in the mid-twentieth century has brought a tremendous growth in international business, international conferences, and associations. Railroads caused a similar revolution in interstate thought and activities in the eastern half of the United States, beginning with the period 1850-1890.

Examples of the advance of organization became more and more numerous. Wisconsin banks had been miserably weak in 1860 but the formation and operation of the Wisconsin Bankers' Association helped bring order and high standards to replace chaos and chicanery. The condition of the banks and the increased regional and national scope of their operations, resulting from the immense wartime expenditures by the government, made unified effort essential.[194] Moreover, as we have noted, the National Bank Act of 1863, along with its many epochal effects, brought banks all over the North into closer relationship and necessitated cooperation, organization, and more or less uniformity in methods. In March, 1865, New York passed an act enabling banks to form associations to

194. Fite, *op.cit.*, 152-154.

qualify under the National Currency Act of June 3, 1864.[195]

Boards of trade or chambers of commerce had long existed in leading cities. The New York Chamber of Commerce was formed in 1768 by twenty businessmen.[196] During the crisis preceding the American Revolution, merchants in Boston, New York, and Philadelphia formed associations for non-importation, another example of organization forced by necessity. However, early in the 19th century the work of such groups declined. By 1858, ten Chambers and twenty boards of trade were said to be active.[197]

By the Civil War period these groups became more energetic. The New York Chamber of Commerce strongly supported Northern principles and President Lincoln at the start of the war, passing resolutions against the anti-war and pacifist elements in New York City as early as April, 1861. It supported the Legal Tender Act and passed numerous resolutions favoring the government, but at the same time pressed hard for better harbor defenses and protested against the depredations of the Confederate naval raiders.[198] Western cities, before Sumter, were already forming boards of trade or chambers of commerce.[199] In 1868, a National Board of Trade was formed.

The predominant position of agriculture naturally limited such groups before the war, but organization had long been essential in various fields. The New York Stock Exchange was established in 1792. The American Iron and Steel Association can trace its beginnings to 1855, and the woolen and cotton industries were also early organizers. But such associations were diverse and scattered, or were brought into being for some special purpose or event. The United States Brewers Foundation of 1862, for instance, helped the Federal government collect liquor taxes.[200]

Besides the exchange of ideas, the early trade associations gave much attention to methods of restricting competition, price-control and similar subjects. However, despite the establishment of some associations, most businessmen were fairly slow to act together. Some men feared disclosure of trade secrets, and it was only reluctantly that certain trade groups finally united. Even the purposes of the National Association of Cotton Manufacturers, said to be the oldest continuous trade association in the nation, were narrowly conceived during the early

195. *Banker's Magazine*, Vol. XIV, No. 10, April, 1865, 344-346.
196. Bradley, Joseph F., *The Rôle of Trade Associations and Professional Business Societies in America*, University Park, Penn., 1965, 41-42; Sturges, Kenneth, "American Chambers of Commerce," *Williams College David A. Wells Prize Essays*, New York, 1915, 3-7, 11-15.
197. Sturges, *op.cit.*, 41.
198. Bishop, Joseph Bucklin, *A Chronicle of One Hundred & Fifty Years, the Chamber of Commerce of the State of New York, 1768-1918*, New York, 1913, 71-72, 74-75, 83-85.
199. Fite, *op.cit.*, 140-141.
200. For survey see Bradley, *op.cit.*, 19-21, and *passim*.

years of the 1850's. Tariff questions often drew some trades together.[201]

State boards of agriculture had also had a limited life. New York had a state board in 1821, but it was short-lived. The U.S. Commissioner of Patents, Henry L. Ellsworth of Connecticut, took over the task of receiving new seeds and plants sent from abroad by government representatives and distributing them.[202]

State governments had done some experimental work such as Georgia's experimental botanical garden in 1733, and South Carolina's work on tropical crops begun in 1669. A bill to set up The American Society of Agriculture failed in 1797. As one writer states, with reference to the institution of a Department of Agriculture in 1862, "It was something of a wonder that the Congress and Mr. Lincoln could find the time to establish a new department to improve agriculture. That might well have been postponed until the war had ended."[203] While the activities of the Department were definitely limited, it marked the organization of one of the first social agencies of government.

In science and the professions, physicians were the most numerous body of truly advanced specialists. But once the railroads made communication more accessible, organization increased. After 1790, a growth in medical societies multiplied and medical literature grew. Between 1830 and 1845 the number of medical societies doubled, and many of them urged an improvement of the term and quality of professional education, which is said to have been only sixteen weeks in many instances. The founding meeting of the American Medical Association is considered to have been the National Medical Convention in Philadelphia in May, 1847.[204]

While the annual meetings heard learned papers, and the Association was endeavoring to lift medical standards and education, its activities and attractions were limited. In 1860 the meeting at Boston attempted to strengthen the group, and as Dr. Shryock writes, "the convention seemed about to resolve itself into the first American public health association when the Civil War put an end to such aspirations."[205] The 930-page transactions of this meeting contained many papers of professional value,[206] but no meetings were held in the next two years. When conventions were resumed in 1863, the transactions were only half as long.

201. Foth, Joseph Henry, *Trade Associations, Their Services to Industry,* New York, 1930, 4-13; Naylor, Emmett Hay, *Trade Associations, Their Organization and Management,* New York, 1921, 23. There are discrepancies in various sources as to the dates of the first trade association and other facts.

202. For summaries, see Shannon, Fred A., *The Farmer's Last Frontier, Agriculture, 1860-1897,* New York, 1945, 269-285; Gates, Paul W., *Agriculture and the Civil War,* New York, 1965, *passim.*

203. Terrell, John Upton, *The United States Department of Agriculture,* New York, 1966, 10-18.

204. Background on medical organizations may be found in Shryock, Richard H., *The Development of Modern Medicine,* New York, 1947, 22, 110, 235; Fishbein, Morris, *A History of the American Medical Association,* Philadelphia, 1947, 19ff; Burrow, James G., *American Medical Association, Voice of American Medicine,* Baltimore, 1963, 2-19ff.

205. Shryock, *op.cit.,* 235.

206. *Transactions of the American Medical Association,* Vol. XIII, 1860, Philadelphia, 1860.

Most papers were highly technical. The war received limited attention. Although a report of the Committee on Military Hygiene appeared in 1864, most papers were mainly applicable to civilian medicine.[207] Thus, it may be said that medicine moved hesitantly toward professional organization.

Early in the 19th century, there were few enduring national scientific societies formed, although local bodies were proliferating. The American Philosophical Society and the American Academy of Arts and Sciences were the major national societies. By the 1830's the need for more national groups increased. The successful satisfaction of some of these needs marked an important advance in the organization of American scientific activity.[208]

By the start of the Civil War, State academies of science could be found in most of the North, and parts of the South. Cities, large and small, had their special museums and academies. While a majority of these were in the East, the West was not far behind. The Chicago Academy of Natural Science, founded in 1856, became the Chicago Academy of Sciences, and has survived to the present day. Louis Agassiz was a popular lecturer in Civil War days. The great Smithsonian Institution, founded in 1846, was exerting a powerful influence upon the American mind and spirit even before Sumter. But, as a direct result of the Civil War, the National Academy of Sciences stands foremost among the radiant intellectual lighthouses of the time. Several temporary organizations had given technical scientific advice in the early days of the war, particularly to the War and Navy Departments. In February, 1863, Gideon Welles appointed a permanent Commission to report on various "matters of science and art" of importance to the Navy. The Commission was fortunate in having expert and dedicated men on its staff such as Joseph Henry, Secretary of the Smithsonian Institution, Alexander Dallas Bache, Superintendent of the Coast Survey, and Charles H. Davis, Chief of the Bureau of Navigation in the Navy Department.[209] Davis, who had a brilliant career early in the war on the Mississippi, wrote in a letter of Frebruary 24, 1863: "The appointment of a permanent Commission was suggested to me by one of my letters, which quoted a passage from the British War Office which spoke of a Select Commission; and when I mentioned it to Bache and Henry they acquiesced, and the latter [Henry] presented the plan to the department."[210]

A bill was introduced in the Senate February 21, 1863, for a National Academy of Sciences. It went easily through Congress, and was signed by Lincoln March 3, 1863.[211] Bache is quoted as saying he felt that an institution of science, supple-

207. *Ibid.*, 1863, 1864, and 1865.

208. Bates, Ralph S., *Scientific Societies in the United States,* New York, 1951, 28.

209. *Ibid.*, 78; True, Frederick W., *A History of the First Half-Century of the National Academy of Sciences, 1863-1913,* Washington, 1913, 1-4.

210. Davis, Capt. C.H., *Life of Charles Henry Davis, Rear-Admiral, 1807-1877,* New York, 1899, 289.

211. True, F.W., *op.cit.*, 5.

mentary to those already existing, was much needed in America, "to guide public action in reference to scientific matters."[212]

The early projects of the National Academy ranged afar, including the possibility of a national university, special research in branches of science little known in the United States, schemes for aiding the government in developing the national domain and resources—even work in political science, literature and art. Bache and Henry felt it especially important "to afford recognition to those men of science who had done original work of real importance, and thereby to stimulate them and others to further endeavors; and to aid the Government in the solution of technical scientific problems having a practical bearing on the conduct of public business . . ."[213] The government at once called on the Academy for advice respecting a number of subjects.[214]

The American Institute of Instruction, founded in 1830, included both teachers and those interested in education. Although limited largely to New England, it met during the war years with five to six hundred in attendance at each annual convention. The National Teachers' Association, founded in 1857, had a much broader membership, but suspended meetings early in the war. Teachers' institutes, and state and local associations were numerous, becoming a great influence in teacher education.[215]

[VI]

One virtue of early organization was its fluidity. Society was versatile and adaptable; the swift new growth of industrial corporations, mercantile businesses, philanthropic undertakings and other enterprises that the war helped spring into existence profited greatly by the ready movement of members from one project to another. Grant could be soldier, farmer, teamster, store clerk, and War Department head within ten years without exciting special wonder.[216] Not until a later era did specialization, professionalism, and group loyalties create barriers between the farmer, the professor, the scientist, the engineer, the worker, and the industrialist that were hard to cross. Men later could no longer be jacks-of-all-trades as in Lincoln's time; versatility became a handicap, not a virtue; and American life lost one of its unique qualities.

As war contracts multiplied, as expenditures of private philanthropic and patriotic bodies increased, and as the impact of the new National Banking system,

212. *Ibid.*, 7.
213. *Ibid.*, 14.
214. *Ibid.*, 17-28, 204-219.
215. Fite, Emerson Davis, *op.cit.*, 247-248.
216. Cf. Gardner, John W., *Self-Renewal: The Individual and the Innovative Society,* New York, 1864, 75-78.

the special grant for a transcontinental railroad, the Homestead and Land-Grant laws, and other wartime legislation was felt, a great body of alert young men pressed forward to inaugurate a new era. Thomas A. Scott, made Assistant Secretary of War in his late thirties, discerned during his Western service opportunities for expanding his Pennsylvania rail system; his much younger protégé Andrew Carnegie, who transported the first brigade of troops to Washington and helped organize the military telegraph system, perceived larger opportunities not in railroads, but in the iron industry. John D. Rockefeller, looking for "something big" to undertake, realized during the war that Cleveland might well dominate the fast-growing business of oil-refining. J. Pierpont Morgan, whose long-misrepresented sale of remodelled carbines to the government was not at all discreditable, and who brought expert knowledge to foreign exchange, was pushing forward to the day when he could outstrip Jay Cooke in financial operations. These names would resound down the half-century after Appomattox; and the spirit of these rising men was the spirit of unnumbered others. As the gates of the new era opened, it was an understanding of organization that did most to swing them wide.

W.E. Channing could write: "In truth, one of the most remarkable circumstances or features of our age is the energy by which the principle of combination or of action by joint forces by associated members is manifesting itself. It may be said, without much exaggeration, that everything is now done by societies ... You can scarcely name an effort for which some institute has not been formed. Would men spread one set of opinions or crush another? They make societies. Would one encourage horse racing and another discourage traveling on Sunday? They form societies. We have immense institutions spreading over the country, combining hosts for particular objects . . ."[217]

The formless, protoplasmic United States of 1861 emerged from the war four years later eagerly groping toward organization, and much more aware of the paths it must take forward. Under the forcing-blast of necessity and opportunity, as well as by government contracts, protective tariffs, and inflation, a thousand businesses doubled or trebled in size. Men's ideas expanded, as government activities swelled to proportions previously incredible, as the national banking system rose, and as the outlines of trunk-line railroads were foreshadowed. Truly national industries, reaching out for regional or continental, as distinguished from local, markets, began to appear—for example in milling, meat packing, and the manufacture of shoes and clothing. Not only capital, but organizing ability was being invested as never before. Half the colonels had learned a great deal in their service about system, celerity, and administrative discipline. As mentioned elsewhere, visitors in large business offices could overhear the manager pointing out

217. Channing, W.E., *Works*, Boston, 1877, 139.

executives with the words: "The man at that desk was a brigadier—that one yonder a major—that one was in the Provost-marshal General's office." The principal fault of these new executives was an overwhelming eagerness for quick results.

Of broad significance in this growth of organization was the instruction Americans had received in the use of credit, along with the new use of the cash system in merchandising practiced by John Wanamaker and others. While the national banking system was being organized, it had joined with the Treasury to sell national government bond issues. Jay Cooke, when the normal market was exhausted, began selling bonds in every street and village. His canvassers sought far and wide for buyers; never before had credit given such a powerful impetus to the industrial revolution and the advance of the machine. A cooperative spirit was hereby engendered that changed the outlook of Americans. While hitherto a nation of "joiners" on strictly local levels, people began to develop a taste for larger voluntary combinations that within a few years ran the gamut from the G.A.R. to the trusts and the Grange. By 1885, one of the most powerful of modern organizers, Rockefeller, was able to make the momentous pronouncement: "The age of individualism has gone, never to return."[218]

This effort to organize the energies of the country harmonized with tendencies in its life already partly formed in 1860, and vigorously growing; tendencies necessitated by the natural increase of population and wealth, and given extraordinary impetus by the conflict. Through this effort, as it was carried forward after Gettysburg and Appomattox, ran a vibrant self-confidence, the exuberance of victory, the pride of a service record. Dr. S. Weir Mitchell struck a characteristic note of elation when, after recalling how his fellow-physicians had built great wartime hospitals, admirably equipped without the help of architects, he described what the gruelling upheaval had done for his calling, leaving it with justifiable pride in its broad achievements.[219]

Multitudes of veterans emerged from the hard lessons of war with this self-confidence born of success, and a pride in duty well-done; the spirit of the Greeks after Marathon, and Britons after crushing the Armada. Tens of thousands of civilians who had built machine-shops, run arms factories, and filled contracts for shovels, canned foods, and blankets, or who had managed recruiting, income-tax

218. Nevins, Allan, *John D. Rockefeller: The Heroic Age of American Enterprise,* New York, 1940, Vol. I, 66ff. Rockefeller's statement was made not in defense of monopoly, which he never completely possessed, but as an opponent of the savagely implacable competition he had found in control of the oil-refining industry until he and his associates reorganized it. Rockefeller's attitude upon the movement toward industrial concentration and belief that it had become invincible is treated in this volume, 66-69. See also: Nevins, Allan, *Study in Power: John D. Rockefeller,* New York, 1953, Vol. II, 383, upon Rockefeller's declaration in 1912 that pure competition was an anachronism and the government must come to terms with industrial combination.

219. Burr, Anna Robeson, *S. Weir Mitchell, op.cit., passim.*

collection, or home relief, felt the same thrill of experience, confidence, and pride. The day of small affairs began to pass; visions of great new ventures became common. Improvisation grew into hardheaded planning, individualism was channeled into disciplined action. In the eight years before the postwar boom had spent itself, the rails of the Union Pacific spanned the continent, Hewitt and Carnegie founded the open-hearth and Bessemer steel industries, the first large industrial pools were formed, and two especially chaotic businesses—oil and tobacco—were taken in hand by Rockefeller and Duke. Research and technology began to be energetically organized.

Of all the changes effected by the war, this replacement of an amorphous, spineless society by a national life even partially organized for efficient action— organized first to win the war, and then to develop the continent—was perhaps the most striking, and as vital in effect as the unification of the nation and the renascence of all its liberal impulses and commitments by the abolition of slavery. As the first two years of the struggle might be called the improvised war, the last two could be termed the organized war. The transition from one to the other was a transition from the old America to the new, and not in material terms alone, but in psychological terms also. Like ore thrown into an Alexander Holley converter, men's ideas were shaken into new patterns with a closer approach to the structure of steel. Americans still detested regimentation, but they had learned the power of voluntary combination for definite objects while leaving themselves free in other relations. "We are *gaining* strength," said Lincoln in his last annual message, and the country was unquestionably gaining strength in a variety of ways, both old and new, both predictable and unexpected.[220]

220. Lincoln, *Collected Works*, VIII, 151.

9

Prison Walls of the Confederacy

ALMOST THROUGHOUT the war, the Confederacy was in a state of siege. Like a medieval fortress, the Southern States had to stand barricaded against the enemy. It was a double siege, by sea and by land, uneven, partial, at times inefficient, but nevertheless a debilitating and disabling siege by the North. Its leaky apertures did not really diminish its eventual strategic effectiveness. Rebel intercourse with the outside world was impossible except by penetration of ever closer cordons of warships on the 3500-mile coastline, waiting outside harbors and paralleling the shores broken by a multitude of bays, inlets and creeks. Evasion was possible by avoiding sentries along the ill-populated portions of the beaches, but on these stretches the lack of port facilities made it less advantageous to bring in supplies. Movement into or out of the Confederacy looked easy to those studying a coastal map of the long, rough shoreline from the Great Dismal Swamp to the Texas line at Brownsville. Actually, it was an increasingly difficult feat for venturesome men to pilot a fair-sized vessel from closely-watched Bermuda or Nassau into the few available harbors, still more intently scanned. The land frontier from Virginia across the Alleghenies, across the Mississippi to the Ozarks, and then south to Mexico, looked penetrable to those who knew nothing of river gunboats, cavalrymen on patrol, guarded railroads, scouts and guerrillas infesting forests and swamps, and vast distances. "Halt! Who goes there?"—a run —a shot—a plunge into the brush—another exhausting day with little sleep and less food! This kind of experience was often as deterrent to enterprise as a stone-wall.[1]

No task before the Union command was more toilsome or important than the establishment and maintenance of this double blockade, half of it on the waves and half of it intercepting the inland channels of trade. It began with hastily improvised forces and policies, for its urgency was manifest from the outset. The South was desperately hungry for money and foreign credit to be had by shipping its superabundant cotton in any quantity, even small, to West Indian ports especially Nassau, or across the Atlantic. The blockade grew tighter and sharper on

1. Capt. James M. Wells, *With Touch of Elbow*, Philadelphia, 1909, 222ff.

332

the coast as naval forces swelled and bases and enclaves multiplied on the sea perimeter of the Confederacy. Simultaneously, it seemed to become looser and laxer inland as Northern armies moved into the wide cotton kingdom. The adventure that accompanied it was more striking, but far less significant than the speculation and corruption that it bred.

Union armies eventually won the war, but the North might have triumphed many months earlier had the blockade, especially by land, been sternly rigorous and efficient. The rebels they met would then have been more gaunt, more ragged, more often shoeless, and more poorly armed. The fact that the Confederacy secured more than 112,000 small arms through the tightening blockade (from October 1, 1862 to the end of the war), with many miscellaneous supplies, is eloquent of the part played by blockade evasion during the war. It greatly relieved the strain on the factories of Virginia and Alabama.[2]

[I]

Then and later, the term "ocean blockade" (for many people were ignorant of the larger inland network of siege) called before men's minds a series of graphic pictures, fanciful images that emphasized the adventurous and perilous aspects of sea duty, a romantic glow that obscured its harsh realities. The primary antagonists facing each other in the blockade were the seagoing steam warship, not the little patrol-vessel, on one side, and the swift blockade-runner, big enough for a substantial cargo, on the other.

On the Atlantic swell, far out between the Bermudas and Wilmington, or on the sea-lanes between England and the Bahamas, swung the U.S.S. *Susquehanna*, a beehive of vigilantly busy officers and men. Lookouts high on the masts conned the horizon; sailors of the watch were cleaning the guns and holy-stoning the decks free of soot and coal dust. Steam propulsion, used but little in the late Crimean War, was being given its first major wartime employment, and it would alter the whole technique of blockade and blockade-running. Marines paced the gangways on sentry duty; some seamen were mending spare sails or moving stores below. Every half-hour a man struck the bell and the pace and direction of activity changed. The sailing-master, busy over the ship's reckoning, halted at times to direct a check of her rigging and sailing gear; the warrant officers, surgeons, sailmakers, and gunners, were intent on their respective duties; the boatswains used their silver whistles, rattan canes, and thunderous voices to pass along orders and maintain discipline. Engineers and stokers below decks were ready with instant steam should the moment of action come. For most blockaders it was still an age of double power—sails for everyday usage and steam when

2. Howe, Caleb, *The Supplies for the Confederate Army*, Boston, 1904, 23ff.

needed. Over all this the captain held sway, or when he was busy below decks, the first lieutenant, both men hawkeyed and sleepless. Every member of the crew had his ship-number, hammock-number, mess-number, and assigned station in battle. Each had to jump to duty on the instant, lest he dislocate the fixity and discipline essential in that tight-packed little world.

It was seldom a heroically exciting duty. It was usually laborious, monotonous, and dull, though blended with a full measure of routine dangers and miseries. Ship-duty had as many accidents—falls, drownings, explosions—as land-duty, and as much illness. A long period of hot weather gave the crew dysentery, despite the surgeons' precautions. Water pumped from the tanks to the butts on deck began to smell abominably. The bread became full of the little gray bugs called weevils. The "salt-horse" or pickled beef grew intolerable. If the ship moved toward shore, snipers' bullets, steel-billed mosquitoes, and sand-flies could be pestiferous. When she steamed out to sea and met a gale, mountain billows would roar as they dashed past; life-ropes had to be rigged at nightfall to prevent men from being carried overboard by deluges sweeping the decks; seamen would watch apprehensively as masses of scud swept wildly over the sky, the wind furiously tearing and twisting it about. To reach the foretop and maintop sails was hard, dangerous work. Unless pains were taken, unless the clew lines were manned and hauled taut, the sail might be slatted to pieces. And yet, with the thermometer a few degrees above freezing and the decks too wet to sit upon, the sailor might find that, with a tarpaulin wrapped about the weather rigging for shelter and an extra jacket, a station in the tops was the least uncomfortable place on the vessel.

But boredom was the worst trial on the big warships, and worse still on the smaller cruisers. Seamen, hungry for action, envied the men of Shiloh and Chancellorsville. The sight of a suspicious craft, an island excursion, a fight in the crew —any break was welcome. If only a ship could be captured, with resulting prize-money; if only the roving *Alabama* would suddenly appear to begin a bloody encounter!

On the other side lay the blockade-runner, matching wits against the warship. The *Banshee*, for example, more than two hundred feet long, only twenty feet in the beam, with mere poles for masts and no yards, boats lowered to rail level, painted the dull white or bluish gray that was hardest to see on a moonless night, had only 220-tons displacement but she boasted deep holds and powerful engines. Here was excitement enough! One Briton who repeatedly ran into blockaded Wilmington tells us that tiger-hunting, wild-boar sticking, and the riskiest steeplechases never compared with it. Not a spark must be seen. The engine-room hatchways had to be cloaked with tarpaulin, the binnacle covered until the compass was almost invisible, and all hands kept below. The ship crept stealthily through the darkness to reach the blockading line; slipped by, close past the cruisers; pointed her prow to the low shore identified by a white line of surf; and at the critical moment put on all steam to swoop over the bar just as the Union gunboats opened fire. Fort Fisher awakened to return the shots, its flashing guns sending shells to keep the gunboats out of range. Soon, if they were lucky, the officers quaffed welcoming champagne ashore.[3] Blockade-running at its best seemed more intoxicating than the wine. A veteran "runner" wrote:

I recall my first day under fire, the trembling knees, the terrifying scream of the approaching shells, the dread of instant death. Again, the notable storm at sea in which our ship was buffeted and lashed by the waves until the straining steel plates cut the rivets and the fireroom was flooded and the engines stopped, while the tempest tossed us helpless upon the mountainous waves, and all hope of our lives was gone, until we were mercifully cast upon a reef which extends about three miles from Bermuda. . . .

And again:

Amidst almost impenetrable darkness, without lightship or beacon, the narrow and closely watched inlet was felt for with a deep-sea lead as a blind man feels his way along a familiar path, and even when the enemy's fire was raking the wheel-house, the faithful pilot, with steady hand and iron nerve, safely steered the little fugitive of the sea to her desired haven. . . . he could get his bearings on the darkest night by a taste of the land . . ."

Another runner wrote:

The men who ran the blockade had to be men who could stand fire without returning it. It was a business in which every man took his life in his hands, and he so understood it. An ordinarily brave man had no business on a blockade-runner. He who made a success of it was obliged to have the cunning of a fox, the patience of a Job, and the bravery of a Spartan warrior. . . ."[4]

A world of adventurous stories could be told by the men of Fort Fisher and the blockade-runners who gained the protection of its Southern commander, Colonel William Lamb. The British speculators acclaimed his services by giving him a battery of six Whitworth guns. Mrs. Lamb lived through one memorable experience after another: the drowning of the famous spy Rose O'Neal Greenhow and the recovery of her body; the rescue of the Canadian plotter James P. Holcombe, half-dead; the battles over blockade-runners driven ashore; the narrow escapes of dozens of vessels and capture of dozens more; the execution of desert-

3. Taylor, Thomas E., *Running the Blockade: A Personal Narrative of Adventures, Risks and Escapes During the American Civil War*, London, 1896, Chs. III, IV.
4. Sprunt, James, *Cape Fear Chronicles*, Raleigh, N.C., 1914, 350, 354, 387.

ers, the onslaught of yellow fever—this was but half of it.[5] When a Confederate agent in Egypt sent Jefferson Davis a valuable Arabian steed, it almost caused the loss of the *Banshee* by neighing loudly when it first smelled land. Another time a pet game-cock suddenly crowed. One unlucky blockade-runner, the *Stormy Petrel*, anchored safely behind Fort Fisher only to settle down on a discarded anchor as the tide went out, with such grave damage that she became a total wreck.

But emphasis on adventurous incident blurs the fact that only hard planning, hard ship-design, hard dirty work, and bold acceptance of wounds and death made blockade-running the peril to the North that it was. When picket-boats poured shot into the *Chameleon* off Charleston, and a boarding party captured the *Ella and Annie* after a collision, men lost their lives. Thousands of hours of drudgery were put into the blueprints of ship designs, machine-shop work, and study of navigational charts, for every half-hour of excitement. The labors of Federal blockading service were still grimmer. At Charleston, for example, winter storms of great severity were common, and ships that could not gain an offing in time were usually driven ashore. The bar here was especially difficult; the channel was narrow with shoaling sides, while the current swept across it diagonally. Small wonder that the blockading fleet was often in trouble. Incessant vigilance was demanded both in the extreme heat of summer and fierce tempests of winter. The picket-boat service here was especially hazardous. Heavy launches full of men were swept in by wind and current to fall under the guns of Sumter or be lost in the surf above the bar; once, four boats were swamped at one time and their personnel left floundering in the sea.[6] It was off Charleston that the monitor *Weehawken* sank with two dozen of her crew. No shot touched her; a strong ebb-tide washed down an open hawse-pipe and hatch, and she simply disappeared.[7]

As we have stated, the notion, long held by some Southerners and many historians, that President Davis could have exported enough cotton in 1861 to Europe to provide a solid basis for the Confederate economy and finances, was for several reasons untenable.[8] To begin with, after the right and proper proclamation of neutrality by Great Britain, no ships adequate for such ocean-transportation were available. In the second place, the South had no warships to break the blockade that Lincoln at once instituted. And finally, this blockade soon became sufficiently effective to balk any large-scale attempt at exportation, making it certain that under the best of circumstances most of the cotton shipped would end in Northern prize-courts. The Southern editor, J.D.B. DeBow, proposed

5. See files of Wilmington *Messenger*, 1863-65.
6. Wait, Horatio I., "The Blockading Service," *Military Essays and Recollections*, Illinois Commandery Loyal Legion, Chicago, 1891, II, 211-252.
7. *Civil War Naval Chronology*, Part III, Philadelphia, 1907, 161.
8. W.E. Dodd enunciated this idea in his *Jefferson Davis*.

early in the war that the Confederate Government obtain control of at least a million bales of cotton, bought with paper, and establish a central office in Montgomery to "arrange, order, and organize" its use in trade.[9] But how to get it to market? And without a market, what use did it have? British cotton-mills at the end of 1860 were four months behind their supply, despite the impetus supplied by high profits for both owners and workers. The Southern crops of 1860 had broken records, and with storm clouds thickening, the planters were in a hurry to sell. One authority tells us that the market was so glutted that many mills actually shut down in 1861, and prices were at a standstill. Britain had bought some 1,650,000 bales just before the war began. By the end of the fiscal year ending August 31, 1861, an estimated 3,127,568 bales had been exported to England and the Continent. By the end of 1861, however, the blockade was more effective, and a pinch was on, but at least at the start of the war considerable cotton was exported and not hoarded.[10]

In answer to the postwar criticisms that Davis had been responsible for holding cotton and had refused to use it to create a sound Confederate financial system, the Southern President quoted a letter of his Secretary of the Treasury, C. G. Memminger, to the editor of the Charleston *News and Courier* on March 27, 1874: "The Confederate Government was organized in February, 1861. The blockade was instituted in May, thus leaving a period of three months in which the whole cotton crop on hand, say 4 million bales, ought, according to this military financier, to have been got into the hands of the Confederate government, and to have been shipped abroad. This would have required a fleet of four thousand ships, allowing one thousand bales to the ship! Where would these vessels have been procured in the face of the notification of the blockade? And was not as much of the cotton shipped by private enterprise as could have been shipped by the government? When so shipped, the proceeds of the sale were in most cases sold to the government in the shape of bills of exchange. . . ." Davis also quoted G.A. Trenholm in the same paper that, of the 1860-61 cotton crop, some 3 million bales had been received at Southern seaports by February 29, 1861. ". . . the great bulk of it had been exported to Europe or sold to the New England spinners. By the 1st of May, 586,000 bales more had been received and sold. England and the Continent took 3,127,000 bales; the New England spinners 650,000. It will thus be seen that before the new government was fairly organized the entire crop was already beyond its reach! Another crop followed, but the exportation in any quantity was an absolute impossibility. . . ."[11]

The first ship to run the blockade wholly on Confederate Government account was the *Fingal*, a Clyde-built steamer with the high speed of thirteen knots,

9. DeBow to C.G. Memminger, January 2, 1862, DeBow Papers, Duke Univ.; Russell, William Howard, *My Diary North and South*, New York, 1863, 52.
10. Scherer, James A.B., *Cotton as a World Power*, New York, 1916, 264.
11. Davis, Jefferson, "Lord Wolseley's Mistakes," *The North American Review*, Oct. 1889, 481-482.

armed with rifled steel guns. The heavy cargo of Enfield rifles, ammunition, and other war materials that she brought into Savannah in the fall of 1861 sent a thrill of elation through the South, and won the Confederate representative in charge of the voyage, J.D. Bulloch, salvoes of applause. The significant fact, however, was that the *Fingal* found it impossible to return. After vainly trying for months to slip out through the blockading cordon with a cargo of cotton, she gave up the attempt. The Confederates transformed her into an ironclad-ram, re-named the *Atlanta;* but when she tried to gain the open sea she was ingloriously disabled and captured.[12]

By the close of 1862, when Gideon Welles had built the Union Navy to a strength of 427 ships, with 28,000 seamen and 3,268 guns, the entire Southern coast was held in an increasingly effective grip. The Navy had captured 390 blockade-runners during the first eleven months of the year, 153 of them between late April and early December, 1861. It and the land forces had taken or closed one strategic port after another: New Orleans, Norfolk, Roanoke Island, Savannah (sealed by the capture of Fort Pulaski), Fernandina, St. Augustine, and New Bern. In addition, new Federal bases had been established such as that at Hilton Head north of Savannah, which enabled the blockaders to be coaled and supplied. The only important ports still open—Wilmington, Charleston, Mobile, Galveston, and Brownsville—were patrolled with partial success by blockaders.[13] Secretary Welles boasted that in no previous war in history had the harbors of an enemy been so largely closed by naval activity. Blockade had played a rôle in the Revolution, the Tripolitan War, the War of 1812, and finally the Mexican War, when it had cut off from the Mexicans munitions and other supplies that they vitally needed. Never, however, had it been half so important as now. Its strength, moreover, was steadily growing. By December, 1864, the Navy had 671 vessels, mustering almost 5,000 guns, and about 471 of these ships were in blockade-service.[14]

At first, Washington had supposed that a small naval force at each of eight or ten points on the Atlantic and Gulf coasts, with the supplementary squadrons steaming up and down, would suffice. It quickly found this idea fallacious. Although the United States was not a party to the Declaration of Paris, it had to accept the rules that the other maritime powers had there laid down. "Blockades, to be binding, must be effective . . ." For reasons both national and international,

12. Bulloch, James D., *The Secret Service of the Confederate States in Europe,* New York, 1959, Vol. I, 110-128.

13. Galveston was recaptured by Magruder from the Union on New Year's Day, 1863. For 1861 Navy figures see Welles report, *Congressional Globe,* 37th Cong., 2nd Sess., Appendix, 19.

14. *Annual Report,* Sec. Navy, 1864, House Executive Document No. 1, Vol. VI, 38th Cong., 2d Sess., *passim.* For 1862 Navy figures see Welles report, *Congressional Globe,* 37th Cong., 3rd Sess., 1862-1863, Appendix, 11-16. Also *Congressional Globe,* 38th Cong., 2nd Sess., 1864-1865, Appendix, 9; and 39th Cong., 1st Sess., Appendix, 20.

the paper blockade of the first few months had to be developed into a blockade by real ships and real guns. The North Atlantic blockading squadron under Goldsborough and its auxiliaries covered the coast from Chesapeake Bay to South Carolina; the South Atlantic squadron under Dupont extended the line past South Carolina, Georgia, and Florida; and two Gulf squadrons, the eastern command being held in 1862 on Key West, and the Western command at Pensacola where Farragut took charge in February, 1862, carried it to the Rio Grande. When Appomattox came, a total of some 1,500 blockade-runners had been captured or destroyed. This figure might not seem significant, for many were still in business. But the fact that cotton exports to Britain and European countries, which in 1861 had soared to about 3½ million bales out of a total production of over 4½ million bales, dropped to a mere 132,000 bales exported in 1862, and 168,000 bales in 1863, was very significant indeed.[15]

The important questions with respect to the ocean blockade were two. Was it effective in terms of international law? Was it effective in economic and commercial terms? In other words, did it meet the general requirements of the other Powers since the Declaration of Paris? And did it meet the general requirement of the Northern public that it contribute heavily to Confederate collapse? The first question was really academic. No blockade could be totally effective, and this was more effective than most predecessors, for Britain and France could have held it ineffective and hence invalid only if they had been willing to go to war. Great Britain was never ready to do this. As for the second question, it must be given a clear affirmative. As the sea blockade, new to the U.S. Navy of that day, grew from early weakness to giant strength, it did accomplish its purpose of slowly strangling and weakening the Confederacy. Pace and energy might be questioned, but not the result. Because of the blockade, thousands of foreign-flag merchantmen did not sail, and those that did ran greater and greater risks.

[II]

Nobody knew better than the Confederates themselves that, by and large, the sea blockade was economically effective. To be sure, blockade-running continued till the very end of the conflict. When the surrender came, no fewer than 150 such vessels were still afloat, but 1,500 had been taken.[16] Perhaps 2,000 would be a reasonable guess as to the total number of blockade-running vessels. The great change in their character took place in the first half of 1862, when what might be called the regular blockade-runners began to emerge on the seas. These were built

15. Hammond, M.B., *The Cotton Industry,* New York, 1897, Appendix I; Owsley, Frank L., *King Cotton Diplomacy,* Chicago, 1931, new edition, 1959, disputes Hammond's export figures, 253-265.

16. Owsley, Frank L., *King Cotton Diplomacy,* Chicago, 1931, 285, 286. (New edition, Chicago, 1959, 262).

for business return, specializing in speed rather than size of cargo, for as prices of goods shipped rose, profits were glittering. It paid to operate fast, slippery vessels, which in large part glided quietly out of hidden wharves near the blockaded ports of Nassau, Hamilton, or Havana. Nassau especially profited from a huge increase in commerce. It was hard to halt such a sly, well-concealed traffic, especially by any resort to negotiations and court action when complete and convincing evidence was lacking. Matamoros, next door to Texan markets, and ostensibly neutral, was an extra tough nut to crack, for technically neutral harbors were outside the blockade. Even New Yorkers plunged their fingers into the money to be made from the flow of contraband to the Confederacy. The South detailed troops and even field artillery to help the ships make harbor.

A few large fortunes were made by some lucky men, and smaller fortunes by a great many. Likewise, there were those who lost heavily. George A. Trenholm of Charleston owned a number of blockade-runners that made successful trips to and from Bermuda early in the war. His light-draught steamer *Herald*, for example, on which Matthew Fontaine Maury made one trip, is said to have taken aboard, in eighteen voyages, $3,000,000 worth of cotton.[17] The *Robert E. Lee* was reported to have carried out $2,000,000 worth in twenty-one ventures. Successful early voyages encouraged Richmond to go into the business to shore up the government finances, and the government had some fourteen vessels built, or building, in England, six of which made one or more trips. The Tredegar Works yielded to the combined influences of patriotism and profit-hunting, and engaged in the trade, but with ultimate loss.[18]

Indeed, successes early in the struggle were followed by increasing numbers of failures later.[19] While the subject must always be shrouded in doubt, our best evidence suggests that in 1861 one blockade-runner in ten was captured; in 1862 one in eight; in 1863 and 1864 one in three; and in 1865, one in two.[20] The later figures were ruinous. Moreover, the biggest steamers were the most easily cap-

17. Morgan, James M., *Recollections of a Rebel Reefer*, London, 1918, 98ff.

18. Knox, Dudley W., *A History of the U.S. Navy*, New York, 1936, 277; Bulloch, James D., *The Secret Service of the Confederate States in Europe*, London, 1883, New York, 1959, II, 239, 242-243.

19. The subject is supplied with interesting additional material by James M. Merrill in "Notes on the Yankee Blockade of the South Atlantic Seaboard, 1861-1865," *Civil War History*, Vol. IV, No. 4, Dec. 1958, 387-397.

20. Owsley's figures with supplemental data, *King Cotton Diplomacy*, 1959 ed., 261-262. Confederate Assistant Secretary of State William M. Browne informed Captain M.F. Maury on April 21, 1862, that customs records recorded that 792 vessels had entered at, or cleared from ports of the Confederate states during the first year of war. If this is anywhere near accurate, it shows that even in its first months the Federal blockade had great effect. For, one survey indicates that about 2,000 vessels entered or cleared Confederate ports in the year from June, 1860 to June, 1861. During entirely peaceful years the figure was even higher. *O.R.N.*, II, Vol. III, 397; Survey of Southern shipping compiled by E.B. Long for notes for Bruce Catton's *Centennial History of the Civil War*, LC and E.B. Long Collection, Univ. of Wyoming.

tured; the small sailing vessels and other light craft that slipped into little-used creeks and inlets accomplished little. One naval authority, J.R. Soley, remarks that until near the end of the war, the captures took only a small margin from the enormous profits netted by shipowners. If this is so, it is not because the successful voyages took very much cargo in or out; it is because the profits on what they took were so egregiously high. A merchant who carried 800 or 1,200 bales of cotton to Europe might make $30,000 over costs, and if he brought back arms, ammunition, salt, and medicines he might double that gain. But a thousand bales of cotton and a hundred bags of salt represented only infinitesimal amounts of international trade, a tiny fraction of what the South needed.[21]

Did blockade-running, as it continued into 1863-65, really assist the Confederate cause? Many people believed that it was damaging, both economically and morally. Too many luxuries—silks, velvets, wines, jewels, watches—were brought in and sold for gold that the government needed. Too much cargo-space was given for superfluities, when drugs, surgical instruments, and machinery were urgently needed. Women wearing dresses made of unbleached cotton-sheeting, dyed with sumach leaves or walnut hulls, gazed grimly at imported Paris gowns; families drinking a decoction of raspberry leaves looked chidingly on cups of Mocha coffee and Ceylon tea. When President Davis noted, as one instance of profiteering, the fact that some cotton that had cost sixpence a pound in the Confederacy was sold at four times that sum in England, people asked why the Confederacy should not impound such margins. In the spring of 1863, the Georgia legislature asked Congress to take direct control of blockade-running for its own benefit.[22] Belatedly, Congress did pass regulatory legislation, approved February 6, 1864, so that the great Southern staples, cotton, tobacco, sugar, naval stores, rice, and molasses, might be exported only under a permit signed by the President, while no articles might be imported except those of necessity and common use. "No more watered silks and satins," trumpeted the Richmond *Examiner*, "no more Yankee and European gewgaws; nothing but Confederate sackcloth!"[23]

Sterner decrees followed. The government almost immediately required all privately controlled blockade-runners to give half their cargo space to the nation at a low charge, while allowing those who gave up two-thirds of their space a somewhat higher return. Any States which held absolute ownership of an entire vessel could employ it as their governments pleased. But as such ownership was seldom practicable, various States joined lustily in the chorus of protest that arose

21. Soley, James R., *The Blockade and the Cruisers*, New York, 1883, 1885, 165-166.
22. Extra Session of 1863, cited by Coulter, E. Merton, *The Confederate States of America, 1861-1865*, Baton Rouge, 1950, 291.
23. Feb. 13, 1864; quoted by Coulter, *Ibid.*

from individual merchants and skippers. The fact was that for some time the coastal States had competed with the Confederacy for chartered space on promising blockade-runners, and one object of the new regulations was to halt this rivalry. The uproar from Georgia, Mississippi, and the two Carolinas compelled Congress to pass a bill that would largely have nullified the new controls. President Davis vetoed it with unanswerable arguments. If the seaboard States claimed special privileges in shipping room, he pointed out, the inland States with no access to blockade-runners would take wrathful measures.

The new regulations thus remained in force. Under the law, two men were appointed with powers that largely controlled foreign trade: Thomas L. Bayne to oversee cotton-purchasing east of the Mississippi; and Colin J. McRae to have charge of the sale of Southern staples in Europe and the purchase of arms there. The new policy was highly successful. President Davis reported that at the end of 1864 the new system had kept the volume of foreign trade intact, had enabled the government to distribute more supplies than formerly, and had put into the Treasury profits that had formerly lined private pockets. But the measures had been taken too late. If the Confederacy could have seized complete control of its railroads, its shipping, and its internal and external commerce early in the war, its position might have been much stronger. The desperation of its struggle might have justified such resolute action, but any such move was impossible in the Confederacy, as it was a matter of principle, and would not have been tolerated earlier, even if tried.

The amount of greed and corruption that attended the business of blockade-running was about what might have been anticipated, and involved not only Southerners and Britons, but some grasping Yankees. When Gazaway B. Lamar, a pre-war smuggler of Africans into the South, headed a company that vigorously operated four steamers, and along with Fraser and Co. of Charleston, and Fraser, Trenholm of Liverpool reported lucrative returns, it is no wonder that some Northerners watched these traders enviously! The contraband commerce had all the attractions of gambling for high stakes. It was reported that fifty vessels left Havana within one three-month period; that in 1864 six ships steamed out of Bermuda within twenty-four hours for Wilmington; and that a half-dozen more sometimes left Nassau in a single night for Charleston or other ports.[24] The stocks of some blockade-running corporations, Southern or British, rose to mountain heights—even $6,000 a share! James Morris Morgan sketched a lurid picture of blockade-runners in Bermuda as he visited the port of St. George during the war:[25]

24. Wait, H.I., *Military Essays and Recollections, op.cit.,* 222-225.
25. Morgan, James Morris, *Recollections of a Rebel Reefer,* Boston, 1917, 101.

Their business was risky and the penalty of being caught was severe; they were a reckless lot, and believed in eating, drinking, and being merry, for fear that they would die on the morrow and might miss something. Their orgies reminded me of the stories of the way the pirates in the West Indies spent their time when in their secret havens. The men who commanded many of these blockade-runners had probably never before in their lives received more than fifty to seventy-five dollars a month for their services; now they received ten thousand dollars in gold for a round trip, besides being allowed cargo space to take into the Confederacy, for their own account, goods which could be sold at a fabulous price, and also to bring out a limited number of bales of cotton worth a dollar a pound. In Bermuda these men seemed to suffer from a chronic thirst which could only be assuaged by champagne, and one of their amusements was to sit in the windows with bags of shillings and throw handfuls of the coins to a crowd of loafing negroes in the street to see them scramble. It is a singular fact that five years after the war not one of these men had a dollar to bless himself with. Another singular fact was that it was not always the speedier craft that were most successful. The *Kate* (named after Mrs. William Trenholm) ran through the blockading fleets sixty times and she could not steam faster than seven or eight knots. That was the record; next to her came the *Herald*.

A closely held South Carolina concern reported selling one of its shares as late as the summer of 1864 for $28,600.[26] More than half the ships and cargoes tried in the New York prize-court were British, but the British name too often concealed Northern interests.[27] Some Yankees were as ready to evade trading-with-the-enemy laws as their fathers had been in 1812. Northern goods, their labels altered to flaunt famous English names, passed through Boston or New York on long roundabout trips, Boston-Bermuda-Wilmington, or New York-Nassau-Mobile, and sometimes were even shipped with bold directness to Charleston or Matamoros.[28]

At its height, the New York trade with Bermuda, Nassau, and Havana was scandalously large. A "ring" of dealers, shippers, and blockade-runners helped organize the traffic and made arrangements with the Custom House for shipments. The extent of the ring's operations, according to the New York *Tribune* early in 1864, could be measured by the fact that about 5,000 Custom House bonds had then been executed. Collector Hiram Barney, a man of integrity, administered the regulations laid down by joint action of the Treasury and State Departments with strictness and wisdom, but the honesty of some subordinates

26. Coulter, E.M., *Confederate States, op.cit.*, 288-290.

27. Robinton, M.T., *An Introduction to Papers of the New York Prize Court, 1861-1865*, New York, 1945, 1ff.

28. Bradlee, F.B.C., *Blockade Running During the Civil War*, Salem, Mass., 1925, 64, 112; Thompson, S.B., *Confederate Purchasing Operations Abroad*, Chapel Hill, 1935, *passim*.

was open to question.[29] In the autumn of 1864, information was given Naval Officer William E. Dennison that blockade-runners had been heard to boast of the ease with which they could clear outward-bound goods through the Custom House. Several men swore that one employee, a son of H.B. Stanton the noted Abolitionist orator, had taken bribes, and he and his father were dismissed. Another officer, who had gone as surety on bonds, was thrown into Fort Lafayette by General John A. Dix.[30]

Morgan Dix, writing in a biography of his father, stated that New York trade with the South "had become a doubtful element in the problems of the day . . . an active, energetic and numerous party was there, capable, in a favorable emergency, of offering open resistance to the Federal authorities; men known to be in sympathy with the Confederates, and suspected of holding treasonable correspondence with them, were domiciled in it. Trade with the blockaded ports was carried on to a considerable extent; traffic and communication by letter and personal intercourse between residents in that city and inhabitants of the insurgent states were constant. . . ."[31] Yet Dix had pressed Washington hard to allow vessels to pass the blockade and open trade with Norfolk in late 1862, after it had been taken by Federals. Welles opposed this so strongly that, as he put it, "it became necessary the President should issue an order. . . ." On Nov. 12, 1862, Lincoln did issue an order for shipping into Norfolk for "military necessities" under approval of the Commandant of the area, John A. Dix, who had headquarters at Fortress Monroe.[32]

In the South some earnest leaders, impatient for the benefits the Confederacy might gain from an exchange of cotton for supplies, resented the restrictions placed upon contraband trade by President Davis and others. So did many traders. C.C. Clay, Jr., informed Secretary Memminger in the spring of 1864 that certain gentlemen of large capital had authorized him to buy a hundred thousand bales of government cotton, if it could be shipped to Mobile within six months under a guarantee by Richmond that it would not be destroyed and might be freely exported. Benjamin had already assured T.C. De Leon that he was sure the authorities would cheerfully sanction the export of cotton on government account if it were done in such a way as to "ensure us against the enemy's reaping profit from the operation." This was a large condition, and the diarist R.G. Kean thought the responsible executives altogether too

29. He was editorially praised in the New York *Tribune*'s article, "Custom House Frauds," January 14, 1864.

30. N.Y *Tribune*, January 14, 15, 1864; no evidence existed against the elder Stanton.

31. Dix, Morgan, *Memoirs of John Adams Dix*, New York, 1883, II, 72.

32. Welles, *Diary*, I, 165, 183; Lincoln, *Works*, V, 495-496.

33. Clay, C.C., to Memminger, April 25, 1864, De Leon Papers, South Caroliniana Library, Univ. of S.C.

exacting. He angrily complained that, when the War Department drew up a set of regulations for the cotton trade and sent them to Davis, they came back so tightened as to make the business impossible. "There are earmarks which show Benjamin's hand, as is usually the case when mischief has been done in the granite building."[34]

Yet Southern officials concerned with efforts to evade or break the sea blockade were in general entirely honest.[35] On the Union side, meanwhile, the conduct of the Navy Department under Gideon Welles and Gustavus V. Fox, and of all the naval officers, was not only above reproach, but marked by exemplary efficiency, honesty, and energy. Indeed, their management of the great work in hand may be termed one of the most praiseworthy parts of the Union war effort. British leaders later declared that they deemed the blockade and its ever more rigid enforcement the greatest single feat of the conflict. Never before had so extensive a line of coast been brought under blockade; never had ports so difficult been so effectively sealed. Never before had a steam-navy so large been kept at sea for such long periods, distant from provisions, general supplies, coal, and even water. Never, even in British history, had naval power, speed, and vigilance been displayed on so large a scale.

It is impossible to state with accuracy the statistical result of the Southern efforts to penetrate or evade this sea-wall. Only rough estimates of the imports in various categories can be ventured. Those given by two historians who, though diligent in research and shrewd in judgment, tended to overrate Southern achievement, are as valid as any. They thought that 600,000 small arms might have come through by sea during the war, 400,000 blankets, and great quantities of clothing.[36] In little more than a year, November 1863 to December 1864, some 550,000 pairs of shoes were imported. During November and December, 1864, some 8,500,000 pounds of cured meat, 500,000 pounds of coffee, and 1,500,000 pounds of lead arrived. Such supplies helped the Confederacy to sustain the struggle as long as it did. Yet the flow of goods had diminished even as the need for them grew more urgent. J.T. Soutter of London had written Lamar on August 10, 1863: "We must have the raising of the siege of Charleston before they will think blockade-running a good business for the future. People here look upon the fall of Charleston and Mobile as certain, and hence we find few willing to talk of running risks with their money in any such scheme as blockade-running." L.C.

34. Kean, *Diary*, University of Virginia, March 13, 1864, "Inside the Confederate Government," 144; Benjamin to DeLeon, March 16, 1864, De Leon Papers, South Caroliniana Library, Univ. of S.C.

35. Exceptions were found chiefly among financial agents abroad. The trader Lamar wrote his father from London, Oct. 18, 1863, that Confederate agents in Europe were a dishonest lot, that swindling in cotton-secured notes and bonds went on steadily, and that "Captain Bulloch is the only one whose name is untarnished," *Captured Letters* in N.Y. *Tribune*, Jan. 16, 1864.

36. Owsley, *King Cotton Diplomacy*, new ed., 266; Cf. Coulter, *Confederate States*, 295.

Bowers, active in the trade, had written from Liverpool, October 2, 1863: "I see the blockade-runners to Mobile have nearly all been caught."[37]

Lord Wolseley later wrote: "I have often pondered over the effect upon the future of the United States that a refusal on the part of Mr. Lincoln to hand us back Messrs. Mason and Slidell would have had. In my opinion, as a student of war, the Confederates must have won had the blockade of the Southern ports been removed by us, as it would have been at once if the North had been ruled by a flashy politician instead of the very able and far-seeing Mr. Abraham Lincoln. It was the blockade of your ports that killed the Southern Confederacy, not the action of the Northern armies."[38]

Even the Southern scholar who labors hardest to find weaknesses in the barrier admits that the Navy laid down a blockade which, for two years at least, made the old-fashioned English blockade of Napoleonic Europe look like a rickety wooden fence.[39]

[III]

Not the ocean blockade, or the land blockade, the manpower shortage, economic weaknesses, or even military conquest, can be singled out as the one most important cause of Confederate impotence. All must be considered, along with the geographical facts of life that made a siege by the North possible. Each one of them has striking features of historical significance. But probably the land side of the "prison" was hardest to maintain, and was fullest of loopholes, yet sufficiently effective in economic terms to have a slow and halting, and in the end decisive result. No attentive reader of that grimly true story, *A Blockaded Family in Alabama During the Civil War,* by Parthenia Antoinette Hague, can doubt, as he turns the pages describing the homespun garments, the parched-corn coffee, the lard candles, the huckleberry-leaf tea, the willow-plaited furniture, the half-empty tables, the general shortages and substitutes in the deep South, that the blockade struck staggering blows upon the Southern economy and morale. Worse than those of the emaciated and ragged at home were the hard deprivations of the soldiers. Miss Hague writes: "My brothers wrote home (without murmur or discontent) that they were living the greater part of the time on parched corn, which they bought or begged; that they were foraging around in the country, on the mountainsides, and in the valleys, for succulent roots, leaves, and berries to allay the pangs of hunger; sassafras bushes were stripped in a trice of leaves, twigs, and bark, and eaten ravenously. They wrote that sometimes for

37. In the captured Lamar Letters, N.Y. *Tribune*, Jan. 16, 1864.
38. McKim, Randolph H., *A Soldier's Recollection, Leaves from the Diary of a Young Confederate,* New York, 1910, 258; letter of Lord Wolseley to Rev. R.H. McKim, Nov. 12, 1903.
39. Owsley, *op.cit.,* 267.

two or three months they never saw so much as a slice of bacon, and then perhaps for a week or two a rasher of bacon the size of a pocket-knife would be issued to each man of their regiment. One of my brothers once drew from his pocket, when asked about his slice of bacon, the pocket-knife which he brought home after the war was over, and said: 'It is a fact; the rasher of bacon was no longer, and about just as thick and wide as this knife.' Such a slice they held over the fire with bread underneath to catch the drippings, so as to lose none. A brother-in-law of mine told me that he, as well as other soldiers of his division, lived on parched corn most of the time; sometimes they had roasting ears, either roasted in the ashes or eaten raw; that if they had money, they would buy the corn; if not, beg it; and at times they would be so crazed with hunger that if neither money nor begging would get it, they would steal it. At first the men were punished for stealing something to eat, but at last the sight of our hollow-eyed and ragged, emaciated soldiers appealed so to the sympathies of the officers that they could not find it in their hearts to punish their men for trying to keep soul and body together with pilfered corn. Times were almost as hard with citizens all over the South the last year of the war, as with our soldiers. Corn was twelve and thirteen dollars per bushel, and our government's pay to its soldiers was only eleven dollars per month; so one whole month's wages would not quite buy a bushel of corn. . . ."[40]

As the Northern armies pressed southward, they carried stern but often confusing restrictions upon trade. Secretary Chase, their author, declared it his policy, as it was Lincoln's,[41] to relax them as fast as was possible without excessive risk of strengthening the hostile forces of the South. Furthermore, there was the immediate built-in difficulty of deciding what was legal, illegal, or extra-legal trade. It was seldom clear, perhaps in the cases of some trades on purpose.

The difficulties were tremendous. Huge quantities of cotton remained in the South, its owners almost desperate to find markets for it. Sales of cotton were often the last barrier between them and utter penury, the final defense against rags and starvation for their families. At the same time, the Yankee cotton-hunger was fierce and insatiable. In certain Southern areas farmers rallied with muskets and pitchforks to halt the cotton-burning that the government at first decreed, while Negroes wept to watch the crop they had toiled so hard to gather mount in black columns of smoke to the skies. Planters realized that the destruction was equivalent to burning the clothes they might have put on their wives' backs, and

40. Hague, Parthenia Antoinette, *A Blockaded Family in Alabama During the Civil War*, Boston, 1888, 133-135.
41. For Lincoln's position see Thos. H. O'Connor, "Lincoln and the Cotton Trade," *Civil War History*, Vol. VII, No. 1, Mar. 1961, 20-35, which lays emphasis upon the President's combination of subtlety and flexibility.

the bread intended for their children's mouths. Meanwhile, workers in the New England mills saw in cotton their one bulwark against bankruptcy and the almshouse.

The problem was one of human need and hope on both sides of the Atlantic; the cotton-chopper bent under the burning Southern sun, the lean loom-tender in the Lancashire factory—and the rifleman standing between them. When late in the war Kirby-Smith proposed to burn all the cotton stored on the Ouachita in Louisiana, the most statesman-like of Southern governors, Henry W. Allen, was vehemently opposed. He knew that while east of the Mississippi the State was under Union occupation, west of the river the people were starving. With the energy that had marked his life since, as a boy of seventeen, he had run away from his Missouri college to study law, he set to work. He gathered together cotton and sugar, exported them to Mexico, and there exchanged them for the mixed goods that Louisiana needed: machinery, cotton and wool-cards, textiles, medicines, and salt. He barred luxuries, and established State stores for the sale of the commodities at fair prices. It was as absurd to burn cotton, he said, as to destroy breadstuffs, meat, livestock, or furniture, and the policy would simply impoverish the people. "If their cotton, their only remaining resource, is destroyed by you," he wrote Kirby-Smith, "they must, in the event of invasion, starve or beg from the enemy and receive Yankee rations at the cost of the oath of allegiance to Lincoln. Will you reduce them to this extremity?"[42]

The imperative reasons for allowing some wartime trade in cotton, as the armies moved into the areas full of it, were thus three, in addition to the pressure for profits. The needs of the North for the staple had to be met; the anxious foreign situation demanded some alleviation of the Anglo-French pressure, while humanitarian considerations required that destitute people be allowed to exchange some cotton for necessities.[43] Secretary Chase declared in 1861 that the best policy was to let commerce follow the flag.[44] This axiom, properly defined, was followed. When Union forces carried the flag into a district, rules were laid down by the Treasury by which the people might trade with the North under Army and Treasury supervision in everything compatible with military safety. The ensuing difficulties seldom sprang from the rules, which so far as Washington was concerned, were clear, severe, and unbending, but often, in practice seemed confusing, contradictory and vague. They arose instead from the inability of certain commanders to gather the proper kind of subordinate personnel. The

42. Dorsey, Sarah A., *Recollections of Henry Watkins Allen*, New York, 1866, 280-284.

43. Roberts, A. Sellew, "The Federal Government and Confederate Cotton," *American Historical Review*, Vol. XXXII, No. 2, Jan., 1927.

44. Schuckers, J.W., *The Life and Public Services of Salmon Portland Chase*, New York, 1874, 319, May 29, 1861.

John Adams Dix, Union General

—author of the famous words: "If any man dare pull down the American flag, shoot him on the spot!"

juxtaposition of large and loosely held supplies of staples over a tremendous area and along fluctuating front lines, with a voracious demand provided with large quantities of money, required a guardian body of Spartan vigilance and honesty. Such a body could not be created by Washington fiat or military command.

The question arises at once: just how firm a land blockade did the Federal government really wish to impose? No question existed as to the sea blockade, but ashore the situation was much different. Lincoln and the Administration had to face a complicated and constantly changing set of conditions. And, as was his habit in many situations, Lincoln seems to have been extremely flexible with respect to trade. At times, the President's own issuance of trade-permits and passes complicated the problem for those in the field. It seems clear that he favored as a war measure the restoration of trade in an occupied or supposedly conquered area as soon as possible. As for extra-legal or illegal trade with the overt enemy, that was a different matter. However, the nature of the war was such that legal and illegal traffic often became so tangled that no one could separate them.[45]

In December, 1864, Lincoln wrote E.R.S. Canby that his policy was "not merely a concession to private interest and pecuniary greed." The President went on: "By the external blockade, the price is made certainly six times as great as it was. And yet the enemy gets through at least one-sixth part as much in a given period, say a year, as if there were no blockade, and receives as much for it as he would for a full crop in time of peace. . . . You know how this keeps up his armies at home, and procures supplies from abroad. For other reasons we cannot give up the blockade, and hence it becomes immensely important to us to get the cotton away from him. Better give him *guns* for it, than let him, as now, get both guns and ammunition for it. . . . Our finances are greatly involved in the matter. . . . And if pecuniary greed can be made to aid us in such effort, let us be thankful that so much good can be got out of pecuniary greed. . . ."[46]

It should be noted that Lincoln opened trade at seaports very rapidly. Port Royal, S.C. was taken in November, 1861; New Orleans in late April, 1862; and Beaufort, N.C. in late April, 1862. With great promptness, Lincoln, on May 12, 1862, relaxed the blockade of all these ports.[47] He opened trade at Norfolk, over the objections of Gideon Welles, who thought the city would become a hive of contraband traffic.[48] Brownsville, Texas, was occupied November 6, 1863, and the following February Lincoln proclaimed trade open with such specific exceptions as arms and other articles which might aid the enemy.[49] He told Congress late

45. For a good summary of Lincoln's rôle, see O'Connor, Thomas H., "Lincoln and the Cotton Trade," *Civil War History*, Vol. VII, No. 1, March, 1961, 20-35.
46. Lincoln, *Works*, VIII, 163-165.
47. Lincoln, *Works*, V, 210, 211.
48. Lincoln, *Works*, V, 495-496; VI, 479.
49. Lincoln, *Works*, VII, 192-193.

in 1864: "It is hoped that foreign merchants will now consider whether it is not safer and more profitable to themselves, as well as just to the United States, to resort to these and other open ports, than it is to pursue, through many hazards, and at vast cost, a contraband trade with other ports which are closed, if not by actual military occupation, at least by a lawful and effective blockade."[50] Two days after Appomattox, Lincoln, however, listed a number of ports as still closed. In this, as in all policies, he was flexible rather than rigid.[51] After all, it had not been until August 16, 1861, after passage of a law by Congress, that he had issued his proclamation against all commercial intercourse, although he had declared the sea blockade on April 19.[52]

From Lincoln's actions and Chase's statements, it seems that he agreed with Chase's policy of permitting trade to "follow the flag" as much as possible.[53] In December, 1862, Chase's annual report reiterated that Treasury regulations authorized trade only in sections of the country where "the authority of the Government has been reestablished by military occupation."[54] But the question of the meaning of the word "occupation" remained adjustable. By the end of 1863, Chase admitted that the duty of regulating commercial intercourse "has been found exceedingly arduous and perplexing. . . ." His first major set of trade regulations of 1863 had been proven so defective that it had to be revised. "The subject is too vast and complicated, the appetite for trade is too eager and exacting, and the impatience of all restraint, however salutary and necessary is too great," he wrote, "to allow any hope of avoiding many and sometimes just complaints. . . ."[55] Congress had passed the necessary acts, but their application remained vexatious.

Once the lower Mississippi Valley lay open, two generals of unbending integrity and strict canons of discipline did their utmost to see that proper rules were enforced—Grant and Sherman. They had no patience with the laxity and corruption that spread about them. By the autumn of 1862 a brisk traffic, half-furtive and half-open, had sprung up, not only in occupied areas but where Union troops faced Confederate troops. Scores of officers intent upon commercial deals, and a much greater number of merchants anxious to trade in cotton, tobacco, and general merchandise flocked down, first to Memphis, then to Little Rock and Helena, and finally to Vicksburg. Every branch of business had its agents, eager to obtain permits from the Treasury and the Army. "I was not long in learning that Grant abominated cotton buyers as a class," declared the war-correspondent Cadwallader. "In private conversations to the end of the war, he always spoke of

50. Lincoln, *Works*, VIII, 140.
51. *Ibid.*, VIII, 396.
52. *O.R.*, III, I, 417-418.
53. *Report of the Joint Committee on the Conduct of the War*, Pt.3, 1863, 562-563, Chase to William P. Mellen.
54. *Congressional Globe*, 37th Cong., 3rd Sess., Appendix 27-28.
55. *Congressional Globe*, 38th Cong., 1st Sess., Appendix, 9-10.

them as a gang of thieves."[56] He did his best to thwart their activities, and if given full authority would probably have forbidden all sales, purchases, and exchanges, but Lincoln and Chase took a wider and more statesmanlike view.

Sherman was equally uncompromising in his antagonism toward commercial activity. When he first moved against Vicksburg, he forbade all trading in cotton, and in his later campaigning in Georgia he restricted purchases to the minimum needed to afford farmers and planters imperative supplies of food and clothing.[57] While moving upon Atlanta and later upon Savannah, he was able to hold some of the predatory elements in check, but in the Mississippi Valley this was impossible. As Lincoln crisply put it: "The army itself is diverted from fighting the rebels to speculating in cotton." Rear Admiral Porter said of the Treasury agents sent down by Chase to control the situation: "A greater pack of knaves never went unhung." Yet his own gunboat crews were equally unscrupulous, one Senator later declaring that they had made a hundred millions during the war. Charles A. Dana wrote: "Every soldier dreams of adding a bale of cotton to his monthly pay." And David Perry of the Fifth Illinois Cavalry, son of a mayor of Bloomington, Illinois, made a yet graver charge.

"Many lives have been sacrificed during the past summer and fall," he informed his father as the year 1862 ended, "that certain high officers might make their fortunes with cotton-trade, and many a poor darkey who had fled to us has been traded off, by officers holding high positions in the army and before the world, for cotton. The truth is, when an impartial history of this war shall be written, it will expose a greater amount of fraud and corruption than the world has ever before seen. Even your Bloomington general, Hovey, traded Negroes for cotton and sacrificed many lives . . . for the sole purpose of making money."[58]

No man-made laws are so inexorable as laws of economics. Hydraulic forces become uncontrollable when pent within permeable dams; the demands of the market are irresistible when vast quantities of goods and tens of millions of dollars are kept apart only by weak bureaucrats and loose Army commands. This fact was evident long before the end of 1862. The capture of Island Number Ten on the Mississippi early in April pried open the gates to the cotton land in the great valley; the seizing of Memphis early in June flung the portals wide. By autumn, a correspondent of the New York *Tribune* was asserting flatly: "One of the causes of the want of discipline, energy, and military power in the Army of the Southwest is the mania for cotton speculation which has seized upon the officers of the Army, from generals down to quartermasters and lieutenants."[59] The story was

56. See Cadwallader, S.C., *Three Years with Grant*, ed. Benjamin P. Thomas, New York, 1955, 22-23.
57. Roberts, A.S., "The Federal Government and Confederate Cotton," *op.cit.*, 263-264.
58. December 29, 1862; Palmer Collection, Western Reserve Historical Society; Dana, Charles A., *Recollections of the Civil War*, New York, 1898, 18; Lincoln, *Works*, VI, 307.
59. "C" writing from the Steamboat *Gladiator*, Helena, Arkansas, October 1, 1862; N.Y *Tribune*, October 13.

the same wherever the Army moved in cotton districts, at all dates, and in all commands. The situation was best under officers as conscientious as Grant, Sherman, and Washburne, but even Grant had unfortunate friends like "Russ" (Joseph Russell) Jones; while his father Jesse Grant was willing to dabble in the trade, and even Sherman and Washburne had to make repugnant concessions.

When General McPherson was at Corinth in the summer of 1862, he had found the corruption appalling. He wrote the equally conscientious Col. L.B. Parsons, who did so much to organize steamboat services on the Mississippi, that he had been compelled to rebuild ten bridges east of Tuscumbia within a fortnight, and that his greatest difficulty was to find good men. "Sutlers and cotton dealers have been trying to bribe everyone on the road almost, and I have been doing my best to stop it . . . the trouble is to catch them."[60] It was the same situation on the Arkansas River after the capture of Helena that angered a *Tribune* correspondent. The town was full of civilian speculators working in connivance with military officers. As cotton could be bought all along the Arkansas for $25-$50 a bale, or seized for nothing, and then resold in St. Louis for $250, steamboats under government contract were being sent out ostensibly on military errands, but really to grab cotton, bearing Army detachments to take it and Army wagons to haul it, while nine dollars in ten went to enrich the illicit partnership of traders and colonels. Loyal Union planters saw their cotton pounced upon by greedy officers who waved papers, talked of the violation of obscure military orders, and shipped the crop away with almost no concealment of the fact of private interest.

Indications exist that the Tennessee River remained a principal artery of the traffic by which Northern supplies were half-openly, half-secretly exchanged for Southern cotton down to the very end of 1864. R.B. Hunt of Jackson, Tennessee, wrote the notorious Confederate trader W.A. Violette of Mobile on January 26, 1865: "The parties north informed me last evening by special messenger that they could deliver at once via Tennessee River one hundred thousand dollars' worth of supplies. The authority is from the very highest source in Federal power with an order from all military commanders to give every facility to the execution of the permit, which amounts in all to the value of twelve thousand bales of cotton."[61] Hunt was anxious that Major L. Mims of Mississippi, who controlled this type of trade, should give firm assurances that as soon as the supplies were delivered he would send the cotton forward. All this is a little vague, but clearly points to a large semi-official exchange.

The ebullient "Russ" Jones of Chicago, close friend both of Grant and Elihu Washburne, made no secret of his activities. He wrote Congressman Washburne at the beginning of 1863, from Holly Springs, Mississippi, that Grant had treated

60. McPherson to Parsons, August 13, 1862, Parsons Papers, Ill. State Hist. Lib.
61. N.Y. *Tribune;* T.C. DeLeon Papers, South Caroliniana Library, Univ. of S.C.

him very kindly. He hoped the army would push farther south, "as I want to get as far into the enemy's country as possible. If we get out safely with what cotton we have bought, I shall clear four or five thousand for my share. . . . If Grant goes south I shall try it again, but there is not enough between here and Columbus or Memphis to make it an object. Foraging teams have to go eight to ten miles for corn and fodder. Planters cannot haul their cotton as their teams have all been gobbled up."[62] The dealers with whom he was operating were pressing him hard for money they had advanced, and were dissatisfied by his results. "If we could have gone to Granada and Jackson and kept the road clear to Memphis or Columbus, I could have cleared $50,000 by spring—but such is life."[63]

Joseph Russell Jones may be taken as more or less a typical case. Even if, so far as can be determined his activities seem legal for the most part, his grandson wrote that Jones had "his eye always on the main chance. . . ."[64] Jones, armed with the proper passes, made two or three trips south in the winter of 1862-1863. As far as we can ascertain, Jones made about $7,500 in two trips.[65] He apparently was able to leave his post as U.S. Marshal in Chicago without jeopardy. Jones even wrote Lincoln of a plan to set up centers of intercourse properly guarded by the army. He suggested the Federals agree not to further invade the interior except in cases of hostility. This would encourage planting and trade, and discourage a renewal of fighting.[66] Jones's adventures in the South show that cotton-trading was not really an easy way to make a killing. Once one bought cotton, it had to be brought out. There was a constant struggle over permits and whether certain areas might be traded in or not.

Jones, former Galena businessman and Republican politician, continued to serve in his patronage post of Marshal. In 1869 he was named Minister to Belgium by Grant, and was very active in Republican politics and Chicago street railroads. At one time he managed some property and investments for Grant.[67]

[IV]

Memphis, immediately after its capture, became a boom-town, the center of the cotton-trade in a long stretch of the Mississippi Valley. At the beginning of the war it had ranked sixth among the trade centers of the Confederacy, proudly wearing the name of "Charleston of the West." After Sumter, all the staples once

62. January 6, 1863; Washburne Papers, LC.
63. *Ibid.*
64. Jones, George R., *Joseph Russell Jones*, Chicago, 1964, 29, and interviews with George R. Jones.
65. *Ibid.* ,31.
66. Holly Springs, Miss., Jan. 7, 1863, Joseph Russell Jones Papers, Chicago Historical Society; also Robert Todd Lincoln Papers, LC.
67. For biographical summary see George Jones, *Joseph Russell Jones*, and Wilson, James Harrison, *Joseph Russell Jones*, typescript of ms., courtesy of George R. Jones, *passim.*

shipped overseas—thousands of bales of cotton, of barrels of molasses, and of boxes of sugar—had been piled up in mounds on the bluff overlooking the city. If left there, they would have been a rich quarry for the Union forces. After Shiloh, Beauregard ordered the bales burned and the barrels emptied on the ground. The advent of the Union flag at first elated many residents. They hoped they could resume their allegiance, restore their commerce, and restock their shops with the necessities of life. Instead, an anomalous situation soon revealed itself. Although the stars-and-stripes floated above public buildings, Memphis stood in a no-man's-land. While Union gunboats patrolled the river and Union cavalry trotted through the streets, a vast terrain inland was traversed by Confederate detachments and rebel guerrillas. Grant, taking command in June, 1862, thought he saw "great disloyalty" among the citizens. Undoubtedly he did, and many disloyal people were eager to smuggle whatever Northern goods they could get to Southern relatives, friends, and soldiers. The stream of Unionist refugees, from Kentucky, middle Tennessee, northern Alabama, and elsewhere, plus the invasions of Northern opportunists, made the situation worse.[68]

The Northern traders who flocked into Memphis brought shipments of salt, flour, coffee, and cloth, selling them at first furtively, but as soon as Sherman took command (July 21) and laid down explicit rules, quite openly. Although Sherman strictly forbade the sale of arms, allowed salt and salt-meat to be retailed only in limited quantities under special permit, and rationed the disposal of drugs and medicines, he soon favored the free entry of other commodities, arguing that as Treasury officials thought it wise to encourage cotton-buying and allow trade, he must not interpose any obstacle.[69] As farmers and planters from inland counties filled the shopping streets, Sherman was pleased to learn that in their sales of cotton they preferred Tennessee banknotes to the new greenbacks. The old commercial channels were being restored. Clearly, some of the trading by such small dealers was quite legal, and in fact healthful for the economy.

Grant tightened his regulations in the autumn of 1862, and again in December, special permits being required for all traders. The new restrictions, however, did nothing to improve the situation. Abuse of the oath of allegiance increased; so did corrupt connections between traders and Army officers; so did smuggling and bribery. A large body of permit-bearing intermediaries or "contact men" emerged, charging high commissions for their services. Charles A. Dana wrote Secretary Stanton: "The mania for sudden fortunes made in cotton, raging in a vast population of Jews and Yankees scattered throughout this whole country, and in this town almost exceeding the regular residents . . .

68. Parks, Joseph H., "A Confederate Trade Center Under Federal Occupation; Memphis, 1862 to 1865," *Journal of Southern History*, Vol. VII, No. 3, Aug., 1941, 289-314.
69. Sherman, *Memoirs*, I, 265-268; *O.R.*, I, xvii, Pt.i, 140-141, 158, 619-20, 868; *OR*, III, ii, Pt.2, 349.

has corrupted and demoralized the army."[70] As matters grew worse, Secretary Chase, in the spring of 1863, ordered all Memphis-bound goods halted at Cairo, and when Lincoln revoked by proclamation all previous trading privileges, and specified districts where they might be restored, Memphis was pointedly omitted.

The opening of the full length of the Mississippi by the capture of Vicksburg and Port Hudson augmented the illicit traffic from all river towns into the Confederacy. Any person who established his loyal status by oath, and got the requisite permits, might use them after the beginning of September, 1863, to trade in almost anything, and in any quantity. A flood of commodities, both legal and contraband, poured into Memphis from the North and immediately poured out again to happy holders of cotton. General Hurlbut, himself probably corrupt and certainly drunken, explained to his superiors the impossibility of imposing controls. "A perpetual flood of fraud, false swearing, and contraband goods runs through the city," he wrote, "—guided and managed by designing men—I am surrounded by hostile forces regular and guerrilla, and they are fed and supplied from Memphis."[71] Even the pickets were bribed. When military restrictions were tightened to stop trade in everything but necessities like food and fuel, evasion remained easy. The wide, sinuous Mississippi, its shores and islands densely wooded, its sloughs ideal for small craft, invited boats sagging with valuable cargoes to slip from the Memphis waterfront nightly, drop down to a convenient base, and spend several weeks in a cruise, getting replenishments from smaller boats.

[V]

It was natural for overworked guardians of the law to lay blame for the prevalent lawlessness at the doors of special groups. Treasury agents were really no more culpable than Army officers, and old cotton-brokers no worse than Chicago commision-men; Yankees and foreigners could be equally unscrupulous. But when Grant issued his sweeping order of December 17, 1862, expelling from the department "the Jews as a class," he was simply expressing the same prejudice that had led Sherman a little earlier to complain of the "swarms of Jews,"

70. Dana to Stanton, Memphis, January 21, 1863, Stanton Papers, LC.
71. Parks, "Confederate Trade Center," *ut supra;* Lyman Trumbull Papers, LC., Joseph Medill, to Trumbull, July 13, 1861: "An awful blunder has been committed in the appointment of Hurlbut Brigadier General. His habits of intemperance wholly unfit him for so high a command. He has been in the city for a week now *drunk every day*—will the Senate inflict this confirmed sot upon the army?" O.H. Browning from Senate Chamber, Washington, July 18, 1861, to Hurlbut, letter in Stephenson County Hist. Soc., Freeport, Ill., courtesy of Gerhard Paul Clausius, is much the same, but more hopeful. Also see Belvidere, Ill. *Daily Review,* May 14, 1909. Various pieces of evidence tend to indicate that Hurlbut was possibly corrupt, though he naturally denied it. See Papers of G.P. Clausius, Belvidere, Ill., private collection.

and condemn "the Jews and speculators here trading in cotton."[72] An instant outcry came from Jewish citizens. The B'nai B'rith of St. Louis passed a resolution of protest and sent it to Attorney-General Bates; Cesar Kaskel of Paducah hurried to Washington and saw Lincoln; and Halleck, on January 4, 1863, peremptorily revoked Grant's order. It seems clear enough that Grant himself was the author, and that it would not have been withdrawn had Kaskel not organized a vigorous protest against it. Some Jewish traders had been troublesome, and may have made mischievous efforts to enlist men possessing influence with Grant. He would quickly react against such efforts—although he never again showed any special animus against Jews. Conventionally, then as later, some men used the word "Jew" loosely to refer to a class or kind of men, not to a race. Sherman's castigations of Israelites had no more validity than D.D. Porter's attacks upon "thievish Illinois lawyers," and those unrivalled "Scamps," the Federal marshals.[73]

On the day of the order, Grant wrote C.P. Wolcott, Assistant Secretary of War, a letter that deserves attention. "I have long since believed that in spite of all the vigilance that can be infused into post commanders, the special regulations of the Treasury Department have been violated, and that mostly by Jews and other unprincipled traders...." Here is indication that Grant lumped "Jews" and traders together. He went on, "So well satisfied have I been of this that I instructed the commanding officer at Columbus to refuse all permits to Jews to come South, and I have frequently had them expelled from the department, but they come in with their carpet sacks in spite of all that can be done to prevent it.... The Jews seem to be a privileged class that can travel everywhere.... If not permitted to buy cotton themselves, they will act as agents for someone else. ... There is but one way I know of to reach this case; that is, for Government to buy all the cotton at a fixed rate and send it to Cairo, Saint Louis, or some other point to be sold. Then all traders (they are a curse to the army) might be expelled...."[74]

It is possible that the unfortunate involvement of Grant's elderly father, Jesse Grant, with a trade permit to transport cotton through the lines on his last visit to the Army, caused General Grant to change his mind on the issuance of such permits—for the order expelling all Jews from the department was issued immediately after the discovery of Jesse Grant's embarrassing conduct.[75]

The demoralizations of the cotton-trade were as deeply felt by the Confeder-

72. Grant's order, dated December 17, 1862, *O.R.*, I, XVII, Pt.2, 424; Sherman's letter of July 30, Rawlins Papers, Chicago Hist. Soc.

73. Korn, Bertram W., *American Jewry and the Civil War*, Philadelphia, 1951, offers a careful exploration, 121ff.

74. *O.R.*, I, Vol. XVII, Pt. 2, 421-422.

75. McCartney, Clarence E., *Grant and His Generals*, New York, 1953, 306.

ate forces as by the Union troops. In the spring of 1864, officers of the State of Mississippi informed President Davis that in the wake of Sherman's raid against Meridian, many citizens of Hinds County had carried on active exchanges with the enemy. They were anxious to complete their transactions before the Confederate cavalry returned. Twenty-three wagonloads of cotton were hauled through the streets of Jackson in one day. Women in nearby towns, their men at the front and their children hungry, rode over the countryside collecting cotton to be traded to the Yankees for miscellaneous supplies. Men with access to Confederate government cotton were meanwhile stealing it, removing official marks, and selling it to Northerners in Vicksburg and other places.[76] The Confederate agent for the purchase or impressment of cotton in Louisiana wrote his superiors that most of the growers around Alexandria held to their cotton with deathlike grip, hiding it and refusing to confess its existence; yet all the while men equipped with Union permits were slipping it out to Northern buyers. One boatload of two hundred or more bales had just been sent away by stealth.[77]

And in Louisiana, where rival forces had swept back and forth across great areas, Governor Henry W. Allen was outraged not only by the corruption attending the traffic across the lines, but by the class discriminations involved. Most of the cotton in western Louisiana that the Confederate Government wished to destroy, he wrote, was the property of small farmers who had nothing else left. The big planters had sold their holdings at high prices to the enemy; a good deal of Confederate government cotton had gone with it. Allen thought it had been wise of the Confederacy to trade it for army supplies. But were not poor farmers justified in selling a few bales for food?[78]

As the coastal blockade grew tighter and let in less and less material, the land blockade had to hold lengthening lines, became looser and more careless, and unquestionably admitted an increasing body of supplies. The land blockade ran from the Kentucky and Missouri boundaries to the Gulf. One of its weakest segments was long the New Orleans area. The capture of this great port had at once involved the inland trade in cotton. Ben Butler, who had held command in 1862, believed in generous trade policies, and one recipient of his generosity was his brother, Andrew Jackson Butler. Andrew remained an active trader as late as January 24, 1864, when he wrote Ben that he had drawn $274,683 for nearly 900 hogsheads of tobacco shipped to New York. The operations of both the Butlers became highly complicated, involving enforcement of the Confiscation Acts of Congress, registration of the property of persons taking the oath of allegiance, orders for the sequestration of property in rebel-controlled areas, and large sales

76. Wharton, T.J., Jackson, Miss., to Jefferson Davis, April 16, 1864, Davis Papers, Duke University.
77. Letterbook of T.D. Miller, CSA Agent, 1864, 1865, LSU Archives.
78. Dorsey, Allen, *op.cit.*, 280-284.

of goods of all kinds. When military expeditions were sent out ostensibly for the chastisement of guerrillas, but with cotton also in view, and shallow-draft steamers began to scour the bayous with the same objectives, the situation became still more tangled.

An impartial investigation and report being needed, Chase's special agent, George S. Denison, who for a time was acting Collector of the Port of New Orleans, provided them. He found that a great deal of contraband material was being shipped to the Confederates in return for cotton, and that military men of high rank who lent their cooperation were reaping large harvests. It was clear, he wrote Chase, that Ben Butler "knows everything, controls everything, and should be held responsible for everything."[79] This was an inadequate statement of the situation. Butler held occupational control of a restricted area where trade was funneled through New Orleans. It seems clear that he knew much about the trading activities that went on around his post of duty, but he had much less complete information and a less rigid sense of responsibility than Grant and Sherman had and used in their areas of command. When the New York *Herald* was reporting that the talk of New Orleans hotels was "cotton, cotton, cotton," and General Richard Taylor was declaring that cotton made more rascals on both sides than anything else, Ben Butler was no more responsible for every nefarious act than Grant or Sherman.[80] His character was of course more questionable, but the charges against him and his brother were vague, and his efficiency and energy were unquestionable. Common report said that the brother had pocketed well over a million dollars between the capture of the city and the end of 1862. Ben Butler denied this, asserting that his brother's profits, all in legitimate trade, amounted to less than two hundred thousand.[81] Denison admitted that while Ben had for a time tolerated speculators in an unfortunate way, he had allowed nothing objectionable since he had received a set of strict regulations from Chase at the end of August, and he added an unequivocal tribute to the General: "He is a man not to be spared from his country's service."

Many well-informed Union officers would have questioned this and Denison's further statement: "Ben Butler has more brains and energy than any other three men in New Orleans."[82] For his record was a clouded one, and he had helped his brother Andrew make money. Andrew also had a rather equivocal record; for example, he had taken control of an abandoned plantation, hired freedmen, demonstrated they could work efficiently, and made a thousand barrels of sugar. But unfortunately, great quantities of salt, among other commodities, had also

79. Chase, Salmon P., "Diary and Correspondence of Salmon P. Chase," *Annual Report of the American Historical Association*, 1902, Vol. II, 320-328.

80. Harrington, Fred H., *Fighting Politician: Major-General N.P. Banks*, Philadelphia, 1948, 135.

81. Denison to Chase, November 14, 1862, in Chase, "Diary and Correspondence," *op.cit.*, 329-333.

82. *Ibid.*, 327.

meanwhile been shipped to the rebels across Lake Pontchartrain along with medicines and other contraband.

On the Red River in the spring of 1864, the carnival of trade and speculation reached its height for a single campaign. It produced such a mass of controversial evidence, cross currents, personal denunciations and insinuations that it could never be straightened out. General Banks, who also had to carry the ignominy of defeat, suffered censure by Admiral Porter and the Navy among others; Porter and the Navy were blamed by the Army and others; Lincoln and Chase came in for their share of criticism owing to charges of loose control over permits, rules and regulations; and the traders themselves did not escape. At the same time, one must not forget the Confederates and local residents of uncertain political affiliation who had their part in the affair as well.[83]

Some attempts seem to have been made, particularly by the Joint Committee on the Conduct of the War, to discredit N.P. Banks and whitewash Porter. A good deal of evidence exists that the Navy exerted every effort to profit by this, its first major chance at trading. Much of what Navy officers seized in the way of cotton was lost through the courts, and much of it undoubtedly was C.S.A. cotton, open to anyone for seizure. On the other hand, the Navy seems to have ranged pretty far from water in some of its cotton transactions. President Lincoln needlessly permitted his office to complicate matters through a somewhat indiscriminate issuance of permits which could not be ignored by the military. Apparently the Navy did not make any real bargain with high Confederate commanders. As for the rôle of the Army, Banks, while in many ways inept in the military phases of this expedition, does not seem to have been personally involved in cotton operations. Reports that "hordes" of speculators accompanied the Army seem exaggerated, but a good many did appear. Undoubtedly some Army officers were involved. Although it is a matter of indefinite opinion, one can surmise that the Army was perhaps less culpable on the Red River than elsewhere.

Early in February, 1864, Banks in New Orleans wrote Lincoln of the increase in questionable trade and the pressures on him: ". . . the profits of an illicit commercial intercourse are so gigantic that it is almost impossible to prevent the subornation of subordinate officers. . . ."[84] Banks testified that, immediately after the start of the Red River expedition, Porter and the Navy "began to capture cotton on both sides of the river. Marines were furnished with a wagon-train, and during the whole of that time they were passing out our lines and returning with loads of cotton . . ." General Banks, supported by other and even stronger

83. Best secondary summary is Johnson, Ludwell H., *Red River Campaign*, Baltimore, 1958; there is a vast amount of primary material in *Report of the Joint Committee on the Conduct of the War*, "Red River Expedition," Vol. II, 1865 Ser., Washington, 1865. This latter is subject to the usual political bias that is inherent in all the Committee's reports.

84. *O.R.*, III, Vol. IV, 68-70.

testimony from Army officers, told of Navy officers boasting about their prize-money. He properly felt he had no authority to take remedial action. Respecting his own activities in the South, he said, "Every dollar's worth of property that was captured by the army was taken down to New Orleans in government vessels, in charge of the quartermaster's department, and turned over to the treasury agent. There was not a dollar's worth of property taken by any individual, or on any private account whatever...."[85] He did write that cotton was taken by the Army on the retreat, with receipts given, to prevent it being appropriated to support rebellion, this cotton then being turned over to the Treasury agents. Often cotton was burned or otherwise destroyed if necessary. From Banks and the other witnesses it clearly appears that as far as cotton goes, the Army's role was very small. Yet, nearly all Army witnesses were bitter against the Navy, perhaps feeling some jealousy because they could not shelter their gains behind any prize law arrangements.[86]

Captain John S. Crosby, aide to Banks, testified that he saw some men he thought might be speculators, but believed they really had Washington permits. A conspicuous figure was one McKee, a former partner of Butler's brother; and as to the Navy, he wrote: "They seemed to turn their whole attention there to getting cotton. Every available vessel that could carry a bale of cotton was taken for that purpose ..."[87]

Banks had no control over speculators like Samuel L. Casey, a Kentuckian, and other merchants who bore Presidential permits. Whether he intended to or not, Lincoln effectively circumvented control of cotton-trading by the issue of such documents.[88] In addition, there seem to have been other traders with the Army, or hanging around the Army, though certainly not in the numbers some avowed. An Illinoisan named William Butler, for instance, or his agents, was active, with permission to ship given by General Banks.[89]

Officer after officer, in testimony that runs for pages despite sharp questions put by Congressmen, charged that the Navy seized wagons and mules right and left, ranging far into the interior away from the Red River and branding cotton "C.S.A." so that they could with impunity then add "U.S.N."

On the other hand, Admiral David D. Porter gave a flatly contradictory account of his record: "Fortunately, neither my name nor that of any officer

85. *Report of the Joint Committee on the Conduct of the War, op.cit.*, 18-19.
86. *Ibid.*, 34ff.
87. *Ibid.*, 71.
88. Lincoln, *Works*, VII, 62-63, 213-214; Banks Papers, LC, copy of presidential permit for Casey, endorsed by Banks; Johnson, *Red River Campaign, op.cit.*, 71-74; Harrington, Fred Harvey, *Fighting Politician, op.cit.*, 161-162.
89. *O.R.*, I. Vol. XXXIV, Pt. I, 269.

under my command has been connected with cotton, which has led so many men astray from their duties; nor do I think it ever will be. . . ."[90] Porter testified that when his fleet reached Red River, the Confederates began burning cotton, and hence the Navy took charge of what lay along the banks and sent it to Cairo for adjudication, if it was the property of the C.S.A., or gave bonds if it was privately owned. This modest estimate is directly opposed to the Army's story of Navy operations. Porter did admit that "I deemed that I had a right to take all rebel government cotton, or that of persons in arms against the Union. . . ." adding "but I am happy to say that not one instance occurred, after we entered the river, where officers or men failed to respect private rights. . . ."[91] Porter went on to attack the Army, writing: "General Banks had come up in the steamer *Black Hawk*, loaded with cotton speculators, bagging, roping, champagne, and ice. The whole affair was a cotton speculation. . . ."[92] Porter took an innocent, holier-than-thou attitude throughout his testimony. He denied that cotton was seized by the Navy as a prize. "It was seized as government cotton, sent to the courts, without any application on the part of the Navy as a prize at all." But, he added: "Where the courts adjudicated it as prize, that was the end of it. . . ."[93]

Yet, all along Porter had considered cotton seized on the river a lawful Navy prize.[94] He even made a report to Welles from Alexandria, La., March 17, 1864, containing "prize lists. . . ."[95] In several documents he showed conclusively his interest in seeing the cotton considered a naval prize.[96] In the spring of 1865 the Supreme Court ruled that prize-law did not apply to inland seizures.[97] The leading authority on the Red River feels "Porter wholly misrepresented the role of the Navy."[98]

At times, in the aftermath of the Red River campaign, it seems that every participant was misrepresenting everyone else. The only definite certainty is that it was a time of bungling, lying, chicanery, corruption, and unprincipled self-seeking, all to the injury of the war effort.

By the last year of the war, the whole Mississippi Valley from St. Louis to New Orleans was deeply involved in the exchange of mixed commodities for cotton, sugar, molasses, and tobacco. A greedy desire for money seemed pervasive. St. Louis merchants, in sharing this appetite, thought themselves entitled to

90. *Report of Joint Committee on Conduct of the War, op.cit.,* 262–263.
91. *Ibid.,* 263.
92. *Ibid.,* 270.
93. *Ibid.,* 272–273.
94. *O.R.N.,* I, Vol. XXV, 506, 607.
95. *Ibid.,* Vol. XXVI, 180.
96. *Ibid.,* 318, 412.
97. *Ibid.,* 287.
98. Johnson, *op.cit.,* 284–288.

a much larger share of this trade than they got. Two-thirds of the rich river-trade properly belonged to them, they declared; in the middle of the war they were not getting one-half, and what of the future? A Treasury agent, who pointed out to them what large cargoes the St. Louis officials had allowed men to send down the river in violation of law and regulations, told them that they had better not talk in such terms to the troops of Ohio, Indiana, Illinois, and Kentucky, who were fighting to open valley commerce to the entire West.[99] Businessmen of Mayfield, Kentucky, complained to the same special agent that Paducah merchants had better treatment than they did. When Louisville grumbled, the same Treasury agent sent that city a tart reply. Her merchants had shipped all they possessed to the South under the arrangements for Kentucky's neutrality for months after the men of Illinois, Indiana, and Ohio had been forbidden any trade whatever. They should keep quiet, he wrote.[100]

Every navigable stream flowing from the cotton kingdom to the Mississippi, whether from the East or the West, contributed to the traffic. The Yazoo, for example, became a heavy source, and was for a time the principal channel of the trade in northern Mississippi. Union purchasing agents came out regularly from Vicksburg to buy. Planters noted that whenever they were reluctant to trade, Federal troops often came out within a few days to confiscate all available farm produce; and taking the hint, they abated their tendency to haggle. When C.C. Washburn visited Helena on the Mississippi, he was scandalized by the stories he heard there of the corrupt practises permitted by two commanders—namely Samuel Ryan Curtis and Willis Arnold Gorman, particularly the latter. The Chicago *Tribune* published a blistering indictment of Colonel Charles E. Hovey of the Thirty-third Illinois for returning Negroes to their Mississippi masters in exchange for cotton, and for sending out troops in an effort to seize 300 bales near Delta, Mississippi, for his own benefit. All along the valley, it declared editorially, "the spectacle is sickening and aggravating beyond description."[101] Some officers were anxious to prolong the war until they had their share.

J.D.B. DeBow, reporting to Richmond on the Yazoo affairs, declared that trade with the Yankee enemy was universal, for the temptations to fraud were overwhelming. Not a few Mississippians who had sold their cotton to the Confederacy re-sold it to the Union when opportunity offered, salving their consciences by saying they would give the next year's crop to Richmond.[102] As the war neared its end, however, the rigors of the land blockade increased. The public outcry against disorganization and corruption, on both the Confederate and

99. Thomas Heaton to Secretary Chase, July 6, 1863, Special Agents' Reports and Correspondence, National Archives.
100. Letters of Thomas Heaton to Treasury Dept., Aug. 4, Sept. 11, Oct. 3, 1863, *ut supra.*
101. See long news stories, with editorial, Feb. 12, 1863; affidavits included.
102. Smith, Frank E., *The Yazoo*, New York, 1954, 131, 132; De Bow Papers, Duke University.

Union sides, had an effect. Stricter regulations were applied by the Treasury Departments and military authorities. The increasing breakdown of Southern transportation also impeded the exchange of commodities.

In Memphis, for example, belated reforms were effected in the spring of 1864. General C.C. Washburn, succeeding Hurlbut, brought not only probity but sobriety and foresight to his position. He testified to the Joint Committee on the Conduct of the War that: "I believe that permitting trade has been of vast assistance to the rebel armies; that it has had a most demoralizing influence upon our army. . . . I know of many disasters of our arms, which, in my judgment, would never have taken place, had not cotton, sugar and trade in general, invited our arms to places where they should not have gone. . . . The extent of the trade daily passing outside of our lines here, into the enemy's country, is estimated by Brigadier-General Buckland, commanding the district at Memphis, at from $40,000 to $50,000 daily. . . . So long as the lines are kept open, it is not possible to prevent large quantities of such articles from reaching the enemy. . . ."[103] Washburn declared indignantly that since Memphis had been occupied by the Northern forces, it had done more to feed, clothe, and arm the Confederacy than all the blockade runners using the Bahamas. At once, while Grant and Meade were beginning their bloody campaign in Virginia, and Sherman was moving upon Atlanta, Buckland issued a set of drastic new orders. After May 15, nobody could leave the city by water, or enter it by land, without his permit, and no boats except those carrying Union troops would be allowed to halt anywhere on the Mississippi between Cairo and the White River. Any vessel found trading would be seized, and all men of service aboard it would be made prisoners-of-war.

These orders, shutting all cotton peddlers out of Memphis, practically ended the cotton-trade. It was estimated that between twenty and thirty million dollars' worth of goods had flowed through Memphis to the support of the Confederacy. Washburn of course arranged that food, clothing, and other necessaries should be allowed all who would take an oath of loyalty, and he permitted the city's stores to do business (up to $2,000,000-a-month) for this purpose. As storekeepers had to swear that they had never violated any of the former trade regulations, a good many businesses had to close their doors. Among those who opened new shops were many Union soldiers, who were given a preferred position. A little smuggling and speculation continued, but the trade was limited and dull, and profits were small. Like other river towns, Memphis and New Orleans were changing fast. Large numbers of Northerners were coming in—soldiers, administrators, speculators, deserters, cripples—and the Negro population was increasing rapidly. In 1860 only seventeen percent of the population of Memphis and

103. *Report of Joint Committee on Conduct of the War*, 1865, *op. cit.*, Vol. III, Misc., 42.

Shelby County had been black, but in 1870 the total had risen to thirty-nine percent.[104]

Confederates had similar problems in trying to halt the Memphis trade. For example, orders were issued at Canton, Mississippi, September 4, 1863, that "All wagons carrying cotton into the lines of the enemy for trade will be taken and the wagons and teams confiscated. All cotton that can be gotten at by the enemy will be destroyed at once. . . ."[105] In May, 1864, General Polk had to write General Chalmers, "I am informed that cotton is passing freely into Memphis. Give instructions to your commands to capture and confiscate all wagons and teams found to be engaged in this business, and to be vigilant. . . ."[106]

It did not suffice even for perfectly legal traders to purchase cotton; the staple had to be taken North. Some traders had permits to take vessels with them, as Lincoln gave permission on the Red River in 1864; others brought along their own transport without permission, taking the risks involved. Confederates—or at least Southerners—often helped by getting their cotton to a river bank or major center. Once cotton arrived at New Orleans, Memphis, or Nashville, the very adequate Northern rail transportation system took it North. But very often there was no railroad available in the trading area.

Some speculators undoubtedly lost cotton because of transportation difficulties. Grant's friend Jones had problems with getting cotton "out." One main source of help was government cooperation, both by the Treasury agents and the military. For instance, on October 6, 1864, Washington ordered that officers of the Quartermaster's Department, upon application of authorized agents of the Treasury Department, "may furnish transportation, by land or water, for collecting and forwarding to market articles of produce within the insurrectionary States. . . ." This should be done only if it were without prejudice to military service and it had to be approved by the local commander.[107] This made it official, but in fact such a practice had been followed for some time. Much of it was considered legal and an implementation of Treasury Department policy. Undoubtedly, however, though specific cases are hard to prove, there were some shenanigans by quartermasters and transportation officers in some localities, or at least a winking at the business. If the government, its agents, a number of military officers, and a host of traders wanted cotton badly enough, transportation could usually be found.

104. *O.R.*, I, Vol. XXXI, Pt.2, 22, 27-28; *Report of Joint Committee on Conduct of the War,* 1865, Vol. III, Misc., 42. Censuses of 1860, 1870; Capers, Gerald M., *The Biography of a River Town: Memphis, Its Heroic Age,* Chapel Hill, 1939, *passim.*
105. *O.R.*, I, Vol. XXX, Pt.4, 593-594, Maj. G.W. Holt to Brig.-Gen. J.R. Chalmers.
106. *Ibid.*, Vol. XXXIX, Pt.2, 575.
107. *O.R.*, IV, Vol. IV, 755.

[VI]

The center that most stubbornly maintained a large flow of goods into the trans-Mississippi Confederacy until near the very end was an entrepôt of unique character—Matamoros. Its trade, which was largely in British hands, with some scattered Yankee participants, remained especially lucrative until the war had closed, for this squalid little port on Mexican soil, just across the Rio Grande from Brownsville, Texas, was comparatively safe. One cotton dealer who braved the wretched hotels with their myriads of gigantic fleas, their Latin ways, and their torrid food, thought the gains hardly worth the price. As Appomattox approached, he welcomed the prospect of peace. Large fortunes have been made here, he wrote, and rumors of peace have cast such gloom on the money-hunters "that it has perfectly disgusted me to think that Man can become so selfish."[108] Tampico and other smaller places shared in the traffic less than Matamoros.

Early in the war, Brownsville became crowded with a cosmopolitan throng. "We have English, French, Germans, people from the East, all talking business," reported the Brownsville *Flag* in the summer of 1861. "We have Mexicans from the West, an infinite number of Cubans, and a large sprinkling of Confederates from the South."[109] The town was treated as neutral territory, Yankees coming and going more freely than some Confederates went in and out of New York. Early in 1863, Greeley's *Tribune* reported seventy vessels waiting in Matamoros for cotton, of which millions of dollars worth was sold monthly there, and the proceeds invested in arms, ammunition, and all kinds of Army supplies.[110] The amount of cotton available in Texas was very large. The crop of 1860 had amounted to more than 450,000 bales, only limited amounts had been shipped in 1861, and the 1862 and 1863 crops, though diminished by the demand for foodstuffs, were substantial, for prices remained high. In these years tens of thousands of Negroes—some observers believed 100,000 in all—were brought into the State as field workers. The New York *Herald* correspondent in Matamoros in the spring of 1864 believed that 50,000 bales might have run the blockade from Galveston and other Texas Gulf ports, and 250,000 might have been exported by way of Mexico.[111]

Three main routes were available for Texas cotton into Mexico. One ran from East and Southeast Texas through the King Ranch to Brownsville, another from Central Texas to Laredo City, and the third from Central and West Texas by way of Austin and San Antonio to Eagle Pass. The Rio Grande was fordable at many points. Kirby Smith asserts that he bought cotton through his Cotton Bureau at

108. Thomas H. Morris to his wife, Matamoros, Feb. 18, 1865, Morris-Sidley Papers, L.S.U.
109. Brownsville *Flag*, August 1, 1861.
110. New York *Tribune*, editorial, "The Relief of Texas," Feb. 7, 1863.
111. New York *Herald*, June 13, 1864.

three or four cents a pound, and sold it at fifty cents in gold, the staple passing in "constant streams" over the river, or in smaller quantities through Galveston.[112] At times great trains of wagons rolled across the Texas plains in clouds of dust, whips cracking and mules braying. The return shipments of goods into the Confederacy continued almost invaluable until after a secure Mississippi River patrol was established. A special correspondent of the New York *Tribune*, writing from the St. Charles in New Orleans in the early weeks of 1863, reported that Richmond had established regular agencies extending into the interior of Mexico as far as San Luis Potosi, only three hundred miles north of Mexico City, and that the blockade at Matamoros, Tampico, and Vera Cruz was a miserable failure. "The rebels obtain by far the greater portion of their supplies through Texas, by way of the Rio Grande or from the Mexican ports. So long as these sources are available, and they have cotton to pay for powder, lead, blankets, cloth, sugar, coffee, and so on, they will never want for them."[113]

The confusions and tensions of international politics facilitated the trade. As usual the British were among the most active. It was important for the United States to support the Mexican insurgent leader Benito Juarez, who in return for recognition by Washington had agreed to Seward's stipulation that he give the Confederacy neither material nor moral support.[114] When the French established themselves in central Mexico, the shipment of arms and munitions to Matamoros could be represented as vital to the Juarez cause. Some war supplies actually were sent to the Mexican patriots. When Juarez issued decrees forbidding trade with the Confederacy, two of the border states, Tamaulipas and Nuevo Leon, undertook to protect commercial intercourse. Mexican governors were often lax, corrupt, and semi-autonomous. Many Mexicans sympathized with the Confederates and were by no means insensitive to the prospect of dollars and pounds to be obtained from cotton. Defying Juarez, they did what they could to send supplies into the Confederacy.[115]

A law unto himself was Santiago Vidaurri, strong-man governor of Nuevo Leon and Coahuila with considerable power in Tamaulipas, Sonora, and Chihuahua as well. His was almost an independent domain. Juan A. Quintero of Texas was the Confederate emissary to Vidaurri. As he was in charge of his government's trade with northern Mexico and influential with Vidaurri, he carried out his operations well.[116]

112. Holladay, Florence E., "Powers of the C. in C. in Trans-Mississippi Dept.," *Southwestern Historical Quarterly*, Jan. 1918, 279-298.

113. Letter in New York *Tribune*, dated Feb. 2, 1863, by T.B.G.

114. Owsley, *King Cotton Diplomacy, op. cit.*, 88ff.; Rippy, J. Fred, *The United States and Mexico*, New York, 1931, 239ff.

115. *O.R.N.*, II, Vol. III, 116, 117, 308, 316-317, 899-902; Richardson, James D., *Messages and Papers of the Confederacy*, Nashville, 1905, Vol. II, 77-80.

116. Thompson, S.B., *Confederate Purchasing Operations Abroad*, Chapel Hill, N.C., 1935, 104, 107-109; Owsley, *op. cit.*, 112ff.

The British role in the Matamoros trade deserves attention. It came to a head on February 25, 1863, when Acting Lieutenant C.H. Baldwin, commanding the U.S.S. *Vanderbilt,* seized the British ship *Peterhoff* anchored near St. Thomas. Baldwin's superior was Charles Wilkes, "hero" of the *Trent* affair, now commanding the West India Squadron. There appeared to be little question that the *Peterhoff* was one of those vessels carrying British goods into Matamoros destined for the Confederacy. But, was she a *bona fide* blockade runner? Britain was quick to denounce the capture. London claimed that the *Peterhoff* and Matamoros trade did not fall within the limits of the "continuous voyage" doctrine approved by Britain. This doctrine held that contraband going to a belligerent via neutral ports could be seized. But in this case, "continuous voyage," according to the British, did not apply to goods transported overland.[117] Lord Russell wrote to Lord Lyons that "The trade to Matamoros is a perfectly legitimate trade. . . . To pretend that some goods carried to Matamoros may be afterwards transported across the frontier to Texas, does not vitiate the legitimate character of that trade. Nor is it possible to say beforehand that certain goods will be consumed in Mexico, and certain other goods will be carried into the so-called Confederate States. . . ."[118]

In the *Peterhoff* affair, Lord Lyons once more had to speak firmly and wrote: "I have given Mr. Seward verbally a warning from H.M. Government that the impression which prevails in England that the United States are systematically endeavouring by fair means and foul to stop our trade with Matamoros is producing very dangerous effect. . . . I told Mr. Seward that I should regard another questionable seizure anywhere of a British vessel bound to Matamoros as little less than a calamity. . . . Many of the naval officers would like a war with England. . . ."[119] The diplomats saw fit to ignore the fact that before the war the foreign trade to Matamoros and the Mexican coast had been miniscule. The war was the only reason for its present size. Courts later ruled that the trade such as carried on by the *Peterhoff* was legal, and no blockade was violated because the United States could not lawfully blockade the Mexican half of the Rio Grande.[120]

General Banks in New Orleans forwarded to Washington a letter of Franklin Chase, U.S. Consul at Tampico, of December 17, 1863, saying that the banking establishment of England was sustaining what he called the "Texas blockade runners." Despite Chase's protestations, his warnings had not been taken seriously in official quarters. He said there was an arrangement by which a runner would hoist the British flag and upon arrival at Tampico "they are promptly

117. *O.R.N.,* I, Vol. II, 97-98; Welles, *Diary,* I, 266; Duberman, Martin B., *Charles Francis Adams,* New York, 1961, 304.

118. Bernard, Montague, *A Historical Account of the Neutrality of Great Britain During the American Civil War,* London, 1870, 214-316.

119. Newton, Lord, *Lord Lyons, A Record of British Diplomacy,* London, 1913, I, 104-105, Lyons to Admiral Sir A. Milne, Washington, May 11, 1863.

120. Bernard, *op. cit.,* 315.

furnished with a British owner, whose only investment is a stretch of conscience by taking and subscribing to the oath of ownership This traffic so successfully carried on impresses the people of this country with the belief that our Navy is too impotent to enforce a blockade, and that our Government has no control over any of the Southern ports—which emboldens them to give our enemies all the aid and comfort in their power. Hence the power and influence of our Government and its agents are daily losing ground, in this distracted part of the Mexican republic. . . ."[121] Chase desired a naval blockade of Matamoros and Tampico.

Several other ships, such as the *Agnes* and the *Magicienne* were seized by the Navy while engaged in Mexican trade, but it was impossible to make a case stick.[122] Welles wrote to Seward "that the condition of affairs on the Rio Grande and at Matamoros was unsatisfactory. . . ." The Navy Secretary wanted a principle established regarding the right of adjoining nations and added, perhaps with some exaggeration, "Our blockade is rendered in a great degree ineffective because we cannot shut off traffic and mail facilities, or exclude commercial and postal intercourse with the Rebels via the Rio Grande. . . ." He claimed there were one or two hundred vessels off the mouth of the Rio Grande compared with six or eight before the war. The crusty Welles as usual was provoked with Seward for not making the power of the United States felt through diplomatic channels.[123]

General Canby in December, 1864, wrote Halleck from New Orleans that the trade was increasing, particularly from New York and northern ports. "Casks and crates of crockery, freighted with rifle and musket barrels; barrels of codfish, with the small parts of the arms; kegs of powder in barrels of provisions; pistols and percussion caps in boxes of soap and barrels of fruit; clothing, shoes, and other army supplies, with scarcely any attempt at concealment, are constantly being received at Matamoros, and are constantly transferred to the insurgents in Texas. . . ." Canby said that all the moves he had made against such trade had been ineffective.[124]

The most remarkable feature of the great Matamoros loophole in the blockade, however, was the vigorous participation of Northerners in its business. In the course of four years, according to the New Orleans *Times,*[125] the exchange of cotton for supplies brought to the once sleepy port more than 20,000 speculators from all parts of the globe. As rents rose to astronomic levels, while an English-language newspaper was born, and a regular packet line to Havana sprang into life, many eager Yankees pushed forward to dip their hands in the Pactolian stream. The trade with New York merchants was heavy and profitable.

121. N.P. Banks Papers, LC.
122. *O.R.N.,* I, Vol. XVII, 401-403.
123. Welles, *Diary,* I, 334-335, June 18, 1863.
124. *O.R.,* I, Vol. XLI, Pt.4, 805.
125. New Orleans *Times,* June 1, 1865.

Naval reports in 1863 revealed that a shipload of army wagons, essential to the Confederate troops, had been cleared by the New York Custom House for direct shipment to Matamoros.[126] Small arms and medicines came in large quantities. Before the war, New York's trade with the city had been minimal, yet in 1862 twenty-odd ships from New York arrived, in 1863 seventy-two, and during only ten weeks of 1864 thirty-two. After the opening of the Mississippi, New Orleans shared in the trading of supplies for cotton, and her merchants angrily resented regulations that seemed to discriminate against them. New York undoubtedly kept its primacy, however. One firm in particular, declared the *Herald* as peace came, had carried on a tremendous contraband business with Matamoros to the last, and had sometimes netted a fortune from a single voyage to Mexico.[127]

To the very end of the war, after Wilmington had been captured and Memphis brought under effective trade controls, Matamoros remained an open gate in the walls raised about the Confederacy. Some high naval officers believed there was not much use in blockading other Gulf ports unless this gate was slammed tight and locked securely. General Lew Wallace wrote Grant early in 1865 that the commercial activity there exceeded that at Baltimore or New Orleans.[128] Texas sent cotton-trading agents to various border points. Even after Lee's surrender and Lincoln's assassination, the agent in Brownsville was acknowledging the receipt of hundreds of bales from various points.[129] Then came the collapse of the Confederacy—and of the recently thriving port. One hundred and twenty merchantmen, it is reported, left Matamoros without any cargo whatever; shutters were closed upon the brokerage houses and shipping offices; the markets were glutted with all kinds of surplus miscellaneous wares; and grass grew under "For Sale" signs.[130]

Opinions vary as to the value to the whole Confederacy of this Mexican trade. It certainly was lucrative and wide open, and these supplies obviously helped the trans-Mississippi Confederacy. However, a relatively small amount, especially after 1863, seems to have reached east of the Mississippi. Distances were vast, railroads non-existent to any useful extent west of the river, and Federal invasion often interrupted whatever trans-shipping was attempted.

It would be a mistake, however, to emphasize only the trading in the trans-Allegheny region. That it was conducted in the East and along the seaboard is unquestionable, though generally such trade does not receive attention comparable to that given the Mississippi Valley or trans-Mississippi. Throughout the war an irregular flow of mail, drugs, cotton, and persons between North and South

126. Delano, Robert W., "Matamoros, Port for Texas," *Southwestern Historical Quarterly*, Vol. LVIII, April, 1963.
127. New York *Herald*, Sept. 17, 1865.
128. *O.R.*, I, Vol. XLVIII, Pt. I, 1279.
129. Letterbook of Capt. T.J. Lynch, cotton-agent, Brownsville, Texas, Tex. State Hist. Library.
130. Delano, *op. cit.*, 456.

continued in Virginia, and especially out of such growing coastal enclaves as that in North Carolina. In the mountains, and along much of the irregular ocean front, trade was carried on both legal and illegal. It is probable that not much cotton was gathered from the southeast, for the simple reason that the main cotton areas were farther west.

As the war continued, and Federal coastal control increased, so did trade. A Congressional committee heard Dr. John R. Winslow of Baltimore testify that he had visited his family home in North Carolina twice. He stated that early in 1863 a good deal of contraband trade was carried on. He told of twenty or more wagons that left Norfolk (a favorite center for trade with the enemy) at the same time he did, all heavily loaded with merchandise and going straight to the rebel lines. The wagons carried groceries and concentrated lye for making soap. Stores in Norfolk had alleged agreements with Confederates, and even with Federal military authorities. Cotton and tobacco came back in return.[131] Navy Captain Melancthon Smith, writing from off Roanoke Island, June 15, 1864, asserted that the steam-tug *Philadelphia* had been there with permits from General Butler, indorsed by the President, "to trade with loyal citizens in Chowan county." Smith had detained the vessel because its destination was not within Union lines, and "There are many articles on the manifest which would afford comfort to the enemy if not properly distributed. . . ." These included dry-goods, groceries, and fifteen barrels of whisky. Lane, master and owner of the vessel, had $45,000 in "North and South Carolina current funds." Admiral S.P. Lee ruled that the permits of Butler and the President must be respected, but Gideon Welles, on June 24, ordered that Lane be forbidden to trade in Chowan county.[132] Many such instances, varying in degree and detail, were recorded.

Grant's problems with trade did not end when he went East. On February 7, 1865, he complained to Stanton that one A.M. Laws had a steamer partially loaded with sugar and coffee and a Treasury Department permit to bring out 10,000 bales of cotton. Grant declared, "I have positively refused to adopt this mode of feeding the Southern army unless it is the direct order of the President. It is a humiliating fact that speculators have represented the location of cotton at different points in the South and obtained permits to bring it out, covering more than the entire amount of the staple in all the cotton-growing States. . . . It is for our interest now to stop all supplies going into the South between Charleston and the James River. Cotton only comes out on private accounts, except in payment for absolute necessities for the support of the war,"[133] Stanton replied, "The

131. "Trade with Rebellious States," 38th Cong., 2nd Sess., House Report No. 24, 23-24.
132. *Ibid.,* 10-11.
133. *O.R.,* I, Vol. XLVI, Pt.2, 445.

President directs that you will regard all trade-permits, licenses, or privileges of every kind, by whomsoever signed and by whomsoever held, as subject to your authority and approval as commander of the U.S. forces in the field, and such permits as you deem prejudicial to the military service by feeding or supporting the rebel armies or persons in hostility to the Government you may disregard and annul, and if necessary to the public safety seize the property of the traders. In short, the President orders that you, 'as being responsible for military results, must be allowed to be judge and master on the subject of trade with the enemy.' "[134] But, clear as the above ruling seemed to be, the matter was not closed. As the war neared its end in the East, the situation became more and more a problem.

A devious character, "General" James Washington Singleton, ostensibly involved in informal peace "negotiations" with the South, made several trips to Richmond late in the war. His "negotiations" were probably a front, for Singleton was associated with O.H. Browning and James Hughes in a plan to buy Confederate products with greenbacks, bring the goods through the lines with the permission of Lincoln, and sell them in the North at substantial profits.[135] Grant, on March 8, 1865, wired Stanton that the permits of Singleton and Hughes should be revoked, and Singleton be ordered back from Richmond. Federal "friends" in Richmond had reported that tobacco was being exchanged for bacon and Singleton was believed "to be at the bottom of it." Grant continued. "I believe there is a deep-laid plan for making millions, and they will sacrifice every interest of the country to succeed. . . ." Half an hour later, Grant wired further that he had stopped supplies going via Norfolk to the rebels, "but information received shows that large amounts still go by way of the Blackwater. They no doubt go on the Treasury permits heretofore given under the act of Congress regulating trade with States in insurrection. I would respectfully recommend that orders be sent to the Army and Navy everywhere to stop all supplies going to the interior, and annulling all permits for such trade heretofore given."[136] Stanton replied at once that the President's passes and permits were subject to Grant's authority and that he could seize goods and stop trade.[137] The same evening, Lincoln wired Grant that he did not think Singleton and Hughes were in Richmond by any authority, "unless it be from you." But the President did quote his letter to Grant of February 7 pertaining to Singleton: "General Singleton, who bears this, claims that he already has arrangements made, if you consent, to bring a large amount of Southern produce through your lines. For its bearing on our finances I would be glad for this to be done, if it can be without injuriously

134. *Ibid.*
135. For brief biography of Singleton, see *D.A.B.*
136. *O.R.,* I, xlvi, Pt.2, 886.
137. *Ibid.*

disturbing your military operations or supply the enemy. I wish you to be the judge and master on these points. Please see and hear him fully, and decide whether anything, and, if anything, what can be done in the premises. . . ." Now Lincoln authorized Grant to get Singleton and Hughes out of Richmond if he so wished and could. Clearly, despite his denials, Lincoln had given Singleton a permit, subject to Grant's authority.[138] Grant did admit to Stanton that "I recognize the importance of getting out Southern products if it can be done without furnishing anything that will aid in the support of the rebellion. . . ." He did sharply restrict Singleton, and on March 10 suspended operations on Treasury permits in the East except along the eastern coast of North Carolina, South Carolina, and Georgia.[139]

Washington kept emphasizing that trade-permits were subject to control of the military and, as Halleck put it, "in no case must be used as a means of furnishing the enemy with either funds or supplies. . . ."[140] In some instances the military authority did try to control things, but all too often the trade went on anyway. In one case, Brigadier General Joseph R. Hawley at Wilmington, N.C., March 20, 1865, wrote of a contractor named Gibbons who, according to Hawley, tried to bribe him. Gibbons was put in the watch-house. But there probably were other officers who did not always act so; at least it was so rumored.[141]

Again, as in the West, no figures on legal or illegal trade are possible, but certainly it was true that along the Atlantic coast, as the sea blockade tightened, the land control slackened.

[VII]

When the war ended, Northerners who chanced to review the double blockade by land and sea perceived that, although the totals of Southern exports and imports could never be ascertained, the land trade had possibly been the more important. Definite statistics which would permit us to make a clear decision are quite unattainable. One authority, admittedly speculating in part, says that about 900,000 bales of cotton were brought into Boston and New York during the war. Of this amount, 160,000 bales were imported from England, but may have been of Confederate origin. Some 250,000 bales were listed as legal. This still left nearly 400,000 bales unaccounted for, or brought in through illegal, extra-legal, or unreported methods.[142] Several authorities accept the figure of $200,000,000 as the

138. *Ibid.*, 885-886.
139. *Ibid.*, 901-902, 915.
140. *O.R.*, I, xlvii, 775-776, Halleck to Q.A. Gillmore, Mar. 10, 1865.
141. *O.R.*, I, xlvi, Pt.2, 926-928.
142. O'Connor, Thomas H., "Lincoln and the Cotton Trade," *Civil War History*, Vol. VII, No. 1, March, 1961, 32.

amount of goods which got through the sea blockade, but this may well be low.[143] The vast seepage in both directions on the Mississippi and the Rio Grande had lacked the dramatic qualities of the trade by way of Havana, Nassau, the Bahamas, and the long Atlantic voyage. But, longer sustained, less easily controlled, and operating through many channels—for even in Virginia, Florida, and Kentucky, Southern staples were illicitly traded for supplies right down to the last shots— the land traffic may have counted for more than the sea voyages.

Channels of information and intercourse between the United States and the Confederate States were never fully interrupted. They were often devious, expensive, and difficult to find and use, but they could be searched out. There were confidential offices in New York where men could leave letters for Southern points nearly as certain of safe delivery as if addressed to Boston or Chicago. During Lee's march upon Gettysburg, it was a matter of common knowledge among military authorities that a daily mail left Baltimore for Richmond. Though military connivance was obviously at work somewhere, nobody could find just how it worked. The Confederates were said on vague authority to have agents in Washington whose information upon most topics was superior to that of a majority of newspaper men.[144] Messages, parcels, and persons were forwarded by underground railway with fair success, though many were intercepted. Federal authorities in the North had the names of Unionists in Richmond with whom they communicated steadily; and they knew the identity of rebel informants in Washington, New York, and Chicago.

It was plain to Southerners after their defeat, as it was to some while the war raged, that their government would have done better to place all shipping under a firm, well organized, central control. The Confederacy could then have fought the ocean blockade more efficiently. But this was politically impossible, for such a move would have encountered a stone wall of resistance in public sentiment friendly to State and local independence. It was equally plain to Northern leaders, after victory was gained, that they could have won more quickly if they had rigidly forbidden all trade across the lines, and punished summarily every infraction of the rules against commercial relations with the enemy. But in war, and particularly a great civil war, a wide gulf lay between policies that were advisable, and those that were feasible.

143. Thompson, S.B., *Confederate Purchasing Operations Abroad*, Chapel Hill, 1935, 44-45; Schuckers, J.W., *The Life and Public Services of Salmon Portland Chase*, New York, 1874, 323.

144. So averred the veteran journalist Noah Brooks in his Washington letter, April 25, 1864, to Sacramento *Union*.

Discouragement and Determination: Southern Morale, 1863

DURING THE winter of 1862-63 and the ensuing spring, the South had had reason to rejoice. Wave after wave of exultation over victory, and of hope triumphant over fears, had swept across the States of the Confederacy. Fredericksburg had seemingly offered a sudden new example of the invincibility of Lee's troops; Union drives on Vicksburg appeared to have been blunted; Murfreesboro had given a check to Northern arms which, even though the successes on the first day were followed by retreat after the second, lifted the Southern heart. Chancellorsville was both a deliverance from fearful peril, and proof that the Army of Northern Virginia could defeat any force which had no abler commander than Hooker. The annual message of Jefferson Davis struck many readers as the best State paper he had produced, and its defiant tone appealed to all valorous hearts.

As one Southern woman recorded in her diary, "Our victories at Vicksburg and Murfreesboro are confirmed. A few Northern papers seem to be violent against the Lincoln Administration, and are said to go so far as to demand that Lincoln and his Cabinet shall be hung . . . . the power of Lincoln's Administration will soon be broken." The diarist continues, ". . . Our people have made for themselves a great name, no people ever made a more glorious record. All the world sees with astonishment their successful struggle against a boastful, powerful, and unscrupulous foe."[1]

But by midsummer of 1863 the barometer of morale stood far lower in the Confederacy. Hope after hope failed: hope for Vicksburg, the hope of revolt in the Northwest, the hope that Lee's thrust into Pennsylvania would end in the fall of Baltimore, the hope of foreign recognition. A contributor to *De Bow's Review* would later criticize the Southern people for excessive volatility. "Defeat creates with them despondency, victory exaltation, and appearances are magnified into realities."[2] When defeats and disappointments came not as single spies, but in

1. McDonald, Cornelia, *A Diary with Reminiscences of the War and Refugee Life in the Shenandoah Valley, 1860-1865,* Nashville, 1934, 132, 137.
2. *DeBow's Review,* Vol. XXXIV, July-August, 1864, 2.

battalions, as they did in the months of Vicksburg, Port Hudson, Gettysburg, Tullahoma, Chattanooga, and Lookout Mountain, despondency was inevitable.

After Chickamauga and Chattanooga, it was plain that the Confederates won some of the battles, but the Union forces won most of the substantial strategic successes. The Confederates had won Chancellorsville and Chickamauga, but the North at Vicksburg, Gettysburg, and Chattanooga had triumphed in the battles that counted.[3] Southern newspapers noted how often the laurels of initial success had been swiftly turned into the willows of defeat. "We trust," remarked the Richmond *Sentinel,* Sept. 22, 1863, "that fortune is not to tantalize us at Chickamauga, as at Shiloh, and Corinth, and Murfreesboro. We trust that this time, at least, the courage of our troops will be rewarded by a complete and glorious victory." But the North had always the stronger reserves. Beauregard, Lee, Johnston, and Bragg, each in turn had been censured for not pressing advantages, recalled the Richmond *Examiner,* September 22, 1863. They simply did not have the reserve strength.

The roseate days of strength through victory were passing away, and the iron days of strength through adversity taking their place. Southerners were learning to substitute grim bravery for bravado, and to remember that this was a war not for military glory, but for national existence. Classical-minded editors and clergymen turned back to the tales of Athenian resistance to the Spartans, Macedonians, and Persians, and of Roman fortitude under the onslaughts of Hannibal, to give their people examples of stubborn courage. Many men and women found that, once they nerved themselves to it, the endurance of privation brought them a fierce joy. A Richmond youth wrote in May, 1863: "The enemy seem to be making an attack on all sides. I still feel undismayed, and pray God to enable us to endure whatever awaits us in the way of evil, with fortitude, and to receive with humble gratitude what may await us in the way of success. . . ."[4]

The nonchalant gaiety of the first months of the war had ended in the East with the carnage of the Seven Days, and in the West with the fearful losses of Shiloh. George W. Cable related how New Orleans, after cheering with exultant pride the erect young men in bright uniforms who marched off to join Albert Sidney Johnston's ranks, wept as the ragged, limping files returned, full of gaps that meant unmarked graves. Sarah Fowler Morgan drew a similar contrast in her diary. That bright April day when the war opened found her at a dance in Baton Rouge for her brother Harry—a scene of music, flowers, and confidence. A year

---

3. *Army and Navy Gazette,* Oct. 2, 1863. Quoted London *Daily News,* Oct. 12, 1863.
4. After Chancellorsville, and the death of Stonewall Jackson, this same youth, Jed Hotchkiss, wrote from headquarters of the Second Corps of Lee's army that Jackson's death had left a void which time could not fill. "We miss him all the time." But he goes on to say that in the Chancellorsville campaign few were killed, and many of the wounded had already returned to the front. "I am very sorry the people despond. I see no reason to do so, but on the contrary, much to cheer and gladden . . . I have not the most distant idea that Virginia will be given up." Jed Hotchkiss to wife, May 19, 1863, Hotchkiss Papers, LC.; Diary of Emma Mordecai, Southern Hist. Coll., Univ. of N.C. Library.

later, all that was changed. "Father is dead, and Harry. Mr. Trevezant lies at Corinth with his skull fractured by a bullet; every young man there has been in at least one battle since, and every woman has cried over her son, brother, or sweetheart . . . The week before Louisiana seceded, Jack Wheat stayed with us, and we all liked him so much and he thought so much of us; and last week . . . he was killed on the battlefield of Shiloah."[5]

The bells and cheers which welcomed the war had not been forgotten two years later, but in retrospect seemed utterly unreal. After months of hardship in the field, soldiers looked back contemptuously to the first drills held by lawyers, mechanics, clerks, and farm lads, half of them unfit for army life; they recalled with derision how the students of the University of Virginia had paraded through Richmond in red shirts and black trousers, unprovided with coats, blankets, or mess kits.[6] On the long border from Norfolk to Little Rock the first sight of the hated Yankee had awakened emotions now impossible. A family in the Shenandoah had sat at breakfast in tears as they heard the blare of "The Star Spangled Banner"; people along the Tennessee had turned rigid in hatred as the smoke of Union gunboats rose above the trees. Alas, the facts of Union advance and Yankee occupation were now familiar.

War by 1863 meant almost every conceivable form of endurance. People could steel themselves to face the long lists of dead, which one Virginia mother described as "the first fruits of the bitter tree that our people had helped to plant and to nourish for so many years"; to endure the return of the mutilated, to watch the burning of homesteads, to meet all the starker penalties of conflict. It was the gnawing anxieties as husbands and sons disappeared into the mist of war, not to be heard of for months at a time, that made the heart ache. The drain upon white manpower by the spring of 1863 was indeed becoming terrible. When Jefferson Davis issued his proclamation early in 1863 urging the people to discard cotton and tobacco and plant food crops, Governor Francis R. Lubbock of Texas said that out of a total white population of a little more than 400,000, Texas had furnished 87,000 men and youths to swell the rebel armies, so that a gravely diminished force was left to grow food.[7] The manpower shortage was rendered more acute by the fact that many slaves were becoming insubordinate, although a large number did remain loyal. Mrs. C. C. Clay, Sr., wrote her son from Huntsville, Alabama, in September of 1863: "The negroes are worse than free.

5. Cable, George Washington, "New Orleans Before the Capture," *Battles and Leaders of the Civil War*, II, 18; Dawson, Sarah Morgan, *A Confederate Girl's Diary*, ed. James I. Robertson, Jr., Bloomington, Ind., 1960, 7.
6. *Mason Smith Family Letters, 1860-1868*, eds. Daniel E. Huger Smith, Alice R. Huger Smith, A.R. Childs, Columbia, S.C., 1950, 4ff; McDonald, Cornelia (Peake), *A Diary with Reminiscences of the War . . .* , Nashville, 1935, 15ff.
7. New York *Herald*, April 17, 1863.

They say they *are* free. We cannot exert any authority. I beg ours to do what little is to be done . . . I have to work harder than I ever did, but am patient, silent, and prayerful. . . . The negroes are so bold that Alfred told me this morning that if your father went to Monte Vista . . . and let the overseer punish him for disobedience, that some one would kill the overseer. I asked him how he knew. He said, 'Stephen, Hannibal, and Sampson said that they would do it if he ever attempted it. . . .' Our people are sad and fearful. So many horses and mules and stock were taken and food taken or destroyed, that all are fearful for the winter. Wood and coal are not to be had at scarcely any price."[8]

The vast displacements of population that took place were a complicating factor. Early in the war great evacuations of slaves took place from Kentucky into Tennessee, the slaveowners going with them or sending overseers, while some slaves on the coast of Virginia and North Carolina were taken into the interior. A little later other slaves were removed from Western Tennessee into Mississippi, and from western Mississippi into Alabama and Georgia. The movement from Virginia southward was slower; still, it occurred. Union seizure of the densest slaveholding region in the South, the sea margin of South Carolina and Georgia, forced large planters there to take their slaves up-country, when possible. Some were taken from Florida.[9] "We believe," recorded a writer in the New York *Times,* August 1, 1863, "that of all the slaves of the eight rebel States this side of the Mississippi River, nine-tenths are in the Carolinas, Georgia, and Alabama."[10]

The widespread opposition to conscription was gravely accentuated by the amendment to the Draft Act which extended the drain upon Southern manpower by making those 18 to 45 liable, and stemmed from many impulses. Some thought that the enlarged draft dangerously weakened State defense; others held that it was leaving insufficient labor on the farms and plantations to support women and children. Some believed that the compulsory enlistment of mere boys might fatally weaken the next generation, leaving a corporal's guard to rear families. Not a few were convinced that conscription was an engine of military tyranny, giving the generals complete control over the South.

Nobody but an oldtime Union leader like himself, Governor Zebulon M. Vance of North Carolina wrote to Jefferson Davis, could have executed the first Draft Act; and even he, with all his popular following, would find it difficult to enforce the second and more severe law. If a West Point general, who knew much less about human nature than Vance knew about military service, were to ride roughshod over the countryside, drag men from their homes, and consign them to strange regiments and commanders without regard for their desire to join a

8. Sept. 5, 1863. C.C. Clay Papers, Duke Univ. Lib.
9. Wiley, Bell Irvin, *Southern Negroes 1861-1865,* New York, 1938, 4-8; Coulter, E. Merton, *The Confederate States of America,* Baton Rouge, 1950, 261.
10. Quoted in London *Daily News,* Aug. 13, 1863.

regiment of their own State, Vance would give up the task. Many of the best men of the various communities had been restrained from enlisting by large and helpless families, poverty, business exigencies, or other valid reasons, and now they should be treated with some consideration.[11] As Vance reminded Davis, North Carolinians had always been jealous of their political rights, and had left the Union after first giving a majority of 30,000 against secession.[12] W. W. Holden, editor of the *North Carolina Standard*, broke into angry denunciation of the Richmond *Enquirer* because "it favors a military despotism like that of France."[13]

In the springtime—the spring seasons of 1863, 1864, and 1865—the instability of soldiers became especially acute, and was transferred to their families. They longed to make sure that crops were being properly planted and tended; they wished to learn how mothers, sisters, and sweethearts had endured the winter; the first flowers made them homesick. They wished to see fences mended, roofs repaired, and livestock tended while colts, pigs, and calves were being born. Many of them came from areas overrun by the Federals. "I think it my duty to say to you that the restiveness of the men under their present restraint is almost irrepressible," Captain C. D. Fontaine wrote Governor Pettus of Mississippi as March sap ascended the trees in 1863. "They will either be disbanded by deserting or by open mutiny unless they are furloughed."[14] Middle-aged men were even more discontented than young men—their homes were dearer to them. The governor's papers contained numerous petitions from officers of Mississippi regiments asking that their men be furloughed a short time to look after their families; especially the middle-aged militiamen. The anxiety of soldiers respecting their homes and families was intensified, as many diaries and letters prove, whenever news reached them that the areas familiar to them had been overrun by the Union hosts.

"I speak the sentiments and wishes of four-fifths of the people of Kemper County," wrote Phil Gully of De Kalb, Mississippi, to Pettus, "when I ask the disbanding of the militia, or giving them an indefinite furlough, at least until they can plant and put their crops in a suitable condition for making a support."[15]

Material deprivations were of slight importance compared with the mental sufferings endured by countless Southerners—the anguish of bereavement, of seeing children and the aged suffering from deprivation and neglect, of feeling

11. Vance in Lefler, Hugh T., *North Carolina History Told by Contemporaries*, Chapel Hill, 1956, 290-291.

12. *Ibid.*, 290.

13. *Ibid.*, 295.

14. Capt. C.D. Fontaine to Gov. Pettus, March 9, 1863, Pettus Papers, Mississippi Dept. of Archives and History.

15. Pettus Papers, March 11, 1863.

that countless thousands were wasting their lives and throwing away their futures. We must think of the constant gnawing anxiety of public officers compelled to look on at the destitution of scores and hundreds of families; destitution so alarming in some areas of Mississippi early in 1863 as to threaten absolute starvation.[16] Or we must try to realize the anguish of mothers and fathers of captured sons in reading a newspaper article—clearly veracious—on prison conditions in Camp Douglas in Chicago, a scene of suffering and death. One returned prisoner estimated that in three months more than 750 Confederate boys had died. The camp lay in a low marshy lakeside plain; every rain left it half submerged; it was full of filth; the ill-clothed, half-starved inmates endured a long desolate confinement without solace. Some were thrown in bitter midwinter cold into quarters with nothing but a damp pallet of straw for a bed, devoid of blankets or other covering. In one stormy interval, twenty-five or thirty men froze to death. It was "a tyranny and cruelty worse than that of the dark ages," wrote one prisoner.[17]

We must consider the anguish of Robert Kells, the head of the Mississippi State Insane Asylum, writing his governor September 14, 1863, that it was plain the institution would soon be seized by the Union forces. What then would become of his poor charges? The Union authorities would at once discredit Confederate currency, and he would have no money to buy supplies, or pay staff and servants. And what then could he do with his poor deranged people? To turn them loose would be a public calamity. He suggested that he be allowed to buy a stock of cotton, to resell to the Union authorities; but what if they seized it without any compensation?[18] We must consider also the anguish of Governor John Letcher of Virginia, recording in his annual message of January 7, 1863, the destruction by Union troops of the College of William and Mary, next to Harvard the oldest seat of learning in the country. This was a deliberate act. The troops removed commissary stores and then applied the match. "Thus," wrote Letcher, "we have another evidence of the vandal spirit which animates the Yankee army. With them nothing is sacred . . . The outrages they have committed, the enormities they have perpetrated, have aroused and inflamed the Southern mind . . . They have 'poured out the sweet milk of concord into hell,' and our future relations must be those of enemies."[19]

John W. Burgess, later one of the revered makers of Columbia University, tells us that his parents had their fortunes wrecked beyond recovery. Burgess was stationed as a soldier in Nashville, his office in a quartermaster depot, overlooking the station. Often he saw wives and daughters of once wealthy planters emerge

16. James H. Rives, Private Secretary of Governor Pettus of Mississippi, to Pemberton, March 9, 1863, Pettus Papers, Miss. Dept. of Archives and History.
17. Richmond *Examiner*, April 14, 1863, copied in Chicago *Post*, May 6, 1863.
18. Robert Kells, State Asylum, Sept. 14, 1863, to J.J. Pettus, Pettus Papers, *op. cit.*
19. Executive Papers, Virginia State Library.

from box-cars, clad in tatters, carrying rolls of bedding, looking about vacantly, at wits' end for food and shelter. "Some of them, were already stricken with famine and disease, and would sink down exhausted in the streets and alleyways, often to die."[20]

Countless Southern children were without education, the schools crumbling into decay. Plans for libraries, for college and university expansion, and for better charitable institutions, had been abandoned.

To all this was added, in the summer of 1863, the anguish of almost crushing defeat. In this dark hour, wrote Kean of the War Department in July, as Lee's veterans completed their withdrawal from Pennsylvania and as whole regiments of Vicksburg prisoners were herded toward the Northern prison-camps, Southerners might well consider whether they ought not to seek a powerful foreign ally even at the expense of some pride and independence. Why not sound out Napoleon III with an offering of large commercial privileges, and control of Southern cotton, naval timber, naval stores, and the acceptance of a French protectorate in foreign affairs? Kean had little hope that the armies could be augmented. Raising the conscription age to 45 would probably not yield more than 50,000 men, and it would take six months to get them into the forces. "We are almost exhausted."[21]

One of the most eloquent voices of the South was raised in Alabama—the voice of Augusta J. Evans, the novelist. She wrote to J. L. M. Curry that he must be acquainted with the insubordination and disaffection rife in the armies, which in her section had become alarming. The press was reticent upon this disgraceful truth, but experienced officers expressed great uneasiness. "The number of desertions in General Pemberton's army and even among the troops stationed in Alabama is appalling, and fears are entertained of painful and disastrous consequences, unless the evil can be promptly remedied. Courtsmartial are everywhere in session, and it chills the blood in my veins to hear the degrading and horrible punishments inflicted on Southern soldiers, who plead in palliation of deserting the cries of hungry wives and starving children. I have been told by officers of unquestioned veracity and prudence that they almost daily see letters received by the privates in their commons, in which the families implore them to come home at every hazard and save them from the pinching penury that scowls at their thresholds."[22]

She denounced "the shameless tribe of speculators and extortioners who swarm in every nook and cranny of the Confederacy," adding that public blame

20. Burgess, John W., *Reminiscences of an American Scholar,* New York, 1934, 31-32.
21. Kean, Robert G.H., *Inside the Confederate Government,* ed., Edward Younger, New York, 1957, 80-82.
22. Augusta J. Evans to Curry, Dec. 20, 1862, J.L.M. Curry Papers, Vol. I, Alabama State Archives.

was laid chiefly on the Exemption Bill, which offers a premium for extortion among "all classes of artificers" instead of compelling them to join the army or raise food.

"Moreover, one unfortunate clause . . . has resulted most unhappily in the creation of an anti-slavery element among our soldiers who openly complain that they are torn from their homes, and their families consigned to starvation, solely in order that they may protect the property of slaveholders who are allowed . . . to remain in quiet enjoyment of luxurious ease."

Everything was running down—deteriorating—in the South, and this fact depressed the people. During 1863 the speed of railroad trains, at their best, was dwindling to fifteen miles an hour. Furthermore, the South was compelled by military needs, Union raids, and shortages of rails and railroad cars to reduce operations sharply. Horseshoes were becoming difficult to procure, whether for farm animals or for Lee's cavalry. Hand-looms, of the kind used in Revolutionary days, were coming into use in some areas; General Arthur M. Manigault told of a fellow soldier in South Carolina who had one on his plantation, worked by a Negro, and who made another for Manigault himself.[23] Under pressure of universal shortages, soldiers in 1863-64 began to steal from each other if strangers. It did not do to leave an overcoat, a parcel of sugar, or a bottle of liquor unguarded on a march or in a train.

How many unyielding Unionists the South contained, we shall never know, but they were numerous. While some suffered for their stand, no mass arrests took place. The Washington correspondent of the New York *Tribune* probably exaggerated the facts when he wrote (1864) that more than three hundred Unionist Virginians were immured in Richmond; some in Castle Thunder, a few in Libby Prison, and many crammed into Winder's Cage, a new prison on 20th Street. The newspapers of Richmond were not permitted to publish particulars of the arrests, and the most important prisoners were not allowed to mingle with others, but were confined by twos and threes. The correspondent added that the South was full of such prisons. In Atlanta, he had visited the Citizens' Prison to see an oldtime friend who had been there nearly two years.

"I found him immured with about 450 others in a building of insufficient capacity for the humane confinement of one-third of that number. The whole place was as filthy as the Augean stable. The inmates were half-covered with tatters and rags, and literally alive with vermin. Their sunken eyes and emaciated forms and faces confirmed too clearly my friend's declaration that they were dying of starvation and despair."[24] That much of this was propagandist writing seems evident. Close research simply does not reveal such extensive persecution.

23. Manigault, Arthur M., ms. Memoirs, Univ. of North Carolina Library.
24. New York *Tribune*, January 25, 1864.

While many Southern Unionists suffered social hostility and abuse, others, like Judge Petigru in Charleston, were respected.

However, the strength of Union feeling became manifest whenever a city or district was securely occupied. In Arkansas, by the beginning of 1864, three Federal regiments had been raised and sent into the field, two more were being enlisted, and Home Guards had been organized. The whole number recruited since October 10, declared the *Tribune,* might be stated at 6,000.[25] This may be high, as Arkansas contributed 8,289 Union men during the whole war. Knoxville, Tennessee, was captured in the late summer of 1863. Rosecrans, in a letter or dispatch to the Nashville *Union* dated September 4, written from Bridgeport, Alabama, wrote that Tennesseans were flocking in daily from the mountains by thirties and fifties to enlist under the Union flag. "Yesterday 85 men came into Stevenson, and the day before 150."[26] Each had his own horse, needed only a musket, and asked immediate mustering-in. Most of these were probably Unionists, but others were probably the kind who seek always to be with a winner.

Northern soldiers soon recorded the fact that hostility and hatred burned higher among women in the South than among men, and higher among young women than their elders. Many women were passionately vindictive and used insulting and taunting language. They presented the soldiers with bouquets containing thorns or pins. One woman, giving coffee to a squad of soldiers, observed: "I hope it will poison you!" Another, seeing Massachusetts volunteers fall into line at the double-quick, cried, "Ashby will make you run faster than that!" The family of Charles Faulkner, former minister to France, called for a guard, but when it came, refused to allow the men to use the kitchen stove to heat their food. One of the women called the guard "poltroons" and "vulgar Yankees" in French, and was taken aback when a soldier told her he knew French well. Again, a woman held out a cake to gaunt, hungry soldiers; then, when one reached for it, threw it to a dog. Younger women were the most spirited (and spiteful) in manner. They would draw their skirts tightly about them as they passed Union men. Ben Butler sentenced one young woman in New Orleans, who had openly expressed glee on hearing of the death of a Union soldier, to a year in an island camp. After New Orleans had been in Union hands more than a year, a soldier passing a small church was attracted by the sound of a choir practicing within, and stepped just inside the door to listen. As soon as the singers espied him, the music and hymn stopped. Every eye glowered at him; and when he asked if he were intruding he received the curt reply, "Yes."[27]

25. *Ibid.,* article dated Jan. 12 in issue of Jan. 20, 1864; Kriedburg, Marvin A., and M.G. Henry, *History of Military Mobilization in the United States Army, 1775-1945,* Washington, 1955, 96.

26. New York *Tribune,* Sept. 8, 1864.

27. Powers, George W., *The Story of the Thirty-Eighth Regiment of Massachusetts Volunteers,* Cambridge, 1866, 59-60.

[I]

A young post-adjutant in the Southern army whose family, fleeing from New Orleans, had taken refuge in Georgia, met some old Louisiana friends in Richmond in July of 1863. "Took a mint julep with them ($15 each)," he noted in his diary. Juleps at $15 were beyond most men.[28] The occupant of the British consulate in Charleston wrote Lord John Russell in April of that year that every article of food in the city except Indian corn had risen to tenfold its normal cost, and every article of clothing twentyfold. "The usual price of flour is three cents a pound; but I paid for it but yesterday thirty-five cents, or nearly twelvefold; and longcloth for shirting, which usually costs twelve cents a yard, cannot be obtained for less than two and a half dollars a yard, a twentyfold advance." Although the value of his sterling had increased sixfold, this was manifestly insufficient to counteract the upward spiral.[29] The British consul in Mobile bore the same testimony. Daily advances were taking place, he wrote Russell in August; the newspapers concealed them, but cotton cloth was $5 a yard, woolen cloth $100 a yard, and boots $100 a pair.[30]

"Of all the high prices we have ever known or heard of," declared the Jackson *Mississippian* on January 24, 1864, "none equal those which were paid at an auction sale in this city yesterday. Glass tumblers brought $12 each; wineglasses $4.50 each; a rocking chair that in former days would scarcely have been carried home brought $105. Even a pillow fetched $20, and a fly-brush $50."[31] C. C. Clay of the Confederate Senate wrote his wife in March, 1863, that general gloom prevailed in Richmond because of the scarcities and cost of living. "In this city the poor clerks and subaltern military officers are threatened with starvation, as they cannot get board on their pay." Apprehension existed that part of the army in Virginia might have to be disbanded for want of provisions. "God only knows what is to become of us, if we do not soon drive the enemy from Tennessee and Kentucky, and get food from their granaries."[32]

From Columbus, deep in Georgia, came an identical plaint. That town by 1863 had become a huge workshop. Mills there, or in the vicinity, were turning out woolen cloth, and thousands of soldiers' wives and indigent women were converting it into uniforms. For making four suits a week the government paid them $8. "Think, seriously, for a moment," G. M. Jones wrote Jefferson Davis, "of $8 a

28. Ms. Diary, Library of Congress. A prominent Richmond resident in August, 1863, wrote of watermelons being offered at eight dollars each, choice. "Pa has just been telling us that he preserved a barrel of brown sugar five hundred dollars a barrel; a short time since he paid seven hundred for a barrel of crushed sugar—we dislike brown sugar in our tea. . . ." (Valentine, E.A. to W.W. Valentine, Richmond, Aug. 7, 1863, Valentine Museum, Richmond, Va.)
29. H. Pinckney Walker to Earl Russell, FO5/908, British Foreign Office.
30. Fred J. Cridland, Aug. 31, 1863; FO5/908, British Foreign Office.
31. Jackson, Miss., *Mississippian*, Jan. 24, 1864.
32. C.C. Clay Papers, Duke Univ. Lib.

week as stipend for the maintenance of a family, with rent at $200 per annum, meal $8, beef $1, wood $40 a cord! Words are useless. You can appreciate the case. Such tales of wretchedness as these women have to tell their husbands in the army make a host of deserters."[33] But to stem the tide of inflation and want was beyond President Davis or anyone else.

Depreciation of the currency went from bad to worse. In Richmond, the French consul reported at the close of 1864 that it took $35 in Confederate paper to buy one dollar in gold; in Charleston that month it took $42. Earlier in 1864 the Richmond Congress had taken action to compel the conversion of its notes, reducing the interest rate and contracting the amount of paper in circulation. Charleston merchants thereupon refused for a time to sell any goods at all, shutting their doors. As a tax was laid on notes of large denomination, smaller ones were hoarded, and nothing could be bought for less than $10. One result was that nearly all Southerners whose savings were in Confederate currency, became accustomed to the idea that they were ruined, and that even if the South triumphed, it would triumph in a state of utter financial collapse. Such men fought on with no fear of financial loss, for such loss had already smitten them.[34]

Shortages and high prices went hand in hand. Because people thought them unconquerable, a violent riot exploded in Richmond in the spring of 1863. This so-called "bread riot" fell upon the government like a clap of thunder. A captive Union officer saw from his prison window a motley throng that he estimated at about 3,000, chiefly women, armed with sticks, stones, and a few guns, breaking open stores and seizing provisions and clothing. They were spurred by desperation and partially led by agitators; the militia, when called, were plainly sympathetic.[35] The rebel war-clerk Jones, who estimated the mob at more than a thousand, ascribed the outbreak to hunger. When he asked where they were going, an emaciated young woman replied they were going to get something to eat. Seizing meal, flour, shoes, and other portables, they loaded them upon carts to be driven off. On Main Street, where all the shops were closed, they smashed plate glass windows, and began helping themselves to silks, jewelry, and other valuables. Foreign-born residents took an increasing hand in the looting. When the mayor threatened to order the City Battalion to fire on them if they did not disperse, they stood defiant.

"About this time the President appeared," wrote Jones, "and ascending a dray, spoke to the people. He urged them to return to their homes, so that the bayonets there menacing them might be sent against the common enemy. He

33. Jones, Jan. 6, 1863, to Davis, Jefferson Davis Papers, Duke Univ. Lib.
34. Wright, Gordon, "Economic Conditions in the Confederacy as Seen by French Consuls," *Journal of Southern History*, May, 1941, 208ff.
35. Statement in New York *Tribune*, April 8, 1863.

told them that such acts would bring famine upon them in the only form which could not be provided against, as it would deter people from bringing food to the city. He said he was willing to share his last loaf with the suffering people, (his best horse had been stolen the night before), and he trusted we would all bear our privations with fortitude. . . . He seemed deeply moved; and indeed it was a frightful spectacle, and an ominous one . . ."[36]

Diseases grown desperate demanded relief by treatment just as desperate. Southern soldiers who took a prisoner soon stripped him of his clothing. One Joseph E. Moody of the Fiftieth Massachusetts, taken prisoner near Petersburg, found that on the way to a Richmond jail he lost his sound uniform, hat, and stout boots, his razor, penknife, and greenbacks, getting instead a faded brown coat, faded gray trousers, a homemade flap-brimmed hat of green cloth, and cow-hide shoes. He had left the country of plenty for the country of want. Once inside Libby Prison, he was fed a limited ration of corn bread, salt beef, and muddy water from the James River. "I felt like a hunted animal," he wrote.[37]

Households all over the South were becoming more and more self-dependent. One large wool-grower of South Carolina, John McRae, explained to a dealer in 1862 why he had sent nothing to market. Steep increases in the price of finished garments, the unsalability of much that he produced, and the increasing inflation of the currency all helped to make it imperative for him to devote what wool and labor he could command to home-manufacture of clothing.[38] The South, cornered, tormented by unending hardships and sufferings, and seeing an iron door closing shut on all its hopes, was becoming ready for acts of material and psychological desperation. The bread-riot previously described was not so much an explosion of hunger and want as an effect of overstrained nerves and of long-pent emotion. This is murkily suggested in one partisan account, that of the Richmond *Examiner* of April 4, 1863: "A handful of prostitutes, professional thieves, Irish and Yankee hags, gallows birds from all lands but our own . . ." took part. Josiah Gorgas, a reliable witness, wrote, "Yesterday a crowd of women assembled on the public square and marching thence down Main, sacked several shoe, grocery and other stores. Their pretence was bread; but their motive really was license. Few of them have really felt want. . . ." The Richmond *Whig* of April 6 told of the women being "led by a virago who is known to have made a fortune by market gardening, and cheered by a rabble of gamblers and ruffians. . . ." The same paper pointed out that there had been fewer applications for charity than

36. Jones, J.B., *A Rebel War Clerk's Diary*, New York, 1935, I, 284-286.
37. Ms. Account of Prison Life, by Joseph E. Moody, 59th Mass., Palmer Coll., Western Reserve Historical Society.
38. McRae, Camden, S.C., June 2, 1862, to F. & H. Fries of Salem, N.C., McRae Letterbooks, State Historical Society of Wisconsin.

in previous winters. Another eyewitness asserted, "Almost every one of them was armed. . . ."[39]

The reign of substitutes had become general throughout the Confederacy. As the shops were swept bare, the people became used to every possible contrivance, from thorns for pins to acorns for coffee. A Tennessee girl has recorded the method of making dresses in her home. Her family grew their own cotton, spun it, and wove the cloth. For a purplish dye they boiled the bark of hard maples and mingled it with copperas to get a clear, bright color. For green dye they boiled peach leaves, mixed with a bit of alum; for black dye the berries of black sumac with copperas; and for gray dye cedar tops.[40] The greatest deficiencies in rural districts, where garden produce, corn-meal, and fruit were often abundant, were tea, coffee, salt, matches, and good candles. Blackberry leaves were used for tea; parched rye, cornmeal, or bits of sweet potato for coffee. Yet the alliance of scarcities and inflation remained unconquerable.

One of the most pathetic documents of the time is the letter which a niece of President Davis, Carrie Leonard of Germantown, North Carolina, sent her "uncle Jeff" on February 9, 1865. "This is my first essay at begging," she wrote, "and you must know I have suffered much when I resort to it." For a long time she had been a drudge, doing all the household work indoors; now she had to carry wood and water in from outdoors, a task beyond her strength. Her husband was teaching the few pupils he could find a little Latin, Greek, French, mathematics, and the lower branches of English for a little corn each month. The cost of fuel and food appalled them; with Confederate money they could buy nothing. She had not heard from her father for many weeks. "I am very sorry to trouble you with my sorrows and trials and would not do so had I anyone to turn to."[41]

Pathetic, too, the cry of Miss Sidney Harding in her diary as 1864 closed. She and her family were refugees from Texas who had found haven in De Soto Parish near Shreveport. Their old home had been burned; cherished music, books, flowers, and other amenities were all gone. Nothing was left "but poor fare and all crowded up." Miss Sidney at twenty-two naturally maintained a show of spirit as she occupied herself with moonlight horseback rides with young Confederate officers, with a few picnics, with visits to neighbors, with straw bonnets, the Sunday sermons, the first peaches. Her diet was bacon and corn bread; her most

39. For modern, careful study, see: Kimball, William J., "The Bread Riot in Richmond, 1863," *Civil War History*, Vol. VII, No. II, June, 1961, 149, and *passim.*; Richmond *Examiner*, Apr. 4, 1863; Davis, Varina Howell, *Jefferson Davis*, New York, 1890, II, 373-376; Gorgas, Josiah, *The Civil War Diary of General Josiah Gorgas*, ed. Frank E. Vandiver, University, Alabama, 1947, 28-29; Dowdey, Clifford, *Experiment in Rebellion*, Garden City, N.Y., 1946, 272-273; Richmond *Whig*, April 6, 1863; Hall Tutwiler to his sister, Southern Historical Collection, Univ. of N.C., as printed in *Virginia Magazine*, April, 1963, 203.
40. *Historical Records Survey*, Records of Middle Tennessee, Civil War Letters, III, 146ff.
41. Jefferson Davis Papers, Duke Univ. Lib.

poignant experience was a visit to a camp-hospital just after Price's men had fought a battle: "Oh the sickening sight; some shot in face, both eyes out, heads bent, arms, legs everywhere." One day a carriage drew up and from it issued four friends. "Poor Ma she sat down in despair and cried. Nothing in the house to eat."[42]

"I recently made a rough calculation to compare the present currency with a sound one in the matter of my household expenses," wrote Robert G.H. Kean of the War Department in March, 1863. "The result is that my salary of $3,000 will go about as far as $700 would in 1860. Flour $28 against $4 then, tea $15 against $1.25, bacon $1.25 against 20 cents, and other things in proportion. A coat cost $120, calico $2.50, unbleached cotton $1, bleached cotton $2 to $2.50, linen $7, and so on."[43] Behind such figures lay endless scrimping and worry; before each harried householder stretched a prospect of deepening anxiety.

To Herschel V. Johnson of Georgia, in this same dark hour just before Chancellorsville, the swollen paper-currency of the South was the gloomiest feature of its situation. The Confederacy had made a great initial blunder by failing to tax the people. Instead, it had resorted to gigantic issues of paper-money. Its next blunder was in paying interest on its loans in irredeemable paper. These errors were avoided by the North, which in the end laid taxes nearly half sufficient to pay war costs, and which made interest on loans payable in gold. By January 1, 1864, Johnson wrote a friend, the Confederate paper-money debt would be more than 1,200 million dollars, and no funding bill which Congress could adopt would absorb more than $300 millions, leaving $900 millions in circulation. Yet the normal demands of internal commerce required less than $150 millions. "Think of it! What prices! What destruction of public confidence! Shall I not say what ruin? All this, and the end not yet."[44]

Class feeling, and resentment against unscrupulous money-makers were aroused by every discussion of revenue measures. Johnson, demanding taxes which would raise a hundred millions, wished to see them laid almost entirely on gross income, not property. "The tax on income takes in nobody who is too poor to have an income, and it will take in the entire body of speculators and extortioners and heartless and bloated corporations."[45] This was an agrarian voice. Yet when the House Finance Committee proposed instead a tax in kind of one-tenth upon agricultural production, Johnson supported it because it would furnish food and materials for the army, and would enable countless penniless

42. Diary of Miss Sidney Harding, Louisiana State Dept. of Archives, La. State Univ.

43. Kean, *Inside the Confederate Government, op. cit.*, 43, Mar. 7, 1863.

44. Johnson, Richmond, March 4, 1863, to A.E. Cochran, Macon, Ga., Johnson Papers, Duke Univ. Lib.

45. Johnson, Richmond, March 25, April 3, 1863, to Alexander H. Stephens, Johnson Papers, Duke Univ. Lib.

soldiers to pay their taxes without money. After the stage of impressment was reached in the Revolutionary War, Washington correctly warned his associates that this resource could not long endure. When that stage was reached in Confederate history, it was equally evident that the power of the government to supply the army with food, clothing, arms, and ammunition was nearing its end. The South pursued ever-elusive victory under the threat of even more imminent financial collapse.[46]

The Virginia legislature greatly impaired popular confidence in the Confederate paper currency when it passed a law providing that no issues preceding April 6, 1863 should be taken for State taxes. This, the Governor declared, was bad legislation. People concluded that the early issues were not good money, and as they seldom recalled the dates on bank notes or looked at them, they began to view all Confederate paper as dubious. Much of this Confederate money had been paid to soldiers; when they sent it home to pay taxes and found it rejected, they felt outraged. They were paid but $11 a month, and that in suspect money! The object of the legislation had been to force holders of early issues of Confederate paper to fund them in Confederate bonds, and thus retire the superabundant paper from circulation. But four-fifths of the people, as the governor pointed out, had no money for bond investments; they needed all the paper they received for pressing needs.[47]

Early in the war, freed Negroes in scattered spots endeavored, without success, to join the Army. Others went to the war as servants with their masters, but the Confederate Congress did not pass an impressment act until March 26, 1863. It limited impressment of slaves according to rules and regulations of the States and with consent of slaveowners in most cases. On February 17, 1864, President Davis signed another law, providing that the Secretary of War should be authorized to employ up to 20,000 slaves, furnishing them with rations and clothing. Owners were to be paid at the rate for privates in the ranks; each owner was to be allowed to keep one slave, at least, at home; and "an equal ratio from all owners" was guaranteed. But weaknesses appeared in the enforcement of the law, and most slaveowners deeply disliked this government seizure of slaves. They feared the Negroes would be maltreated and injured, would be allowed to escape, or would be exposed to capture. As conditions worsened, the Confederate Government did fail to provide the Negroes with adequate food and clothing. Their families at home suffered. General Bragg in North Carolina condemned the treatment of slaves by careless officers. Hence, sporadic opposition to slave impressment came from the governors, Pettus of Mississippi, Vance of North Carolina, and others. Congress in 1864 appropriated money to pay claims for the

46. Schwab, J.C., *The Confederate States of America, A Financial and Industrial History of the South During the Civil War, 1861-1865,* New York, 1968, Chs. III, IV, XIII.

47. Message of the Governor of Virginia, Sept. 7, 1863, *Annual Messages of Governors,* Richmond, 1863.

loss of slaves impressed in Virginia who had been captured or died of disease while working on the Richmond fortifications; the rate was to be $2,000 in Confederate money for each slave lost.[48]

Wherever the Southerner turned he was met by financial anxieties, ending all too often in poverty and ruin. Early in 1863, the Confederate House passed a bill to increase the pay of soldiers, but it was killed in the Senate. Finally, in June, 1864, pay was raised from $11 to $18 a month. As the Treasury could not raise by taxes the twenty to thirty millions a year which this would require, and it would mean new issues of paper money, such leaders as C. C. Clay of Alabama bitterly opposed it. Clay, who expected political defeat in Alabama as a result, actually accused J. L. M. Curry of bad faith in supporting it.[49] Benjamin H. Hill, another opponent, thought the so-called increase worse than useless. The resultant currency depreciation would cost the soldiers more than adherence to the former payment level.[50] Other members of the Confederate Congress took the same view.

If Confederate taxation was weak and disorderly, the tax measures of the various States were yet more confused, uncertain and onerous. It was utterly impossible, Secretary Memminger complained to Howell Cobb, to reduce the different revenue systems to any uniformity. Even the assessment of lands was often haphazardly arbitrary without reference to their real value. Some States levied a poll-tax on slaves, some an *ad valorem* tax. The various items taxed up and down the Confederacy were so numerous and heterogeneous that they could be classified only in the roughest fashion. The census of 1860 had estimated the gross value of property in the Confederacy at $5,202,176,000, so that a low tax of fifty cents upon each hundred dollars' worth of property would theoretically raise $26,000,000. But the States had no rule and no plan, and the Confederate government no clear mode of action.[51]

How could the authorities in Richmond equalize the burdens of the States when no two capitals agreed on what was taxable? Some States taxed slaves of all ages and types but Tennessee exempted all slaves under 12 years or above 45. Then, too, what was a fair assessment? The average value of slaves in Virginia, the Carolinas, and Georgia as ascertained by the directors of tax-collection was about $380 each in 1862. In Arkansas, however, they were rated at lower figures. Tennessee did not assess bank stock, or other corporate stocks. Memminger complained to the authorities of that State in the winter of 1862-63 that they had

48. Trexler, Harrison A., "The Opposition of Planters to the Employment of Slaves as Laborers by the Confederacy," *Miss. Valley Hist. Review*, Vol. XXVII, 211-224. For an example of Negroes seeking to serve the Confederacy, see petitions of free Negroes requesting to be allowed to join the Army. Pickens-Bonham papers, LC., petitions of S. Car. Negroes.

49. Memorandum by Clay Montgomery, Nov. 14, 1863, C.C. Clay Papers, Duke Univ. Lib.

50. Hill to Clay, Nov. 19, 1863, C.C. Clay Papers, *ibid.*

51. July 24, 1861; Memminger Papers, Univ. of North Carolina Lib.

grossly underestimated the war tax due the Confederacy under the Act of August 19, 1861.[52]

Everywhere by 1863, the population was becoming restive under the interminable exactions laid upon them; everywhere defiant men were resisting what they thought arbitrary decrees. When a committee in southwestern Georgia, indignant because Robert Toombs did not send slaves in 1862 to labor on the public works and planted a larger crop of cotton than usual, passed resolutions of censure, he replied from Richmond in bellicose vein. "Your telegram has been received," he telegraphed the committeemen. "I refuse a single hand. My property, as long as I shall live, shall never be subject to the orders of those cowardly miscreants, the committee of public safety of Randolph County and Eufaula. You may rob me in my absence, but you cannot intimidate me."[53] As the months passed, impressment became more and more intolerable. A fellow-Mississippian sent Jefferson Davis in the spring of 1864 a complaint against arbitrary seizures. Little was said, he wrote, about the burden of the tax law, currency law, or draft law, but the "illegal and unjust impressments" were arousing anger. "Hundreds have been forced to give up mules and horses actually required for agricultural purposes, by men claiming to belong to regiments or fragments of regiments and in contempt of the laws of Congress . . . No attention is paid whatever to the wants of the plantation from which the mules or horses are taken . . . Land is forced out of cultivation by these abuses. Women whose husbands are in the army have thus lost the only horse they had for farm work."[54]

As everybody became poorer, and many desperately poor, mutual antagonism developed between classes, and even between the Army and the civilians. Exhibitions of charity became fewer. Early in the war, leaders had eloquently protested that the families of poor soldiers would not be allowed to suffer, but pledges of this sort were soon too often drowned in general apathy. The Georgia legislature empowered the various county courts to impose taxes on the citizens for needy households whose breadwinner was with the colors. Unfortunately, it was found that counties having the least property generally possessed the largest numbers of needy people. While the richest counties had almost no poor, the burden on the few well-to-do people in the poorest counties became well-nigh insupportable.[55] "We all know that great national afflictions harden the heart," remarked the Richmond *Examiner.*[56] Doubtless, class antagonisms would have been more

52. Memminger to J.G.M. Ramsey of Knoxville, Dec. 22, 1862, Davis Papers, Duke Univ. Lib. He held the State Comptroller at fault.
53. Chicago *Morning Post,* July 3, 1862.
54. T.J. Hudson, Morse County, Miss., April 23, 1864, to E. Barksdale; copy to J.D., Davis Papers, Duke Univ. Lib.
55. Fielder, Herbert, *A Sketch of the Life, Times and Speeches of Joseph E. Brown,* Springfield, Mass., 1883, 242-244.
56. Richmond *Examiner,* March 14, 1863.

freely expressed in the South had not much of the public irritation found a vent in hatred for the North.[57]

Never did a country have to cope with so many vicious economic circles as the Confederacy. In the Virginia Senate one member remarked early in 1863 that inflation of the currency was not the cause of the rise in prices, but the effect. As prices rose, so necessarily did the amount of paper money, the government being compelled to double its issues to meet the new costs. The scarcity of goods and the want of transportation were the basic reasons for inflation, the activities of monopolists and extortioners merely contributing to the result. Another vicious circle lay in the fact that malcontents began resisting the government, and even organizing insurrectionary activities; and the resulting confusion produced still deeper discontent. Yet another vicious circle was drawn by those who rashly predicted—as the Jackson *Mississippian* did early in 1863—that the North would soon acknowledge Southern independence. Disillusionment produced a fresh demand for dishonest utterances by editors and politicians.[58]

A correspondent of the Cincinnati *Commercial,* in a long letter at the close of 1863, gave the somewhat exaggerated impressions of an intelligence officer (a well-concealed spy) who had just concluded a four-months' tour of the South from Tennessee through the Carolinas and Georgia, and into Alabama. For weeks before Chickamauga, he declared, the Southern army had to subsist on quarter-rations. When detachments were sent on special duty, they were almost never given rations, but were ordered to live upon the country, the result being indiscriminate pillage. Many families of soldiers were in pitiful straits; wherever he

57. Divided views of the blockade contributed to dissensions among Southerners and between various Southern States. Some financiers in South Carolina were strongly in favor of the blockade; it brought a valuable commerce to Charleston, attracted great numbers of traders from all over the South, and enriched many speculators. A first voyage, according to the French Consul, often paid for cargo and ship, and gave a profit. But Georgia was against the blockade. Many condemned it as the chief source of Southern ills; it augmented the premium on gold, and saved Europe from being forced to recognize the Confederacy. The reason for the attacks, wrote the consul, was "that rivalry which has long existed between Georgia and Carolina." Gordon Wright, *op. cit.,* 201-202.

58. One device constantly used by the Southern press was to talk of certain if delayed peace. The Chattanooga *Rebel* early in 1863 predicted that the men of the West, rude, brave, self-assertive, would yet realize that they had been duped into the war, and cause an earthquake that would topple Lincoln. The Montgomery *Advertiser* felt certain that the war would terminate about the expiration of Lincoln's term. This guess at March, 1865, was close enough—but the *Advertiser* made a wrong guess. The Jackson *Mississippian* meanwhile declared its certainty that an early peace would *dawn* upon the bloodstained country.

But Southern valor was sometimes sustained by unworthy words of hate. Gov. John Letcher of Virginia had admirable qualities, but they disappeared in his violent indictment of the Northern people: "This war has exhibited them in their true character, as murderers and robbers. They have disregarded all the rules of civilized warfare. Their prisoners we take are entitled to no consideration ..." *Message to the Legislature,* Jan. 7, 1863. Nor did incitements to fortitude based upon the everlasting strength of slavery have high moral dignity. The Richmond *Dispatch* of Jan. 6, 1863, declared that "beyond the lines of the Federal Army Slavery will continue intact and impregnable as the Rock of Gibraltar."

went he saw instances of intense suffering. So many women in towns and cities had been driven to prostitution that the term "war widow" commonly implied a life of immorality. In the impressment of property for army use gross discrimination was often practised between rich and poor, the wealthy and influential retaining their provisions and goods while the helpless were plundered. The condition of slaves in many areas was wretched beyond all recent precedent, their masters being unable to feed and clothe them properly. Blockade-running became widely unpopular, for most people thought it depreciated the currency, and it brought in arms, munitions, clothing, and luxuries, but never food.

This report, while in some particulars exaggerated, was in the main veracious, at least as to some areas. The intelligence officer reported that after every battle the Confederates, if they held the field or took prisoners, indulged in a "peeling bee," and that in some engagements shoeless soldiers had been held in reserve at the rear until they could obtain footgear from the dead and wounded, whether Northern or Southern.[59]

Life in Richmond by the second half of 1863 had become highly demoralized. "We were prepared for ugly sights," declared the Richmond *Examiner* of January 9, 1864. "We were prepared for the extortioners and the speculators; for the gamblers; for the painted bawds and bedizened strumpets; for drunken brawls and noonday murders. We were prepared for the madness of crime. But, we confess, we were not prepared for the simpering of the dancing parties which are now the rage."[60]

The fashionable days of the Randolphs and Wickhams, the Carters and Lees, had passed away, lamented the same paper. Instead, the city had the Baltimore plug-uglies, the exuviae of the antebellum federal departments in Washington, the agents who sold substitutes, and the refugees who swarmed in the cellars and lived by a little trading or a lively amount of gambling. Verminous deserters paraded their rags in defiance of civil and military authority alike. Merchants and tradesmen who had anything to sell—such as tough beef at sixty cents a pound, leather at almost its weight in gold, silks, jewels, or furniture, were intolerably arrogant. A fairer picture appeared in the Boston *Journal* of February 16, 1863, for its informant, a gentleman just arrived from the Confederate capital, emphasized the general trust in Jefferson Davis, the bitter determination of most people, and the widespread belief that Northern war-weariness would eventually lead to Southern independence. But this account, too, emphasized the seamy side of life, and the prevalence of lawlessness and violence. "The city is filled with desperadoes, and gambling and drunkenness prevail. The standard of morality is at a

59. Letter in Cincinnati *Commercial,* dated Chattanooga, Dec. 29, 1863; clipped, and printed in New York *Tribune,* Jan. 13, 1864.
60. Richmond *Examiner,* January 9, 1864.

very low point." Places of amusement abounded, and the theatres were never so well filled. The Richmond *Examiner*, recalling the gaiety with which the French noblesse met the lowering menace of jail and the guillotine during the Revolution, found a like temper among the first families of Virginia.[61]

Its gaiety, if the *Examiner* can be believed, was heavily streaked with profligacy. The editor knew of a virtuous deacon arrested in a gambling saloon, and of a cabinet minister who had effected his escape from inner rooms by jumping from a window. The motley population of the city included "the thief and garroter dressed in fine clothes, the seedy and bloated vagabond from Washington in a cheap paradise of free liquor, and the bogus military man of Richmond whose title is but a recognition given him in a brothel."[62] The anxieties of the time, the precarious value of money, and severance of home ties made roulette attractive; at any rate, the *Examiner* thought "the gamblers of Richmond are multiplied as the lice of Egypt."[63] Drinking was so widespread that the editor believed whisky would be master of the Confederacy in place of the Yankees.[64]

Such lurid utterances did injustice to the true spirit of Richmond. From the Seven Days onward the city felt itself in the front lines of the Confederacy, and most people ate their thin fare of corn bread, bacon, and greens with iron determination. Repeatedly, as at the time of Stoneman's raid, they felt that any hour

61. *Ibid.*, Editorial, Jan. 9, 1863.

62. *Ibid.*, Jan. 3, 1863. Governor William Smith in February, 1864, sending the legislature a grand-jury report, deplored the large amount of crime in the city. The principal cause, he thought, was the constant tippling, for in addition to 161 licensed drinking places, it was said that at least 300 unlicensed establishments were selling liquor. They employed a thousand people, and they victimized young and unsuspicious soldiers. He wished all sales of drink, like the sale for medicinal purposes, to be on certificate of a physician. Feb. 26, 1864; Exec. Papers, Virginia State Library.

The Richmond *Examiner* of Feb. 6, 1862, pronounced the rowdyism intolerable. "Acts of brutal violence, vulgar ruffianism, and gross indecency are of momentary occurrence in our streets. No man's life is secure in broad daylight in our most public thoroughfares."

A blank book, with text written by a Virginia Unionist, probably some close friend of John Minor Botts, now in the W.P. Palmer Collection, Western Reserve Historical Society, speaks of the swarm of prostitutes in Richmond. At one time, it said, the government stationed a guard in each hotel in Richmond to prevent Confederate officers and questionable women from entering these inns. It was said that James P. Ballard of the Exchange Hotel had "the most extensive and fashionable house of prostitution ever kept in America."

63. *Ibid.*, Jan. 3, 1863.

64. *Ibid.*, Jan. 22, 1864. Virginia was indeed becoming a bibulous State. In a half-year period in 1861-62 at least 200 new distilleries had sprung up within her boundaries, and they were gradually absorbing much of the corn. They turned out fiery white-mule, a half-dozen drinks of which would make a man drunk for two days. Doubtless you have much drunkenness in Charleston, wrote the corrrespondent of the Charleston *Courier* in Richmond, but even the hardened observer could hardly imagine the daily scene in Richmond. The streets were full of soldiers on furlough; a hundred whisky-shops were busy on Main Street and the side alleys; drunken men reeled about, sprawled over the sidewalks, brandished knives and pistols, and sometimes fell into murderous brawls. *Courier*, Feb. 19, 1862. Gambling was thriving in all the side streets, wrote the same correspondent. (*Courier*, Feb. 10, 1862). When the alarm was given by some scout, a faro table was transformed on the instant into a festive board, with a group of colonels, Congressmen, judges, and minor politicians holding genial converse on the issues of the day.

might see Federal bayonets on their streets. Citizens of the homeguard filed doggedly behind their breastworks to watch through the night hours. The fortifications were strong, with double lines of entrenchments in some places, but so inadequately manned and gunned that at critical moments, as when Lee moved north to Gettysburg, they could not have repelled a determined attack by fifteen thousand Union veterans. Although the poorer people suffered for want of proper food and clothing, they paid a dollar for a bushel of coal, or a quart of potatoes, or a pound of beef, mutton, or pork, with a feeling that they must see the struggle through.[65]

Exaggeration is easily possible from the press or individuals. On the other side of the coin Sallie Putnam, in Richmond in the gloomy summer of 1864, wrote: "Yet the spirits of the people were unconquered. Despondency was unknown. A cheerful submission to these increased inconveniences was everywhere visible, and a more certain hope of prosperity in the Confederate cause indicated in all. . . ."[66]

Observant T. C. DeLeon commented of the early spring of 1864: "Yet there was no *give* to the southern spirit, and as ever in times of deadliest strain and peril, it seemed to rise more buoyant from the pressure. . . ."[67]

[II]

Dissension in high places had troubled the Confederacy even from its beginnings. Jefferson Davis, who had long opposed secession, seemed to radical leaders like Yancey too ready to win conservatives over to the new government by appointing them to office. Punctiliousness and good intentions, thought Yancey, were not acceptable substitutes for superior ability and insight.[68] In the autumn of 1861, men were whispering that both Davis and Alexander H. Stephens were reconstructionists and that as founders of a new nation they would not prove steadfast. Hawk-like observers watched Davis, who was exposed to attacks by multitudinous critics as censorious as Pollard of the *Examiner* and enemies as jealously vindictive, for any sign of vacillation. At the same time, he inescapably came under the fire of champions of State Rights. The efficient prosecution of the war by the President and his executive departments involved a steady pressure toward centralization of authority that offended believers in State sovereignty such as C. C. Clay of Alabama.[69]

65. "An Interior View of Richmond," New York *Tribune*, July 31, 1863.
66. Putnam, Sallie A., *In Richmond During the Confederacy*, New York, 1961, 292.
67. DeLeon, T.C., *Four Years in Rebel Capitals*, Mobile, 1890.
68. DuBose, J.W., *Life and Times of William Lowndes Yancey*, Birmingham, 1892, 628ff.
69. See Ketring, Ruth Anna, *Clay of Alabama: Two Generations in Politics*, Duke University, Ph.D. thesis.

Thus Southern feeling with respect to Jefferson Davis underwent inevitable mutations. When he took office—when William L. Yancey stood beside him before a cheering concourse, announcing, "The man and the hour have met!"—most Confederates felt confidence in him. His eloquent speeches after his selection made many ready to give him implicit trust. Bull Run lifted his prestige to a peak. But then came the disasters in the West; the deterioration of Confederate finances; the tightening of the blockade and paralysis of the Confederate navy. Men began to grumble that Mr. Davis was too slow, was inept, and made bad appointments. In general, Southerners at first blamed the generals; then they blamed Congress; then as Congress retorted that the department heads were culpable, they began to blame President Davis. Here, said the Montgomery *Advertiser* of June 7, 1862, they were right. "We would not cast a doubt upon the patriotism of the President. All his feelings and his hopes are with the South in this struggle. He is only an illustration of the folly of the one-man power."

There had to be an individual to blame, and Davis was the obvious whipping boy as things went down hill. Without question, his was one of the most difficult, nigh impossible, tasks any American political leader ever attempted. Who else was there really, but Davis?

Jefferson Davis's treatment of his generals, his favoritism for some and hostility to others, was the cause of criticism and dissension at the time, and gave birth to enduring rancors. His military fallibility was seen most clearly in his severity toward Joseph E. Johnston. When he abruptly relieved Johnston from command of the army which had just made a masterly retreat from Chattanooga to Atlanta, and had given Sherman a sharp defeat at Kenesaw Mountain, he took a step that pleased Sherman as much as it offended many Confederate officers.[70] For obvious reasons, Davis was reluctant to give up territory. Johnston, however, was anxious to concentrate troops until he had a sufficiently strong army in hand to deliver a stunning blow at an over-extended enemy, no matter how great the area he meanwhile surrendered. Armies were worth more than land, he felt, to the Confederate cause. The question Davis had to ask was: Would Johnston really ever fight? Undoubtedly Davis's favorite, Pemberton, should have followed Johnston's directions in 1863, should have abandoned Vicksburg, and should have fought in the open; that is, should have given up the city and saved the army. Yet Pemberton would have been greatly criticized if he had done so. Davis faced one dilemma after another.

"I think Mr. Davis treated you very badly," Longstreet wrote D. H. Hill long afterward, "but that he treated me much worse, and has pursued me since the

70. Cf. Govan, Gilbert E., and James Livingood, *A Different Valor; The Story of Joseph E. Johnston, C.S.A.,* Indianapolis, 1956.

war. But he seems disposed to be kind towards you in his book.[71] In it he tells falsehoods of me." It was part of Davis's nature, Longstreet concluded, to approve failure and disparage success. He approved of Pemberton and Bragg; he disparaged Longstreet and Johnston.

The primary faults of Davis were narrowness, frigidity, and pride; he had little breadth, little magnanimity, little warmth or imagination—qualities fundamental in his great antagonist in Washington. The basic ideas of Jefferson Davis were, in fact, conventionally Southern, and limited. They were the ideas expressed even after the end of the war to his friend and medical attendant at Fortress Monroe (1865), Lt.-Col. John Craven, reported faithfully by Craven in *Prison Life of Jefferson Davis* (1866). He disliked Joe Johnston, H.S. Foote, and the Rhetts, and Brown of Georgia. He liked Lee, Stonewall Jackson, Bragg, and Pemberton. He thought the Negro needed the fostering care of a superior race. He believed it impossible for white men to grow cotton, rice or sugar. He held the people of the South aristocrats and cavaliers; the people of the North mean, money-grubbing democrats. If we judged him by his preconceptions we should give him a far lower rating than he merits.

He showed favoritism and fickleness in his relations with his departmental heads, and especially his Secretaries of War. Judah P. Benjamin was certainly a great favorite. The circumstances in which Davis had parted with Leroy Pope Walker and George Wythe Randolph pained many people. Randolph applied for field command, but had to resign due to ill health and went to Europe. Why was he not used elsewhere? Kean heard early in the battle-summer of 1864 that Davis was discontented with Seddon, and wished to get rid of him.[72] Later Kean wrote that he thought Seddon should have resigned at this time, when he had good reason and an unclouded record, instead of waiting to be forced out early in 1865. Poor Seddon lost his brother and a 12-year-old daughter late in the war, blows that almost prostrated him. On March 13, 1864, Kean wrote that Seddon was "out of spirits since the enemy burnt his barns and stole his horses." A little later the diarist recorded: "Mr. Seddon is much disgusted with his position. In a conversation with a friend who told me on yesterday, he complained heavily that the President was the most difficult man to get along with he had ever seen. If the President cannot get along with a man as smooth and yielding as Mr. Seddon, nobody can please him."[73]

Friends of Seddon, including Kean, also complained that Davis ignored him, making use of General Bragg instead to execute all kinds of orders. Davis appointed officers, moved troops across the map, and assigned officers to new

71. Greenville, S.C., June 15, 1886, D.H. Hill Papers, Virginia State Library.
72. Kean, *Diary, op. cit.,* 161, June 25, 1864.
73. *Ibid.,* 140, 153-154.

functions without consulting Seddon. His appointment of Bragg to be in charge of "the conduct of military operations in the armies of the Confederacy," was unpopular. "All accounts agree," wrote Kean on June 12, 1864, "that the deepest uneasiness pervades the army, officers and rank-and-file, at Bragg's being in Richmond. They think that if anything should happen to Lee that Bragg would be assigned—which they regard with universal assent as the ruin of the army and the cause."

Davis, however, was sometimes in the right in military affairs. He had truly a justification for his displacement of Beauregard. As he put it: "Beauregard was tried as Commander of the Army of the West and left it without leave when the troops were demoralized, and the country he was sent to protect was threatened with conquest."[74]

But Davis was proudly quarrelsome. In the autumn of 1863, he sent haughty and umbrage-taking letters to Alexander Y.P. Garnett of Virginia because Garnett had written General Henry A. Wise quoting a message that Mrs. Davis had authorized him to transmit. Davis wrote Garnett: "Your statement in regard to myself was untrue and your reference to my wife in connection with it an offensive familiarity."[75] Garnett then explained that his letter to his relative and close friend Wise had been playful. Details elude us, but it is clear that Davis by his stiff proud letters had unnecessarily made enemies of Garnett and Wise. Garnett was left bitter after an acrimonious correspondence. Wise, himself a troublesome character, after declaring he would welcome a break with the insolent Davis, continued typically: "the Davises are a little, low, vulgar people."[76]

Wigfall was continuously violent against Davis; a bitter, vituperative enemy. In a letter to Davis, August 13, 1863, he blamed the President for the fall of Vicksburg. "Had Johnston last November been allowed to march into Tennessee, and uniting with Kirby Smith and Bragg, to crush Rosecrans," the Confederacy would now have both Tennessee and Kentucky.[77] Evidently C. C. Clay, Robert W. Barnwell, R. M. T. Hunter, and Louis Wigfall made up a congenial group, spending much time together; though Clay remained close to Davis.

When Benjamin H. Hill of Georgia supported a bill in the Congressional session of 1863 for the organization of a Supreme Court, it logically met opposition by State Rights men who had long been suspicious of the highest Federal tribunal. It failed in the House partly because many members recoiled from the general idea that John A. Campbell, another moderate, would be made chief justice. A larger reason, however, lay in an apprehension that the proposed

---

74. Davis, Richmond, Oct. 29, 1862, to E. Kirby-Smith, E. Kirby-Smith Papers, Univ. of N.C. Lib.; Kean, Diary, *op. cit.*, 155.

75. Correspondence, Nov. 9, 10, 1863, in Henry A. Wise Papers, Univ. of N.C. Lib.

76. Nov. 17, 1863, Wise Papers, *Ibid.*

77. C.C. Clay Papers, Duke Univ. Lib.

Supreme Court might hand down decisions that would limit the reserved powers of the States and the State courts.[78] Then Clay and Yancey fell out with Davis over the question whether Alabama troops should be placed under the command of officers from other States. A dispute also arose between the executive department and the State Rights men in Congress over the question whether the purchase and export of cotton and other products to gain funds abroad for buying munitions and warships should be handled by the Treasury Department, or by an independent bureau. If the Treasury Department had full authority, Davis would control the use of cotton and tobacco; if an independent bureau were created, Congress would dominate. President Davis used a pocket veto to kill the independent-bureau bill.[79]

Gettysburg, Vicksburg, and other reverses in the summer of 1863 accentuated the public criticism of Davis. Yancey was outspoken in his criticism. His ally C. C. Clay told the President to his face that he had shown personal enmity to Yancey in his appointments to office.[80] At the same time, Clay told Yancey and others that he had lost confidence in Davis. "His official course grows daily more inscrutable, and the more I see of him the less I understand him."[81] Other men felt the same. Kean in the War Department later wrote that the President had shown such a faculty for converting friends into enemies that his administration could not go on for a month, but for wartime pressures. Many members of both houses who had at first been staunch supporters had become alienated. They believed they had suffered personal slights, and they avenged them by systematic attacks.[82] Just after Gettysburg, Wigfall demanded of Clay: "Has it ever occurred to you that Davis's mind is becoming unsettled? No sane man would act as he is acting. I fear that his bad health and bad temper are undermining his reason,

78. T.J. Withers of South Carolina, to C.C. Clay, April 18, 1863; cited by Ketring, *ut supra.*

79. Yearns, Wilfred Buck, *The Confederate Congress,* Atlanta, 1960, 37-38. Yancey's attitude toward Davis developed from mild criticism in the spring of 1862, when he had just returned from Europe, to bitter hostility in July, 1863, when he lay dying. In a joint letter of April 21, 1862, Yancey and C. C. Clay, Jr. complained that Davis was not appointing as many Alabamians to brigadier-generalships as he should. To this Davis returned a very stiff reply. Nominations to generalships were his alone; the Senate could confirm or reject; and he would not argue the propriety of his nominations.

Then on May 6, 1863, Yancey wrote Davis accusing him of personal enmity. He had asked that a commission be conferred upon his son; now he withdrew the request. Davis in reply stated that he had never declared any enmity to Yancey. To this Yancey replied in the most quarrelsome terms. Ever since they had talked about arms purchases abroad, he had noticed a hostile manner on Davis's part; and he had particularly noticed that Davis nominated some of Yancey's most inveterate personal foes in Alabama for office. He bitterly indicted Davis for acts that evinced a settled hostility, and that justified such hostility on his own part.

But it should be noted that Yancey's opposition was essentially petty. He thought that he and his Alabama had been slighted in appointments; that his son had been neglected. He specifically said in this last letter of July 11: "Upon administrative measures of a legislative character I have generally agreed with you." All this in "More Yancey Letters," *Alabama Historical Quarterly,* Fall, 1940, 334-341.

80. Ketring, Ruth Anna, *ut supra.*

81. DuBose, *Yancey, op. cit.,* 751.

82. Kean, *Diary, op. cit.,* 156-157, June 13, 1864.

and that the foundation is already sapped."[83] Howell Cobb, declared Wigfall, would have made a better President.

By the summer of 1863, the diarist Kean was ready to indict the entire government. In relations with the enemy, he noted, the President was infirm. "The benevolence of his disposition would appear to stand in the way of such measures as would have resolved these questions (treatment of prisoners, citizens, and violations of the laws of war) heretofore when the balance of captures was in our hands. I think it is quite clear that he has little skill or knowledge as a publicist, and also that the Secretary of State [Benjamin] is a poor adviser. He is a smart lawyer—a ready, useful drawer-up of papers but perhaps the least *wise* of our public men. The Attorney-General [Thomas Watts], too, while a most amiable gentleman, is hardly qualified to assist to sound conclusions (to judge by his opinions.) He has had but little experience in dealing with large questions of administration and public law, having been conversant only with . . . a provincial sphere."[84]

The most caustic of the many journalistic critics of Davis was John Moncure Daniel, editor of the Richmond *Examiner*, whose attacks took on a more and more personal tone. When Daniel singled out Judah P. Benjamin as target, accusing him of losing large sums in Worsham's gambling rooms, and followed this by attacks on Edward C. Elmore, treasurer of the Confederacy, he went too far. The sensitive Elmore first proved that every cent of Confederate funds had been accounted for, then demanded an apology from Daniel, and finally sent a challenge to a duel. The result was that Daniel was wounded.[85]

The criticism of Davis by the press, by hostile governors, and by that curious quartet Clay, Hunter, Wigfall, and Barnwell, increasingly affected public opinion. Clay, who remained fairly close to the President and often went riding with him, was restrained in his utterances. Hunter never openly attacked Davis. But Wigfall, like Robert Toombs and Yancey, publicly execrated the President, and Toombs carried his arraignment to the people in stump diatribes.[86] Wigfall blamed Davis for the fall of Vicksburg. He continued to express the idea, mentioned earlier, that if Johnston had been encouraged to unite Holmes's army with Pemberton's in the autumn of 1862, their combined forces could have defeated

83. C. C. Clay Papers, Duke Univ. Lib.

84. Kean, *Diary, op. cit.,* 93, August 13, 1863.

85. Capers, Henry D., "Memories of Men and Women," Montgomery *Advertiser,* Jan. 18, 1903; Cappon, Lester J., *Virginia Newspapers, 1921-1935: A Bibliography,* New York, 1936, *passim.;* Patterson, A.W., *The Code Duello,* Richmond, 1927, 55; Richmond *Dispatch,* Aug. 17, 1864; Richmond *Whig,* Aug. 16, 18, 1864; Richmond *Sentinel,* Aug. 17, 1864; Richmond *Enquirer,* Aug. 17, 18, 1864; Wilkerson, A. N., "John Moncure Daniel," *Richmond College Historical Papers,* 1915, Vol. I, 73-95; correspondence, J. Ambler Johnston, Richmond, Va., 1966, and reports from Virginia State Library and Virginia Historical Society.

86. He is speaking "in a terrible manner," Lawrence M. Keitt wrote his wife, Jan. 21, 1864. Keitt Papers, Duke Univ. Lib.

Grant, marched to join Kirby-Smith and Bragg in crushing Rosecrans, and taken control of all Tennessee and Kentucky.[87] This was preposterous, but it made an impression upon some people. So did the discontented talk of Keitt and Yancey. "I have always feared the divisions which I saw would spring up among us," wrote Keitt.[88] Too many revolutions had been shipwrecked on such rocks.

Yet Davis had his well-earned admirers and defenders. One of the ablest was Herschel V. Johnson of Georgia, who had admired him since they first met in the Senate in 1848, and who argued persistently against the disposition of Georgians to unite in parties for and against Davis. The President was a pure patriot, doing his best, and despite a few obvious errors, doing well. He was the leader of the South, who would hold office for his fixed term; the people would succeed or fail behind him; "it is a patriotic duty to sustain him, for in this crisis he is in truth the government."[89] And Johnson urged another Southerner of frail health, A. H. Stephens, to repair to Richmond in the autumn of 1863, and do his duty by presiding over the Senate, a weak body which needed his counsel. "We are in great peril: the country has great confidence in your wisdom, and hence the general feeling is that you ought to be in Richmond."[90]

That Davis was tied to one principle was clear—the principle of independence. Benjamin is quoted as saying in June, 1863, "In order to prepare a treaty of peace, it would only be necessary to write on a blank sheet of paper the words 'self government.' Let the Yankees accord that, and they might fill up the paper in any manner they choose. We don't want any state that doesn't want us; but we only wish that each state should decide fairly upon its own destiny. All we are struggling for is to be let alone. . . ." Nothing had changed. The Confederacy was struggling to be let alone, and the North struggling not to let it alone, or so the South regarded it.[91]

[III]

The war had given Richmond newspapers much the same primacy in Southern journalism that New York newspapers had taken in the North, for Richmond was the fountainhead of news. People all over the Confederacy sent in subscriptions, so that at least one journal was unable in 1862 to meet the demand.[92] The *Enquirer*, which was the oldest of the five dailies, had opposed secession and was edited by Richard M. Smith, an able, moderate man. The editor of the *Whig*,

87. Wigfall, Charlottesville, Va., Aug. 13, 1863, to C.C. Clay, Clay Papers, Duke Univ. Lib.
88. Keitt to wife, Jan. 31, 1864, Keitt Papers, Duke Univ. Lib.
89. Johnson to A.E. Cochran of Macon, Ga., from Richmond, March 4, 1863, Herschel V. Johnson Papers, Duke Univ. Lib.
90. Johnson, Richmond, Nov. 29, 1863, to Stephens, Herschel V. Johnson Papers, Duke Univ. Lib.
91. Fremantle, James Arthur Lyon, *The Fremantle Diary*, ed. Walter Lord, Boston, 1954, 167.
92. Charleston *Courier*, Feb. 12, 1862.

another moderate sheet, was James McDonald, a pungent writer. But the *Examiner* seemed to many the most interesting of the Richmond journals, for its owner and editor, the brilliantly erratic John M. Daniel, made it unfailingly sensational, voiced the opinions of the critical Hunter faction, and kept up incessant attacks on everything and everybody. The writings of Edward A. Pollard added to the *Examiner*'s often shrill voice. The *Dispatch*, with a distribution of about 40,000 copies in 1862, claimed the greatest circulation in the Confederacy.[93] Then there was also the *Sentinel*, somewhat more moderate in tone.

No Richmond newspaper did as much yeoman work for national unity and support of the Adminstration as Henry J. Raymond's *Times* did in New York. Some lesser sheets of the Confederacy were well edited, but struggled against countless difficulties. When John Withers Clay established a journal in Chattanooga in the summer of 1863 in competition with the *Rebel*, he had to ransack the Confederacy for a power press and stocks of paper. A new paper-mill was under construction in Atlanta, and presses were advertised for sale at scattered points. He finally got under way with a press purchased in Augusta for $3000, and coarse paper obtained in Charleston. Soon he began making a small profit, sufficient to support him if he lived in the plainest way. For bed, he had a piece of carpet and a blanket laid on a door; for pillow, two bricks beneath his folded overcoat and haversack; and for cover a Mexican serape. He dined with his office boys on fat bacon bought at $1.50 or $1.75 a pound, greens at fifty cents a head, and potatoes at $12 to $14 a bushel; this diet was varied sometimes by blackeyed peas, beef, corn-bread, and molasses at $9 or $10 a gallon.[94]

A newspaper produced under such hardships could do little to sustain Southern morale. Nor were the newspapers produced by editors on the run, moving from Memphis to Jackson, and from Nashville to Chattanooga and then Altanta, in a position to do better. Most of the dingily printed sheets did well just to keep alive. A picture of the Southern press presented by the Selma (Alabama) *Morning Reporter* on April 15, 1864, gave but lukewarm praise, and that mingled with much censure. It liked the Richmond *Whig* best, conservative as it was. "There is an exquisite pleasure always felt in contrasting its high dignified tone with the *Examiner,* which is as erratic as it is brilliant. The *Dispatch*, too, is an excellent journal, abounding with well written editorials . . ." The Charleston *Mercury* was better than the *Courier,* for it never spared censure. Of the Atlanta journals, the *Confederacy* and the *Appeal* were both good, but the *Register* had become comparatively timid. The Augusta *Chronicle and Sentinel* was conducted by a sturdy patriot, while the Savannah *Republican* abounded in coarse abuse of Governor

93. *Ibid.;* Coulter, *Confederate States, op. cit.,* 499-500, 583-585.
94. John Withers Clay, Chattanooga, July 16, Aug. 16, 1863, to C.C. Clay, Clay Papers, Duke Univ. Lib.

Brown. In Mobile, the *Tribune* and the *Register* were again timid; neither of them spoke out fearlessly on any critical question. In Selma, the *Mississippian* was self-willed and unruly, and the *Dispatch* was as blind as an adder in August. This revealing editorial article was obviously full of half-expressed condemnation. The fact was that Southern journalism, always weak, had fallen by the end of 1863 to a low estate indeed. Not one editor possessed abilities comparable with those of Greeley, Bryant, Raymond, Samuel Bowles, or Murat Halstead.[95]

Both talent and defiance went into the two principal Southern periodicals, the *Southern Literary Messenger* and *DeBow's Review.* When George William Bagby became editor in May, 1860, the *Messenger* was twenty-six years old, with a record of contributions by Poe, Simms, and others of note. It had long avoided sectional prejudice, but Bagby made it one of the first publications in Virginia to predict the certain dissolution of the Union, treating the outbreak of war and the assumption of independence as just and desirable.[96] *DeBow's Review,* the creation of another indefatigable crusader, James Dunwoody Bronson DeBow, was influenced by the fact that much of its advertising revenue came from Northern manufacturers and merchants. It had devoted itself since its establishment in 1846 to a defense of the interests of the South, emphasizing tariffs, internal improvements, foreign trade, and agricultural advancement. DeBow declared in January, 1861, that he had never hesitated an instant in presenting the issues of the time and warning readers of the dangers ahead. Publishing George Fitzhugh's article on "Disunion Within the Union" a year earlier, he had declared that he preferred disunion out of it. The vital question was no longer slavery, he asserted; it was secession.[97]

In 1862, Bagby began to take a vitriolic attitude toward President Davis. Although he had broken precedent by editorial articles urging the election of Davis, in March, 1862, he set down in his private notebook his conclusion that a breach was opening between the people and the leader—the people distrustful, and Davis contemptuous of their opinion. It was Davis who was chiefly to blame; "cold, haughty, peevish, narrowminded, pigheaded, malignant, he is the cause of our undoing. While he lives, there is no hope for us."[98] This antipathy of Bagby toward Davis did not abate. In commenting upon Davis's visit to the Southwest, he noted resentfully his cordiality toward Bragg and Joe Johnston, and his cool

95. The Southern Press Association in 1863 had an office in Atlanta, with J.S. Thrasher its superintendent. The papers of R.M. McKee in the Alabama State Department of Archives and History show that the Association specially valued the journalistic services of an official telegraph operator at headquarters of the Army of Tennessee, and was willing to have him send news letters to various journals.
96. *Southern Literary Messenger,* Sept.-Oct., 1862, 581.
97. *DeBow's Review,* XXVIII, January, 1860, 123.
98. Bagby, George William, private notebook, Bagby Papers, Virginia Hist. Soc., Richmond, Va.

disregard of Beauregard and Price.[99] But DeBow in his *Review* sternly defended Davis. To be sure, he had chosen his commissioners to Europe unskilfully; he had sent men who did not realize the unpopularity of slavery in Europe—however, the situation was most difficult. Perhaps slavery was not more unpopular in 1862 than revolution and republicanism had been in the time of the revolt against George III.[100] All in all, DeBow found no true ground of censure for the government. Late in the struggle he declared that Davis yet stood "brave as Ajax and wise as Ulysses," and "that he had won a name in the annals of his age as proud as that of any of the heroes of old."[101] When he brought the Confederacy into port, coming generations would place him beside Washington.

The *Southern Illustrated News*, begun in September, 1862, gave little space to editorial comment, yet it was as defiant as any other proud Southerner. In the spring of 1863 it devoted a column to asseverations of undaunted resolution. What matter if Lincoln was made dictator in the North and given three million men with which to "pulverize" the Southern armies? What matter if England held to a policy of strict neutrality? They would fight their way through. The President, the generals, the troops, above all, the women, remained serenely confident. "There is in the hearts of the Southern people a sunshine from an unseen source which but brightens and beams more steadily as the clouds get blacker."[102] The *Illustrated News* angrily attacked the Congress in Richmond; it had been blundering along in slow-coach style, as if all eternity were before it. The members were "the most notorious incompetents ever gathered together in a deliberative body." It also attacked the selfishness of blockade-runners, the evasiveness of "hospital rats," and the cowardice of aliens. "Much gold is taken away by departing foreigners—timid, dirty birds, whose absence is hailed by every patriot." But the *Illustrated News*, like *DeBow's Review*, was much more inclined to exhort men to courage than to offer criticism.

Magazines no less than newspapers had grave difficulties in finding paper, ink, and press facilities, and in obtaining circulation. A large crop of war-born periodicals, seedlings in the South's literary garden, rose bravely after Sumter only to die when hardly beyond infancy. DeBow's had to omit several issues, but the number for October-November, 1861, announced that a full supply of paper had been obtained and would prevent further interruptions. The *Southern Literary Messenger*, as a result of the government seizure of paper mills and the interruption of North Carolina supplies also had to issue a double September-October number in 1861, and it ceased publication in 1864.[103] In the month of Chancellors-

---

99. *Southern Literary Messenger*, XXXVI, Jan. 1863, 39-42, 57.
100. *DeBow's Review*, XXXIII, May-August, 1862, 1-9.
101. *Ibid.*, XXXIV, July-August, 1864, 102.
102. *Southern Illustrated News*, Vol. I, March 7, 1863.
103. *Southern Literary Messenger*, XXXV, Sept.-Oct. 1862, Editor's Table.

ville, the editor of the *Southern Illustrated News* told a story of brave struggle against the dangers of the blockade, the rascality of Northern corporations, and the inadequacy of boxwood for paper manufacture.[104] The following year the *Illustrated News* dwindled to a single sheet folded, descended to the use of rough brown paper and makeshift ink, and finally sent its last issue on October 22, 1864, to the remnant of subscribers. Yet, for at least two years, the *Southern Illustrated News*, published in Richmond, gave the Confederacy a gleam of literary and journalistic brilliance. The best Southern writers were enlisted. Announcing early in its career a contest for a prize poem, the *Illustrated News* conducted a spirited competition, Henry Timrod winning the $300 award.[105] While it lasted the *News* was a ray of hope to the Confederacy.

Even more heroic was the struggle conducted by J. D. B. DeBow for his *Review*. What vicissitudes it endured! When New Orleans fell, it had to be removed to the offices of the *South Carolinian* in Columbia, where a May-August issue was brought out in 1862. After the editor removed to Richmond early in the war to join the Confederate Government, his brother B. F. DeBow took his place —a man of journalistic experience who claimed he was the first Southerner in Washington to resign after the secession of South Carolina. But the founder continued writing for the editorial columns, and in the summer of 1864, after an interruption of a year, was again back at the helm. He would continue the magazine, he proclaimed, with a higher mission than before. "Society, institutions, and government are to be established and confirmed, and the editor enters upon the labor of love as if to the manor born."[106] Alas for J. D. B. DeBow! When Sherman swung northward to Columbia after his march to the sea, no editorial harbor was left for the *Review*. Only when the guns were silent and cold did DeBow briefly resume publication of a chastened but still interesting *Review*. [107]

One channel of effort in sustaining Confederate morale was the publication of ballads and music suited to the time. The paper-bound collection of *War Songs of the South* issued in 1862 by "Bohemian," a writer for the Richmond *Dispatch*, was perhaps the best such volume. Its authors included some of the best Southern

104. *Southern Illustrated News*, May 2, 1863.
105. *Ibid.*, Jan. 17, 1863.
106. *DeBow's Review*, July-August 1864, 98.
107. The strongest of the Southern religious periodicals was the *Southern Presbyterian Review*; the strongest of the agricultural journals was the *Southern Planter* (established 1841). Other periodicals included the *Southern Monthly* (Memphis), the *Age* (Richmond), the *Bugle Horn of Liberty* (Georgia), a humorous magazine; *Southern Field and Fireside* (Augusta, Ga.), *The Record*, and *Smith and Barrow's Monthly Magazine* (both Richmond.) A shortlived juvenile publication of Charleston was *The Portfolio*. See Frank L. Mott, *A History of American Magazines*; M. J. Moses, *The Literature of the South*. One shortlived Richmond periodical bore the title of *The Record of News, History, and Literature*, an eight-page magazine, of about the same size as the *Nation* that Godkin began in 1865, well-printed on good paper stock. The first issue was dated June 18, 1863; Columbia University has 17 out of 24 numbers issued to November 26, 1863, *Confederate States, op.cit.*, 515-516, also mentions *The Countryman, Southern Cultivator, Weekly Register, Southern Field and Fireside*.

names: Henry Timrod, Paul Hamilton Hayne, Albert Pike, John R. Thompson, and William Gilmore Simms. The subjects were Sumter, the muster of southern forces, Big Bethel, Bull Run, the battle of the Merrimac and Monitor, Shiloh, and other war events. Not a little denunciation of "caitiff scum" and "despot bands" was mingled with appeals to brave Southerners to "bare to the hilt the heart-avenging knife," and "strike home" in the spirit of '76. Timrod used the word "Huns." Although the verses which had any merit were echoes of Scott, Macaulay, or Tennyson, such songs unquestionably did something to console and inspirit the people.[108]

Music-publishing grew into a profitable business in the South. Before the paper shortage became acute, and Northern invasion extensive, a flourishing industry had been established. The most stirring Confederate song was, of course, James Ryder Randall's "Maryland, My Maryland." Other strictly Confederate ditties were: "You Are Going to the Wars, Willie Boy"; "The Southron's Chaunt of Defiance"; "The Soldier's Suit of Gray"; and "Somebody's Darling." Popular Southern songs with Yankee tunes included: "When This Cruel War is Over," "The Vacant Chair," and "Aura Lee." "Lorena", first published in 1857, was written by the Rev. H. D. L. Webster and set to music by J. P. Webster, who also composed "In the Sweet By and By." "Lorena" was popular both North and South before the war. "Listen to the Mocking Bird" was written in the North in 1855, and "The Girl I Left Behind Me" went back to British sources in the late eighteenth century. "Dixie" had been a Yankee minstrel song, and credit for popularizing the word Dixie as well as writing the tune seems to belong to Dan Emmett. But rather significantly, the most popular Confederate songs were the lachrymose ballads: "Call Me Not Back from the Echoless Shore," "Dear Mother, I've Come Home to Die," "Do They Miss Me at Home?", "I Remember the Hour when Sadly We Parted," and "Just Before the Battle, Mother," though they were not always of Southern origin.

The bard of the Confederacy, the best song-writer and song-composer, was John Hill Hewitt, a graduate of West Point, too old in 1861 for active service, but indefatigable with his pen. His first song-hit was "All Quiet Along the Potomac Tonight," published in Columbia, South Carolina. Harry Macarthy wrote the hugely popular song, "The Bonnie Blue Flag," which, like "Maryland" and the adopted "Dixie," lifted the Southern heart. Inevitably, many patriotic songs— "The Star Spangled Cross," "The Southern Marseillaise," "You Can Never Win Us Back," "God Save the South"—appeared, and inevitably many of them were adaptations, imitations, or plagiarisms of song classics.[109]

Book-publishing in the Confederacy was maintained with creditable vigor

108. Published by West & Johnston, 145 Main Street, Richmond, 216.

109. Harwell, Richard B., "Confederate Carrousel: Southern Songs of the Sixties," Emory University *Quarterly*, VI, No. 2 June, 1950.

amid countless difficulties. It profited at first from a popular conviction that the
new nation should achieve a cultural and educational as well as political independence, but suffered more and more as the years passed from the fact that the war
and the attendant blockade shut off not only Northern, but much European
literary and cultural production, while it steadily diminished the market for
Southern productions. The Confederate Government made immediate attempts
to protect and extend Northern and European copyrights within its borders, and
would have established an international copyright with other countries; however,
never recognizing Confederate independence, these countries could not enter
into the necessary treaties. Southern publishing houses tried to flourish in Richmond, Charleston, Macon, and other cities—even one in Vicksburg, both before
and after the fall of that city. Southern authors were especially prolific in the
production of verse, though not, except for Paul Hamilton Hayne and Henry
Timrod, of poetry; also of chronicles, histories, and polemics. Southern publishing houses reprinted many well-known works both Northern and European.
Some volumes, like John Esten Cooke's early biography of Stonewall Jackson,
apparently became, by Southern standards, best-sellers. A few humorous essays
and sketches also did well, and it was creditable to the Confederate spirit of
wartime endurance under hardship that the periodical *Southern Punch* began
publication in 1863 in Richmond. The South had its own textbooks and textbook
publishers, but as schools and colleges closed their doors, the currency of even
the best texts, like William Bingham's useful *Latin Grammar*, diminished.[110]

[IV]

As the war dragged on, internal dissension increased. Davis is inveterately
obstinate, his obstinacy bred in the bone, wrote one Richmond observer. His
health is so bad that only his patriotic devotion and stubbornness combined could
keep him at his desk; but his death would be one of the direst misfortunes that
could befall the South.[111]

110. This whole large subject, along with the place given the fine arts and related activities in the
Confederacy, is capably treated by E.M. Coulter in *The Confederate States of America, 1861-1865,*
Louisiana State Univ. Press, 1950, Chs. XX and XXI, 482-532. Confederate publishing houses, while
not comparing in number or size with those at the North, managed to supply the nation with
pamphlets and books in considerable quantity. Evans & Cogswell of Charleston and then Columbia,
S.C., was the major private publishing house. Others of note included Ayres & Wade, and West &
Johnston, both of Richmond; Burke, Boykin & Company of Macon, Ga.; S.H. Goetzel & Company
of Mobile; and H.C. Clarke of Vicksburg. See Coulter, *Confederate States,* 508. There was no governmental printing office, and the voluminous printing of the Confederate government was spread
among several firms. Harwell, Richard Barksdale, *Cornerstones of Confederate Collecting,* Charlottesville, Va., 1952, 8. Publishing, of course, suffered from the same shortages as did newspapers and
periodicals.
111. W.B. Machen, April 21, 1863, to R.B. McKee, McKee Papers, Department of Archives and
History, Alabama.

Davis realized that management of the Confederate cause required a firm hand, which its basic philosophy simply would not permit. Seeing that a great war cannot be waged without an approach to dictatorship, perhaps even more than Lincoln, he feared being called a despot. Vice-President Stephens applied that name to him in the same spirit that Ben Wade applied it to the occupant of the White House. "I have no feelings of antipathy, much less of hostility," Stephens wrote of Davis in the spring of 1864. "While I do not and never have regarded him as a great man or statesman on a large scale, or a man of any marked genius, yet I have regarded him as a man of good intentions, weak and vacillating, timid, petulant, peevish, obstinate but not firm." Weak and vacillating? On the contrary! Stephens had allowed his rhetoric to overpower his sober, good judgment. He thought Davis harsh and obstinate because he insisted on pursuing policies of national authority that Stephens abhorred. "He has changed many of his former States Rights principles, as in case of Conscription. His whole policy on the discipline and organization of the Army is perfectly consistent with the hypothesis that he is aiming at absolute power. Not a word has come from him of military usurpation in the order for Martial Law by Bragg and Van Dorn, or the whole system of passports and provost martials, which is utterly wrong and without authority of law."[112]

The Confederacy would have been far weaker without the Conscription Act of 1862 that Stephens opposed from the moment it was suggested. It had good reasons for the Act of February 27, 1862, authorizing suspension of the writ of habeas corpus for spies, Unionists, and traitors. Stephens's belief that volunteering would suffice, and that suspension of habeas corpus would lead to "military tyranny," was absurd. When the Confederacy was first organized, men had supposed that Davis and Stephens would work in close accord. If they had done so, and if Stephens had spent more time in Richmond advising the President, and in touring the South to inspirit the people, Confederate prospects would have been brighter. Instead, he allied himself with the other Georgia leaders, Brown and Toombs. Brown, fretting over the "imperial power" of the President, kept

---

112. Stephens, April 5, 1864, to Herschel V. Johnson, André de Coppet Collection, Princeton. Stephens's speech of Nov. 1, 1862, at Crawfordsville, Ga., was a declaration of war on Davis, for he asserted that the whole policy of the Confederacy had been wrong. "Our strength is in our locks— not of hair or wool, but in our locks of cotton," he declared. If he had been in control he would have exchanged eighty per-cent bonds for cotton at generous prices, would thus have obtained two million pounds of the crop of 1861, would have used government possession of this resource to get a large fleet of ironclads, perhaps fifteen, built in Europe, and would have employed them to break the blockade and convoy the cotton across to Europe. Five ironclads would have been ready by January 1, 1862; they would have done the job. Holding the cotton in Europe until its price reached fifteen cents a pound, he would have sold it for a billion dollars "at least a profit to the Confederacy of 800 millions." This would have sustained the war for years. Stephens's speech is in his *A Constitutional View of the Late War Between the States,* Philadelphia, 1870, II, Appendix, 783. A favorable commentary is in John C. Reed, *The Brothers' War,* Boston, 1905, 286ff.

the Stephens brothers (Linton was influential) closely informed of his ideas. All three men were incensed when Braxton Bragg placed Atlanta under martial law in order to frustrate spies, ensure the safety of railroads, hospitals, and military stores, and facilitate the apprehension of deserters. Bragg's creation of the post of civil governor for Atlanta, wrote Stephens, was "a most palpable usurpation" of power.

Not only did Vice-President Stephens fail to assist Davis in any way, and avoid any public speechmaking that would have lifted Southern hearts; he began in 1863 to circulate letters and issue statements that interfered with the Confederate war effort. He asserted that no power on earth could rightfully declare martial law in the Confederacy, and that every citizen had a right to a speedy trial by jury even though the writ of habeas corpus had been suspended. He informed one Mississippi woman in March, 1863, in a letter widely copied in the press, that all the South found wanting was the brains to manage and mould its resources. When the Confederate Congress took up bills at the beginning of 1864 to widen the scope of conscription and protract the suspension of habeas corpus, Stephens let it be known that he was incensed. "Far better," he wrote R. M. Johnston, "that our country should be overrun by the enemy, our cities sacked and burned, and our land laid desolate, than that the people should suffer the citadel of their liberties to be entered and taken by professed friends."[113] He planned to make a trip to Washington during the summer of 1863 to discuss the exchange of prisoners; this, he thought, might afford an opportunity for opening peace talks.[114]

It was a sore handicap to the Confederacy that its two most prominent civil leaders should be on bad terms with each other, and that one should sow disaffection broadcast. They should have stood shoulder to shoulder in keeping the cotton states a unit, and proving that highminded attachment to the new republic overrode all personal differences. Stephens had accepted the vice-presidency because he believed himself one of the few Southerners with enough integrity, loyalty to principle, and pure disinterested patriotism to guide the government through its early crises. Instead, his jealousies and suspicions befogged his mind with incredibly unreal fantasies, until he moved from a merely passive indifference to Davis to an active hostility. Both men were essentially proud, cold, humorless, and stiff, and instead of correcting each other's faults, they intensified them. Davis, however, labored with intense devotion to do his duty.

113. Johnston, Richard M., and William H. Browne, *Life of Alexander H. Stephens,* Philadelphia, 1878, 453; Stephens, Alexander H., *A Constitutional View of the Late War Between the States,* Philadelphia, 1870, II, 787.
114. Rabun, James Z., "Alexander H. Stephens and Jefferson Davis," *American Historical Review,* Vol. LVIII, 290-321; Rowland, *Jefferson Davis, Constitutionalist, op. cit.,* V, 513-515; Stephens to Davis, June 12, 1863.

When Governor Brown called a special session of the Georgia legislature to sit in Milledgeville in March, 1864, Linton Stephens offered two sets of resolutions. One of them assailed the suspension of the writ of habeas corpus; the other called upon the Davis Administration to proffer peace to the North on all proper occasions, upon the sole condition that the United States recognize the right of the South to self-government. To support these resolutions Alexander H. Stephens made a three-hour speech, his sole oratorical effort of the year. He dwelt upon the tyrannies of conscription and of martial law. Who is safe? he asked. "Tell me not to put confidence in the President."[115]

Georgia and her leaders in fact became a focus of discontent within the Confederacy. Alexander H. Stephens, Linton Stephens, and Robert Toombs shirked the worst hardships and perils of war to devote their tongues and pens to fault-finding, with President Davis their special target. "Aleck" Stephens, frail, wizened, and waspish, had some excuse, not only of ill health but of devotion to the principles of civil and personal liberty. He condemned the suspension of the habeas corpus, the impressment law, conscription, and the funding act as too high a price to pay for Southern independence.[116] But this was far from justifying his valetudinarian rôle when he should have been hard at work in Richmond, or his vituperative questioning of Davis's abilities and courage.[117] Linton Stephens, after brief service in Virginia as lieutenant-colonel, returned home late in 1861 to enjoy his ruddy fireplace, his library and decanters, and the Christmas gaiety. Toombs, whose brief tenure of the secretaryship of state ended on July 25, 1861, was given command of a brigade, but dropped it after Antietam to resume life in his country home. Here he made his study resound with discontented talk, freely cursing everything Confederate, as Mrs. Chesnut observed, from President down to horse-boy.[118] And Governor Brown added to the resentment of all malcontent Georgians.

In all this Georgia criticism of Davis, jealousy was an unacknowledged element. Toombs and Stephens could not forget that they had originally been suggested for the presidential office. They had been as willing as Barkis, but Toombs had been lamed by his elbow-bending, his precipitancy of temper, and the opposition of Howell Cobb whom he had lampooned; while Stephens could muster so few supporters that he was glad to get the vice-presidency.[119] Governor Brown hinted that he should have received the distinction.[120] Had Davis been

115. Rabun, *op. cit.*, 310, quoting Atlanta *Intelligencer*, April 2, 1864.
116. Patrick, Rembert W., *Jefferson Davis and His Cabinet*, Baton Rouge, 1944, 41-42.
117. As in letter to H.V. Johnson, April 8, 1864, *O.R.* IV, Vol. III, 279.
118. Kean, *Diary, op. cit.*, 117.
119. Patrick, *op. cit.*, 28-29; Johnston & Browne, *op. cit.*, 385-390; Hull, A.L., ed., *Correspondence of T.R.R. Cobb, 1860-62*, Washington, 1907, 171.
120. Rabun, *op. cit.*, 290-321.

more conciliatory, and had he taken pains to confer more sedulously with Stephens in particular, he might have soothed the sensibilities of these men—all close friends of each other. Some patient explanation early in 1864 might have convinced Stephens that Davis did not really aim at despotism; that he waged a continuous struggle to prevent his authority from ebbing away altogether. Irretrievable bankruptcy, runaway inflation, and mounting opposition to impressment of supplies were not foundations on which autocracy could be built.[121] Foreign observer Captain Justus Scheibert seems perceptive in his comment: "The fact that an uncritical, partisan madness now besmirches his character, that the rabble scorns him, can not rob him of the place in history which will be given him when calm reason stands in judgment over blind confusion. . . ."[122]

One evidence of the diminishing confidence of the South lay in the spasmodic if futile peace tentatives of 1863-64. When, just before Gettysburg, Southerners discussed a mission to Washington to arrange an exchange of prisoners, Stephens hoped that he might go, and that once in the capital, he might bring up "a general adjustment." He would negotiate only on the basis of a full recognition of the right of each State to determine its own destinies. If repelled, he could explain to the world the Southern thirst for peace, and the flinthearted arrogance of the North. But when he proceeded northward as far as Newport News carrying two letters from Davis to Lincoln, he was halted, for Lincoln and his Cabinet suspected his motives and designs. Stephens in his suspicious way leaped to the conclusion that Davis had taken three steps to frustrate the mission: by sending Lee into Pennsylvania; by arranging Morgan's raid across Indiana and Ohio; and by dispatching a letter to Lee upon Stephens's mission by a route which ensured its capture by Union troops.[123] Such were his feverish fantasies!

Later in 1863, Stephens joined his brother Linton and Governor Brown in a pacifist intrigue which ran parallel with the sour defeatism of W. W. Holden in North Carolina and William W. Boyce in South Carolina. "I tell you we are a doomed people," Linton wrote the Vice-President.[124] The two brothers laid plans, after Congress broadened conscription and maintained the suspension of habeas corpus, for placing Georgia behind a peace movement. Governor Brown was to call a special session and open it with a speech assailing the Davis Administration; Linton was then to introduce a set of resolutions proposing an invitation to peace; and Stephens was to deliver a fiery oration in their support. This scheme was carried out, culminating in a three-hour philippic by Alexander H. Stephens

121. Kean, *Diary, op. cit.*, 118; Nov. 5, 1863, enumerates them all.
122. Scheibert, Captain Justus, *Seven Months in the Rebel States During the North American War, 1863,* Tuscaloosa, Ala., 1958, 126-127.
123. Rabun, *op. cit.*, " Stephens and Davis," 306.
124. Linton Stephens to A.H. Stephens, Oct. 14, 1863, Stephens Papers, Manhattanville College.

against Davis.[125] But all tentative moves toward peace in 1864 broke down.

They broke down because Lincoln and his Cabinet would discuss no terms that failed to embrace restoration of the Union, and Davis and his associates discussed no terms that failed to embrace its disruption. The continuous eruptions by the Stephens brothers, however, and the possibility that Georgia and North Carolina might leave the Confederacy to make a separate peace, did much by the autumn of 1864 to impair Southern morale. Vice-President Stephens wrote Linton in October that if Georgia believed her best interests counselled withdrawal, she should leave; and her action would involve no breach of faith with her sisters or with the Confederacy! This statement was not published. But he did publish a letter to Senator T. J. Semmes of Georgia declaring that Davis apparently preferred Lincoln's reëlection to the election of McClellan, and desired a continuance of the war.[126]

It was the simmering demand for peace, fed by the letters, the talk, and the speeches of the Stephens brothers and Toombs, Governor Brown, W. W. Holden, and others, along with military strategy and morale, that constrained President Davis in the early autumn of 1864 to make a speechmaking trip into Georgia, South Carolina, and Alabama—his third such trip during the war. He told the crowd in Columbia that the surest way to ensure the election of a Northern leader favorable to peace would be by gaining some decisive Confederate victories; victories that would be within grasp if every shirker and absentee joined the armies.[127] But his speeches merely drew from Stephens a new torrent of abuse. By the beginning of 1865, members of Congress and others in Richmond spent much of their time talking about the necessity of depriving Davis of Army control or even of his Presidency; and Davis, who heard about the talk, was declaring that he would resign at once if the Vice-President would go first—but he would never relinquish the government to a man who would immediately hand it over to the enemy.[128]

This was when the last sands of the Confederacy were running out. But as early as the autumn of 1863, Kean in the War Department was expressing a sense of utter discouragement. The loss of Chattanooga, the retreat of the Confederate army into Georgia, and the promotion of Grant with superior forces, augured a black future. "Infatuation rules the hour," he wrote.[129] "I have never actually despaired of the cause, priceless—holy—as it is, but my faith in the adequacy of the men in whose hands we are is daily weakened. Men are getting tired of it. Steadfastness is yielding to a sense of hopelessness of the leaders." North Carolina

125. To R.M. Johnston, January 21, 1864, Johnston and Browne, *op. cit.*, 453.
126. Augusta *Constitutionalist*, Nov. 16, 1864, quoted in Rabun, *op. cit.*, 315.
127. Rabun, *op. cit.*, 315.
128. *Ibid.*, 317; Rowland, Dunbar, *Jefferson Davis, Constitutionalist*, Jackson, 1923, VIII, 213.
129. Kean, *Diary, op. cit.*, 119, Nov. 6, 1863.

had elected several men to Congress on a demand for reconstruction of the Union, and Governor Vance was more and more intimate with supporters of the traitorous *Raleigh Standard.* Perhaps the one road out of the Southern dilemma was to cover Richmond with a single corps of the Army of Northern Virginia, and send the other corps with Lee to help defend Georgia. This was the language of desperation.

A year later, the sense of desperation was much deeper. Davis may have been right when he wrote in July, 1863, "Our people have not generally realized the magnitude of the struggle in which we are engaged . . ." Perhaps its magnitude may have been just too much for anyone to realize or do anything to meet effectively.[130]

130. Rowland, *Jefferson Davis Constitutionalist, op. cit.,* V, 548, to Sen. R.W. Johnson of Arkansas.

11

Under the Trampling Armies: The Tragic Lot of the Freedmen

AS UNION troops crossed the borders of the South, tens of thousands for the first time saw slavery face to face. They gazed at it with intense curiosity. Were the Negroes an utterly ignorant folk, unable even to use the English language? Were they, as many Southerners held, a childlike people? Then, too, questions of their history arose. Were evidences of physical maltreatment numerous? Had they suffered heavily from the separation of families? How deeply had they suffered from repression? And how intense was their consequent thirst for freedom? These questions rose in the minds of countless soldiers as black people, roughly garbed, uncouth in manner, and often hardly intelligible, gazed from slave quarters at the marching columns, crowded in shy knots to the camps, or came singly to beg food and give information. The boom of guns, the song of bugles, and the shouts of drill-sergeants brought them into sight as fast as such sounds sent their owners into hiding.

Along the border, slavery showed an outwardly mild face. A Union officer in charge of contrabands at Fortress Monroe found that with one exception these scores of Negroes made no complaint of severe whippings or systematic cruelty. A locust tree in front of Hampton jail had been used as a whipping-post, and they insisted on chopping it down, but only such flagrant offenses as running away had been punished there. Most masters had never gone beyond rough language and chance blows, and many had shown kindness. Complaints of the sundering of families, however, were numerous. "Where is your wife?" "She was sold off two years ago, and I've not heard of her since." As Virginia was a slave-breeding area, a similar answer was often given about children, who were sold at eight years of age or earlier. Evidence of miscegenation appeared on every hand. Many men put to work on the fortifications appeared as white as the sunburnt troops, and many women trailed children who, in color, features and hair, were semi-Caucasian, sometimes as blonde as the Saxon slaves whom Gregory had met in the Roman markets. All, with great emphasis, wanted freedom: "We want to belong to ourselves."[1]

When opportunity offered, all the way from Virginia to Missouri, they fled in droves within the Union lines. Late in 1862, commissioners appointed to take a census of slaves in King William County, Virginia, reported that while 595 able-bodied males between 18 and 45 remained in the county, 590 had gone to the Yankees, nine-tenths of them able-bodied adult males. "Contrabands in large numbers are fleeing from Missouri into Kansas and especially into Lawrence," a Kansan wrote in the autumn of 1861: "131 came into Lawrence in ten days, yesterday 27 had arrived at two P.M."[2] Not an intelligent slave in Missouri but knew of Lawrence as an ark of freedom, and thousands were determined to get there. Opportunities to escape became easy to find. A Tennessee slave who had suffered from the overseer's cat-o'-nine tails was sent off with a group of others to hunt deer or wild hogs to help the meat shortage. "This was the chance I been wanting, so when we gits to the hunting ground the leader says scatter out."[3] He followed the North Star until he reached Rosecrans's lines, happy amid his hardships, for "I's gwine to the free country, where they ain't no slaves."

Were they ignorant? In the borderland and at favorable points farther south the escaped slaves had learned much from the oratory accompanying Presidential elections, from the talk of their owners, and from a few scattered black men who could read. With rare exceptions, they instantly accepted the Yankees as their friends. When asked if they thought themselves fit for freedom, some answered with rough logic: "Who but the darkies cleared all the land 'round here?" demanded one. "I feed and clothe myself and pay my master $120 a year," responded another. Virginia slaves evinced a general desire to learn to read—a few had been taught clandestinely by white playmates in childhood. They had no monopoly of ignorance, anyway, for of the whites who took the oath of allegiance at Hampton not more than one in fifteen could sign his name. Negroes worked hard on the fortifications there, and faced and dressed the breastworks as well as anybody.[4] John A. Kellogg of the Wisconsin Iron Brigade, escaping from a Charleston prison, was helped on his way by many slaves. "I may be credited with speaking dispassionately," he wrote later, "when I say that in my opinion they were, as a class, better informed of passing events and had a better idea of

1. "The Contrabands at Fortress Monroe," *Atlantic Monthly*, VIII, No. XLIX, November, 1861, 636-637.

2. John B. Wood, Lawrence, Kans., to George L. Stearns, November 19, 1861, Stearns Papers, Kansas Hist. Soc.

3. Botkin, Benjamin A., ed., *Lay My Burden Down: A Folk History of Slavery*, Chicago, 1945, Pt. IV, 198-201.

4. "The Contrabands at Fortress Monroe," *ut supra*, 637.

questions involved in the struggle between North and South than the majority of that class known as the 'poor whites.' "[5]

A future President, campaigning in West Virginia, shared a general opinion that the slaves there would do well in freedom. "These runaways are bright fellows," wrote Rutherford B. Hayes. "As a body they are superior to the uneducated white population of this State."[6] Henry M. Cross of the Forty-eighth Massachusetts thought as highly of the Negroes he encountered at Camp Banks near Baton Rouge early in 1863. "They are smart enough for anyone," he wrote of some casual hands, and he gave a more emphatic verdict on a Negro regiment 1100 strong: "They are not barbarous, or blood-thirsty, but are docile, attentive, and drillable."[7] The first white agents to take charge of Negroes at Hilton Head, S.C., formed a strong impression of "developing manhood." One observer was touched when the refugees there, deciding it was not right for the government to provide free candles, took up a collection to pay for them, and although they earned but pittances, they turned in $2.48. Everywhere the Negroes, when properly supervised, furnished good laborers, stevedores, artisans, bridge-builders, scouts, and guides; the troops often found them responsible and hardworking. "We could never get enough of them," testified Vincent Colyer, in charge of freedmen on Roanoke Island after the fighting early in 1862. They often showed nerve and resourcefulness as spies, but at other times were unreliable. "They frequently went from thirty to three hundred miles within the enemy's lines. . . . bringing back important and reliable information. . . . often on these errands barely escaping with their lives."[8] Southerners learned to fear the scouting capacity of escaped slaves.

Treachery to the Union was practically unknown among the contrabands. "Thousands of soldiers after the war," wrote the historians of the Fifty-fifth Illinois Infantry, "blessed the memory of black men who had given them invaluable aid." If masters tried to frighten them by horrible tales of Yankee cruelty, they were not fooled. Their confidence in "Lincum's sojers" was unshakable. "When, as often happened during the march, information was given by the slaves, it could always be relied upon, and again and again the neighborhood of the enemy was disclosed and the secret hiding places of horses, mules, and forage made known to the great advantage of the army. One day there came into the lines two escaped prisoners bringing with them an aged Negro upon a mule. This freed slave had

5. Kellogg, John A., *Capture and Escape*, Madison, Wis., 1908, 147.

6. Hayes, Rutherford B., *Diary and Letters*, ed. Charles R. Williams, Columbus, Ohio, 1922-1926, II, 188.

7. "A Yankee Soldier Looks at the Negro," ed. by William Cullen Bryant II, *Civil War History*, Vol. VII, No. 2, June, 1961, 133ff.

8. Colyer, Vincent, *Report of the Services Rendered by the Freed People to the United States Army, in North Carolina, in the Spring of 1862*, New York, 1864, *passim*.

hidden them in the swamp and fed them for weeks, and in the warmth of their gratitude the men vowed that the benefactor should ride to freedom and be fed on the best of the land for the rest of his life.[9] Undoubtedly this soldier was extreme when stating slave information could "always be relied upon," for in many cases such information was erroneous, or at least distorted and exaggerated.

In the Lower South, and especially on large plantations, the evidences of mistreatment multiplied. Many slaves appeared with backs ridged and livid from floggings: more of them were scarred by cuts or burns; even mutilation was sometimes visible. The London *Times* correspondent, William H. Russell, visiting the plantation of Governor Roman in Louisiana just as the war began, had been struck by the sadness on the faces of the Negroes, convincing him that deep dejection was the prevailing if not universal characteristic of the race.[10] They all looked downcast; even the aged woman who boasted that she had held the governor in her arms when he was a baby, even the attractive yellow girl with fair hair and light eyes whose child was quite white. A soldier of the Eighty-first Ohio, who examined for enlistment a great body of hands fleeing to the Union lines after Iuka and Corinth, was depressed by the evidence of ill usage.

"One gang that I enrolled," he wrote, "sixty in number, had been so terribly abused, beaten, lashed, and branded that they were little better than beasts, and could hardly tell their own names, and not half of them had any idea about their own age, but all referred me to a bright mulatto girl of more than usual intelligence, who had two children with her that looked to me white. As I put down her name I put the usual question, 'Are you married?' and received the answer, 'no!' 'Whose children are these?' 'Them's mine!' 'Who's their father?' 'My master!' As I enrolled this gang of plantation hands and saw the great ugly seams on their backs, and actually great brands on their thighs, fully four inches long, burned so as to leave a deep red scar, and the embruted and pitiable condition of all of them, I thought Mrs. Stowe's Legree a saint compared with the owner of these slaves."[11] Of course many Southerners rejected such evidence. The author of *The Brothers' War,* the cultivated Georgia attorney John C. Reed, testified that among his father's many slaves not one instance of a family separation had occurred before Appomattox, and that, on the contrary, his father had at much expense and inconvenience bought the husband of one slave, and the wife of another, to keep two couples united.[12] Now and then, he admitted, sales which sundered man and wife, or parent and child, were indeed made, but many slaveholders were poor, and sales were declining in proportion to pop-

9. A Committee of the Regiment, *The Story of the Fifty-fifth Regiment, Illinois Volunteer Infantry,* Clinton, Mass., 1887, 401-402.

10. Russell, William Howard, *My Diary North and South,* New York, 1863, Ch. XXXII, 97-100.

11. "Reminiscences of Edwin W. Brown," *Ohio Archeological and Historical Quarterly,* Vol. XLVIII, 304-323.

12. Reid, John C., *The Brothers' War,* Boston, 1905, 166-167.

ulation under pressure of public opinion. He protested earnestly against Lincoln's suggestion that blood was sometimes drawn by the lash, denying this, and forgetting that Lincoln's eloquent utterance was in symbolic, not factual language.[13]

In the Deep South slavery had brutalized some white men as much as their victims. Henry W. Allen, who was elected governor of Louisiana in 1863, had to send officers through the State to halt the stealing of Negroes (especially children from the river parishes) from plantations whose owners had fled; they were seized by so-called guerrillas, taken into Texas, and sold away from their parents and owners. Allen restored about five hundred of these forlorn little wanderers to their families.[14]

It was universally observed that while the Negroes were highly religious, they had limited canons of morality according to Victorian and disciplined white standards. Many had little respect for the Seventh Commandment. It was also universally observed that while they evinced a bustling industry under supervision, they had shown little initiative, morality, or enterprise under slavery. Yet neither their native life in Africa, nor their life as slaves had been conducive to initiative or enterprise in the American sense. Military demands for labor went far toward occupying the contrabands as long as the war lasted, but no longer. As Union forces penetrated deeper into the South and the number of refugees swelled, it was plain that the freed Negroes needed care and supervision. At Yorktown, when the Peninsular campaign began, and later at Memphis, Jackson, and Nashville, they gathered in thousands, forming long lines for rations. Their gratitude for help was touching; they sang, danced, and prayed exultantly. All the way from Tidewater to the Arkansas, as the war progressed, camps of Negroes grew more numerous, active, and troublesome.

Never had America witnessed such scenes. Sometimes the spectacle was merely picturesque. A New York infantryman reached Falmouth on the Rappahannock in April, 1862. "On the day after our arrival," he recorded, "the Negroes came flocking to the guard line, with baskets of eggs, hoe-cakes, and other luxuries, and proved themselves sharp bargainers, doing a lively business." Every squad soon had Negroes as cooks, waiters, foragers for food, and runners of errands.

On occasion, the efforts of freedmen to make a living combined heroism with pathos. At Beaufort, S.C., for example, where several thousand Negroes were quartered outside the town like sheep, volunteers gazed with respect at the shacks where venturesome freedmen sought to attract customers. "Pyes for Sail Here," ran the signs; "Resturent"; "Fresh Bred"; "Soljur's Home"; and "The American

13. *Ibid.*, 169-170.
14. Dorsey, Sarah A., *Recollections of Henry Watkins Allen*, New York, 1866, 244; Mrs. Dorsey herself had three children stolen. Dudley, T., in *The Sable Arm: Negro Troops in the Army, 1861-1865*, New York, 1966, temperately notes this fact.

Hotel." The record continued: "The wild, fervid religious dances, with their accompanying chants, sometimes beginning with Genesis and giving a complete synopsis of the leading points of Bible history from Adam to Peter . . . were the most weirdly exciting yet ludicrous performances imaginable."[15] But pathos was often predominant. The Englishman Edward Dicey, going with Nathaniel Hawthorne to look at Bull Run, was saddened by a group of some dozen runaway slaves huddled upon a flatcar. "There were three men, four women, and half-a-dozen children. Anything more helpless and wretched than their aspect I never saw. Miserably clothed, footsore, and weary, they crouched in the hot sunlight more like animals than men." He overheard one man remarking to a woman, as he munched some white bread he had picked up, "Massa never gave us food like that."[16]

The story of the freedmen in wartime is one of gross mismanagement and neglect. The problem was neither vigilantly foreseen by the government nor dealt with vigorously and promptly by it or by private organizations. Having upset the social system of slaveholding, the North should have acted more generously and promptly to substitute new devices for meeting the old social needs. Almost the whole country was at fault. The abolitionists who had called so long for emancipation should have foreseen that the mere ending of slavery was far from a solution of the stupendous and many-sided problem of creating an efficient and humane social order to meet the exigent new demands. The Lincoln Administration, coping heroically with a multitude of crowding tasks and needs, might ideally have done something more than it did, even if the social, economic, military and governmental standards which then controlled it would have hindered the President from taking such a far-reaching step. Looking back more than a century after emancipation, it might have seemed logical to have urged the creation of a separate government department of Cabinet rank to study, and as far as possible meet, the needs of the freedmen. The government might well have done more than give general support to Grant's plans for succoring the Negroes who flocked into the Army camps, and might have championed more decisively the organization of a Freedmen's Bureau under Brigadier-General John Eaton in March, 1865. Eaton, acting under Grant's orders, had done magnificent work in caring for the physical wants and education of liberated Negroes. In the Department of the Tennessee, including Arkansas, he had set them to work on abandoned plantations, and at cutting wood for the Army and the river steamboats.[17]

All too often squalor, hunger, and disease haunted the refugees, their camps becoming social cancers that were a reproach to the North no less than the South.

15. Mills, John Harrison, *Chronicles of the Twenty-first Regiment, New York State Volunteers*, Buffalo, 1867, 74, 160ff.

16. Dicey, Edward, *Six Months in the Federal States*, London, 1863, II, 29-30.

17. Eaton, John and Ethel Osgood Mason, *Grant, Lincoln, and the Freedmen*, New York, 1907, *passim*.

Maria R. Mann, the first woman sent by the Sanitary Commission as agent in a contraband camp, wrote of appalling conditions and often cruel treatment. Deaths were frequent, disease was universal, and the future so bleak that many of the refugees talked of returning to their slave masters, and some did so. Writing of the hospital, she said: "I found the poor creatures in . . . such quarters, void of comfort or decency;—their personal condition so deplorable that any idea of change for the better seems utterly impossible. Many of them seem to come there to die, and they do die very rapidly. . . . The carcasses, filth and decay which 40,000 have scattered over this town, will make the mortality fearful when warm weather comes . . . So much formality attends red tape, and so few friends have the negroes among the Officials . . ." It is impossible to learn whether this camp at Helena, Arkansas, was worse or better than others, but assuredly it was a doleful place. Speaking out sharply, Mrs. Mann charged the Army with "barbarities" against the refugees, while on the other hand admitting, "Our soldiers suffer untold privations here. . . . What is to be done for either class of sufferers under these discouragements I know not. . . ."[18] William Todd of the Seventy-ninth Highlanders described in sad terms the thousands scattered along the river, canal, and roads near Vicksburg just before its capture. The aged, lame, and blind were conspicuous, for most vigorous young men had found some form of army service. One hatless and shoeless old slave wore a blue dress coat with brass buttons; others had little to cover their nakedness but plug hats and old blankets. Some women were decently dressed in coarse plantation homespun or cast-off clothing of the whites; the busts of others were scantily covered with old silk waists. Malnutrition was evident in nearly every place "where the government has been obliged to support destitute contrabands." An aide of General Rufus Saxton at Beaufort reported in midwinter of 1863, that the authorities had issued only such portions of the army ration as were absolutely necessary to support life. He added that intoxication was far rarer than among the white troops. But, the "ill-fed, ill-sheltered, ill-clothed, unmedicined" freedmen were an easy prey of the infectious maladies that swept their poor quarters. "What is to become of them?" asked William Todd.[19]

[I]

What, indeed, was to become of them? The answer was long in coming, and was unsatisfactory when it did come. The story of the freedmen in wartime, as we have already noted, remained one of gross mismanagement and neglect, for the provision made by the government was too little and too late. Washington

18. Mann, Maria R., Letters from the Freedmen's Camp, Helena, Ark., LC; Todd, William, *The Seventy-Ninth Highlanders, New York Volunteers*, Albany, 1886, 300-301; "To Emancipation League of Boston, Jan. 6, 1863," New York *Tribune*, Jan. 27, 1863.
19. *Ibid.*

failed utterly to foresee the widespread flight of slaves within the Union lines, to assess their needs realistically, and to make considered provision for their future. Lincoln, the War Department, and other agencies, facing a situation completely new in the history of the republic, clung to the usual American policy of delay and improvisation, and manifested the chronic reluctance of government to interfere with personal life. It speaks well for the Army that Ben Butler, David Hunter, N. P. Banks, and above all Grant, showed great sensitivity to the problem, acting with humanity and common sense. But, as we have said, it speaks ill for the Administration not only that it drifted inertly, but that it permitted the care of the freedmen to become in part a football between the Treasury Department and the War Department. Along with Negroes, the Army took possession of much other real and personal property of the rebels, the custody of which properly belonged to the Treasury. To complicate the situation, the Treasury wished to collect the direct tax of 1861 in the seceded States. It therefore legitimately claimed a share in the management of captured Southern property, and Congress recognized the validity of the claim. With foresight and care, a workable adjustment might have been reached, but it was not.

A few officials in Washington, notably William Whiting of the Treasury Department, argued at an early date that the task of caring for refugee slaves and managing abandoned areas demanded a new department of Cabinet rank. It did, indeed. Had such a department been created, and had Lincoln appointed a shrewd and practical head, the new national authority, although it might have suffered terribly from bureaucracy, could have solved some critical wartime problems and smoothed the path of both races into Reconstruction. But Lincoln could not establish a department; Congress alone possessed the power, and for several reasons Congress was unwilling to take farsighted action in behalf of the four million slaves that the war gradually released.

In the first place, most Democrats and the Bell-Everett moderates of the Borderland wished to retard rather than accelerate emancipation. They raised some terrible bogeys: the Negroes would flock northward and flood the labor markets (a fear felt from St. Louis and Cincinnati to Baltimore); they would prove unruly and dangerous; and frightful expenses, necessitating heavy taxes, would be needed to care for the ignorant, helpless, and often ailing refugees. For another reason, many Radical Republicans within and out of Congress believed with Horace Greeley that Negroes were essentially white men with colored skin, who could rapidly learn to care for themselves. Little tutelage or aid would be needed. Turn them loose, lease them vacant lands, and they would quickly become self-supporting, self-respecting citizens, contributing to the wealth of the nation. In short, Radicals seriously underestimated the problem. A third impediment was lack of executive leadership. Lincoln believed at heart in gradual emancipation, and hoped that the white Southerners would show enough wisdom and generosity, once the war ended, to help the freedmen to their feet. He did not wish to see a great bureaucracy ruling the colored people of the South; he hoped to see whites and Negroes ruling themselves, and helping each other.

The strongest impediment of all to well-planned, well-directed action lay in a natural but excessive deference to the military arm. Men believed that the first task was to win the war; nothing must be allowed to interfere with this objective. Officers in the field had expert information and should be entrusted with full responsibility. This belief possessed such great force that many refused to perceive that it did not cover the whole ground; that the inadequacies of government policy injured the Army, the freedmen, and the entire nation in 1864.

[II]

What was government policy, and how was it hammered out on the anvil of war?

Throughout 1861, as we have seen, the Administration adopted no definite program, while the Army wavered between the eagerness of Ben Butler to use refugee slaves, and the determination of John A. Dix in the East and Halleck in Missouri to discourage their reception. The Cabinet, on May 30, upheld Butler's view that, in conquered territory, fugitive Negroes were to be confiscated as contraband of war, and employed by the army. But the final disposition of these contrabands remained uncertain. Meanwhile, until its repeal June 28, 1864, the Fugitive Slave Act remained operative on behalf of *loyal* masters, who could ask Federal marshals to help them reclaim their runaways. When such owners called on Army officers to return fugitives, altercations sometimes ensued. The colonel of the Ninth New York Volunteers gave a Virginia master permission to take home two slaves who had escaped to the Union lines, and he began leading the Negroes through camp by a well-tied rope. As he passed the guard-house a corporal angrily leaped out, cut the rope with his knife, and bade the slaves to run.[20] Some soldiers went much further, attacking and even killing slave-hunters. Actually, an act of March 13, 1862, prohibited military or naval personnel from using force to return fugitives, and by an act of July 17, 1862, no slave escaping into any State from another State could be delivered up except for crime, unless to a loyal owner.

Although the First Confiscation Act, passed in August 1861, applied only to slaves who had been employed against the United States, and Lincoln held Frémont strictly to its letter, Secretary Cameron at once informed Ben Butler that his contraband policy was still valid. In States wholly or partially under insurrectionary control, he wrote, claims to escaped slaves were forfeited by the

20. Graham, Matthew John, *The Ninth Regiment, New York Volunteers*, New York, 1900, 220-221.

treasonable conduct of claimants. In view of the confusion of war, he thought even loyal owners could make few recoveries, and their best course would be to let fugitives be put into the service of the United States with some form of compensation. The Army was not to encourage the flight of slaves, and not to obstruct their "voluntary return" (an absurdity) to loyal citizens.[21] But how could an overworked, harassed officer distinguish between loyal and disloyal masters, or tell whether his troops were quietly encouraging flight or not? Army policy naturally became more and more liberal.

Conservative commanders, apprehensive of Border State anger, nevertheless hung back. Halleck in the Department of Missouri instructed his officers to bar fugitives from their lines.[22] Dix, as head of the Department of Maryland, issued a proclamation to reassure the eastern shore counties of that State and Virginia. "I ordered my colonels to allow no negroes to come within their encampments," he wrote F. P. Blair, Sr., "and I have had no trouble. We have neither stolen negroes, nor caught them for their masters. In a word, we repudiated Genl Butler's whole doctrine of contraband." The government, he foolishly thought, could not undertake to subsist a mass of freedmen while supporting ever-larger armies, for the burden would be too great. Let slavery, now doomed anyway, die a natural death. "The moment you begin to legislate for the emancipation of slaves, you divide the North and consolidate the South."[23] When owners of thirteen fugitive slaves came to Harpers Ferry in the summer of 1861 to demand their property, General Robert Patterson ordered that they be given full assistance, and the runaways were returned. Bull Run was fought within the week, and some of the owners were in the Confederate army![24]

A large part of the Union officers and troops agreed with these conservative attitudes. Many had an instinctive dislike of Negroes, and many shared the views of the Democratic Party on slavery. They turned the Negroes back with contumely. Dissension on the subject persisted until after the Emancipation Proclamation, and never disappeared.

Lincoln continued to support Ben Butler's policy of taking fugitive slaves into the lines and caring for them as contrabands, but it was not at once a national policy. In revising Secretary Cameron's instructions to General Thomas W. Sherman for the Port Royal expedition in October of 1861, Lincoln toned down the orders considerably, directing that Sherman receive fleeing Negroes and put them to work with such compensation to the masters as Congress might sanction. The President eliminated an assurance that the slaves would not again "be reduced to their former condition," and added that they were not to be used as

21. Cameron to Butler, August 8, 1861, War Office Military Book No. 45, National Archives.
22. Meneely, Alexander Howard, *The War Department, 1861*, New York, 1928, 337.
23. Dix to F.P. Blair, Sr., Nov. 27, Dec. 5, 1861 Blair-Lee Papers, Princeton Univ.
24. Quint, Alonzo H., *The Record of the Second Massachusetts Infantry*, Boston, 1867, 39.

soldiers.[25] As temporary army use of contrabands steadily evolved into permanent harborage, and as Halleck, Dix, and other officers who supported the recovery of slaves were more and more angrily denounced by Republican newspapers, pressure upon Congress to take a definite stand increased. Finally, the radical antislavery members forced it to act. On March 13, 1862, the law was approved making any officer who used soldiers or sailors to return fugitive slaves to their owners subject to court-martial and dismissal from the service. Then in midsummer (July 17, 1862) the Second Confiscation Act underlined this policy. Any member of the armed forces who on any pretext whatever presumed to decide on the validity of a claim to a slave, or who gave up a fugitive slave to an owner, should be dismissed. No more slave-catchers in the uniform of the United States!

Under this Second Confiscation Act, the escaped slaves of disloyal masters would be forever free. Fugitives from loyal masters, on the other hand, might be recovered by a Federal marshal or his deputy. The Judge Advocate-General ruled on August 17, 1863, that the Army must follow a line of absolute non-intervention, neither returning fugitives nor preventing civil officers from reclaiming them under the Fugitive Slave Act.[26] But what did this mean? In practical fact, as the armies pushed south *all* masters were regarded as disloyal. Under the new law, Negroes might be hired at $10 a month plus one ration to build entrenchments, perform camp duties, or do any other naval or military work for which they were competent. Officers treated most refugees as captured property, employed many of them, and gave them certificates of liberation. Theoretically, civil officers might appear to estop any certificate, but in war-torn areas they never did.[27] South of the Border States, the armies were thus great mobile machines of emancipation.

In the Borderland alone did the reclamation of fugitives continue, at least until June, 1864. General Curtis wrote from Missouri in the late fall of 1862 that it was still necessary to respect the legal rights of loyal slaveholders.[28] Nearly a year later General Schofield, while urging the enlistment of able-bodied slaves, recommended that the Army give loyal masters a guarantee that they would be returned; and Adjutant General Lorenzo Thomas proposed the same course with respect to Kentucky slaves. As late as the first months of 1864, General Charles J. Paine not only let loyal Kentuckians repossess their slaves, but took steps himself to return them in defiance of the non-intervention rule, because they would be safer and healthier on their plantations than under army care.[29]

25. Meneely, *op. cit.*, 341-342.
26. Holt to Stanton, August 17, 1863, Judge Advocate General Record Book No. 3, National Archives.
27. *Ibid.*
28. Curtis to Loan, Nov. 1, 1862, Dept. of Missouri Letter Book No. 13, 72, National Archives.
29. L. Thomas to G.H. Thomas, Feb. 27, 1864, Thomas Letter Book No. 2, 49ff, National Archives.

It was in the District of Columbia, with its many slaveholders and slaves, numerous free Negroes, and a steady influx of Negro refugees, that controversy simmered most hotly. From Maryland, Northern Virginia, and even greater distances, fugitive slaves slipped into the capital. After the Emancipation Proclamation they flocked in openly. Seward's daughter Fanny wrote in her diary that as they came from church the first Sunday in 1863, the family lighted upon a procession of Virginia slaves trudging toward the contraband camp, a few soldiers escorting them. Each grown man carried a touching little bundle of worldly goods, each woman a baby, and along with them trotted some half-grown children. "In the rear of the procession was a huge wagon, laden with all kinds of possessions, a lively little black face peeping out from the topmost layers."[30] What should be done with the fugitives? They could be put into temporary camps, the almshouse, or in quarters supplied by charitable citizens. The government also rented space for lodging about two hundred.

As they flocked in, the sharp difference of opinion on Army policy between Ben Butler and Dix was paralleled by even sharper differences on District policy between the Federal marshal, Ward H. Lamon, friend of the President, and the oaken-hearted James Wadsworth of Geneseo, N.Y., who became military governor of Washington in the summer of 1862. From 1861 to 1865, Ward Hill Lamon served as marshal of the District Court, one of whose judges was past eighty, and another so disloyal that, as Senator Henry Wilson said, "His heart is sweltering with treason."[31] A Virginian by birth and a hater of abolitionism, the swashbuckling Lamon, a noisy and exhibitionistic figure in Washington life, set himself to enforce both the Fugitive Slave Act and the District stipulation that any slave distant from his master's house without a written pass was subject to arrest. The fact that owners paid an apprehension fee for fugitives encouraged men to lay hands on errant slaves. Many old Washington residents felt a positive hatred for the contrabands. Their care swelled the tax burden, they contributed to local thievery and vice, and their mere presence was a daily reminder that the old era of Southern gentility and arrogance was dying.

When Wadsworth became military governor he found a frightful situation in the District jails, crammed with four times as many inmates as they had been built to hold, and fed on a starvation system that gave Lamon nearly half of the twenty-one cents a day allowed for each prisoner's keep. The previous winter, antislavery Senators had indicted Lamon so fiercely for his arrests and his mistreatment of refugees that Lincoln had been compelled to intervene. He cut through Lamon's protests with an edict in January that the marshal should release all Negroes held on mere suspicion, that he should thereafter imprison no fugi-

---

30. Fanny Seward ms. diary, Seward Papers, Univ. of Rochester Lib., Jan. 4, 1863.
31. *Congressional Globe,* 37th Cong., 3rd Sess., 1139.

tives except those committed in due legal form, and that he should hold nobody past thirty days.[32] Even so, Wadsworth thought that an undue number of Negroes had been jailed. For those outside the homes that had been improvised for the refugees, many of them ragged, hungry, and wretched, no adequate provision had been made. The callous attitude of many whites was summed up in a statement by T. J. Barnett of the Interior Department: "Among the most disgusting things here is the negro element. They won't work; they infest the town . . ."[33]

Wadsworth gave the weary, helpless runaways more than rations. He found government quarters for them in Duff Green's Row near the Capitol, and he supplied them with clothing, medicines, and other necessities confiscated from blockade runners. He appointed a superintendent to teach them to follow some regular occupation, and find them work. The government used many as laborers at forty cents a day. Wadsworth asserted that of nearly 400 fugitives who arrived during one week in July, employment was found immediately for two-fifths of them. He cooperated with the National Freedmen's Association and other philanthropic bodies in getting schools established and seeing that the Negroes were given instruction in the duties of citizenship.[34] Most important of all, he took a rocklike stand on the rule that no fugitive slave should be restored without a searching inquiry into the master's loyalty. This principle, "the habeas corpus of the contraband," was endorsed by the War Department, and as we have seen, was later incorporated in the Second Confiscation Act.

Altogether, Wadsworth, who returned to field duty after Fredericksburg, stands with Frémont, Ben Butler, and David Hunter as one of the advanced spirits in demanding freedom for escaped slaves, perhaps with less interest in personal and political advancement than Ben Butler, but with Frémont's tinge of impulsive humanitarianism and a little of Stanton's conviction that liberated slaves could be made helpful in winning the war. But the subject remained clouded by equivocal legislation and confused rules. The Fugitive Slave Act was still valid; it was invoked all along the border by owners who protested that they were loyal; Federal marshals and their deputies were subject to heavy fines if they did not execute the law. They had a legal right to search Duff Green's Row, Buell's Louisville, and the army camps of Grant in Kentucky for runaways. Once fugitives were apprehended, it was for civil commissioners, not the military, to decide their fate.[35]

The situation was complicated rather than simplified by the emancipation of slaves in the District of Columbia on April 16, 1862, an act with which Lincoln

32. Pearson, H.G., *James Wadsworth of Geneseo*, New York, 1913, 129ff. Wadsworth returned to field duty in late December, 1862, after Fredericksburg.
33. Barnett, to S.L.M. Barlow, Sept. 23, 1862, Barlow Papers, HEH.
34. Pearson, *Wadsworth, op. cit.*, 133.
35. *Ibid.*, 137-138.

was not in agreement on all details. Anticipating this measure, which Lincoln signed with some reluctance and with personal reflections upon the possible propriety of compensation to the owners, Washington slaveholders had hurried a small army of chattels into Maryland—whence many soon filtered back into the District. Although it was not certain that the Fugitive Slave Act covered these runaways, a deputation of slaveholders obtained from Lincoln what they thought was an intimation that it did. The work of Lamon's deputies in seizing fugitives reached a new intensity, and so did Wadsworth's wrath. When his Negro cook, whose former master he knew to be disloyal, was lodged in the city jail for examination by the civil commissioners, he marched a squad to the prison, took possession, and released all the contrabands inside. Lamon then mustered his own squad of city police at midnight, captured Wadsworth's garrison of two, and held the jail. This conflict of policy continued all summer. The civil authorities of the District, with Southern ideas, tried to enforce the Fugitive Slave Act there; the military authorities under Wadsworth did what they could to nullify it.

This was a conflict which the prompt creation of a strong department for the care and policing of freedmen might have done much to obviate. The Union still had four slaveholding States, wherein the rights of masters had to be protected. The Emancipation Proclamation did not apply to thirteen parishes of Louisiana, the forty-eight counties of West Virginia, or seven counties of Virginia. Here, as everywhere, loyal masters had the right to recover slaves up to the final proclamation. A strong independent agency could have decided which runaways were truly contraband, and which belonged to loyal owners, and could have helped get employment for Negroes arriving in Washington, Cincinnati, Cairo, and other border towns. When Northern speculators tried growing cotton in Kentucky, Missouri, and even Southern Illinois, with Negro hands, an active Bureau might have been of assistance.

Certainly many Negroes, when properly aided, showed a striking capacity for self-help. In Washington, where refugee slaves had increased to perhaps 10,000 by the spring of 1863, with 3,000 more in Alexandria, they were industrious whenever given a real chance. Many men worked as government laborers; the more capable learned crafts, from blacksmithing to shoemaking; and women took positions as cooks and laundresses. A new camp at Arlington, supervised by the Quartermaster's Department, became a well-developed town, with substantial houses, shops, a church, a school and a hospital—the Freedman's Village, quite self-supporting. Most refugees, however, continued to live in the city, mainly in old tenements and shacks, a demoralized people.[36] The tatters, ignorance, and squalor of many of the poor creatures made them seem like beings from another world, their poverty expressing itself in pilfering, and their lack of proper food,

36. Leech, Margaret, *Reveille in Washington*, New York, 1941, 246-247, 250-251.

shelter, and sanitary arrangements exposing them to disease. It is not strange that fashionable women drew their skirts aside when they passed, that urchins jeered and threw stones, and that hoodlums cursed them. Yet the willingness of white soldiers to insult them because they hated the idea that black men should claim the same privileges as themselves, the readiness of white laborers to buffet them because they feared Negro competition, were actually tributes to their potentialities. They were asserting their right to a future.

The general prejudice rose to a climax on the Negro's day of jubilee—New Year's Day of 1863. Freedmen who gathered in the chapel of the Twelfth-Street camp to which many had fled when smallpox broke out in Duff Green's Row, had to mute their rejoicing, for some were afraid that any demonstration might well be the signal for a mob outbreak.[37] Conscious of injustice but too cowed to complain, proud of their freedom but humbly deferential to those who begrudged it, soft-voiced but determined to press on, their demeanor was an augury of their course for a century to come.

[III]

"Oh, you are the man who has all those darkies on his shoulders." So Grant in the autumn of 1862 addressed Chaplain John Eaton of the Twenty-seventh Ohio, a thirty-two-year-old former superintendent of schools in Toledo whom he had just appointed supervisor of the contrabands crowding into the army camps at La Grange, Tennessee.[38] The General directed Eaton to establish his first refuge at Grand Junction hard by. The cohorts of blacks might be transformed into a valuable auxiliary, said Grant, if the men were given camp duties and construction work, and the women were assigned to hospitals and camp kitchens.

As Grant's troops advanced into northern Mississippi through a region dense with Negroes, owners fled their plantations and farms, and slaves thronged into the Yankee camps. The flood of want and misery appalled all observers. It was like the oncoming of cities, wrote Eaton. Women ready to give birth, old men and toddling children, invalids in the last stages of disease, honest and hardworking hands alongside hands lazy and thievish, presented a perturbing problem. Many Northern soldiers, quite unused to color, had more bitter prejudices against it than Southerners. But even the benevolent were nonplused, fearing "the demoralization and infection of the Union soldier and the downfall of the Union cause" if dark hordes swamped the advancing columns.[39]

This Western influx presented graver problems than any encountered in the

37. Ibid., 249-250.
38. The appointment was dated Nov. 11, 1862: Eaton, John, and Ethel Osgood Mason, Grant, Lincoln, and the Freedmen, op. cit., 5.
39. Ibid., Ch. I.

East. After Iuka and Corinth, the refugees poured in by platoons, until about 7,000 had collected in byways and purlieus of the latter town. As the Army was occupied with its wounded, they at first had to shift for themselves without tents or decent clothing, and their demands grew so desperate that (as Grant wrote later) it was impossible to advance until their needs were met. Military tasks would support only a small fraction; what should he do with the rest? He set many to collecting and ginning whatever cotton remained on the abandoned plantations, and gave others tools to erect their own shelter.[40] Citizens remaining at home were allowed to hire them at the government rate of pay. Some refugees had brought teams, farm implements, and cooking utensils with them; others needed everything. Grant might have been held liable for the hundreds of thousands of dollars' worth of Army property distributed among them, but he never hesitated to accept the responsibility. His resourceful confrontation of the situation was characteristic.

And in John Eaton, Grant found so efficient a lieutenant that, as we have noted, just before Christmas in 1862 the General appointed him superintendent of contrabands for the Department of the Tennessee. "In no case will Negroes be forced into the service of the Government," wrote Grant, "or be enticed away from their homes except when it becomes a military necessity."[41] Eaton found most troops reluctant to serve the Negro in any manner, and even parties detailed to guard the contrabands did their work unwillingly. Once Eaton was roughly arrested by a colonel as he gave directions to some wandering Negroes; once his horse, used by a sergeant in foraging for contrabands, was shot by somebody who hoped to kill Eaton himself. But his talent for organization slowly brought order out of chaos.

In Grant's retreat from Grand Junction to Memphis the refugees, though carried by rail, fared badly. In the city, where no quarters had been provided, they met new hardships. Eaton saw shivering groups around campfires on every corner. As soon as possible a refuge was prepared just below town, and large numbers were transferred thither. A Minnesota chaplain named A. S. Fiske had already done much for black fugitives, and Eaton lost no time in enlisting him as superintendent in the Memphis area. At Camp Fiske he created a model town of log huts and gardens, clean, well-drained, well-policed, and comfortable. General Grenville M. Dodge meanwhile organized another camp at Corinth.[42] New settlements of Negroes sprang up steadily all over the Department.[43]

40. Halleck authorized this; Eaton, *op. cit.*, 12.
41. General Order No. 13, Dec. 17, 1862; Eaton, *op. cit.*, 26-27.
42. During 1863 Dodge officered and mustered in two Negro regiments; Personal Records, 56, National Archives.
43. Eaton, *op. cit.*, 30-33.

The fact that two chaplains took charge of the Mississippi Valley refugees gave a strong moral imprint to their care. Strict regulations respecting marriage were enforced, for Eaton and Fiske, determined to allow "no promiscuous inter-mingling," made the family a unit of community life. Many former slaves were eager for legal weddings, and Fiske once married 119 couples in a single mass service. Since the chaplains encouraged religious activities, preachers flourished. One night, Eaton heard a black exhorter addressing the Almighty with emotion: "Oh Lord, shake Jeff Davis over the mouth of hell, but Oh Lord, doan' drop him in!" The superintendents required freedmen to labor or give a good excuse, and reduced the number dependent on the government to the lowest level. Many Negroes, drifting north to Cairo, found it a gateway to larger opportunities in the North. And many, living in Northern communities long enough to acquire new skills and ideas, returned to their old homes fully equipped to make a living.

Like Wadsworth in the East, Eaton became impressed by the capacity of many former slaves. In a report to Grant during the siege of Vicksburg, which the General sent on to Lincoln, he asserted that they were much brighter than their friends had originally supposed, that house servants were more intelligent than field-hands, proving the influence of environment, and that "all learn rapidly". He pronounced them quite fit to bear arms if only good officers were placed over them. Among the many mulattoes, some were as indistinguishable from whites in mental traits as in complexion. "Van Dorn paroled a servant at Holly Springs," he noted, "not suspecting his African descent."[44]

From an early period Grant had foreseen the desirability of arming Negro recruits, and he told Eaton at the outset that when the contrabands demonstrated they could perform Army labor well, it would be easy to put weapons into their hands. As soon as Halleck wrote Grant that all hope of reconciliation was gone and peace must be forced by the sword, Grant was quite ready to support the enlistment of black men. When Lorenzo Thomas arrived on his Western tour for organizing Negro contingents, Eaton accompanied him to the principal Army camps. He recorded that Thomas had a peremptory way of dealing with men reluctant to accept the new policy. After calling a command before him and reading the new War Department order, he would ask those opposed to it to move one step from the ranks. A few would do so—and Thomas would order them to the guardhouse to revise their opinions. The enlistment of Negroes, as we have noted, was a conspicuous success. Probably 70,000 all told were placed under arms in the Mississippi Valley, or nearly one-third of the total of 186,000[45] in all areas taken into the Union service. They often fought bravely in numerous

44. *Ibid.*, 65-68.
45. *O.R.* III, Vol V. 661.

engagements, though, like all soldiers, they at times fell short of the highest soldierly standards.[46]

As Thomas and spring arrived together in 1863, more systematic measures had to be taken to employ those Negroes who could not enlist. After the fall work of harvesting corn and cotton, Eaton had used many in cutting wood. For the new crop season, the cultivation of abandoned lands inside or near the Union lines offered larger opportunities. Thomas instituted a plan for the leasing of plantations, and appointed a commission of three to supervise it. Calls upon Northern benevolence brought in seed and implements—a hundred ploughs at one time. Under his plan, white tenants were to get Negro hands from the government, engaging to feed, clothe, and kindly supervise them until February 1, 1864, and to pay them modest wages according to a stated scale—$7 a month for able-bodied men. Nobody knew as yet how much free Negro labor was really worth, for it was uncertain how efficient the former slave would prove, and still more uncertain how much former masters or Northern speculators could be induced to pay for him. These tenants were to pay the government a rent of $2 for every 400-pound bale of cotton they produced, and five cents for every bushel of corn or potatoes.[47]

By midsummer of 1863, an elaborate if clumsy mechanism had been created to help freedmen in the Mississippi Valley to their feet. Part of it was the leasing system under Lorenzo Thomas's three-man commission. Another part was Eaton's section of the Army administration (sometimes called the Freedmen's Department) which Thomas strengthened by ordering all the generals to appoint provost-marshals who would look after the Negroes scattered over the Army-controlled plantations. A third part was supplied by philanthropic organizations of the North, particularly the various freedmen's aid societies or commissions. Eaton specially praised the helpful activities of H. B. Spelman as head of a Cleveland agency for assisting freedmen, and the generosity of H. B. Claflin & Co. of New York, for the Cleveland group assisted small tenant farmers to sell odd lots of cotton, and Claflin's firm outfitted stores for freedmen at various points with goods at no cost.

As the Army of the Cumberland under Rosecrans advanced upon Chattanooga, tens of thousands of former slaves, men, women, and children, were liberated. Almost without exception they turned to the military for support. The men found employment as servants to officers, cooks to soldiers, teamsters, and work-hands for the Commissary's and Quartermaster's departments. They chopped wood, built roads, and repaired railway lines, while the women cooked and washed. Although destitution was common, a correspondent of the New

46. Randall, James G., *Civil War and Reconstruction*, Boston, 1953, 505.
47. Eaton, *op. cit.*, 60.

York *Tribune* thought they were in better estate than the contrabands about Washington; for while they received less help from charitable societies, they showed more self-reliance and took better care of what they earned. The Army gave them wages, food, and medicine, but no clothing, and little training or discipline.[48]

What the situation most demanded, declared the correspondent, was one man of heart and intelligence as authoritative head of a Freedmen's Department. William Whiting, Solicitor of the War Department (as previously noted) was one of those who vigorously urged a Cabinet post to deal with the many problems of emancipation. When the Freedmen's Bureau was finally created on March 3, 1865, it was not a Cabinet post, but did have wide powers, becoming a political organ as well. A wartime Department would have been effective even though the danger of political meddling in the general wartime government was great. Much would have depended upon the tact and prudence of the head of such a powerful and sensitive new governmental agency. Such a department head, with a proper staff, could have systematized and coordinated the multitudinous activities of a hundred philanthropic organizations, many of them limited in funds, skills, and persistence. He could have met the peculiar difficulties of Negro enlistments in the Border States. In Missouri, General John Schofield, after wrestling with the objections raised by legal masters, and with the governor's stipulation that State laws of Missouri must never be violated, helped see to the mustering-in of all Negroes fit for duty, who had gathered at the army posts, and were clearly entitled to their freedom under the Confiscation Act. Two regiments were thus obtained by the end of the summer of 1863, and another was authorized, although public excitement was generated in the process.

"I believe the able-bodied negroes in Missouri will be worth more to the government than they are to their masters as laborers, and that this is the general opinion among slave owners in the state," Schofield wrote E. D. Townsend, Acting Adjutant-General.[49] "I respectfully suggest that it might be wise policy to enlist all able-bodied negroes in Mo. who may be willing to enter the service, giving to their masters receipts upon which those who established their loyalty may base a claim upon the Government for the value of the services lost." A Freedmen's Department could have decided such questions of policy all the way from Missouri and Kentucky to Maryland.

The farther south the armies penetrated, the greater was the care needed by the released slaves. In the spring of 1863, those reaching Memphis impressed a Chicago journalist as pitiable victims of American heedlessness, greed, and class prejudice. They seemed indeed the mudsills of society described by Dew,

---

48. Spec. Corr., N.Y. *Tribune*, Murfreesboro, Tenn., May 30, 1863, June 8, 1863.
49. Sept. 29, 1863; Dept. of Missouri Letter-Book No. 14, 260-261 National Archives.

Harper, and other slavery apologists. The field-hands, little above animals in appearance, dirty, wretched, and half-naked, shambled along with awkward gait. "Some wear a piece of carpet or matting. A child is perhaps encased in an inverted salt or meal sack, with a hole in the top. . . . Many of the younger girls are arrayed in a single thin article of clothing, too flimsy for a real cover."[50]

When the occupation of Vicksburg and the towns south of it threw upon the government some 30,000 contrabands, their situation became appalling. They were crowded together in utter destitution, two-thirds of them in or near the half-wrecked city, and the remainder on the west bank; hardly one family properly fed, clothed, or sheltered, and many in utter despair. Some died miserably in the streets, without medical or hospital care. Debility, excitement, and confusion unfitted many for sustained labor. Men and women alike, unable to do anything but field work, would take a job and leave it in a few hours. "Housekeepers," Eaton wrote Levi Coffin, the Quaker philanthropist famous for his management of the Underground Railroad, "often had a new cook for each meal in the day."[51] For some time all efforts to establish order in the camps broke down; the sea of misery burst the dykes. Another Quaker, representing Philadelphia philanthropy, reported that the squalor of one camp gave him a feeling that approached despair, and he was told that another close by was even worse.[52]

Yet gradually, as some Negroes enlisted, and others found places on leased plantations, or gathered wood for government steamboats, the skies brightened. The Sanitary Commission supplied medicines in all large refugee camps, and soon a capable Army surgeon was appointed medical director of freedmen, with power to outfit sick-camps and hospitals, and to employ surgeons.[53]

The enlightened attitude of General Grant, manifest as long as he commanded in the West, was as creditable to his humanity as his wisdom. He gave Eaton's measures unwavering support, encouraged the enlistment of capable Negroes, and approved the hiring out of others on leased plantations. "At least three of my Army Corps commanders," he wrote Halleck in the spring of 1863, "take hold of the new policy of arming the Negroes and using them against the rebels with a will. . . ."[54] How different was this attitude from McClellan's hostility to any inroads upon slavery! It was Grant's idea in the autumn of 1862 to use refugees to harvest crops on abandoned plantations; it was he who, while employing freedmen to cut wood for the government, had the surplus sold at higher prices to independent steamboats, which yielded funds for giving housing, hospi-

50. Memphis letters, Chicago *Morning Post*, Feb. 4, 1863.
51. Eaton, *op. cit.*, 105.
52. *Report of F.R. Shipley of Friends Assn. for Relief of Colored Freedmen*, submitted Jan. 12, 1864, pamphlet in New York Hist. Soc.
53. Eaton, *op. cit.*, 130-139.
54. Grant to Halleck, Milliken's Bend, April 19, 1863, Eldredge Papers, HEH.

tals, and various comforts to the Negroes;[55] and it was he who promised these former slaves that, if they fought well, he would give them the right to vote.[56]

He could act the more freely because he did not face the monstrous problems which smouldering hatreds presented in places such as New Orleans. When Secretary Chase urged Ben Butler to treat the Negro in that city with understanding, Butler replied that he would, but added: "I assure you it is quite impossible to free him here and now without a Santo Domingo. A single whistle from me would cause every white man's throat to be cut in this city. Hate has piled up here between master and servant until it is fearful."[57] Although slavemasters in Mississippi quaked over Negro restlessness and took what precautions they could against any uprisings in the Natchez district, in 1861-62, apprehension ran so high that forty Negroes were hanged, and as many more jailed. But the slaves were in general more docile than might have been anticipated, even on plantations left without masters.[58]

[IV]

Permanent policies for the freedmen could not be determined until full evidence was accumulated upon their capacities. Late in 1862, prominent antislavery men, including Moncure D. Conway of Virginia and Washington, and Samuel Gridley Howe of Boston, addressed carefully phrased questions to a number of officers superintending the former slaves.[59] How many could read and write? Were they willing to work hard? What was their record as to honesty, chastity, and temperance? Did they show vengefulness? Two important questions ran: Do they desire to migrate to the North? and, Can they at once take their place in society as a free laboring class, able to support themselves, or do they need preparation?

Witnesses agreed that few could read on arrival at the refugee camps; scarcely one, wrote the superintendent at Fortress Monroe. Officers also agreed that, except to gain freedom, few wished to go North. If emancipated in the South, they would remain there. Their obedience, cheerfulness, and good nature won general praise. So did their desire to learn, their interest in religion (although this was emotional rather than thoughtful), and their industry. They are more pious than moral, wrote one officer; while another declared that they were somewhat given to lying and stealing, as might be expected of any enslaved people. The

55. Eaton, *op. cit.*, 12.
56. Grant, Ulysses S., *Personal Memoirs of U.S. Grant*, New York, 1885, I, 424-426; Eaton, *op. cit.*, 15.
57. Butler to Chase, New Orleans, July 10, 1862; Salmon P. Chase Papers, Pennsylvania Hist. Soc.
58. Bettersworth, John Knox, *Confederate Mississippi*, Baton Route, La., 1943, 159-173.
59. Members of the Emancipation League were responsible for the questionnaire. See Conway, Moncure, *Addresses and Reprints*, New York, 1908, 117-123, on his idea of Negro traits.

head of the contraband depot in Washington declared that they were the most religious people he had ever known, but their religion was entirely divorced from morality.[60]

The superintendents agreed, in general, that contrabands needed education and supervision before they could take a proper place in society. They were "irresponsible", wrote the East Arkansas chaplains. An aide to General Rufus Saxton at Beaufort, S.C., believed that the lack of opportunities for employment would make Union guardianship indispensable until the South was reconstructed and could furnish a healthy demand for free agricultural labor. The head of the Craney Island camp near Norfolk declared, "We can only judge of the capacity of the colored race when a generation shall arise that has had the opportunity of being fitted by education to care for themselves."

Bacon's remark that "a man that studieth revenge keeps his own wounds green" had little application to the Negroes. All witnesses agreed that they showed singularly little ill-will for their former masters. They often manifested an independent spirit, like the Negro girl who told her mistress, "The time for answering bells is gone by," but they seldom showed malice. They were often as harshly treated by Army men as by their oldtime masters. The two chaplains in East Arkansas declared that many of lower rank were "hard, unjust, and cruel," while the ordinary privates treated freedmen "as savages and brutes." General Saxton's aide reported that the generosity of many officers and privates was counterbalanced by the "abuse and injustice" of others. Scanty as the government wage of $10 a month for labor was, callous officers often withheld all or part of it. Fortress Monroe reported more than $30,000 due the black people for work, to say nothing of a great amount of night and Sunday service for which promised payment was never given.[61]

The conclusions of the field superintendents were corroborated by a new Freedmen's Inquiry Commission which shortly afterwards made its first report to Congress, a body organized primarily by three friends of the released slaves, James McKaye of Pennsylvania, Robert Dale Owen of Indiana, and S. G. Howe of Massachusetts. Stanton gave it the necessary authority, appointed Owen chairman, and asked McKaye and others to draw up its instructions.[62] After much investigation, it presented an optimistic view, reiterating the old familiar state-

60. This correspondence, originally published in the *Boston Commonwealth*, an emancipationist journal, was reprinted in the New York *Tribune*, January 27, 1863.

61. The men reporting to the Emancipation League of Boston included E.W. Hooper, aide to General Saxton; C.B. Wilder at Fort Monroe; O. Brown at Craney Island; Samuel Sawyer at Helena; George D. Wise at St. Louis; and Charles Fitch and J.G. Ferman in East Arkansas. Saxton estimated the number of contrabands in the Department of the South at about 18,000; Fort Monroe reported "several thousand" in the "several counties" it controlled; Helena reported about 4,000; St. Louis gave no numbers; the District of East Arkansas reported "about 3,000"; and the Washington Contraband Depot stated that 3,381 had passed through its camp in the previous six months. New York *Tribune*, January 27, 1863.

62. McKaye to Andrew, March 21, 1863, Andrew Papers, Mass. Hist. Soc.

ments upon Negro industry, appetite for knowledge, and piety. It assured Congress that strong local attachments and a preference for the Southern climate would keep most liberated slaves in their home communities. Admitting certain weaknesses of the race, the Commission entered a plea for the defense. Negroes evinced little regard for truth because lies had been a shield against unjust punishment. Yet, the Commission declared, even the most retarded could be quickly elevated by military discipline, regular payment for work done, and access to land —for they longed above all to own a few acres.[63]

Sympathetic Army officers were equally hopeful, as were those who studied the coastal Negroes of the Carolinas. James M. McKim of Philadelphia, who had founded a relief committee for the thousand slaves in the Port Royal (S.C.) area, brought back from the Sea Islands in the summer of 1862 a mass of facts to prove that, in spite of many handicaps, the experiment of hiring freedmen to cultivate the land had been a success. He had found some 3,800 laborers growing good crops of corn, potatoes, and cotton upon 14,000 acres.[64] General Banks wrote from Alexandria, La., early in 1864: "I entertain no doubt whatever of the capabilities of the emancipated colored people . . . I have seen them in all situations, in the last year and a half, and . . . they seem to me to have a clearer comprehension of their position and the duties which rest upon them than any other class of our people."[65]

That destitute white refugees often needed assistance as acutely as the black people was obvious, for many were too young or too old for self-support. Nevertheless, the two grim problems of the white and the black refugees were quite different. Many white folks, fallen into poverty, lacked the ingenuity to find employment and not a few showed that their initiative and industry were dulled by long ease.[66] Their numbers became appalling. "Half the world is refugeeing," wrote one plantation girl late in the war.[67] Many whites, conscious of dignity, were more reluctant than Negroes to ask help, which was given grudgingly. The sufferings of uprooted and impoverished families caught behind the Union lines were often heartrending, for they could not count on community support as could displaced wanderers farther south. John M. Palmer wrote his wife from Nashville in the autumn of 1862 that if she could see the eager competition between refugee white women and Negro women to gain a few dollars by

---

63. 38th Cong., 1st Sess., *Senate Exec. Doc. 53;* Governor John A. Andrew had encouraged the formation of the Commission.

64. McKim's address in Philadelphia, New York *Tribune,* July 18, 1862; see also his book, *The Freedman of South Carolina,* Philadelphia, 1862; Rose, Willie Lee, *Rehearsal for Reconstruction,* Indianapolis, 1964, *passim.*

65. Banks to James McKaye, March 28, 1864, Banks Papers, Essex Institute, now in LC.

66. Massey, Mary Elizabeth, *Refugee Life in the Confederacy,* Baton Route, 1964, 160ff., on shortcomings inside the Confederacy.

67. See Andrews, Eliza Francis, *The Wartime Journal of a Georgia Girl,* New York, 1908, 19-174, for a vivid account of wartime travels.

washing for the soldiers, selling them pies and cakes, or sewing for them, she would find the spectacle harrowing. "Indeed, in this struggle the Negro woman has an advantage over the modest white woman, as she permits the indecent liberties of coarse men, and thus gains employment. It is not uncommon for the colored wench, by a vulgar joke or licentious allusion, to drive her white competitor from the field."[68]

[V]

Dissatisfaction with government fumbling in the care of freedmen steadily rose in 1863-64. Northerners who asked for more effective measures to keep contrabands inside the South were dissatisfied; so were those who wished fuller provision made for all who migrated to the North. President Lincoln did not help matters by clinging to the impracticable idea that many former slaves might be colonized in Central America, the West Indies, or even Africa. This plan offended large numbers, including free Negroes of long standing, the new freedmen, all American idealists, and employers who wished to use Negro labor. The Freedmen's Inquiry Commission, in its second report in May, 1864, emphasized the fact that demand for Negro help both inside and outside the armed forces exceeded supply. Somehow the government was not siphoning such help to the quarters where it was needed most. Meanwhile, the equivocal status of many Negroes in Missouri, Kentucky, and other Border States—not quite slaves and not quite free—might have been corrected by a competent general administration.

Month after month, the cry of anguish rising from helpless refugees wrung the hearts of humane citizens. "You must pardon me again," a friend wrote Elihu Washburne from Cairo early in 1863. "Five hundred contrabands, men, women, and children, have been suddenly thrown in here, since three days ago, and just at this time a severe change in the weather has taken place. A severe snowstorm is raging here at this time, and these poor people are suffering terribly for the lack of fire and even food—and the few who have money are being imposed upon in all kinds of shapes by the money grabbers here . . . There are at this moment, while the snow is falling thick and fast, quite a number of women and little children crowded together in the second story of the Upper Barracks; in these apartments there are no fireplaces, nor stoves."[69]

Radical opinion in the North in 1863 levelled two heavy charges against governmental management of the freedmen. One was that no thoughtful, coherent plan had been studied and applied. The Lincoln Administration, which at first

68. To Mrs. Palmer, Nashville, October 2, 1862, Palmer Papers, Illinois State Hist. Libr.
69. H.O. Wagoner, to Washburne, Jan. 15, 1863, Washburne Papers, LC.

expected gradual emancipation, had been caught unprepared when the events of 1862 made it necessary to decree the immediate emancipation of most of the slaves. It had resorted to a series of stopgap expedients. Only in the Sea Islands area and in part of the Mississippi Valley had government made serious efforts to organize a labor system for the South, based upon a full recognition of Negro rights. Only on the islands and the coast between Charleston and Savannah, where General David Hunter had made his premature and dictatorial effort at emancipation, had an important experiment been carried through in the sweeping reconstruction of social and economic relations between the races, and the permanent establishment of the freedmen on a well-planned basis. This undertaking alone attracted national attention.[70]

More important was the charge that the makeshift expedients carelessly adopted looked toward the wrong goals. Their objects were merely policing the masses of refugees, reducing government expenses in dealing with them, and providing wood, corn, and cotton for government use. The government should have adopted a larger program, which included a new pattern of land ownership and a higher code of race relations.

General Lorenzo Thomas's plan of leasing abandoned plantations to returned owners or Northern speculators, who could employ Negroes at government-controlled wages, brought these complaints to a head. To Northern emancipationists this looked like a timid halfway house, so far as the Negroes were concerned, between slavery and independence. Behind the Union lines in the Mississippi Valley, the tracts abandoned by Confederates exceeded in area the tracts still held by loyal citizens. Why not divide the confiscated estates among those who had done so much, by the unpaid toil of half a lifetime, to make them productive? At least why not give a small homestead to every family of liberated slaves? In many areas the old slate had been sponged half-clean; why not sponge it completely? It was a half-step to raise the Negroes to the wage level; a full step would mean raising them to land-ownership. "I am informed by the planters generally," wrote Thomas W. Carter, head of the bureau of free labor in the Department of the Gulf, reviewing the year 1864-65, that planters "cannot survive the shock which has come upon them with the war, the abolition of slavery, and the . . . loss of their fortunes, their sons, and their hopes . . . They are now preparing to give way to new capital and new proprietorship."[71] Why not give way in part to Negro smallholdings?

---

70. Hunter from March, 1862, until June, 1863, commanded the Department of the South, including the South Carolina islands and coast mentioned, and the towns of Hilton Head, Port Royal, and Beaufort. For national interest, see "The Freedmen at Port Royal," *North American Review*, Vol. 101, July, 1865, 1-28.

71. Carter, Thomas W., *Annual Report for 1864-65*, New Orleans, 1865. In this Department plantations were being cultivated under military administration, with 50,000 freedmen on them.

This was the position taken by the New York *Tribune*. Thomas's system of leasing plantations to white men, it argued, was doubtless good for the government and the lessees, but promised no beneficial results to the Negroes. Like the system instituted by N. P. Banks in Louisiana, it overlooked the fact that the helpless freedmen, as well as the Treasury and occupants of plantations, should be consulted. Was the prospect of a cotton crop in the fall of 1863 of more importance than justice to a half-emancipated people? The Negroes should have secure homes, a permanent footing, and hope for the future.[72] In Rosecrans's army, Brigadier-General Oliver H. Payne (the resourceful officer who later became Rockefeller's partner, and a great capitalist and philanthropist), prided himself on his success in changing slave-labor to wage-labor. "We are hiring the black people to their own masters," he wrote Rosecrans. "We say to the servant that he is to have $8 per month, and is to be faithful and good, and work hard . . . We make written contracts, in which the slave is only known as a hired man."[73] This was a step forward, but men like Greeley believed that a much stronger move was needed.

The government, moreover, failed to protect many of the freedmen from abuse and exploitation by plantation lessees. James E. Yeatman, the eminent civic leader in St. Louis who became head of the Western Sanitary Commission, found in a tour down the Mississippi Valley late in 1863 that many Negroes were resentful and discouraged. He questioned thousands. Large numbers had not been paid real money for months; their employers had given them tickets for their days of actual work, presumably to be redeemed in cash when the crop was sold. Their families sometimes went without bread for days. "They all testify that if they were only paid their little wages as they earned, they could stand it; but to work and get poorly paid, poorly fed, and not doctored when sick is more than they can endure."[74] It was hard for Army men to reproach planters for dilatory payment when the Army itself paid its Negro hands but a tardy pittance.

Many planters who leased land from the government treated the freedmen badly, and were abetted in this by local police officers. "If the freedmen were left to the mercy of those who formerly owned them as slaves, or to the officers of their selection," wrote Thomas Conway of the Department of the Gulf, "we might with one count of the fingers of our hands number the years which the race would spend with us." Conway found that the fairest employers in matters of pay were the Northerners who came to the Gulf States with money and the intention of staying. Long-settled Southern masters were almost as fair; but the get-rich-

---

72. New York *Tribune,* May 27, 1863.
73. Payne, Gallatin, Tenn., June 1, 1863, in New York *Tribune,* June 8, 1863.
74. Yeatman, James E., *Report on the Condition of the Freedmen of the Mississippi to Western Sanitary Commission, 1863,* St. Louis, 1864; Forman, Jacob Gilbert, *The Western Sanitary Commission,* St. Louis, 1864, *passim.;* Hodges, W.R., *The Western Sanitary Commission,* St. Louis, 1906.

quick newcomers were most dishonest. The basic rate of pay was inadequate, even below the level earned by independent Negroes in slavery days. Under Federal regulations, freedmen were hired to lessees for $7 (in some places $8) a month—$84 or $96 a year, less $2 for medical attendance. The $7-hand earned 27 cents a day, and if he worked only ten days a month, his income was $2.70! Yet in antebellum years an able-bodied Negro was often hired out at from $200 to $240 a year, and a woman at from $150 to $180, with food, shelter, and clothing—and this when cotton brought only ten cents a pound! Representative Thomas D. Eliot of Massachusetts commented sharply on Lincoln's recommendation that the freedmen should labor faithfully for reasonable wages.

"So they will, if allowed," he said. "But who is to allow them? Will you let harpies go among them, or white bloodhounds whose scent is keen for prey, whose fangs are remorseless, whose pursuit is for gold at any cost of human life? Such men have been there; they are there now, under cover of government authority; and the abuses practised by them sadden and depress the freedmen."[75]

The situation was complicated in 1863 by the increasing conflict of jurisdiction between the War and Treasury Departments to which we have previously alluded. Much abandoned property everywhere was stolen by Army officers, and they or their accomplices enriched themselves, in the Mississippi Valley in particular, by trade in contraband cotton. Since this seized cotton properly belonged to the Treasury, Congress passed a much-needed law in March, 1863, for the protection of relinquished assets, enabling Treasury agents to take charge of lands and crops left by fleeing Confederates. By a subsequent order of the War Department, Army officers were required to give these agents any assistance they might require in collecting and holding. That is, the Treasury gained very nearly paramount authority, but Army men were often reluctant to recognize it. Such supervisors of the freedmen as Eaton complained that Treasury agents were excessively interested in Negroes and crops as sources of revenue, and lacked a just perception of the position of the former slaves as human beings and citizens, sharing Justice Taney's view of them as potentially profitable chattels.

Nobody could accuse Secretary Chase of indifference to the Negro. When he read Yeatman's report exposing the faults of the leasing system, he gladly agreed to have the Treasury's supervisor of special agents, William P. Mellen, work with Yeatman in drawing up better regulations for the management of abandoned lands.[76] From the beginning of 1864, no lessee was allowed more than one plantation; preference was given to men desiring small tracts; wages were lifted to $25 a month for the best men, $20 for the second-best, and $14-18 for women; and

75. *Congressional Globe*, 38th Cong., 1st Sess., 568.
76. Eaton, *op. cit.*, 145.

payment was made a first lien on crops. Every lessee was now required to pay
the full monthly total whether he employed his help every working day or not,
and he could not withhold more than half of their wages until the crop was sold.
All laborers had to be obtained through the authorized superintendents, and given
clothing and food at low prices.[77]

Although in theory the Yeatman-Mellen regulations marked a happy advance,
difficulties continued. The Treasury was so anxious to encourage cotton-growing
that it rented out lands exposed to guerrilla incursions. Even worse than these,
were the predatory men eager to make money at the expense of both Negroes
and the Treasury. The glittering prices paid for cotton attracted to the Mississippi
Valley a cohort of adventurers utterly without scruples. Some recklessly traded
across the lines, sending quantities of drugs, ammunition, clothing, and other
contraband goods into the Confederacy, bringing out cotton in exchange. Others
used every contrivance to cheat the Negroes of their crops. Many Treasury
agents and Army officers conspired to seize corrupt gains. Although the planters,
whether Northern dollar-hunters or Southerners professing loyalty, included
many honest men, they also included many rogues. Thus, a thick fog of thievery
and chicanery enveloped much of the Valley during 1864.[78]

The regulations, moreover, were so strict that they frightened prudent applicants from the field. A good many Northerners and Border men who had bid for
plantations took one look at the contracts and rules, and fled. The new wage scale
would have been a heartening improvement over the old rates had it been
economically sound, but as Eaton and others saw, it proved impossibly high for
any district where Confederate raids, poor soil, undependable hands, or other
difficulties, made the return precarious. Before the end of February, 1864, Eaton
and Mellen were exchanging protests, Eaton regarding the Negroes as still under
his control, and Mellen assuming they were now his wards to whom he issued
orders. In this dispute between the Army and the Treasury, Lorenzo Thomas
took a vigorous hand, sending Stanton urgent appeals that "The military authorities must have command of the Negroes to avoid endless confusion," and declaring that, if the Treasury insisted on its plan, the Negroes would get no rations.[79]
Lincoln acted instantly:

"I wish you would go to the Mississippi river at once," he wrote Lorenzo
Thomas at Nashville, "and take hold of, and be master in, the contraband and
leasing business." He feared that Mellen's well-intended system would be stran-
gled by its details. "Go there and be the judge."[80]

Unfortunately, administrative confusion persisted throughout 1863 and 1864,

77. *Ibid.*, 146, 147.
78. *Ibid.*, 147-150.
79. *Ibid.*, 152, 153; Feb. 20, Feb. 27, 1864.
80. Feb. 28, 1864: Lincoln, *Collected Works*, VII, 212.

with Lincoln still too much harassed by other problems or too indifferent to give adequate attention to the problem of the freedmen. The Treasury could not legally relinquish its authority over plantations; the Army had full authority over freedmen, but was preoccupied with its military task; and semi-independent workers like Eaton and Fiske sometimes disapproved of the acts of both. Guerrilla forays continued destructive, especially in the districts about Helena, Vicksburg, and Natchez, where Confederate raiders carried off great droves of livestock in the crop season of 1864, and took nearly a thousand Negroes into the interior to be resold as slaves. Agricultural activities in much of the region were demoralized by these hit-and-run tactics. Many Negroes and loyal whites were killed, and many planters escaped ruin only by paying tribute. One investigator found late in 1864 that people in Arkansas and Mississippi were terrorized, that most planters had not made expenses, and that freedmen had flocked into camps again seeking Federal protection and care.[81] Many Negroes toiled hard, and even after repeated guerrilla raids, returned to work in places where no loyal white man dared enter. But in areas without Union safeguards, they suffered from increasing neglect. Wasting the money they earned on foolish trifles, and soon losing interest in the novelty of lawful marriages, they slumped into ignorance and lassitude.

The lack of system became glaringly evident in the vital area of education. Eaton, a professional educator, took a strong interest in schooling the refugees. His Freedmen's Department tried to obtain the services of Army chaplains and specially-trained soldiers for part-time work, welcoming qualified teachers from the North, whether individual volunteers, or agents of philanthropic organizations. The government, beginning in the autumn of 1863, offered such workers transportation, quarters, and rations.[82] Eaton had no authority, however, to superintend the schools, enforce discipline, prescribe uniform texts, or regulate the conduct of teachers, and he could contribute no money to buy books or rent schoolhouses. Inside the camps he had to use wretched quarters, and outside of them usually had none at all, for few planters cared to help educate their workers. Friction and jealousy sprang up among the independent agents working side by side, each anxious to promote the interests of a particular organization, and some eager for the easiest or showiest places.

Belatedly, Lorenzo Thomas issued an order placing Eaton as General Superintendent of Freedmen in effective charge of the schools, with power to appoint heads for his various districts from Vicksburg and Helena to Columbus, Ky., and to use them in directing all details of instruction.[83] Later, Eaton named Dr. Joseph Warren superintendent of Negro schools throughout his jurisdiction. More sys-

81. "Report of A.S. Fiske," late in 1865, as in Eaton, *op. cit.*, 157-159.
82. Lorenzo Thomas, Special Order 63, Sept. 29, 1863; Eaton, *op. cit.*, 194.
83. Sept. 26, 1864. Eaton, *op. cit.*, 196.

tematic work was then undertaken, and some women teachers exhibited a heroic devotion worthy of highest praise. Warren nevertheless had to bring home to Northern friends a sad truth when he reported: "This unfortunate class of people is so unsettled that any permanent plan for the instruction of the children is impracticable."[84] Refugees generally hoped to return to their old homes, and the best that could be done was to seize fleeting opportunities to awaken a desire for education.

It was plain by 1864, East and West, that the conflicts of authority in managing the freedmen should be ended, that their welfare must be made the paramount consideration, that a more practical wage system must be devised, and that a larger force of provost-marshals to supervise them must be put into the field. Meditating on the folly of a divided administration, N.P. Banks made an emphatic statement: "The assignment of the abandoned and forfeited plantations to one department of the government, and the protection and support of the emancipated people to another, is a fundamental error productive of incalculable evils, and cannot be too soon and too thoroughly corrected."[85] It seemed plain to progressive men that the government would do well to seize the opportunity of endowing Negroes of intelligence and industry with small parcels of land. Many of the large plantations seized from Confederates could and should have been broken up, with compensation to the owners to be determined later. Mississippi in 1860 had more than 6,460,000 acres of improved land in farms and plantations, and nearly 12,670,000 of unimproved land, with only 354,000 white inhabitants. Much of the land should have been apportioned to former slaves. Alabama had approximately 6,400,000 acres of improved land, and 12,690,000 unimproved, with only 526,500 white people. The Negro families, who longed for forty acres and a mule, might at least have been allowed twenty acres.

The brightest ray in the dark situation was the fact that freedmen, if given half a chance, prospered as small independent cultivators. They loved the land, proving themselves as expert as most masters in methods of tillage. Having small means, they leased limited tracts and farmed them carefully, and once settled, they clung to these tracts with passion throughout all the storms of war. Grant had been anxious to settle part of the black population in and about Vicksburg on a rich peninsula below the city called Davis or Palmyra Bend, where John A. Quitman, Joseph Davis (the President's brother), and other prominent Southerners had owned plantations. The freedmen who took tracts of five to a hundred acres here did make it something of an Eden. Near Helena, too, a number of Negroes who leased land from the Treasury did well, gathering stock and farm

84. *Ibid.,* 208.
85. Banks, Alexandria, La., to James McKaye, March 28, 1864, in *The Mastership and Its Fruits; The Emancipated Slave Face to Face with His Old Master,* New York, 1864, *passim.*

implements from abandoned plantations, and working alongside their hired hands in the fields. "They make more money than the white lessees when they are placed on the same footing," reported Colonel Samuel Thomas of Ohio, who looked after them.[86]

Largely because of these displays of Negro enterprise, many observers concluded that government wage-fixing should give way as soon as possible to free economic forces. An investigator in the Helena-Natchez-Vicksburg districts, early in 1864, expressed a hope that labor might soon compete in the open market, with payments fixed by supply and demand. Careful supervision, however, would be required, for neither Northern speculators nor quasi-loyal Southerners could be trusted to treat Negroes fairly. "I have no doubt," wrote N. P. Banks, "that many of the planters within our lines, who are protected by the Government in the enjoyment of their property, honestly accept the new situation, and enter into the idea of free labor with sincerity; but this attitude is coupled with an incredulity as to the success of the experiment, natural to . . . the ideas in which they have been educated. This is fostered more by the intractability and brutality of the overseers—the middle class between the laborer and the employer—than it is by an innate disposition of the planter himself."[87] Much evidence was shortly presented by J. T. Trowbridge of the willingness of some Southerners in the Carolinas to deal justly with the freedmen, along with many instances of injustice. A newspaper traveller in the South in 1863-1864 and later, Charles Carleton Coffin, correspondent of the Boston *Journal*, emphasized the strong class divisions among Southern whites. He found that many of the wealthy planter class were less likely to express social and political antagonism toward the liberated Negroes and the Unionists than the poor whites.[88]

[VI]

But a new era in the relationship between the Negro and the government was shortly to be foreshadowed: the era associated with the name of the Freedmen's Bureau. Grant later thought that the idea of the Bureau could be traced to Eaton's work at Grand Junction,[89] but in reality the innovation had many precursors. When Congress met in the closing days of 1863 to listen to Lincoln's plan of general emancipation, the provision of a bureau (which most men thought should be in the War Department) had occurred to many. The first effective bill for the purpose came from Representative Thomas D. Eliot of New Bedford, Massachu-

---

86. Eaton, *op. cit.*, 164; *National Almanac*, 1863, 309, 316.
87. Banks, March 28, 1864, in James McKaye, *The Mastership and Its Fruits, op. cit.*
88. Trowbridge, J.T., *A Picture of the Desolated States*, Hartford, 1868, Chs. LXX & LXXI; Coffin, C.C., *Marching to Victory*, New York, 1889. See especially 342, 365-450.
89. Grant, *Personal Memoirs, op. cit.*, I, 424-426.

setts, whose measure for a Bureau of Emancipation was immediately given two readings, and referred to a committee.[90] He acted for the freedmen's societies of Boston, New York, Philadelphia, and Cincinnati, which had petitioned Lincoln on the subject, and found it easy to demonstrate the need for such legislation, without which the powers of the President himself were limited. In a long February speech, Eliot read statements by Lorenzo Thomas, Yeatman, and others, describing the prevalent abuses and miseries,[91] and in another speech Representative W. D. Kelley of Pennsylvania expanded on the subject. Meanwhile a number of Democrats, including S. S. Cox of Ohio, had criticized the bill, primarily on the ground that it would invade the rights of the States.[92] It barely passed the House on March 1, 1864, by a vote of 69 to 67, with Francis P. Blair, Jr., of Missouri, among those voting in the negative. But it still had to pass the Senate, which was occupied with other matters, and disposed to take its time. The history of this agency was, therefore, to belong to the era of Reconstruction, not to the Civil War.

Few chapters upon the war years are as unhappy as that which deals with the slaves to whom the nation owed so great a debt, and for whom it did so little, both tardily and grudgingly. Years later, the Czar of Russia declared that his nation had treated its serfs with far more generosity than the United States had dealt with its slaves; and although the Russian problem was much simpler, and did not have to be attacked in the midst of a bloody and exhausting war, his statement had a certain amount of truth. If the Union Government had faced its responsibility promptly and squarely, it would have devoted far more planning, effort and money to the helpless people who had been forced to come to America unwillingly, whose labor in clearing and developing the country had been exploited for generations without recompense, who had suffered so many cruelties, and whose temper to the end had remained so patient and tractable. No really valid excuses can be accepted for the shortcomings of the nation's leaders in this field.

90. *Congressional Globe*, 38th Cong., 1st Sess., 19, 21.
91. *Ibid.*, 566-573.
92. *Ibid.*, 708-713, 772-775.

12

Lincoln, Congress, and the Radicals

WITH A feeling that the tide of popular sentiment was flowing in his favor, that the elections proved his possession of the hearts of most patriots, and that the apparent safety of besieged Chattanooga provided a basis for sweeping new advances, Lincoln set out on November 18, 1863, for the dedication of a national cemetery at Gettysburg. Edward Everett, the most renowned orator of the land since Webster, had agreed to deliver the principal address. When David Wills, the prominent Gettysburg citizen who, with Governor Curtin's support, had been in charge of burials and a prime mover in establishing the cemetery, invited Lincoln to attend, he probably anticipated a refusal. The President's duties were so incessant and onerous that he almost never stirred from the vicinity of Washington, except to visit his generals upon some urgent occasion. Doubtless in his acceptance he was influenced by curiosity to see the famous battlefield, by the heartening response to his recent utterances, and by the fact that John Murray Forbes, in praising his recent J. C. Conkling letter, had urged him to expound the great truth that the war was not one of North against South, but of democracy against the foes of democracy.

"Our friends abroad see it!" wrote Forbes. "John Bright and his glorious band of European Republicans see that we are fighting for Democracy. . .The aristocrats and the Despots of the old world see that our quarrel is that of the People against an aristocracy."[1]

The overriding reason for Lincoln's acceptance, however, was that he felt attendance a duty to the brave men living and dead who had fought at Gettysburg and on so many other bloody fields of the half year from Chancellorsville to Chickamauga. It was a duty to say something that might assuage the still fresh

1. Forbes to Lincoln, Sept. 8, 1863, brought to the President by Charles Sumner, Robert Todd Lincoln Papers, LC; Thomas, Benjamin, *Abraham Lincoln*, N.Y., 1952, 400. For extensive and analytical coverage of the Gettysburg ceremonies see: Warren, Louis A., *Lincoln's Gettysburg Declaration*, Fort Wayne, 1964; Mearns, David C., and Lloyd A. Dunlap, *Long Remembered, the Gettysburg Address in Facsimile*, Washington, 1963; Randall, James G., *Lincoln the President*, II, 303-320. Other useful secondary works are: Bullard, I.L., *A Few Appropriate Remarks*, Harrogate, Tenn., 1944; Barton, William E., *Lincoln at Gettysburg*, Indianapolis, 1930.

grief of the kinsfolk of the slain, and uplift the national spirit.

Lincoln left Washington shortly after noon. His coach was transferred in Baltimore from the B.& O. to the Northern Central, and towards evening his special train paused at Hanover Junction to be switched to the Gettysburg line. One report tells us that the President, appearing on the platform, remarked to a knot of onlookers in his quaintly awkward fashion: "Well, you have seen me, and according to the general experience, you have seen less than you expected to see." He reached Gettysburg at dusk, to find it jammed with thousands of visitors, through whom he, Wills, General Couch, and Edward Everett drove to the Wills house on the public square.

He sat down to dine with Seward, the two other Cabinet members who had come with him, the French minister, and some high military and naval officers. Everett, who had just toured the field, spoke sadly of the scarred trees, blasted by battle, the raw graves of men buried where they fell with a bit of wood at head and foot as temporary markers, and the Southern corpses in the Devil's Den with naught but rocks for covering. This was the first occasion on which Lincoln and Everett had met for conversation. Later, when some Boston friends bemoaned the President's lack of social grace, Everett was able to say that Lincoln, as he appeared at David Wills's table, was the peer of any person present in manners, appearance, and conversation.[2]

That evening, the roaming crowds kept up their hubbub. The band of the Fifth New York Artillery serenaded Lincoln shortly after nine o'clock, getting a clumsy little impromptu speech from him in response. Thereupon, it appears, although no searcher has found details of hours and circumstances, he retired to his room and worked on the address which he had begun in Washington shortly before the 18th. It seems likely that he finished or almost finished the address that night, and took it next door to show Seward. Perhaps next morning, the 19th, between nine and ten o'clock, he put the last touches on the document. Two facts are certain: that he gave intense and careful labor, after his wont, to his address; and that it was begun in the White House and completed under the Wills roof —no part of it, contrary to a widely accepted legend, being written on the train.

For the most part, the crowd was not there for a celebration. The battle and its dreadful losses were too fresh in memory, the carnage having been only a few short months before in July. As a reporter put it, describing the visitors: "Most of them were fathers, mothers, brothers, and sisters, who had come from distant parts to look at and weep over the remains of their fallen kindred, or to gather up the honored relics and bear them back to the burial grounds of their native

2. Frothingham, Paul R., *Edward Everett; Orator and Statesman*, Boston, 1925, 452-453; Bancroft, Frederic, *Life of William H. Seward*, N.Y., 1900, II, 402-403.

homes—in relating what they had suffered and endured, and what part their loved ones had borne in the memorable days of July." An old man from Massachusetts said, "I have a son who fell in the first day's fight, and I have come to take back his body, for his mother's heart is breaking, and she will not be satisfied till it is brought home to her." A Pennsylvanian from the midland counties said, "My brother was killed in the charge of the Pennsylvania Reserves on the enemy when they were driven from Little Round-top, but we don't know where his remains are." It was a mournful story of affection and pride which many of the visitors had to tell that bleak November day.

For others, the scene had a different meaning. General John Gibbon and his aide, Frank A. Haskell, who wrote a dramatic account of the battle, toured the field during the ceremonies. They had little interest in what was being said, but a great deal in reviewing the well-remembered terrain. They deplored the moving about and removal of bodies, and the omnipresent cheapjacks who took commercial advantage of the occasion, selling relics from the battle-ground at little stands set up in the streets.[3]

Shortly after mid-morning of the 19th, amid a crowd of fifteen thousand people, the solemn memorial procession formed and set out past the brick shops, the wooden houses, and the gaunt, leafless trees, to the seventeen acres of the battlefield that Wills had bought for the cemetery. A band led the march; then came a military detachment with arms sloped, then the dignitaries (Lincoln looking ungainly to some on a small horse), and finally the visitors and villagers. The day was beautiful, with a bright sun, a cool breeze, a crystal air that brought the blue hills into clear relief. A small platform with chairs, open to the heavens, was provided for the speakers and important guests, but all others had to stand on the bare hilltop, devoid of trees, bushes, or grass. One result was that few women, if any, were among the audience; another was that half the crowd grew tired and restive during Everett's long address, and many wandered away.

A dirge by the band and a well-phrased prayer by the Senate chaplain were followed by Everett's two-hour effort, which he had fairly memorized—a speech worthy of the occasion. It was a polished historical discourse, which employed information furnished by Halleck, Meade, Colonel Theodore Lyman, and others, to give an accurate narrative of the campaign and the battle. Fittingly, Everett closed with an elaborate argument to demonstrate that, as English unity had survived the War of the Roses and the Civil War, as Germany survived the terrible hatreds engendered in that country by the Thirty Years' War, and as French unity had arisen purified from the Revolutionary convulsion, so American unity would be restored on a more rocklike foundation after this war. Lincoln

3. Cincinnati *Daily Commercial*, Nov. 23, 1863; Haskell to his brother, Frank A. Haskell Papers, State Historical Society of Wisconsin, Philadelphia, Nov. 20, 1863.

listened approvingly, for he wished nothing more earnestly than such a revival of the union of hearts as Everett prophesied.

"There is no bitterness on the part of the masses," declaimed Everett. "The bonds that unite us as one people, a substantial community of origin, language, belief, and law (the four great ties that hold the societies of men together); common national and political interests; a common history; a common pride in a glorious ancestry . . . these bonds of union are of perennial force and energy, while the causes of alienation are imaginary, fictitious, and transient. The heart of the people North and South is for the Union."

This was the note that Seward had struck the night before when he made a short speech to the serenaders, partly reported in the Washington *Daily Chronicle* of November 20, 1863, predicting a happy acceptance of national integrity and emancipation. Lincoln might have sounded the same chord. But he chose to speak not to the nation, but to all free men, and not to his own moment in history, but to the centuries.[4]

4. Lincoln's remarks at Gettysburg, on evening of Nov. 18: Lincoln, *Collected Works*, VII, 16-17. Everett's address: Stripp, Fred, "The Other Gettysburg Address," *Civil War History*, June 1955, Vol. I. No. Two, 161-173; Soldiers' National Cemetery Commission, *Revised Report Made to the Legislature of Pennsylvania;* Warren, *Lincoln's Gettysburg Declaration, op.cit.,* 185-214; Washington *Morning Chronicle,* Nov. 20, 1863. Seward's speech night of Nov. 18, Washington *Morning Chronicle,* Nov. 20, 1863; Seward, William H., *The Diplomatic History of the War for the Union, Being the Fifth Volume of the Works of William H. Seward,* N.Y., 1853-1884, 490; Hay, John, *Lincoln and the Civil War in the Diaries and Letters of John Hay,* edited by Tyler Dennett, 119-121, N.Y., 1939.
Eyewitness descriptions of the program and exact details of the whole occasion at Gettysburg are many and vary considerably. The estimates of the crowd, response etc., are variously reported. The sources given in footnote 1 above represent the best in research on the subject. Among the outstanding newspaper descriptions are Washington *Morning Chronicle,* Nov. 20, 1863, and Cincinnati *Daily Commercial,* Nov. 23, 1863. Also of value are various issues of *Lincoln Lore:* No. 762, Nov. 1943; No. 1023, Nov. 15, 1948; No. 1473, Nov., 1960. The files of the Lincoln National Life Foundation, Fort Wayne, Ind., contain vast amounts of material on all aspects of the Gettysburg ceremonies.
For a description of the battlefield at the time of the Address from a soldier's viewpoint, see Frank A. Haskell to his brother, Nov. 20, 1863, Haskell Papers, State Historical Society of Wisconsin. For other details of Lincoln's visit see, Judge David Wills to John G. Nicolay, Jan. 19, 1894, typed memo, Lincoln National Life Foundation.
Ever since the President's trip to Gettysburg, authorities have been discussing the writing of the address, and what text Lincoln actually used. While the legend of writing the address on the train is nowhere seriously credited, there remains controversy over whether the President used the first or second copy, or whether he used any at all exactly. For many years experts accepted generally that he used the second copy supposedly written at Gettysburg. Recently David C. Mearns, General McMurtry and others have expressed the opinion that Lincoln used the first draft. Furthermore, there is some difference of opinion as to the exact words Lincoln delivered. While it is of importance to solve these historical questions, there is little that their solution can add to or detract from the spirit of the Address.
Lincoln, *Collected Works,* VII, 17-23, contains all five texts of the Gettysburg Address in Lincoln's hand, plus the Associated Press version. Sources previously given also contain material on the various drafts. Mearns and Dunlap, *Long Remembered, op. cit.,* contains facsimiles and a discussion of differences. As it represents his last effort on the Address, I have adopted the final or "Bliss" copy for this text. While all versions vary in some details and punctuation, the major change is the insertion of "under God" in the third and succeeding copies, and in the Associated Press report.

Four score and seven years ago, our fathers brought forth upon this continent, a new nation, conceived in Liberty, and dedicated to the proposition that all men are created equal.

Now we are engaged in a great civil war, testing whether that nation, or any nation so conceived, and so dedicated, can long endure. We are met on a great battlefield of that war. We have come to dedicate a portion of that field, as a final resting place for those who here gave their lives, that that nation might live. It is altogether fitting and proper that we should do this.

But, in a larger sense, we cannot dedicate—we cannot consecrate—we cannot hallow this ground. The brave men, living and dead, who struggled here, have consecrated it far above our poor power to add or detract. The world will little note, nor long remember, what we say here, but it can never forget what they did here. It is for us, the living, rather, to be dedicated here to the unfinished work which they who fought here have thus far so nobly advanced. It is rather for us to be here dedicated to the great task remaining before us—that from these honored dead we take increased devotion to that cause for which they gave the last full measure of devotion—that we here highly resolve that these dead shall not have died in vain—that this nation, under God, shall have a new birth of freedom—and that government of the people, by the people, for the people, shall not perish from the earth.

Inevitably, Lincoln's immortal speech, delivered to a crowd numbed with standing, seemed to many an anticlimax after Everett's stirring peroration, with its quotation from Pericles. Few then grasped the fact that, while Everett's function was to celebrate the glories of the field and the heroism of the slain, Lincoln's duty was merely to pronounce a formal dedication of the resting place. That he had done far more; that he had dedicated the nation to the defense and invigoration of free institutions wherever the influence of the republic extended; that he had written one of the noblest prose-poems of the language—this was at first evident to some, but not all. His "little speech," as he termed it, was perhaps five times interrupted by applause, and was followed by a long-continued hand-clapping,[5] but he was disappointed in what he thought its lack of impact. Indeed, an able reporter, John Russell Young of the friendly Philadelphia *Press,* wrote later that, while Everett's discourse had the perfection of "a bit of Greek sculpture —beautiful but cold as ice," and was impressive as "resonant, clear, splendid rhetoric," Lincoln's brief speech, delivered in his high tenor voice with not the least attempt at effect, "made no particular impression at the time."[6]

Yet some perceptive men comprehended the august character of Lincoln's utterance, so eloquent in its appeal to the finest aspirations of the nation, and so completely devoid of any note of partisanship, sectionalism, or ignoble emotion.

5. Associated Press Report; *Lincoln Lore,* No. 762, Nov. 15, 1943; New York *Tribune,* Nov. 21, 1863; Warren, *op.cit.,* 125-127.
6. Young, James Russell, *Frank Leslie's Illustrated Newspaper,* Apr. 10, 1886.

It was unfortunate that newspapers using the Associated Press dispatch had an imperfect version; but others, like the Boston *Daily Advertiser* of November 20, obtained a reasonably correct text. Someone on the staff of the Springfield *Republican*, probably Samuel Bowles or J. C. Holland, hailed it as "a perfect gem." Someone on the Providence *Journal*, perhaps the editor James Burrill Angell, pronounced it beautiful, inspiring, and thrilling. The cultivated George William Curtis declared in *Harper's Weekly* that the President's deliverance, an appeal from the heart to the heart, could not be read without emotion: "It was as simple, and felicitous, and earnest a word as was ever spoken."[7] Edward Everett generously assured Lincoln that he had said more in two minutes than Everett himself had said in two hours—and Everett was too sincere a man to make this comment without meaning it.

Throughout the North, more and more men comprehended that the President was the nation's greatest single asset. Newspapers were advertising "The President's Hymn," written as a response to his Thanksgiving Proclamation of October 3, which had opened with a poetic reference to the blessings of "fruitful fields and healthful skies."[8] and had closed on a deep religious note. Henry J. Raymond's New York *Times* had just declared: "In spite of all the hard trials and hard words to which he has been exposed, Abraham Lincoln is today the most popular man in the Republic. All the denunciation and all the arts of the demagogue are perfectly powerless to wean the people from their faith in him."[9] "Wherever I have been this summer," Schuyler Colfax told the President just after the Gettysburg speech, "I have seen the evidences of a very powerful popular feeling in your favor. . . ."[10] Lincoln was stricken with varioloid, a mild form of smallpox, just after his return, and took to his bed with a characteristic jest: "At last I have something I can give everybody." He was too ill to see a committee of eminent men who were pressing the establishment of a new government bureau to protect and aid the freedmen; the members, who included Edward Atkinson of Boston, Henry Ward Beecher and H.W. Bellows of New York, and Levi Coffin of Cincinnati, had to send him a memorial. The country was not alarmed, but it learned with pleasure on December 1 that he had almost recovered.

7. A goodly number of papers and journals did recognize the merits of the President's address within a few days or weeks of the event. For numerous quotations, see Warren, *op.cit.*, 145-146. Also, Springfield, Mass. *Republican*, Nov. 20, 1863; Providence *Journal*, Nov. 20. 1863; *Harper's Weekly*, Dec. 5, 1863; *Associated Press Dispatch* copy from Lincoln Nat'l. Life Foundation. Chicago *Tribune*, Nov. 21, 1863, "More than any other single event will this glorious dedication nerve the heroes to a deeper resolution of the living to conquer at all hazards. More than anything else the day's work contributes to the nationality of the great Republic."

8. Lincoln, *Collected Works*, VI, 496; VII, 24-25.

9. Thomas, *Abraham Lincoln. op.cit.*, 398.

10. Hay, John, *Lincoln and the Civil War in the Diaries and Letters of John Hay*, 123-24.

Of course, Lincoln could not please everybody. Early in 1862, Greeley's *Tribune* published a brief editorial declaring that he was too exclusive, and was not meeting enough men. Honest Greeley at once wrote Nicolay, stating that Charles Dana had let this slip into the paper without the editor's knowledge and against his judgment—the real trouble with Lincoln was that he saw too many people, including many not worth his while![11] Zachariah Chandler sent the President a bullying letter on the eve of the Gettysburg address, demanding that he stand firm against exhuming the conservatives and traitors buried in the elections, who smelled worse than Lazarus. Lincoln's reply was good-naturedly jocular; he was glad, he wrote, that the elections went well and that neither by natural depravity nor submission to evil influences had he done anything bad enough to prevent the victories. Then he flashed a steel blade in defense of moderation: "I hope to 'stand firm' enough not to go backward, and yet not go forward fast enough to wreck the country's cause."[12] He knew when to keep his temper—and when to lose it, for he could show anger if aroused. He had lost his temper when McClellan let Pope fight Second Manassas without the help so desperately needed; he almost lost it with Rosecrans; he lost it over so poor a creature as Fernando Wood. But however sorely tried by Horatio Seymour on one side and Charles Sumner on the other, he kept his temper with them because he believed them sincere.

"I don't know," he remarked philosophically to the radical Senator Lot M. Morrill of Maine, "but that God has created some one man great enough to comprehend the whole of this stupendous crisis and transaction from end to end, and endowed him with sufficient wisdom to manage and direct it. I confess that I do not fully understand and foresee it all. But I am placed here where I am obliged, to the best of my poor ability, to deal with it. And that being the case. I can only go just as fast as I can see how to go."[13] Perhaps the most revealing glimpse of Lincoln at this time is one that to the casual eye reveals nothing. His prevailing mood, writes his secretary Nicolay, was one of meditation; when official business ended and the door closed, "he would sometimes sit for an hour in complete silence, his eyes almost shut, the inner man apparently as far from him as if the form in the chair were a petrified image."[14] This busiest of presidents took time to think.

11. New York *Tribune*, Dec. 1 and Dec. 3, 1863. Collection of Justin Turner, West Los Angeles, Calif.; Nicolay, Helen, *Lincoln's Secretary, a Biography of John G. Nicolay*, New York, 1949, 83; author feels there is some doubt about Lincoln's statement as to his disease.
12. Chandler to Lincoln, Nov. 15, 1863, Chandler Papers, LC; Lincoln to Chandler, Nov. 20, 1863, Lincoln, *Collected Works*, VII, 23-24.
13. Sen. Lot M. Morrill Papers, Univ. of Maine, Brunswick, Me. Cf. Lincoln's statement to G. Hodges, April 4, 1864, in Robert Todd Lincoln Collection, Item No. 32077-78.
14. Browne, Francis, *The Every-Day Life of Abraham Lincoln*, Chicago, 1913, 361.

[I]

Amid the rejoicings over Lookout Mountain and Missionary Ridge, Lincoln had to prepare for the opening of Congress. He could look back on high constructive achievements: land given to the landless; a system of college endowments provided; the Pacific railway launched; financial measures of the first importance passed. He was quite aware that the tariff legislation, railway legislation, internal revenue law, and other measures had given rise to an ominous growth of lobbying by special interests, and of rumored corruption. He was equally aware that the Republican party structure of 1860 had fallen into chaos, and that as a new creation the ruling party had never really been firm; that the Senate leaders—Henry Wilson, Lyman Trumbull, William Pitt Fessenden, Benjamin F. Wade, Charles Sumner, and others—and the House leaders—Henry L. Dawes, Thaddeus Stevens, George W. Julian, and so on,—would have to face the challenge of radical Republicans, conservative Republicans, War Democrats, Lincoln-men, anti-Lincoln men, and determined representatives of every intermediate shade of opinion. Lincoln remembered that early in the war Joshua Speed, scrutinizing the party confusion, had advised a systematic effort to form a distinct Administration Party in Congress. He knew that such thorny issues as confiscation and civil liberties had baffled the wisdom and justice of the best-intentioned men.

Opinion tended toward two opposed extremes. "We are growing more radical . . . every day," a constituent of Lyman Trumbull's had written in 1862.[15] Northern hatred of slavery as the root of the war beat in waves upon members of Congress, who transmitted the shock to the President until he actually feared, by midsummer in 1862, that if he did not adopt emancipation, the Congressional leaders would cut off appropriations for sustaining the war. At the same time, the men whose relatives and friends might be ruined by harsh measures grew more conservative. They feared the loss of fundamental rights of free speech, jury trial, and peaceable assemblage; the overweighting of the economic balance in favor of corporations and against agrarian interests; the drafting of sons into an Army used to bring Negroes north to compete in the labor market; and the shooting of boys by West Point martinets for minor offenses. To Radicals, the critics of conscription and military trials stood next door to treason; to Conservatives, the advocates of Cromwellian severities were Jacobins of revolutionary hue.

Neither body of extremists had the approval of Lincoln; but he knew well that the Republican Party, which was steadily absorbing most of the War Democrats, was his only support, and that in many areas, the Radicals controlled the party. If only the Conservatives would give him more assistance, T.J. Barnett kept pleading. "The President I have now no doubt," he wrote S.L.M. Barlow, the

15. Lyman Trumbull Papers, Ill. State Hist. Library.

Warwick of the New York Democrats, in September, 1863, "is hard as flint on the Abolition ground, if it be fair to call it so, on which his Emancipation Act and Message are based—and his friends evidently intend to press him hard for another term. Poor Mr. Lincoln! one of the best-hearted, best-meaning, and most patriotic men in the world, as well intentioned as he is unfortunate in being misunderstood! I sincerely and deeply sympathize with him, the more he grows on me—and he would, personally, on you also."[16] It was unquestionably true, as we have said, that the Democrats were missing a great opportunity—the opportunity to play the rôle of a patriotic and constructive opposition party rather than that of an opportunist faction exploiting all the discontents and misfortunes of a democracy undergoing a terrible crisis.

Congress met on December 7, 1863, with Union members (that is, Republicans and War Democrats) holding decisive control of the Senate, and a clear though not emphatic majority of the House. The first important step taken was the election of youthful Schuyler Colfax of Indiana, an early Republican and a South Bend editor who had entered the House in 1855, as Speaker. He received 101 votes. The principal Democratic aspirant, S.S. Cox of Ohio, received only 42 and there were 39 scattered votes. Lincoln had decided not to give Colfax the postmaster-generalship, partly because he thought him already assured of a brilliant future, and partly, we may surmise, because of an instinctive feeling that "Smiler" Colfax, with all his engaging qualities, might be a bit too amiable and too ambitious of preferment and its accompanying emoluments, as the country shortly found he was. Colfax's elevation to the chair was proof that the House would not waste time by attempting, as the New York *Herald* had recommended, a series of investigations into the "plunder, profligacy, corruption, and mismanagement" which James Gordon Bennett alleged to have prevailed throughout the war.[17] As we have noted previously, there was a wide variance in statements of party figures for the first session of the 38th Congress. The New York *Tribune* mistakenly counted 90 Republicans and War Democrats, 72 old-style Democrats and John Bell Whigs, and 14 Border-State men. The New York *Tribune Almanac* for 1864, whose total was less accurate, gave 102 Republicans, 75 Democrats, and 9 Border-State men. The 1864 *National Almanac* stated: "Parties are now so intermingled that a political classification of the members of Congress is a difficult and delicate work." The New York *Herald* had compiled figures which convinced it that the House would muster 96 Opposition-men against 92 Administration-men; but although it was difficult to be precise either in numbers or in definitions of allegiance, the Administration actually held a generally adequate

16. Barnett to Barlow, Sept. 14, 1863, S.L.M. Barlow Papers, HEH.
17. *Congressional Globe,* 38th Cong., 1st Sess., Pt.I, 6; New York *Herald,* Aug. 18, 1863; New York *Tribune,* Oct. 18, 1863; *National Almanac,* 1864, 78; 1865, 18; Rhodes, James Ford, *History of the United States,* IV, 419.

margin.[18] In the Senate, a vote of 36 to 5 for seating the West Virginia members demonstrated the Republican strength.

S.S. Cox, a graduate of Brown University, author of a favorably received travel book (*A Buckeye Abroad*), and a man of pleasing humor as well as liberal political views, made an enlightened Democratic leader. From the beginning of the war, he had steadily helped vote men and money to support it.[19] Although a personal friend of Vallandigham, he took a much wiser view of affairs. Lincoln, in late January of 1865, complimented him on the merits of a speech opposing the appearance of Cabinet officers on the floor of the House. [20] He offered valiant arguments in behalf of civil liberties; he called on the President to do more to arrange the exchange of prisoners; he termed the confiscation legislation "an utter failure," (which came near the truth), at the same time praising Lincoln for trying to bring it into close conformity with the Constitution; and he effectively protested against an attempt to expel from the House a Copperhead Ohioan who had the audacity to suggest recognition of Confederate independence. At the same time, he defended the loyalty and patriotism of the great body of Northern Democrats. His general position earned him the praise of his fellow-member James A. Garfield, and the denunciation of Vallandigham and other extremists.[21]

This first session of the 38th Congress passed some legislation of general social and economic interest. It amended the Homestead Act; it established a postal money order system; it provided a national currency secured by United States bonds; it took steps to encourage immigration; it provided for assisting the construction of a railroad and telegraph line from Lake Superior to Puget Sound; and it voted a law enabling the people of Nevada, Colorado, and Nebraska to take steps toward Statehood. All these subjects were important. They received little attention, however, in comparison with one topic that dominated the attention of the session from its opening until adjournment on July 4, 1864—Reconstruction.

[II]

The Union had hardly broken apart before men began discussing the mode and terms of restoration. Their attitudes varied from the mild euphoria of Seward, who for some months indulged his old dream that kindness might woo the

18. New York *Tribune*, Oct. 18, 1863; New York *Tribune Almanac*, 1864, 24; *National Almanac*, 1864, 78; New York *Herald*, Aug. 27, Dec. 7. 1863; Albany *Evening Journal Almanac*, 1863, 73; Rhodes, *op.cit.*, IV, 419.

19. *Congressional Globe*, 38th Congress, First Session, Pt. I, 2-3; Lindsey, David, *"Sunset" Cox, Irrepressible Democrat*, Detroit, 1959, 44-47, and *passim.*; Cox, S.S., *Three Decades of Federal Legislation*, Providence, R.I., 1885, *passim*.

20. Lincoln, *Collected Works*, VIII, 249, Lincoln to Cox, Jan. 31, 1865.

21. *Congressional Globe*, 38th Congress, First Session, Pt. I, 12, 210-212; Pt. II, 1506-1512; Lindsey, *op.cit.*, 81-83.

Southern daughters back to the ancestral hearth, to the bitter vindictiveness of Unionists who felt that treason merited harsh, peremptory, and long-felt penalties. Antislavery leaders were quick to propose that this punishment take the form of transfers of property to the long-exploited Negro. "The free people of the Union believe that the Southern soil belongs equally to the Southern slaves as it does to the slave-master," declared the Harrisburg (Pa.) *Daily Telegraph,* ungrammatically but earnestly, just after New Year's in 1862. It argued that emancipation, combined with a division of property, would rid the South of an ignorant but insolent aristocracy which had long degraded labor, and finally tried to destroy the government.[22]

While Northerners were still hoping that McClellan's spring advance in 1862 would bring the South to terms, the Washington *National Republican,* a leading organ of Radical opinion, laid down some conclusions of startling rigor. It was clear, it asserted, "that the revolt of a State against the authority of the General Government destroys its political rights under the Constitution, and reduces its territory to the condition of the unorganized public domain. It forfeits all its rights. . . . There is no longer a State of South Carolina, a State of Georgia, etc. The territories and their inhabitants still exist, and the General Government has lost none of its rights of superior jurisdiction over them. . ." A rebellion intended to annihilate the nation, declared the paper, had instead annihilated the State governments. "It is equally clear that the seceded States can never come back into the Union until they have been reorganized and reofficered in all their departments. Every vestige of their treason must be repudiated . . . Having framed Constitutions, it will be competent for them to apply for readmission to the Union, and Congress may receive them or continue to hold them in the condition of Territories until satisfactory assurance shall be given that the people have returned to a sentiment of loyalty."[23]

The hand that wrote these words was probably that of the editor, George M. Weston; but the ideas were those of Charles Sumner in the Senate, Thaddeus Stevens in the House, Salmon P. Chase in the Cabinet, Wendell Phillips on public platforms, and other Radicals. The great debate on Reconstruction was already beginning. A fortnight later the *National Intelligencer* devoted almost the whole editorial page, four-and-a-half columns, to a stern rebuttal entitled "The Work of Restoration." The hand that wrote this counterblast may have been that of the editor, Richard Welling; but he echoed the voices of Montgomery Blair in the Cabinet, Orville Browning in the Senate, John Sherman in the House, and Daniel M. Dickinson on public platforms; the moderates arrayed against the "ironbacks."

22. *Congressional Globe,* 38th Congress, First Session, Appendix, 143, 149-50, 153-154, 162, 169-175, 253-255, 259. Harrisburg, Pa., *Daily Telegraph,* Jan. 4, 1862.
23. Washington *National Republican,* Feb. 11, 1862.

"We deny that any State can go out of the Union," declared the *Intelligencer,* "and therefore there can be no necessity in any event of providing for her 'readmission.' " The seceded States were not dead, it asserted; they still held full rights as States, and were not to be governed as Territories. As soon as Tennessee or Arkansas was liberated, its people should "of their own motion proceed to reorganize the State Government on the basis of the State Constitution which existed prior to the outbreak" of war. This was emphatically Lincoln's view.[24]

The President had declared in his inaugural address that under the Constitution the union of the States was perpetual; that perpetuity is implied if not expressed in the fundamental law of all governments. It followed that no State could of its own volition lawfully leave the Union, and that ordinances of secession were legally void. Lincoln added in his special message the following summer that the States had no legal status outside the Union, and could leave it only by successful revolution. "The action of the government in all its departments," his secretaries noted, "was based upon the idea that the rebellion was the unlawful proceeding of individuals which neither destroyed nor impaired any rights or obligations of Statehood, nor even any rights and obligations of their co-citizens who remained loyal."[25]

The exchange quickly became heated. Bryant's *Evening Post* at once rallied to the moderate cause. Attacking the idea that the seceded commonwealths should be treated as Territories, Bryant declared that the State governments had been perverted, but not annihilated, and were merely in suspense, not annulled. "As soon as enough people loyal to the Federal Constitution are gathered to put their machinery in operation, they will be revived." Any plan of "territorializing" the Confederacy would excite sharp hostility in the North as well as the South.[26] The *National Intelligencer* acutely remarked that the principal object of the Radical proposals was to aggrandize Congress, and bring slavery and the Negro under its authority.[27] A mutual distrust of motives was developing between those whom Bennett's New York *Herald,* with characteristic flippancy, called the Niggerheads and the Copperheads. On the Radical side that inveterate gossip, Adam Gurowski, confessed a fear that McClellan might end the war before emancipation could be accomplished. If he won and humbugged the people into believing him a hero, he would throw off the mask and become a champion of the preservation of slavery, and of general amnesty.[28] Many shared that apprehension, which McClellan's failure shortly dispelled. On the Conservative side,

24. *National Intelligencer*, March 1, March 6, 1862.
25. Lincoln, *Collected Works*, IV, 264-265, 434. Nicolay and Hay, *Abraham Lincoln*, VI, 347-348.
26. New York *Evening Post*, March 7, 1862.
27. *National Intelligencer*, March 1, 1862.
28. New York *Herald*, Aug. 25, 1865; Gurowski to Gov. John A. Andrew, March 1, 1862, Andrew Papers, Mass. Hist. Soc.

Montgomery Blair, hostile to such steps as the creation of a new State in western Virginia,[29] was earning the sobriquet of stormy petrel of the Administration shortly given him by a journalist.

Shriller and shriller grew the voices. Such Border-State conservatives as Senator Garrett Davis of Kentucky were enraged by the cruel proscription of the *National Republican.* One of the radical antislavery men, "Parson" William G. Brownlow, had made Northern cities ring in April and May of 1862 with his vituperation of secessionists. He had left East Tennessee, demanding "grape for the rebel masses, and hemp for their leaders." In Cincinnati he told an immense audience that the property of all rebels should be confiscated, and used to recompense suffering Unionists. In Harrisburg he said he would gladly tie a rope himself about the necks of some of the infernal Southerners; at the Academy of Music in New York he declared that if they remained unregenerate he believed in exterminating them; and at Cooper Institute he asserted that a more Godforsaken set of scoundrels did not live than the Southern preachers of the Gospel. The British journalist G. A. Sala heard him proclaim that he would arm every bear, wolf, catamount and crocodile to put down the rebellion, even if this meant slaying every man, woman, and child below the Mason-and-Dixon line.[30] A Yankee colonel named Sargent wrote John A. Andrew of the desirability of extirpating all rebels: "We are to be a regenerating, colonizing power, or we are to be whipped. . ."[31] More tamely, Greeley's *Tribune* expressed the view that the best way of making sure of the loyalty of Florida would be to plant a Northern colony of ten or fifteen thousand people in it forthwith.

Beneath this acrid quarrel lay a basic difference of opinion respecting Southern psychology. Seward, Montgomery Blair, and other moderates believed that Southern loyalty to the Union could easily be restored. Seward, indeed, told the great lobbyist Sam Ward as late as March, 1862, that he still believed, if the Southern States had been allowed to secede peaceably, they would have come back within two years, and saved the Union all its bloodshed and money.[32] Ward emphatically rejected the foolish idea that they would have returned without coercion, but he did tell Sumner that the North had no alternative but to treat the rebels as wayward children until moral suasion could give them new hearts. Bryant, who had travelled in the South, shared Lincoln's belief[33] that a restoration

---

29. Welles, *Diary,* I, 191, Dec. 4, 1862.
30. *Congressional Globe,* 37th Congress, Second Session, Pt. II, 1757-1763; Pt. IV, 3144-3145; Coulter, E.M., *William G. Brownlow,* Chapel Hill, 1937, Chapt. X; Brownlow, W.G., *Sketches of the Rise, Progress, and Decline of Secession,* Philadelphia, 1862, 289, 413, 438; Sala, George Augustus, *My Diary in America in Midst of War,* London, 1865, I, 403.
31. Lt. Col. H. B. Sargent, to John A. Andrew, Andrew Papers, Mass. Hist. Soc.,
32. New York *Tribune,* Feb. 7, 1863; Ward to Barlow, March 4, March 27, 1862, S.L.M. Barlow Papers, HEH.
33. New York *Post,* March 7, 1862.

of the old union of hearts was possible. Most Border-State leaders took that attitude. So did F.A.P. Barnard, former head of the University of Mississippi and future head of Columbia University. And so did Charles Eliot Norton, who just after the defeat at Chancellorsville assured his friend Frederick Law Olmsted that the destruction of slavery and triumph of the Union were inevitable. Then, although roving bands of guerrillas might remain active in some corners of the South for a time, they would soon submit. The love of order and of profits would be strong inducements to peace. As soon as Union forces were strong enough to offer protection, "the mass of the population" would reassert its Union affections; and Yankee immigrants, attracted by the hope of making money out of cotton-growing, would be strongly Unionist in sentiment.[34]

Olmsted, however, out of his deep knowledge of the South, was skeptical of any rapid secessionist conversion. He believed that the population would fight in the field to the end; then as guerrilla bands in mountains and swamps; and even when this became impracticable, they would resist absorption in the Union by trickery, covert obstruction, and assassination. Peace would come not by a dramatic surrender, or some treaty or compromise, "but by the gradual wearing-out, dying-off, and killing-off—extermination—of the rebels." [35] Thaddeus Stevens, recalling the long struggle of Calhoun and Yancey to educate the Southern mind to disunion, told Congress at the beginning of 1862 that the South would have to taste bitter defeat before its defiance was humbled: "Better lay the whole country waste than suffer the nation to be murdered."[36] Sumner was equally convinced of the "natural diabolism" of slaveholders, and insistent that any return to the Union must be by a long, painful process of tutelage and correction controlled by Congress—if possible, controlled by Mr. Sumner.[37]

While this angry debate proceeded, Lincoln was taking practical steps to make his own plans for Reconstruction effective. Less than a month after his Emancipation Proclamation, he confidentially urged the military and naval authorities in Louisiana to do all they could to assist the efforts toward revitalization of the State being undertaken by John E. Bouligny, a lifelong citizen, and a member of Congress who, when Louisiana seceded, was so brave a champion of the Union that his return home in 1861 would probably have meant his immediate assassination. Bouligny, as Lincoln wrote, hoped to influence those people who desired to regain peace for the State upon the old basis under the Federal Constitution, to make that desire clear by electing members of Congress. Perhaps they might also elect a legislature, State officers, and Senators. "In all available ways,"

34. Barnard, F.A.P., *"Letter to the President of the United States," by a Refugee*, Philadelphia, 1863; Norton to Olmsted, Cambridge, Mass., May 20, 1863, Olmsted Papers, LC.
35. Olmsted to Charles Elliott Norton, April 30, 1863, Olmsted Papers, LC.
36. *Congressional Globe*, 37th Congress, Second Session, Pt. I. 439.
37. *Ibid.*, Pt.I., 736-737; Pt. II, 1449-1451.

ordered Lincoln, "give the people a chance to express their wishes at these elections. Follow forms of law as far as convenient, but at all events get the expression of the largest number of the people possible."[38] When certain Louisiana politicians, on hearing of this, took alarm at the possibility that Federal officers from outside the State might run for Congress, Lincoln reassured them. What the Administration wished, he declared, was conclusive evidence that respectable citizens of Louisiana were willing to enter Congress, and that other respectable citizens were willing to vote for them. It did not want Northerners elected at the point of the bayonet. The President, on November 21, 1862, asked his military governor, a Maine officer named G. F. Shepley, to cut all the knots. "And do not waste a day about it, but fix the election day early enough that we can hear the result here by the first of January."[39]

Before 1862 ended, Louisiana had chosen two Congressmen, but they were not seated until February 17, 1863, toward the end of the 37th Congress. They were Georg Michael Hahn with a small majority out of a total of 5,117 votes, and B.F. Flanders with a large majority out of a total of 2,643 votes. Each district had polled about half its usual pre-war total.[40] The fact that nearly eight thousand white men had taken the oath of allegiance, and assisted in filling two of Louisiana's old-time seats, pleased Lincoln. Thus matters stood when Chancellorsville was fought, in May, 1863. Thus they stood when two organizations sprang up in Louisiana, one of antislavery radicals and the other of conservatives, who wished to organize a complete State government. These rival movements were interrupted by General Bank's Port Hudson campaign and his expedition into Texas, but immediately revived. Lincoln had a clear conception of the next steps to be taken in raising Louisiana to the position of a self-governing State once more.

"I would be glad," he wrote General Banks on August 5, 1863, "for her to make a new Constitution recognizing the emancipation proclamation, and adopting emancipation in those parts of the State to which the proclamation does not apply. And while she is at it, I think it would not be objectionable for her to adopt some practical system by which the two races could gradually live themselves out of their old relation to each other, and both come out better prepared for the new. Education for young blacks should be included in the plan. After all, the power or element of 'contract' may be sufficient for this probationary period; and by its simplicity and flexibility may be the better ....I think the thing should be pushed forward so that, if possible, its mature work may reach here by the meeting of Congress."[41]

38. Lincoln, *Collected Works*, V, 462-463, to Benjamin F. Butler, George F. Shepley and others, Oct. 14, 1862.
39. *Ibid.*, 504, Lincoln to Shepley, Nov. 21, 1862.
40. Nicolay and Hay, *Abraham Lincoln*, VI, 353.
41. Lincoln, *Collected Works*, VI, 364-365, to Banks, Aug. 5, 1863.

Lincoln meanwhile had initiated the first important movements toward the restoration of Tennessee to its old place in the Union. His appointment on March 4, 1862, of Andrew Johnson as Military Governor of the State had been a form of restoration, a step he boldly took, though many men in Congress questioned his constitutional power to create military governorships in the South. [42] A week after his letter asking Shepley to arrange elections for Congress in Louisiana, he sent a substantial copy of it to Andrew Johnson as Military Governor in Nashville, asking him to give the Tennesseeans an opportunity to elect members of Congress, a legislature, and State officers. The result was the promulgation of orders by Johnson and Grant for an election on December 29, 1862, to choose members of Congress for two districts. Unfortunately, a raid by Forrest in West Tennessee as the year 1862 gave way to 1863 made any election impossible; Murfreesboro immediately ensued; and then the long delay of Rosecrans in ordering an advance left Bragg in such a central position in the State that he could paralyze nearly all political activities on the part of Union men. In July, 1863, a Union convention met in Nashville, with forty counties represented, and passed resolutions favoring the early election of a legislature. But it was generally agreed that nothing effective could be done until East Tennessee was liberated, and, in fact, no important action was taken until long after the dawn of 1864.

Words, however, are sometimes more important than acts, and Chattanooga had hardly been taken before the brightening of the skies drew from Lincoln one of his more important early expressions of conviction upon Reconstruction. Seeing that his opportunity to remould Tennessee should be seized forthwith, he wrote Andrew Johnson that not a moment was to be lost. The restoration must be such as to keep the control of the State and its Congressional representation in Union hands. "Exclude all others; and trust that your government, so organized, will be recognized here, as being the one of republican form, to be guaranteed to the State . . . I see that you have declared in favor of emancipation in Tennessee, for which, may God bless you. Get emancipation into your new State Government—Constitution—and there will be no such word as fail in your case. The raising of colored troops I think will greatly help every way."[43]

Much swifter was the course of events in Arkansas. That State had been a little reluctant to secede and had been rather uneasy under Confederate domination. Some of its citizens had greeted the fall of Vicksburg with relief. A former Representative, E. W. Gantt, and a former Senator, William King Sebastian, immediately let Lincoln know that they were ready to repudiate the Confederacy and support the Union. By the end of 1863, a good part of the State was under

42. Stryker, Lloyd Paul, *Andrew Johnson: A Study in Courage*, New York, 1929, 95.
43. Lincoln, *Collected Works*, V, Oct. 21, 1862, 470-471; VI, Sept. 11, 1863, 440; Nicolay and Hay, *Abraham Lincoln*, VIII, 439-440.

complete or nominal Federal control, and nine Arkansas regiments (five white and four black) were either in the field or organizing. It is estimated that Arkansas contributed 50,000 men to the Confederate side and 13,000 to the Federal, the latter including a good many Negroes. Here again Lincoln was eager for action, and gave General Frederick Steele in Little Rock much the same instructions he had sent to Butler and Banks in New Orleans. Some confusion arose from the fact that a popular movement for Reconstruction had gotten under way before Steele could act. All differences, however, were soon ironed out, and full advantage was taken of the adoption of a new Constitution by the convention which the popular leaders had called. The election which loyal groups agreed to hold beginning March 14, 1864, a three-day affair, carried Arkansas well ahead of her liberated sisters. More than 12,000 citizens voted for the Constitution (only those who took the oath could vote), and only a handful against it. 12,430 votes were cast for Isaac Murphy, a former schoolteacher and lawyer and an unbending opponent of secession, in the election for governor; three members of Congress were elected; and a legislature was chosen. With pomp, ceremony, and rejoicing, the new government was installed in power in Little Rock in April, 1864.[44]

In short, by the opening of Congress as the winds of December blew over Capitol Hill in 1863, steps looking toward Reconstruction and reëntrance into the union had been taken in three States. The President was plainly anxious to make it easy for any considerable body of loyal citizens to erect a civil government, and to send men knocking at the door of the House. Two Congressmen-elect, the Bavarian-born Hahn and the New Hampshire-born and Dartmouth-educated Flanders, both of New Orleans, were, as we have seen, admitted to this session. Lincoln was plainly determined to exercise the powers of the Presidency to the fullest in the work of Reconstruction. He was willing to accept Congress as partner; he repeatedly emphasized the fact that although a State might elect Representatives and Senators, Congress alone could admit them. But he was insistent that while rebellion might destroy the old structure of society in a State, and its old Constitution, it could not destroy membership in the Union, which was perdurable. Such was the situation when the debate on methods and principles of Reconstruction engendered fresh animosity just before Congress sat.

[III]

In the great debate on Reconstruction which intensified rapidly in the autumn of 1863, dividing national attention with the elections and the war, the Radicals

44. *Ibid.*, V, 462-463; VII, 108-109, 141-142, 144, 154-156, 161, 173, 189, 190-191, 199; Nicolay and Hay, *Abraham Lincoln*, VIII, 412, 416-417; New York *Tribune*, Jan. 25, 1864; *Arkansas and the Civil War*, pamphlet, Arkansas Civil War Centennial Commission, Little Rock, 1961; Dyer, Frederick H., *A Compendium of the War of the Rebellion*, Des Moines, 1908, 997-1000.

led off the attack. Possibly orders had gone out from some central source to prepare public opinion for the Radical program before Congress met. Some students contend that no cohesive Radical movement existed, but it appears to have been quite cohesive, in character at least. Evidently, too, the Radical leaders were deeply perturbed by the steady, quiet, effective steps Lincoln was taking to implement his moderate scheme for bringing States back into the Union. He must be stopped! It seemed as if almost by preconcerted plan, an attack was opened simultaneously in three publications: the Washington *Chronicle*, published by John W. Forney as the organ of Secretary Chase and "ironback" Senators; the Missouri *Democrat*, organ of Missouri Radicals, largely Germans and followers of Frémont; and the *Atlantic Monthly*, edited by James T. Fields for Bay State Radicals, including the eminent antislavery writers Whittier, Lowell, Longfellow, and Mrs. Stowe.[45] Of these three assailants, the *Atlantic* carried the heaviest guns. Tens of thousands of readers in all parts of the country read excitedly its leading article in the October number, "Our Domestic Relations; or, How to Treat the Rebel States." It was unsigned, but people could see at a glance that it was the work of Charles Sumner.

Stamped by all of Sumner's characteristic pedantry, intemperance, and arrogance—and his bellicose force—it began by denouncing Lincoln's appointment of military governors for Tennessee, the Carolinas, and Louisiana, as if there were any practicable alternative to this provisional measure for reviving and supervising local civil authority in the reclaimed areas. Sumner then resorted to his favorite trick of discovering a portentous hidden threat—a frightful Apollyon to be overthrown by the Bay State Valiant-for-Truth. These governors, he assured his readers, might hold a sway indefinite both in extent and duration and rule over a military empire with autocratic powers derived from one man in Washington. Tremble, oh republic! As if Lincoln were a Caesar or even Cromwell; as if he had not committed himself to as prompt and efficient a restoration of self-government in the Southern States as possible; as if ample precedent did not exist in the previous appointment of military governors in California and New Mexico; and as if all his acts were not subject to review by a Presidential election only a year distant! Sumner embellished his horrific vision of a military despotism ruling half the republic for generations to come with quotations from Hallam, Carlyle, and Ludlow's *Memoirs*.

The point of this labored exordium was clear: Down with Presidential authority; up with Congressional power! "In truth," he wrote, "there can be no opening for military governments which is not also an opening for Congressional govern-

45. Sumner, Charles, "Our Domestic Relations; or, How to Treat the Rebel States," unsigned article, *Atlantic Monthly*, Oct, 1863, Vol.XII, No. LXXII, 507-529.

ments, with this great advantage for the latter, that they are in harmony with our institutions, which favor the civil rather than the military power." Sumner would change the balance of government against the executive and in favor of the legislative branch. For what object? He proceeded to make it clear that he and his Radical associates hoped to destroy the former balance of the Constitution, if they could, in two ways—by making legislative power paramount over executive power, and by substituting national authority throughout the South for State authority. The States had formerly been regarded as sovereign, with rights that were not to be invaded by Congress except in areas specified or implied in the Constitution; hereafter the seceded States were to be regarded as completely under the foot of Congress, without any rights whatever that Congress did not grant them. It was not true that, as Lincoln believed, the Acts of Secession were inoperative and void, and therefore left the States intact in all their rights; the truth, declared Sumner, was that the States ceased to exist constitutionally once they seceded. Again Sumner offered erudite references. One was to Edmund Burke:

"If that great master of eloquence could be heard," he wrote, "who can doubt that he would blast our Rebel States, as senseless communities who have sacrificed that corporate existence which makes them living, component members of our Union of States?"

Under the heading, "Congress the True Agent," Sumner went on to argue that as the former State governments had been *vacated* (a word used by the men who dethroned James I in 1688), the Constitution became for the time being the supreme and only law. "And the whole Rebel region, deprived of all local government, lapses under the exclusive jurisdiction of Congress, precisely as any other territory; the military entitled to govern it while fighting endured, but Congress alone empowered to exercise civil authority." Virginia, Mississippi, and South Carolina were not States—they were merely territory. "The whole broad Rebel region is *tabula rasa*, or 'a clean slate.'" Sumner did not assert that the old State boundaries might be wiped out and the South carved into novel political divisions; on the contrary, he wrote that Congress would blot no star from the flag. But other Radicals were making precisely this threat of new partitions and fresh delimitations.

The South was helpless, concluded Sumner. The President had no rightful power to deal with it; it had no powers of its own left. Happy South! Congress would deal with it. "If we are not ready to exclaim with Burke, speaking of revolutionary France, 'It is but an empty space on the political map,' we may at least adopt the response hurled back by Mirabeau, that the empty space is a volcano red with flames and overflowing with lava-floods. But whether we deal with it as 'empty space,' or as 'volcano,' the jurisdiction, civil and military, centers in Congress, to be employed for the happiness, welfare, and renown of the American people—changing Slavery into Freedom, and present chaos into a Cosmos of perpetual beauty and power."[46]

This exhaustive and exhausting discourse by the inexhaustible Senator, as the New York *Herald* called another equally ill-tempered outburst of his on foreign relations delivered at nearly the same time,[47] would have been more effective but for its venomous and rabid prejudice. Sumner did not reasonably discuss all sides of the most complex question of the day; he poured out denunciation on one side. Lincoln made no reply. It was common knowledge that the Cabinet was divided; that the conservative Seward wished to restore the seceded States as they were, while the radical Chase preferred to treat them as provinces wrested from a foreign enemy, completely at the mercy of the government. But Lincoln wisely kept his peace. With no support from Democratic organizations, he was not anxious to divide the Republican Party; and his suspension of the habeas corpus on September 15, in a broad array of cases throughout the land, had plunged him into criticism enough. People were now discussing Chase's overt manoeuvres to deprive Lincoln of a renomination, manoeuvres said to derive tenfold intensity from Chase's hatred of the President's principal lieutenant, Seward. It was obviously best for Lincoln to wait a few weeks and mature his plans.[48]

But one powerful champion of the President did step forward, and he had other supporters, although they were not so many or so noisy as the Radicals. The Radical bombardment had barely opened when Montgomery Blair appeared on October 13 in Rockville, Maryland, next door to Washington, to deliver a reply that combined argument and fulmination. While he denounced the secessionists as Calhounite conspirators, he still more angrily denounced the doctrine that the Southern States had been annihilated by their secession, or that Congress had any right to regard them as dead political entities simply because their loyal citizens —countless in the aggregate—were in chains. How could the Union, which guaranteed republican governments to every member, admit that any part of it was dead? How in common honesty and justice could loyal citizens be disfranchised because of offenses committed by the disloyal? Did not the flag that floated above the national armies still carry a star for every State in the Union? The Radicals, whom Blair called Abolitionists, had adopted the theory that few loyal people remained in the South. This was false. "Multitudes of magistrates, State and Federal functionaries, are ready to resume their functions the moment that rebel military duress is removed." Blair added that notwithstanding all the plot-

46. *Ibid.*, 507-510, 514-515, 523-524, 529.
47. New York *Herald*, Sept. 11, 12, 1863.
48. Lincoln, *Collected Works*, VI, 451-452, for Proclamation suspending Writ of Habeas Corpus; Pierce, Edward L., *Memoirs and Letters of Charles A. Sumner*, Boston, 1877-1893, IV, 160.

ting and toil of the conspirators against the Union, they could not bring a majority of voters to the polls in any State but South Carolina to sanction their usurpation. Missouri, Kentucky, Maryland, and West Virginia had all been quickly rescued from treason.

The country must turn to Lincoln's program, declared Blair. The President's plan was simple. He would dishabilitate the secessionists and their Confederacy, and rehabilitate the loyal citizens and their State governments. From beginning to end his position, as stated in all his messages and published letters, had been the same. It had been defined in his Emancipation Proclamation: "Hereafter, as heretofore, the war will be prosecuted for the object of practically restoring the constitutional relation between the United States, and each of the States, and the people thereof, in which States that relation is or may be suspended, or disturbed." The State governments would resume their functions under officers chosen by loyal citizens and such others as might be comprehended in an amnesty. But the President was caught between two extremes—two knots of conspiring politicians at opposite poles of the nation representing the schools of Calhoun and Wendell Phillips; both ready to break up the Union so that they might experiment with its reconstruction, and both hostile to the principles of balance in the old Constitution.

In part, Montgomery Blair's speech obviously represented the ideas of his father, old Francis P. Blair, the Jacksonian, and his brother of Missouri experience, Frank, Jr. It was universally accepted in Washington, however, as a direct expression of Lincoln's hopes and intents. The Postmaster-General closed his discourse with a sarcastic thrust. Sumner's article, he said, presented the issue on which the abolition party had resolved to rest its hope of establishing its domination over the country. Was it not a bit impudent for radical abolitionists, who had never attained an ounce of political weight until they threw themselves into the scales of the moderate Republican Party, to announce their plans for giving Congress absolute power over the recovered States, without allowing any representation for them in Washington?[49]

Thicker and thicker grew the reports of smoldering disagreement between Seward and Chase. An article in Greeley's *Tribune* of September 19, castigating Seward for his blunders, was widely regarded as a pronunciamento by Chase against the Secretary; counter-statements by Seward's supporters divided public attention with Rosecrans's defeat and the visit of the Russian fleet. "Meantime the President," remarked the Washington correspondent of the *Herald*, "conscious of all the tricks and conspiracies going on around him, remains an amused and tranquil spectator of the Kilkenny cat-fight which these two high officers are

49. Blair, Montgomery, *Revolutionary Schemes of the Abolitionists*, printed version of speech delivered in Rockville, Montgomery County, Md., Sat., Oct. 13, 1863, Baltimore, 1863.

waging. . . . By the time they get through worrying each other, he thinks, they may be in a frame of mind sufficiently reasonable to acquiesce in the political necessity which imperiously demands his own reëlection. Of evenings he drives up to General Halleck's house on Georgetown Heights, and there discusses political questions, puzzles over military maps and problems, tells anecdotes to Mr. Stanton, or listens to Halleck as he paces the room and mutters, 'Let it work,' 'Let it work,' between the whiffs of Halleck's cigar."[50]

The developments that most interested Lincoln at the moment, apart from military affairs, lay in the South, and lent support to his belief in the possibility of a vigorous revival of Union feeling in most States. Georgia, Mississippi, and Alabama held their annual elections on October 5, and in the first State the contest for the governorship had some national importance. The able Joseph E. Brown, a largely self-educated country lawyer of South Carolina birth, who had presided over Georgia since 1857, was seeking reëlection; his opponent was another able country lawyer named Joshua Hill, who had been in Congress throughout Buchanan's Administration. Brown had been a secessionist fire-eater of the Yancey-Rhett school. Hill had opposed secession to the last, lingered in Washington after other Southern Congressmen had left, and refused to take any part in the war, although he later opposed Northern Reconstruction. He ran on a demand for ending the war. Brown won his fourth straight term partly by virtue of his superior organization, but only after a heavy struggle, receiving 26,558 votes to 18,122 for Hill, and 10,024 for pro-Davis Timothy Furlow; and he won as a Georgian rather than a Confederate, for his passionate attachment to his own State had brought him into persistent and heated conflict with Jefferson Davis and the Confederate Government.[51] Many observers had predicted his defeat, for both peace men and Davis implacables opposed him, and his victory left the political front in Georgia nearly as dangerous to the Confederacy as the military front in Virginia. The relations of Jefferson Davis with the Southern State governors were far more anxious than Lincoln's with even the more temperamental eccentrics in the North, and they gave him no such loyal and helpful support in time of grave crisis as Andrew Curtin, Morton and others who cheered the heart of President Lincoln in his darkest hours. But then, while Davis reinforced divisive principles and movements of opinion by proud and tactless words and acts, Lincoln emphasized the principles and sentiment of Union in the North by restrained and timely action. A case in point was his order for the release of the knavish, troublesome, and altogether preposterous Vallandigham when that

50. New York *Tribune,* Sept. 19, 1863; Bancroft, Frederic, *The Life of William H. Seward,* II, 404-406; Seward, *Works, op. cit.,* V, 115-116.

51. Owsley, Frank L., *State Rights in the Confederacy,* Gloucester, Mass., 1925, 60-61, and *passim.;* *American Annual Cyclopaedia,* 1863, 448; Fielder, Herbert, *A Sketch of the Life and Times and Speeches of Joseph E. Brown,* Springfield, Mass., 1883, 108-110.

worthy was making a clumsy bid for election as Ohio's governor. He followed this wise gesture by a tactful demission of Vallandigham to the South—a move as embarrassing to the demagogue as it was to the Southern leaders who had to receive him. Lincoln was as adroit in making the exhibitionistic, traitorous "Val" an effective liability to the President's opponents in the North as he was in making allies of honest John Brough in the State House at Columbus, and of the other "war governors" in Harrisburg, Indianapolis, Springfield and Madison. Davis had no such skill.

Throughout the South, a current of change in public opinion was running strong. North Carolina, which had left the Union reluctantly and had deposited its windrows of dead at Gettysburg with divided emotions, had elected Zebulon B. Vance governor in 1862; a true statesman, great in vision as in courage. Actually, North Carolina had in a sense two governors, for Lincoln had appointed Edward Stanly to be Military Governor over the Union-occupied areas around New Bern and along the coast. That this Union government had some effect in stiffening Unionist inclinations among North Carolina's more lukewarm Confederates, there can be no doubt. However, Stanly resigned in January, 1863, in opposition to Lincoln's Emancipation Proclamation. As a pre-war Congressman, Vance had supported the Union until secession; as an effective speaker for the Bell-Everett ticket in 1860, he had continued his battle for it; and though, as governor, he gave the Confederacy as much support as State reluctance permitted, he too came into frequent collision with President Davis. North Carolina's reluctance was passionately voiced by the journalist William W. Holden, who swung so decisively toward the Union as to demand peace by separate State action. Vance and his party did not go so far, but they opposed the war to "the last extremity" which the fire-eater William Johnston was advocating when Vance defeated him. For at heart many of them preferred the old national bond to the new sectional allegiance that had cost them so dearly in blood and suffering. In this feeling they found companions across the Alabama line. Here, Thomas Hill Watts, former Confederate Attorney General, a former Whig and staunch Unionist until the battle of Sumter, had been elected governor in the summer of 1863, decisively toppling a fire-eater opponent, John Gill Shorter. The conservative Watts resisted Yankee invasion of Alabama soil and Confederate invasion of Alabama rights with equal energy.

In Texas also, Union feeling was rising. The recent election of Pendleton Murrah as governor over another last-ditch, independence-or-nothing secessionist, was evidence that the spirit of Sam Houston was far from dead. Kentucky, safe within the fold, showed by her elections that she was determined to remain there. The people voted by a fifty thousand majority for the Union on the old basis, repelling the Copperheads on one side and the secessionists on the other.

A multitude of Northern moderates saw in the emergence of a conservative Southern party, represented by such leaders as Vance, Watts, and Murrah, evidence that Lincoln could indeed rally a great body of supporters below the Mason-and-Dixon line to a moderate plan of Reconstruction. At the same time, Northern observers may have missed the point that these men were conservative within the framework of the Confederacy, rather than the Union. Bennett's *Herald* came out emphatically, during the autumn, for the essence of the President's program. It could be pardoned an excessive optimism when it declared: "The leaders and managers of the rebellion are intractable because they fear the consequences of their guilt; but the suffering people whom they have betrayed, and who are not responsible for the crimes of their masters, have ceased to sympathize with their hopeless cause, and, disgusted with Jeff Davis and all his works, are anxiously waiting their day of deliverance."[52]

[IV]

A new America was taking shape as Congress began its work in the closing weeks of 1863. On December 3, ground was broken for the Union Pacific Railroad at Omaha. Upon the approach of Sherman's troops from Chattanooga, Longstreet withdrew his Confederates from Knoxville, where he had been besieging Burnside's Federals. Much of east Tennessee now seemed firmly in Union hands, although Longstreet in the Greenville area was still a threat. This was also the day that veteran abolitionists and free-soilers marked the thirtieth anniversary of the founding of the American Antislavery Society by Lewis Tappan, John G. Whittier, William Lloyd Garrison, Samuel J. May, and others. In New York a hopeful labor movement was gaining cohesion, with almost nightly meetings of workers in one or another industry. A military governor, Andrew Jackson Hamilton, an Alabamian in origin but a staunch Unionist, was in Texas with a fast-enlarging field before him. At Cooper Institute a meeting to promote the raising of volunteers heard a letter from Lincoln expressing his gratification that a part of the Army of the Potomac had shared in the victories just won by men of the Great West.[53]

When Congress gathered on December 7, the coming storm over Reconstruction was presaged by argument over seating of various Border-State Congressmen. Presidential election talk was high on the agenda in the Capitol and elsewhere. Lincoln, of course, was assumed to be the Republican candidate, but

52. New York *Tribune*, June 18, 1862; Tucker, Glenn, *Zeb Vance, Champion of Personal Freedom*, Indianapolis, 1966, *passim.; American Annual Cyclopaedia*, 1862, 660-662; 1863, 447-448, 569, 691-92, 829; New York *Herald*, Dec. 10, 11, 1863; Harper, Robert S., *Lincoln and the Press*, New York, 1951, 318-324.
53. Lincoln, *Collected Works*, VI, 465-466; VII, 32, Lincoln to George Opdyke and others, Dec. 2, 1863; *O.R.*, I, Vol. XXVI, Pt.I, 832; New York *Tribune*, Dec. 3, 1863.

the name of Grant was heard, and McClellan was considered the Democratic leader. It is clear that this talk of candidates could not be separated from restoration and Reconstruction. Very early in the Congressional session a wide variety of resolutions and bills were filed in House and Senate.

Fernando Wood of New York put in a resolution that the President name three commissioners to open negotiations with Richmond to end the war and restore the Union. Green Clay Smith of Kentucky, in contrast, introduced a resolution calling for more vigorous prosecution of the war, opposing any peace, mediation, armistice, or intervention. Joseph K. Edgerton of Indiana introduced a resolution in the House censuring the Administration for invading and occupying States by armed force. Thad Stevens introduced a bill to repeal the Fugitive Slave Act, and Representative James M. Ashley of Ohio proposed a bill to send to the States an amendment to prohibit slavery. Owen Lovejoy in the House had a bill "to give effect to the Declaration of Independence," to end slavery. William H. Wadsworth of Kentucky had a resolution that powers not delegated to the United States by the Constitution were reserved to the States or to the people, and that the President could not exercise such powers thus reserved. Another measure by Aaron Harding of Kentucky set forth that the Union had not been dissolved, and that, as soon as armed rebellion was put down, a State would be restored to all its rights and to full control of its domestic institutions, free from Congressional or executive control. Other subjects were possible repeal of conscription, abridgment of the power of the President to suspend the privileges of habeas corpus, oaths of office, and similar subjects, most of them directly connected with the pattern of Reconstruction.[54]

On December 8, Lincoln's annual message went to Congress. Its first pages were commonplace enough, but its last paragraphs, introducing and explaining a proclamation of amnesty and Reconstruction, had the impact of an exploding bomb. No such paper since Washington's day, wrote the correspondent of Greeley's *Tribune*, had given such general satisfaction; none, Sumner and Thaddeus Stevens would have said, had produced such dismay. Henry J. Raymond's New York *Times* heartily approved of the document as another signal illustration of the practical wisdom of the President; the Copperhead *Daily News* pronounced it a despot's edict.

The message and proclamation offered a full pardon to all those who had participated in the rebellion, except those who had been civil or diplomatic officers of the Confederacy, those who had abandoned judicial stations, seats in Congress, or commissions in the Army or Navy of the United States to aid the rebellion, and those who had been officers above the rank of colonel in the Confederate Army, or lieutenant in the Confederate Navy. Persons guilty of

54. *Congressional Globe*, 38th Cong., 1st Sess., Pt. I, 19-22, 45-47, 57-58.

maltreating prisoners of war were also excepted. This pardon, which carried with it a restoration of all rights of property except as to slaves, and except where the rights of third parties had intervened, was conditional upon the acceptance and maintenance of an oath of allegiance. The statement in the oath that the subscriber would "henceforth faithfully protect and defend the Constitution" contained an important word, for "henceforth" fixed a date which the Radicals tried to override by making their later Radical oath retroactive. The resumption of allegiance and the grant of pardon were steps preparatory to the re-inauguration of loyal State governments. Here lay the crux of Lincoln's great new announcement of policy; here he crossed a Rubicon wider than the Mississippi.

Whenever, in any of the ten seceding States south of Virginia, one-tenth of the total number of persons who had cast votes in the 1860 Presidential election of that State had taken and kept the oath of allegiance, and held each the status of a legally qualified voter, they might reëstablish a republican State government. This should then be recognized as the true government of the State, and should receive all the benefits of the constitutional provision for protecting and safeguarding every member of the Union. "And it is suggested as not improper," added Lincoln, "that, in constructing a loyal State government in any State, the name of the State, the boundary, the subdivisions, the constitution, and the general code of laws, as before the rebellion, be maintained, subject only to the modifications made necessary by the conditions hereinbefore stated. . . ." He pointed out that Congress alone could determine whether members sent from any State could be admitted. Finally, declared the President, "while the mode presented is the best the Executive can suggest, with his present impressions, it must not be understood that no other possible mode would be acceptable."[55]

The generosity of the President's scheme of Reconstruction impressed every fair-minded citizen. It accorded with his attitude in the Gettysburg Address. "Nothing, it must be admitted," wrote William Cullen Bryant in the New York *Evening Post*, "could be more magnanimous or lenient toward the Rebels; they have put themselves beyond the pale of the law by their insanity; their properties are already declared confiscated, and their lives are in jeopardy; and, if they continue contumacious, the whole of the beautiful region they inhabit will be inevitably overrun by our armies, their fields laid waste, their cities and towns desolated, and their homes pillaged. But in this dire strait the President offers

55. New York *Tribune*, Dec. 10 and 11, 1863; New York *Daily News*, as in New York *Tribune*, Dec. 11, 1863; New York *Times*, Dec. 10, 1863; Lincoln, *Works*, VII, Proclamation of Amnesty and Reconstruction, Dec. 8, 1863, 53-56; Message to Congress, Dec. 8, 36-53, 59-60. For reaction see Nicolay & Hay, *Abraham Lincoln*, IX, 109-111; Randall, James G., and Richard N. Current, *Last Full Measure*, Vol.IV, *Lincoln the President*, New York, 1955, 2-10; Dorris, Jonathan Truman, *Pardon and Amnesty under Lincoln and Johnson*, Chapel Hill, 1953, 38-47; Hesseltine, William B., *Lincoln's Plan of Reconstruction*, Tuscaloosa, Ala., 1960, 95-97.

them not only a peace, which shall save them from the miseries of war, but an honorable pardon which shall imbue them with all the attributes of the citizen. The very condition, moreover, on which they are asked to accept these boons, is a beneficent one—the renunciation of that monstrous idol of Slavery, which has been the source of all their sacrifices and sufferings and woes."[56]

At Richmond, Lincoln's proclamation aroused some of the diehards once more.[57] Representative Henry S. Foote of Tennessee proposed a resolution on December 16 proclaiming the resolve of the people of the Confederacy never to relinquish the struggle of arms until liberty and independence be achieved. Foote characteristically wrote of Lincoln as "the imbecile and unprincipled usurper who now sits enthroned upon the ruins of constitutional liberty in Washington city. . . ." In the Virginia House of Delegates a series of resolutions was offered deprecating the amnesty proclamation as "degrading to freemen. . . ."[58]

In Washington at the moment of its delivery, nearly all Republicans seemed in favor of the proclamation and message. Hay could write, "I never have seen such an effect produced by a public document. Men acted as if the millennium had come. Chandler was delighted, Sumner was beaming, while at the other political pole Dixon & Reverdy Johnson said it was highly satisfactory. . . ." Boutwell, Lovejoy, Garfield and others were enthusiastic. The President seemed pleased with the immediate reception, particularly from both Radicals and Conservatives. However, the millennium did not last long, as far as the Radicals especially were concerned. Within a few days or weeks, as the moderate tone of Lincoln's words sank in, the opposition arose. Naturally, the Administration press was complimentary, but the Democratic press, such as the New York *World* and New York *Herald*, were dubious or downright skeptical.[59]

Probably because of the vital import of the proclamation and annual message about Reconstruction, and perhaps because of the rather turgid, uninspired style of the message, other aspects of what Lincoln had to say were overlooked. The message opened with a laborious recounting of foreign relations, including those with secondary nations. The state of the Territories was good, and immigration was thriving. The various departments of government were commented on and operations were found praiseworthy. The natural resources of the nation seemed inexhaustible and had been put to good use. The liberal policy on public lands was stimulating the settlement of the nation, despite the war. Indian problems,

---

56. New York *Evening Post* as in New York *Tribune*, Dec. 11, 1863,
57. Moore, Frank, *Rebellion Record*, Vol. VIII, see the Index for material treating Confederate comment on Lincoln's plan; Moore's *Rebellion Record* "Diary of Events," 21, 24.
58. *Journal of the Congress of the Confederate States of America*, VI, 536-537; Moore's *Rebellion Record*, VIII, 24.
59. Hay, *Lincoln and the Civil War*, 131; Nicolay and Hay, *Abraham Lincoln*, IX, 110-112; Hesseltine, *Lincoln's Plan of Reconstruction*, 95-100; Randall and Current. *Last Full Measure*, 6-10.

communications between the Mississippi and the Northeast, agriculture, all were duly mentioned before the President examined the war itself. Lincoln was displaying his realization that, despite problems of military operations and of Reconstruction, much else was going on that reflected the sound state of the Union.[60]

The message and proclamation of early December, 1863, certainly did not have the sublime inspiration of the address of November 19 at Gettysburg. They were more an amplification and implementation of the principles expressed at Gettysburg, and a practical application of those principles to the real situations of wartime days—and also to further problems which would have to be solved as soon as the war was won.

60. Lincoln, *Collected Works*, VII, 36-53.

13

A New Crisis in Foreign Relations

THE YEAR 1863 had witnessed a series of military turning-points at Gettysburg, at Vicksburg, and in Tennessee, where the great Chattanooga campaign had resulted in a Confederate withdrawal into Georgia. Had it also witnessed a decisive checking of all efforts to align cautious Great Britain and the slightly more venturesome French Government with the Confederate cause?[1] A last display of adventurous romanticism, of readiness to play with edged tools, was offered this year by Napoleon III, always hungry for more prestige and hopeful of Southern victory. A final crisis in Anglo-American relations cost Washington some of its tensest hours of anxiety as two ironclad rams, with which Southern agents hoped to break the blockade, approached completion at Liverpool. But could Confederate leaders really gain the compelling success of foreign recognition?

The international situation was complicated by the fact that in 1863 the coals of war glowed suddenly in two areas of Europe, threatening to spring into a general flame. The Polish torch and the Holstein match, as a British leader termed them, seemed equally capable of igniting a conflagration. While the American armies still lay gripped by winter, armed conflict broke out in Russia's grand duchy of Poland. At the beginning of January 1863, the Czar introduced a general conscription; resistance had flared instantly, and the fighting developed into a bloody insurrection. The proud Polish people, who had never forgotten the era when Poland had been one of the great Powers of Europe, and who saw before them the possibility of a total loss of national identity within the Muscovite realm, fought desperately, but in vain. The watchful Bismarck took advantage of the situation to negotiate a convention with Russia, establishing a virtual entente between the Prussian and Muscovite autocracies. A chorus of indignation rose

---

1. See Joseph M. Hernon, Jr., "British Sympathies in the Civil War," *Journal of Southern History,* August, 1967, for evidence that the legend of British leaning toward the Confederacy was a spurious, exaggerated myth. Many careful students have concluded that the autumn of 1862 witnessed the last grave threat of foreign intervention in the Civil War, and that after Antietam all thought of even mediation was dead. Great Britain quite wisely regarded British interests as primary, as France did French interests.

from liberal Europeans. French opinion was notably enraged, and Napoleon III urged Great Britain to join his government in sending identical notes of protest. Cautious as usual, Palmerston refused. During the spring, while the struggle in Virginia and Mississippi recommenced, Britain and France offered stiff remonstrances to Russia and both—especially France—met humiliating rebuffs. Palmerston went so far as to suggest that Poland might be given independence with an Austrian archduke for King, but Austria did not support the proposal. "Meddle and muddle" was Lord Derby's somewhat unfair characterization of the British handling of the Polish imbroglio.[2]

The Danish question was equally embarrassing and dangerous. "It is a matter not of right but force," growled the Prussian Minister of War, General von Roon, "and we have the force." Since the complexities of the dispute over the possession of Schleswig-Holstein almost defied comprehension, Bismarck meant to cut through them, and to repress Danish liberalism with brutal might. Denmark was determined to resist. At first Palmerston and Russell could hardly believe that Bismarck would rock the European boat by violent action. In June, 1863, Palmerston wrote that Bismarck seemed crazy, for, if he took aggressive action against Denmark, a Franco-Prussian war would probably ensue, and he would get the worst of it. He told the Commons a month later that Britain stood with France and Russia in their anxiety to see the independence of Denmark maintained, and that if the Prussians used bayonets, he was convinced "that it would not be with Denmark alone that they would have to contend." But Bismarck was not bluffed. Late in December, 1863, troops of the German Bund, Saxons and Hanoverians, invaded Holstein, and soon stood on what was at the time clearly Danish territory.[3] Prussian and Austrian troops entered the area in early 1864.

These European conflicts hampered the men who wished to embroil England and France in the American struggle. Many British had reasons of blood, sentiment, and policy for sympathizing with forlorn Denmark, though there seemed

2. As Lord John Russell wrote his ambassador to Russia, the kingdom of Poland had been constituted and placed in connection with Russia by the Treaty of 1815, in which Great Britain was a contracting party. The insurrection was traceable to the fact that Poland had not been given the rights that the treaty required, nor the popular contentment that Czar Alexander I had planned for her, although there were some reforms at the start of the reign of Alexander II. If the revolted Poles were granted an amnesty, and their kingdom a national diet and national administration, this would content them and satisfy European opinion. Here spoke the Russell who had long been champion of liberty in Europe. Russell, Foreign Office, March 2, 1863, to Lord Napier, Archives Affaires Étrangères, Angleterre, vol. 723. The important point is that the Foreign Office was deeply occupied with continental affairs until the end of 1864. A still more important point is that Palmerston was genuinely alarmed by the precarious state of international relations in Europe. He wrote Gladstone Oct. 19, 1864, that the alacrity with which the Commons had voted large defense expenditures, and the readiness with which 170,000 men had formed volunteer corps, pointed to a firm conviction "that in the present state of the world, events may at any time happen, which would expose this country to danger." Gladstone Papers, British Museum.

3. Temperley, Harold and Lillian M. Penson, *Foundations of British Foreign Policy*, Cambridge, 1938, 250-251.

little enthusiasm for direct action; the French perhaps felt more keenly still for Poland. For centuries the Polish frontier had been the coastline of Western civilization, upon which the ocean of Eastern autocracy and barbarism had been steadily encroaching.[4] Frenchmen grew bellicose as they denounced the Russian proconsul, Mikhail N. Muravieff, for his use of the torch, the halter, and the knout. But Great Britain, seeing that she could accomplish nothing by action in Central and Eastern Europe, and remembering only too well the losses in the Crimea, rejected any French impulsiveness.

Would-be troublemakers between Great Britain and the United States were hampered also by certain massive shifts in the economic situation. The anxieties of the world's cotton-textile industry were rapidly relaxing as new sources of raw cotton were opened. Although in 1860 India was sending but small amounts of cotton to Great Britain, by 1863 her shipments were tremendous. Imports from Egypt and Brazil also rose rapidly, while Turkey, Algeria, and parts of Russia made contributions. Altogether, British imports of cotton from non-American sources grew, according to one authority, from 1,445,000 bales in 1862 to 1,932,000 bales the following year, and to 2,587,000 bales in 1864. To be sure, the American staple was in general far better in quality, but some Penang cotton took prizes and fetched high prices.[5]

Furthermore, British industry as a whole had adjusted itself by the summer of 1863 to the wartime situation. Surplus stocks of pre-war cotton had been sold at golden profits; the makers of linens and woolens had garnered an unanticipated harvest of orders; exporters of arms, explosives, and steel had fattened their bank accounts; shipbuilding had expanded vigorously to satisfy the orders of Confederate agents and British blockade-runners; and a goodly share of the American merchantmen driven from the high seas had found refuge under the British flag.

4. *London Illustrated News,* Aug. 8, 1863.
5. New York *Herald,* Apr. 15, 1864; *London Illustrated News,* Aug. 9, 1863; for other figures see: Owsley, Frank L., *King Cotton Diplomacy,* Chicago, 1959, 147, 149, 150ff, 571, 572; (Sources vary on statistics.) Cf. Hammond, M.B., *The Cotton Industry,* New York, 1897, 261, giving following table for British Cotton Imports in 1860:

Year	From U.S.	From Other Countries	Totals
1860	2,580,700 bales	785,000 bales	3,365,700 bales

Later figures from various good sources are:

1861	1,841,600 bales	1,194,000 bales	3,035,600 bales
1862	72,000	1,445,000	1,517,000
1863	132,000	1,932,000	2,064,000
1864	198,000	2,587,000	2,785,000
1865	462,000	2,755,000	3,217,000

These statistics show that imports from other countries began to rise rapidly even in 1861 as well as in 1862. Prices also were much higher for non-American imports. Scherer, *Cotton as a World Power,* 263, points out that in 1860 America furnished 84% of the entire European supply of cotton, and in 1862 only 7%. The quality of various sorts of cotton was a debatable factor.

While it was true that about half the cotton mills of the kingdom remained closed during the year 1863, when only 132,000 bales of American cotton came in, the other half made handsome profits from the higher prices. Although the inferior Indian cotton required far more pains and labor from the operatives, and fluctuations in the market worried the owners, the chief anxieties of both now arose from the fact that any sudden peace would effect a fall in values that would half ruin Lancashire.

"It is easy," wrote one of the principal Manchester experts, "to understand how the peace rumors, with the prospect of a not-distant fall to normal prices, should produce a panic, and how good and honorable men spoke of the probable cessation of the most terrible war of modern times as a thing to be dreaded."[6]

The same facts were evident in France. A visitor to Lille found every mill in that city and its dependent environs in operation— nearly a quarter of all the spindles of France. "Are you really anxious for peace and the opening of the cotton ports?" he asked one of the largest manufacturers. "As a man, yes; as a manufacturer, no," was the reply. "The throwing into the market of the world of a couple of million bales of cotton would cause immense and widespread perturbation and disaster. The same speculative spirit which has now stimulated a rise in cotton beyond its value would equally exaggerate in a contrary sense this supply."[7]

Pauperism still walked the streets of Manchester and Preston, and lay hidden in the black tenements of Ashton and Stockport; groups of unemployed textile workers still wandered the streets of London and Liverpool, singing hymns for pennies, the women cowering in the rear and the sad-faced men sometimes facing backwards to avoid identification. Still, the tooth of want in the cotton-mill districts was felt less painfully. The number of persons needing relief in the mill districts fell until the Christmas season of 1863 found only 180,000 on the rolls, somewhat more than a third as many as a year earlier. By the closing months of 1864, the total was fluctuating between 130,000 and 150,000, as compared with a normal figure of about 50,000 on relief.[8] Meanwhile, British social solidarity and philanthropy had written a memorably lustrous record of patient altruism. Poor-law relief had done its work fairly well, and the provident societies of the various towns had helped. Soup-kitchens had been installed in empty mills. Schools had been opened where idle hands could give their time to study, and long lines of women, under supervision of tailors and seamstresses, had been plying the needle to repair clothing and make bedding.[9] Assistance had poured in from all over the globe. The Mansion House Relief Committee in Manchester received subscrip-

6. Watts, John, *The Facts of the Cotton Famine*, London, 1866, 357-360.
7. Private letter quoted in New York *Tribune*, Feb. 17, 1863.
8. Owsley, Frank L., *King Cotton Diplomacy, op.cit.*, 147; *London Illustrated News*, Jan. 7, 1865.
9. *London Illustrated News*, Nov. 22, 29, 1862, and into 1863 and 1864.

tions from every British colony and every nation, even Haiti and Japan. At the same time thousands of the hardy, self-reliant Lancashire folk emigrated and made new homes in America, Canada, or Australasia.

Happily, too, the apprehensions of a bread famine generated by two years of bad harvest were disappearing. The British position changed dramatically for the better in the late summer of 1863. A year ago, declared the London *Daily News* of August 20, 1863, the grain situation was terrible. "All through the winter and on into the spring the holders of last year's grain were more and more dismayed by the way the crops turned out in the threshing. Both quantity and quality proved to be worse than the lowest estimates. We were saved from the miseries and even all apprehensions of dearth by the prodigious cargoes of grain sent from America as early in the season as possible; but there was a craving desire for a good season this year. . . . We have had the fine season we longed for, and we have the glorious harvest. . . ."

As the economic pressures favorable to intervention thus lost force, those adverse to it grew stronger. By 1863, commercial observers in New York saw that formidable new influences were making themselves felt in Britain. East India shippers, merchants, and capitalists now realized that the blockade of the South was equivalent to a protective tariff on Indian cotton and a bounty on Indian trade and shipping. Let it continue five years longer, they predicted, and England could snap her fingers at American cotton. Some of the businessmen involved even asserted that their groups could afford to take care of the Lancashire toilers thrown out of work. This large East Indian influence was reinforced not only by the munition-makers, shipbuilders, steel and iron workers, and general hardware dealers profiting from the American demands, and the woolen and linen interests, but by importers of American wheat, oats, cured meats, and other foodstuffs.

That British anxiety to maintain the Northern wheat supply was an important consideration in keeping Palmerston's government neutral may well be doubted, and the idea that it was "decisive" can assuredly be rejected. It is true that Great Britain had become an importer of wheat on a large scale, and also true that early wartime wheat harvests were abysmally poor. France also suffered crop failures. It can be shown that at the time of the war Great Britain imported from one-fourth to one-half of her supply of wheat, and that the United States furnished from thirty to forty-five percent of this importation. A good deal of effective argument was naturally based by some British advocates of strict national neutrality upon this reliance on American foodstuffs. John Bright adverted to it, and W.E. Forster, speaking in Parliament on July 18, 1862, declared that if England intervened in the war, "we should stand in danger of a corn famine." But this spectre failed to affright shrewd men, for British dependence was never more than partial. Russia and Prussia remained steady suppliers of wheat to Britain throughout the war years. Most of the British press scoffed at the idea of a crippling shortage, treating the large American importations as a matter of price —the North having abundant supplies to sell at low rates once the Southern market was cut off—rather than necessity. The *Economist,* opposing recognition, made nothing of the wheat argument. It seems clear that if wheat from the Northern States had been withheld, the price would have risen, and that this enhanced price would have led the Continent east of the Rhine, and other countries, to meet the British demand. Most members of Parliament, in debating neutrality, failed even to mention wheat.[10]

[I]

Far more important than specific economic forces in holding the British line against needless meddling in the American war was the disposition of the hard-headed, clearsighted British people to give primacy to British economic and social interests in general, and their preoccupation with the problems of an expanding economy and growing empire in a restless and dangerous world. This national particularism in refusing to take sides in the desperate conflict across the wide Atlantic was reinforced by certain moral considerations arising out of a regard for emancipation, which were increasingly powerful after 1862, and which counselled not only self-interest but a refusal to take any action hostile to fundamental moral values. Britain had long been a land especially attached to freedom, and had forced one of the great emancipation measures of history upon its empire. The government of Palmerston and Lord John Russell, always holding a realistic, not emotional, view of American relations, was actuated by a desire to serve only the best interests of Britain, with which many citizens undoubtedly agreed. It yielded nothing to the prejudiced hatred of democracy felt in some Tory circles and expressed by the *Times, Morning Post,* and *Saturday Review.* By 1863, however, it had yielded a great deal to massive middle-class opinion, that of professional men, ministers, small manufacturers and merchants, shopkeepers, yeomen farmers, and skilled mechanics, who with their wives had in overwhelming numbers an ineradicable moral detestation of slavery. These middle-class people and the workers *were* England. Many of their members well remembered how Great Britain in Byron's day had befriended freedom in Greece; how it had encouraged self-government in Latin America; how Lord John Russell had decisively aided struggling freedom in Italy.

10. For the influence of wheat, see the writings of Schmidt, Louis B., *Readings in the Economic History of American Agriculture,* New York, 1925; Adams, E.D., *Great Britain and the American Civil War,* Gloucester, Mass., 1957; Owsley, Frank, *op.cit.;* the *London Daily News,* July 1, 1863; New York *Tribune,* July 9, 1862; and the judicious article by Eli Ginzberg, "The Economics of British Neutrality During the Civil War," *Agricultural History,* X, 147ff.

Frederick Law Olmsted, the author of our classic analyses of slavery, sagely commented early in 1863 that emancipation had done the Union cause boundless good by winning England's influence on behalf of the Union, as well as Germany's favor, at the same time effectively restraining France from any possible hostile action. Greeley's *Tribune* made the same statement: that people of England of the middle and lower classes were talking of the American war and American slavery in a tone not to be mistaken, influenced by the principles of the Emancipation Society. Huge public meetings in Bristol, where the slave-trade had lasted longest, in Liverpool, the stronghold of Southern sentiment, and in Bradford, a town as hard hit by the loss of cotton as any, had reinforced the unforgettable assertions of the spectacular Exeter Hall gathering in London.

John Bright told an applauding audience in St. James's Hall early in 1863: "Impartial history will tell that, when your statesmen were hostile or coldly neutral, when many of your rich men were corrupt, when your press. . . . was mainly written to betray, the fate of a continent and of a vast population being in peril, you clung to freedom with an unfaltering trust. . . ." He continued in terms of class-war, appealing to the artisans as against the rich and the noble. "Privilege came forth every morning and with blatant voice cursed the American republic. Privilege had beheld thirty million people happy and prosperous, with no emperor or king, nor state bishop nor priest. Privilege shuddered at what would happen in old Europe if that Experiment succeeded. (*Loud cheers*)." It is not strange that Palmerston felt an intense dislike for Richard Cobden and Bright. Cobden was poor, for he had mismanaged his finances, and Palmerston was honorably quick to support a Parliamentary pension for him. But he foresaw difficulties, and his prejudice came out in a letter to Lord Russell. "Nothing can be worse, with the single exception of Bright, than the line which Cobden has taken and the language he has held both in and out of Parliament in the last two years, and. . . . many men in the House of Commons would find it difficult to vote him anything but a censure."[11]

In London the *Daily News* laid emphasis on the loyalty of the toilers to the cause of freedom. "For every man who has a title before his name who has taken the side of the South, there have been ten, twenty, and even a hundred hardworking men who had taken the side of the North and freedom! We are not concerned to accumulate the proofs of a fact which is plain to everyone who has the use of his eyes. . . . The Americans know on whose side have been the great meetings, on whose side the newspapers which are really read by the millions."[12] An address of sympathy for the North, emanating in the first instance from 750 French pastors and endorsed by 4,000 English clergymen, showed that the pulpit,

11. Trevelyan, G.O., *The Life of John Bright*, Boston, 1913, Ch. XIV, *passim*.
12. London *Daily News*, Sept. 25, 1863.

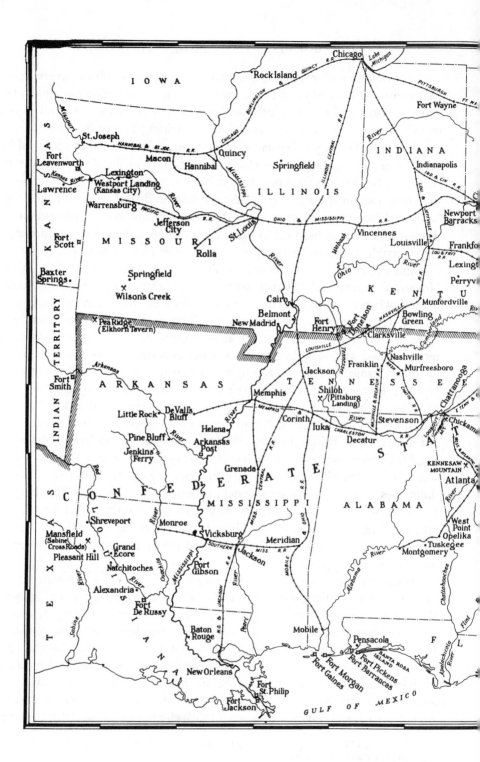

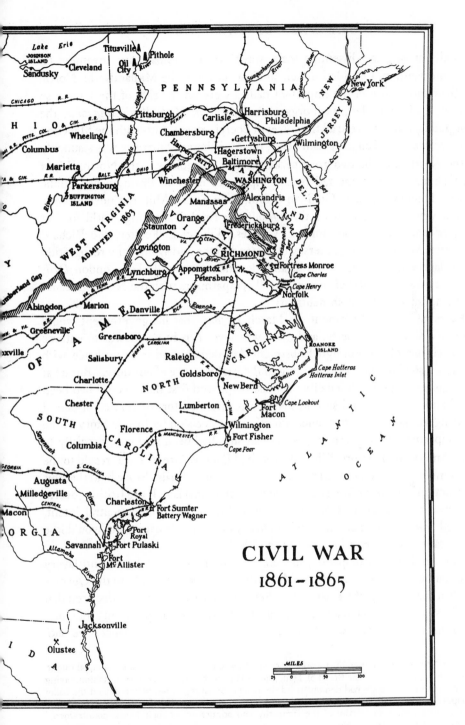

CIVIL WAR
1861–1865

General Map of the Theater of War, 1861-1865

especially among the dissenting sects, was ready to combat any movement toward intervention. Outside London, and especially in the Midlands, the North, and Scotland, many of the important dailies were on the side of the Union; so were most of the ecclesiastical organs, the *Spectator, Macmillan's Magazine,* the labor publications; so were all the voices of liberal reform. Although the Manchester *Guardian* raised an uncertain voice, the Manchester *Examiner* was staunchly for the North, and the two great parliamentary champions of the North, Bright and Cobden, were supported by an impressive array of distinguished public figures. Thomas Hughes, Goldwin Smith, John Stuart Mill, the novelist Mrs. Gaskell who was much loved throughout the English-speaking world for her *Cranford* and other books, John E. Cairnes, William E. Forster, and Richard Monckton Milnes, among others, would stand to the end against any recognition of the slaveholding Confederacy as an independent nation.[13] The London *Daily News* was always a pillar of strength to all sympathizers with the Northern cause and all upholders of British neutrality.

Palmerston told Parliament, on March 27, 1863, that his government would preserve a sincere neutrality, and that "whenever it is in our power to enforce the provisions of the Foreign Enlistment Act, legally and in accordance with justice, we shall not be found wanting in the performance of our duty." But what was required to establish legality? It must be proved first that a vessel had been armed and equipped, and second that it was intended for the service of one of the belligerents. Palmerston called attention to a decision by Justice Story in the U.S. Supreme Court in 1832. An American ship had been sold commercially to South American operators. When she reached Buenos Aires she was resold to the government, which employed her as a warship against Spain. Story held that this was sanctioned by both American law and international law. If the British government lost its case when it detained a vessel on suspicion of unneutral intent, declared Palmerston, it could be held in heavy costs and damages, and would lose its reputation for strict adherence to the law.[14]

One result of emancipation, indeed, was the revival of a broad antislavery movement in Great Britain. When Mr. Althorpe moved the reply to the Queen's speech at the opening of Parliament on February 5, 1863, he not only declared that Lincoln's proclamation made any idea of intervention preposterous, but predicted that it would have worldwide effects. "There was now a chance," he said,

13. One Northern champion, Sir George Cornwall Lewis, died in April. A leader of equal might, Milner Gibson, president of the Board of Trade, spoke Jan. 20, 1863, to the electors of Ashton, saying that the crisis in Lancashire had demonstrated the defects of suffrage laws, which denied the ballot to a population that met the rigors of poverty with such cool bravery. "He favored the extension of the ballot to a people so worthy of the sympathy and admiration of their fellow countrymen." *L'Independence Belge,* Jan. 25, 1863.

14. See report of this speech in the New York *Tribune,* April 13, 1863.

"of the *entire* abolition of slavery if the proclamation were fully carried out, for that proclamation had not been addressed to the Southern States only, but virtually to the Brazils and to Spain as well; for if the slaves should be emancipated in America, but ten years, or certainly not twenty, would elapse before the negroes of Brazil and Spain would be free also."[15] He bade Parliament do all it could to keep the sacred flame of human freedom shining brilliantly. In the same debate, Lord Derby and Disraeli commended the recent determination of the Ministry not to interfere, Disraeli implying a rebuke of Gladstone for his reckless speech at Newcastle;[16] and Lord Russell declared that nobody in England thought of armed intervention.

When in March, 1863, the veteran antislavery leader Sir Fowell Buxton presided over a meeting in London to form a society for assisting the freedmen in America, he and Thomas Hughes prophesied that the imminent death of slavery in America would prove a deadly blow to it in all other lands.

The London *Times*, with its usual capacity for malicious distortions, had predicted soon after the Emancipation Proclamation that Lincoln would do his utmost to excite a servile war. "He will appeal to the black blood of the African; he will whisper of the pleasures of spoil and of the gratification of yet fiercer instincts; and when blood begins to flow and shrieks come piercing through the darkness, Mr. Lincoln . . . will rub his hands and think that revenge is sweet."[17] It was plain in 1863, that no slave rebellion had been initiated and none would take place, although the original apprehension of one yet lingered in some areas. It was equally plain that the *Times* had been preternaturally asinine in declaring, as we have already noted: "Now, we in Europe are thoroughly convinced that the death of slavery must follow as certainly upon the success of the Confederacy in this war as the dispersion of darkness occurs upon the rising of the sun." The fabric of the Confederacy still rested squarely upon slavery.

Buxton's General Freedmen's Aid Society quickly raised £3,000. A similar society in Birmingham collected £4,000 in cash and goods by 1865; Liverpool sent over some money to give charitable aid to freedmen, and other cities generously contributed. The Quakers of Great Britain by a series of drives in 1863-64 obtained more than £8,000 to help the freedmen. Since the abolition of colonial slavery by Great Britain, declared the Society of Friends, no event had occurred which ought more heartily to arouse the energies of every true philanthropist than the

15. Hansard, report in New York *Tribune*, Feb. 24, 1863.

16. Disraeli, when the war began, had thought like most Englishmen that the North would win; but he thought it unwise to take sides publicly in the war, and doubtless thought that Gladstone should have shown the same reticence. Robert Blake, *Disraeli*, New York, 1967, 529. Gladstone described his indiscretion in the Newcastle speech as one of "incredible grossness, a statement as hardly truthful as any that his opponents made." Magnus, Philip, *Gladstone*, New York, 1954, 154. He shortly became a warm friend of the triumphant republic.

17. London *Times*, Oct. 7, 1863.

extinction of Negro bondage in America. The veteran abolitionist, George Thompson, sprang to arms again and took a vigorous part in organizing the new London Emancipation Society, which soon planted branches in the principal British cities.[18]

The combination of a massive middle-class sentiment against slavery with the determination of British workers never to abandon the cause of free labor impressed the men who governed Britain. While professional men, liberal merchants, and churchmen showed a quicker intelligence, the laboring element manifested more courage and wisdom. The British workingmen evinced a deeper sagacity than their social betters, for they had the truer instinct. The Emancipation Society issued in 1863 a pamphlet which, since its sponsors included the mayors of Manchester, Birmingham, and Rochdale, spoke weightily in stating: "Thanks to the intelligence, the integrity, and the foresight of the working men of England, our country has been saved from the sham and humiliation of sympathy with slaveholders." British workmen had manifested the same patient endurance they had shown previously in the Napoleonic struggle, and were to show again in the grim war against Nazi Germany. "Aw wish to God that yon chaps in Amerikay would play th'upstroke, and get done with their bother, so us folks could start working again," one worker told a journalist.[19] But their fidelity to the North was inexhaustible. Every interventionist demonstration was more than countered by speakers who pointed out that recognition of the Confederacy would not bring a pound of cotton unless armed force broke the blockade, which would mean war; that it would be a war in favor of slavery and against freedom; and that whereas the loss in wages to the cotton-mill operatives was ten or twelve millions sterling a year, two years of war with Russia had cost Great Britain more than a hundred millions, and thirty to forty thousand lives.[20]

Yet despite the crystallization of favorable British opinion, Northerners abroad remained uneasy through most of 1863. Their anxiety sprang in part from the glaring want of victories. Charles Francis Adams in the London legation felt that the danger of Anglo-French intervention might become acute when the war approached a close if Union defeat seemed imminent. And he was frankly apprehensive of defeat. "For to us at this distance it looks as if both sides were getting tired of it," he wrote Edward Everett early in the year. "We are groping about for a great commander and they [the Confederates] are evidently at fault for more

18. Korngold, Ralph, *Two Friends of Man*, Boston, 1950, 286-287.

19. Watts, *op.cit.*, p.146.

20. J.B. Priestley, during the Great Depression of the early 1930s, found the impoverished workers of manufacturing towns far gentler, politer, and more generous than the affluent, but selfish people met in fashionable London theatres. "And how often did I hear some wretched unemployed man and his wife say, 'Ay, but there's lots worse off than us.' " Priestley, *English Journey*, London, 1934, 330. The book of Watts may well be compared with that of Priestley.

men. In the meantime, the country is staggering along to some conclusion, the precise nature of which no mortal man can foresee." Chancellorsville deepened his fears, and Everett shared them. If our armies could yet find a competent head, Adams wrote in his diary, all foreign difficulties might be overcome. "It is this deficiency which constitutes the strength of the argument against us in Europe."[21]

[II]

More substantial dangers assailed Adams in his troublous London post as spring came on. British ventures in blockade-running, which angered Northern opinion, were now reaching their height. Thomas H. Dudley, the American consul in Liverpool, told a British acquaintance that he knew of 130 steamers of British origin that were trying to evade the cordon of warships, carry supplies to the Confederacy, and bring out cotton or other valuable Southern materials; he had learned their identity, and that of numerous sailing vessels besides.[22] Still greater anger was aroused by the depredations of the cruiser *Alabama*, which the British authorities had permitted to leave Liverpool July 29, 1862, and arm herself elsewhere for her long oceanic forays. She was in no sense a pirate or privateer, names recklessly applied to her by bitter Americans, but a regularly commissioned warship. But her long cruises with their wake of destruction kindled resentful memories of the British carelessness involved in her escape, and the way she had left the Mersey because the London authorities moved too late.[23]

The *Alabama*, under Captain Raphael Semmes, lifted the work of commerce destruction to a pitch of efficiency never before attained by an individual cruiser in any war. Semmes gave his crew, drawn largely from the Liverpool groggeries, a stern discipline. Having carefully studied the ocean highways, he laid out a well-matured plan of operations. Calculating precisely the time required for news of his presence in any zone of operations to reach Washington, he removed to a new scene before warships could be sent to intercept him. His first two months he spent in the North Atlantic, and the ensuing weeks of the late fall of 1862 in

21. Adams, Charles Francis, *Diary,* May 11, 1863, Ms., Mass. Hist. Soc.
22. Dudley, Thomas H., "Three Critical Periods in Our Diplomatic Relations with Great Britain During the Late War; Personal Recollections by Thomas H. Dudley," *The Pennsylvania Magazine of History and Biography*, XVII, No. 1, 1893, 47.
23. Though the Confederate Government at the commencement of the war issued letters of marque and there were considerable fears of privateers at the North, they never really constituted a major force. The Confederate cruisers *Nashville, Alabama, Florida,* and so on, were no more "pirates" than they were Chinese junks. They were regularly commissioned vessels of war, responsible to the Confederate Government. For a thorough study of Confederate privateers see Robinson, William M., *The Confederate Privateers,* New Haven, 1928. Incomplete records show that there were at least 25 actual privateers, but they captured only 27 prizes, and most of the operations were in 1861. Four were captured or destroyed by the U.S. Navy. *O.R.N.,* I, Vol. I, 818-819; Coulter, *The Confederate States of America, op.cit.,* 296.

the West Indies, finding in both areas many defenseless Northern vessels. On January 11, 1863, off Galveston, Texas, Semmes sank U.S.S. *Hatteras*, an excursion-vessel converted to a warship. Then he placed himself in the narrow passage, hardly more than a hundred miles wide, used near the equator in commerce with South America. Two months on the coast of Brazil followed, and then about two months off Cape of Good Hope, with a bag of several vessels in each place. Semmes then proceeded to the Straits of Sunda in the East Indies, a gateway of the China trade, and found another two months' hunting successful. His movements were interrupted only by stops for coal and repairs, both being supplied at first by ships sent to an appointed rendezvous, and later by prizes. Repair-points and coaling-points were carefully selected for remoteness and privacy; whenever extensive work was required, the captain boldly entered a neutral port with excuses sufficiently ingenious to persuade the authorities to give him full facilities.[24]

Against the miscalled "piracies" of the *Alabama* and *Florida*, the Chamber of Commerce in New York entered a burning protest early in 1863, the merchant A.A. Low declaring that America should hold up these outrages to the ignominy of the whole civilized world.[25] Sumner wrote semi-private letters of the most unreasonable and provocative character to the Duchess of Argyll, declaring petulantly that everyone assumed that England would soon recognize the "slave empire" and that her coöperation with the Confederacy would become open alliance. He smacked his lips, in true Sumnerian style, over the prospect of carnage and destruction. "I feel keenly the force of the remark that war has already begun," he wrote.[26]

Every week seemed to bring a fresh budget of news about some cruiser. Late in May, 1863, the brig *William E. Dodge* put in at Philadelphia fresh from Brazilian waters. It carried Captain Jesse F. Potter of the *Oneida*, a New Bedford ship which, with its valuable cargo, had been destroyed by the *Florida* near the equator in the South Atlantic. "All I saved of my effects," said the captain, "was $15 or $20 worth of clothing."[27] From his deck he had seen the smoke of the burning bark *Henrietta* of Baltimore, and the rebel captain told him that this was the thirteenth vessel the *Florida* had burnt on that cruise. It was on the wave of general Northern resentment of such happenings that Congress,

24. Bigelow, John Jr., *The Principles of Strategy*, 1891, 111 ff; Soley, J.R., *The Blockade and the Cruisers*, New York, 1883, 190-201.

25. New York *Tribune*, Feb. 23, 1863.

26. Sumner to Duchess of Argyll, Washington, April 7, 1863, Sumner Papers, Houghton Library, Harvard Univ.

27. *O.R.N.*, I, Vol.II, 205-206; C.J. Bayley, governor of the Bahamas, vigorously defended himself from Seward's accusation of undue partiality toward the South, and accused Northern warships of flagrant violations of British neutrality in Bahaman waters; Foreign Office, 5/891, Bayley to Lord Lyons, June 26, 1863.

on March 2, 1863, passed a bill, approved by Lincoln March 3, to authorize privateering by Americans, a bill that British shipowners regarded as a direct threat.

Blockade-running was a legitimate activity against which Minister Adams could enter no protest; those who wished to run the risk had every right to do so. Huge sums, partly Confederate, partly from private British sources, and partly, it was said, from Northern speculators, were invested in it. The size of the outlay amazed Adams. Apart from the capital thrown into blockade-running by the British, which was computed by one of the watchful American consuls at nearly fifty millions sterling, Adams found the expenditures in vessels, arms, and munitions steady and unceasing. In time, Nassau had a perfect storehouse of every kind of material needed by the South, awaiting only an opportunity to make the transit. One or two voyages and the owner of a successful blockade runner could boast of the fortune he had made, and retire.

Seward had instructed Adams to use his best judgment in presenting the facts about the ruin wrought by the *Alabama* and *Florida* to the British government, in such fashion as to obtain redress for the public and private injuries sustained by the American mercantile marine. The American minister let the British Government know that a strict account of losses was being kept, and other data collected for the ultimate presentation of a bill. For blockade-running, of course, no damages could be asked, but when the United States came to a final settlement with London, it would weigh in the scale.

On both sides a background of minor irritations, generating suspicion and resentment, made the settlement of major questions more difficult. As the *Alabama* and other cruisers roved about, American seaboard cities grew uneasy. Boston became so fearful of a sudden attack that in the spring of 1863 Governor Andrew implored Secretary Welles to give Massachusetts an ironclad, turreted warship for protection. He called this an "absolute necessity."[28] Lord John Russell for his part resented certain of Seward's tactics. The Secretary repeatedly complained to the Foreign Office of the export of British arms and munitions to the Confederacy, terming this a breach of neutrality. However, it was a recognized principle of international law that citizens of any nation might sell goods freely to belligerents. The United States had long shipped arms to warring lands. For instance, Alexander Hamilton as head of the Treasury in Washington's first Administration had issued instructions for the clearance of war materials, and during the Crimean War President Pierce had insisted, in a message to Congress, that the United States possessed full right to sell arms to both sides. So, also, when the Mexican Minister protested to the State Department that the French were about to buy cannon and other materials in the United States for their

28. Andrew to Welles, April 28, 1863, Edward Everett Papers, MHS.

invasion of his country, Seward had pronounced such purchases legal.

British subjects had actually shipped far more arms and munitions to the North than to the South. In fact, it was said that the North had not only bought war supplies but had sent agents to Britain, and especially Ireland, to find recruits for its forces. Edwin De Leon, visiting Ireland in the late summer of 1863 to discourage the rapid increase in disguised Union recruiting, estimated that up to August, 1862, the North had obtained about 20,000 potential soldiers there. They were taken to America as intended workers on Northern railways, but many knew the real nature of the service required, and their contracts contained a clause that they would take the preliminary oath of renunciation on their arrival, thus making themselves immediately subject to the draft. De Leon despaired of hindering this "cruel and cowardly crimping of recruits" for Northern battle-lines because of the difficulty of getting evidence, and the subservience of Lord Russell to Seward.[29]

Palmerston, telling the Commons that when any political party in America found itself in difficulties, it tried to make capital by attacking England, asserted that his ministry would not be coerced or bullied into any course contrary to British law and dignity. Meanwhile, the risk of some clash in American waters being real, the strictly neutral rôle played by Admiral Sir Alexander Milne as head of the American squadron was creditable. He did his best to minimize friction with American naval commanders. He refused to consider interference with the searching of British blockade-runners by American warships; and he allowed only such repairs of these ships in British dockyards as were absolutely necessary for their safety in continuing their voyages. He felt that neutrality was far more likely to be jeopardized by making repairs than by refusing them. When Milne paid a three-day visit to Washington in the autumn of 1863, he was cordially received along with Lord Lyons by Lincoln and various Cabinet members.[30] After Congress, by the previously mentioned act of March 3, 1863, authorized the President to issue letters of marque, the attitude of British shipping circles toward commerce destruction changed to one of alarm and hostility, and the principal Liverpool shipowners in the summer of 1863 asked Parliament to strengthen its neutrality legislation.

The American voice as raised in newspaper articles and political speeches was often rasping to British ears. August Belmont, visiting London in the autumn of 1863 and finding Parliamentary leaders friendlier to the United States than he had anticipated, wrote Seward that the Administration might well use its influence to get the principal Republican dailies to adopt a more conciliatory tone toward

29. Edwin De Leon to Benjamin, Paris, Sept. 30, 1863, De Leon Papers, Benjamin Papers, courtesy Robert D. Meade.

30. See Baxter, James P., 3rd, "The British Government and Neutral Rights," *American Historical Review,* Vol.34, 9-29; *Lincoln Day by Day,* ed. E.S. Miers, Washington, 1960, entry of October 10, 1863.

England. Greater moderation would be just and useful.[31] The same position was taken by a foreign correspondent of the New York *Tribune*, who, writing on May 1 of Parliament, remarked that the calm, unprovocative tone of Ministers, and particularly Lord Palmerston, had been most notable. They desired to allay irritation, and would take no step in which they were not followed by the chiefs of the Opposition and the great majority of the nation. The same correspondent rebuked "American oratory and editorial eloquence directed against England," for its unfairness made a bad impression abroad. Cassius M. Clay, for example, had just delivered an idiotic speech expressing the hope that France and Russia might unite against Great Britain, though all Europeans knew that Napoleon III neither could nor would act against her.[32]

Congressional deliverances were sometimes outrageous. Commenting on relations with England, the House Committee on Naval Affairs declared early in 1863 that "her government and her governing classes have given us abundant proof of their unfriendly spirit." Actually, the government was striving hard to observe a strict neutrality; it had rudely rebuffed the Confederate envoys; and public meetings in nearly all important cities were at that moment joyously hailing emancipation. The naval committee indicted the British government for permitting the emergence of the "ocean bandit" known as the *Alabama*, although the partly accidental nature of her escape to sea was already known, and she was a Confederate warship, not a bandit. The Committee continued with a threat of armed retaliation "when the pirates now building on the Clyde, the Tyne, the Mersey, and the Thames shall join the *Alabama*"—a combination of wild exaggeration of numbers with a totally unwarranted conclusion respecting the character of the ships on the ways.[33]

[III]

Although the Erlanger loan to the Confederacy, the scheme of a Frankfurt banker living in Paris, ultimately became an international scandal, it was tainted with greed and sharp practice, not with illegality. The United States, which had been born with the aid of French and Dutch loans, could not pretend that anything in national or international law forbade Frenchmen or Britons to sink their money in securities bearing the signatures of Confederate leaders and secured by Confederate promises. Emil Erlanger, a clever financial manipulator, concocted a scheme by which the Confederacy would sell 7 percent bonds in Europe, agreeing to deliver cotton in payment at Southern ports for export six

31. Belmont to Seward, Paris, Nov. 29, 1863, from Belmont, August, *Letters, Speeches and Addresses*, New York, 1890, 100. Belmont had been in London that fall.
32. New York *Tribune*, Paris Corr., May 1, 1863.
33. 37th Cong., 3rd Session, *House Report No. 4;* January 8, 1863.

months after peace, at twelve cents a pound. His plan was laid before a secret session of the Confederate Senate on January 21, 1863. The fact that cotton might be worth twenty cents as soon as the Confederacy won its independence made the scheme attractive to reckless speculators. W.L. Yancey opposed it as a bad bargain for the South, suggesting that the President be empowered to negotiate a $50,000,000 loan, payable either in gold or cotton on the best terms he could make, but his substitute plan was voted down.[34]

Much negotiation took place between Erlanger et Cie. and Judah P. Benjamin, Confederate Secretary-of-State, before the final terms were settled, and the issue was floated in March in Frankfurt, Paris, and London. The amount of the loan was reduced to $15,000,000. Erlanger was required to take the 7 percent bonds at 77 instead of the 70 he had at first offered, and to offer them publicly at 90. The Confederacy would have declined the transaction, Benjamin declared, "but for the political considerations indicated by Mr. Slidell." As the Confederate envoy suggested, large holdings of the bonds by moneyed people would create the right kind of sympathy for the Southern cause.

For a few weeks the loan appeared a success. When the bonds were put on sale they were oversubscribed the first day, and raised to 5 percent premium. James Spence of Liverpool, whom the Confederate Treasury appointed financial agent to assist Fraser, Trenholm & Co. in managing the flotation, threw all his energies behind the work. Buyers had to pay down only 15 percent of the purchase price, so that even a slight rise in the market quotations would more than repay the initial cost. French investors took a goodly share, while in Great Britain orders came pouring in from many quarters—from the owner of the *Saturday Review*, from the aristocratic Tory organizer of the Southern Aid Society, from an agent (apparently) of the Archduke Maximilian of Austria, and from William E. Gladstone.[35] Slidell wrote Benjamin that the "brilliant" reception of the loan was a financial recognition of Confederate independence, and could not fail to have great influence on both sides of the Atlantic. Mason, with the same hasty exultation, asserted it was proof that, despite all detraction and calumny, cotton was king at last. [36]

Yet the terms of the loan, regardless of Benjamin's efforts to better them, were hard upon the Confederacy. Erlanger took so much at its inception that little was left. Although Benjamin's hope had been that the receipts would pay all urgent

34. Yancey Papers, Alabama State Archives, Notes of Secret CSA Senate Proceedings, Jan. 21, 1863.
35. Monaghan, Jay, *Diplomat in Carpet Slippers,* Indianapolis, 1945, 296-297. The French purchases represented in the main the feeling of *legitimistes* for the South—men who did not like American society at all, and who had never accepted the feeling of vague "americanophilism" engendered by Tocqueville's writings, and his idea that the United States was "the continent of the future." Renouvin, Pierre, *Etudes d'Histoire des Relations Internationales,* Paris, 1966, V, *passim.*
36. Monaghan, Jay, *op.cit.,* 296.

bills of the Confederacy, they fell short of the mark, and numerous large creditors went unpaid.

Lee's victory at Chancellorsville improved Southern credit, but not for long; for news of the invasion of Pennsylvania by Lee sent the loan up, while news of the march of the Union army to intercept him sent it down. Predictions that Vicksburg would hold out and counter-predictions that it would fall made the market gyrations even wilder.

On Sunday, July 25, the American consul in Glasgow, frantic with anxiety over the campaigns in Pennsylvania and Mississippi, drove from his suburban home into the city to see if a steamer had arrived. He had scarcely reached the Exchange when a telegram was posted: "Surrender of Vicksburg and retreat of Lee." His heart swelled as a great crowd gathered. "I can assure you," he wrote Hiram Barney, "that if a bombshell had fallen in the Exchange it would have scarcely produced more consternation among the Confederate sympathizers than the intelligence which kept coming in sheet after sheet, for hours, giving the welcome news." Some had expected to hear of the utter rout of Meade's army, and the advance of Lee upon Washington. Now, wrote the Consul, "We have many warm friends here who are rejoicing over the news, and coming in to offer me their hearty congratulations."[37]

That same Sunday the minister of the American church in Paris was in the midst of his sermon when a messenger tiptoed down the aisle to lay a slip of paper on the lectern stating that Vicksburg had fallen. The rector read the bulletin aloud and quietly continued his discourse, but as soon as the benediction was pronounced the organist broke rapturously into "The Star Spangled Banner," and the meeting dissolved amid general enthusiasm.

Gettysburg and Vicksburg brought the Erlanger bonds down with a thud, and they never recovered to high levels. The London *Daily News* headed a leader on July 30, "The Bursting of the Rebel Loan Bubble." Spence's dash to the rescue of the loan in the letter columns of the *Times* merely exposed him to ridicule, and stockbrokers and investors who had been misled by that journal turned savagely upon it.

The shrewd Erlanger himself, whose son married Slidell's lovely daughter Mathilda, was not one of the losers, for his firm did not hold any bonds when the rapid decline came. It had withdrawn in good time. John Bigelow, who inquired into the transaction in 1865, getting all available information in London, tells us that Erlanger's firm finally accounted to McRae, the principal Confederate financial agent, for £1,500,000 face value of bonds sold at 65, or £975,000, less a commission of five percent or £48,750, which made the Southern proceeds £926,250. McRae later issued other bonds at his own option, and broke down the

37. H.E. Stoddard to Barney, Glasgow, July 25, 1863, Hiram Barney Papers, HEH.

market to the damage of trustful investors. James Spence of Liverpool, who asserted that the Erlanger loan was an invasion of his rights as the proper agent of the Confederacy, was bought off by that government with a cash payment exceeding £6,000.[38] We need waste no sympathy on gullible British and French investors, but we can well expend a little contempt on Erlanger and his associates.

"Is it not disheartening," Baron Rothschild asked an American lady in Frankfurt, "to think that there are men in Europe who are lending money for the strengthening of human slavery? None but a converted Jew would do that."[39]

The Erlanger loan, taken in all its aspects, could well be termed one of the disheartening episodes of the war. Meanwhile, one of its most bizarre episodes was being displayed to the gaze of Britons by the two noisiest Confederate sympathizers in Parliament, John A. Roebuck and William S. Lindsay. Roebuck, an independent member who made frequent parade of his hatred of Manchester Liberals and their ideas and of his fierce quarrelsomeness, had been ridiculed in the House by Disraeli and others, and held up to opprobrium in the press. While vituperating Northerners as the scum of every nation, he lauded Southerners as true gentlemen. The *Atlantic Monthly* called him a pocket Diogenes.[40] He represented Sheffield, and Lindsay spoke for Sutherland. The two obtained an interview with Napoleon III at Fontainebleau in the spring of 1863, in which they expressed their anxiety to see the Confederacy recognized as a nation. Napoleon talked rashly, but apparently gave the pair little practical encouragement, beyond suggesting that they sound Palmerston—which, as he knew, would take a long plummet line.[41]

38. Bigelow, John, Ms. *Diary,* New York Public Library, Nov. 6, 1865. There are a number of other estimates. Coulter, *The Confederate States of America,* 169, accepts about $2,599,000. Thompson, S.B., *Confederate Purchasing Operations Abroad,* Chapel Hill, 1935, 71, points out the difficulty of estimates, but states: "... it is not at all impossible that from the first to last approximately $6,800,000 was realized from the Erlanger Loan in one form of credit or another..." The amount of credit the Loan enabled the Confederacy to obtain is really incalculable. Todd, Richard C., *Confederate Finance,* Athens, Ga., 1954, 184, puts the net at $7,675,501.25, or a little over half face value.

39. White, Andrew D., *Autobiography,* New York, 1905, I, 97, 98.

40. *Atlantic Monthly,* Vol. XII, No. LXXI, Sept., 1863, 390.

41. According to our best sources Napoleon was characteristically indiscreet. Roebuck's story was that he had been told late in the spring that Napoleon had changed his mind about intervention, concluding that the opportune time had gone by. He had written Lindsay, who as a large shipping magnate could gain access to Napoleon; and Lindsay had replied, "Let us cross the channel and find out." They saw the Emperor. He said that as soon as he had heard of the rumor in circulation, he had instructed Baron Gros, the French ambassador to Great Britain, to deny it. He told Roebuck: "I have not only done that, but I have done more. I have told Baron Gros to say, not only that my feelings were exactly the same, but if anything still stronger in favor of the recognition of the South; and I have also told him to lay before the British Government my understood wishes upon the matter, and to ask them again if they are willing to join me in that recognition." The account in the London *Daily News* of July 1, 1863, supplements Hansard. *L'Independence Belge,* in a review of the Parliamentary debate July 1, 1863, stated that the *Times* and *Morning Post* played upon words in asserting that no official proposals had come from France. At least "ouvertures officieuses ont-elles du être faites," and the Emperor had certainly ordered his foreign minister Brouyn l'Huys to pursue the matter actively.

Then Roebuck, by a motion that the government should enter into negotiations with other European Powers upon the recognition of Confederate independence, precipitated a debate in Parliament. It was kept on the notice paper of the House until June 30, 1863, a date which some observers later thought significant, for it coincided with Lee's final thrust in Pennsylvania. Roebuck emptied all the gall in his breast upon the North. The Yankees were blustering hypocrites, he declared; they hated slavery, but they hated the Negro still more; had the United States remained united, within a few years it would have become the bully of the world. Before the debate, he had assured L.Q.C. Lamar of Mississippi that he felt no fear of John Bright. "Mr. Bright and I have met before," he said cockily. "It was the old story—the story of the swordfish and the whale. No, Sir, Mr. Bright will not cross swords with me again." The sequel was that Bright, in one of his greatest speeches, tossed Roebuck aside as a whale might toss a sprat. Benjamin Moran of the American legation listened with delight in the gallery. "Roebuck blundered on for a while through a tissue of assertions, slanders, and falsehoods about the United States and Louis Napoleon that caused a great deal of merriment, and showed that Napoleon completely foiled him. . . . He was followed by Lindsay in a long half-mad jumble which the House alternately laughed at and jeered at. Then Palmerston rose and . . . expressed the hope that the unusual proceeding of members of the English Commons constituting themselves envoys to a foreign monarch to induce him to prompt legislation in that body would never be repeated." Palmerston in fact sharply rebuked their utterly irregular proceedings.[42] The chief Southern sympathizers on the Conservative side, Robert Montagu and Lord Robert Cecil, were obviously placed under restraint by their party leaders.

In this memorable debate, Bright was vigorously supported not only by Gladstone as Chancellor of the Exchequer, but by that honest Yorkshireman, William E. Forster—a man of "pure gold, without a trace of base metal," wrote Henry Adams.[43] The two Britons declared that Roebuck's motion amounted to a proposal that the Crown declare war against America, and pointed out the moral and material folly of such a course.

Even if Bright's speech did not impress Palmerston and Russell, the manifest unwillingness of the country and of the majority of the Commons to provoke the North assuredly did; and still more did the course of the war itself. Gladstone, opposing Roebuck's motion, pointed out that if one moment was more inconvenient than another for interference in America, this was it. The war was at its very crisis. "Certainly there has not been a single epoch during the whole period of

42. Moran, Benjamin, *Journal of Benjamin Moran*, Chicago, 1949, II, 1183; Adams, Henry, *The Education of Henry Adams*, Boston, 1918, 186.
43. Adams, *ut supra*, 125.

the war . . . at which there were pending military issues of such vast moment, both in the East and the West—interests so important with reference to . . . both belligerents." He was obviously right. Roebuck made a sorry exhibition of tactless blundering which came near placing the French Emperor in a false position. He had been guilty of a grave impropriety in going to see Napoleon at Fontainebleau without giving notice of his intended visit to the Minister of Foreign Affairs; the Emperor probably granted the interview because he always showed courtesy to visiting Britons. Now guilty of still graver improprieties by betraying the Emperor's confidence, and exaggerating the importance of their conversation, he angered both the Foreign Minister and the Sovereign.[44]

Roebuck lost his motion, covered himself with ridicule, and came near striking a death-blow to Confederate hopes of French demands upon England for joint action. The Foreign Minister, angry at his impertinence, retreated from such cautious attitudes of sympathy as he had shown. Slidell had written Judah P. Benjamin in February, 1862, that nearly everybody in France expressed a marked partiality for the South, and that the Emperor, members of the Ministry, and other high officers were really quite indifferent to the supposed evils of slavery. "The Republicans and Orleanists think that Napoleon III will soon recognize the South, or at least declare the blockade insufficient."[45] Confederate hopes had still run high. August Belmont thought that Lee's invasion, the Roebuck-Lindsay diplomatic manoeuvres, the peace talk by Alexander H. Stephens, and the Draft Riots, were a well-connected effort to bring about foreign recognition.[46] But after Roebuck's humiliation, and the news of Gettysburg and Vicksburg, intervention was impossible. "So the farthing rush-light of hope blinks and goes out once more," exclaimed the Richmond *Examiner.*[47]

With rising chagrin John Slidell, a far abler and more adroit man than his associate James M. Mason, and as quick in his perceptions as in his mastery of Parisian speech, saw the tide of opinion turn against him. Edouard Antoine Thouvenel in the Foreign Ministry, a man of natural reserve and frigid demeanor, had always been chilly toward the Confederate envoy. He bade Slidell be patient and quiet, making it plain that the French Government would not act until Great Britain took the lead or at least acted with her. While not as rude to Slidell as Lord

44. In Paris, *Le Pays* strongly supported the Roebuck motion. On July 1, it declared that it expressed views that Napoleon had long held. *Le Temps*, however, was caustic in its comment of July 6: "The astonishing indiscretion of Mr. Roebuck respecting his interview with the Emperor . . . . has led to a note which appears this morning in the *Moniteur*. . . It is obvious that Mr. Roebuck has in every way compromised the cause he wishes to serve." And the *Journal des Débats* ridiculed Roebuck, declaring (July 8): "We shall never grow weary of repeating that the policy of abstention hitherto followed by Europe is a good and a true policy."

45. Slidell to Benjamin, Feb. 11, 1862, George Eustis Papers, LC.

46. Belmont, August, *Letters, Speeches, and Addresses,* New York, 1890, *passim.*

47. Quoted in *The Southern Sentinel,* Alexandria, La., Sept. 5, 1863.

John Russell was to Mason,[48] he was not encouraging. Slidell could only seek a little comfort in the Duc de Morny, a half-brother of the Emperor and a grandson of Talleyrand, who had a taste for intrigue, diplomatic adventure, and money-making, and who saw that the Confederacy might be induced to abet Napoleon's Mexican schemes. Morny, desirous of an easy fortune and a quiet enhancement of French prestige, believed that Mexico, if seized with French acquiescence, might afford both. Slidell also sought encouragement from another slippery adventurer of the imperial entourage, the Count de Persigny, Minister of the Interior.

But did Morny and Persigny really count for much?

Clearly, Thouvenel held the reins of far greater power, for his ministry was in control of all diplomatic action, and his caution had the approval of responsible men. Slidell was too shrewd to be self-deceived. He cautioned the Confederate government against wasting money on privateers, which the Powers had tried to outlaw by the convention of London; such vessels could do nothing but make enemies, for neutral ports would not accept their prizes. Instead, all the Confederate resources should be put into commerce destroyers. Slidell also urged Benjamin to send him money to buy French journalists, suggesting that a few thousands in gold might bring one of the leading journals aggressively behind the South. But here he was outwitted and outbid by the expert American newspaperman, John Bigelow. This oldtime associate of Bryant, now consul-general and publicity director in Paris, with a longer purse and better cause, executed a series of master strokes in obtaining the support of the most widely-circulated Parisian papers: *Le Temps, Le Siècle, l'Opinion Nationale, La Presse,* and *Journal des Débats.* These sheets persuaded French readers that "Uncle Tom's Cabin" was a faithful picture of the outrages of slavery.[49]

Confederate leaders in Richmond realized as fully as Slidell that the French government offered them far more hope, especially after the Emancipation Proclamation, than the British. Benjamin resentfully compared the brusqueness of Russell with French politeness. "The contrast is striking between the polished courtesy of M. Thouvenel and the rude incivility of Earl Russell." Yet, at the same time Benjamin believed that the two-faced French government had instructed some agents to explore the possibility of detaching Texas from the Confederacy![50] He dismissed the French consul at Galveston for his complicity in this effort, and thought for a time of expelling the consul in Richmond—but still he looked to Napoleon for assistance.

48. Undated Notes by Slidell in Eustis Paper, LC.

49. Paul Pecquet du Bellet, Ms. record, "The Diplomacy of the Confederate Cabinet," LC. Bellet, a native of New Orleans, took notes on affairs in Paris, 1861-1865.

50. Benjamin to Slidell, Oct. 17, 1862, in captured Confederate correspondence in New York *Tribune,* Jan. 19, 1863.

Jefferson Davis hoped throughout 1862 and a great part of 1863 that France would take positive action, even if Britain held back, to break the blockade. When Captain Justus Scheibert of Prussia, who had been sent by his government to observe the defense of Charleston, called in Richmond, Davis made him a confidential proposal. As Scheibert would be going home through Paris, he should seek an interview with Napoleon, and as a neutral military man explain the fighting power of the Confederacy. "If the Emperor delivers me of the blockade, which he can do by a mere stroke of the pen, I guarantee him the possession of Mexico." During the war of 1846, said Davis, Winfield Scott, with 12,000 troops, had forced Mexico to submit; and if the blockade were lifted the Confederacy could afford to detach a corps of 12,000 to 20,000 men to assist Napoleon in completing his conquest. But the Major did not see Napoleon.[51]

For the Northerners, one auspicious event of late spring was the triumph of liberal forces in the French parliamentary elections. A leader who detested Napoleon III, the journalist Provost-Paradol, was so torn by anxiety in May that he questioned John Bigelow as to the possibility of obtaining a 160-acre homestead in the West if reaction triumphed. But as June opened, the Emperor suffered a heavy reverse. Government candidates were defeated for each of the nine Paris seats; Thiers was elected by a large majority over his Bonapartist opponent; and Napoleon found himself facing the necessity of large concessions to popular government.[52] Charles Francis Adams in London rejoiced over this proof that the republican element in France was still powerful. The result will help us, he wrote Edward Everett. "In that country as in this the sympathy of the lower classes with us constitutes our greatest safeguard against unfriendly demonstrations."

And Adams was pleased in the same June season by the friendly tone of Palmerston's remarks upon the pending treaty for the suppression of the slave-trade. "They indicate the prevailing temper of the Ministry," he wrote Everett.[53] He could well forgive occasional asperities from "eighty, rolled up in black-silk handkerchiefs," as one Briton called old Pam.

[IV]

By "unfriendly demonstrations" Adams meant a repetition of such events as the escape of the *Alabama* from British control to prey upon Northern com-

---

51. Scheibert, Justus, *Mit Schwert und Feder: Errinerungen aus Meinen Laben*, Berlin, 1902, 154; Scheibert, *Seven Months in the Rebel States*, Tuscaloosa, Ala., 1958, 12-13, 126-128.

52. *Diary of John Bigelow*, May 13, 19, June 4-20, 1863, Ms. New York Public Library. Lyons, Marseilles, Bordeaux, and other large cities all left the Government candidates in a minority. The movement in favor of Liberal principles and of such reforms as those advocated by M. Casimir Perier, the financier, heartened leaders of the Progressive party in France and throughout Europe. New York *Tribune*, June 23, 1863.

53. Adams, Charles F., to Everett, June 19, 1863, Edward Everett Papers, Mass. Hist. Soc.

merce.[54] The flaming wrecks she made of valuable merchantmen in her wide circuit had set the anger of the North alight, for she put an end to sixty-eight of them. Other cruisers obtained in Great Britain by the Confederacy, the *Georgia*, the *Rappahannock*, and the *Shenandoah*, enjoyed briefer and less important careers.[55]

Upon the insistence of Seward that the nation would have no commerce left if such depredations continued, Adams did complain to the Foreign Office, hinting that the United States might have to send out privateers to protect its merchant marine; though in fact he did not think this necessary, for Britain was apparently becoming more considerate of American rights. Numerous excited public meetings were held in various cities of the kingdom, and some American observers were impressed by the friendliness of the audiences and their exhibition of deep moral convictions.[56] American complaints that still another cruiser designed for Confederate service, the *Alexandra*, was almost ready for departure from Liverpool, bore useful results. The government, in fact, took action which signalized an important change of policy.

By a sudden stroke the Ministry not only seized the *Alexandra* (April 5, 1863),

---

54. Semmes, Raphael, *Memoirs of Service Afloat During the War Between the States*, Baltimore, 1869, 423-424.
55. Bancroft, Frederic, *The Life of William H. Seward*, New York, 1900, 385.
56. *Diplomatic Correspondence*, National Archives, 1863, I, 141-142; Hiram Barney (New York) to A.F. Stoddard (Glasgow), March 2, 1863, Barney Papers, HEH: ". . . Allow me to thank you for your fair and intelligent statement of facts showing the causes of the war and the status of the parties to it, and for your earnest and pertinent appeals to the justice humanity and consistent morality of the people of England and Scotland on this great question.

"The religious people of Great Britain studied well and understood finally the Slavery question in this country. They appreciated I think the enormity of the evil and the difficulties in the way of removing it. They seemed to comprehend how the men of the North and free states could be as innocent of responsibility for its continuance as Englishmen were; and they ought to have seen that British people might by a certain course of policy assume as much responsibility for its triumphs and perpetuity as Northern sympathizers in America have done.

"I have been accustomed so long to respect the moral convictions and philanthropic motives of the British *people* that I have been unwilling to believe that they would retract, or permit their government to retract all the good things they have said and done for freedom. Whatever the politicians and capitalists of England may be, the *people* surely are not hypocrites. But the people ought not to forget that they control their government more directly and certainly than do any other people. Nor ought they to forget that the world is looking at England in this trial of her conscience and consistency, and that History is taking notes. Will they permit the Warships, now nearly completed in their dockyards to follow the *Alabama* and the *Oreto*? Will the British Government record itself a Pirate? If, to drive our commerce from the seas and to secure employment to the operatives and profit to themselves by a monopoly of Southern trade, the capitalists of England urge their government to adopt a hostile policy towards America, if the aristocracy, fearful of the power and example of a prosperous and peaceful republic here, urge their government to a policy which strengthens the rebellion, prolongs the war and exhausts our resources in the hope of dividing and destroying us, then the *people* should besiege Parliament and Downing Street with their remonstrances and give the government no rest till it has established a friendly policy towards the United States. I see not how the people of that country can escape the responsibility for the acts of their government on this question. . . . Our government has remonstrated with that of Great Britain on the subject; but, so far as I am advised, no satisfactory response has been given. . . ."

using evidence furnished by a clerk of the Confederate agent James D. Bulloch, but prosecuted the men behind her construction for their apparent violation of the enlistment law. Six thousand workers met in Manchester to applaud this step. Earl Russell wrote Lord Lyons in Washington that the orders given "to watch, and stop when evidence can be procured, vessels apparently intended for the Confederate service will, it is to be hoped, allay the strong feelings which have been raised in Northern America by the escape from justice of the *Oreto* and *Alabama.* "[57] The prosecution was pressed with energy and ability. Although the Lord Chief Baron gave such hostile instructions to the jury that the government lost its case and had to appeal, the *Alexandra* never entered the Confederate service.[58] Seward recognized the good faith of the Ministry in attempting to prevent delivery of this new commerce destroyer, and expressed confidence that the British judiciary would not uphold a ruling by the Lord Chief Baron that opened the gates to "unlimited employment of British capital, industry, and skill to make war from British ports against the United States."[59]

By mid-July of 1863, however, a new and grave threat was evident. Adams had learned from the alert consul in Liverpool, Thomas H. Dudley, of the construction of two powerful vessels, well-armored and equipped with heavy iron rams.[60] With their double turrets, nine-inch rifled guns, and beaks able to sink any vessel they struck, it was reported that they might be called the most formidable warships in the world. Bulloch had secretly contracted for them with John Laird, who in partnership with his recently deceased brother Macgregor Laird had done as much as any shipbuilder in the world to develop steam navigation and the use of iron vessels. In midsummer they were launched at Birkenhead, the Laird people saying that they were intended for the Egyptian Government, and giving them Egyptian names. When Dudley informed the Collector of the Port of Liverpool that Egypt had no interest in them and they were really built for the South, information was circulated that they belonged to a Parisian named M. Bravay. But by appealing to the French Government, Adams and Dudley found that this was also a lie.[61]

Laying his protest before Earl Russell, Adams minced no words. A portion

---

57. Adams, E.D., *Great Britain and the American Civil War,* Gloucester, Mass., 1957, II, 136; Monaghan, *op.cit.,* 293.

58. Nicolay and Hay, *Abraham Lincoln,* VIII, 256-257; Adams, E.D., *op.cit.,* II, 152.

59. Nicolay and Hay, *op.cit.,* VIII, 258.

60. Adams had other sources of information, stated the *Saturday Review* of May 8, 1863: "The papers which in the autumn of last year were intercepted between the Confederate Government and its representatives in England showed that there were contracts then already entered into for the building of ships for the Confederates in English ports; that the produce of the Cotton Loan was mainly intended to buy more ships. . . . Mr. Adams wrote to explain to Lord Russell that warlike operations were regularly organized in England. . . ."

61. Dudley, "Three Critical Periods in Our Diplomatic Relations with England During the Late War," *op.cit.,* 48.

of the British people, he wrote, were practically waging war against the United States.[62] To this Russell replied that his government must have proof that the rams were being built for the Confederacy before it could take action, and asked Dudley to submit any evidence he could obtain to the port authorities in Liverpool. Evidently he was sensitive to the judicial requirements laid down in the *Alexandra* case. Although resentful, Dudley responded with alacrity.

"It seemed to me," he wrote later, "to be a great hardship for the British Government to throw the burden of vindicating its laws upon the United States, especially when we had no power to compel anyone to give evidence or testify. But . . . I undertook the case and employed counsel to prepare such affidavits as we could procure to make out the case. The great difficulty we had to contend with was . . . [that] those who knew the most were the least willing to give evidence; indeed, they generally were directly interested in concealing from us the facts which they knew. Even those who were not interested and had knowledge, as a rule, would not testify or aid us, because it would injure them in a business point of view in a hostile community such as Liverpool was at that time."[63]

Not only did Dudley lay affidavits before the Collector at Liverpool, but he furnished Adams with duplicates which the Minister sent at once to Earl Russell.[64] Discussion of the rams had meanwhile become universal. Cobden, speaking in the Commons on July 23, 1863, said that their construction was widely known, and that he believed their departure from England would be followed by an American declaration of war. He implored the government to prevent their delivery to Confederate officers. Although Lord Clarendon asserted that he could see no distinction between selling arms to the Union government and selling ships to the Confederates, Cobden made a strong impression. He drove his point home by mentioning that the American government recorded the value of every ship destroyed, and debited the sum to Great Britain. He might also have mentioned that every dispatch concerning the rams set the American press talking of war. Bennett's *Herald* fulminated on August 4, 1863:

62. *Papers Relating to the Treaty of Washington*, Washington, 1872-1874, I, 107.

63. Dudley, "Three Critical Periods," *op.cit.*, 49-50.

64. Did the British Government suppose, Adams asked Russell, that attack upon the United States by these vessels would not provoke retaliatory action? "You have only to listen to the political debates in any part of the country to learn that the United States would accept an unprovoked foreign war now with more unanimity and cheerfulness than at any former period." (*Diplomatic Correspondence*, 1863, I, 365). The *London Illustrated News* reported on Sept. 26 that one ram wanted little to prepare her for receiving her equipment, though the other was less ready. Each was 230 feet in length and 42 feet in beam, of about 1500 tons register. They had iron armor 5.5 inches thick, and each carried four heavy guns in two revolving cylindrical turrets. Built for speed, their beaks made them formidable even without guns. Gustavus V. Fox was urging Ericsson to push forward two strong defensive monitors.

Since the outbreak of the war England has been clandestinely supplying the rebels with men, money, arms, clothing, food, inventions, and vessels-of-war. In other words, England has been actually at war with the United States for the past two years, and by her hypocritical assumption of neutrality has thus far prevented us from retaliating. We have been obliged to see the rebels assisted by English blockade runners, and our commerce destroyed by English privateers, without having had the opportunity to resent and revenge these outrageous insults. . . . The assistance which England has afforded the rebels, and the intolerable intrusion of France in Mexico, have given us great and just cause of offence, and . . . a declaration of war on our part must assuredly end this brief, eventful history, unless circumstances shall compel England and France to offer us satisfactory explanations and reparations.

One evidence of the gravity of the situation lay in the visit which two able business leaders, John Murray Forbes and William H. Aspinwall, paid to England. They came partly to act as Treasury agents in floating United States bonds, but partly also in the hope of buying the most dangerous vessels under construction away from the Confederates. This plan apparently originated with Forbes, was approved by Fox in the Navy Department, and finally gained Cabinet sanction. Sitting with Chase and Welles in New York, the industrialists agreed to make every effort to acquire the rams. Equipped with ten million dollars in government bonds of the new five-twenty issue, they were authorized to use them as security for a loan of a million pounds from Baring Brothers, with which to obtain control of the ships. April found Forbes in London, and Aspinwall soon followed. They were assisted by the astute and witty William M. Evarts, an expert in maritime law whom the State Department hurriedly dispatched to help Adams prepare his arguments. But they were unable to work in the desired secrecy, for both the London *Times* and the Confederate envoy obtained immediate word from New York of their purpose. Moreover, they encountered an unexpected obstacle in the fact that the flotation of the Erlanger loan gave the Confederacy sufficient financial resources to maintain control of the rams. They had to give up their main objective.[65]

The question of the rams, of peace or war, and—it is perhaps not too much to say—of the whole future prospect of Anglo-American amity, with all its profound influence upon world history, came to a head in the first half of September. If the first ram to be finished were left in a position to take to the high seas under the Confederate flag, the gravest consequences to the United States, to Great Britain, and to mankind might ensue. Adams, who was agitated beyond measure with anxiety, and who in the true Adams spirit feared the worst, felt no relaxation of tension when Parliament rose; for Lord Russell set off on a vacation trip to Scotland and delivered an address at Blairgowrie, published in all the newspapers, in which he asserted that the American government must furnish

65. Maynard, Douglas H., "The Forbes-Aspinwall Mission," *Miss. Valley Hist. Rev.*, XLV, 67ff.

not only ample evidence, but "credible evidence." According to Dudley, he used this phrase because he questioned the affidavit furnished by the former purser of the *Alabama,* a disreputable fellow who had married a quadroon from the West Indies.

Russell's speech contained other material, including a denunciation of quarrelsome American utterances, which alarmed Adams, yet it was actually a fairminded speech. Not only did Russell pay a warm tribute to Seward, saying that although they sometimes disagreed, he never questioned Seward's fairness, nor did Seward question his; he also avowed a firm belief that Britain and America ought to be friends—that as they felt the same veneration for law, the same love of liberty, the same respect for free institutions, they ought to stand together to cast their light upon the pathway of civilization. Moreover, Russell added that he believed a majority of Britons sympathized with the North; and as for himself, he considered slavery "one of the most horrible crimes that yet disgrace civilization."

The fact was that Adams had wrought himself into a feverish state of mind. He was exchanging letters with the still more feverish and excitable Charles Sumner which did him no good, for Sumner actually believed that Great Britain's proclamation of neutrality, treating the Confederacy as a belligerent, had been an unfriendly act which had been responsible for the long protraction of the conflict. It was hard for the American Minister to realize that the British Government would risk severe legal and political penalties if it halted the building of great and costly ships on a mere suspicion that they might be used improperly. The elder Laird was a member of Parliament, and thus in a position to make trouble. It was also hard for Adams to give the Government credit for its general regard for the rules of neutrality, and especially for the respect with which it treated the Northern blockade. Plenty of Britons wished to break the blockade. But "in my opinion," Russell had said at Blairgowrie, "the men of England would have been forever infamous if, for the sake of their own interest [in obtaining cotton], they had violated the law of nations and made war with these slaveholding States against the Federal States."[66]

Adams returned from his own Scottish vacation early on the morning of September 3, 1863. It was fortunate that he did, for the stopping of the Laird rams required immediate action; one of them seemed almost ready to sail. Angered by the Ministry's failure to take preventive steps, Adams wrote in his diary: "Their moral blindness culminates in cowardice which acts like the greatest daring." He supposed that Russell's delays arose from secret hostility to the United States, when actually they sprang from the necessity that the Crown substantiate its case before it wrecked the market for the two valuable ships and prove, indeed, the justice of its case. This involved making sure that Egypt was *not* the true con-

66. Most of the speech in *London Illustrated News,* Oct. 3, 1863.

signee of the rams. Yet delay might be dangerous, for if one of the warships shipped out a collision with America was almost certain.

On the day of his return, Adams sent Lord Russell a note about the impending departure of the rams, registering in the name of the American Government "this last solemn protest against the commission of such an act of hostility against a friendly government." His apprehension that it would be of no avail seemed justified when at 4 P.M. next day, September 4, he received a communication dated September 1 which stated that the Ministry could find no evidence justifying it to proceed in stopping the ironclads. "This affected me deeply," he noted in his diary. "I clearly foresee that a collision must now come of it." Not only had Russell's communication dated September 1 declared that "Her Majesty's Government are advised that they cannot interfere in any way with these vessels," but its tone seemed at once defensive and insolent.[67] Adams had learned from Liverpool that the foremost vessel had taken on coal in readiness to steam away. If it left, the assistant secretary in the legation wrote in his diary, war would be as certain as the shining of the sun.[68] "I then gave up all for lost," declared Adams, "and made preparations for the catastrophe."[69] That is, he feared that the change in British policy registered in the *Alexandra* decision in April would not be applied to the rams in September. He could not know that on September 3, the day Adams came back from his vacation, the Under-Secretary for Foreign Affairs, acting on Russell's instructions, had sent word to the Treasury that the rams were under such deep suspicion that if sufficient evidence could be found, Russell believed they ought to be detained. Nor could he know that on September 3 Russell, with such evidence at last in his hands, had ordered that the warships be stopped. For various reasons a communications-barrier existed.

But on Saturday the 5th, an abrupt and happy brightening of the outlook occurred. Adams that day wrote Russell stating his profound regret over the announcement that the rams could not be stopped, and adding ominously: "It would be superfluous in me to point out to your Lordship that this is war." His note was delivered to the Foreign Office that afternoon. But before it arrived, Lord Russell, breaking through the communications-barrier, had sent Adams a new note, declaring that the halting of the rams was under "the serious and anxious consideration of the government."[70] Dudley, who had come down from

67. Nicolay and Hay, *Abraham Lincoln*, VIII, 258-259; Adams, Charles Francis, *Charles Francis Adams* (by his son), Boston, 1900, 340-342.

68. *Journal of Benjamin Moran, 1857-1865, op.cit.*, II, 1202.

69. Adams to Edward Everett, London, Sept. 9, 1863, Everett Papers, Mass. Hist. Soc.

70. Moran, *Journal, op.cit.*, II, 1203. This whole subject is fully treated in E. D. Adams, *Great Britain and the American Civil War*, II, 142-151; Rhodes, *History of the United States*, IV, 377-386; Channing, *History of the United States*, VI; Baxter, J.P. "The British Government and Neutral Rights," *Amer. Hist. Rev.*, XXXIV, 9-29, 77-91. The reasons for imperfect communication between Russell and Adams include the fact that Adams did not get back from vacation until September 3; the fact that

Liverpool to welcome the returning Adams family and confer with the Minister, related the story of the day dramatically, though with a little confusion of dates. He had found Adams in a state of profound depression, regarding war as inescapable.

"I shall never forget how he walked up and down his drawing-room, discussing the gravity of the situation. He said, 'We would have only nineteen more days in England; that he would have to leave as soon as he heard from Washington, which would be in about nineteen days; he could see no alternative but war.' While we were walking up and down the drawing-room I observed through a side window a Queen's messenger approaching the house. The bell rang, and soon Mr. Adams's servant delivered him a dispatch. . . .He opened it and read it aloud. It was to this effect: 'That Her Majesty's government still had the detention of the rams. . . .under consideration.' I said, 'This is a backdown on the part of the English government,' He replied, 'It looks that way.' And in a moment we were both breathing more freely; the crisis had passed."[71]

It had indeed passed. The morning of Monday, September 7th, brought a bright gleam of sunshine in a *Times* leader suggesting that the Ministry was disposed to immobilize the rams. On the 8th the sunshine broadened; the Tory *Morning Post* carried an article announcing that the government had decided to detain the vessels and try the case in court. Although this wore an official look, Adams still worried until late in the afternoon when a note arrived: "Lord Russell

---

Consul Dudley did not get his additional affidavits to Russell (through Adams) until the 3rd, so that they could not be studied until the 4th; and the fact that Russell was pressing the Lairds for information which they would not give him if they thought, from some leak in the American legation, that he had already made up his mind, or that he was acting in collusion with Adams. Russell acted honorably and correctly, never wavered from the *Alexandra* decision of April, and on Sept. 10 was praised by Adams for his "firm stand." *U.S. Diplomatic Correspondence,* 1863, I, 370.

Walpole, Spencer, *The Life of Lord John Russell,* II, 359 footnote: "The conduct of the gentlemen who have contracted for the two ironclads at Birkenhead is so very suspicious that I have thought it necessary to direct that they should be detained. The Solicitor-General has been consulted, and concurs in the measure as one of policy though not of strict law. We shall thus test the law, and if we have to pay damages, we have satisfied the opinion which prevails here as well as in America that that kind of neutral hostility should not be allowed to go on without some attempt to stop it. . . ."

Rhodes IV, 383 also shows that Russell on Sept. 3 wired to have the ironclads stopped "as soon as there is reason to believe that they are actually about to put to sea, and to detain them until further orders.". . . .

71. Dudley, "Three Critical Periods," *op.cit.,* 50ff. Dudley also tells a vague and incorrect story of last-minute intervention by Palmerston. He states that in the absence of Russell, Lord Palmerston came to London from Tunbridge Wells, where he was staying, went to the Foreign Office, and asked how matters stood with the American Government. He was told of the recent correspondence, and of the fact that if the rams sailed, the United States would regard this as an act of war. He then asked to see the correspondence, said that the matter had gone far enough, and directed the dispatch to be prepared telling Adams that the detention of the rams was still under consideration. "After this, steps were soon taken by the government to prevent these vessels from sailing." ("Three Critical Periods," page 54). This story rests upon a misapprehension. Lord Russell was continuously in charge of developments. He had written Palmerston from Scotland September 3 that he was stopping the rams, and that if Palmerston disagreed he should call a Cabinet meeting. Palmerston may indeed have gone to the Foreign Office, but if so, it was to confirm, not override, Russell's policy.

presents his compliments to Mr. Adams and has the honor to inform him that instructions have been issued which will prevent the departure of the two iron-clad vessels at Liveroool." Adams now wrote his friend R.H. Dana, Jr.: "The agony is over, an order has gone to stop both vessels. We may now sail-on a few months longer perhaps."

Adams was wrong in believing that Palmerston and Russell had ever hardened their hearts in hostility to the United States. Respect for British law and precedent gave them powerful reasons for waiting until they had definite evidence of Confederate control of the vessels; and even so it was never fully satisfactory. The Ministry, we repeat, might have paid heavy financial and political penalties had it acted in rash haste on mere suspicion. The Duke of Argyll wrote Gladstone on September 10 from Inverary that the evidence he had seen pointed to a French destination for the rams, and that the French consul claimed them. When he had mentioned this to Adams, the Bostonian replied that he had obtained a denial from the French authorities. "I immediately wrote both to Palmerston and Lord Russell that this circumstance alone amounted to a violent presumption of fraud—and Lord Russell tells me that the determination to detain has followed on a similar disavowal on the part of the Pasha of Egypt as regards another alleged destination to him."[72] The Lairds and the Confederate agents were darkening the air with so many false assertions that Russell had to continue his inquiries of the French and Egyptian governments right up to the day that Adams deemed so critical.

The British representative in Cairo, Consul-General R.G. Colquhoun, whose correspondence went in duplicate to Her Majesty's Ambassador in Constantinople (Egypt being of course ruled by a Pasha of the Sultan of Turkey), found his wires kept warm by messages. The Foreign Office telegraphed him in cipher, August 24: "Have the Egyptian Government purchased two ironclad vessels of war now building in this country? The House of Bravay is supposed to be the agents. Answer as soon as possible." A reply being delayed, the Foreign Office telegraphed again, August 30: "Do the ironclad ships belong to the Pasha of Egypt, or has he sold them, and if so, to whom?" Again the reply was delayed. On September 26, the Foreign Office cabled again: "We are disposed to buy the ironclads to sell them again to the Sultan at cost price if he wishes to have them. Ask the Viceroy to keep his hold over M. Bravay, and he may depend upon Her Majesty's Government that the Sultan shall have the ironclads if he wishes it. If not, the British Government will buy them for their own service." On October 1, the Foreign Office was still trying to clear up the matter. Bravay stated (so it telegraphed Colquhoun) that he was bound by his agreement with the Pasha not

72. Adams to Dana, Sept. 7, 1863, R.H. Dana Papers, Mass. Hist. Society; Gladstone Papers, Add. Ms. 44099, British Museum; Adams, Charles Francis, *Charles Francis Adams* (by his son), 343-344.

to sell until the designs or vessels had been presented for final approval, "and that the Pasha had promised to use all his influence to induce the Porte to take them if he declined to do himself."[73]

Clearly Egypt did assert title to the rams; and this thorny, long-drawn negotiation was made rougher by the fact that Britain was pressing Turkey and Egypt to stop their slave-trading activities. Meanwhile, Russell could not wait on the Pasha.

It was a fact that Russell had taken decisive steps as early as September 3 and 5 to prevent the departure of the rams, this action anticipating the minatory note of Adams to the Foreign Secretary, but a fact hidden from public view. It was not until the 9th that the government placed an official watch upon the warships, and its strict embargo became known. For a long generation, ill-informed opinion in America underrated the vigilance of the Ministry in trying to maintain a true neutrality, and overrated the importance of Adam's threat of war—a threat which followed, not preceded, as a factor in averting hostilities. Russell was well aware of the truth embodied in Evart's comment: "Disastrous as the existence of these ironclads would have been to us, the ultimate reckoning of England for the criminal folly of permitting their departure would have been more disastrous to her interests."[74]

The escape from hostilities had been by too thin a margin for comfort, as Adams wrote Everett, but he realized that the Ministry had acted in defiance of heavy pressure for leaving the Lairds alone, and deserved approbation for its courage. "I am not sure that they may not in the end have to go to Parliament to get an indemnity."[75] Ultimately, the British Government did have to purchase the rams. At no time did Adams really lose confidence in Russell's good faith, though he did lose patience with his caution. He knew that the frostiness of the Foreign Minister almost matched his own frigidity of temper, and that they got along with each other better than if they had been men of softer spirit. As the episode ended, Adams could repeat a statement he had made a little earlier: "Thus far we have always harmonized, and I trust we may to the end of the chapter."[76]

The activity of Cobden behind the scenes had been useful in obtaining a fair treatment of American interests. He had called on Russell in May to read him a nasty indictment of British policy just spewn out by Charles Sumner, and despite Russell's irritation had made him listen to every word. He found Russell alive to the necessity for preventing the emergence of any more *Alabamas.* Cobden's great speech of April 24 in the Commons on the neutrality laws made a tremendous impression. John Bigelow, who had gone to hear it, found that it

73. Foreign Office, 141, Vol. 52, dispatches, No.46-50ff.
74. Evarts to Dudley, Sept. 26, 1863, Dudley Papers, HEH.
75. September 9, Everett Papers, Mass. Hist. Soc.
76. Adams to Everett, April 29, 1863, Everett Papers, Mass. Hist. Soc.

exceeded all his expectations. "No one attempted to answer it. From that day to this the tone of public sentiment in England has been growing daily more tolerant toward America."[77] Throughout the crisis, Cobden and Bright played a rôle even when they were silent.

[V]

The late autumn of 1863 was a season of growing calm in Anglo-American relations. Adams wrote Dana in January, 1864: "The last five months have been the quietest I have passed since I have been here. The corner was turned in the beginning of September. . . . The ministry will now continue steady, I think. . . ." Such troublemakers as were active were held in restraint. The Irish-American malcontents called the Fenians were ready to seize every opportunity for mischief. One well-informed observer wrote Lord Lyons this fall that the Fenian Brotherhood had more than 100,000 members who paid ten cents a week into a common fund; that 18,000 were in the Northern armies; and that during the previous year they had sent about 16,000 rifles, 23,000 revolvers, and other weapons into Ireland. They were ready to attempt border raids into Canada; but as yet they had accomplished nothing.[78]

The utterances of half the American press continued as rasping and ill-tempered as those of the Tory journals in Great Britain. Charles Sumner chose the uneasy moment of Russell's stoppage of the rams for characteristically emotional and splenetic outbursts to British friends.[79] He was bottling up ideas and excitements which he let loose in a New York speech on September 10, two days after Russell halted the rams—a speech as ponderous, pedantically documented, and unwise as his speech of ante-bellum days on "The Crimes against Kansas." His friend Moncure D. Conway thought his inopportune diatribe the greatest error of Sumner's life. "It came at a time when all England was coming to our side, and when the moral unanimity was of practical importance."[80] This hysterical attack not only magnified every British offence, but took the untenable ground that British recognition of Confederate belligerency, which Sumner failed to

77. Bigelow, John, Ms. *Diary*, May 13, 1863, New York Public Library. When the crisis was safely past, Gladstone penned a twelve-page letter to the Duke of Argyll, making objections to any interference with the rams. It was to be printed for the Cabinet. Full of doubts and difficulties, it was based on what Gladstone conceived to be international law. Argyll's proposal to prohibit the export of armed ships, he wrote, was really a proposal to depart from neutrality and take the side of the North. Argyll replied in a moderate and unanswerable letter. Gladstone to Argyll, Sept. 30.; Argyll to Gladstone, Oct. 3, 1863, Gladstone Papers, British Museum.

78. John W. Cullin, Phila. n.d. but autumn 1863, to Lyons, Foreign Office 5/Vol.897; Adams to Dana, Jan. 27, 1864, Dana Papers, Mass. Hist. Soc.

79. Pierce, E.L., *Memoirs and Letters of Charles Sumner*, Boston, 1877-1893, IV, 128ff., gives a number of his letters.

80. Conway, Moncure D., *Autobiography: Memories and Experiences*, Boston, 1904, II, 90-93.

recognize as a correct sequel of Lincoln's proclamation of blockade, had been responsible for the stubbornness of the war. John Murray Forbes, who also condemned the speech, showed Sumner an expostulatory letter from William Rathbone, Jr., of Liverpool. The Senator, of course, insisted that he was right. "He does not shine in the perceptive faculties," Forbes wrote Rathbone; "he has eloquence, scholarship, high principles, and many other good qualities, but he has not the faculty of putting himself in the position of an opposing party. . . ."[81]

The general good temper with which the British had taken the decision of American courts in the case of the ship *Peterhoff* was reassuring. This case had arisen some months before the explosive episode of the rams, but the influence of the good temper shown by the British long maintained a calming sway. The English vessel *Peterhoff* had been captured by the *Vanderbilt*, February 25, 1863, just after she left St. Thomas bound for Matamoros, Mexico. To superficial view, she was engaged in lawful commerce. British-built, her registered owner being an Englishman, she was carrying miscellaneous merchandise to a neutral port. The shippers, all but one of them British, were represented by passengers or supercargoes travelling on the vessel, and the bills-of-lading were correct. But as Matamoros lay cheek-by-jowl with the Texas port of Brownsville, and one Texan had cargo valued at $375,000, everybody divined the real destination of her goods. Russell and the British solicitor-general agreed that the American admiralty courts had acted correctly, mainly following Lord Stowell's historic decisions, in condemning the vessel. The maritime code was severe, but it was primarily a British code.[82] Henry Adams wrote his brother Charles Francis, Jr., that in a base world of politics the English still kept a conscience, though often foggy.[83] What was more, they still kept a strong reverence for law.

The appointment of Sir Roundell Palmer as Her Majesty's Attorney-General, announced at the end of September, also pleased Adams. Though not a man of self-reliant courage, he had executive ability and command of speech, and would do better in the courts than his predecessor Sir William Atherton. His sympathies lay with the Union. Adams freely conceded that Lord Russell was making "something of a struggle" to do the Union justice. Like other sane observers, he thought Sumner's attack on Great Britain unwise—Americans should not "exasperate our people too much against our friends."[84] By Thanksgiving Day, as the new Attorney-General took hold with vigor, he was still more optimistic. The *Times*, realizing that its mischievous correspondent Mackay had made himself hateful to most Northerners, recalled him, and sent Antonio Gallenga of Turin, a cultivated Italian who had been exiled for his hostility to Austrian rule, to the United States

81. Forbes to William Rathbone, Jr., Oct. 31, 1863, Forbes Papers, Mass. Hist. Soc.
82. New York *Herald,* August 3, 1863.
83. *A Cycle of Adams Letters,* II, 83.
84. Adams to Edward Everett, Oct. 1, 1863, Everett Papers, Mass. Hist. Soc.

in his stead. It was a felicitous choice. Gallenga, married to an Englishwoman, contributed to the *North American Review,* and was well known to Longfellow, Prescott, Ticknor, and other eminent Bostonians, and to the publisher George P. Putnam in New York.

The change of front by the London *Times* was a great event. "Now and then, it goes so far as to admit a friendly article, correcting its own views," wrote Adams, who in part credited William Vernon Harcourt for the shift.[85] When the Minister visited the Duke of Devonshire at Chatsworth that fall, the cordiality of his reception delighted him.[86]

One important fact that neither Adams nor the editor of the *Times* knew was that Lord Lyons had told his government in blunt terms that autumn that the United States had become too formidable to be challenged. This was a great historic fact, marking a momentous change in world balance. In 1861, Great Britain had possessed a marked advantage; now the relative position of the two Powers had changed. The United States, he wrote on November 3, 1863, would prove the stronger in any encounter. Bermuda, the Bahamas, and other island possessions would fall at once. "Three years ago Great Britain might at the commencement of a war have thrown a larger number of trained troops into the British provinces in Canada than the United States could have placed there. Now the United States could without difficulty send an army into Canada outnumbering any British force five to one."[87] Lyons did not need to advert to the fact that under the Act lately passed by Congress to authorize privateering, American ships could do enormous damage to the British merchant marine; British shipping men kept the Ministry well aware of the fact.

One striking episode of the autumn, the visit of two of the Czar's fleets in New York and San Francisco, was widely misinterpreted by Americans at the time and later. Their arrival was primarily a result of the Polish crisis. Russia, fearing the possibility of war with Britian and France, was anxious to get her warships out of icebound and British-controlled waters, and into neutral ports whence they could emerge to harry Anglo-French commerce. Many Americans, however, resentful of European attitudes, leaped at the surmise that the visits were a friendly gesture, perhaps to be followed by armed action on behalf of the Union if Britain and France intervened on the side of the South. New Yorkers organized receptions, excursions, and a variety of entertainments, crowds gathering to cheer the visitors. The press did not know why the fleets had come, but hoped it was for the best reasons, and the legend of Muscovite amity in an hour of

85. *Ibid.*
86. Adams, to Everett, Nov. 22, 1863, Everett Papers, Mass. Hist. Soc.
87. Lyons to Russell, Nov. 3, 1863; Foreign Office 6/896.

American desperation grew. In one of his resounding Senate speeches, widely circulated in pamphlet form, Sumner was stimulated by his Anglophobe impulses to make the bold assertion that the visit was intended by the Czar and accepted by the United States as a friendly demonstration. Only the hardest-boiled editors grasped the truth that Russia's motive was purely selfish. Cyncial debutantes, like one bud of the Rufus King family, dared to say that the Russian ball in New York was emphatically "shoddy," that most Russian tars were "small men, badly formed, and not handsome or even intelligent looking," and that the popular enthusiasm was vulgarly naïve.[88]

The autumn brought Henry Ward Beecher to England, making speeches that impressed some people and displeased others. He had gone abroad merely as a private citizen on the generous insistence of his congregation that he get a rest. Many sympathizers with the South resented his arrival, one such sympathizer circulating in Liverpool a handbill attacking him as a political emissary sent to stir up strife and ill-will among the people of Liverpool. This American found an immense crowd, almost entirely men, present to hear Beecher speak, with every square inch of the speaker's platform occupied. Men had been scattered through the audience to act in concert to create a disturbance, which everybody seemed to expect. At first, while Beecher read a prepared discourse, the uproar and disorder were tremendous. But when he turned upon his interrupters, his wit, dignity, and eloquence, reaching the highest moral elevation, made a tremendous impression. At the end he commanded universal respect among all upon the platform. One English gentleman exclaimed, "I was prepared to criticize, and ready to dislike, but I never heard anything like this!" As one American present wrote, "He made the entire assembly feel the greatness of his country, the justice of its cause, and the certainty of its triumph."[89] The British people were adamant in condemning slavery and were turning against intervention. At first, Beecher courted retirement, saying that he wished to keep out of the category of meddlers in foreign affairs, and declining invitations of the Union and Emancipation Society to speak. But his ardent temperament soon carried him to the platform, where he commanded attention chiefly as the brother of the author of *Uncle Tom's Cabin*. The London *Era* spoke of him as delivering showy addresses to immense audiences, and *Punch* published a cartoon by Tenniel exhibiting him as trying

88. Mary A. King to Rufus King, Nov. 16, 1863, King Ms., Indiana University Library; Golder, F.A., "The Russian Fleet and the Civil War," *American Historical Review*, July, 1915, XX, 801-812; Bailey, Thomas A., "The Russian Fleet Myth Reexamined," *Mississippi Valley Historical Review*, Vol. XXXIII, No. 1, June 1951, 81-90. See also Thomas, Benjamin P., *Russo-American Relations, 1815-1867*, Baltimore, 1930, 138.

89. Buckley, J.M., "Beecher at Liverpool in 1863," *The Century Magazine*, November, 1888, Vol. XV, New Series, 240-243.

to feed treacle to an indifferent British lion.[90] But his speeches in Liverpool, Manchester, Glasgow, and Edinburgh, October 9-20, attracted wide notice particularly as the London *Daily News* granted him generous publicity.[91] According to the *Daily News,* which printed several of his discourses in full, his reception was friendly, and several cities gave him almost an ovation. While he was speaking in Free Trade Hall in Manchester, October 10, the crowd rose in exultation over a telegram announcing that the government had sent a warrant for seizing the rams. However, an American who spoke with Beecher wrote of the unfriendly reaction at the Liverpool meeting where the crowd was so antagonistic it became a near riot. Beecher argued and fought verbally with the insulting crowd but managed to finish. Beecher is said to have stated, "I am so mad at the way they talk and act over here that I don't care to see an Englishman."[92]

Beecher emphasized his belief that "the American question is the working-man's question all over the world." After a final plea in Exeter Hall on the 20th, he went home to emphasize the importance of preserving Anglo-American unity "for the sake of struggling mankind." If England is to be judged by her middle class, he told a Brooklyn audience, she is with us, and he listed the able editors —Samuel Lucas of the *Morning Star,* Walker of the *Daily News,* Hutton of the *Spectator,* Masson of the *Westminster Review*—upholding the Union cause. After mentioning John Stuart Mill, Thomas Hughes, Goldwin Smith, J.E. Cairnes, Milner Gibson, Lord Granville, and others, he asserted roundly that the North commanded "the great underlying population of England struggling for larger political rights."[93]

Almost simultaneously with Lord Russell's decision to hold the rams, the Confederacy broke off its exiguous relations with Great Britain. Northern irritation over stumblings in British neutrality was far outweighed by the chagrin of the South over the refusal of recognition, and the curt discourtesy with which it was conveyed. Early in 1863, Secretary Benjamin had written Slidell that public resentment of the slights suffered by Confederate diplomats abroad was growing so strong that President Davis would have to exert all his influence to prevent an explosion. Richmond would unhesitatingly recall Mason, so rudely rebuffed by Lord Russell, were it not that the step would embarrass Slidell in Paris and hamper his preparations for the purchase of "articles" (Benjamin meant cruisers) surely needed by the Confederacy in the war.[94] Southern choler increased as 1863 wore on. The butchery in America was being needlessly prolonged, President

90. *Punch,* Oct. 31, 1863.
91. *London Daily News,* Oct. 6,11,12,15, 1863;
92. Buckley, J.M., "Beecher at Liverpool," *Century,* Dec. 1888, 240-243.
93. Full report, New York *Tribune,* Nov. 20, 1863; cf. Hibben. Paxton, *Henry Ward Beecher, an American Portrait,* New York, 1927, 188-196.
94. Benjamin to Slidell, Jan. 15, 1863; Eustis Papers, LC.

Davis wrote, by European failure to recognize the rightful place of the Confederacy among nations, and European leaders would have to answer for the bloodshed at the bar of history.[95]

In the spring of 1863, Mason, whom Cobden tartly described as "that old slave dealer", for many Britons despised him as author of the Fugitive Slave Bill,[96] lamented that he enjoyed no intercourse, social or otherwise, with any member of the British Ministry, and the Confederate agent L.Q.C. Lamar expressed outrage over the chilliness of the London authorities.[97] What rebel emissaries found hard to endure was the fact that no halfway house existed between recognition and non-recognition. Slidell in Paris, A. Dudley Mann in Belgium, and most of all the proud Mason in London, found themselves treated as outsiders, and Mason particularly was outside shivering in the cold.[98] This most pompous, haughty, and unapproachable of Southern leaders submitted persistent appeals to Lord Russell, holding out the temptation of unlimited shipments of cotton as an argument for action, and getting only a curt response that his communications had been received. When Bulloch persuaded Mason to ask Lord Russell in the spring of 1865 to order British consuls to forbid the Confederate cruiser *Shenandoah* (which had been effectively raiding the American whaling fleet in Arctic waters) to commit acts of war, Russell consented to his communication simply as a message, not as an act involving responsible action.[99]

Meanwhile, friction was certain to arise over the position and activities of the four British consuls in the South, placed at Richmond, Charleston, Savannah, and Mobile. They held a peculiar position in a country to which Great Britain did not accord diplomatic status. As they were responsible to Lord Lyons in Washington, the Confederate Government felt keenly the anomaly of sheltering consuls who were controlled by the Minister at an enemy capital.[100] When confusion and turmoil in the South increased, their efforts to protect British interests became more difficult. Their claim of immunity for British subjects from conscription into the Southern army was met by Confederate denials that they had any right to interfere. Secretary Benjamin accused them of an unwarrantable assumption of jurisdiction, and an offensive encroachment on Confederate sovereignty. George Moore of Richmond, who proved specially irritating, was given several

---

95. *Journal, Confederate Congress*, VII, 251. In his tour of the West late in 1862, Jefferson Davis addressed the Mississippi legislature on foreign affairs. He spoke with bitterness of the European powers which had acted so promptly in behalf of Greece, Italy, and Belgium, but were so cold to the South. France alone had made a friendly gesture; *L'Independence Belge*, Feb. 1, 1863.

96. Cf. Hobson, J.A., *Cobden, The International Man*, New York, 1919, 369-370.

97. *O.R.N.*, II, Vol.III, 715-718.

98. Mann termed their treatment "extremely shabby"; Jan. 16, 1863; *Ibid.*, 659.

99. The New York *Herald*, April 1, 1863, jeered at Mason's submissiveness; Formby, John, *The American Civil War*, New York, 1910, 405-406, 569.

100. *O.R.N.*, II, Vol. III, 923.

warnings in 1863, lost his *exequatur,* and finally was expelled from the country.[101]

As the United States in 1860 had 2,476,130 persons who had been born British subjects, the South naturally contained a good many. At last, Alexander Fuller-ton, acting consul in Savannah, brought matters to a head. He had advised Britons conscripted in Georgia to acquiesce in the enrollment until they were called from their homes, or were asked to meet Northern soldiers in actual combat; then, he said, they must refuse service, for it would be a violation of the Neutrality Act. Benjamin, pronouncing this intolerable, sent all the British consular officials home.[102]

After Gettysburg and Vicksburg, and after the detention of the rams, South-ern leaders saw clearly that all hope of foreign recognition was gone. The dignity of the Confederacy forbade further begging. Early in August, 1863, President Davis decided to cancel the mission of Mason to Britain, and late the following month the stiff Virginian packed up all his records and left for France. A once bright dream had vanished. Davis acridly told his Congress in December that the attitude of the European powers had become "positively unfriendly."[103] There-after, such Southern communications as were made were awkwardly roundabout in method and unfriendly in temper.

Americans and Britons who drew about their firesides on Christmas Day of 1863 could look back on some unhappy pages of diplomatic history written during the year. The kindred nations had come closer to war at the beginning of Septem-ber than either cared to remember. With a little more asperity from Charles Francis Adams and arrogance from Lord Russell, they might have stumbled into battle. The sinkings and burnings by Semmes of the *Alabama,* the secret plots of Bulloch and the Lairds, the passage of the Privateering Act by Congress, the bellicose rant of Charles Sumner, the use of the Erlanger Loan to get Britons enlisted on the Confederate side, the willingness of Napoleon III and the Egyp-tian Pasha to fish in muddy waters, were part of the melodrama of the times; melodrama that might have become tragedy. On the brighter side of the year's history were the sturdy activities of Bright and Cobden, the British change of policy in the *Alexandra* case, the fact that after incredible suspense the Foreign Office did detain the rams, and above all, the clear demonstrations of sound sense and good will by both Adams and Russell. With much justice, Russell told the House of Lords on March 24, 1865, that he must observe that the impartial course, "which Her Majesty's Government has pursued has from time to time been impeded and endangered on the one side by those partisans of the North who

101. *Ibid.,* 789ff., 926.
102. *Ibid.,* 928-930.
103. *Journal Confederate Congress,* VI, 497.

were constantly stating that we were acting in a manner hostile to the North, and on the other, by those who were as constantly violating the neutrality which Her Majesty had proclaimed in the pursuit of their own private ends. But, be that as it may, I am satisfied that there is not the slightest pretense for saying that the course which the Government has pursued has not been strictly Neutral . . ." The immortal Charles Dickens also wrote with much justice in a letter to M. De Cerjat on November 14, 1865:[104] "If the Americans don't embroil us in a war before long it will not be their fault. What with their swagger and bombast, what with their claims for indemnification, what with Ireland and Fenianism, and what with Canada, I have strong apprehensions. With a settled animosity toward the French usurper [Napoleon III] I believe him to have always been sound in his desire to divide the States against themselves, and that we were unsound and wrong in 'letting I dare not wait upon I would.' That Jamaica insurrection is another hopeful piece of business. That platform-sympathy with the black—or the native, or the devil-afar off—and that platform-indifference to our own countrymen at enormous odds in the midst of bloodshed and savagery, make me stark wild."

The ablest recent biographer of Lord Palmerston, H.C.F. Bell, who is critical of Palmerston's views of the North, states in a judicious summation of the tangled and controversial events here related: "In the shaping of Anglo-American relations at this time [he is writing here of 1862] Palmerston's hold on the House of Commons seems to have been . . . not entirely negligible. Considering that the pronounced tendency of many members of Parliament to take some sort of action on behalf of the Southern States was being constantly strengthened by the mounting distress of the cotton operatives, and the mounting dissatisfaction of the commercial and shipping interests; considering the eagerness of the friends of the South on both sides of the English Channel to exploit this tendency, and the sensitiveness of the enemies of the South on the other side of the Atlantic concerning it, one may fairly conclude that a speech or two in the premier's best jingoistic style might have made relations between London and Washington more critical. . . . In private, Palmerston drove Adams to the last point of exasperation and protest; but in public he restrained himself, and in restraining himself did much to restrain Parliament. . . ."

In his private letters he protested that England could not be subjected to 'the scandal and inconvenience of having Federal and Confederate squadrons watching and fighting each other' in the vicinity of her shores; she could not allow her vessels to be overhauled by Federal cruisers 'without rhyme or reason' and sent

104. Villiers, Brougham and W.H. Chesson, *Anglo-American Relations, 1861-1865*, London, 1919, 203,204.

to New York for trial. Seward should be admonished and Adams warned. The letters stand out in sharp contrast to the very cool and correct official pronouncements which were issuing simultaneously from the Foreign Office and the Admiralty. "The [Prime Minister's] testiness concerning the war measures of the Union government may have been in part a reaction to the increased difficulties at home which the American Civil War was helping to bring on him . . ."[105]

Although the escape of the rams with British acquiescence would have precipitated a serious diplomatic crisis and would also have frightened the Northern people with grave doubts of the American future, we may well wonder if the appearance of two such vessels, after a long and dangerous passage of the Atlantic in the stormy autumn, would have been a highly threatening event to the North. Their formidability had often been exaggerated by commentators. They could have been shut up in Confederate ports, and, with coaling and other problems, they would have faced a Federal Navy which by the fall of 1863 was in a much stronger position than it had been. They might well have caused trouble, losses, and excitement, but would it not have taken many more than two ironclads to make much real difference? On the other hand, if these two were even partly successful, would there not have been more?[106]

All the while, in Europe as in America, the progress of emancipation wrought upon the hearts and minds of discerning men. Its influence marched while generals halted and armies went into winter quarters. All the while, too, men caught more of the inspiration of Lincoln's personality and words.

"The more the text of the President's message is considered," declared the *Caledonian Mercury* in December, 1863, "the higher must be our appreciation of its calm thoughtfulness, so different from the rowdyism we were wont to receive from Washington when proslavery Cabinets were in the ascendant. President Lincoln speaks of the attitude assumed toward the United States by European governments without irritation . . . He speaks without acerbity even of the rebels who have done so much to bring calamity upon the country. . . . When we recollect the rancorous hate entertained in this country toward the Indian rebels, we feel humiliated that this 'village attorney, this 'rail-splitter from Illinois,' should have shown himself so superior to the mass of monarchical statesmen."

The day would come, predicted the Edinburgh newspaper, when the character of Lincoln would receive justice in Britain, and when his most rancorous assailants would blush for their part in lampooning a noblehearted man. Truly had he written, that the fiery trial through which his people passed would light them down, in honor or dishonor, to the latest generation. The verdict of the future was certain. "Before two years of his Administration have been completed, he has

105. Bell, Herbert C.F., *Lord Palmerston*, 2 vols., Longmans, London, 1936.
106. Summary from Soley, James R., *Blockade and the Cruisers*, New York, 1883, 218-219.

reversed the whole constitutional action of America upon the subject of slavery. He has saved the Territories from the unhallowed grasp of the slave power; he has purged the accursed institution from the Federal District; he has hanged a slave-trader in New York, the nest of slave pirates; . . . and he has joined Great Britain in endeavoring to sweep the slave trade from the coast of Africa!" His moral stature impressed the world. "Within the light of the fiery trial of which the President speaks, another light has shone clear and refulgent: the torch of Freedom." This anticipated the verdict of history as eloquently as Cobden had anticipated it.

INDEX

PART II

The War for the Union

THE ORGANIZED WAR TO VICTORY
1864–1865

Robert E. Lee

CONTENTS

ILLUSTRATIONS

1

Grant, Meade, and Sherman
Take Command

ON HOW MANY FRONTS, as 1864 opened, did the war drag along at a
snail's pace and with uncertain outlook for the Union! In Virginia, where the
principal news was the ovation that Richmond gave the bold John H. Morgan
after his escape from the Ohio penitentiary; at Charleston, where Beauregard
held his lines while the Union fleet of ironclad monitors and wooden steamships rode out the winter gales; in northwestern Louisiana, where Kirby-
Smith stood firm at Shreveport; in West Tennessee and northwest Mississippi,
where Nathan B. Forrest had raised more than four thousand recruits for fresh
campaigns; and at Knoxville, where Union troops were watching Longstreet.
From Missouri and the Kentucky-Tennessee border had come a stream of
dismal reports of men on both sides murdered in cold blood by guerrillas,
although by the beginning of 1864 such activities had temporarily slackened.
Daily rumors predicted that the Confederates would attempt another invasion
of Pennsylvania, or strike at Little Rock, or win a French alliance. The one
certainty was stated by Greeley's *Tribune:* "The country expects the war to be
resumed with energy the moment it is possible for our armies to move."[1]

That the country's expectations would be met was demonstrated by a
ringing summons from Lincoln on February 1: "Ordered, that a draft for five
hundred thousand men to serve for three years or during the war will be made
on the 10th day of March next, for the military service of the United States."
He had called for 300,000 volunteers the previous October, but despite liberal
Federal bounties ($402 for veterans, $302 for raw recruits), the response had
been unsatisfactory. Recruiting details from field regiments were active in the
North all winter, and the new drafts were expected to fill up the lagging State
quotas.[2]

---

1. New York *Times,* January 28, 1864; Swiggett, Howard, *The Rebel Raider, a Life of John Hunt
Morgan,* Garden City, 1937, Ch. X; Lytle, Andrew Nelson, *Bedford Forrest and His Critter Company,*
New York, 1931, 257ff.
2. Lerwill, Leonard R., *The Personnel Replacement System in th. U.S. Army,* Washington, 1954, 100-112.

Suddenly the opening of February brought a flurry of Union activity—partly successful, partly abortive—at half-a-dozen points. Sherman at Nashville had written Admiral D.D. Porter in December, 1863, regarding his plans which included a move up Red River: "I propose to strike at large armies and large interests." He now made good his words. With 20,000 men, he marched directly toward Meridian, Miss., where he ordered General William Sooy Smith with 7,000 cavalry to join him from Memphis. He would seize Meridian, a town of several thousand people near the eastern boundary of Mississippi, destroy the Confederate railroads and supplies about it, and lay waste the country. If successful, he and Smith could press on east to Selma, with its rich manufacturing facilities in the heart of Alabama, or turn south toward Mobile. Sherman later denied he had ever intended to go to Mobile. Beginning his march on February 3, Sherman reached Meridian with little loss, but Smith utterly failed him. He allowed Forrest to head him off at West Point, Mississippi, defeat him near Okolona, Mississippi, and compel him to retreat to Memphis. Sherman had to content himself with tearing up long stretches of railroad about Meridian, and destroying bridges, buildings, supplies, and farmhouses. "He leaves the country perfectly impoverished wherever he has been," declared Richmond papers.[3] Then he, too, returned to the Mississippi, at Vicksburg.

Early in February, Ben Butler planned a sudden descent upon Richmond, but the officer he sent out on this mission, Isaac J. Wistar, found the defensive lines too strong for an attack. Before the month ended, Kilpatrick's cavalry, with Colonel Ulric Dahlgren (son of the admiral) leading five hundred of its best men, launched another raid on the rebel capital, its primary object the release of Union captives in filthy Libby Prison. While Kilpatrick took prisoners on the outer Richmond lines and destroyed railroad property, young Dahlgren and many of his men were killed, and his command was scattered.[4] The gallant Dahlgren was widely mourned.

Much the most unfortunate development early in 1864, however, was the Red River expedition organized and led on land by N.P. Banks, Butler's successor in command of the Department of the Gulf. The genesis and blame for undertaking this expedition has long been a controversial subject among students. Halleck and Banks are usually censured for what became a first-class blunder, although Banks opposed it in the early stages of the planning, and Halleck, although he appeared to support it, was certainly echoing non-mili-

3. Quoted in New York *Tribune*, March 10, 1864; a good summary of the Meridian campaign is in the New Orleans *True Delta*, March 2, 1864. Sherman brought out huge numbers of mules and Negroes. *O.R.N.*, I, 25, 645.
4. Liddell Hart, Basil H., *Sherman, Soldier, Realist, American*, New York, 1929, 224-226; Wistar, Isaac Jones, *Autobiography*, New York, 1914, 1937, Chaps. VIII and IX.

tary considerations in Washington. Lincoln and others apparently favored some such move as the Red River Campaign in 1863 for three reasons: to bulwark Lincoln's new Reconstruction government in Louisiana; to obtain large amounts of cotton; and by possible movements into Louisiana and Texas to present a show of force to the French in Mexico which might discourage adventures in that area.

French troops had impudently entered Mexico City, June 7, 1863.[5] On July 29, 1863, Lincoln wrote Stanton, "Can we not renew the efforts to organize a force to go to Western Texas? . . . I believe no local object is now more desirable. . . ."[6] Welles was writing of July 31, when he said that Seward wanted a meeting with him and Lincoln to discuss a Texas occupation. The idea having been discussed for some weeks, Seward continued to press for a move into Texas at the Cabinet meeting of July 31, and in a later meeting with Stanton and Halleck.[7] On August 5, Lincoln wrote Banks, "Recent events in Mexico, I think, render early action in Texas more important than ever. . . ." The President then turned his attention to Louisiana politics.[8]

Halleck told Banks on August 6, "There are important reasons why our flag should be restored in some point of Texas with the least possible delay. Do this by land at Galveston, at Indianola, or any other point you may deem preferable. . . . There are reasons why the movement should be as prompt as possible. . . ." This message was sent to Banks by direction of Stanton.[9] Halleck enlarged on the subject August 10, writing that the previous dispatch was by order of Stanton, "the only condition imposed being that the flag of the United States should be again raised and sustained somewhere within the limits of that State. That order, as I understood it at the time, was of a diplomatic rather than of a military character, and resulted from some European complications, or, more properly speaking, was intended to prevent such complications. . . ." Halleck now declared that in his opinion Indianola and Galveston were not proper points of attack, but that the move should be up the Red River to Alexandria, Natchitoches, or Shreveport, with military occupation of Northern Texas.[10]

In response to Halleck's message urging a movement into Texas, Banks agreed upon the expediency of moving into so important a part of the country, adding that, "The rebellion in Louisiana is kept alive only by Texas. . . ."[11]

5. Roeder, Ralph, *Juarez and His Mexico*, New York, 1947: II, 512.
6. Lincoln, *Works*, VI, 354.
7. Welles, *Diary*, I, 287-391.
8. Lincoln, *Works*, VI, 364-366.
9. *O.R.* I, xxvi, pt. 1, 672.
10. *Ibid.*, 673.
11. *Ibid.*, 697-698.

The Texas operations were carried out in the fall, but fell short of expectations, for in September, 1863, an expedition to the Sabine was defeated by Dick
Dowling and his handful of men at Sabine Pass. In October, the Bayou Teche
expedition got to Opelousas and a little beyond. The Union forces landed at
Brazos Santiago on November 2, and Brownsville, Rio Grande City, Aransas
Pass, and Matagorda Island were occupied, but these small gains did not really
constitute a major occupation of Texas. Halleck continued pressing for an
advance, writing Grant on September 9 that if Frederick Steele from Arkansas
and Banks would succeed, "all the Trans-Mississippi must return to the
Union."[12]

In early December, Banks wrote Lincoln that it had been impossible within
reasonable time to gain a foothold in Texas that season. He thought he did not
have enough strength to march to Texas by either the Sabine or the Red.[13]
Halleck maintained his pressure, and Seward congratulated Banks on the
utility of his Texas operations.[14] Lincoln, on December 24, also thanked Banks
for his "successful and valuable operations in Texas . . . ," urging him "now
to give us a free-state reorganization of Louisiana. . . ."[15] The diplomatic
objectives with regard to Texas had apparently been satisfied.

Halleck continued to advise Banks on a Red River operation in concert
with Steele. Other reinforcements would be found.[16] On January 8, 1864, Halleck told Grant that Banks's campaign against Texas had been less for military
than for political reasons. "The President so ordered," he added, "that it might
be better to direct Union efforts for the present to the entire dispersion of rebel
forces west of the Mississippi rather than to divide the Northern force also
operating against Mobile and Alabama. . . ."[17]

Later historians concluded that the plan of operations was Halleck's, and
that Lincoln approved it.[18] Halleck wired Banks on February 11, 1864,[19] that the
substance of dispatches to him on this subject was given to the President and
Secretary of War, and it was understood that, while stating his own views upon
operations, Halleck should leave the general free to adopt such plans of campaign as he might deem best.

At any rate, Halleck, in his message of January 8, again had urged Banks
to undertake a Red River campaign. Banks had long favored operations against

12. *O.R.* I, xxx, pt. 3, 475.
13. *O.R.* I, xxvi, 833.
14. Johnson, Ludwell, *Red River Campaign*, Baltimore, 1958, 41.
15. Lincoln, *Works*, VII, 89-90.
16. *O.R.* I, xxxiv, pt. 2, 15-16; 29-30.
17. *Ibid.*, 46-47.
18. Randall, James G., and Richard N. Current, *Last Full Measure*, New York, 1955, 145; Nicolay
and Hay, *Lincoln*, VIII, 285ff; Williams, T. Harry, *Lincoln and the Radicals*, Madison, 1941, 341.
19. *O.R.* I, xxxiv, pt. 2, 293-294.

Mobile, along with Grant, but in late January he acquiesced. Having finally agreed to try the Red River, Banks sent Halleck a memorandum specifying certain indispensable steps to success. "Not one of these suggestions, so necessary in conquering the inherent difficulties of the expedition, was carried into execution," he later complained.

On March 12, Admiral Porter's fleet of more than twenty ironclads, tinclads, and other vessels entered the Red River and headed toward Alexandria, convoying the three divisions of Brigadier-General A.J. Smith from Sherman's army. Smith's troops captured Fort De Russey near Simsport, La., March 14; the river fleet went on up to Alexandria by March 15. While Banks was detained in New Orleans by the attempts at Union reconstruction of the State, he sent his troops north to Alexandria under William B. Franklin. By March 24, Banks himself was at Alexandria preparing to advance further toward Shreveport, but was now told he would have to return Sherman's troops by April 10. Thus, another obstacle had to be encountered along with low water, inhospitable country, and snipers. Furthermore, Banks really did not have a unified command. Porter and his navy men were quite independent, while A.J. Smith seemed to fancy his troops completely separate from Banks's army. No firm communications were established with Frederick Steele's expedition coming down through Arkansas. The worst impediment of all was the ravenous greed of the naval and the military forces, as well as the speculators, for the seizure of cotton.

The whole force, moving up the Red River, reached the Natchitoches and Grand Ecore area by April 3. At Sabine Crossroads or Mansfield, Louisiana, on April 8, Richard Taylor's Confederates halted Banks and inflicted on him a stunning defeat that ended the whole advance. Banks began to withdraw, and by April 11 he was back at Grand Ecore. He then retreated further down the Red River to Alexandria. According to his own report on the advance from Alexandria and return, including battles, Banks's losses were 289 killed, 1,541 wounded, and 2,150 missing. According to Taylor, the Federals lost 2,500 prisoners, 20 guns, and 250 wagons, but the repulse was conclusive in the general result, coming close to an utter rout.

The gunboats were now in great peril because of falling water in the Red River. Although the Confederates continued to harass the retreat, most of the vessels were brought safely down the river by the masterly construction of dams under the direction of Lt. Col. Joseph Bailey of Wisconsin. These dams permitted the accumulation of sufficient water to keep the gunboats afloat during their passage. By mid-May, the whole enterprise was over. Because neither the Union nor the Confederate forces had conducted themselves with credit, a bitter series of quarrels ensued on both sides. Meanwhile, Steele's

Union column had to return to Little Rock with little if any visible accomplishment.

The moral results were far-reaching, and for the North unhappy. "After the Red River campaign," wrote a participant who became its most effective historian, "no important operation was undertaken by either side in Louisiana. The Confederate forces in that State held out until the end of the war"—the rebel forces, that is, west of the Mississippi.[20] Moreover, the land attack on Mobile upon which Grant had counted so heavily was postponed.

But even as Banks failed, the really important operations of 1864 were about to begin in Virginia and Georgia.

[I]

"When I assumed command of all the armies"—so Grant began a terse chapter of his memoirs. He went on to explain that when he thus took charge, early in 1864, the Union and Confederate forces held much the same Virginia positions as earlier in the war. They stood equidistant between the Northern and Southern capitals, Grant's main forces lying along the northern bank of the Rapidan, Lee's along the southern. Advantage of numbers was with the Army of the Potomac, but advantage of position with the Army of Northern Virginia. Behind Lee the heavily wooded country was intersected by deep streams, difficult to cross until bridged; the roads were narrow and rough, hopelessly miry after rains. Lee was in position to move in response to Grant's expected drive, and back of him had strong defensive lines around Richmond and on the James to which at need he could retreat.

This had been a triumphant winter for Grant. Shortly before Christmas, leaving Thomas in command at Chattanooga, he had moved his headquarters to Nashville, and begun preparing for the spring campaign against Atlanta. Indeed, he took the first step in February, ordering Thomas to march against Dalton, Ga. His home county in Illinois gave him a diamond-hilted sword with a gold scabbard; Congress voted him its thanks for Chattanooga and a gold medal for the victories there and at Vicksburg; and as he rode in bitterly cold weather from Knoxville through Cumberland Gap to Lexington, Ky., he was cheered in every village. Early in 1864, a bill reviving the grade of Lieutenant-General and authorizing the President to confer it upon the Major-General who was most distinguished for courage, skill, and ability, introduced by Grant's patron Elihu Washburne, moved through Congress.

Its passage was by emphatic votes. However, a few critical voices were

20. Irwin, Richard B., "The Red River Campaign," *Battles and Leaders,* IV, 345, 362; cf. Taylor, Richard, *Destruction and Reconstruction,* New York, 1879, Ch. X.

raised: Grimes of Iowa declared that as Grant was already getting $6,000 a year, he was against ramming the hand of Congress into the Treasury to make his pay $13,000 or $14,000. But nearly everybody applauded Fessenden's assertion that if Grant had been at Antietam he would have demolished Lee, and if at Gettysburg the Confederates would never have recrossed the Potomac. The bill passed the House 96 to 41, and the Senate with only six dissenting voices. Lincoln had meanwhile let it be known that he would like to talk with some close friend of Grant. Washburne thereupon had Russell Jones, Federal Marshal in Illinois, call at the White House, where he volunteered an apt remark. "Mr. President," he said, "perhaps you would like to know whether Grant is going to be a candidate for the Presidency." Upon this, he handed Lincoln a letter in which Grant declared that nothing was further from his mind than high political office, and that he meant to support Lincoln in all circumstances and above all other men.[21]

The law providing for the lieutenant-generalship became effective as February ended. Grant was at once nominated, confirmed, and ordered to Washington. At dusk on March 8 he took a room at Willard's Hotel. He was halfway through dinner before guests noted his presence and raised a sudden cheer, for it was easy to overlook the short, slightly-built man with stooping shoulders, brown hair and beard, reddish mustaches, and mild blue eyes. When he went to the White House that evening—a reception evening—he entered the front door through a considerable crowd, the *Republican* having announced that he would attend. The President, gathering from the commotion that he had arrived, said, "This is General Grant, is it?" and received the equally simple reply, "Yes." As they shook hands, the crowd fell back, with no jostling or pushing. After a short conversation, the President turned Grant over to Seward, who took him to pay his respects to Mrs. Lincoln. Then the Secretary and General entered the East Room together, where amid cheer on cheer Grant was compelled to mount a sofa to shake hands with the throng.[22]

Later, Lincoln sat down in the Blue Room with Stanton and Nicolay to give Grant some instructions. "Tomorrow," he said, "at such time as you may arrange with the Secretary of War, I desire to make you a formal presentation of your commission as Lieutenant-General. I shall then make a very short speech, to which I desire you to reply for an object, and that you may be properly prepared to do so, I have written what I shall say, only four sentences

21. *Congressional Globe*, 38th Cong., 1st sess., Pt. I, 431, 798. In the House, James Garfield and Thaddeus Stevens raised objections. For Jones, see Richardson, Albert D., *A Personal History of Ulysses S. Grant*, Hartford, Conn., 1868, 380ff; Jones, George R., *Joseph Russell Jones*, Chicago, 1964, 42-43; Wilson, James Harrison, "Joseph Russell Jones," manuscript in possession of George R. Jones, 12-13.
22. Nicolay, John G., *Ms. Notes*, Nicolay Papers, LC, March 8, 1864.

in all, which I shall read from my manuscript as an example which you may follow and also read your reply; as you are perhaps not so much accustomed to speaking as myself. I therefore give you what I shall say that you may consider it and form your reply. There are two points that I would like to have you make in your answer: first, to say something which shall prevent or obviate any jealousy of you from any of the other generals in the service, and secondly, something which shall put you on as good terms as possible with the Army of the Potomac."[23]

Next day the ceremony took place at one, with the Cabinet, some staff officers, and Grant's oldest son looking on. Grant's speech had been hurriedly written in lead pencil on a half-sheet of note paper, and between his embarrassment and its illegibility, he stumbled badly, making neither of the points Lincoln had mentioned. Nicolay writes that the President had told him he contemplated bringing the general East to see whether he could not "do something with the unfortunate Army of the Potomac." Grant, determined on no account to fix his headquarters in Washington, immediately left to visit Meade's headquarters at Brandy Station.

This journey to the capital was even more important than people supposed. At first Grant had intended to exercise his supreme command from the West, for before his appointment he had written Halleck and others outlining some curious ideas as to the proper operations for 1864. The Western armies, he thought, should push forward from the Chattanooga-Mobile line to Atlanta and beyond, while the Eastern forces assumed a secondary rôle. "I shall recommend," he wrote Thomas from Nashville on January 19, 1864, "that no attempt be made towards Richmond by any of the routes heretofore operated on, but that a moving force of sixty thousand men be thrown into New Bern, or Suffolk, favoring the latter place, and move out destroying the road as far toward Richmond as possible. Then move to Raleigh as rapidly as possible, hold that point, and open communication with New Bern, even Wilmington. From Raleigh the enemy's most inland line would be so threatened as to force them to keep on it a guard that would reduce their armies in the field much below our own." Fortunately this strategy, evidently devised in distrust of the Army of the Potomac and its leaders, was never adopted.[24]

Instead, Grant's initial ideas were quickly revolutionized by pressure from Lincoln and Stanton, acquaintance with Meade and his staff, and a close view of the Eastern battle front. James Harrison Wilson tells us that Grant had intended not only to keep his headquarters in the West, but to make the tall,

23. *Ibid.*

24. *O.R.* I, xxxii, pt. 2, 100-101, 142, 143. Yet the use of a North Carolina bridgehead was not in itself a bad idea.

impressive William Farrar ("Baldy") Smith field-commander of the Army of the Potomac. Wilson ought to have known, for he had sat in conferences with Grant, Smith, and John A. Rawlins in Nashville, but we need more evidence before we accept his story. At any rate, the notion did not last. Grant's national strategy, he wrote Sherman at the beginning of April, was to move all parts of the Army simultaneously in coordinated action—Banks marching as soon as possible upon Mobile; Sigel advancing in the Shenandoah; and Sherman driving against Johnston's army to scatter it, to penetrate the Confederate interior as far as he could, and to do all damage possible to rebel war resources. He did not intend to lay down a plan of operations for Sherman, but to indicate an objective. From the Shenandoah operations Grant did not expect very much, but he borrowed a phrase from Lincoln to say, "if Sigel can't skin himself, he can hold a leg whilst some one else skins. . . ."[25]

Of course, Lincoln clung to his fundamental idea that the prime object of the North was not to close upon Richmond by water, but to close upon Lee's army by land and destroy it. Stanton held the same view. After talking with them, and with Meade and Ben Butler, and reflecting on the situation, Grant decided upon a direct movement from the Rapidan against Richmond. He also decided that Meade should keep command of the Army of the Potomac, while Smith took a lesser role. He would command one corps under Butler in the Department of the James, Q.A. Gillmore taking the other. Butler's force would then be sent from Fortress Monroe up the James in support of the principal army, trying to force the Confederates back along the river and into the entrenchments around Richmond while Meade drove down from the north. This seemed a good plan, but Smith, Gillmore, and Butler—men as ambitious, temperamental, and imperious as Napoleonic marshals—were soon at crippling odds.[26]

In his 1865 final report, Grant was later to say that he believed a continuous and active series of operations on the part of all troops was essential in 1864. He had felt that for far too long the Eastern and Western armies "acted independently and without concert, like a balky team, no two ever pulling together. . . ." Therefore he had determined to keep as coördinated a pressure as possible upon the enemy, now that Federal forces were under his command. He was convinced that the war could not be won "until the military power of the rebellion was entirely broken. . . ."[27]

25. *Ibid*, pt. 3, 245-246.
26. Grant, *Memoirs*, II, 116-117, 129-132; Wilson, James Harrison, *Life and Services of William Farrar Smith*, Wilmington, 1904, 82-83; Dodge, Granville, M., *Personal Recollections of President Abraham Lincoln, General Ulysses S. Grant and General William T. Sherman*, Council Bluffs, Iowa, 1914, 69-70.
27. Grant, U.S., *Report of Lieutenant General U.S. Grant of the Armies of the United States—1864-'65*, no date, no place, Grant's report of July 22, 1865.

Lincoln's exact rôle in setting up this plan is not altogether clear. Grant and Lincoln were conferring frequently, and even before Grant had come to Washington the President had conversed with him by telegraph. Lincoln is quoted as saying he was "powerfully reminded" of his old suggestion to move upon the whole line of the enemy so as to make use of superior Federal numbers.[28]

The simplicity of the plan is deceptive. At its best it was to involve the entire striking force of the Union, and thus keep the enemy more than busy in several widely separated fields. Yet no one part of the plan was dependent directly upon the other. It was not a house-of-cards whereby if one element failed the whole thing failed. It was directed not only against the armies of Lee and Johnston, but, despite later historians, against the inner fortress of the Confederacy combining all military aims, the enemy's armies, his communications, supplies, bases, territory, and people. It was to be a total offensive and the Union had the manpower and the know-how to carry it out.

[II]

Returning West in mid-March, Grant met Sherman, Rawlins, "Baldy" Smith, and other officers in Nashville, turned over his command to Sherman, and made a significant statement. He had accepted the lieutenant-generalship, he told them, on two conditions: that Washington should not interfere with his plans; and that he should control the commissary, quartermaster, ordnance, and other staff men, hitherto largely independent of the line commanders. Lincoln had replied that, while he possessed no legal authority to assign these officers, "nobody but myself can interfere with your orders, and you can rest assured that I will not do that."[29] Grant's news that he would move his headquarters to the Eastern theatre and keep close to Meade in the field must have been a shock to some of the Western group, although he softened it by adding that he intended to take several of the best Western officers with him.

Circumstances made this decision inescapable, as Lincoln and Stanton doubtless pointed out to Grant. The capture of Vicksburg and Port Hudson, the seizure of the whole line of the Mississippi, and the severance of the Confederacy in two, might well be termed the most decisive single operation of the war; but ultimate victory could be achieved only by bringing Lee and the most powerful single army of the South to surrender. The curious fact, if

28. Hay, John, *Lincoln and the Civil War in the Diaries and Letters of John Hay*, ed. Tyler Dennett, New York, 1939, 178-179.

29. Dodge, Grenville, H., Ms. Autobiography, Iowa State Hist. Soc. In his *Memoirs*, II, 123, Grant tells of an occasion when the President submitted some military ideas. Grant listened respectfully, but "I did not communicate my plans to the President, nor did I to the Secretary of War, or to General Halleck."

fact it be, was that Grant should ever have taken a different view. He was now quick to see the true requirements of the situation just as he was quick to perceive the high qualifications of Meade.

What was to become a strong mutual confidence, invaluable in the war effort, was springing up between Grant and Meade. It was the more important because Sheridan, Rawlins, James Harrison Wilson, and "Baldy" Smith all regarded the Pennsylvanian dubiously, and so did many others. The press felt a positive loathing for Meade, who had shown the inability of many professional military men to realize that the war was not their private affair, but a struggle in which the people had a right to full and free information. He was proud, sensitive, and irascible. In his thin-skinned way he had taken offense at a critical paragraph by the Philadelphia journalist Edward Crapsey, given him a humiliating parade through the lines with a placard reading "Libeler of the Press," and sent him off with orders never to return. In retaliation, correspondents had met and resolved to give Meade little publicity and no favor for the rest of the war.[30] The general's ungovernable temper had made countless enemies in the Army; fellow officers spoke of finding him like a bear with a sore head, nobody willing to approach him. Many political leaders had never forgotten his failure to pursue Lee energetically after Gettysburg. Zack Chandler and Ben Wade, the ruling spirits of the Committee on the Conduct of the War, were so hostile that on March 3 they called upon Lincoln, and told him that a sense of duty to the country compelled them to urge Meade's removal.[31]

Grant, however, saw through Meade's pride, touchiness, and irritability to his deeper merits—his mastery of military principles, and a certain cautious, uninspired, but efficient power of Army management that won the reluctant trust of Lincoln, and the readier esteem of Stanton. Grant knew that the man was restrained and safe, whereas "Baldy" Smith, like Hooker, might be impulsively erratic. Before long, in fact, Grant thought so much of him that when Meade was appointed a major-general in the regular Army, the General-in-chief sent a spirited protest to Henry Wilson because Meade's elevation followed that of Sheridan and Thomas instead of preceding theirs.[32] Meade in time came near a place alongside Rawlins as Grant's chief adviser, although he was never so close a friend.

30. Poore, Benjamin Perley, *Reminiscenses of Sixty Years in the National Metropolis*, New York, 1886, II, 126-127. Crapsey was a reputable correspondent, but printed rumors; Andrews, J. Cutler, *The North Reports the Civil War*, Pittsburgh, 1959, 545-548.

31. Patrick, Marsena, *Inside Lincoln's Army, The Diary of Marsena Rudolph Patrick*, ed. David S. Sparks, New York, 1964, and Wainwright, Charles P., *A Diary of Battle*, ed. Allan Nevins, comment on Meade's irascibility. The Committee castigated Meade harshly for the disastrous repulse before Petersburg, on July 30, 1864.

32. Jan. 23, 1865, copy in Meade Papers, Hist. Soc. of Pa.; Wilson was still head of the Senate Military Committee.

The desire of Grant to take able Western officers with him naturally elicited a strong protest from the volatile Sherman. He did not want to be left with second-raters. In the end, Grant had just a few Western stars with him, the chief being Sheridan in command of his cavalry. He also detached James Harrison Wilson, a brilliant topographical engineer by training, who had fought under McClellan and had become a major-general only five years after leaving West Point while head of the cavalry of a key division of Sherman's command. Grant assured Sherman that Wilson would add one-half to the effectiveness of his cavalry. "Baldy" Smith on the James and the ever-faithful Rawlins as heart of his staff were also withdrawn from the West. Sherman kept some of the best officers, of whom two, McPherson and Thomas, could be accounted hosts in themselves, while John M. Schofield, an Illinoisan who had roomed at West Point with McPherson and had seen eventful experience with Lyon in Missouri, possessed administrative gifts of unusual value. (In due course, Schofield and James Harrison Wilson, like Grant and Sherman, were to publish memoirs of exceptional penetration and vigor.)

While still in Nashville, Grant announced to Sherman, Rawlins, and others, that he intended to set all the Northern armies in motion on a given day, and that they must help make certain that Lee could not reinforce Joe Johnston, and that Johnston could not reinforce Lee. His poise and serenity did not fail him as he began preparing orders to his generals. In the East he had studied with concentrated care all the data upon the strength and resources of the chief commands, and had talked with Halleck, who had constantly urged that more troops be raised. Even though we discount somewhat the praise that Sherman later gave to the wonderful precision of Grant's mind and plans,[33] nevertheless, even if the instructions that he gave Sherman in two letters of April 4 and April 19, 1864, were not quite as complete as any of Wellington's to his lieutenants (this was Sherman's comparison), they were remarkably clear and detailed.

On the other side, Lee, who used scouts and spies to keep informed, was perplexed and distressed. "The approach of spring," he wrote Jefferson Davis, "causes me to consider with anxiety the probable action of the enemy and the possible operations of our armies in the ensuing campaign." This was a stiff way of saying, "I am worried about their probable sword-thrust and how we can parry it." He added, "If we could take the initiative and fall upon them unexpectedly, we might damage their plans and embarrass them the whole summer." A big if! The South might strengthen Longstreet in Tennessee for a sudden blow; or—another big if—Lee might draw Longstreet secretly and

33. Sherman, W.T., "The Grand Strategy of the War of the Rebellion," *Century Magazine*, February 1888, XL, No. 4, 591; *O.R.* I, xxxii, pt. 3, 245-246, 409f.

rapidly to his side, and force Meade back to Washington, creating sufficient alarm to weaken any Union offensive. Thus he looked desperately from side to side to escape the coming blow. He had no desire for another Antietam or Gettysburg—"We are not in a position, and never have been in my opinion, to invade the enemy's country with a prospect of permanent benefit."[34]

On March 23, Grant was back in Washington, and three days later made his headquarters at Culpeper Court House. On his passage through the capital the author of *Two Years Before the Mast* glimpsed him, a man with no gait, no manners, no dignity, and a scrubby aspect withal. "He had a cigar in his mouth, and rather the look of a man who did, or once did, take a little too much to drink."[35] Only on closer scrutiny did Richard Henry Dana perceive that the shabby officer, like somebody shelved on half-pay with nothing to do but loaf around Willard's, "had a clear blue eye, and a look of resolution, as if he could not be trifled with, and an entire indifference to the crowd about him." Next morning Dana recorded some fresh impressions. "He gets over the ground queerly. He does not march, nor quite walk, but pitches along as if the next step would bring him on his nose. But his face looks firm and hard. . . ." His air of determination impressed a Yankee colonel, Theodore Lyman, who noted that "he habitually wears an expression as if he had determined to drive his head through a brick wall, and was about to do it." Late in life Grant remarked that a successful general required so much health, resilience, and energy that he would not like to put one in the field past fifty.[36] He was in excellent health, and about forty-two.

[III]

Thus Grant devoted April to his final preparations. In the seventeen different departments under his command he had probably about 535,000 men present for duty. He would have to give direction first of all, of course, to Meade in Virginia, who by conservative estimates at the end of April had in the Army of the Potomac 102,000 present for duty. Burnside's Ninth Corps, operating with this army though for a time not part of it, would participate in the campaign with enough men to give Grant a total of 121,500. Ben Butler's army

34. Lee to Davis, Feb. 3, 1864, A. De Coppet Collection, Princeton Univ. Lee knew that the Army of the Potomac would move in the spring, that it was being reorganized, that every train brought it fresh recruits, that every available regiment at the North was said to be destined to it, and that camps and railroads were guarded with a closeness that pointed to secret preparations. Davis to Lee, *Ibid.*, March 30, 1864.

35. R.H. Dana Jr., to his wife, April 21, 1864, Dana Papers, Mass. Hist. Soc.

36. Lyman, Theodore, *Meade's Headquarters, 1863-1865*, Boston, 1922, 80-83; Young, J.R., *Around the World with General Grant*, New York, 1879, II, 353.

for the advance up the James numbered 53,000.[37] Grant would try to coördinate Butler's movements and those of Franz Sigel's force in the Shenandoah with his own main army. He would have difficulties, for his subordinate generals had their idiosyncrasies.

Butler's abilities were unquestionable, and he was a forcible administrator. He was also a master of quick, clever marches, feints, ruses, and shrewd surprises. He had held difficult posts in Baltimore and New Orleans with great credit, great publicity, and great friction. Nobody ever doubted his energy; nearly everybody doubted his character. He was endlessly useful and endlessly troublesome. Only a Dickens could do justice to his remarkable combination of gifts, faults, and picturesque anfractuosities. Long hampered and limited, he at last rejoiced in an independent and important theatre of action. Compared with him, Sigel, now briefly commander of the Department of West Virginia, was all too simple. This German revolutionary, New York militiaman, and St. Louis school director, journalist, and politician, had two great assets—fiery zeal for high causes, and eloquent power in rallying German-Americans to the Union. He had also two deep-seated defects—bad judgment and general clumsiness. It was not long until Grant pushed him aside for "lack of aggression." As for Burnside of the famous muttonchop whiskers, a handsome failure, an impressive blunderer, he had at last scored his second notable success by capturing Knoxville, the strategic heart of East Tennessee. After this (he entered the city September 2-3, 1863), hardy mountaineers flocked to him in groups of twenty and fifty, with their horses, to enlist. Burnside had then defended the city successfully against Longstreet's thrust later in the fall. It could be said to Burnside's discredit that he was unfit to command an army, and to his credit that he knew it.[38]

Facing Grant stood Lee, with about 62,000 men present for duty after Longstreet rejoined him, and with his unquestioned genius.[39]

In giving some direction to all the armies of the republic, East and West, Grant would have to rely heavily upon the telegraph system as it reached out to all the headquarters. Even with the network that Eckert had established, the task would be difficult, particularly in keeping contact with armies on active operations. Grant would also have to allow a large autonomy to his most trusted generals, especially Sherman, and to work out an amicable *modus ope-*

---

37. According to *O.R.* I, xxxiii, 1036, 1045, 1053. The figures in Humphreys, A.A., *The Virginia Campaign of 1864 and 1865*, New York, 1879, 14-17, and in Porter, Horace, *Campaigning with Grant*, New York, 1897, 36-41, are essentially the same. See also *O.R.* I, xxxiii, 1297-1298.

38. "Burnside in Knoxville," New York *Tribune*, Sept. 8, 1863. See Grant's verdict in his *Memoirs*, II, 539.

39. Freeman, Douglas Southall, *R.E. Lee*, New York, 1934, III, 270, gives the Confederate numbers most authoritatively.

randi with Meade, yokefellow rather than subordinate on the front against Lee. Would the partnership with so sensitive, hot-tempered a man succeed? It was to the credit of both that it ran almost as smoothly as the yoking of Lee and Stonewall Jackson had run, and with almost the same lubricant of mutual respect—though Grant and Meade could never be called men of complementary genius like Lee and Jackson.

Grant's elevation to the chief command meant almost total extinguishment for Halleck. The lamp that had never burned brightly now gave off waning rays. John Hay had erroneously concluded that Halleck was "badly billious" about the new chief and his steady rise, but he really was not, in part because he knew that he had dropped below all license to jealousy. Lincoln had become contemptuously frank, to intimates, about his incapacity. The President recalled that when the government sent for Halleck after the failure of the Peninsular campaign, the general had stipulated that he be given the responsibility and power of a commander-in-chief. He enjoyed that altitude until his selected army commander Pope collapsed at Second Manassas while the thunder of Lee's guns vibrated in the Washington streets. Then, said Lincoln, Halleck lost all nerve and pluck, so that he became little more than a first-rate clerk, evading all large responsibilities. He had been adroit enough to manoeuvre Hooker, just before Gettysburg, into a position where Hooker felt constrained to resign, but to do this he had needed the help of Stanton and of Hooker's own ineptness. From the moment of Grant's elevation he relapsed, with good grace, into the position of a capable office-manager in Washington for the general. Many officers regarded him as scornfully as did Ben Butler.[40]

The destiny of the country now rested upon two Mid-Westerners, Lincoln and Grant. They had sprung from the common people of the Mississippi Valley; they had scanty background of cultivated homes or communities; a dozen years earlier they had been obscure. In fact, they had long seemed without heroic traits. As Lincoln had entered the Presidency untutored in administration and needing to learn countless lessons as he went, so Grant had entered upon high command ignorant of large-scale war. At Belmont he had been an amateur relying heavily upon luck. At Forts Henry and Donelson his luck held, though some of his movements compared dubiously with those of the older, more experienced Charles F. Smith. At Shiloh he was still amateurish, making dire blunders before the battle just as did Sherman. But he enjoyed three blessings: the opportunity to rise gradually from low rank; the capacity

40. Ben Butler exploded this July: "Now there is General Halleck, what has *he* to do? At a moment when every true man is laboring to his utmost, when the days ought to be forty hours long, General Halleck is translating French books [on strategy] at nine cents a page; and sir, if you should put those nine cents in a box and shake them up, you would form a clear idea of General Halleck's soul!" Lyman, *Meade's Headquarters, 1863-1865*, Boston, 1922, 193.

to learn rapidly from his errors; and the assistance of loyal and discerning men who divined his potentialities. Fellow generals helped him; Elihu Washburne helped him; friendly newspapermen in Chicago and New York helped him—and he justified their faith.

His principal gift was that which English-speaking peoples have always esteemed most, strength of character. Intellectually, he must be ranked below the major strategists of the war; below Joe Johnston, Sherman, and Thomas —far below Stonewall Jackson and Lee. Although his memoirs are justly esteemed to be among the ablest of all military reminiscences, and show in the first volume especially (before illness impaired his powers) much lucidity and penetration, they exhibit more soundness of judgment than strength of reflection. They are as devoid of subtlety or imagination as Caesar's, and their conclusions are sometimes defensive rationalizations, after the event, of lines of action ill-planned at the time. They disclose little of the intellectual power of Napoleon, Wavell, or Bradley.

For the work of the fighter, however, he had better qualities than those of the cerebral gymnast. One was logical vision. He was a clear, simple thinker, with the power of sorting out from many facts the few that were vitally important, of seeing in a complex situation the basic outline. He saw how important it was to seize Paducah in 1861, how Donelson could be taken in 1862, how Vicksburg could be captured in 1863 by a flanking march to the south, and how Chattanooga could be made a gateway to Georgia and the Carolinas in 1864. He saw that when he had established a line in Virginia a little longer than Lee's, a repulse could mean simply a swing to the flank. His staff filled him with facts and theories from which he selected the few that counted. Too much imagination about enemy numbers had paralyzed McClellan; too much pedantry about logistics had ruined Rosecrans; but if Grant was sometimes too simple, as when before Shiloh he thought that one battle might mean final victory, his grasp of essentials rested upon an extremely shrewd faculty of elimination.

His soundness of judgment was supported, like Lee's and Wellington's, by traits that helped make him a great captain. First of these was his decisive promptness. Having made up his mind about a situation, he moved. He did not wait for perfection in training and equipment, an impeccable plan, or overwhelming numerical superiority. He marched—on Paducah, Donelson, Grand Gulf, Jackson, Vicksburg, Petersburg. Second, was his nerve; in tight squeezes he kept his head. At Belmont, he coolly waded his horse out of a Confederate trap. At Donelson, he rallied the line and calmly inspected the Confederate knapsacks. After the first day at Shiloh, he waited unperturbed for dawn, for Buell's arrival, and the wavering of the Confederate onset. A third trait was tenacity. He never knew when he was beaten, for he had the bulldog instinct to hold fast.

With some reservations, we may also say that he had an instinctive ability to distinguish between true and false humanitarianism. A man of gentle ways, never angrier than when he saw a horse maltreated, he tried in the main to spare his troops useless bloodshed. Yet he saw that the truest economy in lives was often a temporary ruthlessness in expending them. He would not have hesitated to follow the Confederate repulse at Gettysburg by firm, unhesitating action.

And another invaluable trait was his strong instinct for obedience to the civil arm. Although naïve in civil affairs, seldom fully grasping them, he knew that when the President and Congress ordered, he must obey. And by the word "obey," as he proved in recruiting Negroes, he meant complete obedience. McClellan, Butler, McClernand, Frémont, Hooker, and Banks played politics with the Army, but never Grant.

Much might also be said about his modesty, contrasting with the strut of other generals; his avoidance of loose language and profanity; his Spartan regimen, a weakness for liquor at relaxed moments excepted; and his generosity to the foe, well illustrated by his letter explaining why he dealt so magnanimously with the prisoners taken at Vicksburg. To be sure, he had his share of faults and shortcomings. Generosity was not evident in his jealous attitude toward his rival McClernand or his perplexing treatment of Thomas. Regard for candor came under eclipse when he deliberately obscured the facts by failing to send in a proper report on Shiloh. Conscientiously vigilant in days of crisis, he marred his record by two deplorable sprees on slack days in loose surroundings. Down to Vicksburg he appeared to many comrades in arms simply a resolute soldier of common abilities and impulses—and some thought much too common.[41]

But he had elemental strength when the republic needed precisely that, and needed it above all else. Lincoln summed up this supreme fact in explaining why he preferred Grant to other generals: "He fights." Then, too, Sherman put his finger on another vital point when he wrote that Grant was "a growing general" throughout the war; he grew all the way from Camp Yates to Appomattox.[42]

Such a man could make mistake after mistake, and still profit by his errors. Military associates of Grant pointed to a variety of blunders. At Belmont, they said, he had mismanaged two brigades, let some of his troops become a rabble

41. See Grant, *Memoirs*, I, 570-572, for his fine position on the Vicksburg prisoners. One spree was reportedly at Vicksburg, another in New Orleans.
42. Sherman to a friend Nov. 18, 1879, in *Century Magazine*, April 1897, 821.

of looters, and almost lost a regiment, the 27th Illinois. After that engagement he should have organized a working staff, but neglected it, and let his time be carelessly devoured by details. When he marched after Fort Henry from the Tennessee to the Cumberland, he permitted excessive dispersion of his troops; and some thought after Donelson that he seemed too confused by his unexpected victory to grasp the rich fruits at hand. For his failure to entrench at Shiloh and throw out scouts he might well have been cashiered. His loss of men and stores at Holly Springs could not be blamed entirely upon a stupid subordinate, and his first bloody assault upon the Confederate lines at Vicksburg was a cruel error. But all generals err, Grant profited more than most from error, and as Lincoln declared: "He fights."[43]

Three comments shed some illumination upon the innermost man. Horace Porter believed that Grant's most extraordinary quality was his simplicity, a simplicity so extreme that many overlooked it. A remark by John M. Schofield reinforces the statement of Hamilton Fish that Grant was the most truthful man he ever knew. "He was incapable of any attempt to deceive anybody except for a legitimate purpose, as in military strategy; and above all, he was incapable of deceiving himself." A mail clerk at Grant's headquarters added another perceptive bit. The general was always perfectly self-possessed, giving the impression that he knew what he meant to do without hesitation or fluster. "He was never in a hurry."[44]

[IV]

On May 3-4, 1864, at the same time that Butler commenced moving his troops up the James River, the Army of the Potomac began moving across the Rapidan, using fords and pontoon bridges, and pressed into the wooded country beyond. Sherman was to advance from Chattanooga two days later with the combined Armies of the Tennessee, the Cumberland, and the Ohio. The grand coordinated sweep had begun. The Army of the Potomac was Meade's army, for any orders Grant gave it were delivered through Meade. It was also an Army of tested corps commanders—Sedgwick, longer with this force than any other high officer; Hancock, supervising most of the trains, in the field for the first time since his Gettysburg wound; Warren, one of the first regular Army officers to ask and receive high volunteer command.[45] But the most important fact was that the days of disjointed action, when the armies of the

43. See criticisms by A.L. Conger, "The Military Education of Grant as a General," *Wisconsin Magazine of History*, (1920-21) IV, 239-260.

44. Porter, *Campaigning with Grant, op. cit*; 13-16, 515 and *passim*. Garland, Hamlin, Interview with Schofield, Garland Papers, UCLA, Box 49; interview with M.H. Strong, *ibid.*

45. Page, C.S., New York *Tribune*, May 6, 1864.

West and of the East had acted independently, with confusing complications, were at an end. The Confederates still had the advantage of interior lines, but the Union possessed the greater advantage of superior numbers, managed with centralized control.[46] Colonel G.F.R. Henderson, who praises as warmly the fighting qualities of the Union soldiers as the wisely planned strategy of Grant, points out that after Grant assumed command, Lincoln ceased his anxious and well-meant but often vexatious and unwise interference with Federal military commanders. The spirit of the troops was high. Many familiar place-names reappeared in dispatches: Ely's Ford, Chancellorsville, Thoroughfare Gap, Germanna Ford. As the first advance, with Warren in the rear, gained distances up to a dozen miles, Stanton expressed a hope of "full and complete success." Grant was elated. Although he had crossed the river just where Lee had expected, the formidable Southern army did little to obstruct him, the first movements of Longstreet, who arrived on the 6th, being dilatory. Some Union divisions might have thrust farther south, but this would have exposed them to a flank attack, left their trains insecure, and tired the men on the eve of heavy fighting.[47] The object was not to take Richmond, but to destroy or paralyze Lee's army—a less costly and arduous operation.

Sunrise on May 5 found the Army of the Potomac pushing deep into the fitly-named Wilderness. This was a district of low sandy soil, worthless for agriculture, but covered, save for scattered open patches and swampy spots, with fairly dense thickets of oak, hickory, and pine, stunted to the size of saplings fifteen to thirty feet tall. The dense bushes and half-formed leaves of the hardwood stands shut off the vision at about fifty yards. When the gray skirmishers of A.P. Hill's corps opened fire on some Union troops under G. W. Getty, they were within easy range, but quite invisible.[48] The fighting immediately became fierce, until in many places the battle-lines grappled at almost pointblank range. Inevitably, as smoke filled the woods, the troops desperately wielding axes to fell trees and bushes became confused. Some regiments lost touch with other units of their division; and the contest swayed back and forth, with sharp losses, but no real advantage on either side. The use of artillery or cavalry was impossible, and any manoeuvering extremely difficult. On the second day of the fighting Longstreet was seriously wounded, a heavy blow to the South, while the North lost James S. Wadsworth. The death

46. Cf. G.F.R. Henderson, *The Science of War*, London, 1910, 255-279.

47. Stanton's phrase is in the dispatch of May 8 to Gen. John A. Dix in New York; New York *Tribune*, May 9. See Law, E.M., "From the Wilderness to Cold Harbor," *Battles and Leaders*, IV, 118, and Wolseley, Garnet Joseph, *The American Civil War*, ed. James A. Rowley, Charlottesville, Va., 1964, 197-199; Grant, *Memoirs*, II, 177ff; Humphreys, *The Virginia Campaigns of 1864 and 1865*, 20ff; and Grant's report in *O.R.* I, xxxvi, pt. 1, 18ff.

48. Lyman, Theodore, *Meade's Headquarters*, op.cit., 89.

of this high-minded, intrepid, and patriotic veteran of Gettysburg, shot in the head while rallying troops and expiring next day within enemy lines, caused great grief in his own area of upper New York State. Impetuous attacks, for both Grant's and Lee's armies had resolved to attack, developed into a stern contest of endurance, not unlike the tenacious fighting about Port Arthur in the Russo-Japanese War, or in front of Stalingrad in the Second World War.

Why did the Union army attack in this Wilderness tangle? Grant told the eight senior members of his staff the night before his offensive that he had weighed the question whether he should assault Lee's left, or his right. A movement against the rebel left offered more decisive results if it succeeded, and would best block any attempt by Lee at a northward thrust, but it would cut off the Union army from easy communication with its bases on the Rappahannock and Potomac, and compel transportation of huge quantities of ammunition and other supplies by heavily guarded wagon-trains. A blow against Lee's right would be facilitated by easy water carriage, for materials could be brought up from the junction of the Rappahannock and Rapidan, while wounded men could be taken out by the same smooth water carriage. Troops fighting on Lee's right would also be nearer Ben Butler's army advancing up the James. Though Meade emphatically disagreed, he was overruled.[49]

Hence Grant and Meade had crossed the Rapidan below the main position of Lee's army, Confederate headquarters being at Orange Court House. They hoped to defeat Lee, or at least push him back into the fortifications about Richmond. Grant had no burning desire to take that city, and no desire whatever to make an assault against troops protected by its defenses. He had always comprehended the possibility that he might have to conduct a siege of Richmond or the Richmond-Petersburg axis. If necessary, he had written Meade on April 17, siege-guns, shells, and general equipment could be rapidly brought from the Washington arsenal and Fortress Monroe. Preparations had been made for all types of water transportation, connecting with land carriage. "The means of moving heavy artillery is always at hand with an army as well as the means of constructing batteries. I will take advantage of Gen. Hunt's

49. A friend of Meade's, Henry Carey Baird, set down some reminiscences in his papers in the E. C. Gardiner Collection of the State Historical Society of Pennsylvania. He quoted Meade as saying that he and Grant had only one sharp disagreement. This was just before the Rapidan crossing. "I wanted," General Meade said, "to move by the right flank, while General Grant wished to move by the left." Grant said, "General Meade, I wish you to understand that this army is not to manoeuvre for position." Meade replied, "General Grant, you will find that you have a consummate general to fight, and that you will have to manoeuvre for position." Meade added that the army never did anything but manoeuvre for position, and never got it. *Newsletter* of Ulysses S. Grant Assoc., Vol. III, No. 3, April 1966.

suggestions as to the number, calibre, etc. of guns necessary for it." Yet he looked forward to open battle, not to siege operations.[50]

Tension rose high in the North. Stanton telegraphed Dix on the 9th that the fighting of the previous days had been the fiercest in modern times. Grave anxiety persisted as news of the two-day battle of the Wilderness trickled in. The struggling armies had been introduced to the area in the Chancellorsville fighting; now they were clasped to its thorny bosom. Tangled trees and brush, uneven ground, and numberless pits and gullies, made it impossible for either side to preserve distinct formations, so that men fought by squads, not companies. Only the roar of rifle-fire, as Hancock later wrote, disclosed the position of the troops to those at a distance, the thud of artillery punctuating it, although in this area cannon could be little used.[51] As fighting began, Ewell and Hill moved forward to meet the Union advance. The Southerners profited somewhat from their superior knowledge of the terrain, the Federal maps being inaccurate and confusing, and from the fact that the inhabitants could tell them about the little woods roads, the clearings, the winding streamlets, the shafts sunk in places for iron ore, and the swampy spots left undrained.

The general direction of the Confederate attack was from the southwest, striking the Union flank as Grant moved southeast; and the rebels struck hard.

Grant's aide Horace Porter gives us graphic vignettes of the general in action. Riding forward on May 5th, he found Meade waiting at the intersection of two highways near the deserted Wilderness Tavern and its weed-grown yard. Here he ordered all forces to seize the initiative and attack vigorously, and then rode on with Warren, Grant slouchy in his plain garb, Warren smart in a fresh blue uniform with yellow sash. The fighting that day left Grant fairly satisfied, though as he said, both sides battled against the forest rather than each other. But the combat on the 6th, when it reached its climax, was quite different in outcome. On their right the Union forces got nowhere, in the center they made little progress, and on their left one brigade after another was thrown back in confusion. At one time late that afternoon word came that the enemy had burst entirely *through* Hancock's line. At headquarters Grant and Meade, their backs to a tree, heard the officer bearing the report, sent reinforcements, and listened impassively to the distant battle clamor. Then Grant said with laconic emphasis, "I don't believe it"—and he was right.[52]

50. For the letter to Meade, see Meade Papers, State Hist. Soc. of Pennsylvania. A little later, April 26, Grant had written Halleck, "The Army of the Potomac is in splendid condition and evidently feels like whipping somebody; I feel much better with this command than I did before seeing it." Ill. State Hist. Soc.

51. Humphreys, *op.cit.*, 44 ftn.; Lyman, *Meade's Headquarters, op.cit.*, 90.

52. Porter, *Campaigning with Grant, op.cit.*, 53-54, 59; C.A. Page in New York *Tribune*, May 10, 1864.

During the afternoon of May 6th, General John B. Gordon's brigades captured two Union generals, Alexander Shaler and Truman Seymour, forced their troops into ragged disarray, and took many prisoners. As twilight deepened the Southerners, struggling through the thickets, themselves became disorganized. It was fortunate, Early writes, that darkness fell to close the affray, for the Northerners might have perceived the disorder and taken advantage of it.[53] That daytime battle had been gloomy enough—gloomy with the shadow of death. Trees riddled by the artillery fell with a crash. Forest fires raged, with ammunition wagons exploding, dead bodies roasting, and wounded crawling frantically to escape the flames.

Yet Grant slept soundly that night, and was up at dawn on the 7th to sit by the campfire in foggy air still darkened by smoke. Porter's hero-worshipping book puts some complacent utterances in Grant's mouth. According to Porter, Grant spoke of the previous day as in one sense a drawn battle, but really an advantage for the North. "We remain in possession of the field, and the forces opposed to us have withdrawn to a distance from our front and taken up a defensive position." This alleged comment, published in 1897, thirty-odd years after the event, does not sound like the modest Grant—and it was not accurate. Lee had been substantially on the defensive from the beginning, and the fact that his numerically inferior army had not smashed the Union lines was nothing to boast about. And what of the price of the battle? Men presently ascertained that the Union losses on the 5th and 6th of May had been fearful. The Army of the Potomac, with Burnside's corps, lost 12,485 men killed and wounded, while lists of the missing brought casualties up to 15,500. The Confederate losses were at most 8,000 killed and wounded, and 3,400 missing.[54]

Once more, long rosters of dead and maimed darkened the pages of newspapers North and South. One of the best Union regiments, the Twentieth Massachusetts, had lost about one-third of its men. Philadelphia had a day of mourning as the brave General James S. Wadsworth's body, delivered to Union troops by the Confederates, was brought through the city to be laid at rest in the Genesee Valley. Many a town and hamlet, many a country farmhouse, were draped in black as thousands of families met the shock of bereavement. And how gloomy the scene of the slaughter! Theodore Lyman wrote that most officers had seen no rebels, only smoke, bushes, and blue-clad men tumbling in all directions. Gone were the days of lines advancing, bands playing, and

53. Early, Jubal A., *Autobiographical Sketch and Narrative of the War Between the States*, Philadelphia, 1912, 346-351. See the anonymous "Recollections of Jubal Early," *Century Magazine*, N.S., XLV, 1905, 311-313.

54. Porter, *Campaigning with Grant, op.cit.*, 65-76; Humphreys, *op.cit.*, 53, 54. The figures for Union losses as given in *O.R.* I, xxxvi, pt. 1, 133, are 2,246 killed, 12,037 wounded, and 3,383 missing, a total of 17,666. Freeman, *Lee*, III, 297, states the Confederate losses in killed and wounded at 7,600.

platoons delivering united volleys. Now the officers bellowed, "Left face—prime—forward!"; the muskets went wrang, wr-r-rang for hours; and as brush fires started, the bleeding wounded streamed to the rear.[55]

It was clear to Union observers on the 7th that continued attempts to force through the Wilderness would be bloody futility, and that the Northern army must be swung to a route where it could attack in open country. As Grant sat under a pine tree stoically pondering on the third day, Colonel Lyman heard him say: "Tonight Lee will be retreating south."[56] Lee had no such intention. He had the use of two good parallel roads in holding on—the Orange and Fredericksburg plank-road and the Orange and Fredericksburg turnpike, running east from Orange directly against Grant's advancing line. On the night of the 4th, the front forces of the two armies had made bivouac in close proximity to each other on the roads just named; and on the morning of the 5th, while the Union columns continued their dogged advance, Ewell on the Confederate side, with equal doggedness, went on marching eastward, so that a lively clash was resumed. The Union men who pretended that they had won a strategic success in Lee's failure to fling back their advance upon Richmond claimed too much. Lee *had* momentarily stopped them. His army was more daring and rapid; it showed a fiercer discipline—in part the discipline of desperation, in part the discipline of tremendous faith in its leaders; it made better use of entrenchments. Only dubious consolation could be found in the losses Hancock and Sedgwick had inflicted, for the larger number of fresh graves lay on the Northern side. The real comfort for Grant was that his vastly stronger army held Lee, not so tightly that he could not manoeuvre, but so firmly that he could never advance.

As the battle closed, a Northern Senator, surveying the frightful carnage, exclaimed: "If that scene could have been presented to me before the war, anxious as I was for the preservation of the Union, I should have said: 'The cost is too great; erring sisters, go in peace.' " A Southern Senator would have said, "Ah, what folly to secede!"[57]

At dawn on the 7th, the initiative seemed to lie with Lee. Would he attack

55. Pearson, H.G., *James Wadsworth of Geneseo*, New York, 1903, 289-290; Lyman, *Meade's Headquarters, op.cit.*, 101.

56. Lyman, *op. cit.*, 102.

57. This statement by Henry Wilson, Senator from Massachusetts and Vice-President, known as "the cobbler of Natick" when he entered public life, was characteristic of his humanitarian attitude toward battle costs—an attitude widely shared North and South by both Union and Confederate leaders witnessing the truly appalling mortality on the battlefield. According to Kirkley, statistician of the War Department, the Union army lost 67,058 men killed, and 43,012 died of wounds received on the battlefield. The Confederate rolls justify Thomas L. Livermore in estimating the Confederate losses as 86,886 killed and died of battle action, which he says "must be much below the full number." Livermore, *Numbers and Losses, in the Civil War in America*, 6.

at the center, lie still behind his fortified line, or launch a flank movement?
Union troops quickly ascertained that the Confederate front was so fully
intrenched, with powerful artillery at hand, that a charge was impracticable.
But Grant had already decided upon a night march southeast to Spotsylvania
Court House, between him and Richmond. Detailed orders were issued.
Wagon trains were to move at four in advance of the infantry. At dusk they
were to park, and let Warren's troops pass them, while Hancock's corps held
a screening position. After Warren had gone, Hancock was to follow him.
Grant hoped that, containing Lee's right flank, he could move on toward the
rebel capital.[58]

But Lee, who knew the importance of Spotsylvania, had anticipated the
stroke. In the race for the crossroads he intended to win, again barring Grant's
road—and win he did. By dawn of the 8th, two Confederate divisions under
General Richard H. Anderson were in position to assist Fitzhugh Lee's cavalry
in halting the Union advance. During a morning clash, Northern visions of
an easy progress melted away in the reality of another bloody field with a series
of uncertain battles beyond it.

[V]

Meanwhile, the restlessly energetic Sherman had put his armies on the
march just after Grant's. "We are now moving," he wrote his wife from
Chattanooga on May 4, "I will go to Ringgold tomorrow, and will then be
within five miles of the enemy."[59] His letter breathed the assurance of Nelson's
famous dispatch written "within sight of the combined fleets of France and
Spain." Yet he did not underestimate his task, for he knew that it would
require a strong army to push into a hostile country along a single railroad,
and against his determined opponent, Joseph E. Johnston, leading between
60,000 and 70,000 effective troops. Sherman's three corps commanders,
Thomas at Chattanooga with more than 60,000 men, McPherson in northern
Alabama with about 30,000, and Schofield in eastern Tennessee with around
17,000, could concentrate in a way to give him more than 100,000 troops. In fact,
he soon put his fighting strength at 112,000 including cavalry, and added that
he could not possibly supply more. He had capably equipped his force with
horses, wagons, ammunition, provisions, and forage, and he felt complete
confidence in it. It is a big army and a good one, he wrote his wife, and a little

58. Grant, *Memoirs*, II, 208-212, where Grant asserted that "Lee, by accident, beat us to Spotsylvania;" Meade's Report in *O.R.* I, xxxvi, pt. 1, 189-190.
59. Sherman, William T., *Home Letters of General Sherman*, ed. M.A. DeWolfe Howe, New York,
1909, 288-295.

later, in his exuberant way, he crowed a bit more lustily: "I think I have the best army in the country."[60]

His objectives might be defined as the capture of the vital railway center of Atlanta, the crippling or destruction of Johnston's army, and the further splitting of the Confederacy. He had just told Thomas, "We must whip Joe Johnston wherever he may be."[61] He would have to battle a mountainous country traversed by many streams, its rough, wooded slopes and steeps giving the Confederates many advantages. Johnston had entrenched himself in front of Dalton, a quarter of the way from Chattanooga to Atlanta, and had laid out excellent defensive positions in his rear all the way back. The weather, too, interposed obstacles. At first it was excessively hot; then a fortnight of heavy rains set in. Sherman was certain, however, that he could at least press Johnston close, and prevent his sending any aid to Lee, or to the Confederate defenders of Mobile. Thus he would perform his part in the Grand Plan of the Union high command. Had Banks been able to move against Mobile, this would have prevented Polk from taking strong reinforcements to Johnston in Georgia, where they arrived in time for the Resaca fighting.[62]

The temperamental Sherman, always extreme in opinions and vehement in language, set out on his campaign in a savage frame of mind. The heroic determination that Southerners manifested in fighting on after the loss of kindred, homes, property, and even hope, had given him some harsh convictions. "There is no doubt," he wrote his brother John in Congress, "we have to repeople the country and the sooner we set about it the better. Captured houses and lands must be repeopled by Northern settlers. The whole population of Iowa and Wisconsin should be transferred at once to West Kentucky, Tennessee, Mississippi, and a few hundred thousand settlers should be pushed into South Tennessee." Although such embittered statements were impulsively irrational, the fact that they came from a general leading an armed march into Georgia was ominous. Sherman had been deeply angered by the recent Fort Pillow "massacre" and by the murderous terrorism of irregulars. "You may order all your post and district commanders," he shortly wrote a Kentucky general, "that guerrillas are not soldiers, but wild beasts, unknown to the usages of war."[63]

60. *O.R.* I, xxxii, pt. 3, 468-469; Govan, G.E. and J.W. Livingood, *A Different Valor, the Story of General Joseph E. Johnston, C.S.A.*, Indianapolis, 1956, 250-262; Cox, Jacob D., *Atlanta*, New York, 1882, 26-28.

61. Letter in extra-illustrated copy of *Battles and Leaders*, XIII, HEH.

62. *O.R.* I, xxxii, pt.3, 245ff, 312ff, with Grant-Sherman correspondence; Polk, W.M., *Leonidas Polk, Bishop and General*, New York, 1915, II, Chap. IX.

63. To John Sherman, April 11, 1864, William T. Sherman Papers, LC; to Gen. Stephen G. Burbridge, Cincinnati *Enquirer*, July 12, 1864.

He was resolved to make Southerners *feel* the war. He would shortly write the mayor of Atlanta that it was time for rebels to taste the woes they had inflicted on others. "I myself have seen in Missouri, Kentucky, Tennessee, and Mississippi hundreds and thousands of women and children fleeing from your armies and desperadoes, hungry and with bleeding feet." Army-men were learning that Sherman's mind had more velocity, his emotions a deeper intensity, and his temper a sharper edge than those of any other commander North or South. His nature was a compound of sharply defined and sometimes contradictory traits; if he had the iron will of a Cromwell and the energy of a Hamilton, he had also some of the fierceness of a Tamerlane. When he found some of his foraging troops murdered, he ordered instant reprisals in the shooting of an equal number of prisoners. When he encountered local hostility, his officers were to "enforce a devastation more or less relentless" according to the provocation. His ardor was unquenchable, and his vision far-reaching. But he admitted that his judgment of current situations was faulty. One of his admiring friends made a perceptive observation: "He is a man of immense intellectuality, but his brain is like a splendid piece of machinery with all the screws a little loose."[64]

As the leader of such a military offensive as he now had under way, Sherman was superb, his belief in action, aggressive temper, and impetuosity enabling him to move with a driving vigor that contrasted with the deliberation of his ablest lieutenant, Thomas. He said of himself that he had a "vitality that only yields to absolute death."[65] Endlessly restless and strenuous, vivid in imagination, tireless in talk and gesture, his kinetic qualities expressed his versatility: he was sometimes a dreamer, sometimes a very practical businessman and organizer, and always an intensely combative commander. He did not like fighting and killing. Even success the most brilliant, he wrote, "is over dead and mangled bodies, with the anguish and lamentation of distant families."[66] Yet when aroused he could look upon slaughter, so long as it was for a valid end, with stoic rigor.

He held all his principles fiercely. Fighting for slavery, he said, was fighting against the spirit of the age; to make the navigation of the Mississippi safe, "I would slay millions."[67] And principle distinguished him. Because he had little of Grant's serene equipoise in moments of crisis, or Grant's remarkable self-

---

64. George W. Morgan, Mt. Vernon, O., to H.V. Boynton, Oct. 8, 1892, Boynton Papers, N.Y. Pub. Lib. Cf. Bradford, Gamaliel, *Union Portraits*, New York, 1916, 131-164, and Liddell Hart's penetrating *Sherman, Soldier, Realist, American, op.cit., passim.*

65. *O.R.* I, xlvii, pt. 3, 547.

66. Liddell Hart, *Sherman, op.cit.*, 402.

67. *O.R.* I, xxxi, pt. 3, 459; also Sherman to Logan, Nashville, Dec. 21, 1863, Logan Family Papers, Yale Univ. Lib.

control, he would never have been suited for the control of all the armies. Where Grant tranquillized friction and jealousies, he might have exacerbated them. Moreover, as Gideon Welles puts it, with a more incisive intelligence than Grant's and a wider range of knowledge, he was too often erratic and uncertain. Grant's friends, as Henry Adams observed, sometimes wondered just what processes of thought he followed. Sherman's friends knew that he often followed no logical processes at all, leaping to his results by intuition, and stating not reasons but conclusions. Principles, however, he did have, and one great principle, frequently reiterated, was especially to his credit. "War is only justified among civilized nations to produce peace," he declared; and again, in the sentence inscribed on his statue in Washington, "The legitimate object of war is a more perfect peace."[68]

A bundle of contradictions, occasionally all too vehement of speech, he could be the most stimulating and delightful of men in his relations with associates, and also one of the most irritating. Grant's *Memoirs* are the product of a clear, accurate mind devoted to the truth; Sherman's *Memoirs* were originally in part so inaccurate that Josiah Royce termed the California chapters a violation not only of sound evidence but of antecedent probability, and Gen. H.V. Boynton, who won a Medal of Honor at Missionary Ridge, called them Sherman's historical raid. Yet the corrected *Memoirs* are fascinating. He ended the war the unrelenting enemy of Stanton, but in their angry controversy the just appraisal of their respective attitudes is difficult, and must be deferred till later in the narrative. He ended it the man whom perhaps the South hated most, vying at times in this dubious distinction with Sheridan, Hunter, and Ben Butler, yet to the general Southern population, especially the poor people and, although no abolitionist, to the Negroes, he was a sympathetic and helpful friend. Altogether, he was the most remarkable combination of virtues and deficiencies produced in the high direction of the Union armies. Many soldiers idolized him while distrusting him a little. Many politicians and journalists admired him while distrusting him a great deal. One student who calls him a typical American in his nervous restlessness, quick ideas, energy, and optimism, adds that he was typical too in lacking a depth proportionate to his splendid breadth and variety—the depth, mystery, and humanity that helped make Lincoln immortal.[69]

We have to think of him in this campaign as a man whose measure the Army and the country were slowly taking. He was not one of the great captains of history, but a very effective general whom Liddell Hart, admiring his grasp of logistics and his daring, calls the first modern general; not a great

68. Liddell Hart, *Sherman, op.cit.*, 425.
69. *Ibid.*, 430.

man, but a great soldier.[70] With advantages of numbers and equipment, he knew how best to use them, as McClellan conspicuously did not, and was intent upon realizing the further advantages of calculated audacity.

The Union soldiers set out in high spirits, confident they could thrust the enemy aside. They built or repaired the Chattanooga-Atlanta railroad as they marched, exultantly cheering the whistling locomotive as it caught up with them. They distributed food and clothing from the cars and wagons to the thousands of Negroes and scores of whites flocking to their camps to ask help. The Confederates had stripped the line of march of as much meat, grain, and vegetables as they could carry off, but a good deal was left for Union seizure. Once crystal waters turned into muddy streams as cohorts of thirsty troops clustered about them. Herds of cattle bellowed wildly as men drove them off to commissary corrals; frantic squealing of pigs rent the air as privates pursued them with bayonets; cackling chickens and quacking ducks disappeared; and troopers cracked their whips over flocks of sheep. Aided at first by a little easily-found whisky, the infantry whooped and sang as they pressed on. And all the while, night and day, there was hardly a minute without the eternal pop —pop—bang—bang of the guns.

70. Bradford, *Union Portraits, op.cit.,* 133, 161-163.

2

Midsummer Frustration, 1864

AS GRANT AND SHERMAN launched their simultaneous attacks upon Lee's Army of Northern Virginia and Johnston's Army of the Tennessee, the anxiety of the Northern people was perhaps more intense and anguished than any they had ever before endured. They knew that the war might well be in its final crisis. What had seemed three stumbling years of carnage, sorrow, and miscarriage lay behind them. Victory had appeared delusively certain until First Bull Run came as a sudden stunning shock in 1861. They had again hoped to win when their splendid army advanced up the Peninsula in 1862, until McClellan's humiliating reverses and retreat to the James had been followed by Pope's defeat in the very gates of Washington, whose people listened in anguish as the sullen thunder of Union guns advanced, paused, and receded. Patriotic people had again hoped to win in 1863 after Vicksburg and Gettysburg—and had tasted apples of Sodom at Mine Run and Chickamauga. As Americans thought of two hundred thousand graves of Northern boys staring at the sky, they were aware that another summer of faltering and defeat might be the last. Meanwhile, dwellers in the cities once more opened their newspapers daily to long lists of the slain and maimed; villagers and townspeople bleakly studied the sheets posted on bulletin boards; farm mothers opened War-Department envelopes with trembling fingers. We shall endure, people said, but—and often they did not complete the sentence.

Day by day, the hammer blows fell, and were parried or returned. Greeley's *Tribune* kept a standing headline—*The Great Contest*. It might also have kept standing the subheads that told of terrific battles and of ever-renewed fighting until night ended the slaughter. On May 12, 1864, such a bulletin announced, "Our Losses So Far 40,000," with some, but all too little, exaggeration. This after the first full week of Virginia battle—the drawn battle of the Wilderness! Next night, Senators Doolittle and Green Clay Smith, Representative Isaac N. Arnold, and Governor Richard Oglesby were to speak for the Union Party in New York City at Cooper Institute. Would the mood of the meeting be fitly heroic? Greeley threw down a disheartening pronouncement in his sometimes Roman-spirited but now faltering editorial page. "Our own conviction is that the opening of the Presidential canvass should have been postponed until after the 4th of July, and that it is advisable for the Union Party to nominate for President some other among its able and true men than Mr. Lincoln. We think the events now transpiring in Virginia and Georgia add force to all that has hitherto been urged in favor of postponement of the Presidential canvass."[1]

Behind uneasy headlines and sour editorials, perceptive men saw that three crucial questions were being decided this summer. Could Grant really operate his Grand Plan for coordinated offensive movements by all the principal Union forces, accurately timed? Could he coordinate the armies in Virginia, Georgia, and the Southwest with such unified precision that Lee could not reinforce Johnston, or Johnston send aid to Lee, or either general send help to Kirby-Smith? In the second place, would the campaign show that Northern recruiting had at last reached the stage where preponderance on the battle lines would enable Grant and Sherman, when checked in a frontal advance, to turn the rebels in that dangerous manoeuvre, a flank march? A preponderance would also enable the Union forces to deploy that array of specialized manpower which just now, in mid-May, was being so efficiently used to rescue Porter's stranded gunboat fleet on the Red River—Maine lumbermen felling trees, Yankee stone-cutters opening an old quarry, Negroes seizing timbers from fences, warehouses, and cotton-gins to build dams.[2] The third question was whether the North had at last equipped its armies with material resources —wagons, horses, mules, ambulances, guns, caissons, uniforms, blankets, tents, medicines, muskets, mortars, repeating rifles—that would give them the decisive fire-power and marching-power they needed. And even though many knew that preponderant material had been provided, yet they still asked themselves, would this preponderance be employed promptly, shrewdly, and with the proficiency of a Caesar?

The answers to these three questions nobody knew in May, 1864. Yet the answers would determine the life or death of the Union, for war-weariness was growing as it had grown in America in 1781, and would grow in France in 1917 and Germany in 1918.

Behind these questions, as fiercely menacing as if written in fire on an inky sky, this election-year posed a larger query. Able and true men, Greeley had

1. New York *Tribune*, May 13, 1864.
2. Harrington, Fred H., *Fighting Politician: N.P. Banks*, Philadelphia, 1948, 130. See Adm. D.D. Porter's vivid account in *O.R.* I, xxxiv, pt. 1, 219-221. Irwin, Richard B., *History of the Nineteenth Army Corps*, New York, 1892, Chs. XX-XXIX, covers the whole Red River subject.

written, must head the nation. If the three questions just named were answered in the negative, and if Lincoln's party repudiated him, what chance would there be of finding leaders staunchly true to the ideas of an indissoluble Union and the maintenance of emancipation measures—and strong enough to hold to them? What if discouragement should overcome the adherents of the patient, indomitable Lincoln, and the men who still stood firm in the Union convictions of Jackson, Webster, Benton, and Douglas?

[I]

The repulse of Du Pont's attack on Charleston on April 7, 1863, the worst naval defeat of the Union thus far, had disheartened multitudes and cast a pall of gloom over the North. Du Pont was relieved of command of the South Atlantic Blockading Squadron, and replaced by Rear-Admiral John A. Dahlgren on July 6, 1863. Du Pont, a brave and conscientious admiral, who had begun his service as midshipman in 1815, and had been given the thanks of Congress for gallantly taking his fleet into Port Royal, naturally chafed under an unwarranted sense of disgrace. For he held the conviction (one which naval colleagues shared) that he had been given improper orders to follow at Charleston, and that Secretary Welles had treated him badly. Lincoln had emphasized the need of remaining before Charleston even if it could not be taken. Before Du Pont resentfully left, however, the Confederate ironclad ram *Atlanta* had been captured in Wassaw Sound by two Federal ships.[3] In mid-June, 1863, Quincy Adams Gillmore, twice brevetted for distinguished service, had succeeded David Hunter in command of the Army Department of the South. On July 10, three thousand Union troops landed on Morris Island and captured works at the southern end. The next day, operations were begun against Battery Wagner farther north on Morris Island. Attack after attack was thrown back with heavy casualties, including many borne by Negro troops; a siege was then undertaken. In mid-August, huge Northern Parrott rifles mounted on Morris Island began a devastating bombardment of Fort Sumter. It was successful in knocking the already damaged fort into rubble, but the guns could do no more and Fort Sumter held on. By the end of August, little was left at Sumter but one gun in operation and a couple of others occasionally serviceable. Slowly the sappers brought their works nearer and nearer Battery

---

3. Ammen, Daniel, *The Atlantic Coast*, New York, 1883-1885, 121; Du Pont, H.A., *Rear-Admiral Samuel Francis Du Pont*, New York, 1926, 292. Du Pont's resentment is well shown in his correspondence with his friend and protagonist Henry Winter Davis (mss. in Eleutherian Mills Hagley Foundation, Wilmington, Delaware).

Wagner. The warships joined in. Then, on September 6, after a siege of 85 days, the Confederates evacuated Battery Wagner and Morris Island. Questions could well be asked at the North if the prize had been worth the cost. On September 9, a small boat expedition against Fort Sumter proved a fiasco. After a few quiet weeks, the newly built Federal batteries on Morris Island opened up on Fort Sumter again, with heavy and light bombardments which continued for months. Thousands upon thousands of rounds were poured upon the fort. Dahlgren finally gave up any idea of entering Charleston harbor with his ships. The symbolic defense of Fort Sumter against Union guns was a gallant story, while the failure of the overwhelming cannonade and the ironclads was a frustrating story at the North. One outstanding authority puts the total number of Northern projectiles fired against Battery Wagner at 18,491, and the total number of projectiles fired against Fort Sumter from 1863 to 1865 at 46,053, with an estimated weight of 3,500 tons. The fort was said to have been under 117 days of major bombardment, 40 of minor bombardment, and 280 days under either steady or desultory fire, the Union managing to kill only 52 Confederates and wound 267. Thus, by the start of 1864, Charleston Harbor rankled in the hearts of the Northern military and civilian leaders.

Early in that year, action was limited at Charleston to some secondary skirmishing and the continued bombardment of Fort Sumter. After a daring torpedo-boat raid in mid-February sank the Federal gunboat *Housatonic* off Charleston Bar, pressure on Charleston with bombardment and exploratory operations went on into the spring and summer. Plymouth, North Carolina, had been recaptured by Confederates in April, while their formidable ram, the *Albemarle*, was active along the Roanoke River in North Carolina. Although it appeared now that the Union forces were not willing to risk losses even if they could take Charleston, the blockade of the coast went on, and Confederate troops and supplies were being drained away in defending the city of secession.[4]

As we have already seen, the failure of the Red River expedition was equally frustrating to the North; the rescue of Porter's gunboats had been one of that campaign's few bright spots.[5] On May 19, General N. P. Banks was relieved of his military functions by Canby in greater discredit than had overtaken the abler Du Pont. Banks was full of excuses, but his three months

4. Figures on bombardment of Battery Wagner and Fort Sumter are from Johnston, John, *The Defense of Charleston Harbor, including Fort Sumter and the Adjacent Islands, 1863-1865*, Charleston, S.C., 1890, 273. Same source has "Calendar of Events in the Defense of Charleston, South Carolina," Appendix xi-xx.

5. Success was achieved May 13, 1864. See Harrington, *op.cit.*, 158; Knox, Dudley W., *A History of the United States Navy*, New York, 1936, 300; Bailey's concise reports, *O.R.* I, xxxiv, 402-404.

of marching, fighting, and marauding had cost the government needed men, supplies, time, and prestige. The origins of the expedition had been cloudy, apparently lying partly in Lincoln's anxieties over the future course of Emperor Maximilian in Mexico, partly in Halleck's notions of Texas strategy, and partly in the easy acquiescence of Banks, Sherman, and others in badly laid plans. Maximilian landed at Vera Cruz on May 28, resulting in a Congressional investigation, official censure, much quarreling among both Northern and Southern commanders, a well-grounded suspicion of cotton jobbery, some real injury to Lincoln's chances for re-election, and considerable chagrin to the North as a whole.[6] A blow against Mobile, ordered by Sherman, might have accomplished valuable results in 1864; however, such a blow was not struck until after Lincoln had delivered his second inaugural address in 1865.

For more than two years, wrote Grant, he had tried to get the stroke against Mobile launched when it would have been of great advantage, but it was finally undertaken when it had become worthless. Farragut had been eager to undertake a sea expedition against Mobile just after the capture of New Orleans, when land forces did not appear needed, but Washington had given priority to the Mississippi—although advocating an attack on Mobile as well, either after the river was cleared or as a substitute. By the time Banks was sent on the Red River expedition, the strength of the coastal forts had made a coördinated military effort essential, and his absence placed Mobile beyond reach.[7]

Worse still, the North had to accept the immobility of its best naval commander, Farragut. He had returned to his Gulf station in January, 1864, burning to move against Mobile, but for six months he was sentenced to minor duty. "I am *depressed*," he wrote, "by the bad news from every direction."[8] The

6. Cf. Lt.-Col. Richard B. Irwin, "The Red River Campaign," *Battles and Leaders*, IV, 361ff.

7. Grant, *Memoirs*, II, 519. Grant's impatience had also been forcibly expressed over delays in attacking Forrest in April this year. Sherman telegraphed Mason Brayman on April 16: "General Grant is properly offended at the timidity displayed in and about Memphis and has ordered Gen. Hurlbut to be relieved. I have instructed Gen. McPherson as soon as possible to transport his wagons, mules, etc. to Clifton, and make up a force to strike inland from the Tennessee at Forrest." Brayman Papers, Chicago Historical Soc. Washington and the War Department have often been accused of not supporting the idea of a drive on Mobile. Actually, at the time of the capture of New Orleans in April, 1862, Farragut's orders had been to go on up the Mississippi River, but after that, or in place of it, if necessary, "You will also reduce the fortifications which defend Mobile Bay, and turn them over to the army to hold . . ." *O.R.N.*, I, Vol. XVIII, 7-8, Welles to Farragut, Jan. 20, 1862. This idea was repeated several times. The problem had been that the Mississippi Campaign, including Vicksburg, had been more difficult than foreseen, and had taken long to execute. Thus, Mobile had been delayed, and continued to be delayed.

8. Lewis, Charles Lee, *David Glasgow Farragut, Our First Admiral*, Annapolis, 1943, 236-240; Mahan, A.T., *Admiral Farragut*, New York, 1892, 237-252.

bad news which he and the Northern people had to sustain included dispatches concerning Forrest's slashing raids in Tennessee and Kentucky; accounts of the bloody Confederate capture of Fort Pillow on April 12; and the tale of General Frederick Steele's failure to sweep the Confederate columns in Arkansas with their lurking threat to Union movements, away toward the interior of rebeldom. Steele's delays in starting frustrated the intended capture of Shreveport, and his failure added to the gloom over General Banks's reverses. Another sorry item in the catalogue of Union disappointments was the defeat of General Franz Sigel's attack at Newmarket in the Shenandoah, on a field forever immortalized to Southerners by the heroic stand of 147 young cadets of the Virginia Military Institute, a number of whom gallantly gave up their lives before Sigel retreated. At the same time, Ben Butler let himself be bottled up at Bermuda Hundred on the James, in a way that was both too humiliating and too ridiculous for the country ever to forget.

All eyes were turned to Virginia and Georgia, where men recorded heroic deeds in lines as curt as those William Francis Bartlett wrote in the Wilderness on May 6: "It will be a bloody day. I believe I am prepared to die. God bless my friends at home . . . Went into action about eight. Thick woods. Men behaved well. I was struck in head about eleven. Carried to the hospital in rear. Lay there among the wounded and dying until night." This month might well be called "bloody May," the Richmond *Examiner* shortly remarked. Estimating the total killed in all armies at 70,000, it listed seven general officers slain on each side.[9]

Yet it was only gradually that the realities of the situation were grasped by the Northern public, for the official utterances of Stanton deceived both press and people. On Thursday, May 6, the battle of the Wilderness closed, and on the night of the 7th Grant began his losing race with Lee toward Spotsylvania. He had fought a drawn battle with far heavier losses than his opponent and was still far from Richmond. Yet on the 9th the War Department shouted victory! At 4 P.M. Stanton announced: "Dispatches have just reached here from Gen. Grant. They are not fully deciphered yet, but he is 'On to Richmond.' We have taken 2,000 prisoners." In a supplementary dispatch Stanton added that dispatches from Meade showed Lee's army had "commenced falling back Friday night"; that the Union army "commenced the pursuit" on Saturday, the Rebels being "in full retreat for Richmond by the direct road"; that Hancock had passed through Spotsylvania Court-House at daylight on Sunday the 8th; and that Union headquarters at noon on the 8th were twenty miles south

9. Clipped in Selma, Ala., *Daily Reporter*, June 10, 1864. The *Examiner* listed the Union generals Wadsworth, Sedgwick, Haynes, Webb, Taylor, Joshua T. Owens, and James C. Rice; the Southern generals Stuart, Jenkins, Stafford, Jones, Julius Daniel, Gordon, and Perkins.

of the Wilderness battlefield. Another War Department bulletin, May 9, read: "Our army in full pursuit of the enemy toward Richmond."

No wonder that newspapers blazed with exultant headlines on the 10th! "Victory for the Union—The Rebels Fly by Night—Is it a Race for Richmond?" No wonder that Lincoln on May 9 urged people to repair to their homes and churches, to "unite in common thanksgiving" to Almighty God. After confused news from Spotsylvania, the headlines exulted again on Saturday the 14th. "Glorious Successes—Lee Terribly Beaten on Thursday—He Retreats During the Night—His Army Nearly Hemmed In—Occupation of Dalton by Our Forces—'The End Draws Near.' "[10]

The facts of the situation were utterly different from the Stanton bulletins and the silly headlines. Grant had indeed made a momentous decision when, on May 7, instead of turning back to the Rapidan, he had ordered the night march on Spotsylvania. Sherman later called this one of the decisive strokes of the war, and, in his judgment, the supreme moment of Grant's life. The bold movement electrified the Army. Hancock's troops, watching along the road by the light of torches, suddenly saw Grant and Meade pass by, realized that the army was moving southeast upon Lee's flank toward Richmond, and, springing to their feet, gave cheer upon cheer.[11] The drama of the moment was unforgettable. The Army that had suffered endless humiliation since Bull Run at last had a leader determined upon victory.

But morning gunfire showed that victory might yet be far distant. Instead of being "in full retreat for Richmond," the rebels were fiercely barring the road.

The long night tramp had been desperately fatiguing to Union troops who had fought and marched for almost four days and nights; the check at dawn was infuriating. Tempers wore thin as a fierce sun mounted into a dust-choked sky. One division of the hot, dirty, hungry troops broke ranks as its general, John C. Robinson, was carried from the field with a shot in the knee. About noon, an angry quarrel broke out between Meade and Sheridan over responsibility for delays in the advance. Meade, working himself into one of his towering rages, sent for Sheridan to come to his headquarters, and went after him hammer-and-tongs. Sheridan retorted in hot anger, placing all the blame upon Meade for countermanding his first orders. They threw Billingsgate exple-

10. All headlines from New York *Tribune*, but typical of other papers.

11. Porter, Horace, *Campaigning with Grant*, Ch. V; Badeau, Adam, *Military History of Ulysses S. Grant*, II, 235ff. Frank Wilkerson writes in his *Recollections of a Private Soldier in the Army of the Potomac*, New York, 1887, that Grant's standing with the troops hung on the direction he turned. When he moved to the right, a sigh of relief went up. "Our spirits rose. We marched free. The men began to sing." Sherman, William T., "The Grand Strategy of the War of the Rebellion," Century Vol. XXXV, No.4, Feb., 1888, 592.

tives, spiced with profanity, one at the other. "I will not command the cavalry any longer under such circumstances," roared Sheridan.[12] Eventually Meade apologized, but Sheridan thereafter nursed a truculent Irish grudge toward him and Warren. Late that afternoon, renewed attacks by the jaded Union troops broke down under the angry eyes of Grant, watching within bullet range.

All around the Union troops lay reminders of galling hardships and terrible losses. They were still almost as close to Washington as to Richmond, and the map ahead was strewn with tragic names—Mechanicsville, Gaines' Mill, Seven Pines, White Oak Swamp. Would Spotsylvania add another band of crêpe to this dreary list?

The Confederates were now masters of entrenchment. In taking any position they would hastily form a line of defense. They would collect loose stones, small logs, fence rails, and other materials, pile them into a rampart, and use picks, shovels, and bayonets to cover it with dirt from a trench. Within an hour they had sufficient cover for a kneeling man. "It is a rule," wrote Theodore Lyman, "that, when the rebels halt, the first day gives them a good riflepit; the second, a regular infantry parapet with cannon in position; and the third, a parapet with an abattis in front and entrenched batteries behind. Sometimes they put this three-days' work into the first twenty-four hours." The men inside these fortifications matched the veterans of Caesar, Gustavus Adolphus, and Wellington; "sinewy, tawny, formidable looking," they used bullet and blade with terrible effect.[13]

[II]

The approach to Spotsylvania had ended badly; the battle lay ahead. Beginning May 9, it continued more than a week, one bloody encounter following another. The first day was confined to skirmishing and sharpshooting, and

---

12. Porter, op.cit., 83, 84; Sheridan, Philip, Personal Memoirs, New York, 1888, I, 357-369: this is a characteristic report of the unseemly altercation. He writes that Meade "showed a disposition to be unjust, laying blame here and there for the blunders that had been committed. He was particularly severe on the cavalry, saying, among other things, that it had impeded the march of the Fifth Corps by occupying the Spottsylvania road. I replied that if this were true, he himself had ordered it there without my knowledge. I also told him that he had broken up my combinations, exposed Wilson's division to disaster, and kept Gregg unnecessarily idle, and further, repelled his insinuations by saying that such disjointed operations as he had been requiring of the cavalry for the last four days would render the corps inefficient and useless before long. Meade was very much irritated, and I was none the less so. One word brought on another, until, finally, I told him that I could whip Stuart if he (Meade) would only let me, but since he insisted on giving the cavalry directions without consulting or even notifying me, he could henceforth command the Cavalry Corps himself—that I would not give it another order." The acrimonious interview ended with this remark. Cf. Meade, G.G., Life and Letters of George Gordon Meade, New York, 1913, II, 220-222.

13. Lyman, op.cit., 100, 106, 115.

Sedgwick was killed when struck in the head by a sharpshooter's bullet. Perhaps the most able corps-commander in the Army of the Potomac, Sedgwick's loss was a serious blow. He was replaced in command of the Sixth Corps by Horatio Wright. Cavalry was useless on a terrain so rough and heavily wooded; furthermore, Sheridan departed on May 9 on a lengthy expedition that penetrated to the suburbs of Richmond, where, at Yellow Tavern on May 11, Jeb Stuart was mortally wounded. Yet Stuart's cavalry and the Richmond defense troops checked Sheridan, so he turned east to the Peninsula, not rejoining Grant until May 24. On May 10, at Spotsylvania, the three corps of Hancock, Warren, and Wright were thrown against the Confederate left and left-center. Little was gained, however; Grant was learning how skillful Lee could be in disposing his smaller force.

On the night of May 11-12, Grant massed about 20,000 men to assault the enemy center, springing forward at the glimmer of dawn. The weather had changed. The 11th had been rainy. A chill downpour continued through the night, the troops lying in wet clothes on wetter ground, without shelter. Morning came with dank fog. The main Union attack was directed at a five-sided salient of the Confederate line held by Ewell, projecting into thick brush in the shape (as farm-boys on both sides noted) of a mule-shoe. Hancock's troops, moving against the salient in dense ranks under heavy fire, at first seemed to be gaining a decisive success. Then, inside the outer works, they encountered a second line. It was a heavy abattis, with rear logs banked with clay, the upper timbers raised just sufficiently to enable the defenders to fire from shelter. Openings in the fortified line gave room here and there for the muzzles of cannon. Some of the artillery faced forward; other pieces were placed at an angle to catch advancing lines in the flank. When Hancock was forced back, Wright and the Sixth Corps came in on his right, assaulting the west face of the salient, particularly at the famous "Bloody Angle." Here some of the hottest fighting of the war took place. Farther to the Union right Warren attacked, and on the Union left Burnside drove in, though the fight was not as severe as at the salient.

"The attempt seemed hopeless," wrote one soldier, "but attack, attack everywhere is the word today; no joint in the enemy's harness must be left unsmitten." His unit, after advancing through heavy underbrush, freed itself from the pine thickets, straightened its line, and faced forward just as the earthworks burst into flame. "A brief dash now across the shot-swept open, no firing, the bayonet only, and with thinned ranks, the abattis is reached. . . . Up now the Fifteenth, what is left of you, up over the logs, inside and hand-to-hand, foot-to-foot in deadly mêlée." His regiment forced its way into the earthworks, using the bayonet freely, and took about a hundred prisoners, but too few men were left to hold the place. Moreover, a Southern battery was now sweeping the whole brigade with a flank fire of grapeshot. Like the Light Brigade, they were under fire all the way back. Next morning a roll-call showed that the regiment had lost 116 men.[14]

In his *Memoirs*, Grant stated that two Northern commands, one under Francis C. Barlow and the other under David B. Birney, plunged across the Confederate entrenchments almost simultaneously. Desperate hand-to-hand fighting ensued, the combatants too close to fire, but using bayonets and clubbed rifles. The Union forces, capturing four thousand prisoners and twenty guns, had won such a signal victory that Lee could not afford to leave them in full possession of his works. Bringing up fresh troops, he attacked so furiously that the Northerners under Hancock were compelled to retire. But they retreated slowly, inflicting heavy losses until they stood behind the breastworks they had recently captured. Then they turned, fighting from the new cover, and continued to hold the lines.[15]

"Lee massed heavily from his left flank on the broken point of his lines," wrote Grant. "Five times during the day he assaulted furiously, but without dislodging our troops from their new position. His losses must have been fearful. Sometimes the belligerents would be separated by but a few feet." In one place a tree eighteen inches in diameter was severed and felled by musket balls. All the forest growth between the lines was heavily slashed by artillery and musketry. It was three o'clock next morning before the fighting ceased. "Some [Northern] troops had then been twenty hours under fire." That night Lee took a position in the rear of his former line, fortifying it by breastworks and trenches. On May 13, both exhausted armies rested. That night it again rained heavily, and for nearly a week the general immobility continued, although there was considerable movement and fighting along the battle lines at times. Then, on the 20th, as Lee was inclined to stand fast, Grant ordered a movement toward his left.

The story of the bloody actions that ensued, of Lee's use of interior lines to frustrate Grant, of the stubborn fight on the North Anna in which the armies lost about equal numbers, and of Grant's passage of the Pamunkey River to make a desperate new assault on Lee at Cold Harbor, has long been familiar. Union veterans, in advancing to Cold Harbor, showed an impressive endurance. The New York *Tribune* correspondent C.A. Page wrote that

14. Dodd, Ira S., *The Song of the Rappahannock*, New York, 1898, 245-250.
15. Grant, *Memoirs*, II, 230-232. During a lull at Spotsylvania, Charles Carleton Coffin spent a day in Fredericksburg visiting the hospitals. The city was one vast hospital; churches, public buildings, stores, attics, basements, all full. "There are thousands upon the sidewalk," he wrote. "All day long the ambulances have been arriving from the field." A red flag had been hung out from the Sanitary Commission rooms, a white flag from the Christian Commission. Three hundred volunteer nurses were in attendance, every Northern State having its Relief Committee at work. The Sanitary Commission used fourteen wagons in bringing supplies from Belle Plain. *The Boys of '61*, Boston, 1881, 326, 327.

Wright's Sixth Corps made an especially remarkable showing.[16]

"On Monday [May 30] they marched all day without rations. That night they formed line of battle, and what with the labor of intrenching and several hours of the night getting rations, they obtained no sleep. On Tuesday they were engaged with the enemy more or less all day. That night, on 30 minutes' notice, they marched at midnight, marched till morning, marched till noon, marched till 4 o'clock, and then set to work with all their might intrenching. The day was one of the sultriest I ever knew, and the roads ankle-deep with dust—impalpable Virginia dust, that hung so densely in the air that it became exceedingly palpable. And yet these Corps veterans, hungry for two days, sleepless for three days, fatigued with relentless marching by day and by night, all streaming with perspiration, grim and blear-eyed, their hair dusted to whiteness . . . grasped shovels and axes . . . and sprang to work with never-surpassed vigor, and an hour later exchanged tools for weapons and fought with unequaled spirit and tenacity."

The month of May was one long test of physical fortitude. The men, tired of hard bread and salt meat, craved fresh vegetables so much that one woman, looking at her ravaged garden, exclaimed: "You Yanks don't seem to keer for nothin' but injuns [onions]." Many of the wounded were sent on hospital steamers to Fredericksburg, Washington, or New York, but many suffered in field hospitals. The Topographical Engineers did masterly work in surveying, mapping, and analyzing all the varied pieces of terrain encountered after the crossing of the Pamunkey. One leader, tireless in riding about, questioned Negroes, prisoners, deserters, talked with farmers, and drew sketches of streams, bridges, and roads. This was Captain W.H. Paine, who at Spotsylvania partly found and partly made a road that saved four miles in moving troops. Fifty pioneers improved it for artillery. Nevertheless, the rough country was hard on men and beasts alike. Before Spotsylvania ended, the roads thereabouts were strewn with the carcasses of six thousand horses. Many soldiers were felled by sunstroke. As June began, more than 100,000 of Grant's soldiers had not changed a garment since they started; they had marched, slept, and fought thirty days and thirty nights in the same sweat-stiffened garments. Dense clouds of dust overhung the roads from battlefield to battlefield, filling eyes and lungs. But the fighting spirit of the men never faltered even when they were betrayed by bad generalship.

[III]

For sheer horror of butchery, Cold Harbor, fought June 1-3, can stand beside Fredericksburg. The Union army now faced towards Gaines' Mill, for

16. New York *Tribune*, June 6, 8, et seq., 1864.

it was back near the old battleground of the Seven Days. On the evening of May 31st, Lee made ready to recapture a vital road junction here near the Chickahominy River, for Cold Harbor was not a town or village, but a mere, half-isolated intersection of ways leading to the Pamunkey, York, and Chickahominy fords. A stubborn encounter occurred on June 1, a day of torrid heat. Next day, a heavy downpour fell. Lee, still intent on covering Richmond with his troops, had thoroughly surveyed the familiar terrain and at least partially fortified some of its vital bridges, fords, and other points. Grant, therefore, postponed the general assault he had planned for the late afternoon, but that night orders were given for an attack at 4:30 on the morning of the 3rd, orders that the troops knew would result in terrible loss of life.

The Confederates had entrenched with great energy and efficiency. Before the rain, this had been easy to do for trenches could be dug in the dry, sandy earth with bits of board, tin plates, or any kind of shovel, the dirt heaped alongside; and a few flying axes soon provided enough straight pines to give the breastwork a wall. As dawn broke on the 3rd, a beautiful summer morning, a single cannon pealed the signal for a general assault. The soldiers scanning the area between the armies, an open plain already trampled in many places into fine dust under the baking sun and then turned into a quagmire by the ensuing rain, saw that they had small likelihood of success. Colonel Theodore Lyman, at Meade's headquarters, saw none. "If we could smash them up, the Chickahominy lay behind them," he wrote; "but I had no more hope of it after Spotsylvania, than I had of taking Richmond in two days." Yet, with three corps participating, the men moved staunchly to the charge. Many were so certain of death that they had written their names on slips of paper fastened to their clothes to make identification easier.

This assault, which took place when many officers were out of humor with the costly frontal attacks involved in Grant's strategy, resulted within half an hour in about 7,000 more Union soldiers killed and wounded. "I do think," wrote Theodore Lyman in his journal, "there has been too much assaulting, this campaign. Following our lessons of failure and of success at Spotsylvania, we assault here, after the enemy had taken thirty-six hours to entrench, and that time will cover them over their heads, and give them slashings and traverses besides! The best officers and men are liable, by their greater gallantry, to be first disabled; and of those that are left, the best become demoralized by the failures, and the loss of good leaders; so that, very soon, the men will no longer charge entrenchments, and will only go forward when driven by their officers."[17]

17. Lyman, *op.cit.*, 143-150.

"I am disgusted with the generalship displayed," Peter S. Michie wrote his sister the day after the charge. Michie, a West Pointer of Scottish birth, was a shrewd engineer later brevetted brigadier-general. "Our men have, in many instances, been foolishly and wantonly sacrificed. Assault after assault has been ordered upon the enemy. Thousands of lives might have been spared by the exercise of a little skill." He again wrote his sister on June 5, that the recent assault was murderous. "I say murderous, because we were recklessly ordered to assault the enemy's intrenchments, knowing neither their strength nor position." He went on: "I have seen but little generalship during the campaign. Some of our corps commanders are not fit to be corporals. Lazy and indolent, they will not even ride along the lines; yet, without hesitancy, they will order us to attack the enemy, no matter what their position or numbers. Twenty thousand of our killed and wounded should today be in our ranks."[18] This doubtless paralleled the talk in Nivelle's ranks in 1917, after his grand assault on the fortified German lines from the Aisne Heights was choked in blood. Yet on June 3, almost no Northerner flinched. At the hour prescribed, the men quietly rose from the sloppy trenches they had dug during the night downpour, and moved forward with grim, steady tread. The Confederates were ready for them. "There rang out suddenly on the summer air such a crash of artillery and musketry as is seldom heard in war." All three corps, under Hancock, Wright, and W.F. Smith, were terribly exposed to flank as well as frontal fire, so that each commander complained later to General Meade that the others failed to protect him from an enfilading storm of bullets. The main charge ended in less than half an hour. The ground was soon cumbered with between six and seven thousand Union bodies. Yet so stubborn was the valor of the troops that here and there, where the fire was intolerably heavy and the works in front were plainly impregnable, the men still refused to retreat, lying prone behind some slight ridge and hanging on, though perhaps only two hundred or four hundred feet from the enemy.[19]

After the attack had broken down; after more men had fallen than in any other similar period of brief, intense action in the war; after headquarters in the rear had learned by field telegraph of the opening of deadly enemy fire upon the three corps attacking on diverging lines, new orders came from high command. Orders to retire?—for sharpshooters still swept the field with bullets, and more shells exploded. No. Each corps was directed to attack again, moving directly against the enemy without reference to the action of its fellow corps, thus sacrificing unity. In uneven ranks, troops that had retired to protected areas renewed their plunge forward, as again other detachments, hug-

18. Michie, Peter S., *Life and Letters of Emory Upton*, New York, 1885, 108, 109.
19. McMahon, Martin T., "Cold Harbor," *Battles and Leaders*, IV, 213-220.

ging the muddy ground, loosed ragged but futile volleys. After fresh lines of dead and wounded recorded another total failure, Grant sent his insensate order for a general assault. But this third time not a soldier moved. Everyone knew that a fresh charge would be suicidal. Some volleys were loosed by the prone ranks, but that was all.[20]

Union valor now met the same reward as at Second Manassas and Vicksburg, a callous abandonment of the wounded to hours and days of agony. The field was a horrifying sight, with windrows of the immobile dead and writhing injured marking each stage of the advance. No man on it dared rise to face certain bullets; no stretcher-bearer behind it dared venture into the open.

"When night came on," wrote Martin T. McMahon, the Canadian-born officer who was Wright's chief of staff, "the groans and moaning of the wounded, all our own, who were between the lines, were heartrending." It was like the freezing night of stricken men after Fredericksburg. Morning and noonday brought no relief. "Some were brought in by volunteers from our intrenchments, but many remained three days uncared for beneath the hot summer suns and the unrefreshing dews of the sultry summer nights. The men in the works grew impatient, yet it was against orders and was almost certain death to go beyond our earthworks."[21]

Without care for three days! Without a drop of water, a bandage, a morsel of food, a helping touch—and this fell short of the truth. The troops had begun to fall at dawn on June 3. That hot day passed, and that night; then an equally hot June 4 and its night. The responsibility for action was Grant's; his had been the main losses. An armistice of two hours would have been sufficient. Yet not until June 5 did Grant open with Lee a correspondence which he self-righteously paraded in his *Memoirs*. It is reported to me, he stated, that wounded men "probably of both armies" are lying exposed between the lines. He could see the field of wounded for himself; he knew well that the great majority were Union soldiers—McMahon says "all our own." Grant proposed that each side be authorized to send unarmed litter-bearers out after an action to pick up its dead or wounded. Lee replied this same June 5 that men should be sent "immediately" to collect the dead and wounded, but that a flag of truce should be accepted before such parties were dispatched. Not until June 6 (he does not state the hour) did Grant accede to Lee's demand for use of a flag of truce, and

    20. *Ibid.*, 218-219; Swinton, William, *Campaigns of the Army of the Potomac*, New York, 1866, 481-487. Meade in his unrevealing account of Cold Harbor writes: "I had immediate and entire command on the field all day" (Meade, George, *op.cit.*, II, 200). He adds, "Up to this time our success has consisted only in compelling the enemy to draw in toward Richmond; our failure has been that we have not been able to overcome, destroy, or bag his army."
    21. McMahon, *op.cit.*, IV, 219.

Union Cavalry Commanders:
second from left, standing, Philip Sheridan;
third from left, seated, Alfred Pleasonton;
seated at right, George Custer.

General Grant and Staff, Spotsylvania, 1864

to his strict limitation of the ground to be covered; for Lee feared that stretcher parties might spy out the strong and weak sections of his line. At 7 P.M. on June 6 Lee then wrote, fixing an immediate time for removal of the casualties. But somehow his message did not reach Union headquarters until 10:45 P.M., when the allotted hour had expired.[22] Thus it was not until June 7 that parties were sent out from the Union lines to collect men who had lain on the field since the morn of the 3rd—more than four days earlier. A hundred hours of burning thirst and agony had intervened!

But it was not so long for most of the casualties. In the interim, as Grant succinctly stated, "all but two of the wounded had died."[23] And what had their lives purchased? Grant gave the answer in his *Memoirs:* "No advantage whatever was gained for the heavy loss we sustained."[24] We may well believe his statement late in life that, "I regret the assault more than any I have ever ordered."[25] Inadequate as this statement seems, it was a greater admission of fault than any that Meade, quick to lose his temper but slow to admit fault, ever made.[26]

[IV]

Grant's Cold Harbor attack, blundering and seemingly callous though it was, had behind it a thoughtful plan and design characteristic of the reflective, studious general. It did not have behind it the egoistic hardness of David Hunter, discarding prudence in Missouri and rules of Army authority in Georgia to better himself, or the blind impetuosity of Hooker at Chancellorsville. Still determined upon erosion of Confederate strength and numbers even by an unequal trading of manpower and positions, Grant looked ahead. He must push inexorably forward against Richmond whatever the cost. He knew that the marshy Chickahominy, often called "a wet ditch, in front of the outer fortifications of the capital," still lay before him. Had he won Cold Harbor, two bridges over it would have lain open, and he could have used the full strength of McClellan's old position, lying secure behind breastworks, as he besieged the city. But he had failed to force the passage of the Chickahominy—and now what? If he persevered in "fighting it out on this line. . . . all summer," his next

---

22. This Grant-Lee correspondence is in Grant's *Memoirs*, II, 273-275.
23. Why the delay? Because, McMahon declares, "An impression prevails in the popular mind, and with some reason perhaps, that a commander who sends a flag of truce asking permission to bury his dead and bring in his wounded has lost the field of battle. Hence the reluctance on our part to ask a flag of truce." *Battles and Leaders*, IV, 219.
24. Grant, *Memoirs*, II, 276.
25. Cf. *Battles and Leaders*, IV, 220.
26. Cleaves, Freeman, *Meade of Gettysburg*, Norman, Okla., 1960, 151.

advance by the left would carry his army not toward Richmond, but away from it.

His first impulse was to try again to force the Chickahominy line, not by hammer blows, but by the regular approaches of a siege operation. With Lee's army still intact, however, and Lee's genius undimmed, and with strong fortifications available to rebel use, a breach of one line in front of Richmond would simply bring the Union army up against another even more formidable. When a rebel newspaperman suggested that Grant might move down the Chickahominy to try crossing in the vicinity of White Oak Swamp, he found Lee's veterans exultant in the thought of the earthwork defenses the Union troops would have to assail.[27]

Grant, however, had learned his lesson. Long afterward, he admitted in his *Memoirs* that the ghastly Union losses at Cold Harbor had been without "adequate compensation"; he might have said without *any* compensation. He also admitted that the battle had elevated Confederate morale, and depressed the Union army and people. Like Shiloh, mention of Cold Harbor always pained him.[28]

Now he wrote Halleck on June 5 that after thirty days of trial he had decided that "without a greater sacrifice of human life than I am willing to make, all cannot be accomplished that I had designed outside of the city" of Richmond; that is, Lee could not be defeated north of that city. He must embrace the only real alternative, transferring his army south of the James. In the darkness of June 12-13, his frustrated force took up its march from Cold Harbor to the lower reaches of the James, the Harrison's Landing shore where McClellan had once ensconced himself under naval guns. On the 14th, Grant's advance reached the river, and immediately pressed across to march against the defenses of Petersburg beyond. On June 15, when General William Farrar Smith (whose corps had been moved from the Peninsula by water) began an assault on these works, the whole battle front suddenly and dramatically changed.

Well it was for Grant that in the very week of Cold Harbor the Republican National Convention diverted a portion of the nation's attention by opening its sessions in Baltimore. Grant had hoped, nay, had expected, to defeat Lee decisively between the Rapidan and the James, but had failed. Many observers thought that his strategy might be summed up in one word: "Butchery." He had told Meade in the hearing of one press correspondent, "I never manoeuvre," and the result proved it.[29] Various high officers blamed him, and

27. Swinton, *op.cit.*, 481; Tyrone Power in Selma *Dispatch*, June 6, 1864.

28. Grant, *Memoirs*, II, 264-278; here he turned abruptly to discuss the Vicksburg assaults.

29. Note statement of G.F.R. Henderson, *The Science of War*, London, 1910, 7: "Grant knew not only how to command an army, but how to teach an army, how to form skilled leaders, strategists, and technicians . . ." For the remark to Meade, see Swinton, William, *op.cit.*, 440.

Meade, and others including his aide Comstock who was credited with the aphorism "smash them up!", for the fearful loss of life. His inexorable thrust against Lee rested upon the same basic advantage that enabled the Russian armies to move as inexorably in 1944-45 against the Germans: heavily superior numbers, greater length of line, and utterly heedless sacrifice of lives.[30] We may accept an English estimate that the total cost of Grant's attrition policy from the Wilderness through Cold Harbor exceeded 52,000 casualties, the Confederates losing slightly over one-third as many.[31]

Attrition at this rate was too costly. If three Union men died for one Confederate, the North would give up sooner than the South. The patriotic press put the brightest face possible on matters: Grant's overland movement had kept Lee from threatening Washington, he had taken twice as many prisoners as Lee, his wounded and ill would recover more rapidly than Lee's, and after all, it was relative, not positive, losses that counted.[32] Forlorn comfort! The gloom that thickened over a great part of the Union as people read of Cold Harbor and of new exploits by Nathan Bedford Forrest in crushing a raid by General "Sooky" Smith into North Mississippi, mingling with the news of Lincoln's renomination, made Republican victory dubious. The close observer Swinton declares that while the morale of Lee's army now reached its highest point, Northern depression produced "great danger of the collapse of the war."[33]

Yet Grant had accomplished much. He had bled the South to weakness, especially its échelons of command. He had compelled Lee to accept the defensive once and for all. Grant now had a stranglehold on Lee, and by virtue of his tenacity as well as his superior numbers, was firm in maintaining his iron grip. The public at large could not see this; they were more aware of the depressing surface manifestations of failure. Grant had proved the merits of his (and Lincoln's) fundamental plan. If he had taken his army at the outset by water to the James River landings below Richmond, then Lee on the Rapidan might have retained a dangerous freedom to lunge at Washington. Now he could not consider any such advance. Had Grant flanked Lee's army on its left, moving southwestwardly, he would have limited the flow of his

30. In Virginia, Meade's official return of Union casualties for May 5-12 was 29,410, and for May 12-21 was 10,381, a total of 39,791. At Cold Harbor on June 1-3 about 12,000 more were killed or wounded. Official returns for the period May 5 through June 15, including Wilderness, Spotsylvania, North Anna, and Cold Harbor, totaled 52,789 casualties, including 7,407 killed, 37,264 wounded, and 8,118 missing. Confederate total losses are estimated at something around 20,000.

31. *O.R.* I, xxxvi, pt. 3, 598, Grant to Halleck, June 5, 1864. Pt.I, 133, 149, 164, 180, gives a complete return of casualties from the Rapidan to the James. See also Livermore, T.L., *Numbers and Losses in the Civil War in America, 1861-1865*, Boston, 1901, 114-115; Burne, Col. Alfred H. *Lee, Grant and Sherman*, New York, 1939, 50-52; and Long, A.L., *Memoirs of Robert E. Lee*, New York, 1886, 348.

32. New York *Tribune*, July 2, 1864. But Greeley actually was disheartened.

33. Lytle, A.N., *Bedford Forrest and His Critter Company*, New York, 1931, 259ff; Swinton, *op.cit.*, 492.

essential supplies. Instead, he had kept in easy communication with vital
sources of transport, arms, food, and forage, and still had moved steadily closer
to Richmond.

[V]

Having formed his new plan, Grant stuck to his central aim. In vain had
Halleck proposed, just after Cold Harbor, that the army invest Richmond from
the north. Grant's superiority in numbers would have made this feasible, and
it would have given Washington a continued sense of security; but it would
have entailed bloody new assaults on lines of tremendous strength, while
leaving Richmond in possession of all the arteries of supply below the James.
Grant therefore threw his army across that river. Union engineers chose the
vicinity of Wilcox's Landing as the best point, for it was covered on the west
by Herring Creek, with eminences at hand to protect the rear. Fortunately,
no better military engineers could be found in the world than those of the
Army of the Potomac. According to the historian of the Fifth Corps, Lieut.-
Col. William H. Powell of the regular Army (an Ohio manufacturer of Welsh
birth who won the Medal of Honor, and was wounded at Wytheville, Virginia,
and became brigadier-general of volunteers in October, 1864), the engineers of
the Fifth Corps built in this campaign no fewer than thirty-eight bridges,
aggregating 4,458 feet in length.[34]

"To cross so wide and deep a river with so large an army," writes the ablest
Union engineer, A.A. Humphreys, "with all its artillery, together with its
ammunition, subsistence, quartermaster, ambulance, and hospital trains, was
a difficult operation, and exposed the army to attack under disadvantages while
crossing."[35] But Lee could not attack without moving so far from Richmond
as to imperil his own line. The building of a great pontoon-bridge over the
James, one of the engineering triumphs of the war, the passage of the army,
and deployment on the south bank, were swiftly and expertly managed. By
June 16, Grant had his main force on the south bank. Whether he completely
deceived Lee by his rapidity of movement is a question much debated by
strategists. At one moment he seemed to have a decisive victory within his
grasp in the capture of ill-defended Petersburg or even Richmond itself. He
had been deprived of this triumph, however, by the fumbling of Ben Butler
and William Farrar ("Baldy") Smith.

Fumbling is an inadequate word for the failure of Butler and Smith, which
had about it more the quality of *opéra bouffe* than of war. It will be remembered

---

34. *The Fifth Army Corps of the Army of the Potomac*, New York, 1896, 678.
35. Humphreys, *op.cit.*, 199.

that part of the Grand Plan for coordination of the Union drive against Lee's army and Richmond was a movement by Ben Butler and his Army of the James. This force of about 39,000 infantry and cavalry, and 82 guns, was expected to march at the same time that Grant left the Rapidan, occupy City Point on the south bank of the James near the mouth of the Appomattox, and then advance along the river toward Richmond, getting a foothold as far upstream as possible. If the Confederates fell back upon the city, the Army of the Potomac would try to unite with the Army of the James in the area which Butler had reached. Whenever Butler should learn that the Confederates were sustaining an attack by Grant or feared it, he was himself to attack with all possible vigor. Was this a good plan? An officer of the Royal Engineers, Captain E.H. Steward, who watched operations, declared that it was "thrusting in a division between Petersburg and Richmond, before the main Confederate army could fall back to cover the capital, while the garrison at Petersburg was held in check by fear of the advance of the Federal army," and that it "was one of the boldest pieces of Grant's strategy, and deserved success . . . It is possible that, had less reliance been placed on the fleet, the advance on the Confederate capital and its capture when almost denuded of its defenders, might have been effected according to Grant's plan."[36]

On May 5-6, Butler's main force had landed at Bermuda Hundred on the north side of the mouth of the Appomattox, across from City Point, which was seized by Negro troops. At this time, Confederate defences were very thin, but Beauregard was attempting to organize an adequate force. The night of May 5, Butler proposed to take what ship-weary troops had landed, and advance on Richmond! The proposition was turned down by both corps commanders, Smith and Gillmore, because of the darkness, unfamiliar terrain, and confusion natural upon landing. On May 6, Butler sent his army forward toward the important Richmond & Petersburg Railroad and the Richmond-Petersburg road. Despite very light opposition, they did not get there. On May 7 and 9, operations against the railroad were a little more successful, but the line was not held. On May 9, Gillmore and Smith proposed to Butler that they cross the Appomattox and enter Petersburg, but Butler refused, saying that his cavalry was operating against the railroads near Petersburg.

Then on May 12, Butler began an advance northward toward the outer works of Richmond. Painfully slow, the Army of the James invested Drewry's Bluff on the James, the main Confederate defensive position south of Richmond, but a proposed general assault was abandoned. On May 16, the Confederates themselves advanced, and after some furious fighting, Butler's army

36. *O.R.* I, xxxiii, 904-905; Steward, *Royal Engineers Professional Papers*, War Office, London.

retired. A heavy rain fell, and early in the evening the Army of the James withdrew to its Bermuda Hundred lines. Butler was now cooped up tightly by a much inferior force on the narrow peninsula about fifteen miles from Richmond and seven from Petersburg. Grant, learning of the defeat of the Army of the James, ordered Smith's corps to move north in aid of Grant's own efforts. Butler as late as June 9 sent Gillmore and his cavalry to try against Petersburg, but Gillmore soon gave up the effort. At one time or another, Butler, W.F. Smith, Gillmore, cavalry commander August V. Kautz, and Rear-Admiral S.P. Lee, delayed movements, muffed opportunities, and failed miserably. Tempers became ragged, everyone blamed everyone else, and everyone was to blame. The Confederates under Beauregard scraped together troops from here and there and managed, with the help of Federal asininities, to hold Richmond, Petersburg, and the vital communications between, while at the same time penning up the much superior Army of the James. A comedy of errors and general ineptitude combined with a skillful Southern leadership to prevent a Northern success, one that might have obviated ten months of siege at Petersburg.[37]

For the final failure to overrun Petersburg on June 15th, when capture might still have been relatively easy, most observers placed immediate blame upon "Baldy" Smith, a stain upon the record of the short, portly, roundheaded officer that obliterated the memory of all his proud services in the Seven Days, at Antietam, and Chattanooga. The military historian, Colonel Thomas L. Livermore, pronounced Smith's timid inaction at the critical moment quite inexcusable. Others censured Butler for not following orders on June 15, and attacking between Petersburg and Richmond. Then, too, Hancock is also criticized. His Second Corps was slow in arriving at Petersburg from the crossing on the James River pontoon bridge because of poor maps and other handicaps. Many feel that when he did arrive, a night attack in the moonlight would have been effective. Grant, too, has been criticized. Busy supervising the James crossing, he and Meade could not oversee all the operations at Petersburg. In fact, enough faultiness existed for twenty men, and controversy over its distribution proved endless. It was Smith whom Grant shortly cashiered, and his presumed reasons for relieving that officer generated another controversy. No part of a sad campaign was sadder than these delinquencies.[38]

37. Basic correspondence, both Union and Confederate, *O.R.* I, xxxvi, pt. 3, 722-903, for June 10-30, 1864. See *Butler's Book*, Boston, 1892, Chs. XV, XVI: West, Richard S., Jr., *Lincoln's Scapegoat General, Benjamin Butler*, Boston, 1945, Chs. XX, XXI; *Private and Official Correspondence of Gen. Benjamin F. Butler*, Norwood, Mass., 1917, III, 155-452, containing spirited letters by Mrs. Butler.

38. Livermore, Thomas A., *Days and Events*, Boston, 1920, 353-364; Gray, John C., and John Codman Ropes, *War Letters, 1862-1865*, 185, 202ff., 461-490; Francis A. Walker, *History of the Second Army Corps*, New York, 1891, 525-538; Kautz, Gen. A.V., *Battles and Leaders*, IV, 533-535; R.E. Colston and G.T. Beauregard, *ibid.*, 536-544; and Meade, *op.cit.*, II, 198 ff. Smith's defensive letter of July

And alas, on the heels of the blunders of the Bermuda Hundred Campaign and June 15 at Petersburg, ensued the commission of more errors by high commanders. On June 16, General Meade, who had arrived before Petersburg, ordered Hancock, who had now taken command of all the forces facing the city, to attack at six in the evening. In the spirited assault that followed, driving the Confederates back at some points, the Union troops suffered severely. At dawn on the 17th, another assault, delivered so stealthily that the command "Forward!" was passed along the line in whispers, made so much fresh ground that Beauregard withdrew to a shorter, stronger line in his rear. Here, on the 18th, more fighting brought the two sides to another deadlock, but when night fell, Grant at last declared himself satisfied, and ordered his troops under cover for some rest. Their losses for the three desperate days, June 15-18, in killed, wounded, and missing, had aggregated 10,586. Thus ended six weeks of blood-drenched marching from the Rapidan to the James.[39]

The final assaults had proved that it was almost impossible to storm Petersburg, no matter how many men were flung against it. And now that Lee could tighten his grip upon it, storming Gibraltar would be as easy. The Confederate positions from Petersburg to Richmond defied such attacks as had been made. While fortified lines were not impregnable, they were proof against assaults so imperfectly coordinated as those Grant's army could deliver. One officer who vividly described a repulse at Petersburg—"it was beyond human endurance to stand such an iron rain;—our men broke and came back a broken, bleeding, routed body"—emphasized the lack of harmony in troop movement.[40] Besides, the Army of the Potomac was now fairly exhausted. Its almost incessant marches day and night, the close grapples with the enemy for more than six weeks, the repeated attacks on trenches defended by brush entangle-

30, 1864, to Senator H.S. Foote of Vermont is in the *Century Magazine*, XXXII, No. 4, Aug., 1897, 636-638. The Walter Wilgus Collection, private, contains correspondence upon Smith's contention that Butler employed a "hold" upon Grant to get Smith ousted, the "hold" being that Butler had seen Grant in his cups. The New York *Independent*, June 16, 1864, carried a vigorous editorial defense of Butler's strategy. Cyrus Comstock in his Journal (LC) writes on July 17 that "Some time ago Smith criticized in his ex-cathedra way this campaign as having been a series of useless slaughters. The General heard of it and told me he did not know which to do, relieve him or talk to him. . . . Smith has declared he will not serve with Butler, and as Butler is to stay for the present, Smith will probably be relieved." Smith had also criticized Meade harshly, apparently for "useless slaughters." But then Meade got on badly with other officers. "Meade and Burnside managed to quarrel again," writes Comstock on July 30. See also Livermore, Thomas L., "The Failure to Take Petersburg June 15, 1864," *Papers of the Military Historical Society of Massachusetts*, V, 33-74; Smith, William F., "The Movement Against Petersburg," *ibid.*, 75-115.

39. Freeman, *Lee*, IV, 444, footnote, remarks that "the actions of June 15-17 were as much mismanaged as any that Grant ever fought in Virginia"; A.H. Burne writes in *Lee, Grant, and Sherman*, 62, that for these three days Grant had "the best opportunity open to him throughout the campaign of winning a great victory," but missed it. His prestige in the North sensibly declined. Humphreys, *op.cit.*, 216-225.

40. Carter, Robert and Walter, *War Letters from the Battlefront* (Ms. Letters), II, 743-744, HEH.

ments and heavy embankments, the discouragement as ranks wilted under hot musket and artillery fire, had worn it out. A considerable number of the officers, dauntlessly leading the men into battle, had been slain or wounded; great numbers of privates were in their graves or in the hospitals. Rest and reanimation were badly needed.

It was a spent and shaken body of men who, realizing by the opening of July that the campaign from the Rapidan had ended in disillusionment, contrasted their present ragged ranks with the ardent hundred thousand who had plunged into the shades of the Wilderness. They would need time to recuperate, and reinforcements to supply their depletions. At this date, with Lincoln's Presidential battle just beginning, great numbers of voters felt tired and shaken too. As Senator Lyman Trumbull wrote, they "fear he is too undecided and inefficient to put down the rebellion."[41]

When the so-called siege of Petersburg began (not a true siege for the town was never invested, but a beleaguerment, resembling that of Stalingrad in the Second World War), a new phase of Grant's campaign also opened. In reality, the Federals were besieging both Petersburg and Richmond. By midsummer, the lines ran about 26 miles from north of the James to south of Petersburg. Grant had been hammering away incessantly at the enemy; now he would try instead the use of military science and strategic combinations. He had varied his flank marches with frontal assaults; now he would move against the enemy communications at Petersburg—the Richmond & Petersburg, the South-Side Railroad to Lynchburg, the Norfolk & Petersburg which immediately fell, and the Weldon Railroad running south out of Petersburg, thin webs of iron reaching west and south. In his hammering operations, his able quartermaster-general, Rufus Ingalls, had shifted his base of supplies from Aquia Creek to Port Royal on the Rappahannock, then to White House on the Pamunkey, and finally to City Point where the Appomattox River empties into the James. He had done this with such skill and precision that the troops had never lacked food, ammunition, or other essential supplies a single half-day. As new lines were laid out, the men put down their rifles for the axe, spade, and pick with which they rapidly built trenches and covered ways. City Point became an ant-hill humming with activity.

"Steamboats and sailing vessels, transports and lighters of all kinds," wrote one brigade commander, "encumbered the river near the improvised wharves on which they were still working. Higher up, toward Richmond, the eye could

---

41. White, Horace, *Life of Lyman Trumbull*, Boston, 1913, 218. See Field Marshal Wolseley's judgment that the military balance in 1864 up to and beyond Cold Harbor was with the South; Wolseley, Garnet J., ed. James A. Rawley, *The American Civil War: An English View*, Charlottesville, 1964, 205.

distinguish at a distance the turrets of the monitors, which appeared to stand out of the water, and the gunboats, on which enormous pivot guns were visible. The river bank, rising up high, had been cleared and levelled, so as to make room for storehouses, . . . and for a station for the railroad. All this had sprung out of the earth as if by magic . . . All was activity and movement. Legions of Negroes were discharging the ships, wheeling dirt, sawing the timber, and driving piles. Groups of soldiers crowded around the sutlers' tents; horsemen in squadrons went down to the river to water their horses." On the plateau above the James, a small city of huts and tents leaped into sleepless animation.[42]

While the Army of the Potomac and the Army of the James had been playing the most prominent roles in the Federal advance, the third prong in Grant's thrust had been frustrated in the Shenandoah. On May 9, Sigel left Winchester heading south, or up the Shenandoah Valley. He met little opposition until he arrived near New Market, where, on March 15, outnumbered Confederates under John C. Breckinridge smashed him. This was the battle, relatively small, in which the youths of the Virginia Military Institute won great and enduring fame. A few days later, Sigel was relieved and replaced by the controversial David Hunter. A new Union advance aimed at Charlottesville was begun. Hunter defeated Confederates at Piedmont on June 5, burned the VMI building at Lexington, and spread destruction in the Valley. Grant ordered Sheridan to take his cavalry and operate on the Virginia Central from Hanover Junction to Charlottesville where he was to join Hunter. On June 11-12, Sheridan was defeated by Wade Hampton's Southern cavalry at Trevilian Station, and forced to call off his raid. Jubal Early now took over for the reinforced Confederates in the Shenandoah, and planned to attack Hunter June 19 at Lynchburg, only to find the Federals pulling out. Hunter retreated into the Kanawha Valley of West Virginia, leaving the Shenandoah open to Early who headed north toward the Potomac. Grant's plans for the cooperating movement in the Shenandoah had gone awry.

A war of greater organization, ingenuity, and strategic skill had now commenced in Virginia, but its results could not be immediately registered, and its first heavy stroke continued the disheartening tale of bungling and disaster. On July 30, the great mine under the Confederate works at Petersburg, which had been planned by Lt. Col. Henry Pleasants, a civil engineer commanding a regiment (the 48th Pennsylvania) made up largely of former coal miners, was exploded. In the ensuing Battle of the Crater, Union casualties reached a total of about 3,800 while the Confederate casualties were about 1,200. As Grant

---

42. De Trobriand, Gen. Regis, *Four Years with the Army of the Potomac*, Boston, 1889, 594.

put it, the effort was "a stupendous failure," adding to the midsummer sense of gloom and frustration.[43]

[VI]

Meanwhile, a livelier kind of history was being written by William Tecumseh Sherman as commander of the military division of the Mississippi, though it too had tragic interludes, and ran into mid-July without decisive result. He and his subordinates, Thomas, McPherson, and Schofield, had to press their campaign from the Tennessee simultaneously with Grant's from the Rapidan. His army of a hundred thousand, with 254 guns, had gotten under way with a promptness that heartened everybody, and, as we have seen, had quickly thrust Johnston's army from its positions at Dalton and Resaca, for it was large enough to outflank its smaller adversary with ease.

Yet the disparity of strength was not as great as it appeared. Johnston might have counted a ratio of three-to-five, far from hopeless for a defensive position in rough and confusing country. Ahead of Sherman lay a mountainous, thickly wooded, ill-roaded district, with three potentially difficult rivers, the Oostenaula, the Etowah, and the Chattahoochee, in his path. Before him also stood a general who was not only a strategist of stubborn skill, but a vivacious, warmhearted, determined leader, most of whose veterans loved him and would follow him to death with implicit confidence.[44]

Mid-May found Sherman's army pushing beyond the Oostenaula, after taking the two strong Dalton-Resaca positions at a cost of only 6,805 casualties compared with Johnston's 5,245. By the 20th, the rapidly advancing flank marches of Sherman had compelled Johnston to retreat across the Etowah, a stream that he later regretted he had not attempted to defend. Johnston had listened to the advice of two of his three corps commanders, Polk and Hood, in making the withdrawal. Sherman was not confident of his future. "I shall

43. See articles on the Crater by W.H. Powell, C.H. Houghton, and H.G. Thomas, *Battles and Leaders*, IV, 540-567. The vigorous account in Munroe, J.P., *Life of Francis Amasa Walker*, New York, 1923, 266-268, emphasizes Hancock's vigilant competence as contrasted with Burnside's incompetence. The story, possessing suspense and drama, but little military significance, has been too often told to require retelling. This may also be said of Jubal Early's foray toward Washington (best recounted in *Jubal's Raid*, New York, 1960, by Frank E. Vandiver), which reached an outer fort of the capital on July 11, but failed in all its main objects and did the Confederacy as much harm as good. It weakened neither Grant's army nor his determination to fight doggedly ahead. For its effect upon Lincoln see Nicolay and Hay, *Lincoln, op.cit.*, X, 165-171.

44. Govan, Gilbert E., and James W. Livingood, *A Different Valor, The Story of General Joseph E. Johnston*, New York, 1956, give an appreciative view of Johnston; Foote, Shelby, *The Civil War*, New York, 1963, II, 618ff., 622, 623, 646, 647, is judicious; Bradford, Gamaliel, *Confederate Portraits*, Boston, 1914, Ch.I, is balanced. The best edition of Johnston's *Narrative of Military Operations* is edited by Frank E. Vandiver, Bloomington, 1960.

give two days' rest to replenish and fit up," he telegraphed Washington. "On the 23rd I will cross the Etowah and move on Dallas. This will turn the Allatoona Pass." He had managed his operations with skill, taking advantage of the fact that no matter how far Johnston extended his flanks, he could extend his own farther. In his reminiscences he scoffed at the claim of some Southerners that Johnston had deliberately planned to give up his strong points in order to draw the Union army farther south. On the contrary, he wrote, Johnston evacuated these towns only because it was unsafe to wait another hour lest the Northern pincers close.[45]

While he advanced, scattered troops had to guard the railway lines all the way back to Chattanooga, back to Nashville, back to Louisville—they and the railwaymen shouldering a dangerous task. While they maintained the flow of supplies in heat and dust, or more often in pouring rain and mud, they had to fight off the hornet attacks of cavalry, guerrillas, and snipers. Whenever the Southerners could not set a bridge afire or derail a train, they struck other blows. They burned thousands of tons of munitions and stores on the long lines through Tennessee and Kentucky, and captured thousands more. The Tennessee Unionist, John W. Burgess, later noted as a scholar, declared that after a year of watching, and fighting, he was physically almost ruined.[46]

To ensure the efficiency of the long rear lines, Sherman placed them under iron military control with civilian assistance. He restricted trains, subsequently cutting down forage and camp equipment to a minimum; he impounded locomotives and rolling stock from Northern railroads. Later he recalled his satisfaction in seeing cars from distant lines (such as the Lackawanna) hauling his supplies. When the impoverished inhabitants of East Tennessee clamored for food, especially around Chattanooga, he made them grow vegetables with the energy of hunger.

These measures might have excited violent opposition had Sherman not sternly denied his own soldiers aught but necessities. He ordered that each regiment and battery should be restricted to one wagon, and the officers of each company to one pack-animal, for supplies; that the headquarters of each corps, each division, and each brigade should have only a single wagon apiece; and that all remaining transportation should be organized into ordnance and supply trains, carrying twenty days' rations per man for each command. When

---

45. *O.R.* I, xxxvii, pt. 4, 533-595, contains Sherman's dispatches of June 20-25, 1864; see also his revised *Memoirs*, 4th ed., Chs. XVI-XVIII, and M.A. DeWolfe Howe, ed., *Home Letters of General Sherman*, New York, 1909, 296-308. Stone, Henry, "The Atlanta Campaign" (Pt.I, *Papers of the Military Historical Society of Mass.*, VIII) covers the opening of the campaign, and gives the casualties noted here.

46. See Grenville M. Dodge, Ms. *Autobiography*, Iowa State Hist. Lib., for railway duty; Burgess, John W., *Reminiscences of an American Scholar*, New York, 1934, 32-33.

practicable, the soldiers were to carry three days' provisions with them. "This made our ordnance and supply trains pretty heavy," wrote General Grenville M. Dodge, "but the rest of the transportation was very light." Troops began the campaign with 140 rounds of infantry ammunition for each man, 100 rounds of artillery ammunition for each gun, and no tents whatever. Most of the officers in the Army of the Tennessee followed this order literally, and when Sherman took the field he himself stuck to it rigidly.[47]

The Confederates defending the craggy passage from Ringgold into Atlanta were also tied to the same single railway line, the old Western & Atlantic, long owned and operated by the State. The country through which they retreated was steadily being drained of able-bodied men, supplies, and horses. It was so rough and hilly, largely covered by thick woods and brush, and channeled by swift streams, that bodies of troops dared not venture far from the rails, and had little room for manoeuvering, so that Sherman, with far superior forces, was able to compel Johnston to make retreat after retreat by simply moving around one flank or the other. Thus, until Kenesaw Mountain, no great battles marked his early progress. Brisk, fierce engagements took place, confined to one or two corps on each side. The Union Army could always extend its line beyond the Confederate positions on one side or both, making any stand by Johnston impossible. Thus, neither Johnston's defensive situation nor his ability to fortify his lines helped him very much.

Sherman summarized his advance to Atlanta in a few sentences. He declared that Johnston, who in time had 62,000 men, was confident that he could draw the Union forces far from their base, and then turn and destroy them. "We were equally confident and not the least alarmed," asserted Sherman. Johnston fell back by June 21 to just west of the vicinity of Marietta, with the bold and striking peak called Kenesaw Mountain marking his center, and his line extending approximately ten miles. As this was too long, he contracted his flanks and concentrated on Kenesaw, repairing the railroad up to his camps, and preparing for the contest. "Not a day, not an hour or minute," wrote Sherman, "was there a cessation of fire."[48]

Finally, on June 27, Sherman made the mistake of ordering a general assault. Thomas had objected to this, suggesting an advance by systematic sapping trenches, but the commander could not be restrained. Word had just come that Forrest, at Brice's Crossroads, Mississippi, had defeated S.D. Sturgis (the incompetent cavalry officer supposed to help protect Sherman's outer com-

47. Dodge, *ut supra;* also *Personal Recollections of President Abraham Lincoln, General Ulysses S. Grant, and General William T. Sherman,* Council Bluffs, Iowa, 1914, 143ff; Perkins, J.R., *Trails, Rails, and War; The Life of General G.M. Dodge,* Indianapolis, 1929, 91-94.
48. Sherman, *Memoirs,* II, Chs. XVI, XVII, XVIII.

munication in Tennessee) and had driven him back into Memphis. This bad news may have contributed to Sherman's impetuosity. At eight in the morning, he began the fighting all along the high, narrow, and extremely steep front of Kenesaw, its three-mile ridge crammed with batteries and rifle-pits. The battle soon became one of the hottest of the war, with nearly 35,000 men engaged on the two sides. "We have no words to describe this awful day," wrote one Middle Westerner engaged. He found the roar of artillery, explosion of shells, crash of small arms, and yells and groans of the combatants, positively sickening.[49]

"The infantry next to us made a splendid charge and partially took a strong line of works, but were driven back with terrible slaughter," he continued. "So the battle raged all along the west side of the mountain, and so it rolls away down to the right along a line of flame and smoke and blood. But on the extreme right our men are more successful and drive the rebels back . . . Our men on the south have taken three lines of the enemy's works and hold two of them, but are driven from the third with fearful slaughter. This has all occurred before ten A.M., and it has become apparent even to Sherman that the assault is a failure." On the hot days following, the stench of corpses, clouds of flies, and hosts of maggots made the Union position almost intolerable. The total Northern losses were put by Sherman himself at 3,000, a rough figure.[50]

At the end, Sherman did what he should have done at the beginning. The night of July 2, he began to move his main forces by the right flank around Johnston. Part of these troops were now armed with Spencer repeaters, which enabled a single company to fire as effectively as a regiment with the old Springfields. The result was inevitable; Johnston had to pull out to new defences near Smyrna Church. Union troops soon marched past line after line of substantial earthworks, now useless and empty, to enter Marietta on July 3. By July 4, Johnston had pulled back to the bridgeheads across the Chattahoochee, and Sherman pushed him fairly beyond that stream by the 10th. The river, he wrote, was "covered and protected by the best line of field entrenchments I have ever seen, prepared long in advance." These flanking movements were spirited and effective. "I begin to regard the death and mangling of a

49. Magee, E.F., *History of the 72d Indiana Volunteer Infantry*, Lafayette, Ind. 1882, 324ff. S.R. Watkins, in his history of the First Tennessee Regiment, *"Co.Aytch," Maury Gray's First Tennessee Regiment*, Nashville, 1882, 151-164, writes that the Southerners shot down "column after column" until weary of killing. Among the dead were Gen. C.S. Harker, half-a-dozen years out of West Point, and Daniel J. McCook, a former law-partner of Sherman's, just thirty, who recited Macaulay's "Horatius at the Bridge" to his men before the attack.

50. Livermore, *Numbers and Losses*, 121, puts the Union killed and missing at 2,051 on the day of the Kenesaw charge, June 27. O.R. I, xxxviii, pt. 3, 703, 870, gives Confederate losses as 270 for killed and missing.

couple of thousand men as a small affair, a sort of morning dash," he wrote home. [51]

In this advance upon the Chattahoochee and Atlanta the impatient Sherman had to proceed, as he informed Halleck, by the slow tactics of movement upon a long line of fortified positions. "The whole country is one vast fort, and Johnston must have at least fifty miles of connected trenches, with abattis and finished batteries." Sherman kept his army well in hand, reproving Hooker sharply on June 23 for his tendency to separate his Twentieth Corps from the armies under Thomas, McPherson, and Schofield so that he might win a little special glory for himself. Hooker was jealous of these three commanders, all younger and in his view less experienced and capable.[52]

The loss of perhaps three thousand men at or near Kenesaw Mountain in the last ten days of June, however, remained a sore point in the Northern consciousness. Were the attack and repulse unavoidable?

As his troops were approaching the impregnable slopes, Sherman had declared that "we cannot risk the heavy losses of an assault at this distance from our bases." Yet three days later, he telegraphed Halleck that he had changed his mind and now inclined to thrust at the enemy center, although "it may cost us dear." Why the shift? Sherman explained that the results of a frontal drive "would surpass any attempt to pass around." The sequel proved the opposite. In his report he gave a fuller and franker statement of his reasons for a direct attack. "I perceived that the enemy and our own officers had settled down into a conviction that I would *not* assault fortified lines. All looked to me to out-flank. An army, to be efficient, must not settle down to one single mode of offense, but must be prepared to execute any single plan that promises success. I wanted, therefore, for the moral effect, to make a successful assault on the enemy behind his breastworks." The moral effect of uselessly throwing away lives![53]

The soldier-journalist Donn Piatt, who had been made General R.C. Schenck's chief-of-staff, later offered an explanation even less creditable to Sherman. Quoting John A. Logan, he told how on the night before the assault, after reading a newspaper full of news about Grant's fighting, Sherman had looked up from it to say that the whole attention of the country was fixed on the Army of the Potomac, while his army was forgotten. Now *he* would fight; next day he would order the assault. McPherson quietly commented that no necessity existed for this step, since Johnston could again be outflanked. To this Sherman replied that "it was necessary to show that his men could fight

51. Sherman, *Home Letters*, 299.
52. See Sherman's report, *O.R.* I, xxxviii, pt. 1, 61-85.
53. *Ibid.*, also Greeley, Horace, *The American Conflict*, Hartford, Conn, 1879, II, 629.

as well as Grant's." This was hearsay evidence. Yet it was a fact that Sherman had telegraphed Grant the previous week that he was out of patience with Thomas, that the Army of the Cumberland was dreadfully slow, and that "I have again and again tried to impress on Thomas that we must assail and not defend."[54]

The bloodshed at Kenesaw was made harder to bear by the fact that McPherson's subsequent flanking movement on the right (July 2) was an instant success. After reaching the Chattahoochee, Sherman paused. Realizing that his men needed rest, and that Johnston's army was still intact with numbers practically equal to those he had led out of Dalton, Sherman gave the Union forces a breathing-spell to make ready for the next move. He remained quiet until July 16, and on the 17th the main crossing of the Chattahoochee began. Also in July, Farragut was still outside Mobile Bay, its fortifications untested; the national debt was mounting toward two billions of dollars; and the Democrats were preparing for the August Convention that was shortly to nominate McClellan for the Presidency amid cries that the war was a failure.

54. Piatt, Donn, *Memories of Men Who Saved the Union*, New York, 1887, 248-255; Lewis, Lloyd, *Sherman, Fighting Prophet*, New York, 1932, 374-375.

3

Cement of the Union

AS A war becomes rougher, internal politics get rougher too. Throughout the spring and summer of 1864, Lincoln's most anxious efforts, aside from military affairs, were devoted to holding a majority of Northern voters in sufficient harmony to maintain his prestige and moral power. Unity and patience!— these were his fundamental demands. If impatience grew, if men gave way to fear and anger, party disruption would open the gate to national destruction. In June he urged the Yankee journalist Noah Brooks, who sent Washington correspondence to various journals East and West, to do all he could to correct the optimistic delusion that "the war will end right off victoriously." It would not, and people must steel themselves for a cruel endurance of stubborn exertion. Although the North was further ahead than he had anticipated, he stated: "as God is my judge, I shall be satisfied if we are over with the fight in Virginia within a year." As the strain of war increased, he had to meet one domestic crisis after another. Subjected to constant vicissitudes in his relations with the Cabinet, Congressional leaders, editors, governors, and political adventurers, he fought always a central battle for balance, compromise, and an overriding insistence upon unity. If he struck a hard blow here, it was for harmony; if he yielded there, it was for harmony.

[I]

Nobody knew better than Lincoln that the prospect for his reëlection that fall was anxiously uncertain. A democracy always feels the failures of a leader more sharply than his successes. In political sagacity, adherence to principle, and vision of the national future, Lincoln rose superior to his contemporaries. The people of Civil War days, however, saw incomplete lineaments of his wisdom, generosity, and eloquence. What they did see clearly were his deficiencies in executive energy and skill. Some agreed with George Bancroft that he was self-willed and ignorant—ignorant of finance, economic forces, foreign governments, and military necessities. Others thought with Lyman Trumbull that he had drifted when decision was needed. Still others held with Charles

Francis Adams, Sr., that in the storm then raging a stronger hand was needed on the tiller.

Lincoln's prestige had sunk to its nadir after the failure of the Peninsular Campaign and Pope's defeat just outside Washington at Second Manassas. The Democrats were embittered by his decisive removal of McClellan, and Radical Republicans had fallen into the deep depression that inspired fierce demands after Fredericksburg for a reorganization of the Cabinet. Had the United States possessed a government of British type, its Ministry might have fallen. Antietam and the Emancipation Proclamation had lifted the President's standing; Chancellorsville unquestionably depressed it again. Gettysburg and Vicksburg raised it anew; the drama of Missionary Ridge lifted men's hearts like a sudden burst of martial music. Chickamauga hurt Lincoln's prestige but Chattanooga restored it; the first bloody checks of May and June, 1864, sank it once more, and even though Grant was at the gates of the Confederate capital, many in the North did not consider that a victory.

Lincoln and the Administration, knowing the value politically of war news, kept the Baltimore Union Party convention delegates well posted, so that when the news of Hunter's victory at Piedmont (June 5, 1864) came in, there was great cheering. Stanton is credited with having sent these dispatches. Such oscillations of elation and despair were natural and understandable, but they struck many observers as unworthy of a great people with the traditions of the Seven Years' War, the long Revolutionary struggle, and of Valley Forge in its past. Surely Americans had the Spartan valor of their ancestors who had crossed the stormy seas and had subdued a rocky continent to found a nation. It was confidence that he could appeal to the deep, latent tenacity of the American people, complete faith in their chilled-steel devotion to ancient principles, which had inspired Edward Everett Hale to publish in the *Atlantic Monthly* for December, 1863, his unexpected yet clearly inspired tale "The Man Without a Country," which was more than a short story, soon soaring to a mass circulation—which was a trumpet peal lifting the national heart. It was in the same faith that the deep national fealties and convictions of the American people rose superior to the fluctuations of victories and defeats, that another gifted author, the economist and veteran journalist David A. Wells, published *Our Burden and Our Strength* (1864), which was worth as much to the Union cause as a resounding battlefield victory. This book, like Hale's imperishable story, represented the true devotion and tenacity of the Northern people, and helped nerve their arms to strike. So did another telling book of 1864, Charles J. Stillé's *How a Free People Conduct a Long War*, a study of British resolution in combating Napoleon, that helped fortify countless readers. Was this really the spirit of the majority of Northerners?

Lincoln's military missteps, beginning with War Order No. 1 for a general advance on Washington's Birthday in 1862, and his occasionally maladroit interferences with generals, were more evident than the soundness of his basic strategic ideas. Suspension of the habeas corpus, military arrests, and spasms of press censorship offended multitudes who revered the Bill of Rights. As the conflict lengthened, it was saddening to think of the battlefield agonies of tens of thousands of young men, the myriad of bereaved homes, and the coarsening of the national character which were among its effects. Little stories illuminated the popular tension—the story, for example, of a speculator who said exultantly in a crowded car, "Well, I hope the war may last six months longer; in the last six months I've made a hundred thousand dollars." Instantly a woman slapped him, crying "Sir, I had two sons—one was killed at Fredericksburg, the other at Murfreesboro!"; and the indignant spectators hustled him out the door.[1]

Few events of the war aroused such a feeling of mingled anger and anguish in the North as the April "massacre" at Fort Pillow already mentioned. The facts of this occurrence, in which 231 Union soldiers, largely Negroes, were killed while only 14 Confederates fell, have provoked some disputation. Northerners, however, saw only one side. They read headlines announcing "Attack on Fort Pillow—Indiscriminate Slaughter of the Prisoners—Shocking Scenes of Savagery"; dispatches from Sherman's army declaring "there is a general gritting of teeth here"; reports from the Missouri *Democrat* detailing the "fiendishness" of rebel behavior; and editorials like that in the Chicago *Tribune* condemning the "murder" and "butchery." Senator Henry Wilson published in the New York *Tribune* a letter from a lieutenant-colonel in the Army of the Tennessee giving gory particulars, while others poured in from survivors in the Mound City (Ill.) hospital. All this made a heavier impression because of the unquestionable facts that Confederates had previously killed some Negro soldiers after capture, and had exchanged not a single Negro private of the many captured at Battery Wagner, Port Hudson, and Olustee. Was Lincoln doing enough, men asked, to prevent such ebullitions of the barbarism of slavery and to punish them when they took place?[2]

People were now aware that the fast-lengthening casualty-rolls confronted the nation with one of the saddest tragedies of modern history. They had taken

---

1. Nevins, Allan, *The New York Evening Post*, New York, 1922, 320-321.
2. For Fort Pillow, see files of newspapers April 16-30, 1864; Castel, Albert, "The Fort Pillow Massacre: a Frank Examination of the Evidence," *Civil War History*, IV, No. 1, March, 1958, 37-50, a careful examination which reaches the conclusion that a massacre did occur; and the papers in the Chicago Historical Society of Gen. Mason Brayman, commanding this summer at Natchez, which support the charge of an inhuman massacre. Brooks, Noah, *Washington in Lincoln's Time*, ed. Herbert Mitgang, New York, 1958, 138. There is great conflict between various Confederate reports and the *Report of the Joint Committee on the War*, "Fort Pillow Massacre," Washington, 1964, 39th Cong., 1st Sess., House Report No. 65.

deaths hard when Elmer Ellsworth and Theodore Winthrop fell in the first weeks; they took them still harder as the graves of young men numbered hundreds of thousands. And at last the moral costs were all too evident. The war had so many heroic aspects that at first it had been easy to ignore the moral erosion. But now men comprehended that the conflict was accentuating some of the baser features of a society too full of frontier crudities, too casually addicted to neighborhood violence, and too often ready to let the dollar prove or excuse wrong acts. Civil wars often have a Cain-Abel savagery, and this one had sent large armies trampling across defenseless communities. Guerrilla warfare on both sides sometimes became mass-murder, as in Quantrill's raid on Lawrence, Kansas. All along the indefinite warring fronts, and in tenuously-held Federally-occupied areas, bands of outlaws, often irrespective of North or South, were busy ambushing sentries, slaying householders, and perpetrating outrages that made the blood run cold.

The treatment of prisoners of war on both sides was often a story of neglect. Financial corruption spread like some valley fog along ill-cleared waterways —graft in illicit cotton traffic, contracts, appointments to office, bounty-jumping, and tax-evasion. It was small wonder that, while the nation's sacrifices were sullied by so much rascality, sensitive men, anxious to protect the nation's character, sometimes lost heart. Some criticism of Lincoln was healthy, but the danger was that licentious criticism might lead a majority to falter in the war. "Jefferson Davis is perhaps in some respects superior to our President," Charles Francis Adams wrote from the London legation in the spring of 1863. When a perceptive man, snobbishly class-conscious, could write this, public sentiment might take any turn. James Gordon Bennett, who had little education or insight, but a good deal of hard Scotch common sense, was arguing in the *Herald* that Lincoln's vacillations had already gravely prolonged the war, and "will cause it to be interminable if another sort of man, independent of political factions and true to the Constitution, is not soon placed in the President's chair."[3]

A majority of Republicans not only saw that the party must stand or fall with Lincoln, as governors like Andrew, Morton, Curtin, and Yates of Illinois did, but admired his record and personality. Yet a powerful body of the Radicals, who had supported Frémont's emancipationist ideas, were so dissatisfied with Lincoln's conciliation of Border settlement and ten-percent plan for Reconstruction, that they were ready to revolt.[4] Among the War Demo-

3. New York *Herald*, quoted in Detroit *Free Press*, Jan. 7, 1864, C.F. Adams to R.H. Dana, Jr., Apr. 8, 1863, R.H. Dana Papers, Mass. Hist. Soc.
4. Welles, Gideon, "The Opposition to Lincoln in 1864," *Atlantic Monthly*, March, 1878, No. CCXLV, Vol. XLI, 366-376.

crats, indispensable to a Union Party, a large number adhered to Lincoln. They shrank from the Copperheads, respected the President's abilities, and rejoiced over his charitable attitude toward conquered Southerners. Yet here, too, some would prefer another man. They parroted the cry: "The Constitution as it is and the Union as it was," which sounded patriotic and was actually defeatist. They accepted the argument, pleasing to Lincoln-haters, that the principle of one-term Presidencies ought to be firmly established. Nobody since Andrew Jackson had served two terms, and eight men in succession had held the White House four years or less.

The Radical opposition to Lincoln might have been less formidable if he had treated members of Congress, who now included more than the usual proportion of vain, jealous, and fanatical men, with greater tact. He never concealed his contempt for "politicians" and their "sophisms." In conversation he sometimes gave the names, with biting comment, of men he thought foolish or rascally. He took pains, to be sure, to maintain his friendship with Charles Sumner, Thaddeus Stevens, Henry Wilson, Lot M. Morrill, James W. Grimes, Galusha Grow, and other influential figures. He tried to handle a few men he really despised, such as coarse Ben Wade and serpentine Henry Winter Davis, with gloves. He was ready to give Congressional leaders the patronage they wanted. But he could be as hostile to enemies like the New York Peace Democrat Ben Wood as they were to him; and, having sat in Congress himself, he had no awe of it. He was no more disposed to let Congress manage the war than when he had refused to call a special session after Fort Sumter, and he was still less willing to let it manage the peace.

He had been aloof in his relations with some of his Cabinet. To the two principal departments, State and War, he gave close attention, but Welles, Chase, Montgomery Blair, Caleb Smith, and Bates were expected to run their machines to suit themselves. His Administration remained a loose coalition, never unified, seldom harmonious. Chase still complained to friends that no coordination of the departments existed, and so little consultation that when he wished to know how the war was getting on he had to consult newspapermen. While the Cabinet is not historically a consultative body, Lincoln might have made fuller use of it for the exchange of information; it was important for Welles to know what moneys Chase could provide for ships, and for Blair to know what naval vessels might carry mail. Lincoln visited Stanton every day, saw Seward frequently, and sometimes consulted Montgomery Blair, but neglected the others. The fact was that the country did not wish a highly centralized government, and he could make no greater error than to strive to give it one.

Gideon Welles, grumbling that he had little of Lincoln's confidence, thought that Seward and Stanton got too much of it. He suspected that Seward, by his devious ways and loose talk, risked pushing some States into the Democratic column. He was equally distrustful of acid-tongued Senators like Lyman Trumbull and William Pitt Fessenden, who seemed trying to destroy confidence in the President. Their criticisms too often reached critical editors like Greeley, Medill, and Bennett. "If, therefore, the reëlection of Mr. Lincoln is not defeated, it will not be owing to them."[5] When Welles wrote this, Greeley believed that Rosecrans might be a more popular Presidential candidate than Lincoln.[6]

Secretary Chase held no stronger position in the Administration than that of financial specialist. Yet he was not only an able fiscal administrator, the creator of the national banking system and a military organizer of some limited experience within his State, but also the ambitious head of one fairly numerous wing or faction of the Republican Party in the Middle West. Chase believed that Lincoln's conception of the Executive was too constricted, but Lincoln's instinct in this matter was sound. Nevertheless, some careful enlargement of the Administration to include a bureau of transportation and supplies, the partial equivalent of the War Industries Board in the the first World War, and a bureau for the freedmen, might have strengthened it immediately, and helped it cope with the grave problems of 1864-1866. Other men agreed with Chase that Lincoln's gifts simply did not include distinction as an administrator.[7] In political acumen he was unexcelled; his sense of timing—his patient instinct for the occasion, or as Nicolay and Hay put it, his *opportunism*—was remarkable; his breadth of view was statesmanlike. But his haphazard, unsystematic ways were sometimes the despair of associates.

All spring, visitors found Lincoln painfully altered in looks and manner; as April ended, the Ohio Congressman A.G. Riddle found him worn and harassed.[8] The almost endless war, the grief and anxiety were proving an intolerable burden. Others in and outside Congress were equally worried, and nerves were growing taut. Washington, no longer close enough to battlefields to hear the guns, was still a huge receiving-station for the wounded. As boatloads of casualties steadily arrived on the Potomac waterfront, and trainloads rumbled in by rail, cohorts of ambulances jolted through the streets to the twenty-one hospitals. People from the North and West, betraying hurry, anxiety, and grief, thronged through the city on their way to hospitals in Freder-

5. Welles, *Diary*, II, 130-131.
6. Gilmore, James Robert, *Personal Recollections of Abraham Lincoln and the Civil War*, London, 1899, Chs. X-XII, especially 103, 145-46.
7. See Maurice, Sir Frederick, *Statesmen and Soldiers of the Civil War*, Boston, 1926, Ch.V, on the penalties Great Britain and the United States have both paid for lack of system in war.
8. Riddle, Albert G., *Recollections of War Times*, New York, 1895, 266-267.

icksburg or Culpeper. Details of clerks from government departments who had volunteered for half-month duty as nurses and orderlies came back with tales of the suffering they had seen. Night after night, men with anguished faces, and women who wilted at the sight of bloody forms, viewed the changing procession. Those watchers in the May or June moonlight who saw two or three thousand casualties landed at a time on the Sixth-Street Wharf never forgot the ghastly lines of shattered men, the clumps of tearful spectators, and the rigid shapes of those who had died in transit, outlined against the flowing river and distinct shores. Meanwhile, letters written in the midst of amputations, hemorrhages, and death were scattered far and wide across the country.

"There are many very bad now in hospital," ran one letter signed Walt Whitman, "so many of our soldiers are getting broke down after two years, or two and a half, exposure and bad diet, pork, hard biscuit, bad water or none at all, etc., etc., so we have them brought up here. Oh, it is terrible, and getting worse, worse, worse. I thought it was bad; to see these I sometimes think is more pitiful still."[9]

[II]

The cement of the nation had been furnished since Federalist-Republican allegiances by its political parties; what if the cement began to crumble? In the spring of 1864, it seemed to be disintegrating, for the two main parties were both more deeply riven than ever. Peace Democrats were willing to end the war even without saving the Union; War Democrats were determined to end the war on a full restoration of the Union and on no other fixed condition whatever. In opposition to them the Moderate Republicans stood for the Union, Emancipation, and a rapid Reconstruction on mild terms; the Radical Republicans demanded Union, Emancipation, and a delayed Reconstruction on steel-hard terms or rather penalties. A variety of shades of opinion might be distinguished under these four areas, but they suffice for a broad classification. If the Peace Democrats ever gained overwhelming strength in the North and Northwest, the Union was lost. If the Radical Republicans conquered majority opinion, they would insist upon nominal union in spiritual disunion.

Lincoln, the chieftain and animating spirit of the Moderate Republicans, provided by his moral leadership the truest national cement of all. He stood for a party of the Center, uniting the War Democrats and Moderate Republicans in the new Union Party. Clearly, he had two battles to fight. In the first,

9. Walt Whitman to his mother, Washington, Apr. 5, 1864; *The Wound Dresser*, New York, 1949, 160-161.

he must enforce sufficient harmony within this Union Party to gain and hold the nomination with a strong chance of election. This did not appear easy in April, and looked still harder in August, when many discontented members clamored for a new convention. In his second battle he must defeat the Democrats, who were expected to nominate McClellan. All the while the war would be a mighty tide bearing the ship of state and the several parties in unpredictable directions. Waves of hope would lift the vessel forward. Waves of dejection would stop it, spin it into eddies, or throw it upon the rocks. Was shipwreck a real danger? Very real, indeed, for a few more defeats in late summer might possibly have swept the country into an irrational demand for peace at almost any price. All spring, all summer, Lincoln and his adherents had to confront ever fluctuating difficulties and perils, while the dragging, wearisome war itself, with its inevitable drain upon national morale, was a far more important factor than the changing ideologies of the stormy time.

The Administration, though numbering old Jacksonian leaders like Welles and Blair, could do little for the Democratic rank-and-file. It offered a haven in the Union Party for staunchly individualistic War Democrats like John A. Dix and Andrew Johnson, and that was about all. To Peace Democrats it could only assert a defiant, unremitting opposition. Lincoln expressed this defiance in an April address at the Sanitary Fair in Baltimore, drawing a line between liberty as defined by wolves and defined by sheep, and coupling his use of colored troops with the general advance of emancipation.[10] On the Republican side the Moderate Republicans presented no problems of grave perplexity, but the Radical Republicans offered Lincoln nearly as much hostility as the Peace Democrats, and were as refractory and treacherous.

These Radicals showed no lack of resolution. Initially their movement had possessed four principal objects. They meant, first, to insist on a more energetic prosecution of the war; second, to require that no great army be entrusted to a general who did not believe in complete victory and emancipation; third, to persuade the President to get rid of lukewarm Cabinet members like Montgomery Blair; and fourth, to induce him to make more efficient use of his Cabinet. Later, they added another object, governmental adoption of a Reconstruction policy that would keep the South subjugated until all roots of rebellion were dead, and this they soon regarded as the most important of all. Radical critics made some mistaken assumptions. They thought that Seward and the Blairs led while Lincoln followed, when the opposite was the fact. They believed that Ben Butler would make a better military adviser than Halleck or Stanton. Nevertheless, they held a few correct ideas upon the need

10. Lincoln, *Works*, VII, 301-303.

for such firm war leadership as Grant and Sherman and Farragut were soon to supply.[11]

Lincoln never lacked humility, and this spring gave it emphatic expression. His political difficulties were brought home to him when Governor Thomas E. Bramlette of Kentucky faced a tempest over the compulsory enrollment of male slaves of twenty to forty-five for military draft. As Border State slaveholders saw Federal officers take down names, they trembled for their property. The governor hurried to Washington to talk with Lincoln, and the President thereupon explained in a letter to the Frankfort *Commonwealth* why he believed that Negro enlistments were a necessity. These enlistments, he wrote, had cost the government nothing in foreign embarrassments or in popular strength at home; they had helped the freedmen; and they had given the nation fully 130,000 soldiers, seamen and laborers. To this he added a characteristic comment. "I claim not to have controlled events, but confess plainly that events have controlled me. Now, at the end of three years struggle the nation's condition is not what either party, or any man devised, or expected. God alone can claim it. Whither it is tending seems plain. If God now wills the removal of a great wrong, and wills also that we of the North, as well as you of the South, shall pay fairly for our complicity in that wrong, impartial history will find therein new cause to attest and revere the justice and goodness of God."[12]

Feeling in Kentucky nevertheless remained so inimical to a slave-arming Administration that the self-styled Unionists there shortly took action which made it certain that the State in the fall would cast her electoral vote against Lincoln. Provost Marshals meanwhile enlisted Negroes in large numbers, for Kentuckians, seething with discontent and hatred, refused to fill the State quotas with volunteers.[13]

Beyond doubt, the astute young Maine politician, James G. Blaine, was right in believing that the prevailing judgment of the Union-Republican Party pointed to Lincoln's renomination. The party would fatally cripple itself if it repudiated the Administration. Moreover, the President's faith had fortified the national heart, for he saw as nobody else the American Idea. But would the party battle for him in a fervent or a lukewarm spirit?

Among the men whose jealous ambition impaired party harmony, the able, self-righteous Salmon P. Chase held a conspicuous place. Although he maintained with Chadband rhetoric that he never used the Treasury to build a personal machine, its staff supplied active workers on his behalf. Friendly with

11. See the exchange of opinion among Stanton, Chase, and Welles in Oct. 1862, on Lincoln's deficiencies, Welles, *Diary*, I, 160-169.
12. Lincoln, *Works*, 281-283; to Albert G. Hodges.
13. Coulter, E.M., *The Civil War and Readjustment in Kentucky*, Chapel Hill, 1926, 198-207.

all Radicals, he had given them energetic assistance in the State elections of 1862 in the hope of winning their support. In his financial labors he had taken pains to conciliate such leaders of industry and banking as Erastus Corning, George S. Coe, W. M. Vermilye, and George Opdyke, at the same time wooing the principal Republican editors and officers of the Union League. While pretending throughout 1863 that he was not anxious for the Presidency, he was actually burning for the office.[14]

When Lincoln at the close of 1863 announced his liberal plan of Reconstruction, Chase did not need to warn his friends that the hour for action had struck. His diary tells us nothing. But an impetuous Kansas politician of erratic judgment, Senator Samuel Clarke Pomeroy, a former Amherst student full of New England Radicalism, helped form a "national committee". Pomeroy and his Radical associates dealt just one blow—but it proved a fatal blow to Chase's aspirations. They issued a pamphlet entitled "The Next Presidential Election", and a shorter statement soon known as the Pomeroy Circular. These were at once summarized by the press and franked widely over the country by Radical Congressmen, so that Washington's Birthday in 1864 found the entire North acquainted with them. They offered an offensively phrased argument that aroused widespread irritation and derision. The reëlection of Lincoln, they declared, would be a national calamity; only an advanced thinker, versed in political and economic science, could guide the ship of state through the rapids ahead; and fortunately this advanced thinker was at hand—nobody needed to be told that Secretary Chase was the man; he even was named. Chase assured Lincoln on February 22 that he had known nothing about the circular or a formal committee, although he admitted he had consented to the use of his name to "several gentlemen" who had called on him. Ten years later, his statement that he had no prior knowledge of the circular was contradicted by its author, James M. Winchell, who declared flatly that Chase had been informed of the proposed action and approved it fully.[15]

14. Lincoln, *Works*, VII, 200-201; Schuckers, J.W., *The Life and Public Services of Salmon P. Chase*, New York, 1874, 356-489; Donald, David, ed. *Inside Lincoln's Cabinet*, New York, 1954, 179, 190, 208-209. Chase esteemed Lincoln, but personal uneasiness tinged his attitude, for he suspected that the virulent attack that Frank Blair made upon him in the House at the end of April might have had Lincoln's sanction. It did not; Lincoln was distressed to learn that Blair had kicked over another beehive. But the circumstances of the attack, made as Blair departed to resume his commission as major-general with the 17th Corps in the Atlanta campaign, were highly irritating; and Blair's charges, impugning Chase's honesty, were so outrageous that the Secretary's Radical friends had advised an immediate and abrupt resignation. Much annoyed, Lincoln considered cancelling his orders restoring Blair to the army. Chase accepted the President's disclaimer of any connection with the attacks, brought to him by two Ohio politicians (Riddle, *Recollections of War Times*, Chs. XXXVII, XXXVIII), but he and his friends resented more than ever Lincoln's friendliness to the Blair clan. Congressional Globe, 38th Cong., 1st Session, Appendix, 50, 51, and Pt. II, 1829.

15. New York *Times*, Sept. 15, 1874; Schuckers, *Chase, op.cit.*, 497, 499-501.

This movement was so premature and ill-supported that John Sherman, one of Pomeroy's helpers, instantly retreated.[16] The country, in fact, received the circular with general hostility. Moderate Republicans, War Democrats, and most uncommitted voters, however critical of Lincoln, regarded him as decidedly preferable to Chase. "The Pomeroy Circular has helped Lincoln more than all other things together," wrote one of John Sherman's friends.[17] As Welles put it, the Chase gun had been far more dangerous in its recoil than its discharge. Lincoln kept a dignified silence.[18] How little strength Chase possessed was demonstrated when the Ohio legislature passed a resolution in favor of Lincoln's reëlection.

But although this first Radical foray against Lincoln quickly collapsed, an alarming amount of ill-humor was evident in the country. The New York *Times*, declaring the House had done nothing for nineteen weeks but dawdle over empty speechmaking with an utter neglect of urgent financial legislation, accused Congress of "flagrant unfaithfulness."[19] Sensible men were aghast at the Senate's passage of a bill against speculation in gold, a measure certain to defeat its object by raising the price of gold. When it did rise on June 23 to 208 in greenbacks, Congress saw that the new law must be repealed. Publication of the President's letter to Montgomery Blair, suggesting that his brother Frank let his commission as major-general lie dormant while he returned to the House, and have it revived when he wished to rejoin the army, seemed to many a flagrant evasion of the Constitutional provision that "no person holding any office under the United States shall be a member of either House of Congress during his continuance in office," and repugnant to a sentiment that in English-speaking lands went back to the "Self-Denying Ordinance" of Puritan Commonwealth days.[20]

In May, Henry Winter Davis carried through the House a Reconstruction Bill that was designed to make mincemeat out of Lincoln's policy as laid down in his annual message. Much talk was meanwhile heard about the "rotten boroughs" that might figure in Lincoln's reëlection—Arkansas, Delaware, Louisiana, Maryland, West Virginia, statehood for Nevada, and so on—and the possible perversion of democracy by manipulation of their votes.

At the same time, a sinister interpretation was placed on the government's impetuous suppression of two New York newspapers, the *World* and *Journal*

16. Details in Schuckers' *Chase*, 497-500; Zornow, W.F., "The Kansas Senators and the Reëlection of Lincoln," *Kansas Historical Quarterly*, May, 1951; letters of Philip Speed and J. Gibson to Lincoln, Feb. 22, 1864, Lincoln Mss., LC.
17. Zornow, *op.cit.*, 137.
18. Welles, *Diary*, I, 525, 533.
19. As cited in New York *World*, May 5, 1864.
20. Lincoln, *Works*, VI, 554-555; New York *World*, May 5, 1864.

of Commerce, on what turned out to be no grounds at all. In mid-May they had been hoaxed into publication of a fictitious Presidential proclamation appointing a day of national fasting, humiliation, and prayer, and announcing an imminent draft of 400,000 more men. This was the work of a would-be stockmarket manipulator, whose forged proclamation, foisted upon the two newspapers in the dead of night, was quickly repudiated. Sales of papers were stopped, and bulletins announcing the imposture were posted. A dispatch boat that was hurried down New York Bay caught the *Scotia* before she cleared the Narrows for Europe with the forgery. Although in the temporary excitement gold shot up ten percent, little real harm was done. The suppression was indefensibly abrupt and harsh. Democratic spokesmen wildly asserted that civil liberties were dead, and lamented that the United States had no Thiers who dared denounce its despot. The editors of the two injured newspapers, when these dailies were restored to their owners on May 22, were left boiling with anger, and denouncing the Administration for both its arbitrary action and its tardiness of release. Gideon Welles agreed that the suppression, for which he correctly blamed Seward and Stanton, had been "hasty, rash, inconsiderate, and wrong."

This suppression gave Horatio Seymour an opportunity to attack the Administration afresh, and to instigate legal proceedings in the local courts against General Dix and his subordinates, all of which only deepened the general conviction that Seward lacked judgment. Worst of all, it reminded the country of numerous other instances in which editors had been disciplined and their papers stopped on charges that they were interfering with enlistments or otherwise hampering the war effort. And the fact that three of the ablest newspapermen of the country, Henry Villard, Adam Hill, and Horace White, were needlessly harassed—Villard ordered under arrest by Stanton, and White sharply questioned—added to the general feeling of uneasiness.[21]

John G. Nicolay, talking with Thurlow Weed at the end of March, had found him gloomy. "His only solicitude," Nicolay wrote the President, "was for yourself. He thought if you were not strong enough to hold the Union men together through the next Presidential election . . . the country was in the utmost danger of going to ruin." Actually, Weed doubted that Lincoln *could* hold the Union men together. The Cabinet, he pointed out, was so notoriously discordant and jangling that it gave the President little support and set the

---

21. The New York *World, Herald, Tribune,* offer full accounts in late May issues. For general studies, see Randall, James G., *Constitutional Problems under Lincoln,* Urbana, 1951 pp. 396-499; Nicolay and Hay, *Lincoln,* IX, 47-50; Rosewater, Victor, *History of Cooperative News-Gathering in the United States,* New York, 1930, pp.104-105. The man guilty of the forgery, Joseph Howard, then city editor of the Brooklyn *Eagle,* was quickly run down, but Henry Ward Beecher pleaded for him with Lincoln, and he escaped lightly. Welles, *Diary,* II, 37-38.

nation a bad example. "Welles is a cipher, Bates a fogy, and Blair at best a dangerous friend."[22] This lack of harmony was all too obvious. Seward and Stanton were openly gleeful over Chase's discomfiture, laughing about it in a corner chat at a Cabinet meeting, while Montgomery Blair frankly delighted in every buffet that Stanton took. Judicious men feared that even though Chase and Frémont were weak candidates, their fractious followers might disrupt the party and cripple the national war effort.[23]

Everybody knew, as spring advanced, that Lincoln would be renominated by the national Convention to meet in Baltimore on June 7. Decisive majorities in both houses of the Maryland, Minnesota, Kansas, and California legislatures had called for him; so had most Union and Republican members of the New Jersey, New York, Connecticut, and New Hampshire legislatures. Republicans of diverse views knew that, all in all, he was the best candidate available.[24] But this was not the important point: the danger was that he would be named without deep conviction, and that factional quarrels would then defeat him and weaken the battle power of the North. Greeley had offered a fresh demonstration of folly in a rumbling editorial declaring that Chase, Frémont, Butler, or Grant would be better.[25] Chase made it plain in letters to friends that, while he was ready to withdraw his own name, he was far from ready to advocate the reëlection of an indecisive President subject to the influence of such political schemers as Thurlow Weed and Montgomery Blair, and leaning toward a soft Reconstruction policy.[26]

Factionalism rode higher and higher in the party. It was astonishing how much sordid greed and personal malice pervaded the organization that had seemed so happily idealistic four years earlier. Gideon Welles, resentful of stinging attacks on the Navy Department that he ascribed to contractors, claim agents, corrupt newspapermen, and such unprincipled members of Congress as John P. Hale, thought that Chase abetted his harassment. They exchanged blistering letters, and glared at each other in Cabinet meetings.[27] Blair, Chase, and Stanton, indeed, hardly concealed their mutual detestation. When Montgomery Blair wrote later that he believed Chase was the only man Lincoln ever really hated, he spoke for himself; it was Blair who nursed the hatred, for Lincoln based hatreds only on principle, not on personal feeling.[28] As for Frémont, few people except his wife Jessie and the extreme Abolitionists

22. Nicolay to Lincoln, Mar. 30, 1864, Nicolay Papers, LC.
23. Welles, *Diary*, I, 536.
24. New York *Tribune*, Feb. 23, 1864.
25. *Ibid.*, Feb. 2, 1864; he used the one-term argument.
26. Chase, Feb. 29, 1864, to James A. Hamilton, *Chase Papers*, New York Public Library.
27. Welles, *Diary*, I, Chs. XV, XVI.
28. Blair to Samuel J. Tilden, June 5, 1868; *Letters and Literary Memorials of Samuel J. Tilden*, ed. John Bigelow, New York, 1908, I, 232-233.

thought him really fit for the presidency. Yet when the Missouri House rejected 46 to 33 a resolution endorsing the Administration, the St. Louis press explained that most Republicans of German blood favored the election of Frémont.[29]

"Stanton has a cabinet and is a power in his own Department," growled Welles. "He deceives the President and Seward, makes confidants of certain leading men, and is content to have matters move on without being compelled to show his exact position. He is not on good terms with Blair, nor is Chase, which is partly attributable to that want of concert which frequent assemblages and mutual counselling on public measures would secure. At such a time the country should have the combined wisdom of all." In May, 1864, R.H. Dana, Jr., wrote his wife, "The cabinet is disjointed. There is more hate, more censure uttered by members of the cabinet against each other than I supposed possible. I speak for what is said directly to me." In another letter, to Motley, Dana said: "The cabinet is at sixes and sevens . . . They say dreadful things about one another. . . ." Blair was quite critical of Welles, for example, but not of Seward.[30]

While the Union Leagues rallied to Lincoln's side, and Henry J. Raymond brought the New York *Times* into a supporting position, two of the most powerful Republican editors, Bryant and Greeley, refused to endorse him; independent-spirited governors like John A. Andrew and Oliver P. Morton, and critical-tempered Senators like Sumner and Fessenden stood coldly aloof. Wisely, Lincoln refused to antagonize the doubtful ones by aggressive measures in his own behalf. He was receptive, but avoided any grasping eagerness. He discouraged Carl Schurz from leaving the army to work for him,[31] and evinced no anxious uneasiness lest Grant might seek the White House. Though glad to hear from Rufus Jones that Grant spurned politics, he remarked with philosophic magnanimity that, if Grant took Richmond, we should let him have the office.[32] Whatever men talked about in politics interested Lincoln keenly, but he lifted himself above appetite or animosity. As Noah Brooks told California readers, he took almost no thought of his own future. "But, patient, patriotic, persevering, and single-hearted, he goes right on with his duty, pegging away just as though, as he has said to me, his own life was to end with

29. Among Frémont's supporters were some Radical Republicans, some Abolitionists, some Germans, and some War Democrats; 350 to 400 all told.

30. Welles, *Diary*, II, 17-18; Dana to his wife, May 3, 1864 and to Motley, May 7, 1864, Dana Papers, Mass. Hist. Soc.

31. Nicolay and Hay, *Abraham Lincoln*, IX, 56, 59, 60.

32. Grant was simply not interested. He wrote from Nashville, Jan. 20, 1864, to a politician who tried to tempt him (I.N. Morris) that election as the next President was the last thing in the world he desired. "I would regard such a consummation as being highly unfortunate for myself, if not for the country." Grant Papers, Illinois State Hist. Library.

his official life, content to leave his earnest labors and conscientious discharge of duty to the disposal of God and country." To which Brooks added: "A nobler and purer nature than his never animated man."[33]

Frémont was the first possible nominee pushed into the arena. A "people's provisional committee" of Radical origin invited like-minded lovers of freedom to gather in Cleveland on May 31, and about 350 self-chosen men from fifteen states and the District of Columbia met that day in Cosmopolitan Hall.[34] Since the really important Radicals like Henry Winter Davis, Zach Chandler, and Ben Wade had stood coldly aloof, the calls were signed by such relatively obscure Missouri politicians as B. Gratz Brown, Emil Preetorius, Friedrich Kapp, and James Redpath. Although some observers believed the movement had the covert sympathy of John A. Andrew, Schuyler Colfax, and David Dudley Field, they had sense enough to keep quiet.[35] Wendell Phillips, Frederick Douglass, and Elizabeth Cady Stanton were the principal personages of some national renown to stand up for the Pathfinder, or to support the call for a convention. The proceedings were short and businesslike, for everyone present agreed that Frémont should be nominated, and everyone believed that more emphasis should be thrown upon repudiation of Administration policies than upon condemnation of the rebellion.

The brief platform, Radical from beginning to end, promised a sweeping reversal of Lincoln's policies, and an acceleration of government action against slavery. One resolution, insinuating Administration indifference to governmental integrity and economy, promised strict regard to both. It contained a forcible assertion that as the war had destroyed slavery, the Federal Constitution should now be amended to prohibit its reëstablishment, and "to secure to all men absolute equality before the law." Another plank demanded that civil liberties be protected against infringement outside of areas under martial law. A third called for a constitutional amendment restricting Presidents to a single term. The most important resolutions declared that control of Reconstruction

---

33. Letter dated Oct. 6, 1863, in Sacramento *Daily News*.

34. Blaine, James G., *Twenty Years of Congress*, Norwich, Conn., 1886, I, 516, says *150*. *American Annual Cyclopaedia*, 1864, 786, says *500*.

35. Nevins, Allan, *Frémont*, New York, 1955, 574-575. Frémont later wrote: "The Cleveland Convention was to have been the open avowal of that condemnation which men had been freely expressing to each other for the past two years, and which had been fully made known to the President. But in the uncertain condition of affairs, leading men were not found willing to make public a dissatisfaction and condemnation which could have rendered Mr. Lincoln's nomination impossible; and their continued silence and support established for him a character among the people which leaves now no choice." The New York *World* commented Sept. 20: "Frémont alone of all the recognized leaders of the Republican Party dared to stand forth as the public opponent of a man who has been for two years the object of their freely expressed private scorn. . . ." McPherson, Edward, *The Political History of the United States of America During the Great Rebellion*, Washington, 1865, 410-415.

belonged to the people through their representatives in Congress, not the Executive, and asked that the lands of rebels be confiscated and distributed among soldiers and actual settlers. Clearly, the document was not a practical program of action, but an extremist manifesto. This tiny splinter-party hoped not to elect any man, but to ally itself with malcontent Republicans in defeating Lincoln and his moderate aims. The vital question to most members was the adoption of a Radical plan of Reconstruction. Others were actuated by devotion to the Pathfinder, memories of Administration hesitancy in Kentucky and Missouri, sympathy for the freedmen, and disgust with the protracted war effort.

Frémont, now fifty-one, restless, ambitious, and erratic as ever, had neither liking nor aptitude for politics. Living in New York surrounded by Radical antislavery men who had bitterly resented his removal from command in Missouri, influenced by his impatient wife, and bruised by what that judicious corps-commander Jacob D. Cox believed to be the Administration's negligent treatment of himself and his soldiers in the West Virginia campaign, he had longed for restoration to military authority. If nearly everybody mistrusted the calculating Blairs, he had special reason for dislike in their enmity and the malicious stories they had circulated about him; if the Wades, Sumners, and Chandlers criticized Lincoln, Frémont was still more critical when he heard that Lincoln had called him a "bespattered hero." When nominated for President by acclamation, he felt reluctance, for he knew he was a mere figurehead. To his discredit, his letter of acceptance on June 4 betrayed personal animus toward the Administration, being full of shopworn Radical phrases about military dictation, usurpation, executive feebleness, incapacity, and imminent bankruptcy. But to his credit, he repudiated the platform declaration upon the confiscation of Confederate lands, and with more promptness than McClellan showed this summer, resigned his army commission.

John Cochrane, chosen for Vice-President, was neither stronger nor weaker than most such nominees. A graduate of Hamilton College, a hard-working Congressman in Buchanan's time, a former State-Rights Democrat, a patriotic brigadier-general who had himself raised a regiment, he had been elected Attorney-General of New York State on the Union-Republican platform in 1863. He had been an early advocate of the enlistment and arming of Negro troops. So astute an observer as Gideon Welles pronounced him a leader of ability and principle.

The Cleveland nominations utterly failed to impress the country. While most Moderate Republicans thought the convention a motley assemblage of weak and erratic political vagrants, the War Democrats and Peace Democrats for quite divergent reasons disdained it and its choice. Lincoln packed his condemnation into a neat quotation from the Old Testament (II Samuel, 22) about the four hundred Adullamites who withdrew from Gath into a cave. Lincoln is said to have read these words; "And every one that was in distress, and every one that was in debt, and every one that was discontented, gathered themselves unto him, and he became a captain over them; and there were with him about four hundred men."[36] Yet the Convention could not be lightly dismissed. Although in May nobody would have given a copper cent for Frémont's chances of a substantial presidential vote, in a close contest even a small poll might prove as important as James G. Birney's Liberty Party vote had been in 1844; and the full story of his rôle in the election was yet to be written.

[III]

So certain was it that Lincoln would be nominated at Baltimore and control the platform that David Davis, the President's closest Illinois friend, did not deem it worthwhile to leave his Bloomington home for the Convention. The opposition was utterly routed, he assured Lincoln, and if a spokesman for their State was needed, Leonard Swett would suffice.[37] Most of the party, indeed, demanded the renomination. As Bryant wrote, the plain people believed Lincoln honest, the rich people believed him safe, the soldiers believed him their friend, the religious people believed him God's choice, and even the scoundrels believed it profitable to use his cloak.[38] When the Convention opened on June 7 with ex-Governor William Dennison of Ohio as permanent chairman (tactfully selected as a prominent friend of Chase), more than 500 delegates were present. Louisiana, Tennessee, and Arkansas had sent representatives who were unconditionally admitted, while Virginia and Florida men were seated without a right to vote, and South Carolina was rejected.[39]

The gathering met in the Front Street Theatre, festooned with flags and soon densely packed. At the outset, a rugged Kentucky parson, Dr. Robert J. Breckenridge of a ruling border-family, made a speech awesomely Radical in temper. Fortunately, few took him seriously when he said that the government must use all its powers to "exterminate" the rebellion, and that the cement of free institutions was "the blood of traitors." Former Governor Morgan of New York called for a constitutional amendment abolishing slavery. The platform, which received perhaps less note or discussion than usual, called upon citizens

36. Nicolay and Hay, *Abraham Lincoln*, IX, 40.
37. Davis to Lincoln, June 2, 1864, David Davis Papers, Chicago Hist. Soc. (photocopies).
38. New York *Evening Post*, June 3, 1864.
39. *American Annual Cyclopaedia*, 1864, 788.

to discard political differences and center their attention upon "quelling by force of arms the Rebellion now raging." No compromise must be made with Rebels and the demand was laid down for unconditional surrender of "their hostility and a return to their just allegiance . . ." Slavery was the cause of the rebellion and thus there should be an amendment to the Constitution ending slavery. In addition to usual platitudes, harmony in national councils was called for. Discrimination in the armies was to be ended; there was to be speedy construction of the Pacific Railroad; and, of course, there was to be economy and responsibility by the Administration. Then came the ballot for President. Only Missouri voted for General Grant, and Lincoln received a renomination on the first ballot by a vote of 506 to 22. A Missourian moved that the nomination be made unanimous. Then, suffering fearfully from heat, humidity, and overcrowded hotels, the politicians concentrated their attention upon the one undetermined question—the Vice-Presidency.[40]

"Things are going off in the best possible style," Nicolay had written John Hay from Baltimore on the 6th. With only a shadow of opposition to Lincoln visible except for the Missouri Radicals, the Convention seemed too docile under Administration leadership to be exciting. When Nicolay added that Hannibal Hamlin would in all probability be renominated, he might be forgiven his bad guess, for there were as many opinions about the proper selection as factions.[41] Hannibal Hamlin, Joseph Holt, Ben Butler, Simon Cameron, John A. Dix, W.S. Hancock, Edwin D. Morgan, Andrew Curtin, and William S. Rosecrans all had advocates. Even the sixty-three-year-old War Democrat, Daniel S. Dickinson, who had done so much to rally New York after Sumter, was lustily supported by Middle State Radicals, and more slyly by Sumner and some New Englanders who saw that, if Dickinson were elected, Lincoln would

40. McPherson, *op.cit.*, 406-407. Talk about the Vice-Presidency had been going on all spring. Ben Butler later asserted that he had been approached by emissaries professing to speak for Chase and Lincoln, as they inquired whether he would accept a vice-presidential nomination. "Vice Presidential Politics in '64," *North American Review*, Vol. CXLI, No.3, Oct. 1885. He doubtless heard random questions from slandering busybodies, but his story concerning Lincoln is certainly untrue.

41. A.K. McClure says in *Abraham Lincoln and Men of War Times*, Philadelphia, 1892, 444, that Lincoln discreetly but earnestly favored Andrew Johnson's nomination. George Jones, owner of the *Times* and one of Raymond's closest friends, says Raymond was influenced by Lincoln, as McClure was. Nicolay states that, on the contrary, Lincoln's personal feelings were for the renomination of Hamlin, but he persistently withheld any opinion calculated to influence the convention. Nicolay and Hay declare: (*Abraham Lincoln, op.cit.*, Vol. IX, 72-73): "It was with minds absolutely untrammeled by even any knowledge of the President's wishes that the convention went about its work of selecting his associate on the ticket."

Out of these statements grew a controversy to which McClure gives an appendix of nearly fifty pages in his *Lincoln and Men of War Times*. It offers much personal vituperation on both sides; a few statements of historical significance; and, on the whole, a substantiation of Nicolay. McClure's recollections in 1891 of what happened in 1863 are not impressive. Nicolay, Helen, *Lincoln's Secretary, a Biography of John G. Nicolay*, New York, 1949, 207-208.

have to drop Seward from the Cabinet. Sumner was in fact suspected of being a general marplot. He would rejoice if he could get Seward out of the Cabinet by the election of Andrew Johnson. At the same time, Seward, consistently filled with a desire to protect the rights of the freedmen, and in favor of a reorganization of parties that would attract the support of both Southerners and Northern Democrats, also showed a leaning toward Johnson.[42] If the shelving of Hamlin resulted in his running against Fessenden for the Senate in Maine's next Senatorial contest, Sumner would rejoice again, for he hated Fessenden. Seeing a plain threat to Seward, the latter's friends vehemently opposed Dickinson.[43] Hence, the situation became highly confused.

Many men who would really have preferred Hamlin conceded that, as the Republican Party, a sectional organization in 1860, now claimed to possess a national character, a Southern man would better befit it than a Maine down-easter.

Hamlin deserved renomination, for he had been a dignified, salty, right-minded Vice-President, and if he had given little impression of force or stature, his office made it almost impossible to make any impression at all. The son of a poor farmer, deprived of a college education, he had steadily grown as he rose from a law office through legislature, House, and Senate. A gentleman of the old school, a six-footer of blandly courteous manners, he had clung to a stock and black swallow-tailed coat after most men abandoned them. He was punctilious in the discharge of duty; his speech had terse Yankee pungency, but also judgment and tact; and he held some firm convictions—one that amnesty ought to be granted all Southerners sincerely converted to loyalty, and another that the Negro could be developed into a useful citizen just as surely as he had been developed into a soldier.[44]

Lincoln, declared Welles, would have liked Hamlin renominated, despite his personal fondness for Andrew Johnson. But he kept his hands off, and a curious combination of circumstances gave Johnson the victory. For one, Sumner rallied most of New England against Hamlin.[45] For another, the day before

---

42. Cox, Lawanda and John H., *Politics, Principle and Prejudice, 1865-1866*, London, 1963, 220-223.

43. Glonek, James F., "Lincoln, Johnson and the Baltimore Ticket," *Abraham Lincoln Quarterly*, Vol.VI, No.5, Mar., 1951, 261 and *passim*; Hamlin, Charles E., *The Life and Times of Hannibal Hamlin*, Cambridge, 1899, 462-466.

44. Hamlin, *Hamlin, ut supra*, 461ff., and Jellison, Charles A., *Fessenden of Maine*, Syracuse, N.Y., 1962, 178ff., offer full materials.

45. Simon Cameron wrote Senator Fessenden after the convention: "I strove hard to renominate Hamlin, as well for his own sake as yours, but failed only because New England, especially Massachusetts, did not adhere to him." Lot M. Morrill bore the same testimony that the hostility of Massachusetts (i.e. Sumner) had crushed his own efforts for Hamlin. See Hamlin, *Hamlin, op.cit.*, 461-488; Noah Brooks, letter of June 7 from Baltimore in Sacramento *Union*; Charles A. Dana, Jr., in his Journal of a Trip to Washington in January, 1862, has a good characterization of Hamlin, Dana Papers, Mass. Hist. Soc.

the Convention met, the Illinois delegates conferred in Barnum's Hotel upon the attitude they should take toward two rival Missouri groups that were asking admission—a body of Radicals hotly opposed to the Blairs and hence to Lincoln, and some Conservative Republicans who would join everybody else in making the nomination of Lincoln unanimous. The Illinois men were about to vote to debar the anti-Blair contestants, an action which other States would reluctantly ratify, when suddenly a slight, thin-visaged young man arose, and announced that he wished to say a word for himself alone. In his opinion, he went on, Illinois had better favor the admission of the Missouri Radicals. He was John G. Nicolay, Lincoln's secretary! He gave no argument; it was not necessary. Next day Illinois voted as Nicolay suggested. Delegations hostile to the Blair faction joyously took their seats and, as we have noted, the 22 votes of Missouri went on the first ballot to Grant.[46]

This action reflected Lincoln's sagacity, for if the Radicals had been excluded they would have raised a damaging cry of tyranny. But the admission of Missouri Radicals had to be balanced by letting in Lincoln Moderates from Louisiana, Tennessee, and Arkansas. When Tennessee was admitted, Johnson became available. Henry J. Raymond, head of the national committee, had for months argued that a War Democrat should be nominated, and had come to Baltimore convinced that Johnson, with his record as a hot opponent of secession, an effective military governor, and a Radical with some Lincolnian ideas, was the right man. When men whispered that Lincoln must have told Raymond to take this position, the editor said nothing to dispel the idea. It was in such clever management of political movements and manoeuvres that Lincoln excelled.[47]

The Grand National Council of the Union League held a meeting on June 8, and adopted a declaration of principles or quasi-platform, pledging the Union League to vigorous prosecution of the war, to the backing of an anti-slavery amendment, support of the Monroe Doctrine, and championship of the principle that every person bearing arms in defense of the flag is "entitled, without distinction of color or nationality, to the protection of the government . . ." But the Union League's statement of principles differed from the Union platform in declaring "that the confiscation acts of Congress should be promptly and vigorously enforced, and that homesteads on the lands confiscated under it should be granted to our soldiers and others who have been made indigent by the acts of traitors and rebels."[48]

46. Carr, Clark E., *My Day and Generation*, Chicago, 1908, 133-144; Hume, John F., *The Abolitionists*, New York, 1905, Ch. XXI, tells how he cast the votes.
47. Brown, Francis E., *Raymond of the Times*, New York, 1951, 252-253. Cf. George H. Mayer, *The Republican Party, 1854-1964*, New York, 1964, 518, 519.
48. McPherson, Edward, *The Political History of the United States*, Washington, 1864, 410.

The first ballot showed Johnson, Hamlin, and Dickinson far in the lead—Johnson 200, Hamlin 150, Dickinson 108. Instantly Iowa shifted its vote to Johnson, and the avalanche began. For the credit or discredit of this decision we must turn primarily to honest Raymond, who some thought at the time had read Lincoln's mind, but more probably had just followed his own. Hamlin accepted the result with good humor, ready to work hard for both candidates.

The day after the Convention, a committee under Dennison called on Lincoln to inform him of what had been done, and hand him the first copy of the resolutions that he had seen. "I know no reason to doubt that I shall accept the nomination tendered," he replied, "and yet, perhaps, I should not declare definitely before reading and considering what is called the platform." This definite answer he delivered in writing on June 27, sounding a note of warning to the French Emperor in the remark that he would sustain the positions of the State Department and the Republican Convention respecting Mexican affairs. Andrew Johnson's acceptance carried some foolish rhetoric to the effect that treason was "worthy of the punishment of death."[49]

[IV]

As the last delegates from Baltimore reached their distant homes, a thunderbolt fell upon the Radical wing of the party in the resignation of Chase from the Treasury. Washington was dismayed by the announcement (June 30) that he had stepped down, and still more by the news that Lincoln would nominate David Tod, first war governor of Ohio, as his successor. Tod was a notorious dunderhead. When the Senate met in executive session on July 1, Chase's admirers were livid with wrath, asserting that he had been driven out by the machinations of the Blair family, that Tod was unfit, and that the quarrel would cost Lincoln his reëlection.[50] Old Francis P. Blair was jubilant. Chase, he wrote his son Frank, had first tried to bully Lincoln, and then astonished himself and everybody else by dropping off like a rotten pear.[51] This analysis was shrewd and sound. The Secretary had gone too far, for the President must control executive appointments; and once more Lincoln's shrewd managerial tactics had triumphed.

The head of the Sub-Treasury in New York, John J. Cisco, had offered his resignation several weeks earlier, to take effect July 1. Chase, after vainly inviting several others, told Maunsell B. Field, a Yale graduate and literary

49. Seward, Frederick W., *Seward at Washington, 1861-1872*, New York, 1891, III, 226; Stryker, Lloyd Paul, *Andrew Johnson, a Study in Courage*, New York, 1929, XI; Hamlin, *Hamlin, op.cit.*, XXXVI; Lincoln, *Works*, VII, 380-382.
50. Noah Brooks, letter dated July 1, 1864, Sacramento *Daily Union*.
51. Smith, William E., *The Francis Preston Blair Family in Politics*, New York, 1933, II, 271.

figure of some small note, then Assistant-Secretary in Washington, that he would get him transferred to the office, which was only less important in the Treasury than Chase's own. The Secretary lobbied for Field among Senators, and was assured that he could easily be confirmed. But Lincoln objected. The New York Republicans were deeply divided, and he dared not offend the Moderates under ex-Governor (and now Senator) Edwin D. Morgan by naming Chase's protégé to the vacancy. This, he later told Field, "would have been another Radical triumph, and I could not afford one." In correspondence with Chase, the President made it plain in his considerate way that, after offending the New York Moderates by keeping Hiram Barney in control of the Custom House, and making John T. Hogeboom general appraiser there—that is, giving Radicals control of two vital patronage centers—he could not put Field into a high metropolitan post without outraging many friends.[52]

But Chase was obdurate. As Field himself wrote, it was his nature to command, not obey.[53] Chase had refused to consider three other names for the New York post. Instead of yielding graciously, he told the President that he had recommended Field as the best-qualified man willing to take the place, and for that reason alone. "This, especially in these times, should be a controlling reason."[54] With this lecture to his superior, he enclosed a note. Lincoln did not at first see it, for he was hurried that day. Then, after forgetting lunch until three o'clock, he seized Chase's letter to read it in full before answering. "I took it out of the envelope for that purpose," he later wrote, "and, as I did so, another enclosure fell from it upon the floor. I picked it up, read it, and said to myself, 'Halloo, this is a horse of another color!' It was his resignation. I put my pen into my mouth, and *grit my teeth* upon it. I did not long reflect. I very soon decided to accept it."[55] This, he noted, was the fourth time that the irritating Mr. Chase had offered to resign.

Another consideration played its part in the affair. The House Ways and Means Committee had refused to support Chase's request that Congress, soon to adjourn, should pass a supplemental tax law for a hundred million to meet various appropriations which had already been authorized, but which the estimates of the Treasury Department had failed to cover. Lincoln declined to send a special request to Congress for this tax bill. Presumably, the President's patience with the much-demanding Secretary was exhausted.

Chase retired in the self-righteous mood so characteristic of him. "No man

52. Lincoln, *Works*, VII, 413-414. Barney, a man of character, had lost public confidence by letting the unscrupulous J.F. Bailey, special Treasury agent in New York, usurp many of his powers; *op.cit.*, VII, 181.
53. Field, Maunsell, *Memories of Many Men and of Some Women*, London, 1874, 305.
54. Lincoln, *Works*, VII, 414 ftn., Chase to Lincoln, June 29, 1864.
55. Field, *ut supra*, 302.

has labored more earnestly to promote the welfare of the country than I have," he wrote an old Ohio friend,[56] "and I cannot see, on looking back, that I could have done better than I have. I . . . felt sure that if I could have the full support of Congress and the hearty sympathy of the President I could carry the country safely through the financial embarrassments of the present as I did through those which attended the adjournment of Congress last year. Unfortunately, I had neither . . . But what was really wanting was the sympathy and good will of Mr. Lincoln. We have never seen public duties through exactly the same glasses; and within the last year he has allowed Mr. Blair, without the least grounds that I am aware of, to assail me in the most shameful manner, when a Jacksonian command from him would have silenced him. But all this alone would not have moved me." He further complained of the rebuff to Maunsell B. Field, and Lincoln's implied demand that Chase accept the necessity of placating New York Moderates. "It was impossible to hold office with this understanding. It would be degrading to me and dangerous to the country."

Chase did not reflect that it might be degrading to Lincoln, whose view embraced facts and interests not seen by the Secretary, to ignore the fourth resignation and submit to Chase's demand for full control of Treasury appointments. "Of all I have said in commendation of your ability and fidelity, I have nothing to unsay," Lincoln wrote him June 30; "and yet you and I have reached a point of mutual embarrassment in our official relation which it seems can not be overcome, or longer sustained consistently with the public interest."[57]

Nearly everybody squirmed at the name of Tod. Happily, he alleged uncertain health and business cares, and declined the appointment.[58] Lincoln, after vainly offering the Treasury to the able and popular Governor John Brough of Ohio, who was in Washington,[59] resolved upon appointing William Pitt Fessenden, Chairman of the Senate Finance Committee. Early on July 3, the President prepared the nomination and handed it to his secretary, John Hay. When told that Fessenden was then waiting in the anteroom, Lincoln made a quick, shrewd decision.

"Start at once for the Senate," he ordered, "and then let Fessenden come in." The gray-whiskered, thin-faced Yankee, on entering, launched into a discussion of the vacancy and suggested Hugh McCulloch, only to be met by Lincoln's reply that it was too late—he had just sent Fessenden's own name to the Senate. "You must withdraw it," exclaimed Fessenden, leaping to his

56. Chase to W.T. Coggeshall, July 8, 1864, Illinois State Hist. Libr.
57. Cisco on June 28 offered "temporary withdrawal" of his resignation; Lincoln, *Works*, VII, 414.
58. Lincoln, *Works*, VII, 419; Wright, G.B., "Hon. David Tod," *Ohio Archeological and Historical Publications*, Columbus, 1900, Vol.III, 107-131.
59. Reid, Whitelaw, *Ohio in the War*, Cincinnati, 1868, I, Chs. XIV-XIX.

feet. But when Lincoln explained that he would not, Fessenden thereupon softened his refusal, and as news that the Senate had instantly confirmed the nomination was followed by the entrance of happy friends, he saw that he must yield. After extracting from Chase a promise of help and advice, he accepted.[60]

First, however, Fessenden and Lincoln came to a clear understanding.[61] Its tenor indicates that the President had learned something from his recent collision with Chase. They agreed that Lincoln would keep no officer in the Treasury against the Secretary's express will, and also that in filling Treasury vacancies the Secretary would bow to Lincoln's wishes whenever they were made known. Lincoln further explained, in a memorandum for Fessenden, his ideas upon proper Cabinet procedure: that questions affecting the whole country should be given full and frequent consultations, and that no action particularly affecting any department should be taken until after a consultation with its head. Fessenden obviously knew all about Chase's complaints, and Lincoln plainly was trying to satisfy him that due heed would be given to their substance. The President would retain control over his appointments, but would recognize the desire of Cabinet members for fuller information, explanation, and consultation.[62]

Chase returned by way of New England to Ohio, licking his wounds, and showing resentment over the treatment he had received. This was resentment partly of Lincoln's acts, but more largely of the malignant course of the Blairs, the attacks of Thurlow Weed, and the inability of many people to understand his financial policies. He was in a dangerous mood. He did not head an open revolt against the Administration, for he lacked the strength. But he did temporarily support the idea of a new Republican Convention, refusing to drop it until it was clearly doomed to failure. Later he wrote that as soon as he learned

60. Jellison, *Fessenden of Maine, op.cit.*, 181-182. He faced a difficult Treasury situation, for at least fifty millions of money were urgently needed to meet demands on the government, and he had to hurry to New York to try unsuccessfully to get bankers to loan him the funds. *Ibid.*, 184.

61. Fessenden had criticized Lincoln freely. He had been part of the Senate caucus committee that tried to force Seward out of the Cabinet. Later he had written J.S. Pike; "Unhappily the President began by thinking Seward and Wood the great wise men of the nation and the delusion still continues." Still more recently he assured Pike that he felt no faith in the men in charge of affairs—he thought Ben Butler more the man of the hour than anybody else—but he believed the weight of the North would crush the South. Fessenden, April 5, 1863, March 4, 1864, to J.S. Pike, Fessenden Papers, Bowdoin College. One reason for Fessenden's reluctance was that he suffered from dyspepsia and irritability; Jellison, *op.cit.*, Ch.XIII. Fessenden had arraigned the Administration in Congress on Dec. 21, 1863, for hamstringing the Conscription Act of March by excessively liberal exemptions, and by continuing and increasing bounties for volunteers. Stanton had taken offense and protested. Fessenden had also attacked Lincoln's amnesty proclamation of Dec. 8, 1863, grumbling: "Think of telling the rebels that they may fight as long as they can, and take a pardon when they have had enough of it." He criticized Lincoln's Reconstruction policy, and had voted against admitting Fishback and Baxter to Senate seats.

62. Lincoln, *Works*, VII, 423; mem. dated July 4, in Fessenden Papers, Bowdoin College.

of the nominations and platform of the Democrats, he devoted all his energies to Lincoln's reëlection. In stating this he exaggerated. He did belatedly take the stump, perhaps realizing that party loyalty might later help him gain the post of Chief Justice in succession to Taney. The final verdict upon his devious path must be that given by the candid Ohio journalist William H. Smith:

"When the true history of the differences between President Lincoln and Secretary of the Treasury Chase shall be written, it will not redound to the credit of the Secretary or his indiscreet and ambitious friends. The persistent effort of these men to break down the President during a great civil war were discreditable in the extreme."[63]

As the Convention ended, observers could truly say that its delegates, fresh from the people, had expressed one central sentiment. The speeches, the platform, the hotel talk had all breathed patriotic devotion to the Union, a determination to crush the foes attempting its disruption, and an intention to rebuild it on the rock of universal freedom. The harmony of the assemblage had been almost complete; its avowed aims had been lofty beyond cavil. Nevertheless, under the florid speeches of those early summer days, and the professions of harmony, lurked the serpents of dissension. Lincoln had been named with apparent unanimity. Yet, as the members caught outgoing trains, they read not only new accounts of futile assaults north of the Chickahominy, but acrid comments by Democratic politicians and recriminations among Republicans that boded ill for the election.

"The life of the republic is still in imminent peril," declared Horace Greeley, "and its bitterest enemies are of its own household." He pointed to a formidable party in the loyal States who were at heart enemies to the national cause. Saying this, Greeley understated the peril. Several such parties existed and he himself headed one; his editorial vacillation and defeatism played into the hands of the Confederates as much as Montgomery Blair's gift for sowing dissension, or Seward's naive idea that traitors could be coaxed back, or Vallandigham's fondness for playing with fire. All the divisive factions, continued Greeley, make their assaults under cover of hostility to the Administration. "And the renomination of Mr. Lincoln will inevitably intensify their efforts and rebarb their arrows. A Presidential election implies dissent, difference, criticism—nay, license, assault, and open hostility.... These charges will often convert passive into active and efficient hostility to the prosecution of the war."[64]

This was all too true. And the first heavy spear launched at Lincoln and

63. Undated note, W.H. Smith Papers, Ohio Hist. Soc. Smith was a friend of Whitelaw Reid.
64. New York *Tribune*, June 9, 1864.

at united effort for the Union came from two champions of a Radical Reconstruction policy.

[V]

During the spring of 1864 Lincoln's program for Southern Reconstruction had made progress in Louisiana and Arkansas, and as it moved forward, had evoked violent dissent from the Radical wing of Congress. When Arkansas sent William M. Fishback and Elisha Baxter to apply for admission to the Senate, the door was slammed in their faces. After some delay, the Senate asserted 27 to 6 that the rebellion had not been so far suppressed in Arkansas as to entitle the State to representation in Congress. Sumner would have gone further. He offered a resolution that any State in arms against the Union must be regarded as subject to military occupation, and without right of representation until readmitted by vote of both Houses. Although this motion was shelved, both Chambers were clearly ready to do battle with the President.

A momentous conflict over national policy impended, recalling the historic combats of Hamilton and Jefferson, Jackson and Clay, Buchanan and Douglas, but weightier far than the old struggles over Jay's Treaty, the Bank, and Lecompton. The President was coolly, tactfully adamant. He had not settled the details of his Reconstruction program; he was ready to modify them as time and circumstance dictated; but he was determined to do everything in his power to restore a fraternal Union, never stooping to vengeance or malice. Far different was the stand of the Radical leaders, athirst for party advantage, sectional domination, and the sating of old hatreds and new economic greeds. They turned from their Arkansas decision to throw down the gage of battle to the White House.

Three preliminary demands for Reconstruction must be met, they declared in a bill which Ben Wade and Henry Winter Davis, as chairmen of the Senate and House Committees on the Rebellious States, pressed through both Chambers. First, the President should appoint a provisional governor for each State declared to be in rebellion. Second, as soon as military resistance ended, the governor should enroll the white male citizens and offer them an oath to support the United States Constitution. Finally, when a majority of registrants had signed the oath, the governor should arrange the election of a State constitutional convention. This was perhaps a reasonable program, although Lincoln thought of inaugurating Reconstruction on a ten-percent basis rather than a majority basis. But the Wade-Davis legislation proceeded to lay down additional tests of penalizing character.

One, a requirement that the new constitutions cancel all debts incurred in aid of the rebellion, was perfectly equitable. It would impoverish some Southerners, but they deserved their losses. Quite different was a Draconian stipulation that the constitutions should forbid all men who had held high civil office under the Confederacy, or military rank above a colonelcy, to vote for a legislator or governor, or occupy these positions. No former office-holder or person who had voluntarily borne arms against the United States could take the oath, and no one who did not take the oath could vote for the constitutional convention. This would proscribe the ablest and most experienced leaders in the South. Worse still, in theory and practise, was a demand that the constitutions abolish slavery. This was plainly unconstitutional, for Congress had no power to deal with slavery inside the States. It was also unwise, for if slavery were thus abolished by national action, the nation might be expected to take steps to aid and protect the freedmen for which it had made no preparatory study, and possessed no adequate machinery. The Wade-Davis bill provided that, whenever a State constitution embodying these iron provisions had been adopted by a majority of the registered voters, the President, with prior Congressional assent, should recognize the government so established as competent to send men to Congress and choose Presidential electors.[65]

This legislation had originally been prepared by Henry Winter Davis, an active Marylander whose emotional instability reflected his intense ambition for national prominence and personal advancement. He had allied himself in succession with the Whigs, Know-Nothings, Republicans, Bell-Everett men, and Radical Republicans, consistent only in seeking to further his own career. He had never failed to cherish the dream that he might ultimately become President. Why not? He came of aristocratic parents, his father a president of St. John's College in Annapolis; he had gained a good education at Kenyon College and the University of Virginia; tall, handsome, eloquent, he had a flair for bold action. Sitting in Congress since 1855, except for one term 1861-63, he had inspired powerful friendships and hatreds. He had come to detest Montgomery Blair, idolize Thaddeus Stevens, and distrust Lincoln, his feeling about the President being tinged by disappointment that he was not appointed to Lincoln's Cabinet in 1861. Left out of Congress by the Maryland election of 1861, Davis employed the next two years in delivering anti-Administration speeches all over the East. He resumed his diatribes as soon as he reëntered the House in 1863. It was not the Blairs and Lincoln alone that he attacked, for he indicted Seward, Gideon Welles, and all moderate editors, governors, and Congressmen as hotly.[66]

Davis had persuaded John Sherman to introduce his first bill on Re-

65. Blaine, *Twenty Years*, II, 41-42, gives an account of the bill; *Congressional Globe*, 38th Cong., 1st Sess., Pt.4, 3448-3449.

66. Steiner, B.C., *Life of Henry Winter Davis*, Baltimore, 1916, *passim*; Welles, *Diary*, I, 505, 531; II, 30, 95ff. Gideon Welles characterized him as a man of cultivation who was eccentric, unreliable, and given to intrigue—"restless and active, but not useful"; *Diary*, II, 408-409.

construction just before he returned to Congress, when it was blocked by a counter proposal. Now he offered it anew, with Wade as sponsor in the Senate.[67] Davis was riding the wave of Radical feeling, and riding high.

To this Wade-Davis bill, supported by Sumner and opposed by Thaddeus Stevens only on the ground that it was insufficiently severe, Lincoln had invincible objections. It practically scrapped all the work of Reconstruction he had done under his fluid ten-percent plan proclamation the previous December, and showed a hard retaliatory spirit which he believed altogether the wrong attitude toward the defeated and humbled South. He would have accepted Winston Churchill's dictum on the proper approach of a victorious nation to a vanquished enemy. We should help the foe to his feet, said Churchill, and we should remember only so much of the past as is useful for the future. Lincoln believed that to see the hopeful governments already created in Arkansas and Louisiana roughly flung aside would inevitably discourage loyal men in other States. Looking to the early destruction of slavery by constitutional amendment, he was unwilling to repudiate his oft-stated contention that Congress had at the present no power to touch the institution within the States. Of course, he would let any State adopt the Wade-Davis plan if it liked, but he would not close the gate on milder plans.

The bill came to Lincoln in the anxious hour before Congress adjourned on July 4, 1864. Rejecting heavy pressure to sign it, he put it to death by a pocket veto.

The scene, as the President thus squarely confronted the Radicals who intended to destroy his Reconstruction program, was one of the most dramatic in wartime history. The House had occupied its last minutes with a reading of the Declaration of Independence. Sitting in the President's room in the Capitol, Lincoln had been signing final bills. Sumner entered with characteristic vehemence, his fanatic mind centered on the measure. George S. Boutwell, equally nervous and angry, raised a voice of lamentation. Zach Chandler made a scene by buttonholing the President, threatening him with the prospect that loss of the Wade-Davis Bill would cost the Republicans Ohio and Michigan in the fall election, and denouncing his constitutional objections. Secretary Fessenden reminded the excited group that Republicans had always agreed that Congress had no power over slavery inside the States. With his manifest approval and the support of Seward and Usher who looked on, Lincoln then delivered a pointed speech.

"This bill and this position of these gentlemen," he said, "seems to me to make the fatal admission (in asserting that the insurrectionary States are no longer in the Union) that States whenever they please may of their own motion

67. Sherman, John, *John Sherman's Recollections of Forty Years in the House, Senate, and Cabinet*, Chicago, 1895, I, 359-360.

dissolve their connection with the Union. Now we cannot survive that admission, I am convinced. If it be true, I am not President, these gentlemen are not Congress. I have laboriously endeavored to avoid that question ever since it first began to be mooted. . . . I thought it much better, if it were possible, to restore the Union without the necessity of a violent quarrel among its friends as to whether certain States have been in or out of the Union during the war: a merely metaphysical question and one unnecessary to be forced into discussion." John Hay stated that Lincoln, after they left the Capitol, said: "If they choose to make a point upon this, I do not doubt that they can do harm. They have never been friendly to me and I don't know that this makes any special difference as to that. At all events, I must keep some consciousness of being somewhere near right; I must keep some standard of principle fixed with myself." He was concerned about the constitutional issue, and still more deeply concerned over a harshly vengeful formula of Reconstruction. If it were adopted, farewell to his dream of a fraternal Union! The Wade-Davis Bill was in effect a stinging censure of his course. Lincoln admitted no right of Congress to censure him, or to thwart his settled policy by last-minute legislation. He was determined to maintain all the dignities and powers of the Presidency.[68]

We may well believe the assertion of contemporaries that Henry Winter Davis was beside himself with rage that afternoon, for his boiling-point was low.[69] But we must reject both the statement of young James G. Blaine that Republican members of Congress almost unanimously dissented from Lincoln, and Sumner's preposterous assertion that Lincoln later expressed regret that he had not signed the Wade-Davis Bill.[70] In disregard of precedent, Lincoln on July 8 issued an explanatory proclamation giving with brevity and point his main reasons for refusing his assent.[71] Some members of Congress sided with him and Seward and Fessenden. More rallied to him later when Henry Winter Davis wrote a caustic arraignment which, signed also by Wade and published in the newspapers, became famous as the Wade-Davis Manifesto. Its averment that the Presidential veto was a blow at the rights of humanity and the principles of republican government could be dismissed as sophomoric rhetoric. But it went beyond rhetoric; it was a chal-

68. Lincoln, *Works*, VII, 433-434; Hay, John, *Lincoln and the Civil War in the Diaries and Letters of John Hay*, *op.cit.*, 204-206.

69. *Ibid.*; W.E. Dodd's article on Henry Winter Davis in *Dictionary of American Biography*, Vol. V, 119-121.

70. Blaine, *Twenty Years*, *op.cit.*, II, 42; Sherman, *Recollections*, I, 361. Blaine had entered Congress in 1863 and as yet knew its membership imperfectly; while the speedy dispersal of members all over the North after the veto forbade any systematic inquiry into sentiment. Sumner's alleged assertion is a bit of stale hearsay contradicted by the facts.

71. Lincoln, *Works*, VII, 433-434; July 8, 1864.

lenge of force and power, the most direct that Republican leaders ever gave Lincoln.

Lincoln's proclamation and the Wade-Davis Manifesto at once transformed the Republican campaign; it became in great part a referendum upon the issue of Reconstruction. The Manifesto, addressed to supporters of the government, declared it their duty "to check the encroachments of the Executive on the authority of Congress and to require it to confine itself to its proper sphere." English Tories had never been more emphatic in assailing the aggressions of Whig Ministries, followers of Adams and Clay never so bitter in resisting Andrew Jackson. The President, declared the Manifesto, "must understand that our support is of a cause and not of a man; that *the authority of Congress is paramount* and must be respected; that the whole body of Union men in Congress will not submit to be impeached by him of rash and unconstitutional legislation; and if he wishes our support, he must confine himself to his executive duties—*to obey and to execute,* not to make the laws—to suppress by arms armed rebellion, and leave political reorganization to Congress." In conclusion, it implored citizens to "consider the remedy of these usurpations and, having found it, fearlessly to execute it."[72] This was flat defiance! It asserted the doctrine of the Radicals that Congress held paramount authority in rebuilding the nation, and it laid down principles which reached their logical conclusion within four years in the impeachment of a President.

Such declarations suggested a possible disruption of the government and the whole Union effort, but fortunately the authors overshot their mark. Their paper, as Blaine observes, was so extreme that it recoiled upon itself, and its indictment of Lincoln "rallied his friends to his support with that intense form of energy which springs from the instinct of self-preservation."[73] It helped defeat Winter Davis's efforts for a renomination, so that soon he was once more out of Congress.

Reconstruction was now a subject for national debate in which the Radical Republicans were outnumbered and outgunned by the combined forces of the Moderate Republicans and War Democrats. Simultaneously the position of the War Democrats was well defined by James W. Sheehan's Chicago *Post*, the oldtime organ of Stephen A. Douglas. It maintained that, as the government had always denied the right of any State to leave the Union, the ordinances of secession were null. No State can commit treason, it argued, and no State can give its citizens authority to commit treason. The war was therefore a struggle not to reduce States to submission, but to compel the obedience of rebellious individuals. While War Democrats took a variety of constitutional

72. *American Annual Cyclopaedia,* 1864, 307-310.
73. Blaine, *op.cit.,* II, 44.

views, they would all stand with Lincoln in battling the Wade-Davis extremists.

As for Moderate Republicans, the feelings of a majority were tartly expressed by the Maine newspaperman, now Washington correspondent of the Sacramento *Union*, Noah Brooks. "It is a matter of regret," he declared, "that a man of so much oratorical ability and legal sharpness as Henry Winter Davis should be so much of a political charlatan as he is; but he is, like the Blairs, insatiate in his hates, mischievous in his schemes, and hollow-hearted and coldblooded." Most Republican newspapers agreed. So did *Harper's Weekly*, which had remarked of Lincoln's letter of acceptance that, "like all he says and does," it would appeal "to the heart of the people whom he serves so faithfully and well." George William Curtis, editor of this now powerful organ, growled: "We have read with pain the manifesto of Messrs. Wade and Winter Davis, not because of its envenomed hostility to the President, but because of its ill-tempered spirit, which proves conclusively the unfitness of either of the gentlemen for grave counselors in a time of national peril."[74] Most people refused as yet to grow excited about Reconstruction. Let's win the war for the Union first, and talk about its rehabilitation later, they said. Meanwhile, Lincoln's mild attitude, tentative and pragmatic, offended few and satisfied many. It had ambiguities, but then the situation was ambiguous.

Meanwhile, although the heavy Virginia carnage darkened men's spirits, now and then a ray of light glimmered along the horizon as possible augury of coming dawn.

The Union commander in West Virginia, David Hunter, who had taken control after Sigel's defeat in May at New Market, had the task of holding down the ebullient Jubal A. Early, who headed an aggressive segment of Lee's army in the Shenandoah Valley. Hunter was a stodgy, ill-tempered man with a passion for assisting the Negro, but little military skill. When he retreated into West Virginia to reorganize and refit, he left the Shenandoah wide open. At the beginning of July, Early seized the opportunity to throw his veterans northward in the Valley and into Maryland behind Washington. Had not Lew Wallace gallantly delayed him for a few days on the Monocacy (July 9), he might conceivably have penetrated the city's fortifications. As it was, he destroyed part of the Philadelphia, Wilmington & Baltimore Railroad, did some damage to the Baltimore & Ohio, and Northern Central, and sent his troops within sight of the Capitol dome, killing men of the city garrison.[75] Public anxiety rose high in Washington on the 10th. Then, in the nick of time, it was relieved on the 11th, as cheering crowds gathered by the Potomac shore to

74. See Chicago *Post*, July 10-25, 1864, for Sheehan's view; *Harper's Weekly*, July 9, 30, August 20, for Curtis; and Noah Brooks's letter, July 1, 1864, in Sacramento *Union*.
75. Vandiver, Frank E., *Jubal's Raid*, New York, 1960, 122-179.

watch transports discharging long lines of blue-coat reinforcements. These troops headed for Fort Stevens, where on both July 11 and 12 Lincoln himself mounted the ramparts to see rebel sharpshooters firing in his direction, and hear Captain Oliver Wendell Holmes shout, "Get down, you fool!"—Holmes not recognizing the President.[76]

Great if brief excitement had seized both Baltimore and Washington as they realized that they were momentarily cut off from the North except by sea; no trains, no Northern newspapers, no fresh food, prices soaring, and courage dropping! As Early's men pulled back, people were left fuming with rage and humiliation. That at this late date it should be possible for more than 12,000 rebels to swarm across the Potomac, capture trains, force Stanton to send a carriage in haste to bring the President's family back from the Soldier's Home, and take south great stocks of horses, cattle, and general supplies, was outrageous. Some secession sympathizers displayed impudent delight in Washington streets, crying "At last, at last! Thank God." In Maryland, disloyalists plundered many houses, including that of one of the governors, and the Blair family home in Silver Spring. Early had gathered part of the Shenandoah harvest for Lee's army. He had lifted the sagging Confederate prestige abroad.[77]

But at last he had been repelled! And his gains were offset by losses and disappointments so important that the Richmond press gave his raid as much criticism as praise.

While the disturbance over Early was at its height, a refreshing breeze blew in from the English Channel. On July 6 came news that the United States sloop-of-war *Kearsarge* had fought a short naval duel June 19 with the *Alabama* off Cherbourg, and destroyed that world-famous cruiser. No vessel under the Confederate flag was so hated by Northerners as Raphael Semmes's "pirate." Moreover, this battle seemed as much an encounter between Britain and America as between South and North. The *Alabama* had been built in England, manned largely by Englishmen and Irishmen, armed with British guns, and driven by British coal. It refreshed Americans, smarting under Tory gibes, to hear how completely she had been vanquished.

Considerable advantages, to be sure, had lain with Captain John A. Winslow's *Kearsarge*. She had a makeshift armor of sheet-chains which her adversary lacked, and the merits of which are disputed; she had held frequent target practises which a shortage of ammunition had denied the Confederates; she carried a heavier armament—two 11-inch Dahlgrens together with other guns.

76. Howe, M.A. DeWolfe, *Justice Oliver Wendell Holmes: The Shaping Years, 1841-1870*, Cambridge, Mass., 1957, 168-169.

77. Early, Jubal, *Autobiographical Sketches and Narratives of the War Between the States*, ed. Frank E. Vandiver, Bloomington, Ind., 1960, 455-456, for his boastful account of his achievements; Riddle, *op.cit.*, 291.

The action lasted sixty-two minutes, during which the *Kearsarge* was but slightly injured by the twenty-eight shots she received.[78] At the end, Semmes, with thirty men killed and wounded, vainly tried to regain the French shore. He charged in his official report to the Confederate agent, J.M. Mason in London, that the *Kearsarge* had been deplorably slow in sending boats to save lives after the *Alabama* went down. He himself was picked up, with others, by the English yacht *Deerhound*.[79] Nevertheless, Winslow paroled more than sixty prisoners. At news of the battle, Americans exultantly recalled the days of the *Constitution* and the *Guerrière*. The seas were now freer for American shipping.

The *Alabama*, no privateer but a properly commissioned naval vessel, was to become a brilliant part of Confederate legend, and Semmes unquestionably had gallant traits. When the ship's log was published in London, however, readers found that the seemingly heroic cruise had not really been "glorious." The story had little interest and less dignity.[80] From the time *Sumter* (her original name) first sailed out of the Mississippi until she was sunk as the *Alabama*, not a speck of real danger enlivened the narrative. Hunting and fleeing, fleeing and hunting, made up the monotonous tale. It recorded mainly a series of efficient chases of helpless prey, stained by unscrupulous but not unprecedented or unusual use of the flags of the United States and of neutral nations. Only once did the *Alabama* get involved in a true sea-fight, and then her superiority over the *Hatteras* lifted her so far above peril that but two men were slightly wounded. The story had no touch of Marryat or Cooper or Conrad.[81]

For Northerners, Winslow's exploit was a much-needed ray of sunshine in a dark hour. It was particularly welcomed by merchants, for Semmes had spread ruin far and wide, capturing sixty-five vessels worth more than six million dollars, Confederate raiding was one factor, though a relatively short-lived one, influencing and affecting the long decline of the American carrying-trade.

[VI]

But alas for Lincoln in this hot, bloody, and gloomy summer! The resignation of Chase and the Wade-Davis insurrection were heavy shocks. So far as

78. Captain Winslow in London *Daily News*, June 27, 1864.

79. John Lancaster, the owner, acted at Winslow's request, saving Semmes, thirteen officers, and twenty-six men; see London *Daily News*, June 24, July 2-22, for the ensuing controversy. Also *O.R.N.* I, iii, 649-651.

80. For the log, see *Cruises of the Sumter and the Alabama*, London, 1864; Roberts, Walter Adolphe, *Semmes of the Alabama*, Indianapolis, 1938, *passim*.

81. The story is best told in Semmes, Raphael, *Memoirs of Service Afloat*, Baltimore, 1869.

we can judge, public sentiment sustained them well, while they gave many Republicans a desperate sense that they must close their ranks or be ruined. Yet they deepened the general impression of political disorganization and Administration uncertainty, and helped convince weak-kneed men that if military defeats continued the party would face disaster. The seven weeks from Independence Day until late August, weeks with Atlanta still untaken and Lee's army still formidable, saw the spirits of Republican fainthearts at their lowest point. Whitelaw Reid, war correspondent of the Cincinnati *Gazette* and librarian of the House, travelling in these weeks from Cincinnati through Washington to Kennebunk, Maine, gathered from available reports that Lincoln's reëlection under existing circumstances was an impossibility. Attorney-General Bates was telling friends that the prime need of the country was a competent leader.[82]

When ex-Mayor George Opdyke of New York signed letters in mid-August inviting Republican leaders to a meeting to discuss the withdrawal of Lincoln in favor of a stronger candidate, he met a remarkable body of support. This honest but commonplace clothing merchant was of course merely a catspaw. The real movers, of whom Winter Davis was the most determined, stood behind him.

His letters went out to Lyman Trumbull, Zach Chandler, Charles Sumner, Jacob Collamer, Ben Wade, and other Senators, to War Democrats like Daniel S. Dickinson, to various governors, and to leading party editors.[83] The meeting, originally fixed at Opdyke's house on August 19th, was soon postponed until early September with David Dudley Field as host. The responses to Opdyke struck a sullen chord. Chase, of course, warmly approved the proposed gathering, writing that the Republicans were never more in need of wise counsel and fearless action. Dickinson, a compromiser by nature, long wavering between men and parties, expressed his belief that if Lincoln were fully advised of the dismal state of party affairs, he might withdraw. "Mr. Lincoln is already beaten," declared Horace Greeley. "He cannot be elected. And we must have another ticket to save us from utter overthrow. If we had such a ticket as could be made by naming Grant, Butler, or Sherman for President, we could make a fight yet." John Jay proposed a letter asking Lincoln to cancel his acceptance of the Baltimore nomination. Ben Wade, as Winter Davis ascertained, was hopeful of getting a stronger candidate, but wished to wait—like other men whom Davis called "snails."[84]

82. Reid to Chase, Aug. 22, 1864, Chase Papers, Hist. Soc. of Pennsylvania; Bates to Orville H. Browning, *Diary of Orville Hickman Browning*, ed. T.C. Pease and James G. Randall, Springfield, Ill., 1925-33, I, 676.
83. All this correspondence is printed in New York *Sun*, June 30, 1889.
84. Brown, Francis, *op.cit.*, 260ff.

Word of this letter-writing quickly got around. It contributed to an atmosphere in high party circles as chill and clammy as a Labrador fog. When the
Republican National Committee met at the Astor House on August 22, the
chairman, Henry J. Raymond, exuded the sepia gloom of a cuttlefish. Despair,
he reported, glowered from every corner of the horizon. As editor of the *Times*,
he possessed information that seemed decisive—information that men everywhere had a deep longing for peace and a conviction that Lincoln could not
or would not furnish it. Other committeemen shared his impression. In despair, he wrote Lincoln that all seemed lost, for Elihu Washburne had told him
that if an election were held immediately in Illinois, the Republicans would
be worsted. Cameron had sent word that Pennsylvania would go Democratic,
and Oliver P. Morton had declared that only the most strenuous fighting could
save Indiana. As for New York, Raymond thought that in an early election
Lincoln would lose the State by 50,000.[85] Such pessimism had seized some
party leaders that Raymond, usually clearheaded and determined, persuaded
the National Committee to support him in laying a preposterous suggestion
before the President.

This suggestion was that Lincoln should send a commission to propose
peace to Jefferson Davis on the sole condition that the South give up its demand
for independence and accept the Constitution, all other questions—including
slavery—to be settled in a national convention![86] Davis would reject this,
argued Raymond, and Northerners would thus be aroused to a new passion
of loyalty. It did not occur to him that millions might be aroused to a new sense
of bewilderment, disgust, and discouragement.

And what of Lincoln while defeatism and hostile conspiracy swirled about
the White House? He knew of the general pessimism. Thurlow Weed and
others had assured him that his reëlection was impossible.[87] When Raymond
came to Washington to tell him that all seemed lost, and his close friend
Leonard Swett offered the same opinion, the President felt that McClellan (for
the Democrats would certainly nominate him) would be the next occupant of
the White House. At a Cabinet meeting on August 23 he therefore asked the
members to endorse the back of a memorandum which he did not show them,
but sealed and laid away.

"This morning, as for some days past," he had written, "it seems exceedingly probable that this Administration will not be reëlected. Then it will be

85. Seward, F.W., *op.cit.*, 244, for Seward's admission that as late as August 29 the American
people "seemed vacillating and despondent."
86. Brown, Francis, *op.cit.*, 260-261; cf. Nicolay and Hay, IX, 218-219; Raymond to Lincoln, Aug.
22, 1864, Robert Todd Lincoln Papers, LC.
87. Lincoln, *Works*, VII, 515-516; Weed so recalls in a letter to Seward Aug. 22.

Pledge Signed by President Lincoln and his Cabinet, Prior to the 1864 Election

my duty to so coöperate with the President-elect as to save the Union between the election and the inauguration; as he will have secured the election on such grounds that he cannot possibly save it afterward."[88] The plan on which Lincoln had solemnly resolved was to confer with President-elect McClellan, and ask him to raise as many troops as he possibly could for a final effort to save the Union before March 4, 1865.

Raymond's recommendation of a peace offer requiring the return of the South to the Union, but omitting any stipulation respecting emancipation, was certain not only to dismay Lincoln, but to fill him with mingled chagrin and resentment. The idea that he might repudiate his slavery policy was worse than insulting; it was odious. It meant that he would surrender all claim to principle. Such a course would break national faith with the host of Negroes serving under the Union flag; it would antagonize all Radicals and most moderate Republicans; it would disgrace the nation in the eyes of the world. Lincoln told Judge Joseph T. Mills on August 19 how deeply he felt on the subject. "There have been men who proposed to me to return to slavery the black warriors of Port Hudson and Olustee to conciliate the South. I should be damned in time and eternity for so doing. The world shall know that I will keep faith to friends and enemies, come what will."[89] His enemies said he was fighting an Abolition war. It would be carried on, as long as he was President, for the sole purpose of restoring the Union, but no human power would subdue the rebellion without using the weapon of emancipation. "Freedom has given us control of 200,000 able-bodied men, born and raised on Southern soil. It will give us more yet."[90]

Charles A. Dana, then in the War Department, had made an emphatic statement in connection with some recent delusive negotiations at Niagara with professed Confederate agents exploring a possible peace. The President had made no pronouncement suggesting a relinquishment of his measures against slavery in connection with these peace talks, said Dana. If he had, he would have done irreparable harm to his party; he would have convicted himself of insincerity upon a supreme issue of the war; and he would have shown readiness to let Southern leaders return to Washington with all their former power.[91] In short, he would not have been Lincoln had he done this, for, as Dana wrote long afterward: "His strongest point was judgment— soundness of judgment—not making any mistakes as to the nature of the thing he had to deal with. . . . The great thing about him was a great, wide and solid

88. Lincoln, *Works*, VII, 514, 515.
89. Lincoln, *Works*, VII, 506-508, gives this same note from the Mills Diary in correct form; see also *Conversations with Lincoln*, ed. Charles M. Segal, 338-339, quoting from Mills's Diary.
90. *Ibid.*
91. Undated letter to Raymond cited in Brown, *Raymond*, 260.

judgment."[92] Ever since his Cooper Union speech he had proved how effectively he had trained himself to think—to think problems through with precision and clarity, keeping his thought on a high and disinterested plane.[93]

While doubt still reigned, Lincoln took a step to placate the Moderate Republicans in New York under Thurlow Weed's leadership. He was well aware that the Albany editor, wielding tremendous political influence upstate, felt irritated by Hiram Barney's continued tenure of the Collectorship of the Port of New York. For months the President had worried about it. He did not wish to offend Chase, long a protector of Barney, or to be unjust to a hardworking, honest official not at all responsible for the corruption that plagued the Custom House. Yet he knew that Barney was running the place in the interest of the Radicals. His initial plan for getting Seward to transfer the Collector to a diplomatic post had been balked by Chase. Finally, a few weeks after Fessenden took Chase's place (August 31), the President asked for the resignation of Barney, who gave way to one of Weed's oldest friends, Simeon Draper.[94] The choice was sound, for Draper was able and independent, but it left the Radical wing more convinced than ever that Weed, Seward, Montgomery Blair, and Senator James Dixon of Connecticut held what Zach Chandler fatuously called full possession of Lincoln.[95]

Nobody less intemperate and abusive than Zach Chandler would have accused Lincoln of letting himself fall into the possession of one faction. His independence and impartiality never wavered. Aware that he must reconcile disparate groups, keep the party balanced, and shut the door against extremism, he knew that in accepting Chase's resignation he had not completed the task of remodelling his Cabinet. The Radicals who hated Montgomery Blair were quite as numerous as the Moderates who hated Chase, and their detestation was quite as fervent. The judicious Fessenden had fairly well represented the idea of party harmony. Could Lincoln find a replacement for Blair who would equally typify restraint and unity? The President felt liking and respect for Blair, just as he felt respect (though not liking) for Chase, but he did not approve the man's quarrelsome and malignant streak. Once when Blair was

92. Dictated Memorandum in Tarbell Collection, Allegheny College.

93. In the "Miscellaneous Mss. Civil War 1861-1865" in the New-York Historical Society is a sheet of note-paper headed "Executive Mansion" on which are pencilled figures in Lincoln's handwriting, allotting the electoral vote in the contest of 1864 to himself and McClellan. The memorandum is not signed, but is indubitably Lincoln's. The date is uncertain, but must have been at a time when the probable result seemed very close, and when three crucial Northern States could be assigned to the Democrats. In McClellan's column Lincoln put New York 33; Pennsylvania 26; Illinois 16; Missouri and Kentucky 11 each; New Jersey and Ohio 21; Indiana 13; Michigan, Wisconsin, and Iowa eight each; and five other States to bring the total to 117. This was a dangerously close result.

94. Barney Papers, HEH.

95. Chandler Papers, LC; undated scrap on Dixon.

denouncing the Radicals as selfish and vindictive, Lincoln rebuked him: "It is much better not to be led from the region of reason into that of hot blood, by imputing to public men motives which they do not avow."[96]

In late summer a Damoclean sword hung over Blair's head, and it was certain that Lincoln, in his deep concern for party and Union harmony, would soon sever the thread holding it.

As the first half of August wore on, the military outlook continued discouraging for the North, with Grant immobile at Petersburg and Sherman's progress checked by such equivocal battles as Kenesaw Mountain. The front of domestic affairs was equally gloomy, as published in a summary of the situation by Greeley in the *Tribune* of July 7, with news that gold had risen to 270. "Gold goes up like a balloon; so that $4,000 of it will buy $10,000 of United States six percents, payable principal and interest in coin! The business of the country is all but fatally deranged; all nominal values are so inflated and unsettled that no one knows what to ask or how to trade; the Laboring Class are stinted in spite of ample work and large wages; and there is danger of Social Convulsion from the artful, inflammatory incitements addressed to Ignorance by Treason. . . . Avarice and Gambling, engineered by Disloyalty, ride the whirlwind and direct the storm. . . . Every necessity of life grows hourly dearer; and the congregated Traitors who burrow in this city here scheme and struggle to paralyze the raised right arm of the nation." Nor did the political outlook seem happier.

When mid-August came, the Republican Party had not yet pulled itself together, or made a final decision upon its candidate, and the Democratic Party had made no decision whatever. All seemed confusion. Militant Radicals might yet force Lincoln to retire in favor of a stronger nominee; copperish elements might yet set McClellan aside for a wilder man. Connecticut Democrats were proposing a demagogic defeatist in Thomas H. Seymour of Hartford, who had come near gaining the governorship on a negotiated-peace platform, and who steadily denounced efforts to restore the Union as atrocious and abominable. Lincoln, in view of the deepening calamities and perils, designated August 4 as a Day of Fasting, Humiliation and Prayer. Friendly editors pronounced this very fitting; the public burdens were fearful, the taxes enormous, the debts, State and national, almost crushing. Conscription and volunteering were

---

96. This characteristic utterance of Lincoln's is too general in terms to be directly identified with any specific date or political episode. Lincoln consistently emphasized the unity in Republican or Union Party ranks, and deplored the schismatic personal denunciations of conservative or moderate Republicans by associates and followers of Thaddeus Stevens or Charles Sumner, along with the vendetta that some of the Jacobins waged against Secretary Seward as a spineless "moral and physical coward." In such intemperate language Lincoln saw national division and ruin. Randall, J.G., *Lincoln, the President*, New York, 1945, Vol.III, 241, 242.

more and more painful, discontent and sedition increasingly flagrant.

But, courage countrymen!, cried the ablest editors, Bryant, Raymond, and even Greeley; "the darkest hour is just before the dawn!" It was even so.

[VII]

In this crisis—"this great trouble," as the President called it—the cement of the Union was furnished from three main sources besides the nation's historic memories, traditions, and principles. It came from Lincoln's tact, sagacity, and patience; from such victories as the preponderant Northern armaments could now win; and from the nation's party system, which bound Americans together in adherence generally to patriotic clarification of political principles as laid down in the exalted arguments of Hamilton, Jefferson, Jackson, Clay, and Webster. The American party system ever pitches and sways like a wagon traversing rough ground. It gives forth ominous cracks and groans, and threatens to crash on the rocky hillside. Nevertheless, as the generations struggle forward, it endures. It must remain a viable wagon to reach its goal and deliver its straining load of offices, honors, and power. Whatever the rude strains and torsions, all the main groupings, the radicals, moderates, and conservatives, must consent to be held in one fabric; it must not give way to the far right, the far left, or the sudden ideological eruption. Keeping crazily, illogically intact, one party cannot differ too sharply from the opposite party, which feels the same stresses but responds to the same demand for a working degree of unity. Thus holding groups of varying opinions and interests together, the parties become a strong ark and essential chariot of national unity. Americans in 1864 had fresh in mind the catastrophic results of the temporary disintegration of one party by extremist demands in 1860.

The Presidential campaign would really begin when the Democrats made their nomination in the final days of August. Actually, the Republicans came up to that point with fair unity; a battalion of shortsighted dissenters might clamor for a new chieftain, but the main army marched forward unperturbed behind Lincoln. If the Democratic Party made a strong campaign, it too would have to conquer its divisions, show a workable unity, and convince the North that it was safe. As delegates began to flock to the Chicago Convention, the chances were two to one that it would do this. Meanwhile, the other essential source of cement for the Union was at last, after harrowing delays, coming into play. Sherman was moving forward. Grant was holding on like a bulldog. On Tuesday, August 16, 1864, the front page of the New York *Tribune* blazed with a huge map, taking up two-thirds of its space, labelled: "Map of the Bay of Mobile——THE SCENE OF FARRAGUT'S VICTORY."

Victory at last, on a tide that was just beginning to swell!

4

Lincoln, McClellan, and the Presidential Battle

ON SEPTEMBER 3, 1864, every steeple throughout the North was clangorous with bells. From every staff and window rippled the stars-and-stripes; in city squares, batteries of guns set the hills echoing, and on every village green a brass nine-pounder barked its joy. Every face wore a look of happy triumph. Atlanta had fallen; the news had reached Washington on the first day of the month. Yet amid these exultant scenes, posters, handbills, and newspaper columns reminded the public that the Democratic Party had just been bewailing "four years of failure to restore the Union by the experiment of war," and had just called for "a cessation of hostilities, with a view to an ultimate convention of the States." Four years of struggle, according to the Democratic chieftains, had resulted in failure and ignominy.

How was it that the great party of Jefferson, Jackson, and Polk had put itself in so abysmal a posture? How could it possibly extricate itself?

By the beginning of September, other resounding victories had been won.

"I am going into Mobile in the morning, if God is my leader," Farragut had written his wife on August 4 from his flagship *Hartford*. At daybreak he had quietly remarked to the captain, "Well, Drayton, we might as well get under way." By a few minutes after seven on August 5 his fleet of four monitors and fourteen wooden warships was engaged with Fort Morgan and other defensive works on Mobile Bay. At 7:40 the leading monitor in the starboard column, *Tecumseh*, hit a torpedo (or mine) and almost immediately sank. *Hartford* now took the lead by passing *Brooklyn*, while Farragut himself, aloft in the rigging to keep a better watch through the billows of smoke, was lashed fast there by subordinates who feared he might fall. By ten o'clock the battle was substantially ended when the rebel ironclad *Tennessee*, formidably gunned but with weak engines, struck her flag. At a critical moment, warned that mines strewed the channel ahead, Farragut is said to have uttered his historic exclamation, "Damn the torpedoes! Four bells!"—the signal for high speed ahead. The three-hour action had given the Union fleet the mastery of the most important

97

port left to the Confederacy on the Gulf coast, although the city of Mobile itself remained in Confederate hands. Casualties were heavy, the Union fleet losing about 315 men killed or wounded, including 93 lost on the *Tecumseh*, but the glory won was great. How much Farragut had done to lift the Northern heart was made evident when he returned soon afterward to one of the most enthusiastic welcomes New York had ever given a popular hero.[1]

Meanwhile, the beleaguerment of Petersburg dragged its slow way along with a tardiness that tried Northern patience, but was not without its dramatic gains. In the battle of Globe Tavern or Weldon Railroad in mid-August, for example, a bloody four-day engagement, Warren's Fifth Corps bit deeper than before into the vital rail and road communications of Petersburg and Richmond with the south and southwest, and held firm under the most ferocious attacks that Lee and A. P. Hill could launch. Late in September, Federals pushed west of the Weldon Railroad at Peebles' Farm, while on October 27 at Burgess Mill a Federal advance against the Southside Railroad was repulsed.

[I]

The Democratic Convention had opened on August 29 in Chicago amid tumultuous and meaningless enthusiasm. Eleven railroads had poured delegations and excitement-seekers into the city, until it housed a hundred-thousand strangers; parades with bands of music filled the streets and fired salutes at intersections; hotel lobbies and barrooms were choked. Everyone knew that McClellan would be nominated, behind whom stood a half-dozen influential New Yorkers—S.L.M. Barlow, Samuel J. Tilden, Dean Richmond, August Belmont, Peter Cagger, Manton Marble. They were reinforced by such veteran leaders as S. S. Cox of Ohio, James Guthrie of Kentucky, and Ex-Governor William Bigler of Pennsylvania.

The two opening speeches were floridly rhetorical. August Belmont, national chairman, predicted that Lincoln's reëlection would mean "the utter disintegration of our whole political and social system," while Bigler lamented that the land was "literally drenched in fraternal blood." Then Horatio Seymour seized the gavel of permanent chairman for another burst of sound and fury.[2]

1. Lewis, Charles Lee, *David Glasgow Farragut, Our First Admiral*, Annapolis, 1943, Chs. XXII and XXIII; Farragut Papers, Huntington Library; *Official Records, Navy*, Ser. I, Vol.XXI, 405-407, 422-423; Farragut, Loyall, *The Life of David Glasgow Farragut*, New York, 1879, 422-423.
2. New York *World*, Aug. 29, 30, 31, 1864. The men named had dignity and ability, and deserved kindlier descriptions than Noah Brooks gave them. He contrasted August Belmont, "pale, sleek-headed, dapper and smooth," with Dean Richmond, who had done much to create the New York Central system, and this year succeeded Erastus Corning as president, "a tall, potbellied, bottle-nosed man, austere and arbitrary." He spoke ill of Fernando Wood, sour because he hated McClel-

The delegates had braced themselves for a deadly struggle between War Democrats who would keep on fighting for Union and emancipation, and Peace Democrats who would compromise. One side talked of McClellan as a leader who would give fresh energy to the war; the other talked of a speedy arrangement with Jefferson Davis to end the bloody struggle. McClellan's strength lay chiefly in the New England, New York, and Pennsylvania delegations, while peace sentiment ran highest among men of the Middle West and Border. Yet it was a curious fact that, although the principal champion of peace by submission was Vallandigham, his staunchest allies came from the raffish element in New York City, where Fernando Wood and Ben Wood led the unwashed myrmidons of Tammany Hall; and it was another curious fact that, although New England was full of wartime zeal, the handsome, ever-popular Thomas Hart Seymour of Connecticut—a talented reactionary of exhibitionist tendencies, often called traitor by Republicans—held views as disloyal as Vallandigham's.

In this situation, with the two wings of the party sternly hostile to each other but with a measure of unity essential for success, talk sprang up of mixing oil and vinegar on a simple formula—the War Democrats to name the candidate and the Peace Democrats to write the platform. The compromisers would have liked to nominate T. H. Seymour, but McClellan's fame was so great that they were abruptly stopped in their tracks. Moreover, Seymour protested that he did not want the post. The Peace Democrats, seeing that they had to accept McClellan, helped nominate him on August 31 by a moderately greater vote than that given Seymour. They resolved, however, to control the Convention in every other respect.

They managed this so smoothly that hardly a ripple disturbed the surface harmony as the oil blended with the vinegar. Men who had predicted a fierce battle could hardly believe their eyes and ears when nobody objected to McClellan except two delegates who accused him of measures unfriendly to civil liberties in Maryland early in the war. George H. Pendleton was unanimously nominated for the Vice-Presidency, and the defeatist platform was adopted with but four dissenting votes. Observers guessed that all this was done by clever pre-arrangement, and the advantages lay so clearly with the Peace Democrats that cynical men surmised that Vallandigham had dominated those who had made the pre-arrangement.

Perhaps this was true, perhaps not. But it was apparent that when the

lan and knew he would be nominated, but was more respectful of Horatio Seymour, "smooth, oily, dignified, and serene," who came in with a knot of small politicians "over whom he towers head and shoulders mentally and physically." De Alva Stanwood Alexander, in *A Political History of the State of New York*, New York, 1906-1909, III, *passim*, treats these leaders accurately.

platform spoke of "four years of failure" in the war effort and the prostration of "public liberty and private right," it took a submissionist view. Men realized that when the platform called for cessation of hostilities "with a view to an ultimate convention," it was suggesting unconditional surrender of the main differences between North and South. The platform did not come out directly for Confederate independence, but for restoration of the Union and rights of the States unimpaired. The Democrats also opposed alleged interference by military authorities in elections in Kentucky, Maryland, Missouri, and Delaware; opposed subversion of the civil law by military law in States not in insurrection; condemned arbitrary military arrests; arraigned suppression of speech and press; and defied employment of "unusual test oaths." The word slavery was not mentioned in the platform. It was rumored that at one of the secret meetings Dean Richmond had waged a desperate battle for a plank proposing an attempt at negotiation first, and then if necessary a war to the knife, but Vallandigham fought so angrily to strike it out that nobody dared interfere.[3] Actually Vallandigham had much to do with drafting the vital planks of the platform, and it was generally known that Pendleton was one of the most unyielding Copperheads in the country. Inheriting the prestige and opinions of a great Virginia family, although a native of Ohio, he had opposed the war from the beginning, voted against supplies to carry it on, and denounced all Northern leaders involved. He had in fact never concealed his desire to see the South gain its independence.

Nor did anyone lose sight of the fact that McClellan's nomination received the enthusiastic adherence of Vallandigham, Pendleton, Fernando Wood, T.H. Seymour, and other politicians of equivocal loyalty.[4] It was also noted that Manton Marble's New York *World* and other Copperhead publications took immediate pains to republish McClellan's letter to Lincoln in June, 1862, from Harrison's Landing. They repeated, as being still his views, his protests against

3. The War Democrat, Amasa J. Parker, wrote S.L.M. Barlow on Sept. 5: "You have seen the platform adopted at Chicago; but you do not know what difficulty we had in modifying it to its present shape, and how fain were our efforts to still more improve its phraseology." Barlow Papers, HEH. The platform asserted "that, after four years of failure to restore the Union by the experiment of war, during which. . . . the Constitution itself has been disregarded in every part, and public liberty and private right alike trodden down. . . . justice, humanity, liberty, and the public welfare demand that immediate efforts be made for a cessation of hostilities, with a view to an ultimate convention of the States . . ." Stanwood, Edward A., *History of the Presidency from 1788 to 1897*, Boston, 1912, I, 304-305; McPherson, Edward, *The Political History of the United States of America During the Great Rebellion*, Washington, 1865, 423.

4. Men disloyal to Jackson's principle, "Our Federal Union: It Must be Preserved." Senator James A. Bayard's views about the struggle had not changed since 1860, he wrote S.L.M. Barlow on Feb. 4, 1864. "I cannot but look upon the idea of many Democrats that a govt. such as ours can be restored by war, as a sheer hallucination." He had stayed in the Senate wishing to be of public use. "I have however lost all hope and look forward to a far more disastrous condition of affairs than the people dream of." They would see tyranny, then revolution, and then entire disintegration of the Union, all largely the fault of New England. Barlow Papers, HEH.

attacks upon slavery, and against any confiscations of property, any territorial reorganization of States, or any military arrests outside the area of actual hostilities. They readvertised his belief of 1862 that any declaration of radical attitudes toward slavery would "rapidly disintegrate" the Union armies.

It was also noted that Pendleton said nothing to modify his old position that the government should allow the erring sisters to go in peace. In the Congressional session beginning in July, 1861, he had declared, "I will heartily, zealously, gladly support any honest effort to maintain the Union and reinvigorate the ties which bind these States together." But somehow he had then found every practical Union effort dishonest. He had voted against increasing the regular Army, against the draft, against the Legal Tender Act, and against the important revenue bills; he would later propose to redeem United States bonds, not in gold but in greenbacks—thus combining inflationary ideas and financial dishonesty in a single measure. In short, men of conviction found him to be a gentleman of unstained private reputation, but untrustworthy in principles respecting the Union.[5]

The Richmond *Examiner* accurately estimated the situation. Reporting that Peace Democrats and War Democrats had compromised on McClellan, it commented that the platform "is half peace and half war; it floats between peace and war, being constructed in such a way as to drift to either side, and settle down next March in a war or peace policy as circumstances may require. Armistice will certainly be a feature in the new policy; armistice with a view to negotiation." If Washington should negotiate under McClellan with Richmond, Confederate independence might be safe, but if Washington should negotiate separately with the several States, Southern independence would be imperilled. In either event, thought E. A. Pollard's *Examiner*, negotiations for peace under the Constitution would mean the preservation of slavery.[6]

But the Democratic position, in view of recent events at Atlanta and Mobile, was asinine. If the party went before the voters with asseverations that the war was a failure while every week loosed fresh jubilations over victory, its own defeat was certain. If the Democratic Party stood for negotiations with the Confederacy embracing possible disunion and the certain restoration of slavery, angry desertions from the Democratic ranks would become general. Some people supposed that McClellan had given clear intimations of the kind of platform he wished built for him, and had promised to stand squarely upon it.[7] They thought that Vallandigham was aware of this when he told a crowd on reaching home from Chicago: "That convention has met every expectation

5. See New York *World*, Sept. 6, 1861, for summary and comment. Horace Greeley, in his *Tribune*, shared this opinion of Pendleton.
6. Richmond *Examiner*, Sept. 1, 1864.
7. See New York correspondence dated Sept. 13, London *Daily News*, Sept. 27, 1864.

of mine; the promises have all been realized." Others thought that the Peace Democrats were merely counting on McClellan's well-understood malleability. Whatever Little Mac's intentions, whatever the expectations of spineless peace-men, the storm of disgust and anger that met the platform gave intelligent and patriotic Democrats a shock they could not mistake.

"The whole thing can be put right with McClellan's letter of acceptance," the New York jurist Amasa J. Parker wrote Barlow,[8] meaning that McClellan must repudiate the "failure" plank and sound anew the slogan of Union. McClellan's letter of acceptance, which Barlow helped him write, was blazoned throughout the North on September 9. In spite of this brilliant opportunity given him to rebuke defeatism, he was, instead, weakly equivocal. To be sure, he rejected the idea that the war could be called a failure. "I could not look in the face my gallant comrades of the army and navy, who have survived so many bloody battles, and tell them that their labor and the sacrifice of so many of our slain and wounded brethren had been in vain. . . ." But he cravenly yielded to the platform in asserting that whenever the South showed a disposition to reënter the Union on any terms, he would negotiate. After Chancellorsville, Gettysburg, and the Wilderness, he would return to Buchanan and to the Union of 1859! No unity! He surrendered to the defeatists again in emphasizing the national longing for peace, and to the compromisers by declaring that if "any one State is willing to return to the Union, it should be received at once, with a full guarantee of all its constitutional rights."[9]

A chorus of approval from many leading War Democrats which greeted McClellan's rejection of the plank declaring the war a failure drowned out resentful growls from Ben Wood's semi-traitorous New York *Daily News* and Washington McLean's Cincinnati *Enquirer*. Yet the damage done the Democratic Party by the platform could not be undone. Its silly and evil stigmatization of the heroic war effort as worthless gave the Northern millions an image of the Democratic Party they could never forget. That phrase upon the failure of the war was to echo down the coming decades as the pronouncements of the Hartford Convention had echoed for decades, and would cost the party votes for a generation.

The issues were now crystal clear. Lincoln would entertain no proposal for a return to the Union by the rebellious States which did not include the abandonment of slavery by the whole Confederacy. McClellan would receive into the Union any State, restoring immediately all its constitutional rights, including the right to hold slaves, while other States yet remained in rebellion.

8. London *Daily News, ut supra;* Parker was a founder of the Albany Law School.
9. The Barlow Papers, HEH, contain both a rough draft of the letter in Barlow's handwriting, and a final draft; McClellan to Barlow, June 17, 1864.

Yet, ever since the days of Van Buren and Wilmot, a host of Northern Democrats had been antislavery men, and they still recoiled from the idea of embracing the foul hag slavery, even if paired with the beautiful maiden peace.

Thus, as the wind of sentiment shifted to favor Lincoln, McClellan's letter gave his party only the slenderest chance of success. To Peace Democrats, it promised almost nothing, to War Democrats nothing that the moderate Lincoln did not offer. In experience, Lincoln's four years in the White House gave him an overwhelming advantage. In personal popularity, he held a better place than McClellan in most towns and cities outside New York, while in rural areas his strength was unconquerable. The acute correspondent of the London *Daily News* pointed out that while country folk cared nothing about his defects of dress and manners, "his logic and his English, his jokes, his plain common sense, his shrewdness, his unbounded reliance on their honesty and straightforwardness, go right to their hearts." No important peace party really existed, the correspondent declared, and now that a brief interval of national weariness and depression was being overcome, no Administration would dare to cease fighting as long as the Confederacy was in existence.

"I think of Lincoln's chances at this moment," wrote the correspondent on September 10, "as five to three."

[II]

Although the voting was yet to come, by the end of September the campaign was indeed over. The wave of popular disgust with Vallandigham's platform flung tens of thousands of Democrats out of their party, and hundreds of thousands of wavering Republicans back within their own. Seldom has so swift a change occurred in the political situation of the great republic. No sooner did the country learn of the Chicago platform than Bryant, Greeley, Charles Sumner, John A. Andrew, Richard Yates, Lyman Trumbull, and other influential Republican dissidents, one by one, fell in behind Lincoln, declaring they would put every ounce of strength into the fight against McClellan. After Mobile Bay and Atlanta, gold came down with a rush, easing the pressure on national finances and prices. Volunteers pressed forward. Seward, delivering his annual address to his fellow townsmen of Auburn on September 3, made the welcome announcement: "We shall have no draft, because the army is being reinforced at the rate of five to ten thousand men a day."[10]

More significant still, Washington dispatches early in September included news that informed Republican circles expected Frémont to withdraw in the next ten days, and Ben Wade to take the stump immediately. Uneasiness would

10. Seward, Annual Address, Sept. 3, 1864.

persist until the Frémont splinter and the Chase factions disappeared completely. And the echoes of earlier successes had not ceased when the press carried jubilant new headlines late in September: "Victory! Another Glorious Triumph in the Shenandoah Valley!" Sheridan had smashed Early's forces at Fisher's Hill, capturing twenty guns and eleven hundred prisoners. This thrilling news of victory reached the public together with intelligence of the third battle of Winchester (September, 1864) in which Sheridan's forces drove Early's army in full retreat up the Shenandoah Valley, with substantial losses. General James A. Garfield wrote his wife from Cincinnati, September 23, 1864, that Sheridan had just made a speech in the Shenandoah more powerful and helpful to the Union cause than all the speeches the Union stump-orators could make; "our prospects are everywhere brightening."[11]

Lincoln had been unfortunate early that summer in that the war had moved so tardily, defeats appeared to outnumber victories, and Grant's losses had proved so poignant. What tragedies from the Wilderness to the Crater were registered in the Northern memory! Yet he had been politically fortunate in that no victorious chieftain had arisen in the North. What if the handsome, plausible Hooker had defeated Lee at Chancellorsville?—what if he had pressed on to destroy the Confederate army at Gettysburg? He might have been politically invincible. The efforts of men like Greeley to galvanize the unfit Rosecrans and Ben Butler into political leadership in the spring of 1864 indicate the perils that might have existed. Happily for Lincoln and the nation, inept generals possessed no appeal. As has been seen, a successful general like Grant had taken himself out of the picture. Now it was fortunate that Democratic blunders, recent military and naval victories, and the dissipation of the last foreign threats coincided to furnish a background for Lincoln's climactic efforts to unify the party and nerve the nation for the final critical months.

The last dangerous breaches in Republican ranks were healed when a sudden Radical assault upon Montgomery Blair accomplished his downfall. Chase and his friends regarded the retention of Blair in the Cabinet as an affront, for (as Lincoln told Gideon Welles) they considered it a condemnation of themselves and an endorsement of the whole Blair clan. Stanton's hostility had deepened as he heard stories about Montgomery's aspersions on his character, and a special incident had fanned the coals of his anger into flame. When Early's troops, in their raid north of Washington, burned Blair's mansion "Falkland" at Silver Spring, the postmaster-general had been stung into a bitter comment: "Nothing better could be expected while politicians and cowards have the conduct of military affairs." He termed the commanders

11. Freeman, Douglas S., *Lee's Lieutenants*, III, 577ff.; Garfield to his wife, Cincinnati, Sept. 23, 1864, Garfield Papers, LC.

about Washington "poltroons." Halleck wrote Stanton that if this accusation could be substantiated, the commanders should be cashiered; if not, the slanderer should be dismissed from the Cabinet. Stanton laid the letter before Lincoln. Meanwhile Gideon Welles was irritated by Blair's efforts to get the navy yards made cogs in the Republican machine.[12]

Beyond question the multifariously malicious Blair family was imperiling party unity and Northern cohesion. Montgomery was distrusted by Moderate Republicans, hated by such Radicals as Schuyler Colfax and Thaddeus Stevens. Henry Wilson, who thought his Rockville speech an insult to the Administration, told Lincoln that Montgomery Blair would cost the Administration tens of thousands of votes. The Union League and Loyal Legion refused him membership. A host of German-Americans in the Middle West, adhering to Frémont and recalling that all three Blairs had been Democrats, disliked him. Such Radical Congressmen as George S. Boutwell and John Covode urged Lincoln to dismiss him, and as September wore on, men anxious for success in November—Washburne, Senator James Harlan of Iowa, James M. Edmunds of the Union League, and Zach Chandler—became active in a two-headed undertaking. By getting Montgomery Blair ousted they would placate Chase and his allies, and at the same time persuade Frémont to withdraw his third ticket. Frémont flatly denied, with every evidence of sincerity, that he had made a political bargain in return for an assurance that Blair would be dropped, and although any final statement on the subject is impossible, we may well accept his statement. The final dénouement came with startling swiftness. On September 23, Blair astonished Gideon Welles and Edward Bates as they left a Cabinet meeting by announcing: "I suppose you are both aware that my head is decapitated—that I am no longer a member of the Cabinet." Lincoln had reminded him that morning of an earlier promise to keep his resignation available. "The time has come," wrote the President.

Since this followed by one day the withdrawal of Frémont, many people erroneously connected it with that event. The connection was tenuous. Frémont, a lifelong Abolitionist at heart, had withdrawn primarily because he thought that McClellan's candidacy on a platform which offered longer life to slavery must at all cost be defeated. "The Chicago platform is simply separation," he wrote. "General McClellan's letter of acceptance is re-establishment with slavery." Both were intolerable. "The Republican candidate, on the contrary, is pledged to the re-establishment of the Union without slavery . . ." Frémont would do what he could to prevent a Democratic victory, and he

12. Seward, Frederick W., *Seward at Washington, op.cit.,* 243; Riddle, A.G., *Recollections of War Times,* New York, 1895, Chs. XXXVII, XXXVIII; Welles, Gideon, *Diary,* New York, 1960, II, 136ff; Nevins, *Frémont* (1961 ed.), 581.

realized that Republican unity was a paramount necessity. In saying this, he did not yield his conviction that the Lincoln Administration had been "politically, militarily, and financially a failure," and that, "its necessary continuance is a cause of regret for the country." Years later Frémont was to write in his own hand: "I resigned [from the army] when I entered the political contest against Mr. Lincoln himself. In that contest I was strongly supported by the West, and the North East. So strongly that it became evident that Mr. Lincoln could not be elected if I remained in the field. In order therefore to save the Republican party, as they alleged, an appeal was made to me by Mr. Lincoln and his friends to withdraw. A council was held at the President's house and a committee appointed to wait upon me in New York for this purpose. Upon our meeting, which was at the office of a lawyer . . . in New York I took a week to consider the appeal. At a second meeting, in the same place, I had concluded to withdraw and so informed the Committee and withdrew accordingly. By this act I offended and alienated many friends, especially in the West. The Com. brought me offers, of patronage for my friends, and of disfavor to my enemies. I refused both; my only consideration was the welfare of the Republican party. I cannot permit my withdrawal to be placed otherwise than upon the sole ground—as it was alleged by the Com., 'vital to the party.' "[13]

In the complicated talks that preceded his retirement, Frémont had heard directly or indirectly from spokesmen for Seward, Weed, Chase, Ben Wade, Zach Chandler, and others. He later said he had been promised that if he withdrew he would get rewards for himself and punishment for his foes, the rewards apparently being reinstatement in active military command or a Cabinet appointment, the punishment Blair's dismissal; and he had refused both as insulting. This statement may be accepted as quite honest. Zach Chandler in particular was frantically zealous to bring all Radicals back to the flock.[14]

13. Lincoln, *Collected Works*, VIII, 18; New York *Herald, Tribune, Times*, Sept. 23, 1864; Nevins, *Frémont* (1961 ed.), 659ff; Frémont Papers, Bancroft Library, Univ. of Calif. Berkeley, manuscript corrections in Frémont's hand of his memoirs, written largely by his wife and sons.

14. Nevins, *Frémont*, op.cit., 578-582, 659-661. Zach had a blunt way of shouldering himself into any office, even Stanton's, to demand action. According to the Detroit *Post* and *Tribune*, he went first to see Ben Wade, then Lincoln and Henry Winter Davis, and then "the leaders of the Frémont organization." Before seeing Lincoln a second time, about mid-September, while at the Astor House in New York, he learned that William Cullen Bryant was about to publish an editorial urging Lincoln's withdrawal and the assembling of a convention to name a new candidate. It was in type, but "by instant and earnest efforts, he obtained its withholding until the result of his labor could be known." (Detroit *Post* and *Tribune*), *Zachariah Chandler*, New York, 1880, 275.

Winter Davis, in a letter of Sept. 28 to Admiral DuPont, gives a more sensational story of Chandler's machinations to get rid of Montgomery Blair. "Chandler says he began when things looked very hopeless four or five weeks ago, everybody telling him success was hopeless. He did not go to Lincoln, but found out who his boon companions are, the men who crack jokes Sunday night till 1 A.M.—not politicians or Cabinet members, but the President's *familiar spirits*. [He] imbued them with the darkest views of Lincoln's prospects and sent them night after night to regale him with some new tale of defection or threatened disaster, never appearing himself for eight days till Lincoln was in the condition of a child frightened by ghost stories and ready to take

"If Montgomery Blair left the Cabinet, Chase and his friends would be satisfied, and this the President thought would reconcile all parties, and rid the Administration of irritating bickerings." So Lincoln later explained his course to Welles.[15] He did not bargain directly with Chase; he did not bargain directly with Frémont. When he threw Blair overboard he pleased not only both of them but Stanton and Halleck, Greeley and Bryant, Sumner and Wade, and a thousand other leading Republicans. Chase said nothing. Frémont should have said less, for his diatribe against Lincoln showed a poor spirit and poor taste. But Frémont, who might have reached for benefits by bargaining, had lost much. And there was real truth in the remark of Bennett's *Herald* as it recalled how recently leading Republicans had abused Lincoln as "a tyrant," "a failure," and "imbecile." "He (Frémont) does not act the cowardly, treacherous, and hypocritical part of Greeley, Chase, Pomeroy, Wade, Opdyke, and the rest. He does not deny his principles and eat his words."[16]

The hypocrisy of various Republican politicians and editors had in fact been unconcealed until the very opening of the Democratic Convention. The meeting that the hastily-assembled Opdyke political camarilla called to discuss a possible new convention had duly taken place at the house of David Dudley Field on August 30. This snake-cold attorney, aggressive in temper and sometimes careless of ethics in conducting dubious legal cases, had been chairman of the New York delegation to the Peace Conference of 1861, had since leaned toward a compromise peace, and would yet rejoin the Democrats. He was no friend to Lincoln. Henry Winter Davis had come to distil his poison into the discussion, and George Wilkes, a conservative newspaperman, had asserted that Grant alone could be elected. Francis Lieber had sent Charles Sumner a

refuge anywhere.... Next morning Chandler called and Lincoln said if Frémont could be induced to withdraw by giving up Blair, he would do it. Chandler went to New York; no Wade. He went to Massachusetts [and] saw Frémont, who was told the condition on which Lincoln would remove Blair. Frémont took time to consult his friends, met Chandler: 'But I wish a conditional one to get Blair out.' Fremont: 'I will make no conditions; my letter is written and will appear tomorrow!'

"So Chandler jumped into the cars, was in Washington next morning, saw Lincoln, and told him the condition on which he had promised to remove Blair had been complied with, and he claimed the performance of his promise. Lincoln: 'Well, but I must do it in my own way to soften it.' Chandler: 'Any way so it be done.' Exit Chandler. In the evening he called to see if it were done, when lo! Frémont's letter was before the President, who was excited at the form of it, and showed symptoms of flying from the bargain. Chandler recalled to him that the form of the withdrawal was not a condition, and offensive as it was, still it was a substantial advice to support Lincoln. So Lincoln yielded and wrote to Blair, 'The time has come.' Sic transit Blair! Stanton knew nothing of it yesterday when it was done!" H. W. Davis's Letters to S.F. DuPont, Eleutherian Mills, Hagley Foundation, Wilmington, Delaware.

For a modern analysis, see Trefousse, H.L., "Zachariah Chandler and the Withdrawal of Frémont in 1864; New Answers to an Old Riddle," *Lincoln Herald*, Winter, 1968, Vol. 70, No. 4, 181-187. Trefousse concludes that Frémont did act independently, but "it also becomes manifest that Chandler played an important part in the negotiations...." Trefousse feels the evidence shows Chandler prevailed upon Lincoln to carry out the bargain when the President hesitated.

15. Welles, *Diary, op.cit.*, II, 158.
16. New York *Herald*, Editorial, Sept. 23, 1864.

report. Numerous States were represented, he wrote: "All agreed that Lincoln cannot be re-elected, unless great victories can be attained soon, which is next to impossible on account of the worn-out state of the armies of the Potomac." Henry Winter Davis told Admiral DuPont about the meeting, adding, with a note of sour Radical vindictiveness, "Those who think Lincoln came down from Heaven will soon be convinced he was on his way lower down and was not intended to stop here much longer and having been found out he will be sent on his way rejoicing. There was but one opinion among *all* the persons consulted—that the Chicago nominee must be selected unless Lincoln be withdrawn; and we hope people enough will act on that opinion to make it effectual. . . ."[17]

This was just before the Chicago platform and the capture of Atlanta put a new face on affairs. Three editors—Greeley, Parke Godwin of the *Evening Post,* and Theodore Tilton of the *Independent*—had undertaken to sound the opinion of other Republican leaders. In the swiftly changing situation they obtained answers that set them running to board the Lincoln wagon—an ignoble but edifying spectacle.

By October, as we have seen, the Presidential battle was virtually over. On September 29-30, Federal troops on the Petersburg front pushed west and north once more beyond the Weldon Railroad at the battle of Peebles' Farm. At the same time, north of the James, Grant's men captured Fort Harrison on September 29, and other ground, forcing Lee to pull back, build new intrenchments, and actually extend his already lengthy lines. Most spectacular of all had been the aforementioned movements of Sheridan in the Shenandoah where, after victories at Third Winchester September 19, Fisher's Hill September 22, and Tom's Brook October 9, Federal forces continued to press Early farther southward in the Valley.

By this time Phil Sheridan had become one of the best-loved Northern leaders, his picture and exploits familiar to all. Driving the defeated, ill-equipped Confederates before him, he began, it seemed to sanguine Northerners, to threaten Lee's lines from the Northwest. The many-fronted Union advances had several noteworthy results. Lincoln's reputation being inextricably bound up with the success or failure of the armed forces, the gains burnished his reputation as war leader to new lustre. They helped men peer through the battle-smoke in expectation of a sunrise of cheerful postwar activites. Meanwhile, so intense was the suspense over daily dispatches headed "The Gulf," "Atlanta," or "The Valley," that everybody forgot about ordinary issues. No national task stood paramount but one—the grim task of war.

17. Wilkes to Elihu Washburne, Aug. 31, 1864, Washburne Papers, LC.; H.W. Davis to S.F. DuPont Letters, Aug. 31, 1864, Eleutherian Mills-Hagley Foundation, Wilmington, Del.

The battle news now wrote an increasingly sardonic commentary upon the phrase "four years of failure," which Bennett's *Herald,* after long standing cynically on the sidelines, now called the most stupid, impudent, and detestable phrase coined by any conclave since Valmy had ended one of the severest defeats of the French revolutionary wars.[18] On October 21-22, Northern newspapers blazed again with the news of Cedar Creek, fought on October 19. Stanton's bulletin curtly summarized one of the most dramatic encounters of the war, long to be celebrated and translated into legend in prose, poetry, and drama. "Another great battle was fought yesterday at Cedar Creek, threatening at first a great disaster," he wrote, "but finally resulting in a victory for the Union forces under General Sheridan more splendid than any heretofore achieved."

Fuller accounts told how the Confederates under Early had been the assailants; how they intended, as Longstreet wrote Early, to "crush Sheridan out of the Valley at once and at all hazards"; how they struck when Sheridan had been called to Washington for a consultation with Stanton and was returning; how, at dawn in Winchester where he had unaccountably delayed over night, he heard the boom of cannon in the distance; how he galloped out of Winchester at seven-thirty, and how two hours later he reached the field of battle twenty miles away. Actually an officer reported hearing firing about 7:00 A.M., but Sheridan later admitted he paid no attention to it and "was unconscious of the true condition of affairs until about 9:00, when having ridden through the town of Winchester, the sound of the artillery made a battle unmistakable. . . ."[19] Furthermore, the distance was under the legendary 20 miles to the battlefront. Here the incipient panic caused by Early's stunningly effective surprise attack had already been checked by General H. G. Wright, but Sheridan's dramatic entrance made the Union recovery quick and complete. To Northern observers it seemed that from the jaws of defeat, like Napoleon at Marengo, he had snatched means to parry a desperate Confederate stroke that might have altered the entire face of the war in Virginia in favor of Lee, and to convert it into a stunning blow to the South. The stampede of the rebel troops was followed by another stampede of the gold gamblers and the supporters of McClellan.[20]

The Richmond press was carrying material of quite different import. It made room for letters written by Alexander H. Stephens, Governor Joseph E.

---

18. New York *Herald,* Oct. 20, 1864. Lincoln reputedly offered Bennett about this time the post of minister to France; Harper, Robert S., *Lincoln and the Press,* New York, 1951, 320-321.

19. *O.R.* I, xliii, pt. 1, p.52.

20. Merritt, Wesley, "Sheridan in the Shenandoah Valley," *Battles and Leaders,* IV, 500-521; Early, Jubal A., "Winchester, Fisher's Hill, and Cedar Creek," *Battles and Leaders,* IV, 522-530; *O.R.*, I, xliii, pt. 1, 52, 561.

Brown of Georgia, James P. Boyce of South Carolina, and Herschel V. Johnson, which caught eagerly at the idea of a national convention, Johnson sagaciously and courageously writing that the sooner the issue could be transferred
from the field of blood to the forum of rational discussion the better for both
sides.[21]

[III]

Both parties were deficient in organization. But the veteran editor Henry
J. Raymond as the Republican national chairman was more resourceful and
dexterous than the Democratic national chairman, the capitalist-politician August Belmont, and the fact that the Republicans were in power gave him a clear
advantage. In 1862 the Democratic organization had been stronger in most
States than the Republican; now the Republican was as good, if not better. In
raising money for speakers, pamphlets, and a thousand other purposes, the
Republicans fell back upon the well-established process of assessing Federal
officeholders for contributions. With some exertion Raymond obtained the
assistance of the War Department, Treasury, and Post Office, but the Navy
under the stern moralist Gideon Welles remained impregnable. Regarding
Raymond as a journalistic mercenary, Welles was disgusted by his attempt to
use navy yards to elect candidates instead of build ships. He stigmatized the
collectors of assessments as harpies who put into their own pockets much of
the money they extorted. Nevertheless, Raymond finally succeeded in getting
the Brooklyn navy yard to dismiss men because they supported McClellan.
He collected money so brazenly in the New York Post Office and (after
Hiram Barney left) the Custom House, that the *Herald* and *World* emitted
indignant growls. When Phelps, Dodge, the metal dealers, gave him $3,000,
and he tightened the screws on other contractors, the *World* snorted that
every man who sold the government a pound of pork or bottle of quinine was
expected to walk into the National Committee offices and plank down his
greenbacks.[22]

Welles was the only cabinet member who objected to the general levy upon
officeholders, five percent being the accepted amount. A committee under
Senator James Harlan of Iowa looked after this shabby screw-tightening.
Montgomery Blair had given $500 to the campaign fund, and when workers
in the New York post office objected to paying tribute, his successor William
Dennison told them he thought the levy was right. Lincoln had a hard-headed
sense of the importance of parties and elections, but also a hard-headed conviction that party demands must not pervert the standards of honesty and effi-

21. Summary in Richmond *Whig*, Oct. 18, 1864.
22. Brown, Francis, *Raymond of the Times*, New York, 1951, 362-364.

ciency in government. He took no position on assessments except to refuse to permit coercive pressures on officeholders. He rejected the request of a Congressman that he bring official influence to bear to compel assistance from a reluctant postmaster, and rebuked the Philadelphia postmaster because his employees displayed a suspiciously Republican unanimity. In August and September the party was straitened for funds,[23] but by October the prospect of victory had loosened purse strings.

Some dubious methods of rallying the party were well illustrated even in distant California. "I went to the Navy Yard today," wrote Richard Chenery of the Naval Agent's office in San Francisco on September 22, "to induce the commandant to put in 200 more men, that we may carry that county and assist in saving the district, but he is timid and feared he might be censured if he did so. . . . I told him that the Administration expected him to do such a thing." The subject of politics was dominant in Presidential councils. Attorney-General Bates was at an October 28 cabinet meeting "and was not a little surprised to hear nothing talked of but election matters, and those minor points. Neither great *principles*—nor great *facts* seem, at present to have any chance for a fair consideration. . . . I wish the election was over. . . ."[24]

On the Democratic side, Manton Marble of the New York *World* was put in charge of publicity by August Belmont and Dean Richmond, gathering funds and paying speakers, publishers of pamphlets, and distributors of government documents. On one September day, five men contributed a thousand dollars apiece for his work, one of them that shrewd businessman, collector, and party-indefatigable, Sam Barlow. Yet he found his task arduous. "It looks ugly," the sensible Congressman "Sunset" Cox wrote him from Ohio on October 12. "The Vallandigham men have done just enough for us to damn us. Medary's paper put up McClellan's name—a little bit—and damned him with faint praise." At the end Marble referred bitterly to the difficulties of a contest "against an administration disbursing millions daily, employing one-third of the active industries of the whole population, and directing the interested energies of a whole army of stipendiaries scattered through every city, town, and village in the land. . . ."[25]

Each party had its loyal phalanx of speakers and writers, the Republicans leading. To be sure, the Democrats could call upon such intelligent stalwarts as William R. Morison of Illinois, Thomas A. Hendricks of Indiana, John V.L. Pruyn of New York, Reverdy Johnson of Maryland, S. S. Cox of Ohio, Samuel

23. Fowler, Dorothy Canfield, *The Cabinet Politician: The Postmasters-General, 1829-1909*, New York, 1943, 119-122; Brown, *Raymond of the Times, op.cit.*, 264.

24. Chenery to Senator Cornelius Cole, Cole Papers, UCLA Library; Bates, *Diary, op.cit.*, 422.

25. Cox in Manton Marble Papers, LC. Samuel Medary's *Crisis* was so obnoxious to Union men that an angry mob had wrecked its press in 1863; he died that fall. Marble in New York *World*, Nov. 10, 1864.

J. Randall of Pennsylvania; men who had served in Congress, made their mark in debate, and begun careers that would later be noteworthy. But how many seats in Congress once filled by eloquent Southern members were now marked "vacant"! And how many prominent Democrats would do the party more harm than good by public speeches! To place Bayard of Delaware, Voorhees of Indiana, or Ben Wood of New York upon a platform would be to invite a disastrous bolt of lightning, or cause a vast secession of honest men from the party. They would attract mobs more quickly than adherents. Among editors, such figures as Wilbur F. Storey of the Chicago *Times*, William Wright of the Newark *Journal*, and Washington McLean of the Cincinnati *Enquirer* wielded two-edged swords, as dangerous to friend as to foe. The manly activities of James Sheehan of the Chicago *Post*, George Lunt of the Boston *Courier*, Manton Marble of the *World*, and James C. Welling of the *National Intelligencer*, undaunted champions of civil liberties and political moderation, suffered heavy damage from wild party associates.[26]

Greatest of all was the disparity of literary strength in this party contest. Had Nathaniel Hawthorne, the devoted friend of Franklin Pierce, not died this spring, he might possibly have raised a voice for consideration of the Democratic position, though his single essay on wartime affairs had irritated many by his neutralism.[27] Some writers were as little concerned with politics as Herman Melville or Walt Whitman. A few were as inefficiently on the Democratic side as George Ticknor Curtis, the biographer of Webster and Buchanan. A staunch phalanx of authors, however, with the most famous names in America—Lowell, Longfellow, Whittier, Holmes, Emerson, Mrs. Stowe—took the field for Lincoln. When Bryant's seventieth birthday practically coincided with election day, it evoked from Lowell one of his happiest war poems, vibrant with the feeling of the Republican host behind the President. His spirited lines, beginning "Our ship lay tumbling in an angry sea," rose to a climax in his tribute to the much revered poet-editor:

> But now he sang of faith to things unseen,
> Of freedom's birthright given to us in trust;
> And words of doughty cheer he spoke between,
> That made all earthly fortunes seem as dust,
> Matched with that duty, old as time and new,
> Of being brave and true.

26. The Boston attorney, George S. Hillard, friend of Hawthorne and Sumner, esteemed Lunt highly. "Lunt wants tact, discretion, and temper," he wrote Manton Marble on May 4, 1864, "but on the other hand, he has dauntless courage, and that fidelity to conviction which is the rarest quality in our people, and for want of which the country is going to the devil." Manton Marble Papers, LC.

27. Hawthorne, Nathaniel, "Chiefly About War Matters," *Atlantic Monthly*, July, 1862.

Undoubtedly Lowell was the most effective literary champion of Lincoln. He made embattled America seem greater, just as Milton and Wordsworth had once made embattled Britain rise to higher grandeur. He was contemptuous of the Democrats, who in his opinion had not a single principle on which to keep afloat the great party of Jefferson and Jackson. His article in the *Atlantic* of October, 1864, "McClellan or Lincoln?" not only proved that McClellan was committed to an untenable policy of conciliation, but provided a summary of the President's traits. "Mr. Lincoln, in our judgment, has shown from the first the considerate wisdom of a practical statesman. If he has been sometimes slow in making up his mind, it has saved him the necessity of being hasty to change it."[28] A message from Whittier to Frémont, "There is a time to *do* and a time to *stand* aside," helped influence the explorer to withdraw from his race.[29] Some young writers showed especial zeal. A young clerk in Washington named John Burroughs, who often glimpsed Lincoln from his Treasury window, went to vote this fall. Hearing some disparaging comments on Lincoln from a farmer who gave him a ride, he angrily leaped from the wagon, shook his fist, and declared that he would be damned if he rode farther with such a damned Copperhead.[30]

The young French journalist August Laugel, visiting Boston in the last stages of the campaign, found Sumner and Henry Wilson aroused, and Edward Everett, Josiah Quincy, George Ticknor, John G. Palfrey, and Longfellow exerting all their influence. The two Abolitionist leaders, Garrison and Wendell Phillips, were at odds, for though Garrison spoke and wrote for Lincoln, Phillips stubbornly refused his aid. The President's reëlection was certain, he said, but it would make the task of friends of the slaves hard. "We have constantly to be pushing him from behind."[31] But otherwise all was unity.

Not all the pamphlets, speeches, and other writings were on such a high plane by any means. The 1864 election was little different from previous ones in its fulminations, except that the war lent a somewhat unusual context. For instance, *Harper's Weekly* in late September printed a list of terms which were said to be applied by the friends of General McClellan to the President: "Filthy Story-Teller, Despot, Big Secessionist, Liar, Thief, Braggart, Buffoon, Usurper, Monster, Ignoramus Abe, Old Scoundrel, Perjurer, Robber, Swindler, Tyrant, Fiend, Butcher, Land Pirate, A Long, Lean, Lank, Lantern-Jawed, High-Cheek-Boned-Spavined-Rail-Splitting Stallion."

28. Scudder, H.E., *James Russell Lowell*, Boston, 1901, 56-57.
29. Pickard, A. T., *Life and Letters of John Greenleaf Whittier*, Boston, 1907, II, 487.
30. Barrus, Clara, *Life and Letters of John Burroughs*, Boston, 1925, I, 99-100.
31. Laugel, Auguste, *The United States During the Civil War*, ed. Allan Nevins, Bloomington, Ind., 1961, 311-325.

Pamphlets played their usual important role. For the Democrats there were such as "The Future of the Country by a Patriot," "Corruptions and Frauds of Lincoln's Administration," "The Lincoln Catechism whereby the eccentricities and beauties of despotism are fully set forth," "Lincoln's Treatment of Grant, with Lincoln's Treatment of McClellan and The Taint of Disunion," "Mr. Lincoln's Arbitrary Arrests." From the Republican side came Isaac N. Arnold's "Reconstruction; Liberty the corner stone, Lincoln the architect," "The Chicago Copperhead Convention: The Treasonable and Revolutionary Utterances of the Men Who Composed It," D. S. Coddington's "The Crisis and the Man," "The Copperhead's Prayer, containing remarkable confessions by a degenerate Yankee," the Chicago *Tribune*'s "Issues of the Campaign, Shall the North Vote for a Disunion Peace?" "Proofs for the Workingman of the Monarchial and Aristocratic Design of the Southern Conspirators and Their Northern Allies," "Spirit of the Chicago Convention—a surrender to the rebels advocated—a disgraceful and pusillanimous peace demanded—the Federal government savagely denounced and shamefully vilified and not a word said about the crime of treason and rebellion," "Letters of Loyal Soldiers," "How Douglas Democrats will vote." Many others of a like nature, along with speeches and campaign biographies, clog the archives of that time.

A few quotes suffice. "Corruptions and Frauds of Lincoln's Administrations," claimed that there had been fraud after fraud, and described "the wretched schemes of speculation and plunder into which the prominent partisans of Mr. Lincoln have embarked." Charges are based on the New York Custom House case and alleged corruptions in selling of cargo of captured blockade runners. "The Lincoln Catechism," one of the most vicious, has a devilish-looking colored face on a bright yellow cover. The publisher advertises such songs as "Ballads of Freedom and Abraham Africanus I." The text of the Catechism goes, "What is the Constitution? A compact with hell—now obsolete. By whom hath the Constitution been made obsolete? By Abraham Africanus the First. To What end? That his days may be long in office—and that he may make himself and his people the equal of the negroes. . . . What is the meaning of the word 'patriot?' A man who loves his country less, and the Negro more. What is the meaning of the word 'traitor?' One who is a stickler for the Constitution and the laws. What is the meaning of the word 'Copperhead?' A man who believes in the Union as it was, the Constitution as it is, and who cannot be bribed with greenbacks, nor frightened by a bastille. . . ."

The Republicans were not far behind, if behind at all, in such trash. From "The Copperhead's Prayer", we quote: "To the great and the mighty, the terribly feared, and the wonderfully adored Jefferson Davis, . . . Thou who are exalted so high above the common people—thou more than mortal whom we delight to deify, and worship as a God—knowing thou art DEVIL! Thou Aristocrat, professing Democracy—thou who hatest the poor white man, and whose mission it is to establish the only slave government the world ever saw. . . . It is not so much for the consideration of any natural affection which we have for you personally, O, immaculate Davis! but because we know that we are necessary to each other's political salvation. . . . It has been our prayer by day and our comfort by night that the time is not far distant when we shall be permitted to greet you as conqueror—and as the head of a great, independent, and glorious SLAVE CONFEDERACY. . . . I have joined the enemies of my country, and I must go with my party."

On a somewhat different level, Francis Lieber and his Loyal Publication Society distributed widely: "Report of the Judge Advocate General, on the 'Order of American Knights,' or 'Sons of Liberty'—A Western Conspiracy in Aid of the Southern Rebellion." This report of Judge Advocate General Joseph Holt presented a series of wild and exaggerated stories on the Copperhead menace.[32]

It was truly a Union Party in great parts of the North that faced the Democrats, a coalition of War Democrats and Republicans. A Union Convention was held in New York; the Union Party in Indiana took strength from the fact that Governor Oliver P. Morton had appointed Joseph A. Wright, a Democrat, to a Senatorship; Governor Buckingham in Connecticut called himself a Union Party man, and owed his spring victory largely to the support of Ex-Governor James T. Pratt, long a loyal Democrat. In Maine, town and county tickets uniting Republicans and Democrats were placed in nomination, and in Wisconsin the same procedure was followed. This alliance made it easier for Raymond's helpers to collect money, for by placing their pleas on a Union Party basis they could appeal to contributors of former Democratic allegiance. John Hay used White House stationery in acknowledging the receipt of a non-partisan contribution from a Federal attorney.[33] When Nicolay spent a mid-October week in Missouri he did it to obtain a full and harmonious combination of Union voters there and wrote Lincoln that "with the exception of very few impracticables, the Union men will cast their votes for you."[34]

The last weeks found the tide setting in one direction. "I have just had a conversation with a prominent New York politician and McClellan man,"

32. The Chicago Historical Society possesses an outstanding collection of these campaign documents, from which we have mentioned or quoted only a few. For a more readily available selection see Freidel, Frank, ed., *Union Pamphlets of the Civil War*, Cambridge, Mass., 1967, particularly Vol. II.

33. Hay to Raymond, Oct. 17, 1864, George E. Jones Papers, NYPL.

34. Oct. 18, 1864; Hay Papers, Illinois State Hist. Library.

Halleck wrote Lieber on October 22. "He says they expect to carry New York, New Jersey, Delaware, and Kentucky, and hope to get Pennsylvania and Missouri, but have given up all hope of electing McClellan. What they now want is to roll up as large a vote against Lincoln as possible, so as to preserve their party organization for the next election." Here and there a nervous Congressman like Schuyler Colfax feared local defeat, but the State elections on October 11 revealed an unmistakable trend. In Indiana Morton was reëlected governor for four years by nearly 21,000 majority over Joseph E. Macdonald, and Ohio also registered large Union Party gains. In Pennsylvania the result was at first in doubt. Democratic leaders had made heroic efforts in McClellan's former home State, where irritation had been excited by frauds connected with the recruiting system. But after several days of uncertainty the soldier vote gave the Union Party a clear majority.[35]

In an astonishingly close election, the voters of Maryland meanwhile approved 30,174 to 29,799 a new Constitution which provided for the emancipation of all slaves, without compensation to owners. Vehement opposition was made to this destruction of a property right that some citizens declared existed by divine authority as well as laws passed in accordance with the national Constitution. Voters were required to take an oath that they had never given aid or countenance to the rebellion, and nearly a hundred men refused it; as they would have voted against emancipation, the real majority for it was only about 270. But this margin gratified Lincoln, who made a special plea for approval two days before the election. "I desire it on every consideration," he wrote. "I wish all men to be free. I wish the material prosperity of the already free, which I feel sure the extinction of slavery would bring. I wish to see in process of disappearing that only thing which ever could bring this nation to civil war."[36]

35. Halleck in Lieber Papers, HEH; Colfax to Raymond, Oct. 8, 1864, Jones Papers, NYPL; New York *Herald, Times,* Oct. 11-16, 1864; *American Annual Cyclopaedia,* 1864, 436-438, 629-632, 648-652.
36. Lincoln to Henry W. Hoffman, Oct. 10, 1864, *Collected Works,* VIII, 41.

5

The Triumph of Lincoln

AS MEN of the Union Party read the encouraging State returns in October, 1864, Lincoln had a new opportunity to augment the strength and unity of his followers. On October 12 Roger B. Taney died, scion of an old Roman Catholic family of Maryland, graduate of Dickinson College in 1795, cabinet member under his friend Andrew Jackson, and successor of John Marshall in the Chief Justiceship. Even those who most detested his part in the odious Dred Scott decision could not deny his erudition and courage, nor the dignity and impartiality, apart from a pro-slavery bias, with which he had conducted the business of the tribunal. For years he had been a walking skeleton, kept alive, said some, by his annual visits to White Sulphur Springs, and by his determination, said others, to maintain a judicial citadel against Republican policies. Ben Wade had made a rough joke about him: during Buchanan's Administration he was fearful that Taney would die any day and "Old Buck" name his successor, but after Lincoln came in his fear was that Taney would manage to hang on into a new Democratic regime.[1]

The Supreme Court needed a firm hand, for peace was certain to bring before it important questions of finance, State rights, and the new status of the freedmen. For a time after taking office, Lincoln had hesitated to fill three vacancies. Two of the outgoing justices had been residents of seceded States. Appointments from the same area, even if possible, could not serve the vacated circuits; and he did not like to make all selections from the North, thus impeding justice to the South when peace was won. Early in 1862, however, he named Noah H. Swayne, a Virginia-born Ohioan, to one vacancy, and later that year appointed Samuel F. Miller of Iowa, and his old friend David Davis of Illinois. In 1863, Stephen J. Field of California was appointed, making a total of ten justices. This move was made by the Administration and Congress primarily to insure a "safe," strongly pro-Union Court. Now, who would guide the vessel thus partially remanned and enlarged?

1. Nicolay and Hay, *Lincoln*, New York, 1890, IX, 386.

The week after Taney's death, well-informed newspapers predicted that Salmon P. Chase would probably be made his successor.[2] Great was his friends' rejoicing—and great the anxious chagrin of Montgomery Blair, then conducting a characteristically devious movement to obtain the office. Instigated by the Blair family, William Cullen Bryant, John M. Forbes, and other men of influence had written Lincoln in Blair's behalf, while editors like Joseph Medill had made representations for him. When Mrs. Lincoln mentioned to Francis P. Blair, Sr., that the pressure of lawyers was giving Chase the advantage, the old politician hurried to the White House to lobby for his son. Montgomery himself tried to enlist Senator E. D. Morgan. "There is one consideration which I hope you will bring to the President's attention to prevent Chase's appointment," he wrote. "He is known to be so vindictive towards me for supporting the President, that no one would employ me as counsel to the Court if he were Chief Justice. Now the President cannot consent not only to turn me out of his Cabinet, but to drive me from the bar for life, because I supported him for the Presidency."[3]

Lincoln, however, had his own ideas about the Chief Justiceship. He told old Blair that he could not resist the general will of the bar. "Although I may be stronger as an authority, if all the rest oppose I must give way." He knew that Montgomery Blair's promotion would be politically divisive. When Chase's appointment was finally announced on December 6, Charles A. Dana astutely appraised Lincoln's reasons: "That appointment was not made by the President with entire willingness. He is a man who keeps a grudge as faithfully as any other living Christian, and consented to Chase's elevation only when the pressure became very general and very urgent. The Senate especially were resolved that no second-rate man should be appointed to that office, and if Mr. Montgomery Blair had succeeded in presenting his programme to that body, I have no doubt it would have been smashed to pieces in a moment. Mr. Blair's idea was that one of the existing justices, as for instance Judge Swayne, should be appointed Chief Justice, and that he himself should be made an Associate Justice . . ." Later he could step up. It was

2. Lincoln had repeatedly told friends earlier of his willingness to appoint Chase if a vacancy occurred; Nicolay and Hay, *Lincoln*, *op.cit.*, IX, 387. Chase's advice to him on constitutional questions like West Virginia, emancipation, and Negro enlistment, had been careful and weighty; Schuckers, *Chase*, New York, 1874, 459-464. For Lincoln's judicial appointments see King, Willard L., *Lincoln's Manager David Davis*, Cambridge, Mass., 1960, 192ff.; Silver, David, *Lincoln's Supreme Court*, Urbana, Ill., 1957, 83-93.

3. F.P. Blair, Sr., to John A. Andrew, *Massachusetts Historical Society Proceedings*, 1930, 88-89; Blair to E.D. Morgan, Nov. 20, 1864, Morgan Papers, New-York Hist. Soc.; J.M. Forbes to Bryant, Nov. 21, 1864, Bryant-Godwin Papers, NYPL. Montgomery Blair's wire-pulling was neither honest nor dignified.

fortunate for the country that this seat-warming arrangement for Blair never eventuated.[4]

It was still more fortunate that the opportunity for service went to Chase. Though regarded by the bar with some doubt as to the completeness of his professional training (graduating from Dartmouth without distinction, he had studied law sketchily under William Wirt before being admitted to practice), Chase had such eminent gifts that in due course he took rank among the great American jurists. Nobody could foresee that he would have to deal with the proposed trial of Jefferson Davis for treason, and the impeachment of an American President, but everyone knew that he would have to meet critical tests. William M. Evarts, who was delighted by his nomination, lived to deliver a judicious, if eschatological, judgment upon him. He compared Chase, as a financial statesman, with Alexander Hamilton. He laid emphasis upon Chase's deep religious convictions and his stern sense of duty, but most of all he praised his vision as a jurist intent upon making the government of the republic one not of men, but of laws.[5] Lincoln, faced with one of his weightiest decisions, had disregarded personal feeling and unwise counsel to choose aright. No other man suggested—Blair, Bates, David Davis, Stanton, Swayne, or William M. Evarts—had the stature of Chase. Lincoln appointed him with but one apprehension, that in his exalted new seat he might still look covetously at the Presidency.[6]

[I]

The main issue of the Presidential contest as it moved into its final month had little to do with the party platforms, for after McClellan published his letter of acceptance both candidates stood on the same central demand, the maintenance of the Union at all costs. The question was which man and which party could best assure this goal. Some voters doubted McClellan's sincerity in asserting that "reëstablishment of the Union in all its integrity is and must be the indispensable condition in any settlement." They were relatively few

4. Segal, Charles M., editor, *Conversations with Lincoln*, New York, 1961, 360-361; Dana to James S. Pike, Dec. 12, 1864, Pike Papers, Columbia Univ. Lib. The unscrupulous Montgomery Blair, meeting Senator Henry Wilson, told him that, unless Blair got the place, it would go to "one of the old fogies on the supreme bench, and so he ought to help Blair." Nicolay Papers, Illinois State Hist. Lib.

5. *Arguments and Speeches of William Maxwell Evarts*, edited by his son Sherman Evarts, New York, 1919, Vol.III, Ch.III, "Eulogy on Chief Justice Chase," 59-92.

6. *Ibid.*, 78-82. Lincoln told Henry Wilson: "I fear if I make him C.J. he will simply become more uneasy and neglect the place in his strife and intrigue to make himself President. He has got the presidential maggot in his head, and it will wiggle there as long as it is warm." Nicolay Papers, Illinois State Hist. Lib.

in number, however, for the Democrats now stood no possible chance of winning the election except on such firm pledges. As Bennett's *Herald* said on September 24, the salvation of the Union was the all-absorbing issue with the masses of both parties in all the loyal States. They might elect Lincoln or elect McClellan, but only as a Union man. This meant war to complete victory, for not only Davis, Lee, and Toombs, but the six Southern governors who met at Augusta on October 17 were still stubbornly demanding Confederate independence.[7]

With every passing day, moreover, the question of slavery retention became more unreal. The institution had been too far mutilated and undermined to recover. John J. Crittenden had said it would go out like a candle, and it was now guttering. Missouri was on the point of abolishing it as Maryland did. The only question was whether emancipation there should be gradual, as the State convention of 1863 had provided, or immediate, as the so-called Radicals, demanding a new convention, urged. Farther South, hundreds of thousands more who had heard Sherman's bugles and Farragut's cannon would tolerate slavery no longer. If McClellan were elected, it would be by the votes of men who knew that slavery was moribund, but would try to write into the peace arrangements a few mild stipulations on the subject. If Lincoln were elected, it would be by the votes of men who knew that slavery was dead and would write into constitutional amendments steel-clad guarantees of a new political and social order. Which man, which party, could best be trusted with a future certain to be utterly different from the past?

A new spirit was in the air which made platform declarations, and such vague assurances as those in McClellan's acceptance letter, quite meaningless. McClellan promised economy without saying when or where; "a more vigorous nationality" in foreign affairs without telling how it would be gained; "a return to a sound financial system" without defining "sound." The new spirit appeared when a crowd serenading Seward in Washington rose enthusiastically to his assertion that Sherman and Farragut had knocked the bottom out of the Chicago nominations, and somebody recited lines from Thomas Buchanan Read's poem "Sheridan's Ride."[8]

On nearly every front the conditions we have listed as precedent to victory were now being fulfilled. Was the coordinated and unified command of all the armies operating so efficiently that it interdicted Confederate attempts at exchanging army reinforcement on interior lines? Lee, aware of how desperately

7. McPherson, Edward, *The Political History of the United States of America During the Great Rebellion*, Washington, 1864, 421. Some governors possibly came in subversive mood: Coulter, E.M., *Confederate States*, Baton Rouge, 1950, 400.

8. Shotwell, W.G., *The Civil War in America*, London, 1923, II, 300.

the Western armies and other forces of the Confederacy needed men, was helpless to aid them. He was pinned down, with his hands overtaxed in Virginia. Did the Northern commanders at last have such heavy superiority in numbers and fire-power as permitted a steady outflanking of the enemy and continual pressure in lieu of costly frontal assaults? Grant's movements since before Cold Harbor and nearly all Sherman's movements answered this query affirmatively. Their strategy anticipated that of the Russian leaders in driving back the German armies in 1944-45. Finally, did the superiority of the North in medicines, equipment, transportation, artillery, and cavalry lend force to truly shattering blows and give the fighters irresistible confidence in the future? Nearly every week some engagement proved it did.

The superior power of the Union forces was being used, in the last weeks before election, to tighten the noose about Petersbrug, or rather to extend the beleaguerment of the little city. Hancock, who had been sent to the north bank of the James to harass Lee's lines before Richmond, and prevent Lee from sending further reinforcements to Early in the Shenandoah, remained there until August 20, when he was recalled. Warren, as has been mentioned at the start of the preceding chapter, had been ordered on August 16 to move against the Weldon Railroad, to cut it, and to renew the pressure upon Lee. This vital line, only three miles from Grant's flank, was obviously a prize of the first importance—the road running straight south through Weldon to Wilmington, with a lateral connection in North Carolina to Raleigh, and in South Carolina to Florence. The tracks, locomotives, and cars on this cluttered artery were in deplorable condition, but it and the Southside Railroad running to Danville and the North Carolina Piedmont still carried indispensable supplies and men. By noon on August 18 Warren had reached the railroad. Sharp battles filled several days, Henry Heth and A. P. Hill fighting hard to keep control of the lines. But Warren held tenaciously to his position, permanently ousting the Confederates, and compelling Lee to haul his supplies thirty miles by wagon around the break.[9]

This was a telling Union gain although made at high cost. A few days later in a separate operation, Hancock enlarged the Northern hold, although the Confederacy was temporarily successful in an attack on the Federals at Ream's Station, August 25. Cyrus Comstock of Grant's staff wrote in his diary on August 27 that he had visited the new line. "Hancock has destroyed the road for five miles below Ream's Station, but lost 9 guns and 2,000 prisoners. He says Gibbon's division behaved disgracefully . . . It is disgusting—Warren lost 3,000 the other day and now Hancock 2,000." Official figures were a total of 4,279

9. Freeman, Douglas S., *R.E. Lee*, New York, 1934, III, Ch.XXVII; Humphreys, Andrew A., *Virginia Campaign*, New York, 1883, 273-279.

Federal total casualties for Weldon Railroad and 2,742 for Ream's Station. Comstock added later, on September 10, that the Union position has been further improved. "Our line now runs across the Weldon R. R., then down its western side, then across it again on a line nearly parallel to the front, giving a large entrenched camp. A railroad is nearly completed in rear of our line from the City Point to the Weldon R. R. . . . Meade returned today and his staff report the feeling of the North very much improved by the successes at Atlanta, Mobile, and the Weldon R. R."[10]

On September 29, in conjunction with the Union attack on Fort Harrison north of the James, Federals moved out against Petersburg once more. The battle of Peebles' Farm, September 29 to October 1, failed to take the Southside Railroad, but did extend the lines three miles westward. Losses were again heavy, totaling 2,889. On October 27, Grant made another thrust to the left in an effort to outflank Lee and seize the now indispensable Southside Railroad. The drive known as Burgess' Mill, Boydton Flank Road, or Hatcher's Run failed, but the Union nevertheless had made considerable fall gains in the Petersburg fighting. As election day impended, a long lull began at Petersburg, a lull that meant enhanced strength to the North and growing weakness to the South. The winter about to begin proved a season of unusual severity. The Confederate soldiers, poorly clad, meagrely fed, and scantily sheltered, suffered terribly, having almost no meat, little bread, and no coffee, tea, or sugar. Rickety railway cars and wagons could not haul sufficient rations to the front. "Ten days ago the last meat ration was issued and not a pound remained in Richmond," Robert G. H. Kean was soon writing in his diary. An emergency supply had to be borrowed from the navy. "The truth is we are prostrated in all our energies and resources." Men shivering in bitter winds, living mainly on coarse corn-bread, and receiving piteous appeals from wives and children, were deserting in large numbers.[11]

These last weeks of the Presidential campaign found the situation in Georgia and Tennessee also in rapid transformation. The familiar events that led up to the capture of Atlanta will not be recounted here, save to note that they included President Davis's transfer of the Western army from Joseph E. Johnston to John B. Hood, a Kentucky West Pointer. Hood, who had taken command of the "Texas Brigade" early in 1862, had proved himself an aggressive fighter in engagement after engagement, from the Seven Days through

10. *O.R.* I, xlii, pt. 1, 128, 131; Comstock Papers, LC; cf. Willcox, O.D., "Actions on the Weldon Railroad," *Battles and Leaders*, IV, 568ff.

11. *O.R.* I, *ut supra*, 143; Humphreys, *Virginia Campaign, op.cit.*, 290-292; 294-303; Kean, *Inside the Confederate Government, op.cit.*, 181; Taylor, Walter H., *Four Years with General Lee*, ed. J.I. Robertson, Bloomington, Ind., 1962, 141-144.

Chickamauga, and during the campaign and siege of Atlanta, where he failed to drive back Sherman's forces. Then followed a Confederate repulse at Jonesboro (August 31 and September 1, 1864), demonstrating that Hood's troops would be enveloped if he did not evacuate the place, and his retreat a few miles south of Jonesboro to Lovejoy's Station on the railroad that connected Atlanta with Macon. Hardly a week after the Union entry into Atlanta, Sherman issued his edict that the whole population must remove; those who preferred it going South, and the others North. And on the day after the occupation General W. J. Hardee, at Hood's suggestion, sent President Davis a piteous telegram:

"Unless this army is speedily and heavily reinforced, Georgia and Alabama will be overrun. I see no other means to arrest this calamity. Never, in my opinion, were our liberties in such danger. What can you do for us?"[12]

The story of the Atlanta campaign, if narrated in detail, is an engrossing story, but it has been told too often to bear full review except in works primarily military. The important facts are that Davis made one of his worst mistakes when he removed the wary Johnston, who was following the only strategy that offered his weaker army a vague chance of success against Sherman's host, in favor of the rashly impetuous Hood; that in the final fighting around Atlanta the Union troops managed for the most part to take advantage of entrenched lines while the Confederates did the assaulting; that the loss of General James B. McPherson on July 22 at the Battle of Atlanta, a vigorous, able, and lovable leader only thirty-five years old, was one of the worst blows in leadership the Union army suffered; and that Sherman's removal of the people of Atlanta, while naturally assailed by Southerners as cruel, was justified by the situation and the laws of war. After taking Atlanta, Sherman rested his men for a time. He held not only an important rail center but a cluster of manufactories that had given the Confederacy a goodly stock of munitions. He had finished a considerable amount of the work of again cutting the Confederacy in twain, this time by a line from Memphis through Chattanooga and Atlanta to Mobile. Little military resistance southwest of this line was henceforth feasible.

Whither now should Sherman march? Forward! Forward into new eastern areas! The decision to go was his own, and one he conditionally made soon after taking Atlanta. While Sherman made the decision, the idea had been prevalent for some time, and was obvious to anyone who glanced at a map. Apparently Thomas had been urging a campaign south from Atlanta with his own army. Grant had wired Sherman as early as September 10, "As soon as

12. September 4, 1864; Hood, John Bell, *Advance and Retreat*, New Orleans, 1880, 245.

your men are sufficiently rested and preparations can be made, it is desirable that another campaign should be commenced. We want to keep the enemy constantly pressed to the end of the war. If we give him no peace while the war lasts, the end cannot be distant. Now that we have all of Mobile Bay that is valuable, I do not know but it will be the best move to transfer Canby's troops to act upon Savannah, whilst you move on Augusta. . . ."

Thus began a lengthy correspondence. At first Sherman favored moving if he could find provisions at Augusta or Columbus, Ga. He felt he could make such a march if another Federal force would take Savannah and move up the Savannah River as high as Augusta or up the Chattahoochee as far as Columbus. Otherwise, the risk would be too great. This line of thought continued with variations until early October when Hood moved north and westward. It could not be a final decision, of course, until he knew more about Hood's intentions, and about Grant's wishes. But he sent Grant his plan for destroying Atlanta as a base, and that part of its rail connections with Chattanooga that might be perilous to Union forces in the future. When this work was done, he suggested, he might push on through the heart of Georgia. The Confederacy would thus be dissevered not only to the Gulf but to the Atlantic. While Sherman rested and made plans, Jefferson Davis was visiting Hood's army, and making speeches to the disheartened troops and the people of several cities. Frankly admitting that the loss of Atlanta had been a heavy blow and that gloom enshrouded the future, he bade no one despond. "If one half the men now absent without leave will return to the front, we can defeat the enemy." When he added in Montgomery, "Let us win battles," Sherman knew that Hood would undertake a new offensive.[13] He was convinced of this six weeks before election day.

As early as September 18, in fact, Hood was shifting his army from the Macon Railroad and his base at Lovejoy's Station westward to the West Point Railroad, obviously hoping to cut Sherman's communications with the bases behind him. That is, he moved his forces from interior Georgia toward the western boundary. This backward movement was in effect, as Sherman later wrote, "stepping aside and opening wide the door for us to enter Central Georgia." Grant in his City Point headquarters far away saw the situation somewhat differently. He thought on September 26 that the next logical step for Sherman would be to turn back to Middle Tennessee in order to drive out the troublesome Forrest, who had just won a smart new victory at Athens in Northern Alabama. Sherman, however, had few fears about enemy forces at

13. Van Horne, Thomas B., *The Life of Major-General George H. Thomas*, New York, 1882, 255; *O.R.* I, xxxix, pt. 2, 355-356, 364-365, 411, 432, 464; Strode, Hudson, *Jefferson Davis, Tragic Hero*, New York, 1964, III, 94.

the rear. He knew that it would be safe if he were to send Thomas back to Tennessee, reinforced by an extra division, and by reserves which Grant had ordered to be sent him. Much of this movement was accomplished by rail and march by early October; whereupon, Sherman telegraphed Grant on October 1 an all-important question. As Hood had moved behind Atlanta, would it not be best to leave Thomas to cope with him, set fire to the city, "and march across Georgia to Savannah and Charleston, breaking roads and doing irreparable damage?" Receiving no immediate assent, on October 9 he telegraphed Grant more insistently. He must move forward to the sea. "I propose that we break up the railroad from Chattanooga forward, and that we strike out with our wagons for Milledgeville, Millen, and Savannah. Until we can repopulate Georgia, it is useless for us to occupy it; but the utter destruction of its roads, houses, and people will cripple their military resources . . . I can make this march, and make Georgia howl!" Grant still demurred, thinking it best to destroy Hood's army first. But by November 2 he had decided that Thomas could take care of Hood, and that Sherman would lose valuable territory by pursuing him. "I say, then, go on as you propose."

Hood, having reached Sherman's rear early in October on the railroad between Atlanta and Chattanooga, occupied several points, and on October 5 attacked a fortified Union post at Allatoona Pass. Sherman pulled part of his force out of Atlanta to go after Hood. From this movement rose the legend about Sherman sending a dispatch by signal to John M. Corse, defending Allatoona, "Hold the fort for I am coming." The courageous defense of Allatoona captured the imagination of the nation. Hood swung westward and then hit the railroad again, taking Dalton on October 13 before moving over to Gadsden, Alabama, October 22. By the 31st, he was at Tuscumbia preparing for his move into Tennessee. Then came Grant's decision of November 2 to let Thomas handle Hood.

Public attention had also been called to the Trans-Mississippi area once again, where Sterling Price had invaded Missouri from Arkansas, swinging up through Pilot Knob to the outer environs of St. Louis, and then westward across the State. General Samuel R. Curtis gathered what forces were available at Kansas City and Westport, while a force under Pleasonton was following Price. After several preliminary actions at Lexington and the Little Blue River, Curtis's troops defeated Price's Confederates in the battle of Westport, just south of Kansas City, on Sunday, October 23, 1864. Price was forced into a somewhat headlong and disastrous retreat southward.

These events took place only a few days before the election. The stir of preparations in Georgia for a lusty new stroke—guns and wagon-trains being readied, munitions collected, and sick and wounded sent back to Chattanooga

—was known throughout the North as men prepared to vote. It heartened everybody. The day before election, Bennett's *Herald* summarized the situation in an inaccurate but influential editorial note. "General Hood has been defeated with considerable loss in his first attempt to cross the Tennessee River. . . . It appears from our correspondence that General Sherman has sent the Fourth Corps to Decatur to operate against Hood, while, with the remaining five corps of his army, he has moved to Atlanta, and is, in all probability, about to inaugurate an offensive campaign from that point."

Meanwhile, did national questions which looked beyond the restoration of the Union without slavery receive the attention they needed in the Presidential contest? Far from it. The war obliterated every other topic, and men on both sides skirted every controversial subject that risked votes. Wendell Phillips complained that even the pending Thirteenth Amendment received no attention; "it is avoided as a subject which, too freely handled, may endanger the election." The exigent social, economic, and legal issues plainly lying ahead were ignored.[14]

Reconstruction was too prickly a subject to be gripped. The President having declared his tentative policy, and Wade, Sumner, and Winter Davis having momentarily retreated from their defiance, most Republicans were content to let that tiger doze. War Democrats and Peace Democrats were also sharply divided on the advisability of imposing probationary tests upon the rebel States, and content to hold their tongues.

Bennett's *Herald*, ostensibly neutral between McClellan and Lincoln, supported the kind of straddle that appealed to every corner-grocery loafer with bellicose prejudices. Smash the Confederate armies completely; hold seats in both Houses ready for the return, no questions asked, of any Senators and Representatives whom the Southerners chose to elect; hold a friendly national convention later; demand that France instantly vacate Mexico, and Britain instantly foot the bill for her "piratical depredations"—these were Bennett's terms.[15] A Peace Democrat from Boston, Robert C. Winthrop, one of the old money-minded cotton Yankees, his long, bony bespectacled face owlishly shortsighted, had an even easier formula of evasion. Elect McClellan to arrange a peace with restoration of the Union the only object; drop not only all attacks on slavery but all tests for Reconstruction as well; pass a sponge over the secession folly, and swing the door wide for return of the South, its staples, and its markets—these were his dollar-hungry conditions. Should they treat the Southern sisters as subjugated provinces? "Are we deliberately bent on having an American Poland?"

14. Cooper Institute speech October 26, 1864, New York *Herald, Tribune, Times;* Bartlett, Irving H., *Wendell Phillips,* Boston, 1961, Ch. XV; *O.R.*I, xxxix, pt. 2, 48; pt. 3, 3, 162, 594.
15. New York *Herald,* October 25, 1864.

For making speeches of this tenor in Massachusetts, Connecticut, and New York, Winthrop was angrily assailed by various journals and hooted at the Harvard Commencement. Some wealthy Yankees like William Amory and William H. Gardiner, and rich New Yorkers like William B. Astor, James T. Brady, and James Gallatin, agreed in part with him, but not many. Such other important business and professional men as R. B. Roosevelt, Moses Taylor, Henry G. Stebbins, and the Stewarts and Wadsworths, calling themselves War Democrats or Jacksonian Democrats, stood for enduring safeguards of the Union. At a mass-meeting in Wall Street just before election, wealthy men like Moses H. Grinnell, Hiram Walbridge (head of the Produce Exchange), and even David Dudley Field, who was at last reconciled, spoke for Lincoln.[16] The rich were feeling the income tax, which this year rose to five-percent on incomes above $600. But of real discussion upon either Reconstruction in the South, or long-term fiscal measures in the North, little as yet emerged.

The fact was that the country could not debate Reconstruction intensively until it made perfectly certain of defeating the Confederacy; until it knew more about the Negroes, their masters, and economic prospects North and South; until the temper of the people and the new Thirty-ninth Congress was more clearly defined; and until certain Cabinet changes now being adumbrated took reality. The best time and place for debating Reconstruction were doubtful, but certainly the hustings in a heated Presidential campaign were the worst. Sensible men realized that McClellan had good reasons for omitting the platform demand for a national convention from his acceptance speech. They knew that Winthrop's notion of blotting out secession with a sponge of forgiveness was asinine. If they had any insight, they knew that the groping country could best trust to Lincoln's fluid, experimental approach to Reconstruction.

Nor was the issue of civil liberties discussed with proper vigor, although Democratic spokesmen gave it noisy partisan treatment. Lincoln had proclaimed on September 15, 1863, that the privileges of the writ of habeas corpus should be suspended throughout the United States in cases where persons were held under the authority of the government as spies, prisoners of war, aiders and abettors of the enemy, or as soldiers or deserters, or for offenses against the military service. This proclamation remained in effect during the remainder of the war. Under it, officers in various departments created military commissions from time to time to try persons who fell under government suspicion. They did not necessarily deal with specific offences or charges, and their purpose was not necessarily to judge and convict. The suspicions they explored might be vague. They might find it more important to amass evidence

16. New York *Herald*, October 28-Nov. 5, 1864; Boston *Advertiser*, September 21, 1864; New York *Times*, November 5, 1864; Winthrop, Robert C. Jr., *Memoir of Robert C. Winthrop*, Boston, 1897, 235-262.

by inquiry, and develop the outlines of a situation, than to prove anybody guilty of a crime. These commissions were quite different from courts martial, which tried military personnel alone, and only for specific offences under strict rules fixed by law and precedent.[17]

This sweeping proclamation, as we have said, was one of Lincoln's most unfortunate acts. Under it, numerous men were arrested and tried during 1864, in circumstances imperiling the basic civil liberties long held sacred in Anglo-American tradition and law. The editor of the Newark *Evening Journal* was prosecuted before a military commission for an article on the draft; the editor of the Bangor *Republican Journal* for a similar offense; the editor of the New York *Metropolitan Record* for advising resistance to conscription; and the editor of the Indianapolis *Daily Sentinel* for criticizing a Mid-Western military commission. Arbitrary arrests, according to the New York *Journal of Commerce*, became so numerous that a mere list would fill eighteen columns of the paper. No one will ever be able, probably, to come up with a narrowly accurate figure on the number of political arrests at the North or the total number of papers suppressed. Figures as to arrests range from 38,000 as a top to 13,535 which may be too low. Many of these persons were held for short terms. Perhaps a good estimate of the number of papers suppressed for any period is 300.

As the campaign drew to a close, many men were jailed on charges of cheating soldiers out of their votes, or making false returns of soldier votes. Kentucky witnessed particularly flagrant violations of civil liberties on the scantiest evidence, the lieutenant-governor and chief justice being imprisoned, and the former temporarily banished beyond Union lines. In Missouri, Congressman William A. Hall was arrested for his denunciation of the President.[18]

Although Lincoln's secretaries later defended his course vigorously, declaring that he took the greatest care to restrain officers from abusive acts,[19] he and his subordinates were repeatedly open to grave criticism. Attorney-General Bates said so emphatically. He remained in office, he wrote his friend James O. Broadhead in August, to perform a painful and almost hopeless duty. "When the nation wakes up from its present revolutionary delirium, and begins to remember that it once had principles and laws, I do not mean that it shall be truly said, that *all* of us were guilty of that disloyalty which consists in trampling down the law. I am resolved that the records of my office shall

---

17. See the able article, "Habeas Corpus," *American Annual Cyclopaedia*, 1864, 421ff.
18. All this is summarized in the *American Annual Cyclopaedia*, 1864, 422-423; Rhodes, James Ford, *History of the Civil War*, New York, 1917, IV, 230-232; Randall, James G., *Constitutional Problems under Lincoln*, Urbana, Ill., 1951, 152; Eaton, Clement, *A History of the Southern Confederacy*, New York, 1954, 231; Thomas, Benjamin P., and Harold Hyman, *Stanton, The Life and Times of Lincoln's Secretary-of-War*, New York, 1962, 375-377.
19. Nicolay and Hay, *Lincoln, op.cit.*, VIII, Chs. I and II.

bear testimony that at least *one* member of the government did sometimes resist capricious power and the arbitrary domination of armed forces." Lincoln, he continued, saw clearly the good of the nation. "O! that he could *act* as well as *see!*" His intentions were upright, but he "lacked the faculty to control—the will to punish the abuses of his power, which rampant and unrebuked, are rapidly bringing him and this good cause to sorrow and shame."[20]

Lincoln's own defense of his general course in the long, careful letter which he had sent to Erastus Corning and other agitated New Yorkers on June 12, 1863 (first reading it to the Cabinet), included his arguments for the constitutionality of his acts, his prediction that he might yet be censured for having made too few arrests instead of too many, and his agonized question, "Must I shoot a simple-minded soldier who deserts, while I must not touch a hair of a wiley [*sic*] agitator who induces him to desert?" This and other papers from his pen offered an able and earnest plea for his precautionary measures. The men who abused him for "executive usurpations" and called him "another Genghis Khan" deserved no attention.[21] With reason, he sometimes felt that he sat on a powder-barrel. Francis Lieber, for example, wrote Halleck in the spring of 1864 that it was the universal conviction of the best citizens of New York that new riots of the worst kind were certain if any military disaster occurred.[22] Two Ohioans warned Governor Dennison early that year: "Camp Dennison is surrounded with perhaps the most violent Butternut population in Southern Ohio, and in several localities it was, during the summer, unsafe for Union people to hold public meetings for the promulgation of loyal sentiments. This subtle disloyalty entered into camps and the hospital. . . ."[23] Honest officers of the law, and the President in particular, had to walk a razor's edge between rigorous severity and culpable laxity. With the nation's life at stake, they preferred to err on the side of safety.

Stanton in particular, who had been given military control of state prisoners, leaned to severity, for he regarded the judiciary as exasperatingly indifferent to his security measures. In 1863, asking Seward to urge the Federal district attorney in New York City to help enforce the law, he complained: "There never has been any assistance rendered by civil officers of the government in this war where they could get a tolerable pretext for withholding it."[24] We may suspect that Stanton had the least judicial mind in the Cabinet, and that he was

---

20. Bates to Broadhead, Aug. 13, 1864, Broadhead Papers, Missouri Hist. Soc.
21. Lincoln, *Collected Works*, VI, 260-269. These phrases are from the Hon. Levi Bishop's pamphlet, "Mission of the Democracy, An Address, Cincinnati, Feb. 4, 1864."
22. April 20, 1864, Lieber Papers, HEH.
23. J. C. Dunleavy and G.R. Sage, Lebanon, O., Jan. 21, 1864, Mason Brayman Papers, Chicago Hist. Soc.
24. Flower, Frank A., *Edwin McMasters Stanton*, Akron, Ohio, 1905, 135.

much too tardy in laying down explicit lines of policy. An overburdened man, ill-tempered and abrupt, he allowed confusion to envelop the subject. Excessive zeal by officers who based arrests on flimsy tale-bearing was sometimes followed by carelessness in getting cases scrutinized, and too much buck-passing when a final decision was sought. Thus when Dennis A. Mahony of the Dubuque *Herald* was jailed, the buck went from hand to hand until the fall elections of 1862 halted it and gave Mahony justice. Although Stanton eventually introduced more order into procedures and moderated their rigor, because of great and dangerous provocations some harshness persisted.[25]

It is not strange that the Cincinnati *Enquirer*, edited by a Peace Democrat, burst out during the summer of 1864 in fierce denunciation. How, it asked, can men celebrate Independence Day "with the habeas corpus suspended by fiat of the President—with our prisons and dungeons filled with men guilty of no offense except holding opinions different from the Administration—punished without trial and without law, simply because the President so willed it—the press existing only by sufferance of the government, and under a censorship as rigid as that of Austria or France—with elections carried by the bayonet, and the whole civil power prostrated at the foot of the military?" Nor is it strange that Edward Bates later lamented to Gideon Welles the subversion of ancient principles. "You and I were taught in our youth to respect and honor the Revolutionary fathers. . . . because they were brave, wise, and good enough to establish for themselves and for us a just Government of Law—a government—all of whose powers and duties are specified by law." The Constitution and laws, he concluded, must be obligatory upon all officials, civil and military.[26]

Many Americans, however ill-schooled in literature, science, and economics, were well versed in the principles of liberty and equality before the law that they had inherited from vigilant forebears. They could trace them back to the Bill of Rights penned by George Mason, the Petition of Right, and Magna Carta, and felt an instinctive reverence for every line of them. The embattled Democrats of 1864 neglected a plain opportunity in not making a more spirited appeal against infractions of these principles. Why didn't they? Because they would at once be placed in a defensive position. The troublesome Vallandigham, who had returned to Ohio in time to make speeches denouncing "King Lincoln," did far more harm to the Democratic Party than to the Union, but he was a standing menace to the Northern cause nonetheless.

The safety of the nation was the primary consideration to be kept in view.

25. Cf. the treatment of this subject in Nevins, *War Becomes Revolution, 1862-63*, New York, 1960, 309-318.
26. Bates to Welles, Oct. 23, 1866, Welles Papers, Claremont Graduate School.

During the summer of battle-thunder on the Georgia hills and of blood-soaked fields and trenches along the Rapidan, the James, and the Appomattox, while fresh cohorts of volunteers pressed forward to drill-grounds throughout the North, every patriot knew that the temporary humiliation, hardship, and suffering of a few thousand men suspected of sedition and disloyalty was a small price to pay for the assured preservation of the republic. A few traitors, left to perfect their plots, might cost tens of thousands of lives; they might endanger the future of tens of millions. The traitors were there. The question was, how numerous were they, and how effective were their operations. Briga-dier-General Henry B. Carrington, a Yale-trained Abolitionist, spoke simple truth when he said of the Knights of the Golden Circle: "Their oaths are disloyal. They have used their influence to protect deserters. They have passed resolutions to defy United States law."[27] Carrington, whose management of a military commission was sharply criticized, and who was accused of making political capital, was upheld not only by Lincoln, but by public sentiment, and certainly deserved warm commendation for the protection he gave to Indiana citizens threatened with Copperhead incendiarism and violence.

[II]

During the summer and fall, reports and rumors of sinister conspiracies in the Middle West filled the air, becoming more alarming after the Democratic Party had adopted the Chicago platform, and more definite in character when various officers and members of the new Copperhead organization called "Sons of Liberty" were put on trial before a military commission in Indianapolis, set for September 22. The wide-spread despondency that seized the North in the summer months of defeat and deadlock seemed especially acute in the Great Valley, so long and closely tied to the South by the Mississippi River. Currency inflation, protective tariffs, rising railroad rates, and high farm-mortgage charges fed popular resentment over conscription, and fears of a suffocating influx of freedmen kept apprehensions of the future keyed high.

Panicky governors like Oliver P. Morton demanded troops to forestall armed outbreaks, Copperhead businessmen like Cyrus McCormick talked wildly of a union of the South and Northwest, and the nervously anxious Joseph Medill of the Chicago *Tribune* even told Congressman Elihu Wash-burne that the last desperate expedient might be to concentrate all Union armies to clear the Mississippi as a prelude to a ten-year armistice with the Confederacy! Fright and folly stalked abroad. Most people were above such

27. General Order No. 6, April 9, 1863, HQ District of Indiana.

panic—nevertheless, violent draft-resistance and deserter-protection remained endemic diseases in southern Indiana and Illinois. Copperhead zealots like Lambdin P. Milligan would gladly turn foxes with flaming tails (and skunks and weasels) into inflammable areas, and rebel agents lurked and schemed along the Canadian boundary. Plotters faced plotters, spies faced spies, and officers ready to hang traitors confronted fifth columnists ready to murder their opponents.[28]

It was a tangled, murky situation, full of darkness and prowling bogeys. The summer gloom of 1864 had shrouded dangerous subversives, scheming politicians, blundering Dogberries, rumor-mongers, lovers of disorder, conceited paranoiacs, sensational journalists and irresponsible crackpots as well as the mass of sincere patriots. It in fact affected all manner of men—from Dr. Samuel Bowles, chief of the Copperheads' Military Department of Indiana, laboring to drill his followers in minuteman tactics, to the patriotic General Carrington, who dispersed the "Sons of Liberty" in time to rejoin the army before Nashville.

The two centers of genuine peril were Chicago and lower Indiana. Lieutenant-Governor William Bross of Illinois later published a melodramatic and doubtless weirdly exaggerated story of the Camp Douglas plot.[29] Going east early in August to retrieve the body of a brother killed in the battle of the Crater, he had told Lincoln of the deep Western depression and its purplish hues of subversion. "Well," responded Lincoln sadly, "they want success and they haven't got it; but we are all doing the best we can. For my part, I shall stay right here and do my duty." Bross had learned of a newly hatched Copperhead conspiracy for liberating eight or nine thousand rebel prisoners in Camp Douglas, arming them, and seizing the city of Chicago. He learned also that the Copperheads had secreted ten thousand stand of arms downtown near the Tremont House. He and Colonel Benjamin Sweet, commander of Camp Douglas, a sharp, incisive young man, searched and found the arms. Colonel Sweet then placed his spies adroitly in various conclaves of the Knights of the Golden Circle or the Sons of Liberty, had every leading rebel who came from the South or Canada spotted and trailed, and took steps to cope with the uprising which, according to serpentinely devious rumors, they had arranged to coincide with the Democratic Convention.

On Saturday, August 26, the politicians began to arrive, and among them, according to Bross, milled numerous thugs and desperadoes. "As day after day

28. See the studies of disloyal activities in Milton, George Fort, *Abraham Lincoln and the Civil War,* New York, 1942; Gray, Wood, *The Hidden Civil War: The Story of the Copperheads,* New York, 1942; and Klement, Frank L., *The Copperheads in the Middle West,* Chicago, 1960.

29. Bross, William, pamphlet, "Biographical Sketch of the Late B.J. Sweet, and History of Camp Douglas," Chicago, 1878.

passed, the crowd increased till the whole city seemed alive with a motley crew of big-shouldered, blear-eyed, bottle-nosed, whisky-blotched vagabonds, the very excrescence and sweepings of slums and sinks of all the cities in the nation. I sat often at my window on Michigan Avenue, and saw the filthy stream of degraded humanity swagger along to the Wigwam on the lake shore, and wondered how the city could be saved from burning and plunder . . ."[30] Then on Monday morning the authorities heard that the danger was over. The New York leaders, Seymour, Dean Richmond, and Tilden, had arrived, taken counsel together, and put their feet down. They declared that if any riot or disorder took place, it would ruin the party—and the convention proved one of the most sedate in history. The humiliated conspirators left Chicago, their whole elaborate effort a pitiful debacle.

A new presumption of peril to the Union Government raised its dragon-head when a second conspiracy was formed to mature on election day. The plan this time was to release the Camp Douglas prisoners, seize the polls, stuff the ballot boxes, and then sack the city. Only about 800 Union troops guarded the 60-acre camp. Knights of the Golden Circle began to arrive from Fayette and Christian Counties, two Copperhead centers of Illinois. But when reckless men filtered in from Missouri and Kentucky, Southern sympathizers from Indiana, and Confederate officers from Canada, Colonel Sweet was ready. Two days before election he arrested Colonel G. St. Leger Grenfell, who had been adjutant to the Confederate raider John H. Morgan; Vincent Marmaduke, brother of General John S. Marmaduke; Captain George E. Cantrill of the Confederate Army; Charles Walsh of the Sons of Liberty, at whose house 349 revolvers, 189 shotguns, 30 carbines, powder, and cartridges were found, and others. Twenty-seven well-armed plotters were seized in one hotel, while others brought the total to a hundred. The conspiracy, which in great part reflected Confederate desperation, collapsed.[31] How much of this whole baleful story was a gin-bottle miasma, how much of it was an emanation of the Sunday Supplement sensationalism of the period, and how much of it had some slippery bases in fact, we shall never know. Probably little of the huge concocted fable can ever be substantiated, and that little inextricably mingled a few facts with a barrage of wild inventions. Plots and conspiracies may have had some transient political utility to various party irresponsibles, but in

30. *O.R.* I, xlv, pt. 1, 1077-1080. There are many conflicts in the several accounts, and what actually transpired is hard to pin down in details. For instance, Bross's and Sweet's accounts differ considerably from Ayer, Col. I. Winslow, *The Great Treason Plot in the North During the War*, Chicago, 1895. In this, Ayer gets most of the credit as "The Preserver of the City of Chicago." Among secondary accounts, Klement, *The Copperheads in the Middle West*, 199-202, deprecates the whole plot.

31. Gray, Wood, *op.cit.*, 206-222; Milton, *op.cit.*, Chs. XI-XV; Bross, Sweet, *op.cit.*, *passim*.

general they had never done the Confederacy, the Copperhead movements, or the valid Democratic organizations aught but harm. Some plotting of course did take place at the time, covert, clumsy, and ineffective; the so-called "Lake Erie Conspiracy", supposedly organized to seize "strategic points on or in the Erie", is one of the best-known instances.

Indiana, where the Indianapolis *Sentinel* cheered on the Copperheads, where the temperamental and voluble "Sycamore of the Wabash," Daniel Voorhees, preached peace at any price, and where the Sons of Liberty organized members in forty counties, had possessed seditious areas ever since Jesse D. Bright had been expelled from the Senate for disloyal activities. The vigilant Carrington, with headquarters in Indianapolis, found a resourceful aide in an energetic and imaginative young infantryman named Felix Grundy Stidger. It is probable that Stidger exaggerated his rôle and the strength of the Indiana Copperheads. Many of his recounted details are suspect. But he did organize an elaborately efficient system of espionage which soon put him in possession of seditious plans and secrets in Kentucky and Indiana, and undoubtedly he enlarged upon them in reports. Worming his way into the heart of the conspiracy, Stidger said he found the leading Knights communicating by two direct lines with Confederate leaders, experimenting with Greek fire and hand grenades, planning assassinations, and using Southern money channeled through Canada for a variety of violent purposes. The true facts probably will never be known.

Thanks largely to Stidger, Carrington soon laid the so-called Northwest Conspiracy in ruins, seized large caches of arms and piles of treasonable materials, and haled the leading plotters to trial before a military commission. Three of the accused, of whom the most notorious was Lambdin P. Milligan, a Copperhead who liked to talk about the "pecuniary vassalage" of the agrarian West to the industrial East, were found guilty and sentenced to be hanged, but appealed to the Federal Courts, and after the famous decision in *ex parte Milligan*, were released on the ground that military commissions were unconstitutional in peaceful districts. This was right and proper, but it cast no shadow upon the achievement of the four unsleeping watchers, Bross, Sweet, Carrington, and Stidger, who had brought the miscreants to bay.

In addition to the Chicago plot and activities in Indiana there was also the Lake Erie Conspiracy, perhaps the most sensational of all. The basic idea was for Confederate agents operating out of Canada to free prisoners at Johnson's Island in Lake Erie off Sandusky and at Camp Chase, Columbus, Ohio. To do this it would be necessary first to capture the Federal gunboat *Michigan* and then release the Johnson's Island prisoners. A train would be commandeered to go to Columbus for the prisoners there. Sandusky would be captured and the released prisoners would set up a Confederate army and department on the shores of Lake Erie. Main agents for this wild scheme were Charles H. Cole of Forrest's cavalry and Captain John Yates Beall of the Confederate Navy. Cole visited Sandusky, making plans and enlisting help, while Beall gathered men in groups at several Canadian ports. On September 19, Beall and his followers seized the steamer *Philo Parsons*, and also took possession of another vessel, the *Island Queen*, which they later scuttled. The *Philo Parsons* moved to a point near Johnson's Island and the U.S.S. *Michigan*. Cole, who had carefully ingratiated himself with the officers, was aboard the gunboat. During the evening, *Michigan* received word that Cole was a spy and he was arrested before he could give any signal to the *Philo Parsons*. Beall's crew, becoming apprehensive, mutinied and Beall had to steam away and destroy the vessel. Beall was later captured and hanged; but Cole was later pardoned.[32]

It was military men who blighted these budding conspiracies. Military commissions, however, contributed little to the work, and the conspirators might better have been haled before civil courts of law. The so-called Northwest Conspiracy had benefited neither the Confederacy nor the Peace Democrats, had injured McClellan's candidacy, and had ruined various circles of unknightly Knights. Republicans made good use of the conspiracies and rumors of conspiracies, exaggerating them considerably. The Democrats involved (as previously noted) would have done more for their party if they had spent time and energy in a reasoned indictment of the Administration infringements of civil liberties. The issue, however, like those presented by the tariff, inflation, inadequate taxes, and the excessive wartime profits of manufacturers, was fumbled. On this subject McClellan in particular exhibited what the diarist George Templeton Strong called "his uncommon faculty of brilliant silence."[33]

[III]

Much was heard, as election day approached, of the soldier's vote. Republicans had been hostile early in the war to the proposal that soldiers be allowed the ballot in national elections. The three leading Union generals at the opening of the war—McClellan, Halleck, and Buell—were Democrats, and McClellan achieved a remarkable popularity with the Eastern troops. In January, 1863, the Republican Congressional caucus decided against supporting soldier enfranchisement. Then, however, came the emergence of Grant, Sherman, Rosecrans, and Meade, who clearly supported Lincoln, while the President himself

32. See the report of Adj.-Gen. W.H.H. Terrell of Indiana (1869), in 1890 reissue, 288-393.
33. Strong, George Templeton, *A Diary of the Civil War*, ed. Allan Nevins, New York, 1962, 297.

gained an ever-larger place in the volunteers' hearts. By the beginning of 1864 the Republican leaders were exerting themselves to give fighters the ballot. The rising Republican Speaker of the New Hampshire House, William E. Chandler, indeed, published a pamphlet in which he not only claimed party credit for this, but accused the Democrats of selfish opposition.[34]

Some states had made provision before the war for the votes of soldiers absent on military duty. Others now made due arrangements, until eleven in all (out of twenty-five) allowed participation by the troops. The list did not include New York, where Horatio Seymour had vetoed a suffrage bill and impromptu alternative measures proved cumbrous and uncertain. Both parties devoted much time and effort to courtship of the soldiers. In this the Union Party gained a lead, for Secretary Stanton barred practically all Democratic campaign material from the camps until a month before the election. Moreover, Union men had the larger campaign funds, and the distributor of their campaign circulars, George T. Brown, showed special enterprise, boasting later that he had sent nearly a million documents to the troops.[35] Influential men of both parties visited all the larger camps, and badges for the candidates were sold at many sutlers' stores.

In Sheridan's command at Cedar Creek an old ambulance was outfitted as a polling place, and a thousand-ball cartridge box was set up as receptacle for the ballots.[36] Other arrangements were as crudely efficient. They were not always impartial. Brigadier-General Clinton B. Fisk in Missouri issued General Order No. 195, directing officers to see that "no rebel, traitor, bushwacker, or Southern sympathizer touches the sacred ark of our liberties," and the commander in the Hannibal district specially charged field officers to see that this order was in the hands of all officers at the polls when they opened. Theodore Lyman noted that in Meade's command Lieut.-Col. Martin T. McMahon, who had talked openly and strongly in favor of McClellan, was mustered out of the service in October without warning. "You would scarcely credit the number of such cases as this," he added.[37]

In October, eyes were turned upon the three States, Pennsylvania, Ohio, and Indiana, which held elections that month for State offices. In Pennsylvania the result was at first in doubt, but was eventually turned in favor of the Republicans by the soldier vote. This had been McClellan's home State. The

34. Chandler, William E., "The Soldier's Right to Vote," Washington, 1864.
35. Zornow, William F., "Lincoln Voters Among the Boys in Blue," *Lincoln Herald*, Vol. LIV, No. 3 (Fall issue, 1952).
36. Taylor, James E., Ms. Diary, "An Artist with Sheridan in the Shenandoah Campaign, 1864," Palmer Coll., Western Reserve Hist. Soc.
37. Fisk's order was dated St. Joseph, Nov. 5, 1864; copy in Broadhead Papers, Missouri Hist. Soc. Cf. Greeley, Horace, *American Conflict*, Hartford, 1867, II, 671; Lyman, Theodore, *Meade's Headquarters*, Boston, 1922, 247-248.

bounty system had painfully strained the resources of some counties, and the draft was unpopular among laboring folk; hence the narrowness of the majority. In Ohio and Indiana, however, the Republicans won sweeping victories, a portent of the November result. Ohio elected 17 Republicans and two Democrats to Congress in comparison to the old lineup of 14 Democrats and five Republicans. Pennsylvania was now 15 Republicans to nine Democrats, compared to the previous 12 and 12. Lincoln's role is shown by his message of September 19 to Sherman stating, "The State election of Indiana occurs on the 11th of October, and the loss of it to the friends of the Government would go far towards losing the whole Union cause. . . . Any thing you can safely do to let her soldiers, or any part of them, go home and vote at the State election, will be greatly in point. They need not remain for the Presidential election, but may return to you at once. This is, in no sense, an order, but is merely intended to impress you with the importance, to the army itself, of your doing all you safely can. . . ."

For various good reasons Lincoln remained apprehensive until the end. He vividly recalled the cold douche he and his party had received in 1862, when the Democrats had elected legislatures in Illinois, Indiana, and Pennsylvania, and a governor in New York. Next year, to be sure, Brough had defeated Vallandigham in Ohio, and Curtin had beaten Woodward in Pennsylvania. Still, few if any could see that these two States had then passed from a generation of Democratic ascendancy into a long generation of Republican dominance. Lincoln knew that many of his own party deeply resented his refusal to give effective enforcement to the Confiscation Act. If he opened a newspaper it was likely to be the New York *Herald*, and on October 26 he could read a *Herald* editorial declaring: "The imbecility of Old Abe, his mismanagement of the war and total incompetency exhibited at almost every stage of the present struggle, have alienated many whose sympathies are with the Republican Party." He knew that some officers in his own camp were as uncertain supporters as the double-tongued Speaker, Schuyler Colfax, who could be flatterer and obstructor at the same time, or the House overlord, Thaddeus Stevens, of imperious will.[38]

As campaign excitement mounted to a climax on November 7 and 8, a host of voters scurried home to cast their ballots. Many Pennsylvania regiments

---

38. Lincoln, *Works*, VIII, 11; or Ben Wade to Zach Chandler, October 2: "As for the election of Lincoln, I never had a doubt of our ability to reëlect him by an overwhelming majority. I only wish we could do as well for a better man. . . . Were it not for the country there would be a poetical justice in his being beaten by that stupid ass McClellan, whom he persisted in keeping in the service. . . . That stupid wilfulness cost this nation more than a hundred thousand men, as you well know, and when I think of these things, I can but wish the devil had Old Abe." Chandler Papers, LC.

were sent back on furlough, and New York troops, distrusting the machinery for casting their ballots by proxy, also got leaves. Hospitals and convalescent quarters in and about Washington discharged thousands more into the home-ward-bound throng, and a swarm of civilians from government departments swelled the ranks. "The railroad is blocked up with trains going north," wrote Noah Brooks on the 7th, "and more than once during the past week there were not cars enough to make up the regular train for Baltimore." This stream angered the Democrats, who knew that a great majority of the men would vote for Lincoln. Since Indiana had no provision for letting soldiers vote in the field, the War Department specially favored the return of her troops. Schuyler Colfax had written Lincoln that the State might be lost unless whole regiments were sent back, and one Hoosier commented sarcastically upon the fearful "sickliness" of the men, crowds of whom flocked home on invalid leave. Charles A. Dana long afterward recalled how busy he was kept in the War Department responding to telegrams asking that soldiers on detached service be sent home.[39]

Everywhere, as the final returns showed, the soldiers stood ready to vote in overwhelming strength for Lincoln; everywhere except in Kentucky, where his stand on slavery was resented. In California and Iowa, the soldier vote was more than ten to one for Lincoln, and in Wisconsin, Vermont, Maine, Mary-land, and Ohio nearly five to one; yet in not a single State was it the decisive factor in the result. Countless soldiers were of course too busy or preoccupied to vote.

Election Day was filled with anxiety and tension in the largest cities, especially in New York, where memories of riots mingled with warnings of coming incendiarism that Secretary Seward helped circulate. This incendiar-ism would become a reality on November 25-26, when eight men sent by Jacob Thompson, that egregiously unprincipled member of Buchanan's cabinet now plotting in Canada, made a futile effort to start blazes in the St. Nicholas, Fifth Avenue, Metropolitan, St. James, and Belmont Hotels, the Astor House, and four others; their mixtures of camphene and phosphorus smoldering feebly and going out while firebells clanged. Barnum's Museum had a fire and there were alarms in two theaters. But on November 8, fog and rain beset the long

39. Colfax to Lincoln, July 25, 1864, Nicolay Papers, LC; Dana, Charles A., *Recollections of the Civil War*, New York, 1898, Ch.XVIII. Democratic leaders in States like Illinois and Indiana, which did not permit voting in the field, sent agents to the South to see that convalescent soldiers in the hospitals were returned to the front lines; Republican agents meanwhile acted to get them inval-ided or furloughed home! Because the uproar interfered with military duty, Grant ordered all electioneers out of his army. In the West, Col. James T. Davidson of the 73d Illinois wrote that the politicians were manipulating surgeons, who in turn manipulated the soldiers—especially on Lincoln's side. "One lot passed through Nashville this morning of several hundred, and others are coming." Davidson to his wife, Oct. 27, Davidson Papers, Alabama State Archives.

lines that waited patiently in the streets to deposit their ballots. The grog-shops were tightly closed, and disorder was unknown, save for a little street-fight in one ward. Hardly a soldier could be seen, and the police kept a quiet mien. General Dix, commanding the department, had of course taken full precautions. The Hudson and the East River were lined with vessels full of troops which could be landed at any point if needed, and the armories held detachments armed with bayonets. August Belmont's vote was challenged on the ground that he had laid bets upon the election! When night fell people began thronging to the hotels and newspaper offices, still quiet and orderly.[40]

In Washington, only two members of Lincoln's official family attended the Cabinet meeting that dull, gloomy, rainy day. Stanton was sick abed with chills and fever, Seward, Usher, and Dennison were voting at home, and Fessenden was consulting with New York financiers, leaving Welles and Bates on duty. The President showed manifest anxiety. He had said before the session: "I am just enough of a politician to know that there was not much doubt about the result of the Baltimore Convention, but about this thing I am far from certain."

First returns came from Indianapolis at half-past six. Lincoln had made a gain of 1,500 votes in that city. At seven he went with a friend to the War Department to listen to telegrams, but it was nearly nine before he had definite news. Then Baltimore reported that he had a majority of more than 10,000, and Massachusetts a majority of 75,000. After a long interval New Jersey sent news of a Union gain of one Congressman. As the President was telling a story about this Congressman, a family friend, he was interrupted by a New York dispatch stating that he had carried the State by 10,000. He expressed doubt, and when Greeley presently reported that he should have a margin of 4,000, he accepted that as more reasonable. By midnight he was sure of Pennsylvania, the New England States, Ohio, Indiana, Michigan, Wisconsin, and Maryland, while it appeared he would also have Delaware, which he eventually lost in a close vote. He was especially concerned to hear from his own State, and was cheered about one o'clock by a New York dispatch stating that he had carried Illinois by 10,000. A bad storm then shut off further news from the West.[41]

Later intelligence from Missouri revealed that Lincoln had defeated McClellan there by more than two to one, that the Radical Union candidate for governor had triumphed, and that a great majority had approved a constitutional convention certain to decree the immediate abolition of slavery. Francis Lieber said he hoped the event would go down in history as the Great and Good Election of 1864. The President, happy that both Maryland and Missouri

40. The *London Illustrated News*, Dec. 3, 1864, has a good account.
41. Noah Brooks's letter, Nov. 11, 1864, in Sacramento *Union*.

were "secure to Liberty and Union for all the future," turned his thoughts to further steps in Reconstruction, which he would announce in his Annual Message the next month, and to plans for implementing the Constitutional amendment abolishing slavery. McClellan wrote his friend S.L.M. Barlow: "I suppose I must make up my mind now to shake the dust off my shoes and go elsewhere. So be it." He was soon in Italy. Horace Greeley packed into a letter of December to the elder Blair more wisdom than he had lately shown: "There is yet much work before us, and we are in great danger of being betrayed by divisions. I look to you, as the oldest in political experience of our men at Washington, to mediate and moderate and bring about a good understanding among all our true men. I am sure you realize that we cannot afford to have such true men as Sumner, Wade, and Julian alienated from the Administration, and yet there is danger of it if you do not interpose to calm the fury of faction."[42]

In a total vote counted of about 4,175,000 Lincoln's majority was in excess of 500,000. He had an electoral vote of 212 against 21 for McClellan, who had carried only Kentucky, New Jersey, and (rather narrowly) Delaware. Out of slightly more than 154,000 soldiers' votes Lincoln received 119,754. The Union Party victory was decisive. The two States of Louisiana and Tennessee, which had held elections deemed valid by the President but invalid by Congress, offered their votes when the electoral college met, but Vice-President Hamlin, who presided, declined to present them.[43]

[IV]

The election of 1864 was not so great and refreshing but that it left the country many lessons to ponder, and some to take deeply to heart. It was perfectly true that, as Lincoln told his serenaders on the day his confirmation in office was announced, the people of the North had proved the strength of democracy by holding a free election, with an untrammeled discussion of a still new party's principles, in the midst of a terrible civil conflict.[44] They had demonstrated that a people's government could sustain and renew itself; had

---

42. McClellan, Nov. 18, 1864, in Barlow Papers, HEH; Horace Greeley in Blair-Lee Papers, Princeton Univ. According to Thomas D. Drake of Missouri, the magnitude of the victory of Lincoln and the Radical element in that State could be ascribed to Rosecrans's Order No.135 for using troops at the polls "to prevent illegal voting." Gates wrote this order and Rosecrans issued it after Gates had written Lincoln an urgent letter on the necessity of the step, and Nicolay had paid a special visit to Rosecrans. What Gates called "military interposition" thus helped assure the immediate eradication of slavery in Missouri—and eleven electoral votes for Lincoln. Gates, Ms. Autobiography, Ch. XXXVII, Missouri State Hist. Soc.

43. Stanwood, Edward, *A History of the Presidency*, Boston, 1912, I, 307-312.

44. Lincoln, *Collected Works*, VIII, 100-102, Nov. 10, 1864.

shown how sound and how strong they were; and had found that they possessed more men—"living, brave, patriotic men"—than when the war began. The orderliness with which a decisive verdict had been rendered did much to prove to the world, as Lincoln said in his December message this year, a quiet firmness of purpose that was highly creditable to the much-suffering people.

Some considerations far less happy, however, had to be weighed. The Republican hesitations early in the year, the willingness of many governors. senators, and editors to cast Lincoln aside and seek another candidate, and the tentative approaches to Grant and Rosecrans, showed how fortunate the country was that no military hero had gained wide popular acclaim by the summer of 1864. A victorious general of strong political ambitions could have unseated the President. The vacillations of many of the Republican as well as Democratic chieftains proved that the political leaders of the North were much too erratically responsive to the tides of victory and defeat. Had the record of bloody repulse and lost battles continued into the autumn, McClellan might have won after all, while Union resolution might have grown flabby and uncertain. The defeatism rife in New York, Philadelphia, parts of the Middle West, and the Borderland was the spirit of the Hartford Convention, not Valley Forge. It seemed to contrast shamefully with the devotion of soldiers who at Gettysburg and Cold Harbor exulted in giving an eye, a leg, or life itself for their cause.

We do not know how widespread that spirit was, for not even the crudest modes of appraising public opinion existed. We can only trust that it was not really pervasive; that the politicians and editors had underrated the courage and tenacity of the plain folk of the land. We can only trust that Greeley may have been right when he had exhorted Lincoln, much earlier, to "lean upon the mighty heart of the people," and that the correspondent of the London *Daily News* may have been correct when he wrote in September that great as was the credit he had given to Northern fortitude, he believed that he had underestimated it.

"I have always scouted the idea," this correspondent wrote, "that there was any large class of people at the North, outside the scum of the towns, who were prepared to make any peace with the South which would divide the United States into two nations; but I have always acknowledged that I see limits to this devotion. Today I do not think I can see any. I am astonished the more I see and hear of the extent and depth of the determination which seems to pervade the farmers to fight to the last. . . . The men may be infatuated, but they are in earnest in a way the like of which the world never saw before, silently, calmly, but desperately in earnest; and they will fight on, in my opinion, as long as they have men, muskets, powder, and corn and wool, and would fight on, though the grass were growing in Wall Street, and there was not a gold dollar on this side of the Atlantic."[45]

Henry Winter Davis commented in his usual serpentine way on the re-election of Lincoln—"that the people now know Lincoln and voted for him to keep out worse people—keeping their hands on the pit of the stomach the while! No act of wise self-control—no such subordination of disgust to the necessities of a crisis and the dictates of cool judgment has ever before been exhibited by any people in history. . . ."

Confederate comments varied from disgust to the belief that Lincoln's election would strengthen the Southern will to resist. The Richmond *Sentinel* stated: "It is the official declaration of a great people, that they will not only have war against us, but war in its most barbarous and malignant form. . . . We say it is sad that the evil design entertained against us should be marked by such deliberate depravity in the attempted execution. But perhaps this, also, is for good. It deepens and widens the gulf between us, and renders our success more certain by rendering failure more dreadful and intolerable. . . ." The Richmond *Dispatch*, just before the election: "Give us Lincoln with his brutalities—those inhuman measures and persecutions which have united our people, given vigor to our resistance, and must finally establish our independence. . . ." After the election, the *Dispatch* stated that the victory of Lincoln had done away with any hesitation. "Had McClellan been elected, our danger would have been much greater than it is likely to be under the rule of Lincoln. . . ." Various observers agreed that the election was a confirmation that the war would go on until the subjugation of the Confederacy.[46]

The time came when people would recall with shame the responsiveness of so many of the strong men of the republic, even Charles Sumner and William Cullen Bryant, to the call for arranging a new convention and the selection of a new candidate; when Chase's bid for power would seem pitiably eccentric and unrealistic; when Henry J. Raymond would blush to remember that he had told Lincoln his reëlection was impossible, and had thus stung Lincoln into writing a secret memorandum on the course to be pursued after his defeat. The time came when the distrust and dissension so rife in the Cabinet during the summer of 1864 would seem a bad dream, and the utterances of Winter Davis as foully malign as those of Vallandigham. These unhappy episodes of a deeply troubled time could not be forgotten. They would

---

45. London *Daily News*, Sept. 27, 1864; a paper as admirable as the *Times* was wretched.

46. Henry Winter Davis-S.F. DuPont Letters, Eleutherian Mills-Hagley Foundation, Nov. 1864, no date, but after election; Richmond *Sentinel*, Nov. 12, 1864; Richmond *Dispatch*, Nov. 7 and Nov. 10, 1864; Kean, *Inside the Confederate Government, op.cit.*, 177; Jones, *Rebel War Clerk's Diary*, Philadelphia, 1866, 448; Gorgas, Josiah, *The Civil War Diary of General Josiah Gorgas*, ed. Frank Vandiver, University, Ala., 1947, 150.

have to be pondered even when final victory helped people to conclude, with that acute observer from England whom we have previously quoted, that the fighters and toilers of the North were in earnest in a way which the world had never seen before, and would battle on to the last cartridge and last drop of blood to save the Union of their fathers, and to save it purged of the foul blot of slavery.

6

Sherman's March to the Sea: The Disruption of the South

DURING THE second half of 1863, the Union forces had for the first time definitely seized a winning strategic position in the war. In great part, the way had been opened for a final advance against Southern forces by the capture of Vicksburg, and the stunning checkmate administered to Lee's bold Confederate invaders at Gettysburg. The tenacity with which the Union army under Banks maintained the bloody struggle (after Vicksburg's surrender) to capture Port Hudson was also of cardinal importance, although disappointing use was made of that capture. Grant would have preferred to turn the entire army against Mobile just after the fall of Port Hudson, thus completing the clearance of the Mississippi. Banks also favored this movement, but Halleck once more made the inept blunder of dispersing the Union armaments which might have been kept concentrated for use against an important objective. Then, too, Lincoln was filled with such lurking suspicions of Napoleon III that he desired a stronger grip upon Texas; and to the dismay of Grant, who saw that Union sea-power at Brownsville would adequately protect Texas from the French, the newly-released Union strength was squandered without permanent result. Happily for the North, however, the Confederates also made mistakes, so that at Chattanooga (as we have seen) Rosecrans was able for a time to out-general Bragg, who had equal or even superior forces. The spectacular Union victories at Lookout Mountain and Missionary Ridge that followed freed Grant and Sherman to move forward upon Atlanta, Dalton, and other industrial towns of Georgia. The North had suffered a humiliating defeat at Chickamauga, but it had placed its armies in a situation where they could sweep into the heart of the South, and if they took bold decisions, even farther still.

The achievement of a decisive strategic advantage by the North was attributable also in part to non-territorial gains—to progress unconnected with the full control of the Mississippi, the Gulf Coast, the vital rail center of Chattanooga, and the mountains looking down on central Tennessee, the

Tennessee River, North Alabama and North Georgia. These great and important advantages were now safe. But the Union had achieved advances of equal importance in the experience and skill of its generals, in the recruiting and organization of its armies, and in the contributions of invention, technology, and growing industrial resourcefulness to the power of its now seasoned and determined ranks of fighting men.

Lincoln's proclamation calling out a half-million more men (the draft to take place on March 10) had been a measure of obvious necessity; and it was one of the vital facts of the war that Washington by late 1863 had comprehended this necessity.

"To secure the permanence of our conquests in Tennessee," declared *The Army and Navy Journal* on February 5, 1864, "our army under General Grant should be doubled." The heavy losses in the Wilderness, at Spotsylvania, Cold Harbor, and before Petersburg, emphasized the need thus stated for more recruits. The country had the men—and difficult though it was to enforce the vague, loosely-worded draft law of 1863; distressing as were the endless instances of fraud, bribery, and evasion; costly as was the gigantic bounty system erected by national, State, and local governments to cajole civilians into uniform; and undemocratic as was the substitute system,[1]—the men steadily if unevenly, and not altogether reluctantly, moved into the armies. Conscription stimulated volunteering. Provost-Marshal General James Barnet Fry, a brave field officer and an efficient administrator, served ably as director of the drafts. Struggling against political pressures, the incompetence or dishonesty of his subordinates, and the shifting winds of public sentiment, this Illinoisan product of West Point training, despite inevitable errors, carried through an admirable piece of work for his country. He also helped arrest and return to their commands many thousands of deserters and other absentees.[2]

The draft riots in New York, the scandals of the substitute-brokerage system, and the crimes of the bounty-jumpers stained the shield of the nation in a way that could never be erased. But Fry's courageous activities helped fill the depleted ranks, and kept on filling them. The draft of 1863 had furnished 35,850 men; the draft calls of February and March, 1864, furnished 12,321; and that of July, 1864, yielded 37,577.[3] The early drafted men, with very few exceptions, were sent to existing regiments as replacements for lost manpower, and thus the draft law became immediately beneficial.[4] But conscription did not provide enough men by far—it did not come anywhere near maintenance of

1. Murdock, Eugene C., *Patriotism Limited, 1862-1865*, Ms., Ohio Hist. Soc., 1-172.
2. Williams, Kenneth P., *Lincoln Finds a General*, New York, 1959, II, 557. states that more than 76,325 were returned.
3. *O.R.*, III, iv, 927, 928; v, 486-487.
4. Lerwill, Leonard L., *The Personnel Replacement System in the United States Army*, 97.

existing units at effective strength. In consequence, volunteering furnished most of the replacements in the two last years of the war.[5] The War Department followed faulty policies of placement. It could have insisted that the State governments assign all volunteers, as they enlisted, to regiments then in being. Instead, it gave governors permission to raise new regiments—fifteen at first in Pennsylvania, and then others until forty in all had been authorized— regiments largely of green troops, often ill-officered. Happily, however, the veteran regiments themselves prosecuted effective recruiting activities, not only by sending agents back to home areas, but by inviting loyal men in such occupied districts as East Tennessee and Western North Carolina, to join.[6]

Meanwhile, the effectiveness of the troops was enhanced by closer attention to drill and instruction. The institution of training camps can be traced back to a camp that was ordered established at Annapolis in June, 1862, under General John E. Wool, who had learned military skill in Taylor's campaigns against Mexico, and exhibited his shrewdness and celerity at Buena Vista. General Wool was given facilities for fifty thousand men or more.[7] The pressing need for elementary instruction was emphasized in Charles S. Wainwright's fascinating *Diary of Battle*.[8] To pitch shelter tents; to march steadily under the burden of heavy knapsacks, blankets, and accoutrements; to make meals of fat pork, molasses, and cornmeal, and to keep watch vigilantly—all required training and experience. The high command, however, found it more convenient to send new recruits, along with drafted men and substitutes, directly to regiments in the field, expecting that they would master the craft and bearing of the soldier most effectively in simple association with veteran troops and experienced officers. As General Thomas wrote, "Recruits added to old regiments are at once under the hand of discipline, learning how to take care of themselves, and by mingling with their comrades who have seen service, readily learn their duties, and in a short time become almost as efficient and reliable as the old troops."[9]

The main failures of the Union armies in 1862 had arisen from deficiencies of leadership in Washington and also in the field, the quality of the brains, character, experience, and training of commissioned officers and non-coms being lower in the Union armies than the Confederate, and too low for a conflict so unexpectedly fierce and trying. Many of the failures in 1863 had resulted from want of adequate numbers, organization, and discipline.

5. Lerwill, *Ibid.*, 97.
6. Lerwill, *Ibid.*, 99, 100.
7. *O.R.*, III, ii. 108.
8. *A Diary of Battle: The Personal Journals of Col. Charles S. Wainwright, 1861-1865*, ed. Allan Nevins, New York, 1962, viiff.
9. *O.R.*, I, xlv, pt. 2, 344-345, quoted in Lerwill, *op.cit.*, 102.

The system of regimental recruiting instituted in the summer of 1863—that is, the dispatch of details from existing regiments to bring back from home communities as many veterans as possible—was continued during the winter of 1863-64 with enhanced effectiveness.[10] Distribution of troops according to Army needs was also improved by the creation of well-managed depôt camps or pools for recruits of all kinds. Thus, in the latter part of 1864, young Middle-Westerners who were wanted in the Department of the Gulf or in one of Sherman's armies were collected at Cairo, to be sent by steamboat down the Mississippi or up the Tennessee. Those marked for the Army of the Mississippi were likely to arrive at a training camp established at Nashville. Large contingents, however, were sent to the Army of the Ohio, and the Army of the Tennessee.[11]

In short, the Federal government had at last taken measures for enlisting, organizing, distributing, and training troops which met the urgent necessities of the military situation. Armies that were too small, armies constantly reduced by battle casualties, sickness, and (most deplorably of all) by desertions and absences without leave, were now being built to formidable strength. More and more commands were being "veteranized" by the recall of experienced soldiers, subalterns and officers to serve alongside raw volunteers, drafted men, and substitutes. An army of accomplished and tenacious fighters was coming into being, an army ready for any hardship, any ordeal of fire and steel, any sacrifice. The importance of able, careful, efficient officers to good training and effective fighting is noted in many regimental histories. Captain Thomas H. Parker, for example, tells how Major Edwin Schall trained his men under the scorching Carolina sun until they were able to make a hot dusty march of forty-two miles and fight a long battle under murderous grape, canister and musket fire at Currituck Court House until victorious. Later, Schall (now a Colonel) and many of his men were killed charging dauntlessly at Cold Harbor.[12]

Could a supreme Western commander be found, as Lincoln thought he had at last found one in Grant for the East, of high skill, relentless determination, endless patience and courage, and deep resourcefulness—one worthy of the new legions, better armed, better organized, better officered—one who would not fail the national government and his armies of brave men as John Pope had failed at Second Manassas, who would not be found lacking in vigilance at a critical moment as even Grant had lacked vigilance at Shiloh, and who would not hesitate in the pursuit of an undoubted advantage as Meade had hesitated

10. Lerwill, *op.cit.*, 104.
11. *O.R.*, I, xxxiii, pt. 3, 488ff., cited in Lerwill, *op.cit.*, 105.
12. Parker, Thomas H., *51st Pennsylvania Volunteers*, Philadelphia, 1869, 542-569.

after Gettysburg? This was a critical question asked by every high official in Washington, every corps commander in his camp, and every plain citizen sitting distressed and worried beside his fireside.

Nobody knew the answer. It was encouraging, however, to read the thoughtful encomium upon William Tecumseh Sherman that William Conant Church, founder and editor of the *Army and Navy Journal*, penned at this moment—September 10, 1864—under the title "Atlanta Ours." He wrote that a leader of remarkable ability and strategic skill had suddenly emerged.

"The progress and result of the Georgia campaign, in our judgment, stamp Sherman as a thorough soldier . . . That his plan at the outset was good, success, the final criterion, has demonstrated. His combinations have been sound, and he has been fertile in expedients. The country he traversed was unfriendly to military manoeuvres. Arduous and abrupt mountains, hazardous ravines and ridges, were constantly interposed across the path of the army into central Georgia. His march, nevertheless, had been steady, without a single retrograde. Sherman has fought his campaign, in some respects unlike any of his others, displaying more maturity, greater power, skill learned from experience, observation, and history, and no little coolness, method, and deliberation. Heretofore promptness, rapidity, and brilliancy were the chief qualities the majority of the American people saw in him. Now he has exhibited caution, sound judgment, and pertinacity." In one assault, Kenesaw Mountain, Church added, Sherman had revealed his impetuosity, but he had then turned to flanking.

One very noticeable trait in the campaign was the skill with which Sherman's line of communications had been protected. This long line was not a little precarious, and more than once aroused the anxiety of the nation.

"His base was, in one sense, not at Chattanooga, but at Nashville, with the former railway center as the secondary base. The rebels did their best not only to break the line Atlanta-Ringgold, but to raid the road from Chattanooga back to Nashville. From Atlanta to Nashville the railroad is 145 miles long, from Chattanooga to Nashville only a little less. With this line of 250 miles stretched across the great Allegheny chain from flank to flank, in a disputed country filled with guerrillas and hostile inhabitants, with nooks and eyries in the mountainous region apt for the assemblage and protection of marauding bands, with that attenuated line infested by many squadrons of the best cavalry in the Confederacy, long accustomed to be victorious everywhere, under such bold and skilful leaders as Morgan, Forrest, Wheeler, Stephen Lee, and James Chalmers. In spite of all, Sherman has been able to keep his line strong and clear."[13]

13. *Army and Navy Journal*, "Atlanta Ours", Sept. 10, 1864.

But Sherman did not stand alone. Around him in the West stood other Union generals of elevated intellectual and moral qualities, a band who recalled, if not Napoleon's resplendent marshals, at least the type of keen and steadfast officers who were assembled about Wellington in the Peninsular and Belgian campaigns.[14]

[I]

To understand the memorable march that Sherman, as the foremost Union leader in the West, was now about to begin from Atlanta across the State of Georgia to Savannah—from the rugged Appalachians to the heaving Atlantic —readers should keep in mind a number of basic facts.

We start with the fact that he was attempting not a raid, but a much more important strategic movement—a new bisection of the Confederacy, supplementing the north-south bisection on the line of the Mississippi, and involving an eventual exchange of his inland base for a more secure base on the ocean, commanded and supplied by Northern sea-power. His object was not primarily the capture of a great city, although he did capture several; it was not primarily the destruction of a powerful army, though his campaign did encompass such a destruction. It was the disruption of the Confederacy by a great march, leaving ruined farms, shattered factories, and uptorn and severed railroads and highways behind it. It was a demonstration of the validity of a belief increasingly held by Northern war-leaders, that the South was to a great extent an empty shell, which could be seized and broken by bold Federal strokes.

A second important fact is that he commanded not a single relatively compact army, like that which Grant had thrust down and across the Mississippi, or like Meade's Army of the Potomac, but a great loosely composite force, really three or four armies linked together, under as many comradely leaders, for the North now had that many able and experienced commanders.

Three or four armies? The list is readily summarized.

On succeeding Grant as prime military commander in the West, Sherman had combined the Eleventh and Twelfth Corps to form a new Twentieth Corps. This was under the athletic, red-faced, rather seedily handsome Joseph Hooker, who bore (along with his wounds from Antietam, and his letter of thanks from Congress for his defense of the capital) a sense of humiliation for

---

14. Sherman tells us that in Thomas, McPherson, and Schofield he had three officers of education and experience, admirably qualified for the work before them. Each, he adds, possessed special qualities of mind and character which fitted him in the highest degree for his tasks. *Memoirs*, II, 15ff.

his share in several costly defeats and for bad conduct that had drawn from Lincoln early in 1863 such a letter of mingled kindliness and severity as Lincoln seldom penned. History would long remember Lincoln's reproach of over-cautiousness,[15] yet thousands still admired Hooker. Sherman had also arranged for the respected Oliver Otis Howard, who had lost an arm at Fair Oaks but continued to serve with gallantry through subsequent campaigns, to command the Fourth Corps. Grant, in addition, had seen to the formation of a new cavalry corps.

Under Sherman now stood likewise the Army of the Cumberland, led by George H. Thomas, the Virginia-born patriot who had fought well at Mill Springs in the dawn of 1862, and in Buell's advance across difficult country to Pittsburgh Landing. Thomas had been made a major-general in the spring of 1862 over forty-two of the fifty-five brigadiers senior to him, had fought ably at Murfreesboro, and had especially distinguished himself at Chickamauga where he had held the battle-line with an immovable corps while less steely troops were routed. He had then risen to command the Army of the Cumberland, with its recent infusion of veteran fighters from Potomac ranks, and had been in general charge of Union forces when they pinned the glory of Lookout Mountain and Missionary Ridge to their banners. Thomas had conspicuously displayed his qualities of poise, coolness, and imperturbable tenacity, which Grant came in time (though some thought tardily) to appreciate. Some observers thought that Grant might have given Thomas the Western command that he assigned to Sherman.[16]

Beside these contingents, Sherman numbered among his forces the Army of the Tennessee with its brilliant but ill-fated leader James B. McPherson, a clean-cut West Pointer who had aided Grant in the Tennessee campaign of 1862, playing a sturdy part in the operations that raised the national colors over Vicksburg. In the spring of 1864 McPherson would take energetic charge of the Army of the Tennessee, which included one able Illinoisan, John A. Logan, a histrionic figure with flowing hair and bellowing voice, who remembered standing with Lincoln to hear Douglas address a Chicago crowd. Defying the Copperhead elements in southern Illinois, Logan had helped rally that region to support the North. He had played a determined part in taking Donelson, and later had distinguished himself in the fighting before Atlanta.

Finally, Sherman's officers included John M. Schofield of the Army of the Ohio, another West Pointer who, after long and difficult service in Missouri, had become a corps commander early in 1864, just in time to take part in

15. *O.R.*, I, xix, pt. 1, 13.
16. Livermore, Col. Thomas L., *Sketches of Some of the Federal and Confederate Commanders*, Boston, 1895, 238-243, does not agree on this.

Sherman's victorious Atlanta campaign. He was a more mature officer than McPherson, though only thirty-three years old in the summer of 1864. Sherman, born in 1820, was much his senior—"old Uncle Billy," who had not reached his forty-fifth birthday!

"What a a galaxy of commanders!" men later said.[17]

Another cardinal fact to be remembered in following Western movements is that the rough, ill-roaded terrain of Sherman's operations played a dominant role in affairs, laying down stern topographical laws that he had to obey. South of Chattanooga, the Allegheny range ran in a great diagonal roughly NNE and SSW, throwing out lower ranges eastwardly, ending in an expanse of chaotically broken country.

It is equally important to remember that the railroads were an essential factor in Sherman's activities—in this first great railroad war of world history. He was tied to them, their iron bands vital to his operations. If he ever attempted to make any point north of central Ohio his base, he would leave the vital State of Tennessee uncovered and open to a rebel thrust. Thomas's protective Army of the Cumberland had its natural base on the Ohio, just as Schofield's Army of the Ohio found its natural base in Cincinnati.

This being so, the most important railroad of the area to Sherman and Thomas was the Louisville & Nashville, running down from the Ohio River to the capital and central city of Tennessee, 135 to 140 miles from Chattanooga. Sherman, with the support of James Guthrie, the loyal president of the L & N, had boldly taken control of the railroads of the area himself in April, 1864, and had soon brought together enough rolling stock to carry his campaign against Johnston to the gates of Atlanta. Within a short time (as previously noted), the Union forces had equipment from almost every line north of the Ohio, and were amused to see far down in Georgia cars marked "Pittsburgh & Fort Wayne," "Delaware & Lackawanna," or "Baltimore & Ohio." "I have always felt grateful to Mr. Guthrie," Sherman wrote, "who had sense enough and patriotism enough to subordinate the interests of his railroad company to the cause of his country."[18] The usefulness of railroads in the war (and far greater use was being made of them than ever before in any conflict) was just being grasped by American and foreign observers. They drew their value from the great distances of the shaggy, unkempt continent, the slovenly marking of the highways and byways, and the rapidity with which rain and summer dust made roads a horror to man and beast. They could be quickly destroyed, as Sherman had demonstrated, but even more quickly repaired if needed materials were at hand. A single railroad in good order, with sidings, rolling stock,

17. Sherman, *Memoirs*, II, 15.
18. *Ibid.*, II, 11, 12.

and junctions, was sufficient for the ordinary supply of an army in the field. Sherman, assuming the strength of the army with which he moved from Chattanooga into Georgia to be a hundred thousand men, with 35,000 animals for cavalry and transport to be fed, while beef cattle were driven on the hoof, had calculated his resources shrewdly. He had decided that even a daily movement of 130 cars of ten tons each into Chattanooga would not meet the army's needs unless he dispensed with a normal amount of hay, oats, and corn for his horses and mules, but that he could do this by feeding his livestock in large part from growing crops.[19]

A British observer, Captain H.W. Tyler of the Royal Engineers, laid down shrewd military rules based on his American observations.[20] He declared that railroads built for strategic purposes and intended for troop conveyance should be given a double row of rails. Every soldier should be trained both to destroy and repair railroads; the officers must remember that railroads were of much greater advantage in defensive than offensive warfare. A commander should in no instance rely upon a railroad for communication in a hostile country, and should not rely too much upon a long railroad, subject to enemy attack, in any country. He praised Sherman for the fact that the establishment of depots of supplies in his immediate rear was part of his plan for any forward movement, thus making himself in large degree independent of communications.

The grand disruptive movement began, inevitably from Atlanta. But first, Sherman had to deal with the Confederate commander and forces there.

[II]

The battle of Atlanta had been fought on July 22, 1864, with General Hood, who had succeeded Johnston by order of Jefferson Davis, observing it from the Confederate entrenchments.

As the Union army approached Atlanta, Sherman had placed the troops of Thomas on the right, moving southward toward it, while McPherson's command on the left drove against the city from the east. Schofield's command was in the center, approaching from the northeast. Sherman, McPherson, and Schofield had talked together on the climactic morning about the prospects of a battle—both McPherson and Schofield having been in the same class with Hood at West Point, their class also including Sheridan. They had agreed that they should be prepared for sharp Confederate thrusts from the defensive lines about Atlanta, for Hood was by temperament a bold, aggressive leader, and

19. Sherman, *Memoirs*, II, 23.
20. *Army & Navy Journal*, June 11, 1864.

everybody knew that he had been given his command because the Confederate government was out of patience with Johnston's caution and his repeated Fabian retreats.[21] It was true that Hood had given orders for an attack, which opened about noon on July 22nd, falling upon the left wing of the Union advance. At this point, McPherson, riding intrepidly along his lines without escort, was shot dead, a heavy loss to the Army and the nation. The battle developed so fiercely that Sherman himself felt it necessary to visit his endangered left wing, but his guidance and a timely use of part of Schofield's artillery retrieved the position, and the battle of Atlanta turned decisively against the South.[22] The skillful maneuvering of Sherman was the principal factor in this Union victory, but Hood later attempted to throw the blame upon his subordinates Cheatham and Hardee. In his book, *Advance and Retreat*, he placed his finger upon what he wished identified as the fatal moment in the battle.

A considerable time had elapsed when I discovered, to my astonishment and bitter disappointment, a line of battle composed of one of Hardee's divisions advancing directly against the entrenched flank of the enemy. I at once perceived that Hardee had not only failed to turn McPherson's left, according to positive orders, but had thrown his men against the enemy's breastworks, thereby occasioning unnecessary loss to us, and rendering doubtful the great result desired. In lieu of completely turning the Federal left, and taking the entrenched line of the enemy in reverse, he attacked the retiring wing of their flank . . . I then began to fear that his disregard of the rule in war that one danger in rear is more to be feared than ten in front—in other words that one thousand men in rear are equal to ten thousand in front—would cause us much embarrassment and place his corps at a great disadvantage.[23]

Immediately thereafter, Sherman executed one of the masterly strokes which gave justification to the high praise by Church in the *Army and Navy Journal*. He struck the railroad above Jonesboro and was thus able to interpose his forces between Hardee and Atlanta, placing the Union army between two main parts of a divided rebel army. It was necessary for the Confederates to give up both Jonesboro and Atlanta. Hardee retired in confusion. Early next day, Hood, destroying his munitions and stores, fled from Atlanta which Sherman at once entered.

The effect of this achievement upon the Northern people was tremendous. Lincoln had ardently desired Sherman's success, for he knew well that it would decisively affect the Presidential election, then hanging in the balance.

But Sherman himself was by no means completely satisfied. He had not

21. Sherman, *Memoirs* (old edition), II, 74, 75.
22. Hoehling, A.A., *Last Train from Atlanta*, New York, 1958, 125-145.
23. Hood, *Advance and Retreat*, New Orleans, 1880, 179ff.

accomplished all he desired, for Hood's army, his principal objective, had eluded him.

In moving from Chattanooga to Atlanta he had expertly directed one of the great campaigns of the war. His loss, to be sure, had been about 30,000 men; but the Confederates had lost about 40,000. Hood as always had his excuses. The fault was Joseph E. Johnston's. "My failure on the 20th and 22nd to bring about a general battle," he wrote later, "arose from the unfortunate policy pursued from Dalton to Atlanta, and which had wrought such demoralization amid rank and file as to render the men unreliable in battle."[24]

On September 21, Hood shifted his forces from Lovejoy's Station on the Macon Railroad, to the West Point road at Palmetto Station, seemingly toward the Alabama line. Here he made systematic preparations for an aggressive campaign against Sherman's communications, hoping that he might thus compel the Union leader to abandon Atlanta. Here, too, at Palmetto Station, President Jefferson Davis paid Hood another visit, in the course of which he delivered a speech, assuring the Confederate army and the Southern people that their troops would soon compel Sherman's army to begin a retreat from Georgia which would prove more disastrous to them than Napoleon's retreat from Moscow had proved to the French armies. This gave Sherman the information he needed, and spurred him to take vigorous action. "Forewarned," wrote Sherman later, "I took immediate measures to thwart his plans. One division was sent back to Rome, another to Chattanooga, and the guards along our railroad were reinforced and warned of the coming blow. General Thomas was sent back to the headquarters of his department at Nashville, Schofield to his at Knoxville, and I remained in Atlanta to await Hood's initiative. This followed soon."[25]

Hood had the cooperation of the indomitable and enterprising cavalry leader, Forrest, who began playing havoc with the Union forces and lines in West Tennessee, raiding all the way from the Mississippi border north to Kentucky. Both the Davis Administration and public sentiment in the South brought the heaviest pressure to bear upon Hood, to see that all his available forces took determined offensive action early in September, Davis had written Hood that he had exhausted his resources for reinforcing Hood's army. It was also essential that all Confederate absentees be brought back into the ranks, and that the means at hand be used with an energy proportioned to the needs of the country.[26] Hood, therefore, weighing the situation carefully with his force of only 40,000 men, decided to continue operating in Sherman's rear. By

24. Hood, *Advance and Retreat*, 123.
25. Sherman, *Memoirs*, II, 144-155.
26. Hood, *op.cit.*, *passim*.

effectively threatening his communications, he believed he could draw Sherman after him into Tennessee, and eventually into Kentucky, or could force the Union army back into the mountains of North Georgia as General Lee had on two different occasions transferred the fighting from Virginia into Maryland, and on northward.[27]

Hood's whole plan to halt Sherman's march into central Georgia and southward was a desperate gamble, as he well knew. He made some changes in the organization of his forces to improve their efficiency, while Sherman was sending General Thomas back to Chattanooga and Nashville to keep the situation in his Department under control, and to prepare to meet Hood's expected invasion. Receiving information that Sherman had gathered large supplies of stores at Allatoona, Hood sent General Samuel Gibbs French with his division to seize the place and the stores—French beginning his attack on October 5, but meeting stiff resistance from General Corse and his Union veterans. On October 7, Hood telegraphed General Richard Taylor to send Forrest at once to operate in Tennessee, and on the 11th Hood's army crossed the Coosa, marching directly towards Rosecrans and Dalton. In his *Memoirs*, Hood wrote: "If Sherman would cut loose and march south, as I believed he would do after I left his front without previously worsting him in battle, I would occupy Richmond, Kentucky," and as this was a position of great advantage, Sherman would have to take defensive action for the rescue of Kentucky and Ohio. He might follow Hood directly into Tennessee and Kentucky. Alternatively, Sherman might choose to march directly to the support of Grant in Virginia. If he did take this bold step, stated Hood, "I could pass through the Cumberland gaps to Petersburg, and attack Grant in rear at least two weeks before he, Sherman, could render him assistance. This move, I believed, would defeat Grant, and allow General Lee, in command of our armies, to march upon Washington, or to turn upon and annihilate Sherman. Such was the plan which, during the 15th and 16th (October), as we lay in bivouac near Lafayette, I maturely considered and determined to carry out."[28] It will be seen that Hood looked at the situation in a large, loose way, and laid his plans with more of wishful thinking than of a sober study of possibilities.

There were others, too, who took a large and reckless view of the possibilities of the situation for the Confederacy. Benjamin H. Hill, for example, thought that Davis's removal of Joseph E. Johnston had been right and that this drastic step should have been taken a month earlier. He wrote his friend Herschel V. Johnson that the appointment of Hood had been quite a venturesome experiment, but that he did not see how, under all the circumstances,

27. See John P. Dyer, *The Gallant Hood*, Indianapolis, 1950, 272.
28. Cf. *Battles and Leaders*, IV, 425ff.

President Davis could have done otherwise. Atlanta had virtually been lost when Hood took command, but it had been important to delay the final fall of the city so as to discourage Sherman from attempting any further progress into Georgia that season. Hill added:

Hood's new movement is more than was originally anticipated and thus far is most promising. I warmly approved it from the beginning, and have great hopes of the result. I am now a little afraid Hood will go back too fast and too far. It is now intimated he is going directly to Nashville. It is urged by some that he can go on *to the Ohio*. The idea is that he will get 50,000 soldiers in Tennessee and Kentucky. I think he may get these men if Lincoln should be elected, and in that event also the appearance of our army, strong and increasing, in Kentucky, may encourage a revolution in the North itself.

All these ideas are in the calculations. Price seems to be helping the movement in poor Missouri—I mean 'poor' because of her sufferings.

Hill wished to find a safe place for his family; but what place nowadays was really safe?

The way was now open for the culminating battles which were to wreck Hood's elaborate Tennessee campaign, and would not only bring all his ambitious plans to naught, but would leave his armies in so shattered a condition that Sherman need feel no further anxiety respecting his movements and might lay secure plans for his own southward thrusts. October 5 found Sherman near Marietta, with Atlanta still securely in Union hands. General Schofield, who held a position at the rear where he might delay Hood's movements, and had been chafing over what he regarded as lost opportunities to achieve the grand goal of the destruction of Hood's army, was deeply disappointed. Jonesboro seemed to him the place to deliver the final decisive blow. "So anxious was I that this be attempted that I offered to go with two corps, or even with one, to intercept Hood's retreat on the McDonough road, and hold him until Sherman could dispose of Hardee."[29] Schofield remained near Marietta until a smart action at Spring Hill enabled him to move his troops to Franklin, Tennessee, ready to defend that position against any further advance by Hood. This was just south of the Harpeth River. He decided to stay there with his 32,000 men and organize a strong defense against Confederate attack.

Hood had telegraphed President Davis early in September that the soldiers were much in need of rest. His men had since endured even further trials. Not only were they wearied out by their efforts to maintain a fighting front against Sherman; they were deeply discouraged after their defeats, retreats, and evasive movements to avoid outflanking, and disheartened by what they knew of

29. Schofield, John M., *Forty-Six Years in the Army*, New York, 1897, 159.

General William Tecumseh Sherman

General John Bell Hood

the quarrels within the Confederacy itself. They were in large part ragged, shoeless or ill-shod, and without money to send their families, not having been paid for ten months.[30] The Confederate Army was being weakened as steadily by desertions as the Union Army was being strengthened by drafting and volunteering.

But Sherman also had his perplexities. He had suffered from some of the attacks the Confederates under Forrest and others had launched at him and his lines of communication. Deep in hostile territory, exposed to cavalry thrusts, his army of about 82,000 had to deal with Hood from its precarious position at the end of the long line of rails running back to Chattanooga and thence to Nashville. He could not sit still while enemy forces manoeuvered recklessly behind him, and he soon recognized that but one course was really open to him. In his march from Chattanooga into north Georgia he had discovered that his large army, carrying with it all necessary stores and baggage, could actually overtake and bring to bay an inferior enemy force in its own country. He saw that with an army, including communications forces, of nearly a hundred thousand men and 254 guns, he could not safely hold the long supply line from Louisville to his troops if he advanced into Tennessee in pursuit of Hood, while at the same time trying to protect middle Tennessee from invasion. The safest course would therefore be to turn not northeast, but southwest. He would divide his forces into two parts, using one to take the offensive, while with the other he would act on the defensive and invite the enemy to attack him. Thus it was that a curious military situation suddenly revealed itself to the country. Almost immediately upon the capture of Atlanta by the Union forces, the main armies, which had been battling each other at close quarters, had separated and moved in opposite directions. Sherman was now well on his way through the wide, fertile tract between Atlanta and Waynesboro, the garden of Georgia. Down from the mountainous and hill country of north Georgia the army moved into the area of the rivers, all flowing toward the sea.

The great March to the Sea began in a spectacular and memorable scene on November 16, 1864. That day Sherman sat astride his horse on a small eminence just outside Atlanta, and with stern mien but exultant heart watched the foremost detachments of his army, some 60,000 fighting veterans, encumbered by as little impedimenta as possible, swing past, some shouting exultantly, and some chorusing "Glory, Glory, Hallelujah!" They were on their way to the sea—perhaps even to be first into Richmond and to achieve a junction with Grant.[31]

Sherman's intrepid decision to transfer his army to Savannah and the

30. Dyer, *The Gallant Hood*, 272.
31. Liddell Hart, B.H. *Sherman, Soldier, Realist, American*, New York, 1929, 308ff.

seacoast made many Northerners catch their breath. General Thomas, commanding one wing of Sherman's army, advised against it. Lincoln was dubious, and even apprehensive. General Grant thought that the safest course would be to destroy Hood before pushing the army farther to the south. But Sherman believed that it might be impossible to destroy Hood—that no single army could catch him.[32] He was determined that he would not let himself be manoeuvered out of Georgia.

A half-dozen objectives dawned upon Sherman at once. Cutting his army free from his communications with Tennessee, he would march through the country, living upon it as he went. He would create a new base on the coast, with a shorter supply line, protected in part by the Navy as Nelson's fleet had protected Wellington's fast-moving columns in Spain after Trafalgar. In slicing across Georgia, he would strip that State of its summer crops, so that Hood's army would lack sustenance until the next harvest-time. He was confident that he could entrust the defense against Hood to Thomas. By shrewd and systematic retreats, Thomas could draw Hood well up into Tennessee, meanwhile concentrating on strengthening his own army until the moment when he could turn decisively about and destroy or fatally cripple Hood.[33]

"I was thereby left," wrote Sherman in his final report to the War Department, "with a well-appointed army, to cut the enemy's only remaining rail communications eastward and westward."

[III]

The Federal army that moved out of Atlanta in mid-November numbered some 60,000 infantry and 5,500 cavalry, and they were stripped down for action. Quantities of necessary supplies had been gathered, and all needless baggage eliminated. This elimination was generally easy, for by this time the veterans had learned how to travel light, carrying only a well-packed knapsack, tightly rolled blankets, and arms. They usually bore with them rations for two days, had supplies in wagons for a longer period, and drove cattle before them; but their main dependence for food, and particularly for forage, was to be upon the countryside.

In bare figures the Union army lost in the great movement at least 103 men killed, 428 wounded, and 278 missing for a remarkably low total of 809.[34] As Sherman put it, his men and animals "consumed the corn and fodder in the region of the country thirty miles on either side of a line from Atlanta to

32. Sherman, *Memoirs*, II, 165.
33. *O.R.*, I, xliv, 13.
34. *Ibid.*, 15, and Sherman, *Memoirs*, 221.

Savannah, and also the sweet potatoes, cattle, hogs, sheep and poultry, and have carried away more than 10,000 horses and mules, as well as countless numbers of their slaves." He declared that several hundred miles of railroad were destroyed and that the damage inflicted upon the State of Georgia aggregated a hundred million dollars—"at least, $20,000,000 of which has inured to our advantage, and the remainder is simple waste and destruction." This, he commented, ". . . may seem a hard species of warfare, but it brings the sad realities of war home to those who have been directly or indirectly instrumental in involving us in its attendant calamities."[35] For one instance, for the four infantry corps which had 3,476 cattle on hand at Atlanta when the march started, 13,294 more were captured en route, and 6,861 were available when they reached Savannah.[36] Sherman had indeed carried out his threat to make Georgia howl, or as he wrote General Schofield as early as October 17, "I will then make the interior of Georgia feel the weight of War."[37]

In the actual march, Sherman's object was not to capture important strategic towns, but to place his army between Macon and Augusta, the two towns where he was likely to encounter strong defensive forces. Thus he would force the Confederates to defend both cities, along with the sorry hamlet of Millen where lay a noisome Southern prison-camp almost directly south of Augusta in the Savannah River valley; the Confederates, meanwhile, would have also to maintain a tight grip upon Savannah and Charleston. Kilpatrick, with grim eyes, hawk nose, and bristling side-whiskers, marshalled his cavalry with Howard's right wing, moving against the Oconee. He carried out his orders to make a feint against Macon, keeping on the right flank of the main force until it passed that city, and cutting a swath of destruction as he moved on. At Griswoldville the Northern infantry and cavalry had to fight a sharp battle, Kilpatrick losing about 2,000 men, according to hurried reports. Then Slocum's left wing, which included troops under Gen. A.S. Williams and Gen. Jefferson C. Davis, moved on against the capital of the state, Milledgeville, and the crossing of the Oconee.

On November 22, Slocum occupied Milledgeville, from which the legislature had fled precipitately a few days earlier on learning of the Union army's proximity, revealing panic that quickly infected the people as they evacuated their shops, factories, and houses to join outgoing vehicles. But a few Union soldiers entered the city. Factories, warehouses, and depots were burned, but few private dwellings were touched, and civilians were treated with courteous respect. Sherman, who had marched with the left wing, occupied the executive

35. *O.R.* I, xliv, 7-14, Sherman's report.
36. *Ibid.*, 65.
37. Sherman, William T., *Sherman's Home Letters*, New York, 1909, 300.

mansion of Governor Brown, protecting its contents. Slocum then pushed on over the Oconee, dispersing some Confederate horsemen under General Joseph Wheeler. Kilpatrick paused in his progress to break the railway from Augusta to Millen, and Northern journals soon carried ghastly pictures of emaciated prisoners just released, and of the clay mounds in the prison-pen under which they had crawled to find refuge from burning sun and beating rains. Some unburied corpses lay near the graves of 700 dead.[38]

The only organized opposition had come from Joe Wheeler's cavalry, G.W. Smith's 3,000 Georgia militia (made up of exempts from Confederate enlistments), scattered groups of men not in rebel military service,[39] and a few local volunteers at various points. Generals were plentiful, with Beauregard, Richard Taylor, Toombs, Cobb and Hardee figuring prominently in the operation. But generals were not enough. Delaying and harassing operations were all that were possible, and even these were not telling except in nuisance value. After Milledgeville, Sherman in person moved to Howard's right wing. Now the whole force was marching southeasterly between the Savannah river on the left and the Ogeechee River on the right, although one corps was south of the Ogeechee. Destruction of railroads and bridges was continued under light opposition. Wheeler hung around the edges and occasionally attacked isolated elements, but could deal no substantial blows.

By December 3, Sherman's main forces were in the Millen area and thereabouts. Orders were given to march on toward Savannah. As they approached the sea, the country became lower and more marshy; marching difficult. Additional obstructions were presented by trees chopped down across the roads, particularly near creek, swamp and causeway crossings, but Sherman's able workers, under the skilled engineer Col. Orlando M. Poe, a West Pointer (1856) of frontier experience, rapidly removed them. By the time the army was within fifteen miles of Savannah, opposition thickened and so did the barricades, while supplies became shorter. By December 10, the Confederates were forced back into the fortifications of Savannah. Here Hardee was protected by swamps, creeks, and flooded rice fields. In investing the city, Slocum's columns were supported by Davis's corps on the left on the Savannah River, while other troops on the right extended the siege line toward the sea where Admiral Dahlgren's fleet was awaiting Sherman.

Five narrow causeways ran through formidable swamps into the city—two carrying railways and the others mere dirt roads; these were all well defended. So Sherman wisely turned his attention to the necessary opening of communication and supply lines with the warships waiting off shore in the sounds south

38. *Harper's Pictorial History of the Rebellion,* New York, 1866, 687.
39. Confederate Records of Georgia, III, 647ff.

of Savannah. Hardee himself was partially trapped in the city, with railroad connections cut both north to Charleston and to the south.

Sherman determined that the mouth of the Ogeechee River south of the city was the proper place to establish communications with the supply fleet. The river was well defended by a huge earthwork, Fort McAllister, with 200 men, 23 guns, and one mortar, but its main defences were toward the river and the sea rather than on the land side. Late on the afternoon of December 13, Hazen's division stormed the works at three points and was everywhere successful. Sherman watched the storm from a neighboring rice mill. Soon afterward he went out in a small boat to the tug *Dandelion*. After talking with Dahlgren about opening supply lines, he returned to the siege to prepare for an assault, aided now by improved bases on the Ogeechee.

To the north in South Carolina, General Foster from his position at Port Royal had failed to break the railroad from Savannah to Charleston, though he had placed guns to command it. The Confederates, therefore, continued to run trains to Savannah.

On December 17, Sherman demanded Hardee's surrender with his 10,000 men. But Hardee had decided against surrender and was planning an escape by way of the one causeway still open across the Savannah. Realizing that he could no longer delay evacuation, he completed the movement on the 20th. At daybreak next day, the Twentieth Corps entered Savannah. Sherman himself followed on the 22nd, and he wrote: "I was very much disappointed that Hardee had escaped with his garrison, and had to content myself with the material fruits of victory without the cost of life which would have attended a general assault." [40]

Sherman comprehended the full import of his dramatic triumph and electrified the nation with his famous telegram from Savannah, December 22: "His Excellency President Lincoln: I beg to present you, as a Christmas gift, the city of Savannah, with 150 heavy guns and plenty of ammunition, and also about 25,000 bales of cotton." [41]

We may take as typical of the exultation felt by Union soldiers that Christmas season in 1864, a report made by Brigadier-General William B. Hazen, commander of the Second Division of the Fifteenth Corps, at the beginning of 1865. He recalled that on November 15, "every preparation being completed," his division had broken camp at Atlanta and set out on its march through Georgia. It had an effective strength of 4,426 officers and men, and comprised 17 regimental organizations. He recalled how the troops moved

40. *O.R.*, I, xliv, 7-14, Sherman's report. Cox, Jacob D., *The March to the Sea: Franklin and Nashville*, New York, 1882, 21, 61; and Gibson, John M., *Those 163 Days*, New York, 1961, *passim*.
41. *O.R.*, I, xliv, 783.

forward rapidly, crossing the Ocmulgee River on November 19, and reaching Clinton, Ga., on the 21st. He related how they left a brigade here to cover the Macon roads, and had engaged in some skirmishing with a few casualties. On November 22, the Macon and Augusta Railroad was crossed, and the march continued past the Oconee River and Bell's Ferry on the 25th. Here the column encountered the enemy, but pressed on through continuous pine forests, crossing low, marshy branches of another river, and reaching Summerville on November 30. He followed this with a typical entry: "On Dec. 1 the march was resumed in the direction of Statesborough along the right branch of the Ogeechee River. The remainder of the march was impeded by low, broad marshes which it was invariably found necessary to corduroy." From Summerville to the Canauchee River, which they reached on December 7, the Second and Third Divisions formed a separate column under Hazen's command which, he writes, was "somewhat exposed to annoyances from the enemy," endeavoring to reach Savannah before the Union army could get there. On December 3, the Fifty-third Ohio lost twenty-seven men captured and eight wounded.

This narrative is characteristic of the record of many organizations which participated in the march. They executed a long, wearying, military advance, diversified seldom by battles, but often by adventurous incidents, with the constant possibility that a soldier or officer would be killed, wounded, or captured, if he strayed far off the main path or was involved in the numerous small skirmishes, clashes, and impromptu duels that occurred. But the bare facts convey only a fragmentary and inadequate impression of the great martial feat accomplished by Sherman and his veterans, and only a partial intimation of the tremendous consequences, some of them physical and material, but others of far larger significance, spiritual and moral, which sprang from this exhibition of national planning, daring, and determination in one of the most spectacular enterprises of modern war. The unconquerable industrial and military strength of the Union, and the surpassing skill of its most experienced commanders, were at last plain. A new confidence had entered the American spirit, and a fresh and brightly-colored panel of pictures had been impressed upon the national consciousness. The pictorial sweep and color of Sherman's march across Georgia to the Atlantic at Savannah worked upon the national imagination in a way which, while obscuring his grand strategic purpose of disrupting Southern railroads, roadways, and other communications, emphasized his ability to cut a swath of ruin across the granary of the South, while proving that his army could subsist and move at will upon the wide countryside.

Before the Federal army left Atlanta, it had been treated to a scene which was at once dramatic, uplifting, and terrible. All the while that Sherman's men were setting the torch to the "workshop of the Confederacy," the band of the Thirty-third Massachusetts rendered "John Brown," heard even above the din. "The men took up the words wedded to the music, and, high above the roaring flames, above the crash of falling walls, above the fierce crackling of thousands of small-arm cartridges in the burning buildings, rose the triumphant refrain, 'His truth is marching on!' "[42]

The following description of a typical marcher by one who made the march has a convincing vigor: "He was fertile of resources, and his confidence was unbounded. His careless, swinging gait when on the march was the impersona-tion of a determination to 'get there,' although he knew absolutely nothing of his destination. Of that he was careless. His confidence in the longheadedness of the 'old-man' was such that he did not disturb himself on that score. He was heading south instead of north, and this was ample assurance that Thomas was taking care of Hood, and that Grant was 'holding Lee down.' He went into action as unconcernedly as he took the road in the morning for a day's march; or, if not ordered into the conflict, he would sit on a fence, or lie down in the road, the image of peaceful contentment, within hearing of a fierce engage-ment, apparently wholly indifferent as to the result. . . . He waded swamps, made corduroy roads, and pulled wagons and cannon out of ruts from which the bottom had seemingly dropped. But there was one thing he did not know, that in all this magnificent effort he was making immense drafts upon his reserve energy, and that the day was sure to come when he would find himself far older than his years by reason thereof. . . ."[43]

The real achievement of Sherman in this march across Georgia to Savannah did not lie in the physical endurance shown, nor in the show of arms which accompanied it, although all such feats were recorded. His achievement was primarily moral, not physical. It is not to be compared with such a heroic march as that of Field Marshal Hugh Henry Rose (Baron Strathnairn) across India during the Great Mutiny of 1858, storming cities and engaging formida-ble forces as he went; or with some of the fighting marches of the Russian armies or of Field Marshal Wavell during the Second World War. Sherman defeated the enemy by strength of will, dexterity of movement, and uncon-querable fixity upon a few grand purposes, culminating in the achievement of important goals. Seldom have the soldierly virtues of foresight, determination, patience and skill been better illustrated in a single campaign. To comprehend the value of Sherman's stroke, we must realize that it had been, in his own phrase, long contemplated. As we have already seen, during the campaign for

---

42. Hedley, F.Y., *Marching Through Georgia, Pen-Pictures of Every-day Life in General Sherman's Army, from the Beginning of the Atlanta Campaign Until the Close of the War*, Chicago, 1890, 257-258.
43. *Ibid.*, 259-263.

Atlanta he, and others, had realized two great facts: first, that a hostile force operating over long distances and a rugged terrain had endless capacities for delaying and diverting an invading army; and second, that in a State rich enough to support such a population as Georgia's the invaders could never really be threatened with starvation unless they tarried too long in one location. We must realize, too, that the Atlanta campaign had also taught him the great value of elasticity of operation, and the possibility of adapting his plans to ever-changing circumstances.[44]

While dismemberment of the Confederacy had been a part of the Federal strategy since near the beginning of the war, the cardinal questions were always *where*, *when*, and *how* to invade the inner fortress of the South. Grant had been unable to get his proposed campaign against Mobile effectively launched. Undoubtedly many men had hit upon the general idea of invading Georgia. Its advantages were clear to anyone who glanced at a map, but implementing the idea was far more difficult. For instance, early in May, 1864, Sherman had told the Inspector-General of the Union army of his plan for seizing Atlanta. That officer was nonplused for, as he pointed out to Sherman, when he reached Atlanta he would be 450 miles from his base of supplies and dependent upon a single precarious railroad. To keep his communications open and well protected would absorb all his military strength. How could he solve the problem of further movement? Sherman snapped out a concise reply in the words: "Salt water!" He obviously meant that he would exchange his Chattanooga base for one at Savannah or possibly Charleston. He would cross Georgia to the Atlantic, living on the country as he went, without worrying about his own base of communications. But until October it was not clear what Hood and his army would do. The Confederate army had to move, for the morale of the Army of Tennessee was declining, and the Southern people expected it to act.

We have already noted the part that the defiant speech which Jefferson Davis delivered at Macon, Georgia, played in shaping Sherman's purposes. The angry Davis served rash notice that the Rebel generals would do their utmost to force Sherman to quit Atlanta, and would then try to visit upon his retreating army the same fate that had overtaken the French during Napoleon's retreat from Moscow. This was nonsense, for Sherman's movement from Atlanta would be in reality anything but a "retreat". He would leave the city and push boldly to the sea and new supply lines, and in doing so his withdrawal would in reality be carefully planned and a well-organized offensive.

Sherman had not been the only leader anxious to deliver so clearly effective

44. Liddell Hart, B.H., *Sherman, op.cit.*, 317.

a stroke at the heart of the South. Early in September, General Thomas reportedly asked Sherman to allow him to move to Andersonville, Georgia, to release the prisoners there and go on to the sea coast, while Sherman looked after the Confederate army in the area. Thomas is said to have proposed to Sherman: "Now you have no more use for me, let me take my little command and go eastward to the sea." Sherman replied that he would take it up with Grant, but nothing more was heard until Thomas was ordered to face the Confederate armies in the neighborhood of the Georgia capital, while Sherman himself set out for the Atlantic.[45]

But Sherman might well have had hesitations, especially at first. In late September he wrote Silas F. Miller: "I've got my wedge pretty deep and must look out that I don't get my fingers pinched." [46] About the same time he wrote: "I fear elevation, as a fall would be the harder." If the draft is successful, "we should make big strikes to that end for which I know the loudest Peace men of the land do not yearn with more solicitude than you and I." "When this only question of sovereignty is settled by war and nothing else can settle it, all else is easy." For himself, although pained to undertake it, Sherman had "warmed to the work."[47]

Confederate Joshua Hill, who had several interviews with Sherman in September, quoted Sherman as expressing regret over the inhumanities of war, but "I shall be forced to march to the sea, touching it somewhere in Georgia or South Carolina. Hood keeps cutting my communications with Chattanooga, endangering my supplies, and I shall be forced to move."[48]

On September 10, Sherman wrote Grant: "I am perfectly alive to the importance of pushing our advantage to the utmost. I do not think we can afford to operate farther, dependent on the railroad. . . ." If he could be sure of finding provisions and ammunition at Augusta, or Columbus, Georgia, he could march on Milledgeville, the capital, and compel Hood to give up Augusta or Macon. He was aware of the major problem of any march. "The country will afford forage and many supplies, but not enough in any one place to admit of a delay." So he proposed, "If you can manage to take the Savannah River as high as Augusta, or the Chattahoochee as far as Columbus, I can sweep the whole State of Georgia. Otherwise, I would risk our whole army by going too far from Atlanta."[49] For some weeks Sherman continued to propose to march from

45. Chicago *Tribune*, Dec. 24, 1894, from Gen. Fullerton in St. Louis *Globe-Democrat*; Van Horne, Thomas B., *The Life of Major-General George H. Thomas*, New York, 1882, 255, and footnote quoting Thomas in letter of Gen. W.F. Smith to Van Horne.

46. Letter from Sherman to Silas F. Miller, Filson Club, Louisville.

47. Sherman to Theodore S. Bell, Sept. 18, 1864, Sherman Papers, HEH.

48. Hill, Joshua, article in Atlanta *Daily Herald*, Feb. 28, 1875, typed copy in W.T. Sherman Papers, Ohio State Museum, Columbus.

49. *O.R.*, I, xxxix, pt. 2, 335, Sherman to Grant, Sept. 10, 1864.

Atlanta, providing he could be met by a column coming in from the coast, probably from the Hilton Head, South Carolina, area, held by Federal forces since the fall of 1861.

Sherman had other problems too. There had been furores over his evacuation of the civilian population of Atlanta, a policy for which he was violently condemned by General Hood, by other Confederate leaders, and the citizens themselves, Further, he felt that with his old troops "I have never felt a waver of doubt," but he was opposed to having Negro troops with him. There had been some talk of Sherman for President: "If forced to choose between the penitentiary and the White House for four years, I would say the penitentiary. . . . "[50] Through many of his letters there shows, though subtly, a doubt of his own ability, a wonder that he was where he was.

But at the same time, he was forthright as to war. In a statement that was to reverberate for more than a century in a somewhat different and stronger form, Sherman wrote Halleck, September 4; "If the people raise a howl against my barbarity and cruelty, I will answer war is war, and not popularity seeking. If they want peace, they and their relatives must stop war."[51] In answer to a protest by the Mayor of Atlanta regarding the evacuation order, Sherman replied: "War is cruelty, and you cannot refine it; and those who brought war into our Country deserve all the Curses and Maledictions a people can pour out."[52]

Grant wrote Sherman concerning future plans as early as September 12, showing that he understood his subordinate's position and difficulties. He had hoped to have sent him more men, but Price's raid in force in Missouri had prevented it. Grant had felt that these extra troops should have been sent half to Mobile and half to Savannah. The latter group would then have tried to come up and meet Sherman as he moved down from Atlanta.[53]

By September 20, Sherman was still thinking of having Savannah taken from the sea, and "if once in our possession, and the river open to us, I would not hesitate to cross the State of Georgia with 60,000 men, hauling some stores and depending on the country for the balance. . . . But the more I study the game, the more am I convinced that it would be wrong for me to penetrate much farther into Georgia without an objective beyond. . . . If you can whip Lee and I can march to the Atlantic, I think Uncle Abe will give us twenty days' leave of absence to see the young folks."[54]

50. *O.R.*, I, xxxviii, pt. 5, 791-794, Sherman to Halleck, Sept. 4, 1864.
51. *Ibid.*, 794, Sherman to Halleck, Sept. 4, 1864.
52. Sherman's reply to the Mayor of Atlanta, Sept. 12, 1864, ms. Houghton Library, Harvard Univ., Cambridge, Mass.
53. *O.R.*, I, xxxix, pt. 2, 364-365, Grant to Sherman, City Point, Va., Sept. 12, 1864.
54. *Ibid.*, 411-413, Sherman to Grant, Sept. 20, 1864.

In October, however, Sherman had his hands full diverting Hood's offensive movement between Chattanooga and Atlanta, and trying to keep his lines of supply and communication open.[55]

Grant was never opposed to Sherman's march. He left its development to the field commander in large part, but he wanted to make sure what the objectives were and that they could be kept as targets of action. On October 13, he wrote Stanton: "On mature reflection I believe Sherman's proposition is the best that can be adopted. With the long line of railroad in rear of Atlanta Sherman cannot maintain his position. If he cuts loose, destroying the road from Chattanooga forward, he leaves a wide and destitute country for the rebels to pass over before reaching territory now held by us. . . . Such an Army as Sherman has, (and with such a commander) is hard to corner or capture. . . ."[56]

Any intelligent professional officer might well have conceived of such a move as the March to the Sea, although he would have wisely asked questions during the planning stage. That able soldier and keen observer, Jacob D. Cox, felt that the march had been commonly misunderstood: "There has been a singular tendency to treat the conception of a march from Atlanta to the Gulf or to the ocean as if that were an invention or a discovery. People have disputed the priority of the idea, as if it were a patent right. . . ." Cox felt that Sherman's final decision and plan were highly creditable. A weak general might have followed Hood, but Sherman had the determination to take the opposite course. Cox added that "Grant's sympathies were never lacking for a bold and decided course, but in this instance he had less faith than Sherman that all would go well in Tennessee." Lincoln, too, was "anxious, if not fearful."[57] Grant confirmed the apprehensions of Lincoln, and there was certainly a momentary bit of hesitation in Washington, though never any basic disagreement.[58]

In his letters Grant wrote: "I was in favor of Sherman's plan from the time it was first submitted to me."[59] Sherman was later to identify November 2 as the first date on which General Grant assented to 'march to the sea.' . . ."[60] Sherman also asserted that he "saw" the move in his "mind's eye," when after the fall of Atlanta Hood shifted from Lovejoy's Station to Palmetto, and he was more positive in his determination after President Davis's speeches. The ques-

55. Sherman, *Memoirs*, II, 157ff.

56. Grant to Stanton, Oct. 13, 1864, City Point, Va., Ulysses S. Grant Letters and Papers, Illinois State Hist. Libr.

57. Cox, Jacob D., *The March to the Sea: Franklin and Nashville*, New York, 1882, 2-6.

58. Grant, *Memoirs*, II, 374-376.

59. *Ibid.*

60. Sherman, *Memoirs*, II, 166.

tion was time and manner. We have evidence, however, that as early as September 10 Grant told Sherman that, after rest and preparation, "it is desirable that another campaign [against the Confederate leader] should be commenced . . . If we give him no peace while the war lasts, the end cannot be distant." Grant thought it best to send Canby's men to advance upon Savannah while Sherman moved on Augusta.[61] Sherman replied, as we have seen, that if a force could be pushed up from Savannah, he could come southeast and meet it.[62] A lengthy correspondence shows that the overall planning did not spring into existence at once, or from any one person. It developed slowly and steadily, although the basic aim and conception remained the same.

Sherman kept pressing for help from the coast.[63] By October 1, he was proposing to send Thomas to Nashville and to undertake his march, if Hood would go over toward Alabama, for "We cannot remain on the defensive."[64] Sherman's famous message of October 9 spelled out his plans in greater detail and dropped the idea that Savannah should be taken first. He felt that it would be "a physical impossibility to protect the roads, now that Hood, Forrest, and Wheeler, and the whole batch of devils, are turned loose without home or habitation." He proposed breaking up the line from Chattanooga to Atlanta, abandoning it and then marching directly on Savannah. "Until we can repopulate Georgia, it is useless to occupy it, but the utter destruction of its roads, houses, and people will cripple their military resources . . . I can make the march, and make Georgia howl. . . ."[65] Grant foresaw that Hood would go north of the Tennessee, and wrote Sherman, "If there is any way of getting at Hood's army, I would prefer that, but I must trust to your own judgment." Grant also declared he could not send a force to act against Savannah in concert with Sherman.[66] The same day, Sherman, who was now at Kingston, Georgia, informed Grant of Hood's manoeuver to the north, adding, "but I believe he will be forced to follow me. Instead of being on the defensive, I would [then] be on the offensive; instead of guessing at what he means to do, he would have to guess at my plans. The difference in war is full 25 per cent. . . ."[67] Immediately thereafter, shortly before midnight on October 11, Grant replied: "If you are satisfied the trip to the sea-coast can be made, holding the line of the Tennessee firmly, you may make it, and destroy all the railroad south of Dalton or Chattanooga, as you think best. . . ." [68]

61. O.R., I, xxxix, pt. 2, 355, Grant to Sherman, City Point, Sept. 10, 1864.
62. Ibid., 355-356, Sherman to Grant, Atlanta, Sept. 10, 1864.
63. Ibid., 464, Sherman to Halleck, Sept. 25, 1864, and passim.
64. O.R., I, xxxix, pt. 3, 3, Sherman to Grant, Atlanta, Oct. 1, 1864.
65. Ibid., 162, Sherman to Grant, Atlanta, Oct.9, 1864.
66. Ibid., 202, Grant to Sherman, City Point, Oct. 11, 1864.
67. Ibid., Sherman to Grant.
68. Ibid., Grant to Sherman, Oct. 11, 1864.

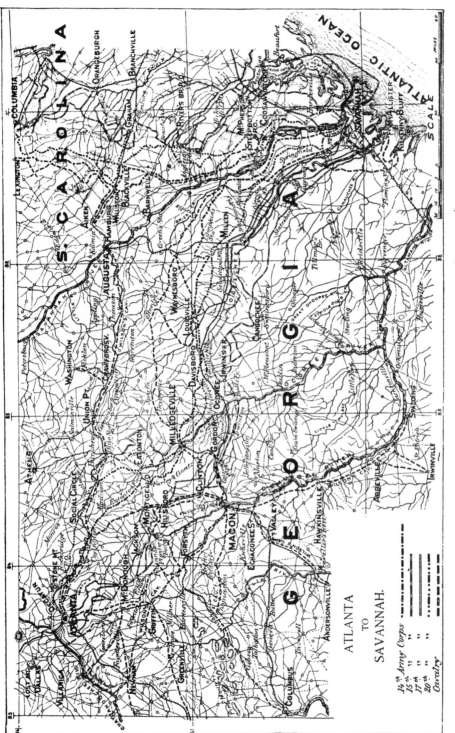

Map of Sherman's March from Atlanta to Savannah

Thus the two generals had worked out a program together by use of the telegraph, and Grant had fully approved the specific plan. Still, the President felt some additional "solicitude" and Grant had again to give his approval.[69] Grant had to understand what the manoeuver was intended to accomplish; in addition to giving his approval, he had to ship south stores and vessels ready to meet Sherman when he should break out upon the coast.

Even then, however, certain doubts seemed to have arisen in Sherman's mind, for as late as November 2, he telegraphed Grant from Rome, Georgia: "If I could hope to overhaul Hood, I would turn against him with my whole force . . . If he ventures north of the Tennessee I may turn in that direction and endeavor to get between him and his line of retreat . . ." But the same day he also wired: "I am clearly of the opinion that the best results will follow me if I hold to my contemplated movement through Georgia."[70] Grant, in fact, had to embolden Sherman, writing: "I see no present reason for changing your plan . . ."[71] Very soon Northern papers outlined Sherman's plans despite War Department efforts to keep them secret.[72] One source of information on these plans was furnished by officers who went North before the campaign. A number actually resigned and others tried to. One officer commented on these absentees: "They are being laughed at by the whole army here . . . I can't see why they are so much afraid of this campaign, for I regard it as one of the easiest campaigns I have engaged in. . . ."[73]

[IV]

The essentially triumphant character of Sherman's march, producing a tremendous popular effect upon both the North and the South, would have been shattered and its moral effects would have been reversed had it encountered any staggering check, compelling it to retreat, and resulting in an augmentation of Confederate confidence. This would have been sweeping in nature and consequences if Hood's Tennessee campaign had succeeded, and if he had occupied Nashville and the surrounding mid-South and crushed Thomas's army. Tennessee and Kentucky would then have lain open to the Confederacy with little immediate opposition in front of its columns, while Hood's army could have been supplied from the region. Conceivably, he could have pushed even to the Ohio, and the moral encouragement given to the

69. *Ibid.*, 222, Stanton to Grant, Oct.12, 1864, and Grant to Sherman, Oct.12, 1864.
70. *Ibid.*, pt. 3, 594-595, Sherman to Grant, Nov. 2, 1864.
71. *Ibid.*, 679, Grant to Sherman, Nov. 7, 1864.
72. *Ibid.*, 740, Grant to Stanton, and Stanton to Grant, Nov. 11, 1864.
73. Connolly, Major James Austin, Major Connolly's Letters to His Wife, 1862-1865, *Transactions of the Illinois State Hist. Soc., 1928*, Springfield, 1928, 370, Nov. 11, 1864.

Confederacy thereby would have been even greater than the North experienced through Sherman's successful march. While the outcome of the war itself would probably not have been jeopardized, unquestionably the history of 1865 would have been drastically changed if Hood had succeeded in Tennessee. But this is one of the colossal and unprofitable "ifs" of history, along with "if Napoleon had taken a winning stand against Wellington." Nothing of the kind happened because Hood and his army possessed weaknesses that even on the first glance appeared disabling compared with the strength possessed by Sherman and his veterans; because a courageous, although heedlessly impetuous Confederate commander led an army which fatigue and losses were rendering impotent; because the great industrial strength of the North was growing more and more overwhelming, and because the incalculable fortunes of war always favor the better-prepared, better-trained, and more thoughtfully directed forces.

Even before the threat delivered by Hood and his army, Sherman worried about the safety of the middle South and the area to his rear at Atlanta. In fact, besides trying to bring Forrest to bay, he even suggested that the guerrillas and malcontents in Kentucky and elsewhere be put aboard troop-ships and exiled to Honduras, British or French Guiana, or San Domingo, or even Madagascar or Lower California would do. "But one thing is certain," he declared, "there is a class of people, men, women, and children, who must be killed or banished before you can hope for peace and order, even as far south as Tennessee."[74] Stanton seemed to approve this flint-hearted scheme, but nothing came of it.[75]

In addition to the guerrillas, and Wheeler's cavalry operations in Sherman's neighborhood, the Union troops had repeatedly encountered Forrest, all summer and on into the fall. Forrest at Brice's Crossroads and Tupelo; Forrest raiding even into the Federal stronghold of Memphis itself in late August; Forrest moving up from Mississippi to Pulaski, Tenn., and back into Alabama and Mississippi in late September and early October. In this exploit, the brilliant Confederate master of raiding operations reported that in sixteen days he captured 86 Yankee officers, 67 government employees, 1,174 noncommissioned officers and privates, 933 Negroes, and killed a thousand others of the enemy. He captured 800 horses, 7 guns, 2,000 small arms, 50 wagons and ambulances, several hundred saddles, medical, commissary, and quartermaster's stores. In addition, Union forces had to bear the destruction of the Duck River railroad bridge in Tennessee and other depredations. Forrest's army was now well supplied with boots, shoes, hats, blankets, overcoats, and other kinds of equipment.[76]

74. *O.R.*, I, xxxix, pt. 2, 131-132, Sherman to Stanton, June 21, 1864.
75. *Ibid.*, 157, Stanton to Sherman, July 1, 1864.
76. *O.R.*, I, xxxix, pt. 1, Forrest's report, 542-549.

Forrest was not yet through. Fortunately for the North, when Hood's army marched west and north from the vicinity of Atlanta, eventually reaching northern Alabama, Forrest was not on the scene to meet him and to augment immediately the Army of Tennessee. Indeed Forrest was some 300 miles away from Hood at the time Hood most needed him, executing a raid into Tennessee that was spectacular but by no means necessary to the Confederacy. Cavalry under Forrest had moved to the Tennessee River, capturing a gunboat and several transports. He manned some of them with crews, fought a river gunboat battle, burned and sank nineteen vessels at the wharf at Johnsonville, Tenn.; he also destroyed immense Union stores. All this was in late October and early November. Of course, Thomas had to send troops to Johnsonville. Sherman angrily wrote that "that devil Forrest was down about Johnsonville and was making havoc among the gun-boats and transports . . ."[77]

By October 21, Hood was at Gadsden, Alabama, some 30 miles southwest of Sherman's pursuing forces who were at Gaylesville on the Georgia-Alabama line. By this time Hood had abandoned his campaign against the Chattanooga-Atlanta railroad and was formulating other plans. This new scheme was to cross the Tennessee at or near Guntersville, Alabama, drive first toward Stevenson and Bridgeport, Alabama, and then against Thomas and Schofield, hoping to beat them before they could fall back to Nashville. He would then take Nashville and operate from that city, boldly threatening Cincinnati.[78] Hood moved on, threatening Decatur, Ala., then withdrawing to the west to Tuscumbia. Sherman continued to send troops to Thomas in Tennessee, and to make plans for the Great March. Thomas had been quite weak before the 9th of November when he received Schofield's 10,000-man Twenty-third Corps to add to the Fourth Corps of David S. Stanley. With a strong field force now, Thomas was in a good position to shift his troops and defend Tennessee against Hood's promised advance. Previously he had been handicapped by the necessity of garrisoning a number of important posts with inferior or raw troops.

By early November, Hood had already failed in his main effort. Unable to move north promptly, because of deficient supplies and the absence of Forrest who was away at Johnsonville, Hood had lost the opportunity to strike into Tennessee against Thomas's garrisons, a move that quite possibly would have forced Sherman to give up his own plans for the grand march.[79] Thomas now sent Schofield down to Pulaski, Tenn., and on November 14 the thoughtful careful Schofield took over command of the major Union field force of about

77. *Ibid.*, 859-60, Thomas to Sherman, Nov. 4, 1864; *O.R.*, I, xxxix, pt. 3, 658-661, Sherman to Grant, Nov. 6, 1864.
78. Hood, John Bell, *Advance and Retreat*, New Orleans, 1880, 267; and Stone, Henry, *The Battle of Franklin, Tennessee, Nov. 30, 1864*, MHSM, Vol. VII, 435-437.
79. Stone, *op.cit.*, 439.

17,000. By the time Hood crossed the Tennessee, Thomas's available force totaled about 29,000, in addition to various garrisons.[80]

One military critic, it may be noted, feels that Sherman misrepresented to Grant the large numbers Thomas had, and that he actually neglected Thomas while taking more than 60,000 on "a holiday march."[81] Sherman did at least order A.J. Smith's corps to Nashville from the Mississippi, but this force was delayed by the advance of Price's impetuous expedition into Missouri during October, essentially a great raid against that Northern area.

Altogether, Thomas as of November 20 had 54,240 infantry present for duty, and an aggregate strength of 65,615 foot-soldiers. To this might be added 17,563 cavalry, making a total of 71,803. But garrison duties and detachments employed more than half of this. So, as far as field forces are concerned, Hood actually outnumbered Thomas at the start. Thomas had about 29,000 in the field, whereas Hood's aggregate effective force was about 35,000, with some more than 40,000 total present.[82] Hood did not begin his northward advance into Tennessee from Tuscumbia until November 21, nearly a week after Sherman left Atlanta for the sea. He maintained that the failure of Forrest to join him caused the long delay in Alabama.[83] Beauregard, who conferred with Hood, later claimed that if his ideas of the campaign had been followed "without undue delay and modifications and with vigor and skill, Sherman most probably would have been compelled to return to Middle Tennessee to repair and protect his line of communications . . . " and that the disasters of Franklin and Nashville would not have occurred.[84] It is quite possible that Sherman would have been forced to make new decisions if Hood had crossed the Tennessee before the Federals left Atlanta, and before Sherman gave up his communications with the North.

When he did move, Hood hoped to place his army between the Union field force at Pulaski, Tenn., and Nashville. He attributed his failure to reach Columbia, Tenn., before the Federals to deep mud and lack of maps.[85] Actually, however, the Union troops themselves frustrated Hood's first move. Hearing of Hood's movement, Schofield sent Jacob D. Cox with two divisions towards Columbia. Despite the rain, Cox moved rapidly, arriving within ten miles of that town the night of November 23. On the 24th, he reached Columbia just in time to frustrate Forrest's move. One critic surmises that in another

80. Stone, op.cit., 440; O.R., I, xlv, pt. 1, 590.
81. Stone, op.cit., 441-442.
82. O.R., I, xlv, pt. 1, 590. Important Article on Comparative Union and Confederate Strength in New York, Nation, February 23, 1905, 149, 150.
83. O.R., I, xxxix, pt. 1, 801-803, Hood's Report
84. O.R., I, xlv, pt. 1, 649-651, Beauregard's Report.
85. Ibid., 652-653, Hood's Report.

half-hour the Confederates would have taken lightly garrisoned Columbia, and the crossings of the Duck River.[86] Skirmishing was frequent until the night of November 27 when Schofield's force was pulled north of the Duck River, and the bridges destroyed. That same night, Hood was making plans with Forrest to seize Spring Hill, about halfway between Columbia and Franklin, the possession of which was vital to any Federal withdrawal toward Franklin.

Forrest started out on the 28th but was encountered by Federal cavalryman James Harrison Wilson, who informed Schofield that Forrest was moving toward Spring Hill, having pushed aside feeble defenders. Schofield at Columbia was in close touch by telegraph with Thomas at Nashville. Thomas told Schofield that if Wilson's Federal cavalry could not hold off Forrest, the Union infantry would have to withdraw from their Duck River position and fall back to Franklin behind Harpeth River. But Schofield was reluctant to pull out. Early on the morning of November 29, Thomas again wired Schofield to fall back to Franklin, leaving forces at Spring Hill to deter the enemy advance.[87] Schofield delayed a few hours more before his army was sent back up the road from Columbia to Spring Hill.

The scene was being set for one of the most controversial and mystifying events of the war in the West—the Spring Hill affair. Students have long debated the events of that November night in 1864 when Schofield's army managed to go right up the road from Columbia to Franklin through Spring Hill, even though the Confederate Army of Tennessee had beaten them to the area and was encamped along the Franklin Pike. The incident has been so thoroughly investigated that it is doubtful that any new material will now appear to give a definitive answer to the puzzle. But the vital fact is that Thomas's field force was not cut off from Franklin and Nashville. It did get back to defend the approaches to the Tennessee capital while Thomas was building his defences and awaiting the arrival of A.J. Smith's corps from Missouri.

The fact that it accomplished its return by a thin margin was certainly the second of the major events that frustrated Hood, the first having been his failure to seize Columbia before its occupation in strength by the Federals. Schofield's duty was to impede Hood, avoid imperilling his own force, and keep in touch with Nashville, where Thomas was directing the general defense of Tennessee and preparing his army to repulse Hood's moves against obvious objectives. Schofield's delay for a few days at Columbia could have resulted in Union disaster.[88]

86. Stone, *op.cit.*, 444-445.
87. *Ibid.*, 450-451.
88. Wilson, James Harrison, *Under the Old Flag*, New York, 1912, 39-40.

Forrest and his horsemen arrived at Spring Hill at about the same time as Stanley's Union infantry from Columbia. Sharp fighting ensued as more Confederates came in, but Stanley's men succeeded in holding the main highway. That night, the 29th, Schofield's entire force passed through Spring Hill and on up to Franklin.[89] In discussing this question of the true blame for failures on either side, the shrewd General Jacob D. Cox, who acquitted himself very ably in this campaign, later asserted that Hood was wrong in trying to shift the blame for the escape of Schofield to the shoulders of B.F. Cheatham, and adds: "Had his own confidence not wavered, and had he not begun to yield to the belief that much more than one division stood facing him, [Hood's] own energy would have carried his subordinates with him, and [they] would have made the assault," unavoidably desperate though it was, the next day. Cox felt that Hood lacked the grasp of mind and will to seize upon the situation, despite his earlier record of quick, vigorous action.[90] Another critic feels it was not until about 3:00 on the afternoon of November 29 that Schofield realized Hood was trying to cut him off, and even then he also failed in energy.[91] This same observer describes the confusion in Hood's army as to which officer should have taken some undefined action during the 29th, and then attributes this confusion to the alleged fact that there "was music and dancing and feasting [in Hood's ranks] and other Gods than Mars were worshipped."[92]

One Union soldier describes the night with grateful relief; "Straight past a thousand gleaming fires, around which were bivouacked the soldiers of Hood's army, had marched the Federal column, and those two gallant corps were saved. When it was known that the peril was past, a hearty 'Thank God!' escaped from many lips unused to prayer. The star of 'good-luck' twinkled upon Schofield's army out of the midnight sky!"[93]

Hood later maintained that if Cheatham had carried out his instructions, "there is no doubt that we should have possessed ourselves of the road . . ."[94] The Confederate general does not explain why he did not see to it that the orders were carried out. He writes a simple admission of the disastrous Southern failure: "The enemy continued to move along the road in hurry and confusion, within hearing nearly all the night." Thus was lost a great opportunity of "striking the enemy for which we had labored so long—the greatest this campaign had offered, and one of the greatest during the war . . . The fruits

89. For a good account, see Cox, Jacob D., *The Battle of Franklin, Tennessee*, New York, 1897, Ch.II, 21-36.

90. *Ibid.*, 79.

91. Stone, *op.cit.*, 455.

92. *Ibid.*, 462.

93. Hinman, Wilbur F., *The Story of the Sherman Brigade*, privately published, 1897, 643-644.

94. *O.R.*, I, xlv, pt. 1, 652-653, Hood's report.

ought to have been gathered at that point . . ."[95] Hood's report was dated February 15, 1865. In it and other reports,[96] he seemed correct in attaching great importance to the Spring Hill fiasco, but he persisted in shifting the responsibility to others, as was too often his wont. Each of Hood's accounts varied a little.[97] In fact, the narratives of Hood, when compared with Cheatham and others, are not easily reconciled with each other.[98]

Some, or many, in the Confederate high command, had blundered. One recent writer lays the Confederate failure to the lack of "a definite and well-organized plan of action." He writes that Hood either failed to work out a plan, or, if he had one, "he failed to brief adequately his subordinate commanders." Hood at the time seemed "to have failed to grasp the full significance of the situation as it developed at Spring Hill." Furthermore, the "entire group of Confederate generals seems to have been permeated with a paralyzing lack of initiative. . . ."[99] These reasons certainly are part of the explanation, although they seem somewhat superficial. Whatever the reasons, the fact remains that "the Yankees lit their pipes by the campfires of the Rebs. . . ."[100]

When Schofield with most of his national troops arrived at Franklin and the south bank of the Harpeth River in the early morning of November 30, following their escape at Spring Hill, the Union commander found that the pontoons he had ordered had not arrived. Busying himself with repair of bridges and improvement of fords, Schofield turned over his corps to General Jacob D. Cox, who organized an infantry line south of the Harpeth, facing down the road to Spring Hill. The line ran in a rough semi-circle from the river above the town to the river below. Quickly the tired and hungry infantrymen began to dig. In half-an-hour they expected to have an earthwork behind which they could at least rest a bit. By noon, the two-mile line was nearing completion.

Meanwhile, a chagrined and angry Hood had ordered his whole army to move in pursuit from Spring Hill. When, about four miles south of Franklin, Hood came upon the Yankee rearguard, he attempted to outflank them, but the Federals retired. This retreat caused some delay, and it was about 3:30 P.M. when the seven Confederate divisions of the Army of Tennessee formed along

95. *Ibid.*, 653-655.

96. *O.R.*, I, xlv, pt. 1, 652-654, Hood's Report, Feb. 15, 1865.

97. See also Hood, J.B., "The Invasion of Tennessee," *Battles and Leaders*, IV, 425-37, in comparison with his reports in *O.R.*, I, xlv, and also in Hood, John Bell, *Advance and Retreat*, 284-291.

98. See Campbell Brown Books, Southern Historical Collection, Univ. of N.C. Library, interview of Brown with Gov. Isham G. Harris of Tenn., May, 1868; Cheatham, B.F. "General Cheatham at Spring Hill," *Battles and Leaders*, IV, 438-439.

99. Crawford, W.T., "The Mystery of Spring Hill," *Civil War History*, Vol.I, No.II, June, 1955, 101-126.

100. Buck, Irving, *Cleburne and His Command*, Jackson, Tenn., 1959, 269.

the Winstead Hills south of Franklin. As the gray line swung forward two-and-a-half miles to Cox's main position, the whole advance being in full sight, Schofield occupied a fort north of the river, overlooking the entire field. An advanced Union position was overrun as the retiring Federals and advancing Confederates poured into the main works at about the same time. At first it appeared that the hot Confederate upsurge made Union disaster imminent, but Colonel Emerson Updycke saw the emergency and, according to at least one critic, "saved the army from the threatened destruction" by the quick deployment of his brigade.[101] In a few moments, the Confederates who had entered the works were killed, captured, or forced back. Thirty-two battle flags were taken. Around the Carter House and the Columbia Pike the fighting became sanguinary in the extreme. A locust grove was almost cut down by rifle fire. At sunset, the field was "lighted up to redness" by the hot exchange of fire.[102]

Hood, his commanders, and his army had delivered a blow expressing their desperate frustration in a hot fury of anger and determination, but it was a blow struck in passion without sufficient serious consideration of the defenses to be met. By midnight, the battle of Franklin was over, and Schofield, withdrawing his troops across the river, urged them on their way to Nashville. Out of some nearly 28,000 troops possibly engaged, the Yankees lost only 189 killed, 1,033 wounded, and 1,104 missing—a total of 2,326. The effective Confederate strength employed in the action was a matter of dispute, but it probably was well over 20,000 infantry. Of this force, a staggering casualty-roll had to be reported: 1,750 killed, 3,800 wounded, and 702 missing, to make a total of 6,252.[103]

We must ask, first of all, should such a dreadful blood-bath as Franklin ever have stained the pages of history. Schofield felt that he was protecting his transportation by keeping his infantry south of the Harpeth, but in fact his transportation was over the river before 1 P.M. It would seem that Schofield made his mistake in ordering Cox to prepare and maintain an unnecessarily exposed and dangerous position with his back to a river because of a misunderstanding of the situation, perhaps deepened by sheer fatigue.[104] If he had placed himself on the high ground north of the Harpeth, Hood could not have attacked.

At the same time, most authorities feel that Hood should never have attacked such a formidable position, or at least not so directly as he did. Little or no strategic skill or tactical ability was exhibited on the part of the Confeder-

101. Stone, *op.cit.*, 469-470.
102. *Ibid.*, 471.
103. *O.R.*, I, xlv, pt. 1, 343; Livermore, *Numbers and Losses*, 131-132; Hood, *Advance and Retreat*, 298; Crownover, Sims, *The Battle of Franklin*, reprinted from Tennessee Hist. Quarterly, Vol.XIV, No.4, December, 1955, 26; Cox, *op.cit.*, 96.
104. LeDuc, William G., *Memoirs*, ms., HEH.

ates. Lower commanders on both sides shone in the fighting—Jacob D. Cox, Stanley and Updycke for the Federals; Cleburne, Forrest, and others for the Confederates. On Hood's side, the defeat was not only a lamentable display of rashness, but costly both in manpower and morale. The Federals sustained losses, and drew off, but they had achieved their object in impeding Hood. For the third time within a few days, the Confederate army had been frustrated.[105]

Personal recollections of the conflict were many and vivid. A Wisconsin soldier wrote: "It is impossible to exaggerate the fierce energy with which the Confederate soldiers, that short November afternoon, threw themselves against the works, fighting with what seemed the very madness of despair." He spoke of thirteen assaults including one in which he saw General Patrick Cleburne with his staff ride up onto the works, until "horse and rider and some of his Staff went down to death."[106] The stark, deadly simplicity of the Battle of Franklin impressed those who participated. Many of them could see it all from the Winstead Hills to the Carter House; and one can survey the tragic and memorable field today, virtually unchanged without the intrusion of monuments or modern memorials.

As Schofield moved on up toward Nashville and the Confederates who survived sullenly followed, post-mortem analyses were volunteered, particularly on the Confederate side. Cheatham, Cleburne, and Forrest, among others, had opposed the attack, and now Cleburne, with five other general officers, was dead.[107] Hood was once more full of excuses, including a plea that Schofield had been instructed to hold Franklin, and for this reason he wished to attack before the Federals were solidly intrenched.[108] In his book *Advance and Retreat*, Hood makes much of the Confederate disappointment at Spring Hill as an impelling motive for the bloody charge at Franklin. He says nothing about opposition to the attack from his generals,[109] maintaining that the attack "became a necessity as imperative as that which impelled General Lee to order the assault at Gaines's Mills."[110] On the other hand, Confederate Lieut. Gen. A.P. Stewart wrote: "To assault was a terrible proposition to troops who, during Johnston's long retreat, had been trained to avoid charging breastworks."[111] Another officer commented: "The truth is, the failure at Spring Hill was General Hood's own failure. . . . The loss at Spring Hill could have been fully

105. Cox, *op.cit.*, 81-98; Horn, Stanley, *The Army of Tennessee*, 394-404; Van Horne, T.B., *History of the Army of the Cumberland*, II, 198 and *passim*; Hood, J.B., *Advance and Retreat*, 292-300; Hay, Thomas Robson, *Hood's Tennessee Campaign*, New York, 1929, 119ff.
106. Atwater, M.B., *Reminiscences*, ms. State Hist. Soc. of Wisconsin.
107. Hay, *op.cit.*, 120-121.
108. *O.R.*, I, xlv, pt. 1, 652, Hood's report.
109. Hood, *Advance and Retreat*, *op.cit.*, 292-300.
110. *Ibid.*, 294.
111. Quoted in Buck, *Cleburne and His Command*, *op.cit.*, 287.

retrieved at Franklin by crossing the Harpeth River by fords above Franklin and getting a strong position among the Brentwood hills in the rear of the enemy."[112] One Southern eyewitness frankly declared: "Our men were flushed with hope and pride and all thought they fought for Tennessee. They felt that the eyes of the men and women all over our country as well as in Tennessee were upon them, and the Yankee army which they had followed so long was before them. . . . The chivalry of the South did charge. . . ."[113] But despite the courage of that charge and the frightful carnage, Hood had lost the battle, a battle that probably should never have been fought.

By the second day of December, Hood had approached Nashville. He found the handsome city ready to meet his onset. Strong Union lines ran from the Cumberland River on the west, or right, around the south side of the city to the river on the left, or east. There were three Union corps under Thomas along with an extra division, and the cavalry under James H. Wilson. Hood placed his own troops on high ground, but they actually circled less than half the city. Forrest, of course, commanded the cavalry. There they stood, adamantly waiting. This waiting was extended when, for the entire half-month ending December 14th, the two armies were icebound. Cox tells us that from the 7th to the 13th, "the slopes in front of the lines were a continuous glare of ice, so that movements away from the roads and broken paths could be only with the greatest difficulty and at a snail's pace. Men and horses were seen falling whenever they attempted to move across country. A man slipping on the hillside had no choice but to sit down and slide to the bottom."[114] Rain, snow, and sleet had begun on the 8th and prevented any action whatsoever. One officer later said that the ice problem "was so exceptional that it was not appreciated or fully understood at the East."[115] The weather did not improve until December 14, when Thomas was able to issue afternoon orders to his corps commanders for an advance. His 50,000 men, now fully in hand, were impatient to go. Hood, for his part, felt confident of the result if the Union army took the offensive. "I felt," he wrote in his official reports, that if Thomas attacked him in his works, "I would defeat him and thus gain possession of Nashville, with abundant supplies for the army. This would give me possession of Tennessee." Meanwhile, the leaders in Washington and Virginia did not share Thomas's hopefulness, for as time passed the situation appeared more and more anxious. Sherman and his 60,000 troops were busy somewhere in Georgia. Grant and Meade were held fast at Petersburg, while Hood had

112. *Ibid.*, 287.
113. William D. Gale to his wife, Jan. 14, 1865, in Gale-Polk Papers, Southern Historical Collection, Univ. of N.C.
114. Cox, Jacob D., *Military Reminiscences of the Civil War*, II, New York, 1900, 352-353.
115. *Ibid.*, 354.

marched into central Tennessee to Nashville. And it was about Hood that they were deeply concerned.

For his part, Thomas, by noon of December 1, had Schofield's two somewhat battered corps back from Franklin, along with Wilson's cavalry. A.J. Smith's veteran corps had come in from Missouri, so by the tenth of December Thomas's total force was 70,272 present for duty, many in garrison duty rather than at Nashville.[116] That city had been strongly fortified since early in the war, and the defenses several times enlarged until a formidable series of forts and entrenchments encircled its southern half and guarded the eight primary pikes that led into the place. Nashville had served since 1862 as a major, if not the major, base of the Union in the West. The eight miles of new lines held 44,000 infantry and there were 10,000 more men of the post garrison and quartermaster's department. They were ready but they continued to improve their defensive positions. Thomas still had a lot to do when the inclement weather set in.

Hood was up to Nashville and in position by December 3, with about 37,000 infantry present for duty although he maintained that he had but 22,000.[117] The Army of Tennessee was very well posted as were their opponents; Hood had a string of detached, self-supporting redoubts helping him hold an extremely strong position. So secure did Hood feel that he sent Forrest out toward Murfreesboro with a considerable part of his cavalry and an infantry division which the inexperienced Federal garrison ably repelled. Meanwhile he made a strong position stronger by fortifying Montgomery Hill near the Union center and other lines paralleling the northern exposures. He could do little with his left, however, which, widely separated from the swollen river, remained weak enough to be easily flanked. The central question remains whether he should have entrenched at all! Might it not have been possible for him to move around Nashville and head north, weather permitting? This would have forced Thomas into action, a different action than was taken at Nashville.

But the Southern idea was that if Hood forced Thomas out of Nashville, the Confederates could resist and repulse the attack. At a council of war with his generals, Hood exclaimed that Thomas's strength had been exaggerated, and "that we must take Nashville and we *shall* take it! And then, gentlemen, how we shall feast off the rich Yankee spoils!"[118]

Meanwhile, Thomas's problems mounted—problems that for the most part should never have arisen. He had not wanted to go back to Tennessee and felt

116. Stone, *op.cit.*, 483.
117. *Ibid.*, 487-489.
118. N.Y. *Herald*, Dec. 22, 1864, dispatch of D.P. Conyngham.

that he was not liked by Grant (as was Sherman), though at the same time he did not know why he should not be equally trusted.[119] Smith's troops and others had reached Nashville lacking transport, and the horses and mules of the other two corps, like those of the cavalry, were in bad shape after the fighting withdrawal from Pulaski to Nashville. While men, arms, ammunition, and rations were sufficient, many other needed items were in very short supply. Furthermore, this was not an Army in the best sense; it was a command put together in a hurry and needed shaking-down. The Union leader did his utmost. As an officer who was there put it, Thomas knew what his job was, and "he realized too keenly the importance of victory to allow anything that might help secure it to be neglected."[120] Nashville became a busy workshop of preparation, day and night. Every draft animal within many miles was gathered in, and even those of a storm-bound circus were appropriated.

But an anxious Washington was growing more and more impatient. Grant, far distant and unaware of the biting cold that impeded Thomas's ill-clad troops, on December 6 peremptorily ordered an attack. Thomas called in his corps commanders, but they decided it would be impossible before the 10th. Grant tells us in his official report that before the battle of Nashville he grew restive over what he thought of as the unnecessary Union delay. This impatience was increased upon learning that the enemy had sent a force of cavalry across the Cumberland into Kentucky, for he feared that Hood might cross with his whole army, and create a vexatious situation there. He was ready to start west himself to take general command in person, but when he arrived in Washington from Petersburg, he found there a dispatch from Thomas announcing his attack upon the Confederates and its initial progress. "I was delighted," his report recalls. "All fears and apprehensions were dispelled." He still thought that Thomas should have moved out earlier as soon as Hood approached Nashville, but now he realized that Thomas had made his plans and completed his preparations with a quiet, consummate skill stamped by the deliberate, tenacious genius he had shown at Chickamauga.

Grant had heard nothing in Virginia of the attack, so he had wired Stanton recommending that Thomas be replaced with Schofield! A very observant officer called this attempt to displace Thomas an "unprecedented and unmerited indignity."[121] In retrospect, it is difficult to regard it otherwise. On the other hand, Lincoln, Stanton, and Grant were seeing the situation from the East, in Washington and Petersburg, and affairs did hold a different aspect from that distance and at that time. Still, the doubts respecting Thomas and

119. Stone, *op.cit.*, 492.
120. *Ibid.*, 496.
121. *Ibid.*, 500.

the movement toward his replacement were in many ways puzzling.

Defenders of Thomas feel that he had been left by Sherman with an inferior army to accomplish a huge task, given scattered detachments of troops from which to create an adequate force, ordered to hold a position which he did not seek, given promises of support which were never fulfilled—and then on the eve of the crucial battle was threatened with the loss of his command to a subordinate whose actions in the campaign up to that time had been somewhat questionable.

Actually, larger elements entered the situation than the natural and not altogether impulsive (though excessively hasty) anxiety shown by Grant. The President himself felt the deepest uneasiness. Secretary Stanton had telegraphed Grant as early as December 2 that "The President feels solicitous about the disposition of Gen. Thomas to lay in fortifications for an indefinite period 'until Wilson gets equipments.' This looks like the McClellan and Rosecrans strategy of do nothing and let the rebels raid the country. The President wishes you to consider the matter."[122] It may seem strange that Washington could not perceive the difference between a McClellan or a Rosecrans and Thomas! But Washington received only bits of authentic intelligence from the front mingled with conclusions and guesses. Little was known about the weather and other logistical impediments, and the indifference shown by Thomas to any success less than decisive had naturally reawakened Lincoln's mistrust of commanders with the "slows". That same December 2, Grant told Thomas that he should attack because if the Federals did not, Hood could inflict "incalculable injury upon your railroads . . ."[123] Thomas retorted that Smith had just arrived along with another division, that he lacked cavalry and "it must be remembered that my command was made up of the two weakest corps of General Sherman's army and all the dismounted cavalry except one brigade, and the task of reorganizing and equipping has met with many delays, which have enabled Hood to take advantage of my crippled condition. I earnestly hope, however, that in a few more days I shall be able to give him a fight."[124] Grant continued to bait Thomas who replied that he would possibly attack on the 7th.[125] Then came the order of December 6 at 4 P.M., "Attack Hood at once, and wait no longer for a remount of your cavalry. There is great danger of delay resulting in a campaign back to the Ohio River."[126] At 9 P.M. on the 6th, Thomas replied: "I will make the necessary dispositions and attack Hood at once, agreeably to your order, though I believe it will be hazardous

122. O.R., I, xlv, pt. 2, 15-16.
123. Ibid., 17, Grant to Thomas, Dec. 2, 1864, City Point, Va.
124. Ibid., 17.
125. Ibid., 29, 55.
126. Ibid., 70.

with the small force of cavalry now at my service."[127] The next day, the 7th, Stanton continued to bring pressure upon Grant, writing: "Thomas seems unwilling to attack because it is hazardous, as if all war were anything but hazardous. If he waits for Wilson to get ready, Gabriel will be blowing his last horn."[128] Then, at 1:30 P.M. the chafing Grant informed Stanton that if Thomas did not attack promptly, "I would recommend superseding him by Schofield, leaving Thomas subordinate . . ."[129] Late in the afternoon of the 8th, Grant burst out to Halleck: "If Thomas has not struck yet, he ought to be ordered to hand over his command to Schofield. There is no better man to repel an attack than Thomas, but I fear he is too cautious ever to take the initiative." Grant was completely out of patience, and adding that he feared Hood would reach the Ohio, he asked if it was not advisable "to call on Ohio, Indiana, and Illinois for 60,000 men for thirty days."[130]

Then and even later, Thomas was regarded as a defensive general addicted to a type of Fabian warfare at which he had excelled. At the same time, it was and still is too often forgotten that he had repeatedly shown capacities for the offence, both in action and in planning. But Halleck now entered the situation. He reluctantly told Grant—at 9 o'clock in the evening of December 8—"If you wish General Thomas relieved from command, give the order. No one here will, I think, interfere. The responsibility, however, will be yours, as no one here, so far as I am informed, wishes General Thomas's removal."[131] Grant now retreated a little, telling Halleck he wished Thomas "reminded of the importance of immediate action," but he would not say relieve the general until he heard further from him.[132]

More messages were exchanged, and then on December 9, through presidential instructions and by direction of the Secretary of War, orders were given to relieve Thomas.[133]

But Halleck delayed transmitting them, apparently because of news of the bad ice storm.[134] Grant had even repeated his order for removal. Yet, on the evening of December 9, in a message to Halleck, he stated: "I am very unwilling to do injustice to an officer who has done so much good service as General Thomas has, and will, therefore, suspend the order relieving him until it is seen whether he will do anything."[135] This was judicious. Halleck, then, by his advice and by his delay in acting had prevented Thomas's supercession.

127. *Ibid.*, 70.
128. *Ibid.*, 84, Stanton to Grant, 10:20 A.M., Dec. 7, 1864.
129. *Ibid.*, 84, Grant to Stanton, Dec. 7, 1864.
130. *Ibid.*, 96.
131. *Ibid.*, 96.
132. *Ibid.*, 96.
133. *Ibid.*, 114.
134. *Ibid.*, 97, 114, 115, 116.
135. *Ibid.*, 116, Grant to Halleck 5:30 p.m., Dec. 9.

Meanwhile, that General was keeping Washington informed of the hazardous state of the weather and the impossibility of moving over the icy hills. By the 11th, however, Grant's impatience once more burst out: "If you delay attack longer the mortifying spectacle will be witnessed of a rebel army moving for the Ohio River, and you will be forced to act, accepting such weather as you find. Let there be no further delay. . . . I am in hopes of receiving a dispatch from you today announcing that you have moved. Delay no longer for weather or reenforcements."[136] Of course, Hood's army would slip and slide about on the ice just as much as Thomas's so that nobody was moving, and Thomas was quite aware of the possibility of Hood's heading north. He replied to Grant late on the 11th that he would obey the order promptly "however much I may regret it, as the attack will have to be made under every disadvantage. The whole country is covered with a perfect sheet of ice and sleet, and it is with difficulty the troops are able to move about on level ground. It was my intention to attack Hood as soon as the ice melted, and would have done so yesterday had it not been for the storm."[137] On the 12th, Thomas sent Halleck word that he was ready as soon as the ice melted sufficiently.[138]

But it seemed almost too late, for on December 13 Grant sent orders from City Point that General Logan should proceed immediately to Nashville, reporting by telegraph his arrival at Louisville, and also his arrival at Nashville.[139] Halleck, in a less strenuous way, urged Thomas to act. He replied on the evening of December 14 that, the ice having melted away that day, "the enemy will be attacked tomorrow morning. Much as I regret the apparent delay in attacking the enemy, it could not have been done before with any reasonable hope of success."

Grant himself then rushed up to Washington, bound for Nashville, but he was still in the capital city when he heard the news of the Union success on December 15.[140] Logan stopped at Louisville and went no further. Students must study pages of official dispatches and other material to analyze satisfactorily this seeming crisis in Union command, which was actually but a transiently dramatic episode. The telegrapher David Homer Bates tells us that Grant wrote three orders removing Thomas, and that Lincoln suspended the first, that Logan did not deliver the second because of the attack, and that Eckert suppressed the third.[141] Bates believed that Halleck intensified Grant's doubts respecting Thomas, but the official dispatches indicate rather that Halleck softened the removal order. Bates asserts that the order made out in the

---

136. *Ibid.*, 143, 4 P.M., Dec. 11.
137. *Ibid.*, 143, Dec. 11, 10:30 P.M.
138. *Ibid.*, 155.
139. *Ibid.*, 171.
140. *Ibid.*, 195.
141. Bates, David Homer, *Lincoln in the Telegraph Office*, New York, 1907, 310.

name of the President was not sent because Lincoln halted it. Bates also reports
a conference in the War Department on the evening of December 15 with
Lincoln, Stanton, Grant, and Halleck present. Grant then wrote his third
order although Lincoln and Stanton were opposed. Telegraph director Eckert
delayed sending it more than an hour, and by that time news of the first day's
battle came. Lincoln and Stanton quickly approved Eckert's action.[142]

Lincoln's secretaries emphasize the tension in Washington, adding that
Grant exhibited his impatience much more strongly than the civil authorities.[143] But we must not overlook the second message of Stanton to Grant,
noting that the President "feels solicitous about the disposition of General
Thomas to lay in fortifications for an indefinite period . . ."[144] The secretaries
also criticized Grant for sending Logan west to relieve Thomas and in starting
for Nashville himself.[145] But they recognized that Halleck's delays saved
Thomas for a few vital days.[146] Cavalry commander James Harrison Wilson
writes that Thomas told him with deep emotion on the night of Dec. 10:
"Wilson, they [meaning General Grant and the War Department] treat me as
though I were a boy and incapable of planning a campaign or fighting a battle.
If they will let me alone I will fight this battle just as soon as it can be done,
and will surely win it; but I will not throw the victory away nor sacrifice the
brave men of this army by moving till the thaw begins. I will surrender my
command without a murmur, if they wish it; but I will not act against my
judgment when I know I am right, and in such a grave emergency."[147]

Grant in his *Memoirs* is unduly critical of Thomas, employing such phrases
as: "Thomas made no effort to reinforce Schofield at Franklin . . ." and "Hood
was allowed to move upon Nashville and to invest that place almost without
interference . . ."[148] Neither statement is accurate and both are distortions.
Hood did not "invest" Nashville, the word "allowed" is inaccurate, and how
could Thomas have reinforced Schofield at Franklin when he did not know
that Hood would attack and had already properly ordered Schofield back to
Nashville? The Tennessee capital was the only place for Thomas to organize
and watch and prepare to oppose Hood. Grant admits the weather was bad,
writing, "But I was afraid that the enemy would find means of moving, elude
Thomas and manage to get north of the Cumberland River . . ."[149] Perhaps

142. *Ibid.*, 315-317.
143. Nicolay and Hay, *Lincoln*, X, 23.
144. *O.R.*, I, xlv, pt. 2, 15-16.
145. Nicolay and Hay, *Lincoln*, X, 28.
146. *Ibid.*, 24.
147. Wilson, James Harrison, "The Union Cavalry in the Hood Campaign", *Battles and Leaders*,
IV, 467.
148. Grant, *Memoirs*, II, 379.
149. *Ibid.*, 380.

Hood, as we have said, should have moved north, but Thomas was watching and would have undoubtedly taken action if the Confederates had done so. Grant gives the traditional picture of Thomas's slowness (another distortion at least at Nashville) and he does not mention the orders for Schofield to take over.[150] He does mention sending Logan west and his own going to Washington, and he is very critical of the follow-up after the victory at Nashville. It is difficult to defend Grant in his actions at the time, and even more difficult to justify the comments in the *Memoirs* which were written after a lapse of time sufficient to have provided a clearer recollection of the facts.

Schofield states that no anxiety was felt at Nashville, that Hood's operations were closely watched every day, and that the Federals awaited the attack with confidence. "The anxiety felt elsewhere, especially by General Grant, was probably due to some doubt of the wisdom of Sherman's plan of going off with his main army before disposing of Hood . . . as well as to lack of confidence in General Thomas on account of his well-known deliberation of thought and action. . . ."[151]

The ice was gone on the 15th of December (although the weather was foggy and drizzly, but fairly warm) when the guns boomed out from Fort Negley and other points, awakening the people of Nashville to the fact that a great battle was going on to the south of their city. The Union troops were in line of battle waiting for the offensive to begin. On the Federal left, General James B. Steedman's troops including two brigades of black soldiers advanced against Cheatham, an operation to conceal the real attack which would be on the Confederate left. A reporter found one black warrior who made light of a seeming injury: "Oh, Lor, cannon struck me right on the breast and rolled me over." [152] Steedman's men did well, making the proper simulation of an assault. But the principal action was on the Federal right, where Union troops overlapped the Confederate line on a slanting advance. A.J. Smith's corps moved into position, and by the time the fog lifted, Wilson's cavalry was also ready for battle. The Confederate left was driven back and several redoubts fell. Schofield's corps and then Wilson's cavalry advanced further around Hood's left. Montgomery Hill was captured. Once when the charge seemed to falter, a timely burst of cheering heartened the assailants. "That is the voice of the American people," exclaimed Thomas.[153] About four o'clock in the afternoon,

150. *Ibid.*, 380-382.
151. Schofield, *op.cit.*, 236-237.
152. New York *Herald*, Dec. 22, 1864, dispatch by D.P. Conyngham.
153. Stone, *op.cit.*, 517.

another general charge was made with success, until further progress was halted by the early December darkness. Thomas's plan of attack against the weak Confederate left flank was paying off. Meanwhile, Steedman threatened Hood's right, holding new troops in that quarter.

Hood could have retired, but he did not; he simply withdrew his battered troops into a shorter two-mile position, well entrenched. Meanwhile, Thomas and his generals conferred and determined to continue the conflict.

The 16th was warmer and cloudy, with some gleams of sunlight followed later by showers. The Federal hosts were ready for the fight and moved forward. The plan was much the same, to hit Hood's left, but now the Union army could operate more as a single force, the enemy line being much shorter. In the great assault on Shy's Hill the Federals were more than successful. Beset in front and rear, "the rebels broke out of the works at a bound and ran down the steep hill toward their right and rear as fast as their legs could carry them. It was more like a scene in a spectacular drama than anything in real life. The steep hill, its top crowned with trees through which the enemy's works and movements could be dimly seen, and its sides still green with patches of moist grass—the waving flags, the smoke slowly rising through the leafless branches, the wonderful outburst of musketry, the still more ecstatic cheers, the multitude racing for life, the eager and rapid pursuit—so exciting was it all the lookers-on involuntarily clapped their hands as at a splendid and successful transformation scene; as indeed it was just that, for in those few minutes the whole elaborate structure of the rebellion in the Southwest was utterly overrun by one crash, and even its very foundations destroyed."[154]

As Thomas rode with his staff to the crown of Overton's Hill at the battle's end, he lifted his hat and said, "Oh, what a grand army I have! God bless each member of it."[155] As for the victorious General himself, he had planned well, struck when ready, and struck hard with great skill. Later he was to confess what he called a "grave error of judgment," remarking that at the close of the first day he should have detached a force and sent it round to Hood's rear to cut off his retirement. Had he done so, he might have captured nearly or quite the whole of Hood's army. Instead Hood was enabled to effect his retreat, with the help of Forrest, who made a timely appearance upon the scene, throwing a large body of cavalry westward at the rear of the defeated Confederates, and shielding them from J. H. Wilson's force. Thereafter, Forrest, together with some infantry reinforcements, protected Hood's final retreat to the Tennessee, and his successful crossing of that river on December 27th. The really important charge against Thomas, however, remained that of excessive caution in

154. *Ibid.*, 531.
155. Johnson, Richard W., *Memoir of Maj. Gen. George H. Thomas*, Philadelphia, 1881, 195.

forming a concentration against Hood, with consequent risks to the Union army.[156]

Thomas probably had a force in the field of approximately 50,000, which lost 387 killed, 2,562 wounded, and 112 missing, or total casualties of 3,061. Confederate statistics are much more difficult to ascertain because the demoralization of Hood's army made accurate returns impossible. Hood probably had nearly 23,000 men engaged.[157]

Hood's broken army fled southward in the December darkness. Units were split into fragments, nobody quite sure where they were going. A heavy rain added to the misery and confusion. The night bivouac was sorrowful and painful, but a small semblance of order was restored.

The total character of Hood's defeat has been exaggerated. His army had suffered heavily, and its fighting power was shattered for at least the moment. But the commander, the staff, and part of the manpower were still in the field. Wilson's dismounted cavalry were not in condition or position to pursue the Confederates on the evening of December 16, and not ready for action until the morning of the 17th.

A Confederate effectively described one good reason for the Southern defeat. "We could see the whole line in our front, every move, advance, attack, and retreat. It was magnificent, if our men had only fought. I could see the Capitol all day and the churches. What a grand sight it was! The Yankees had three lines of battle everywhere I could see, and parks of artillery playing upon us and raining shot and shell for eight mortal hours . . ." This mighty force broke and routed the Confederate defenders. " 'Tis impossible to give you any idea of an army frightened and routed. Some brave effort was made to rally the men and make a stand, but all control over them was gone, and they flatly refused to stop, two out of three throwing away their guns, and, indeed, everything that impeded their flight, and fled every man for himself. 'Sauve qui peut' actuated and urged all officers and men, who poured over the fields and hills in wild confusion, all trying to be first towards Franklin."[158]

A few Federals pursued the fugitives down the Franklin Pike on the night of December 16, taking prisoners by whole squads; the darkness, however, prevented more effective pursuit at the moment.[159] In fact, on the 17th, Hood found himself able to march rapidly with the forces he still possessed, unhampered by artillery, wagon trains, or wounded. As they passed safely through

156. Van Horne, Life of Gen. George H. Thomas, op.cit., 344, 345; Formby, John, The American Civil War, London, 1910, 365, 366.

157. Livermore, op.cit., 132-133; O.R., I, xlv, pt. 1, 105, 679.

158. Gale-Polk Papers, So. Hist. Coll., Univ. of N.C. Library, William D. Gale to his wife, Jan. 29, 1865.

159. New York Herald, Dec. 22, 1865.

Franklin behind Wilson's cavalry, Stephen D. Lee's men held off attacks as a rearguard. By nightfall of December 17, they were around Spring Hill, of bitter memory, and on the 18th were concentrating near Columbia, delayed by high water in the streams. But these adverse conditions also impeded the pursuing Federal cavalry and foot-soldiers. By the 19th, Hood was fleeing across the Duck River, rejoined by Forrest, who now furnished cover. The main forces crossed the Tennessee at Bainbridge, December 26-28. The sufferings of the army had been deplorable, but at least a remnant still existed. The heavy rains, more cold, mud in the atrocious roads, added to the difficulties of both sides. Everyone was exhausted. The Federals wisely halted their advance and Hood's sullen army limped on westward through Tuscumbia toward Iuka.[160] The Confederate army concentrated January 3, 1865, at Tupelo, Mississippi. On January 17, Richard Taylor was ordered to replace a now useless Hood, who resigned. As one historian puts it, "The once powerful army of Tennessee was all but a mere memory."[161]

Jacob D. Cox vividly sums up the campaign: "Hood's retreat from Nashville to the Tennessee and Thomas's pursuit were almost equally arduous for their armies, though very different in their effect upon the spirits of the troops. The roads were in horrible condition, even those which had been macadamized being almost impassable. The ordinary country roads were much worse, and after passing Pulaski, till the Tennessee was reached, the wrecks of wagons and carcasses of animals filled the way. . . ."[162] One writer states that the men captured in the battle and pursuit included one major-general, seven brigadier-generals, 14 colonels, and many lesser officers, with more than 8,600 fighting men in all. In engagements preceding Nashville, some 75 field guns, over 60 colors, more than 300 wagons, a thousand mules, and countless amounts of equipment were captured by the Union forces.

[V]

In the view of the government, the Atlantic coast, from Fortress Monroe to Florida, was never really a secondary front, and it was in the news almost constantly. During most of the war the Federals had held a lodgment on the North Carolina coast around Roanoke Island and New Bern. This back door to Virginia had not been sufficiently utilized, but it remained ajar. Now, after Nashville, late in 1864, the time had come for the North to turn belated attention to the last major port of the South open to blockade runners—Wilming-

160. For a good summary, see Hay, *op.cit.*, 171-178.
161. *Ibid.*, 181.
162. Cox, *The March to the Sea, op.cit.*, 124-130.

ton. There was another reason for coastal action. If Sherman was to come north from Savannah and the Georgia coast, he certainly would need help from an operational Federal base at Wilmington.

The key to Wilmington was Fort Fisher, a typical wartime coastal defense, largely of sand, erected on the right or west bank of the Cape Fear River south of Wilmington. From the summer of 1862 until December, 1864, Colonel William Lamb had been strengthening Fort Fisher to the point where he hoped "it could withstand the heaviest fire of any guns in the American Navy...."[163] That he did not make an effective defense was not his fault. He certainly made a gallant effort. The fort had been built with the sole view of receiving naval fire, and it withstood, uninjured except for its armament, two of the fiercest bombardments the world had thus far known.[164]

In the end, Fort Fisher was to fall, like Fort McAllister, to an attack by land. Up to that time it had ably protected Wilmington and the blockade runners, proving that a sand fort was difficult if not impossible for naval guns to destroy completely, while at the same time revealing once more the vulnerability of any fort when attacked by mobile columns. By 1864 Union officers referred to Fort Fisher as the "Malakoff of the South." Strong works supported heavy coast defense guns, though there was no moat with scarp and counterscarp. These defences against storming were nullified by shifting sands. Bomb proofs, magazines, passageways, traverses and other military engineering construction added to the strength of the fort as did land mines across the peninsula and a palisade of sharpened logs, both intended to stave off land assaults.

Slowly the blockade around the mouth of Cape Fear tightened, but despite some 65 captures and destructions of vessels, numerous runners got through. New Inlet, protected by Fort Fisher, soon became the major gateway to the port.

In the fall of 1864, Bragg took over comprehensive command of the North Carolina defense, with General W.H.C. Whiting as second. On the morning of December 20 the Federal fleet was seen off Fort Fisher. The garrison had been cut to not more than 500 men. A severe gale impeded the fleet, however, and by the 23rd reinforcements came in; the defenders now mustered 900 men and boys.

Colonel Lamb reported that on the night of December 23 he was awakened by a gentle sway of his small brick house followed by a slight explosion. No one took it very seriously, on the Confederate side at least.[165] On the 24th,

163. Lamb, William, "Defence of Fort Fisher, North Carolina," *Operations on the Atlantic Coast, 1861-1865,* Vol.IX, Papers of the Military Hist. Soc. of Mass., Boston, 1912, 350. See also: Lamb's article in *Battles and Leaders,* IV, 642-654.
164. *Ibid.,* 350.
165. *Ibid.,* 361.

Porter's great armada approached the fort. His bombardment was soon at thunderous height, the "most terrific bombardment from the fleet," declared Lamb, "which war had ever witnessed."[166] Many Union shots fell in the parade ground without harming the garrison. After two hours the flag was shot away, but despite the rain of shot and shell, no casualties occurred. Damage was slight and by 5:30 the fleet withdrew. The warships had not tried to get inside the bar where they could have taken the fort in reverse. Colonel Lamb estimates the Federals fired 10,000 shot to his 672. Probably never, since the invention of gunpowder, had so much of it been so harmlessly expended as in this first day's attack on Fort Fisher.[167]

On Christmas day, the Yankee fleet moved in to mount another heavy bombardment. Lamb, losing two 7-inch rifles by explosion, maintained a slow, deliberate, economical return-fire. Some quarters were destroyed and earthworks penetrated, but damage remained trivial. By now, Lamb had 1,371 men, including 450 Junior Reserves. Late in the afternoon, a heavy fire against the land-face commenced, and skirmishers advanced upon the fort. Lamb opened upon them with grape and canister. But no real assault was undertaken, and casualties for the day continued light. The Federal landing party avoided capture.

The project of a Union attack upon Wilmington and Fisher had long been considered. Gideon Welles had told Farragut that fall that the Navy Department had desired an amphibious attack on the Cape Fear defences since the winter of 1862, but the Army had refused. Welles believed that Grant was now ready to spare troops and that Farragut could command the naval forces. But Farragut rejected the assignment because of deficient health.[168] Rear-Admiral David Dixon Porter was then given the task, and the command of the North Atlantic Blockading Squadron. Grant named Major General Godfrey Weitzel, one of Butler's officers, to the Army command; but, to the annoyance of Grant and Porter, Butler took over the land forces in person.[169]

Butler had heard of a tremendous accidental explosion near London which had destroyed buildings, and he wished to try such an explosion before Fort Fisher. An old hulk filled with two or three hundred tons of gunpowder would be towed near the fort, run aground, and detonated, and the troops sent ashore without further preparation. Porter finally took the old powder-ship *Louisiana* and exploded her early on the morning of December 24 (about 1:00 A.M.) in one of the most ludicrous fiascoes of the war. "It was terrible," exclaimed one defender later. "It woke up nearly everybody in the fort!" Only a slight shak-

166. *Ibid.*, 362.
167. *Ibid.*, 364-365.
168. Farragut to Welles, no date, Farragut Papers, HEH.
169. King, Capt. Joseph E., *The Fort Fisher Campaigns, 1864-1865*, U.S. Naval Institute Proceedings, August, 1951.

ing was felt on the walls at Fort Fisher. On December 24-25 the naval expedition opened another immense cannonade, and helped land some 2,000 troops. When, on approaching within about fifty yards of the palisades, they were met with a heavy burst of canister, the Yankees withdrew to their lines! Porter tried to get Butler to try again, but he sullenly took his men and sailed northward to Virginia. Grant was chagrined; Washington was mortified. This was Butler's last explosion, however, for on January 7, 1865, he was relieved.[170] Grant told Lincoln on the 28th: "The Wilmington expedition has proven a gross and culpable failure . . ."[171]

The powder-ship experiment had been absurd enough, but Grant and others were more critical of Butler's failure to sustain the assault. In the end, Fort Fisher remained in Confederate hands, and Wilmington was still open to blockade runners. To the Federals, it was clear they could not let this blot on their military-naval record stand. Besides, Wilmington was needed.

Hence, in January, about two weeks after the first expedition had failed, Porter's fleet was again off Fort Fisher, with 8,000 troops under Major General Alfred H. Terry, an unspectacular soldier up to now, but a sound one. On January 13 the bombardment began, and expeditionary forces were landed. On January 14, the attack continued from land and sea, and on January 15 the fort was assaulted and captured. The Army put 4,700 men ashore in entrenchments to watch for an attack by Bragg from the north, or Wilmington. Terry took 3,300 men against Fort Fisher itself. When the land attack was launched in mid-afternoon of January 15, some 400 marines and 1,600 sailors assailed the fort from the beachside, despite heavy fire. The sailors and marines were forced to retreat in disorder, but their charge served as a decoy, and the Federal infantry fought their way into the fort. The combat was hand-to-hand, and fighting continued well into the evening until the Confederates surrendered at ten o'clock. The Union army lost 955 men killed, and about 1,700 wounded or missing. Bragg with 6,000 men to the north did not get involved.[172]

Confederate Colonel Lamb, still in command of the fort, had been aware the Yankees would return. As soon as the lights of the armada were seen, he had prepared for action. Daylight of the 13th had "disclosed the return of the most formidable fleet that ever floated on the sea," shortly raining upon the fort and beach a storm of shot and shell which, he wrote, "caused both earth and sea to tremble." When the naval bombardment ceased, suddenly the steam whistles of the fleet sounded a charge by the Federal army and the sailors and marines. Lamb's men held and repelled the naval force, but shouts of triumph

---

170. King, op.cit., 844-848, Grant's Memoirs, II, 387-395; O.R., I, xlii, pt.3, 1085, Butler to Grant, Dec. 27, 1864.

171. Ibid., 1087; Report of the Joint Committee on Conduct of the War, Vol.II, 1865, Fort Fisher Expedition, 51-56.

172. Battles and Leaders, IV, 661-662.

arose, and Lamb espied Federal flags upon the land-side ramparts. The naval guns continued to aid the Union land attack, driving the defenders from the parapets. The scene in the galleries "was indescribably horrible. Great cannon broke in two, their carriages wrecked, and among their ruins the mutilated bodies of my dead and dying comrades. Still no tidings from Bragg! . . ."[173] Lamb was wounded, but the fight continued until there was nothing to do but surrender.

Bragg was to say that, "To have assaulted the enemy behind his intrenchments, covered by his fleet, with inferior numbers, would have exhausted our means to aid the fort, and thereby not only have insured its ultimate fall, but have opened the country behind it."[174] General William H.C. Whiting, who was mortally wounded, in his report while a prisoner wrote: "I think that the result might have been avoided, and Fort Fisher still held, if the commanding general had done his duty. I charge him with this loss . . ."[175] Bragg had still more to say in his own defense: "Believing myself that Grant's army could not storm and carry the fort if it was defended, I felt perfect confidence that the enemy had assumed a most precarious position, from which he would escape with great difficulty . . ." But "such was the configuration of the country and the obstacles, that he would have accomplished his object with the force he had. Our only safe reliance was in his repulse . . . The defense of the fort ought to have been successful against *this* attack, but it had to fall eventually. The expedition brought against it was able to reduce it in spite of all that I could do. . . ."[176] One naval officer called the Fort Fisher operation and landings the most important and most instructive of the Civil War.[177] Cooperation of a high degree was achieved between Porter and Terry, an important factor.[178]

With the fall of Fort Fisher and the end of Wilmington as a sanctuary for blockade runners, the city itself remained intact, waiting to be opened to the Federals. On January 14, Schofield's Twenty-third Corps was ordered east from Tennessee. Down the Tennessee, up the Ohio, and by rail to Washington and Alexandria, they went, and before February 1st were ready to sail. Bad weather delayed them until February 4 when they were well started.[179] Gales off Hatteras hampered progress, but the new force landed safely at Fort Fisher

173. Lamb, *op.cit.*, 370-382.
174. *O.R.*, I, xlvi, pt. 1, 433.
175. *Ibid.*, 441.
176. Bragg, Braxton, Letter to His Brother, Southern Hist. Soc. Papers, X, 346, Jan. 21, 1865. Terry's report, *O.R.*, I, xlvi, pt. 1, 396-397; Ames, Adelbert, "The Capture of Fort Fisher, Jan. 15, 1865," Papers of the Military Historical Society of Mass., Vol. IX, 402-407.
177. Soley, John C., "The Naval Brigade," Papers of the Mil. Hist. Soc. of Mass., Vol.XII, 247.
178. Harkness, Edson J., "The Expeditions Against Fort Fisher and Wilmington," *Military Essays and Recollections, Illinois Commandary*, Chicago, 1894, II, 163; *O.R.*, I, xlvi, pt. 2, 155-156, Stanton to Lincoln, Fort Monroe, Jan. 17, 1865.
179. Cox, Jacob D., *The March to the Sea, op.cit.*, 147-162.

on February 9, joining Terry's men. The intention was that, after Wilmington surrendered, Schofield would open a route from Wilmington and New Bern to Goldsboro in time to meet Sherman coming north from Savannah. This was a wise plan, reminiscent of Sherman's original idea at Atlanta that he might be met by a force from the coast.

The Union campaign against the city of Wilmington was complicated by the wildness of the area, which included inlets, sands, swamps, ponds, lakes, and numerous other water deposits.[180] Yet the indefatigable General Jacob D. Cox led two brigades on a by-pass, forcing the Confederates to abandon their strong positions. The Union troops moved up both the left and right banks of the Cape Fear River, and despite stubborn opposition the two-pronged Union attack made a steady successful advance. By February 21, the Federals saw huge columns of smoke arising from the city of Wilmington, and on the morning of Washington's birthday, the Northern army entered it. In the long run, however, New Bern proved more valuable as a base for Sherman than Wilmington. Its adjacent harbors were better, and its rail facilities more efficient.

The Confederates had found their defensive efforts fruitless. Once Fort Fisher fell, Wilmington was of little use. One analyst of the evidence believes that the Southern troops should have been evacuated from the city sooner, with all forces concentrated and made available in the Carolinas and Georgia nearer the Savannah River. "Bragg, with the independent command of North Carolina, remained in Wilmington . . . until he was pushed out, frittering away his strength in skirmishes and letting the dry rot of desertion unchecked by vigorous action gnaw into his army, until in a few weeks he had no troops left but Hoke's division and a regiment of cavalry. . . ."[181]

It is doubtful that such concentration against Sherman would have been successful, but certainly it would have been a far more promising military policy than an inert submission to the dissipation of the discouraged, ill-supplied, and more and more desperate Confederate forces that remained. To be sure, a confessed failure to resist Federal invasions would have had its own debilitating effects on the Army and the population. Either way, by February 1865, little hope could be found in the Carolinas except in adherence to the policy of grimly hanging on.

[VI]

The bare statistics of miles marched, days and weeks spent, and men killed and wounded on both sides, convey only a fragmentary and inadequate impression of the great martial feat accomplished by Sherman and his veterans. Long

180. *Ibid.*
181. Hagood, Johnson, *Memoirs of the War of Secession*, Columbia, S.C., 1910, 329-331.

columns of statistics give us only a partial and hazy intimation of the tremendous consequences, some of them physical and material, but others of far larger significance, spiritual and moral, which sprang from this exhibition of national planning, daring, and determination in one of the most spectacular enterprises recorded in the history of modern war. For generations to come, Americans would view the feat with all the accompaniments of color and drama to be found in a great historical narrative by Thucydides, or in a romanticized and poetic canvas by J. M. W. Turner when he was most chromatic and imaginative. They would see again Sherman's serried lines of bayonets and snake-like files of covered wagons, his foam-flecked cavalry pressing southward along the yellow-clay roads, past pine-clad hills, while Atlanta flamed behind them. Their vision would pursue the march as the blue-clad soldiers met ragged battlers in gray, as they moved past forlorn groups of refugees, black and white, male and female, fleeing with bellowing cattle and squealing pigs in front of Yankee squads which fired farmhouses and whole towns as they drove inexorably on—toward the State House of Milledgeville, toward the long bridges which betokened the approach to the seacoast. Accompanying this vision would be the flash of flags flying, the sound of bands playing, or the sullen boom of artillery as a new action was begun against the unpredictable Hood or the dashing Forrest.

The country would never forget Sherman's fierce determination, his repeated demands for total war against a section that he described as "simply one big fort." It would never lose its memory of the grim tenacity of Thomas, the gallant immovability of the "hold-the-fort" course, nor the dash and velocity of Kilpatrick's bodies of cavalry. The march had effected many pragmatic results, but by no means its least gifts were those it had given the American vision and imagination. It had imparted to the sodden, bloody, exhausting and immeasurably depressing conflict some touches of rhetoric, of a grim poetry that would linger in the popular mind of the republic long after the gallant leaders had died, long after the phrase "Sherman's bummers" had lost its undertones of meaning for North and South alike, long after men ceased to feel the thrill that so long nerved millions on hearing the bands strike up clangorously the strains of "Marching Through Georgia."

[VII]

Elsewhere the war continued, but at a much more diminished pace. After the battle of Burgess Mill, October 27, 1864, little movement of any importance was undertaken on the Petersburg front until February. Intermittent sniping took place. Grant and Meade sustained their unwearied pressure. Lee was forced to defend a front of roughly thirty-five miles, from east of Richmond down to Hatcher's Run lying southwest of Petersburg, his effective force reduced to a mere 57,000 men.

On February 5, Meade's men, two corps, moved out toward Hatcher's Run and took the Boydton Plank Road. The Confederates fought back but were unable to dislodge the enemy. Although the road itself proved none too important, the action did extend the Federal line to the west, and once more Lee was forced to defend a longer line, now up to thirty-seven miles. Furthermore, his army was steadily draining away.

In the Shenandoah Valley, Sheridan was reaping the rewards of the October victory at Cedar Creek. There were numerous small raids and actions, and Early had to send a good portion of his troops to Richmond. Late in February, Sheridan left Winchester in the direction of Staunton, forcing Early back to Waynesborough. On March 2, Sheridan easily defeated the mere 1,800 men Early had left at Waynesborough, dispersing and capturing them. Destruction and devastation were rife in the Valley, and Sheridan was free to rejoin Grant at Petersburg.

A great deal had happened in the field since the reëlection of Lincoln in November. Sherman had completed his destructive march across Georgia and taken Savannah. Hood's offensive movement into Tennessee, the last major campaign by any Confederate army, had been frustrated, and his forces no longer required primary consideration. The last principal port for blockade-runners had been closed by capture and occupied, giving the Union an enlarged foothold in North Carolina. The Shenandoah Valley was at last placed completely at the mercy of the North, and Lee's army could not move at Petersburg, but remained stretched out upon a rack that steadily grew more agonizing.

Leadership had shown growing proficiency under Sherman, Thomas, Grant, Schofield, Porter, and Terry. Only once had a high commander really failed—Butler, in the first attempt upon Wilmington. The leadership had profited more and more from the experienced and vigorously supplied body of troops with which it could operate. The North could take the initiative freely now while the Confederacy had to respond. And it was even growing late for any vigorous response. By February it was plain on every front that the springtide would bring more than mild showers and lilacs and breezes.

7

The Second Administration Opens

"IT HAS long been a grave question whether any government, not *too* strong for the liberties of its people, can be strong *enough* to maintain its own existence in great emergencies." The President-elect thus began his response to the jubilant serenade given him by Lincoln and Johnson Clubs of Washington the day after the election of 1864.

He frankly told John Hay, his secretary, that his comments were "not very graceful," adding, "but I am growing old enough not to care much for the manner of doing things." No extempore response by a tired man to an excited audience is likely to be graceful, and Lincoln may well have felt that, after election night, propriety counselled him to speak with modest restraint. He did not attempt to approach the literary achievement of Gettysburg, and with an instinctive sense that he spoke to a nation above and beyond any section, merely refused to sound the strident notes of national triumph or victory that might have wounded many. Indeed, he said just the fitting words with a suitable combination of gravity and sober decorum. He told his hearers and the waiting country that the rebellion had placed the republic under wholly unprecedented tensions, and the presidential contest had added not a little to the strain. Nevertheless, "the election was a necessity. We cannot have free government without elections; and if the rebellion could force us to forego or postpone a national election, it might fairly claim to have already conquered and ruined us." He urged men to study the incidents of the election as examples of human nature and "as philosophy to learn wisdom from," rather than to be corrected or "prevented."

Furthermore, he continued, the election "had demonstrated that a people's government can sustain a national election in the midst of a great civil war." This had not previously been certain. The contest at the polls, added the President, had shaken the country, but "it shows also how *sound*, and how strong we still are." Evidences a-plenty appeared of that strength. And now that the election was over, he asked, "May not all, having a common interest, be re-united in an effort to save our common country?" With three cheers for the soldiers, seamen, and commanders, the brief speech was over. Perhaps Lincoln's ideas were not then sufficiently comprehended; perhaps they have not since been sufficiently studied.[1]

The festive campaign clubs listened in an atmosphere curiously unattuned to so serious a pronouncement as the President's. Gay banners lit with lanterns and transparencies danced over the huge crowd in front of the main entrance of the White House. Cannon roared, bands played, and Tad Lincoln ran from room to room lighting his own "illuminations." As the concourse thickened, a few windows were broken by the sweeping movements of the crowd. When the President did appear, it was many minutes before he could speak. "And then," wrote Noah Brooks, "in all probability the listeners were more entranced with the event they were celebrating than the words of the successful candidate."[2]

The Northern press, for the most part, applauded the victory, though some stubbornly partisan journals accepted the decision reluctantly. The widely read *Harper's Weekly*, for instance, spoke for many when its editor, George William Curtis, declared exultantly: "This result is the proclamation of the American people that they are not conquered; that the rebellion is not successful; and that, deeply as they deplore war and its inevitable suffering and loss, yet they have no choice between war and national ruin, and must therefore fight on. . . . One other of the most significant lessons of the election is that the people are conscious of the power and force of their own Government. . . . Yet the grandest lesson of the result is its vindication of the American system of free popular government. No system in history was ever exposed to such a strain directly along the fibre as that which ours has endured in the war and the political campaign, and no other could possibly have endured it successfully. The result is due to the general intelligence of the people, and to the security of perfectly free discussion. . . . Thank God and the people, we are a nation which comprehends its priceless importance to human progress and civilization, and which recognizes that law is the indispensable condition of Liberty."[3]

The happy military leader, Henry Wager Halleck, in one of his thoughtful letters to Francis Lieber, wrote on November 13, "Besides its general effect upon the country, its effect upon our armies in the field will be most excellent. Had the Marshal of Salt River been elected, the tone of the army would have rapidly changed through the influence of his military partisans, and we should

1. Lincoln, *Collected Works*, VIII, 100-102.
2. Brooks, Noah, "Lincoln's Reelection," *Century*, Vol. XLIX, No.6, Apr. 1895, 866-867.
3. *Harper's Weekly*, Nov. 19, 1864.

have had no more victories under this administration. . . ."[4] In this, he greatly exaggerated McClellan's possible influence.

Yet while the opposition had to lie quiescent perforce for the moment, scattered malcontents and resentful individuals were quick to express disappointment and pessimism over the election. S.L.M. Barlow, for instance, burst out to McClellan, "I see little prospect of anything, but fruitless war, disgraceful peace, and ruinous bankruptcy. . . . The fearful responsibility to be assumed by a President next March, with an empty treasury, a wasted army, and a defiant and apparently ill-united people in rebellion, is enough to appall anyone. . . ." Barlow and perhaps, indeed, McClellan were relieved that the general did not have to accept what Barlow termed a burden "greater than ever before borne by any man. . . ."[5]

Manton Marble, editor of the Democratic *World*, wrote McClellan, "I never have despaired of a constitutional restoration of things at the South; the election shows that we had more reason to despair of a constitutional restoration of things at the North. The coming calamities will teach even the North their bitter lessons; suffering pierces at last the most obdurate heart and finds some secret access at length to the most pervert understanding . . . the North in its secret soul is still stubborn and stiff—in its refusal of constitutional right to those who saw its temper and sought a lawless and wicked remedy, therefore the time is not ripe for our success. . . . We must never despair of the Republic; yet how impossible it is to hope. . . ."[6]

To a sympathetic friend in Washington, T. J. Barnett, Barlow declared that though the President's words had sometimes been smooth, no proof existed that Lincoln would be anything but "a radical fanatic." Barlow predicted that the results of the election would enable the Confederates to unite and "divide the people of the North as they have never been divided since the war began."[7]

In the capital of the Confederacy, press comment following the election was about what well-informed men expected. After all, Lincoln's re-election proclaimed with thunderous emphasis that the policies of the Northern government would remain adamant. Any misty expectation that he might give way to a new President vanished. All the heady dreams of a friendly armistice or of some vague arrangement for putting Southern independence into a magic pill that credulous Yankees might swallow in a coma, vanished. The Richmond *Sentinel*, as noted earlier, acknowledged the realities confronting the Southern people when it raised a Pecksniffian lament that ". . . perhaps this, also, is for

4. Lieber Papers, HEH.
5. Barlow to McClellan, Nov. 9, 1864, Barlow Papers, HEH.
6. Marble to McClellan, Nov. 13, 1864, Manton Marble Papers, LC.
7. Barlow to Barnett, Nov. 15, 1864, Barlow Papers, HEH.

our good. It deepens and widens the gulf between us, and renders our success more certain by rendering failure more dreadful and intolerable. Every charred homestead is a fresh warning to our people that they must never be conquered, but must rather fight forever. . . ."[8]

The Richmond *Dispatch* was still more hypocritically abusive: "What other men on the habitable globe would have chosen an ignorant and vulgar backwoods pettifogger for their Chief Magistrate: or having incurred the loss of the richest portion of their territory, more than a million of men, and two billions of money, in penalty of their folly, would have worked for his re-election with every energy of soul and body? What other men would expect anything else from another four year's experiment but a double amount of debt and dead men! What other men would find occasion for thanksgiving in such a past and such a future! . . ."[9] The *Dispatch* also pretended to think that the danger would have been greater to the Confederacy had McClellan been elected: "He would have insisted on conducting the war in a spirit more humane and more nearly approaching the rules recognized and binding among Christian and civilized communities."[10]

Such a perceptive Confederate as Josiah Gorgas saw the bitter truth, and exclaimed, "Lincoln has been reëlected President of the United States by overwhelming majorities. There is no use in disguising the fact that our subjugation is popular at the North, and that the War must go on until this hope is crushed out and replaced by desire for peace at any cost."[11] Robert Kean of the Confederate War Department, to his credit, made an honest entry in his diary. "The Yankee election," he wrote, "was evidently a damper on the spirits of many of our people, and is said to have depressed the army a good deal. Lincoln's triumph was more complete than most of us expected."[12] The rebel war-clerk Jones also admitted, "This makes many of our croaking people despondent. . . . The large majorities for Lincoln in the United States clearly indicate a purpose to make renewed efforts to accomplish our destruction."[13]

While he felt obvious personal satisfaction over his re-election, Lincoln continued to pursue his routine tasks unemotionally, following his laborious daily round of interviews, correspondence, and frequent inquiries respecting military and naval progress, and exchanges with the South. Many of the

8. Richmond *Sentinel*, Nov. 12, 1864, Virginia State Library.
9. Richmond *Dispatch*, Nov. 10, 1864, Virginia State Library.
10. *Ibid.*
11. Gorgas, Josiah, *Civil War Diary*, ed. Frank E. Vandiver, University, Alabama, 1947, entry of Nov. 17, 1864, 150.
12. Kean, Robert Garlick Hill, *Inside the Confederate Government*, ed. Edward Younger, New York, 1957, 177, Nov. 20, 1864.
13. Jones, John B., *A Rebel War Clerk's Diary*, ed. Earl Schenck Miers, New York, 1958, 448, Nov. 14, 15, 1864.

applications made to him had political as well as military and economic undertones, while other interruptions might be regarded as trivial. For instance, the
day after election, Lincoln sent Secretary Stanton a request that Ella E. Gibson
be appointed Chaplain of the First Wisconsin Heavy Artillery; but, perhaps
wisely, because of her sex, Stanton rejected the proposal.[14]

At the first Cabinet meeting after the election, on November 11, the President did astonish his associates. In the midst of the Presidential campaign, on
August 23, he had asked Cabinet members to sign a document which they had
not read, and which had since remained sealed. "Gentlemen," he asked, "do
you remember last summer I asked you all to sign your names to the back of
a paper of which I did not show you the inside? This is it. Now, Mr. Hay, see
if you can get this open without tearing it." Lincoln then read the memorandum.

"This morning, as for some days past, it seems exceedingly probable that
this Administration will not be reëlected. Then it will be my duty to so
cooperate with the President-elect as to save the Union between the election
and the inauguration; as he will have secured the election on such grounds that
he cannot possibly save it afterward." This incident shows not only the despondency of the President for a time regarding his re-election, but also his
conviction that the Democrats and McClellan, pursuing their probable policies
after election day, could not or would not win the war.[15]

At the meeting on November 11, the President remarked, after reading the
memorandum, "You will remember that this was written at a time six days
before the Chicago nominating Convention, when as yet we had no adversary,
and seemed to have no friends. . . ." He added that he had resolved, if McClellan
were elected, to see him and talk things over and try to reach an agreement
on a policy intended to bring a rapid termination of the war. Seward caustically interposed: "And the General would answer you 'Yes, Yes'; and the next
day when you saw him again and pressed these views upon him, he would say,
'Yes, Yes'; and so on forever, and would have done nothing at all." Lincoln,
however, retorted: "At least, I should have done my duty, and have stood clear
before my own conscience. . . ."[16] Probably we shall never know whether
additional facts going beyond the limited information which this account
provides were then revealed. Although there is clear evidence that in August,
1864, Lincoln did entertain grave doubts about the election, many people will
still ask what was the precise character of these doubts, and how deep was his

14. Lincoln, *Collected Works*, VIII, 102-103; for day-to-day activities a useful summary is presented
in Miers, E.S., *Lincoln Day by Day; A Chronology*, Washington, D.C., 1960.

15. Hay, John, *Lincoln and the Civil War in the Diaries and Letters of John Hay*, ed. Tyler Dennett,
New York, 1939, 237; Lincoln, *Collected Works*, VII, 514.

16. Hay, *op.cit.*, 237-238.

apprehension that he would not be elected, and how seriously did he fear that the policies of his successor would involve the defeat of the Union and the ruin of its previous constitutional principles.

Amid all the excitement of the election and its results, the routine occupations and duties of life continued in Washington, on the battle fronts, and at home. As November waned, Sherman, as we have seen, had begun his thrust into the half mysterious terrain from Atlanta to the sea; Hood's Confederate Army of Tennessee was moving northward into Tennessee; and Grant was still stubbornly gripping Lee's forces before Richmond and Petersburg. In the Trans-Mississippi area, operations had become quieter after the October defeat of Sterling Price at Westport, Missouri. Troops exchanged shots and fought minor engagements all along the Army fronts, while the blockade tightened its silent but deadly hold upon the Gulf and Atlantic coasts of the Confederacy.

In Northern homes the majority of the war-worn people could glimpse more and more tokens of hope. The wistful longing that throbbed in the bars of "When This Cruel War Is Over," seemed ever closer to fulfillment. More and more confidently the press, politicians and people began discussing the great practical questions of the future. What new course would public and private life follow after the silencing of the guns and bugles? Might the war possibly go beyond the summer of 1865? Mr. Lincoln, now elected for four more years, had been the patient, sagacious leader in war. What would he do to meet the even more perplexing problems of peace?

[I]

As congratulations upon the election came to Washington, there came also a communication from General McClellan. He was resigning from the army! While a decision undoubtedly motivated by a feeling of defeat, pique and purely personal chagrin, the resignation, accepted November 14, did at least remove the controversial Democratic leader from the public scene. McClellan spent the next three years abroad, quite aloof from the political and military conflicts in which he had so conspicuously been a participant. In 1878, he was elected governor of New Jersey, but he never again assumed the stature of a national figure. His polemical and defensive memoirs, *McClellan's Own Story*, published after his death, provoked a controversial renewal of various old disputes which have never quite died,[17] but the man himself remained impotent and, ere many years, became totally disregarded.

17. The literature, all of it exuding heat both for and against McClellan, is vast and continuing. A full unbiassed biography is badly needed.

On November 21, in the course of his usual attention to individual matters, the President wrote a letter to a Mrs. Lydia Bixby which was printed in the Boston *Transcript* of November 25, 1864, a beautiful tribute to the mother of five sons "who have died gloriously on the field of battle." Celebrated thereafter, reprinted and anthologized as the Bixby letter, the manuscript original has never been found. Some historians have conjectured that John Hay may have written this miniature masterpiece, while others maintain that it is Lincoln's own, and forged facsimiles have continued to be numerous. It may be noted that Lincoln was given inaccurate information regarding Mrs. Bixby's sons by the Adjutant General's Office. Two sons only were killed, another was captured and reported to have deserted to the enemy, a fourth was listed as a deserter, and the fifth was honorably discharged December 17, 1864, after this letter was written. But even the official records are not completely certain. The whole matter has been blown up into a mystery of Lincolniana.[18]

Re-election would also require readjustments in the cast of characters, both major and secondary. The Chief Justiceship had been an object of fervent competition among men and parties since the death of Roger Taney in mid-October. Several Cabinet posts would undoubtedly be open; lesser posts would be available as well; and a new flood of office-seekers would base their claims on tasks performed or assertedly performed during the recent campaign.

Since the opening of the Lincoln Administration in 1861, four of the seven Cabinet positions had changed hands; only Secretary of State Seward, Secretary of the Navy Welles, and Attorney-General Bates remained. The incompetent Cameron, the colorless Caleb Smith, the ambitious Chase and the contriving, though astute, Montgomery Blair were gone. Now it was time for the conservative Missouri lawyer Bates to step down. Long a target of the Radicals, accused then and later of being stuffy and pedestrian, Bates had brought a following to the Administration, and had shown himself to be a solid bulwark of Union policies and of social justice in the Cabinet, particularly during the early years of the war. Slowly his influence had lessened, and Bates had, himself, felt unhappy in opposing some of the Administration's policies. He had never been congenial with Stanton, Seward, or Chase. Back home in Missouri, the political struggles of State factions, won eventually by the Radicals, had undermined his prestige and influence. Government by sound legal principles, as he conceived them, had been for Bates an unchanging ideal, a difficult ideal to pursue.[19]

18. Bullard, F. Lauriston, *Abraham Lincoln and the Widow Bixby*, New Brunswick, N.J., 1946, *passim.*

19. Cain, Marvin R., *Lincoln's Attorney-General, Edward Bates of Missouri*, Columbia, Mo., 1965, is the only modern biography of this neglected public figure.

Dejected over the course which plans for Reconstruction were following, and believing the Radicals were gaining an unfortunate control in the nation, Bates had indicated to the President early in October his desire to resign. Upon the death of Chief Justice Taney, he sent Lincoln a request for appointment to the post. Nothing came of this application, for Bates was no longer close to the President. By November 1, he had determined to leave, and on the 24th, sent a formal letter of resignation to Lincoln, quitting his office December 1.[20]

Seeking an able attorney to replace him, the President asked Judge-Advocate-General Joseph Holt, a former member of Buchanan's cabinet, to take his place as Attorney-General. Holt refused in a letter of November 30,[21] and suggested the appointment of James Speed of Kentucky. Lincoln therefore telegraphed Speed on December 1: "I appoint you to be Attorney-General. Please come on at once." Speed promptly arrived.[22] From the same western State as Holt, Speed had been prominent in politics and law and had turned into a strong Lincoln supporter after (in 1861) favoring the Union though anxious to avoid war. Speed, a brother of the President's close friend Joshua Fry Speed, who had often advised Lincoln on Kentucky affairs, was deemed a worthy successor to Bates. In the Johnson Administration, he soon fell out with the new President and moved closer and closer to the Radicals, until he stood in violent opposition to Johnson and became a leader of the Kentucky Radicals. By appointing him to office, the President kept a Cabinet seat for a western Border State man, border politics being never far from his attention.

The cardinal question was that of the next Chief Justice of the United States. Although the decision to appoint Chase has been already discussed in Chapter 5, it will be reviewed here more particularly from the point of view of Lincoln's reasons for making the appointment. Taney had died October 12, but Lincoln had waited until after the election to name a successor. The list of those who sought the post, or had friends urging their elevation, was formidable. The former Treasury Secretary, Chase, cherished ambitions from the outset, even before Taney's death. Attorney-General Bates had forthrightly and promptly asked for the appointment. Two justices, Noah H. Swayne and Lincoln's close Illinois friend David Davis, were seriously considered. Other men duly scrutinized were Postmaster-General Dennison, Secretary Stanton, Judge William Strong of Pennsylvania, and the eloquent attorney, William M. Evarts. The Blair family was urging the President not to overlook former Postmaster-General Montgomery Blair. The vacancy occurred as the Presi-

20. Summation and details in Cain, op.cit., 310-315. Also see Robert Todd Lincoln Papers, LC, Bates to Lincoln, Nov. 24, 1864; Bates, Edward, Diary, ed. Howard K. Beale, Washington, 1933, 428.
21. Robert Todd Lincoln Papers, LC, Nov. 30, 1864.
22. Lincoln, Works, VIII, 126-127.

dential contest coincided with the last phases of war, and the opening of the struggle over Reconstruction. It was therefore regarded in a partisan rather than a judicial or really national light.[23]

We have some evidence (although secondhand) confirming the supposition that the President had thought of naming Chase as Chief Justice some time before Taney's death. According to Orville H. Browning, Secretary of the Treasury Fessenden told him on the morning after Taney died that he knew the post would be Chase's. Fessenden tells us that after Chase resigned, Lincoln refused to reinstate him in the Cabinet despite Fessenden's plea that he do so. Lincoln spoke of his respect for Chase, adding that if the Chief Justiceship was now vacant, he would appoint him to that place.[24] When, a few days later, Browning called on Mrs. Stanton, she asked him to see the President about naming the Secretary of War as Chief Justice. Browning wrote in his diary that he feared the appointment of Chase, and was anxious to prevent it.[25]

Chase himself recorded in his diary at the end of June that the President had spoken of intending to appoint him Chief Justice if a vacancy occurred. Chase had learned this from Congressman Samuel Hooper of Massachusetts, who received the intelligence from Lincoln in the midst of the Cabinet crisis.[26]

Thus, it seems that by the middle of 1864, Chase was the foremost candidate for Chief Justice, while all Washington was engaging in a political death-vigil over Taney. And Lincoln's comments upon the matter had certainly not been kept secret. The scramble of various men to seize the position at the time of Taney's death was inspired both by personal ambition and by a desire to keep Chase out of an office which was certain to be powerful during Reconstruction and later. Montgomery Blair's activities can be attributed without question to his wish to keep the conservatives stronger than the Radicals.

Hard upon the demise of the old Chief Justice, Sumner led the Radical movement in behalf of Chase. He immediately wrote Lincoln an argument for Chase's appointment.[27] It may be asked why, if Chase had had assurances in mid-1864 from the President, did he take part in the late-summer plotting to overturn Mr. Lincoln as a Presidential candidate. To be sure, Taney was still alive, and the Radicals might turn to Chase to replace Lincoln. It could be that

---

23. Little primary research has been done upon the true motives of Lincoln in making the appointment, or the pressures exerted upon him. Estimable secondary narratives include Randall, J.G., and Richard N. Current, *Lincoln the President, Last Full Measure*, 270-276; Carman, Harry J., and Reinhard H. Luthin, *Lincoln and the Patronage*, New York, 1943, 315-320; and Silver, David M., *The Supreme Court During the Civil War*, Urbana, 1956, *passim*.

24. Browning, Orville Hickman, *Diary*, ed. Theodore Calvin Pease, Springfield, Ill., 1925, 686-687.

25. *Ibid.*, 687-688.

26. Schuckers, J.W., *The Life and Public Services of Salmon Portland Chase*, New York, 1874, 509-510. Also, Hay, *Lincoln and the Civil War*, 203.

27. Robert Todd Lincoln Papers, LC, Sumner to Lincoln, Oct. 12, 1864.

Chase was simply playing all horses, or that the rumors of his becoming Chief Justice were exaggerated. A few days later, the President let Chase know through Fessenden that, while he had not forgotten what he had earlier said, he thought it best to delay action until after the election.[28] Chase, meanwhile, was campaigning in Ohio for Lincoln. Whether this helped him gain the appointment is uncertain, but it certainly did him no injury; indeed, rumors of a bargain soon cropped out, although no specific evidence of one has been found. After the election, Sumner and other Radicals evinced pique over the delay.

How inevitable was the appointment, and how nearly had it ever been certain? We can never know, for the secret lay with the President. Gideon Welles was not sure that Chase would obtain the place—but then, Welles did not always possess authentic information. As of November 26, he wrote: "I have not much idea that the President will appoint him, nor is it advisable that he should." Lincoln had told Welles that he would delay a choice until Congress met, and he also spoke of Evarts. Welles, who vainly championed Montgomery Blair, wrote of the "host of candidates."[29] He concluded that Chase would obtain the post, although he confided to his diary a wry comment on the possibility: "The President sometimes does strange things, but this would be a singular mistake, in my opinion, for one who is so shrewd and honest,—an appointment that he would soon regret. . . ."

On the same day that his message went to Congress, Lincoln sent a two-line nomination of Chase to the Senate, where he was at once and unanimously confirmed.[30] Welles reported that not a word had been spoken in the Cabinet about it. He continued to feel "apprehensions" about the appointment of Chase, and feared that the man would use it for "political advantage." He set down a caustic estimate of Chase, pronouncing him "selfishly stubborn at times, and wanting in moral courage and frankness, fond of adulation, and, with official superiors, inclined to play the sycophant."[31]

Historians may still inquire why Lincoln selected Chase. Did he have some perception that Chase would, as he did, make a more than distinguished record in the post? Did he feel the Radicals needed appeasing? Was this selection part of the old manoeuvre, used so often and so effectively to reward and keep in official posts those who had been replaced or those who might be more troublesome as political enemies, if kept outside of the government? The answers elude us.

28. Randall-Current, *op.cit.*, 271, from Fessenden to Chase, Oct. 20, 1864, Chase Mss., Historical Society of Pennsylvania.
29. Welles, *Diary*, II, 181-184.
30. Lincoln, *Collected Works*, VIII, 154.
31. Welles, *Diary*, II, 192-193.

According to Congressman George S. Boutwell, of Massachusetts (a Radical), Lincoln appointed Chase because he was a prominent leader with impressive backing, because he would uphold the Administration, and because the office required a man whose opinions were known. Furthermore, although Lincoln realized that the former Secretary of the Treasury nursed most irritating and discreditable ambitions to grasp the Presidency, this did not prevent the appointment.[32] Lincoln might have felt that the appointment would put an end to such ambitions. However, it did not.

Other men possessed high qualifications, equalling Chase's by Lincoln's severe standards. Blair, in particular, had great gifts and merits, but his appointment to the Chief Justiceship would have produced a revolt among the Radicals. Lincoln had given this important subject careful study, had patiently considered the rivalries of the men who guessed, contrived, and schemed, had waited until their emotions and appetites cooled, and had at last named the man most acceptable to the Radical Republicans. Who can doubt that once more Lincoln had exhibited consummate political skill, and in the end had given the country a Chief Justice whom history would accord high rank as a jurist and statesman.

He had again proved, moreover, his majestic qualities of balance. His annual message, which comprehended much of his legislative programme for 1865 on controversial and sensitive subjects, received more patient attention from the Radicals than would otherwise have been accorded it. As might be expected, the abolitionist voice of Henry Ward Beecher was raised in the New York *Independent*, expressing raptures over the naming of Chase.[33] A voice from the past even approved. In a private letter, James Buchanan, rusticating at Wheatland near Lancaster, Pa., wrote: "I think Mr. Lincoln made the best selection from his party for the office of Chief Justice. Mr. Chase is a gentleman; and although extreme in his views on the abolition question, I have no doubt he will worthily fill the place of his eminent predecessors. . . ."[34]

The second session of the Thirty-eighth Congress met in Washington on December 5, 1864—the same Congress that had witnessed the rise of Radical antagonism to Lincoln, that still held a little anti-war group, along with many supporters of the President. The election could not prevent the gathering of this rather out-of-date assemblage. The new Congress would not meet until the following December, more than a year after election, unless called in special session. This new Congress would have a heavily preponderant majority of Republicans and Unionists, two-thirds of the members. Meanwhile, results of

32. Boutwell, George S., *Reminiscences*, II, 29.
33. New York *Independent*, Dec. 15, 1864, E.B. Long Collection, Oak Park, Ill.
34. Buchanan Papers, Hist. Soc. of Penn., Philadelphia, Buchanan to Joseph C. G. Kennedy, Dec. 23, 1864.

the election in November, 1864, would certainly be felt, albeit indirectly, in the fresh session of the old Congress, now beginning.

As was customary, the President's Secretary, this time John G. Nicolay, appeared before the Senate and the House (separately) on December 6th, to deliver the written Presidential message. It was a longer and more factual message than Lincoln usually wrote, devoid of the inspiring and thoughtful passages of his greater documents. Nevertheless, the message expressed his firmness of purpose, fixity of policy, comprehension of the profound importance of the long-continued struggle for the Union. These all-important aspects of the document were only partially concealed by the fact that the President plunged at once into a rehearsal, not of the state of the war or wartime policies, but of foreign affairs which he termed "reasonably satisfactory." Relations with Mexico, Costa Rica, Nicaragua, Colombia, Venezuela, Peru, Chile, all received treatment. In every instance, except the comment on Mexico, the exposition dealt with matters of distinctly secondary or tertiary importance. Lincoln then turned to Liberia, and to the proposed overland telegraph between America and Europe by way of the Bering Straits. Covering developments the world over, he even discussed at length affairs in Egypt, China, and Japan.

After this rather dull review, Lincoln turned to trade, mentioning that Norfolk, Fernandina, and Pensacola had been opened as ports by proclamation November 19, and that it was hoped foreign merchants would trade there to avoid the blockade. Because of the series of disturbances on the Canadian line, and particularly the raid upon St. Albans, Vermont, by Confederates in October, the President felt constrained to notify Canada that it would be necessary to increase naval armaments on the Great Lakes, although this, by no means, implied any unfriendliness towards Canadians.

Turning to finances, the President said that they had been so successfully administered that on July 1, 1864, the Treasury balance reached $96,739,905.73. The War Department was spending $690,791,842.97, while the Navy was costing $85,723,292.77. This came out to well over two million dollars a day in Federal operating expenditures. The public debt was $1,740,690,489.49, and was undoubtedly increasing. He asked Congress to turn its attention to increased taxation, but made no specific recommendations. By November 25, the United States had 584 national banks, and the President found that the system was proving acceptable to capitalists and to the people.

As usual the reports of the various secretaries were submitted as accompanying documents. Lincoln gave special attention to the Navy, however, outlining the great increase in the number of vessels, praising their construction, and in general paying tribute to the efficiency of naval operations.

It was noteworthy, he wrote, that the steady expansion of population, improvement and governmental institutions over the unoccupied new parts of the country had scarcely been arrested, much less impeded or halted by the war, which at first glance might seem to have absorbed almost the entire energies of the nation. As was being proved in many fields, the Federal Union could fight a civil war while the normal progress of social and economic life was largely maintained. The message touched on the Western States and territories, public lands, the transcontinental railroad, noted discoveries of precious metals, recommended revision of the Indian Administration, a grant of pensions to invalid soldiers and sailors with their families, and the work of the new Agriculture Department.

Somewhat lost in the laconic array of facts was a statement that, despite economy of words, displayed a strength that proved well for the years to come. "The war," said Lincoln, "continues."

The advance of the Federal armies did not have to be recorded in detail, but the President happily declared that the liberation of Missouri, Kentucky, Tennessee, and other areas, gave the promise of fair crops. He called the "attempted march" of Sherman from Atlanta to the sea "the most remarkable feature of the military operations" but did not mention Grant's campaign to the gates of Richmond. Two brief paragraphs were all that were devoted to the land military operations!

The strongest emphasis in the message was in the last pages dealing with "important movements (that) have also occurred during the year, to the effect of moulding society for durability in the Union." He emphasized, in this regard, the organization of loyal State governments in Louisiana and Arkansas, and similar movements in Missouri, Kentucky and Tennessee. He held up Maryland as the happiest example of all, now "secure to Liberty and Union for all the future."

The crux of the policy for the future, however, was the "proposed amendment of the Constitution abolishing slavery throughout the United States." He pointed out that the amendment had passed the Senate but failed of the two-thirds needed in the House. Even though this was the same Congress, the President said he recommended reconsideration and passage of the measure at the current session, stating that while the abstract question had not changed, the election had decisively shown that the new Congress would pass the measure. "And, as it is to so go," he asked, "may we not agree that the sooner the better?" He reasserted that the voice of the people, as expressed in the election, had unmistakably declared for passage of the amendment.

Even the opposition, he urged, had not been in favor of giving up the Union. And so, although means and modes of action had been argued with

The Union Army Entering Richmond

heat, the election had been of tremendous value in proving once and for all that no popular division existed on the issue of union or disunion.

Coming back to the theme of Western advance, Lincoln found that the recent political campaign had taught people the enormous importance of the fact that America had not been drained of its most important resource—manpower. While the grave and casualty lists had been melancholy, indeed, "it is some relief to know that, compared with the surviving, the fallen have been so few." The soldier vote had proved that the nation had more men in 1861 than in 1865; that we were not exhausted, "nor in the process of exhaustion; that we were *gaining* strength," and might, if necessary, maintain the contest indefinitely. Material resources, too, he believed, were "more complete and abundant than ever," even inexhaustible. Only the manner of continuing the national effort remained to be chosen.

The President specified some of the courses desirable, and some he then rejected. For instance, he wrote, "no attempt at negotiation with the insurgent leader could result in any good," (although within two months he would try such negotiations at Hampton Roads), for nothing less than severance of the Union would satisfy the Southern leader—"precisely what we will not and cannot give. . . . He cannot voluntarily reaccept the Union; we cannot voluntarily yield it." This issue was "distinct, simple and inflexible."

But while the Southerners in revolt could not yield, wrote Lincoln, "some of them, we know, already desire peace and reunion." He hoped this number would increase and said, "They can, at any moment, have peace simply . . . by laying down their arms and submitting to the national authority under the Constitution." If any questions remained, they should be adjusted by legislation, conferences, courts and votes. In view of the bitter realities, this idea seems naïve. However, the President did admit that some questions such as admission of members to Congress or appropriation of money would not be for him to decide; indeed, he foresaw that executive power would be "greatly diminished by the cession of actual war." Pardons and remissions of forfeitures would remain within Presidential power, nonetheless, and the temper controlling the exercise of this power might be fairly adjudged by past history. The difficulty was that, although Lincoln regarded past policies as lenient, the people of the South did not!

The door of general pardon and amnesty had been open for a year. "It is still so open to all," stated the President. "But the time may come—probably will come—when public duty shall demand that it be closed; and that, in lieu, more rigorous measures than heretofore shall be adopted." In declaring that abandonment of armed resistance was the only indispensable condition to ending the war, Lincoln added, "I retract nothing heretofore said as to slavery." He would plainly maintain the Emancipation Proclamation and the Acts of Congress. And, in conclusion, he mildly stated that the government's peace condition was simple: ". . . the war will cease on the part of the government, whenever it shall have ceased on the part of those who began it."[35]

No comprehensive new policy was defined in the speech, which rather combined a somewhat curious recital of the state of the Union with some indications of future action. That Lincoln keenly desired to incorporate the Thirteenth Amendment in the Constitution was no secret, but he now made it absolutely clear. The extinction of slavery in the United States had not been in doubt for some time, but it was well to have it once more made a fundamental object. The plan of appealing to influential individuals and groups in the South, rather than to the oldtime Confederate leaders, had also been given careful trial for a year. The threat of ending the period of moderation in the South was now given firmer statement. All those loyal to Confederate ideas and authority were still summoned by Lincoln to absolute surrender. His emphasis upon foreign relations at a time when such relations were in no critical state, struck some as odd, but was perhaps useful in warning Paris and Madrid to be watchful. The attention he gave to westward development encouraged many people by reminding them of our untapped wealth, and drew the attention of others to the organization of railroads, mining ventures, and cattle-ranching; it was also a refreshing diversion from political squabbles and sectional dissensions.

Open Confederate comment on the message was what might be expected. The Richmond *Dispatch* noted that Southerners, determined to have peace on any terms, must now realize that they could have it only by unconditional submission. The editor tried some feeble sarcasm. If they so yielded, people without a record of active disloyalty would be allowed to breathe, but after acquiescing in all the legislation of the Yankee Congress and proclamations of President Lincoln, they would be left no property of any kind whatever. "Their estates, real and personal,—the whole vast territory of the Confederate States has been declared confiscated, and Congress is called on to abolish slavery. . . ."[36] The Richmond *Sentinel* took the same attitude, angrily telling peacemen that they faced "absolute, unqualified submission, to be followed by spoliation of our property and the Africanization of our country, all this superciliously laid down as the only terms of 'peace' . . ."[37]

The rebel Chief of Ordnance, Gorgas, felt much the same, "Lincoln's

35. Lincoln, *Works*, VIII, 136-152.
36. Richmond *Dispatch*, Dec. 10, 1864, Virginia State Library.
37. Richmond *Sentinel*, Dec. 10, 1864, Virginia State Library.

message spawns nothing but subjugation."[38] War-clerk Jones recorded that "President Lincoln's message to the Congress . . . produced no marked effect. His adherence to a purpose of emancipation of the slaves, and his employment of them in his armies, will suffice for an indefinite prolongation of the war, and perhaps result in the employment of hundreds of thousands of slaves in our armies. The intimation, however, that all applications for 'pardon,' etc., have been and are still favorably entertained, will certainly cause some of our croakers who fall into the lines of the United States forces to submit . . ."[39]

On the Union side, *Harper's Weekly* was enthusiastic about the message, terming it a "calm, simple, concise statement of public affairs—this firm, manly expression of the noblest national aspiration for equal justice. . . . The prospects of peace as set forth by the President are exactly what every faithful citizen supposed them to be. When the men who began this war upon the Government lay down arms, and yield to the Constitution and the laws and acts in accordance with it, the war will end. . . ."[40] Seward found the statement of the President "generally satisfactory."[41]

In the House, however, a long debate arose over the message. Representative James Brooks of New York brought up the subject on December 14 in true Copperhead vein, by denouncing Lincoln's policies and making Biblical references to the tolerance of slavery. When George S. Boutwell of Massachusetts interrupted him, asking if he really understood that the institution of slavery was dead, Brooks replied, "Why should you try to kill a dead body?" In a customarily tart retort, Thaddeus Stevens drily advised him, "we ought to bury it lest it become noxious." Brooks, by now ferocious, cried: "The whole country has become intoxicated on this subject of slavery, and in the midst of the intoxication, this civil war is kept up. . . . Centralization and consolidation is nothing but unlimited despotism. There is no freedom for the people, no self-government, no municipal government, no household government, under such a system."[42]

Representative Hiram Price of Iowa thought that the entire aim and intent of Brooks's speech and the desire of the man himself were to aid the enemies of our country. Amos Myers of Pennsylvania hotly declared: "We are told that we must have an armistice, negotiation, must exhaust all the arts of statesmanship and have a national convention. Sir, we *have* peace Commissioners. They are Grant, Sherman, Sheridan, Thomas, and Farragut. We have our national convention, and the delegates to it are the invincible soldiers and sailors of the

38. Gorgas, *Diary, op.cit.*, 155.
39. Jones, *A Rebel War Clerk's Diary, op.cit.*, 458.
40. *Harper's Weekly*, Dec. 24, 1864.
41. Seward, Frederick W., *Seward at Washington*, III, 253.
42. *Congressional Globe*, Second Session, 38th Cong., Pt.I, 38, 39, 42.

Union, clothed in the royal purple of the nation, the Union blues; and they are now debating that question. . . ." Debate followed on the issue of calling a national convention and setting up an armistice. For the moment, it was obvious that argument would be the order of the hour. The issues were too deep, too intertwined with personal ambition and politics to permit agreement.

[II]

For approximately two years, the Emancipation Proclamation had been in effect; for two-and-a-half years the Second Confiscation Act had been a law. Other measures had contributed to the disintegration of slavery, yet the issue as a permanent national question had not been met! It could not be met clearly except by means of a constitutional amendment. The slavery issue was so completely involved with the fabric of the war in all its phases that it was almost a sentient part of it. At the same time, extending above and beyond the war itself, and far beyond slavery, was the question of what to do about the Negro. But perhaps, as many thought at the time, the truly supreme issue was that of local government versus Federal. Desirable as the end of slavery might be to many, what would a constitutional amendment do to the rights of States, local governments and the people? Could the Federal Union rule on property, could it intrude into the field of social reform? What was done about all this, or was not done, would clearly decide the principles of national action for long decades to come.

It was an issue not properly to be decided in the heat of a Civil War, nor with an eye to partisan politics and personal gain, nor in the give-and-take of economic life, but on the loftier level of philosophic principle. Few men considered it in that light.

The climactic issue of the disposition of slavery, however, had arisen. What would be the scope of the decision; how much would it solve? Few, regardless of their feelings, were really clear on this issue. Slavery was, indeed, moribund —it could not be restored—nevertheless, it was not yet dead. "The rebellion, instigated and carried on by the slaveholders, has been the death-knell of the institution." Representative James A. Rollins of Missouri, a former slaveholder himself, deprecated the refusal of Border State men to accept compensated emancipation, and further said that the "American sentiment is decidedly anti-slavery," and, "we never can have an entire peace in this country as long as the institution of slavery remains as one of the recognized institutions of the country."[43]

43. *Congressional Globe*, 38th Cong., 1st Sess., Vol.I, 259-260.

Resolved by the Senate and House of Representatives of the United States of America in Congress assembled, (two-thirds of both Houses concurring), that the following article be proposed to the legislatures of the several States as an amendment to the Constitution of the United States, which, when ratified by three-fourths of said legislatures, shall be valid, to all intents and purposes, as a part of the said Constitution, namely: Article XIII, Section 1. Neither slavery nor involuntary servitude, except as a punishment for crime whereof the party shall have been duly convicted, shall exist within the United States or any place subject to their jurisdiction. Section 2. Congress shall have the power to enforce this article by appropriate legislation.

So read the proposed new "Amendment"—the first to be added to the Constitution since the Twelfth Amendment of 1803, ratified in 1804. Nor was this an amendment in the strictest sense of the word. It was, in a larger sense, an expansion of the Constitution, permitting entrance into a new field of social control and reform by the Federal government.

That Lincoln perceived the larger implications of the action now to be taken we cannot doubt. Some Radicals thought he was too deliberate in dealing doom to the institution, as some Democrats declared that he was an intemperate abolitionist. Not only was he convinced that, even if emancipation had become "an indispensable necessity," events had not conferred upon him "an unrestricted right" to act in accordance with his feelings;[44] he felt a firm though still unformulated conviction that the North had entered upon a course of enlarging social and racial equality that would require cautious if courageous definition.[45]

On the last day of January, 1865, the Thirteenth Amendment came before the House for vote. After debating throughout the morning, the vote was taken that afternoon—the result being 119 "aye", 56 "no", 8 not voting.[46]

One publication declared that even up to noon the issue had been in doubt.[47] The direction of the wind was indicated when applause greeted the Democrats, James English of Connecticut, and John Ganson of New York as they voted "aye." The four Democrats who had previously voted in favor did so again, to be joined now by thirteen others. In addition, eight Democrats were reported absent without pairs, a result which Lincoln's secretaries admit was "perhaps not altogether by accident."[48]

Leading Democrat S.S. Cox of Ohio later wrote of a "fund which was said

44. Randall, J. and Richard N. Current, *Lincoln the President, Last Full Measure*, New York, 1955, 298.

45. Quarles, Benjamin, *The Negro in the Civil War*, Boston, 1953, 255ff.

46. *Congressional Globe*, 38th Cong., 1st Sess., Pt.I, 531.

47. Nicolay and Hay, *Lincoln*, *op.cit.*, X, 85, from Report of Special Committee of the Union League Clubs of New York.

48. *Ibid.*, X, 83.

to be ready and freely used for corrupting members. Can anything be conceived more monstrous than this attempt to amend the Constitution upon such a humane and glorious theme, by the aid of the lucre of office-holders?"[49] As is usual in such cases, proof of corruption is lacking, but rumors abounded. Cox clearly believed it, and had personal experience. Other Congressmen made allusions to job deals as well.[50]

The *Congressional Globe*, which seldom reveals strong feeling, states that, "The Speaker called repeatedly to order, and asked that the members should set a better example to spectators in the gallery . . ." Finally, the Speaker announced that the constitutional majority of two-thirds having voted in the affirmative, the joint resolution was passed. The announcement was received by the House and by the spectators with an outburst of enthusiasm. "The members on the Republican side of the House instantly sprang to their feet, and, regardless of parliamentary rules, applauded with cheers and clapping of hands. The example was followed by the male spectators in the galleries, which were crowded to excess, who waved their hats and cheered long and loud, while the ladies, hundreds of whom were present, rose in their seats and waved their handkerchiefs, participating in adding to the general excitement and intense interest of the scene. This lasted for several minutes."[51]

Carl Schurz, who was present, wrote his wife, "The scene that followed the announcement of the result of the vote was worthy of the great event. . . . All arose as at a word of command . . . they embraced, they shook hands, and ten minutes passed before the hurrahing and the enthusiastic racket ceased. The House immediately adjourned and the news of the action spread through the city. Cannon were brought out to greet with their thunder this great step on Freedom's path. It is worth while to live in these days. . . ."[52]

[III]

The election, the reaction to it, the appointment of Chase, the Cabinet changes, the message to Congress outlining policy, the fight for and final passage of the Thirteenth Amendment, the various peace efforts, were all events of the fall and winter of 1864-1865 in which the role of the military was intermingled.

At the Christmas season, General Ben Butler had once again occasioned embarrassment (as we have seen) by a defeat in his blundering effort to take Wilmington. In January, after pressure by Grant, he was removed, thus alter-

49. Cox, S.S., *Three Decades of Federal Legislation*, San Francisco, 1885, 329.
50. Riddle, Albert Gallatin, *Recollections of War Times*, New York, 1895, 324-325.
51. *Congressional Globe*, 38th Cong., 2nd Sess., Pt.I, 531.
52. Carl Schurz to his wife, Feb. 1, 1865, Carl Schurz Papers, State Hist. Soc. of Wis.

ing the temporary relationship between Lincoln and the Radicals. Once more, Lincoln had bided his time and then, at the most opportune moment, had removed one of his most troublesome thorns.[53]

The President, still watching the military movements at Petersburg, Wilmington, and elsewhere, sent Stanton down to Savannah to confer with Sherman. Lincoln, who had been worried about the march to the sea in December, was now anxious that Sherman should move forward as "the enemy is wavering," going down hill, and he should be kept going that way.[54]

Legislative action between December, 1864, and March 4, 1865, reflected the war and the peace to come. Early in the session, among other bills, Congress passed and the President approved an act to establish the highest naval rank, that of Vice-Admiral, to honor Rear-Admiral Farragut. An act of February 25, 1865, made it unlawful for Army and naval officers to have troops at election places unless necessary to repel armed enemies or keep the peace. There was also a bill to aid Western railroads financially, several measures relating to Indian affairs, and a measure to end any disqualification by reason of color in carrying the mails, as well as a resolution providing that wives and children of any person in the military or naval service should be free.[55]

But the major legislation of the session was "an act to establish a Bureau to serve one year for the Relief of Freedmen and Refugees." Abandoned lands and, indeed, all subjects relating to refugees and freedmen were to be handled by this Bureau.[56]

In the Senate, Sumner said that to end slavery was not enough. "The debt of justice will not be paid if we do not take them by the hand in their passage from the house of bondage to the house of freedom; and this is what is proposed by the present measure. The temporary care of the freedmen is the complement of emancipation; but the general welfare is involved in the performance of this duty. . . ."[57] And so, appropriately enough, the Congress began debate on the most crucial aspect of national Reconstruction—the status of the soon-to-be-free black man—as Washington prepared for the second inauguration of Abraham Lincoln.

[IV]

On March 4, 1865, the great bronze statue of freedom by Thomas Crawford, crowning the Capitol dome, looked down upon a murky, muddy, confused scene. According to Welles, "All was confusion and without order—a

53. See Chapters I, II, and IX, this volume.
54. Lincoln, *Works*, VIII, 201, Jan. 5, 1865.
55. *Congressional Globe*, 38th Cong., 2nd Sess., Vol.II, Appendix, Laws of the United States, 113ff.
56. *Ibid.*, Vol.II, 141; Vol.I, 988.
57. *Ibid.*, Vol.I, 768.

jumble."[58] The mud in the streets was worse than usual, and the atmosphere warm and smoky, while from dun-colored clouds there broke occasional light showers. About 11 A.M. a curious celestial phenomenon occurred whereby a small, sharp, pointed diamond or star of light could be seen directly at the zenith.[59]

Mud hampered the procession on its way to the Capitol, where the President labored over last-minute business. There were the usual "bands of music". Two regiments of the Invalid Corps, a squadron of cavalry, a battery of artillery, and four companies of black troops were in the military escort, as well as visiting dignitaries, firemen of Washington and Philadelphia, groups of Odd Fellows and Masons, including members of a Negro Masonic Lodge.[60]

As General Halleck wrote later: "The Inauguration passed off well. Thanks to abundant preventions we had no disturbances, no fires, no raids, or robberies. I was out on the *qui vive* all day and night and consequently did not join in the proceedings. There were a large number of rebel deserters here who excited some suspicion of wrong intentions, but they were closely watched. New York and Philadelphia also sent their quotas of roughs and rowdies, but they were completely overawed."[61]

Lincoln and Johnson had been declared elected by 212 votes, with 21 for McClellan. Thus the first order of the day was the swearing-in of the new Vice-President in the Senate Chamber, an unfortunate occasion, later much belabored by his political opponents. Johnson, having suffered from a severe illness, had arrived late in Washington, where, indisposed because of restoratives he had been obliged to take, he indulged in rambling talk punctuated with maudlin, ill-timed, and inappropriate comments. The brilliant gathering was dutifully shocked, believing him to be intoxicated; Lincoln waited patiently for it to be over, while others were not so patient. Consequently, reports, which ignored Johnson's illness, were exaggerated by those who were already his political enemies.[62]

After Johnson's speech, everyone proceeded from the Senate Chamber to the portico for the swearing-in of the re-elected President. About the time of the ceremonies the sun came out, to give a feeling of hope to the assembled throng. One free Negro wrote in his diary ". . . and on the fourth of March 1865 on Saturday the hon Abraham Lincoln taken his Seat. Before he came out on the porch to take his the wind blew and it rained with out intermission and as soon as Mr. Lincoln came out the wind ceas blowing an the rain ceased

58. Welles, *Diary*, II, 251.
59. Riddle, Albert Gallatin, *Recollections of War Times*, New York, 1895, 229-230.
60. New York *Times*, March 5, 1865.
61. Halleck to Francis Lieber, Mar. 5, 1865, Lieber Papers, HEH.
62. Thomas, Lately, *The First President Johnson*, New York, 1968, Chap. I, 268-269, 289, 295-303.

raining and the Sun came out and wear as clar as it could be and calm and at the mean time there near a Star made its apperence west rite over the Capitol and it Shined just as bright as it could be. . . ."[63]

This Inauguration Day was vastly different from that of March 4, 1861, when people awaited the words of the newly elected President on the crisis momentarily descending on the nation. Now a tremendous shout, "prolonged and loud, arose from the surging sea of humanity" that spread in waves from the specially built platform on the east front of the Capitol, out to the foliage of the Capitol grounds.[64] With few preliminaries, Lincoln, "rising tall and gaunt among the groups about him," advanced with a single sheet of paper in his hand. A roar of applause greeted him and at this moment the sun burst forth in full splendor.

This second Inaugural was very brief; one of the shortest on record. In his opening words, the President admitted that little new could be presented. The progress of arms was well known and, "I trust, reasonably satisfactory and encouraging to all. . . . Both parties deprecated war; but one of them would *make* war rather than let the nation survive; and the other would *accept* war rather than let it perish. And the war came. . . . Neither party expected for the war, the magnitude, or the duration, which it has already attained. Neither anticipated that the *cause* of the conflict might cease with, or even before, the conflict itself should cease. Each looked for an easier triumph, and a result less fundamental and astounding. Both read the same Bible, and pray to the same God; and each invokes His aid against the other . . . but let us judge not that we be not judged. The prayers of both could not be answered; that of neither has been answered fully. The Almighty has His own purposes. . . . If we shall suppose that American Slavery is one of those offences which, in the providence of God, must needs come, but which having continued through His appointed time, He now wills to remove, and that He gives to both North and South, this terrible war, as the woe due to those by whom the offence came, shall we discern therein any departure from those divine attributes which the believers in a Living God always ascribe to Him? Fondly do we hope—fervently do we pray—that this mighty scourge of war may speedily pass away. Yet, if God wills that it continue, until all the wealth piled by the bond-man's two hundred and fifty years of unrequited toil shall be sunk, and until every drop of blood drawn with the lash, shall be paid by another drawn with the sword, as was said three thousand years ago, so still it must be said 'the judgments of the Lord, are true and righteous altogether.' With malice toward none; with charity for all; with firmness in the right, as God gives us to see

63. Shiner, Michael, *Diary*, LC. (Spelling is his own.)
64. Brooks, *Washington in Lincoln's Time, op.cit.*, 212-213.

the right, let us strive on to finish the work we are in; to bind up the nation's wounds; to care for him who shall have borne the battle, and for his widow, and his orphan—to do all which may achieve and cherish a just, and a lasting peace, among ourselves, and with all nations."[65]

The crowd listening to the President's "ringing and somewhat shrill tones," broke in with applause several times, interrupting the continuity. At the close, cheers burst forth from many who had been moved, accompanied even by the tears of those who had grasped the solemn impact of the most religious of American state papers.[66]

The youthful-looking Chief-Justice Chase, almost as tall as Lincoln himself, delivered the oath; the President kissed the Bible; the artillery boomed, and Lincoln retired. But in that vast concourse of people stood a sullen group of men, their minds closed to the moving eloquence of the President, the simple pageantry of the scene, intent only on dark thoughts of revenge.

Harper's Weekly termed the address "characteristically simple and solemn. He neither speculates, nor prophesies, nor sentimentalizes...."[67] Others called it "noble," and one Congressman pronounced it "most masterly, and regarded by some as the best of his many remarkable utterances...."[68]

In contrast to the loud applause, the New York *Herald* ventured to comment, "It was not strictly an inaugural address.... It was more like a valedictory.... Negroes ejaculated 'bress de Lord' in a low murmur at the end of the almost every sentence. Beyond this there was no cheering of any consequence. Even the soldiers did not hurrah much." But the Boston *Evening Transcript* said, two days later, "The President's Inaugural is a singular State paper—made so by the times. No similar document has ever been published to the world.... The President was lifted above the level upon which political rulers usually stand, and felt himself 'in the very presence of the very mystery of Providence.' " Charles Francis Adams, Jr., wrote his father, "That rail-splitting lawyer is one of the wonders of the day.... This inaugural strikes me in its grand simplicity and directness as being for all time the historic keynote of this war...." The London *Times* called it, "an address full of a kind of Cromwellian diction and breathing a spirit very different from the usual unearnest utterances of successful politicians." Gladstone said, "Mr. Lincoln's words show that upon him anxiety and sorrow wrought their true effect. The address gives evidence of a moral elevation most rare in a statesman, or indeed in any man." According to James Grant Wilson, "Emerson said he thought it

65. Lincoln, *Works*, VIII, 332-333.
66. Brooks, *op.cit.*, 213-214.
67. *Harper's Weekly*, March 18, 1865.
68. Brooks, *op.cit.*, 213-214; Riddle, Albert G., *op.cit.*, 329-330.

was likely to outlive anything now in print in the English language."[69]

"The Last Inaugural" was at once seen to breathe an elevation of soul worthy of a great people in a climactic moment of its history. Its influence upon the events in 1865 which closely followed it was slight. But this immortal admonition was designed for the decades and the ages, not for the immediate moment, for many men were still far from ready to forget their hot malice or adopt the golden maxim of charity for all in a land so long rent by resentments and hatreds. The nobility of Lincoln's words, however, gripped the national consciousness with a force that moulded thought and action as nothing had done since Washington's Farewell Address—a force that still lifts and shapes the American purpose.

69. Lincoln Lore, Fort Wayne, Ind., No.1212, June 30, 1952.

8

Net and Trident: The Growth of Southern Desperation

IN THE Punic Wars, the Seven Years' War, and the Napoleonic Wars, a time came when the vital question was not which of the combatants would win the next victory, but which nation would exhibit the sterner resolution and grimmer persistence. Commanders could do little without the support of their embattled people. Would the Romans, in the discouraging days before Cannae, continue harassing Hannibal's seemingly unhaltable army, and would they, in the yet darker hours after Cannae, rally their men as unflinchingly as ever to the standard of Scipio? The brilliant younger Pitt saw one coalition after another wrecked by Napoleon's genius. Would he again set indomitably to work, people and Parliament behind him, to build new bulwarks? Much later, in 1918, a year of alternate victories and defeats on each side, would the reeling Allies or the reeling Central Powers first give way?

The familiar drama was playing itself out on the American stage in 1864. By late summer the test of endurance, the ordeal of fortitude North and South, was the same risk that so many leaders from Pericles to Churchill have had to run. Not the next battle, but the last battle, would be decisive, and skill in arms would count less than dogged persistence behind the fighting lines. At the same time the fact that the Confederacy was besieged and that it was fighting a war of desperation had to be considered. In courage, tenacity, and resourcefulness, the North and the South were well matched. Nobody could say which was superior. On the other hand, the disparity in material resources constantly intruded into the picture. Since circumstances tried the combatants unequally, the fortunes of war swayed back and forth; and down to Lincoln's reëlection few could feel sure which antagonist would win.

The South was of necessity the more daring fighter, armed with the swifter sword—the sword of Lee and earlier that of Jackson, now dead, but inspiring millions from his grave. The North was a slow, cool battler, a gladiator armed with the net of blockade and the trident of three powerful armies in Virginia,

in Georgia, and in the Mississippi Valley. Nerve and endurance must ultimately fail somewhere; but on which side?

Late in August, 1864, William E. Dodge, Jr. sent Greeley's *Tribune* a letter
by Brigadier-General Truman Seymour, a veteran of the Mexican and Seminole Wars who, after being taken prisoner in the Wilderness, had just returned
from Charleston. Having talked with old Army friends there, he set down an
honest impression. "The rebel cause is failing fast from exhaustion," he wrote.
"Their two grand armies have been reinforced this summer from the last
resources of the South. From every corner of the land every old man and every
boy capable of bearing a rifle has been impressed. . . . Lee's army was the first
to be strengthened; it was at the expense of Hood's. Governor Brown told the
truth with a plainness that was very bitter, but it was nonetheless the truth."[1]
Blunt Joseph E. Brown, whose devotion to the Confederate cause was surpassed only by his devotion to State Rights, had told his Georgians before the
fall of Atlanta that Jefferson Davis was giving all his energies to the protection
of Virginia; that he would leave to Georgia itself the main task of saving
Atlanta and Johnston's army; and that their hopes lay in themselves alone.
Governor Brown added ominously: "If General Johnston's army is destroyed,
the Gulf States are thrown open to the enemy, and we are ruined."[2] General
Seymour added that the Southern people realized the desperate weakness of
a government that could not reinforce Lee and Johnston at the same time. He
had copied a letter by one leading Georgian, which he gave in an apparently
authentic text.

"Very few persons are preparing to obey the call of the Governor," it ran.
"His summons will meet with no response here. The people are soul-sick and
heartily tired of the hateful, hopeless strife. They would end it if they could,
but our would-be rulers will take good care that no opportunity is given the
people to vote against it. . . . We have had enough of want and woe, of cruelty
and carnage, enough of cripples and corpses. There is an abundance of weeping parents, bereaved widows, and orphaned children in the land."

It was perhaps Herschel V. Johnson, a State Rights Unionist, who wrote
thus from Georgia. He had feared disaster and defeat from the beginning, and
he informed several Georgians about this time that he longed for peace as the
hart pants for the cooling waterbrooks.[3] In Richmond, Mary Boykin Chesnut
noted in her diary late in July, 1864, that talk of defeat had been rife for weeks.
"How they dump the obloquy on Jeff Davis now, for no fault of his but because

1. New York *Tribune*, Aug. 22, 1864.
2. Fielder, Herbert, *A Sketch of the Life and Times and Speeches of Joseph E. Brown*, Springfield, Mass.,
1883, 255-334.
3. Flippin, Percy S., *Herschel V. Johnson of Georgia*, Richmond, 1931, 261-263.

the cause is failing. A ruined country! Who can bear it?" Another observer who scrutinized the whole South closely, the soldier-journalist T. C. DeLeon, declares that as early as the fall of 1863 the people were utterly losing faith for a variety of reasons. The government was hopelessly divided, for the weak Congress which President Davis had once led by the nose had turned dead against him. The blockade had become so thoroughly effective that blankets and shoes had almost given out, and a large proportion of the army was barefoot, with old rugs cut up by patriotic women for overcoats.[4] At every point the North was superior, its armies stronger, its navy in command of the seas, its artillery more powerful, its supplies seemingly inexhaustible. All the old Southern illusions were dying: the illusion that France and Britain would intervene; the illusion that Union finances would utterly break down; the illusion that a seditious Northwest would break away from the selfish, canting New Englanders.

The American correspondent of the London Daily News, who kept a close eye on the South, wrote on August 21 that he saw "the apparent commencement of the debacle in the Confederacy—the signs of it in Mississippi and North Carolina are very strong."[5] They were in fact overwhelming. Governor Zebulon Vance had written President Davis as 1864 began that after a careful examination of all the sources of discontent in North Carolina, he had concluded that the people wanted peace, and that some effort at negotiation with the North was desirable. Offering of terms without retreat from principles would strengthen the Southern cause, Vance believed.[6] Davis replied with his usual defiance, but with a significant admission that he comprehended the danger of a revolt in the State. He feared from the news he received "that an attempt will be made by some bad men to inaugurate movements . . . which all patriots should combine to put down at any cost. You may count on my aid in every effort to spare your State the scenes of civil warfare which will devastate its homes if the designs of these traitors be suffered to make head."[7] He urged Vance, a former Whig of the Henry Clay school who had stubbornly opposed disunion until Lincoln's call for troops, to avoid conciliating malcontents, for otherwise "you will be driven to the use of force to repress treason." Efforts to communicate with the North had failed, Davis added.

As for once-fiery Mississippi, which out of her 92,000 white males aged sixteen to sixty-five in 1861 had put about 78,000 into uniform by 1865, even her

4. DeLeon, Thomas Cooper, Four Years in Rebel Capitals, Mobile, Ala., 1892, 316-319, 341, 348; Chesnut, Mary Boykin, A Diary from Dixie, New York, 1905, 424, July 26, 1864.
5. London Daily News, Sept. 5, 1863.
6. Vance, Gov. Zebulon, Dec. 30, 1863, a letter Davis received early in 1864; Rowland, Dunbar, Jefferson Davis Constitutionalist, Jackson, Miss., 1923, VI, 141-142.
7. Ibid., 143-146, January 8, 1864.

military ardor was chilled after Vicksburg and paralyzed after Atlanta. The northwestern district from the upper waters of the Big Black and Pearl to the Alabama boundary, an area of pineland and hills where much of the land was poor, the farms very small, and slaves but few, became by 1863 a "disloyal country"—disloyal to the Confederacy. One county that year had so many absentee soldiers that runaway slaves found themselves crowded out of their refuges by runaway white men. Other counties were "deluged with deserters."[8] When the people grew hungry, many women openly encouraged sedition. They danced at news of the fall of Vicksburg, they urged men in the army to return and join the "swamp service." Union sympathizers of Attala County, denouncing the Confederate demagogues who were ruining the land, began to escape to the Yankee lines. In the prevalent discontent, a story sprang up that men of the piney woods in Jones County had seceded from Mississippi as the "republic of Jones."[9] In October, Senator James Phelan wrote Davis that only a Spartan band retained their firm loyalty, "whilst the timid, the traitor, and the time-server are legion."[10]

Yet if evidences of defeatism were most obvious in Mississippi, so heavily invaded, and in North Carolina, so reluctant to secede, so little attached to slavery, and so sorely stricken by battle losses, they could be found everywhere by the autumn of 1864. In Richmond gloom grew thick during September. That month had barely begun when loud cheers from the Union lines around the city heralded the fall of Atlanta. This calamity created general Southern dismay. Angry denunciation fell upon the head of Joe Johnston, and bitter reproaches were heaped upon Jefferson Davis for not removing him sooner. The discontent was naturally greatest in the Confederate capital. "You could hear the loungers growl as you pass along the street," writes one Richmond annalist.[11] Everyone knew that the capture of the vital railroad center of Atlanta with its invaluable machine shops and foundries was a sore blow to the Confederacy and provided an open portal for possible further invasion of Georgia. At the same time, some in the South were hopeful and others in the North fearful that Sherman's army was over-extended and that he could or would be cut off from his tenuous supply lines running clear back through Chattanooga to Nashville. Sherman's ensuing march across the State to Savannah seemed to Pollard of the Richmond *Enquirer* an annunciation of the end.[12] Already bisected north and south and ringed by fire, the Confederacy would now be cloven east and west.

8. Bettersworth, John K., *Confederate Mississippi*, Baton Rouge, 1943, 218ff.
9. *Ibid.*, 226-227.
10. *O.R.*, IV, pt. 3, 707-710.
11. Bill, A.H., *The Beleaguered City: Richmond, 1861-1865*, New York, 1946, 234.
12. Pollard, Edward A., *The Lost Cause*, New York, 1967, 645-646.

Everywhere in the South, in fact, discontent boiled to the surface as people lost their last shreds of confidence in the Davis Administration. Many, anguished by their mounting deprivations and losses, felt that since defeat was now inevitable, the sooner it came the better. Congress made some clumsy efforts to allay the general despondency, but these simply revealed that it had neither a plan nor determination enough to meet the crisis. People began to look desperately for any way out. "Now, for the first time," wrote T. C. De Leon, "they began to speculate upon the loss of their beloved capital. It was rumored in Richmond that General Lee had told the President that the lines were longer than he could hold; that the sole hope was to evacuate them and collect the armies at some interior point for a final struggle. . . . And the rumor added that Mr. Davis peremptorily and definitely rejected this counsel; declaring that he would hold the city at any cost and any risk." However, "even now there was no weak relaxation—no despairing cry among the Southern people."[13] Where was the interior point, the fortress, to use for a last stand? Chattanooga? It was gone. Montgomery? It was surrounded. Lynchburg? It was too weak. And what was the use of throwing lives away in a last stand?

One index of Southern desperation was the preposterous character of some of the last-minute expedients proposed. Robert G. H. Kean of the War Department thought that the government might well try to obtain the help of a foreign power even at the expense of its pride and independence. Why not sound out Napoleon III upon his willingness to come to the aid of the Confederacy? It might be made a French protectorate, with French control of its foreign policy, special French access to its cotton, ship timber, and naval stores, and French security in the occupation of Mexico. Of course the South would retain complete autonomy in domestic affairs. Kean embodied this harebrained idea in a memorandum to Secretary Seddon, in July, 1863, who gave it with a grimace to the Secretary of State![14]

[I]

The Southern will to resist was heroic; it had such iron strength that well into the last year of the war it still seemed almost unconquerable. The hardships of the Southern people, taken alone, would perhaps never have fatally sapped it. Whatever their sufferings, they might well have fought on. It was the interaction of three principal forces that brought Southerners to the point where they began to accept the idea of defeat. These forces were the heavier and heavier loss of life—the drawing of an ever-deeper stream of blood from

13. DeLeon, Thomas Cooper, *op.cit.*, 348.
14. Kean, Robert G.H., *Diary*, New York, 1957, 82, July 12, 1863.

veins that could not be replenished; the ever sharper bite of a hundred steel teeth of internal privation; and the growing conviction that all the Southern losses would be in vain, that no matter what the struggles of the people or the feats of the armies, superior Northern strength and organization would ultimately win.

For Southern leaders knew that as the spirits of the Confederacy fell, the spirits of the North rose. They learned from stray Yankee newspapers after Atlanta fell that Grant had recently telegraphed Lincoln (July 19, 1864) suggesting a draft of 300,000 more men because the Confederacy "now have their last men in the field. Every depletion of their army is an irreparable loss—desertions from it are now rapid." They learned that the day before Grant telegraphed, Lincoln had anticipated him by calling for a full half-million recruits. And if at all well informed, Southern leaders knew that although the total raised under this call was not large, a steady current of fresh soldiers did flow into all the Northern armies from August onward.[15]

Grant reiterated on August 16, 1864, his conviction that the Southern armies were becoming disastrously weaker. "The rebels have now in their ranks their last men. The little boys and old men are guarding prisoners, railroad bridges, and forming a good part of their garrisons for intrenched positions. . . . They are now losing from desertions and other causes at least one regiment per day."[16] A great body of Southerners must have guessed that such statements were being made by Northern generals. They may even have suspected that Lee was making statements that tallied with Grant's. "Unless some measure can be devised to replace our losses," Lee wrote Seddon on August 23,[17] "the consequences may be disastrous. Without some increase of strength, I cannot see how we are to escape the natural military consequences of the enemy's numerical superiority." And early in September he wrote President Davis that immediate measures must be taken to reinforce the Army of Northern Virginia. "The necessity is now great, and will soon be augmented by the results of the coming draft in the United States. As matters now stand, we have no troops disposable to meet movements of the enemy . . . without taking them from the trenches and exposing some important point."[18]

The death's head of defeat grinned and grimaced at dejected Southerners, while a spectral hand wrote under every death-roll the burning question: "To what end?"

And what black rolls these were! The deepest grief of the South, the pro-

---

15. Lerwill, L.L., *The Personnel Replacement System in the United States Army*, Washington, 1954, 165.
16. To Elihu Washburne, *Grant Papers*, Illinois State Hist. Libr.
17. *O.R.*, I, xlii, pt. 2, 1199-1200.
18. *Ibid.*, 1228.

foundest source of disheartenment, sprang from the continuous losses by death, mutilation, and sickness, and the harsh measures taken to repair them. Even more than in the North, every town and village shuddered at the long casualty lists posted in public places. The slow, jolting trains brought home anguished huddles of the sick, exhausted, and maimed, crowding ever more thickly alongside piles of officers' coffins; then bore away the reluctant conscripts. "It was not unusual to see at the railroad stations long lines of squalid men, with scraps of blankets in their hands, or small pine boxes of provisions, or whatever else they might snatch in their hurried departure from their homes, leaving for training camps."[19] These recruits were what a British observer termed "poor old Dixie's bottom dollar." They could never fill up the depleted ranks. At every point the Northern strength was now vastly superior. Even the Yankee cavalry was now stronger. The days when the Stuarts, Wade Hamptons, Forrests, and Fitzhugh Lees had outridden and outfought the Pleasontons and Griersons were gone forever. Southern horses were worn out, and Southern horsemen had lost some of their dash and pride; that the Yankees had learned to fight was comprehensible, but that they had also learned to ride was a fact harder to grasp.[20]

The scanty Southern successes were meanwhile won upon the same old costly terms as at Chickamauga; once more a terrible exertion, a ghastly loss of life—more than 2,300 men killed, 14,600 wounded,[21] and nearly 1,500 missing. Once more a merely nominal victory, and a disheartening failure to grasp its fruits. Like Sisyphus, the South toiled up hill after hill to meet exhausting defeats or equally exhausting triumphs that dissolved into new chagrins. In the bloody shambles of the Wilderness, Lee's army of just over 61,000 effectives was believed to have lost about 7,750 men slain and wounded. The Union loss was much greater, but it could be repaired; the Confederate casualties could not. In the heavy combat at Spotsylvania on May 8-12, Confederate losses were placed by Generals Hancock and Humphreys at 5,000 to 6,000. In the fighting at Petersburg on June 15-18, Humphreys pronounced the Southern losses "severe." The battling along the Weldon Railroad on August 18-25 cost the Confederates 1,200 killed and wounded. Meanwhile, Hood's futile assault at Atlanta on July 22, when the South threw 37,000 men into what Hardee termed one of the most desperate and bloody encounters of the war, left about 7,000 Confederates killed or wounded.[22]

19. Pollard, op.cit., 646-647.
20. DeLeon, op.cit., 318-319.
21. Livermore, Thomas L., Numbers and Losses in the Civil War in America, Boston, 1901, 106.
22. Ibid., III, 113, 118, 123; Humphreys, A.A., The Virginia Campaign of 1864 and 1865, 106, 225; O.R., I, xxxvi, pt. 1, 337; O.R.,I, xxxviii, pt. 3, 75, 699. As usual, such casualty figures are subject to much dispute as to accuracy, particularly on the Confederate side.

What a wealth of talent these and other similar cold figures represent, what a load of grief they laid upon Southern homes, and how terribly the losses crippled coming generations! Longstreet, badly wounded in the Wilderness, mentions in his memoirs that Micah Jenkins, son of a leading planter family in South Carolina, was slain the same day: "intelligent, quick, untiring, attentive, truly faithful to official obligations, abreast of the foremost in battle." He was but one of a thousand; and as the Southern historian Douglas Freeman notes, in all the commands fewer and fewer brilliant juniors were left to fill gaps.[23] One man who was promoted from a captaincy to a brigadiership in a single jump was killed before he had served a fortnight in his new rank. As this gory summer of 1864 wore on, Southern officers took more desperate personal risks to stiffen wavering troops against Union soldiers who fought better and better. Valor endured, but frequently inexperienced troops had to be placed under incompetent captains and colonels, and untested generals.[24]

While bloodshed had a limited effect upon Grant, it grieved Lee so intensely that Pollard and others accused him of excessive tenderness.[25] When Pemberton proposed a useless charge against the Yankee lines before Richmond, Lee silenced him with cutting words.[26] It seems clear that by the last weeks of 1864, he realized that further fighting would be hopeless. After the war a Southern woman, finding him pensive and depressed, asked the reason. He was thinking, he replied, of the men who had died under the Confederate banner after all prospect of victory had vanished. "Why didn't you tell them?" asked his questioner. "They had to find it out for themselves," he responded. Unquestionably, however, many Southerners knew after Lincoln's reëlection, after the terrible carnage of Franklin left 1,750 Confederates dead and around 3,800 wounded on the field, and after Sherman's army approached the defenses of Savannah, that the lives thereafter lost were a senseless sacrifice to Moloch. Many a devoted Southern officer reproached himself as he gave fatal orders. Yet still a Spartan sense of duty bound the President, the high civil officers, and the generals as in bands of steel.

"It is agonizing to see and hear the cases daily brought into the War Office," wrote Kean as the screws of the conscription were tightened; "appeal after appeal, and *all* disallowed. Women come there and weep, wring their hands, scold, entreat, beg—and almost drive me mad. The iron is gone deep into the heart of society."

Countless Southerners felt, during this last year of the war, as if they were

23. Longstreet, James, *From Manassas to Appomattox*, Philadelphia, 1896, 566; Freeman, Douglas S., *Lee's Lieutenants*, New York, 1955, III, 546-548.
24. *Ibid.*, 556.
25. Bradford, Gamaliel, *Lee the American*, Boston, 1927, 176.
26. Sorrel, G. Moxley, *Recollections of a Confederate Staff Officer*, New York, 1905, 265.

walking in a nightmare. And yet, busy people might momentarily forget the
almost universal grief over the extinction of bright young lives; they might put
out of mind for an hour other sources of anxiety and anguish. Many gradually
became accustomed to the abnormal situation. They had interludes of reconciliation with fate, exhilaration over good fortune, and even bursts of gaiety.
The churches were flower-trimmed for bridals; dining-rooms were now and
then lighted for school-commencement suppers of fruits, ices, and cakes.
Judith McGuire, returning from a hospital where she had seen a young girl
mourn by her dying brother, passed a house bright with music and dancing,
and thought of the ball in Brussels the night before Waterloo.[27] Some young
people held "starvation parties" to laugh at their privations; some crippled
soldiers went courting with a jest over "Cupid on Crutches." Yet the sword
seemed to flash in the lamplight of parlors, the whine of shells seemed to pierce
bars of the lightest music, and the tramp of distant battalions echoed through
wedding marches. The iron pressures of a hundred deprivations never relaxed
their grip; if the throbbing pain was eased at one point, it struck at another.

The phrase "a hundred deprivations" could be taken literally. The young
wife with market-basket on her arm felt that the growing inflation was beyond
human tolerance; how could people endure such costs? Sewing ugly frocks of
unbleached Macon calico in place of wornout gowns, nursing children without
medicines, or learning that a son's amputation had been without benefit of
anaesthetics, older women writhed in the grip of the blockade. A hardworking
farmer who saw the steel ploughshare of invasion rip through his plantation,
his buildings burned, his cotton seized, his poultry, cattle, and pigs butchered,
his slaves urged to flee, realized that war must mean utter impoverishment.
And if this was only individual tragedy, the long lines of smashed railroads,
the wrecked bridges, the dilapidated public buildings, the sacked stores, the
decaying factories, meant the ruin of whole communities. Everywhere in
northern Virginia, western Mississippi, Tennessee, half of Georgia, and much
of Alabama and Louisiana, such sights had become familiar. The loss of lives,
the loss of property; who did not know their ruth and pang? And whenever
men glimpsed a gutted library, a shattered college, or a ruined church like St.
Finbar's Cathedral in Charleston, they realized how deadly a blow the war had
struck at cultural and moral progress.

Was inflation worse than invasion and devastation? Who could answer such
an inquiry? Some would have said that the steady breakdown of the Southern
railroads was more painful in its social and economic consequences than the
blockade, but the imponderables in such an equation defy measurement. The

---

27. Freeman, *Lee, op.cit.*, III, 496; McGuire, Judith White, *Diary of a Southern Refugee*, New York,
1867, 328, and *passim.*; Kean, *Diary, op.cit.*, 174.

shortages of salt, medicines, and cutlery, of tea, coffee, and sugar, of silverware, china, and fine textiles, and of a thousand luxuries that had become almost necessities, were galling in the extreme. So were the demands of the impressment system, which placed as inexorable a hand upon all war-needed commodities as conscription laid upon the able-bodied men of the land. Was the problem of refugee-crowding in some areas worse than the problem of loneliness in others when all wonted modes of communication and intercourse failed? Nobody could say. The important fact was that the South suffered from all these ills. By the autumn of 1864 it was an aching void, and the typical Southerner regarded himself at times as but a hungry aggregation of bruises, aches, and unsatisfied wants.

"It is impossible to say precisely when the conviction became general in the South that we were to be beaten. . . . It was a part of our soldierly and patriotic duty to believe that ultimate success was to be ours, and Stuart only uttered the common thought of army and people, when he said, 'We are bound to believe that, anyhow.' We were convinced, beyond the possibility of a doubt, of the absolute righteousness of our cause, and in spite of history we persuaded ourselves that a people battling for the right could not fail in the end. And so our hearts went on hoping for success long after our heads had learned to expect failure. . . . It was our religion to believe in the triumph of our cause, . . ."[28] Take away the Southerner's belief in ultimate victory and substitute a gnawing anxiety for the welfare of family and friends, and his valor grew steadily staler and limper.

It was not the hardships of war-bound life in a hundred socio-economic respects, not the widening devastation, not even the steady splash of blood of multitudes of young men, that sapped the Southern spirit. The people would have fought on despite all this as their grandfathers had fought on under Washington. It was, we repeat, the combination of a sickening conviction of ultimate defeat along with such adversities and losses that broke down the will to endure.

[II]

Then and later many were willing to say that the greatest single cause of demoralization lay in inflation—in the flood of paper currency choking the Confederacy. Treasury Secretary Memminger and his associates had really possessed no choice. They had been compelled to finance the war on credit. It was impossible to obtain a sufficient revenue from tariffs, the blockade

28. Eggleston, George Cary, *A Rebel's Recollections*, Bloomington, Ind., 1959, 172.

shutting off imports and exports more and more completely; from taxation, no considerable collections being possible; or from the sale of lands, there being no cash customers. The monetary resources of the South had been slender. No stocks of gold and silver existed, and no Confederate coins could be minted. After secession about twenty million dollars in United States coins, it was estimated, remained in the possession of the people, who in considerable part jealously hoarded the money. The only basis for borrowing lay in the staple crops, which could not be exported in any appreciable quantity, and lay increasingly at the mercy of invading armies.[29]

The history of Confederate finance is a record of prolonged failure, but failure attributable far more to hard circumstances than human short-sightedness or error. Tariffs, taxes, produce loans (that is, contributions in cotton, tobacco, sugar and the like in exchange for bonds), tax-in-kind or tithe, loans floated abroad—all were tried, and all proved false lights; will-o'-the-wisps glimmering over the depths of a fiscal quagmire. The story of the tariffs can be briefly dismissed. At the very outset (February 9, 1861) the Confederate Congress voted temporary adoption of the tariff of 1857; the next month it erected the first distinctly Confederate tariff; and within two months more it voted the second—a low tariff devoid of protective duties, which were in fact prohibited by both the temporary and permanent Constitutions. But the tariffs on imports amounted to very little. All told, the customs receipts of the Confederacy came to less than $3,481,000, for the whole war period.[30] As for export duties, which were permissible under the Confederate Constitution, they yielded practically nothing. The total amount collected on shipments of cotton, tobacco, and naval stores came to just over $39,000![31]

Taxes also proved a frail support. Secretary Memminger realized perfectly well that theoretically they were much better means of gathering resources for government use than the floating of loans; but practically, he faced mounting and almost insuperable difficulties. The first $15,000,000 loan, authorized nearly a fortnight before the firing on Fort Sumter, and bearing eight per cent interest payable in specie, was a success. This was because the banks gave it full support, throwing their resources into the effort so loyally that they lost control of a great part of the specie held in the South; much of it went abroad for the purchase of munitions and satisfaction of other needs. Almost at once in the spring of 1861 Congress had to authorize the Secretary to issue another $50,000,000 bond issue, payment this time coming not from the banks in specie,

29. Todd, Richard C., *A History of Confederate Finances*, Athens, Ga., 1954, Ch. I.
30. Reports of Secretary of the Treasury to Congress, Mar. 14, 1862-Nov.7, 1864; Summary, Todd, R.C., *op.cit.*, 121-130.
31. Todd, R.C., *op.cit.*, 127.

but from the agricultural population in salable produce. Then issue followed issue, Memminger perforce turning to sales of bonds as the main source of revenue.

Although the exchange of government paper for produce was the logical expedient of an agricultural society for paying its way, vexatious problems of storage and marketing arose, and acrimonious controversy followed. As the blockade tightened, many subscribers to loans complained that the stipulation that crops be turned over on a fixed day carried the seeds of their ruin. The government could compel a sale on that date even though prices had fallen abysmally low.[32] When Congress refused to guarantee the growers any relief, various States followed Mississippi in issuing notes and bonds for cotton; and the States thus drifted into speculations in cotton in competition with the Richmond government. These activities, carried on abroad as well as at home, led to embarrassing conflicts between State and Confederate authorities.

Efforts to raise money abroad were of little avail. Obtaining title to large quantities of cotton, the Treasury issued 1,500 Cotton Certificates valued at $1,000 each, which Secretary Memminger regarded as the most hopeful implement for obtaining funds from abroad. The results were very far below those he anticipated. The certificates sold so slowly on a reluctant market that the field soon had to be cleared to give sole possession to the Erlanger Loan. As we have seen previously, the house of Emile Erlanger & Co. agreed, under a contract with the Confederacy signed October 28, 1862, and perfected on January 8, 1863, to market $15,000,000 worth of cotton-secured bonds. James Spence of Liverpool, who had been authorized to sell as many of the Cotton Certificates as he could, had to stand aside. By the time that the Confederacy began to collapse, the Erlanger loan had slumped lower and lower. Henry Hotze wrote Judah P. Benjamin on August 17, 1863, that "the slightest causes affect it sensibly without adequate reasons"—as if Vicksburg and Gettysburg were trivial matters! When the Confederate financial authorities submitted a final report (February 11, 1865), it showed total receipts of about seven-and-one-half millions, a little more than half the face value of the loan.[33] Actually, the true net figure is not known.

The failure of tariffs, taxes, and foreign borrowings, with the emission of greater and greater quantities of paper money, meant a rapid drop into the abyss of inflation. By midsummer of 1863 a gold dollar would buy $10 in Confederate notes; by August it would buy $12; and by November it would purchase $15, so swift was the descent into the financial Avernus! Peering

32. See letters in *Correspondence of the Treasurer CSA*, IV, V, *passim*.
33. Report on the Erlanger Loan, showing receipts to Oct. 1, 1864; *Confederate Treasury Reports*, III, 435, 436. For further details see Nevins, *War for the Union* (Vol. 7, Chap. 13), "Foreign Relations."

ahead, people could wonder whether even $25 in Confederate notes would obtain a gold dollar a year later. As a matter of fact, in the month of Lincoln's reëlection, about $35 in rebel money was asked for one dollar in gold, or $150 for a sovereign.[34] As Pollard bitterly wrote, a soldier's monthly pay (if he received it) would hardly buy him a pair of socks as Christmas of 1864 approached. When hostilities began, the amount of Federal currency circulating in the Confederacy had been estimated at $85,500,000. By the beginning of 1863, however, about $290,000,000 in Confederate Treasury notes not bearing interest were circulating; $121,500,000 in interest-bearing notes; and at least $20,000,000 in States notes and banknotes.[35] The consequences were inevitable.

As in the North, the premium on gold in exchange for paper money bore no close relationship to the amount of paper in circulation. It was governed rather by popular hopes and fears, expectations and disappointments, over the probable outcome of the war. The amount of Union greenbacks in circulation did not rise greatly after midsummer in 1863, and not at all after midsummer in 1864, yet the gold valuation assigned to greenbacks fluctuated sharply in value even while increasing in volume. It is significant that Union credit rose and Confederate credit fell decidedly in the summer of Vicksburg and Gettysburg; that quotations on Northern greenbacks fell in the militarily anxious weeks preceding and following Chancellorsville, but rose that fall and winter while Treasury notes of the Confederacy slumped; and that from May through August, 1864, as Grant's army suffered heavy losses, greenbacks were again low. But, beginning in October, Confederate credit sank, and in January, February and March of 1865 it dropped tragically lower. By February, indeed, it took $58 in Confederate Treasury notes to buy a dollar in gold.[36]

It would be tiresome and pointless to recapitulate the list of Confederate funding acts and their amendments; to repeat the oft-told story of the growing Southern demand for Union greenbacks; or to rehearse the tale of Southern speculation in gold, and of the chorus of opprobrious epithets rained upon the speculators. Gambling in specie ran parallel with gambling in cotton. The search for scapegoats, as usual in such situations, was hotly pursued. They were found in certain Army officers—and indeed, Lee aimed some general orders against soldiers who bought supplies for a speedy resale;[37] in certain Jews whom the diarist Jones accused of profiteering on shoes, and of buying real estate because they had no faith in Confederate money; in turncoat Yan-

---

34. Schwab, J.C., *The Confederate States of America, 1861-1865; A Financial and Industrial History*, New York, 1901, 167. This gives a full wartime table.
35. Pollard, *Lost Cause, op.cit.*, 647; *Confederate Treasury Reports*, III, 59-70; 90-115.
36. Schwab, *op.cit.*, 167.
37. General Orders, Department of Northern Virginia, Nov. 14, 1862.

kees; and in blockade runners.[38] Trade with the enemy across the lines, nominally illegal but winked at even by the Secretary of War,[39] profited the Confederacy by bringing in supplies; it profited the speculators by bringing in foreign money. Such speculation had a demoralizing effect which invited the condemnation of Lee and other leaders, and of the press. But the opinion of some of the ablest generals was a bit more moderate; they said that it was essentially outrageous,[40] but that it could not be stopped.

The excessive paper money issues, the appalling rise in the cost of living as measured by paper, and the destruction of all confidence in the future value of paper money, government securities, bank deposits, and industrial shares, meant much more than a decay of normal financial standards. That would have been bad enough in the feeling of helplessness, and sometimes even despair, which it often created. But far worse was an accompanying degeneration in the moral tone of the Southern people. When money changed its value overnight, men used it in reckless speculation. As in France during the Revolution, and much later in inflation-riddled Germany after the First World War, rising markets led people to turn money into goods with frenzied haste. And as in various countries at numerous times, many observers blamed gamblers for the speculation, when actually speculation bred the gamblers. Extravagance was a natural consequence of inflation. Holding fortunes real or fictitious, the *nouveaux riches* used them in fast living; they seized on all available luxuries— gay dress, handsome houses, fine carriages, and glittering fêtes. Gambling halls, which rose overnight in Richmond, Charleston, and other cities, were crowded with men. Soldiers gambled because they did not know whether they would live another month, government contractors gambled because they could not be sure of next week's orders, and bankers, lawyers, and merchants because their money was fairy gold.[41] "Speculation is running wild in this city," wrote the Rebel War Clerk in April of 1863. From gambling and extravagant spending sprang crime. Cupidity became general, so that one observer remarked: "Every man in the community is swindling everybody else."[42]

Currency inflation, in fact, was a contributory agency in the breakdown of social discipline and self-control which became so marked as the war continued, and which we had a glimpse of previously in 1863. It helped bathe much of the South in an atmosphere of laxity, self-indulgence, and blind resignation. The section had always displayed an excessive fondness for whisky and rum, toddies, and juleps; now drunkenness became frequent inside and outside the

38. Jones, John B., *A Rebel War Clerk's Diary*, Philadelphia, 1866, I, 150, 289ff.
39. Schwab, *op.cit.*, 264.
40. *Ibid.*, 264ff.
41. Jones, *A Rebel War Clerk's Diary*, *op.cit.*, I, 288.
42. Quoted in Schwab, *op.cit.*, 230.

Army—until after 1863 the scarcity of intoxicants cut it down. The South had always been too much addicted to duelling, street affrays, and rural feuds of the kind described in *Huckleberry Finn*; now violence, sanctioned in battle, grew familiar behind the lines. "With the imposing and grand displays of war," writes Pollard in describing Richmond life, "came flocks of villains, adventurers, gamblers, harlots, thieves in uniform, thugs, tigers, and nondescripts. The city was soon overrun with rowdyism."[43] Statements of the same kind can be found in all newspapers. It was with good reason that, a quarter-century after the war, the principal historian of Confederate finance included in his book a section headed, "The Moral Decadence of the South."[44]

Many were the wails that arose from impoverished Southerners as they saw not only their property but their pride in character and principle vanishing in the smoke of inflation, speculation, and extravagance. It was not the Richmond government alone that was responsible. States, cities, and smaller local units issued notes; the total became at the end purely conjectural, but it must have approached if it did not exceed a billion dollars.[45] Private businesses added their petty shinplasters valued at from five to fifty cents. "Virginia is flooded with trash," exclaimed one irate citizen of the Old Dominion, while a Mississippi editor cried out against the financial mismanagement that cursed the people with 250 different kinds of paper promises, and not one silver dime to give them weight. The Confederacy itself printed fifty-cent notes. As the currency became debased, a resort to barter (as in the exchange of corn for nails, cotton for cloth) became general. Payments were made in kind, just as taxes were collected in crops.

Counterfeiting of the badly executed Confederate notes soon became rampant. Some unscrupulous Southerners engaged in it, though scarcity of paper and rarity of engraving tools and skills limited their nefarious activities, but most of it was the work of Northern hands, the notes being smuggled from New York, Philadelphia, and Louisville into the Confederacy. Near the end of the war some counterfeits were made in Cuba, and slipped through the blockade to Mobile or Texas ports. Although the Confederacy established a detective bureau in Atlanta,[46] efforts to identify the counterfeits were largely abortive, and when persons who passed them were arrested, they could usually plead ignorance. The most famous of the Northern counterfeiters, Samuel Upham of Philadelphia, later boasted that he had printed, in all, twenty-eight

43. Pollard, Edward A., *Life of Jefferson Davis*, Philadelphia, 1869, 152-153.

44. Schwab, *op.cit.*, Ch. XII; cf. material on Southern morale in Nevins, *War for the Union: The Organized War*, Ch. 10.

45. Schwab, *op.cit.*, 165.

46. *Correspondence of C.S.A. Treasury*, IV, 381; Col. G.W. Lee was head of the bureau; Todd, *op.cit.*, 99; Schwab, *op.cit.*, 159-161.

different facsimiles of Confederate notes and shinplasters; that Senator Foote had credited him with doing more to injure the Confederate effort than McClellan's army; and that President Davis had offered a reward of $10,000 for him dead or alive.[47] But it was not until late in the war that the government engaged a London firm to prepare plates of new design, with "chemiograph" engraving hard to counterfeit; and then some if not all the plates were intercepted by the blockade, passing into the hands of Northerners who cheerfully used them.[48]

[III]

Only less painful than the conscription of men, and well-nigh as strong a contributor to general demoralization as the growing rottenness of the currency, was the military seizure of all manner of goods and supplies. Impressment had swiftly become a dread word in the Confederacy. By 1864 it fell on men's ears like a pronouncement of doom. Early in the conflict army officers had begun to distrain commodities, and they expanded their grabbing as necessity or convenience prompted them. As it was not until March, 1863, that the Confederate Congress voted some systematic regulations for the collection of materials, arbitrary action long held full sway and set unhappy precedents. Military men attached crops, meat, flour, salt, hardware, horses, and wagons on the simple plea that necessity knew no law. Nor did the new law introduce evenhanded justice or really judicious procedures. It provided that, in every State, President Davis and the governor were each to appoint a commissioner, and these two were to try to agree on fair prices for goods impounded. If they disagreed they were to call in an umpire. In fixing the general scale, producers or men who kept supplies for their own consumption were to get preferential treatment over those who kept them for sale. The farmer and householder, that is, fared better than the merchant or speculator. If any holder disputed the price given him, he might appeal to two citizens of the neighborhood or an arbiter of their choice. This was a hit-or-miss procedure, full of holes. It had to be applied in a loosely organized society undergoing rapid deterioration, by army men acting under more and more desperate strain.

It worked wretchedly. Neither in theory nor in practise can much be said at any time for military impressment of the goods of a people carrying on a war. Efforts to seize supplies during the Revolution, in an effort to thwart "forestallers," speculators, and monopolists, and to help ragged veterans, had

47. Lee, William, *The Currency of the Confederate States of America*, Washington, 1875, 24-25; Todd, *op.cit.*, 100-101.

48. Chase, Philip H., *Confederate Treasury Notes*, Philadelphia, 1947, 123ff.

done more harm than good. Now, in the Confederacy, even the conscription of young men was hardly more detested, for *that* was acknowledged a necessity, at least by some. The system would have been regarded as abusive in the hands of men as honest as Lee and as conscientious as Stonewall Jackson, whereas the impressment officials were in fact sometimes knavish, often incompetent, and always under shaky supervision. Impressment reached deep into the rural areas and hamlets where the war had not been quite directly felt, and where any government supervision was generally resented. No other single exercise of power, declares a thorough investigator, produced such sullen discontent and sharp resentment.[49]

At first the general complaint was that the prices fixed were too low; later in 1863-64, that they were lifted too high.[50] Efforts by State commissioners to agree on a uniform scale east of the Mississippi broke down. Six States met in Montgomery in September of 1863 for the purpose, but got nowhere. The various impositions and abuses suffered by the people in the name of impressment authority aroused a rebellious temper and created an angry confusion that had no counterpart in the North. The activities of well-accredited agents were irritating enough. In addition, false officers appeared, brandishing their weapons before farmers and shopkeepers, signing worthless receipts, and filling their wagons by barefaced imposture. Various States passed laws to punish these cheats. The Louisiana legislature, for example, instructed Governor Henry W. Allen early in 1864 to call on Confederate troops to assist him in stopping illegal seizures, recovering unlawful confiscations, and making impostors suffer proper penalties.[51] In Georgia the Supreme Court pronounced a portion of the Impressment Act unconstitutional, and Governor Brown tried to make rascals who had taken property under false pretences subject to thirty-nine lashes and ten years' imprisonment.[52]

The interminable losses and harassments, in fact, aroused bitter antagonism throughout the whole South. When impressment officers lost good corn in the mud, and let bacon spoil in the sun, whole countrysides grew angry. Lack of planning accentuated local and regional disparities of supply, so that while one district had an excess, another sixty miles distant felt painful want. Farmers found it hard enough at best, what with lack of horses, broken-down railways, and uncertain steamboat service, to get their crops to market; they were rebellious when, on reaching town, they had their produce impressed at prices flagrantly below market rates. Indeed, as the governors of Virginia and

49. Ramsdell, Charles William, *Behind the Lines in the Southern Confederacy*, Baton Rouge, 1944, 117.
50. Coulter, Ellis M., *The Confederate States of America, 1861-1865*, Baton Rouge, 1950, 252.
51. Bragg, J.D., *Louisiana in the Confederacy*, Baton Rouge, 1941, 268.
52. Bryan, Thomas Conn, *Confederate Georgia*, Athens, Ga., 1953, 92.

the Carolinas complained, military detachments often seized commodities on the roads to market.[53] And what tremendous volume the seizures attained! During 1863, as Seddon admitted, the government was compelled to rely almost exclusively on impressment to meet its needs.[54] As 1864 began, this was "its only reliance." It has been estimated that at the end of the war the Confederacy owed half-a-billion dollars to citizens whose goods it had taken with promises to pay; and much more had been taken with fraudulent promises or none. Seddon gave Jefferson Davis a frank view of the matter.

"Impressment is evidently a harsh, unequal, and odious mode of supply," he wrote. "With the utmost forbearance and consideration even its occasional exercise is harassing and irritating; but when it has to prevail as a general practise, to be exercised inquisitorially and summarily in almost every private domain, by a multitude of subordinate officers, it becomes beyond measure offensive and repugnant to the sense of justice and prevalent sentiment of our people. It has been, perhaps, the sorest test of their patriotism and self-sacrificing spirit afforded by the war, and no other people, it is believed, would have endured it without ... resistance. It has caused much murmuring and dissatisfaction, but a knowledge of the necessities which alone justified it has caused the outcry to be directed rather to the mode and ... occasional excesses of its exercise than against the system itself."[55]

The universal hatred of impressment became commingled with the widespread hostility to President Davis, and the fear of a military despotism headed by the Secretary of War and leading generals. The personal resentments of some Confederate chieftains gained depth from the property seizures. When Senator A. G. Brown asserted that in Mississippi impressment was sheer robbery, when Governor Vance of North Carolina made the same charge, and Governor Brown of Georgia issued a proclamation in the fall of 1864 warning the people against rascals who made impressment a veil for robbery, they accentuated the feeling of an unbridgeable gap between State and Confederate governments. Impressment seemed part of the centralizing tendency that excited the wrath of Toombs and Stephens, and the waspish Richmond *Examiner* dwelt on the theme no more acridly than the moderate Richmond *Whig.*[56]

Property seizures of course extended to slaves, and the impressment of Negroes became more and more general in 1863-64, as we have seen in an earlier volume of this work. Here too, sporadic irregular activity gave way to a clumsy approach to system under legislation of March, 1863. Congress required that

53. Schwab, *op.cit.*, 208.
54. *O.R.*, IV, ii, 1009; Report Nov. 26, 1863.
55. *Ibid.*
56. Owsley, Frank Lawrence, *State Rights in the Confederacy*, Gloucester, Mass., 1961, 112ff.; Schwab, *op.cit.*, 208-213.

appropriations of slave labor must conform to State laws, or if none existed, to regulations laid down by the Secretary of War. Although these regulations were fairly simple, public necessities made their application steadily harsher. The paucity of labor in the South by 1863 was painful, and such workers as were available—over-age men, free Negroes, men unfit for fighting but able to do limited manual labor—demanded excessive wages. They were reluctant to leave home to go to distant mines, saltpeter caves, or factories.[57] Owners of slaves resisted hiring them to the government. They feared they would be exposed to battle, enemy seductions, or temptations to vagrancy if sent away from personal supervision. Congress had provided in 1862 for the use of Negroes as teamsters, cooks, and other camp employees, but here also the opposition of owners forbade hiring. Impressment had become a necessity.[58]

By 1864, indeed, the labor shortage became truly desperate. The Tredegar Iron Works in Richmond wanted a thousand men whom it would pay $25 a month with keep; the government shoe factory in Columbus, Georgia, wanted 200 cobblers; armories, salt works, and lumber mills needed help at once in large numbers. The cotton manufacturer William Gregg maintained a twelve-hour day in his workshops, and offered double wages to those who would toil fourteen hours.[59] Efforts to attract workers from Europe were largely fruitless; the hardships of inflation, and the threat of conscription, repelled foreigners, and of the few who came a great many soon departed. Inside the Confederacy the adaptability of labor to new conditions and environments was slight. It was noted that among the multitudinous refugees, many tilled the soil for the first time, buying or renting farms. But comparatively few farmers and planters could enter mechanic or mercantile employment with satisfaction or profit.

The Confederate government tried to be fair to owners in impressing slaves. It paid an agreed wage, or, failing agreement, $30 a month; it cared for the slaves in illness, and offered full compensation for those who died. But, above all other forms of property, this was the one whose impressment hurt. On December 30, 1863, Wigfall spoke in the Senate contrasting the early willingness of Southerners to make heavy sacrifices with their subsequent angry reluctance. In 1861 an appeal by Beauregard for corn and provisions to feed his army at Manassas had been read in every church on Sunday, and next day sixty wagonloads had been delivered to him without charge. But now farmers burned their wheat rather than sell it to the government at $5 a bushel, and haggled about the price of pork while their sons in the army went hungry. It was the refusal of owners to lend their slaves to the cause, however, that most

57. Seddon, in *O.R.*, IV, ii, 998, 999.
58. *Ibid.*
59. Coulter, *op.cit.*, 235-236.

irked Wigfall. "Singular to say, they think a great deal more of their negroes than of their sons and brothers." A friend had encountered a slave on a train to Richmond who reported that his master had felt worse to give him up than to have his five sons enlist. The planters, said Wigfall, would willingly put their own flesh and blood into the army, but asking for a Negro was like drawing an eyetooth.[60]

Such was the pressure for slave labor that in February, 1864, Congress made all male Negroes between 18 and 50 liable for work upon fortifications, in factories, or in army hospitals. This included freed Negroes. It further authorized the War Department to employ not more than 20,000 male Negro slaves. Owners were to receive compensation in case of death or escape to the enemy. If the Secretary of War should be unable to procure sufficient slaves for service then he was authorized to impress slaves not to exceed 20,000. This measure warned the South of more severe action impending! Sure enough, in the last desperate days of the war the States were required to furnish more Negroes (but not more than one in every five male slaves from a single owner) for rear service, while some officers talked of giving them front-line action. This, too, came about, for in the act approved March 13, 1865, the use of slaves as soldiers was authorized. If sufficient troops were not raised through request the President was authorized to call on each State for a quota, though not more than a fourth of the male slaves should be called. Although the act did not grant the slave his freedom if he served in the army, there appeared to be that tacit understanding. A few Negro troops were organized in Richmond, but time ran out before they could see any real action.[61]

To invest government officers with authority to seize supplies and labor was to give them power of economic life and death over whole communities. The South, which had taken up arms to achieve a larger liberty, was falling under the most arbitrary tyranny. It was becoming, in large areas, a police state. War has always been arbitrary, and always increasingly harsh. Southerners were finding that it poured its heaviest broadsides into individual freedom and local independence. They were learning what Napoleon's marshal had meant when he growled to a Franconian town: "We battle for liberty and equality—and the first person who moves without permission will be shot!"[62] The worst scars of the conflict, moreover, were not physical, but moral and psychological.

This fact was illustrated in the vein of callous inhumanity that by 1863-64 streaked the refugee life now becoming a broader and broader part of Southern

60. *American Annual Cyclopaedia*, 1863, 231-232.
61. Schwab, *Confederate States, op.cit.*, 193-195; O.R.,IV, iii, 208, 1114-1116, 1161.
62. Montross, Lynn, *War Through the Ages*, New York, 1944, 509.

existence. Just how many of the four million Southerners became wartime fugitives nobody can say, but it is certain that they finally numbered in hundreds of thousands. All Southern States passed laws to provide relief for indigent dependents of soldiers, and in many these laws applied to families on the run from the foe.[63] Their need was often pitiful. Old men, women, children, abandoning their homes all the way from Galveston and Memphis to Atlanta and St. Augustine, found the refugee camps ugly, crowded, and comfortless; the shelters offered by friends dreary and chill; the bankruptcy they carried with them a grievous burden to ruined communities. When they came into countrysides dotted with burned homes and desolated fields, they looked in vain for a cabin or an onion. To travel in dilapidated buggies behind skeleton horses, to beg a slave for some hoe cakes, and to take refuge in roofless walls covered with canvas, or even in caves, was a depressing experience.

A grandniece of Jefferson Davis, who found a dreary haven in Tuscaloosa, wrote bitterly: "What mockery to call this home! We are poor refugees. How suggestive that word refugee is to my poor heart of sorrows past, present anxieties, and future misery." Her grandfather, Joseph Davis, had lost all—his handsome mansion burned, his plantation confiscated; and he never returned home again, for he had none.[64]

Many refugees were forced to exchange their most prized personal possessions, including family heirlooms, for subsistence. They saw their children go with random education or none. Sensitive ladies learned to beg for help from men wearing ragged overalls with homemade galluses, and women able to expectorate tobacco juice ten feet. They met rudeness, insult, and occasional violence along with kindness and aid—the extremes of generosity and meanness. Many of them showed remarkable resourcefulness and courage in hewing out new pursuits; but many encountered suspicion and jealousy, finding that Virginians looked down upon Alabamians, and South Carolinians upon Georgians. When Dr. Joseph LeConte of South Carolina College sent off his carefully packed laboratory equipment for safe-keeping, it got only as far as Greensboro before it disappeared forever; whether into Southern or Northern hands nobody knew.

Yet these distressed folk, who showed so much courage, devotion to duty, and patriotism, got far less sympathy and aid than they deserved. High Confederate officials said little in their behalf, and did less; well-to-do people closed their hearts and purses so tightly that Kate Stone of Louisiana laid down an accurate generalization: "it is not the rich who are most generous." Charleston newspapers with reason denounced residents of the interior who leeched coastal refugees by steep rents and commodity prices; people of North Georgia

63. Massey, Mary Elizabeth, *Refugee Life in the Confederacy*, Baton Rouge, 1964, 244-246.
64. *Ibid.*, 269-270.

assailed the residents of Augusta and other southern towns for their greedy exactions. Those who plundered refugees, wrote an Atlanta editor, might yet meet *"their* day of tribulation." Pollard called the dispossessed Tennesseeans who came to Richmond for assistance "vultures who are now preying upon the community." The pressures of the time, in short, made inhumanity, ill-will, and selfishness familiar in all communities. It was a rare citizen who showed the spirit of Thomas Dabney, publishing in the Vicksburg press a notice that any and all citizens quitting the city might take refuge on his estate.[65] Much more common were the people who regarded refugees first as a nuisance, and then as foes.

The woes of displacement, the gloom of homelessness, the frictions of exile, were a cancer that ate into not merely the endurance of Southerners, but their very soul. Hundreds of thousands were never the same afterward. By the final winter of their struggle they felt the price they were paying for its maintenance almost unendurable, and knew that it would leave marks they would carry to the grave.

[IV]

Inevitably, the rising Southern discouragement and desperation found outlets in two fatal movements: an organized demand for peace among the civilians, and a spasmodic impulse toward desertion among the soldiers. A rough logic lay behind both impulses. On every side stretched a stormy sea of confusion and disorder. Look at the commissary service under the hated Northrop, so clear a failure in collecting and storing indispensable supplies! Look at the quartermaster department under that unstable South Carolinian, Abraham C. Myers—by no means so generally disliked, but somehow never truly effective in allotting and distributing supplies until he gave way in August, 1863, to an equally hampered West Point graduate, General Alexander R. Lawton. Look at the railroads! The flagging circulatory system of the Confederacy was managed first by William S. Ashe, an attorney and planter who had become a Congressman, and then a railroad president; later by William M. Wadley, a burly, self-made man of New Hampshire birth; and later still by a Georgian named F. W. Sims—all three floundering in a swamp of difficulties. Had the Confederacy established a railway dictatorship under an autocrat ruling all the lines, he might have delivered the South from its worst transportation troubles for a short time; but he also might have created new difficulties, and such a dictatorship was for many reasons impossible.

Month by month, year by year, the tracks, the rolling stock, the mechanical

65. *Ibid.,* 152.

facilities for overhaul, and the railroad force decayed. Even a vitally needed forty-mile stretch of rails between Greensboro, North Carolina, and Danville, Virginia, which Davis urged early in the war, remained unlaid until the spring of 1864. Railway companies were so jealous that they balked at uniform gauges. And worse than that, they refused to join their lines at junction points like Petersburg even when gauges were uniform. The Southern railroads had found that when Northern workers went home, they were left with employees so inexperienced that they wrecked trains and ruined locomotives; they learned that when they applied to the Tredegar works, the Atlanta rolling mills, and the Macon machine-shops for iron materials, these facilities had been preëmpted by more urgent demands. Under Sims, the most dynamic action and the most stubborn defiance of red tape were of but trifling and transient value in relieving the railroad system from the unrelenting pressures of Northern military effort and the demon decay. Destruction from without and wastage from within left the South with but a feeble, halting, much-interrupted, and precarious service.

An example of the way in which ruin overtook service is afforded in a page from the records of the eastern Mississippi railroads early in 1864. W. T. Sherman ordered a detachment of 7,000 cavalry under William Sooy Smith south from Tennessee along the Mobile & Ohio toward Meridian, Miss., where he was to meet Sherman's main army of 20,000 infantry. This presumably swift and secret stroke miscarried. Smith barely got across the Mississippi boundary before Forrest stopped him. Sherman's columns did penetrate to Meridian, but made so much noise in the process that the Confederates under Leonidas Polk, with Major George Whitfield as chief of transportation, promptly parried the stroke. Whitfield frenziedly used all the resources of the Mobile & Ohio and the Alabama & Mississippi Rivers line to evacuate a large amount of government stores and rolling stock from Meridian. But Sherman settled down then in Meridian for a full week while his troops roamed the surrounding districts and played havoc with railroad property.

They smashed and burned all the bridges and trestles on fifty miles of Mobile & Ohio track, tearing up twenty miles of rails. They destroyed tracks, bridges, and other facilities on the Alabama & Mississippi Rivers and smashed nineteen locomotives, many cars, and a great stock of car-wheels in the region of Jackson on the Mississippi Central. It was necessary for Whitfield, as soon as Sherman retired, to gather gangs of laborers, obtain rails, ties, and bridge timbers (collecting from other roads whatever materials they could spare) and set frantically to work to restore communications.

"Thereafter, the railroads serving Jackson operated upon a day-to-day basis only," writes the historian of Confederate railroads. "Military supply routine had been broken asunder. As late as May, quantities of bacon were stranded in both north-central and southwestern Mississippi, while heavy shipments of salt, just arrived from Virginia, could find no satisfactory places of storage." Any substantial Union force could now occupy Mississippi at its leisure. Sherman did not attempt this, for he was busy farther east, but other men did.

Evidences that the railroads were falling deeper and deeper into exhaustion multiplied. During 1864, their ability to meet emergency demands for trains of troops at one point, and trains of corn and bacon at another, became more and more dubious. When in May, some Federal troops briefly seized and tore up a short stretch of the Richmond & Petersburg Railroad, Confederate officials tore their hair in anxiety. It required weeks to repair this indispensable link.[66] Already, early in May, the creaky lines south of Richmond had been strained to their utmost as Lee strove to bring troops from Florida and South Carolina up to Petersburg. It took eight days to get about 300 men of the 21st South Carolina to the defenses.[67] In June, the command under Jubal Early had to be brought from Charlottesville to Lynchburg, sixty miles, to reinforce General John C. Breckinridge. The trains were delayed in starting; their average speed was twelve miles an hour; and they arrived in time to save Lynchburg, but not to stage a counterattack that might have staggered David Hunter's army.

By Christmas that year the situation had worsened until the railways were in a pitiable state. When a Union raid created a new emergency in the Shenandoah Valley, Longstreet met the greatest difficulty in moving two brigades from Richmond to repulse it, and the troops were exhausted before they were thrown into the battleline.[68] A tragic occurrence in Georgia late that summer illustrated both the deplorable condition of the railroads and the mismanagement in operation. General Hood's chief-of-staff had noted that the rickety line from Atlanta southeast into central Georgia caused great suffering and loss of life among the casualties it carried. Trains took seventy hours from Atlanta to Macon. Yet the men had to be transported. On September 1, a large number of wounded men were sent off on jammed cars. Part way down to Macon the train collided with another coming north with commissary supplies. Both engines were smashed, cars were demolished, many men were seriously injured, and thirty were killed.[69]

Everything was running down. Even before the capture of Saltville, Va.,

66. Freeman, *Lee's Lieutenants, op.cit.*, III, 464-466; Black, Robert C., III, *The Railroads of the Confederacy*, Chapel Hill, 1952, 238-244; *O.R.*,I, li, pt. 2, 899-900.
67. Black, *op.cit.*, 244-245.
68. *Ibid.*,247; Eckenrode, H.J., and Bryan Conrad, *James Longstreet, Lee's War Horse*, Chapel Hill, 1936, 324-325.
69. Black, *op.cit.*, 253.

with its invaluable mines, late in 1864, the shortage of this indispensable commodity was alarming. The preservation of meat without it was impossible; the boiling of sea-water was a slow process; inland sources were few; and salt, heavy to carry at best, deteriorated rapidly in quality and became useless when wet. A shudder ran through the Confederacy when Saltville fell. Only less distressing was the want of drugs. Quinine and calomel were needed to conquer malaria. The cruel Northern embargo upon shipments of chloroform meant needless anguish not only for Southerners in and outside armed service, but for many Northern prisoners-of-war as well. Everywhere, necessities as well as luxuries were disappearing. And as want strode through half the Southern communities, robbery and marauding strode alongside it. In all parts of the land, trustworthy Confederate officers reported that bogus impressment officers, undisciplined squads of cavalry or mounted militia, and bands of outlaws were roaming the roads, sowing terror and disloyalty with the same hand. Two letters to Governor Vance of North Carolina in 1863 sounded the same note.[70] One from the northern area ran: "There is a degree of Penury & Want in this county, and others no doubt that is truly distressing, & under existing circumstances I do contend that our Government and Legislature should interfere. . . . Now just let the news reach our Soldiers in the Army whose families are thus oppressed, & I should not be surprised to hear any day that many of them had laid by their arms and marched off home." And one from the southern area declared: "the time has come that we the common people has to hav bread or blood & we are bound boath men and women to hav it or die in the attempt. . . . We are willing to give . . . two Dollars a bushel but no more for the idea is that the Slave oner has the plantations & the hands to rais the brad stufs & the common people is drove off in the war to fight for the big mans negro. . . . if there is not steps taken soon necessity may drive us into measure that may proove awful. . . ." Men who wrote thus were near the end of the tether—the breaking point of desperation.

Civilians reached the end of the tether when they joined an organized agitation for peace; soldiers reached it when they deserted. To some extent the two evidences of desperation stood in the relation of cause and effect. Pacifism and defeatism at home, conveyed to soldiers by letters or grapevine telegraph, led to desertion in the field.

The rise of scattered but increasingly large and determined peace organizations in the South in 1864-65 registered forever the fact that, while the people of the Confederacy were able to build a highly effective military machine, they failed to solve the problem of sustaining the welfare and morale of the entire

---

70. Quoted in Ramsdell, Charles W., *Behind the Lines in the Southern Confederacy*, Baton Rouge, 1944, 46-48.

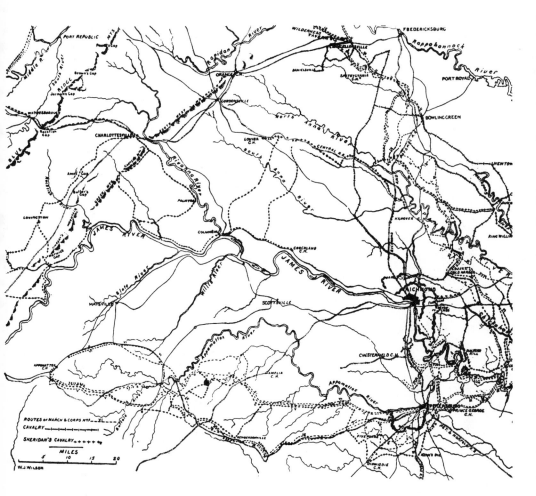

Map of Grant's Campaign against Richmond, 1864-1865

civil population. Governor Vance declared early in the autumn of 1864 that the heart of the people had never been in the war; that it was an attempted "revolution of the politicians, not the people."[71] War-weariness made the defects of public spirit plainly evident. Napoleon's observation that morale is three-fourths of battle-power found larger and larger illustration. President Davis did his utmost to rally the people, making three long speaking and inspection tours of the country east of the Mississippi, during which he held numerous conferences with military and political leaders. Some governors lent him assistance. As late as March 9, 1865, General Lee wrote: "While the military situation is not favorable, it is not worse than the superior numbers and resources of the enemy justified us in expecting from the beginning. Indeed, the legitimate military consequences of that superiority have been postponed longer than we had reason to anticipate. Everything, in my opinion, has depended and still depends upon the disposition and feelings of the people. Their representatives can best decide how they will bear the difficulties and sufferings of their condition and how they will respond to the demands which the public safety requires."[72] But all was in vain.

The hard core of peace movements within the Confederacy was inevitably found in the many thousands of Union men of the South who felt that they had been betrayed into a detestable and disastrous war.[73] Amid its first heady enthusiasms, its swirling banners, thumping drums, and squealing fifes, they had dumbly hoped for a negotiated peace and a restoration of the oldtime republic. As Southern blood was poured out like wine spilling from some mighty press, as defeat followed defeat from Shiloh to Gettysburg, as half the Carolina coast was occupied and starry flags blossomed deep in Georgia, clandestine organizations appeared wherever men kept the memory of the day on which a Southern President of the United States had risen at a dinner in honor of Jefferson to propose the immortal toast: "Our Federal Union: it must be preserved." Their names, as they arose in different parts of Dixie, were various—The Heroes of America; the Peace and Constitutional Society; the Peace Society. But their objects were everywhere the same: to aid each other in passive or active resistance; to impede enlistments; to send information to Union forces; to encourage desertion from the Confederate ranks; to help men get into the Union Army, and assist that Army wherever it invaded the South. Some were pacifists. Some were malcontents. But others were men of iron

71. Quoted in Silver, James W., "Propaganda in the Confederacy," *Journal of Southern History*, XI, No. 4, Nov., 1945, 487-503.

72. Dowdey, Clifford, and Louis H. Manarin, *The Wartime Papers of Robert E. Lee*, Boston, 1961, 913. (See Lee to John C. Breckinridge, Sec. of War.)

73. *O.R.*,I, xlvi, 1295; see Tatum, Georgia Lee, *Disloyalty in the Confederacy*, Chapel Hill, 1934, *passim*.

conviction, who meant to be in at the death of the Blatant Beast—the death of Disunion.

The earliest body to achieve a strong organization, the Peace and Constitutional Society, emerged in the hilly northwestern counties of Arkansas, where slaves were few and nationalist sentiment had true Western strength. It was a natural growth in a section of Arkansas that had voted almost solidly against secession.[74] Stronger and more widely diffused was the Peace Society, which arose in 1862 in two other areas full of Union feeling, East Tennessee and North Alabama—the valley of the Tennessee as it flows down from Knoxville into the Huntsville district, and the Cumberland Gap country. Here Federal agents lent a hand as it grew in vigor, penetrating Georgia and Alabama, and even "contaminating" some Confederate regiments. Strongest of all was the Order of the Heroes of America, which grew lusty enough in North Carolina, southwestern Virginia, and East Tennessee to interfere materially with the Southern war effort. A Confederate agent who reported on it in the fall of 1864 summarized the inducements to membership in a sentence: exemptions from military service, protection to persons and property during the war, and at the end, participation in a division of captured property.[75]

It was with good reason that North Carolina became a center of disaffection. The heroic commonwealth sent into the war about one-fifth of all the Confederate fighters, though it had only a ninth of the Southern population, and it contributed about one-fourth of those killed in action—some 40,000 men. Lee wrote Seddon at the opening of 1863: "I have relied much on the troops of that State." But throughout 1863 resentment grew. A statement issued anonymously complained that conscription and the tithe law were stripping Old North bare; that they took all the fighting men and a great part of the production. "Seizures of persons and property have become as common as they are in France and Russia."[76] The writer added: "Our patient, uncomplaining, heroic soldiers have been placed in the van of every battle and in the rear of almost every retreat." Most of the State held firm. But riotous disturbances by hungry people took place at several points, most conspicuously Salisbury, where a mob of soldiers' wives armed with hatchets assailed warehouses and carried away flour, molasses, and salt. The boldly intransigent editor, W. W. Holden, whose press, the Raleigh *Standard*, was destroyed by soldiers in 1863, was a born fighter whose State Rights feeling made him sternly hostile to the Confederate cause. Early in 1864 he suspended the *Standard* for several months, and ran for governor. It was understood that if elected he would open direct

74. *American Annual Cyclopaedia, 1861*, 25.
75. *O.R.*,IV, iii, 814-815; N.F. Bocock to Secretary Seddon.
76. *American Annual Cyclopaedia, 1863*, 691-692.

negotiations with Washington, or call a convention to leave the Confederacy, or both. But he lost.[77]

"The one great demand of the people in this part of the State," wrote one leader, "is peace—peace upon any terms that will not enslave and degrade us." Most people wanted Southern independence, but if it could not be obtained, "then they are for any terms that are honorable." Throughout 1863-64 a revolt against the authority of Richmond simmered just under the surface in North Carolina. One bloody occurrence filled people with horror. After a raid by Unionists on the mountain town of Marshall, a band of alleged disloyalists was seized in the Laurel area by Lt.-Col. James A. Keith and his Confederate command. Crime and violence had become common along the French Broad. A judicial officer reported to Governor Vance that thirteen captives had been shot, that other men had been seized unarmed in their homes, and that women had been whipped. Vance asked Secretary Seddon to cashier Keith for his brutality. "This heartless execution," writes one chronicler, "aroused the whole section to white heat."[78]

Thus the virus spread. We are not astonished to learn that so many North Carolina soldiers received letters from home urging them to desert, especially after Chief Justice William Mumford Pearson pronounced the conscription law unconstitutional, that they began quitting the ranks in squads.[79]

The peace movements and desertion, it is clear, were firmly linked. Toward the end of the struggle losses in battle, heavy as they became, were more than matched by losses from absenteeism. Soldiers had all too many reasons for leaving the colors anyway. The excitements of battle were rare. Ill-fed, ill-clothed, unpaid for long stretches, alternating weary hours of marching with wearier hours of drill, verminous, enduring fierce summer heat, sharp winter cold, and soaking rains, they suffered from loneliness, homesickness, and above all boredom. The thought in spring of fields to be seeded, in summer of harvests spoiling for want of labor, in winter of pinched wives and crying children, became insupportable. Desertion sometimes seemed an overpowering duty, not an offense. When the fighting spirit ebbed away among the old people, the wives, sisters, sweethearts, and neighbors left at home, and when letters begged not for heroism but for an end of the hopeless carnage, then hearts sank and desertion, always endemic among both Northern and Southern troops, became epidemic.

Statistics of desertion in areas of the Mississippi Valley were highly de-

77. Dowd, Clement, *Life of Zebulon B. Vance*, Charlotte, N.C., 1897, 447ff; Tucker, Glenn, *Zeb Vance, Champion of Personal Freedom*, Indianapolis, 1966, Chap. XXIII.

78. Tatum, *op.cit.*, 11ff; *O.R.* I, xviii, 881; Tucker, Vance, *op.cit.*, 307-311.

79. *O.R.*, IV, iii, 975-979, H.W. Walter of Inspector-General's Dept. to J.W.C. Watson, Dec. 29, 1864.

pressing. In 1863, two hundred men marching to Arkansas left one regiment. All but forty dropped out of an Arkansas regiment within ten days; the First Alabama lost almost a hundred men; and sixty Texans abandoned the colors. For one reason, Vicksburg had filled the troops with a deep distrust of their commanding general, Pemberton. "I have seen a great many of the officers and men who were under him at Vicksburg and have conversed freely with them," Governor Joseph E. Brown wrote Secretary Seddon on August 10, 1863, "and have never yet found one of them who has confidence in him.... Without some change to inspire the troops with confidence, General Pillow or anyone else who attempts to carry them back will need a heavy and an active force."[80]

The shock of Gettysburg to army morale, if less serious than Vicksburg, was great; so was Chattanooga. In Virginia in midsummer of 1863, deserters daily tramped the roads homeward, almost invariably bearing their arms. If asked for papers authorizing absence, they patted their guns, saying defiantly: "This is my furlough." When garrison troops of General Samuel Jones, a West Pointer, were sent to reinforce Lee after Gettysburg, desertions were heavy because they felt the new duty a breach of implied contract.[81] Some of John Daniel Imboden's troops deserted for the same reason. Moreover, the general attitude toward desertion was changing. At first it had been regarded as a crime almost equivalent to treason, but in the late summer of 1863 an officer in Columbia, South Carolina, reported that disaffection had reached such a height that all sense of shame was lost. Many recruits in upland counties came from poor, ignorant backgrounds; the mountain coverts furnished them conceal-ment; the success of the boldest in gaining immunity encouraged others, until scarcely a family did not have a deserter husband, son, brother, or cousin hiding in the mountains. "The tone of the people is lost; it is no longer a reproach to be known as a deserter; all are ready to encourage and aid the efforts of those who are avoiding duty."[82]

Six weeks after Gettysburg, Lee wrote President Davis that the number of desertions had become so great that unless they could be checked, "I fear success in the field will be seriously endangered." He had hopes that an amnesty granted to absentees would bring many of them back. After all, it was impossible to define the term deserter with accuracy; men might be absent from illness, exhaustion, imperative family duties, or simple negligence about dates. Americans North and South in Civil War days, like Australians in the First World War, were too individualistic to accept discipline tamely. Self-

80. O.R., IV, ii, 753.
81. Freeman, Lee, op.cit., III, 254; O.R., IV, ii, 721.
82. C.D. Melton, Aug. 25, 1863, to Col. John S. Preston, Supt. of Conscription in South Carolina; O.R., IV, ii, 769.

assertion was so general, the line between straggling and desertion was so thin, and the difficulty of keeping commands intact in the wide shaggy American countrysides was so pronounced, that it was impossible to maintain a harsh attitude.[83] On both sides, moreover, political leaders realized that harshness would defeat itself People who heard that their boys were dying at the hands of martinets in charge of firing squads would refuse to support the struggle.

The Southern army had to be more severe than the Northern. Furloughs were less frequent in the South than the North. Homesick soldiers got little chance of seeing parents, wives, and children unless they strayed when the fortunes of war took them near their hearths. Hence it was that about 4,000 men absented themselves after Shiloh,[84] and large numbers after Vicksburg and Chattanooga. Inferior in manpower, Southern leaders had to strain every nerve to keep their echelons strong. Yet even so, they inflicted the death penalty with reluctance. A table submitted by the Second Corps in the last months of the war tells its own story: tried for desertion, 29; found guilty, 6; shot, 1.[85] Men were too precious to be executed. Sometimes, the array of deserters was so great, running into several thousands, that death sentences were unthinkable, although some executions did take place.[86]

Davis had expected much from his offer on August 1, 1863, of an amnesty to deserters and others absent without leave if they returned within twenty days, provided they were not second offenders.[87] Instead, his gesture encouraged many to remain at home, or to join some partisan corps. General Imboden wrote Lee that many deserters in the Shenandoah successfully hid from the squads sent to arrest them. Lee had to inform President Davis that as the amnesty offer had not borne fruit, he had changed his mind. He believed that all the requirements of mercy and forbearance had been met; and he was now convinced that he must exact a "rigid enforcement of the death penalty in future cases of conviction."[88] His subordinates learned of his views and executions duly took place—without avail.

Early in 1864 Congress passed a law for the punishment of anyone who advised or aided desertion,[89] but the penalties were mild, and it was difficult to enforce them. A wife might write: "The children are hungry, and crying for bread. If only you could come home!" Who would punish her for the

83. Cf. Stephen Crane, *The Red Badge of Courage*; Dowdey, Clifford, and Louis Manarin, eds., *The Wartime Papers of R.E. Lee*, Boston, 1961, 591.
84. Coulter, *Confederates States, op.cit.*, 463.
85. Lonn, Ella, *Desertion During the Civil War*, New York, 1928, 60.
86. *Ibid.*, 57.
87. Coulter, *op.cit.*, 468; it extended to men under punishment; *O.R.*, IV, ii, 687-688.
88. Dowdey and Manarin, *op.cit.*, 591.
89. Coulter, *op.cit.*, 466.

poignant statement? In February, 1864, Congress tried to reward soldiers for resisting the temptation to straggle, desert, or otherwise go absent without leave. If they stuck grimly to the post of duty for six months from April 1, each of them would be given a hundred-dollar bond. When Davis visited Georgia and Alabama in the autumn to hearten the people, he urged men and women alike to persuade deserters to return to the Army of the Tennessee. "Can they see the banished, can they hear the wail of their suffering countrywomen and children, and not come?"[90] "If one-half the men now absent without leave will return to duty," he added, "we can defeat the enemy." When he got back to Richmond on a bright, warm October day, he found the capital depressed, conscription lagging, and desertion increasing. "The dead come in, and the living do not get out so fast,"[91] wrote Varina Davis. By the beginning of 1865 desertions were more alarming than ever. "I have endeavored to ascertain the causes," Lee wrote Seddon, "and think that the insufficiency of food and nonpayment of the troops have more to do with the dissatisfaction. . . . than anything else."[92] But the causes were many—and imperative.

On February 11, 1865, Lee renewed the offer of an amnesty to all absent soldiers who would return within twenty days. It was a final gesture, reinforced by a last appeal to patriotism. Brave men with arms in their hands, he declared, could never barter manhood for peace, nor the right of self-government for life or property.[93]

By the latter half of 1864 great numbers of deserters and draft-evaders had gathered in countless safe refuges in the Southern mountains, swamps, and forests. The fastnesses of Eastern Tennessee, the hills and caverns of North Carolina, the swampy sections of Virginia and Florida, were full of pockets where concealment was easy, escape rapid, and defensible nooks abundant. Lawless men banded to protect themselves from scouting parties, to secrete cotton, and to prey at will upon farms and hamlets. Unionists throughout the lower Appalachians had always been ready to shelter escaped Northern prisoners, help runaway Negroes, and resist Confederate authorities. Some units, like the Independent Union Rangers of Florida, grew to a strength of several hundred.[94] In the West and Southwest, crews of deserters, jayhawkers, and guerrillas, along with mere robbers and desperadoes, terrorized whole counties, seized horses, food, and clothing wherever they could, and became—as

90. Strode, Hudson, *Jefferson Davis*, III, New York, 1964, 93-94; Rowland, *Jefferson Davis Constitutionalist*, *op.cit.*, VI, 342-344.
91. Strode, *op.cit.*, III, 106; to Mrs. Chesnut.
92. Dowdey and Manarin, *op.cit.*, 886-887.
93. *O.R.* I, xlvi, pt. 2, 1230-1231.
94. Lonn, *Desertion*, *op.cit.*, 65-66.

General Gideon Pillow said of some Alabama gangs—as vicious as rattle-snakes.

It added to the distress and discouragement of Southerners to realize that in spite of all their efforts to enforce the conscription laws, to encourage volunteering, to bring deserters back into the ranks, and to heal the sick and lightly wounded, the strength of their armies steadily fell. This fact had been emphatically pointed out to them in Secretary Seddon's report of November 26, 1863. The whole able-bodied male population from 18 to 45 had been made liable to military service although exemptions were numerous during most of the war. Substitution had been repealed by the Act of December 28, 1863. It was difficult to state accurately the number brought into the service, and the number who might still be called into the field. The law gave men the privilege, before being enrolled for conscription, of volunteering, and it was supposed that three volunteers had entered the army to every conscript. Seddon believed that, in the year just ending, about 20,000 volunteers and conscripts had entered the army from Virginia, and 80,000 men from the whole South. "Yet with so serious an addition our armies have not fully maintained their strength in numbers. This affords a startling, but, it is feared, not an incorrect view of the waste by sickness, casualties of battle, captures, desertions, and discharges."[95] Still less did the Confederate armies maintain their strength during 1864. By 1865 the last sands were running out.

[V]

The South was paying the penalty for its involvement in total war. War was its single all-engrossing occupation; war caught up the energies not only of its half-million white men but its boys, its women, its Negroes, its aged. The North looked to many objects—industry, trade, speculation, pleasure; the South had but one, the war. In the North the seashore and mountain resorts were crowded, the theatres, bookshops, and racetracks kept their votaries, and the Western rails and steamboats carried throngs to new homes. In the South people had but one business, war. The South held a small and diminishing number of fighters, and it used nearly the whole, putting into the field beside them beardless youths and white-haired elders. The South was poor, but the Confederate authorities seized whatever they could find; pork, flour, forage, cloth, leather, corn, sugar, tobacco—all were taken by the government, receipted for in worthless paper, and used or sold, no excuse being heard, no

95. *O.R.*, IV, ii, 995.

grumbling tolerated. At the same time there had been considerable amounts of material voluntarily contributed at various times and places.

"Look at this war; it has come to everybody," wrote the tempestuously brilliant South Carolinian, Lawrence Keitt, soon to lay down his life. "States, towns, villages, firesides—all feel it and share in it."[96] Total mobilization and total war, something new in the world, was to mean in the end almost total ruin.

The epic struggle, the war of brother against brother, was not a quadrille in a drawing room; it was a chronicle of endless personal tragedies, many of them enacted far behind the battle-lines and in dim obscurity. "Its interior history," wrote Walt Whitman, "will not only never be written—its practicality, minutiae of deeds and passions, will never be even suggested." True, and truest of all to those who looked within. To Whitman it was the illustrations of character and fortitude on the battlefield and in the hospitals that were most impressive. "The actual soldier of 1862-65, North and South, with all his ways, his incredible dauntlessness, habits, practises, tastes, languages, his fierce friendship, his appetite, rankness, his superb strength and animality, lawless gait, and a hundred unnamed lights and shades of camp, I say, will never be written. . . ." But this was less than half the story. Behind the camps and exploding shells, in caravans of refugees, in desolated homes, at gravesides of mothers and wives just as truly killed by the war as if struck down by a bullet, were found exhibitions of character and devotion as impressive as any in the field. The wide Southern land from the Virginia sounds and Florida beaches to Galveston Bay and Eagle Pass had become, indeed, a land of multi-faceted drama, and it was the domestic drama that was most poignant.

Yet the dragon of desolation that ravaged the South in the last year of war carried, like Shakespeare's ugly and venomous toad, a precious jewel in its head. It cleared a field for new tillage; it did a work of transformation that, however brutal, had to be done. The Northern columns brought torch and sword, but they also brought fresh ideas wherever they tarried. The thousands of refugees who wearily trailed their way from lodging to lodging suffered much, but they gave galvanic activity to a section that had been all too largely torpid. Half of the land under the flail of war had needed a flail to awaken it; it was the land where Frederick Law Olmsted had found houses without a book or paper, and people who were not sure whether New York was a free State or not, or whether Iowa was beyond "the Texies." The tale of wartime destruction was shocking, yet less agonizing when we recall that Olmsted had

---

96. Sullivan's Island, Feb. 11, 1864, to his wife; Keitt Papers, Duke Univ. Libr.

found in Virginia itself "an essentially frontier condition," with beasts, birds of prey, forests, and marshes increasing while, in areas where slavery had existed longest, bridges, shops, schools, and churches were diminishing.[97] Much was being destroyed in the South, but much had to be destroyed if a better land, with better institutions and ideas, was to be born.

97. Olmsted, Frederick Law, *A Journey in the Back Country*, New York, 1860, Chs. VII, VIII, IX, X; Whitman, Walt, *Walt Whitman's Civil War*, ed. Walter Lowenfels, New York, 1960, 293-294.

9

Final Triumph of Union Arms

AN ARMY of more than 600,000 men present for duty, and with more than half as many more in reserve, making a total Union force of nearly 960,000, stood poised and ready after exceptionally heavy winter snows and rains for what was clearly going to be the last campaigning of the war. Optimism had marked each of the preceding four springs, but confidence was greater in 1865. A million men exerting the tremendous economic and logistical energy of the North simply could not be halted, especially now that the opposing forces had dwindled to an aggregate army of about 160,000 men present for duty in a total force of 358,000.[1]

Not only were the manpower odds three or four to one against the South and the odds in war materiel many times greater still, but the Federal armies were deep in the heart of the Confederacy, chopping the hostile country into smaller and smaller bits, while at the same time the Army of the Potomac held fast, pinning the main Confederate force down tight in the Richmond-Petersburg area. The Union now had the advantage of movement. No longer could Confederate armies strike out suddenly in a bold attempt to throw their opponents off balance. They could only hang on—and for what? Many Southerners were still courageous, but knowledge of practical realities could not but affect the total morale.

First of all, the strongest Southern army, that of Northern Virginia led by Lee, could now do nothing but stand the long watches in the trenches of Petersburg and wait, chilled by the inclement winter and the steady approach of impending doom. In Georgia it was well known that the drenching rains and swollen streams would not long halt Sherman in his well-planned northward sweep into the Carolinas, a march that would be like the irresistible point of a sword thrusting its antagonist back against the high wall of Grant's forces. There was no logical escape.

The western legionaries of the Union had just completed the most success-

---

1. Troop figures are approximate.

254

ful march of the war, Sherman meeting little opposition from Atlanta to the sea.

[I]

In less than a month from the time his troops entered Savannah, Sherman had worked out and put into effect an efficient yet humane plan of occupation for the city. As he later wrote, not without pride in his achievement: "No city was ever occupied with less disorder or more system than this of Savannah, and it is a subject of universal comment that though an army of 60,000 men lay camped around it, women and children of an hostile people walk its streets with as much security as they do in Philadelphia. I attach much importance to these little matters. . . ."[2] But he placed major emphasis on the push northward from Georgia into the Carolinas. This would be quite a feat, and vastly different from the march through Georgia. Lengthy and laborious preliminaries had gone into the assembly of the fleet off shore; arms and ammunition had been gathered, food stocks accumulated, horses fattened, men rested, and accoutrements of all kinds readied. At Savannah, in January, supply problems still persisted. One officer felt that his men were being less well fed than at any time during the war. For lack of fodder horses were on short rations too. It took time to organize new supply routes from the north via ships; the area around Savannah, unlike the richer areas of inner Georgia, simply could not support the army. In time, however, the problem was conquered, but much suffering was endured, perhaps more so than on the march through Georgia.[3]

The four corps of Sherman's field force still numbered around 60,000, including cavalry and artillery, and in addition, the Union had in John G. Foster's Department of the South nearly 23,000 troops.[4] To oppose this host of battle-tempered veterans, the estimated enemy strength available was put at a little over 33,000 soldiers of all service branches, and with some units greatly scattered. Even this estimate was much too high.[5] Confederate generals P. G.

2. Sherman, William T., *Home Letters*, ed. M.A. DeWolfe Howe, New York, 1909, 319-322, letter Dec. 31, 1864, to Thomas Ewing. At Savannah Sherman received an official visit of Secretary of War Stanton, and believed at the time that Stanton was pleased with what he saw. Later, however, after the imbroglio with Stanton over the Johnston surrender, Sherman wrote: "The Great War Secretary came to Savannah to 'betray me.' Of this I am more than convinced—I admire his great qualities, but despise his mean ones." Sherman, *Home Letters*, *op.cit.*, 327, Jan. 15, to his wife; also Sherman's handwritten comments in his copy of Boynton, H.V., *Sherman's Historical Raid*, Sherman Collection, Northwestern Univ. Library.

3. Williams, Alpheus S., *From the Cannon's Mouth, The Civil War Letters of Gen. Alpheus S. Williams*, Detroit, 1959, 335.

4. *O.R.*, I, xlvii, pt.2, 192-193; Cox, Jacob D., *The March to the Sea*, New York, 1897, 239.

5. Cox, *op.cit.*, 239-240; Barrett, John G., *Sherman's March Through the Carolinas*, Chapel Hill, N.C., 1956, 49-50.

Beauregard, Hardee, D.H. Hill, G.W. Smith, and others met in a somewhat bleak atmosphere near Augusta to try to see what force they had and what could be done with it. Remnants from the Army of Tennessee were being brought east from Mississippi in bits and pieces. New recruits were scarce, the militia of little use. An ailing Beauregard had to take command over what force remained, but faced a discouraging outlook. Sherman's route north was uncertain to the Confederates, rendering the use of their depleted troops even more dubious. It was finally decided that probably Hardee should not attempt to defend Charleston if pressed strongly, as that would take 20,000 men, and the assembling of such numbers was out of the question. Beauregard, however, continued to oppose abandoning Charleston.[6] Hardee told President Davis in late January that "The people of Charleston, though in many respects to be admired, are so entirely wrapped up in their own State and city as to be unmindful of the wants of other portions of our country—to them Charleston is the Confederacy, and to save Charleston they are willing that Lee should give up Richmond, or any other section of the Confederacy so that their selfish ambition might be gratified. . . ."[7]

There were increased calls for the reassignment of Joseph E. Johnston to command. Johnston himself was reluctant in view of his long-standing disagreements with President Davis.[8] The truth was, and the generals were aware of it, that mere leadership was not enough. They simply lacked the troops, the materiel, the transportation, to oppose Sherman or even effectively to delay him.

By January 15, Sherman had sent Howard by sea with the right wing up to Beaufort, S.C., to make a lodgment on the railroad from Charleston to Savannah. Slocum with the left wing and the cavalry of Kilpatrick were to cross the Savannah River on a pontoon bridge and the Union causeway into the swamps and rice fields north of Savannah. Slocum's move was seriously delayed by the heavy January rains which overflowed the bottom lands, flooded the causeway, and swept away part of the pontoon bridge. It was not until the first week of February that he could cross three miles up the Savannah River from his previously planned transits, which were now flooded land. On January 18, Sherman turned Savannah over to Foster, while he himself went to Hilton Head and Beaufort. From Beaufort he made a demonstration toward Charleston, but later said he never had any intention of actually approaching that city.[9]

6. Roman, Alfred, *Military Operations of General Beauregard*, New York, 1884, II, 336-340, including notes on meeting.

7. Hardee to Davis, Jan. 29, 1865, Davis Papers, Duke Univ. Library.

8. Johnston to Mackall, Jan. 26, 1865, Columbia, S.C., Mackall Papers, Southern Historical Collection, Univ. of N.C.

9. *O.R.*, I, xlvii, pt.1, 17-18, Sherman's report.

In the march straight north from Savannah toward Columbia the army at times moved in four columns, and other times in three, so as to keep the Confederates off balance and inhibit their concentration.

However, the main obstacle was not the rebel forces but the natural geography of the area, made even more difficult by the excessive downpours, the felling of trees along the route, and the removal of obstructions set up by Wheeler's Confederate cavalry. The Union pioneer battalions performed yeoman service in clearing roads, rebuilding bridges, and replacing causeways over the almost continuous lowlands and waterways of southeastern South Carolina. By February 11, the army was fairly close together, occupying a position dividing the enemy, who were thus forced to watch both Charleston on the coast and Augusta to the northwest.

Something of a change came over Sherman's army when it sensed it was heading northward in the general direction of home in what must be its last major campaign. "It now seemed as if every soldier felt he was in the heart of the enemies' country, and it was a portion of his duty to do all the damage possible to the enemy. There were fires in every direction, many times houses were fired so near the road we were marching on that it became so hot in the road that our ammunition trains were obliged to go out in the fields to pass. If we halted to rest in a little town it would be but a short time before houses all about seemed to be in flames. . . . These fires were kept up all across the state. No one had orders to do this work of destruction; but on the contrary, it was strictly forbidden. But in a large family it is always difficult to keep all members on the right track. At any house where the inhabitants had remained, neither they nor their property was molested."[10] Countless eyewitnesses agree that burning, looting, and bumming increased sharply as the Yankees moved en masse into South Carolina, which they regarded as the heart of rebellion and secession.

One member of the 195th Illinois wrote his mother of "the treasonable soil of South Carolina." In one instance a whole brigade rushed pell mell upon a few houses grouped together, and within half-an-hour "not a vestige of them remained save the chimneys and one house for head-quarters. They made us excellent fires and warmed us thoroughly. Such was our entrance into the state. . . ."[11] An officer proclaimed, "We must go, for there are rebel flags flying and rebel guns between us and our Nation's capital, and we must cut our way through to where our banner waves over our war-worn comrades on the James; . . . I want to see the long deferred chastisement begin. If we don't purify

10. Memoirs of Richard Edward May, ms., HEH.
11. Letter from Loring Armstrong, Elmhurst, Ill., Jan. 5, 1865, George F. Cram letters, Loring Armstrong Private Collection, Oak Park, Ill.

South Carolina it will be because we *can't get a light*. . . ."[12] This same major said in March that, "The army burned everything it came near in the State of South Carolina, not under orders, but in spite of orders. The men 'had it in' for the State and they took it out in their own way. Our track through the State is a desert waste. Since entering North Carolina the wanton destruction has stopped." At the same time he was sickened by the "frightful devastation our army was spreading on every hand. OH! it was absolutely terrible! Every house except the church and the negro cabin was burned to the ground; women, children and old men turned out into the mud and rain and their houses and furniture first plundered then burned. I knew it would be so before we entered the State, but I had no idea how frightful the reality would be. . . ."[13]

At first, part of Sherman's army, fearing the new march would be more dangerous, expressed concern lest Lee should confront them. But that did not stop them in their march of destruction. One eyewitness of the columns of black smoke meeting their gaze, stated, "South Carolina has commenced to pay an instalment, long overdue, on her debt to justice and humanity. With the help of God, we will have principal and interest before we leave her borders. There is a terrible gladness in the realization of so many hopes and wishes."[14] Building materials were to be long in demand along the path of Sherman's army. Fire, ashes, and desolation followed the army, but a goodly portion of the army felt South Carolina was only meeting with the fate she deserved.[15] Some soldiers stated that in Georgia few homes had been burned, but in South Carolina few escaped. "The middle of the finest day looked black and gloomy, for a dense smoke arose on all sides, clouding the very heavens. At night the tall pine trees seemed so many huge pillars of fire. . . . Vandalism of this kind, though not encouraged, was seldom punished. . . . Foragers and bummers heralded the advance of the army, eating up the country like so many locusts. . . ."[16] Even the generals were aware of it all. General Alpheus S. Williams wrote to his daughter, "We swept through South Carolina, the fountainhead of rebellion, in a broad, semi-circular belt, sixty miles wide, the arch of which was the capital of the state, Columbia. Our people, impressed with the idea that every South Carolinian was an errant Rebel, spared nothing but the old men, women, and children. . . . The soldiers quietly took the matter into their own

12. Connolly, Major James Austin, *Diary, Transactions of the Illinois State Historical Society*, Springfield, 1928, 375.
13. *Ibid.*, Letters of March 12 and 21, 379, 381.
14. Nichols, George W., *The Story of the Great March*, New York, 1865, 131.
15. *Ibid.*, 140.
16. Conyngham, Capt. David P., *Sherman's March Through the South*, New York, 1865, 310-311.

hands. Orders to respect houses and private property not necessary for the subsistence of the army were not greatly heeded. Indeed, not heeded at all. . . ."[17]

When Confederate military leaders protested, Sherman wrote the Southern cavalry officer, Joe Wheeler, on February 8, that "I hope you will burn all cotton and save us the trouble . . . All you don't burn I will. As to private houses occupied by peaceful families, my orders are not to molest or disturb them, and I think my orders are obeyed. Vacant houses being of no use to anybody, I care little about, . . . I don't want them destroyed, but do not take much care to preserve them. . . ."[18] Earlier, Sherman had told Halleck that he realized "the whole army is burning with an insatiable desire to wreak vengeance upon South Carolina. I almost tremble at her fate, but feel that she deserves all that seems in store for her."[19] Halleck, too, in Washington, had written Sherman thus: "Should you capture Charleston, I hope that by some accident the place may be destroyed, and if a little salt should be sown upon its site it may prevent the growth of future crops of nullification and secession . . ."[20]

Sherman charged the Confederates with what he termed the murder of several foragers and threatened severe reprisals.[21] Wade Hampton replied he knew nothing of the cases, but did say he had ordered his men "to shoot down all of your men who are caught burning houses. This order shall remain in force so long as you disgrace the profession of arms by allowing your men to destroy private dwellings. . . ."[22] Yes, in many ways it was a more devastating march than that through Georgia, at least for those still at home in the Confederacy.

Sherman had given his marching orders as of January 19 with the goal of reaching Goldsborough, N.C., about March 15. Much preliminary movement and fortification took place in the latter half of January, but the real march began February 1, when Slocum was able to cross the flooded Savannah. Northward the four corps moved toward the state capital of South Carolina at Columbia, a route that really detoured Charleston, leaving it stranded. After crossing the Savannah, they reached the Salkehatchie where the right wing fought to control the bridges, part of the troops wallowing through a three-mile swamp sometimes in water up to their shoulders. In weather turning steadily colder, after numerous skirmishes along the way, the Fifteenth Corps

17. Williams, Alpheus S., op.cit., 373, Mar. 12, 1865.
18. O.R., I, xlvii, pt. 2, 342, Sherman to Wheeler, Feb. 8, 1865.
19. O.R., I, xliv, 798-800, Sherman to Halleck, Dec. 24, 1864.
20. Ibid., 741, Halleck to Sherman, Dec. 18, 1864.
21. O.R., I, xlvii, pt. 2, 546, Sherman to Wade Hampton, Feb. 24, 1865.
22. Ibid., 596-597.

reached the south bank of the Congaree opposite Columbia on February 16, but were unable to capture the bridges before they burned.[23]

The men were proud of their "semi-amphibian" march to Columbia, and discussed with professional intelligence the decisive moves of the campaign.[24] Once more, pioneers and engineers alike were operating superbly.

At the same time, the capital city, Columbia, South Carolina, was paying the penalties of the State's recalcitrance. As Federal troops arrived on the south bank of the Congaree on February 16, people could be seen excitedly thronging the streets of Columbia and occasional groups of Southern cavalry boldly emerged. The next day Sherman himself was at the newly laid pontoon bridge when a Confederate major drove up in a carriage and formally surrendered to the Twenty-fifth Iowa. Soon a few Union soldiers of the Seventeenth Corps arrived. Sherman had ordered that troops were to destroy all arsenals and public property not needed for Federal use, and all railroads, stations and useful machinery, but that dwellings, colleges, schools and "harmless private property" should be spared. Sherman rode rapidly into the city, where, he reported later, a "perfect tempest of wind was raging."[25] A brigade of Northern men was vigilantly posted. Some heaps of cotton in the street were said to be on fire and blowing loosely around, their flames only partially extinguished. Most of the Federal troops were bivouacked outside the city.

Under circumstances like these, a catastrophe was inevitable. That night the handsome capital of South Carolina burned with a completeness more total than the destruction of any other city during the war. And even more furious than the flames was the resentment felt by the people of the South in widening circles about the ruined city. During the decades since then, scholars and angry or lurid Southern writers have chanted "Who burned Columbia?" until it has become a stale refrain like "Who sank the Maine?" No answer can be given that seems completely convincing. Masses of evidence have been assembled, but still the problem remains insoluble. Three main theories have found support: first, the fires spreading from burning cotton were ignited by irresponsible vagabonds and some drunken, retreating troopers;[26] second, that Sherman willfully ordered the city burned, an allegation that he sternly denied and that seems incredible; third, that released prisoners, emancipated slaves, and/or intoxicated Union soldiers or vagrant Southerners were responsible. For each hypothesis some circumstances can be found to offer partial support except the

23. *Ibid.*, pt. 1, 18-21, Sherman's report; *Sherman Letters, Correspondence between General and Senator Sherman from 1837 to 1891*, ed. Rachel Sherman Thorndike, London, 1894, 245-246.

24. Nourse, Henry, "The Burning of Columbia," *Military Historical Society of Massachusetts Papers*, IX, 440-441.

25. *O.R.*, I, xlvii, pt. 1, 20-21, Sherman's report.

26. Wade Hampton strongly denied such fires.

allegation that Sherman deliberately fired the city. Some observers reported fires breaking out in homes in widely scattered sections of Columbia at about the same time, indicating incendiarism. Others told of drunken soldiers and Negroes breaking into homes and setting blazes.[27]

About two-thirds of Columbia was in ashes when the sun rose on February 18. The homeless gathered in the suburbs, or in open parks or lots around vestiges of furniture and household goods.[28] During the night, a large majority of the city's population, swelled by war from its normal 8,000 to about 20,000, were driven into the streets or engaged in combatting fires and looters. The worn-out fire apparatus was ineffective, hoses often being chopped to pieces by riotous marauders. Wade Hampton's splendid residence was among the first to go. By morning blackened chimneys and an occasional half-ruined building marked the sky-line of Columbia. The new state capitol building itself was razed, as well as the entire business district. Looting of shops had been extensive, particularly the liquor stores. The ringing cheers and martial music of the entry into Columbia were silenced. The neat, little city with its upland Southern charm of frame and brick buildings was a wreck. While mothers sought terrified children among the ruins, and invalids lay exposed in the streets, shots frequently rang out. The Federal guards proved too few or impotent, a lack of responsibility that may be charged to Sherman.

A Federal captain wrote later that the fires could have been kept under control but for "the folly of its inhabitants and military rules."[29] This captain recorded as one tragic instance of loss that the home and library of the novelist William Gilmore Simms, though intact when he and other Federals left, were burned the following day, and blamed the Negro servants. Simms himself bitterly blamed the Yankees for the destruction of his home and library of eight to nine thousand volumes, many of them autographed, along with volumes of manuscript letters from many distinguished personages.[30]

For the Confederates the situation was desperate, if not hopeless. But Lee, now General-in-Chief, had to try. On February 19, from Petersburg, he wrote Secretary of War Breckinridge that "General Beauregard does not say what he proposes or what he can do. I do not know where his troops are, or on what lines they are moving. . . . He has a difficult task to perform under present circumstances, and one of his best officers (General Hardee) is incapacitated by sickness. I have also heard that his own health is indifferent, though he has never so stated. . . . General J.E. Johnston is the only officer whom I know who

27. *O.R.* I, xlvii, pt. 1, 22, Sherman's report; Sherman, *Memoirs*, II, 286-288.
28. *Ibid.*, 191-199, 242-244; Hedley, Fenwick Y., *Marching Through Georgia*, Chicago, 1890, 389.
29. Nourse, Henry, *op.cit.*, IX, 435-437.
30. *Ibid.*, 445-446.

has the confidence of the army and people, and if he was ordered to report to me I would place him there on duty. It is necessary to bring out all our strength, and, I fear, to unite our armies, as separately they do not seem able to make head against the enemy. Everything should be destroyed that cannot be removed out of the reach of Generals Sherman and Schofield. . . . I fear it may be necessary to abandon all our cities, and preparation should be made for this contingency. . . ."[31]

Although Beauregard was undoubtedly humiliated by the move, he agreed to serve under Johnston; thereafter, however, his duties were primarily routine. As a matter of fact, the Confederacy in the Carolinas now had a surplus of generals, when they really needed soldiers with guns.

Johnston said he took command "with a full consciousness on my part, however, that we could have no other object, in continuing the war, than to obtain fair terms of peace; for the Southern cause must have appeared hopeless then, to all intelligent and dispassionate Southern men. I therefore resumed the duties of my military trade with no hope beyond that of contributing to obtain peace on such conditions as, under the circumstances, ought to satify the Southern people and their Government. . . ."[32] Johnston estimated his available troops to number about 17,000 including cavalry,[33] but the figures kept changing, and no one was ever sure just how many Confederates were available. Believing, with Lee, that the remaining Confederate forces should be concentrated, if possible, to strike Sherman, Johnston even suggested that Lee send him half of his army so Sherman could be crushed near Roanoke, thus enabling them to turn on Grant together.[34] However, Lee was unable to reduce his force and still hold the Petersburg-Richmond axis. The General-in-Chief told Johnston, "If you are forced back from Raleigh, and we be deprived of the supplies from East North Carolina, I do not know how this army can be supported. Yet a disaster to your army will not improve my condition, and while I would urge upon you to neglect no opportunity of delivering the enemy a successful blow, I would not recommend you to engage in a general battle without a reasonable prospect of success. . . ."[35] Lee continued, "I shall maintain my position as long as it appears advisable, both from the moral and material advantages of holding Richmond and Virginia. If obliged to abandon it, so far as I can now see I shall be compelled to fall back to the Danville road for subsistence, . . ." But he felt there could be no fixed rules or plans, for too much clearly depended on the enemy; the Yankees were in control.

31. O.R., I, xlvii, pt. 1, 1044, Lee to Breckinridge.
32. Johnston, J.E., Narrative, 371-373.
33. O.R., I, xlvii, pt. 1, 150.
34. Ibid., 1051; pt. 2, 1256-57.
35. Ibid., pt. 2, 1395-96, Lee to Johnston, March 15.

At Raleigh on March 14, Johnston was slowly concentrating the troops of Bragg, of Hardee, and of the Army of Tennessee.

Sherman, realizing full well that Johnston would have to try something, ordered Kilpatrick's cavalry out in front. Slocum on the left was traveling light with four divisions; Howard, on the right, with another four divisions, was ready to give support to the left if attacked. Sherman was with Slocum. Schofield at New Bern, and Terry at Wilmington, were to move towards Goldsboro. The rains continued and the mud increased, but on the morning of March 16, Sherman moved toward the troubled area.

The road to Goldsboro ran through a narrow, swampy neck between the Cape Fear and South Rivers, where Hardee had set up a blockade. The skirmish which followed at Averysboro was not a major engagement, but it was sharp and hard while it lasted. Furthermore, it showed that the Confederates, even though weak, could still be dangerous.

In letters home, Sherman gave rein to just a modicum of emotion late in March: "Soldiers have a wonderful idea of my knowledge and attach much of our continued success in it. . . . I don't believe anything had tended more to break the pride of the South than my steady, persistent progress. My army is dirty, ragged, and saucy. . . . I would like to march this army through New York just as it appears today, with its wagons, pack mules, cattle, niggers and bummers, and I think they would make a more attractive show than your fair. . . ."[36] Later, on April 5, he told his wife, "I will challenge the world to exhibit a finer-looking set of men, brawny, strong, swarthy, a contrast to the weak and sickly fellows that came to me in Kentucky three years ago. . . . Whilst wading through mud and water, and heaving at mired wagons, the soldiers did not indulge a single groan, but always said and felt that the Old Man would bring them out all right; . . . If we can force Lee to abandon Richmond and can whip him in open fight, I think I can come home and rest and leave others to follow up the fragments. . . ."[37] Many felt that the Carolina campaign was much more arduous than that in Georgia. General Alpheus Williams, for example, said that the labor and fatigue were far greater.[38]

Sherman was proud of the job he had done, proud of the adulation he was receiving, but at the same time, he was still the same Sherman who had probably not changed much except perhaps for being more confident than ever. The statement of one observer that Sherman's brain was "a splendid piece of machinery with all the screws loose" is familiar.[39] What such critics

---

36. Sherman to his wife, Mar. 23, 1865, Goldsboro, N.C., *Home Letters*, 334-336.
37. *Ibid.*, 339-341.
38. Williams, *From the Cannon's Mouth, op.cit.*, 377.
39. George W. Morgan, Mt. Vernon, to Boynton, Oct. 8, 1892, H.B. Boynton Papers, N.Y.P.L.

did not realize was that during these months in Georgia and the Carolinas all of the screws had been tightened.

After the capture of Fort Fisher, the high command decided that New Bern was a more useful base of supply for Sherman than Wilmington. Harbors were better, there were some usable railroads that could be repaired toward Kinston through the Dover Swamp. Schofield undertook the task of setting up the lines from New Bern toward Goldsboro with Wilmington as a secondary base.[40]

At first, Schofield's advance encountered little opposition, but from March 8-10, his men were forced to fight for control of the slight ridge that carried the roads through this swampy area. Confederates under Bragg did achieve some element of surprise at the battle of Kinston, but Federals under Cox came up and easily repulsed additional attacks. After some severe fighting, Bragg withdrew to Goldsboro on the night of March 10.[41] Schofield's troops pressed on, occupying Kinston on March 14, while Terry was also advancing toward Goldsboro from Wilmington. The men in this "Campaign of the Carolinas" could hear the dull pounding of distant cannonading from Bentonville as they hurried on, building bridges and removing obstructions in the Neuse River. Schofield's well-organized force reached Goldsboro on March 21, within one day of the time indicated by Sherman.[42]

[II]

A vastly different war was fought in Virginia, ever since the preceding June. Critics were to say that Grant was doing nothing with his huge armies of the Potomac and of the James.

The Union forces on the Petersburg-Richmond front were squeezing as in a slowly-closing vise the last major army of the Confederacy, led by the greatest of the South's leaders. This never-ending pressure even increased in February, 1865, when the Federals extended their lines farther westward. Heading toward Hatcher's Run, two Union corps gained the Boydton Plank Road where the resistance was ineffective, though fighting endured for three days. After taking the Boydton Plank Road, the Union troops decided not to hold it as it was no longer a vital supply route. However, they did set up new lines to Hatcher's Run, thus extending their front a distance of 37 miles if men counted the irregularities in the entrenchments. Furthermore, by March 1, Lee's army had

40. Cox, J.D., *The March to the Sea, Franklin and Nashville,* New York, 1882, 154-156. This is really first-hand as Cox was in the North Carolina operations.
41. *Ibid.,* 156-160.
42. Schofield, John M., *Forty-six Years in the Army,* New York, 1897, *passim.*

been reduced to 46,398 men present for duty, of an aggregate of soldiers present of 56,895.[43]

It was an extremely severe winter for Virginia, and still cold at the time of the February action. Despite snow and frozen ground, the Confederates continued to dig and build their entrenchments. Immobile defense alone remained—no longer the dashing offensive-defensive movements of past years. Earthworks would help compensate for lack of manpower and materiel.

Lee was perhaps not so much concerned with the extension of Federal lines in early February as with the condition of his own army. "If some change is not made and the commissary department reorganized, I apprehend dire results. The physical strength of the men, if their courage survives, must fail under this treatment. Our cavalry has to be dispersed for want of forage . . ."[44] Earlier, Lee had told the Secretary of War, "There is nothing within reach of this army to be impressed. The country is swept clear. Our only reliance is upon the railroads. We have but two days' supplies."[45] Appeals were made to farmers for supplies.

The manpower problem was manifest in Lee's inability to send troops from Virginia to South Carolina. "I do not know where to obtain the troops," he wrote.[46] Desertion was increasing, and Lee's discouragement was contagious.

Despair in countless long-tried homes, and disaffection in the government offices of Southern Congressmen and the State legislatures, was strengthened by the steady flow of reports upon diminishing supplies, failing transportation, and an inadequate supply of employable men and women for households, farms, or factories. Worst of all, the boundaries of the Confederacy were constantly diminishing, as was the population, so that by the closing days of March, 1865, but one army truly worthy of the name existed to defend the various fronts. The rising crisis seemed beyond all the resources of the leaders.

More and more, Lee kept emphasizing the debilities of the Confederate forces and issuing warnings. He predicted dire results if rations were not improved. In one of many such messages, he wrote Secretary of War Seddon on February 8 that in view of these facts of general exhaustion in connection with the paucity of their numbers, the public must not be surprised "if calamity befalls us. . . ."[47]

Lee's assumption of the rank of General-in-Chief on February 9 made no

---

43. *O.R.*, I, xlvi, pt. 1, 390; Humphreys, Andrew A., *The Virginia Campaign of '64 and '65*, New York, 1883, 310.

44. *O.R.*, I, xlvi, pt. 1, 381-382.

45. Lee, R.E., *The Wartime Papers of R.E. Lee*, ed. Clifford Dowdey and Louis H. Manarin, Boston, 1961, 881, Lee to Seddon, Jan. 11, 1865.

46. *Ibid.*, 885-886, Lee to William P. Miles, Jan. 19, 1865.

47. *Ibid.*, 890.

real difference. By February 21 he gave warning that he expected Grant to move within a week, "and no man can tell what may be the result." Sherman and Schofield, he wrote his wife, "are both advancing, and seem to have everything their own way, but trusting in a merciful God who does not always give the battle to the strong, I pray we may not be overwhelmed. I shall, however, endeavor to do my duty and fight to the last. Should it be necessary to abandon our position to prevent being surrounded, what will you do?" He added, with more anguish than resignation, "It is a fearful condition . . ."[48] Repeatedly, he told correspondents that Richmond might have to be given up and that the most important duty was to save the army. It took no great insight to predict that Grant was going to advance, although the time and exact character of his movements could not be divined. These honest comments upon the growing crisis were not like the frightened outcries of the generals who were easily thrown into panic, and who lacked courageous determination. They were the candid appraisals of an almost hopeless situation by a leader of iron persistence and restrained utterance. To the Secretary of War (now Breckinridge), Lee felt constrained to write: "I fear it may be necessary to abandon all our cities, and preparation should be made for this contingency."[49] While the North was celebrating recent successes on Washington's birthday, Lee was informing Longstreet of the difficulties of resisting both Sherman and Grant. He felt that the Confederate line of defenses was already excessively long and that a point for concentration should be picked if retreat became necessary. He and his aides were already devising plans for specific moves to be taken as circumstances dictated and permitted.[50]

As the war in Virginia wore on, Lee became more deeply alarmed, in his taciturn, unemotional, and resolute way. By March 9 he felt obliged to tell Breckinridge, sadly but with a sense that unity, and the Spartan temper of Fabius after Cannae, must be preserved, that the time was "full of peril and requires prompt action," meaning action to hold on with bulldog tenacity. He added a philosophic tribute to the unyielding valor with which the Confederate nation and fighters had confronted the superior strength of the well-equipped Northern hosts. The consequences of that superiority "have been postponed longer than we had reason to anticipate. . . ."[51]

One illustration of the fatal postponement of much-needed practical reforms lay in the replacement early in February of Commissary-General Northrop by the more competent Capt. I.M. St. John. St. John proved able to

48. To his wife, Feb. 21, 1865, Papers of R.E. Lee, LC.
49. Dowdey, *Wartime Papers of R.E. Lee, op.cit.*, 904, Feb. 19, 1865.
50. *Ibid.*, 907-909.
51. *Ibid.*, 913.

augment the supplies sent to the Army of Virginia, and to place increased reserves in subsistence depots.[52] Quartermaster-General F.W. Sims reported that just where transportation was most badly needed, in Virginia and North Carolina, "the roads are least able to furnish it."[53] The number of railroads available to the Confederacy had been so reduced that the fragile facilities remaining had to carry an intolerable load to deliver even the barest minimum of supplies. Sims also reported that, like everyone else, he had to deal with insoluble shortages of manpower. "Not a single bar of railroad iron has been rolled in the Confederacy since the war, nor can we hope to do any better during its continuance." The main lines were robbing the tributary lines of their rails and rolling stock.[54]

[III]

As the winter approached its end, Southern discontent inevitably increased in the gravest degree, though no one can measure it precisely. The War Clerk Jones formed the opinion that "the disaffection is intense," but thought that all the leadership in the world would not have produced a difference by 1864 or 1865 in delaying the final termination of the struggle.[55]

The familiar dreary tale of rising prices, painful shortages on every hand, and what seemed to be blundering in the government's measures, is conclusive, and need not be detailed at length here. President Davis's letters show that he was groping to find a way out of the Confederate difficulties, and to enlarge his supply of men and workers. But what little reinforcement he could obtain for the army was by this time necessarily drained away from some essential industry; at the same time, to assist industry he had to rob the army of some of its troops.

Various people were propounding possible methods of assisting the Confederacy, none of them practical. Governor A.G. Magrath of South Carolina sounded other Southern governors upon a shadowy plan to invigorate the Confederate Constitution, and along with it the dignity and efficiency of the State governments.[56] Howell Cobb wrote Davis lamenting the "deep despondency of the people," which too often extended to disloyalty. He wished to have Joseph E. Johnston restored to command, as countless others did, and

52. St. John, Gen. I.M., *Resources of the Confederacy in 1865*, Southern Historical Society Papers, III, No.3, Mar., 1877, 98-100; Coulter, E.M., *The Confederate States*, Austin, 1950, Ch.XVIII, "Progress and Decay," *passim*.

53. St. John, *ut supra*, report of Sims, 121-122.

54. *Ibid.*

55. Jones, J.B., *A Rebel War Clerk's Diary*, Philadelphia, 1866, 471-472.

56. A.G. Magrath to Gov. Brown of Georgia, Jan. 26, 1865, LC.

more of the zeal of volunteers imparted to an army more and more filled with conscience.[57] One soldier urged Davis to take the field command in the West.[58]

John A. Campbell, in the War Department, seemed to see the situation more clearly, but even his suggestions proved impossible. In early March he sent Breckinridge a long report full of sorry details upon the condition of the forces and the Confederacy as a whole: "The armies in the field in North Carolina and Virginia," he declared, "do not afford encouragement to prolong resistence. . . . The political situation is not more favorable. Georgia . . . may properly be called insurrectionary against the Confederate authorities . . ." In other areas the situation was equally deplorable. "Virginia will have to be abandoned when Richmond is evacuated and the war will cease to be a national one from that time." He concluded that the South might succumb, "but it is not necessary that she should be destroyed. I do not regard reconstruction as involving destruction . . ."[59]

Late in January, James Seddon resigned as Secretary of War, after serving as capably as any man could have under the restrictions of President Davis, and in the face of the nation's many limitations and adversities. His successor was John C. Breckinridge, who had served as a general during much of the war. Davis accepted the retirement of the never-vigorous Seddon, but deprecated Seddon's acceptance of the view of the Virginia Congressional delegation that the Cabinet could not then be completely reorganized.[60]

Lincoln, unwavering in his purpose of preserving the Union, and restoring the authority of the United States Government in the rebellious States, had little faith in "peace movements," for he was familiar with Jefferson Davis's grim determination not to surrender.[61] However, in spite of several abortive efforts between 1862 and 1865, a peace mission did materialize early in 1865, through the unofficial efforts of Francis Preston Blair, Sr., 73-year old patriarch of the politically-minded Blair family. On the pretext of searching for some missing papers, lost when his home in Maryland had been burned by General Early's men in July, 1864, Blair received a pass to go South in January, 1865. Lincoln was unaware of Blair's true mission,[62] which was really to sound out Davis on the possibilities of negotiating a peace. Davis finally agreed to send a commission, as he thought, to Washington, consisting of Vice-President

57. Cobb to Davis, Jan. 6, 1865, Howell Cobb Papers, Duke Univ. Libr.

58. M.W. Phillips to Jefferson Davis, Richmond, Jan. 28, 1865, Confederate Mem'l. Literary Society.

59. John A. Campbell to John C. Breckinridge, Mar. 5, 1865, Campbell-Colston Papers, Univ. of N.C. Library.

60. Rowland, Dunbar, ed., *Jefferson Davis, Constitutionalist*, Jackson, Miss., 1923, VI, 458-461, Davis to Seddon, Feb. 1, 1865.

61. *O.R.N.*, Ser.II, Vol.3, 1190-1194.

62. Nicolay and Hay, X, 94, 95.

Alexander H. Stephens, Senator R.M.T. Hunter, and Assistant Secretary of War John A. Campbell, none of whom could be termed to be in close relationship with Davis, either personally or in principle.[63] After a few days' delay, and induced by a dispatch from General Grant[64] at Fortress Monroe, Lincoln and Seward made a hasty trip from Washington to meet the Southern representatives at Hampton Roads aboard the *River Queen* on the morning of February 3, 1865, with the idea of carrying on informal talks.[65] No clerks, secretaries, or witnesses attended, and nothing was written or read at the meeting, which was informal, calm, courteous, on both sides. Accounts of the meeting, however, are found in the memoirs of the various participants.[66] Campbell, who had hoped for some agreement on peace measures even if based on preservation of the Union,[67] was greatly disappointed in the outcome of the mission, which ended where it began, with no yielding on the part of either Lincoln or Davis.[68]

The Confederate President, having consistently devoted most of his attention and very real talents to the alarming military situation, did join in the attempted resuscitation of the Confederate spirit during February. Even such a vitriolic enemy as Edward A. Pollard, editor and historian, could on occasion appreciate the unperceived gifts of the President. In one of his last public appearances, Davis arrived unannounced at a public hall just after the Hampton Roads Conference. In a worn gray suit, wrote Pollard, the thin figure stalked into the hall. "It appeared that the animation of a great occasion had for once raised all that was best in Mr. Davis; and to look upon the shifting lights on the feeble, stricken face, and to hear the beautiful and choice words that dropped so easily from his lips, inspired a strange pity, a strange doubt, that this 'old man eloquent' was the weak and unfit President . . ." He held the audience an hour, speaking extemporaneously, and pausing frequently to recover his strength. There were tremendous cheers, "and a smile of strange sweetness came to his lips as if the welcome assured him that, decried as he was by the newspapers and pursued by the clamor of politicians, he had still a place in the hearts of his countrymen . . ." The tone of his address was that of "imperious unconquerable defiance to the enemy." But Pollard concluded:

63. Davis, *Rise and Fall of the Confederate Government, op.cit.*, II, 612-620.
64. Lincoln, *Collected Works*, VIII, 282.
65. *Ibid.*, VIII, 277-282.
66. Seward, Frederick, *Seward at Washington*, III, New York, 1891, 260-261; Campbell, John A., memo on Hampton Roads Conference, Campbell-Colston Papers, Southern Hist. Collection, Univ. of N.C.; Hunter, R.M.T., "The Peace Commission of 1865," Southern Hist. Soc. Papers, III, 170-171; Stephens, Alexander, *Constitutional View of the War Between the States*, Philadelphia, 1870, II, 619-623.
67. *Diary of Robert Kean*, ms. Univ. of Virginia Library, Feb. 18, 1865.
68. Lincoln, *Collected Works*, VIII, 284-285; S.S. Cox to H.N. Marble, Feb. 5, 1865, Manton Marble Papers, LC.

"There was no depth in the popular feeling thus excited; it was a spasmodic revival, or short fever of the public mind."[69]

To an audience at the African Church, Davis "emphatically asserted that none save the independence of the Confederacy could ever receive his sanction. He had embarked in this cause with a full knowledge of the tremendous odds against us, but with the approval of a just Providence which he conscientiously believed was on our side, and the united resolve of our people, he doubted not that victory would yet crown our labors. . . ."[70]

That Davis was not oblivious of the attacks upon him, is borne out by a letter he wrote on March 30 to Mrs. Howell Cobb: "Faction has done much to cloud our prospects and impair my power to serve the country." He thought that this was not the purpose of his detractors, and he cherished the hope that when his enemies realized their attacks injured not only the President but also the cause, of which he called himself "a zealous though feeble representative, they might alter their course, and make an earnest effort to repair the mischief done it."[71]

That usually accurate observer, General Gorgas, had commented some weeks earlier: "People are almost in a state of desperation, and but too ready to give up the cause." This was not from a lack of patriotism, but because "there is a sentiment of hopelessness abroad—a feeling that all our sacrifices tend to nothing, that our resources are wasted, in short, that there is no leadership." Hence, many were "ready to despair. . . . The President has alas! lost almost every vestige of the public confidence," Gorgas added. "Had we been successful," he thought, "his faults would have been overlooked, but adversity magnifies them." He ended by striking an unflinching note: "We cannot lose the cause, and the President will perhaps show his strength of character in sustaining it when others have lost all hope."[72]

Lee did all he could to strengthen General Johnston, whom he had again placed in command, but, as we have seen, his efforts met with little success. The desertion problem was no better and Lee now, in late February, blamed friends and families of soldiers at home "who appear to have a very bad effect upon the troops who remain and give rise to painful apprehension. . . ."[73]

One of Lee's officers wrote in February: "Truly, matters are becoming serious and exciting. If somebody doesn't arrest Sherman's march, where will he stop? They are trying to corner this old army, but like a brave lion brought to bay at last, it is determined to resist to the death, and if die it must, die game.

69. Pollard, Edward A., *Life of Jefferson Davis*, Philadelphia, 1869, 468-470.
70. Richmond *Dispatch*, Virginia State Library, Richmond, Feb. 7, 1865.
71. Rowland, *op.cit.*, VI, 524-525.
72. Gorgas, Josiah, *Diary*, University of Alabama, 1947, 172, Mar. 2, 1865.
73. Lee, *Wartime Papers*, 910, Lee to Breckinridge, Feb. 24, 1865.

We are to have some hard knocks, we are to experience much that is dispiriting, but if our men are true (and I really believe that most of them are) we will make our way successfully through the dark clouds that now surround us. *Our people must make up their minds to see Richmond go*, but must not lose spirit, must not give up."[74]

On March 2, Lee told the President he had proposed to Grant that they have an interview, but was not sanguine of results. "My belief is that he will consent to no terms, unless coupled with the condition of our return to the Union. Whether this will be acceptable to our people yet awhile I cannot say. . . ."[75] It had come about because of conversations between Longstreet and E.O.C. Ord over prisoner exchange. Lee proposed that he and Grant talk about submitting the subjects of controversy to a convention.[76] Grant replied on March 4 rather curtly that, "in regard to meeting you on the 6th instant, I would state that I have no authority to accede to your proposition for a conference on the subject proposed. Such authority is vested in the President of the United States alone. . . ."[77]

The officers of Lee's army seemed to be aware of their plight and the grave threats all around them. By March 5, a change for the worse in public sentiment was noted by at least one pessimistic officer who spoke of the increased talk of *"terms and reconstruction."*[78]

The new Confederate General-in-Chief warned the new Secretary of War Breckinridge, March 9: "It must be apparent to every one that it is full of peril and requires prompt action . . . it seems almost impossible to maintain our present position with the means at the disposal of the Government. . . . Unless the men and animals can be subsisted, the army cannot be kept together, and our present lines must be abandoned. Nor can it be moved to any other position where it can operate to advantage without provisions to enable it to move in a body. . . . If the army can be maintained in an efficient condition, I do not regard the abandonment of our present position as necessarily fatal to our success. . . . While the military situation is not favourable, it is not worse than the superior numbers of resources of the enemy justified us in expecting from the beginning. Indeed, the legitimate military consequences of that superiority have been postponed longer than we had reason to anticipate. Everything in my opinion has depended and still depends upon the disposition and feelings of the people. . . ."[79]

74. Taylor, Walter H., *Four Years with General Lee*, New York, 1878, 43, notes for Feb. 20, 1865.
75. *Ibid.*, 911.
76. *Ibid.*, 911-912, Lee to Grant.
77. *O.R.*, I, xlvi, pt.2, 825.
78. *Ibid.*, 144.
79. Lee, *Wartime Papers*, 912-913, Lee to Breckinridge, Mar. 9, 1865.

The hammer, the anvil, and strangulation had done their work! From the spring of 1864, the Federal strategy had been clearly open for all to see, but not everyone had scrutinized it accurately. Grant and Meade had seized upon the Army of Northern Virginia and had tightened their grip in the desperate battles of the Wilderness, Spotsylvania, and Cold Harbor, and would tighten it still further in the battles to follow until the final victory at Appomattox. Although several of Grant's other campaigns had proved disappointing and an early movement against Mobile had largely gone awry, Sherman had performed his great thrust magnificently. In the West the Confederacy had found little ground for hope since the period preceding Vicksburg in 1863. The outer fortress walls of the Confederacy had been breached before 1864, and now the inner works were being carried. To the east and south on the Atlantic and Gulf coasts the blockade had stiffened until near the end it was perhaps the major element in garroting the South. Through the use of enclaves and invasions, all the ports of any significance to the South had been first sealed and then captured. To the west the Trans-Mississippi was, after 1863, at best a useless appendage, although it did divert some Confederate energies and resources.

10

Victory

THE EXULTATION of victory filled all loyal breasts as April covered the land with blossoms in 1865. The end that all believers in the Union regarded as inevitable had come. It could be no other way! The question among all men was still, "When would the South lay down its arms?" The dragging conflict had long since dissipated the optimistic dreams held by many Northerners in the fever after Sumter. The conflict they had hoped would be short, quick, and glorious had turned into nearly four years of agony and grief, but the endurance of harrowing anxiety and defeat had taught the people grim lessons in fortitude and intellectual realism. They knew that the Confederacy could endure but a few months longer. Mangled and suffering by the sword thrusts of Sherman in the Carolinas, lightning invasions on the Atlantic and Gulf coasts, and Union marches in the West, the Confederacy, manacled by the ever-tighter grip of the blockade, was stumbling to its doom. Cardinal attention was still fastened upon Richmond and Petersburg, where the growing strength of the blue ranks under Grant and Meade held an increasingly clear mastery of the area where the last real army of the South, feebler and more discouraged day by day, struggled to hold its ground.

In the wide domain once so proudly ruled by the Confederacy, the economic and social erosion had become ruinously destructive. Much land had been conquered or depleted. Many people were dead or in exile. Large districts had been lost or rendered unproductive, and what remained was insufficient and often could not be utilized. Yet the South largely retained its old principles and its fealty to its special concepts of sectional liberty and State rights. As so often in the history of English-speaking peoples, some long-embattled men and women had made the sad period of desperation and defeat their finest hour of spiritual renewal and philosophic resolution; so, now, they exhibited a spirit that their descendants could remember with respect and even an alloyed admiration. Their doctrines might be subject to question, to much revision, and even to condemnation, but the spirit of Dixieland had aspects and qualities that would be cherished along with the memory of Robert E. Lee.

Many at the North had, during the dark months and years, broadened their view of both the war and the peace. The President had been re-elected, re-inaugurated, and, without disturbance, would have four years to deal with the imminent tasks of pacification and reconstruction. For the moment, however, as blossom and leaf unfolded and showers began to ease, most eyes and ears were tuned to the sound of the guns southward. This was the spring of 1865.

[I]

By March, the Administration could distract its attention from the war and its multitudinous labors and prepare to resume the long-postponed tasks required by national recovery and growth, and by governmental and social reorganization. All too many responsibilities demanded action by the President, Congress, and the States.

Lincoln once more faced a cohort of office-seekers, including many Republican politicians clamorous for favors ever since the November election. As more and more of the South came under partial or full Northern control, traders, both honest and dishonest, lifted noisy demands for commercial permits. Important Cabinet positions, including the Secretaryships of State, of the Treasury, and of the Interior, had to be filled with circumspect care. Happily, the care-worn President had a brief interval—all too brief, as it soon appeared —to concentrate upon the most exigent labors. Fortunately for him and the country, Congress was not in session, and he was free from the criticisms, denunciations, exhibitions of jealous spleen, and ebullitions of malicious plotting that would otherwise have come from Capitol Hill. In his last Cabinet meeting, on April 14, Lincoln frankly remarked that he "thought it providential that this great rebellion was crushed just as the Congress had adjourned, and there were none of the disturbing elements of that body here to hinder and embarrass us. . . ."[1] The war had begun without the benefit or interference of Congress in the administration of the government, and now it was to end the same way.

Although the pressure of office-seekers was still almost intolerable, Lincoln now seemed a little more resigned to it, and more hopeful of the government's future than he had been before, with most Northerners sharing his sanguine outlook. While many citizens, and especially politicians, were pondering the future with concern, national confidence was growing steadily, giving rise to expressions of relief and to a certain exuberance. As historians of the war have said, it is impossible to determine just when the people realized that a trium-

1. Welles, Gideon, typescript of article, "Lincoln and Reconstruction in April, 1865," John Hay Library, Brown Univ., Providence, R.I.,

phant close was inevitable. The belief in imminent victory had been spreading since the fall of 1864, which had brought victories in Georgia, Tennessee, and the Shenandoah.

On Washington's birthday, 1865, the North had thrilled to the headlines, "Charleston evacuated!" The city where the rebellion started was once more in Union hands![2] The New York *Tribune* correspondent on the scene described the fires, explosions, and the destruction of stores, bridges, and warships. The national colors once more floated over Sumter, a shapeless mass of rubble in the harbor. No American heard the news without emotion.[3] At the same time dispatches from Admiral Porter's flagship, the *Malvern*, in Cape Fear River, confirmed that Fort Anderson had fallen. The way to Wilmington at last lay open; the public, however, did not know as they read the news on February 22 that the city had been evacuated that day.

New York, like other parts of the North, was in a festive, holiday mood under sunny skies, the air soft and springlike. "We never saw Broadway so utterly jammed with human beings," reported the *Tribune*. The shipping in the harbor was gaily dressed, and at noon, guns began firing from all the forts, while the chimes of Trinity deepened the clamor. Veterans of the War of 1812 paraded, and the armories turned out the proudest militia regiments to join in the procession. The Seventh led the way, its band playing patriotic airs while the crowd cheered. At night the most elaborate fireworks the city had yet seen lighted up the skies. A huge audience pressed into the Brooklyn Academy of Music to hear Wendell Phillips speak on "Our Country, Our Whole Country." Greeley had declared in a *Tribune* editorial that the fate of the rebellion hung by a thread which a single decisive Union victory could sever. Next day, February 23, another headline, "Fall of Wilmington," blazed in the New York press over Navy Department dispatches announcing that national forces had entered the last Confederate port of importance left open.[4] Then, day by day, the newspapers offered fresh tidings of Union advances. Dispatches from Sherman in the Carolinas, Terry outside Wilmington, and Sheridan in his last victories over the remnants of Early in the Shenandoah, were especially gratifying, for they were popular heroes.

But even with the thrill of victory abounding, some faint-hearts still strove for a negotiated peace. Horace Greeley would not forsake his dream of fashioning an end to bloodshed. He wrote S.L.M. Barlow, March 15, that he was willing to go to Richmond and talk with the Confederates if Lincoln "will indicate in confidence the most favorable terms" which he was prepared "to accord to the insurgents, stating what he must require and what he is ready

2. For description of the fall of Charleston, see Chap. 9, "The Final Triumph of Union Arms."
3. New York *Tribune*, Feb. 22, 1865.
4. *Ibid.*, Feb. 23, 1865.

to concede with regard to the Union, Emancipation, confiscation, amnesty, restoration to political equality in Congress, etc. . . ."[5]

But cheering crowds, parading troops, and pounding bands did not express the deep earnestness of the people. In Washington departments and bureaus the grim work of conducting the war kept desk-lamps burning from midnight until dawn. Countless details required attention. For example, Grant had objected to the President's liberation of prisoners after merely taking the oath of allegiance. Lincoln responded that he had freed about fifty men a day recently. This was a greater number than he liked, but they were names brought to him mainly by Border State Congressmen, and vouched for by various sponsors. The President argued that in only one or two instances had his trust been betrayed.[6] As if he intended continuing this policy of calculated leniency, on March 11 he issued a proclamation giving deserters sixty days within which they might be pardoned if they came back and reported. Wilful absentees might incur severe penalties.[7]

It was often Lincoln's habit to make a memorable statement on what was ostensibly some merely perfunctory occasion. Addressing the 14th Indiana Regiment, he pithily remarked: "I have always thought that all men should be free; but if any should be slaves, it should be first those who desire it for *themselves*, and secondly, those who *desire* it for *others*. Whenever [I] hear anyone arguing for slavery, I feel a strong impulse to see it tried on him personally." He went on to remind his listeners that if the Negro fought for the rebels, he could not at the same time "stay at home and make bread for them."[8] In fact, he tolerantly held the view that, as he quaintly put it, "We have to reach the bottom of the insurgent resources; and that they employ, or seriously think of employing, the slaves as soldiers, gives us glimpses of the bottom." Lincoln, of course, was more correct than he thought, as to the glimpse of the bottom —not merely the bottom of the immediate Southern resources of white manpower, but the bottom of the age-old Southern exploitation of black manpower in all departments of life and activity.[9]

On the surface, March appeared to offer the President a quiet month, but it actually proved busy and harassing. All the old problems remained, and were growing more urgent and complex, while the President's minor tasks also made increasing demands on his time and strength. On March 20, Grant telegraphed that he wished to see the President, and thought a rest would do him good. Lincoln replied that he had been thinking of such a visit.[10] In

5. Greeley to Barlow, Mar. 15, 1865, Barlow Papers, HEH.
6. Lincoln, *Collected Works*, VIII, 347-348, Mar. 9, 1865.
7. *Ibid.*, 349-350.
8. *Ibid.*, 361.
9. *Ibid.*, 362, March 17, 1865.
10. Lincoln, *Works*, VIII, 367.

consequence, on the afternoon of March 23, Lincoln, Mrs. Lincoln, Tad, a maid, and two bodyguards left on the *River Queen* for City Point, arriving at that vital Virginia base at nine on the evening of the next day. The President had been slightly ill on the trip. He did not even have a secretary with him, and Stanton for the interim seemed to be the unofficial Washington substitute for Lincoln, the two keeping in communication by wire.

One of Lincoln's motives for the trip was apparently to escape the hectic atmosphere of the capital and the pressure of trivial details, so that he might better concentrate his attention on the military climax soon to come in Virginia. Earlier Sherman had repelled Johnston's desperate attacks at Bentonville in North Carolina with ease, and on March 22, the able young cavalry commander, James Harrison Wilson, had led his Union forces into Alabama to threaten Selma and defeat Forrest's worn troopers. On the Gulf Coast, meanwhile, Union pressure entered upon a bolder phase as Canby began an energetic movement against Mobile.

All could see that great events impended on the Virginia battlefront, and, in fact, they began to disclose themselves on March 25, the morning after Lincoln's arrival. The weary President, looking unwell, boarded a special train from City Point to the Petersburg line. He toured the field of the recent engagement at Fort Stedman, viewing the burial of men slain in that abortive Confederate attack. The cars returning to City Point bore wounded soldiers.[11]

A few miles away from the point where Lincoln had surveyed the smoke-wreathed lines, but in the grip of a mood much darker and more perturbed, President Davis, Lee, and their Confederate associates faced an ominous future. No attempts to muster a transitory optimism could conceal the ugly realities of their plight. The most exhausting efforts had proved unavailing to check the steady decline in Southern strength and spirit during 1864; instead, almost everything had grown worse.[12]

There were ardent Southerners who held, or pretended to hold, a belief that some hope of success still remained. But shrewder or more practical men could not blind themselves to the harsh fact that not even a miracle could now save the sinking cause.

In January, 1865, Lee had written letters urging the use of Negroes as soldiers. Much as he disliked this measure, it now seemed unavoidable to him if he was not to overtax the white population.[13] Lee, therefore, after describing the Northern preponderance of strength, continued with a suggestion which many people considered ghastly: "I think, therefore, we must decide whether

11. *Lincoln Day by Day: A Chronology, 1809-1865*, Lincoln Sesquicentennial Commission, Washington, 1960, 322.
12. See the previous Chapter.
13. Lee to Andrew Hunter, "Lee's View on Enlisting the Negroes," Memoranda of the Civil War, *Harper's Monthly*, Vol. XXXVI, No. 4, Aug. 1888, 600-601.

slavery shall be extinguished by our enemies and the slaves used against us, or use them ourselves at the risk of the effects which may be produced upon our social institutions. . . ."[14] As early as February 20, one of Lee's staff-officers wrote: "Our people must make up their minds to see Richmond go. . . ."[15] And in Richmond itself, the laggard Confederate Congress, on March 13, finally completed passage of a measure approving the enrollment of Negroes for army service on a voluntary basis, involving the free action both of slaveholders and slaves. Davis signed this measure immediately after Lee had pressed him hard to give his assent. Lee was now more anxiously urging prompt action upon it. Negroes might not be made available in season for the spring campaign, but "no time should be lost in trying to collect all we can."[16]

Under the law of March 13, the Confederate Congress authorized the President to call upon slaveowners to seek volunteers of 18 to 45 in age among their Negroes. However, the new legislation did not require owners to volunteer the slaves, nor did it specifically give those slaves who volunteered to serve their freedom. It was nevertheless tacitly understood that the States would emancipate such slaves. Negro troops were to be willing to go as volunteers, and would receive the same pay, rations, and clothing as other troops. Recruiting thus began in the Richmond area amid considerable early excitement, and in the last weeks of the war a few Negro troops were seen parading in Richmond.[17]

A number of officers, all white, saw the opportunity for gaining a higher rank. By March 24, the Richmond Sentinel reported that enlistments were continuing.[18] On March 22, the Richmond Dispatch had begged Virginians to give the call their support, and reported that a devoted group of farmers in Roanoke County had offered to liberate any of their slaves who volunteered.[19]

Davis, however, later recorded that insufficient time remained to obtain any result from the enactment.[20] This was not the true explanation, for the underlying problem was lack of support by any considerable number of slaveholders. Davis frankly wrote Lee on April 1 that, "I have been laboring, without much progress, to advance the raising of negro troops . . . ,"[21] to which Lee replied that he had been willing to detach recruiting officers.[22]

In the War Department, on March 23, Robert Kean wrote the following

14. Ibid.
15. Taylor, Walter H., Four Years with General Lee, New York, 1878, 143.
16. Lee to Davis, Mar. 10, 1865, Lee Papers, Duke Univ. Libr.
17. American Annual Cyclopaedia, 1865, 194.
18. Richmond Sentinel, Mar. 24, 1865.
19. Richmond Dispatch, Mar. 22, 1865.
20. Davis, The Rise and Fall of the Confederate Government, New York, 1881, I, 518.
21. O.R., I, xlvi, pt. 3, 1370.
22. Lee to Davis, Apr. 2, 1865, Lee Headquarters Papers, Virginia State Hist. Soc.

illuminating paragraph: "This measure was passed by a panic in the Congress and the Virginia Legislature, under all the pressure of the President indirectly, and General Lee directly, could bring to bear. My own judgment of the whole thing is that it is a colossal blunder, a dislocation of the foundations of society from which no practical results will be reaped by us. The enemy probably got four recruits under it to our one. . . ."[23]

The fact is that slaveowners simply did not respond. Robert Toombs, even stronger in disapproval, felt the Negro unfit to be a soldier or at least a Confederate soldier. He believed they would rapidly "abandon their flag. . . . In my opinion the worst calamity that could befall us would be to gain our independence by the valor of our slaves . . . instead of our own. . . . The day that the army of Virginia allows a negro regiment to enter their lines as soldiers they will be degraded, ruined, and disgraced."[24]

One of Lee's officers wrote General Ewell that Lee "directs me to . . . say that he regrets very much to learn that owners refuse to allow their slaves to enlist. He deems it of great moment that some of this force should be put in the field as soon as possible, believing that they will remove all doubts as to the expediency of this measure. He regrets it the more in the case of the owners about Richmond, inasmuch as the example would be extremely valuable, and the present posture of military affairs renders it almost certain that if we do not get these men, they will soon be in arms against us, and perhaps relieving white Federal soldiers from guard-duty in Richmond."[25]

Though of small consequence in the actual life of the Confederacy, this legislative admission that Negro troops were needed and the approving actions of some in recruiting them, revealed that powerful social stresses were at work in the Confederacy, operating under duress but nonetheless important.

By March 6 it had become evident in the War Department that plans were being made to evacuate Richmond.[26] Conditions in Richmond for the average citizen had declined from bad to worse. In addition to worrying about the future of the armies and his country, the ordinary citizen had many daily hardships to encounter. Prices had risen steadily. One Richmond minister, on March 27, reported beef at $15 a pound, bacon $20, meal $100 a bushel; potatoes were $100 a bushel, and even turnip greens $10 a peck. There was another problem—what to do when the Yankees arrived—a problem which became daily more anguishing. "If we should evacuate Richmond," wrote the Reverend Mr. Alexander Gustavus Brown, "I do not know what is to become of us.

23. Kean, Robert G.H., *Inside the Confederate Government*, New York, 1957, 204.
24. Robert Toombs, Washington, Ga., to "Dear Dudley," March 24, 1865 (probably Dudley Mann), Charles A. Dana Papers, LC.
25. Lt.-Col. Charles Marshall to Ewell, Mar. 30, 1865, George Washington Campbell Papers, LC.
26. Jones, John B., *A Rebel War Clerk's Diary*, Philadelphia, 1866, 512, Mar. 6, 1865.

I have made up my mind to stay here, and take the chances."[27]

It was evident to all that the fall of Richmond must herald the beginning of the end. Some had tried to pretend otherwise. Lee, for instance, in January, in testimony to the Joint Committee on the Condition of the Army, is said to have replied to the question, "Will the Fall of Richmond end the war?": "By no means, sir, by no means. In a military point of view I should be stronger after than before such an event, because it would enable me to make my plan of campaign and battle. From a moral and political point of view the abandonment or loss of Richmond would be a serious calamity, but when it has fallen I believe I can prolong the war for two years upon Virginia soil. Ever since the conflict began, I have been obliged to permit the enemy to make my plans for me, because compelled to defend the capital. . . ."[28]

But even Lee's ideas had apparently changed. Reporting to Davis March 26 on the failure at Fort Stedman, he wrote, "I fear now it will be impossible to prevent a junction between Grant and Sherman, nor do I deem it prudent that this army should maintain its position until the latter shall approach too near."[29]

The Richmond *Sentinel* printed, as late as April 1, 1865, the statement of one unconquerable Southerner who proclaimed gallantly, if unwisely: "We are very hopeful of the campaign which is opening, and trust that we are to reap a large advantage from the operations evidently near at hand. . . . As for ourselves, *nothing* could equal, in its horror, the dreadful calamity of Yankee domination of our land. Awful as have been the four years of conflict through which we have passed, they have been four years of joy compared with what they would have been with the heel of Lincoln on our necks."[30]

But far sooner than that writer was willing to admit, the tramp of Lincoln's soldiers would make the campaign of which he was so hopeful nothing more than the last stand of the few fanatical rebels who remained staunch in spirit though weak in strength.

[II]

With Grant's two huge armies, those of the Potomac and the James, stationed around Richmond and Petersburg, Lee could really do nothing except await the now almost certain end. At the same time, Grant, impatient as he really was, had good reasons for waiting. He believed, as did most everyone,

27. Letters of the Rev. Alexander Gustavus Brown, Virginia State Hist. Soc.
28. Clipping from the New Orleans *Democrat*, July 5, 1881, interview with former Confederate Senator Benjamin Hill, Alfred Roman Papers, LC.
29. Lee, *Wartime Papers, op.cit.*, 916-918.
30. Richmond *Sentinel*, April 1, 1865.

that the spring campaigning would close the war. It had been a severe winter, making roads impassable in the early Virginia spring. As Grant put it in his *Memoirs*, "It was necessary to wait until they had dried sufficiently to enable us to move the wagon trains and artillery necessary to the efficiency of any army operating in the enemy's country." Sheridan, with the cavalry in the Shenandoah, had to move his force down to Petersburg by a long circuitous route. As early as March first, Grant issued orders to keep a sharp lookout for any move by Lee.[31]

On March 3, Grant outlined his ideas to Meade,[32] proposing an attack, when rumor came that Lee was moving, but Lee was *not* moving. Therefore, Grant decided: "It is better for us to hold the enemy where he is than to force him South. . . . To drive the enemy from Richmond now would be to endanger the success of Sherman and Schofield." At the same time he warned, "It is well to have it understood where and how to attack suddenly if it should be found at any future time that the enemy are detaching heavily. My notion is that Petersburg will be evacuated simultaneously with such detaching as would justify an attack. . . ."[33]

To the west and north of the Petersburg-Richmond position in the Shenandoah, major warfare, army against army, had almost ceased. Sheridan's cavalry had a free hand in the Valley now, except for isolated local opposition. Jubal Early in the Waynesboro-Staunton area had what was called a division, though by March the infantry was well under 3,000 men. He had a few cavalry units left, but they had much too wide an area to watch. The hard winter had not helped. Morale was low, and Early himself came under severe criticism.

By March 27, Lee became convinced from all reports available that Grant was about to move. Furthermore, he was sure that Grant would move westward from his existing line now extended to the area of Five Forks and Dinwiddie Court House. No possibility of deception existed. If the Confederate lines were lengthened by the four miles that seemed required, they would be overstrained. The only troops that Lee could possibly find to move were Pickett's division of about 5,000, suffering as all were from exhaustion.[34] Upon learning of Federal troop movements westward on the 28th, Lee prepared to shift Pickett from his position north of the James to the Five Forks area. No real attempt would be made to cover the whole new extension of the lines, but

31. Grant, *Memoirs*, II, 427, 430.

32. Grant had secondary problems on his hands as well, such as attempting to have Meade confirmed as major-general in the regulars, and the continuing problem of both legal and illegal trade with the enemy. Grant to Henry Wilson, Jan. 23, 1865, and Grant to Elihu Washburne, Jan. 23, 1865, Meade Papers, Hist. Soc. of Pennsylvania.

33. Grant to Meade, City Point, Mar. 3, 1865, Meade Papers, *ut supra*.

34. Freeman, *Lee, op.cit.*, IV, 24-27; an excellent analysis of Lee's troop problem.

rather one to provide a movable force to meet the enemy thrust. Orders were sent out on the 29th for Pickett to move forward, collect his isolated units and join the cavalry on the extreme Confederate right. Fitzhugh Lee was in command of the hastily convoked cavalry units, numbering about 4,200. Lee next gave Pickett some help from the force on the far Confederate right, bringing his infantry to 6,400.[35]

As Pickett and the cavalry moved toward Five Forks on the night of March 29 and the morning of the 30th, the rain fell in blinding sheets.[36] Forces of both armies marched in the rain through the broken country with its narrow roads, the terrain broken in places by swamps studded with alder thickets, briars and stunted pines.[37] Despite the rain and the rough terrain Lee at this critical time kept fairly good intelligence. On March 28 he learned that Sheridan had reached Grant's left, and on the 29th that both Union infantry and cavalry were in motion.[38]

On the night of March 27, E.O.C. Ord's Army of the James, three divisions strong taken from two corps, began to march westward, reaching their position near Hatcher's Run on the morning of March 29. That morning Warren's Fifth Corps began its march. Other troops shifted position, and Sheridan's cavalry now reached Dinwiddie Court House.[39] Grant felt, "Everything looked favorable to the defeat of the enemy and the capture of Petersburg and Richmond, if the proper effort was made." And despite the rain, delays, and other impediments, great exertions were pressed, showing that the troops that had fought from the Rapidan to the James and Petersburg, and then engaged in a siege, now remained sufficiently resilient to mount another offensive drive. In fact, another move spurted on the left flank, resembling the movement Grant had carried out in the campaign of the preceding May and June.

At the same time, many shifts had been made in the corps and division commanders, and two armies were operating together. On the 31st, Sheridan pushed out from Dinwiddie Court House, while Pickett and the Confederates were moving toward Dinwiddie. In the restricted fighting that ensued Sheridan suffered a tactical defeat, and the Confederates drove to a point near the Court House. Pickett asserts that with a half hour of daylight they would have reached Dinwiddie; others declare that Pickett failed to push the drive and presently halted.[40] Grant had decided to extend his lines no farther, but to turn north toward the enemy, believing Southern lines were now thin enough to

35. See also reports of Confederate generals in Lee Headquarters Papers, Virginia State Hist. Soc.
36. Munford, Thomas T., "Five Forks," mss. article, Virginia State Hist. Soc.
37. Ibid.
38. O.R., I, xlvi, pt. 3, 1363, Lee to Early, March 28, 1865, and Lee to Breckinridge, March 29.
39. Ibid., pt.1, 52-53.
40. Lee Headquarters Papers, Virginia Hist. Soc.

permit his general offensive to succeed. Warren, with the Fifth Corps, was impeded by bad roads, darkness, rain, and mud, while an enemy attack had thrown him back severely. Later, Grant and others charged Warren with slowness, faulty alignment and failure to keep his troops together.[41] But now, every assertion relating to Warren is subject to so much controversy that historians conclude their examination with opposite opinions upon him and his actions. Details of the events of these days on the Petersburg front may be left to the specialist, for they require detailed explanations which render full narratives unwieldy.

By the night of March 31, Lee had on his right 10,600 cavalry and infantry to oppose more than 10,000 Union cavalry and as many as 43,000 infantry that could be called upon. On April 1, Lee told Davis, "The movement of Genl. Grant to Dinwiddie Court House seriously threatens our position, and diminishes our ability to maintain our present lines in front of Richmond and Petersburg. . . . It also renders it more difficult to withdraw from our position, cuts us off from the White Oak Road, and gives the enemy an advantageous point on our right and rear. . . ."[42] He feared the South Side and the Danville railroads would be cut, and therefore preparations should be made if it became necessary to evacuate positions on the James. Some critics feel that Lee should have retreated while he still had time, after the failure at Fort Stedman, near Petersburg.[43]

After hearing of the action at Dinwiddie Court House and the withdrawal of Pickett's men to Five Forks, he issued firm orders. To Pickett he wrote, April 1: "Hold Five Forks at all hazards. Protect road to Ford's Depot and prevent Union forces from striking the South-side Railroad. Regret exceedingly your forced withdrawal, and your inability to hold the advantage you had gained."[44]

At about 4 p.m. on April 1, Sheridan's attack, delivered by both cavalry and infantry, came later than he had intended, but through considerable confusion in orders, bridges being out, and difficulties over roads and numerous other impediments, Warren's Fifth Corps had been delayed. After some brief, ill-directed moves, with the cavalry striking on the left toward Five Forks and the infantry on the right, the attack finally succeeded in forcing the Confederates to fall back in confusion.

The Union actions, or lack of them, at Five Forks were no better nor worse than those of many others in battle, and can even be justified by the facts of

41. *O.R.*, I, xlvi, pt. 1, 53-54.
42. *Wartime Papers of R.E. Lee, op.cit.*, 922-923.
43. Livermore, Col. Thomas L., "The Generalship of the Appomattox Campaign," *Military Hist. Soc. of Mass. Papers*, VI, 474.
44. Pickett, La Salle Corbell, *Pickett and His Men*, Philadelphia, 1913, 386.

the situation and the orders Warren received. Grant and others later suggested that Warren's difficulty stemmed from peculiarities of temperament, or defects of personality.[45] At any rate, the sacrifice of one corps commander could not minimize the striking importance of the Union victory at Five Forks, won by both the cavalry and infantry. On April 1, a Union witness wrote: "Sheridan is a tiger, up with the front line always, and in the heat of battle. . . . All of us fought on our own hook. . . . I never saw a fight before where the victory was so well followed up. Indeed, I think I never saw a perfect victory before. . . ."[46]

One cavalry officer, Thomas J. Munford, in his lengthy analysis of Five Forks from the Confederate side, was critical in the extreme of Pickett, Rosser, and Fitzhugh Lee "talking" two miles back of the line of battle. He claimed his 1,200 "carbines" faced 12,000 infantry and 2,000 cavalry. "It was indeed a glorious target. But what could we do? A handful to a houseful! We could do nothing but shoot and run. At their first fire the smoke enveloped them completely and as soon as it drifted so that we could see them advancing again we poured into them our salute of death—then turned and scooted through the woods like a flock of wild turkeys. . . . Shells went shrieking and screeching through the air or dropped with a long, mellifluous *wh-o-o-o-m!* into the tops of the mourning pines. Soon came the great bursting fusilade of Pickett's whole line; then the roar of gallant Pegram's thunderous guns and the crashing of Torbert's ten thousand carbines gave volume to the tumultuous voice of battle. The earth trembled under the shocks of the thundering guns; rolling volumes of sulphurous smoke wreathed the trees in ghostly, trailing garments. The low sun showed faintly through the smoke-clouds like a pale moon and the woods were stifled in their sulphurous draperies. No enemy was in sight, because of the smoke, but the hellish din of war arose on every hand, the deadly balls spat against the boughs or whined like pettish voices above our heads. Occasionally a man crumbled down in his place and a little rivulet of blood trickled away on the ground. . . ."[47] The battle did not last long. In the rough, broken, boggy country, cut up by creeks, and covered with a heavy growth of briars and brambles, the Confederates were breaking up. Finally Pickett came

45. An immense secondary and primary literature exists on the Warren case. Among them are: Higginson, T.W., "Five Forks: The Case of General Warren," *Contemporaries*, Boston, 1899, 317-321; Catton, Bruce, "Sheridan at Five Forks," *The Journal of Southern History*, Vol.XXI, No.3, Aug. 1955, reprint; Stern, Philip Van Doren, *An End to Valor*, Boston, 1958, 129-152. The Warren Papers in the N.Y. State Library, Albany, contain countless important documents. Grant, *Memoirs*, II, 213-215, 313, 445. The Sheridan Papers in LC are limited in value due to the destruction by fire of most of his papers. *O.R.*, I, xlvi, pt. 1, has numerous reports pertaining to this.
46. Fowler, William, *Memorials of William Fowler*, New York, 1875, 129-131.
47. Munford, Thomas T., "Five Forks—The Waterloo of the Confederacy," mss., Virginia State Hist. Soc., Richmond.

galloping up. Everything was in confusion among his retreating men and the General had to stave off "utter rout."[48]

Lee told Breckinridge late on April 1 that Pickett's present position was not known, but painted a gloomy picture.[49] On April 2, Lee told Breckinridge, "I see no prospect of doing more than holding our position here till night. I am not certain that I can do that. If I can I shall withdraw to-night north of the Appomattox, and, if possible, it will be better to withdraw the whole line to-night from James River. . . . Our only chance, then, of concentrating our forces, is to do so near Danville railroad, which I shall endeavor to do at once. I advise that all preparation be made for leaving Richmond to-night. . . ."[50] The move to Dinwiddie Court House and the Battle of Five Forks disrupted all the Confederate plans.

Sheridan's pursuit of the Confederates continued well into the evening of April 1, before he took up secure positions. That night from the well-placed Federal guns in the Petersburg siege lines, shells pounded the Confederate trenches and forts, landing within the city itself. Grant had constantly alerted his forces to be ready when the crisis came—and here it was at Five Forks.

Even before the success was fully known, orders had been issued for an attack at 4 A.M. on April 2 by the Sixth, Ninth and Twenty-fourth Federal Corps, clearing the way for the Second Corps. Troops were not sanguine; they had been in the trenches too long, facing abattis, chevaux-de-frise, tangled telegraph wire, stakes driven in the ground at a forty-five degree angle, and other defensive gadgets in front of the formidable Confederate earth works. Enemy guns clearly swept the front, along which attack must come. Curt remarks were common, such as, "Well, good-bye, boys, that means death."[51]

Early morning fog shrouded the land, hiding the slight rises that supported Confederate entrenchments. It took some prodding and urging, and smothered oaths to launch the attack when the signal gun was finally heard. For a time the Federals advanced in the sil ence of the fog until the shots of the enemy pickets rapped out, followed immediately by the rolling surge of full musket fire. Enemy guns roared; but with mighty cheers the Yankees rushed ahead. Formations were lost, a few men shrank from the task, but in the main they rolled ahead. Tearing away the obstacles, leaping over some and smashing into others, the Federals vaulted over one parapet after another, scattering the thinned ranks of Confederate defenders. The Sixth Corps did not even stop there, some plowing on in pursuit of the fleeing Southerners.[52]

48. *Ibid.*
49. *O.R.*, I, xlvi, pt. 1, 1263-1264.
50. *Ibid.*
51. Stevens, Hazard, "The Storming of the Lines of Petersburg," MHSM, VI, 422.
52. *Ibid.*, 423-424.

Grant knew that Lee had now been forced to the breaking point, and that the risk had become materially slighter than it had been only a few days before.[53] Grant kept close control over activities at Petersburg on April 2, making sure that Lincoln was fully informed at City Point. The President in turn wired Stanton in Washington the results as their news reached headquarters. At 11 A.M. Lincoln informed Stanton: "Dispatches frequently coming in. All going fine. Parks, Wright, and Ord, extending from the Appomattox to Hatcher's Run, have all broken through the enemy's intrenched lines. . . ." At 2 P.M. the President relayed Grant's message of 10:45 A.M. to Washington: "Everything has been carried from the left of the Ninth Corps. The Sixth Corps alone captured more than 3,000 prisoners. The Second and Twenty-fourth Corps both captured forts, guns, and prisoners from the enemy. . . . We are now closing the works of the line immediately enveloping Petersburg. All looks remarkably well. . . ."[54]

By 4:30 Grant telegraphed Lincoln: "We are now up, and have a continuous line of troops, and in a few hours will be intrenched from the Appomattox, below Petersburg, to the river above. . . . All seems well with us, and everything quiet just now." Lincoln, grasping the magnitude of the day's operations, sent Grant the following message: "Allow me to tender to you and all with you the nation's grateful thanks for this additional and magnificent success."[55] Grant, however, was not going to be rash at such a time, but ordered a heavy bombardment early on April 3 to be followed by a 6 A.M. assault, "only if there is a good reason for believing the enemy is leaving."[56] But at 8:30 on the morning of April 3, Lincoln telegraphed Stanton: "This morning General Grant reports Petersburg evacuated, and he is confident Richmond also is. He is pushing forward to cut off, if possible, the retreating army. I start to him in a few minutes. . . ."[57]

While the message carried the essential news, the situation was not quite as simple as it seemed to indicate. The Sixth Corps under Wright penetrated the lines *en masse*, on the morning of April 2, as did two Twenty-fourth Corps divisions of Ord's command. Another division of Ord had forced the lines near Hatcher's Run. Ord and Wright moved to the right toward Petersburg to try to hold the enemy in. Parke with the Ninth and Humphreys with the Second moved ahead as well. Parke penetrated the main line but failed to carry the inner defenses. After considerable fighting, Gibbon seized two strong enclosed works, thus shortening the Federal attack line considerably, while other Fed-

53. *O.R.*, I, xlvi, pt. 3, 422.
54. *Ibid.*, 447, 466.
55. *Ibid.*, 447-449.
56. *Ibid.*, 458, Grant to Meade, Apr. 2, 1865, 7:40 P.M.
57. *Ibid.*, 508.

eral troops harassed and harried the broken Confederate units. Grant later learned that Lee had evacuated Petersburg on the night of April 2,[58] being fortunate to have kept the Federals out of town until darkness covered his retreat.[59]

From the news of the defeat at Five Forks onward, it was clear that the only course the Confederates could take was to delay at Petersburg until they could evacuate the city and salvage whatever supplies and guns they could. In one of several messages to the Secretary of War, Breckinridge, Lee wrote on April 2: "It is absolutely necessary that we should abandon our position tonight, or run the risk of being cut off in the morning. . . . It will be a difficult operation, but I hope not impracticable. . . . The troops will all be directed to Amelia Court House."[60] This would not be an orderly, organized withdrawal. Under such heavy Federal pressure, the Confederate units were too widely disposed on the long defense lines to be brought together. Lee recognized this, ordaining that Amelia Court House be the concentration point. It was then that he sent to President Davis a similar message: "I think it is absolutely necessary that we should abandon our position to-night. I have given all the necessary orders on the subject to the troops, and the operation, though difficult, I hope will be performed successfully. I have directed General Stevens to send an officer to Your Excellency to explain the routes to you by which the troops will be moved to Amelia Court House, and furnish you with a guide and any assistance that you may require for yourself."[61] Lee issued rather specific orders to his various commanders regarding routes to Amelia Court House, but in spite of his well-laid plans, the withdrawal did not go as smoothly as expected. As transportation was rapidly falling into chaos, the already long-standing supply problem became steadily worse.[62] In order to secure needed forage, for months Lee had been obliged to separate cavalry and artillery units at points too distant from the lines. In this crisis of supplies, arms orders became confused, or were not properly issued.

Reports of Lee's principal generals, forwarded later to their commander, including many not appearing in the *Official Records*, told the same doleful story of the breakdown of their positions at Petersburg and Richmond.[63]

On the morning of April 3, it was uncertain whether Lee's retreating army,

58. *O.R.*, I, xlvi, pt. 1, Grant's report, 54-55.

59. Meade, George G., *Life and Letters of General Meade*, II, 269, to his wife, Apr. 3.

60. *O.R.*, I, xlvi, pt. 1, 1265.

61. *Ibid.*, pt. 3, 1378.

62. For a good summation, see Vandiver, Frank, "The Food Supply of the Confederate Armies," *Tyler's Quarterly Historical and Genealogical Magazine*, Vol.XXVI, 77ff.

63. Taylor, Walter H., *Four Years with General Lee*, op.cit., 150; Gordon, John B., *Reminiscences of the Civil War*, New York, 1903, 418-419.

which crossed the Appomattox River at Goode's Bridge during the night, or his Union pursuers, would be first to reach the Danville Road. Early on the morning of the 6th, Lee reached Amelia Court House, where he found not a morsel of food, and had to halt and scour the surrounding area for supplies— a fatal delay, for Sheridan's cavalry pushed ahead of him, and reached the railroad at Jetersville, where the Army of the Potomac began to concentrate. The avenue for the retreat of Lee's hungry and exhausted army lay on the narrow line between the Appomattox and James Rivers. When night was falling, the head of Lee's columns reached Appomattox Station, where, as the tired veterans lay down to rest, Custer's cavalry burst like a thunderbolt upon them. The scene was set for the last act in the great drama.[64]

[III]

The strains of "Dixie" echoed from the seven hills of Richmond as marching columns climbed the streets toward the capitol. But, alas, the oncoming troops wore blue, and the regimental band pouring forth the familiar notes preceded a Negro regiment. Cavalry thundered past at a furious gallop. Worn army horses labored up the incline, dragging heavy cannon. Through the smoke of the burning city, men caught glimpses of flaming walls. Now and then they heard the report of repeated explosions. They forced their way through an hysterical crowd of dancing, shouting Negroes, some of whom were busy plundering the rapidly burning shops of ham, shoes, flour, dry-goods, bolts of cloth, chairs, and even sofas. Some of the gratefully exalted freedmen called out "Saviors, our Saviors!" to the Yankee troops. As blue-clad horsemen dashed up to the City Hall, an officer threw open the doors. Above the capitol dome two soldiers had unfurled a tiny flag. One Richmond lady sank to her knees, and, as she wrote later, "the bitter, bitter tears came in a torrent."[65]

The heart of a nation and a people was being deeply torn that April Monday in 1865. The burning of the city and scenes of anguish might have been anticipated for months; perhaps for four years. But, however it might have been foreseen, the surrender was a shock to all. For some days, great events had been occurring, and more were anticipated. Since President Lincoln had arrived in City Point, he had been indulging in the role of military tourist, or observer, combining long postponed vacation hours with a half-anxious, half-

---

64. Dowdey & Manarin, eds., *The Wartime Papers of R.E. Lee*, Boston, 1961, 901.
65. Letters of Mrs. Mary A. Fontaine to Marie Burrows Sayre, Confederate Memorial Literary Society, Richmond; and others felt equally stricken. See Letters of Emmie Sublett (age 13), Confederate Memorial Literary Soc., Richmond.

relieved watch over the death throes of the Confederacy from his *River Queen* headquarters.[66] On March 26, he saw Sheridan's troopers from the Shenandoah cross the James to add dash and strength to the irresistible panoply under Grant, Meade, and Ord, about to hew through Lee's army and advance upon Richmond. That afternoon, he attended a review of Ord's Army of the James, an occasion marked by Mrs. Lincoln's disclosure of open pique over the President's courteous attention to Mrs. Ord—a minor incident that had unfortunate social sequels.

However, national leaders were dealing with serious problems. For two days an earnest conference occupied an able group on the *River Queen*. Lincoln, Grant, and Admiral Porter conferred with Sherman, newly arrived from the Carolinas. Their decisions were expected to influence the future of the nation, but no one can be certain just what was concluded.

Sources are limited on what was said at this conference (unlike Hampton Roads) for we must depend primarily on memoirs, and on Sherman's accounts which may be colored and exaggerated. Much later, Grant was to write carefully in his own *Memoirs* that Sherman "had met Mr. Lincoln at City Point while visiting there to confer with me about our final movement, and knew what Mr. Lincoln had said to the peace commissioners when he met them at Hampton Roads, to wit: that before he could enter into negotiations with them [the Confederate agents] they would have to agree to two points: one being that the Union should be preserved, and the other that slavery should be abolished; and if they were ready to concede these two points, he was almost ready to sign his name to a blank piece of paper and permit them to fill out the balance of the terms upon which we would live together . . ."[67] The subject was to come up a few weeks afterward in the dispute over Johnston's terms of surrender to Sherman, upon which Grant wrote that Sherman doubtless thought he was following the President's wishes. It should be noted, however, that Grant stated Sherman came to the conference primarily to discuss military movements with him.

Lincoln's secretaries also dismissed the President's action as "a hasty trip to confer with Grant."[68] Yet, informal discussions in the cabin of the *River Queen* gave Lincoln, Grant, Sherman, and Porter an opportunity for a frank exchange about the prospects of early and final victory. Porter and Sherman reported that the President expressed some liberal views on the restoration of State governments in the conquered South which did not seem altogether

66. George Merryweather to his parents in England, March 26, 1865, George Merryweather Letters, property of grandson, John Merryweather, now in Chicago Hist. Soc.
67. Grant, *Memoirs, op.cit.*, II, 514-515.
68. Nicolay and Hay, *Abraham Lincoln, op.cit.*, X, 215.

compatible with the guarded language which Lincoln used elsewhere. We may presume that their private opinions sometimes colored their recollections, though we may well believe that he repeated his willingness to be generous to the verge of prudence, and let them understand that he would not be displeased by the escape from the country of Davis and other rebel leaders.[69] After the conference Sherman hurried back to North Carolina, where Schofield had been left in charge.

Sherman modestly assured his father-in-law as March closed: "It is perfectly impossible for me in case of failure to divest myself of responsibility, as all from the President, Secretary-of-War, General Grant, etc. seem to vie with each other in contributing to my success," adding that Ewing need not fear he would commit a political mistake, for he well realized that he would imperil the government by any unwise concessions. He had repelled all political advances made, and would continue to do so.[70] He thought he had "a clear view of another step in the game," a statement as dubious as it was cloudy.[71]

Sherman's *Memoirs* give a full and naturally somewhat defensive account of the meeting with Lincoln. He recalled that he was received by Grant "most heartily" and that they discussed the situation fully. When he went aboard the *River Queen* with Grant, he found the President highly curious about the incidents of the great march, and quick to enjoy its more ludicrous aspects, such as the activities of the bummers, and their eager devices to collect food and forage when many Americans supposed the invaders to be starving. At the same time he expressed anxiety lest some misfortune should befall the army in North Carolina during Sherman's absence. Sherman assured him Schofield could handle anything that came up. Clearly the assemblage on March 27 had its cheerful social moments.

The next day, after talks with Meade and others, Grant, Sherman, and Porter returned to the *River Queen*, where a more discursive conversation was held on such military topics as Federal operations, and Lee's possible activities. Many expected a bloody battle, and Lincoln inquired anxiously if it could not be avoided. "During this interview," relates Sherman, "I inquired of the President if he was all ready for the end of the war. What was to be done with the rebel armies when defeated? And what should be done with the political leaders? . . . He said he was all ready; all he wanted of us was to defeat the opposing armies, and to get the men composing the Confederate armies back to their homes, at work on their farms and in their shops. As to Jeff. Davis, he was hardly at liberty to speak his mind fully, but intimated that he ought to

69. *Ibid.*, X, 215-216.
70. Howe, M.A. DeWolfe, ed., *Home Letters of General Sherman*, New York, 1909, 337-338.
71. *Ibid.*

clear out, 'escape the country,' only it would not do for him to say so openly...."
After Lincoln told an apropos story, Sherman remarked that he "... inferred
that Mr. Lincoln wanted Davis to escape, 'unbeknown' to him."

Sherman made no notes, later using those of Admiral Porter, and with
some confusion over the dates. He continued: "Mr. Lincoln was full and frank
in his conversation, assuring me that in his mind he was all ready for the civil
reorganization of affairs at the South as soon as the war was over; and he
distinctly authorized me to assure Governor Vance and the people of North
Carolina that, as soon as the rebel armies laid down their arms, and resumed
their civil pursuits, they would at once be guaranteed all their rights as citizens
of a common country; and that to avoid anarchy the State governments then
in existence, with their civil functionaries, would be recognized by him as the
government *de facto* till Congress could provide others ...." Grant does not
mention this, nor does Porter; and Porter has no record of the last vital clause
respecting final Congressional provision as an important part of the utterance
thus somewhat hazily attributed to Lincoln.

Sherman also tells us: "I was more than ever impressed by his kindly
nature, his deep and earnest sympathy with the afflictions of the whole people
resulting from the war.... His earnest desire seemed to be to end the war
speedily, without more bloodshed or devastation, and to restore all the men of
both sections to their homes...."[72]

The recollections written by Admiral Porter[73] in 1866, despite their gossipy
and often inaccurate character, may also merit brief quotation. His statement
that Lincoln visited City Point "with the most liberal views toward the rebels,"
partially confirms Sherman's account. He seems less clearly credible when he
writes: "Mr. Lincoln did, in fact, arrange the (so-considered) liberal terms
offered General Jos. Johnston, and, whatever may have been General Sherman's private views, I feel sure that he yielded to the wishes of the President
in every respect...."[74]

In another account, written to Isaac N. Arnold of Chicago, Sherman expressed himself cautiously upon this meeting with Lincoln, and his talk with
him of the experience of the campaign. He also says that General Grant and
himself explained their next moves to Lincoln, though various leaders often
said that Grant never told Lincoln of his plans in advance. Lincoln is said to
have deprecated the probable necessity of one more bloody battle. Of the
second visit Sherman wrote: "I ought not and must not attempt to recall the
words of that conversation.... Though I cannot attempt to recall the words

72. Sherman, *Memoirs, op.cit.*, II, 324-328.
73. *Ibid.*, 328-331, written in 1866.
74. *Ibid.*

spoken by any one of the persons present, on that occasion, I know we talked generally about what was to be done when Lee and Johnsons [sic.] armies were beaten and dispersed. . . ." Sherman recalls that Lincoln remarked that he hoped there would be no more bloodshed, that the men of the Rebel armies would be disarmed and sent back home, and "that he contemplated no revenge —no harsh measures—but quite the contrary, and trusted that their suffering and hardships in the war would make them now submissive to law—I cannot say that Mr. Lincoln or any body else used this language at the time, but I know I left his presence with the conviction that he had in his mind, or that his cabinet had, some plan of settlement, ready for application the moment Lee and Johnston were defeated. . . ."[75]

The conference of the President and his generals was the last quiet moment in national events. That same day, Lee wrote his daughter: "Genl. Grant is evidently preparing for something. . . ."[76] He was correct in a conjecture that sprang naturally from the expectation (which he had held all spring) of an advance by Grant.

On March 29 Lincoln asked Grant, as he had asked other generals for four years: "How do things look now?" And on the 30th the President told Stanton he felt he should be back in Washington, but disliked to leave without seeing nearer to the end of Grant's movement. Stanton did not object, and Seward came down for a day or two. But most of the time Lincoln was without his official family. By March 31, as the battle news from Petersburg came in, Lincoln seemed depressed, and on April 1 he walked the deck of the *River Queen* most of the night. One of his bodyguards wrote: "I have never seen suffering on the face of any man as was on his that night."[77]

Indeed, the last campaign against the Army of Northern Virginia had begun. For twelve days, as we have seen, Grant extended his lines to the westward, stretching Lee's to the breaking-point and beyond. Union troops moved in rainy weather against Lee's far right, tearing away one of the last mobile forces in the Confederate defenses. On April 2, observers of the Petersburg line watched the Federal masses break the enemy.

Perhaps twenty miles distant from Lincoln, the scene was quite different. In Richmond a congregation quietly gathered in Lee's church to hear the service, a scene that is indelibly imprinted in Civil War history.

Lee had told Breckinridge on April 2 that he despaired of doing more than hold his position at Petersburg until night, and that preparations should be

75. Sherman to Arnold, Nov. 28, 1872, Isaac N. Arnold Papers, Chicago Hist. Soc. Cf. Naroll, Raoul S., "Lincoln and the Sherman Peace Fiasco Another Fable?" *Journal of Southern History*, Vol.XX, No.4, Nov. 1954, 459-483.

76. *Wartime Papers of R.E. Lee, op.cit.*, 919.

77. Lincoln, *Works*, VIII, 376-377; *Lincoln Day by Day*, III, 323-324; Crook, William H., "Lincoln's Last Day," compiled by Margarite S. Gerry, *Harper's Monthly*, Vol. CXV, Sept., 1907, 520.

made to quit the capital. Life in the city during the most recent days had gone on much as before, with the clouds of war ever darker, but not yet oppressive. Southerners were familiar with St. Paul's Episcopal Church, where the Reverend Dr. Charles Minnigerode now lifted his last prayer for the President of the Confederacy.[78] The waiting concourse watched in awed suspense as a messenger from the War Department slipped down the aisle, and the President quietly walked out of the church.

As Davis himself said, "the congregation of St. Paul's was too refined to make a scene at anticipated danger."[79] Hastening to his office, Davis summoned the heads of departments and bureaus, and gave instructions for removing the government. The news spread rapidly and, as Davis proceeded from his office to his house, many personal friends ventured questions. "The affection and confidence of this noble people in the hour of disaster," he declared, "were more distressing to me than complacent and unjust censure would have been. . . ." Mrs. Davis had already left.[80]

One resident later recalled: "The hours I remained in Richmond on that melancholy Sunday, after leaving St. Paul's, were among the saddest of my life. I felt that our cause was the Lost Cause. Many of the scenes . . . were heartrending. The bad news had spread with lightning speed all over town. . . . The men, generally, were on the street, and large numbers of the ladies stood in the doors and on the steps of their houses, many bathed in tears, making inquiries and giving utterance to woeful disappointment and anguish. . . ."[81]

It was a lovely spring Sunday "when delicate silks that look too fine at other times seem just to suit . . ." wrote one woman. "I have never seen a calmer or more peaceful Sabbath morning, and alas! never a more confused evening. . . ."[82] "Then Mr. Davis, oh, so bowed, and anxious, came. When he told us he feared Richmond must be evacuated by midnight, the truth was forced upon us. . . ."[83]

By afternoon of April 2, officials started leaving on the Richmond & Danville Railroad. Sixty midshipmen under Captain William H. Parker escorted what remained of the Confederate treasury.[84]

Secretary Mallory wrote of the final scene in Richmond: "As usual the

78. Note the minister's name is often misspelled Minnegerode. St. Paul's and the Richmond Civil War Centennial Committee confirm the correct spelling.

79. Davis, Varina, *Jefferson Davis, a Memoir by His Wife*, New York, 1890, II, 582-584.

80. *Ibid.* For other accounts of the scene in St. Paul's, see Longstreet, *From Manassas to Appomattox*, Philadelphia, 1896, 607, his wife's account; Bruce, H.W., "Some Reminiscences of the Second of April, 1865," Southern Historical Society Papers, IX, No.5, May 1881, 206-207.

81. Bruce, *op.cit.*, 206-207.

82. Letters of Mrs. Mary A. Fontaine to Mrs. Marie Burrows Sayre, Confederate Mem'l. Literary Society, Richmond, Apr. 30, 1865.

83. *Ibid.*

84. Hanna, A.J., *Flight into Oblivion*, Richmond, 1938, contains secondary account of the flight of the Confederate government.

President's face was closely scrutinized as he entered St. Paul's alone . . . but its expression varied not from the cold, stern sadness which four years of harrassing mental labour had stamped upon it. . . . the cold, calm eye, the sunken cheek, the compressed lip, were all . . . impenetrable. . . ." Dull, booming sounds of the distant guns could be heard.[85]

At the President's office, Davis explained to his Cabinet the necessity for evacuation, and each pursued his duties, including the transfer of important papers to the depot. Mallory saw Secretary Benjamin, impeccably dressed and calmly carrying his habitual cigar, walking to his office, and caught sight of Mayor Mayo, spotless in white cravat, ruffles, and waistcoat, busy with plans to protect the people. "The African church had, at an early hour, poured its crowded congregation into the streets; and American citizens of African descent were shaking hands and exchanging congratulations upon all sides. Many passed through the confused streets," writes Mallory, "with eager faces, parted lips, and nervous strides, gazing about for friends and helpers."[86]

The government train finally got under way about 11 P.M. Hundreds sought to leave on it, but only those whose services were essential to the government were allowed, some women excepted. The train moved off "in gloomy silence over the James River," continues Mallory. "A commanding view of the riverfront of the city caught their sad and wistful gaze; and as the last flickering lights died away, many spoke with sad and philosophic frankness upon the hopes, achievements, errors, and tragic final collapse of the Confederate Cause, until all relapsed into silence."[87] But one man retained a sense of cheerful detachment. Even at the end, Benjamin's epicurean philosophy and inexhaustible good humor cropped out in well-informed discussion of other lost causes, and he munched his sandwich and puffed his cigar with unconquerable poise.[88]

Slowed by the bad roadbed, the train did not make the 140 miles to Danville, Virginia, until mid-afternoon April 3. Government operations were reorganized, and continued in Danville until the evening of April 10. No substantial evidence supports the assertions made later that the movement of the official train prevented the collection of supplies at Amelia Court House for Lee's retiring army. Davis denied that he or the president of the railroad, who was with him, knew anything about supply plans.[89]

85. Mallory, S.R., *Diary*, Southern Historical Collection, Univ. of N.C. Library. His story of the last days of the Confederacy is one of the best records, though apparently written sometime afterward.
86. *Ibid.*
87. *Ibid.*
88. *Ibid.*
89. Davis, Jefferson, *op.cit.*, II, 675-676.

A large crowd met the party at the Danville station as the train came in, "and the President was cordially greeted. There was none of the old, wild, Southern enthusiasm, however, and there was that in the cheers which told almost as much of sorrow as of joy. . . ."[90]

Elsewhere the scene was different. One Confederate soldier, moving through the falling city of Richmond, said: "the men, as usual, light-hearted and cheerful round the fire, though an empire was passing away around them. . . ."[91] As they renewed their march, a tremendous explosion took place toward the James, probably a gunboat going up; others followed which "told, in anything but a whisper, the desperate condition of things. . . ." Passing through the Richmond suburb of Rockets, the soldier found a different atmosphere. "The peculiar population of that suburb were gathered on the sidewalk; bold, dirty-looking women, who had evidently not been improved by four years' military association, dirtier-looking (if possible) children, and here and there skulking, scoundrelly looking men, who in the general ruin were sneaking from the holes they had been hiding in. . . ." The rebel soldier continued: "The great crowd, as we soon saw, were . . . pillaging the burning city. . . . The roaring and crackling of the burning houses, the trampling and snorting of our horses over the paved streets . . . wild sounds . . . through the cloud of smoke that hung like a pall around him, made a scene that beggars description. . . . the saddest of many of the sad sights of war—a city undergoing pillage at the hands of its own mob, while the standards of an empire were being taken from its capitol, and the tramp of a victorious enemy could be heard at its gates. . . ."[92]

War refugees, particularly in recent months, had gathered in Richmond, which, it was believed, held about 5,000 deserters. The passage of Confederate troops westward April 3 was hindered by the flames. "As we sat upon our horses on the high hill on which Manchester stood, . . . a suburb south of the James," wrote one observer, "we looked down upon the City of Richmond. By this time the fire appeared to be general. Some magazine or depot for the manufacture of ordnance stores was on fire about the centre of the city; it was marked by the peculiar blackness of smoke; from the middle of it would come the roar of bursting shells and boxes of . . . ammunition. . . . On our right was the navy yard at which were several steamers and gunboats . . . burning in the river, from which the cannon were thundering as the fire reached them. . . ."[93]

90. Mallory, *Diary*, *op.cit.*
91. Boykin, Edward M., *The Falling Flag, Evacuation of Richmond, Retreat, and Surrender at Appomattox,* New York, 1874, 9.
92. *Ibid.*, 11-12.
93. *Ibid.*, 15.

Most of the residents of Richmond remained in the city, along with many refugees from Petersburg and nearby towns. General Alexander wrote that on April 3, Irish, Germans, and Negroes—men, women and children—crowded the city, "carrying off bacon, corn, bedding, saddles, harness, and every variety of army stores . . ." Nearly every shop on Main Street was plundered.[94]

A Richmond lady, describing the night of April 2-3, relates: "All through that long, long night we worked and wept, and bade farewell, never thinking of sleep; in the distance we heard the shouts of the soldiers and mob as they ransacked stores; the rumblings of wagons, and beating of drums all mixed in a confused medley. Just before dawn explosions of gunboats and magazines shook the city, and glass was shattered, and new houses crumbled beneath the shocks. Involuntarily I closed the shutters, and then everything had become still as death, while immense fires stretched their arms on high all around me. I shuddered at the dreadful silence. Richmond burning and no alarm. . . . I watched those silent, awful fires; I felt that there was no effort to stop them, but all like myself were watching them, paralyzed and breathless. After a while the sun rose as you may have seen it, a great red ball veiled in a mist."[95]

Among the refugees who did leave Richmond were men in broadcloth— politicians, members of Congress, and prominent citizens, nearly all on foot, but a few in carriages. One observer thought the ladies generally calmer than the men.[96]

Another resident of Richmond was struck by the burning of government offices, all the major newspapers, and other business establishments. Most of the windows were broken in her house and a shell from an exploding ordnance depot entered the library.[97]

The first major fires had been set by order of Confederate authorities, though some officers opposed this needless loss. Mrs. LaSalle Corbell Pickett described the scene as a saturnalia, saying that some law-officers fled from the frenzied mob. Liquor added to the excitement.[98] General Ewell, commanding in Richmond, admitted destroying military stores, but maintained that in many instances the mobs set fire to business and other buildings.[99]

One family feared their large, convenient house would be taken over by the Yankees, but their free colored man, Peter, said: "Don't you be scared, Miss

94. Letter of April 3, 1865, E.P. Alexander Papers, Southern Hist. Coll., Univ. of N.C.
95. Letters of Mrs. Mary A. Fontaine, Confederate Mem'l. Literary Soc., Richmond, April 30, 1865.
96. Blackford, Lieut.-Col. W.W., War Years With Jeb Stuart, New York, 1945, 283.
97. Diary of Miss Lelian M. Cook, Virginia State Historical Society, Richmond.
98. Johnson, Rossiter, ed., Campfire and Battlefield, New York, 1896, containing article by Mrs. LaSalle Corbell Pickett, "The First United States Flag Raised in Richmond after the War," 453-454.
99. O.R., I, xlvi, pt. 1, 1292-1295.

May. I done tell 'em you is a good Union woman." This of course aroused indignation, and the young girls could hardly be restrained from hanging out a Confederate flag.[100]

Thirteen-year-old Emmie Sublett told of Confederate troops passing through the city the night of April 2-3, with friends in the army dropping by to say farewell. The family hid their jewelry, even covering ten gold pieces with green to make them buttons. In the murky red light of the next morning the Yankees came, "and first of all placed the *horrible stars and stripes* (which seemed to be to me so many slashes) over our beloved capitol. O, the horrible wretches! I can't think of a name horrible enough to call them. It makes us fifty times more southern in our feelings to have them here; . . ." But the fiery teenager did admit that the Yankees "have behaved very well indeed. No private property has been touched, and no insults have been offered to any of the citizens. . . ." Emmie noted that the Richmond girls went around the streets coolly, thickly veiled and without noticing the Yankees. "It seems a dreary life for one who is just setting out in life. . . ."[101]

Youthful Emma Mordecai, who lived just outside the city, came in April 4 and wrote that Richmond "could no longer be recognized. Yankee officers on fine horses dashing down Broad St., and the sidewalks thronged with people I never saw before, and negro soldiers, drunk and sober. The Screamersville population looked truly joyous, and seemed to be delighted at the new order of things. . . ." She spoke of general rubble and streets strewn with fragments of paper. To her the city was "desecrated, desolate and defiled."[102]

While it was obvious most of the white population were proudly sensitive, all evidence indicates that the Union forces occupied Richmond in an orderly manner, and without giving offense. One woman reported shortly after the occupation that they could no longer afford to keep Negro servants. "We now see what idle lives they must have led. We love the colored people and shall always love them, yet believe they have kept many families poor. We all prefer German servants. . . ."[103]

Two small Federal cavalry guidons were raised over the Confederate capitol by Major Atherton H. Stevens, Jr., Fourth Massachusetts Volunteer Cavalry, and Lieut. Johnston S. de Peyster of New York raised a larger flag.[104]

General Godfrey Weitzel with troops of the Army of the James promptly

100. Papers of Emmie Crump Lightfoot, Confederate Memorial Literary Society, Richmond.
101. Letter of April 29, 1865, Letters of Emmie Sublett, Confederate Mem'l. Lit. Soc.
102. Letters of Emma Mordecai, Confed. Mem'l. Lit. Soc., Richmond, April 5, 1865.
103. Benetta Valentine to her brother, E.V. Valentine, April 21, 1865, Valentine Family Letters, Valentine Museum, Richmond.
104. Maj.-Gen. G. Weitzel to the Governor of New York, Nov. 5, 1865, *Battles and Leaders*, extra-illustrated ed., HEH; Langdon, Loomis L., "The Stars and Stripes in Richmond," *Century*, May-October, 1890, 308-309.

took charge, extinguishing fires and partially restoring order. However, by April 14, War Clerk Jones thought that Weitzel's rule became "more and more despotic daily. . . ."[105]

The brigade under Edward H. Ripley was ordered to lead the way in for the infantry. "The bands had arranged a succession of Union airs which had not been heard for years in the streets of the Confederate capital," wrote Ripley.[106] He described the "surging mob of Confederate stragglers, negroes, and released convicts" that seemed in full control from the moment Ewell crossed the James, burning bridges behind him. "The air was darkened by the thick tempest of black smoke and cinders which swept the streets, and, as we penetrated deeper into the city, the bands were nearly drowned by the crashing of the falling walls, the roar of the flames, and the terrific explosions of shells in the burning warehouses. Densely packed on either side of the street were thousands upon thousands of blacks, . . . They fell upon their knees, throwing their hands wildly in the air and shouted 'Glory to God! Glory to God! Massa Linkum am here! Massa Linkum am here!' while floods of tears poured down their wild faces. . . ." Ripley's brigade had immediate command of the city. Other troops were cleared out although there was some disorder from the Negro troops. Regiments went to work fighting the fires, primarily by blowing up and pulling down buildings in the flames' path. Prisoners were released, Confederates rounded up, streets were patrolled and order brought from chaos. "This was done well, as even Confederates admitted."[107]

Charles A. Dana arrived shortly to preserve as many Confederate records as he could. He wrote Stanton that, "The malignity of the thorough rebel here is humbled and silenced, but only seems the more intense on that account. . . . there is a great throng of people after victuals. Confederate money is useless and they have no other."[108]

Reporters came in with the troops, for the public at the North was avid for news from this strange capital of rebeldom. One leading journalist wrote: "There were swaying chimneys, tottering walls, streets impassable from piles of brick, stones, and rubbish. Capitol Square was filled with furniture, beds, clothing, crockery, chairs, tables, looking-glasses. Women were weeping, children crying. Men stood speechless, haggard, woebegone, gazing at the desolation. . . ."[109] The capitol several times caught fire from cinders. "If it had not been for the soldiers the whole city would have gone. . . ." Another reported:

105. Jones, *A Rebel War Clerk's Diary*, op.cit., 357.
106. Eisenschiml, Otto, ed., *Vermont General; The Unusual War Experiences of Edward Hastings Ripley, 1862-1865*, New York, 1960, 301.
107. *Ibid.*, 296-306.
108. Dana to Stanton, April 6, 1865, Stanton Papers, LC.
109. Coffin, Charles Carleton, *The Boys of '61*, Boston, 1881, 508.

Scene in the House of Representatives, January 31, 1865, after Passage of the Thirteenth Amendment.

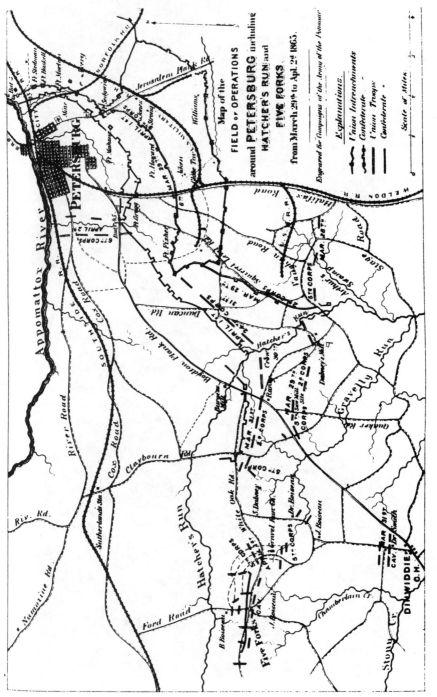

Map of Operations around Petersburg, March 29–April 2, 1865

"This town is the Rebellion; it is all that we have directly striven for; quitting it, the Confederate leaders have quitted their sheet-anchor, their roof-tree, their abiding hope. Its history is the epitome of the whole contest, and to us, shivering our thunderbolts against it for more than four years, Richmond is still a mystery. . . ."[110] However, "no people in their subjugation wear a better front than these brave old spirits, whose lives are not their own. Fire has ravaged their beautiful city, soldiers of the color of their servants guard the crossings and pace the pavement with bayoneted muskets. But gentlemen they are still, in every pace, and inch, and syllable,—such men as we were wont to call brothers and countrymen. . . ."[111]

Another Northern reporter was struck by the number of Negroes abroad and their exultant bearing. Not less than a thousand were promenading the State House grounds which they had never before been allowed to enter. One colored man was heard to exclaim, "We-uns kin go anywhar, jist anywhar we wanter. No passes!" A white citizen reported that three of his former slaves had told him they were a committee to inform him that the twenty-seven he had owned were free, but would continue to work for him on condition that they were *paid in greenbacks!* He took the news hard. Not a Negro in the city, it was reported, had failed to learn that he was free, and to count on the fact.[112]

In Washington there was the expected rejoicing. "Today is one long to be remembered in the annals of our country, for today we have occupied Richmond, the boasted stronghold of rebellion. . . ."[113] A large crowd assembled at the War Department and there were speeches by Stanton, Seward, Vice-President Johnson and others. News came in of rejoicing throughout the country, and on the night of April 3, there was a "grand illumination" all over Washington.[114] The news had come in about 10 A.M., April 3, with newspaper extras being sold throughout the city. "From one end of Pennsylvania Avenue to the other the air seemed to burn with the bright hues of the flag. The sky was shaken by a grand salute of eight hundred guns, fired by order of the Secretary of War—three hundred for Petersburg and five hundred for Richmond. Almost by magic the streets were crowded with hosts of people, talking, laughing, hurrahing, and shouting in the fullness of their joy. Men embraced one another, 'treated' one another, made up old quarrels, renewed old friendships, marched through the streets arm in arm, singing and chatting in that happy sort of abandon which characterizes our people when under the influ-

---

110. Townsend, George Alfred, *Campaigns of a Non-Combatant,* New York, 1866, 330.

111. *Ibid.,* 331.

112. New York *Tribune,* April 10, 1865.

113. Ms. Diary and Journal, David Homer Bates Collection, Stern Collection, Rare Book Room, LC.

114. *Ibid.*

ence of a great and universal happiness. The atmosphere was full of the intoxication of joy. . . ."[115]

Stanton read to the throng Grant's despatch telling of the capture of Richmond, and the fact that the city was burning. The War Secretary asked the
crowd what they could reply. Some shouted "Let her burn!" "Burn it!" "Burn
it!" and another, "Hold Richmond for the Northern mudsills!"[116] In fact,
reporter Noah Brooks, said: "a more liquorish crowd was never seen in Washington than on that night."

In a remarkably few days, the Orange & Alexandria Railroad was opened
and steamers were plying from Washington to Richmond. The Richmond
post-office was opened by Federal authorities almost at once. These were
outward tokens of restoration, though some deep scars of the war would
remain for decades.

On April 2, Lincoln had spent the day inspecting lines and entrenchments.
He also telegraphed to Stanton in Washington, Mrs. Lincoln, and Grant, and
relayed messages from the General-in-Chief.

Monday, April 3, as Lee's disorganized and scattered troops were straggling
toward Amelia Court House, as President Davis was traveling to Danville, and
as Richmond was being occupied, President Lincoln went into Petersburg. He
reviewed the passing troops, and conferred for an hour-and-a-half with Grant
in a house vacated by a fleeing resident,[117] Grant having requested the meeting.
The town was nearly deserted when the general and the President met. The
correspondent of the New York *Tribune*, riding through Union lines at Petersburg on the morning of April 3, found the troops all astir, with knapsacks being
slung, blankets rolled, and every preparation made for an immediate advance.
Some units had occupied the town a few hours earlier, and a general fusillade
was resounding, with bands playing "Hail, Columbia," "Yankee Doodle,"
"Kingdom's Coming," "We'll All Drink Stone Blind," and one striking up
"Old Hundred." Although the enemy had removed his dead and wounded,
many evidences of his heavy casualties were visible. The correspondent saw
one dying Confederate, emaciated, half-clad, and pallid, with a wound in the
side of his head red with clotted gore. Doors were closed and window-blinds
shut in parts of the city not wrecked by the siege. But its whole eastern half
showed how much shot and shell had been poured into it. Chimneys were
smashed, windows splintered, walls toppled, porches knocked to bits, and even
whole buildings obliterated. Before the war, Petersburg had been one of the
neatest, most attractive Southern centers. Now it was an expanse of ruin.[118]

115. Brooks, Noah, *Washington in Lincoln's Time*, New York, 1895, 219.
116. *Ibid.*, 220.
117. Nicolay and Hay, *op.cit.*, X, 216.
118. New York *Tribune*, April 10, 1865.

It was here that Lincoln was said to have congratulated Grant, saying, "Do you know, General, that I have had a sort of sneaking idea for some days that you intended to do something like this?"[119] Grant was anxious that the Eastern armies should get the credit for vanquishing their long-time enemies. He wanted no bickering over the laurels and Lincoln agreed. The General is quoted as saying: "I had a feeling that it would be better to let Lee's old antagonists give his army the final blow and finish up the job. The Western armies have been very successful in their campaigns, and it is due to the Eastern armies to let them vanquish their old enemy single-handed. . . ."[120] Lincoln had informed Stanton of his plans to visit Grant. The Secretary expressed concern for the President's safety. Lincoln then told him of plans to go to Richmond, adding: "I will take care of myself. . . ."[121]

However, the truth is that Lincoln did not seem to take adequate good care of himself in his visits to Richmond on April 4 and 5. On the morning of April 4, the President started up the James on the *River Queen*, escorted by Admiral Porter's flagship, a transport, another small vessel and a tug. But, because of the obstructions in the river, the President went on in the twelve-oared barge of the Admiral. They landed, with no one to meet them, about a block above Libby Prison.

We still may wonder why Lincoln made such a hazardous trip so soon to the former enemy capital. Its propagandist value was no longer important. It is true he held some vital political talks, but was it necessary to go into Richmond to do this? Possibly the President was chiefly curious to see the now lifeless heart of the Confederacy. Perhaps he wished to demonstrate the restoration of a united country in which people could move about freely. His secretaries correctly wrote: "Never in the history of the world did the head of a mighty nation and the conqueror of a great rebellion enter the captured chief city of the insurgents in such humbleness and simplicity."[122]

Up the streets of Richmond the small party of ten armed sailors, a contraband guide, Admiral Porter, three officers and Lincoln, walked toward the capitol. The newly-freed Negroes crowded around, and continual risk was evident. The streets abounded with drunken rebels, liberated Negroes and onlookers. Confusion reigned and fires still blazed.[123]

Lincoln and his escort proceeded to the White House of the Confederacy, now used as General Weitzel's headquarters, which Davis had quitted less than forty-eight hours earlier. In the afternoon, the President took a drive about the

119. Grant, *Memoirs*, II, 459-460.
120. Coolidge, Louis A., *Ulysses S. Grant*, 2 vols., Boston, 1924, Vol.I, 193.
121. Lincoln, Works, VIII, *op.cit.*, 384-385.
122. Nicolay and Hay, *op.cit.*, X, 216-218.
123. Penrose, Major Charles B., "Lincoln's Visit to Richmond," *Century*, June, 1890, Vol. XL, No.2, 307.

city. A youthful Confederate girl, who wrote vividly of the fall of the city, stated: "You know Lincoln came to Richmond Tuesday the 4th and was paraded through the streets in a vehicle very much like an ambulance, only a little nicer, but *very common indeed*, attended by a bodyguard of about one hundred horsemen and dashing through the streets like the horses were wild. The 'monkey show' came right by here, but we wouldn't let them see us looking at them, so we ran in the parlor and peeped at them. . . ."[124]

During this first visit to Richmond Lincoln did see, upon his own request, John A. Campbell. Thus, for the third time during the Civil War, the former Associate Justice of the Supreme Court of the United States was to play a prominent, though controversial, part in national affairs. Twice before, as the intermediary between the Confederate commissioners and Seward during the crisis immediately preceding Sumter, and again at Hampton Roads in February, 1865, this highly-respected jurist had been involved. Even though he had been Assistant Secretary of War of the Confederacy, he had not fled Richmond.[125]

At their first meeting in Richmond, Campbell told the President that he was no official spokesman for Confederate leaders, but that obviously the war was over, "and all that remained to be done was to compose the country." Campbell said later: "I spoke to him particularly for Virginia, and urged him to consult and counsel with her public men and her citizens as to the restoration of peace, civil order, and the renewal of her relations as a member of the Union. . . ." Campbell informed Lincoln that prominent men in the state were ready to work for pacification. It must be remembered that at Hampton Roads Campbell had not been adamant in refusing Lincoln's terms for settlement. Of this new meeting he later made a brief record. Campbell declared that in referring to his remarks on Virginia, Lincoln "answered that my general principles were right; the trouble was how to apply them. . . ." The President wanted another talk with Campbell, and would stay in Richmond overnight.[126]

124. Letters of Emmie Sublett, *op.cit.*

125. As in so many events, controversy surrounds the identity of the men who attended two Lincoln-Campbell conferences, and the question of precisely what was said or meant. The following account is primarily based on Nicolay and Hay, *op.cit.*, X, 219-228; Connor, Henry G., *John Archibald Campbell*, Boston, 1920, 174-182; Letter of John A. Campbell to Horace Greeley, April 26, 1865, unsent, Southern Historical Collection, Univ, of N.C., Campbell-Colston Collection; Campbell, John A., "A View of the Confederacy from the Inside; a Letter from Judge John A. Campbell, July 20, 1865," *Century*, October, 1889, 952; Welles, *Diary*, II, 279; Lincoln, *Collected Works*, VIII, April 5, 1865, 386-387 (to Campbell); Lincoln to Grant, April 6, 1865, 388; Lincoln to Weitzel, April 6, 1865, 389; Lincoln telegram to Weitzel, April 12, 1865, 405; Lincoln to Weitzel, April 12, 405-408; *O.R.*, I, xlvi, pt.3, 655, 656, 657, 724. For worthy secondary accounts, see Randall-Current, *Last Full Measure*, New York, 1955, 346-347, 353-356; Hesseltine, William B., *Lincoln's Plan of Reconstruction*, 137-139.

126. Connor, *op.cit.*, 174-176.

Lincoln spent the night on the *Malvern* in the James; he saw Campbell again the morning of April 5. Again, the details and even the substance of who said what, and what was understood and not understood, is confused and debatable. Campbell and a lawyer, Gustavus Myers, saw the President and Weitzel. The President, now prepared, read and commented on a paper or memorandum. In this, as he had so often done, Lincoln called for restoration of national authority, and promised no retreat by the executive on the slavery question, and no cessation of hostilities short of an end to the war, plus the disbanding of all hostile forces. He stated that other propositions not inconsistent with the major points would be considered by the North. Lincoln said that confiscated property would be returned to the people of a State which should immediately withdraw its troops and halt its support of the rebels. Of course, that did not refer to slaves.[127]

Campbell said he did not believe there would be any opposition to the terms, and further stated: "Mr. Lincoln told me that he had been meditating a plan, but that he had not fixed upon it, and if he adopted it, would write to General Weitzel from City Point. This was to call the Virginia Legislature together, 'the very Legislature which has been sitting up yonder,' pointing to the Capitol, 'to vote the restoration of Virginia to the Union.' He said he had a government in Virginia—the Pierpont Government—but it 'had a very small margin,' and he was not 'disposed to increase it.' " There are many accounts, all of them after the event, as to what Lincoln said, or Campbell thought he said, and the nuances are important, though too lengthy to chronicle here.

Campbell later wrote to Greeley in an unsent letter: "My intercourse with President Lincoln both here and at Hampton Roads impressed me favorably and kindly to him. I believe that he felt a genuine sympathy for the bereavement, destitution, impoverishment, waste, and overturn that war had occasioned at the South. . . . "[128]

Campbell went on that Lincoln, in the conversation regarding the Virginia Legislature, "had expressed his object in desiring them to meet and to vote. . . ." Is this what Lincoln really said? Or did he, in exacting, carefully-chosen words, qualify the rôle of the Virginia Legislature? Certainly, at any rate, it was a departure in policy to suggest making use of the Virginia Legislature in any form.

Back at City Point on April 6, Lincoln wrote Weitzel the well-known statement: "It has been intimated to me that the gentlemen who have acted as the Legislature of Virginia, in support of the rebellion, may . . . now desire

127. Lincoln, *Collected Works*, VIII, 386-387.
128. John A. Campbell to Horace Greeley, April 26, 1865, Campbell-Colston Papers, Southern Historical Collection, Univ. of N.C.

to assemble at Richmond, and take measures to withdraw the Virginia troops, and other support from resistance to the general government. If they attempt it, give them permission and protection, until, if at all, they attempt some action hostile to the United States, in which case you will notify them and give them reasonable time to leave; and at the end of which time, arrest any who may remain. Allow Judge Campbell to see this, but do not make it public. . . ."[129]

Campbell gathered together a group of the legislators in Richmond, along with others, and issued a call for the legislature to meet. Lee surrendered April 9. On April 12, Lincoln wrote Weitzel calling the whole thing off. On April 14, Campbell and R.M.T. Hunter wired for permission to visit Lincoln. Thus, we have the second incident within a few days—the first involving Lincoln and Sherman, the second involving Lincoln and Campbell—in which confusion and misunderstanding abound.

Lincoln may not have placed high expectations upon the Virginia legislature, for the same day that he wrote Weitzel, April 6, he told Grant, "I do not think it very probable that anything will come of this; but I have thought best to notify you, so that if you should see signs, you may understand them. From our recent dispatches it seems that you are pretty effectually withdrawing the Virginia troops from opposition to the government . . ."[130]

In his letter of April 12 to Weitzel, Lincoln seems to take a tortuous dialectical approach in order to end the possibility that the Virginia Legislature would meet. He stated that Campbell "assumes, as appears to me, that I have called the insurgent Legislature of Virginia together, as the rightful Legislature of the State, to settle all differences with the United States. I have done no such thing. I spoke of them not as a Legislature, but as 'the gentlemen who have *acted* as the Legislature of Virginia in support of the rebellion.' I did this on purpose to exclude the assumption that I was recognizing them as a *rightful* body. I dealt with them as men who have power *de facto* to do a specific thing, to wit, 'to withdraw the Virginia troops, and other support from resistance to the General Government,' for which in the paper handed Judge Campbell I promised a specific equivalent, to wit, a remission to the people of the State, except in certain cases, of the confiscation of their property. I meant this and no more. Inasmuch, however, as Judge Campbell misconstrues this, and is still pressing for an armistice, contrary to the explicit statement of the paper I gave him; and particularly as Gen. Grant has since captured the Virginia troops, so that giving a consideration for their withdrawal is no longer applicable, let my letter to you, and the paper to Judge Campbell both be withdrawn or counter-

129. Lincoln, *Collected Works*, VIII, 389.
130. *Ibid.*, VIII, 388.

manded, and he be notified of it. Do not now allow them to assemble; but if any have come, allow them safe return to their homes. . . ."[131]

It may or may not be true that Campbell misconstrued Lincoln's full meaning, and it certainly was true that the surrender at Appomattox had taken the Virginia troops out of the war. But it also appears from his language and action that, after consultation with his Cabinet and its disapproval, Lincoln manoeuvered his course out of what had become an embarrassing situation.

It has long been assumed, and probably with a correct interpretation of the limited evidence available, that the Cabinet on April 11 was unanimous against the proposal of Lincoln to use the Virginia Legislature. Two days later, Welles had a talk with Lincoln in which the President said that as all Cabinet members had taken a view differing from his own, "he concluded he had perhaps made a mistake, and was ready to correct it if he had. . . ."[132] Stanton and Speed were the men most determined against the plan, while Dennison also was quite firm. Lincoln possibly said, as Welles reported, that "Their decisive opposition . . . was annoying him greatly . . ."[133] Welles pointed out to the President that the North had never recognized any of the Confederate "organizations."

Despite some intervals of anxiety, these days at the end of the war constituted a fairly happy interlude in the melancholy life of Lincoln, with plenty of good news, particularly from the military fronts. According to the New York *Tribune* correspondent, he returned to the capital much stronger "in body and soul" than he had left.[134] How could he fail to feel joyful on entering Richmond to behold Negroes, wild with delight, shouting, "Glory to God! Glory! Glory!"

On the other hand, the Campbell meeting had been a disappointment. Lincoln was indignant over accounts of it in the Richmond *Whig*, repeated in the Washington *Chronicle*. A paragraph appeared in Greeley's *Tribune*, on April 10, headed "Peace Rumors," which said: "R.M.T. Hunter and Judge Campbell were the leading spirits in the recent Richmond conference on peace." It added that they had admitted the hopelessness of their cause, the wickedness of a further waste of life in a fruitless struggle for independence, and were primarily anxious that such generous terms should be conceded by the government that continuance of the struggle would be impossible. "This and many other statements are afloat tonight, but beyond the fact that the President has returned with the deliberate purpose of issuing some sort of an address to the common masses of the South, all is sheer conjecture." Yet

131. *Ibid.*, VIII, 406-407.
132. Welles, *Diary*, *op.cit.*, II, 279-280.
133. Welles, Gideon, Typed Mss. of article, "Lincoln and Reconstruction," John Hay Library, Brown University.
134. New York *Tribune*, April 10, 1865.

Greeley, one of the foremost advocates of what he termed "magnanimity in victory," continued hopeful. On his editorial page of April 11, he declared: "We had hoped to print herewith the President's proclamation of amnesty and oblivion to the partisans of the baffled rebellion, and we do not yet despair of receiving it before we go to press." He went on to present a forcible argument against the indulgence of passion, and in behalf of a prompt restoration of the Union. In an editorial April 14 he wrote: "We entreat the President promptly to do and dare in the cause of magnanimity! The Southern mind is now open to kindness, and may be majestically affected by generosity." Thus, Lincoln's meeting with Campbell aroused the hopes of those who advocated generosity toward the South.

At 11 P.M. on April 8, the Lincoln party had left City Point for Washington. He had heard late on the 5th, after returning from Richmond, that Secretary Seward had fallen from his carriage and had suffered serious injuries. Mrs. Lincoln, Senator Sumner and others had come down from Washington for a visit to Richmond. Haunting the headquarters offices, Lincoln was keeping as close touch as possible on the progress of the Union armies as they sought to bring Lee to bay. He was intensely interested in the skirmishing near Amelia Court House, Sheridan's movements to cut Lee off from North Carolina, the engagement at Sayler's Creek April 6, and, of course, the question of how soon and in what way the war in Virginia would end.

On the 7th, Lincoln sent his well-known telegram to Grant: "Gen. Sheridan says 'If the thing is pressed I think that Lee will surrender.' Let the *thing* be pressed."[135]

Concerned over Seward's condition, Lincoln then turned back for the capitol and should have been content in knowing that his generals were pressing the "thing", indeed.

[IV]

"We have Lee's army pressed hard, his men scattering and going to their homes by thousands. He is endeavoring to reach Danville, where Jeff Davis and his Cabinet have gone. I shall press the pursuit to the end. Push Johnson [sic] at the same time and let us finish up this job at once." Thus, Grant wrote Sherman from Burkeville, Va., April 6, 1865.[136] Grant had been pressing since May of the previous year, and he was not about to stop.[137]

Now, however, had come the time to combine personal messages to Lee

135. Lincoln, *Collected Works*, VIII, 392.
136. *The History of America in Documents*, Rosenbach Company Catalogue, 1951, pt.1, 69-70.
137. For military events of the campaign from Richmond to Appomattox, see Chap.IX.

along with the use of military force against him. Appraising the losses to Lee's army at Sayler's Creek, in other fighting and in general attrition, Grant believed the situation of the Army of Northern Virginia utterly hopeless, and on April 7, opened correspondence with the Confederate general. From Farmville he wrote Lee that he regarded it his duty "to shift from myself the responsibility of any further effusion of blood, by asking of you the surrender of that portion of the C. S. Army known as the Army of Northern Virginia. . . ."[138]

Lee, in the field, read the communiqué, handed it to Longstreet, who read it and returned it, saying, "Not yet."[139] Lee formally replied to Grant: "Though not entertaining the opinion you express on the hopelessness of further resistance on the part of the Army of Northern Virginia, I reciprocate your desire to avoid useless effusion of blood, and therefore, before considering your proposition, ask the terms you will offer, on condition of its surrender. . . ."[140]

Grant had already received Lincoln's instructions of March 3 not to treat of anything but surrender, even if his tendency had been otherwise. He, therefore, sent Lee a firm and careful response on April 8 from Farmville: "I would say that, peace being my great desire, there is but one condition I would insist upon, namely that the men and officers surrendered shall be disqualified for taking up arms again against the Government of the United States until properly exchanged. . . ." He reiterated that any meeting would be for surrender. About midnight the same day, Grant received the reply, also carefully worded. Lee did not think the emergency was great enough for surrender, but he was interested in "restoration of peace." For this purpose he would be glad to talk with Grant.[141]

The verbal sparring of the two military leaders was worthy of diplomatic usage. Grant, on the morning of April 9, as his army nearly ringed Appomattox Court House, replied that he had no authority to treat on the subject of peace, but that he and the entire North desired peace. "By the South laying down their arms they will hasten that most desirable event, save thousands of human lives, and hundreds of millions of property not yet destroyed. . . ."[142]

After the war, Grant declared that "I saw clearly, especially after Sheridan had cut off the escape to Danville, that Lee must surrender or break and run into the mountains—break in all directions and leave us a dozen guerrilla bands to fight. My campaign was not Richmond, not the defeat of Lee in actual

138. *O.R.*, I, xlvi, pt.1, 56.
139. Longstreet, James, *From Manassas to Appomattox*, Philadelphia, 1896, 619.
140. *O.R.*, I, xlvi, pt.1, 56.
141. *Ibid.*, 56-57.
142. *Ibid.*

fight, but to remove him and his army out of the contest, and if possible, to have him use his influence in inducing the surrender of Johnston and the other isolated armies. . . ."[143]

Grant's staff secretary, Badeau, wrote a friend that, after the assault at Petersburg, "there was no pause, no hesitancy, no doubt what to do. He commanded Lee's army as much as he did ours; caused and knew beforehand every movement that Lee made, up to the actual surrender. . . . There was no let up; fighting and marching, and negotiating all at once. This accounts for the change in Lee's views; at the beginning of the correspondence you remember, he said he didn't agree with Grant that a surrender was inevitable, and he didn't think so till the very morning it occurred."[144]

The night of April 8 from Appomattox General Pickett wrote his wife: "It is finished. Oh, my beloved division! Thousands of them have gone to their eternal home, having given up their lives for the cause they knew to be just. The others, alas, heart-broken, crushed in spirit, are left to mourn its loss. Well, it is practically all over now. We have poured out our blood, and suffered untold hardships and privations, all in vain. And now, well—I must not forget, either, that God reigns. . . ."[145]

Learning of the condition of his army and the Union positions on the morning of April 9 in the Appomattox area, Lee requested a suspension of hostilities until terms of surrender could be arranged.[146] Later, Lee wrote Davis that "The apprehensions I expressed during the winter, of the moral condition of the Army of Northern Virginia, have been realized. . . ."[147] The disintegration of the rebel army had reached such a point that, on the 9th, Lee had only 7,892 effective infantry, and how truly effective even these were is dubious.

Many accounts exist of the last days of Lee's army and of what the General did and said.[148] A staff officer close to Lee related that on the morning of April 9 the General asked him, "Well, Colonel, what are we to do?" The officer replied that if they could abandon the trains, the army might escape. "Yes," said the General, "perhaps we could; but I have had a conference with these gentlemen around me, and they agree that the time has come for capitulation."

143. "Grant as a Critic," New York *Herald*, July 24, 1878, interview with Grant by John Russell Young.

144. Adam Badeau to James H. Wilson, May 27, 1865, J.H. Wilson Papers, LC.

145. Pickett, George E., *Soldier of the South: General Pickett's War Letters to His Wife*, ed. Arthur Inman, Boston, 1928, 128-133, letter of April 8, 1865.

146. *O.R.*, I, xlvi, pt.1, 1266, Lee's report; Ibid., 57, Grant's report.

147. Lee to Davis, April 20, 1865, *Wartime Papers of R.E. Lee*, 938-939.

148. Freeman, D.S., *R.E. Lee*, New York, 1935, IV, *passim*, for details and analysis.

"Well, sir," said the officer, "I can only speak for myself; to me any other fact is preferable. . . ." "Such is my individual way of thinking," interrupted the General. "But," added the officer, "of course, General, it is different with you. You have to think of these brave men and decide not only for yourself but for them." "Yes," he replied; "it would be useless and therefore cruel to provoke the further effusion of blood, and I have arranged to meet General Grant with a view to surrender, and wish you to accompany me."[149]

That morning of April 9, Lee was described "as calm and cool as at any time since he took command of the army, just as if the army was to pass in review before him. His face denoted great self-command and his dignity was conspicuously grand. He spoke out in his usual tone of voice, nor did it portray in the slightest the fierce conflict going on within. . . ."[150] The same soldier depicted Lee as clad in his best and newest uniform, with elegant cavalry boots, gold spurs, shining sword and accoutrements.

As for the army, another officer described the men as gathering as usual, on clear, cool, fresh mornings, around fires for breakfast. Noises from the distance of the approaching enemy seemed not to bother them. The responsibility lay with the officers.[151]

The final council-of-war held the night of the 8th, with what top officers were left, had come to the only conclusion possible. The absence of so many familiar names and faces was proof of the exhaustion of the Army of Northern Virginia. The discussion included the fate of the Southern people after surrender. There in the woods around the small fire, some spoke of the possibility of forcing a way through Grant's lines and saving a fragment of the army which would continue "a desultory warfare until the government at Washington should grow weary and grant to our people peace, and the safeguards of local self-government. . . ." But that was just chatter. As General Gordon later wrote: "If all that was said and felt at that meeting could be given, it would make a volume of measureless pathos. In no hour of the great war did General Lee's masterful characteristics appear to me so conspicuous as they did in that last council. . . ."[152] The conference did decide that they might attempt on the 9th to break through the Federals and ultimately join Joseph E. Johnston in North Carolina, but this was a forlorn hope and came to naught. General Gordon had a staff officer ask Lee where he should camp, to which Lee replied, "Yes, tell General Gordon that I should be glad for him to halt just beyond

149. Taylor, Walter H., *Four Years with General Lee*, New York, 1877, 151-152.
150. Transcript narrative of J.H. Sharp, 13th Virginia Artillery Battalion, Henry T. Sharp Papers, Southern Hist. Collection, Univ. of N.C.
151. Boykin, Edward M., *The Falling Flag*, 55-56.
152. Gordon, John B., *Reminiscences of the Civil War*, New York, 1904, 433-436.

the Tennessee line." Of course, that was 200 miles away, so Lee had had his grim joke.[153]

As General Grant's messenger was seen bringing news of the arrangement for the surrender, Longstreet is quoted by Gen. E.P. Alexander as saying to Lee: "General, unless he offers us honorable terms, come back and let us fight it out."[154] Alexander, admittedly overwrought, wanted to attempt to break out. He reported that Lee answered: "I appreciate that the surrender of this army is, indeed, the end of the Confederacy. But that result is now inevitable, and must be faced. And, as Christian men, we have no right to choose a course from pride or personal feelings. We have simply to see what we can do best for our country and people. Now, if I should adopt your suggestion and order this army to disperse, the men going homeward would be under no control, and moreover, would be without food. They are already demoralized by four years of war, and would supply their wants by violence and plunder. They would soon become little better than bands of robbers. A state of society would result, throughout the South, from which it would require years to recover. The enemy's cavalry, too, would pursue to catch at least the general officers, and would harass and devastate sections that otherwise they will never visit. Moreover, as to myself, I am too old to go to bushwhacking, and even if it were right to order the army to disperse, the only course for me to pursue would be to surrender myself to General Grant. . . ."[155]

The scene at the house of Wilbur McLean in Appomattox Court House on April 9, 1865, has been depicted many times in words, and often, though less accurately, in paintings, on the screen, and by television. No matter how familiar the scene, it will always conjure in the minds of millions of Americans historic memories and profound reflections. It will always inspire the imaginations of these millions to recreate a vivid vision of the impeccable Lee in his new uniform and the somewhat shoddy figure of Grant, who had been suffering from a severe headache for several days, and who looked half-sick in his shabby, field-worn private's uniform.

Many were to describe the physical and moral statuesqueness with which Lee loomed through these stormy hours. George Cary Eggleston wrote of the General at Amelia Court House as bearing a "heart-broken expression" on his face, and with "still sadder tones of voice."[156] "Lee's carriage no longer is erect; the troubles of those last days had already plowed great furrows in his forehead. His eyes were red as if with weeping; his cheeks sunken and haggard;

153. *Ibid.*, 436.
154. Alexander, E.P., *Military Memoirs of a Confederate*, New York, 1907, 609.
155. Alexander, E.P., "Lee at Appomattox," *Century*, April, 1902, 921-926.
156. Eggleston, George Cary, *A Rebel's Recollections*, with Introduction by David Donald, Bloomington, Ind., 1959, 130.

his face colorless. No one who looked upon him then, as he stood there in full view of the disastrous end, can ever forget the intense agony written upon his features. And yet he was calm, self-possessed, and deliberate. Failure and the sufferings of his men grieved him sorely, but they could not daunt him, and his moral greatness was never more manifest than during those last terrible days. . . ."[157]

It is well remembered that Grant and Lee chatted for a while, probably a bit awkwardly, about the weather, their Mexican War experiences, and several minor matters. Finally, Lee brought up the subject of their meeting. Grant wrote out the terms on field paper, on a little knobbed-legged table. Presently, Lee, sitting at the side of the room at a marble-topped table, rose and went over to read Grant's paper, which was addressed to General Lee:

"In accordance with the substance of my letter to you of the 8th instant, I propose to receive the surrender of the Army of Northern Virginia on the following terms, to wit: Rolls of all the officers and men to be made in duplicate, one copy to be given to an officer to be designated by me, the other to be retained by such officer or officers as you may designate. The officers to give their individual paroles not to take up arms against the Government of the United States until properly exchanged; and each company or regimental commander sign a like parole for the men of their commands. The arms, artillery, and public property to be parked and stacked, and turned over to the officers appointed by me to receive them. This will not embrace the side-arms of the officers, nor their private horses or baggage. This done, each officer and man will be allowed to return to his home, not to be disturbed by U. S. authority so long as they observe their paroles and the laws in force where they may reside. . . ." Lee accepted in writing.[158]

It all sounded so simple—just surrender and few details. Lee seemed satisfied with the terms that officers were to retain side arms and baggage. Turning to Grant, he explained that Confederate cavalrymen owned their own horses, which would be needed for plowing and planting, to which Grant replied that he would give orders to allow every man who claimed to own his horse or mule to take the animal with him. This was not put into the final terms, but Grant did carry out his word. During the copying of the documents,

157. *Ibid.*, 130-131.
158. *O.R.*, I, xlvi, pt.i, 57-58. Many and repetitious are the accounts of the scene of Lee's surrender. Among the more important original accounts are: Marshall, Charles, *An Aide-de-Camp of Lee*, ed., Sir Frederick Maurice, Boston, 1927, 268-275; Adam Badeau to Wilson, May 27, 1865 (typescript), J.B. Wilson Papers, LC; Pamphlet, "General Ely S. Parker's Narrative of Appomattox," Benjamin Harrison Papers, LC; "Lee's Surrender," endorsed by Grant as being accurate, Orville E. Babcock Papers, Chicago Hist. Soc.; "Grant as Critic," New York *Herald*, July 24, 1878; Grant, *Memoirs*, II, 483-496. For excellent secondary sources, see Freeman, *Lee*, IV, 117-148; Stern, Philip Van Doren, *An End to Valor*, Boston, 1958, 257-270; Catton, Bruce, *Grant Takes Command*, Boston, 1968, 404ff.

he arranged for supplying Lee with 25,000 rations. Grant signed his letter to Lee, stating the terms, and Lee signed a letter of acceptance to Grant. Thus, simply and briefly, without emotion or display, the war was ended.

General Lee, no longer in command of the Army of Northern Virginia or the remaining scattered remnants of other Confederate armies, stepped into the front yard of the McLean House. Union officers saluted by raising the hat; Lee returned the salute in like manner. Then, looking into the distance toward the encamped Confederates, he "smote the palms of his hands together three times, his arms extended to their full length. . . ."[159]

General Grant rode away toward his headquarters. Staff Officer Horace Porter asked the General if he did not think he should notify Washington of what had taken place. Grant exclaimed that he had forgotten it momentarily, and asking for note-paper, he wrote out a telegram while sitting on a roadside stone.[160]

As one Confederate artilleryman noted, many pathetic incidents occurred. Some men were crying, overcome by grief over the crushing defeat and their dread uncertainties, whether they should return home or try to join the effort to reach Johnston.[161] Others ran down the hillsides, wildly cheering, to express their relief.[162] Breaking ranks, many tearfully bade Lee goodbye.[163]

Staff-Officer Walter Taylor writes that no description could do the scene justice, as Lee returned to his army. "Cheeks bronzed by exposure in many campaigns, and withal begrimed with powder and dust, now blanched with deep emotion and suffered the silent tear; tongues that had so often carried dismay to the hearts of the enemy in that indescribable cheer which accompanied the charge, or that had so often made the air to resound with the paean of victory, refused utterance now; brave hearts failed that had never quailed in the presence of an enemy; but the firm and silent pressure of the hand told most eloquently of souls filled with admiration, love, and tender sympathy, for their beloved chief."[164]

One officer was seen to break his sword over his knee, others to rip their insignia from their collars.[165] "Men, we have fought through the war together;

159. Merritt, Maj.-Gen. Wesley, "Note on the Surrender of Lee," *Century*, April, 1902, 944.

160. Badeau, Adam, Letter to the Editors of Century Magazine, Sept. 2, 1885, Western Reserve Hist. Soc., Cleveland; Grant notebook with letter of W.D. Thomas, June 5, 1902, Rosenbach Foundation, Philadelphia.

161. Reminiscences of George W. Shreve, Virginia State Library, Richmond.

162. Boykin, *The Falling Flag*, op.cit., 63.

163. Stinson, Thomas A., "War Reminiscences from 1862 to 1865," in *The War of the Sixties*, compiled by E.R. Hutchins, New York, 1912, 341.

164. Taylor, Walter, *Four Years . . .* , op.cit., 153.

165. A Private, *Reminiscences of Lee and Gordon at Appomattox Courthouse*, Southern Hist. Soc. Papers, Vol.VIII, No.1, January 1880, 38-39.

I have done my best for you; my heart is too full to say more," Lee told Gordon's men.[166]

Federal soldiers, for the most part, treated the Confederates considerately. "Success had made them good-natured," said one Southerner. "Those we came in contact with were soldiers—fighting men—and, as is always the case, such appreciate their position and are too proud to bear themselves in any other way. . . . The effect of such conduct upon our men was of the best kind; the unexpected consideration shown by the officers and men of the United States army toward us; the heartiness with which a Yankee soldier would come up to a Confederate officer and say, 'We have been fighting one another for four years; give me a Confederate five dollar bill to remember you by,' had nothing in it offensive. . . ."[167] General Alexander wrote later, "In common with all of Grant's army, the officers and soldiers of our escort and company treated the paroled Confederates with a marked kindness which indicated a universal desire to replace our former hostility with special friendships. . . ."[168] Another soldier testified that the Union troops were very friendly, "in fact almost oppressively so. . . ."[169]

A Union veteran from the West drew the final scene in memorable paragraphs:

"Out of the dark pine woods, down the rock-strewn road, like a regiment of whirlwinds they come; Meade, bareheaded, leading them, his grave scholarly face flushed with radiance, both arms in the air and shouting with all his voice: 'It's all over, boys! Lee's surrendered! It's all over now! . . .' The men listen for a moment to the words of their leaders, and then up to the heavens goes such a shout as none of them will ever hear again. . . . The air is black with hats and boots, coats, knapsacks, shirts and cartridge-boxes, blankets and shelter tents, canteens and haver-sacks. They fall on each others' necks and laugh and cry by turns. Huge, lumbering, bearded men embrace and kiss like schoolgirls, then dance and sing and shout, stand on their heads and play at leapfrog with each other. . . . The standard bearers bring their war-worn colors to the center of the mass and unfurl their tattered beauties amid the redoubled shouts of the maddened crowd. The bands and drum corps seek the same center, and not a stone's throw apart, each for itself, a dozen bands and a hundred drums make discordant concert. . . . All the time from the hills around the deep-mouthed cannon give their harmless thunders, and at each hollow boom the vast concourse rings out its joy anew that murderous shot and shell

166. Lee, Fitzhugh, *General Lee*, New York, 1894, 377.
167. Boykin, *The Falling Flag* . . , *op.cit.*, 65.
168. Alexander, *Military Memoirs*, *op.cit.*, 614.
169. Haskell, John, *The Haskell Memoirs*, ed. Gilbert Govan and James W. Livingood, New York, 1960, 100.

no longer follow close the accustomed sound. But soon from the edges of the surging mass, here and there, with bowed heads and downcast eyes men walk slowly to the neighboring woods. Some sit down among the spreading roots and, with their heads buried in their hands, drink in the full cup of joy till their whole being feels the subtle influence of the sweet intoxication. Others in due and ancient form, on bended knees, breathe forth their gratitude and praise, while others still lie stretched among the little pines, and cry and sob and moan because their natures cannot contain the crowding joy. . . . For a brief moment, now and then, the clamor rounds itself into the grand swelling strains of 'Old Hundredth,' 'The Star-Spangled Banner' or 'Marching Along.' And the waving banners keep time to the solemn movement. . . ."[170]

In Chattanooga an artilleryman, destined to become one of the most eloquent church leaders of Chicago, recorded in his diary how he heard the news from a telegraph bulletin. Two hundred guns fired in rapid succession. There were the huzzahs of troops. "How the thought of peace and tranquility throbs in each soldier's breast when he thinks of the home and associates he left so reluctantly to follow the path of duty, soon to be restored to him. No wonder his spirits should be exuberant, aye, even intoxicated with delight. . . ."[171]

On Monday, April 10, Grant and Lee met again. Lee's aide relates that Grant wanted Lee to go and meet President Lincoln. He quotes Grant as saying, "If you and Mr. Lincoln will agree upon terms, your influence in the South will make the Southern people accept what you accept, and Mr. Lincoln's influence in the North will make reasonable people of the North accept what he accepts, and all my influence will be added to Mr. Lincoln's." Lee was apparently pleased, but said that as a Confederate soldier he could not meet Lincoln. He did not know what President Davis was going to do, so could not make terms.[172]

At this meeting, Lee held a friendly conversation with Meade and others. He told Meade that the years were telling on him, to which Meade replied: "Not years, but General Lee himself has made me gray."[173]

Meanwhile, Lee's aide, Charles Marshall, was composing the General Orders, No. 9. This, Lee's farewell to his men, was brief, stating that they had been compelled to yield. "You will take with you the satisfaction that proceeds from the consciousness of duty faithfully performed; and I earnestly pray that

170. Lee, Major Henry, "The Last Campaign of the Army of the Potomac from a Mud-Crusher's Point of View," California Commander Mollus, War Paper No.10, San Francisco, 1893, 8-10.
171. Jones, Jenkin Lloyd, An Artilleryman's Diary, Wisconsin History Commission, Madison, Wis., 1914, 321.
172. Marshall, An Aide-de-Camp of Lee, op.cit., 274-275.
173. Gordon, Reminiscences . . . , op.cit., 443.

a merciful God will extend to you his blessing and protection. With an increasing admiration of your constancy and devotion to your country, and a grateful remembrance of your kind and generous considerations for myself, I bid you all an affectionate farewell."[174]

On the morning of April 12 came the stacking of arms and colors. Rarely has there been such a scene! "Great memories arose," wrote Joshua L. Chamberlain, a Maine veteran. "Great thoughts went forward. We formed along the principal street . . . to face the last line of battle, and receive the last remnant of the arms and colors of that great army which ours had been created to confront for all that death can do for life. We were remnants also: Massachusetts, Maine, Michigan, Maryland, Pennsylvania, New York; veterans, and replaced veterans, cut to pieces, cut down, consolidated, divisions into brigades, regiments into one. . . ."[175]

General Gordon gathered the pitiful remains of his command, "wholly unfit for duty." "As my command, in worn-out shoes and ragged uniforms, but with proud mien, moved to the designated point to stack their arms and surrender their cherished battle-flags, they challenged the admiration of the brave victors." Gordon relates that the Union troops marshalled in line to salute their late foes, and that "when the proud and sensitive sons of Dixie came to a full realization of the truth, that the Confederacy was overthrown and their leader had been compelled to surrender his once invincible army, they could no longer control their emotions, and tears ran like water down their shrunken faces. The flags which they still carried were objects of undisguised affection. . . . Yielding to overpowering sentiment, these high-mettled men began to tear the flags from the staffs and hide them in their bosoms, as they wet them with burning tears . . . some of the Confederates . . . so depressed, so fearful as to the policy to be adopted by the civil authorities at Washington, that the future seemed to them shrouded in gloom. They knew that burnt homes, . . . poverty and ashes, would greet them on their return from the war. . . ."[176]

General Chamberlain, who ordered the final salute to the Confederates, wrote later that the moment affected him deeply. "Before us in proud humiliation stood the embodiment of manhood; men whom neither toils and sufferings, nor the fact of death, nor disaster, nor hopelessness could bend from their resolve; standing before us now, thin, worn, and famished, but erect and with eyes looking level into ours, waking memories that bound us together as no

174. Marshall, *An Aide-de-Camp of Lee, op.cit.*, 275-278; *O.R.* I, xlvi, pt. 1, 1267.
175. Chamberlain, Joshua L., *The Passing of the Armies*, New York, 1918, 258.
176. *Ibid.*, 447-448.

other bond . . . was not such manhood to be welcomed back into a Union so tested and assured?"[177]

"What visions thronged as we looked into each other's eyes! Here pass the men of Antietam, the Bloody Lane, the Sunken Road, the Cornfield, the Burnside Bridge. . . . The men who left six thousand companions around the bases of Culp's and Cemetery Hills at Gettysburg; the survivors of the terrible Wilderness, the Bloody Angle at Spotsylvania, the slaughter-pen of Cold Harbor, the whirlpool of Bethesda Church! . . . Here are the men of McGowan, Hunton, and Scales, who broke the Fifth Corps lines on the White Oak Road, and were so desperately driven back on that forlorn night of March 31st by my thrice-decimated brigade. . . ."

Lincoln spent the whole of April 9 aboard the *River Queen*. As the vessel steamed up the Potomac, the President diverted himself by reading, chiefly from Shakespeare, and by conversation on literary subjects. Some of his companions long remembered the feeling with which he recited the immortal lines from *Macbeth:*

> Duncan is in his grave;
> After life's fitful fever he sleeps well;
> Treason has done his worst: nor steel, nor poison,
> Malice domestic, foreign levy, nothing,
> Can touch him further.

He seemed in excellent health, though tired, with an outlook both philosophic and cheerful.[178] Passing Mount Vernon as the *River Queen* neared Washington, the President, probably inspired by a companion's remark, mused, "Springfield! How happy, four years hence, will I be to return there in peace and tranquility!"[179] Upon arrival in Washington, he visited the injured Secretary Seward, and received the news from Appomattox. Crowds in front of the White House called for Lincoln, and he briefly responded.

On the rainy morning of April 10, 1865, great booming noises shook the city, breaking windows in Lafayette Square. Five hundred guns fired in all. Quickly the crowds, as on a few days before when Richmond fell, formed again. Actually, a few newsmen and others up late had already heard the news, and sent it over the wires to the nation. The enthusiasm was not quite as great over the news from Appomattox as that of Richmond. Perhaps the mud dampened things, but slowly the implications of what had happened grew on the people.

177. Chamberlain, *op.cit.*, 260-261.
178. Chambrun, Marquis de, "Personal Recollections of Mr. Lincoln," *Scribner's*, XIII, No.1, January 1913, 34-35.
179. *Ibid.*

The Federal departments had the day off. Treasury employees gathered in the hall of their building singing "Old Hundredth" before marching across to the White House to serenade the breakfasting President with the "Star Spangled Banner." Impromptu processions sprang up everywhere, the whole converging on the White House, where the President, serenaded repeatedly, responded with brief sentences. When one of the larger processions appeared, young Tad Lincoln was seen waving a captured flag from a White House window. At this point, the President spoke briefly and promised them remarks at more length the next day, then asking the band to play that "captured" tune —"Dixie."[180]

Across the land the rejoicing was the same everywhere. In Chicago the people manifested a characteristic exuberance. On the stroke of midnight, one hundred guns were fired by the Dearborn Light Artillery, their echoes arousing the sleepers who had not left their beds at the stroke of the bell. Throughout the night the popular jubilation reigned unchecked, bonfires burned brightly, and cheers and laughter rose higher. At early dawn the streets were still crowded, and grew fuller and more joyously animated as the day wore on, with people giving no thought to business or meals in their abandonment to relief and exultation. Thousands of guns were fired, and a huge surge of fireworks poured upward in broad daylight, the more splendid pyrotechnical displays being reserved for evening. The people realized that the "four years of failure" had at last closed triumphantly, and felt that the menacing coils and fangs of the secession serpent had been crushed into dust. Thus the Chicago *Tribune*, on April 11, 1865, so often uncertain in the past but now so completely exultant, proclaimed.

New York diarist George Templeton Strong was aroused by the ringing of his doorbell on the night of April 9. A friend gave him the glad tidings of Appomattox. Unable to hold his hand steady, with wet eyes, he wrote the epitaph of the Army of Northern Virginia. "There is no such army any more. God be praised!" A hard rain dampened the celebration, but the guns kept firing all day.[181]

For at least three days after April 9, Washington was said to be "a little delirious," as it really had been since the fall of Richmond. Everyone celebrated and "The kind of celebration depended on the kind of person. . . ."[182]

Richmond, on Sunday night, heard volley after volley of artillery, as Federal troops celebrated the surrender of Lee. Emma Mordecai pathetically re-

180. Lincoln, *Works*, VIII, 393-394; Brooks, *Washington in Lincoln's Time, op.cit.,* 222-224.
181. Strong, George Templeton, *Diary of the Civil War,* ed. Allan Nevins, New York, 1962, 578-579.
182. Crook, William H., "Lincoln's Last Day," compiled and written down by Margaret Spalding Gerry, *Harper's Monthly,* Vol. CXV, Sept. 1907, 525.

corded that, for her circle, "this was agony piled on agony—Rose sat on the floor before the fire, weeping bitterly. . . . When Richmond fell I had given up all hope, so this was scarcely a new blow to me."[183]

Then a lightning bolt struck, and once more it was demonstrated that the unexpected, irrational, and fortuitous event has a larger place in history than the planned, expected, and rational occurrence.

183. Mordecai, Emma, *Diary*, Southern Hist. Coll., Univ. of N.C. Library.

11

Assassination of Lincoln

AMERICANS MAY reflect that it was perhaps fortunate for the future psychology of the nation, and for its national memories during long decades to come, that the war, which had filled four years with sullen rumblings and confused clamor, should end with a clap of thunder in the sudden murder of the Chief Magistrate, an event which caught the horrified attention of the civilized world, writing "finis" to America's agonizing years of violence and bloodshed, and lifting the dead President to a position where he would be apotheosized by later generations, the influence of his deeds and words deepened by the tragedy. The murder was clearly a sequel of the war, product of its senseless hatreds, fears, and cruelties. A fitting climax of the years of anger and butchery, it would help impress upon the American mind the terrible nature of the conflict. Although in its immediate results it was a long-felt disaster, its larger consequences were not so unhappy, for it seemed to give fuller meaning to the long contest, and enabled people to view their fallen Chief in a more heroic light, as William Cullen Bryant realized when he wrote in his elegiac poem that the assassination had placed Lincoln "among the sons of light."

The day after the informal serenades of April 10, Lincoln was apparently working on the remarks he had promised for that evening. He also presided, on April 11, over a Cabinet meeting devoted to the cotton problem, also talking for a time with Ben Butler on the position of the freedmen. Finally, that evening, he delivered to a great crowd on the White House lawn one of the most important addresses of his presidential years, for it dealt with the tasks of Reconstruction which the government must now assume. Since he knew that many who heard him were hostile to the plans that he believed should be followed, he was more intent upon speaking with care for the record (he read his remarks from script) than upon delivering a persuasive or eloquent plea, or upon paying tribute to people or chieftains, or upon hailing the victory. That very day Chief Justice Chase, after dining with a body of Maryland Radicals headed by Henry Winter Davis, had written a letter admonishing the

President that it would later be counted equally a crime and a folly if the freedmen in the lately rebellious States were left to the control of restored rebels who were "not likely to be either wise or just."[1]

By the victory being honored that night, Lincoln declared, "The reinauguration of the national authority—reconstruction—which has had a large share of thought from the first, is pressed much more closely upon our attention." The President admitted that "it is fraught with great difficulty," especially because of the fact that "there is no authorized organ for us to treat with. . . . We simply must begin with, and mould from, disorganized and discordant elements. Nor is it a small additional embarrassment that we, the loyal people, differ among ourselves as to the mode, manner, and means of reconstruction."[2]

Lincoln remarked that he was aware he had been censured for his Louisiana plan, and he defended it though admitting that other plans for Reconstruction were possible. He dismissed the question whether the lately rebellious States were in or out of the Union as a pernicious abstraction, declaring that the States were certainly out of their proper relation to the Union. Then he turned to a very practical and immediate problem, that of Louisiana, where he had been under heavy fire for his support of the new State government under Michael Hahn, based upon only ten percent of the voters.[3] Here Lincoln made the significant statements that the new government would be better if the electorate were larger, adding that, "It is also unsatisfactory to some that the elective franchise is not given to the colored man. I would myself prefer that it were now conferred on the very intelligent, and on those who serve our cause as soldiers. . . ." But, he declared, "The question is 'Will it be wiser to take it as it is, and help to improve it; or to reject, and disperse it?' 'Can Louisiana be brought into proper practical relation with the Union *sooner* by *sustaining*, or by *discarding* her new State Government?' . . ." He emphasized the advances toward Reconstruction of the Union already made, which included "giving the benefit of public schools equally to black and white." Lincoln went on: "Now, if we reject, and spurn them, we do our utmost to disorganize and disperse them. We in effect say to the white men, 'You are worthless, or worse—we will neither help you, nor be helped by you.' To the blacks we say, 'This cup of liberty which these, your old masters, hold to your lips, we will dash from you, and leave you to the chances of gathering the spilled and scattered contents in some vague and undefined when, where, and how.' " If this course, discouraging and paralyzing both white and black, has

1. Lincoln, *Collected Works*, VIII, 399.
2. *Ibid.*, 399-405.
3. Hahn had resigned March 4, upon election to the U.S. Senate.

"any tendency to bring Louisiana into proper practical relations with the Union, I have, so far, been unable to perceive it."

By sustaining the new government the Union would encourage the hearts and strengthen the arms of the 12,000 Unionists. The Negro also would be aided. And then, "What has been said of Louisiana will apply generally to other States. And yet, so great peculiarities pertain to each State; and such important and sudden changes occur in the same State; and withal, so new and unprecedented is the whole case, that no exclusive, and inflexible plan can safely be prescribed as to details and collaterals. . . ." While plans must be flexible, "Important principles may, and must, be inflexible . . ."[4]

As the journalist Noah Brooks described it, "Outside was a vast sea of faces, illuminated by the lights that burned in the festal array of the White House, and stretching far out into the misty darkness. It was a silent, intent, and perhaps surprised multitude. Within stood the tall, gaunt figure of the President, deeply thoughtful, intent upon the elucidation of the generous policy which should be pursued toward the South. That this was not the sort of speech which the multitude had expected is tolerably certain. In the hour of his triumph as the patriotic chief magistrate of a great people, Lincoln appeared to think only of the great problem then pressing upon the Government —a problem which would demand the highest statesmanship, the greatest wisdom, and the firmest generosity. . . ."[5]

The speech was bound to arouse much speculation and controversy and still does. Contemporaries could not agree whether Lincoln was moving closer to the Radicals or breaking with them. Most later historians feel that the lines were being drawn more sharply.[6]

For instance, Chief Justice Chase, in his long, rambling letter of April 11, told the President of his desire for Negro participation in the new State governments. In discussing Louisiana, Chase wrote: "I knew that many of our best men in and out of Congress had become thoroughly convinced of the impolicy and injustice of allowing representation in Congress to States which had been in rebellion and were not yet prepared to concede equal political rights to all loyal citizens. They felt that if such representation should be allowed and such states reinstated in all their former rights as loyal members of the Union, the colored population would be practically abandoned to the disposition of the white population, with every probability against them; and this, they believed would be equally unjust and dangerous. . . ."[7]

4. Lincoln, *Collected Works*, 399-405.
5. Brooks, Noah, *Washington in Lincoln's Time*, New York, 1895, 225-227.
6. For summations see Randall-Current, *Last Full Measure*, New York, 1955, 361-362, and Williams, T. Harry, *Lincoln and the Radicals*, Madison, 1941, 370-373.
7. Lincoln, *Collected Works*, VIII, 399-401, footnote.

The Marquis de Chambrun, who was a friend of Charles Sumner and sympathetic with Radical Republican ideas, heard Lincoln's speech. "I do not hesitate to say," he wrote later, "that the plan for reorganization was quite insufficient. On that day, Mr. Lincoln seemed to limit his view to the horizon of a material restoration; he did not seem to see that an entire moral and social transformation of the South was the only safeguard for a peaceful future. I only see in that enunciation of ideas an effort made to fathom the depths of public opinion, with a view perhaps to awake contradiction. . . . I do not in that speech find Mr. Lincoln's personal ideas expressed fully. . . ."[8]

The day after his speech of April 11 on practical Reconstruction, Lincoln discussed the subject with various persons, and mentioned the coming struggles. On this April 12, he telegraphed General Weitzel in Richmond, as we have seen, revoking the convocation of the Virginia legislature. On the 13th, he went over to the telegraph office and conferred with Stanton and Welles before a horseback ride out to the Soldiers' Home. He is said to have appeared weary and sad.[9] Stanton, on April 13, halted the manpower draft, curtailed a number of purchases, reduced the number of officers, and removed numerous military restrictions.

April 14, destined to be Lincoln's last day on earth, found him busier. His son Robert, who had been with the army, reached Washington in time for breakfast with the President. He had talks with Schuyler Colfax of Indiana and former Senator John P. Hale of New Hampshire, with members of Congress, and others. It was this day that Lincoln is said to have told several Cabinet members about his recurrent dream of being aboard a ship moving with great rapidity toward dim, indefinite shores—a dream which had several times presaged a great turning-point. As it had just occurred again, he thought some event of importance might be impending.[10] In near mid-afternoon, Lincoln lunched with Mrs. Lincoln, and in the afternoon saw various men on routine business. When Charles A. Dana informed him that the unprincipled Jacob Thompson, a Confederate agent recently busy in Canada, was in the United States preparing to sail for Europe, Lincoln made it clear that he should be allowed to leave.[11]

Late in the afternoon, the President and Mrs. Lincoln went for a drive, stopping at the Navy Yard to look at three monitors that had been damaged

8. Chambrun, Marquis de, "Personal Recollections of Mr. Lincoln," *Scribner's*, Jan. 1893, XIII, No.1, 36.
9. *Lincoln, Day by Day, op.cit.*, III, 328.
10. Lamon, Ward H., *Recollections*, 118-119; Seward, Frederick W., *Reminiscences*, New York, 1916, 255.
11. Dana, C.A., *Recollections of the Civil War*, New York, 1898, 172.

off Fort Fisher. He spoke happily to his wife of the time when they could return to Illinois to lead a quiet life. On his return to the White House, Lincoln found the genial Dick Oglesby, Governor of Illinois, and other home friends there. To Oglesby and others he read with warm appreciation several chapters from Petroleum V. Nasby's *War Papers*, which had appeared the previous year.[12]

Several items in the record of the morning are important and merit special mention. One is that Lincoln, visiting the Cipher Room of the War Department, told Thomas T. Eckert, who had ably organized and administered the United States telegraph system during the war, that he expected to go to the theatre that night, and invited him to go along, the President feeling that he would be a valuable guard. But Eckert declined the invitation, pleading that Secretary Stanton needed him for some special work. Another point of interest is that Lincoln wrote General James Van Alen, "I thank you for the assurance you give me that I shall be supported by conservative men like yourself in the efforts I may make to restore the Union so as to make it, to use your language, a Union of hearts and hands, as well as of States. . . ."[13] Van Alen had written him, incidentally, urging Lincoln, for the sake of his friends and the nation, to guard his life, and not expose himself to assassination.[14] Also on April 14, the President talked in mid-afternoon with Vice-President Johnson for the first time recorded since the inauguration.

But most important of all was the protracted Cabinet meeting at mid-day. Grant attended this meeting, and so did Frederick Seward, sitting in for his badly injured father. According to the younger Seward, the President had "an expression of visible relief and content upon his face." There was talk of what would happen to the leaders of the Confederacy. All agreed it was best to have as few "judicial proceedings" as possible. Yet could they go completely unpunished? Dennison, the Postmaster General, is quoted as asking the President, "I suppose, Mr. President, you would not be sorry to have them escape out of the country?" Mr. Lincoln replied slowly, "I should not be sorry to have them out of the country, but I should be for following them up pretty close, to make sure of their going."

Stanton came in late, and then Grant came and told of the surrender. Frederick Seward records that, "Kindly feelings toward the vanquished, and hearty desire to restore peace and safety at the South, with as little harm as possible to the feelings or the property of the inhabitants pervaded the whole

---

12. *Lincoln Day by Day*, III, 329-330.
13. Lincoln, *Collected Works*, VIII, 413.
14. *Ibid.*

discussion." Such questions arose as the proper identification of State authorities. Would Southern legislatures be continued in office? Should new elections be ordered by the General Government? Seward quotes the President as saying, "We can't undertake to run State governments in all these Southern States. Their people must do that,—though I reckon that at first some of them may do it badly." Stanton outlined his plan of Reconstruction. The Treasury, through the customs houses, should collect revenues. The War Department should occupy or destroy forts in the South, the Navy Department should seize navy yards, ships and ordnance, and in courts and other mechanisms the Federal authority should be reimposed. Violence or insurrection should be put down, but citizens should remain unmolested.[15]

Welles wanted a proclamation setting forth the plan to be pursued, and announcing that trade should be opened, while Stanton is said to have thought trade should not go beyond military lines. The President, glad that Congress was not in session, asked the Cabinet members to consider the issues, as they must soon begin to act. The question of Virginia and its government was discussed.[16]

Stanton, who was later to say that he proposed his plan "with a view of putting in a practical form the means of overcoming what seemed to be a difficulty in the mind of Mr. Lincoln as to the mode of reconstruction," prepared a rough draft form or "mode by which the authority and laws of the United States should be reestablished and governments recognized in the rebel States under the Federal authority, without any necessity whatever for the intervention of rebel organization or rebel aid. . . ."[17]

Secretary Usher of the Interior Department told his wife that the last Cabinet meeting was entirely harmonious, "and the President never appeared to better advantage. He was inspired with the hope that the war and strife was nearly over, and the meeting was assembled to consider the ways and means to restore to the troubled states government and security. He was full of charity to all and only thought of dealing with those who had led the people into the rebellion. . . ."[18]

Secretary McCulloch of the Treasury Department later recorded: "I never saw Mr. Lincoln so cheerful and happy as he was on the day of his death. The burden which had been weighing upon him for four long years, and which he had borne with heroic fortitude, had been lifted; . . . the Union was safe. The

15. Seward, Frederick W., op.cit., 254-257.

16. Welles, Diary, New York, 1909, II, 281-282; Welles, Lincoln and Reconstruction, ms. in Welles Papers, LC.

17. Flower, Frank Abial, Edwin McMasters Stanton, 301-302. For good summations of this meeting, see Randall-Current, op.cit., 362-364; Nicolay and Hay, Lincoln, X, 281-285.

18. John P. Usher to his wife, April 16, 1865, Miscellaneous Papers, LC.

weary look which his face had so long worn . . . had disappeared. It was bright and cheerful . . ."[19]

After supper on April 14, the fourth anniversary of the formal surrender of Fort Sumter, Lincoln talked with Schuyler Colfax of Indiana about a special session of Congress. Then he exchanged a few words with former Representative Isaac N. Arnold of Chicago, while climbing into his carriage to go to the theatre. Accompanied by Mrs. Lincoln, Miss Clara Harris, daughter of Senator Harris of New York, and Major Henry R. Rathbone, he was going to see Laura Keene in a performance of "Our American Cousin." The rest is one of the most tragic and thoroughly studied chapters of our American history.

It had long been clear to Lincoln himself, as to his friends and associates, that assassination was a possibility. Threats had been made upon his life before he left Springfield for Washington, and had thickened as the conflict proceeded. He had penetrated the meshes of an alleged conspiracy in Baltimore. He constantly received threatening letters, and thrust many into a special envelope. He said several times that in a country as free as the United States any man could kill the President who was ready to give up his own life in exchange. "If they kill me," he once remarked, "the next man will be just as bad for them." His attitude was not so much one of fatalism as of indifference. It was difficult for him to comprehend the vengeful malice that would find expression in so terrible a crime. Perhaps he felt that when tens of thousands were bravely giving up their lives for the country on the battlefield, he ought to possess the fortitude to face the possibility of his own murder. He walked to and from the War Department with complete freedom. On summer nights he rode out to the Soldiers' Home, his summer residence, with little or no escort. Once a bullet was fired through his hat as he rode. He sometimes drove to and fro in an open carriage. A striking illustration of the risks to which Lincoln was exposed may be found in the manuscript reminiscences of Robert Brewster Stanton. He had attended a military review where Lincoln was present. When it ended, he wrote, "our buggy was standing close to where the President's open barouche was waiting for him to enter for the return trip to the city." The buggy wheeled into line right behind the barouche, which it followed all the way into Washington and up to the White House gates. "Strange to say, there was no military or other [guard], which was remarkable considering the long miles through the country we had to go, the latter part of the distance after dark. But of this I am sure for this reason. The President's carriage was simply one of a long line of vehicles, before and after, and was frequently stopped by a line in front. On the back seat of the open barouche beside Mr. Lincoln was seated John Hay, his secretary. . . . We were driving

19. McCulloch, Hugh, *Men and Measures of Half-a-Century*, New York, 1888, 222.

quite fast, and Col. Corcoran's old war horse was most eager to go. As each jam occurred the President's carriage was obliged to stop, John Hay would turn around and put his hand up to warn us from running into the Presidential party. Several times our fiery steed could not stop quick enough, and his nose would push over the lowered top of the barouche and strike the President's back. We drove in this way to the very gate of the White House. . . . Remembering the many threats against Mr. Lincoln's life, and the manner of his death, it seems to me remarkable that on such a notable occasion the President of the United States had no military escort as Commander-in-chief of the Army to and from the great review."[20] Even in Europe, reported John Bigelow, plots were formed against him.[21]

Countless authors then and ever since record the events of Good Friday, April 14, 1865, and the following Saturday morning. Every nook and cranny of the assassination and of matters involved even remotely has been investigated. Even yet a few bits and pieces may be found. Some students have found discrepancies and raised legitimate questions. Others have carried their zeal so far as to find a possible conspiracy among anti-Lincoln Republican Radicals, and Secretary of War Stanton in especial has sometimes been vaguely implicated. Part of this historical research has admirable aspects, and within limits may be encouraged, but it has become increasingly frequent for some writers to strain the use of evidence, perhaps even for the sake of sensationalism. In fact, most of the modern writing on Lincoln's assassination is far from objective. Recent assassinations have only added to the legends, folklore, and fabrications of the events of April, 1865.

However, the consensus of serious historians is that the basic facts of the assassination are clear. Abraham Lincoln was shot in Ford's Theater in Washington shortly after 10 P.M., April 14, 1865, by the actor John Wilkes Booth. William H. Seward was viciously assaulted. It is known that Booth had collaborators, but that perhaps the role of one or two accused associates has been exaggerated, and that at least Mrs. Surratt and Dr. Mudd were falsely punished. It is generally agreed today that there was no plot made by President Jefferson Davis or anyone else in high position in the Confederacy to assassinate Lincoln, and that Booth and his array of miscreants acted on their own initiative. Most students agree that it was John Wilkes Booth who was killed in the Garrett barn in Virginia. Nothing in the flood of words written on the assassination seems really to contradict these general conclusions.

Much attention has properly been given to the emotions shown by the

20. Reminiscences in Civil War Times Section, 1861-1866, Manuscript Division, New York Public Library.
21. Holland, James Gilbert, *Life of Abraham Lincoln*, Springfield Mass., 1866, 517.

public and their response to the horror of the event. The pathos, the heartrending tragedy of such accounts affect all readers. Yet, a good many of the more popular writers never or seldom consider the deeper meanings of this event for the people both then and in the years to come. What impact did this first really major assassination of a political figure in this country truly make upon the national mind and heart? Violent deaths had previously attended duels, and many shootings or knifings had marked local political contests. But the assassination of Lincoln was the first deliberately plotted murder of a figure so eminent.

Further, the assassination of Lincoln needs to be regarded more closely as part of the fabric of its time. It is not an isolated episode, or a set eruption of violence upon a detached stage as in a melodrama. The psychological tensions of that spring of 1865 should properly be measured and weighed—the force of the interrelated series of blows upon emotions North and South produced by Sherman's great march, Appomattox, the fall of the Confederacy, and the disbandment of armies. These formed the background of the irresponsible crime—all contributing together to test the country's moral fortitude and inner faith in itself.

Part of the importance of the sad assassination chapter in American history is the severe test that it suddenly imposed upon the American government and people—a fourfold test, all the more gruelling because it came on the very heels of victory, when men were feeling the first sense of true relief and relaxation in years.

The first great question was whether the government could be transferred in such abrupt and harsh circumstances from one leader, fully tested, internationally admired, and popularly beloved by many (though not by all), to a much newer national leader, inexperienced, and mistrusted alike by some Northerners who did not relish his demagogic speeches in East Tennessee, and many Southerners who regarded him as a turncoat. Could such a transfer be effected without disturbance or disorder? The second question was whether the murder of the President could be viewed as the essentially senseless, impulsive and unanticipated crime that it was, and be cast into the gulf of malign fortuitous events, without any deepening of the long-felt hatred of many Northerners for the South, or the smouldering bitterness among Southerners against the North.

The third question, the most momentous of all, was whether the murder of so mild, magnanimous, and statesmanlike a leader, with the words "malice toward none and charity for all" so recently upon his lips, would divert national thought upon the problem of Reconstruction into sinister channels, and perhaps poison the politics of the country for years to come.

A relatively minor test now at hand, but one of importance to the dignity of the nation and to its sense of self-esteem, sprang from the necessity of conducting a careful inquiry into the antecedents of the assassination, including the possibility that it involved a conspiracy of a political or a sectional character; and along with this, the necessity of punishing the participants in any conspiracy in a strictly legal manner, after a just, dispassionate, and decorous trial. American judicial procedures, both State and national, had not escaped sharp censure at home and abroad, and now that the most heinous of all crimes had been perpetrated at the conclusion of a passionate and sanguinary civil conflict, the possibility of some form of judicial perversion seemed all too evident. The law should be vindicated with lofty dignity and decorum, untainted by prejudice, unsullied by violent antagonisms. Could the country give the principal accused participants in so foul a crime a fair trial, and a set of verdicts clearly judicious and just?

Here the nation did not emerge in so happy an aspect. Immediately identified, the foremost culprit was too rapidly removed from the scene to stand trial. John Wilkes Booth had been shot to death in the barn, or more properly tobacco-house, on the Garrett farm. Some details of his death remain controversial or obscure, but the primary fact was that Booth could not answer the charges against him.[22]

[I]

The trial of the seven men and one woman accused of conspiring with or assisting Booth in the assassination was, unfortunately, by no means so creditable to the country as the decorum with which Johnson entered upon his duties, or the courteous good feeling manifested by a majority of the Southern people and their leaders. It opened on May 9, 1865, in an improvised courtroom in the Washington Arsenal Penitentiary, only twenty-two days after the arrest of Mrs. Surratt.[23] Most of the accused had then been under arrest less than three weeks, or but a little more. Almost penniless, generally friendless, and held practically incommunicado in solitary confinement, they were pitiably helpless in preparing their defense. During the trial the seven men wore handcuffs

22. Many summaries of the repulsive plotting against Lincoln, his murder, and the subsequent pursuit and arraignment of those held guilty have been written, among which may be named: Roscoe, Theodore, *The Web of Conspiracy*, Englewood Cliffs, N.J., 1959; Eisenschiml, Otto, *Why Was Lincoln Murdered?*, Boston, 1939; Stern, Philip Van Doren, *The Man Who Killed Lincoln*, Cleveland, 1939; Kunhardt, Dorothy Meserve, and Philip B. Kunhardt, Jr., *Twenty Days*, New York, 1965. These are, however, only a few of the numerous secondary sources.

23. Roscoe, *op.cit.*, 431. The accused were; John Wilkes Booth, George A. Atzerodt, Mrs. Mary E. Surratt, Edward Spangler, John Surratt, Lewis Payne, Dr. Samuel A. Mudd, David E. Herold, Michael O'Laughlin.

fixed to a stiff metal bar, and ankle shackles with ball and chain. Much of the time they were forced to wear hoods. Gen. John F. Hartranft was in charge of the prisoners.

The tribunal was not a civil court, but a military commission hastily assembled on the theory that the slaying of the Commander-in-Chief of the armed forces of the country was a military crime. Although Secretary of War Stanton unhesitatingly supported the propriety of a military trial, President Johnson, to his credit, felt serious doubts. Before giving his approval, he asked Attorney-General James Speed for an opinion. Speed decided that the conspirators not only could, but should, be tried before a military tribunal, an opinion that unhappily was not published until after the trial opened.[24] The tribunal included three major-generals, David Hunter, Lew Wallace, and August V. Kautz, with four brigadier-generals and several lesser officers. Not one of them had received a sound legal training, or possessed any experience of a judicial character. Those who knew David Hunter, the presiding officer, regarded him as a stern military martinet. A descendant on his mother's side from a signer of the Declaration of Independence, and a graduate of West Point in the Class of 1822, Hunter had first come into wide public notice when, on superseding John C. Frémont in Missouri in 1861, he had annulled Frémont's agreement with Sterling Price for the suppression of guerrilla activity. He was a disciplinarian with a rigid conception of patriotic duty.[25] He had served in Kansas in 1860 when that State was full of animosities, and had later shown a special zeal for the liberation of slaves and the organization of Negro regiments. Lincoln had negatived one of his orders in the spring of 1862 as transcending his due authority. He could certainly not be termed a man of judicial temperament.[26] Neither could Lew Wallace, later celebrated as author of the somewhat melodramatic novel *Ben Hur*, but as yet best known for his service at Shiloh. One of the brigadiers on the Commission, Gen. T. M. Harris, later wrote a small book, *The Assassination of Lincoln: A History of the Great Conspiracy*, marked by prejudiced references to some of the defendants.[27]

The chief prosecutor was Joseph Holt, whom Lincoln had appointed Judge Advocate-General of the Army in the autumn of 1862, with the duty of taking, revising, and getting recorded the proceedings of all courts martial and military commissions. He had been an attorney in Kentucky and Mississippi, and had served briefly as Postmaster-General and Secretary of War. Associated with him in the prosecution were two striking figures. One was Henry Law-

24. *Ibid.*, 432.
25. Cullum, G.W., *Biographical Register, 1809-1892*, New York, 1868, *passim*.
26. Roscoe, *op.cit.*, 463.
27. *Ibid.*, 434.

rence Burnett who had been prominent in the trials of various Middle-Western Copperheads, and who was not especially active in the preparation of evidence against the alleged conspirators.[28] The other was a veteran Ohio politician and stump-speaker, John A. Bingham, who had climbed into Congress in 1854, the year of the Kansas-Nebraska Act. He had gained a reputation as a master of partisan speech, clever retort, and loose rhetoric, stuffed with historical allusions. Later he was to play a loud and self-confident part in the impeachment of President Johnson. In the conspiracy trials, according to one careful student, his role was "to bully the defense witnesses," and to assert in his summary of the evidence that "the rebellion was simply a criminal conspiracy and a gigantic assassination," in which Jefferson Davis was "as clearly proven guilty as John Wilkes Booth, by whose hand Jefferson Davis inflicted the mortal wound upon President Lincoln."[29] Such extravagance of speech was all too typical of Bingham, but a great deal of loose talk and writing was inescapably part of the hysteria of the time. The report of the assassination in even the temperate New York *Tribune* termed the assassin "the murderous emissary of the slave power," and stated without substantiation that "Booth's papers in his trunk fully prove a plot," and that the trunk contained the uniform of a rebel colonel—though Booth had never entered the Southern forces.[30]

The conspirators were tried under a blanket indictment drawn in the loosest terms. Not one of the accused was informed of the right to employ counsel. Several, including Mrs. Surratt and Dr. Mudd, made approaches to lawyers which were rebuffed.[31] All this was too obviously in contravention of Anglo-Saxon principles and precedents to be long tolerated, and various public-spirited men took appropriate remedial action. After vexatious delays and impediments had been overcome, a panel of defenders was finally assembled. It included the Hon. Reverdy Johnson of Baltimore, who had shown his courage as a devoted Unionist in a State full of secessionists, and had held that secession was treason. Long a Whig, though later a Democrat, and a member of the United States Senate from 1845, he had supported the War with Mexico, but opposed any annexation of Mexican territory. From his service in the Dred Scott case down to his support of Andrew Johnson's Southern policy, he showed himself a man of principle. He had been Attorney-General under Taylor, and later became minister to Great Britain under Johnson. In short, he was a man of character, moral valor, and intellectual distinction. He was supported by Thomas Ewing, Jr., another man of sterling character and re-

28. Burnett, Alfred, "Assassination of President Lincoln," *History of the Ohio Society of New York*, 1906, passim.
29. Pitman, Benn, *Assassination of President Lincoln*, Cincinnati, 1865, 351, 380.
30. New York *Tribune*, April 19, 1865.
31. Roscoe, *op.cit.*, Chap.XXII, offers the best general account.

cord, who had been one of President Taylor's secretaries for a time, after which he had practised law in Leavenworth, Kansas, with his foster-brother William Tecumseh Sherman and Daniel McCook. Early in the war, Ewing was named the first chief justice of the Kansas Supreme Court. Taking a command with the Kansas cavalry, he was appointed a brigadier-general of United States volunteers early in 1863. In the autumn of 1864, he commanded in St. Louis at the time of Sterling Price's invasion. His record and connections ensured that he would be treated with a respect greater than Hunter and others accorded Reverdy Johnson.[32] But counsel for the defense labored under serious difficulties. They had to prepare their cases and write their briefs while the trial was proceeding, and were given no opportunity before it began to confer with the accused, conduct investigations, or consult law libraries. While thus busy, moreover, they had to seek out friendly witnesses, whom it was very hard to find. The atmosphere and temper of the trial have been sharply criticized by a number of respected persons. Representative J. A. Rogers of New Jersey, a member of the House Judiciary Committee, later commented: "Since the trial of Cranbourne in 1690, no prisoner has ever been tried in irons before a legitimate court anywhere that English is spoken."[33] New fetters appeared. Henry R. Douglas, who had been a member of Stonewall Jackson's staff in Virginia, and who watched the proceedings closely from the room where he was held prisoner, opening into the courtroom, tells us that in its defiance of every principle of law and justice, the tribunal went beyond any rival since the days of the infamous Jeffreys.[34]

In vigorous yet restrained language, Douglas declared:

If justice ever sat with unbandaged, bloodshot eyes, she did on this occasion. The temper, the expressions, the manners, the atmosphere pervading the Court made it an unprecedented spectacle. The Commission illustrated the very spirit and body of the times; and passion decided everything. Of judicial decorum, fairness, calmness, there was absolutely none. Even the Judge Advocates, of whom it can be said, their quality of mercy was not strained, were sometimes compelled to interfere for the appearance of judicial decency. Counsel for the prisoners must have had a hard time to submit in patience to their daily trials. I suppose there is no case on record where a distinguished attorney was compelled to submit to such indignities as General Hunter and several of his Court put upon the venerable Reverdy Johnson. Although the Court was organized to convict, the trial need not have been such a shameless farce. As Judge Elbert H. Gary, before whom the Chicago anarchists were tried in 1886, said, 'The end, however desirable its attainment, excuses no irregular means

32. Ibid., 342.
33. House of Representatives Report, No. 104.
34. Douglas, Henry R., I Rode with Stonewall, Chapel Hill, 1940, 342.

in the administration of justice.' Lewis Payne, and all the men in the conspiracy with Booth, merited death, and would have been convicted in any
court in the land. The Majesty of the Law could have avenged a President's
death—as it did in the case of Charles J. Guiteau, the assassin of President
Garfield; and the record of the trial would have been open for inspection of
the world. The grief of the nation at the death of the gentle and merciful
Lincoln would have had no touch of shame; it was due to his memory that in
avenging his death passion should not depose reason. The administration of
justice should not be degraded, and no unnecessary blood should be spilled at
his grave. The range and character of the investigation indicated why a military commission and not a civil court was selected to try the murders.

So wrote Douglas. But, as he adds, another object, hardly secondary, was in
view. This disreputable and deplorable object was to connect the Confederate
government in some fashion with the conspiracy.

The charge and specifications levelled against the prisoners asserted that
the principal figures, Herold, Atzerodt, Lewis Payne, Mrs. Mary E. Surratt,
Dr. Samuel Mudd, and others "had conferred with, confederated with, and
conspired together with John Wilkes Booth, Jefferson Davis, . . . Jacob Thompson, Clement C. Clay, and others" to kill President Lincoln, a statement made
without qualification, just as the subsequent proceedings showed that it was
presented without any shred of real evidence. Thompson, one of the leading
planners of the outrageous attempt to set fire to New York hotels, was capable
of infamous acts; C. C. Clay was by no means a man of elevated character. But
neither of them had conspired with Booth, and Jefferson Davis would have
shrunk with horror from assassination, or indeed any lesser crime of violence.
Yet, besides making this foul charge, the Military Commission took pains to
fill its proceedings with allegations upon the funds used by Booth and others
intended to suggest that the Confederate Government had financed the conspiracy; and it also brought into its proceedings inflammatory testimony upon
the maltreatment of Union prisoners in Confederate prisons.[35] As the trial
went on, its cruel and unjust character became more evident. Representative
Rogers of New Jersey did not exaggerate when he wrote later, in a report
published by the House, that the persons alleged to have been incited to
murder by Jefferson Davis were "held in constrainment and in pain, with their
heads buried in a sort of sack, devised to prevent their seeing." He adds that
"in this plight they were brought out from dark cells to be charged with having
listened to incitements by Davis," and they pleaded not guilty.[36] When witnesses for the defense appeared, they were compelled to undergo cross-exami-
nation while facing the glowering hostility of the grim officers of the

35. Pitman, Benn, *op.cit.*, 18, and *passim*.
36. *House of Representatives Report* No. 104, 32.

Commission, and were not permitted even a questioning glance at the defense attorneys.[37]

For a time it appeared possible that the trial would be held *in camera*, under the strictest cloak of secrecy. The chief Army officers would have preferred this, but some of the generals saw the possible value of publicity in bringing themselves popular notice and praise.[38] Judge Advocate-General Holt favored a secret trial. But Secretary Stanton perceived that public opinion would regard any furtiveness or concealment with suspicion and resentment. On May 10, he said that he thought that the charges and specifications should go to the Associated Press, with a summary of the proceedings of the day, but asked Holt's assistant, General Burnett, to consult the Advocate-General upon the subject. Holt opposed any publication of the charges, and at first deemed that a very brief synopsis of the proceedings would suffice. But on fuller consideration, comprehending more clearly his responsibility, he gave way. The press obtained not only the charges, but a full synopsis of the proceedings, and next day the doors of the trial room were thrown open. Great crowds gathered at the penitentiary gates, and the demand for tickets was insatiable.[39] Yet, when the leading defense counsel, Senator Reverdy Johnson, attended the trial in order to make a plea for Mrs. Surratt as a citizen of Maryland, he was received with hostile objections and subjected to such insult that he drew himself up indignantly, shut his dispatch case, and withdrew.[40]

The trial of Mrs. Surratt excited especial interest because she stoutly protested her innocence, and bore herself with dignity in the most trying circumstances. A number of witnesses, some of them Catholic clergymen (for she was a Roman Catholic), and including also several colored people of transparent honesty, testified to her character, Christian piety, and readiness to befriend Union soldiers during the war. She had clearly been a Confederate sympathizer, but no substantial evidence was offered that she had participated in any murder plot. The most effective government witness testified only that he had boarded for a time at Mrs. Surratt's house; that on April 22 she had asked him to tell J. Wilkes Booth that she wished to see him "on private business;" and that several days before the assassination she sent him to the National Hotel to see Booth "for the purpose of obtaining his buggy."[41] This was quite inconclusive. Weichmann, who testified that he met Herold at Mrs. Surratt's, also declared: "During the whole time I have known her, her character, so far as I could judge, was exemplary and ladylike in every particular, and her conduct

37. Roscoe, *op.cit.*, 442.
38. *Ibid.*, 443.
39. *Ibid.*, 444.
40. Pitman, *op.cit.*, 316; Roscoe, *op.cit.*, 446-447.
41. Pitman, *op.cit.*, 113ff.

was in a religious and moral sense altogether exemplary."[42] One boarder, who testified that he had seen Wilkes Booth three or four times at Mrs. Surratt's house, said that Booth came to see her son, John Surratt.[43] Gen. Lafayette C. Baker, a notorious fabricator of evidence in trials, later alleged that Mrs. Surratt had made a confession of guilt to him after the trial, but his word is flimsy. Equally trivial, on the other side, is the sworn statement of Lewis Payne to Gen. Hartranft that Mrs. Surratt was innocent of the murder of the President, or any knowledge thereof. The one safe assertion is that guilt was not proved.[44]

On June 30, the Military Commission pronounced sentence. Mrs. Surratt, David E. Herold, and Lewis Payne were to be hanged. Samuel B. Arnold, Dr. Samuel Mudd, and Michael O'Laughlin were to be imprisoned for life at hard labor. Edward Spangler was to get six years' imprisonment at hard labor. In due course, these sentences were carried out. Mudd and Spangler were confined on the Dry Tortugas. John Surratt, after hiding for a time in Canada, went first to England and then to Rome, where he enlisted in the Pontifical Zouaves. Public sentiment generally approved of the verdicts. But the hanging of Mrs. Surratt by no means closed her case, for long after she was in her grave many judicious men believed that, although she had been a Confederate sympathizer, she had not participated in the plot against Lincoln.[45] The story of Dr. Mudd was also to have a dramatic sequel.

Indeed, so many facets of the trial and execution of the conspirators were open to question, that the dubiously legalized excesses of the case have been widely investigated and in most instances harshly criticized by historians and legal scholars. The record and many pronouncements upon it, some learned and many amateurish, have become a well-known body of evidence and attempted judgments. It is a deeply deplorable fact that part of this body of material later had to be scrutinized for possible use in the cases of assassination that have all too frequently horrified the American people during the period of more than a century since Lincoln was murdered.

[II]

The South was in utter confusion; rebel troops still held the field, and a perplexing disarray confronted the former tailor of East Tennessee. Johnson also had to play his part in helping to guide and express the sweeping public

42. *Ibid.*, 115.
43. *Ibid.*, 122-123.
44. Roscoe, *op.cit.*, 492.
45. *Ibid.*, Chs. XXIII-XXV.

response to the assassination; a wave of emotion, a manifestation of grief on a nationwide scale that made maximum demands upon his composure and his power of expressing sympathy with a stricken and bewildered people. In the days and weeks following the dreadful murder, the nation, rendered highly sensitive and emotional by the staggering events of the war, slowly and half-incredulously began to comprehend this final tragedy and to measure its manifold consequences.

The wave of sorrow that overspread the North, universal and heartfelt, was heightened by the sense of contrast with the jubilant victory cries which resounded only a few days before. People wept in the streets; crowded meetings and church services in every city, town and hamlet expressed poignant distress, and emblems of mourning appeared everywhere. The greatest writers of the republic spoke with an eloquence worthy of the sad occasion. Millions read Emerson's restrained but sensitive tribute, William Cullen Bryant's stately lines, "O slow to smile and swift to spare, gentle and merciful and just," and, in due course, Walt Whitman's greatest poem, "When Lilacs Last in the Dooryard Bloom'd," with a grateful feeling that, as so often before in the history of the English-speaking nations, the exalted bards and prophets of the land had fulfilled their mission. Manifestations of sorrow were prolonged as the funeral train moved from Washington to New York, and thence across the country, pausing again and again for processions with bands playing dirges, and mourners filing past the hearse. As in ancient Egypt, wrote Henry J. Raymond in the *Times*, in every house there seemed one dead.[46]

The Southern response to Lincoln's assassination was naturally less emotional than that of the North. It ran a wide gamut of emotion, from deep mourning and regret at one extremity, through callous indifference, to relief and rejoicing at the other extreme. Although many thoughtful people realized that the future lot of the defeated Southern people might be more troubled and unhappy now that a President, well known to be patient and conscientious, had been assassinated, others were willing to await events in a mood of perplexity and submission to the repeated blows of fate. One of the most creditable responses to the news of the murder came from the headquarters of Gen. Joseph E. Johnston, who was then intent upon negotiating the surrender of his army to Sherman.[47] As he wrote in his memoirs, he told Sherman that the deplorable event was in his opinion the greatest possible calamity to the South.[48] According to Sherman, he was even more explicit. "The perspiration came out in large drops on his forehead, and he did not attempt to conceal his

46. New York *Times*, Apr. 7, 1865.
47. For summary, see *Abraham Lincoln Quarterly*, Vol. VII, Sept., 1952, III-127.
48. Johnston, Joseph E., *Narrative of Military Operations*, New York, 1874, 402.

distress. He denounced the act as a disgrace to the age, and hoped that I did not charge it to the Confederate Government."[49]

Jefferson Davis, then in flight, had an opportunity to place himself in a happy aspect with Americans of the time and with posterity by some similar declaration. But his actual utterance was somewhat cold. Speaking to Mallory, the Confederate Secretary of the Navy, he is quoted as remarking, "Certainly I have no special regard for Mr. Lincoln, but there are a great many men of whose end I would rather hear than his; I fear it will be disastrous to our people, and I regret it deeply."[50] In his later book, Davis spoke of the event as sad and portending evil. "For an enemy so relentless in the war for our subjugation, we could not be expected to mourn; yet, in view of its political consequences, it could not be regarded otherwise than as a great misfortune to the South. He had power over the Northern people, and was without personal malignity toward the people of the South; his successor was without power in the North, and the embodiment of malignity toward the Southern people, perhaps the more so because he had betrayed and deserted them in the hour of their need. . . ." Nothing of leniency was to be expected from the "renegade" who succeeded Lincoln.[51]

The Confederate Vice-President, Alexander H. Stephens, was more deeply touched. Confined at Fort Warren in Boston Harbor, he later wrote in his journal that the fate of the South would have been much different had Lincoln been spared.[52] When June 1, 1865, was fixed as a fast-day and day of mourning for Lincoln, Stephens requested the corporal attending him to bring nothing but a cup of hot coffee and a roll.[53] He also related in his diary that he had passed a restless night, with dreams and visions. "My whole consciousness, since I heard of President Lincoln's assassination, seems nothing but a horrid dream." Even more touching was the statement made by the vitriolic Louis T. Wigfall, a former Senator of both the United States and the Confederacy, who told some officers, on hearing the news, that he was damned sorry. "It is the greatest misfortune that could have befallen the South at this time. I knew Abe Lincoln, and with all his faults, he had a kind heart."[54]

One Confederate diarist, the Louisiana girl Sarah Morgan Dawson, condemned Booth's act in her diary as a foul murder, adding "and I hardly dare pray God to bless us, with the crepe hanging over the way."[55] Mrs. C. C. Clay of Alabama records that "a kind of horror" overcame her husband. This former

49. Sherman, *Memoirs, op. cit.*, II, 348.
50. Mallory, S.R., *Diary*, Southern Hist. Coll., Univ. of N.C. Library.
51. Davis, Jefferson, *Rise and Fall, op.cit.*, II, 683-684.
52. Avary, Myrta L., *Recollections of Alexander H. Stephens*, New York, 1910, 401.
53. *Ibid.*, 142-143.
54. Abbott, Martin, *op.cit.*, 113.
55. Dawson, Sarah Morgan, *A Confederate Girl's Diary*, ed. James I. Robertson, Jr., Bloomington, 1960, 437.

Senator was soon to be confined at Fortress Monroe. When he heard the news of the assassination confirmed, he exclaimed, "God help us! It is the worst blow that has yet been struck at the South."[56] Eliza Frances Andrew notes in her wartime *Diary of a Georgia Girl* that wise Southerners were gravely silent. She deemed the murder a terrible blow to the South, placing the "vulgar renegade" Johnson in authority, and enabling Yankees to charge the Confederacy with a crime actually committed by an irresponsible man.[57] It is doubtless true that the great majority of the Southerners who expressed their opinions publicly denounced the assassination, though of course sometimes with mixed motives.[58] Mass meetings to express regret were held not only in New Orleans, Nashville, and Savannah, where the Union banner waved, but in other cities, and one of the most generous of all estimates of Lincoln, appearing in the Galveston *Daily News* of April 27, was widely reprinted in Texas.[59]

On the whole, the reception of the news of the murder, North and South, was creditable to American minds and hearts. Few gave way to an ignoble burst of resentment. General Sherman watched closely the effect upon the army in the field near the capital of North Carolina, for he feared that some foolish man or woman in Raleigh might drop some utterance that would madden the troops, and that the city would suffer a fate worse than that of Columbia. But the Southerners behaved well, and his veterans refused to indulge in a single display of anger. In a special field order, Sherman seized the opportunity to denounce "any exhibition of wild passions in murder, violence, and guerrilla warfare."[60]

From Fort Warren in Boston Harbor, imprisoned Confederate officers, including Ewell, wrote Grant, April 16, that "of all the misfortunes which could befall the Southern people or any Southern man, by far the greatest . . . would be prevalence of the idea that they could entertain any other than feelings of unqualified abhorrence and indignation for the assassination of the President of the United States. No language can adequately express the shock produced upon myself. . . ." Ewell and all the other generals confined with him united in condemning 'the occurrence of this appalling crime" and deploring any tendency in the public mind "to connect the South and southern men with it."[61] Ben Crampton, a prisoner at Fort Delaware, wrote that he had not met any officers in the barracks who approved the act of the assassin. "For my

56. Clay-Clopton, Mrs. Virginia, *A Belle of the Fifties: Memoirs of Mrs. Clay of Alabama*, ed. by Ada Sterling, New York, 1905, 245.
57. Andrews, Eliza Frances, *The War-time Journal of a Georgia Girl, 1864-1865*, New York, 1908, 172-173.
58. Abbott, Martin, |op.cit., 117.
59. *Ibid.*, 126-127.
60. Sherman, *Memoirs*, II, 350-351.
61. "Confederate Officers," in Civil War Centennial Display, National Archives, (Ewell and others to Grant, Apr. 16, 1865).

part," he declared, "I think it is a most unfortunate affair, particularly at this time." "If the worst comes," he asserted, he would much prefer Lincoln to Andrew Johnson.[62]

[III]

The transfer of national authority to a new Administration headed by Andrew Johnson was effected quietly, decorously, and with an elevated dignity creditable to the republic.

As soon as Lincoln died on April 15, 1865, four of the seven Cabinet members, in a formal message, called on Andrew Johnson to assume the office of President.[63] "The emergency of the Government," they wrote, "demands that you should immediately qualify according to the requirements of the Constitution, and enter upon the duties of the President of the United States . . ."

At shortly after 10 A.M. in the Kirkwood Hotel in Washington, Chief Justice Chase, standing in the presence of the Cabinet (with of course the exception of the injured Seward) and several members of Congress, administered the oath of office. Chase had just written friends that he feared Lincoln was so anxious for the restoration of the Union "that he will not care sufficiently about the basis of representation."[64] He had been delighted, when he wrote to Lincoln on April 12, that the President in his Reconstruction speech of the 11th had expressed a wish that the very intelligent Negroes, and those who had been in the armed services, should be allowed to vote, although the Chief Justice was sorry that he was not yet ready for universal or at least equal suffrage. At first eager to talk with Johnson about universal suffrage in Reconstruction, on second thought he had been reluctant to call on him lest his talk do more harm than good.[65] On his way to the Kirkwood House he picked up Secretary Hugh McCulloch of the Treasury and Attorney-General Speed. In his diary Chase briefly describes the ensuing scene. "The Vice-President solemnly repeated the oath after me. He was now the successor to Mr. Lincoln. I said to him, 'May God guide, support, and bless you in your arduous duties.' The others came forward and tendered their congratulations."[66]

As Secretary McCulloch recorded, the ceremony was simple; "the circumstances were painful and alarming" after the night of horrors. Fear of additional violence gripped the gathering, and rumors were omnipresent, but there

---

62. Capt. Ben Crampton to his sister, April, 1865, Ben Crampton Papers, Maryland Hist. Soc.
63. *American Annual Cyclopaedia*, 1865, 800; Stryker, Lloyd Paul, *Andrew Johnson, A Study in Courage*, New York, 1930, 195.
64. Chase, Salmon, *Inside Lincoln's Cabinet*, ed. David Donald, New York, 1954, 262.
65. *Ibid.*, 266.
66. *Ibid.*

was to be no interregnum. The Government was without an official head for only about twelve hours. "The conduct of Mr. Johnson favorably impressed those who were present when the oath was administered to him," McCulloch wrote. "He was grief-stricken like the rest, and he seemed to be oppressed by the suddenness of the call upon him to become President of the great nation which had been deprived by an assassin of its tried and honored chief; but he was nevertheless calm and self-possessed . . . He appeared to be relieved when he was assured that, while we felt it to be our duty to place our resignations in his hands, he should have the benefit of such services as we could render until he saw fit to dispense with them. Our conference with him was short, but when we left him, the unfavorable impression which had been made upon us by the reports of his unfortunate speech when he took the Vice-President's chair had undergone a considerable change. We all felt as we left him, not entirely relieved of apprehensions, but at least hopeful that he would prove to be a popular and judicious President. . . ."[67]

Secretary Usher, head of the Interior Department, wrote his wife that Johnson was not exalted but subdued and he had every reason to hope that his Administration would be successful. "In the murder of Lincoln the rebels have killed their best friend, they may expect in the President a rigid inforcement of the law and the leaders but little mercy. . . ."[68]

Johnson's statement upon taking office, his sole approach to an inaugural address, was, quite properly, devoted in the main to a careful acknowledgment of duty. After admitting that he was almost overwhelmed by the assassination, he went on, "I feel incompetent to perform duties so important and responsible as those which have been so unexpectedly thrown upon me." As for his policies, he declared that they must be left for development as the Administration progressed. The message or declaration must be made by the acts as they transpire. The only assurance that he could now give for the future is "by reference to the past." He spoke of his long efforts to ameliorate and alleviate the condition of the masses. "Toil, and an honest advocacy of the great principles of free government, have been my lot. The duties have been mine—the consequences are God's. . . . I feel that in the end the Government will triumph, and that these great principles will be permanently established . . ."[69] Some men wondered about his failure to mention the last President, and his pious generalization, "the duties have been mine, the consequences are God's" —a statement too conventional, oratorical, and ill-developed to have any real meaning.

67. McCulloch, Hugh, *Men and Measures of Half-a-Century*, *op.cit.*, 375-376.
68. John P. Usher to his wife, Apr. 16, 1865, Personal Papers, Miscellaneous, "U" Box, LC.
69. *American Annual Cyclopaedia*, 800.

Johnson, a man now fifty-seven, sprung from the plebeian background that he so often stressed—his father a poor immigrant, a casual laborer, from England—had risen slowly but far. First, a "bound-out" worker, then a humble and illiterate tailor, then a local politician who, by dint of strong convictions, unresting activity and a rough but sincere eloquence, reached a seat in Congress, he could well call himself a champion of the common people of East Tennessee; a hard-working, self-respecting population passionately devoted to freedom and instinctively hostile to all class pretensions of superiority based upon money or birth. His character, opinions, and early rise can be best understood by some thoughtful use of Charles Kingsley's classic novels, *Yeast*, and *Alton Locke.*

With the aid of his devoted wife, Eliza McCardle, herself at first illiterate, but a woman of great ability and fine spirit, Johnson had learned to read, and had provided himself with books. He had then steeped himself not only in some masters of British eloquence, but in the writings of the fathers of the republic. By the time Lincoln made him military governor of Tennessee, he knew the works of our best early statesmen almost as well as did the Lincoln of the Cooper Union address. As befitted a tailor, he dressed with neat distinction; and as befitted a rising popular leader, he carried himself with dignity, his firm chin, piercing eyes, and evident pride in his climb from lowly beginnings adding to his air of distinction. He was a man of action as well as of stiff and unyielding adherence to his beliefs, and in his difficult position as governor of the much-divided, tempestuous State of Tennessee, he upheld the principles of emancipation and the Union, as enunciated by Lincoln, with a firmness and vigor that were worthy of comparison with the course of such greater States executives as John A. Andrew of Massachusetts, Curtin of Pennsylvania, and Oliver P. Morton, Governor of Indiana.

In taking office as President, he neither said nor did anything that would arouse sectional feeling or partisan emotions. The immediate questions in the public mind concerned the opinions of the new President, and the plans he would follow in the reorganization and reconstruction of the Union. Delegations from various States, and eager individuals hastened to propound these questions to Johnson, and present their officious views. But he was too shrewd to be stampeded.

Inevitably, much distrust of the new President and apprehension concerning his probable course of action appeared. It was obvious that as Vice-President he had not been intimate with the President, nor privy to the operations of the Administration, except on a limited scale. Vice-Presidents of that era had far less influence and importance than they were to achieve a century later;

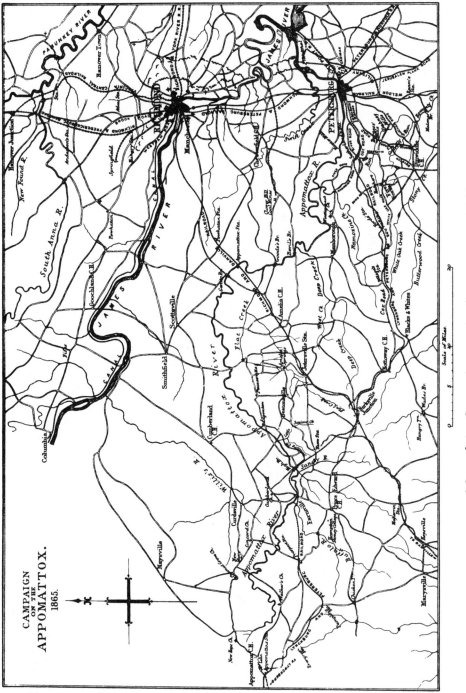

Map of the Campaign on the Appomattox, 1865

even then many men still felt that the office was a thankless position. But, though such samplings of opinion as are available perhaps offer an inaccurate indication of the public judgment, it is clear that many people felt a hesitant mood, not so much of opposition or hostility, as of perplexity and uncertainty.

Even among the Radicals, many of whom felt erroneously cocksure that Johnson was on their side, some men were waiting before deciding on the new President. Carl Schurz, for instance, wrote a friend in German, "Lincoln indeed was not the enlightened mind who could instantly grasp the whole tendency of a period, but through close observation and slow decision he always at last came to the right view. Besides, he was definite and inflexible. Johnson, I fear is a narrower mind. He is not devoid of talent but we shall have to see whether he possesses clearness and decision . . ."[70] The prominent Democrat S.L.M. Barlow could observe in late April, "I hope Mr. Johnson's policy will be such as to give us a speedy peace with all its attendant blessings and a Government of law, and his friends here all believe that he will secure these things." After all, Johnson was a Democrat![71]

General Halleck, whose letters often display more discernment than do some of his acts or his historical image, wrote his confidant, the intellectual Francis Lieber, April 16, "Matters here are settling down more calmly today. The new President has quietly entered upon his duties, and the great governmental machinery, notwithstanding the fearful shock, is working firmly and regularly in its accustomed channels. No cabinet changes will be made for the present, and all will work harmoniously. This sad event may have the effect to open the eyes of all to the danger of the times and the absolute need of a strong and firm policy, but not a cruel one towards our unscrupulous enemies. But our greatest danger is that popular demagogues may take advantage of the present excitement to do things which we shall all wish undone . . ." Two days later Halleck wrote again, "I have known President Johnson for some three years and have had considerable intercourse with him. I like him very much, and think he will make a firm and judicious chief magistrate. He was the only civil-military governor of a rebel state who gave us no trouble and who had the good sense to always act right. This speaks volumes for him. . . . Probably his policy will not be as lenient towards rebels as that of Mr. Lincoln, but, perhaps after all, it may be the better."[72]

The Peace Democrat, James A. Bayard, wrote Barlow that while he would

70. Schurz to Frederick Altheus, June 25, 1865, Carl Schurz Papers, State Historical Society of Wisconsin, (translated from German.)
71. Barlow to T.J. Barnett, Apr. 28, 1865, S.L.M. Barlow Papers, HEH.
72. Halleck, to Lieber, April 16 and 18, 1865, Lieber Collection, HEH.

not prejudge Johnson, "I have more fears than hopes as to his course. . . ." On the other hand, Montgomery Blair, an opponent of the Radicals, informed Barlow: "In my view of the matter, the Democracy, if they are true to their own principles, must sustain Andrew Johnson. . . . There is no issue now in our politics but reconstruction."[73]

Ben Wade, as Chairman of the Committee on the Conduct of the War, a body controlled by the Radical Republicans, had written the President on April 15 that they had just returned from Richmond, where they had seen and heard much which they wished to impart to him at once.[74]

Although a few eccentrics or bitter Copperheads braved the peril of assault to express hostility to the memory of Lincoln, some Radical Republicans, who remembered the Wade-Davis Manifesto and felt alarmed by the Hampton Roads Conference and the speech of April 11, betrayed their mean-hearted satisfaction that the way now lay open for such measures as Thad Stevens, Ben Wade and Sumner were known to demand. Representative George W. Julian of Indiana, then a prime Radical, spent most of the afternoon of the day of Lincoln's murder at a political caucus held to consider "the necessity for a new Cabinet, and a line of policy less conciliatory than that of Mr. Lincoln;" and while everybody was shocked at the murder, the feeling was universal, Julian wrote later, "that the accession of Johnson to the Presidency would prove a godsend to the country." He added that, "aside from his known tenderness to the rebels, Lincoln's last public avowal, only three days before his death, of adherence to the plan of reconstruction he had announced in December, 1863, was highly repugnant to the extremists in Congress." The Radical leaders believed that Johnson was now ready to follow a very different course of action.[75]

In response to Wade's request, the President on April 16 met the Committee on the Conduct of the War in the Treasury Department. Julian relates that an illuminating colloquy took place: "He received us with decided cordiality, and Mr. Wade said to him: 'Johnson, we have faith in you. By the gods, there will be no trouble now in running the government!' The President thanked him, and went on to define his well-remembered policy at that time. 'I hold,' he said, 'that robbery is a crime; rape is a crime; murder is a crime; treason is a crime, and the crime must be punished. Treason must be made infamous, and traitors must be impoverished.' "[76] It is possible that the Radicals, in their desire to control Johnson, had misunderstood their man, or that in the sad aftermath of

73. James A. Bayard to Barlow, Apr. 18, 1865, S.L.M. Barlow Papers, HEH.
74. M. Blair to Barlow, Apr. 18, 1865, S.L.M. Barlow Papers, HEH.
75. Julian, George W., *Political Recollections*, Chicago, 1884, 225.
76. *Ibid.*, 260-261.

Andrew Johnson

the assassination Johnson was reacting from his first deep emotions. But it is clear that the Radicals were placing the President under the heaviest pressure. The impetuous and strong-tempered Zach Chandler of Michigan wrote his wife on April 23, "As there is to be a struggle for the supremacy in the future, much depends upon the formation of the Cabinet of Mr. Johnson. The Blairs are trying their utmost to get control and to turn out Stanton, while we want to clean out the whole Blair tribe. . . . Johnson is *right*. He now thinks just as we do and desires to carry out radical measures and punish treason and traitors, but much depends upon his surroundings. Preston King eats and sleeps with Johnson and is all right except upon Seward. But he stands by Seward and is not right upon that point. Had Mr. Lincoln's policy been carried out, we should have had Jeff Davis, Toombs, etc., back in the Senate at the next session of Congress, but now their chances to stretch hemp are better than for the Senate of the U. S. So mote it be. I have had several conferences with Mr. Johnson and *all* were satisfactory, [he] having been associated with us on the Committee on the Conduct of the War. Our relations *were* perhaps as intimate as any others, but after the 4th of March trouble the Blairs rushed in and took possession, and what the result may be God knows. . . ." In another letter, also dated April 23, Chandler informed his wife, "The Blairs are making a desperate effort to control President Johnson; but thus far I think without success. This morning I called upon the President and found Mr. Blair there. He and I took up Sherman's surrender and the President listened for half-an-hour when B. left *and then* the President took hold of the matter and condemned it worse than I did. . . . We are running our Committee on the Conduct of the War every day. . . ."[77]

Montgomery Blair also told of this meeting with the President and Chandler. He accused Stanton of hoping "to get hold of Johnson as he did of Lincoln by making himself a leader in attacking and denouncing the supposed rival of Johnson's for the succession as he did with Lincoln in attacking McClellan. . . . It is plainly an attempt to take advantage of a blunder of Sherman to recommend themselves (Stanton and Halleck) to Johnson as the great antagonists of the Copperhead Candidate, as they already call him, for Succession. I met Chandler of Michigan, one of Stanton's satellites, at Johnson's room on Sunday morning, and he said to Johnson a lady had just told me I ought not to complain of Sherman's doings. It was a providential blunder as it destroyed the Copperhead candidate for the Presidency. . . ."[78]

One of the most penetrating comments on the consequences of the assassination was made by the journalist Noah Brooks in a newspaper letter from

77. Chandler to his wife, Apr. 23, 1865, Zachariah Chandler Papers, LC.
78. M. Blair to Barlow, Washington, April 28, 1865, S.L.M. Barlow Papers, HEH.

Washington, dated April 27, 1865, and headed "A Radical President."[79] "The radicals in Washington," he wrote, "appeared to think that they have drawn an elephant in the new President. When the late President was alive, they omitted no opportunity for criticism, and no chance which promised success to an attack was neglected. Now that the radicals have their President, however, they are not altogether satisfied. . . . Lincoln used to say that the responsibilities of office had the effect to make men conservative, and Johnson's friends begin to fear that such will be the result upon him. There are now several little cliques of the ultra men who are attempting to get control of Johnson just as some such men tried to get control of President Lincoln when he came into office. It remains to be seen into whose hands Johnson will fall, or whether he will, like Lincoln, offend and anger those who are thereby to be made his opponents by refusing to be controlled by any. Certain it is, however, that the men who are near the new President and who have any designs upon him are those whom we are wont to call radical; they will at least nominally have the control of the administration. It will afford us, who have stood by the former president against captious criticism and ill-natured attacks, some sort of satisfaction to see how they will manage matters with their former champion, who is radical if nothing else. Many think that if Seward should recover and stay in the Cabinet, he will virtually control Johnson. Seward is sagacious and sound, but Preston King would like his place and is at work to secure it. It should not be understood that any new feud is likely to arise from the sudden change in the presidency." Rather, he saw a continuation of the old feud which had almost resulted at one time in a drastic reconstruction of the Cabinet, intended to eject the moderate Seward and to place Chase and the extremists in control. He realized that these feuds might become much more intense.[80]

To a delegation from New Hampshire, the President talked of the trial and suffering of the war, but said he could not forecast his future policy. However, "The American people must be taught to know and understand that treason is a crime. . . . It must not be regarded as a mere difference of political opinion. It must not be excused as an unsuccessful rebellion, to be overlooked and forgiven. It is a crime before which all other crimes sink into insignificance; and in saying this it must not be considered that I am influenced by angry or revengeful feelings. Of course, a careful discrimination must be observed, for thousands have been involved in this rebellion who are only technically guilty of the crime of treason. They have been deluded and deceived and have been

79. The letter caption probably had a question-mark, "A Radical President?"—but the question-mark dropped out.
80. Brooks, Noah, mss., LC.

made the victims of the more intelligent, artful, and designing men, the instigators of this monstrous rebellion. The number of this latter class is comparatively small. The former may stand acquitted of the crime of treason—the latter never; the full penalty of their crimes should be visited upon them. To the others I would accord amnesty, leniency and mercy . . ."[81]

Saturday, April 22, a group of citizens of Indiana, led by Governor Morton, called upon Johnson in the Treasury building offices. Indiana Republicans held Johnson in considerable esteem because of his rôle in Tennessee, and the cordial amity between him and Morton. The Governor addressed the President, declaring in severely combative tones, "Each rebel is politically and criminally responsible for his action, without regard to the number who may have united with him. Nor is there any power to punish rebels collectively by reducing a State to a territorial condition, or declaring its municipal character forfeited. . . ." He called for support of the loyal elements in the rebel States and declared suffrage should be intrusted only to them.[82]

Johnson, in his reply, once more denounced treason and called for the punishment and impoverishment of traitors. However, going further, he expressed a cautionary fealty to the doctrine of State integrity and the rights of the States, saying emphatically: "Some are satisfied with the idea that the States are to be lost in territorial and other divisions—are to lose their character as States. But their life-breath has only been suspended, and it is a high constitutional obligation we have to secure each of these States in the possession and enjoyment of a republican form of Government. A State may be in the Government with a peculiar institution, and, by the operation of rebellion, lose that feature. But it was a State when it went into rebellion, and when it comes out without the institution it is still a State. I hold it as a solemn obligation in any one of these States where the rebel armies have been driven back or expelled —I care not how small the number of Union men, if enough to man the ship of State—I hold it, I say, a high duty to protect and secure to them a republican form of government. . . . If a State is to be nursed until it again gets strength, it must be nursed by its friends, and not smothered by its enemies. Now permit me to remark that, while I have opposed dissolution and disintegration on the one hand, on the other I have opposed consolidation—or the centralization of power in the hands of a few. . . ."[83] This was a refreshing statement indeed to those who wished to retain the old balance of government, and to follow in the moderate path of the resolute but magnanimous Lincoln.

A Negro delegation which called at this time told the President, "The

81. *American Annual Cyclopedia*, 1865, 800-801.
82. Foulke, William Dudley, *Life of Oliver P. Morton*, Indianapolis, 1877, I, 440-441.
83. *American Annual Cyclopedia*, 1865, 801-802.

colored American asks but two things. He asks, after proving his devotion to his country in responding to her call in the hour of her sorest trial, and after demonstrating, upon many hotly-contested battlefields, his manhood and valor, that he have, first, complete emancipation, and secondly, full equality before American law. Your past history, as connected with the rebellion, gives us full assurance that in your hands our cause shall receive no detriment, and that our liberty and rights will be fully protected and sustained."

Johnson made a friendly reply. He declared that the Negroes would find in his and their past history the guaranty of his future conduct toward them. "Where the colored people know me best, they have confidence in me. No man can charge me with having proved false to the promises I have made to any class of the people in my public life. . . ." He added the generous statement that, although it was hard for the Negro to understand that they had friends on the south side of the line, "they have, and they are as faithful and staunch as any north of the line . . ."[84] This was refreshing, too, and breathed the very spirit of Lincoln.

Johnson received other delegations, and to a South Carolina group later on he said, "The policy, now that the rebellion is suppressed, is not to restore the State through military rule, but by the people." Thus, within a few weeks of Lincoln's death, the new President had publicly demonstrated that he repudiated one of the most brutal and evil Radical ideas, that the former Confederate states were no longer part of the Union. The schism between Johnson and the Radicals is generally dated later by most students, but the incipient division, with portents of future conflict, was at least visible within days of his ascendancy.

On Sunday, April 16, the Cabinet had met and Stanton brought up his draft of a Reconstruction plan, much the same that he had presented to Lincoln only two days before, though with some changes. That evening at the War Department, Stanton read his document to Welles and a number of Congressmen. Secretary Welles wrote that Senator Sumner interrupted and "requested Mr. Stanton to stop, until he could understand whether any provision was made for enfranchising the colored man. Unless the black man was given the right to vote, Mr. Sumner said his freedom was a mockery." Stanton replied that differences existed among their friends on this subject, and it would be unwise in his judgment to press the proposal just then. Thereupon Sumner blustered that "he would not proceed a step unless the black man had his rights. . . ."[85] But apparently Stanton held to his objection.

The general welcome given Andrew Johnson on his accession, outside of

84. *Ibid.*, 801-802.
85. Welles, Gideon, "Lincoln on Reconstruction," typescript, John Hay Library, Brown Univ., Providence, R.I.

the politically prejudiced men, pleased many observers. "He grows steadily in public confidence and esteem," commented the New York *Tribune* on April 22. Old stories were recalled of the sad but brave persistence with which, after never enjoying the advantage of a school for a single day, he had obtained an education by his unwearied exertions and the assistance of his devoted wife. It became widely realized that he had never practised law because, after his election to the Legislature, he had insisted upon remaining in the public service. Men began to perceive that he possessed some rare qualifications for his vast responsibilities. In the Reconstruction struggles now at hand he could never be attacked as "Yankee," for he was a Southerner born and bred. Indeed, he had never lived in a free State until he helped make Tennessee free, though he had held a few slaves. The poor whites of the South would regard him as a natural ally. Since he had always voted against protective tariffs, again a prospective issue, it would be hard to make anybody believe that he favored special favors to industry or trade. He knew the rebellion, its leaders and their objects as few men did. Having never manifested any special regard for the colored people, he could not be taunted as a "nigger-lover." He had nevertheless shown that he was not antagonistic to the black folk.

Yet Johnson faced an angrier crisis, and more difficult problems than perhaps any other successor to the Presidency would have to meet until Vice-President Harry Truman suddenly succeeded Franklin D. Roosevelt.

Prompt action upon Reconstruction was plainly needed. The Southern people were anxiously awaiting some announcement of terms, and the Northerners were eagerly awaiting the opportunity to resume a more normal life. While the planting season at the South was rapidly expiring, enterprises there remained disorganized and apprehensive. Many former Confederates were not certain that they could safely return to their families. Numerous freedmen were still deserting plantations where they were needed, and fleeing to towns where they were idle. A typical news dispatch of April 13, 1865, from Raleigh, N. C., declared, "Great anxiety prevails everywhere among the people. The State is thoroughly impoverished, and distress and starvation must overtake them unless an immediate cessation of hostilities affords the opportunity to plant a crop during the present spring. Days, even hours, are now more precious than gold to those who must depend upon this year's crop for support for themselves and families."[86]

One of the first problems of the Johnson Administration was to bring about the surrender of other Confederate forces in the field, especially that of Joe Johnston in North Carolina, and also to effect the capture of the fleeing

86. New York *Tribune*, April 27, 1865.

Confederate government and its complete dissolution. By April 15, Sherman was advancing from Goldsboro, N. C., and his cavalry held Chapel Hill and Durham Station. Johnston was pulling back on roads from Hillsboro to Greensboro. Halleck, shortly to be in command of the armies around Richmond and in southern Virginia, blocked Johnston to the North. Stoneman's cavalry was to the West. On April 14 Johnston had written Sherman regarding "a temporary suspension of active operations . . . the object being to permit the civil authorities to enter into the needful arrangements to terminate the existing war. . . ."[87]

Sherman at once replied from Raleigh that he was empowered "to arrange with Johnston any terms for the suspension of hostilities . . . and would be willing to confer with him for that object. . . ." Already, it is evident that Sherman was going further than Grant had done at Appomattox and certainly his reply showed a marked departure from the policy indicated in Grant's letters to Lee, calling for surrender alone. Sherman did add, "I undertake to abide by the same terms and conditions as were made by General Grant . . ."[88] Altogether, his message was less firm and decisive than Grant's communication to Lee.

On the 15th, Stanton telegraphed Sherman of Lincoln's assassination. Sherman had assured Grant and Stanton the previous day that he would adhere to the terms that Grant had given Lee, and be careful not to "complicate any points of civil policy. . . ."[89] But it became clear within a few days that he would "complicate" the civil policy of the government a great deal.

In a conference at Greensboro, N. C., with Davis, Breckinridge, Mallory, and Reagan, Johnston persuaded Davis to outline a proposal for a meeting to discuss the terms of an armistice. Johnston signed his letter and sent it, as we have noted, to Sherman on April 14.[90] Then Sherman and Johnston met at the Bennett house near Durham Station on April 17 in what would prove a monotonous and controversial conference. At the outset, Sherman informed the Confederate general of the assassination, news which elicited from Johnston the statement that this was a national calamity, which we have already quoted. Later, Johnston wrote that Sherman added, "in a manner that carried conviction of sincerity," that he earnestly wished to protect the South from such devastation as the prolongation of the war would make inevitable; and, as a means of hastening its termination so far as the armies they commanded could be helpful, "he offered me such terms as those given to General

87. *O.R.*, I, xlvii, pt. 3, 206-207.
88. *Ibid.*, 207.
89. *Ibid.*, 221.
90. Johnston, Joseph E., *Narrative of Military Operations, op.cit.*, 399; Mallory, *Diary, op.cit.*, April 14.

Lee. . . ."[91] In this Sherman was undoubtedly taking the correct course, and following the example of Grant. He was later to declare, it seems quite correctly, that he had not received Lincoln's instructions of March 3 to Grant suggesting that no conference be held with the enemy except for "capitulation."[92] Nevertheless, Sherman began by demanding that Johnston accept the same terms as Lee. Johnston refused, pointing to the difference in relative positions as a reason why such a capitulation would not be justified. Johnston tells us in his autobiography that he intimated to Sherman that "instead of a partial suspension of hostilities, we might, as other generals had done, arrange the terms of a permanent peace. . . ."[93] Johnston and Sherman proceeded to discuss possible terms and, according to Johnston, agreed on most points, except that Sherman did not consent to an amnesty for President Davis and officers of his Cabinet.

Before daybreak on April 18, the Confederate Cabinet members, Breckinridge and Reagan, met with Johnston. After Reagan wrote down the terms discussed the previous day, Johnston and Breckinridge then met with Sherman, who listened to Reagan's record, and then made his own written list of the terms, which differed from Johnston's only in being fuller. When the generals signed, a copy was sent to both Presidents. Davis approved these terms within a few days.[94]

Thus it appears, and the conclusion is not really contradicted by Sherman's later comments, that the meeting at the Bennett house produced not only a talk on army surrender, but a discussion of the nature of the final peace, involving negotiations between the two warring peoples. This discussion went to such lengths that it was submitted to the Confederate President as well as to Washington! After all, Davis had not been consulted as to Lee's surrender at Appomattox, even though it had been a political and not merely a military event, so that the Durham Station arrangements would have amounted to a peace treaty between the Union and the Confederates, involving the future of the nation.

Sherman's accounts of this transaction actually do not differ substantially from the account here given, except that they assign to Sherman a larger rôle than appears in Johnston's own records. In his formal report, written with bitter overtones, Sherman called the talks frank and soldierlike. Sherman said that Johnston admitted the terms given Lee were "magnanimous and all that

91. Johnston, ut supra, 134.
92. Lincoln, Collected Works, VIII, 330-331. The message to Grant is in Lincoln's script, though signed by Stanton.
93. Johnston, Narrative, op.cit., 403.
94. Ibid., 404-407; Johnston to "My Dear Maury," March 21, 1879, Chicago Hist. Soc., J.E. Johnston Papers; Letter Mar. 30, 1868, Western Reserve Hist. Soc., Cleveland.

he could ask, but he did want some general concession that would enable him to allay the natural anxieties of his followers, and enable him to maintain control over them" until they could be returned to the area of their homes, thereby saving North Carolina the devastation that would be inevitable if he dispersed his troops then and there without providing for their urgent wants, and subjecting them to possible pursuit as they scattered over the broad State. He also wished to have some general provision made to alleviate the fate of all the Confederate armies that remained. Sherman tells us that, "I never made any concession as to his own army, or assumed to deal finally and authoritatively in regard to any other, but it did seem to me that there was present a chance for peace that might be deemed valuable to the Government of the United States. . . ."[95]

In their second talk on the 18th, Sherman says Johnston satisfied him as to the power of the Confederate general to disband other forces than his own. Sherman went on to explain that his consent to Johnston's points was based upon Lincoln's message of 1864, his proclamation of amnesty, Grant's terms to Lee, the invitation to the Virginia legislature, and "a firm belief that I had been fighting to re-establish the Constitution of the United States;" and finally, but not least, upon the universal desire to close a war which was now without means of organized resistance. These, he declared, were the leading facts that "induced me to pen the 'memorandum' of April 18."[96]

Sherman elaborated his testimony when he spoke to the Joint Committee on the Conduct of the War, stating: "I had had frequent correspondence with the late President of the United States, with the Secretary of War, with General Halleck, and with General Grant; and the general impression left upon my mind was that if a settlement could be made consistent with the Constitution of the United States, the laws of Congress, and the proclamation of the President, they would be not only willing but pleased thus to terminate the war by one single stroke of the pen. . . ."[97]

In the discussion of April 18, Sherman testifies that the points raised included: the question whether the States were to be dissevered; the question whether their people were to be denied representation in Congress, so that, as some Southern extremists put it, they might become slaves to the people of the North. Understandably, but unwisely, the impulsive Sherman states that he answered "No; we desire that you shall regain your position as citizens of the United States, free and equal to us in all respects, and with representations, upon the condition of submission to the lawful authority of the United States

95. *O.R.*, I, xlvii, pt. 1, 31-32.
96. *Ibid.*, 33.
97. *Report of the Joint Committee on the Conduct of the War*, Washington, 1865, Vol.III, 3-4.

as defined by the Constitution, the United States courts, and the authorities of the United States supported by those courts." It seems strange that by the time he gave his testimony, Sherman had not realized that these questions were beyond his province to decide on or even discuss.[98] To the Committee Sherman reported that he had rejected Reagan's memorandum "at once." But the record hardly supports this statement. He told the Committee that the talk went on in the conference at the Bennett place. "There was universal assent that slavery was dead as anything could be; that it was one of the issues of the war long since determined. . . . As to reconstruction, I told them [the Confederates] I did not know what the views of the administration were. Mr. Lincoln, up to that time, had in letters and by telegrams to me, encouraged me, by all the words that could be used in general terms, to believe in not only his willingness but his desire that I should make terms with civil authorities, governors, and legislators, even as far back as 1863. . . ."[99] In the light of all we now know, this later statement seems extreme. There is no firm evidence that Lincoln wished Sherman to make such terms, and the idea that he did stands in opposition to all known evidence.

In time, the supposition grew that Lincoln had told Sherman what to do concerning peace during their conference on the *River Queen* in late March. Neither Grant nor Lincoln, nor Admiral Porter, indicates that this was true, and Sherman himself never said so. In his Committee testimony, Sherman admitted that the talk about terms contained "Nothing definite; it was simply a matter of general conversation; nothing specific and definite." His official report does not mention the conference. In fact, in this report Sherman states, "Up to that hour I had never received one word of instruction, advice or counsel as to 'plan of policy' of Government looking to a restoration of peace in the rebel States of the South. . . ."[100] In a long letter to Lincoln's friend, Isaac N. Arnold, however, Sherman describes the *River Queen* meetings at length. Most of the discussion there concerned military plans. Sherman admits that he ought not to attempt reproducing the words of that conversation. "I know we talked generally," he wrote, "about what was to be done when Lee and Johnston's armies were beaten and dispersed." On this point Lincoln was very full, and said that he wanted the rebels disarmed and sent home. Lincoln also declared that he contemplated no revenge or harsh measures, but quite the contrary, and that the suffering and hardships of the Southern people in the war should make them now submissive to law. Sherman tells us that "I cannot say that Mr. Lincoln or anybody else used this language at the time, but I know

98. *Ibid.*, 4.
99. *Ibid.*, 5.
100. *O.R.*, I, xlvii, pt. 1, 33.

I left his presence with the conviction that he had in his mind, or that his Cabinet had, some plan of settlement, ready for application the moment Lee and Johnston were defeated. . . ."[101]

It is clear that Sherman and his defenders do not say that Lincoln had dictated the controversial terms. In fact, it is clear that the Confederates had a more specific role than did Lincoln. But Sherman, over and over again, says his terms were within the spirit of what he thought Lincoln wanted.[102] It would be tedious and needless to extend any treatment of this controversy. We may merely note that in his later *Memoirs* Sherman stated that Lincoln, speaking fully and frankly, assured him "that in his mind he was all ready for the civil reorganization of affairs at the South as soon as the war was over; and he distinctly authorized me to assure Governor Vance and people of North Carolina that, as soon as the rebel armies laid down their arms, and resumed their civil pursuits, they would at once be guaranteed all their rights as citizens of a common country; and that to avoid anarchy the State governments then in existence, with their civil functionaries, would be recognized by him as the government *de facto* till Congress could provide others. . . ."[103] This is as close to being specific as Sherman came about the talks with Lincoln.

What about these terms? The "Memorandum or basis of agreement" arranged was between Joseph E. Johnston, "commanding the Confederate Army," and Sherman. First, the existing status of armies in the field was to be maintained until further notice was given by either commanding general. Second, the existing Confederate armies were to disband and be conducted to their various State capitals where they would deposit arms and public property in the arsenal. Each officer and man would execute and file an agreement to terminate martial activities, and to abide by the action of both State and Federal authority. Available arms would be used to maintain order within the State. In the third place, the Federal executive would recognize the several State governments as soon as their officers and legislatures would take the oaths prescribed by the Constitution of the United States. Wherever conflicting State governments arose from the war, the question of legitimacy would be submitted to the Federal Supreme Court. In the fourth place, the Federal courts were to be re-established. As a fifth part of the agreement, the people and inhabitants of all the States were to be guaranteed, so far as the Executive could do so, their political rights and franchises, as well as their rights of person and property, as defined by the Constitution of the United States and

101. Sherman to Arnold, Nov. 28, 1872, Isaac N. Arnold Papers, Chicago Hist. Soc.

102. Naroll, R.S., "Lincoln and the Sherman Peace Fiasco Another Fable?", *Journal of Southern History*, Vol.XX, No.4, Nov., 1954, 459-483; Lewis, Lloyd, *Sherman, Fighting Prophet*, New York, 1932, 536ff.

103. Sherman, *Memoirs, op.cit.*, II, 327.

of the States respectively. The sixth article of agreement was that the authorities of the United States would not disturb any of the people "by reason of the late war so long as they live in peace and quiet, abstain from acts of armed hostility, and obey the laws in existence at the place of their residences." Not only was the war to cease, but it was to be followed by a general executive amnesty on condition that the Confederate armies disbanded, their arms were scattered, and peaceful pursuits were resumed by the officers and men of these forces. Not being fully empowered by their respective principals to fulfil these terms, the parties to the agreement pledged themselves, individually and officially, to obtain promptly the necessary authority and to execute the above programs. A comparison of this document, as drawn by Sherman, with the provisions listed by Reagan, Postmaster-General of the Confederacy, reveals no substantial or even minor difference. Sherman's document was somewhat longer and fuller in wording, that is all.[104]

So many points here given vary from the known policies of Lincoln, and show such political naiveté, that the whole document may easily be questioned. First of all, it is labeled both a "memorandum" and "basis of Agreement." Both principles admitted they were not fully empowered to make such an agreement, and would have to submit it to their governments. The document thus virtually recognized the Confederate government and its President, something Lincoln had never done and no responsible officer could be expected to do now. The military commanders concerned had gone too far. Lincoln had always opposed an "armistice," which is what the first provisions really implied. To send the Southern armies home with their arms appeared an open invitation to guerrilla tactics, to which Sherman and Lincoln were implacably opposed. The soldiers would await action of both State and Federal authorities and yet Sherman's plan carried a seeming recognition of the existing Confederate State governments, until their officials took the oath of allegiance. These Confederate State governments might also come into collision with Union governments already set up in several States. Parts of the agreement seemed to concede a recognition of the validity of the Confederate State governments. There could be little quarrel with the idea of re-establishing Federal courts, providing that citizens were in a state of peace. But the guarantee of political, personal and property rights could be interpreted as a re-imposition of the rights of slavery, and sometimes was, although the memorandum did not mention slavery. At this point, Sherman departed more than ever from Lincoln, who had never retreated from his determination that slavery must die. No grant of amnesty was specifically extended, but was given a broad applica-

---

104. *O.R.*, I, xlviii, pt. 3, 243-244; Ms. "Synopsis of the Agreement between Generals Johnston and Sherman," Western Reserve Hist. Soc., Cleveland.

tion. Although nothing was said about Confederate debts, the agreement might have been interpreted as allowing their possible recognition as valid.

In short, little was here stated that Lincoln or any Federal government could have accepted as it stood without abrogating the Administration's war aims. Although we can never know, from Lincoln's many statements and actions it seems clear that he would have done just as Johnson did in rejecting this almost puerile document.

Sherman manifested enthusiasm in sending this agreement to Washington, stating that, if approved by the President, it would produce peace from the Potomac to the Rio Grande. He boldly informed Grant or Halleck, "if you will get the President to simply indorse the copy and commission me to carry out the terms, I will follow them to the conclusion...."[105] Thus a field commander was asking the President to give him authority to carry out terms to which the President had never agreed.[106]

The subsequent results of this controversial episode belong primarily to the personal biography of Sherman, but are important to history at large because of their effect on the relations of Sherman with Stanton, Andrew Johnson, Halleck and others, and because the terms, when revealed to the whole nation, had a striking effect on public sentiment, both North and South.

As Sherman later wrote in his official report, he felt certain that Lincoln would have assented to the agreement had he lived. To many it seems more probable that Lincoln would have been emphatic in his rejection of it. On April 24, a messenger with dispatches arrived at Sherman's headquarters and with him, to everyone's surprise, came General Grant. Sherman was ordered to give Johnston forty-eight hours' notice to accept surrender on the terms which prevailed at Appomattox, or hostilities would be resumed.[107]

Grant told Stanton at the time that Sherman was not surprised by this repudiation of his arrangement, but rather expected it.[108] Sherman then resumed his negotiations with Johnston on grounds comprehending the surrender of his army alone, on the same terms that Grant had given Lee. While remaining at headquarters, Grant did not humiliate Sherman by joining in the talks at the Bennett house. On the afternoon of April 26 the terms were signed.

Sherman went to Hilton Head, where on May 2 he saw in the New York papers of April 28 a dispatch of the 27th from Stanton to General Dix, and a

105. *O.R.*,I, xlviii, pt. 3, 243, Sherman to Grant or Halleck, Apr. 18, 1865.

106. For able, though controversial, secondary accounts, see Naroll, *op.cit.*; Barrett, John G., *Sherman's March Through the Carolinas*, Chapel Hill, 1956, 226ff.; Lewis, *op.cit.*, 526-572; Randall-Current, *op.cit.*, 352-353.

107. *O.R.*,I, xlvii, pt. 1, 34.

108. *Ibid.*, 293.

dispatch of Halleck's. Halleck had told Stanton April 26 from Richmond that Meade, Sheridan and Wright were acting under orders not to consider any truce, or any orders of Sherman suspending hostilities. Their troops were ordered to push forward.[109] Halleck further urged other commanders to ignore the truce. Sherman on May 7 telegraphed Halleck, "After your dispatch to Mr. Stanton of April 26 I cannot have any friendly intercourse with you. I will come to City Point tomorrow, and march with my troops and I prefer we should not meet. . . ."[110] Halleck replied, "You have not had during the war, nor have you now, a warmer friend and admirer than myself. If, in carrying out what I knew to be the wishes of the War Dept. in regard to your armistice, I used language which has given you offense, it was unintentional and I deeply regret it. If fully aware of the circumstances under which I acted, I am certain you would not attribute to me any improper motives. It is my wish to continue to regard and receive you as a personal friend. With this statement, I leave the matter in your hands. . . ."[111] Actually, Sherman and Halleck had been quite friendly, but now Sherman was hotly repulsing a presumed slur upon his actions. He accused Halleck of going beyond the due limits of his authority and intimated that Stanton was guilty of offenses which he left vaguely undefined. Even in his official report he wrote that Stanton's attitude was "too much," adding: "I turn from the subject with feelings too strong for words, and merely record that so much mischief was never before embraced in so small a space as in the newspaper paragraph headed 'Sherman's truce disregarded,' authenticated as 'official' by Mr. Secretary Stanton, and published in the New York papers of April 28. . . ."[112]

Sherman apparently let loose to anyone who would listen. Admiral John A. Dahlgren was a sympathetic listener. On May 3, Dahlgren wrote that the General exploded "instanter" and "said Halleck had not been under fire once, that he could whip him and the Army of the Potomac; . . . All the little dogs are loose on Sherman. How they bark! He is a great sinner against the mass of respectable mediocrities,—the fossils, and the smooth trimmers . . ." The Admiral felt Sherman was "in a magnificent passion. . . ."[113]

Sherman later wrote Schofield of snubbing Stanton at the Grand Review by refusing to shake hands; "the matter being more than official, a personal insult, and, I have resented it and shall continue to do so. No man I don't care who he is shall insult me publicly or arraign my motives. . . ."[114]

109. *Ibid.*, 311.
110. Sherman to Halleck, May 7, 1865, Sherman Papers, HEH.
111. Halleck to Sherman, May 9, 1865, Richmond, Nicholson Collection, HEH.
112. *O.R.*,I, xlvii, pt. 1, 38.
113. Dahlgren, M.V., *Memoir of Admiral John A.Dahlgren*, Boston, 1882, 510-511.
114. Sherman to Schofield, May 28, 1865, Sherman Papers, HEH.

The dispatch of Stanton to Dix which so deeply pained and irritated Sherman described his terms to Johnston, adding that after he had entered into this so-called "basis for peace," with the rebel general, in the presence of the rebel general Breckinridge, a Cabinet meeting was held at which the President, Grant, Stanton, and the entire Cabinet disapproved the terms. Grant was sent South.[115]

Grant at the time wrote that he read the agreement carefully before submitting it to the President and Stanton, "and felt satisfied that it could not possibly be approved. . . ." The Cabinet meeting, as Grant informed Sherman late in April, resulted in "a disapproval by the President of the basic terms laid down, in a disapproval of the negotiations altogether, except for the surrender of the Army commanded by Johnston . . . the rebels know well the terms upon which they can have peace and just when negotiations can commence, namely: when they lay down their arms and submit to the laws of the United States. Mr. Lincoln gave them full assurance of what he would do, I believe, in his conference with commissioners met in Hampton Roads. . . ."[116]

Sherman had to explain the situation to commanders under him. To General Thomas he wrote that his terms had been misconstrued, and that Johnston had asked him to help "to prevent his army and people breaking up into Guerrilla Bands . . . But the more I reflect the more satisfied I am that my dealing with the people of the South magnanimously will restore 4/5 of them at once to the condition of good citizens, leaving us only to deal with the remainder. . . ."[117]

Stanton wrote Grant on April 25: "The arrangement between Sherman and Johnston meets with universal disapprobation. No one of any class or shade of opinion approves it. I have not known as much surprise and discontent at anything that has happened during the war. . . . The hope of the country is that you may repair the misfortune occasioned by Sherman's negotiations." Grant did take some remedial steps, but vestiges of ill-feeling persisted.

Beyond much doubt, Sherman acted upon an impulse of generous good will for the Southern people, and a humane desire to halt the spilling of blood. His intentions had been completely honest, patriotic and high-minded. The President had dealt with him fairly; though he may have felt, as we must, that it is difficult to understand how Sherman could have been so misled by his own inclinations and by the opposing generals.

One glimpse into the reasons which inspired Sherman's course is perhaps afforded by a letter he wrote to Chase on May 6: "I am not yet prepared to

---

115. *O.R.*, I, xlviii, pt. 3, 285-286.
116. Grant to Sherman, April 21, 1865, J.P. Morgan Library, New York.
117. *Battles and Leaders*, Extra-illustrated ed., HEH, Vol.XVII, Sherman to Thomas, May 2, 1865.

receive the Negro on terms of political equality," he declared, "for the reasons that it will arouse passions and prejudices at the North, which, superadded to the causes yet dormant at the South, might rekindle the war whose fires are now dying out, and by skillful management might be kept down. . . . I, who have felt the past war as bitterly and keenly as any man could, confess myself afraid of a new war, and a new war is bound to result from the action you suggest of giving to the enfranchised Negroes so large a share in the delicate task of putting the Southern States in practical working relations with the general Government. . . ." [118] One difficulty was that Sherman apparently overestimated his own powers of "skillful management." Later he told a fellow officer: "I believe if the South had been promptly allowed some approximate representation as a concession to principle, they would have been so impressed with the honesty and fairness of the thing that a fair proportion would have acted from the beginning with the republican party."[119]

Not a few men were deeply disconcerted by Sherman's action. A Union officer from Virginia wrote: "I hope Sherman will be relieved for offering such terms to Johnston. What Gen. Grant gave Lee is sufficient for traitors, and they ought not to have as good since the murder of Mr. Lincoln."[120]

Montgomery Blair could not understand the occurrence; "It is the most incomprehensible thing that Sherman should have committed such a *faux pas.* He talked altogether in a different vein and was too much disposed to severity, I thought, when he met the President and Grant at City Point lately. . . ."[121]

The able and temperate Jacob D. Cox was highly resentful of the course taken by Stanton and Halleck. He particularly emphasized the fact that Stanton's dispatch did not mention that the memorandum had no binding force without the approval of the President, and sharply termed the Stanton account "ignorant, biased and very prejudicial to Sherman."[122]

We may also hazard a guess that Sherman's personal attacks upon Stanton and Halleck were perhaps his way of giving vent to his chagrin and vexation, although the central target of his wrath and disappointment was the rejection of his plan by everyone in Washington, including Grant and the President.

During the long halt or pause of Sherman's army, and as news of the capture of Richmond and surrender of Lee came in, rumor upon rumor swept the Union forces in North Carolina and the civilians of the area, reaching the

118. *O.R.*, I, xlvii, pt. 3, 410-411, Sherman to Chase, May 6, 1865.

119. Sherman to Maj. Willard Warner, Jan. 18, 1866, William T. Sherman Papers, Illinois State Hist. Libr., Springfield.

120. John M. Berry to Barlow, April 27, 1865, S.L.M. Barlow Papers, HEH.

121. M. Blair to Barlow, Apr. 26, 1865, S.L.M. Barlow Papers, HEH.

122. Cox, Jacob D., *Military Reminiscences of the Civil War*, New York, 1900, II, 495-508.

credulous ears of many excited men and especially influencing them in predicting new troop movements—half of them suggesting a direct march home by
way of Richmond, and half of them a fresh offensive against Joe Johnston.[123]
The news of Lincoln's assassination struck many suspicious soldiers as possibly another hoax.[124] When it was confirmed, some Union soldiers angrily
forgot the truce, seized their arms and forgetful of orders, and heedless of
officers, advanced to the front. "A single gun might have opened a conflict
involving the whole army, in which no quarter would have been asked or
given." But as wiser counsels prevailed, the hotheads went reluctantly to the
rear.[125]

The North Carolinians were reported in "pitiable condition," but Northern soldiers came to the aid of at least those who professed Union leanings.[126]
The Confederate soldiers were in equally pitiable plight. They had a full share
of manly hardihood, and of devotion to what they deemed their convictions;
by their valor as soldiers they had won general esteem and admiration. In their
butternut jeans, which by courtesy were known as a uniform, and their broad-
brimmed, gray, slouchy hats, wrote the historian Headley, "they looked anything but soldierly. . . . Yet amid all these hardships and discouragements they
were courageous, self-reliant, even hopeful. . . ."[127] When news of Johnston's
final surrender came, many of them were utterly dejected. "They scarcely had
anything to say all day," wrote one man in his diary.[128] A Union veteran wrote,
however, that when the birds awoke him with the day, "I never heard them
sing so sweetly, and never saw them flit about so merrily." He added that "the
green groves in which we were camped, had a peculiar beauty and freshness,
and as the sun rose above the [Raleigh] steeples, it seemed as if we could float
right up with it."[129]

A young refugee in Hillsboro made a spirited entry in her diary: "Gen.
Johnston *has surrendered his army!* We have no army now—we have been overpowered—outnumbered, but thank God we have not been whipped—Did I
ever think to live to see this day: After all the misery and anguish of the four
past years—Think of all our sacrifices—of broken hearts, and desolated homes
—of our *noble, glorious dead*—, and say for what? *Reconstruction!* how the very
word galls—Can we ever live in peace with the desecrators of our homes

123. Capt. Robinson to Charlie Abbott, William Culbertson Robinson Papers, Illinois State Hist.
Soc., and courtesy of Ralph G. Newman, Apr. 25, 1865, Holly Springs, N.C.
124. *Ibid.*
125. Headley, F.Y., *Marching through Georgia*, Chicago, 1890, 427.
126. Robinson Papers, Illinois State Historical Society.
127. Headley, *op.cit.*, 433.
128. Porter, Albert Quincy, Mississippi Archives, Jackson, Miss.
129. Loring Armstrong to G.F. Cram, Elmhurst, Ill., April 28, 1865, and to his mother on same
date, Armstrong Letters in private collection, Oak Park, Ill.

and the murderers of our fathers, brothers and sons—*Never*—We are bound to rise again—My God, is it thy will that we should be *Conquered?* . . ."[130]

General Johnston had to telegraph to what remaining Southern governors he could reach: "The disaster in Virginia; the capture of all our workshops for the preparation of ammunition and repairing of arms; the improbability of recruiting our little army, opposed by more than ten times its number; or of supplying it except by robbing our own citizens, destroyed all hope of successful war. I have therefore made a military convention with General Sherman to terminate hostilities in North and South Carolina, Georgia and Florida. I made this convention to spare the blood of the gallant little army committed to me, to prevent further sufferings of our people by the devastation and ruin inevitable from the marches of invading armies, and to avoid the evils of waging hopeless war."[131]

The collapse and surrender of other Confederate pockets may be briefly dismissed, but their resistance had an emotional significance, and the memory of the stand they made affected the future of the district and section. A lamentable amount of confusion often appeared. As late as April 26, a Louisiana cavalryman sent his wife word from Alabama that his detachment had just received glorious news to the effect that Lee had fought a great battle with Grant and had killed a great number of Yankees; also that Grant had asked for an armistice, to which Lee had agreed. He reported the further "news" that since the death of Lincoln a hundred thousand of Grant's army had deserted. To cap the climax, intelligence had come that Johnston and Beauregard had whipped Sherman badly.[132] Just how could such preposterous canards circulate in the defeated West?

A Yankee soldier, furious over Lincoln's death, wrote of the dire abuse of Northern prisoners at Andersonville, while in Macon, Ga., Confederates were being paroled at a great pace.[133] By May 6, this Yankee found that in Augusta, Ga., the Northern and Southern soldiers already were mingling freely, smoking and chatting. Another Yankee in Georgia, near Columbus, described a jubilee meeting of Negro camp-followers.[134]

A few miles north of Mobile, the Confederate General Dick Taylor met E.R.S. Canby of the Union forces on April 30, and within a few minutes agreed on a truce. When news shortly came in of Johnston's surrender, Canby and

---

130. Diary of Elizabeth Collier, Southern Hist. Coll., Univ. of N.C. Library.
131. J.E.Johnston, Greensboro, N.C., to Govs. Brown, McGrath, and Milton, Apr. 30, 1865, HEH Miscellaneous.
132. Edwin Leet letter to his wife of Apr. 26, 1865, Edwin Leet Letters, Louisiana State Univ., Dept. of Archives.
133. Gilpin, E.N., Diary, LC.
134. Mitchell, C.D., Extract from *Field Notes of the Civil War*, ms. LC.

Taylor met again on May 4 to make their agreement official. Taylor dated his surrender May 8, when paroles were accepted at Citronelle, Ala., some forty miles north of Mobile. The terms were identical with those of Appomattox, although Taylor retained control of railroads and steamers to expedite the task of returning troops home. Many farewells were delivered. General Forrest issued his in the tone that might have been expected: "That we are beaten is a self-evident fact, and any further resistance on our part would be justly regarded as the very height of folly and rashness . . . The cause for which you have so long and so manfully struggled, and for which you have braved dangers, endured privations and sufferings, and made so many sacrifices, is today hopeless. The Government which we sought to establish and perpetuate is at an end . . . Fully realizing and feeling that such is the case, it is your duty and mine to . . . submit to the 'powers that be,' and to aid in restoring peace and establishing law and order throughout the land . . . Civil war, such as you have just passed through, naturally engenders feelings of animosity, hatred, and revenge. It is our duty to divest ourselves of all such feelings toward those with whom we have so long contested, and heretofore so widely but honestly differed . . . Whatever your responsibilities may be to Government, to society, or to individuals, meet them like men . . . You have been good soldiers, you can be good citizens. . . ."[135]

Elsewhere, rebels were laying down their arms in small batches and units from Florida to Missouri. Facing a hopeless situation, despite some demands that he continue the fight, E. Kirby-Smith beyond the Mississippi surrendered his forces on May 26 when General Buckner brought the summons approved by General Osterhaus in New Orleans;[136] and Smith signed the terms on June 2. Finally, out near lonely Fort Towson in Indian Territory, just north of the Texas line, Brigadier-General Stand Watie, three-quarters Cherokee, surrendered his ragtail remnant, the last significant Confederate land detachment to yield. On July 4, the spectacular cavalry raider, Jo Shelby, led his men across the Rio Grande to inflict new losses in final adventurous blows before allowing their flags and guidons to sink beneath the waters.

At last, all the gray hosts were gone—hosts that had numbered in all perhaps three-quarters of a million or more. No precise figure is possible. They had made a record of gallant devotion, self-sacrificing valor, and intelligently directed effort and ability that commanded the admiration of a host of historians, orators, and poets who later chronicled their deeds.

While the Southern army was collapsing, the Confederate government was in flight. Following its departure from Richmond by train, Davis had set up

135. O.R., I, xlix, pt. 2, 1289-1290.
136. O.R., I, xlviii, pt. 2, 600-601.

the semblance of a capital in Danville, Va., with headquarters in a Main Street mansion. Official word of Lee's surrender did not arrive in Danville until the afternoon of Monday, April 10. The government would have to shift again. As rumors were rife in the North[137] as to Davis's whereabouts, and as Lincoln hinted he would not mind if the Confederate President got away, the ever more diminished Southern government left for Greensboro, N.C. When the news from Appomattox had come in, at first those who read the message were mute, comprehending the solemnity of the hour, and the gravity of the trials facing them. Then, disconsolate, resigned to suffering, but still resolute in spirit, they turned to the responsibilities just ahead. Trudging through darkness, rain, and mud, the disorganized Confederate government boarded the cars, leaving behind disgruntled civilians and soldiers who could not board the train. On its way to Greensboro the train narrowly missed being taken by Federal cavalry. Arriving at that town, the refugees could not find adequate accommodations. A bed was found for the unwell President, but others had to adjust themselves to a "dilapidated passenger-car."[138] The Secretary of the Treasury, Trenholm, who was very ill, was cared for in a fine private home. Despite this, Greensboro was an hospitable exception in the long and somewhat aimless trek of the fleeing Confederate "government."

The "Confederate treasure," as it is called, of some $500,000 under a naval guard, stayed only a day in Greensboro and then went on, eventually arriving at Washington, Ga.[139] Here the funds from Richmond banks were deposited in vaults, and the rest paid out for various expenses and to soldiers. Mrs. Davis joined her husband near Dublin, Ga.

Davis had written his wife from Charlotte on April 23 that the issue before him was very painful, for he must choose between "the long night of oppression" certain to follow the return of the South to the Union, and the carnage and suffering to ensue if resistance continued, such resistance certain to be useless unless the people rose *en masse.* "I think my judgment is undisturbed by any pride of opinion," wrote this proud, self-willed man. "I have prayed to our Heavenly Father to give me wisdom and fortitude equal to the demands

137. Mallory, S.R., *Diary*, Southern Hist. Coll., Univ. of N.C. Library.
138. *Ibid.*
139. Hanna, A.J., *Flight Into Oblivion*, Richmond, 1938. For other accounts, see Mallory, S.R., *op.cit.*, Reagan, John H., "Flight and Capture of Jefferson Davis," *Annals of the War*, Philadelphia, 1879, 147-159; Harrison, Burton K., "The Capture of Jefferson Davis," *Century*, Vol.XXVII, No.1, Nov., 1883, 130ff.; Wood, Capt. John Taylor, C.S.N., *Diary*, Southern Hist. Coll., Univ. of N.C.; Davis to Reagan, Aug. 9 and Aug. 21, 1877, Davis-Reagan Papers, Dallas Hist. Soc., Texas; Davis, Jefferson, *Rise and Fall of the Confederate Government, op.cit.*, II, 675ff. This is only a small part of the rather large body of material available on the flight. For a reasonable explanation of the so-called "Confederate treasure" see Hanna, *op.cit.*, 90-92, 115-116, 264-265; Stutler, Boyd, "The Last Confederate Payroll," *Civil War History*, Vol. VII, No. 2, June, 1961, 201-204.

of the position in which Providence has placed me. I have sacrificed so much for the cause of the Confederacy that I can measure my ability to make any further sacrifice required, and am assured there is but one to which I am not equal—My wife and my children." He was anxious only to see them saved from ignominy or want. "For myself," he concluded, "it may be that a devoted band of Cavalry will cling to me, and that I can force my way across the Mississippi, and if nothing can be done there which it will be proper to do, then I can go to Mexico, and have the world from which to choose a location. Dear Wife, this is not the fate to which I invited [you] when the future was rosecolored to us both; but I know you will bear it even better than myself, and that, of us two I alone will ever look back reproachfully on my past career. . . . Farewell, my dear, there may be better things in store for us than are now in view, but my love is all I have to offer, and that has the value of a thing long possessed, and sure not to be lost. . . ."[140]

Near dawn of May 10, not far from Irwinville, Ga., the career of Davis as President of the Confederacy ended. His capture had been almost certain, and was merely a matter of time. A rather shabby dispute followed among Northerners at once over the question whether Davis had been disguised as a woman in trying to escape,[141] and over the disposal of credit among claimants for the distinction of seizing the fugitives. All this history may well ignore. The all-sufficient fact is that Davis and many other Confederate leaders were finally in Union hands. Vice-President Stephens was arrested at his home, Liberty Hall, in Crawfordville, Ga. Davis, after being delivered to General James Harrison Wilson at Macon, Ga., was taken by sea to Norfolk, Va. Then came his detention in the famous casemate-cell in Fortress Monroe, part of the time in irons, followed by efforts of leading Federal editors and others to improve his lot, and discussion of a trial. By the summer of 1866 Davis and his family were allowed rooms at Fortress Monroe. The ridiculous supposition that possibly Davis had something to do with Lincoln's assassination was dropped. Finally, in May, 1867, Davis was taken to Richmond for a hearing on the question of a pardon. He had refused to request one, but it proved to be wise

140. Rowland, Dunbar, *Jefferson Davis, Constitutionalist*, Jackson, Miss., 1923, VI, 560-561.

141. Davis, Varina, *Jefferson Davis*, II, 641; Davis, *Rise and Fall, op.cit.*, II, 701-702; Harrison, Burton K., "The Capture of Jefferson Davis," *op.cit.*, 142-143; Reagan, "Flight and Capture of Jefferson Davis," *op.cit.*, 156-158; Diary of John Taylor Wood, Southern Hist. Coll., Univ. of N.C.; letters of Davis to Reagan, Aug. 9 and Aug. 21, 1877, in Davis-Reagan Papers, Dallas Hist. Soc.; Walthall, Major W.T., "The True Story of the Capture of Jefferson Davis," *Southern Historical Society Papers*, Vol.V, no.3, Mar. 1878, 118-121; Hanna, *op.cit.*, 100-102; Wilson, James Harrison, *Under the Old Flag*, New York, 1912, II, 297-337; *O.R.*, I, xlix, pt. 1, 370-380, for Wilson's report, and 534-539 for report of Lt.-Col. Benjamin D. Prichard, 4th Mich. Cavalry, ranking officer present at the capture; Wilson, James Harrison, "Pursuit and Capture of Jefferson Davis," *Century*, Feb. 1890, 591; Stedman, William P., "Pursuit and Capture of Jefferson Davis by an Eyewitness," *Century*, Feb. 1890, 594-596, and other sources too numerous to list.

for the Federal government to free him, a particularly politic move, in the early days of Reconstruction.

It was clear that the President, as well as the people, desired the nation's return to peaceful pursuits and a normal frame of mind as rapidly as possible. On May 10, the same day Davis was taken in Georgia, Johnson proclaimed that "armed resistance to the authority of this Government in the said insurrectionary States may be regarded as virtually at an end." Another step which displayed his sagacious anxiety to promote the nation's future and its steady return to prosperity and growth, was his May 22nd proclamation that on July 1, 1865, all seaports, with the exception of four in Texas, were to be open to commerce, and that civilian trade in all parts of the country east of the Mississippi was to be resumed with no limitations except for contraband of war. These proclamations were issued even before Confederate forces west of the Mississippi had actually surrendered.[142] On May 27, the President also ordered the discharge of all persons imprisoned by military authorities, with but few exceptions.

142. Richardson, James D., *Messages and Papers of the Presidents*, 1897, VII, 3504-3512.

12

Martial Demobilization

I read last night of the Grand Review
In Washington's chiefest avenue,
Two hundred thousand men in blue,
    I think they said that was the number—
Till I seemed to hear their tramping feet,
The bugle blast and the drum's quick beat,
The clatter of hoofs on the stony street,
The cheers of people who came to greet. . . .
Till I fell in a revery, sad and sweet,
    And then to a fitful slumber.

And I saw a phantom army come,
With never a sound of fife or drum,
But keeping time to a throbbing hum,
    Of wailing and lamentation;
The martyred heroes of Malvern Hill,
Of Gettysburg and Chancellorsville. . . .

SO WROTE Bret Harte after the Grand Review of the returning armies of the North on May 23rd and May 24th, 1865. The same note of lamentation that he sounded over the more than half-a-million men lost as mortal casualties of the sad conflict was sounded by Henry Howard Brownell in a still more comprehensive poem published in the *Atlantic Monthly*, a requiem deeply appealing in its vision of a spiritual review of the dead heroes held on celestial ground under Lincoln's august eye. Henry Mills Alden (later editor of *Harper's Magazine*), called this poem "certainly the greatest of the many called forth by the war."[1] Overly sentimental, perhaps, to the modern ear, it struck just the right contemporary note of loss mingled with hope, recalling most vividly to that generation the glory, and the tragedy, and the promise.

1. Brownell, H.H., in *Harper's History of the Rebellion*, April, 1865, 789.

The colors ripple o'erhead,
　　The drums roll up to the sky,
And with martial time and tread
　　The regiments all pass by—
The ranks of our faithful Dead,
　　Meeting their President's eye.

With a soldier's quiet pride
　　They smile o'er the perished pain,
　　For their anguish was not vain—
'For thee, O Father, we died!
　　And we did not die in vain.'

March on, your last brave mile!
　　Salute him, Star and Lace!
Form round him rank and file,
　　And look on the kind, rough face;
But the quaint and homely smile
　　Has a glory and a grace
It never had known erewhile—
　　Never, in time and space. . . .

Their task completed, the Volunteer Armies of the Union gathered in Washington more than 200,000 strong on the bright, sunny spring days of May 23 and 24, 1865. For the first time since the death of the President in April, the capital seemed really alive again. The war was over, even though the Trans-Mississippi Confederacy did not formally surrender until May 26. The new President was gripping the reins and a wholly novel chapter of national history was being opened, but before this new series of events could unfold, the armies must march once more, duly ordered by Stanton and Grant.

Down Pennsylvania Avenue they came—on the first day the Army of the Potomac. Nearly continuous lines of grandstands, bleachers, and seats had been erected from the Capitol to the White House. The city swarmed with visitors, the schools were dismissed, and the jubilant populace donned gay attire to welcome home the victors. Viewers perched on lamp posts and crowded windows and roofs along the route. Near the White House special covered stands had been erected for the President, the Cabinet, Generals, diplomats, the press, and just commonplace politicians. One special stand, built at his own expense by a Boston gentleman, was reserved for the use of those who could not march—the crippled and the convalescent. Outlying parts of the city were nearly deserted.

The flags waved everywhere, some faded and in shreds. A few staffs bore no banners, for they had been entirely shot away. Bands blared; the cheering and the weeping were fervent; school children, dressed in white, strewed flowers and sang patriotic songs, while some held aloft such signs as: "The Public Schools of Washington Welcome the Heroes of the Republic." The parade included celebrities, too. The onlookers knew their names and faces, and had their favorite generals, heading corps, divisions, and even brigades.

In front of President Johnson, Secretary of War Stanton, and General Grant, the cavalry clattered past for a full hour. Some disappointment was expressed that the popular Phil Sheridan did not lead the horse troops of the Army of the Potomac, but he was already in the South with occupation forces. One critical observer stated that Sheridan's absence was due primarily to his reluctance to appear under Meade's command.[2] His nonappearance had a partial compensation when, near the reviewing stand, the bugle sounded "Charge" and the cavalry of George Armstrong Custer, each man wearing a red kerchief, thundered past with their youthful, blonde-haired leader in the van. His horse even managed to seize attention by running away briefly until the spectacular Custer reined him in.[3]

The engineer corps appeared with its cumbersome implements of service, including pontoons; the brigades of infantry were accompanied by six ambulances each; and the Zouaves marched proudly in gaudy uniform. The Irish brigade had sprigs of green in their hats; the Ninth Corps excelled in marching precision; many one-armed soldiers found places, each with a wreath over his empty sleeve. The youthfulness of the generals as they took their places in the reviewing stand impressed the watchers. As Sherman joined them, even louder cheers arose. The conqueror of Georgia and the Carolinas saluted the President and then pointedly declined the proffered hand of Secretary Stanton, for the controversy over Johnston's surrender terms was fresh, and Sherman had a nature that nursed old grudges.

The second day, May 24, furnished a contrast: at 11 A.M. Sherman and Howard led forth the soldiers of the West in their first review, before thousands of onlookers. The Western men, wearing their field uniforms, no matter how faded and camp-worn, were taller, strode in a long loose type of swinging step, and were said to have "magnificent physiques."

It was not merely an extraordinary pageant or a gigantic spectacle, such as

2. Wainwright, Charles S., *A Diary of Battle*, ed. Allan Nevins, New York, 1962, 525. Wesley Merritt led the cavalry of the Army of the Potomac.

3. There are many ample descriptions of the Grand Review, some with conflicting details. Brooks, Noah, *Washington in Lincoln's Time*, ed. Herbert Mitgang, New York, 1958, 271-283. For another description of Custer see Papers of Albert H. Prescott, personal notes for May 23, 1865, mss. HEH; newspaper reports such as New York *Tribune*, May 24, 25, 1865, and New York *Herald*, May 24, 25 and 27, 1865.

Libby Prison in 1865, after the Release of Union Prisoners

would probably never be seen again; it was the spectacular expression of "a deep, glorious, solemn sentiment," all patriots feeling deep pride in the "youthful strength of a republic tried and found stead-fast."[4]

Now the volunteer army had to be disbanded, dispersed—a task that could not wait. Four days after the surrender of Lee, the War Department directed that all recruiting and drafting in all States be discontinued. Thus, the machinery of army mobilization was thrown into reverse. By April 28, orders had been issued for reducing expenses of "the Military Establishment," and expenditures were cut as rapidly as was prudent. Purchases of horses, mules, wagons, and much forage were halted, ocean and river transports not required to bring troops home were disposed of, and all requisitions for railroad construction and transportation were stopped. The Commissary-General, and the Chief of Ordnance cut down on buying guns and supplies, and reduced production at government arsenals; engineers ceased work on field and other fortifications; all bureaus, in fact, were to curtail operations sharply, except those needed to maintain the regular army and to aid in disbanding the volunteer force. In addition, the number of general and staff officers was to be reduced, and military restrictions upon trade and commerce were to be removed, "so far as might be consistent with the public safety."[5]

After a conference of not more than an hour-and-a-half, Stanton and Grant on May 11 approved orders, only about a page-and-a-half in length, formulating plans for demobilization of the Union army. Thus was begun what Ida M. Tarbell called "the greatest feat in handling men which this or any government has ever performed."[6]

For months the War Department would be as active as during hostilities. On May 1, 1865, the volunteers in the army totaled 1,034,064. By August 7, 1865, in something over two months of processing, 640,806 troops had been mustered out. By November 15, 1865, nearly four-fifths of the total, or 800,963, had been demobilized. On July 19 the final regiment of the Army of the Potomac was sent home from Washington and by August 1 the last of Sherman's regiments left Louisville. A year later, on November 1, 1866, the army had still left in service only 11,043 volunteer soldiers, of whom 8,756 were U. S. Colored Troops.

General Grant felt the collapse of resistance "rendered a large part of our military force unnecessary," because by July, 1865, it was apparent that the necessity of surrender was being accepted by the South without any apprecia-

---

4. *Harper's Weekly*, June 10, 1865.
5. *O.R.* III, iv, 1263, 1280-1281; v, 509-510.
6. *Ibid.*, 1-3; Tarbell, Ida M., "Disbanding the Union Army," *McClure's Magazine*, March, 1901, 408.

ble reaction. The Regular Federal Army remained, and although it was over three times as large as the pre-Civil War Army, it was a long way from the million under arms in May, 1865. By fall of 1866, the aggregate strength was set at 54,302, a number below the maximum of 75,382 authorized by Congress. During the last year of the war the Army had cost the United States over a billion dollars; two years later that cost was under a hundred million.[7]

The Federal Navy began its gradual reduction of forces used on blockade duty even before the army started demobilization. After the fall of Fort Fisher in North Carolina in January and Wilmington in late February, 1865, steps were taken to cut down naval forces. This reduction was accentuated after Charleston, Mobile, and Galveston were taken over by the Union. The main purpose of the cutbacks seems to have been to reduce expenses. Commanders were ordered to send north purchased vessels needing extensive repairs and naval stores no longer required. Around May 1, squadrons in home waters were reduced by half, and near the end of May even greater cuts were made. The Potomac Flotilla and the Mississippi Squadron were discontinued, so that from a fleet of 471 vessels on blockade duty alone, in January, 1865, there remained only thirty steamers and receiving ships of the blockaders by mid-July.

The total Union Navy had 530 vessels with 2,000 guns in commission at the start of 1865, and was reduced to 117 with 830 guns by December of that year. Foreign squadrons were re-established in European, Brazilian, and East Indian waters, and a new one set up for the West Indies. The Pacific squadron had never been discontinued.

As for manpower, the Navy had grown from 7,600 in 1861 to 51,500, plus 16,880 artisans and laborers in the navy yards, with a like number employed in private shipyards under government contract. By December, 1865, these numbers were substantially reduced to 12,128 men.

The renowned ironclad vessels, mainly monitors, which had proved, according to Secretary Welles, "so formidable in war, but unsuited for active service in peace," were now laid aside, "ready to be brought forward at any time for active duty should circumstances require." Since March 4, 1861, of a total of 418 vessels purchased at a cost of nearly eighteen-and-a-half million dollars, some 340 had been sold by December 1865 for a mere five-and-one-half million.[8]

Thus the demobilization of men and material was accomplished without

7. Oberholtzer, Ellis Paxson, *A History of the United States Since the Civil War*, Vol. I, New York, 1917, 26; *O.R.*, III, v, 1033.
8. Welles, Report, Dec. 4, 1865, *Cong. Globe*, 39th Cong., 1st. Sess., Appendix, 19-23; Richardson, James D., *A Compilation of the Messages and Papers of the Presidents*, New York, 1887, Vol. VII, 3561.

severe disruption, and the world viewed with mixed emotions the return of the war-weary veterans to peacetime civilian life.

No separate reviews, however, were held by certain other elements in the long stormy struggle, who well merited the salutes and homage of crowded streets and cheering people—the women, who, as resolute wives and mothers, unwearied workers, and nurses, had sustained and comforted the fighters; the worn files of unpaid men who had enlisted in the Sanitary and Christian Commissions; the humble trudging Negroes who had donned the uniforms of the Republic and risked obloquy and bullets in order to wield bayonets and trench-shovels. Silent and nameless in their devotion, they fittingly melted away into the throngs of patriotic citizens returning to their habitual labors and duties. But the nation would never forget them or their priceless services —never cease to reverence their memory.

13

Mobilization for Peace

MUCH MORE thoughtful planning and effort were involved in demobilizing the American people from their widely varied war efforts, and in reorganizing their thinking, energies and resources to meet the multitudinous problems of peace, than were expended in merely disbanding the armies and selling unneeded parts of the naval armada. The fact that these exigent tasks were accomplished with speed and efficiency contributed immeasurably to post-war economic stability and growth. A disorderly and delayed dispersal of the armies, while guerrilla activities continued, and coastal trade remained weak and inadequate to help meet the nation's commercial needs, would have resulted in sufficiently widespread friction and bitterness to cripple all American activities for decades. Meanwhile, the morale of the nation might have suffered heavily from years of internal dissension and uncertainty.

If we can imagine the possibility of the type of civil war known at times in various parts of Europe, where the sinking flames of internal conflict were blown into a more destructive blaze by neighboring countries pursuing malevolent or greedy aims, and where the victorious as well as the vanquished elements in the population were forced to live in close proximity while their passionate hatreds and increasingly disparate cultural and economic systems generated a succession of angry new collisions, then we can better picture the malign possibilities facing the weary, bewildered people, North and South, in 1865.

Fortunately, the background of the conflict was American, not European; and still more fortunately, both Northerners and Southerners had long been committed to the fundamental Anglo-Saxon principle of compromise, and were at last ready to turn to mutual concessions to readjust their differences. Another important fact was that the successful North had suffered no crippling injuries, either material or moral, except for human casualties. Few of its areas had been invaded, and it was gaining tremendously in economic strength through development of its resources, and full organization of its manpower to meet the demands of the conflict. Fortunately, also the defeated Confederacy had been seeking not to overthrow the United States, but simply to vindicate what it believed to be the right of secession.

With the opening of the West and its accompanying railroad expansion, broad areas all the way to the Pacific became available to absorb the expanding population of the older States, ready to receive the great flood of immigration about to come. For the most part, too, the victorious North was sufficiently separated geographically from the South so that the defeated Confederates were not obliged to live in neighborhoods with their victors. Above all, the veterans of the North, the West, and the borderland returned home to a civilian economy full of enterprise and growth.

The dual strength of the American economy, its ability to carry on a great war, and at the same time achieve a growth in wealth, business enterprise, and cultural vigor that impressed the world, enabled the nation to quickly bridge the gap from the war era to the post-war period now opening. The Northern stamina and resilience so evident throughout the conflict were undiminished, and now served equally well in peace. The whole nation moved valiantly forward, bringing even defeated sections to at least partial recovery.

Clearly great new developments would have taken place in the 1860's, in spite of the war,[1] for American ingenuity and business genius were definitely manifesting themselves at the outset of the industrial revolution. Railroads would have gone racing over the prairies, mountains, and deserts. Petroleum, still largely a novelty, was becoming a popular topic of conversation; new processes in iron-making were evolving, and Bessemer steel would soon be introduced. The emergence of iron vessels entirely powered by steam would have been certain; telegraph and cable wires would have extended communication both within and without the country; business capital would have proliferated; immigration would have surged forward; new inventions would have abounded; expansion westward was as natural as the passage of time. These and many other striking new changes would have taken place. Indeed, these and many other marvelous changes did appear! But it is a certainty that the war altered and helped reshape some of these developments.

Numerous observers both anticipated and reported these progressive trends at the time.[2] The influential *American Railroad Journal* early in 1865, optimistically believing that peace was at hand, declared: "We may . . . look forward to a brilliant future, when our present difficulties are settled, and an advance in all our material interests, at a rate hitherto unknown. . . ."[3]

1. See Chapter 7, "The Great Boom" in Nevins, *The War for the Union: The Organized War.*
2. Nevins, Allan, *The Emergence of Modern America*, 290.
3. *American Railroad Journal*, Jan. 7, 1865.

The *Scientific American*, at the start of 1865, pronounced: "There is nothing more illustrative of the national energy and genius than the indomitable spirit exhibited under adverse circumstances. If in any other country than our beloved America, faction should arise and threaten the national existence, the plow would stand idle in the furrow, the threads of the loom swing listless from the frames, and anvils clink only to the sharpening of swords. The arts have not languished with us though the war still goes on. . . ."[4]

Later in the year, the New York *Tribune* stated: "The country may be compared to a great ant-hill, of which the swarming inhabitants rapidly and wisely repair damages, and speedily return to the work of provision. . . . There is no suspicion of insolvency. There is no fear of depreciation. There is confidence everywhere among a people proverbially sharp and suspicious in all matters of money. . . ."[5] For example, in early spring before the war ended, when there was a temporary drop in the health of the economy, financial circles remained optimistic. Creditors had never before been so accommodating.[6]

The perceptive economist, Sir S. Morton Peto, who observed much of this near-phenomena, wrote: "Even under all the effects of Civil War—with a population diverted from her labour fields, with her commerce impeded, and the country labouring under a burden of taxation, rendered the more onerous because it could only be applied to a section of the population—even under all these disadvantages, America is shown to have progressed. I have already observed that there is nothing to correspond with this in the records of history." He continued: "Throughout the war the nation gave evidence of rapidly increasing wealth . . . America, which in so many respects has shown herself superior to ordinary rules, has, in regard to the effects of the war, shown that the heaviest and most costly conflict can be borne not only without exhaustion, but even with an increase of national prosperity. . . . In my travel through the United States in the autumn of last year, (1865) the abundant resources of the country . . . struck me most forcibly . . . the key to everything else . . . was the wonderful elasticity of the *resources of the United States.*"[7]

A usually conservative and often pessimistic financial publication wrote in

4. *Scientific American*, Jan. 2, 1865.
5. New York *Tribune*, Sept. 28, 1865.
6. *Merchants Magazine and Commercial Review*, Vol. XLII, April, 1865, 288; New York *Independent*, March 30, June 15, 1865.
7. Peto, Sir S. Morton, *The Resources and Prospects of America*, London, 1866, 391-392, 395. Sir Morton's book is undoubtedly significant, being the observations of a British capitalist, or perhaps the observations of a group of capitalists and investors. Peto led a junket of British gentlemen interested in investment on a tour of the United States in late 1865. Expenses were charged to the Atlantic & Great Western Railroad. His book, published in 1866, caused quite a stir and might well be interpreted as a brochure on the glories of the United States, extolling it as a fine ground for investment. See Jenks, Leland Hamilton, *The Migration of British Capital to 1875*, Thomas Nelson & Sons, Ltd., London, Knopf edition, 1963, 258-259.

July, 1865: "[It is] with a feeling of relief that we perceive ourselves almost upon the eve of the last change from the abnormal to the normal, from the day of battles and proclamations to those of legislation and law. The probable flow of capital, the rate of interest, the signs of future movements, all these soon may be within the compass of practical experience and scientific knowledge, and not as of late totally subject to the chances of war or official caprice. And when the drama is ended, and the dawn of peace and constitutional government ripens into bright morning, the mists of deficit revenues, national poverty and repudiation . . . will disappear."[8]

Senator John Sherman of Ohio wrote his brother, General William T. Sherman, "The truth is, the close of the war with our resources unimpaired gives an elevation, a scope to the ideas of leading capitalists, far higher than anything ever undertaken in this country before. They talk of millions as confidently as formerly of thousands. . . . Our manufactures are yet in their infancy, but soon I expect to see, under the stimulus of a great demand and the protection of our tariff, locomotive and machine shops worthy of the name."[9]

These predictions were perhaps excessive in their optimism, but such an outlook reflected the thinking and hopes of the vast majority of the populace, at least in the North.

[II]

Thanks to the dual strength of the Northern economy the vast majority of returning Union veterans slipped back into old familiar niches, or found new ones with a minimum of trouble and confusion. For instance, perceptive specialized journals of economics have very little to say about demobilization in general.[10] Inevitably, a few weak spots and some pockets of temporary unemployment appeared, particularly in the cities. While many men returned to former jobs or kindred trades, four years had witnessed numerous changes in business, and often old-time jobs were no longer open. Furthermore, many of the youngest veterans had never been gainfully employed before the war, so jobs had to be found for them. Many simply returned to the farm to help ease the wartime load of those left at home, while countless able and venturesome men set out for the West.

Newspapers and other journals continued to urge businessmen to find

8. *Merchants' Magazine and Commercial Review*, Vol. LIII, July, 1863, 53.

9. Nevins, *The Emergence of Modern America*, 31-33; *The Sherman Letters, Correspondence between General and Senator Sherman from 1837 to 1891*, edited by Rachel Sherman Thorndike, London, 1894, 258.

10. *Merchants' Magazine*, 1865-1866, *passim.*, hardly mentions the problem of the returning soldiers in either its articles or in monthly summaries of the economic situation; see also *Prairie Farmer*, 1865-1866, *passim; American Railroad Journal*, 1865-1866, *passim.*

places for the "heroes." In late July in New York, thousands of men were reported "out of work" during the slack season, though the reliability of such reports is hard to verify. In August, 1865, a meeting was held in New York by the "Discharged Soldiers and Sailors' Employment Agency" on Canal Street, where a large number of veterans gathered "for the purpose of forming an association that might urge their claims upon the community with greater force than individuals were capable of doing."[11] In some areas employers were reluctant or refused to hire the one-armed or one-legged men, or rejected crippled veterans entirely, a fact reported by the Sanitary Commission in Philadelphia.[12] The Pension Act of July 14, 1862, which was revised in 1864, provided pensions for veterans disabled by wounds or disease contracted while in line of duty.[13] As yet no pension was provided for mere service in the Union forces.

The majority of the enlisted men seemed to have little trouble fitting into the post-war picture. They were young, adaptable and most of them had not tied themselves down to any single trade or locality. In addition, a large number of them were as yet unmarried. Very often the veterans received the somewhat preferential treatment which most people believed to be their just due, often at the expense of men who had not seen service.[14]

Officers of high rank, especially former West Pointers, found a world of opportunity awaiting them in both national and local politics, in Federal jobs, in engineering, particularly in railroad operation, and in construction work of all kinds, while many veterans continued to serve in the regular Army. It was apparent that the promotional value of having been an officer of any rank in the war far outweighed in value whatever ground had been lost to the men who had stayed at home. Generally the people at home wished to assist the returning soldiers, even after the glitter had worn thin and become tarnished. Moreover, many a veteran would not forget his service "comrade" when it came to setting up a new business.

Officers in the lower echelons apparently did encounter some difficulties, in many instances finding it impossible to return to their pre-war occupations for a variety of reasons. On the other hand, they were often content to take positions which at first glance seemed to be a step down for a captain or major who had commanded fighting men. Sir Morton Peto may have exaggerated the situation slightly in writing that by the end of 1865 no one was without employment; but he did feel that one reason the veterans did not overcrowd the

11. New York *Tribune*, July 22, Aug. 21, 1865.
12. Maxwell, William Quentin, *Lincoln's Fifth Wheel*, New York, 1956, 287.
13. *Congressional Globe*, 37th Cong., 2nd Sess., Appendix, 405-406.
14. Rogers, Joseph, *The Development of the North Since the Civil War*, Vol. XVIII, and Barrie, George, *The History of North America*, Philadelphia, 1906, 33.

country was *"because their several occupations afforded them superior rewards for their labour."* He recalls having visited a printing establishment in Chicago where the owner had employed 47 former soldiers as compositors. One man was a major, another a captain, a third a lieutenant, and another an ex-sergeant. After all, it was explained, the employees received four dollars for every dollar they had received in the army. This employer had kept jobs open for those who had joined the colors. Sir Morton further concluded: "This was the means by which a reign of terror from disbanded soldiers was prevented in America at the conclusion of the Civil War." If there had been no employment for the people, anarchy would have reigned throughout the country. "How entirely inconsistent was all this," wrote Peto, "with our European notions of the consequences of military success!"[15]

What sort of a world did these veterans and their families face in the summer of 1865? While the conclusion of the war had been imminent for some months, no one was really ready for the actual event, especially with the sudden shock of the assassination.

While most of the veterans arrived home in fairly wholesome estate, physical and moral, and were easily absorbed into the civilian body, and while business made its readjustment to peace with a minimum of disruption, a great civil war of four-years' length could not but leave a heritage of profound social consequences, even though some of them might lie beneath the surface.

A myriad of novel social and psychological reactions had arisen from the endlessly varied tensions and passions of the long and feverish war; how deeply penetrating and masterful they were is a question no one can really answer. One commentator of the time spoke of a "certain public frenzy" that characterized the nation's thought and action in the tumultuous year 1865 as the period opened, finding expression in "enormous speculations, losses, and consequent frauds; an increase of crime, a curious and tragic recklessness in the management of railroads and steamers; a fury of extravagance at public watering-places . . . all observable the first months of peace." This ungoverned emotionalism was attributed to several causes, such as sudden fictitious wealth from large issues of paper money; the rapid and wonderful development of America's new Golconda Petroleum; the fact that war inevitably erodes old standards of public morals; the thirst for excitement during the war which had now to be satisfied with new sensations. "The public must have its startling [headlines], its exclamation points, its heavy type; and if there are no battles in Georgia or Virginia to authorize their use, a murder, or a defalcation, or a riot

15. Peto, *op.cit.*, 387, 404, 405.

must suffice. . . ." The theory was enunciated that "a great civil commotion is always followed by a deranged state of society." Perhaps all the above phenomena can be explained as part of the natural readjustment that had to take place before society could settle down to a new "normal condition." The "momentum" of a war is hard to stop or alter.[16]

For one memorable instance, the Fourth of July celebration at the North in 1865 seemed bigger, more frantic and raucous than ever; the country was letting off steam. General Grant appeared at Albany; a cornerstone was laid for the soldiers' monument at Gettysburg Cemetery; a gigantic parade enlivened New York City, and mobilized thousands of happy marchers celebrated elsewhere, while private homes and public buildings displayed "illuminations" emblazoned with patriotic slogans. "There never will be another such Fourth of July—whence it behooved us to make the most of this. There can never be another on which we shall for the first time celebrate at once the Salvation and the Emancipation of the Republic. . . ."[17] After the holiday, Greeley's *Tribune* commented, "The newspapers from all parts of the land are bringing us depressing tidings of homicides, of houses burned, of gunners killed by their own guns, of broken bones, of casualties in dreadful profusion and variety. We are the most impetuously festive people in the World. . . . Upon other days of the year the railway companies conspire with reckless switch-tenders to help the community upon its way to another and a calmer world; but upon the Fourth of July, we, ourselves, mount the locomotive and rush rapturously into the jaws of destruction. Dreadful bells fright us from our propriety; inopportune explosions communicate the mania to our horses; fireworks stimulate in the evening the frenzies of the morning; cocktails, smashes, juleps, slings, and punches keep up the conflagration; great crowds of jostling men, of weary women and of frightened and feverish children eating what they should not eat, drinking what they should not drink, standing where they should not stand, and moving on when safety required them to remain stationary."[18] Additional excitement was contributed on July 14 when Barnum's famous Museum in New York burned down, permitting the escape of a black bear from the menagerie into Wall Street.[19]

Beyond question, the year 1865 beheld an increase in both public and private laxity and corruption. Growth unshackled by the war, in addition to widespread confusion and the overthrow of many old standards, created new uncertainty and instability. Numerous established classes of society in many

16. Curtis, George William, *Harper's Weekly*, Sept. 2, 1865, 546.
17. New York *Tribune*, July 6, 9, 1865.
18. *Ibid.*, July 10, 1865.
19. *Ibid.*, July 14, 1865.

areas were being remoulded. What William Sumner later called the "cake of custom" had been broken in many spheres of conduct and business. Excessive speculation in both financial and personal activities was visible on every hand, and in every community. Men were becoming addicted to taking "chances."[20]

The underlying soundness of the people was coupled with a tendency that has usually been discernible in America in times of sharp crisis or profound change. Even when expected, as peace was in 1865, the majority of the population is seldom quite prepared for the alterations in the national life that such a shift brings about. A sudden feeling of vacancy, or insecurity, overtakes people as they suddenly realize how much of their lives will be altered in color, texture, and feeling. So it was in 1865. The multitudes North and South rushed into their new state of peace with a kind of startled frenzy, which endured until they felt a new serenity in the lifting of a long-sustained load of general anxiety and private sorrow. Yet there remained the new life, new enlarged opportunities for most, new jobs for others, along with national problems such as a new President, the fate of the freed slaves, what would happen in the South, and a host of other difficulties. Just as they had not been prepared for the end of the war, so were they unprepared for the reopening of peace, in a totally free society.[21]

[III]

The returned war veteran faced the harassing consequences of the conflict in the inexorable rise of the costs of living which outpaced all increases in wages, and the same grinding difficulties met by all veterans and civilians during the war years. Clearly, the inescapable inflation was endured by the people with much belt-tightening and some real distress, but happily it did not reach such calamitous depths as in England in the trough of depression or in Germany in the years of wild inflation after the first World War.[22]

By mid-1866, "the chief obstacle to the restoration of [the United States] . . . to its former prosperity, the obstacle which must be removed as soon as practicable, is the high rate of prices upon all the necessities of life."[23] It was of comparatively small consequence that colossal fortunes were amassed, and

20. For analysis of this trend, see Nevins, Allan, *The Emergence of Modern America*, Chap. VII, "The Moral Collapse in Government and Business, 1865-1873," p. 179: "Corruption had been far from unknown before the war; yet the impetus which the conflict gave to evil tendencies was alarming."

21. *Ibid.*, 190-191.

22. *Ibid.*, 225-227.

23. *Merchants' Magazine*, Vol. LV, July, 1866, 61-62.

that many people seemed able to make extravagant exhibitions of wealth, while others suffered hardship. The nation, compelled to pay exorbitantly for whatever necessities were eaten and worn, was fast becoming truly impoverished. The burden of inflation fell primarily on laborers and mechanics in the cities, and especially on "female operatives" and seamstresses. The war had diverted some private building, population in urban centers continued to swell, and there was a scarcity of dwellings in some areas. It was believed that property value would soon be enhanced twofold. For instance, in Massachusetts in 1868 nine more males were living in every hundred houses than had dwelt there in 1860, most of these being heads of families.[24]

Sir Morton Peto showed his characteristic sympathy and effervescence when he declared that the feature of the people that struck him most forcibly was "the absence of pauperism." In comparison with some areas of Europe, like southern Italy, perhaps he was right; at least when he emphasized the fact that in America "You see no rags, you meet no beggars." And he certainly made a telling observation when he stated, "Every one has the means before him of improving his position." He was also generally correct in asserting that "the wealth of America is diffused;" that is, it was well distributed, without areas of sore congestion. Though perhaps not true quite to the extent he implied, this was a statement reasonably sound respecting the roomy nation. He felt that the British had not fully appreciated "the American character . . . its energy, its enterprise, its independent spirit."[25]

Deeply affecting the price structure in postwar days was the excessive issuance of greenbacks and other paper money, the heavy taxation, the difficulties of readjustment from war production to the manufacture and use of civilian goods, the necessity of helping markets to re-arrange themselves. One critic explained the principal reasons why the British observers saw no beggars in the United States; incomes were larger and those who did feel the pinch of necessity practiced retrenchment and economy. Little absolute want existed; "The poor of the United States were not then and are not now identical as a class with the poor of Great Britain and Europe. In the United States, poverty, as a general fact, means simply deprivation of comforts and luxuries, and rarely, if ever, implies a want of necessities or a possibility of starvation . . ."[26] People kept up appearances in the majority of instances.

Within a year after the war, however, the long-anticipated economic trends

24. New York *Tribune*, Sept. 28, 1865; Wells, David A., "The Recent Financial, Industrial and Commercial Experiences of the U.S.," *Cobden Club Essays*, 2nd Series, 1871-72, London, 1872, 483-484.
25. Peto, *op.cit.*, 386-387, 389-390.
26. Wells, David A., "The Recent Financial, Industrial . . . ," *op.cit.*, 482.

resumed their course as affecting the life of the average worker. The situation was again becoming normal, although not all features of the return to normal economic life were entirely pleasant for everyone.

[IV]

A brief fall in economic activity appeared in March, 1865, as similar declines had occurred in previous wartime springs. The premium on gold dropped, the prices of commodities were depressed, a tighter money-market appeared, and an increase took place in mercantile failures. But this relapse had no lasting importance, except to prick some of the gold and silver-mining bubbles and increase the transfer of capital to government securities. One authoritative periodical declared that it made "people a little more careful for a few months."[27] Another factor in the decline was that, since the fall of Atlanta in the autumn of 1864, people had been anticipating peace, and now came the Northern victories of early 1865. These affected commercial transactions, as did "the rapid absorption of nearly $160,000,000 by the Government, mainly through the seven-thirty loans. . . ."[28]

By April the situation and economic factors remained in general unchanged. *Merchant's Magazine* recorded that "events of the most important historical character have since come to pass. . . . but none of them had any perceptible effect upon prices. . . . The daily life of the people is seen to throb with a pulse as regular as though it were passing through the most placid and peaceful portion of its history."[29] In other times far less striking occurrences had caused great cataclysms in trade and commerce; but nothing of the kind now happened in the Federal Union, which had apparently become somewhat inured to transient turbulence. Currency was the main agency used in moving Western Produce to coastal markets in the usual spring trade along the Atlantic; and in making government purchases. Subscriptions to the seven-thirty loan were termed "colossal" in May and the loan attracted more and more capital. Little concern was felt over the withdrawal of capital from industry for the loan, for expert opinion believed that would be replaced by foreign capital. In one day $40,000,000 was subscribed, and during the month ending May 14, 1865, subscriptions reached $300,000,000.[30]

The record of the prices of gold at New York is a primary barometer in

27. *Merchants' Magazine and Commercial Review*, Vol. LII, April, 1862, "Commercial Chronicle and Review," 287.
28. *Ibid.*, 288.
29. *Ibid.*, May, 1865, 380.
30. *Ibid.*, June, 1865, 444-445.

judging the financial conditions of these post-war days. From a high point in July, 1864, of 276-285, gold had dropped fairly steadily to a figure in May, 1865, of 128½-131¾. In the summer of 1865 a small rise occurred, with the price remaining in the mid-140s for the rest of the year and showing a firm post-war stability.[31] Another gauge used at that time was that of "treasure," i.e. gold especially held by the banks and the Sub-Treasury. By an early date in 1866, the condition in respect to this treasure was "one of unusual strength. The supply of gold held at the close of 1865 being thirteen million dollars larger than at the same period of any of the last seven years . . . ," declared the *Merchants' Magazine and Commercial Review.*[32]

The responsible *Merchants' Magazine* in the last half of 1865 mentions numerous factors affecting capital and the market such as Mexican complications, the exodus of Negroes from the South, state tax laws, greenback issues, the opening of communication with the South, as well as the changing political and economic scene. But there is no emphasis on the impact of demobilization.

By September, 1865, even fewer stirring events took place, and commercial activity seemed more stable. "It is less spasmodic in its modes of manifestations," stated the *Merchants' Magazine and Commercial Review.*[33] Economic activity was not lessened, however, and observers noted "we have the slower but infinitely more extensive, though less attractive, operations of a legitimate foreign commerce and domestic traffic." Crops were good this summer and fall of 1865, except for wheat, and a normal peacetime economy was taking hold. This did not mean, however, an unvarying market; "Change, incessant change, is the order of the day,"[34] declared the *Merchants' Magazine.*

Violent agitations affected the prices of many commodities except gold, such as the great politico-economic forces of the time, including the tariff, the expansion and contraction of the currency, the activities of the newly-reopened South, the emergence of hoarded capital at home as well as foreign capital. Leading price increases in all textiles, whiskey, and other liquors, played a part in the general shake-up.[35]

The clamor for resumption of specie payments was increasing in some circles and was certain to continue. The New York *Tribune* was one of the leaders in calling for resumption.[36]

That American finances were in a relatively healthy state is testified by Sir Morton Peto, who states that one of the most remarkable features of the war

31. *Annual Cyclopaedia,* 1865, Vol. V, New York, 1865, 346-347.
32. *Merchants' Magazine,* Vol. LIV, Feb. 1866, 98.
33. *Ibid.,* Vol. LIII, Sept. 1865, 224.
34. *Ibid.,* Oct. 1865, 306.
35. *Ibid.,* Vol. LIV, Feb. 1866, 123 and *passim.*
36. New York *Tribune,* October 23, 1865.

was "the marvellous sustentation of credit in the North, throughout the whole period of the rebellion."[37]

A favorable response by capital to the ending of the war was a cardinal necessity. Peto deplored the fact that when the Civil War threatened, British capital was diverted from the North, and loans were made to Austria, Greece, Turkey, and Egypt, not to mention the Confederacy. He felt that this was a gross mistake, for, as he wrote, what could those countries pay Britain "compared with what America can pay us, where in the course of a few months, the army has been restored to a peace establishment, and the navy has been converted into a commercial marine?" He urged putting British money into securities of a country now at peace rather than where countries "are perpetually threatening their neighbors, . . ." Knowing that considerable amounts of German capital had come into the North during the war, Peto deplored the fact that British capitalists did not take similar action. The fear that filibustering enterprises might be undertaken by some Americans worried the British economist, but he felt that the chances of this could be mitigated by a healthy American economy and affording "them no excuse for taking up arms in illegitimate and piratical enterprises."[38]

British capital certainly responded.[39] However, in the sixties railroads were the main interest of British capital in the United States. A flurried eruption of articles, pamphlets and short books appeared in Britain during the latter part of the war and just after the close, all intended to influence the foreign market.[40] However, balance of payments during the war and the immediate post-war years was adverse to the United States.[41] There seems to have been no major outflow of capital during the war, despite reports to the contrary.[42]

On the Federal level, President Johnson, like Lincoln, appears to have taken very little interest in finance, and possessed little experience in such matters. Financial affairs were left pretty much to the new Secretary of the Treasury, Hugh McCulloch, who had the support of many influential men, despite significant opposition to his policy of elimating greenbacks from the currency.[43]

37. Peto, op. cit., 3-4.
38. Ibid., 392-393, 401-403.
39. Jenks, Leland Hamilton, The Migration of British Capital to 1875, London, 1963, 426.
40. Hazard, R.G., Our Resources, a Series of Articles on the Financial and Political Condition of the United States, London, 1864, passim.; Walker, George, op.cit., passim.
41. Simon, Matthew, "The United States Balance of Payments, 1861-1900," Trends in the American Economy in the Nineteenth Century, op. cit., 699-700.
42. Historical Statistics of the United States, op.cit., 563.
43. Sherman, John, Recollections of the Forty Years in the House, Senate and Cabinet, Chicago, 1895, I, 384; McCulloch, Hugh, Men and Measures of Half-a-Century, New York, 1888, 377; Dunning, William Archibald, Reconstruction, Political and Economic, 1865-1877, New York, 136-137.

The war had been costly, especially when wartime disbursements were compared with the expeditures of the government in the pre-war years, and national deficits worried many. Total wartime costs were estimated to be over three billion dollars for both Army and Navy.[44]

Although taxation was undoubtedly burdensome, some patriotic business-men "not only *endured,* but welcomed the burdens which the great war effort imposed upon them."[45] The diffuse and overlapping wartime taxes were con-sidered a primary cause of the increase in prices and of reductions in produc-tion and consumption, according to the Federal Revenue Commissioners in their report for 1866. The government levied and collected from eight to fifteen percent, and even twenty percent, on most finished industrial products.[46] Thus, careful revision downward was needed to release the national economy from unnecessary and repressive restrictions.

Secretary of the Treasury McCulloch managed to reduce internal taxes, but made little progress in cutting tariffs.[47] Yet, despite the wide array of facts demonstrating both the strength and weakness in the financial situation, both of private citizens and of the government, it was undoubtedly the venturesome spirit, the expansive and confident drive for new sources of wealth, that carried the nation forward in many original and exciting fields of activity. Demobi-lized war veterans, along with countless other citizens, now flung themselves into a new and highly competitive, though more impersonally strenuous strug-gle, mobilizing themselves into corporations for personal gain.

[V]

The disbanding of the Northern military power brought considerably more with it than just the return of a million men to civilian life. The already badly stricken American carrying-trade was reduced to sad levels by 1865. The loss of scope and vigor in the nation's merchant marine had begun long before the Civil War. Restrictions and injuries brought about by the exigencies of the conflict hastened and intensified that decline to an almost disastrous extent.[48] Of the fifteen lines of sea-going steamers out of New York before the war, only three survived the conflict—one to Panama, one to Maine, and one to Cuba.

44. Dewey, Davis Rich, *Financial History of the United States,* New York, 1934, 299, 329-332, for an accurate general summary; "Report of the Secretary of the Treasury," December 4, 1865, *Cong. Globe,* 39th Cong., 1st Sess., Appendix, 39.

45. *Report of the United States Revenue Commission,* Treasury Dept., Washington, 1866, 19.

46. *Ibid.,* 19-20.

47. Dewey, *op.cit.,* 332, 340, 343, 395; Dunning, *op.cit.,* 136-142, for summaries.

48. Wells, David A., *Our Merchant Marine, How it Rose, Increased, Became Great, Declined and Decayed,* New York, 1890, 20-21.

During the war, it was estimated that some 600 American vessels transferred to the British flag alone, and that trade between the North and Europe
was placed almost wholly in the hands of foreigners, while trade to South
America and the Far East was in nearly as disadvantageous a situation.[49] A
leading trade journal stated in February, 1865: "It is a well known and not very
agreeable fact, that our foreign commerce has, during the last four years, been
conducted almost entirely under foreign flags . . . and unless some radical
measures are taken, even the return of peace will not be attended with the
immediate return of our lost commerce."[50] The writer further noted the obvious fact that if you multiply the means of communication, you increase trade.
He also called upon the government to use surplus naval ships as mail packets
to all parts of the world. Others were likewise alarmed; the *Scientific American*
in 1864 had bemoaned the fact that, "the American ocean-carrying-trade has
been almost destroyed for want of fast steamers: for if we had a sufficient
number of these they would bid defiance to the *Alabama* and all its conquerors,
and would have maintained our ocean trade in its integrity."[51] Editors of
another publication, writing in 1863, lamented: "In a war like the present, of
course every interest must suffer, and yet it seems strange that two or three
privateers should have been able to almost destroy our shipping interests."[52]
Certainly the highly publicized Confederate raiders had caused some destruction and much consternation in the American merchant fleet sailing to foreign
shores. The coastal fleet also had been sadly depleted by the needs of the
blockade, cutting off most shipping south of Maryland. All of these factors
increased maritime debilitation in the late sixties.

The Union Navy had actually preserved a considerable portion of the
merchant marine by its construction, purchase, and leasing of vessels for
various war purposes, as the army had done by its active management of its
transports. The return of these vessels to private ownership at very reasonable
prices was a great boon to the entire merchant marine. Men trained in the
shipyards during the war turned to the new ship-construction in 1865, although
rising wages hampered their activities. "The demand for steamships is more
active than it ever was," stated *Harper's Weekly* in the fall of 1865.[53]

The war was not yet fully over when the coastal trade, then a major part
of the entire marine business, began to revive, with passenger and freight
vessels leaving for Charleston and other ports. This trade was especially welcome to New York. "The close of the war, and the release of many new and

49. *Ibid.*
50. *American Railroad Journal,* Feb. 4, 1865.
51. *Scientific American,* Jan. 2, 1864, Vol. X, No. I, 9.
52. *Merchants' Magazine,* Dec., 1863, 435-439.
53. *Harper's Weekly,* Oct. 7, 1865.

finely equipped steamers from government service, have given our enterprising merchants ample opportunity to resume this great trade . . . and they have
embarked in the business with an enterprise and energy that demonstrate their
ability to successfully carry it on, and in a manner never before attempted.
. . .." Vessels were also being constructed in New York for the French and
Pacific trade.[54] Plans were well afoot, also, for American carriers on the North
Atlantic,[55] and coastal trade made a startling recovery, enhanced to a very
appreciable extent by the American Navy's sale of vessels.[56]

Among other valuable assets dumped on the general market by the government at the close of the war were horses and mules, frequent sales being held
in major cities.[57]

Of transcendent importance in restoring the country as a whole was the
improvement in communications by the telegraph. Telegraphic connections
were rapidly completed so that by early June, 1865, New York again had a
direct rapid communication link with New Orleans, Charleston and other
principal Southern cities.[58] In the middle of 1865, when the Great Eastern began
laying a cable across the Atlantic, widespread disappointment was felt when
it broke after about two-thirds of the line had been laid. Early attempts before
the war in 1857 and 1858 had failed, and a seemingly successful second effort in
1858 had operated less than a month. The failure in 1865, however, found
compensation in 1866 when a very effective cable linked Europe in almost
magical proximity with the eastern coast of the United States, and thence even
with the Pacific.

The story of the swift spread of our railroads with the efficiency of a great
spinning-machine, is a subject too large to explore in this study of the closing
of the great conflict. Moreover, the expansion of the railroads is well known.
Railroad construction which had been getting into full stride just before the
war had added a new dimension to war itself. Everyone foresaw that they
would be for decades by far the principal commercial carriers of the expanding
inland domain of the continent.

Capital was still absorbed in railroad financing during and after the war,
many plans being laid for new truck- and branch-lines, with fresh tunnels,
renovated equipment, and novel methods of operation.[59]

The efficiency and experience gained by railroad management and operation during the war was an invaluable legacy. The rapid movement of such

54. New York Tribune, July 4, 1865.
55. Harper's Weekly, Oct. 7, 1865.
56. Wells, op.cit., 23.
57. New York Tribune, July 18, 1865.
58. New York Herald, June 4, 1865.
59. Historical Statistics of the U.S., op.cit., 427.

large bodies of troops as Hooker's two corps from Virginia to the proximity of Chattanooga in the fall of 1863, shipment of Schofield's corps from the West to the East in 1864, and the steady transfer of smaller bodies of men, taught lessons in logistics that could be well applied to commercial activities. Huge quantities of supplies, picked up in various places, and moved about, involved new methods of freight handling that in peace would have taken years to learn. Skillful modes of repairing damaged track and equipment had been mastered of necessity, while need for uniform gauges, standard time, and a rapid interchange of cars, was emphasized by the war. In short, the country's railroad management had learned how to operate great lines swiftly and efficiently.

Wartime tests of equipment in service proved that new, larger, and more durable rolling-stock was needed. Iron rails were soon to be replaced by steel rails, the first being rolled by the Bessemer process in Chicago in May, 1865. In 1867, the Baldwin locomotive works, the nation's largest, were producing twelve steam engines of 25 to 38 tons apiece each month.[60] The use of horse-drawn street railroads, steadily developing before and during the war, was quickly enlarged in immediate postwar years.

Southern railroads, on the other hand, were in appalling condition by the end of the war. Whatever rolling stock still remained in use was worn and battered, many lines were heavily disrupted and almost all at least partially wrecked. Recovery took time, but the market for railroad equipment of all kinds was extremely high, and Northern capital soon became available to the dilapidated railroads of the South, as well as to the opening of the new West.[61]

[VI]

One of the principal sources of the general economic optimism prevalent in 1865 was a belief in the "Fountains of Wealth." The New York *Tribune* commented in October, 1865, upon the "tide of returning prosperity which now rolls across the country" and added, "we must not forget that wonderful legacy of nature to which we fell heirs at the beginning of the war; we mean the Petroleum fields." "Prince Petroleum," had become a recognized potentate creating a whole new industry which would soon dominate many others.[62]

Oil had created frenzied excitement and speculation during the last years of the war, but with peace, oil prices went down along with the value of oil stock. The New York *Tribune* warned its readers that well-managed money

60. Oberholtzer, Ellis Paxson, *A History of the United States Since the Civil War*, I, 240; Clark, Victor S., *History of Manufactures in the U.S.*, New York, 1929, II, 74.
61. Black, Robert C., III, *The Railroads of the Confederacy*, Chapel Hill, 1952, 289-293.
62. New York *Tribune*, July 12, Oct. 6, 1865.

should seek refuge in United States Securities, where it was safe, and should keep clear of speculations, particularly oil speculations. For two months after the war ordinary oil stocks were not worth carrying to market, but, during this time the oil regions had not been idle. Speculators, stated the *Tribune*, had been banished, but "the borers have been unremittingly at work." New wells appeared in the Pennsylvania fields, while others increased their output.[63]

By June, 1865, the oil fever appeared to have subsided, and no longer was there talk of paying off the national debt with petroleum profits, for immense sums of money had been lost through reckless over-speculation. Millions of dollars represented in paper shares, were swept out of existence.

Scientific American declared that "Nothing in the history of this country, if we except the furor that followed the opening of the gold fields of California, has caused so much excitement in business circles as the rapid development of the petroleum oil interests. There are oil stock exchanges, oil stock journals, and all the other appliances of regular commercial and financial operations. Oil cities even have sprung into existence, and speculation is running up to fever heat. . . ." Although many companies were substantial, caution in investing was advised to avoid losses.[64] A few speculators would get control of a patch of land in the oil region, and then try to sell a prodigious amount of stock, giving rich commissions for the sales. Productive value of the land may or may not have been hypothetical. "The stock speculative fever is now raging throughout the whole community to alarming degree—and when the reaction comes on, many an unfortunate dupe will suffer a most prostrating debility."[65] And the break in the oil bubble came in 1865. Abandoned wells and discarded machinery stood dolefully in the Pennsylvania fields.

But the market slowly rose as people made increased use of petroleum as an illuminant. The attractions which oil held for speculators and inventors would not cease to attract venturesome men and bold pioneers even though life in the oil fields was rough. One observer of the miracle of the Oil Creek branch of the Allegheny River stated: "A perplexing maze of derricks is woven thickly along both sides of the stream, from the banks to the bases of the hills. Engine-houses, shanties, offices, tanks, groceries, taverns, embryo villages, give the whole valley an air of activity which surrounds the machine-shops and manufactures of large cities. . . . Men on horseback and men on foot—hundreds of them throng the crooked ways or linger besides the derricks. . . ."[66] But although destructive fires and disastrous accidents were still common-

63. *Ibid.*, June 27, 1865; *Merchants' Magazine and Commercial Review*, Vol. 53, July 1865, 49; *Scientific American*, Jan. 2, 1865, Vol. XII, No. 1, 19.
64. *Scientific American*, Jan. 2, 1865, p. 8.
65. *Ibid.*
66. *Ibid.*, Mar. 25, 1865, 192.

place, the observer noted that speculation and recklessness were less serious.[67] The land value and the oil itself represented actual value, and these were soon to rise. The search for oil continued across the country from Pennsylvania until oil became a world-commodity, a vital force in the wartime and post-war scene.[68]

Meanwhile, the mineral fields of the West still beckoned men imperiously. The appetite for iron, the developing use of steel, the demand for railroads, ships, and a thousand other needed products and implements indicated that mining would face vigorous expansion and command a bright future. For example, although the precise statistics can be disputed, the production of gold and silver in the West in the year 1866 was said to exceed in value all the gold and silver in the national treasury plus all banks throughout the country.[69]

From the famous Comstock lode of Nevada, with its fluctuations at the close of the war, great fortunes were made and lost. A fall of fifty percent or a rise of two hundred percent in the market value of a large mine within the space of six months was a common occurrence.[70]

Industry and manufacturing in the North perhaps encountered the greatest post-war economic adjustment in all its facets, while in the South it had to undergo complete reconstruction. The sudden termination of war contracts was at first a severe blow to a number of manufacturing fields but most areas made the readjustment rather easily. Naturally those industries connected with armament were particularly hard hit, though there was still a demand for weapons in the post-war domestic life. And in spite of a large government surplus of gunpowder, companies like Remington, Sharp & Colt, and Winchester survived and prospered, while others, equally famous, disappeared.[71]

The famous muzzle-loading repeating Spencer rifle, known as the "Horizontal Shot-Tower" developed by tool-maker Christopher Miner Spencer now became a legend,[72] and Spencer turned to other interests.

As to industry in general, the war produced no startling changes in the location of industrial centers. During the immediate post-war years, New England continued to be a mighty, diversified manufacturing area. Textiles were restored to their near-normal balance as soon as cotton became available

67. *Ibid.*, Jan. 2, 1865, 19.
68. *Ibid.*, Jan. 2, 1865, 19; good summation is found in Oberholtzer, *op.cit.*, 249-266.
69. Browne, J. Ross and James W. Taylor, *Reports upon the Mineral Resources of the United States*, Washington, 1867, 9.
70. Browne and Taylor, *op.cit.*, 35.
71. Edwards, William B., *Civil War Guns*, Harrisburg, 1962, 158, 195-196; Winchester was really a war-born concern, taking its name in 1866 from the New Haven Arms Company. It had manufactured the well-liked Henry rifle, most of them sold privately to soldiers. Winchester went on to become a name familiar to all. Sharps and Colt also had a successful post-war career.
72. *Ibid.*, 156-157; Buckeridge, J.O., *Lincoln's Choice*, Harrisburg, Pa., 1956, *passim*.

in quantity once more. Manufacturing was stimulated in the mid-Atlantic and Great Lakes states. Philadelphia remained the leading center of manufacturing. Industries in upper New York State, Cincinnati, St. Louis and Chicago continued to develop after the war. The most accurate figures available show that the country's manufacturing product rose between 1860 and 1870 about 52 percent, nearly twice as rapidly as the population.[73]

Records were set in the great majority of industries during the five years after the war, the market for most products remaining high, sustained by some wartime shortages, demands of returning soldiers with their new activities, immigration, rebuilding in the South, and the westward movement. Because of lack of shipping, local needs and energies, the war had broken down whatever dependence had existed upon European manufacturing and had stimulated national industry. This was possible because the nation found it could simultaneously support a great war and a burgeoning civilian economy too.[74]

Feeling the stimulus of the Civil War, "iron and steel industries at once entered upon a period of extraordinary development." Blast-furnace procedures were revolutionized by more powerful blowing engines and improved hot-blast stoves, by larger furnaces, general use of bituminous coke and richer and purer ores, mainly from the Lake Superior region.[75]

Steel manufacture was in its infancy, but rapidly expanding into wider fields of usage. Production of all kinds of crude steel in the United States trebled from 1863 to 1866, the Bessemer process, invented in England in 1856, having at last begun to dominate steel-making.[76]

In other fields of manufacture changes were equally startling, some of them resulting from the influences of war. Development of machinery for making shoes and ready-made clothing persisted. Demand was tremendous, and while these innovations were bound to emerge sooner or later, the war certainly accelerated the production of daily necessities. Thus, Northern industry, generally immune to wartime damage, moved into the late sixties in a very healthy and energetic condition, with markets available, and capital, manpower and brains ample.

[VII]

The problems in the South were many. The war-torn section had a long, hard path to traverse before economic restoration and readjustment to peace

73. Clark, Victor S., *History of Manufactures in the United States, op.cit.*, II, 145-153, for summary.
74. For a summation see Nevins, *Emergence of Modern America*, Chap. II.
75. Swank, James M., *Notes and Comments on Industrial, Economic, Political, and Historical Subjects, American Iron and Steel Association from 1872 to 1897*, Philadelphia, 1897, 145-146.
76. Swank, James M., *History of the Manufacture of Iron in All Ages*, Philadelphia, 1892, 511.

would be complete. Conditions varied widely from Texas to Virginia; the states faced dissimilar problems, and the political aspects of Reconstruction were naturally affected by numerous economic difficulties. Most assuredly conditions were dismal enough, but it is easy to exaggerate their grimness.

The New York *Tribune*, for example, regarded the "bugaboos" of "Southern industry" as greatly exaggerated. It criticized journals that alleged the Negroes refused to work; that masters refused or were unable to employ them; that fields were standing idle and that danger of general famine threatened the section. These, declared the *Tribune*, "are gross and misleading exaggerations; while stories of Negroes crowding into the cities to die of famine, vice, exposure, and pestilence, are even worse. . . ." The *Tribune* contended that many Negroes stayed peaceably on the farm and plantation and went to work not for cash, but for a share of the crop. For the most part, except when they dealt with severe or unkind masters, the Negroes accepted employment with their former owners. The *Tribune* felt that the South would necessarily remain poor for the foreseeable future and should not revert to its old ways of buying luxuries from the North on credit. Meanwhile, it thought that crops were inevitably suffering for want of teams, livestock, and fences.[77]

While no one can give any accurate figures on the number of displaced Negroes who had left the plantation slave home to follow the armies or those who had gathered in the city, it does seem clear that the total of the uprooted came nowhere near the four-million Negroes who had been held in slavery.

Southern buyers in New York City did not lag far behind the Western customers in numbers during the early fall of 1865. "Notwithstanding all that has been said about the poverty of the South, purchasers from that section are arriving here in droves," declared *Harper's Weekly*, "and all seem able to pay for what they want." Of course, it added, "merchants are not over-anxious to sell on credit to the men who made the rebellion an excuse for cheating their Northern creditors. But everyone is willing to sell for cash; and this, or cotton, which amounts to the same thing, Southern buyers seem to possess to an amount entirely unexpected." Even in areas overrun by Sherman, trade was brisk, with cash and cotton abundant. No longer did buyers emphasize the luxury-trade of silks, laces, wines, and jewels. Now it was coarse dry goods and essential farm implements that they demanded. Furthermore, "The white trash, for the first time in history, are making themselves felt in the market," in place of rice planters and slaves who had vanished.[78] A bale of cotton in 1865 would buy fifteen barrels of flour instead of five. Another factor affecting trade was the large emigration from North to South by enterprising businessmen.

77. New York *Tribune*, July 4, 1865.
78. *Harper's Weekly*, Sept. 16, 1865.

Coastal passenger steamers before the war did a light trade, but now, at much higher passage fares, the steamers were full. The same fact was true respecting railroads running south through Ohio and Kentucky. Mechanics such as masons, carpenters, and bricklayers, were now commanding good wages. The work of common day-laborers was still assigned mainly to Negroes, and skilled labor was in such demand that a worker's market appeared. The need for rebuilding in the South was tremendous—and some of the people had the means for it in the form of cotton.

The year 1865 was a fairly good crop year, although yields were spotty. Wheat production fell below expectation in quality. However, as one authority put it, "So vast is the extent of the country . . . , and so varied its climate, that with our abundant and constantly multiplying means of communication, a deficiency of a particular crop in one section is readily made up by its excess, or at least abundance, in another."[79]

It was to cotton, however, that many minds turned even before the end of hostilities. Within a few days of Johnston's surrender Grant told commanders Schofield and Gilmore in the South: "Give every facility and encouragement to getting to market cotton and other Southern products. Let there be no seizure of private property or searching after Confederate cotton. The finances of the Country demand that all articles of export should be got to market as early as possible."[80]

Little new cotton was put in because planting time came just as the South was in the throes of surrender. Some planters, although late, did plow up young corn and plant cotton instead, hoping for a late frost.[81] Nevertheless, since cotton is a crop that does not deteriorate materially when stored for a reasonable length of time, it was not surprising that a large amount of old cotton came out of storage in time to make a good market.

[VIII]

The sudden surplus of manpower and energy released by the end of the war found an outlet apart from the normal life of the nation—in a great Westward surge. The press promoted this movement, enjoining returning soldiers to "turn their faces westward and colonize the public lands. Thanks to the beneficient policy of the Homestead Law, land is open to all. . . ."[82]

Many looked upon the American West as the nation's greatest resource. Sir

79. *American Annual Cyclopaedia*, 1865, 2-9.
80. Grant to Schofield and Gilmore, Ms., May 29, 1865, Ohio State Museum, Columbus.
81. New York *Tribune*, July 4, 1865.
82. New York *Tribune*, July 11, 1865.

Morton Peto, among others, felt that the resources of the United States were inexhaustible, and would insure prosperity.

Federal land policy offered advantages to the ex-soldier as well as to everyone else. The Homestead Act of May 20, 1862, made possible the ownership of a quarter section of land free-of-charge, except for filing fees, for any head of family who was over 21 and a citizen. An act of March 21, 1864, made it possible for men in the service whose family or a member of his family was residing on the land to make an affidavit to his commanding officer rather than having him file personally at the district land office.[83]

A new belt of wheat-farming had developed in Ohio, running west through Iowa, Missouri, Kansas, Nebraska, and Minnesota, enticing a host of veterans to rush there in time to prepare a crop for harvest in 1865. Others went into Wisconsin and Michigan, and this movement kept its momentum as it reached farther and farther into the West.

Western land, indeed, opened a new world of opportunity to the excess manpower, North and South, after the war. Without it, the absorption of thousands into the normal stream of life would have been much more difficult, or perhaps even impossible without severe economic dislocation.

83. *Congressional Globe*, 38th Cong., 1st Sess., Appendix, 149-150.

14

Toward a Mature Nation

FROM THE flame and ashes of the Civil War emerged, not instantaneously as in the Oriental fable, but slowly and gradually, a phoenix-like apparition— a new country, in the main a creation of evolution rather than revolution, its golden wings and feathers mingled with more familiar and time-tested adjuncts of flight and splendor.

The shock of the conflict had obscured the old gnomic sentiments on the irresistible destiny of the nation; had banished the idea that a shining new chariot could and would replace the heavy-laboring wagon of the past. The long years, seemingly endless, of loss, grief, and almost intolerable strain, had discouraged aspiration in thought and reflection.

Now succeeded a sense of release and relief. It was tinged with less exultation than men had anticipated; rather, it expressed simply a deep sense of happiness that the American people had regained their former sense of grandeur and beauty in their country—the sense that James Russell Lowell expressed in his exclamation, "Ours once more!"

As we have indicated, the changes of the Civil War period, like those which had overswept the country during the War of 1812, and the war with Mexico, sprang largely from internal forces that were not directly connected with the war itself. These included the westward movement that had marked American development from the infancy of New England in Plymouth, of Virginia and the Carolinas in Jamestown; they included the march of invention and technology from the time of Eli Whitney and Fulton and their ever-heightened application; they included also the diffusion of population, the increased productivity of agriculture, mining, and industry, and the accumulation of capital.

Such a war, like the classic Greek tragedy, which in some aspects it closely resembled, had a purgative value, clearing the mind of the nation, as it cleansed the bosom of the people of old prejudices, misunderstandings, and passions which would have yielded to no less powerful and painful a medicine.

The question whether the war was inevitable can never be settled, for our conclusion depends upon the positing and evaluation of too many mutable facts and forces. It is essentially a useless question, for its study involves too many vague and imponderable factors to permit of an answer. What is certain is that, inevitable or not, the war had become in the long period from Jackson to Buchanan a spiritual necessity for the healthy future of the American people. Once it was ended, the country could dismiss the ghastly struggle into its past, with a sense that it had been a necessity even if a cruel one, as other countries had been compelled to dismiss even more costly and anguishing wars as an integral incident of growth and reorientation. It could face the coming centuries with a lightened heart and fuller sense of freedom. This emotional gain might seem imponderable, but was actually far weightier than any ponderable result from the conflict. It was not to be expressed in statistics nor ledger balances; not, alas, in any music that came out of the war, nor in any major contemporary literary productions. Apart from a handful of verses—Herman Melville's "March into Virginia;" Walt Whitman's "When Lilacs Last in the Dooryard Bloomed," "Come Up from the Fields, Father," and "Cavalry Crossing a Ford;" H. H. Brownell's stanzas as quoted in Chapter 13; and Lowell's "Commemoration Ode"—a few bits of fiction, like Thomas Nelson Page's "Burial of the Guns", J. W. DeForest's *Miss Ravenel's Conversion from Secession to Loyalty*, and Ambrose Bierce's short tales—and Whitman's vivid prose recollections of ardors and endurances—the major literary performances inspired by the war were some of Lincoln's best letters (such as those to J. B. Conkling or Erastus Corning) and the President's Second Inaugural Address and his words at Gettysburg.

The republic emerged from the struggle, as men enjoying a little perspective of time later realized, in the grip of some heady new impulses of vast extent and irresistible force. One lay in the truly titanic impulse given to all enterprise in America by the rapid extension of the railroad and the telegraph throughout the continent; another lay in the discovery in every scenic reach, from the gold mines of Nevada to the oil fountains of Pennsylvania, of incalculable natural wealth; still another lay in the more and more unshakable confidence of the civilized world in the permanence of American institutions. Less obvious, but of enormous forcefulness, was the impetus to development lent by the availability of huge quantities of stored capital, which could no longer find a profitable employment in Europe, or safe investment in Asia, Africa, and other uneasy lands. This was added to the huge accumulations of capital already to be found in America in the hands of millionaires, mechanics, and all the intermediate men of property in the country. Of great significance in connection with this tidal flow of dollars and sterling was the fact that it could be used in America by groups which E.L. Godkin correctly termed, "the shrewdest and most indomitable speculators the world has ever seen."

All these forces in combination inevitably created an eager hunger for labor, attracting as by a gigantic magnet an inflow of workers, ranging from the skilled artisans of Britain and Germany to the uninstructed throng of pigtailed Chinese whose incourse excited alarm on the Pacific Coast. The importance of this avid national hunger for labor was the greater because the abolition of slavery had removed from America a great body of manual workers equipped for servile tasks, but without higher social ambition. And as immigration thus poured in, the throngs from the Shannon to the Vistula fed swelling towns and cities in another germinal movement the war had encouraged—that of urbanization. These six forces: first, the explosive expansion of communications; second, the discovery of new treasures of natural resources; third, the growing confidence of the civilized world in the perpetuity of the American political system and its social institutions; fourth, the accumulation of capital ready to be poured into the New World; fifth, the demand for labor; and sixth, the irresistible progress of urbanization, the movement of an always-mobile people from rural environments to the towns and cities, were creating a new America.

As a new and far-stronger nation thus emerged from the war, students at home and abroad searched earnestly for means of identifying the basic ideas and characteristics of the American people which might be deemed responsible for their irresistible and headlong emergence into a position of power, dominating the New World and gradually but surely outstripping nations and alliances of the Old World. These students recognized the error of Lord Macaulay in his famous letter predicting a future time of dire trial and turmoil for America. They measured the shortcomings of Tocqueville in his masterly book, *Democracy in America*, laying altogether too heavy an emphasis upon the egalitarian element in American life; they were ready to discount sharply the criticisms of men abroad and at home who had exaggerated the defects and shortcomings contributed to American society by the heavy immigration of the mid-century era. A surer and far more interesting analysis of the central force of American growth and character was supplied by E.L. Godkin, who, anticipating Frederick Jackson Turner, declared that the vigor and power of American life, unique in its philosophy and ideology, were rather to be connected with what he called "the frontier spirit" and cast of thought in America, as the frontier had moved westward from the Atlantic to the Rockies, and was still moving onward. The temper of pragmatic individualism in America had been partly inherited, and partly nurtured by environment as the pioneer folk engrossed their energies in dealing with raw nature and savage beasts and peoples. Godkin saw that the frontier was not so much conquered by the pioneer as made effective by conquering the pioneer, and imparting its tone and ethos to American life.

Probably the greatest single change in American civilization in the war period, directly connected with the conflict, was the replacement of an unorganized nation by a highly organized society—organized, that is, on a national scale. Various students had remarked before the war that the United States made organization an important goal and had striven toward it with marked success. But they perceived that organization was to a large extent local and regional in character, not yet national. The South, in especial, which was rural and in large part crudely developed, had been in 1860-61 as yet ineffectively organized.

Still lagging behind in this regard when Southern cannon opened against Sumter, the United States had frantically to pull itself together, raise armies East and West which ultimately reached nearly a million in numbers, to move them to the fighting fronts, and to throw them into battle; at the same time collecting a colossal and, for the New World, a totally unprecedented sum of money, about four billions of dollars. Meanwhile, it had to take steps to maintain the devotion and ardor of its people; it had, by gigantic industrial effort, to provide its armies with weapons and ammunition, ships and other armaments; it had to build and sustain railroads in campaign areas behind the lines; it had to furnish pontoon bridges, balloons, telegraphs and hospitals with the latest equipment; for the first time it had to make Herculean exertions in the field of welfare; to pay pensions to disabled and ill veterans; to maintain the families of soldiers called to the front; and to take care of widows, orphans and other dependents. All this required a degree of organization that the country had never before contemplated.

Even the South had its special achievements in the field of organization, such as the work of the Mining and Nitre Bureau, the Quartermaster's Office, and other services of supply. The growth of organization in the South would be better understood if prompt and comprehensive attention had been given to the subject in Southern memoirs and monographic histories, and if records of the bureaus mentioned had been better preserved. The unfortunate nature of the gap left by neglect of the subject is briefly noted by Douglas Freeman in his volume, *The South to Posterity: An Introduction to the Writing of Confederate History.* Unhappily, only by groping among manuscript letters, autobiographies, and in the 128 volumes of the *Official Records of the Union and Confederate Armies,* can some of the requisite information be obtained. Meanwhile, one of the saddest chapters of Southern history is the counter-record of disorganization written by the overwhelming array of refugees, including fighters, prisoners, deserters, demobilized veterans, and displaced Negroes who, by hundreds of thousands, swept back and forth during the war over the whole terrain between the Canadian line and the Gulf. At times, as when Sherman ordered noncombatants out of Atlanta, and Beauregard bade much of the civil population leave Charleston, a whole city seemed to join the despairing concourse of refugees.

The war, beginning so suddenly and unexpectedly for many, and conducted with innumerable mischances and startling developments unforeseen even by the most astute, proved far more protracted than anyone had expected. At the outset, many men had predicted that it would end within weeks. Numerous Southerners had expected and even boasted that secession would bring about a process of negotiation between Northerners and Southerners that would end in the grant to the seceding States of terms for a continuance of national life in a renovated Union, in which the States would find guarantees of a better position and a more amicable nation. Many Northerners, underrating Southern fighting-power, had believed that a few battles might decide the contest and bring peace. Instead, the war proved a contest not in valor, quickly mobilized bodies of troops, or strategic skill, so much as a contest in Spartan endurance—as did the first World War. The requirement of stoicism, which tried national and sectional character to the utmost, tested the institutions of the two peoples even more searchingly.

Most important of all, the prolonged duration of the conflict produced results in the thought, feeling and practises of the people proportionate to its length and multi-faceted force. At its end, Americans who looked about for its consequences, good and bad, found plenty of both. Some were elementary and superficial, such as the firm knotting of the Union tie, and the shattering of the many glaring myths which had marked Southern thought and conduct. And some of the most striking and obvious of the elementary consequences were written into the new Thirteenth, Fourteenth, and Fifteenth Amendments to the Constitution, which in effect constituted the terms of a treaty of peace between North and South, and had all the effect of a far-reaching and adamantine compact.

One prime result was a better understanding by the people of the nation of the true character of the huge American continent, so variegated, so radiantly beautiful, so well-stored with aesthetic as well as economic wealth. By tens and hundreds of thousands, American farm-boys, mill-hands and clerks had moved across prairie, mountain, lake or coastal beaches, from Iowa grain fields or Indiana prairies to the Carolina headlands; those who remained home had read of these diverse geographic expanses in thousands of newspaper columns.

How rich in new experiences of nature was this war! Many a Yankee or Western lad had fancied he knew all about nature. Nevertheless, he would never forget the totally new rapture he felt as he and his comrades broke camp one frosty morning on a long march; as he experienced with clearer senses than ever before the warming light of the sunshine, and saw with sharper vision than in past days the beauty of the dawn, throwing rose-tints into the trees overhead; as he happily felt the comradeship of lines of young men falling in unison into light, springy step. In many a Grand Army gathering he would later recall with delight the youthful exertions of campaigning as in some novel countryside he strode down a dew-spangled slope, or, turning another of nature's pages, inhaled the unaccustomed perfume of pine boughs stretching over tansy-beds in the Great Smokies. He might recall a glimpse of distant goldenrod-clad vistas in Virginia, Ohio, or Tennessee; or, as recruits met a more laborious challenge, the fatigue of city volunteers in struggling through the viscid dampness of sloughs of gumbo mud in Missouri that gripped their army brogans like the hydras of Asia Minor clinging to Xenophon's exhausted Greeks; or the delight of hungry marchers as, in the gleam of new campfires, they sensed the sound and aroma of saltpork frying in a treasured camp-pan over a glowing trench.

For the first time, thousands of troops realized that the long panhandle of Virginia stretched northward over stony crags and dales almost to the gleam of the Great Lakes. But it was not the new land alone, from the chugging steamers on the Yazoo and the moss-draped oaks of Florida to the sandy capes above Wilmington that were a novel revelation to millions of Americans. New continents in psychology and manners were also explored as troops gained a better understanding of the land and its natural life; the wandering armies achieved a fuller comprehension of the intellectual, emotional, and aesthetic variegations of life in a population which could produce a fiery Rhett at one extreme of thought, and a morosely egotistical Sumner at the other. The war, to hundreds of thousands, unlocked an understanding of the intellectual, psychological, and artistic wealth of talent increasingly available to the people of the land, and of their ever-growing achievements.

Another profoundly important moral sequel of the Civil War, which originated during the conflict, was the enlargement and liberalization of attitudes toward the Negro, both North and South. No reflective American could doubt that, as Reconstruction began, the problem of race relations was not only still one of the greatest, but the most urgent, that the country faced. No thoughtful man who had seen anything of plantation life or freedmen's camps could doubt that both sections would have sooner or later to discharge old prejudices and antiquated varieties of ignorance. It was plain, also, after Appomattox and the new Amendments, that this complicated and difficult problem, full of social, economic and political implications, would have to be solved on a national basis, overriding local, sectional and political limitations; and that a solution would have to make use of the latest scientific findings in every sphere, dispelling the dark miasmas of ignorance and prejudice. The most important, tenacious, and morally and socially mischievous of the many expressions of stupidity and bias was the belief held widely in the North, and almost universally in the South and borderland, that the Negro required a special position and treatment because of congenital inferiority; because he was, as even a friend put it, "lower in the scale of development than the white man, his inferiority being rooted and inherent." This postulate respecting Negro inferiority was reinforced by a misreading of Darwin and writers on anthropology. It was reinforced also by a historical sensitivity of many Southerners. They had cultivated the myth that women held a specially exalted status in Southern society and thought. It was natural for many to believe that this myth justified the South in throwing special protections about women, and that loyalty to the heroic memories of the Southern people called for a perpetuation of the myth as one relic of the Confederacy that could be preserved. This attitude played its part in the erection of a defensive shield even around such a flagrant wrong to all people of the South—both white and black—as lynching. Yet, here and there in the South, the war was quickly followed, if not accompanied, by a change in racial attitudes, and by the emergence in some areas of individuals and groups demanding "a reasonable and responsible program of action." Ferments were at work which were to bring forward such courageous men as John Spencer Bassett of Trinity College, later Duke University in North Carolina, and Andrew Sledd, a Methodist minister and teacher of Latin at Emory College in Georgia.

It is not strange that the *Atlantic Monthly* from 1900 through 1905 should publish seventy-two articles dealing with the race problem. But it is strange that only one of the seventy-two articles should depart from the "Southern" point of view in its treatment. This was the article by Andrew Sledd in the *Atlantic* for July, 1902, entitled, "The Negro, Another View." As Henry W. Warnock writes, it not only repudiated the natural-inferiority assumption but implied, in a caustic account of the intolerable condition of the Negroes, that black people should be treated courteously on the streets, and allowed to use waiting-rooms, restaurants, and hotels on the same basis as white people.

The Civil War had brought the country emancipation from slavery, an institution deeply harmful to the white and the black alike, and the 14th Amendment had brought the beginnings of a too-long-deferred acceptance of the principle of equality. But America had fallen in important respects behind

Russia. When Tzar Alexander II freed the serfs, or land-ascribed peasants, in 1861, the serfs were granted sharply limited allotments of land. Serf-emancipation was but part of a larger program of legal and consequently social equality, to which the Tzar, in assuming his throne as the Crimean War ended, had announced the adherence of his government. That program deserved American study, both countries being rich in numerous varieties of class-consciousness and tyranny.

The Southern type of slavery, and the segregation on which it was based, tended, as Frederick Olmsted had observed, to bring Negroes toward equality with domestic animals. But wartime experience had done more to implant the beginnings of a new order than many at first realized. The United States had a complex society that was certain to become more and more pluralistic. In this society, equality must be religious, political and racial. Wartime experience had taught some previously doubtful or indifferent men much-needed lessons on the benefits the Negroes could give the country through their warm appreciation for music, which some developed into a passion; through their social responsiveness to friendly people of all kinds, and through their emotional spontaneity. Many Northerners came to believe that, although the retarding effects of servitude might last for a number of years, they could be alleviated or largely abolished by education. Hence, the zeal with which many Abolitionists flung themselves into educational work both under and outside the Freedmen's Bureau.

A significant myth exploded by the war was the belief of great numbers of men, North and South, that abolition of slavery would in effect mean the destruction or confiscation of a great part of the wealth of the Southern people. On the contrary, within a quarter-century it was abundantly evident that the Southern people prospered much more generously and completely from the labor of the liberated Negroes as freedmen than it could ever have prospered from their assistance as slaves. As men looked about them in 1865 and later, the fact became plain that the abolition of slavery, while terminating an infectious national malignancy, did not reduce the wealth or income of the South. This fact was irrefutably evident by 1884, the year of Cleveland's election, when a Republican alarmist of the South, a prominent Southern plantation owner, wrote in the *Nation* that even if such a step as the restoration of slavery would be tolerable to the North, it would be overwhelmingly defeated if put to popular vote in the South. For "the labor of the Negro, once held as property by a small class, has now become a source of profit to a much larger one, and generally one that never owned, or would have owned one under the old system, or would ever have been the employer of labor at all; a class, too, in whose hands the labor of the Negro, since emancipation, has been much more profitable than to his former owners. Those and others equally interested in Negro freedom would trample any effort at curtailment of freedom under foot at the polls."

The Negro's eagerness for education was pathetic. Although the hopes of some white workers were inflated and patronizing, other men under General Rufus Saxton held realistic ideas. As education increased the number of well-informed Americans, especially in the cities, responsiveness to the Negro and sympathy with his elevation increased. During the war, 178,185 Negroes are recorded as having served in Union armies. They served well, making good soldiers, on the march, in camp, and in battle. They were somewhat more dependent upon white officers than the white troops, but in other respects not essentially different. One entire corps, General Weitzel's Twenty-fifth Corps, was all black, except for its officers.

As succeeding generations after Appomattox studied the history of the war, they had to conclude that in valor the two sides were equally matched. If it was a Northern statesman who extolled the fighters who gave "the last full measure of devotion," it was a Southern poet who, with a heart too full after the death of Pelham to bear the sound of a funeral dirge played by a band, exclaimed: "The living are brave and noble, but the dead were the bravest of all." It is impossible to read unmoved the long lists of soldier-dead in newspaper columns or regimental histories, each with its curt line, "Killed in Battle at Gettysburg," or "Died from Wounds at Dallas, Ga.," and there comes at once to mind John Masefield's challenging lines written of World War I, "The Sinister Spirit said, 'It had to be.' But still, the Spirit of Pity whispered, 'Why?' "

The war more or less directly affected every one of the 35,000,000 men, women, and children in the two sections, Northern and Southern, of the United States. It happily exploded many suppositions that Americans had long held and dreaded as probable results of a stubborn conflict. For example, it totally failed to leave the country a heritage of military ideas, traditions, and impulses, which some had feared. It did not in the least "militarize" the people as various pacifists had anticipated. The best proof of this fact did not lie in the fact that it failed to lead to adventures in foreign conquest, overseas interventions, or filibustering forays, which would have been totally uncharacteristic of the American character. Proof rather lay in the fact that, when Reconstruction came, although one broad course of policy in treating the defeated and restless Southern States was certainly open and many thought inviting, the policy of holding these States in subjugation as territories policed to maintain peace and protect the freedmen in their new rights was never adopted, and was barely approached by the Military Reconstruction Act. On the contrary, the opposed policy was chosen of readmitting the Southern States, while the army was being disbanded, to equal membership in the Union. The military policy would have been a death-knell for the political system which the American people, under wise leadership, had inaugurated in 1789, and which had since then been the admiration of the civilized world. The peaceful policy proved an unassailable success to both North and South, to black and white alike, and vindicated the whole purpose of the founders of the Republic and the men who, from Hamilton and Jefferson to Lincoln, had maintained it. The spirit of the republic in the year of victory was good. It was not boastful or arrogant, for repeated checks and defeats had taught lessons of humility. No outburst of militaristic feeling occurred. Wendell Phillips declared in a speech in Boston that the old farming and reading republic was at an end, and that a strong military and predatory nation might take its place; but he was completely mistaken.

The prevalent foreign criticism of American civilization for decades had been that the republic was the land of the commonplace, and that its democracy inevitably gave emphasis to a code favoring the mediocre average—that its life tended to be dull. One foreign visitor after another touched this chord of criticism, until James Russell Lowell voiced American resentment in his essay "On a Certain Condescension in Foreigners." But Americans were not wont to give way either to bursts of petulance or displays of braggadocio. Their characteristic mood was that of Walt Whitman's "Song of the Banner at Daybreak," a mystical chant over a banner of effort and labor, not of war. His vision was of a land ever higher, stronger, and broader. Americans were well aware that what their land most lacked was high excellence, and distinction.

The United States in the year of Appomattox was a country without a single true university, without any art gallery of wide scope and true eminence, with but few museums of merit in any field (although Natural History was beginning to assert its claims to attention), and with no well-organized library that would satisfy both general students and specialists. The colleges in the State of North Carolina did not offer a single course in English literature worthy of the name. The many and glaring cultural deficiencies of the country were just beginning to receive the attention they demanded. New books were much too few in number, and too poor. The *American Publisher's Circular* listed only 681 works issued in the United States in the second half of 1865 (July 6 through December); and the New York *Nation* thought that only about 140 of them were really substantial books. More distressing than quantitative poverty, however, was the poor quality of American letters during this half-year. The only important volumes of poetry were Walt Whitman's *Drum Taps*, which included "When Lilacs Last in the Dooryard Bloomed," commonly esteemed his greatest single poem; and H.H. Brownell's small book of war verse, which Theodore Roosevelt later praised for its spirited celebrations of the "River Fight" before New Orleans, and the "Bay Fight" before Mobile. In literary criticism Richard Grant White produced some studies of Shakespeare that merited attention. Various chronicles of the war came out, but the writer was correct who asserted that to call them histories would be an abuse of the language. One novel of quality appeared, Elizabeth Stoddard's *Two Men*, and one estimable work of theology, Horace Bushnell's *Vicarious Sacrifice*. In general, however, the crowning year of the war was relatively barren in American letters.

Thoughtful Americans knew well that the pursuit of distinction by production of highly superior works of art, music, and letters, is still more eagerly competitive in democratic than aristocratic societies, other avenues to preëminence being closed. They knew that in a young and struggling and long-impoverished country, the principal prerequisites to the production of real excellence included time, leisure, accumulations of materials of study, the collection of high models, and the clash of active minds in a stimulating environment. They knew that, young and strenuously preoccupied with imperative material tasks as the United States had been, it was already yielding to the world's gaze examples of high excellence, with gleams of distinction that held rare qualities of inspiration. They knew that every year added to the list. One of the many touches of distinction that began to appear in the American scene lay in the vigorous estate of the American Oriental Society, under a president, S. Wells Williams, who stood as high as any other scholar in the world in opening a knowledge of China, the Chinese language, and Chinese letters to the Occident. He had accompanied Commodore Perry as interpreter on his expedition of 1853-54 to Japan; had become secretary and interpreter to the American Legation in China, remaining at that post until 1876; had helped negotiate important treaties; and had become professor of the Chinese language and literature in Yale (1877), writing books of preëminent merit on China and her culture.

The generation of men which read with excited astonishment about the revelations of the ancient past, made by Schliemann in his excavations at the sites of Troy and Mycenae, found equal astonishment and excitement in the revelation of wonders in the Far West as Othniel Charles Marsh built up palaeonto-logical collections in Washington and at Yale of equal significance to the extension of human knowledge.

America had long been a nation of dauntless explorers, and inventive pragmatists. Much of distinction in American life now logically found varied practical expressions, and the mechanical field admitted as high endeavors as any area of the arts and letters. Distinction was given a striking new opening, for example, when the Civil War called young Henry M. Leland, an ardent volunteer in the excitement after Sumter, into government service as a machinist in the Crompton Works in Worcester, Mass., making the Blanchard lathe for turning gun-stocks. In Eli Whitney's day in America, uniformity of machine parts had been brought to the one-hundred-thirty-second part of an inch, after which much filing was required to make machine-joints even.

This would not do. By the labors of artisans such as Leland, precision of machine tools—the cutters, borers, and milling-machines which made the parts of a final mechanism before they were assembled—was steadily improved until uniformity was brought to one-half-thousandth part of an inch. No truer artist was to be found in any land than Blanchard, the lathe-maker, or Leland, the finisher of gauges, jigs, cutters, borers, and other tools that contributed to the development of what men in time called "American industry," preëminent for the combination of delicacy, precision, and adaptability to quantity-manufacture. No truer artists existed in the world than Joseph R. Brown, a clockmaker by origin, who in 1851 introduced the Vernier Caliper, able to make measurements to one-thousandth of an inch.

For all the general poverty of the American cultural scene by the end of the war, it had some aspects of undeniable distinction. Among scholars and writers of high international repute in 1865, the roster included Henry C. Lea, who, already known for his historical articles, published his volume, *Superstition and Force*, in 1866; Frances Parkman, who brought out his *Pioneers of France in the New World* in 1865, and Adolf F. Bandelier, who knew more about Mexican antiquities than any other scholar in Europe or the Americas. A.F. Hall, who had spent years in England studying Sanskrit, Hindustani and Indian jurisprudence, was equally distinguished; Charles F. Peirce, mathematician and philosopher, would have done honor to any country. So would the greatest champion of scientific studies in America, Louis Agassiz, who was laboring along a wide front, his activities respected abroad as well as at home. We find Emerson writing in his journal for March 26, 1864, in the grimmest days of the war, that Agassiz had just returned to Boston from a lecture tour, having created a Natural History Society in Chicago for which 19 persons had subscribed $4,500. Agassiz, with equal enterprise, also took steps to create the Harvard University Museum where he was a pioneer who loved to embark upon costly undertakings with no apparent means of carrying them through —usually with success. William James later summed up his career as that of "a leader who lived from month to month and year to year with no relation to prudence, but on the whole, achieved his aims, studied the geology and fauna of our continent, trained a generation of scientists, founded one of the chief museums of the world, gave a new impetus to scientific education in America, and died the idol of the public."

Another heartening fact was that, with the triumphant close of the war, the American people began to realize that they had larger destinies than those of a purely national character. In 1865 they learned that Mazzini had written the London agent of the Sanitary Commission that the United States had done more in four years for the cause of Republicanism than had been accomplished in Europe in fifty years of discussion. Mazzini added that her task had hitherto been that of self-realization, of vindicating within her own boundaries the ideals that she had erected before herself, the abolition of slavery being her last main achievement. Now she faced a larger body of duties, for the republic must turn from responsibilities that were merely American to purposes of a cosmopolitan and international character. Mazzini hoped she would now assume the leadership in the stern battle rising in all lands between tyranny and liberty, between privilege and equality, furnishing sympathy, moral encouragement, and the support of a successful, enduring, republican society, consistent in all its aims.

The sense of Americans in 1865 that they stood at the close of one era and the beginning of another, a sense which gave millions a new hopefulness and a more convinced belief in the national destiny, was confirmed and strengthened by the evident fact that the perspective of all mankind had been sharply and decisively revolutionized by Union victory in the war. To multitudes the world lost its constricted and limited appearance, and wore a new freshness. It was suddenly evident to the American people that the United States had swiftly and unexpectedly, but undeniably, become one of the principal world powers, with a new set of responsibilities, challenges, and opportunities.

BIBLIOGRAPHY

MANUSCRIPT SOURCES

The author specially thanks Mrs. Pierre Jay for access to the papers of Robert Gould Shaw, and Robert D. Meade for use of the Judah P. Benjamin Papers, as well as Mrs. August Belmont for use of the August Belmont Papers. He thanks E. B. Long, and many others who have supplied transcripts of valuable documents.

In this list, and in the footnote citations throughout the text, the following abbreviations have been employed:

ASA – Alabama State Archives
CHS – Chicago Historical Society
CMLS – Confederate Memorial Literary Society
CUL – Columbia University Library
DU – Duke University
HEH – Henry E. Huntington Library
HSP – Historical Society of Pennsylvania
IHS – Illinois State Historical Society
KHS – Kansas Historical Society
LC – Library of Congress
LSU – Louisiana State University Library
MHS – Massachusetts Historical Society
NA – National Archives
NYHS – New York Historical Society
NYPL – New York Public Library
OHS – Ohio Historical Society
UCLA – University of California, Los Angeles
UNC – University of North Carolina Library
VHS – Virginia Historical Society

MANUSCRIPT COLLECTIONS

Alcorn, James L. Papers, UNC
Allan, Col. William Collection, UNC
Andrew, John A. Papers, MHS
Armstrong-Loring Papers, Private Collection, Oak Park, Ill.
Atwater, M.B., Ms. Reminiscences, State Hist. Soc. of Wisconsin
Babcock, Orville Papers, CHS
Banks, General Nathaniel P. Papers, LC
Barlow, S.L.M. Papers, HEH
Barney, Hiram Papers, HEH
Bates, David Homer Papers, Stern Collection, LC
Belmont, August Papers (Mrs. August Belmont, New York)
Benjamin, Judah P. Papers (Courtesy Robert D. Meade)
Blair-Lee Papers, Princeton University Library
Boynton, H.B. Papers, NYPL
Brayman, Mason Papers, CHS

British Foreign Office Correspondence, London
Broadhead, James O. Papers, Missouri Historical Society
Brooks, Noah Papers, LC
Brown, Campbell Collection, UNC
Brown, Rev. Gustavus Papers, VHS
Bryant, William Cullen Papers, NYPL
Buchanan, James Papers, HSP
Campbell-Colston Papers, UNC
Chandler, Zachariah Papers, LC
Chase, Salmon P. Collection, HSP
Clay, Clement Papers, LC
Collier, Elizabeth, Diary, UNC
Comstock Papers, LC
Connolly, Major James Austin, Letters, IHS
Coppet, Andre de Collection, Princeton University Library
Cram, George F. Papers, Armstrong Collection, Elmhurst, Ill.
Crampton, Capt. Ben Papers, Maryland Hist. Soc., Baltimore
Curry, J.L.M. Papers, ASA; LC
Dana, Charles A. Papers, LC
Davidson, James I. Papers, ASA
Davis, David Papers, IHS
Davis, Henry Winter Papers, Eleutherian Mills Hagley Foundation, Wilmington, Del.
Davis, Jefferson Papers, DU; CMLS, Richmond
Davis-Reagan Papers, Dallas Hist. Soc.
De Bow, J.D.B. Papers, DU
De Leon, T.C. Papers, South Caroliniana Library
Dodge, Grenville M. Papers, Iowa State Hist. Soc.
Dodge, Theodore A. Papers, LC
Doolittle Papers, State Hist. Soc. of Wisconsin
DuPont, H.A. Papers, Eleutherian Mills Hagley Foundation, Wilmington, Del.
Eldredge Collection, HEH
Eustis, George Papers, LC
Forbes Papers, MHS
Fox, G.V. Papers, NYHS
Gale-Polk Papers, UNC
Gardiner, E.C. Papers, HSP
Garland, Hamlin Papers, UCLA
Gay, S.H. Papers, CUL
Gettysburg College Civil War Papers, Gettysburg, Pa.
Gilpin, E.N., Diary, LC
Gladstone Papers, British Museum
Grant, Ulysses S. Papers, IHS; OHS, Columbus, O.
Grant-Halleck Papers, Eldredge Collection, HEH
Grant Notebook, Rosenbach Foundation, Philadelphia
Harding, Sidney, Ms. Diary, LSU
Harrington, George Papers, Missouri Hist. Soc.
Harrison, Benjamin Papers, LC
Hatch, O.M. Papers, IHS
Hay, John Papers, IHS
Heintzelman, Samuel P., Ms. Diary, LC
Hill, D.H. Papers, VHS
Historical Records Survey, Civil War Letters, Records of Middle Tenn.

Hotchkiss, Maj. Jed. Manuscript and Map Collection, LC
House Executive Documents, Washington, D.C.
Howard, Oliver Otis Papers, Bowdoin College Library
Jones, Joseph Russell Papers, CHS
Judge Advocate General Record Books, NA
Keitt, Laurence M. Papers, DU
King, Rufus and Mary Papers, Indiana Univ. Library
LeDuc, William G., Memoirs, HEH
Lee, Robert E. Papers, LC; VHS
Leet, Edwin Papers, LSU
Letcher, John Papers, VHS
Lieber, Francis Papers, HEH
Lightfoot, Emmie Crump, Letters, CMLS
Lincoln, Robert Todd Papers, LC
Long, E.B. Collection Civil War Letters and Mss., Oak Park, Ill.
Mackall Papers, UNC
Madigan, Thomas F., Catalogue of Papers
Mallory, S.R., Diary, UNC
Manipault, Arthur M., Ms. Memoirs, UNC
Marble, Manton Papers, LC
McClernand, Gen. John A. Papers, IHS
McKee, R.M. Papers, ASA
Meade, Gen. George G. Papers, HSP
Meigs, Montgomery C. Papers, LC
Memminger, C.G. Papers, UNC
Meredith, Roy Papers, HSP
Military Historical Society of Massachusetts Papers, Boston
Miller, T.D., Letterbook, C.S.A. Agent, LSU
Moody, Joseph E., Mss. Palmer Collection, Western Reserve Hist. Assoc.
Mordecai, Emma Papers, CMLS
Morgan, E.D. Papers, NYHS, State Library
Morrill, Lot M. Papers, Univ. of Maine, Brunswick, Maine
Morris-Sidley Papers, LSU
Murdock, Eugene C., Ms. "Patriotism Limited," OHS
Nicolay and Hay Papers, IHS
Oral History Collections, CUL
Palfrey, John C. Papers, Military Hist. Soc. of Mass., Boston
Palmer, John M. Papers, IHS
Palmer Collection Civil War Papers, Western Reserve Hist. Soc.
Papers Relating to Treaty of Washington, LC
Parsons, Lewis B. Papers, IHS
Pemberton, John C. Papers, NYPL
Pettus, J.J. Papers, Alabama and Mississippi State Archives
Pickens-Bonham Papers, LC (Petitions of S.C. Negroes)
Pickett, George E. Papers, DU
Porter, Albert Quincy, Diary, Mississippi Archives, Jackson, Miss.
Prescott, Albert H. Papers, HEH
Provost-Marshal General's Records, NA
Quartermaster General's Miscellaneous Letters, LC
Rawlins, John A. Papers, CHS
Records of Relief Commission, CHS
Register of Letters Received, War Records, NA

Reynolds, T.C. Papers, LC
Robinson, Capt. William Culbertson Papers, IHS
Rosecrans, Gen. William S. Papers, UCLA
Royal Engineers Professional Papers, British War Office, London
St. John, Gen. I.M. Papers, NA
Schurz, Carl Papers, State Hist. Soc. of Wisconsin
Secretary of the Interior Reports, Washington
Secretary of the Navy Reports, Washington
Seward, William H. Papers, LC; Univ. of Rochester, N.Y.
Sharp, Henry T. Papers, UNC
Shaw, Robert Gould Papers (Property of Mrs. Pierre Jay)
Sherman, William T. Papers, LC; (Nicholson Collection) HEH; IHS; J.P. Morgan Library, New
    York; Houghton Library, Harvard Univ.
Shreve, George W., Ms. Reminiscences, Virginia State Library, Richmond
Smith, E. Kirby Papers, UNC
Smith, W.H. Papers, OHS
Southern Historical Collection, UNC
Southern Historical Society Papers, NA
Special Agents' Reports and Correspondence, *Censuses of 1860*, NA
Stanton, Edwin M. Papers, LC
Stearns, George L. Papers, KHS
Stephens, Alexander H. Papers, Manhattanville College, N.Y.
Stiles, Joseph Clay Papers, HEH
Sublett, Emmie Papers, CMLS
Tarbell, Ida Collection, Allegheny College
Trescot, William H. Papers, South Caroliniana Library
Trumbull, Lyman Papers, LC
Valentine Family Letters, Valentine Museum, Richmond, Va.
War Papers (1893), San Francisco Archives
Washburne, Elihu Papers, LC
Welles, Gideon Papers, LC; Brown Univ., Providence, R.I.
Wigfall, Louis T. Papers, Univ. of Texas Library
Wilson, J.H. Papers, LC
Wise, Henry A. Papers, UNC
Wood, Capt. John Taylor, Diary, UNC
Woodman, Horatio Papers, MHS
Yancey, William L. Papers, ASA

NEWSPAPERS AND PERIODICALS

Abraham Lincoln Quarterly
Agricultural History
Alabama Historical Quarterly
Alabama Review
Albany *Evening Journal*
Albany *Evening Journal Almanac*
American Historical Review
American Iron and Steel Association Reports
American Journal of Pharmacy
American Pharmaceutical Association Proceedings
American Railroad Journal
Army and Navy Gazette

Atlanta *Daily Herald*
Atlantic Monthly
Bankers' Magazine
Belvidere, Illinois *Daily Review*
Boston *Advertiser*
Boston Board of Trade—Annual Reports
Boston *Commonwealth*
Boston *Transcript*
Bugle Horn of Liberty (Georgia)
Bulletin of Business Historical Society
Century Magazine
Charleston *Courier*
Charleston *News*
Chicago *Morning Post*
Chicago *Tribune*
Cincinnati Chamber of Commerce and Merchants Exchange Annual Reports
Cincinnati *Commercial*
Cincinnati *Daily Gazette*
Civil War History
Commercial and Financial Chronicle
Confederate Inflation Charts
Congressional *Globe*
Contemporaries, Boston
The Country Gentleman
Cultivator Magazine
Genesee Farmer
Harper's Weekly Magazine
Harrisburg, Pa. *Daily Telegraph*
Hartford *Press*
Hartford *Times*
Historical Statistics of the United States, Washington, D.C.
Hunt's Merchant's Magazine and Commercial Review
L'Indépendence Belge
Journal des Débats, Paris
Journal of the Congress of the Confederate States of America, Washington, D.C.
Journal of Negro History
Journal of the Royal United Service Institution
Journal of Southern History
Kansas Historical Quarterly
Le Pays, Paris
Frank Leslie's Illustrated Newspaper
Lincoln Herald
Lincoln Lore
Abraham Lincoln Quarterly
London Daily News
London Illustrated News
London Saturday Review
London *Times*
Louisiana State Historical Quarterly
Massachusetts Historical Society *Proceedings*
Massachusetts *Ploughshare*
McClure's Magazine

Military Surgeon
Mississippi Historical Society Publications, Centenary Series
Mississippi Valley Historical Review
Mississippian, Jackson, Miss.
Missouri Historical Review
Montana, the Magazine of Western History
Montgomery Advertiser
National Almanac
New England Farmer
New Orleans Democrat
New York Evening Post
New York Herald
New York History
New York Independent
New York Journal of Commerce
New York Nation
New York Tribune
New York Tribune Almanac
North American Review
Norwich, Conn. Aurora
Ohio Archeological and Historical Quarterly
Pennsylvania Magazine of History and Biography
Philadelphia Weekly Times
The Portfolio (Juvenile Publication of Charleston, S.C.)
Prairie Farmer
Public Personnel Review
Punch (London), 1861–1865
Register of Officers and Agents, Civil, Military and Naval, in the Services of the U.S. 1865, Washington
    (1861–1870, published biennially)
Richmond Age
Richmond Dispatch
Richmond Enquirer
Richmond Examiner
Richmond Record of News, History and Literature
Richmond Sentinel
Richmond Whig
Rural Annual, Rochester, N.Y.
Sacramento Daily Union
St. Louis Globe-Democrat
Scientific American
Selma, Alabama Daily Reporter
Selma, Alabama Dispatch
Smith and Barrow's Monthly Magazine (Richmond)
Southern Cultivator
Southern Field and Fireside (Augusta)
Southwestern Historical Quarterly
Southern Literary Messenger
Southern Monthly (Memphis)
Southern Planter
Southern Presbyterian Review
Southern Sentinel (Alexandria, La.)

Tennessee Historical Quarterly
Toronto *Globe*
Transactions of the American Medical Association, Philadelphia
Tyler's Quarterly Historical and Genealogical Magazine
United States Naval Institute Proceedings
Virginia Magazine
Washington *Morning Chronicle*
Washington *National Intelligencer*
Washington *National Republican*
Wilmington *Messenger*
Wisconsin Magazine of History
Yale Review

BOOKS

Abbot, H.L., *Memoir of Andrew Atkinson Humphreys,* Nat'l. Acad. Sci. *Biog. Memoirs* (New York, 1865)
Abbott, Lyman, ed., *Henry Ward Beecher* (New York, 1883)
Abrams, A.S., *A Full and Detailed History of the Siege of Vicksburg* (Atlanta, 1863)
Adams, Charles Francis, *Charles Francis Adams, 1835–1915: An Autobiography* (Cambridge, 1916)
Adams, Charles Francis, *Richard Henry Dana: a Biography* (2 vols., Boston, 1891)
Adams, Charles Francis, Jr., *Charles Francis Adams* (Boston, 1900)
Adams, Ephraim D., ed., *Great Britain and the American Civil War* (2 vols., Gloucester, Mass., 1957)
Adams, George W., *Doctors in Blue* (New York, 1952)
Adams, Henry, *The Education of Henry Adams: an Autobiography* (Boston, 1918; 1961)
Agassiz, Elizabeth C., *Louis Agassiz, His Life and Correspondence* (2 vols., Boston, 1885)
Agassiz, George R., ed., *Meade's Headquarters, 1863–1865* (Boston, 1922)
Ages of United States Volunteer Soldiers—a Report (New York, 1866)
Aid Societies in the Civil War (Special volume of pamphlets bound together in the Newberry Library, Chicago)
Alexander, De Alva Stanwood, *A Political History of the State of New York* (New York, 1906–1909)
Alexander, Edward Porter, *Military Memoirs of a Confederate* (New York, 1907)
Ambler, Charles H., *Francis H. Pierpont: Union War Governor of Virginia* (Chapel Hill, 1937)
American Annual Cyclopaedia (New York, 1862–1875)
Ames, Blanche Butler, ed., *Chronicles from the Nineteenth Century: Family Letters of Blanche and Adelbert Ames* (Clinton, Mass., 1957)
Ammen, Daniel, *The Atlantic Coast* (New York, 1883–1885)
An English Merchant, *Two Months in the Confederate States* (London, 1865)
Andreano, Ralph, ed., *The Economic Impact of the American Civil War* (Cambridge, Mass., 1962)
Andreas, A.T., *History of Chicago* (Chicago, 1884–1886)
Andrews, Eliza Frances, *The Wartime Journal of a Georgia Girl, 1864–1865* (New York, 1908)
Andrews, J. Cutler, *The North Reports the Civil War* (Pittsburgh, 1955)
Annual Messages of Governors (Richmond, 1863)
Annual Reports of the Sanitary Company of the New York Police Department (New York, 1862)
Aptheker, Herbert, *A Documentary History of the Negro People in the United States* (2 vols., New York, 1968)
Arkansas Civil War Centennial Commission, *Arkansas and the Civil War* (Pamphlet, Little Rock, 1961)
Armstrong, William M., *E.L. Godkin and American Foreign Policy* (New York, 1957)
Association for Improving the Condition of the Poor; Report (New York, 1865)
Atkins, Gordon, *Health, Housing and Poverty in New York City* (Ann Arbor, 1947)

Avary, Myrta L., ed., *A Virginia Girl in the Civil War* (New York, 1903)

Avary, Myrta L., *Recollections of Alexander H. Stephens* (New York, 1910)

Ayer, Col. I. Winslow, *The Great Treason Plot in the North During the War* (Chicago, 1895)

Badeau, Adam, *Military History of Ulysses S. Grant* (3 vols., New York, 1868–1881)

Baker, George E., ed., *The Works of William H. Seward* (5 vols., New York, 1853–1884)

Baker, L.W., *History of the Ninth Massachusetts Battery* (South Farmington, Mass., 1888)

Bancroft, Frederic, *Life of William H. Seward* (2 vols., New York, 1900)

Bancroft, Frederic, ed., *Speeches, Correspondence, and Political Papers of Carl Schurz* (6 vols., New York, 1913)

Barksdale, Richard, *Cornerstones of Confederate Collecting* (Charlottesville, Va., 1952)

Barnard, Harry, *Rutherford B. Hayes and His America* (Indianapolis, 1954)

Barnes, Thurlow Weed, *Life of Thurlow Weed: Memoir by His Grandson* (2 vols., Boston, 1884)

Barrett, John G., *Sherman's March Through the Carolinas* (Chapel Hill, 1956)

Barrie, George, *The History of North America* (Philadelphia, 1906)

Barrus, Clara, *Life and Letters of John Burroughs* (Boston, 1925)

Bartlett, Irving H., *Wendell Phillips* (Boston, 1961)

Barton, William E., *Lincoln at Gettysburg* (Indianapolis, 1930)

Barton, William E., *Life of Clara Barton* (2 vols., Boston, 1922)

Basso, Hamilton, *Beauregard, the Great Creole* (New York, 1933)

Bates, David Homer, *Lincoln in the Telegraph Office* (New York, 1907)

Bates, Ralph S., *Scientific Societies in the United States* (New York, 1951)

Baxter, James P., *The Introduction of the Ironclad Warship* (Cambridge, Mass., 1933)

Baxter, James P., *Orville H. Browning: Lincoln's Friend and Critic* (Bloomington, 1957)

Beale, Howard K., ed., *The Diary of Edward Bates* (Washington, 1933)

Bearss, Edwin C., *Decision in Mississippi* (Jackson, Miss., 1962)

Belden, Thomas Graham and Marva Robins Belden, *So Fell the Angels* (Boston, 1956)

Bell, Herbert C.F., *Lord Palmerston* (2 vols., London, 1936)

Bellows, Henry W., *Historical Sketch of the Union League Club of New York* (New York, 1879)

Belmont, August, *Letters, Speeches, and Addresses of August Belmont* (New York, 1890)

Bemis, Samuel Flagg, *A Diplomatic History of the United States* (New York, 1936)

Bemis, Samuel Flagg, *The American Secretaries of State and Their Diplomacy* (10 vols., New York, 1928; 1958)

Bennett, A.J., *Story of the First Massachusetts Light Battery* (Boston, 1886)

Bentley, George R., *A History of the Freedmen's Bureau* (Philadelphia, 1955)

Bernard, Montague, *A Historical Account of the Neutrality of Great Britain During the American Civil War* (London, 1870)

Bernath, Stuart L., *Squall Across the Atlantic* (Los Angeles, 1970)

Bettersworth, John Knox, *Confederate Mississippi* (Baton Rouge, 1943)

Bickham, William D., *Rosecrans's Campaign* (Cincinnati, 1863)

Bidwell, Percy W. and John I. Falconer, *History of Agriculture in the Northern United States* (Washington, 1925)

Bierce, Ambrose, *Battle Sketches* (London, 1930)

Bigelow, Maj. John, Jr., *The Principles of Strategy* (New York, 1891)

Bigelow, John, ed., *Letters and Literary Memorials of Samuel J. Tilden* (New York, 1908)

Bigelow, John, *The Life of Samuel J. Tilden* (2 vols., New York, 1895)

Bill, A.H., *The Beleaguered City: Richmond, 1861–1865* (New York, 1946)

Billings, John D., *History of the Tenth Massachusetts Battery of Light Artillery* (Boston, 1881)

Billington, Ray Allen, *America's Frontier Heritage* (New York, 1966)

Binney, C.C., *Life of Horace Binney* (Philadelphia, 1903)

Binney, Horace, *The Privilege of the Writ of Habeas Corpus Under the Constitution* (Philadelphia, 1862)

Bishop, Joseph Bucklin, *A Chronicle of One Hundred and Fifty Years, the Chamber of Commerce of the State of New York, 1768–1918* (New York, 1913)

Black, Robert C., III, *The Railroads of the Confederacy* (Chapel Hill, 1952)

Blackford, William W., *War Years with Jeb Stuart* (New York, 1945)

Blaine, James G., *Twenty Years of Congress: From Lincoln to Garfield* (2 vols., Norwich, Conn., 1884–1886)

Blair, Montgomery, *Revolutionary Schemes of the Abolitionists* (Baltimore, 1863)

Blake, Henry N., *Three Years in the Army of the Potomac* (Boston, 1865)

Blake, Robert, *Disraeli* (New York, 1967)

Blochman, Lawrence G., *Doctor Squibb* (New York, 1958)

Boatner, M.M., *Civil War Dictionary* (New York, 1959)

Bodart, Gaston, *Losses of Life in Modern War* (London, 1916)

Bokum, Herman, *Wanderings North and South: the Testimony of a Refugee from East Tennessee* (Philadelphia, 1863)

Bolles, Albert S., *Industrial History of the United States* (Norwich, Conn., 1879)

Borcke, Heros Von, *Memoirs of the Confederate War for Independence* (Edinburgh, 1866)

Borthwick, J.D., *Three Years in California* (Edinburgh, 1857)

Bosson, C.P., *History of the 42d Massachusetts Volunteers* (Boston, 1886)

Boston Board of Trade, *Tenth Annual Report for 1863* (Boston, 1864)

Botkin, Benjamin A., ed., *Lay My Burden Down: A Folk History of Slavery* (Chicago, 1945)

Boulding, Kenneth F., *The Organizational Revolution* (New York, 1953)

Boutwell, George S., *Reminiscences of Sixty Years in Public Affairs* (New York, 1902)

Bowen, James Lorenzo, *History of the Thirty-seventh Regiment Massachusetts Volunteers* (Holyoke, Mass., 1884)

Bowers, Claude G., *The Tragic Era; The Revolution After Lincoln* (Cambridge, 1929)

Boykin, Edward M., *The Falling Flag: Evacuation of Richmond and Surrender at Appomattox* (New York, 1874)

Boykin, Edward C., *Ghost Ship of the Confederacy* (New York, 1957)

Boynton, H.V., *Sherman's Historical Raid* (Cincinnati, 1875)

Boynton, H.V., compiler, *Dedication of the Chickamauga and Chattanooga National Military Park* (Washington, 1896)

Boynton, Percy H., ed., *Poems of the Civil War* (New York, 1918)

Bradford, Gamaliel, *Confederate Portraits* (Boston, 1914)

Bradford, Gamaliel, *Union Portraits* (Boston, 1916)

Bradford, Gamaliel, *Lee the American* (Boston, 1927)

Bradlee, F.B.C., *Blockade Running During the Civil War* (Salem, Mass., 1925)

Bradley, Joseph F., *The Rôle of Trade Associations and Professional Business Societies in America* (University Park, Pa., 1965)

Bragg, J.D., *Louisiana in the Confederacy* (Baton Rouge, 1941)

Brigance, William N., *Jeremiah Sullivan Black, a Defender of the Constitution and the Ten Commandments* (Philadelphia, 1934)

Brigham, Johnson, *James Harlan* (Iowa City, 1913)

Brinley, Thomas, *Migration and Economic Growth: a Study of Great Britain and the Atlantic Economy* (Cambridge, 1954)

Brodie, Fawn M., *Thaddeus Stevens: Scourge of the South* (New York, 1959)

Brooks, Noah, *Washington in Lincoln's Time* (New York, 1895); ed., Herbert Mitgang (New York, 1958)

Brooks, Robert P., *Conscription in the Confederate States of America, 1862–1865* (Athens, Ga., 1917)

Brooks, Van Wyck, *Makers and Finders: A History of the Writer in America, 1800–1915* (5 vols., New York, 1936–1952)

Bross, William, *Biographical Sketch of the Late B.J. Sweet and History of Camp Douglas* (pamphlet, Chicago, 1878)

Brown, Dee A., *Grierson's Raid* (Urbana, 1954)

Brown, Ernest Francis, *Raymond of the Times* (New York, 1951)

Browne, Francis, *The Every-Day Life of Abraham Lincoln* (Chicago, 1913)

Browne, J. Ross and James W. Taylor, *Report upon the Mineral Resources of the United States* (Washington, 1867)

Browning, Orville H., *Diary*, ed., T.C. Pease and James G. Randall (Springfield, Ill., 1925–1933)

Brownlow, W.G., *Sketches of the Rise, Progress, and Decline of Secession* (Philadelphia, 1862)

Bruce, Kathleen, *Virginia Iron Manufacture in the Slave Era* (New York, 1930)

Bruce, Robert V., *Lincoln and the Tools of War* (Indianapolis, 1956)

Bryan, George S., *The Great American Myth: The True Story of Lincoln's Murder* (New York, 1940)

Bryan, Thomas Conn, *Confederate Georgia* (Athens, Ga., 1953)

Bryant, Sir Arthur, *Years of Victory* (New York, 1945)

Buck, Irving, *Cleburne and His Command* (Jackson, Tenn., 1959)

Buckeridge, J.O., *Lincoln's Choice* (Harrisburg, Pa., 1956)

Buckmaster, Henrietta, pseud. (Henrietta Henkle), *Let My People Go* (New York, 1941)

Buell, Augustus, *The Cannoneer* (Washington, 1890)

Ballard, F. Lauriston, *A Few Appropriate Remarks: Abraham Lincoln and the Widow Bixby* (New Brunswick, N.J., 1946)

Bulloch, James D., *The Secret Service of the Confederate States in Europe* (New York, 1959; London, 1883)

Burgess, John W., *Reminiscences of an American Scholar* (New York, 1934)

Burn, James Dawson, *Three Years among the Working Classes in the United States During the War* (London, 1865)

Burne, Col. Alfred H., *Lee, Grant and Sherman* (New York, 1939)

Burr, Anna Robeson, *Dr. S. Weir Mitchell, His Life and Letters* (New York, 1929)

Burrow, James P., *American Medical Association, Voice of American Medicine* (Baltimore, 1963)

Burtis, Mary E., *Moncure Conway, 1832–1907* (New Brunswick, Me., 1952)

Burton, Theodore E., *John Sherman* (Boston, 1906)

Butler, Benjamin F., *Autobiography [Butler's Book]* (Boston, 1892)

Butler, Pierce, *Judah P. Benjamin* (Philadelphia, 1907)

Byers, S.H.M., *With Fire and Sword* (New York, 1911)

Cadwallader, Sylvanus C., *Three Years With Grant*, ed., Benjamin P. Thomas (New York, 1955)

Cain, Marvin R., *Lincoln's Attorney-General, Edward Bates of Missouri* (Columbia, Mo., 1965)

Capers, Gerald M., *The Biography of a River Town: Memphis, Its Heroic Age* (Chapel Hill, 1939)

Capers, H.D., *The Life and Times of C.G. Memminger* (Richmond, 1893)

Cappon, Lester J., *Virginia Newspapers, 1921–1935, a Bibliography* (New York, 1936)

Carmon, Harry J. and Rembard H. Lytkin, *Lincoln and the Patronage* (New York, 1943)

Carpenter, John A., *Sword and Olive Branch* (Pittsburgh, 1964)

Carr, Clark E., *My Day and Generation* (Chicago, 1908)

Carr, William H.A., *The DuPonts of Delaware* (New York, 1964)

Carter, Robert and Walter, *War Letters from the Battlefront, 1861–1865* (Ms. Notebooks, HEH)

Carter, W.C., *History of the First Regiment of Tennessee Volunteer Cavalry* (Knoxville, 1902)

Caskey, Willie M., *Secession and Restoration of Louisiana* (University, La., 1938)

Casson, Herbert N., *Romance of Steel* (New York, 1907)

Catton, Bruce, *Grant Moves South* (Boston, 1960)

Catton, Bruce, *Grant Takes Command* (Boston, 1968)

Catton, Bruce, *Mr. Lincoln's Army* (Garden City, 1951)

Catton, Bruce, *Glory Road* (Garden City, 1952)

Catton, Bruce, *A Stillness at Appomattox* (Garden City, 1954)

Catton, Bruce, *U.S. Grant and the American Military Tradition* (Boston, 1954)

Chadwick, J.W., *Henry W. Bellows; His Life and Character* (New York, 1882)

Chamberlain, Joshua L., *The Passing of the Armies* (New York, 1915)

Chambers, William N., *Old Bullion Benton* (Boston, 1956)

Chandler, William E., *The Soldier's Right to Vote* (Washington, 1864)

Channing, Edward, *History of the United States* (Vol. VI), *War for Southern Independence* (New York, 1925)

Chase, Philip H., *Confederate Treasury Notes* (Philadelphia, 1947)

Chase, Salmon P., *Diary and Correspondence of Salmon P. Chase* (Washington, 1903)

Chesnut, Mary Boykin, *A Diary from Dixie* (Boston, 1949; 1st ed. 1905)

Church, William Conant, *Grant* (New York, 1897)

Civil War Centennial Commission, *Tennesseans in the Civil War* (Nashville, 1964)

Civil War Naval Chronology (Washington and Philadelphia, 1907)

Claiborne, John F.H., ed., Life and Correspondence of John A. Quitman (2 vols., New York, 1860)

Clapham, John Harold, *An Economic History of Modern Britain* (Cambridge, Eng., 1930–1938)

Clark, Victor S., *History of Manufactures in the U.S.* (New York, 1929)

Clarke, Grace J., *George W. Julian* (Indianapolis, 1923)

Clay, Victor S., *History of Manufactures in the United States, 1607–1860* (New York, 1929)

Clay-Clopton, Mrs. Virginia, ed., Ada Sterling *A Belle of the Fifties; Memoirs of Mrs. Clay of Alabama* (New York, 1905)

Cleaves, Freeman, *Meade of Gettysburg* (Norman, Okla., 1960)

Cleaves, Freeman, *Rock of Chickamauga; the Life of General George H. Thomas* (Norman, Okla., 1948)

Cleveland, Henry, *Alexander H. Stephens, in Public and Private* (Philadelphia, 1866)

Clews, Henry, *Twenty-eight Years in Wall Street* (New York, 1887)

Cobden Club Essays (London, 1872)

Cochran, Hamilton, *Blockade Runners of the Confederacy* (New York, 1958)

Cochran, Thomas and William Miller, *The Age of Enterprise* (New York, 1942)

Coddington, Edwin B., *The Gettysburg Campaign: A Study in Command* (New York, 1968)

Coffin, Charles Carleton, *Marching to Victory* (New York, 1889)

Coffin, Charles Carleton, *The Boys of '61* (Boston, 1881)

Coit, Margaret L., *John C. Calhoun* (Boston, 1950)

Cole, Arthur Charles, *The Irrepressible Conflict* (New York, 1938)

Cole, Arthur Charles, *The Era of the Civil War, 1849–1870* (Springfield, Ill., 1919)

Cole, Arthur Harrison, *The American Wool Manufacture* (Cambridge, Mass., 1926)

Coleman, Ann Mary Butler, *The Life of John J. Crittenden*, ed. by his daughter, Mrs. Chapman Coleman (Philadelphia, 1871)

Colyer, Vincent, *Report of the Services Rendered by the Freed People to the U.S. Army in North Carolina in the Spring of 1862* (New York, 1864)

Commager, Henry S., *Theodore Parker* (Boston, 1936)

A Committee of the Regiment, *The Story of the Fifty-fifth Regiment, Illinois Volunteer Infantry* (Clinton, Mass., 1887)

Commons, John R. and others, eds., *A Documentary History of American Industrial Society* (10 vols., New York, 1910–1911)

Commons, John R. and others, eds., *History of Labor in the United States* (4 vols., New York, 1918–1935)

Comte de Paris, *History of the Civil War in America* (Philadelphia, 1875–1888)

Conger, A.L., *The Rise of U.S. Grant* (New York, 1931)

Connolly, Major James Austin, *Diary* (Springfield, 1928)

Connor, Henry G., *John Archibald Campbell, Associate Justice of the United States Supreme Court, 1853–1861* (Boston, 1920)

Conrad, Earl, *The Governor and His Lady: the Story of William Henry Seward and His Wife Frances* (New York, 1960)

Conway, Moncure, *Addresses and Reprints* (New York, 1908)

Conway, Moncure, *Autobiography: Memories and Experiences* (Boston, 1904)

Conyngham, Capt. David P., *Sherman's March Through the South* (New York, 1865)

Cook, Sir Edward, *Delane of the Times* (New York, 1916)

Cooke, John Esten, *Wearing of the Gray* (New York, 1867); new ed., Philip Van Doren Stern (Bloomington, 1959)

Coolidge, Louis A., *Ulysses S. Grant* (2 vols., Boston, 1924)

Copeland, Melvin T., *The Cotton Manufacturing Industry of the United States* (Cambridge, Mass., 1912)

Cornish, Dudley T., *The Sable Arm: Negro Troops in the Army, 1861–1865* (New York, 1956)

Cortissoz, Royal, *The Life of Whitelaw Reid* (2 vols., New York, 1921)

Coulson, Thomas, *Joseph Henry: His Life and Work* (Princeton, 1950)

Coulter, E. Merton, *The Confederate States of America, 1861–1865* (Baton Rouge, 1950)

Coulter, E. Merton, *William G. Brownlow, Fighting Parson* (Chapel Hill, 1937)

Coulter, E. Merton, *The Civil War and Readjustment in Kentucky* (Chapel Hill, 1926)

Courtney, W.L., *Life of John Stuart Mill* (London, 1889)

Cox, Jacob Dolson, *Military Reminiscences of the Civil War* (New York, 1900)

Cox, Jacob Dolson, *Atlanta* (New York, 1882)

Cox, Jacob Dolson, *March to the Sea, Franklin and Nashville* (New York, 1882)

Cox, Jacob Dolson, *The Battle of Franklin, Tennessee* (New York, 1897)

Cox, Lawanda and John H., *Politics, Principle and Prejudice, 1865–1866* (London, 1963)

Cox, Samuel S., *Three Decades of Federal Legislation* (Providence, 1885)

Cramer, Jesse G., ed., *Letters of U.S. Grant to His Father and His Youngest Sister* (New York, 1912)

Crane, Stephen, *The Red Badge of Courage* (New York, 1896)

Craven, Avery, *The Coming of the Civil War* (New York, 1942; 1947)

Craven, Avery, *Repressible Conflict* (University, La., 1939)

Craven, Avery, *Civil War in the Making* (Baton Rouge, 1959)

Craven, Avery, *Edmund Ruffin, Southerner* (New York, 1932)

Crippen, Lee F., *Simon Cameron: Ante-Bellum Years* (Oxford, Ohio, 1942)

Croffut, W.A., ed., *Fifty Years in Camp and Field, Diary of Major-General Ethan Allen Hitchcock, U.S.A.* (New York, 1909)

Crownishield, Benjamin W., *A History of the First Massachusetts Cavalry* (Boston, 1891)

Crownover, Sims, *The Battle of Franklin* (reprint, Nashville, 1955)

Cruises of the Sumter and the Alabama: Log (London, 1864)

Cudworth, Warren Handel, *History of the First Regiment Massachusetts Infantry* (Boston, 1866)

Cullum, G.W., *Biographical Register of the Officers and Graduates of the U.S. Military Academy, at West Point, N.Y.* (New York, 1868)

Cumming, Kate, *Kate: the Journal of a Confederate Nurse*, ed., Richard Harwell (Baton Rouge, 1959)

Cunningham, Edward, *The Port Hudson Campaign, 1862–1863* (Baton Rouge, 1963)

Cunningham, H.H., *Doctors in Gray* (Baton Rouge, 1958)

Current, Richard N., *Pine Logs and Politics* (New York, 1950)

Current, Richard N., *The Lincoln Nobody Knows* (New York, 1958)

Current, Richard N., *Old Thad Stevens, a Story of Ambition* (Madison, 1942)

Curti, Merle E., *The Growth of American Thought* (New York, 1943)

Curtis, George T., *The Life of Daniel Webster* (2 vols., New York, 1870)

Curtis, George William, *From the Easy Chair* (New York, 1892–1894)

Curtis, George William, ed., *The Correspondence of John Lothrop Motley* (2 vols., New York, 1889)

Curtis, Newton Martin, *From Bull Run to Chancellorsville* (New York, 1906)

Daggett, Stewart, *Railroad Reorganization* (New York, 1966)

Dahlgren, M.V., *Memoir of Admiral John A. Dahlgren* (Boston, 1882)

Dana, Charles A., *Recollections of the Civil War* (New York, 1898)

Dasent, A.I., *John Delane, 1817–1879, ed. The Times* (London, 1908)

Davis, Burke, *Jeb Stuart, the Last Cavalier* (New York, 1957)

Davis, Burke, *Gray Fox: Robert E. Lee and the Civil War* (New York, 1956)

Davis, Burke, *To Appomattox; Nine April Days, 1865* (New York, 1959)

Davis, Capt. C.H., *Life of Charles Henry Davis, Rear-Admiral, 1807–1877* (New York, 1899)
Davis, Charles E., Jr., *Three Years in the Army; the Thirteenth Massachusetts Volunteers* (Boston, 1894)
Davis, Jefferson, *The Rise and Fall of the Confederate Government* (New York, 1881)
Davis, Rebecca Blain Harding, *Bits of Gossip* (New York, 1904)
Davis, Reuben, *Recollections of Mississippi and Mississippians* (Heston, Miss., 1889)
Davis, Varina Howell, *Jefferson Davis . . . A Memoir by His Wife* (New York, 1890)
Dawson, Sarah M., *A Confederate Girl's Diary*, ed., James I. Robertson, Jr. (Bloomington, 1960)
De Chenal, Francois, *The American Army in the War of Secession* (Ft. Leavenworth, 1894)
DeForest, John William, *A Volunteer's Adventures* (London, 1946)
DeLeon, T.C., *Four Years in Rebel Capitals* (Mobile, 1890)
Dennett, Tyler, *Lincoln and the Civil War, in the Diaries and Letters of John Hay* (New York, 1939)
Dennett, Tyler, *John Hay: From Poetry to Politics* (New York, 1933)
De Trobriand, Regis, *Four Years with the Army of the Potomac* (Boston, 1889)
Detroit *Post* and *Tribune, Zachariah Chandler* (New York, 1880)
Dew, Charles B., *Ironmaker to the Confederacy: Joseph R. Anderson and the Tredegar Iron Works* (New Haven, 1966)
Dewey, Davis R., *Financial History of the United States* (New York, 1903; 1934)
Dicey, Edward, *Six Months in the Federal States* (2 vols., London, 1863)
Dix, Morgan, ed., *Memoirs of John Adams Dix* (2 vols., New York, 1883)
Dodd, Dorothy, *Henry J. Raymond and the New York Times* (New York, 1936)
Dodd, Ira S., *The Song of the Rappahannock* (New York, 1898)
Dodd, William E., *Robert J. Walker, Imperialist* (Chicago, 1914)
Dodge, Maj. Gen. Grenville M., *The Battle of Atlanta* (Council Bluffs, 1911)
Dodge, Maj. Gen. Grenville M., *Personal Recollections of President Abraham Lincoln, Gen. Ulysses S. Grant and Gen. William T. Sherman* (Glendale, Calif., 1914)
Donald, David, ed., *Inside Lincoln's Cabinet: the Civil War Diaries of Salmon P. Chase* (New York, 1954)
Donald, David, *Charles Sumner and the Coming of the Civil War* (New York, 1960)
Donald, Henderson H., *The Negro Freedman* (New York, 1952)
Dorfman, Joseph, *The Economic Mind in American Civilization, 1606–1918* (3 vols., New York, 1949)
Dorris, Jonathan Truman, *Pardon and Amnesty Under Lincoln and Johnson* (Chapel Hill, 1953)
Dorsey, Sarah A., *Recollections of Henry Watkins Allen* (New York, 1866)
Doubleday, Abner, *Chancellorsville and Gettysburg, Campaigns of the Civil War* (New York, 1882)
Dowd, Clement, *Life of Zebulon B. Vance* (Charlotte, N.C., 1897)
Dowdey, Clifford, *Experiment in Rebellion* (Garden City, 1946)
Dowdey, Clifford, *Death of a Nation* (New York, 1958)
Dowdey, Clifford, *Lee's Last Campaign* (Boston, 1960)
Dowdey, Clifford and Louis H. Manarin, eds., *The Wartime Papers of Robert E. Lee* (Boston, 1961)
Downey, Fairfax, *Storming of the Gates: Chattanooga, 1863* (New York, 1963)
Duberman, Martin B., *Charles Francis Adams* (New York, 1961)
DuBois, James T. and G.S. Mathews, *Galusha A. Grow, Father of the Homestead Law* (Boston, 1917)
DuBose, J.W., *Life and Times of William Lowndes Yancey* (Birmingham, 1892)
Duke, Basil W., *A History of Morgan's Cavalry* (Bloomington, 1961)
Dulles, Foster R., *Labor in America* (New York, 1949)
Dumond, Dwight L., ed., *Letters of James Gillespie Birney* (New York, 1938)
Dumond, Dwight L., *Antislavery Origins of the Civil War in the United States* (Ann Arbor, 1939)
Dunbar, Seymour, *A History of Travel in America* (4 vols., New York, 1915)
Duncan, Capt. Louis C., *The Medical Department of the U.S. Army in the Civil War*
Dunning, William Archibald, *Reconstruction, Political and Economic,* (New York, 1907)
DuPont, H.A., *Rear-Admiral Samuel Francis DuPont* (New York, 1926)
Dupuy, Richard E. and Trevor N. Dupuy, *The Compact History of the Civil War* (New York, 1960)
Durden, Robert F., *James Shepherd Pike: Republicanism and the American Negro, 1850–1882* (Durham, 1957)
Dutton, William S., *DuPont, One Hundred and Forty Years* (New York, 1942)

Dyer, Brainerd, *Zachary Taylor* (Baton Rouge, 1946)

Dyer, Frederick H., *A Compendium of the War of the Rebellion* (Des Moines, 1908)

Dyer, John P., *The Gallant Hood* (Indianapolis, 1950)

Dyer, John P., *"Fightin' Joe" Wheeler* (University, La., 1941)

Early, Jubal A., *Autobiographical Sketch and Narrative of the War Between the States* (Philadelphia, 1912); new ed. titled *War Memoirs* . . . , with introduction by Frank E. Vandiver (Bloomington, 1960)

Eaton, Clement, *A History of the Southern Confederacy* (New York, 1954)

Eaton, John and Ethel O. Mason, *Grant, Lincoln, and the Freedmen* (New York, 1907)

Eckenrode, H.J. *George B. McClellan, the Man Who Saved the Union* (Chapel Hill, 1941)

Eckenrode, H.J. and Bryan Conrad, *James Longstreet, Lee's War Horse* (Chapel Hill, 1936)

Edwards, William B., *Civil War Guns* (Harrisburg, 1962)

Eggleston, George Cary, *A Rebel's Recollections* (Bloomington, 1959)

Eisenschiml, Otto, ed., *Vermont General: The Unusual War Experiences of Edward Hastings Ripley, 1862–1865* (New York, 1960)

Eisenchiml, Otto, *Why Was Lincoln Murdered?* (Boston, 1939)

Elliott, Charles W., *Winfield Scott: the Soldier and the Man* (New York, 1937)

Emilio, Louis F., *History of the Fifty-fourth Regiment of Massachusetts Volunteer Infantry, 1863–1865* (Boston, 1891)

Evarts, Sherman, ed., *Arguments and Speeches of William Maxwell Evarts* (3 vols., New York, 1919)

Everhart, William G., *Vicksburg National Military Park, Mississippi* (Washington, 1954)

Fahrney, Ralph R., *Horace Greeley and the Tribune in the Civil War* (Cedar Rapids, 1936)

Falls, Cyril, *A Hundred Years of War* (London, 1954)

Farley, Porter, *Reminiscences of the 140th Regiment New York Volunteers* (Rochester, N.Y., 1944)

Farragut, Loyall, *The Life of David Glasgow Farragut* (New York, 1907)

Ferleger, Herbert R., *David A. Wells and the American Revenue System* (New York, 1942)

Fessenden, Francis, *Life and Public Services of William Pitt Fessenden, United States Senator from Maine, 1854–1864* (Boston, 1907)

Field, E.A., *Record of the Life of David Dudley Field* (Denver, 1931)

Field, Maunsell, *Memories of Many Men and of Some Women* (London, 1874)

Fielder, Herbert, *Sketch of the Life and Times and Speeches of Joseph E. Brown* (Springfield, Mass., 1883)

Fishbein, Morris, *A History of the American Medical Association* (Philadelphia, 1947)

Fisher, Sidney G., *The True Daniel Webster* (Philadelphia, 1911)

Fite, Emerson Davis, *Social and Industrial Conditions in the North During the Civil War* (New York, 1930; 1963)

Fladelander, Betty L., *James Gillespie Birney; Slaveholder to Abolitionist* (Ithaca, N.Y., 1955)

Fleming, W.L., *The South in the Building of the Nation* (Richmond, 1909–1913)

Fleming, W.L., *The Freedmen's Savings Bank* (Chapel Hill, 1927)

Fleming, W.L., *Civil War and Reconstruction in Alabama* (New York, 1905)

Flick, Alexander C., *Samuel Jones Tilden* (2 vols., New York, 1895)

Flippin, Percy S., *Herschel V. Johnson of Georgia* (Richmond, 1931)

Flower, Frank A., *Edwin McMasters Stanton* (Akron, 1905)

Foner, Philip S., *History of the Labor Movement in the United States* (New York, 1947)

Foote, Henry S., *Casket of Reminiscences* (Washington, 1874)

Foote, Shelby, *The Civil War* (New York, 1958)

Ford, James, *History of the Civil War* (New York, 1917)

Ford, Worthington C., ed., *A Cycle of Adams Letters* (2 vols., Boston, 1920)

Ford, Worthington C., ed., *Letters of Henry Adams* (Boston, 1930–1938)

Ford, Worthington C., ed., *War Letters of John Chipman Gray* (Boston, 1927)

Formby, John, *The American Civil War* (New York, 1910)

Foth, Joseph Henry, *Trade Associations, Their Services to Industry* (New York, 1930)

Foulke, William Dudley, *Life of Oliver P. Morton* (Indianapolis, 1877)

Fowler, Dorothy Canfield, *The Cabinet Politician: the Postmasters-General, 1829–1909* (New York, 1943)

Fowler, William W., *Ten Years in Wall Street* (Hartford, 1870)

Fowler, William W., *Memorials of William Fowler* (New York, 1875)

Fox, William F., *Regimental Losses in the American Civil War* (Albany, 1889)

Franklin, John H., *The Diary of James T. Ayers, Civil War Recruiter* (Springfield, 1947)

Freeman, Cleaves, *Meade of Gettysburg,* (Norman, Okla., 1960)

Freeman, Douglas Southall, *Robert E. Lee, A Biography* (4 vols., New York, 1934–1935)

Freeman, Douglas Southall, *Lee's Lieutenants* (New York, 1946)

Freeman, Douglas Southall, *Lee's Dispatches* (New York, 1915; 1957)

Freidel, Frank, *Francis Lieber, Nineteenth-Century Liberal* (Baton Rouge, 1947)

Freidel, Frank, ed., *Union Pamphlets of the Civil War* (Boston, 1967)

Fremantle, Lt. Col. James Arthur Lyon, *Three Months in the Southern States, April–June, 1863* (New York, 1864), new ed. by Walter Lord, titled *The Fremantle Diary* (Boston, 1954)

Frothingham, Paul R., *Edward Everett: Orator and Statesman* (Boston, 1925)

Fry, James B., *New York and the Conscription of 1863* (New York, 1885)

Fry, James B., *Military Miscellanies* (New York, 1889)

Fuess, Claude, *Carl Schurz, Reformer, 1829–1906* (Port Washington, N.Y., 1963)

Fuess, Claude, *Daniel Webster* (2 vols. Boston, 1930)

Fuller, J.F.C., *The Generalship of Ulysses S. Grant* (New York, 1919; 1958)

Fuller, J.F.C., *Grant and Lee* (London, 1933; Bloomington, 1957)

Gabriel, Ralph H., *The Course of American Democratic Thought* (New York, 1940)

Gallman, Robert E., *Trends in the Size Distribution of Wealth in the 19th Century* (New York, 1969)

Gardner, John W., *Self-Renewal: The Individual and the Innovative Society* (New York, 1864)

Gates, Paul W., *Agriculture and the Civil War* (New York, 1965)

Gates, Paul W., *The Farmer's Age* (New York, 1960)

Gerrish, Theodore, *Army Life, a Private's Reminiscences of the Civil War* (Portland, Me., 1882)

Gibson, John M., *Those 163 Days* (New York, 1961)

Giddens, Paul H., *The Birth of the Oil Industry* (New York, 1939)

Gilchrist, David T. and W. David Lewis, eds., *Economic Change in the Civil War Era* (Greenville, Del., 1965)

Gilder, Rosamond, *Letters of Richard Watson Gilder* (Boston, 1916)

Gilmore, James Robert, *Personal Recollections of Abraham Lincoln and the Civil War* (London, 1899)

Godkin, Edwin Lawrence, *Unforeseen Tendencies of Democracy* (Westminster, England, 1903)

Goodrich, Lloyd, *The Graphic Art of Winslow Homer* (New York, 1968)

Gordon, John B., *Reminiscences of the Civil War* (New York, 1903)

Gorham, George C., *Life and Public Services of Edwin M. Stanton* (2 vols., Boston, 1899)

Gosnell, Harpur A., ed., *Rebel Raider: . . . Raphael Semmes's Cruise in the C.S.S. Sumter* (Chapel Hill, 1948)

Gosnell, H. Allen, *Guns on the Western Waters* (Baton Rouge, 1949)

Govan, Gilbert E., ed., *The Haskell Memoirs* (New York, 1960)

Govan, Gilbert E., *The Chattanooga Country 1540–1951* (New York, 1952)

Govan, Gilbert E. and James W. Livingood, *A Different Valor: the Story of Gen. Joseph E. Johnston, C.S.A.* (New York, 1956)

Graham, Matthew John, *The Ninth Regiment New York Volunteers* (New York, 1900)

Grant, Ulysses S., *Personal Memoirs of U.S. Grant* (New York, 1885)

Gray, John Chipman, *War Letters, 1862–1865, of John Chipman Gray . . . and John Codman Ropes . . . with portraits* (Boston, 1927)

Gray, Wood, *The Hidden Civil War: the Story of the Copperheads* (New York, 1942)

Greeley, Horace, *The American Conflict* (Hartford, 1867)

Greeley, Horace, *Recollections of a Busy Life* (New York, 1868)

Green, Fletcher M., ed., *I Rode with Stonewall* (Chapel Hill, 1940)

Greene, F.V., *The Mississippi* (New York, 1882)

Grodinsky, Julius, *Jay Gould: His Business Career* (Philadelphia, 1957)

Grossman, Jonathan, *William Sylvis, Pioneer of American Labor* (New York, 1945)

Guernsey, Alfred H. and Henry M. Alden, *Harper's History of the Civil War* (Chicago, 1894–1896)

Hagood, Johnson, *Memoirs of the War of Secession* (Columbia, S.C., 1910)

Hague, Parthenia Antoinette, *A Blockaded Family in Alabama During the Civil War* (Boston, 1888)

Hale, William H., *Horace Greeley, Voice of the People* (New York, 1950)

Hall, Clifton R., *Andrew Johnson, Military Governor of Tennessee* (Princeton, 1916)

Hall, Newman, *A Reply to the Pro-Slavery Wail* (London, 1868)

Hamilton, Holman, *Zachary Taylor* (2 vols., Indianapolis, 1941–1951)

Hamlin, Charles E., *The Life and Times of Hannibal Hamlin* (Cambridge, Mass., 1899)

Hammond, Bray, *Banks and Politics in America* (Princeton, 1957)

Hammond, M.B., *The Cotton Industry* (New York, 1897)

Handlin, Oscar, *Boston's Immigrants* (Cambridge, 1941)

Handlin, Oscar, ed. with others, *Harvard Guide to American History* (Cambridge, 1954)

Hanna, A.J., *Flight Into Oblivion* (Richmond, 1938)

Hannaford, Ebenezer, *The Story of a Regiment* (Cincinnati, 1868)

Hansen, Marcus Lee, *The Immigrant in American History* (Cambridge, 1940)

Harlow, Ralph V., *Gerrit Smith: Philanthropist* . . . (New York, 1939)

Harper, Ida H., *The Life and Work of Susan B. Anthony* (2 vols., Indianapolis, 1898–1908)

Harper, Robert S., *Lincoln and the Press* (New York, 1951)

Harper's Pictorial History of the Rebellion (New York, 1866)

Harrington, Fred H., *Fighting Politician: Major-General N.P. Banks* (Philadelphia, 1948)

Hart, Albert B., ed., *Salmon Portland Chase* (Boston, 1899)

Harwell, Richard B., *Cornerstones of Confederate Collecting* (Charlottesville, Va., 1952)

Haskell, Franklin A., *The Battle of Gettysburg* (Boston, 1898); new ed. by Bruce Catton (Boston, 1958)

Hassler, Warren W., Jr., *General George B. McClellan* (Baton Rouge, 1957)

Haupt, Herman, *Reminiscences* (Milwaukee, 1901)

Hay, Mrs. John, ed., *Letters of John Hay and Extracts from his Diary* (3 vols., Washington, 1908), selected by Henry Adams

Hay, Thomas R., *Hood's Tennessee Campaign* (New York, 1929)

Hayes, Rutherford B., *Diary and Letters*, ed., Charles R. Williams (Columbus, Ohio, 1922–1926)

Hazard, R.G., *Our Resources* (London, 1864)

Hebert, Walter H., *Fighting Joe Hooker* (Indianapolis, 1944)

Hedley, F.Y., *Marching Through Georgia: Pen Pictures of Every-day Life in Gen. Sherman's Army* (Chicago, 1890)

Henderson, G.F.R., *The Science of War* (London, 1910)

Henderson, G.F.R., *The Civil War: A Soldier's View*, ed., Jay Luvaas (Chicago, 1958)

Hendrick, Burton J., *The Life of Andrew Carnegie* (2 vols., Boston, 1932)

Hendrick, Burton J., *Statesmen of the Lost Cause* (Boston, 1939)

Henry, Robert S., *"First with the Most" Forrest* (Indianapolis, 1944)

Henry, Robert S., ed., *As They Saw Forrest* (Jackson, Tenn., 1956)

Hertz, Emanuel, *Abraham Lincoln: A New Portrait* (New York, 1931)

Hesseltine, William B., *Ulysses S. Grant, Politician* (New York, 1935)

Hesseltine, William B., *Lincoln and the War Governors* (New York, 1949)

Hesseltine, William B., *Lincoln's Plan of Reconstruction* (Tuscaloosa, 1960)

Hibben, Paxton, *Henry Ward Beecher, an American Portrait* (New York, 1927)

Higginson, Mary T., ed., *Letters and Journals of T.W. Higginson* (Boston, 1921)

Higginson, Thomas Wentworth, *Army Life in a Black Regiment* (Boston, 1870)

Hill, Louise Biles, *Joseph E. Brown and the Confederacy* (Chapel Hill, 1939)

Hinman, Walter F., *The Story of the Sherman Brigade* (Alliance, Ohio, 1897)

Historical Statistics of the United States (Washington, 1949)

History of the DuPont Company's Relations with the U.S. Government (Wilmington, 1928)

Hoar, George F., *Autobiography of Seventy Years* (2 vols., New York, 1903)

Hobart-Hampden, Augustus Charles, *Hobart Pasha*, ed., Horace Kephart (New York, 1915)

Hobart-Hampden, Augustus Charles, *Sketches from My Life* (New York, 1887)

Hobson, J.A., *Cobden, the International Man* (New York, 1919)

Hodges, W.R., *The Western Sanitary Commission* (St. Louis, 1906)

Hoehling, A.A., *Last Train from Atlanta* (New York, 1958)

Holbrook, Stewart H., *Yankee Exodus* (New York, 1950)

Holland, Cecil F., *Morgan and His Raiders* (New York, 1942)

Holland, James Gilbert, *Life of Abraham Lincoln* (Springfield, Mass., 1866)

Holst, Hermann E. Von, *Constitutional and Political History of the United States* (9 vols., Chicago, 1889–1892)

Holzman, Robert S., *Stormy Ben Butler* (New York, 1954)

Hood, John Bell, *Advance and Retreat* (New Orleans, 1880); new ed. by Richard N. Current, 1959

Hooker, Richard, *The Story of an Independent Newspaper* (New York, 1924)

Hopkins, Owen J., *Under the Flag of the Nation*, ed., Otto F. Bond (Columbus, O., 1961)

Horan, James D., *Mathew Brady: Historian with a Camera* (New York, 1955)

Horgan, Paul, *Songs After Lincoln* (New York, 1960; 1965)

Horn, Stanley F., *The Decisive Battle of Nashville* (Baton Rouge, 1956)

Horn, Stanley F., *The Army of Tennessee* (Norman, Okla., 1953)

Horner, Harlan H., *Lincoln and Greeley* (Urbana, 1953)

Howard, Leon, *Victorian Knight Errant; A Study of the Early Literary Career of James Russell Lowell* (Berkeley, 1952)

Howard, Oliver O., *Autobiography* (2 vols., New York, 1907)

Howe, Caleb, *The Supplies for the Confederate Army* (Boston, 1904)

Howe, M.A. DeWolfe, *The Life and Letters of George Bancroft* (New York, 1908)

Howe, M.A. DeWolfe, *Justice Oliver Wendell Holmes* (Cambridge, 1957)

Howe, M.A. DeWolfe, ed., *Marching with Sherman* (New Haven, 1927)

Howe, M.A. DeWolfe, ed., *Home Letters of General Sherman* (New York, 1909)

Hubbard, Charles Eustis, *The Campaign of the Forty-fifth Regiment, Massachusetts Volunteer Militia* (Boston, 1882)

Hughes, Sarah F., ed., *Letters and Recollections of John Murray Forbes* (2 vols., Boston, 1899)

Hume, John F., *The Abolitionists* (New York, 1905)

Humphreys, A.A., *The Virginia Campaign, 1864 and 1865* (New York, 1883)

Humphreys, H.A., *Andrew Atkinson Humphreys, a Biography* (Philadelphia, 1924)

Hungerford, Edward, *Men of Erie* (New York, 1946)

Hunt, Gaillard, *Israel, Elihu, and Cadwallader Washburn* (New York, 1925)

Hunter, Louis C., *Steamboats on the Western Rivers* (Cambridge, 1949)

Hutchins, E.R., ed., *The War of the Sixties* (New York, 1912)

Hutchinson, William T., ed., *The Marcus W. Jernegan Essays* (Chicago, 1937)

Hutchinson, William T., *Cyrus Hall McCormick* (2 vols., New York, 1930–35)

Hyde, Thomas W., *Following the Greek Cross* (Boston, 1894)

Illinois Commandery, *Military Essays and Recollections* (Chicago, 1894)

Illinois Infantry, *Military History and Reminiscences of the Thirteenth Regiment of Illinois Volunteer Infantry* (Chicago, 1892)

Inman, Arthur C., ed., *Soldier of the South: General Pickett's War Letters to His Wife* (Boston, 1928)

Irwin, Richard B., *History of the Nineteenth Army Corps* (New York, 1892)

Isely, Jeter A., *Horace Greeley and the Republican Party* (Princeton, 1947)

Jackson, W. Turrentine, *Treasure Hill: Portrait of a Silver-Mining Camp* (Tucson, 1963)

James, Marquis, *The Raven: A Biography of Sam Houston* (London, 1929)

Jarrell, Hampton M., *Wade Hampton and the Negro* (Columbia, S.C., 1949)

Jellison, Charles A., *Fessenden of Maine* (Syracuse, 1962)

Jenks, Leland Hamilton, *The Migration of British Capital to 1875* (London, 1963)

Johnson, Allen, *Stephen A. Douglas* (New York, 1908)

Johnson, Allen and Dumas Malone, eds., *Dictionary of American Biography* (New York, 1928–1944)

Johnson, Ludwell H., *Red River Campaign* (Baltimore, 1958)

Johnson, R.U., and Buel, C.C., *Battles and Leaders* (New York, 1887–1888)

Johnson, Richard W., *Memoir of Major-General George H. Thomas* (Philadelphia, 1881)

Johnson, Rossiter, *Campfire and Battlefield* (New York, 1896)

Johnston, John, *The Defense of Charleston Harbor* (Charleston, 1890)

Johnston, Joseph E., *Narrative of Military Operations* (New York, 1874)

Johnston, Richard M. and William H. Browne, *Life of Alexander H. Stephens* (Philadelphia, 1878)

Jones, Archer, *Confederate Strategy from Shiloh to Vicksburg* (Baton Rouge, 1961)

Jones, George R., *Joseph Russell Jones* (Chicago, 1964)

Jones, Jenkins L., *An Artilleryman's Diary* (Madison, 1914)

Jones, John Beauchamp, *A Rebel War Clerk's Diary* (2 vols., New York, 1866; 1935; 1958)

Jones, Maldwyn Allen, *American Immigration* (Chicago, 1961)

Jones, Rufus M., ed., *The Record of a Quaker Conscience: Cyrus Pringle's Diary* (New York, 1918)

Jordan, Donaldson and Edwin J. Pratt, *Europe and the American Civil War* (Boston, 1931)

Josephson, Matthew, *The Robber Barons: the Great American Capitalists* (New York, 1934)

Julian, George W., *Political Recollections* (Chicago, 1884)

Kamm, Samuel R., *The Civil War Career of Thomas A. Scott* (Philadelphia, 1940)

Kean, Robert Garlick Hill, *Inside the Confederate Government: the Diary of R.G. Hill Kean*, ed. Edward Younger (New York, 1957)

Kellogg, John A., *Capture and Escape* (Madison, 1908)

Kennedy, Joseph A., *Population of the U.S. in 1860* (Washington, 1864)

Ketring, Ruth A., *Clay of Alabama: Two Generations in Politics* (Duke Univ. Ph.D. Thesis, 1934)

Kibler, Lillian A., *Benjamin F. Perry, South Carolina Unionist* (Durham, 1946)

King, Willard L., *Lincoln's Manager David Davis* (Cambridge, 1960)

Kirke, Edmund (pseud. J.R. Gilmore), *Among the Pines* (New York, 1862)

Kirkland, Edward C., *Men, Cities, Transportation: A Study in New England History* (Cambridge, 1948)

Kirkland, Edward C., *Business in the Gilded Age* (Madison, Wis., 1952)

Kirkland, Edward C., *Dream and Thought in the Business Community, 1860–1900* (Ithaca, N.Y., 1956)

Klement, Frank L., *The Copperheads in the Middle West* (Chicago, 1960)

Knox, Dudley W., *A History of the U.S. Navy* (New York, 1936)

Koerner, Gustave, *Memoirs* (2 vols., Cedar Rapids, 1909)

Korn, Bertram W., *American Jewry and the Civil War* (Philadelphia, 1951)

Korngold, Ralph, *Two Friends of Man* (Boston, 1950)

Kriedberg, Marvin A. and Merton G. Henry, *History of Military Mobilization in the U.S. Army, 1775–1945* (Washington, 1955)

Kunhardt, Philip B., Jr., *Twenty Days* (New York, 1965)

Lamers, William E., *The Edge of Glory: a Biography of General William S. Rosecrans, U.S.A.* (New York, 1961)

Lamon, Ward Hill, *Recollections of Lincoln* (Washington, 1911)

Lane, Wheaton J., *Commodore Vanderbilt* (New York, 1942)

Larkin, Oliver W., *Art and Life in America* (New York, 1949)

Larson, Henrietta M., *Jay Cooke: Private Banker* (Cambridge, 1936)

Laugel, Auguste, *The United States During the Civil War*, ed. Allan Nevins (Bloomington, 1961)

Leach, Jack F., *Conscription in the United States* (Rutland, Vt., 1952)

Lebergott, Stanley, *Trends in American Economy in the Nineteenth Century* (New York, 1964)

LeConte, Joseph, *'Ware Sherman: A Journal of Three Months' Personal Experience in the Last Days of the Confederacy* (Berkeley, Calif., 1937)

Lee, Fitzhugh, *General Lee* (New York, 1894)

Lee, Robert E., Jr., *Recollections and Letters of General Lee* (New York, 1904; 1924)

Lee, William, *The Currency of the Confederate States of America* (Washington, 1875)

Leech, Margaret, *Reveille in Washington* (New York, 1941)

Lefler, Hugh T., *North Carolina History Told by Contemporaries* (Chapel Hill, 1956)

Lerwill, Leonard L., *Personnel Replacement System in the U.S. Army* (Washington, 1954)

Letterman, Jonathan, *Medical Recollections of the Army of the Potomac* (New York, 1866)

Lewis, Charles Lee, *David Glasgow Farragut, Our First Admiral* (Annapolis, 1943)

Lewis, Lloyd and Henry Justin Smith, *Chicago: The History of Its Reputation* (New York, 1929)

Lewis, Lloyd, *Captain Sam Grant* (Boston, 1950)

Lewis, Lloyd, *Sherman, Fighting Prophet* (New York, 1932)

Liddell Hart, B.H., *Sherman, Soldier, Realist, American* (New York, 1929)

Lincoln, Abraham, *Collected Works* (New York, 1886)

Lindsey, David, *"Sunset" Cox, Irrepressible Democrat* (Detroit, 1959)

Livermore, Col. Thomas L., *Numbers and Losses in the Civil War in America* (Boston, 1901)

Livermore, Col. Thomas L., *Sketches of Some of the Federal and Confederate Commanders* (Boston, 1895)

Livermore, Col. Thomas L., *Days and Events, 1860–1866* (Boston, 1920)

Lloyd, Arthur Y., *The Slavery Controversy, 1831–1860* (Chapel Hill, 1939)

Locke, Alain, *The Negro and His Music* (New York, 1969)

Lodge, Henry C., *Daniel Webster* (Boston, 1883)

Lomask, Milton, *Andrew Johnson: President on Trial* (New York, 1960)

Long, A.L., *Memoirs of Robert E. Lee* (New York, 1886)

Longstreet, James, *From Manassas to Appomattox: Memories* (Philadelphia, 1896; new ed., Bloomington, 1960)

Lonn, Ella, *Foreigners in the Union Army and Navy* (Baton Rouge, 1951)

Lonn, Ella, *Foreigners in the Confederacy* (Chapel Hill, 1940)

Lonn, Ella, *Desertion During the Civil War* (New York, 1928)

Lord, Francis A., *Civil War Collector's Encyclopedia* (Harrisburg, 1963)

Lord, John, *History of the Twenty-second Massachusetts Infantry* (Boston, 1887)

Lord, Walter, ed., *The Fremantle Diary* (Boston, 1954)

Lossing, Benson J., *The Pictorial Field Book of the Civil War* (Hartford, 1881)

Lossing, Benson J., *The Civil War in America* (3 vols., Hartford, 1868)

Lurie, Edward, *Louis Agassiz* (Chicago, 1960)

Luthin, Reinhard H., *Lincoln and the Patronage* (New York, 1943)

Luvaas, Jay, *The Military Legacy of the Civil War* (Chicago, 1959)

Lyman, Theodore, *Meade's Headquarters* (Boston, 1922)

Lyons, Capt. W.F., *Brigadier-General Thomas Francis Meagher* (New York, 1870)

Lytle, Andrew Nelson, *Bedford Forrest and His Critter Company* (New York, 1931)

Mabee, Carleton, *Black Freedom* (New York, 1970)

Macartney, Clarence E., *Grant and His Generals* (New York, 1953)

Macartney, Clarence E., *Mr. Lincoln's Admirals* (New York, 1956)

MacGill, Caroline E., and others under direction B.H. Meyer, *History of Transportation in the United States* (Washington, 1917)

Mack, Edward C., *Peter Cooper, Citizen of New York* (New York, 1949)

Magee, E.F., *History of the 72d Indiana Volunteer Infantry* (Lafayette, Ind., 1882)

Magnus, Philip, *Gladstone* (New York, 1954)

Mann, Albert W., *The Campaign of the Forty-fifth Regiment Massachusetts Volunteer Militia* (Boston, 1882)

Marshall, Charles, *An Aide-de-Camp of Lee*, ed. Sir Frederick Maurice (Boston, 1927)

Marshall, Helen E., *Dorothea Dix: Forgotten Samaritan* (Chapel Hill, 1937)

Marshall, Jessie Ames, ed., *Private and Official Correspondence of General Benjamin F. Butler* (5 vols., Norwood, Mass., 1917)

Martin, Robert F., *National Income in the United States* (New York, 1939)

Marwick, Arthur, *The Deluge* (London, 1965)

Massachusetts Soldiers' Relief Association (Washington, 1863)

Massey, Mary Elizabeth, *Bonnet Brigade* (New York, 1966)

Massey, Mary Elizabeth, *Refugee Life in the Confederacy* (Baton Rouge, 1964)

Mathews, Lois K., *The Expansion of New England, 1620–1865* (Boston, 1909)

Maurice, Sir Frederick, *Robert E. Lee, the Soldier* (Boston, 1925)

Maurice, Sir Frederick, *Statesmen and Soldiers of the Civil War* (Boston, 1926)

Maxwell, William Q., *Lincoln's Fifth Wheel* (New York, 1956)

Mayer, George H., *The Republican Party, 1854–1964* (New York, 1964)

McCaleb, Walter F., ed., *Memoirs of John F. Reagan* (New York, 1906; 1936)

McClellan, George B., *McClellan's Own Story* (New York, 1887)

McClellan, H.B., *The Life and Campaigns of Major-General J.E.B. Stuart* (Boston, 1885)

McClure, Alexander K., *Lincoln and Men of War-Times* (Philadelphia, 1892)

McClure, Alexander K., *Recollections of Half a Century* (Philadelphia, 1902)

McCulloch, Hugh, *Men and Measures of Half-a-Century* (New York, 1888)

McDonald, Cornelia, *A Diary with Reminiscences of the War and Refugee Life in the Shenandoah Valley, 1860–1865* (Nashville, 1935)

McGuire, Judith White, *Diary of a Southern Refugee* (New York, 1867)

McIlvane, Mabel, *Reminiscences of Chicago During the Civil War* (Chicago, 1914)

McKaye, James, *The Mastership and Its Fruits: The Emancipated Slave Face to Face with His Old Master* (New York, 1864)

McKim, James M., *The Freedman of South Carolina* (Philadelphia, 1862)

McKim, Randolph H., *A Soldier's Recollections; Leaves from the Diary of a Young Confederate* (New York, 1910)

McKitrick, Eric L., *Andrew Johnson and Reconstruction* (Chicago, 1960)

McMaster, John Bach, *History of the People of the United States During Lincoln's Administration* (New York, 1927)

McNamara, Daniel George, *The History of the Ninth Regiment Massachusetts Volunteer Infantry* (Boston, 1899)

McPherson, Edward, *The Political History of the United States of America During the Great Rebellion* (Washington, 1864–1865)

McWhitney, Grady, *Braxton Bragg and Confederate Defeat* (New York, 1969)

Meade, George G., *The Life and Letters of George Gordon Meade* (New York, 1913)

Meade, Robert D., *Judah P. Benjamin and the American Civil War* (Chicago, 1944)

Mearns, David C. and Lloyd A. Dunlap, *Long Remembered, the Gettysburg Address* (Washington, 1963)

Medberry, James K., *Men and Mysteries of Wall Street* (Boston, 1879)

Medical and Surgical History of the War of the Rebellion, ed. Surgical-General's Office (Washington, 1875)

Meigs, William M., *The Life of Thomas Hart Benton* (Philadelphia, 1904)

Melville, Herman, *The Works of Herman Melville* (London, 1924)

Mende, Elsie Porter and H.G. Pearson, *An American Soldier and Diplomat* (New York, 1927)

Meneely, Alexander Howard, *The War Department, 1861* (New York, 1928)

Mercier, Alfred, *Biographie de Pierre Soulé, Sénateur à Washington* (Paris, 1948)

Meredith, Roy, ed., *Mr. Lincoln's General: U.S. Grant* (New York, 1959)

Meredith, Roy, *Mr. Lincoln's Camera Man, Mathew B. Brady* (New York, 1946)

Merriam, George S., *Life and Times of Samuel Bowles* (New York, 1885)

Merrill, James M., *The Rebel Shore: The Story of Union Sea Power in the Civil War* (Boston, 1957)

Michie, Peter S., *General McClellan* (New York, 1901)

Michie, Peter S., *Life and Letters of Emory Upton* (New York, 1885)

Miers, Earl Schenck, ed., *Lincoln Day by Day; a Chronology, 1809–1865* (Washington, 1960)

Miers, Earl Schenck, *Web of Victory; Grant at Vicksburg* (New York, 1955)

Miers, Earl Schenck, *The General Who Marched to Hell, William Tecumseh Sherman* (New York, 1951)

Miers, Earl Schenck and Richard A. Brown, *Gettysburg* (New Brunswick, N.J., 1948)

Mill, John Stuart, *Political Economy* (London, 1847)

Mills, John Harrison, *Chronicles of the Twenty-first Regiment, New York State Volunteers* (Buffalo, 1867)

Milton, George F., *The Eve of Conflict: Stephen A. Douglas* (Boston, 1934)

Milton, George F., *Abraham Lincoln and the Fifth Column* (New York, 1942)

Milton, George F., *The Age of Hate, Andrew Johnson and the Radicals* (New York, 1930)

Mitchell, Broadus, *William Gregg, Factory Master* (Chapel Hill, 1928)

Mitchell, Broadus, *Frederick Law Olmsted, a Critic of the Old South* (Baltimore, 1924)

Mitchell, Dr. Silas Weir, *Catalogue of the Scientific and Literary Work of S. Weir Mitchell* (New York, 1852)

Mitchell, Stewart, *Horatio Seymour of New York* (Cambridge, 1938)

Mitchell, Wesley Clair, *Gold Prices, and Wages under the Greenback Standard* (Berkeley, 1908)

Mitchell, Wesley Clair, *History of the Greenbacks* (Chicago, 1903)

Monoghan, Jay, *Diplomat in Carpet Slippers* (Indianapolis, 1945)

Monoghan, Jay, *Civil War on the Western Border, 1854–1865* (Boston, 1955)

Montgomery, James S., *The Shaping of a Battle: Gettysburg* (Philadelphia, 1959)

Montross, Lynn, *War Through the Ages* (New York, 1944)

Moore, Albert Burton, *Conscription and Conflict in the Confederacy* (New York, 1924)

Moore, Frank, ed., *The Rebellion Record: A Diary of American Events* (New York, 1861ff)

Morford, Henry, *Days of Shoddy: The Great Rebellion* (Philadelphia, 1863)

Morgan, James M., *Recollections of a Rebel Reefer* (London, 1918)

Morrell, Daniel J., *The Manufacture of Railroad Iron, 1866* (Philadelphia, 1866)

Morrow, Curtis H., *Politico-Military Secret Societies of the Northwest* (Worcester, Mass., 1929)

Moss, Rev. Lemuel, *Annals of the U.S. Christian Commission* (Philadelphia, 1868)

Mott, Frank L., *A History of the American Magazines, American Journalism* (Cambridge, 1950)

Munroe, James Phinney, *Life of Francis Amosa Walker* (New York, 1923)

Murrell, William, *A History of American Graphic Humor* (New York, 1933–1938)

Muzzey, David S., *James G. Blaine* (New York, 1934)

Myers, Margaret G., *The New York Money Market* (New York, 1931)

Nason, Elias and Thomas Russell, *The Life and Public Services of Henry Wilson* (Philadelphia, 1876)

Naylor, Emmett Hay, *Trade Associations, Their Organization and Management* (New York, 1921)

Nevins, Allan, *The Evening Post, a Century of Journalism* (New York, 1922)

Nevins, Allan, *The Emergence of Modern America, 1865–1878* (New York, 1927)

Nevins, Allan, ed., *The Diary of Philip Hone* (2 vols., New York, 1927)

Nevins, Allan, ed., *The Diary of the Civil War*, by George Templeton Strong (New York, 1962)

Nevins, Allan, ed., *Selected Papers of Abram S. Hewitt* (New York, 1935)

Nevins, Allan, *Abram S. Hewitt with Some Account of Peter Cooper* (New York, 1935)

Nevins, Allan, *Hamilton Fish* (New York, 1936)

Nevins, Allan, *John D. Rockefeller: The Heroic Age of American Enterprise* (New York, 1940)

Nevins, Allan, *Ordeal of the Union, 1847–1857* (New York, 1947)

Nevins, Allan, *The Emergence of Lincoln* (New York, 1950)

Nevins, Allan, *Study in Power: John D. Rockefeller* (New York, 1953)

Nevins, Allan, *Frémont, Pathmaker of the West* (New York, 1955)

Nevins, Allan, *The War for the Union: The Improvised War, 1861–1862* (New York, 1959)

Nevins, Allan, *The War for the Union: War Becomes Revolution, 1862–1863* (New York, 1960)

Nevins, Allan, *The Origins of the Land-Grant Colleges and State Universities* (Washington, 1962)

Nevins, Allan, James I. Robertson, Jr., and Bell I. Wiley, eds., *Civil War Books: A Critical Bibliography* (2 vols., Baton Rouge, 1969)

Nevins, Allan, *The War for the Union: The Organized War, 1863–1864* (New York, 1971)

Nevins, Allan, *The War for the Union: The Organized War to Victory, 1864–1865* (New York, 1971)

Newell, Joseph Keith, *"Ours," Annals of the 10th Regiment Massachusetts Volunteers* (Springfield, Mass., 1875)

Newman, Bertram, *Edmund Burke* (London, 1827)

Newman, Ralph G. and E.B. Long, *Civil War Digest* (New York, 1956)

Newton, Lord, *Lord Lyons; a Record of British Diplomacy* (London, 1913)

Nichols, Edward J., *Toward Gettysburg: a Biography of Gen. John F. Reynolds* (University Park, Pa., 1958)

Nichols, George W., *The Story of the Great March* (New York, 1865)

Nichols, James L., *Confederate Engineers* (Tuscaloosa, 1957)

Nichols, Roy F., *Franklin Pierce: Young Hickory* (Philadelphia, 1931; 1958)

Nicolay & Hay, eds., *Collected Works of Abraham Lincoln* (New York, 1886)

Nicolay, Helen, *Lincoln's Secretary: A Biography of John G. Nicolay* (New York, 1949)

Nye, Russell B., *George Bancroft* (New York, 1944)

Nye, Russell B., *William Lloyd Garrison and the Humanitarian Reformers* (Boston, 1955)

Nye, Russell B., *Fettered Freedom* (E. Lansing, Mich., 1949)

Oberholtzer, Ellis Paxson, *Jay Cooke, Financier of the Civil War* (2 vols., Philadelphia, 1907)

Oberholtzer, Ellis Paxson, *A History of the United States Since the Civil War* (New York, 1917)

Oliphant, Mary C. Simms and others, eds., *The Letters of William Gilmore Simms* (2 vols., Columbia, S.C., 1952–1956)

Olmsted, Frederick L., *A Journey in the Back Country* (New York, 1860)

O'Neill, Edward H., *Biography by Americans, 1658–1936* (Philadelphia, 1939)

Osterweis, Rollin G., *Judah P. Benjamin* (New York, 1933)

Overdyke, William Darrell, *The Know-Nothing Party in the South* (Baton Rouge, 1950)

Owsley, Frank Lawrence, *King Cotton Diplomacy* (Chicago, 1931; 1959)

Owsley, Frank Lawrence, *State Rights in the Confederacy* (Gloucester, 1925; 1961)

Paine, Albert B., *Thomas Nast: His Period and His Pictures* (New York, 1904)

Palmer, George T., *A Conscientious Turncoat: the Story of John M. Palmer, 1817–1900* (New Haven, 1941)

Parker, John Lord, *History of the Twenty-second Massachusetts Infantry* (Boston, 1887)

Parker, Theodore, *Collected Works* (Centenary ed., 15 vols., Boston, 1907–13)

Parker, Capt. Thomas H., *51st Pennsylvania Volunteers* (Philadelphia, 1869)

Parker, William B., *The Life and Public Services of Justin Smith Morrill* (Boston, 1924)

Parks, Joseph H., *General Edmund Kirby Smith, CSA* (Baton Rouge, 1954)

Parrington, Vernon L., *Main Currents in American Thought* (3 vols., New York, 1927–1930)

Parsons, Gen. Lewis B., *Reports to the War Department* (Washington, 1867)

Parsons, Gen. Lewis B., *In Memoriam General Lewis Baldwin Parsons* (private, 1909)

Parton, James, *General Butler in New Orleans* (New York, 1864; 1892)

Patrick, Rembert W., *Jefferson Davis and His Cabinet* (Baton Rouge, 1944)

Patrick, Rembert W., *The Fall of Richmond* (Baton Rouge, 1960)

Patterson, A.W., *The Code Duello* (Richmond, 1927)

Patton, James W., *Unionism and Reconstruction in Tennessee, 1860–1869* (Chapel Hill, 1934)

Paullin, Charles O., *Atlas of the Historical Geography of the United States* (New York, 1932)

Pearce, Raymond J., Jr., *Benjamin H. Hill, Secession and Reconstruction* (Chicago, 1928)

Pearson, Henry G., *The Life of John A. Andrew* (Boston, 1904)

Pearson, Henry G., *An American Railroad Builder, John Murray Forbes* (Boston, 1911)

Pearson, Henry G., *James S. Wadsworth of Geneseo* (New York, 1913)

Pellet, Elias P., *A History of the 114th New York State Volunteers* (Norwich, N.Y., 1866)

Pember, Phoebe Y., *A Southern Woman's Story* (New York, 1879)

Pemberton, John C., Jr., *Pemberton: Defender of Vicksburg* (Chapel Hill, 1942)

Pepper, George W., *Personal Recollections of Sherman's Campaigns in Georgia and the Carolinas* (Zanesville, 1866)

Percy, William A., *Lanterns on the Levee, Recollections of a Planter's Son* (New York, 1950)

Perkins, Jacob R., *Trails, Rails and War, The Life of Gen. G.M. Dodge* (Indianapolis, 1929)

Peto, Sir S. Morton, *The Resources and Prospects of America* (London, 1866)

Phelps, Mary M., *Kate Chase, Dominant Daughter* (New York, 1935)

Phillips, Ulrich B., *The Life of Robert Toombs* (New York, 1913)

Phillips, Wendell, *Speeches, Lectures and Letters* (2 vols., Boston, 1863–1891)

Piatt, Donn, *Memories of Men Who Saved the Union* (New York, 1887)

Pickard, Samuel T., *Life and Letters of John G. Whittier* (2 vols., Boston, 1894; 1907)

Pickett, La Salle C., *The Heart of a Soldier* (New York, 1913)

Pickett, La Salle C., *Pickett and His Men* (Philadelphia, 1913)

Pierce, Edward L., *Memoirs and Letters of Charles A. Sumner* (4 vols., Boston, 1877–1893)

Pitman, Benn, *Assassination of President Lincoln, 1865* (Cincinnati, 1865)

Pleasants, Samuel A., *Fernando Wood of New York* (New York, 1948)

Plum, William R., *The Military Telegraph During the Civil War* . . . (Chicago, 1882)

Polk, William M., *Leonidas Polk: Bishop and General* (New York, 1915)

Pollard, Edward A., *Life of Jefferson Davis* (Philadelphia, 1869)

Pollard, Edward A., *The Lost Cause* (New York, 1967)

Pollard, John A., *John Greenleaf Whittier, Friend of Man* (Boston, 1949)

Polley, J.B., *Hood's Texas Brigade* (New York, 1910)

Poore, Benjamin Perley, *Reminiscences of Sixty Years in the National Metropolis* (New York, 1886)

Porter, David D., *Incidents and Anecdotes of the Civil War* (New York, 1885)

Porter, Horace, *Campaigning with Grant* (New York, 1897)

Porter, Kirk H. and Donald B. Johnson, eds., *National Party Platforms* (Urbana, 1966)

Potter, David M., *People of Plenty* (Chicago, 1954)

Pound, Roscoe, *The Lawyer from Antiquity to Modern Times* (St. Paul, 1953)

Powell, William H., *Fifth Army Corps of the Army of the Potomac* (New York, 1896)

Powers, George W., *The Story of the Thirty-eighth Regiment of Massachusetts Volunteers* (Cambridge, 1866)

Pratt, Fletcher, *Stanton: Lincoln's Secretary of War* (New York, 1953)

Proceedings of the American Pharmaceutical Association (Cincinnati, 1864)

Pryor, Mrs. Roger A., *Reminiscences of Peace and War* (New York, 1904)

Putnam, George Haven, *Some Memories of the Civil War* (New York, 1924)

Putnam, George Haven, *A Memoir of George Palmer Putnam* (New York, 1903)

Putnam, Sallie A., *In Richmond During the Confederacy* (New York, 1961)

Quaife, Milo M., ed., *From the Cannon's Mouth; Civil War Letters of Gen. Alphous S. Williams* (Detroit, 1959)

Quarles, Benjamin, *The Negro in the Civil War* (Boston, 1953)

Quarles, Benjamin, *Frederick Douglass* (Washington, 1948)

Quint, Alonzo H., *The Record of the Second Massachusetts Infantry* (Boston, 1867)

Radcliffe, George L.P., *Governor Thomas H. Hicks of Maryland and the Civil War* (Baltimore, 1901)

Rains, Col. George W., *History of the Confederate Powder Works* (Augusta, 1882)

Ramsdell, Charles W., *Behind the Lines in the Southern Confederacy* (Baton Rouge, 1944)

Ranck, James B., *Albert Gallatin Brown* (New York, 1937)

Randall, James G., *Lincoln the President* (New York, 1945)

Randall, James G., *Last Full Measure* (New York, 1955)

Randall, James G., *Civil War and Reconstruction* (Boston, 1953)

Randall, James G., *Constitutional Problems under Lincoln* (Urbana, 1951)

Rawley, James A., *Turning Points of the Civil War* (Lincoln, Neb., 1966)

Reid, John C., *The Brothers' War* (Boston, 1905)

Reid, Whitelaw, *Ohio in the War* (Cincinnati, 1868)

Renouvin, Mélange Pierre, *Études d'Histoire de Relations Internationales* (Paris, 1966)

Rhodes, James Ford, *History of the United States* (New York, 1917; 1928)

Richards, Laura E. and Maude H. Elliott, *Julia Ward Howe* (2 vols., Boston, 1915)

Richardson, Albert D., *A Personal History of U.S. Grant* (Hartford, 1868)

Richardson, E. Ramsey, *Little Aleck: a Life of Alexander H. Stephens* (Indianapolis, 1932)

Richardson, James D., *Messages and Papers of Jefferson Davis and the Confederacy* . . . with Introd.
by Allan Nevins (New York, 1966)

Richardson, James D., *Messages and Papers of the Presidents, 1789–1902* (New York, 1903)

Richardson, Leon B., *William E. Chandler, Republican* (New York, 1940)

Riddle, Albert G., *Recollections of War Times* (New York, 1895)

Riddle, Albert G., *Life of Benjamin F. Wade* (Cleveland, 1887)

Rippey, J. Fred, *The United States and Mexico* (New York, 1931)

Risch, Erma, *Quartermaster Support of the Army: a History of the Corps, 1775–1939* (Washington, 1962)

Roberts, Walter Adolphe, *Semmes of the Alabama* (Indianapolis, 1938)

Robinson, Johan, *The Accumulation of Capital* (London, 1956)

Robinson, Solon, *Selected Writings*, ed. Herbert Anthony Keller (Indianapolis, 1935–1936)

Robinson, William M., *The Confederate Privateers* (New Haven, 1928)

Robinton, M.T., *An Introduction to Papers of the New York Prize Court, 1861–1865* (New York, 1945)

Roeder, Ralph, *Juarez and His Mexico* (New York, 1947)

Rogers, Joseph, *The Development of the North Since the Civil War* (Philadelphia, c. 1906)

Roman, Alfred, *The Military Operations of General Beauregard* (New York, 1884)

Ropes, John Codman, *The Story of the Civil War* (New York, 1933)

Roscoe, Theodore, *The Web of Conspiracy* (Englewood Cliffs, N.J., 1959)

Rose, Willie Lee, *Rehearsal for Reconstruction* (Indianapolis, 1964)

Roseboom, Eugene, *History of Presidential Elections* (New York, 1947; 1964)

Rosenbach Company Catalogue, *The History of America in Documents* (Philadelphia, 1951)

Rosewater, Victor, *History of Cooperative News-Gathering in the United States* (New York, 1930)

Ross, Ishbel, *First Lady of the South* (New York, 1958)

Ross, Ishbel, *Angel of the Battlefield* (New York, 1956)

Rowland, Dunbar, *Jefferson Davis, Constitutionalist* (10 vols., Jackson, Miss., 1923)

Russell, William Howard, *My Diary North and South* (New York, 1863)

Sage, Leland L., *William Boyd Allison: A Study in Practical Politics* (Iowa City, 1956)

Sala, George Augustus, *My Diary in America* . . . (London, 1865)

Sala, George Augustus, *America Revisited* (3 vols., London, 1883)

Salter, William, *The Life of James W. Grimes* (New York, 1876)

Samuels, Ernest, *The Young Henry Adams* (Cambridge, 1948)

Samuels, Ernest, *Henry Adams: the Middle Years* (Cambridge, 1958)

Schafer, Joseph, *Carl Schurz, Militant Liberal* (Evansville, Wis., 1930)

Schafer, Joseph, ed., *Intimate Letters of Carl Schurz* (Madison, 1928)

Scherer, James A.B., *Cotton as a World Power* (New York, 1916)

Schiebert, Captain Justus, *Seven Months in the Rebel States During the North American War, 1863*
(Tuscaloosa, 1958)

Schiebert, Captain Justus, *Mit Schwert und Feder: Erinnerungen aus Meinen Leben* (Berlin, 1902)

Schmidt, Louis B., *Readings in the Economic History of American Agriculture* (New York, 1925)

Schofield, John M., *Forty-Six Years in the Army* (New York, 1897)

Schouler, James, *History of the United States* (Washington, 1880–1913)

Schuckers, J.W., *The Life and Public Services of Salmon Portland Chase* (New York, 1874)

Schurz, Carl, *Reminiscences* (New York, 1907)

Schwab, J.C., *The Confederate States of America, 1861–1865; a Financial and Industrial History* (New York, 1901; 1968)

Scott, Winfield, *Memoirs of Lieut.-General Scott* (2 vols., New York, 1864)

Scudder, Horace E., *James Russell Lowell.*(2 vols., Boston, 1901)

Sears, Louis M., *John Slidell* (Durham, 1925)

Segal, Charles M., ed., *Conversations with Lincoln* (New York, 1961)

Seitz, Don C., *Braxton Bragg, General of the Confederacy* (Columbia, S.C., 1924)

Seitz, Don C., *Horace Greeley, Founder of the New York Tribune* (Indianapolis, 1926)

Seitz, Don C., *The James Gordon Bennetts, Father and Son, Proprietors of the New York Herald* (Indianapolis, 1928)

Semmes, Raphael, *Memoirs of Service Afloat During the War Between the States* (Baltimore, 1869)

Seward, Frederick W., *Reminiscences of a War-time Statesman and Diplomat* (New York, 1916)

Seward, Frederick W., *Seward at Washington, 1861–1872* (New York, 1891)

Seward, Frederick W., ed., *William H. Seward: an Autobiography* (3 vols., New York, 1891)

Shannon, Frederick A., *Organization and Administration of the Union Army, 1861–1865* (Cleveland, 1928)

Shannon, Frederick A., *The Farmer's Last Frontier, Agriculture, 1860–1897* (New York, 1945)

Sharkey, Robert P., *Money, Class, and Party* (Baltimore, 1959)

Sheridan, Philip, *Personal Memoirs* (New York, 1888)

Sherman, John, *Memoirs* (New York, 1875)

Sherman, John, *John Sherman's Recollections of Forty Years in the House, Senate and Cabinet* (Chicago, 1895)

Sherwin, Oscar, *Prophet of Liberty: Life and Times of Wendell Phillips* (New York, 1958)

Shotwell, Walter Gaston, *The Civil War in America* (London, 1923)

Shryock, Richard H., *The Development of Modern Medicine* (New York, 1947)

Sievers, Harry, *Benjamin Harrison, Hoosier Warrior* (2 vols., Chicago, 1952)

Silver, David, *Lincoln's Supreme Court* (Urbana, 1957)

Silver, David, *The Supreme Court During the Civil War* (Urbana, 1956)

Simms, Henry H., *A Decade of Sectional Controversy, 1851–1861* (Chapel Hill, 1942)

Simon, John Y., *The Papers of Ulysses S. Grant* (Carbondale, Ill., 1967–1969)

Skipper, O.C., *J.D.B. DeBow, Magazinist of the Old South* (Athens, Ga., 1958)

Smith, Charles William, *Roger B. Taney, Jacksonian Jurist* (Chapel Hill, 1936)

Smith, Daniel E., and others, eds., *Mason Smith Family Letters 1860–1868* (Columbia, S.C., 1950)

Smith, Donnal V., *Chase and Civil War Politics* (Columbus, O., 1931)

Smith, Rev. Edward P., *Incidents of the U.S. Christian Commission* (Philadelphia, 1869)

Smith, Rev. Edward P., *Christian Work on the Battle-Field* (London, 1870)

Smith, Elbert B., *Magnificent Missourian* (Philadelphia, 1958)

Smith, Elbert B., *The Death of Slavery* (Chicago, 1967)

Smith, Frank E., *The Yazoo* (New York, 1954)

Smith, George Winston, *Medicines for the Union Army* (Madison, Wis., 1962)

Smith, Theodore Clarke, *The Life and Letters of James Abram Garfield* (2 vols., New Haven, 1925)

Smith, William E., *The Francis Preston Blair Family in Politics* (New York, 1933)

Soley, James R., *The Blockade and the Cruisers* (New York, 1883)

Soley, James R., *Admiral Porter* (New York, 1903)

Sorrel, G. Moxley, *Recollections of a Confederate Staff Officer* (New York, 1905)

Sparks, David S., ed., *Inside Lincoln's Army: The Diary of Marsena Rudolph Patrick* (New York, 1964)

Speed, James (grandson), *James Speed: a Personality* (privately printed, Morton, 1914)

Spiller, Robert E. and others, eds., *Literary History of the United States and Supplement* (New York, 1948)

Sprout, H. and M., *The Rise of American Naval Power* (Princeton, 1942)

Sprunt, James, *Cape Fear Chronicles* (Raleigh, 1914)

Stackpole, Edward J., *They Met at Gettysburg* (Harrisburg, 1956)

Stampp, Kenneth M., *Indiana Politics During the Civil War* (Indianapolis, 1949)

Stanton, H.S., *Random Recollections* (New York, 1881)

Stanwood, Edward, *A History of the Presidency from 1788 to 1897* (Boston, 1912)

Steere, Edward, *The Wilderness Campaign* (Harrisburg, 1960)

Steiner, Bernard C., *Life of Reverdy Johnson* (Baltimore, 1914)

Steiner, Bernard C., *Life of Henry Winter Davis* (Baltimore, 1916)

Steiner, Bernard C., *Life of Roger Brooke Taney* (Baltimore, 1914)

Stephens, Alexander H., *The War Between the States* (2 vols., Philadelphia, 1868)

Stephens, Alexander H., *A Constitutional View of the Late War Between the States* (Philadelphia, 1870)

Stern, Philip Van Doren, *The Man Who Killed Lincoln* (Cleveland, 1939)

Stern, Philip Van Doren, *The Assassination of President Lincoln* (New York, 1954)

Stern, Philip Van Doren, *An End to Valor; the Last Days of the Civil War* (Boston, 1958)

Steward, T.G., *The Colored Regulars in the U.S. Army* (New York, 1969)

Stewart, George R., *Pickett's Charge* (Boston, 1959)

Stiles, Robert, *Four Years Under Marse Robert* (New York, 1904)

Stille, C.J., *History of the U.S. Sanitary Commission* (Philadelphia, 1866)

Stoddard, Henry L., *Horace Greeley: Printer, Editor, Crusader* (New York, 1946)

Storey, Moorfield and Edward W. Emerson, *Ebenezer Rockwood Hoar . . . a Memoir* (Boston, 1911)

Stowe, Charles E. and Lyman B. Stowe, *Harriet Beecher Stowe: the Story of Her Life* (Boston, 1911)

Stowe, Harriet Beecher, *The Lives and Deeds of Our Self-made Men* (Boston, 1889)

Strode, Hudson, *Jefferson Davis: Confederate President* (New York, 1959)

Strode, Hudson, *Jefferson Davis, Private Letters . . .* (New York, 1966)

Strode, Hudson, *Jefferson Davis, Tragic Hero* (New York, 1964)

Strong, George Templeton, *The Diary of the Civil War*, ed. Allan Nevins (New York, 1962)

Struik, Dirk J., *Yankee Science in the Making* (Boston, 1948)

Stryker, Lloyd Paul, *Andrew Johnson: A Study in Courage* (New York, 1929)

Swanberg, W.A., *Sickles the Incredible* (New York, 1956)

Swank, James M., *Notes and Comments on Industrial, Economic, Political and Historical Subjects; American Iron and Steel Association from 1872 to 1897* (Philadelphia, 1897)

Swank, James M., *History of the Manufacture of Iron in All Ages* (Philadelphia, 1892)

Swiggett, Howard, *The Rebel Raider: A Life of John Hunt Morgan* (Garden City, 1937)

Swinton, William, *Campaigns of the Army of the Potomac* (New York, 1882)

Swisher, Carl B., *Roger B. Taney* (New York, 1935)

Symonds, H.C., *Report of a Commissary of Subsistence* (New York, 1888)

Tate, Allan, *Jefferson Davis: His Rise and Fall* (New York, 1929)

Tatum, Georgia Lee, *Disloyalty in the Confederacy* (Chapel Hill, 1934)

Taylor, Emerson G., *Gouverneur Kemble Warren: Life and Letters* (Boston, 1932)

Taylor, George R., *The Transportation Revolution, 1815–1860* (New York, 1951)

Taylor, Richard, *Destruction and Reconstruction* (New York, 1879)

Taylor, Thomas E., *Running the Blockade* (London, 1896)

Taylor, Walter H., *Four Years with General Lee* (New York, 1877)

Temperley, Harold and Lillian M. Penson, *Foundations of British Foreign Policy* (Cambridge, 1938)

Terrell, John Upton, *The United States Department of Agriculture* (New York, 1966)

Tharp, Louise H., *Adventurous Alliance: the Story of the Agassiz Family* (Boston, 1959)

Thayer, William R., *The Life and Letters of John Hay* (2 vols., Boston, 1915)

Thomas, Benjamin P., *Abraham Lincoln* (New York, 1952)

Thomas, Benjamin P., *Russo-American Relations, 1815–1867* (Baltimore, 1930)

Thomas, Lately, *The First President Johnson* (New York, 1968)

Thompson, Robert L., *Wiring a Continent: The History of the Telegraph Industry in the United States, 1832–1866* (Princeton, 1947)

Thompson, R.M. and R. Wainwright, eds., *Confidential Correspondence of Gustavus Vasa Fox* . . . (2 vols., New York, 1918–1919)

Thompson, S.B., *Confederate Purchasing Operations Abroad* (Chapel Hill, 1935)

Thorndike, Rachel Sherman, *The Sherman Letters: Correspondence Between General and Senator Sherman from 1837 to 1891* (London, 1894)

Ticknor, George, *Life, Letters and Journals of George Ticknor* (Boston, 1876)

Tilburg, Frederick, *Handbook on Gettysburg* (National Park System, Gettysburg)

Todd, Helen, *A Man Named Grant* (Boston, 1940)

Todd, Richard C., *Confederate Finance* (Athens, Ga., 1954)

Todd, William, *The Seventy-ninth Highlanders, New York Volunteers* (Albany, 1886)

Towne, Marvin W. and Wayne Rasmussen, *Trends in American Economy in the Nineteenth Century* (Princeton, 1960)

Townsend, George A., *Campaigns of a Non-Combatant* (New York, 1866)

Trent, William P., *William Gilmore Simms* (Boston, 1892)

Trevelyan, George M., *The Life of John Bright* (Boston, 1913)

Trimble, Bruce R., *Chief Justice Waite* (Princeton, 1938)

Trowbridge, J.T., *A Picture of the Desolated States* (Hartford, 1868)

True, Frederick W., *A History of the First Half-Century of the National Academy of Sciences, 1863–1913* (Washington, 1913)

Tucker, Glenn, *Chickamauga: Bloody Battle in the West* (Indianapolis, 1961)

Tucker, Glenn, *Zeb Vance, Champion of Personal Freedom* (Indianapolis, 1966)

Tupper, Henry Allen, *A Thanksgiving Discourse* . . . (Macon, Ga., 1862)

Turner, Carol, *Life of Turner* (Urbana, 1911)

Turner, Frederick Jackson, *The Frontier in American History* (New York, 1920)

Turner, George E., *Victory Rode the Rails* (Indianapolis, 1953)

Tyler, William S., ed., *Recollections of the Civil War* . . . *by Mason W. Tyler* (New York, 1912)

Upton, Emory, *The Military Policy of the United States* (Washington, 1912)

Vallandigham, James L., *A Life of Clement L. Vallandigham* (Baltimore, 1872)

Van Deusen, Glyndon G., *Horace Greeley: Nineteenth-Century Crusader* (Philadelphia, 1953)

Van Deusen, Glyndon G., *William Henry Seward* (New York, 1967)

Van Deusen, Glyndon G., *Thurlow Weed: Wizard of the Lobby* (Boston, 1947)

Vandiver, Frank E., *Ploughshares into Swords: Josiah Gorgas and Confederate Ordnance* (Austin, 1952)

Vandiver, Frank E., *Rebel Brass; the Confederate Command System* (Baton Rouge, 1956)

Vandiver, Frank E., ed., *Confederate Blockade Running Through Bermuda* (Austin, 1947)

Vandiver, Frank E., *Jubal's Raid* (New York, 1960)

Van Horne, Thomas B., *History of the Army of the Cumberland* (Cincinnati, 1875)

Van Horne, Thomas B., *The Life of Major-General George H. Thomas* (New York, 1882)

Van Oss, S.F., *American Railroads as Investments* (New York, 1893)

Van Tyne, Claude H., ed., *The Letters of Daniel Webster* . . . (New York, 1902)

Villard, Henry, *Memoirs of Henry Villard* . . . (2 vols., Boston, 1904)

Villiers, Brougham, and W.H. Chesson, *Anglo-American Relations, 1861–1865* (London, 1919)

Wainwright, Col. Charles S., *A Diary of Battle*, ed. Allan Nevins (New York, 1962)

Walcott, Charles Folsom, *History of the Twenty-first Regiment Massachusetts Volunteers* (Boston, 1882)

Walker, Francis A., *History of the Second Army Corps* (New York, 1891)

Walker, George, *The Wealth, Resources and Public Debt of the United States* (London, 1865)

Walker, Peter F., *Vicksburg: A People at War, 1860–1865* (Chapel Hill, 1960)

Wall, Joseph F., *Henry Watterson, Reconstructed Rebel* (New York, 1956)

Wallace, Irving, *The Fabulous Showman* (New York, 1959)

Wallace, Sarah A., and F.E. Gillespie, eds., *The Journal of Benjamin Moran* (Chicago, 1948–1949)

Wallace, Lew, *Lew Wallace: An Autobiography* (New York, 1906)

Wallace, Willard M., *Soul of the Lion: A Biography of General Joshua L. Chamberlain* (New York, 1960)

Walpole, Spencer, *The Life of Lord John Russell* (London, 1899)

Ward, A.W. and G.P. Gooch, eds., *The Cambridge History of British Foreign Policy, 1783–1919* (Cambridge, 1922–1923)

Warden, Robert B., *An Account of the Private Life and Public Services of Salmon P. Chase* (Cincinnati, 1874)

Ware, Capt. Eugene F., *The Indian War of 1864* (Lincoln, Neb., 1960)

Ware, Norman, *The Industrial Worker, 1840–1860* (Boston, 1924)

Warmoth, Henry C., *War, Politics, and Reconstruction* (New York, 1930)

Warner, Ezra J., *Generals in Blue* (Baton Rouge, 1964)

Warren, Charles, *A History of the American Bar* (Boston, 1911)

Warren, Louis A., *Lincoln's Gettysburg Declaration* (Fort Wayne, 1964)

Watkins, S.R., *"Co. Aytch," Maury Gray's First Tennessee Regiment* (Nashville, 1882)

Watts, John, *The Facts of the Cotton Famine* (London, 1866)

Wealthy Citizens of New York (New York, 1845)

Weber, Thomas, *The Northern Railroads in the Civil War, 1861–1865* (New York, 1862)

Weed, Thurlow and Harriet A. Weed, eds., *Life of Thurlow Weed* (2 vols., Boston, 1884)

Weigley, Russell F., *Quartermaster-General of the Union Army: a Biography of M.C. Meigs* (New York, 1959)

Weiss, John, *Life and Correspondence of Theodore Parker* (2 vols., New York, 1864)

Welles, Gideon, *Diary of Gideon Welles, Secretary of the Navy . . .* (Boston, 1911)

Wellman, Manly Wade, *Giant in Gray: a Biography of Wade Hampton of South Carolina* (New York, 1949)

Wells, David A., *Our Burden and Our Strength* (Norwich, Conn., 1864)

Wells, David A., *The Recent Financial, Industrial and Commercial Experiences of the United States . . .* (New York, 1872)

Wells, David A., *Our Merchant Marine, How It Rose, Increased, Became Great, Declined and Decayed* (New York, 1890)

Wells, H.G., Introduction to *The Outline of History* (New York, 1927)

Wells, Capt. James M., *With Touch of Elbow* (Philadelphia, 1909)

Werner, M. R., *Barnum* (New York, 1923; 1926)

West, Benjamin F., *Lincoln's Scapegoat General: a Life of Benjamin F. Butler, 1818–1893* (Boston, 1965)

West, Richard S., Jr., *Gideon Welles: Lincoln's Navy Department* (Indianapolis, 1943)

West, Richard S., Jr., *The Second Admiral: a Life of David Dixon Porter* (New York, 1937)

Wharton, Vernon L., *The Negro in Mississippi, 1865–1890* (Chapel Hill, 1947)

White, Andrew D., *Autobiography* (2 vols., New York, 1905–1907)

White, Horace, *The Life of Lyman Trumbull* (Boston, 1913)

White, Laura A., *Robert Barnwell Rhett; Father of Secession* (New York, 1931)

White, Leonard D., *The Jacksonians* (New York, 1956)

Whitman, Walt, *Specimen Days in America* (London, 1932)

Whitman, Walt, *The Wound Dresser* (Boston, 1898)

Wiley, Bell, *The Life of Johnny Reb* (Indianapolis, 1943)

Wiley, Bell, *The Life of Billy Yank* (Indianapolis, 1952)

Wiley, Bell, *Southern Negroes, 1861–1865* (New York, 1938)

Wiley, Bell, ed., *This Infernal War: Confederate Letters of Sgt. Edwin H. Fay* (Austin, 1958)

Wiley, Bell, ed., *Fourteen Hundred and 91 Days in the Confederate Army: a Journal Kept by W.W. Heartsill, for Four Years, One Month, and One Day* (Marshall, Tex., 1876)

Wilkerson, Frank, *Recollections of a Private Soldier* . . . (New York, 1887)

Williams, Charles Richard, ed., *Diary and Letters of Rutherford B. Hayes* (5 vols., Columbus, O., 1922–1926)

Williams, Charles Richard, *The Life of Rutherford Birchard Hayes* . . . (2 vols., Boston, 1914)

Williams, Kenneth P., *Lincoln Finds a General* (New York, 1959)

Williams, T. Harry, *Lincoln and the Radicals* (Madison, 1941)

Williams, T. Harry, *Hayes of the Twenty-third; the Civil War Volunteer Officer* (New York, 1965)

Williams, T. Harry, *P.G.T. Beauregard: Napoleon in Gray* (Baton Rouge, 1955)

Williamson, Harold F., ed., *The Growth of the American Economy* (New York, 1951)

Willson, Beckles, *John Slidell and the Confederates in Paris* (New York, 1932)

Wilson, Forrest, *Crusader in Crinoline, the Life of Harriet Beecher Stowe* (Philadelphia, 1941)

Wilson, James G., *The Life and Public Services of Ulysses Simpson Grant* (New York, 1885)

Wilson, James Harrison, *Under the Old Flag* (2 vols., New York, 1912)

Wilson, James Harrison, *The Life of Charles A. Dana* (New York, 1907)

Wilson, James Harrison, *Life and Service of William Farrar Smith* (Wilmington, 1904)

Winks, Robin, *Canada and the United States: the Civil War Years* (Baltimore, 1960)

Winslow, Col. I., *The Great Treason Plot in the North* (Chicago, 1895)

Winston, Robert W., *Andrew Johnson, Plebeian and Patriot* (New York, 1928)

Winthrop, Robert C., Jr., *Memoir of Robert C. Winthrop* (Boston, 1897)

Wise, Jennings, C., *The Long Arm of Lee* (New York, 1959)

Wise, John S., *The End of an Era* (Boston, 1899; 1902)

Wistar, Isaac Jones, *Autobiography of Isaac Jones Wistar, 1827–1905* . . . (New York, 1914; Philadelphia, 1937)

Wolseley, Viscount Garnet Joseph, *The American Civil War, an English View*, ed., James A. Rawley (Charlottesville, 1964)

Woodward, W.E., *Meet General Grant* (New York, 1928)

Woolfolk, George R., *The Cotton Regency: the Northern Merchants and Reconstruction* (New York, 1958)

Worthington, George, *Doctors in Blue* (New York, 1952)

Wright, Edward N., *Conscientious Objectors in the Civil War* (Philadelphia, 1931)

Wright, Lt. Howard C., *Port Hudson, Its History from an Interior Point of View* (Baton Rouge, 1861)

Wyeth, John A., *Life of General Nathan Bedford Forrest* (New York, 1899)

Yates, Richard E., *The Confederacy and Zeb Vance* (Tuscaloosa, 1958)

Yearns, Wilfred Buck, *The Confederate Congress* (Atlanta, 1960)

Yeatman, James E., *Report on the Condition of the Freedmen of the Mississippi to Western Sanitary Commission, 1863* (St. Louis, 1864)

INDEX

About the Author

Allan Nevins was born at Camp Point, Illinois, on May 20, 1890. An editorial writer for the New York *Evening Post* during the period 1913–23, Nevins also wrote for *The Nation*, the New York *Sun*, and other newspapers and magazines. While enjoying a distinguished career in journalism, Nevins was also intrigued with history. A leading American historian, he taught at Columbia University (1928–58), becoming the DeWitt Clinton Professor of American History in 1931. In 1948 Nevins established Columbia's "Oral History Program," a cause he was much devoted to for the rest of his life. The prolific Nevins's most famous works included *Grover Cleveland* (1932) and *Hamilton Fish* (1936), both of which won Pulitzer prizes, as well as *The Emergence of Modern America* (1927), *John D. Rockefeller*, 2 Volumes. (1940), and his famous trilogy on Ford with Frank Hill: *Ford: The Lines, the Man, the Company* (1954); *Ford: Expansion and Challenge* (1957); and *Ford: Decline and Rebirth* (1963). President of the American Historical Association and President of the American Academy of Arts and Letters, Nevins also went on to help found *American Heritage* magazine. He died on March 5, 1971, and was posthumously awarded the National Book Award for his last installments of *Ordeal of the Union*. Lamented C. Vann Woodward, in his elegiac review of the posthumous volumes, "We are not likely to see more history of this character and scope for some time to come."

Other Titles in Our Civil War Library